W9-AZV-365

prentice-hall, inc.,
englewood cliffs, new jersey 07632

Philip Kotler

Northwestern University

PRINCIPLES of MARKETING

Library of Congress Cataloging in Publication Data

KOTLER, PHILIP.
Principles of marketing.

Includes bibliographical references and index.
1. Marketing. I. Title.
HF5415.K636 658.8 79-22895
ISBN 0-13-701557-7

To My Students—Past, Present, and Future

Editorial/production supervision by Linda Stewart
Interior/Cover Design by Linda Conway
Art Director: Lorraine Mullaney
Cover Illustration by Reginal D. Wickham
Copyeditor/Proofreader: Marie Lines
Page Makeup: York Graphic Services
Acquisition Editor: John Connolly
Manufacturing Buyer: John Hall

Printed in the United States of America

10 9 8 7 6 5 4 3 2

PRENTICE-HALL INTERNATIONAL, INC., London
PRENTICE-HALL OF AUSTRALIA PTY. LIMITED, Sydney
PRENTICE-HALL OF CANADA, LTD., Toronto
PRENTICE-HALL OF INDIA PRIVATE LIMITED, New Delhi
PRENTICE-HALL OF JAPAN, INC., Tokyo
PRENTICE-HALL OF SOUTHEAST ASIA PTE. LTD., Singapore
WHITEHALL BOOKS LIMITED, WELLINGTON, New Zealand

CONTENTS

preface
xvii

PART ONE
MARKETING'S ROLE IN THE ECONOMY

chapter one
marketing and human needs
3

Marketing has Different Meanings 4 *Marketing Affects Everyone* 5
Marketing is Controversial 6

□ THE RAPID ADOPTION OF MARKETING 7
In the Business Sector 7 *In the International Sector* 8
In the Nonprofit Sector 8

□ WHAT IS MARKETING 9
Needs 10 *Wants* 10 *Demands* 11 *Products* 11
Exchange 13 *Transactions* 14 *Market* 16 *Marketing* 17

□ MARKETING MANAGEMENT 18

□ MARKETING MANAGEMENT PHILOSOPHIES 20
The Production Concept 20 *The Product Concept* 21
The Selling Concept 21 *The Marketing Concept* 22
The Societal Marketing Concept 24

□ THE GOALS OF A MARKETING SYSTEM 26
Maximize Consumption 27 *Maximize Consumer Satisfaction* 27
Maximize Choice 28 *Maximize Life Quality* 28

□ SUMMARY 30

chapter two

the structure of marketing systems
35

☐ NATIONAL MARKETING SYSTEMS 36
Structure of a National Marketing System 37
Participants and Forces in a National Marketing System 38
How to Research a National Marketing System 39
☐ INDUSTRY MARKETING SYSTEMS 42
Magazine and Paperback Book Industry Marketing System 43
Paint Industry Marketing System 44
☐ COMPANY MARKETING SYSTEMS 44
The Company 45 *Marketing Channel Firms* 47 *Markets* 49
Competitors 51 *Publics* 52 *Macro-environment* 55
☐ SUMMARY 56
Case 1. Ronco Teleproducts, Inc. 58
Evaluating Products We Could Probably Live Without
Case 2. U.S. Postal Service 60
Analyzing Who Does Marketing Work and Why
Case 3. Great Waters of France, Inc.: Perrier 61
Analyzing a Marketing Success

PART TWO
MARKETING'S ROLE IN THE COMPANY

chapter three

strategic planning and the marketing process
65

☐ THE AGE OF ORGANIZATIONS 67
Types of Organizations 67
☐ ORGANIZATION/ENVIRONMENT ADAPTATION 68
Environmental Change 69 *Opportunity and Threat Analysis* 70
Organizational Response 72
☐ STRATEGIC PLANNING 74
Company Mission 74 *Company Objectives and Goals* 76
Company Growth Strategy 77 *Company Portfolio Plan* 80
☐ MARKETING PROCESS 85
Marketing Opportunity Analysis 85 *Target Market Selection* 86
Marketing Mix Strategy 88
Marketing Management Systems Development 91
☐ SUMMARY 92

chapter four
the marketing planning and control system 97

☐ MARKETING PLANNING 99
Benefits of Planning 99
How Business Planning Evolves in Organizations 100
Steps in the Business- and Marketing-Planning Process 102
The Components of a Marketing Plan 103
Developing the Marketing Budget 109
☐ MARKETING CONTROL 114
Annual Plan Control 115 *Profitability Control* 120
Strategic Control 124
☐ SUMMARY 129

chapter five
the marketing information system 133

☐ THE CONCEPT OF A MARKETING INFORMATION SYSTEM 135
Internal Reports System 136 *Marketing Intelligence System* 138
Marketing Research System 139 *Analytical Marketing System* 142
☐ MARKETING RESEARCH PROCEDURE 143
Research Objectives and Problem Definition 144
Exploratory Research 145 *Formal Survey Research* 146
Experimental Research 149
Data Analysis and Report Presentation 151
☐ MEASUREMENT OF MARKET DEMAND 152
Key Concepts in Market Demand Measurement 152
Methods of Estimating Current Demand 156
☐ MARKET AND SALES FORECASTING 160
Surveys of Buyer Intentions 160
Composites of Sales-Force Opinions 161 *Market-Test Method* 162
Time-Series Analysis 162 *Statistical Demand Analysis* 163
☐ SUMMARY 165

chapter six
the marketing organization 169

☐ THE EVOLUTION OF THE MARKETING DEPARTMENT 172
Simple Sales Department (Stage One) 172
Sales Department with Ancillary Functions (Stage Two) 172
Separate Marketing Department (Stage Three) 173

Modern Marketing Department (Stage Four) 173
Modern Marketing Company (Stage Five) 173
□ WAYS OF ORGANIZING THE MODERN MARKETING DEPARTMENT 174
Functional Organization 174 *Geographical Organization* 175
Product Management Organization 175
Market Management Organization 179
Product Management/Market Management Organization 180
Corporate/Divisional Organization 182
□ MARKETING'S RELATIONS WITH OTHER DEPARTMENTS 182
The Question of Marketing's Importance in the Organization 182
Types of Interdepartmental Conflict 184
Strategies for Building a Companywide Marketing Orientation 186
□ SUMMARY 188
Case 4. The Maytag Company 190
Review of Marketing Strategy for a Growing Product Line
Case 5. The Pillsbury Company: Totino's Pizza 192
Evaluating Strategy for a New Crisp Crust
Case 6. Hanes Corporation: From L'eggs to Faces 195
Adopting vs. Adapting a Successful Plan

PART THREE
TARGET MARKET ANALYSIS

chapter seven
the marketing environment
201

□ DEMOGRAPHIC ENVIRONMENT 204
Worldwide Explosive Population Growth 204
Slowdown in U.S. Birthrate 204 *Aging of U.S. Population* 205
The Changing American Family 205
The Rise of Nonfamily Households 206
Geographical Shifts in Population 206
A Better-educated Populace 207
□ ECONOMIC ENVIRONMENT 209
Slowdown in Real Income Growth 209
Continued Inflationary Pressure 210

Changing Savings and Debt Patterns 210
Changing Consumer Expenditure Patterns 210
□ECOLOGICAL ENVIRONMENT 211
Impending Shortages of Certain Raw Materials 211
Increased Cost of Energy 212 *Increased Levels of Pollution* 212
Increasing Government Intervention in Natural Resource Management 212
□TECHNOLOGICAL ENVIRONMENT 212
Accelerating Pace of Technological Change 213
Unlimited Innovational Opportunities 214 *High R & D Budgets* 215
Concentration on Minor Improvements Rather Than Major Discoveries 216 *Increased Regulation of Technological Change* 216
□POLITICAL ENVIRONMENT 217
Increasing Amount of Legislation Regulating Business 217
More Vigorous Government Agency Enforcement 218
Growth of Public Interest Groups 221
□CULTURAL ENVIRONMENT 222
Core Cultural Values Have High Persistence 222
Each Culture Consists of Subcultures 223
Secondary Cultural Values Undergo Shifts through Time 223
□SUMMARY 226

chapter eight

consumer markets and buying behavior

229

□WHO IS IN THE CONSUMER MARKET? (BUYING POPULATION) 232
□WHAT BUYING DECISIONS DO CONSUMERS MAKE? (BUYING DECISIONS) 233
Three Classes of Buying Situations 234
Major Subdecisions Involved in the Buying Decision 235
□WHO PARTICIPATES IN THE CONSUMER BUYING PROCESS? (BUYING PARTICIPANTS) 237
□WHAT ARE THE MAJOR INFLUENCES ON CONSUMER BUYERS? (BUYING INFLUENCES) 238
Cultural Characteristics 239 *Social Characteristics* 241
Personal Characteristics 243 *Psychological Characteristics* 246
□HOW DO CONSUMERS MAKE THEIR BUYING DECISIONS? (BUYING PROCESS) 252
Problem Recognition 252 *Information Search* 253
Information Evaluation 254 *Purchase Decision* 257
Postpurchase Behavior 258
□SUMMARY 260

chapter nine

organizational markets and buying behavior 265

□ THE PRODUCER MARKET 267

Who Is in the Producer Market? (Buying Population) 267

What Buying Decisions Do Producers Make? (Buying Decisions) 270

Who Participates in the Producer Buying Process? (Buying Participants) 271

What Are the Major Influences on Producer Buyers? (Buying Influences) 272

How Do Producers Make Their Buying Decisions? (Buying Process) 275

□ THE RESELLER MARKET 280

Who Is in the Reseller Market? (Buying Population) 280

What Buying Decisions Do Resellers Make? (Buying Decisions) 280

Who Participates in the Reseller Buying Process? (Buying Participants) 281

What are the Major Influences on Reseller Buyers? (Buying Influences) 282

How Do Resellers Make Their Buying Decisions? (Buying Process) 283

□ THE GOVERNMENT MARKET 284

Who Is in the Government Market? (Buying Population) 284

What Buying Decisions Do Government Buyers Make? (Buying Decisions) 284

Who Participates in the Government Buying Process? (Buying Participants) 284

What Are the Major Influences on Government Buyers? (Buying Influences) 285

How Do Government Buyers Make Their Buying Decisions? (Buying Process) 286

□ SUMMARY 288

chapter ten

market segmentation and targeting 291

□ MARKET SEGMENTATION 294

The General Approach to Segmenting a Market 294

Bases for Segmenting Consumer Markets 296

Bases for Segmenting Industrial Markets 307

Requirements for Effective Segmentation 308

Evaluating the Attractiveness of Different Market Segments 309

□ TARGET MARKETING 309

Undifferentiated Marketing 311 *Differentiated Marketing* 312

Concentrated Marketing 313

Choosing among Market Selection Strategies 314

SUMMARY 314
Case 7. Fotomat Corporation 317
Adjusting to Major Environmental Changes
Case 8. Henry F. Ortlieb Brewing Company 319
Formalizing Marketing in a Small Brewery Serving a Declining Market Segment
Case 9. American Cyanamid, Inc. 324
Analyzing Consumer and Industrial Uses for Chemical Light

PART FOUR MARKETING MIX STRATEGY

chapter eleven new-product development and product life-cycle strategies 329

NEW-PRODUCT DEVELOPMENT STRATEGY 332
Idea Generation 335 *Idea Screening* 338
Concept Development and Testing 339
Marketing Strategy Development 341 *Business Analysis* 341
Product Development 343 *Market Testing* 343
Commercialization 345
PRODUCT LIFE-CYCLE STRATEGIES 347
Introduction Stage 348 *Growth Stage* 350 *Maturity Stage* 351
Decline Stage 352
SUMMARY 355

chapter twelve product, branding, packaging, and service strategy 359

PRODUCT MIX DECISIONS 361
PRODUCT LINE DECISIONS 363
Product Line Length 364 *Line-Stretching Decision* 365
Line-Filling Decision 367 *Line Modernization Decision* 367
Line-Featuring Decision 368
PRODUCT ITEM DECISIONS 368
Core, Tangible, and Augmented Product 368
Classification of Goods 369

☐ BRAND DECISIONS 374
Branding Decision 374 *Brand Sponsor Decision 377*
Brand Quality Decision 380 *Family Brand Decision 381*
Brand Extension Decision 382 *Multibrand Decision 382*
Brand Repositioning Decision 382
☐ PACKAGING DECISIONS 384
☐ SERVICE DECISIONS 387
The Service Elements Decision 387 *The Service Level Decision 388*
The Service Form Decision 389
The Customer Service Department 390
☐ SUMMARY 390

chapter thirteen

pricing strategy 395

☐ SETTING PRICE 399
Target Market Objectives 399 *Marketing Mix Strategy 401*
Pricing Policies and Constraints 402 *Pricing Strategy 402*
Pricing Tactics 409
☐ INITIATING PRICE CHANGES 412
Initiating Price Cuts 412 *Initiating Price Increases 412*
Buyers' Reactions to Price Changes 413
Competitors' Reactions to Price Changes 414
☐ RESPONDING TO PRICE CHANGES 414
☐ PRICING THE PRODUCT LINE 416
☐ SUMMARY 417

chapter fourteen

marketing channel and physical-distribution strategy 421

☐ THE NATURE OF MARKETING CHANNELS 423
Why Are Marketing Intermediaries Used? 424
Marketing-Channel Functions 425 *Number of Channel Levels 426*
Types of Channel Flows 427 *Channels in the Service Sector 427*
Growth of Vertical Marketing Systems 429
Growth of Horizontal Marketing Systems 432
Growth of Multichannel Marketing Systems 432
Roles of Individual Firms in a Channel 433
Channel Cooperation, Conflict, and Competition 433
☐ CHANNEL-DESIGN DECISIONS 434
Identifying the Major Channel Alternatives 435
Evaluating the Major Channel Alternatives 437

☐CHANNEL-MANAGEMENT DECISIONS 439
Selecting Channel Members 439 *Motivating Channel Members* 440
Evaluating Channel Members 441
☐CHANNEL-MODIFICATION DECISIONS 441
Adding or Dropping Individual Channel Members 442
Adding or Dropping Particular Marketing Channels 422
Modifying the Whole Channel 442
☐PHYSICAL-DISTRIBUTION DECISIONS 442
Nature of Physical Distribution 443
The Physical-Distribution Objective 445 *Order Processing* 446
Warehousing 447 *Inventory* 448 *Transportation* 449
Organizational Responsibility for Physical Distribution 451
☐SUMMARY 452

chapter fifteen

retailing and wholesaling strategy 455

☐RETAILING 458
Nature and Importance of Retailing 458 *Types of Retailers* 459
Retailer Marketing Decisions 480 *The Future of Retailing* 483
☐WHOLESALING 484
Nature and Importance of Wholesaling 484
Types of Wholesalers 486 *Wholesaler Marketing Decisions* 490
The Future of Wholesaling 492
☐SUMMARY 493

chapter sixteen

marketing communications strategy 497

☐STEPS IN DEVELOPING EFFECTIVE COMMUNICATIONS 501
Identifying the Target Audience 502
Clarifying the Response Sought 502 *Choosing a Message* 504
Choosing Media 506 *Selecting Source Attributes* 507
Collecting Feedback 507
☐SETTING THE TOTAL PROMOTIONAL BUDGET AND MIX 508
Establishing the Total Promotional Budget 508
Establishing the Promotional Mix 509
Responsibility for Marketing Communications Planning 514
☐SUMMARY 514

chapter seventeen

advertising, sales promotion, and publicity strategy 517

□ ADVERTISING 519

Major Decisions in Advertising 524 *Objectives Setting* 524
Budget Decision 527 *Message Decision* 530
Media Decision 533 *Campaign Evaluation* 538

□ SALES PROMOTION 541

Major Decisions in Sales Promotion 543
Establishing the Sales Promotion Objectives 543
Selecting the Sales Promotion Tools 544
Developing the Sales Promotion Program 546
Pretesting the Sales Promotion Program 548
Implementing and Controlling the Sales Promotion Program 548
Evaluating the Sales Promotion Results 548

□ PUBLICITY 549

Major Decisions in Publicity 522
Establishing the Publicity Objectives 552
Choosing the Publicity Messages and Vehicles 552
Implementing the Publicity Plan 554
Evaluating the Publicity Results 554

□ SUMMARY 556

chapter eighteen

personal selling and sales management strategy 561

□ ESTABLISHING SALES-FORCE OBJECTIVES 566

□ DESIGNING SALES-FORCE STRATEGY, STRUCTURE, SIZE, AND COMPENSATION 567

Sales-Force Strategy 567 *Sales-Force Structure* 568
Sales-Force Size 570 *Sales-Force Compensation* 570

□ RECRUITING AND SELECTING SALES REPRESENTATIVES 572

Importance of Careful Selection 572
What Makes a Good Sales Representative? 572
Recruitment Procedures 573 *Applicant-Rating Procedures* 573

□ TRAINING SALES REPRESENTATIVES 574

Principles of Salesmanship 575

□ SUPERVISING SALES REPRESENTATIVES 579

Directing Sales Representatives 579
Motivating Sales Representatives 582

□ EVALUATING SALES REPRESENTATIVES 583

Sources of Information 583 *Formal Evaluation of Performance* 584

□ SUMMARY 587

Case 10. King-Cola Corp. 589

Evaluating a Marketing Plan for a New Cola Beverage from Various Points of View
Case 11. Loctite Corporation 591
Identifying and Developing New Consumer and Industrial Markets for a Small Speciality Chemical Company's "Wonder Glues"
Case 12. Texas Instruments Incorporated: Consumer Products Group 593
Developing a Marketing Plan for Low-Priced Learning Aid Products

PART FIVE
MARKETING'S ROLE IN SOCIETY

chapter nineteen
international marketing
599

□ APPRAISING THE INTERNATIONAL MARKETING ENVIRONMENT 603
The International Trade System 603 *Economic Environment* 604
Political-Legal Environment 605 *Cultural Environment* 606
□ DECIDING WHETHER TO GO ABROAD 606
□ DECIDING WHICH MARKETS TO ENTER 607
□ DECIDING HOW TO ENTER THE MARKET 608
Export 608 *Joint Venturing* 610 *Direct Investment* 611
□ DECIDING ON THE MARKETING PROGRAM 612
Product 612 *Promotion* 613 *Price* 614
Distribution Channels 614
□ DECIDING ON THE MARKETING ORGANIZATION 616
Export Department 616 *International Division* 616
Multinational Organization 617
□ SUMMARY 617

chapter twenty
marketing of services, organizations, persons, places, and ideas
621

□ SERVICES MARKETING 623
Nature and Characteristics of a Service 624
Classification of Services 626

The Extent and Importance of Marketing in the Service Sector 627
Marketing Mix Decisions for Service Firms 628
□ ORGANIZATION MARKETING 630
Image Assessment 631 *Image Choice* 632
Image Planning and Control 633
□ PERSON MARKETING 634
Celebrity Marketing 634 *Political Candidate Marketing* 635
Personal Marketing 636
□ PLACE MARKETING 638
Domicile Marketing 638 *Business Site Marketing* 638
Land Investment Marketing 638 *Vacation Marketing* 639
Nation Marketing 639
□ IDEA MARKETING 639
□ SUMMARY 642

chapter twenty-one
marketing and society
647

□ SOCIAL CRITICISMS OF MARKETING 649
Marketing's Impact on Individual Consumer Welfare 649
Marketing's Impact on Society-as-a-Whole 656
Marketing's Impact on Other Businesses 659
□ CITIZEN ACTIONS TO REGULATE MARKETING 660
Consumerism 660 *Environmentalism* 662
□ PUBLIC ACTIONS TO REGULATE MARKETING 663
□ BUSINESS ACTIONS TOWARD SOCIALLY RESPONSIBLE MARKETING 664
A Concept of Enlightened Marketing 666 *Marketing Ethics* 669
□ PRINCIPLES FOR FUTURE PUBLIC POLICY TOWARD MARKETING 672
The Principle of Consumer and Producer Freedom 672
The Principle of Curbing Potential Harm 673
The Principle of Meeting Basic Needs 674
The Principle of Economic Efficiency 675
The Principle of Innovation 675
The Principle of Consumer Education and Information 676
The Principle of Consumer Protection 677
□ SUMMARY 677
Case 13. STP Corporation 680
Evaluating Domestic and International Marketing Activities in a Changing Environment
Case 14. John Drew, Attorney 682
Mass Merchandising a Professional Service to Consumers
Case 15. Consumers Union of the United States, Inc. 683
Reappraisal of a Nonprofit Organization's Efforts to Serve Consumers and Retain Credibility

appendix 1 marketing arithmetic A1

appendix 2 a career in marketing? A7

glossary

index

PREFACE

Marketing is an old subject and a new subject. Its roots go back to the first appearance of trade among people. Before trade or exchange, people obtained what they needed either by producing it themselves, taking it away forcefully from others, or begging for it. The emergence of trade allowed people to specialize in producing particular goods and services and exchange them in markets for other goods they needed.

Marketing is a new subject in the sense that the formal study of the forces and conditions that make for successful exchange became an organized academic discipline only in the twentieth century. Before this century, scattered writings could be found on selling, advertising, pricing, product design, packaging, branding, physical distribution—but they were neither treated in an integrated way nor scientifically developed. It is only in the last seventy years that various scholars and practitioners have attempted to put together a formal science of marketing.

Marketing consists of a set of principles for choosing target markets, measuring their needs, developing want-satisfying products and services, and delivering them at a value to the customer and a profit to the company. Many of the most successful companies in the world owe their success to practicing a thoroughgoing marketing orientation. McDonald's owes its success to meeting people's needs for fast food service; Kodak to meeting their needs for inexpensive reliable cameras; and Avon to meeting their needs for personal advice on cosmetics. Enterprises such as Procter & Gamble, Gillette, Revlon, General Foods, Sears, IBM, Caterpillar—are exemplary practitioners of the marketing concept. They see consumer problems as company opportunities.

A major surprise that students experience in studying marketing is how universally applicable it is. Marketing is relevant not only to economic institutions such as manufacturing companies, wholesalers, and retailers, but to every organization "that has something to sell." Lawyers, accountants, and management consultants are increasingly using marketing ideas to expand their practices. Colleges, hospitals, museums, and performing arts groups are turning to marketing in the face of low or declining demand for their services. No politician can get the required votes, and no resort area can get the needed tourists, without developing and carrying out marketing plans. And students, when they enter the job market, must do "marketing research" to determine the best opportunities and the best way to "market themselves" to prospective employers. Students report that their study of marketing is an "eyeopener" and they see familiar things in an entirely new and challenging way.

major features of this book

More students than ever before are studying marketing. It therefore should come as no surprise that many different textbooks (brands) are available. Each textbook bears the imprint of the author's particular mindset, style, and enthusiasm for the subject. This text is built on five principles:

COMPREHENSIVE

The student's first exposure to marketing should present the subject primarily in its breadth. This book covers the major marketing topics of interest to marketing students and practitioners. Readers will read about the *major institutions* that are involved in the marketing process—manufacturers, wholesalers, retailers, advertising agencies, marketing research firms, banks, shippers, storage warehouses, and many others. Readers will also examine the *major tools* used by modern marketers—product design, packaging, branding, ancillary services, pricing, advertising, sales promotion, publicity, and personal selling. Finally, readers will examine the *major environmental forces* affecting the marketing process—demographics, economics, ecology, technology, politics, and culture.

SYSTEMATIC

Marketing can easily become overwhelming in its multitude of topics, concepts, theories, and examples. The great need is to present this abundant material in a systematic framework so that readers know where they have been, where they are, and where they are going in the subject. This text utilizes a five part structure. Part I introduces the reader to *marketing's role in the economy.* It explains how marketing is the link between consumer needs and industrial activity, how marketing systems are organized on the national, industry, and company levels, and how marketing practices affect society and are in turn affected by society. Part II introduces *marketing's role in the company.* Marketing contributes critically to the company's growth strategy and is supported by certain planning, information, and organizational structures. Part III introduces the first major step in company marketing planning, namely *target market analysis.* This consists of analyzing the opportunities and threats in the environment, the dynamics of buying behavior in consumer and industrial markets, the segmentation of markets, and the choice of target market segments to serve. Part IV examines the second major step in company marketing planning, namely *marketing mix strategy.* The various chapters in this Part discuss new product development, product life cycle strategies, product design, branding, packaging, service, pricing, distribution, advertising, sales promotion, publicity, and personal selling. Finally, Part V returns to examining *broader marketing issues,* specifically the role of international marketing, the role of nonprofit marketing, and the various controversies surrounding marketing that have led to citizen action, public regulation, and constructive marketing responses by business.

SCIENTIFIC

To the extent possible, this text presents concepts, generalizations, and theories of marketing that are supported by scientific research and evidence. Marketing is treated as an applied science built on the foundations of *economic science, behavioral science, and modern management theory.* Economic science reminds us that marketing involves the use of scarce resources to satisfy competing ends and therefore these resources must be allocated carefully. Behavioral science reminds us that marketing is about people—people who make up markets and who run organizations—and it is essential to understand their needs, motivations, attitudes, and behavior. Finally, management theory reminds us that our approach has the practical purpose of answering how people and organizations can best achieve the marketing objectives they set for themselves.

PRACTICAL

Every marketing situation is unique. The decision maker has to know how to analyze a marketing problem and apply the relevant marketing theory to solve it. This book describes numerous situations in which well-known, as well as little-known, companies applied marketing to solve the marketing problems they were facing—whether there was too little demand for their products or services, the wrong kind of demand, or even too much demand. The situations are illustrated in indented examples running through the text, in special exhibits appearing in boxes, and in longer case studies. They illustrate marketing problems faced by actual companies and the actions taken by these companies to solve their problems.

LIVELY

A book has to be lively or else it cheats the reader. It must not read like a telephone book or an encyclopedia. Marketing is a fascinating subject and the author must be able to communicate enthusiasm for the subject. Almost every chapter starts with a vignette about a company involved in a particular marketing problem that will be discussed in the chapter. Throughout the chapter, important points are illustrated by timely and interesting examples.

Thus the author's intention in writing this book is to present marketing in a comprehensive, systematic, scientific, practical, and lively manner. Whether the intention has been achieved will be determined by the market—how satisfied the users are, and how much use they can make of its ideas.

pedagogical aids

This book employs the latest pedagogical aids to facilitate its use by students and teachers. The main ones are:

1. *Opening Vignettes.* Each chapter opens with a vignette to engage the reader's interest and attention.

2. *Major Chapter Issues.* Following the vignette, each chapter describes the major issues that will be examined in the chapter.
3. *Figures and Tables.* Important points in each chapter are abundantly illustrated with strong visual materials.
4. *Boxed Exhibits.* Some material of unusual interest is set off in specially boxed exhibits.
5. *Summary.* Each chapter ends with a summary that outlines the chapter's major contents.
6. *Review Questions.* Each chapter summary is followed by a list of questions that review the major points made in the chapter.
7. *Case Studies.* The text includes 15 cases for class and/or written discussion. They challenge the reader to apply marketing thinking to actual situations. The cases are grouped at the end of each major part and deal with the issues raised in that part of the book.
8. *Appendixes.* The book contains two appendixes of practical interest, one on *marketing arithmetic* and the other on *marketing careers.*
9. *Glossary.* The book contains an extensive glossary of terms for quick reference.
10. *Indexes.* The book contains author and subject indexes to facilitate finding information.
11. *Supplements.* A Study Guide is available to the student who wishes to review and apply major concepts, principles, and theories of marketing. A separate Instructor's Manual is available to the instructor along with a Test Item Bank and a set of Transparency Masters.

acknowledgments

A textbook, although seeming to be an individual product, is really a team product. It owes its existence to many dedicated people. A great debt is owed to the pioneers of marketing who first raised the field's major issues, clarified marketing's purpose and scope, and contributed major ideas to its development. *Any textbook writer stands on the shoulders of giants.*

The team also includes the author's immediate colleagues at Northwestern University who are a constant source of new ideas and critical insights: Bobby Calder, Richard Clewett, John Hauser, Sidney J. Levy, Louis W. Stern, Brian Sternthal, Alice Tybout, and Andris Zoltners. Thanks also go to my Dean and long time friend, Donald P. Jacobs, for his generous support of my research and writing efforts.

Believing that all new products should be pre-tested, my publishers arranged a "focus group" meeting with several fine teacher-scholars to review the manuscript. They dissected the book chapter by chapter and excellent suggestions came through which influenced the substance and styling of the book. Here I want to acknowledge the fine contributions of Peter D. Bennett (Pennsylvania State University), Robert Drezs (University of Notre Dame), Bernard Katz (Oakton Community College), Patrick E. Murphy (Marquette University), and Albert L. Page (University of Illinois—Circle Campus). In addition, several colleagues elsewhere wrote helpful reviews of the manuscript as it progressed: William Bell (California State Fullerton), Peter Bennett (Penn State University), Bixby Cooper (Michigan State University), Robert Drezs (University of Notre Dame),

Ronald E. Frank (University of Pennsylvania), Edward Hackelman (University of Connecticut), James Hansz (Lehigh University), Frank Houston (Temple University), Arun Jain (Sony, Buffalo), Bernie Katz (Oakton Community College), Thomas Kinnear (University of Michigan), Don Kirchner, L. Lee Manzer (Oklahoma State University), Patrick Murphy (Marquette University), Al Paige (University of Illinois, Chicago Circle), James Petersen (California State Polytechnic), Neil Schiffler (Bucknell University), and William Zeigler (Seton Hall University).

I want to single out two marketing scholars who contributed specific material to this book. Professor Richard Clewett, my distinguished colleague at Northwestern University, prepared the cases for this book, drawing on his vast experience in case teaching and writing. The cases are timely, lively, and challenging. Professor Patrick E. Murphy (Marquette University), with whom I share common research interests in public and nonprofit marketing, wrote the appendixes on Marketing Arithmetic and Marketing Careers, as well as end-of-the-chapter questions.

I had the good fortune to benefit from the research assistance of four able Ph.D. students at Northwestern University, namely Amy Seidel Marks, John Martin, Elias G. Rizkallah, and Ravi Singh, and an M.B.A. student, Robert Philiotis.

A book is not a book without a publishing company. And the company that I most enjoy working with—and have since 1967—is Prentice Hall. They are the "publishing professionals." John Connolly, my editor, deserves the strongest praise for inspiring the book to be written and orchestrating the complex resources needed for its production. I also want to acknowledge the fine editorial work of Linda Stewart, college production editor and the creative graphic design of Linda Conway, assistant art director.

Thanks are also due to my supportive secretaries at Northwestern University who helped me successfully meet each deadline, Marion Davis and Phyllis T. Van Hooser.

My family deserves the greatest thanks for their complete support during the writing of this book. My gratitude goes to my loving and beautiful wife Nancy and our three wonderful daughters, Amy, Melissa, and Jessica.

dedication

One other group—my students—made a great contribution to my development in the field of marketing. I most happily dedicate this book *to my many past students who have also been my teachers, and to my future students.*

PART 1

marketing's role in the economy

MARKETING AND HUMAN NEEDS

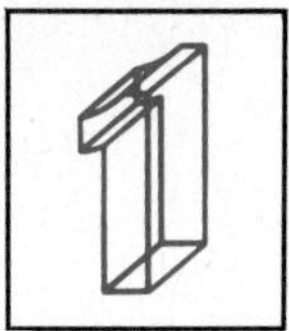

Marketing touches all of us every day of our lives. We wake up in the morning to a Sears radio alarm clock, which begins to play a Barbra Streisand song followed by a commercial advertising a United Airlines vacation flight to Hawaii. We move to the bathroom where we brush our teeth with Colgate, shave with Gillette, gargle with Listerine, spray our hair with Revlon, and use various other toiletries and appliances produced by manufacturers around the world. We put on our Calvin Klein jeans and shirt and Bass shoes. We enter the kitchen and pour some Minute Maid orange juice, and prepare a bowl made up of Kellogg's Rice Krispies and a sliced Chiquita banana in Borden milk. After this, we drink one or two cups of Maxwell House coffee with two teaspoons of Domino sugar accompanied by a slice of Sara Lee coffee cake. We are the personal beneficiaries of oranges grown in California, coffee imported from Brazil, a newspaper made of Canadian wood pulp, and radio news coming from as far away as Australia. All of these goods ended up in our homes. The marketing system has made all this possible without effort on our part. It has designed and delivered to us a standard of living.

☐In starting our discussion of marketing, we should recognize that marketing means different things to different people, affects everyone, and is highly controversial.

Marketing Has Different Meanings

What does the term *marketing* mean? This question was recently put to three hundred educational administrators whose colleges were in trouble because of declining enrollments, spiraling costs, and rising tuition.[1] Sixty-one percent said that they saw marketing as a combination of *selling, advertising,* and *public relations.* Another 28 percent said that it was only one of these three activities. Only a small percentage suggested that marketing had something to do with *needs assessment, marketing research, product development, pricing,* and *distribution.* Most people think of marketing as being synonymous with selling and promotion.

No wonder. Americans are bombarded with television commercials, unsolicited mail advertisements, newspaper ads, and sales calls. Someone is always trying to sell us something. It seems that we cannot escape death, taxes, or selling.

Therefore it may come as a surprise to many people that the most important part of marketing is not selling! Selling is only the tip of the marketing iceberg. It is only one of several functions that marketers perform, and often not the most important one. If the marketer does a good job of identifying consumer needs, developing appropriate products, and pricing, distributing, and promoting them effectively, these goods will sell very easily. The amount of promotion and hard selling will not have to be intense.

Everyone knows about "hot" products to which consumers flock in droves. When Ford designed the first Mustang, when Eastman Kodak designed its instamatic camera, and when Mazda introduced its RX-7 sports car, these manufacturers were swamped with orders because they had designed the "right" product. Not me-too products, but distinct offers that outshone the others.

Peter Drucker, one of the leading management theorists, puts it this way:

- The aim of marketing is to make selling superfluous.[2]

This is not to say that selling and promotion are unimportant, but rather that they are part of a larger "marketing mix" or set of marketing tools that must be finely orchestrated for maximum impact on the marketplace.

Marketing Affects Everyone

Marketing affects everyone. It affects the buyer, the seller, and the citizen. This is illustrated in the following examples.

The buyer. John Smith, a college student, wants to buy stereo equipment and he therefore visits a large stereo retail outlet. He sees many stereo components. As he examines them, the following questions come to his mind:

- Is the brand selection wide enough?
- Is there a brand that has the features I want?
- Is the price fair?
- Is the salesperson helpful, pleasant, and honest?
- Is the service good and is there a warranty?

John Smith and other buyers want the marketplace to provide good-quality products at reasonable prices at convenient locations. The kind of marketing system found in an economy will make a great difference to people's satisfaction as buyers and consumers.

The seller. Bill Thompson is the marketing manager in a company that manufactures stereo equipment. To do his job well, he must decide on a number of issues:

- What do consumers want in stereo equipment?
- Which consumer groups and needs should my company try to satisfy?
- How should the product be designed and priced?
- What guarantees and service should we offer?
- What types of middlemen should we use?
- What types of advertising, personal selling, promotion, and publicity would be cost-effective in selling this product?

Thus the seller faces a whole set of challenges in trying to develop an attractive offer for the market. The market is very demanding. The seller must apply the most modern marketing tools available to arrive at an offer that attracts and satisfies customers.

The citizen. Jane Adams, a state senator, has a special interest in business's performance in the marketplace. As a citizen and legislator, she is concerned with the following questions:

- Are manufacturers making safe and reliable products?
- Are they describing their products accurately in their ads and packaging?
- Is competition working in this market to keep quality high and prices low?
- Are the retailers and service people behaving fairly toward consumers?
- Are the manufacturing or packaging activities hurting the environment?

Jane Adams spends her time acting as a watchdog of consumer interests and trying to improve consumer education, information, and protection. The marketing system has a major impact on the lives of U.S. citizens, and they and their representatives will want to make it work as well as possible.

Marketing Is Controversial

Marketing affects so many people in so many ways that it is inevitably controversial. There are persons who intensely dislike modern marketing activity, charging it with doing such things as ruining the environment, bombarding the public with inane ads, creating unnecessary wants, teaching greed to youngsters, and committing several other sins. Consider the following charges:

- For the past 6,000 years the field of marketing has been thought of as made up of fast-buck artists, con-men, wheeler-dealers, and shoddy-goods distributors. Too many of us have been "taken" by the tout or con-men; and all of us at times have been prodded into buying all sorts of "things" we really did not need, and which we found later on we did not even want.[3]
- What does a man need—really need? A few pounds of food each day, heat and shelter, six feet to lie down in—and some form of working activity that will yield a sense of accomplishment. That's all—in a material sense. And we know it. But we are brainwashed by our economic system until we end up in a tomb beneath a pyramid of time payments, mortgages, preposterous gadgetry, playthings that divert our attention from the sheer idiocy of the charade.[4]

There are others, however, who vigorously defend marketing as being society's savior. Consider the following:

- Aggressive marketing policies and practices have been largely responsible for the high material standard of living in America. Today through mass, low-cost marketing we enjoy products which once were considered luxuries, and which still are so classified in many foreign countries.[5]
- Advertising nourishes the consuming power of men. It creates wants for a better standard of living. It sets up before a man the goal of a better home, better clothing, better food for himself and his family. It spurs individual exertion and greater production. It brings together in fertile union those things which otherwise would not have met.[6]

It is clear that various social commentators have vastly different views on the meaning and contribution of marketing. We will consider these issues later in the book after we have gained a deeper understanding of how marketing works. We will largely deal with marketing from the seller's point of view, since the seller is trying to put together marketing programs that are profitable and that create value for the consumers. At the same time, no seller can make long-run profits without taking the buyers' and citizens' point of view into account. In fact, the major ideological breakthrough in the last thirty years has been the recognition that sellers not only must take the buyers' wants into account but must start with them.

What is now happening is that business is going through another learning phase and is discovering that it must also take the citizens' interests into account. Marketing, at its highest level of practice, is a balanced serving of the combined interests of *sellers, buyers,* and *citizens.* This book is oriented toward helping sellers see the importance of formulating and carrying out marketing practices that are grounded in consumer and citizen interests as well as self-interest. It is not only a matter of doing what is right but also a matter of ensuring business's long-run profitability and survival in an increasingly competitive and turbulent marketplace.

the rapid adoption of marketing

Most people think marketing is something practiced only by large companies in highly capitalistic countries, companies like Procter & Gamble, IBM, Eastman Kodak, McDonald's, Gillette, and Coca-Cola. The fact is that marketing is spreading rapidly, both within and outside the business sector.

In the Business Sector

In the business sector, marketing entered into the consciousness of different industries at different times. A few companies, such as General Electric, General Motors, Sears, and Procter & Gamble, saw its potentialities almost immediately. Marketing spread most rapidly in consumer packaged goods companies, consumer durables companies, and industrial equipment companies—in that order. Industrial commodity companies—steel, chemicals, paper—came later to marketing consciousness, and many still have a long way to go. Within the last decade consumer service firms—especially airlines and banks—have opened themselves to marketing. Airlines began to study travelers' attitudes toward different features of their service—schedule frequency, baggage handling, in-flight service, friendliness, seat comfort. Soon afterward they shed the notion they were in the air carrier business and finally began to operate as if they were in the total travel business. Bankers initially showed great resistance to marketing, but in the end they embraced it enthusiastically. Marketing has begun to attract the interest of the insurance and stock brokerage companies, although it is still poorly understood in these industries.

The most recent business groups encountering marketing have been the professional service providers, such as lawyers, accountants, and physicians. Although various professional societies have generally prohibited their members from engaging in price competition, client solicitation, and advertising, the U.S.

antitrust division has recently called these restraints illegal. Accountants, lawyers, and some other professional groups are now allowed to advertise and to compete on price.

- The fierce competition engendered by the new limits on corporate growth is forcing accounting firms into aggressive new postures. . . . The accountants insist on referring to their efforts to drum up business as "practice development." But many of the activities that fall under this euphemism are dead ringers for what is called "marketing" in other fields. . . . Accountants speak of "positioning" their firms and of "penetrating" unexploited new industries. They compile "hit lists" of prospective clients and then "surround" them by placing their firms' partners in close social contact with the top executives of the target companies.[7]

In the International Sector

Marketing is practiced not only in the United States but in the rest of the world. In fact, several European and Japanese multinationals—companies like Nestlé, Siemens, Toyota Motor, Hitachi—have in many cases outperformed their marketing counterparts in the United States.[8] Multinationals, in general, have been a force that is introducing and spreading modern marketing practices throughout the world. As a result, management in smaller companies is beginning to ask: What is marketing? How does it differ from plain selling? How can we introduce marketing into the firm? Will it make a difference?

In socialist countries such as the USSR and those of Eastern Europe, marketing has traditionally had a bad name. However, various functions of marketing, such as marketing research, branding, advertising, and sales promotion, are now spreading rapidly. In the USSR, for example, there are now over one hundred state-operated advertising agencies and marketing research firms.[9] Several companies in Poland and Hungary have marketing departments, and several socialist universities teach marketing.

In the Nonprofit Sector

Marketing's most recent entry has been in the nonprofit sector of the economy. Such diverse organizations as colleges, hospitals, police departments, museums, and symphonies are currently taking a look at marketing. Consider the following developments:

- More than 170 private colleges have closed their doors since 1965, unable to get either enough students or funds or both. Tuition at the top private universities is now over $6,000. If college costs continue to climb at the current rate, the parents of a child born today will have to put aside $82,830 to enable that child to obtain a bachelor's degree at one of the top private colleges.[10]
- Hospital costs continue to soar, leading to daily room rates of $300 or more in some large hospitals. Many hospitals are experiencing underutilization, particularly in the maternity and pediatrics sections. Some experts have predicted the closing of 1,400–1,500 hospitals in the next ten years.
- The Catholic Church drew as many as 55 percent of all adult Catholics under thirty years of age to church in a typical week in 1966. By 1975 the figure had fallen to 39 percent, and further declines in weekly attendance were expected.
- Many performance groups cannot attract large enough audiences. Even those that have seasonal sellouts, such as the Lyric Opera Company of Chicago, face huge operating deficits at the end of the year.

- Many non-profit organizations that flourished in earlier years—the YMCA, Salvation Army, Girl Scouts, and Women's Christian Temperance Union—are now reexamining their mission in an effort to reverse membership declines.

These organizations all have marketplace problems. Their administrators are struggling to keep them alive in the face of rapidly changing client attitudes and diminishing financial resources. Many of these institutions have turned to marketing as a possible answer to their problems. As a sign of the times, the Evanston Hospital of Evanston, Illinois, recently appointed a vice-president of marketing and was the first hospital in the world to do so.

In addition, U.S. government agencies are showing an increasing interest in marketing. The U.S. Postal Service and Amtrak have developed marketing plans for their respective operations. The U.S. Army has a marketing plan to attract recruits and is one of the top advertising spenders in the country. Other government agencies are becoming involved in marketing energy conservation, anti-smoking, and other public causes.

what is marketing?

We have said many things about marketing without defining it. Marketing has been defined in a number of ways. The American Marketing Association's official definition of marketing is:

- Marketing is the performance of business activities that direct the flow of goods and services from producer to consumer or user.[11]

This definition, unfortunately, makes marketing sound largely like a distribution activity. It fails to indicate marketing's role in determining what goods are to be produced. It does not indicate the specific business activities constituting marketing.

Another way to describe marketing is as follows:

- Marketing is getting the right goods and services to the right people at the right place at the right time at the right price with the right communication and promotion.

This definition supplies an idea of the specific activities that marketers carry out. However, it fails to define marketing activity broadly enough in that other things besides goods and services can be marketed. Furthermore, it defines marketing as a business firm process rather than a social process.

Here is a very thought-provoking definition of marketing:

- Marketing is the creation and delivery of a standard of living.[12]

In contrast to the previous definitions, this definition takes a macro or social view of marketing. However, it does not reveal the fundamental and universal nature of marketing.

We would like to propose the following definition of marketing:

- **Marketing** is human activity directed at satisfying needs and wants through exchange processes.

To understand this definition, we have to define the following more basic concepts: *needs, wants, demands, products, exchange, transactions,* and *markets.*

Needs The most fundamental concept underlying marketing is that of *needs.* Inanimate objects do not have needs, but living matter does. Plants require water and sunlight to survive. Animals require air, water, and food to survive. Higher animals have emotional as well as biological needs. We define *human need* as follows:

- A **human need** is a state of felt deprivation in a person.

Human needs are plentiful and complex. They include basic physiological needs for food, clothing, warmth, and safety; social needs for belongingness, influence, and affection; and individual needs for knowledge and self-expression. These needs are not created by Madison Avenue but are a basic part of human makeup.

When a need is not satisfied the person is unhappy, this being greater the more intense and central the need. An unhappy person will do one of two things—undertake steps to obtain an object that will satisfy the need or try to extinguish the desire. That is, need reduction can occur in two ways:

$$\text{Need reduction} = \frac{\text{Obtaining desired goods or services}}{\text{Extinguishing the desire}}$$

People in Western industrial societies tend to follow the numerator; they manage their needs by trying to find objects that will satisfy them. People in Eastern societies, however, have traditionally followed the denominator; they try to eliminate or reduce their needs whenever possible.

Wants *Human wants* are the expression of human needs as they are shaped by a person's culture and individual development. Suppose someone is hungry. If that person lives in Bali, the need is expressed as a want or desire for mangoes, suckling pig, and beans. If that person lives in the United States, the same need may express itself as a want for a hamburger, French fries, and a coke. Wants always have a reference to culturally defined objects that will satisfy the need. Within the same culture, there will be some variation in individual wants because of individual life experiences and tastes.

As a society becomes more complex, the wants of that society's members expand. First, its members are exposed to more objects, some of which pique their curiosity, interest, and desire. Second, producers undertake specific actions to build desire for the things they produce. The surest way to do this is to try to form a connection between a given object and people's preexisting needs. The object is promoted as a satisfier of one or more particular needs. The marketer does not create the need; it is there. If marketers are successful, however, they can create a want.

Sellers often confuse wants and needs. A manufacturer of drill bits may think that the customer needs a drill bit, but what the customer really needs is a hole. In this sense, there are no products; there are only services performed by products. If another product comes along and can provide the service better or cheaper, the customer will have a new want but the same need. Manufacturers who focus only on existing wants and fail to recognize the need structure underlying these wants are in danger of one day waking up to no demand. They suffer from "marketing myopia."[13] These sellers are so enamored of their products that they lose sight of the customers' needs. They forget that a physical object is a tool to solve a consumer problem.

Demands

People have numerous wants, many of which they cannot satisfy. Every person has a finite set of resources (income, savings, time, energy) and must make choices of what things are affordable and will make him or her feel better off. A want becomes a *demand* when the person is *able* and *willing* to buy the object he or she desires.

It is very easy to list the demands that are found in a given society at a given point in time. In the late 1970s for example, 200 million Americans purchased 67 billion eggs, 250 million chickens, 5 million hair dryers, 133 billion domestic air travel passenger miles, and over 20 million lectures by college English professors. These consumer goods and services led to a derived demand for more than 150 million tons of steel, 4 billion tons of cotton, and many other producer goods. These are a few of the demands that get expressed in a $1.3 trillion economy.

A society could plan next year's production by using this year's mix of demand. The USSR and other centrally planned economies plan production on this basis. Demands, however, are not that reliable. People get tired of some things they are currently consuming; they seek variety for its own sake; and they make new choices in response to changing prices and incomes. Kelvin Lancaster has pointed out that products are really bundles of attributes and people choose the products that give them the best bundle of things they are seeking.[14] Thus a Volkswagen represents a benefit bundle of basic transportation, low purchase price, fuel economy, and European ride; and a Cadillac represents a benefit bundle of high comfort, luxury, and status. The automobile that a person chooses is the one that packages the best bundle of attributes for the money that he or she is willing to spend.

Products

The existence of human needs, wants, and demands implies the concept of products. We define *product* as follows:

- A **product** is something that is viewed as being capable of satisfying a need or want.

Suppose a woman feels a need to enhance her appearance. What products are available? Let us call all the products that are capable of satisfying a certain need the *product choice set.* This product set includes cosmetics, new clothes, a

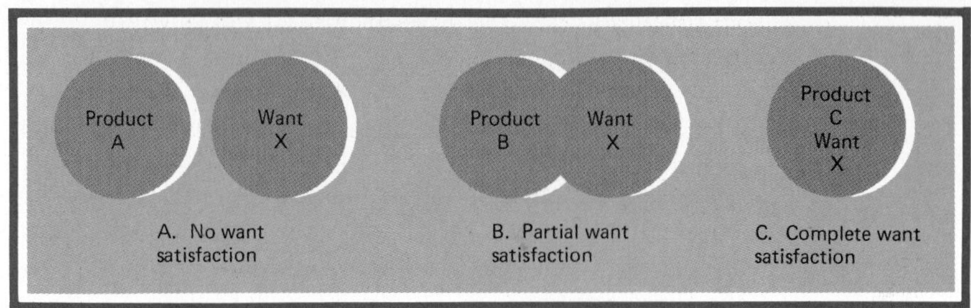

Figure 1-1
Three Degrees of Want Satisfaction

Florida vacation, a beautician's services, plastic surgery, and so forth. These products are all competitive but are not all equally desirable. The more accessible product satisfiers such as cosmetics, clothing, and a new haircut are more likely to be purchased first.

Another way to indicate this is to represent any specific product as a circle and ask how much it would satisfy the person's want also represented as a circle. Figure 1-1A shows that product A has no want-satisfying ability relative to the person's want X. Figure 1-1B shows that product B has partial want-satisfying ability (it may be minimal or substantial). Figure 1-1C shows that product C has virtually complete want-satisfying ability. Product C would be called an *ideal product.*

The concept of an ideal product can be made more rigorous. Suppose the product is vanilla ice cream. We choose a set of important product attributes—say, "creaminess" and "sweetness"—and ask the consumer how much of each attribute he or she would ideally want. Suppose the consumer's answer is represented by "ideal" in Figure 1-2. Now the consumer is asked to taste various existing brands of vanilla ice cream and describe their respective levels of creaminess and sweetness. These are also represented by points in Figure 1-2. Suppose we had to predict which brand of ice cream the consumer would buy. We would predict brand B because it comes closer than the other brands to "packaging" the ideal levels of the two attributes the consumer wants. We are assuming that price and the other attributes of ice cream are not important to the consumer. We are

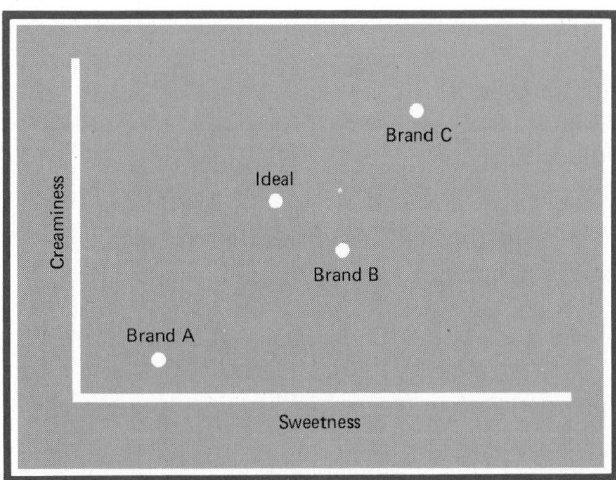

Figure 1-2
Vanilla Ice-Cream Brands in a Brand Space Made Up of Creaminess and Sweetness

also assuming that purchase situation factors do not alter this consumer's choice, such as out-of-stock conditions, a damaged container, or simply a desire to try something different.

It is important not to limit our concept of product to physical objects. The key thing about a product is the service that it renders. Anything capable of rendering a service—i.e., satisfying a need—can be called a product. This includes *persons, places, organizations, activities,* and *ideas.* A consumer makes a decision among different entertainers to watch on television, different places to go to on a vacation, different organizations to contribute to, and different ideas to support. From the consumer's point of view, these are alternative products. If the term *product* seems unnatural at times, we can substitute the term *satisfier, resource,* or *offering.* All of these terms describe something of value to someone.

Exchange

The fact that people have needs, wants, and demands and there are products capable of satisfying them is necessary but not sufficient to define marketing. Marketing exists when people decide to satisfy needs and wants through exchange.

- **Exchange** is the act of obtaining a desired object from someone by offering something in return.

Exchange is one of four ways in which individuals can obtain a desired object. Let us again suppose that someone is hungry. This person can try to obtain food in the following ways:

1. *Self-production.* The hungry person can relieve this hunger through personal efforts at hunting, fishing, or fruit gathering. There is no necessity to interact with anyone else. In this case there is no market and no marketing.
2. *Coercion.* The hungry person can forcibly wrest or steal food from someone else. No benefit is offered to the other party except the chance not to be harmed.
3. *Supplication.* The hungry person can approach someone and ask or beg for food. The supplicant has nothing tangible to offer except gratitude.
4. *Exchange.* The hungry person can approach someone who has food and offer some resource in exchange, such as money, another good, or some service.

Of these four ways of satisfying individual needs, exchange has a great deal in its favor. The person wanting a specific product does not have to prey on others or depend on alms from others. Nor does this person have to produce every necessity, regardless of skill. It is possible to concentrate on producing those things for which he or she has the greatest comparative advantage and trade them for needed items produced by others. The members of a society end up specializing in production, thus leading to much more total output than under any alternative.

Specialization in production, however, does not always lead to a society that uses exchange as the major principle for distributing goods. Goods may be distributed in a society in one of three ways:[15]

1. *Reciprocity.* In some societies, each producer supplies goods or services to whoever wants them and in turn goes to others for whatever is needed. A cobbler will repair shoes for others and will in turn go to the butcher, the baker, and the candlestick

maker for the things he needs. The modern family works on this principle, with each member freely providing services to the other members without formal exchange arrangements.

2. *Redistribution.* In other societies, producers turn over some part of their output to a chief or a central depot. The output is subsequently redistributed to persons according to their needs, status, or power.
3. *Exchange.* In most modern societies, producers offer to sell their goods to others in exchange for money. Exchange is the core concept of the discipline of marketing. For exchange to take place, five conditions must be satisfied:
   a. There are at least two parties.
   b. Each party has something that might be of value to the other party (or parties).
   c. Each party is capable of communication and delivery.
   d. Each party is free to accept or reject the offer of the other party (or parties).
   e. Each party believes it is proper to deal with the other party (or parties) in this way.

These five conditions set up a potential for exchange. Whether exchange actually takes place depends upon the parties' coming to an agreement on the *terms of exchange.* If they agree, we conclude that the act of exchange leaves all of them better off (or at least not worse off) because each was free to reject or accept the offer. In this sense, exchange is a value-creating process. Just as production creates value, so does exchange create value through enlarging the consumption possibilities facing any individual.

It should be noted that exchange is a sophisticated human activity, one without a counterpart in the animal kingdom. Ant colonies and gorilla societies show some division of labor but little evidence of formal exchange. Adam Smith observed that

- Nobody ever saw a dog make a fair and deliberate exchange of one bone for another with another dog. Nobody ever saw one animal by its gestures and natural cries signify to another, this is mine, that is yours; I am willing to give this for that.[16]

Whereas man, according to Adam Smith, has a natural "propensity to barter, truck, and exchange one thing for another." Anthropologists have cast doubt over whether exchange is a natural human propensity or a learned disposition. But, in any case, exchange seems to be a uniquely human activity. (See Exhibit 1-1).

Transactions

If exchange is the core concept of the discipline of marketing, what is the discipline's unit of measurement? The answer is, A *transaction. A transaction consists of a trade of values between two parties.* We must be able to say, A gives X to B and gets Y in return. Thus Jones gives $400 to Smith and obtains a television set. This is a classic *monetary transaction,* although transactions do not require money as one of the traded values. A *barter transaction* would consist of Jones giving a refrigerator to Smith in return for a television set. A barter transaction can also consist of the trading of services instead of goods, as when lawyer Jones writes a will for physician Smith in return for a medical examination.

A transaction involves several measurable entities: (1) at least two things of value, (2) conditions that are agreed to, (3) a time of agreement, (4) a place of agreement. Usually a legal system arises to support and enforce certain behavior on the part of the transactors. Transactions can easily give rise to conflicts based on misinterpretations or malice. Without a "law of contracts," people would approach transactions with some distrust and everyone would lose.

Business firms keep records of their transactions and sort them by item, price, customer, location, and other specific variables. *Sales analysis* is the name given to the activity of trying to analyze where the company's sales are coming from by product, customer, territory, and so on.

A *transaction* should be distinguished from a *transfer*. In a transfer, A gives X to B but receives nothing explicit in return. Transfers include gifts, subsidies, and altruistic acts. It would seem to follow that marketers should confine their study to transactions and not to transfers. However, a little more thought suggests that transfer behavior also includes a concept of exchange. The transferrer gives a gift in the expectation of some immediate or eventual benefit, such as gratitude, a good feeling, relief from a sense of guilt, or the wish to put the other party under an obligation. Professional fund-raisers are acutely aware of the "reciprocal" motives underlying donor behavior and try to supply the utilities being sought by the givers. If they neglect such donors or show no gratitude, they will soon lose them. As a result, marketers have recently broadened the concept of marketing to include the study of transfer behavior as well as transaction behavior.

EXHIBIT 1-1

THE ORIGIN OF TRADE

Since exchange is the basic idea underlying marketing, we might ask how exchange or trade originated in human society. Exchange is so pervasive an idea in modern society that we are blind to the idea that it is a human invention and not an inevitable human practice. For example, there is no evidence of trade behavior among certain groups, such as the Incas, Eskimos, and early Polish peasants. Eskimos, in fact, consider the idea of exchange vulgar. They believe that a person should give another person something without expecting anything in return.

Scholars are not in agreement as to the origins of trade. Several years ago, George Robbins ably summarized seven different theories as to how trade began.

1. *Trading is instinctive.* This theory holds that human beings have an inborn instinct to "truck and barter." While this instinct is not as strong as those of self-preservation and sex, it nevertheless will appear in much of human society. A modification of the theory holds that this trait will appear more strongly in certain people than others. Every society will spawn certain people who are instinctive traders or "born salesmen" who get their kicks from swapping goods.
2. *Trading grew out of warfare.* This theory holds that many primitive tribes resort to warfare in order to gain the economic goods they need or want. But the casualties of war lead these tribes to search for other ways to obtain the needed goods. They eventually hit upon the idea of trading with the other tribes. Trading thus becomes a sublimation of warring behavior.
3. *Trading originated in predation.* This theory holds that much of human history is filled with tribes and individuals who extracted tribute from others by conquering them. Those collecting tribute eventually offered something in return, such as security or small gifts, to keep the tributees from rebelling. It is held that trading may have

picked up some of its negative overtones to the extent that it grew out of tribute.

4. *Trading grew out of friendly gift-giving.* The practice of friendly gift-giving has appeared in many societies. Through receiving gifts, people may have learned the utility of exchange. Through becoming habituated to giving and receiving gifts, the next step was to transform this into trading behavior.
5. *Trading originated with the "silent trade."* Anthropologists have noted many tribes which have engaged in "silent trade," where one tribe leaves its goods on a promontory and retires from sight to permit another group to come out of hiding to take these goods and leave something in return. Silent trade took place primarily between tribes of very different cultures and languages who wished to obtain certain goods without resorting to war on the one hand or building friendship on the other.
6. *Trading arose from surpluses.* A popular theory holds that trading developed from an early division of labor that resulted in certain families or tribes having a surplus of certain goods. They looked for others who had a surplus of needed goods, and proposed to offer some of their goods in return.
7. *Trading grew out of the development of the property concept.* People discover that possession of certain scarce goods gives them power or status. This leads to a concept of ownership and property. Those who want something belonging to another must make a strong offer, hence leading to the concept of trading.

All of these theories have elements of truth and yet none applies to all societies where trading has been observed. Trading can be found in societies that never went to war, that did not practice gift giving, and that did not have a strong concept of property. The question of how trading originated, like the question of how the solar system was formed, may never be fully answered but nevertheless leads to many interesting speculations.

Source: Adapted from George W. Robbins, "Notions about the Origins of Trading," *Journal of Marketing,* January 1947, pp. 228–36.

Markets

The concept of transactions leads to the concept of a market.

- A **market** is the set of all actual and potential buyers of a product.

To understand the nature of a market, let us imagine a primitive economy consisting of four persons: a fisherman, hunter, potter, and farmer. Figure 1-3 shows three different ways in which these tradesmen could meet their needs. In the first case, *self-sufficiency,* each person relies completely upon himself to gather the goods he needs for living. Thus the fisherman spends most of the time fishing but also takes time to hunt, make pottery, and farm to obtain the other goods. He is therefore less efficient at fishing, and the same is true of the other tradesmen. In the second case, *decentralized exchange,* each person sees the other three as potential "buyers" of his product and therefore making up a market. Thus the fisherman may make separate trips to trade his goods with the hunter, potter, and farmer in exchange for their goods. In the third case, *centralized exchange,* a new person called a merchant appears, and he locates in a central area called a marketplace. Each tradesman brings his goods to the merchant and trades for the things he needs. Thus the fisherman now transacts with only one "market" to obtain the goods he needs, rather than transact with three other persons. The emergence of a merchant substantially reduces the total

Figure 1-3
Evolution toward Centralized Exchange

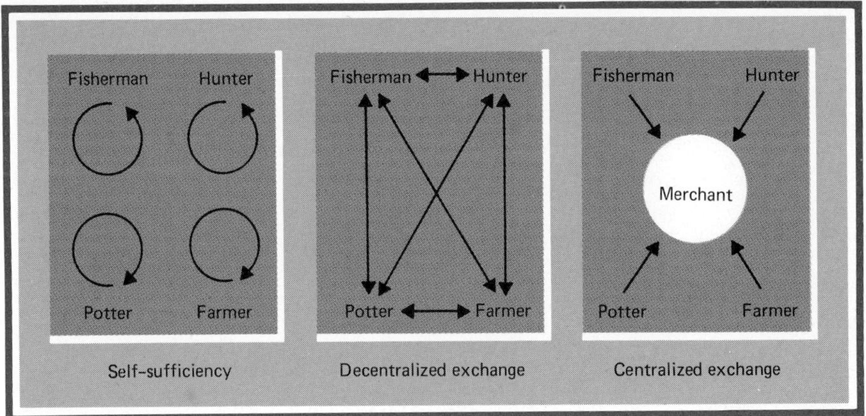

number of transactions required to accomplish a given volume of exchange. In other words, merchants and central marketplaces increase the transactional efficiency of the economy.[17]

As the number of persons and transactions increases in a society, the number of merchants and marketplaces also increases. In advanced societies, marketplaces need not be physical places where buyers and sellers interact. With the development of modern communications and transportation, a merchant can advertise a product on late evening television, take orders from hundreds of customers over the phone, and mail the goods to the buyers on the following day without any physical contact or effort on the part of the buyer.

A market can grow up around a product, a service, or anything else of value. For example, a labor market exists when there are persons ready to offer their labor to others in return for wages or products. Various institutions will grow up around a labor market to facilitate its functioning, such as employment agencies, job advertising, and job-counseling firms. The money market is another important market that emerges to meet the needs of people so that they can borrow, lend, save, or safeguard money. And the donor market emerges to meet the financial needs of nonprofit organizations so that they can carry out their work.

Marketing

The concept of markets finally brings us full circle to the concept of marketing. Marketing means human activity that takes place in relation to markets. *Marketing* means working with *markets,* which means attempting to actualize *potential exchanges* for the purpose of *satisfying human needs and wants.* Thus we return to our definition of *marketing* as *human activity directed at satisfying needs and wants through exchange processes.*

Exchange processes involve work. The seller has to search for buyers, identify their needs, design appropriate products, promote them, store and transport them, negotiate, and so on. Such activities as *product development, search, communication, distribution, pricing,* and *service* constitute core marketing activities.

Although it is normal to think of marketing as consisting of the activities of "sellers," buyers also carry out marketing activities. The housewife does her "marketing," that is, she searches for the goods she needs at prices she is willing to pay. The purchasing agent who needs a commodity in short supply has to track down sellers and offer attractive terms. A *sellers' market* is one in which the buyer is the more active "marketer," and a *buyers' market* is one in which the seller is the more active "marketer."

In the early 1950s the growing supply of goods created a buyers' market, and marketing became identified with sellers trying to find buyers. This book will take this point of view and examine the marketing problems of sellers in a buyers' market. However, it will occasionally allude to the marketing done by buyers to produce desired exchanges.

marketing management

Those who engage in exchange learn how to do it better over time. In particular, sellers learn how to professionalize their marketing management. We define *marketing management* as follows:

EXHIBIT 1-2

VARIOUS APPROACHES TO THE STUDY OF MARKETING

Any phenomenon can be studied from several points of view. This is very true of marketing. The following approaches have been prominent in the history of marketing, and they are listed in the rough order of their appearance.

1. *Commodity approach.* The commodity approach focuses on particular commodities and classes of products to determine how they are produced and distributed to intermediate and ultimate consumers. The major product classes studied are farm products, minerals, manufactured goods, and services.
2. *Institutional approach.* The institutional approach focuses on the nature, evolution, and functions of particular institutions in the marketing system, such as producers, wholesalers, retailers, and various facilitating agencies. For example, an institutionalist might study an institution such as a department store to determine how it has evolved over the years and where it seems to be headed.
3. *Functional approach.* The functional approach focuses on the nature and dynamics of various marketing functions, such as buying, selling, storing, financing, and promoting. A functionalist studies how these functions are carried on in various product markets and by various marketing institutions.
4. *Managerial approach.* The managerial approach focuses on the use of marketing in successfully positioning organizations and products in the marketplace. Managerial marketers are especially interested in marketing analysis, planning, organization, implementation, and control.
5. *Social approach.* The social approach focuses on the social contributions and costs created by various marketing activities and institutions. This approach addresses such issues as market efficiency, product obsolescence, advertising truthfulness, and the ecological impact of marketing.

- **Marketing management** is the analysis, planning, implementation, and control of programs designed to create, build, and maintain mutually beneficial exchanges and relationships with target markets for the purpose of achieving organizational objectives.

The popular image of the marketing manager is that of someone whose task consists primarily of stimulating the demand for the company's products. This, however, is too limited a view of the range of marketing tasks carried out by marketing managers. Marketing managers are concerned not only with the creation and expansion of demand but also with its modification and possible reduction. *Marketing management has the task of regulating the level, timing, and character of demand in a way that will help the organization achieve its objectives.* Simply put, marketing management is *demand management.*

The organization forms an idea of a *desired level of transactions* with a market. At any point in time, the *actual demand level* may be below, equal to, or above the *desired demand level.* This leads to eight distinguishable marketing tasks:[18]

1. *Conversional marketing.* This is the task of trying to get people who dislike something to like it. For example, many people have a fear of flying, and the airline industry tries to convert them into willing flyers. Conversional marketing is a difficult marketing task and it is suspect, since it tries to change people's wants rather than serve their wants. One's attitude toward conversional marketing depends on whether the "cause" is seen as worthwhile.
2. *Stimulational marketing.* This is the task of trying to stimulate a want for an object in people who initially have no knowledge or interest in the object. An example would be trying to get people to buy "pet rocks."
3. *Developmental marketing.* This is the task of trying to develop a new product or service that meets a clear market need. For example, developmental marketing characterizes the effort to develop an efficient electric car.
4. *Remarketing.* This is the task of trying to rebuild interest in a stable or declining product or service. For example, remarketing describes the various steps that church groups are taking to rebuild interest in churchgoing in the face of growing competition from secular activities and interests.
5. *Synchromarketing.* This is the task of trying to alter the time pattern of demand so that it will better match the time pattern of supply. Synchromarketing would describe the effort of public transportation companies to encourage more riders to travel during off-peak periods to reduce the amount of equipment needed during rush hours.
6. *Maintenance marketing.* This is the task of trying to maintain the existing level of sales against the erosive forces of competition. The maintenance marketer monitors the environment continuously and is ready to make necessary changes in the interest of protecting the sales level.
7. *Demarketing.* This is the task of trying to reduce the demand for a product or service on a temporary or permanent basis. For example, energy conservationists are using pricing and promotion techniques to encourage consumers to reduce their energy consumption. Demarketing calls for using the normal marketing tools in reverse, such as reducing availability, advertising, and service and increasing prices.[19]
8. *Countermarketing.* This is the task of trying to destroy the demand or interest in a particular product or service. For example, antismoking groups are engaged in a countermarketing campaign to get people who like smoking to stop smoking. Countermarketing is a difficult marketing task in that the aim is to get people who like something to give it up.

marketing-management philosophies

We have described marketing management as the conscious effort to achieve desired exchange outcomes with target markets. Now the question arises, What is the philosophy that guides these marketing efforts? That is, What is the relative weight given to serving the interests of the *organization,* the *customers,* and *society*? Very often these conflict. It is desirable that marketing activities be carried out under a clear concept of responsive and responsible marketing.

There are five alternative concepts under which business and other organizations can conduct their marketing activity: the production, product, selling, marketing, and societal marketing concepts.

The Production Concept

The production concept is one of the oldest concepts guiding sellers.

- The **production concept** is a management orientation that assumes that consumers will favor those products that are available and affordable, and therefore the major task of management is to pursue improved production and distribution efficiency.

The implicit premises of the production concept are:

1. Consumers are primarily interested in product availability and low price.
2. Consumers know the prices of the competing brands.
3. Consumers do not see or attach much importance to nonprice differences within the product class.
4. The organization's task is to keep improving production and distribution efficiency and lowering costs as the key to attracting and holding customers.

The production concept is an appropriate philosophy of management in two types of situations. The first is where the demand for a product exceeds supply. Here consumers are ready to buy any version of the product they can find. The second situation favoring a production orientation is where the product's cost is high and has to be brought down through learning how to produce it more efficiently. Henry Ford's whole philosophy was to perfect the production of one car model (the Model T) so that its cost could be brought down and made more affordable. He joked about offering people any color car they wanted as long as it was black. Texas Instruments is a prime contemporary practitioner of putting major effort into achieving production volume and lower costs in order to bring down prices. It succeeded in winning a major share of the American hand calculator market with this philosophy and is applying it again in the manufacture of digital watches—it recently introduced a $10 model and hopes to bring this price down to somewhere around $5 during the early 1980s.[20]

Some service organizations also follow the production concept. Many medical and dental practices are organized on assembly-line principles, as are some government agencies such as unemployment offices and license bureaus. While this results in handling many cases per hour, this type of management is open to the charge of impersonality and consumer insensitivity.

The Product Concept

The product concept is another major concept guiding sellers.

- The **product concept** is a management orientation that assumes that consumers will favor those products that offer the most quality for the price, and therefore the organization should devote its energy to improving product quality.

The implicit premises of the product concept are:

1. Consumers buy products rather than solutions to needs.
2. Consumers are primarily interested in product quality.
3. Consumers know the quality and feature differences of the competing brands.
4. Consumers choose among competing brands on the basis of obtaining the most quality for their money.
5. The organization's task is to keep improving product quality as the key to attracting and holding customers.

Many a manufacturer believes that if he can build a better mousetrap, the world will beat a path to his door.[21] But he is often rudely shocked. In the first place, buyers are looking for a solution to a mouse problem and not necessarily a mousetrap. The solution might take the form of a chemical spray, an exterminating service, or something that works better than a mousetrap. In the second place, the inventor of the better mousetrap will get nowhere unless positive steps are taken to design, package, and price this new product attractively, place it into convenient distribution channels, bring it to the attention of persons who need it, and convince them that it has superior qualities.

Companies that operate on a product concept can be found in all fields. Railroad management was so sure that it had a superior form of transportation that it overlooked the emerging challenge of the airlines, buses, trucks, and automobiles. Colleges assume that high-school graduates will continue to want their product. Churches, police departments, and the U.S. Post Office seem to feel that they are offering the public the right product and that the public should be grateful.

The Selling Concept

The selling concept (also called the sales concept) is another hallowed way in which many producers guide their exchange activity.

- The **selling concept** is a management orientation that assumes that consumers will either not buy or not buy enough of the organization's products unless the organization makes a substantial effort to stimulate their interest in its products.

The implicit premises of the selling concept are:

1. Consumers have a normal tendency to resist buying most things that are not essential.
2. Consumers can be induced to buy more through various sales-stimulating devices.
3. The organization's task is to organize a strong sales-oriented department as the key to attracting and holding customers.

The selling concept is practiced most aggressively in the instance of "unsought goods," those goods that buyers normally do not think of buying. Examples would be insurance, encyclopedias, and funeral plots. These industries have perfected various sales techniques to track down prospects and hard sell them on the benefits of their product.

Hard selling is also practiced by manufacturers and resellers when they have a surplus of goods on their hands. Auto dealers often are prime practitioners of the selling concept:[22]

- From the moment the customer walks into the showroom, the auto salesman will engage in "psyching him out," and exaggerating the car's virtues. If the customer likes the floor model, he may be told that there is another customer about to buy it and that he should decide on the spot. If the customer balks at the price (which is artificially high to begin with), the salesman offers to talk to the manager to get a special concession. The customer waits ten minutes and the salesman returns with "the boss doesn't like it but I got him to agree." The aim is to "work up the customer" to buy then and there.

The sales concept is also practiced in the nonprofit area. A perfect example is the political party seeking votes for its candidate. Having chosen a candidate, it will vigorously sell this candidate to the voters as being a fantastic person for the job.[23] The candidate stomps through voting precincts from early morning to late evening shaking hands, kissing babies, meeting power brokers, making breezy speeches. Countless dollars are spent on radio and television advertising, posters, and mailings. Any flaws in the candidate are shielded from the public because the aim is to get the sale, not worry about postpurchase satisfaction.

The Marketing Concept

The marketing concept is a more recent idea in the history of exchange relations.[24]

- The **marketing concept** is a management orientation that holds that the key to achieving organizational goals consists of the organization's determining the needs and wants of target markets and adapting itself to delivering the desired satisfactions more effectively and efficiently than its competitors.

The marketing concept has been expressed in more colorful ways, such as "Find wants and fill them"; "Make what you can sell instead of trying to sell what you can make"; "Love the customer and not the product"; "Have it your way" (Burger King); and "You're the boss" (United Airlines).

The underlying premises of the marketing concept are:

1. Consumers can be grouped into different market segments depending on their needs and wants.
2. The consumers in any market segment will favor the offer of that organization that comes closest to satisfying their particular needs and wants.
3. The organization's task is to research and choose target markets and develop effective offers and marketing programs as the key to attracting and holding customers.

The selling concept and the marketing concept are frequently confused by businesspeople and the public. Levitt draws the following contrast between these two orientations:

- Selling focuses on the needs of the seller; marketing on the needs of the buyer. Selling is preoccupied with the seller's need to convert his product into cash; marketing with the idea of satisfying the needs of the customer by means of the product and the whole cluster of things associated with creating, delivering and finally consuming it.[25]

The marketing concept replaces and reverses the logic of the selling concept. The two concepts are contrasted in Figure 1-4. The selling concept starts with the firm's existing products and considers the task as one of using selling and promotion to stimulate a profitable volume of sales. The marketing concept starts with the firm's target customers and their needs and wants; it plans a coordinated set of products and programs to serve these needs and wants; and it derives profits through creating customer satisfaction. In essence, the *marketing concept* is a *customer needs and wants orientation* backed by *integrated marketing effort* aimed at generating *customer satisfaction* as the key to satisfying *organizational goals.*

The marketing concept is the company's commitment to the time-honored concept in economic theory known as *consumer sovereignty.* The determination of what is to be produced should not be in the hands of the companies or in the hands of government but in the hands of consumers. The companies produce what the consumers want, and in this way they maximize consumer welfare and earn their profits.

Have many companies adopted the marketing concept? We know that the marketing concept is the basis of the success of such companies as Procter & Gamble, IBM, Avon, and McDonald's. We also know that the marketing concept is more prevalent in consumer goods companies than in industrial goods companies, and in larger companies than in smaller companies.[26] In many cases the

Figure 1-4
The Selling and Marketing Concepts Contrasted

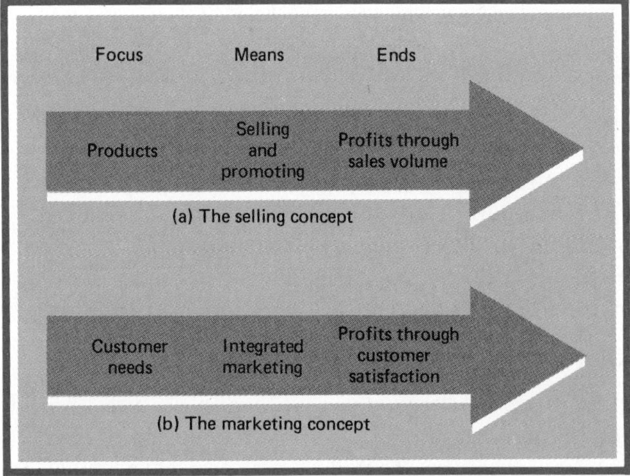

EXHIBIT 1-3

MCDONALD'S CORPORATION: ILLUSTRATION OF THE MARKETING CONCEPT

Among the prime practitioners of the marketing concept is McDonald's Corp., the fast-food hamburger retailer. In its short twenty-five years, McDonald's has served Americans and citizens of several countries over 27 billion hamburgers! With over 4,200 outlets, it commands a 20 percent share of the fast-food market, far ahead of its next rivals, Kentucky Fried Chicken (8.4%) and Burger King (5.3%). Its current annual sales are running $4.6 billion. Credit for this leading position belongs to a thoroughgoing marketing orientation. McDonald's knows how to serve people well and adapt to changing needs and wants.

Before McDonald's, Americans could get hamburgers in restaurants or diners, but not without problems. In many places, the hamburgers were poor in quality, service was slow, decor was poor, help was uneven, conditions were unclean, and the atmosphere noisy. In 1955, Ray Kroc, a fifty-two-year-old salesman of malted milk machines, became interested in a particular restaurant owned and managed by Richard and Maurice McDonald. He liked their concept of a fast-food restaurant and proposed a program of selling franchises to others. This was the beginnings of the fabulously successful McDonald's system. McDonald's was formulated as an alternative, where the customer could walk into a spotlessly clean outlet, be greeted by a friendly and efficient order-taker, receive a good-tasting hamburger in a minute after placing the order, with the chance to eat it there or take it out. There were no jukeboxes or telephones to create a teen-age hangout, and in fact, McDonald's became a family affair, particularly appealing to the children.

As times changed, so did McDonald's. The sit-down sections were expanded in size, the decor improved, a very successful breakfast item called Egg McMuffin was added, and new outlets were opened in high-traffic parts of the city. McDonald's was clearly being managed to evolve with changing customer needs and profitable opportunities.

In addition, McDonald's management knows how to efficiently design and operate a complex service operation. It chooses its locations carefully, selects high-qualified franchise operators, gives complete management training at its facility called Hamburger University, supports its franchisers with a high-quality national advertising and sales promotion program, monitors product and service quality through continuous customer surveys, and puts great energy into improving the technology of hamburger production to simplify operations, bring down costs, and speed up service.

marketing concept, although professed, is not practiced in any thoroughgoing way. The company may have the forms of marketing—such as a marketing vice-president, product managers, marketing plans, marketing research—but not the substance.[27] It takes several years of top-management determination to turn a sales-oriented company into a truly market-oriented company.

The Societal Marketing Concept

In recent years some people have begun to question whether the marketing concept is an adequate philosophy for business in an age of environmental deterioration, resource shortages, explosive population growth, worldwide inflation, and neglected social services.[28] The issue is whether the firm that does an excellent job of sensing, serving, and satisfying individual consumer needs is necessarily acting in the best long-run interests of consumers and society. The marketing concept sidesteps the conflict between consumer wants, consumer interests, and long-run societal welfare.

As a concrete instance, consider the Coca-Cola Company. Its worldwide image is that of a fine trustworthy corporation concerned with the public good. Its products do an excellent job of meeting the wants of people for good-tasting soft drinks. But is it really serving their long-run interests? Here are some criticisms that have been leveled against the company by consumer and environmental groups:

1. Coke is a product from which customers derive little nutritional benefit.
2. The sugar and phosphoric acid are not beneficial for people's teeth.
3. The brominated vegetable oil in colas has been removed from the Federal Drug Administration's (FDA's) list of products "generally recognized as safe."
4. The caffeine in colas has been found to produce tremor, insomnia, gastrointestinal disorders, and possible cellular damage in the drinker or the unborn fetus.
5. The saccharine in Coca-Cola's diet soft drink, Tab, may be banned by the FDA.
6. The soft-drink industry has catered to the American demand for convenience by increasing the use of one-way disposable bottles. The one-way bottle presents a great waste of resources in that approximately seventeen containers are necessary where one two-way bottle would have made seventeen trips before it could no longer be used; many one-way bottles are not biodegradable; and these bottles often are a littering element.

This and similar situations have led to the call for a new concept that goes beyond the marketing concept. Among the proposals are "the human concept," "the intelligent consumption concept," and "the ecological imperative concept,"[29] all of which get at different aspects of the same problem. We would like to propose "the societal marketing concept," defined as follows:

- The **societal marketing concept** is a management orientation that holds that the key task of the organization is to determine the needs, wants, and interests of target markets and to adapt the organization to delivering the desired satisfactions more effectively and efficiently than its competitors in a way that preserves or enhances the consumer's and the society's well-being.

The underlying premises of the societal marketing concept are:

1. Consumers' wants do not always coincide with their long-run interests or society's long-run interests.
2. Consumers will increasingly favor organizations that show a concern for meeting their wants, long-run interests, and society's long-run interests.
3. The organization's task is to serve target markets in a way that produces not only want satisfaction but long-run individual and social benefit as the key to attracting and holding customers.

Societal marketing involves four considerations in marketing decision making: *consumer needs and wants, consumer interests, company interests,* and *society's interests.* The major question facing companies is how societal marketing will affect their profitability. Companies cannot be expected to absorb losses

EXHIBIT 1-4

DOES THE SOCIETAL MARKETING CONCEPT PAY OFF?

One example of the potential in viewing social movements as opportunities rather than problems is afforded by the supermarket industry where a small group of regional chains (King Soopers in Denver, Jewel in Chicago, and Giant Foods in Maryland, Virginia, and Washington, D.C.) have been outcompeting larger, national companies. A primary tool in the recent successes of these three companies has been sensitive and sincere investment in the changing climate of the 1970's, particularly consumerism and environmentalism. The three chains have consistently been the first in their respective markets to innovate on behalf of the consumer—e.g., unit pricing, open dating, nutritional labeling, and consumer education through advertising, booklets, and leaflets. In addition, King Soopers has maintained a vigorous role in the ecology movement by sponsoring tree planting and waste product recycling programs, among others.

Recent market results achieved by the three chains are noteworthy. For example, in Denver, an annual market survey published by a major newspaper there reveals that with respect to "grocery store preference," the percentage of shoppers naming King Soopers has risen from 24% in 1969 to 36% in 1972. In the same time frame, the percentages for all other major chains in the area have either dropped or remained about the same. In Chicago, Jewel's market share has climbed from 21% in 1969 to 30% in 1973, while National Tea slipped from 16% to 14% and A&P from 11% to 7%.

Source: Leonard L. Berry, "Marketing Mistakes That Businesses Make," *Atlanta Economic Review*, July-August 1974, p. 362.

or lower profits in the pursuit of societal marketing. Fortunately there are many companies that have increased their profits by practicing the societal marketing concept. To the extent that societal marketing appears profitable, companies can be expected to give it serious consideration.

the goals of a marketing system

This brings us to the final question in the chapter, What should society seek from its marketing system?

The question is particularly pertinent, as various governments around the world are increasing their regulation of the normal marketing activities of firms. Some of the interventions seem quite extreme:

- Government officials in India are considering prohibiting the *branding* of certain staple products such as sugar, soap, tea, and rice. The allegation is that branding is inevitably accompanied by costly packaging and high advertising and promotional expenditures, which push up prices to consumers.
- Government officials in the Philippines are talking about solving the same problem through *socialized pricing*. Certain staples consumed heavily by the poor would have their prices held down either through subsidy or through price control.
- Government officials in Norway are considering proposals to ban certain "luxury" goods from the market, such as private swimming pools, tennis courts, airplanes,

and luxury automobiles. They think Norway's resources are too limited to permit their use for these purposes, even though such "luxuries" are affordable by certain wealthy individuals. These officials want to promote the idea of "collective consumption" of expensive goods and services.

- To promote "truth-in-advertising," the Federal Trade Commission experimented with three new measures in the early 1970s. *Advertising substantiation* requires firms to stand ready to provide documentary evidence backing any claim they make in an ad. *Corrective advertising* requires a firm found guilty of a false claim to spend 25 percent of its subsequent advertising budget to announce the error to the public. *Counter advertising* encourages groups that have a different view about the social value of a product class (such as an antismoking group) to have easy access to the media to voice their opinion.

The recent proliferation of marketing legislation and regulation throughout the world raises a fundamental question, What are the proper goal(s) of a marketing system? Any policy interventions in a marketing system should be guided by a clear image of what marketing is supposed to contribute to that society.

At one time or another at least four alternative goals have been suggested as being proper for a marketing system: maximize consumption, maximize consumer satisfaction, maximize choice, and maximize life quality.

Maximize Consumption

Many business executives view marketing as a business function charged with the task of maximizing the amount of goods and services that the public buys and consumes. This will maximize consumption, production, employment, and wealth. This business goal can be inferred from typical headlines in the business press: "Wrigley Seeks Ways to Get People to Chew More Gum"; "Opticians Introduce Fashion in Glasses to Stimulate Demand"; "Steel Industry Maps Strategy to Expand Sales"; "Car Manufacturers Try to Hypo Sales."

The underlying societal assumption is that the more people buy and consume, the happier they are. This is captured in the phrase "More is better" and has been a driving force in the American economy. Yet another group has begun to doubt that increased material goods means more happiness. They see too many affluent people leading unhappy lives. This has resulted in a small countercultural group's denying that the good life is achieved through continuous and conspicuous consumption. Their personal philosophy is "less is more" and "small is beautiful."

Frederick Pohl, in a science fiction story called *The Midas Touch,* dramatizes the possible dire consequences of too much consumption. In this story, society has reached a point where factories are completely automated. Goods roll out continuously, and people are required to consume as much as they can so that they will not be buried under these goods. Ordinary people are given high consumption quotas while the elite are excused from having to consume so much. Furthermore the elite are given the few jobs that still exist so that they will not have to face the bleakness of no work.

Maximize Consumer Satisfaction

Most marketers see the goal of marketing as that of maximizing not consumption but consumer satisfaction. Chewing more gum or owning more cars is significant only if these objects bring about real increases in consumer satisfaction.

Unfortunately, consumer satisfaction as a goal of the marketing system poses some formidable conceptual and measurement problems. First, no welfare economist has figured out how to add up the satisfaction of different persons on a meaningful scale so that the total satisfaction created by a particular product or marketing activity can be evaluated. Second, the direct satisfaction that individual consumers obtain from particular "goods" fails to take into account some of the "bads" created in the process, such as pollution and environmental damage. Third, the satisfaction that people experience when consuming certain goods, in this case status goods, depends precisely on how few other people have these goods. For these and other reasons, it is difficult to evaluate a marketing system in terms of how much satisfaction it delivers.

Maximize Choice

Some marketers believe that the ideal marketing system is one that maximizes consumer choice. It would be a system that produces a great variety of products and brands enabling consumers to find those goods that precisely satisfy their individual tastes. In such an economy, individual consumers are able to maximize their life styles and, therefore, their satisfaction.

Maximizing consumer choice, unfortunately, also has some flaws. First, goods and services will be more expensive, since the great variety will call for shorter production runs and higher levels of required inventories. The higher cost of goods will reduce the consumers' real income and their ability to buy a greater quantity of goods. Second, the gain in consumer satisfaction from the great variety of goods will be offset by the greater cost of search time and effort. Consumers will have to spend more time learning about the features of different versions of a product, more time making an evaluation, and possibly more time traveling to the location of the specific dealer carrying the product they finally choose. Third, an increase in the number of brands will not necessarily mean an increase in the consumers' range of *real choice*. There are dozens of brands of beer in the United States and yet most of them taste the same. When a product category features many brands with few differences, this is called *product proliferation* and the consumer faces *false choice*. Finally, the presence of great variety will not always be welcomed by all consumers. Some will feel that there is overchoice in certain product categories that causes consumer frustration and anxiety.

Maximize Life Quality

The aim of a marketing system must transcend a narrow hedonistic conception of consumer satisfaction. In a complex technological society, many different forces affect the happiness of its citizens. The concept of "life quality" appears to be a useful way to capture these various forces.

People everywhere try to improve the quality of their lives. The quality of life is a function of (1) the quantity, quality, range, accessibility, and cost of goods; (2) the quality of the physical environment; and (3) the quality of the cultural environment. In the future, marketing systems will be judged not solely by the amount of direct consumer want satisfaction that is created but also by the impact of marketing activity on the quality of the physical and cultural environment.

EXHIBIT 1-5

WHAT IS THE DIFFERENCE BETWEEN ECONOMICS AND MARKETING?

We might think that the concerns of marketing are the same as those of economics. True, economics is the parent discipline of marketing. At the same time, marketing has gone beyond economics in some of the questions it raises, and it has gone into other questions more deeply.

Economics is a two-hundred-year-old science whose core concept is that of *scarcity*. Economists have noted that human beings have infinite needs but nature is niggardly. Given scarce resources, a society must make decisions on which needs to satisfy. Economists study the following three major problems: (1) What goods and services should the society produce? (2) How should these goods and services be produced? (3) Who should get them?

The answers to these questions differ depending on whether the society is organized under capitalist, communist, or other principles. All of these questions revolve around the issue of economic efficiency in resource allocation; that is, how to make resources go as far as possible in producing want satisfaction in a society.

Free-enterprise economists start with the two goals of consumer sovereignty and economic efficiency. These economists assume that consumers strive to maximize their economic satisfaction, that they have reasonably full information about the quality and price of the available goods, and that they are able to move easily to where the best buys can be found. These economists also assume that producers and sellers maximize their economic profit, know the costs of different resources and technologies at different scales of operation, and know how to put all of this information together to achieve the maximum profit. The free interaction of rational consumers and rational producers is assumed to produce maximum economic output and satisfaction.

Marketing had its beginnings only seventy-five years ago as an attempt to understand certain questions that economists had neglected or oversimplified. Whereas economists tried to explain, say, food prices through demand and supply curves, marketers were interested in tracing the complex sequence of activities that led to final price and consumption levels of food, including farmers' decisions to plant certain crops and purchase certain seed, fertilizer, and equipment; the selling of their crops to grain elevators; the purchase of the grain by food processors, who sold the processed food to wholesalers, who in turn sold it to retailers, who in turn sold it to consumers. During this complicated marketing process, several functions were carried out, including several levels of *buying and selling, assembly, sorting, grading, storing, transporting, risk bearing,* and *financing.* The final price reflected these many operations and the overall efficiency of the marketing process. This was a far cry from the economists' oversimplified picture of price setting.

Thus marketing started out as an effort to develop a richer description of distribution institutions and processes. Marketers were interested in exploring the "whys" of consumer and seller behavior and were not willing to assume simple utility and profit maximization explanations. This inevitably led to less reliance on economic concepts and more use of the findings of modern psychology, sociology, and anthropology. Today marketing is essentially an applied behavioral science rather than a branch of economic science.

Students of marketing are interested in three analytical questions:

1. What are the needs and wants of consumers, how are they formed and influenced, and how do consumers go about satisfying these needs and wants? (Consumer behavior)

2. How do providers or sellers go about trying to supply and influence the wants and buying behavior of consumers? (Seller behavior)
3. What institutions and activities come into being to facilitate exchange and the satisfaction of human wants? (Market channel behavior)

The answers to these questions provide the key to actions that can be taken to improve the performance of the marketing system and therefore consumer welfare. Students of marketing are also interested in the following normative questions:

1. How can consumers be helped to become better buyers?
2. How can providers be helped to become better sellers?
3. How can marketing institutions be improved to increase consumer satisfaction and welfare?

This leads to the normative purpose of the marketing discipline. The purpose of the marketing discipline is to help sellers sell better, buyers buy better, and government agencies regulate better in the interest of promoting efficiency, consumer satisfaction, and life quality through the marketplace.

■ summary

Marketing is a subject that touches everyone's life. It is the means by which a standard of living is developed and delivered to a people. It involves a large set of activities, including marketing research, product development, distribution, pricing, advertising, personal selling, and a number of other functions. Too many people mistakenly believe that marketing consists of only one or a few of these functions, whereas marketing is actually a high-level integration of several functions designed to sense, serve, and satisfy consumer needs while meeting the goals of the organization.

Marketing practices have been both praised and criticized because of their major impact on people in their roles as buyers, sellers, and citizens. Marketing controversy is likely to continue and possibly intensify as more and more institutions in the business sector, on the international scene, and in the nonprofit sector apply marketing concepts and techniques in the pursuit of improved performance.

Marketing can be defined as the study of how various parties go about satisfying their needs and wants through exchange and market processes. The key concepts that make up the subject of marketing are needs, wants, demands, products, exchange, transactions, and markets.

Marketing management is the conscious effort of one or both parties to manage the exchange process to secure desired outcomes. It involves analysis, planning, implementation, and control of programs designed to create, build, and maintain mutually beneficial exchanges and relationships with target markets for the purpose of achieving organizational objectives. The major marketing tasks are conversional marketing, stimulational marketing, developmental marketing, remarketing, synchromarketing, maintenance marketing, demarketing, and countermarketing.

Five alternative philosophies can guide organizations in carrying out their exchange activity. The production concept assumes that consumers will readily respond to products that are available and affordable and therefore management's major task is to improve production efficiency and bring down prices. The product concept assumes that consumers will respond favorably to quality products that are reasonably priced and therefore little additional marketing effort is required. The selling concept assumes that consumers will normally not buy enough of the company's products unless they are reached with a substantial selling and promotion effort. The marketing concept assumes that the main task of the company is to determine what a chosen set of customers' needs, wants, and preferences are and to adapt the company to delivering the desired satisfactions. The societal marketing concept assumes that the main task of the company is to generate customer satisfaction and long-run consumer and societal well-being as the key to satisfying organizational goals and responsibilities.

Different goals have been proposed for a marketing system, such as maximizing consumption, or consumer satisfaction, or consumer choice, or life quality. The orientation of this book is that the goal of the marketing system is to maximize the quality of life.

questions for discussion

1. How does *marketing* differ from *selling*? Do you think that marketers have done a good job of educating the public as to the difference between the two?
2. Discuss how marketing affects the buyer, the seller, and the citizen with regard to the Chevrolet Citation.
3. Why has marketing been embraced by many nonprofit organizations in recent years? Elaborate on a specific example.
4. What distinguishes the definition of *marketing* used in this text from all others?
5. Compare and contrast needs, wants, and demands. How does the consumer reconcile these three concepts? Relate them to a recent purchase of yours.
6. You are planning to go to a fast-food franchise for lunch. Apply the notions of products, exchange transactions, and a market to this situation.
7. How can the marketing management philosophies of the product concept and the production concept be contrasted? Give an example of each.
8. Why has the societal marketing concept superseded the marketing concept for some organizations?
9. What four alternative goals of a marketing system were discussed? Which one do you feel is the best and why?

references

1. PATRICK E. MURPHY AND RICHARD A. MCGARRITY, "Marketing Universities: A Survey of Student Recruiting Activities," *College and University*, Spring 1978, pp. 249–61.

2. PETER F. DRUCKER, *Management: Tasks, Responsibilities, Practices* (New York: Harper & Row, Pub., 1973), pp. 64–65.

3. RICHARD N. FARMER, "Would You Want Your Daughter to Marry a Marketing Man?" *Journal of Marketing,* January 1967, p. 1.

4. STERLING HAYDEN, *Wanderer* (New York: Knopf, 1963).

5. WILLIAM J. STANTON, *Fundamentals of Marketing,* 5th ed. (New York: McGraw-Hill, 1978), p. 7.

6. SIR WINSTON CHURCHILL.

7. DEBORAH RANKIN, "How C.P.A.'s Sell Themselves," *New York Times,* September 25, 1977.

8. RALPH Z. SORENSEN II, "U.S. Marketers Can Learn from European Innovators," *Harvard Business Review,* September-October 1972, pp. 89–99.

9. THOMAS V. GREER, *Marketing in the Soviet Union* (New York: Holt, Rinehart & Winston, 1973).

10. DONALD L. PIKE, "The Future of Higher Education: Will Private Institutions Disappear in the U.S.?" *Futurist,* December 1977, p. 374.

11. *Marketing Definitions: A Glossary of Marketing Terms,* Committee on Definitions (Chicago: American Marketing Association, 1960).

12. This definition was originally proposed by Paul Mazur and was modified by Malcolm McNair. See MALCOLM P. MCNAIR, "Marketing and the Social Challenge of Our Times," in *A New Measure of Responsibility for Marketing,* ed. Keith Cox and Ben M. Enis (Chicago: American Marketing Association, 1968), p. 2.

13. See THEODORE LEVITT's classic article, "Marketing Myopia," *Harvard Business Review,* July-August 1960, pp. 45-56.

14. KELVIN J. LANCASTER, "A New Approach to Consumer Theory," *Journal of Political Economy,* 14 (1966), 132–57.

15. CYRIL S. BELSHAW, *Traditional Exchange and Modern Markets* (New York: Prentice-Hall, 1965).

16. ADAM SMITH, *The Wealth of Nations,* 1776 (New York: Crowell-Collier and Macmillan, 1909), p. 19.

17. For more discussion, see WROE ALDERSON, "Factors Governing the Development of Marketing Channels," in *Marketing Channels for Manufactured Products,* ed. Richard M. Clewett (Homewood, Ill.: Richard D. Irwin, 1957), pp. 211–14. The number of transactions in a decentralized exchange system is given by $N(N-1)/2$. With four persons, this means $4(4-1)/2 = 6$ transactions. In a centralized exchange system, the number of transactions is given by N, here 4. Thus a centralized exchange system reduces the number of required transactions to accomplish a given volume of exchange.

18. See PHILIP KOTLER, "The Major Tasks of Marketing Management," *Journal of Marketing,* October 1973, pp. 42–49.

19. See PHILIP KOTLER AND SIDNEY J. LEVY, "Demarketing, Yes, Demarketing," *Harvard Business Review,* November-December 1971, pp. 74–80.

20. "Texas Instruments Shows U.S. Business How to Survive in the 1980s," *Business Week,* September 18, 1978, pp. 66ff.

21. See "So We Made a Better Mousetrap," *President's Forum,* Fall 1962, pp. 26–27.

22. See IRWIN J. REIN, *Rudy's Red Wagon: Communication Strategies in Contemporary Society* (Glenview, Ill.: Scott, Foresman, 1972).

23. See JOSEPH MCGINNESS, *The Selling of the President* (New York: Trident Press, 1969).

24. See JOHN B. MCKITTERICK, "What Is the Marketing Management Concept?" *The Frontiers of Marketing Thought and Action* (Chicago: American Marketing Asso-

ciation, 1957), pp. 71–82; Fred J. Borch, "The Marketing Philosophy as a Way of Business Life," *The Marketing Concept: Its Meaning to Management,* Marketing Series, No. 99 (New York: American Management Association, 1957), pp. 3–5; and Robert J. Keith, "The Marketing Revolution," *Journal of Marketing,* January 1960, pp. 35–38.

25. Levitt, "Marketing Myopia."

26. Carlton P. McNamara, "The Present Status of the Marketing Concept," *Journal of Marketing,* January 1972, pp. 50–57.

27. Peter M. Banting and Randolph E. Ross, "The Marketing Masquerade," *Business Quarterly* (Canada), Spring 1974, pp. 19–27. Also see Philip Kotler, "From Sales Obsession to Marketing Effectiveness," *Harvard Business Review,* November-December 1977, pp. 67–75.

28. Laurence P. Feldman, "Societal Adaptation: A New Challenge for Marketing," *Journal of Marketing,* July 1971, pp. 54–60; and Martin L. Bell and C. William Emery, "The Faltering Marketing Concept," *Journal of Marketing,* October 1971, pp. 37–42.

29. Leslie M. Dawson, "The Human Concept: New Philosophy for Business," *Business Horizons,* December 1969, pp. 29–38; James T. Rothe and Lissa Benson, "Intelligent Consumption: An Attractive Alternative to the Marketing Concept," *MSU Business Topics,* Winter 1974, pp. 29–34; and George Fisk, "Criteria for a Theory of Responsible Consumption," *Journal of Marketing,* April 1973, pp. 24–31.

THE STRUCTURE OF MARKETING SYSTEMS

Every eight seconds a new American is born. He is a disarming little thing, but he begins to scream loudly in a voice that can be heard for seventy years. He is screaming for 56,000,000 gallons of water, 21,000 gallons of gasoline, 10,150 pounds of meat, 28,000 pounds of milk and cream, 9,000 pounds of wheat, and great storehouses of all other foods, drinks, and tobaccos. These are lifetime demands on his country and its economy.[1]

□When one stops to think about it, the amount of material needs of a people over the span of their lives is incredible. If individuals had to produce all the things they needed, they would not get very far. Their standards of living would be abysmally low. Modern society, fortunately, has discovered three efficient principles for producing and distributing all the goods and services that people need. The first principle is the *division of labor* whereby each person becomes skilled in making one or a few things that can be traded to obtain all the other necessities. The second principle involves the *market,* which creates organized arenas for the efficient trading of goods and services. The third principle is the invention of *money,* which becomes a common denominator of value that facilitates the operation of trade and markets.

Modern society consists of many interlinked marketing systems that carry on the work of meeting people's material needs. In this chapter we examine the concept of a marketing system, which is the first step on the way to understanding the marketing process. We define *marketing system* as follows:

- A **marketing system** is a set of interacting participants, markets, and flows that are involved in an organized arena of exchange.

A marketing system comprises three levels: the national level, the industry level, and the company level. We will illustrate each of these, devoting most of our attention to the company level.

national marketing systems

Every nation develops a particular set of institutions and practices to bring desired goods into existence and to distribute them to the various consumers. Although the number of national marketing systems is tremendous, they can be classified into three broad groups:

1. *Tradition-directed systems.* In this type of economy, the society's methods of production and distribution are fairly primitive and are governed by ancient

customs. Goods may be distributed on the basis of reciprocity, or redistribution, or primitive market systems.

2. *Market-directed systems.* In this type of economy, people freely decide on their production and consumption activities on the basis of their self-interest. Products and prices are determined by demand and supply. The United States, Japan, and several Western economies operate market-directed systems, although they are experiencing increased government regulation and control.
3. *Command-directed systems.* In this type of economy, economic activities are planned and managed by a central authority. This system is found in the Soviet Union, mainland China, and other socialist countries.

Structure of a National Marketing System

We will now examine the structure of a national marketing system as found in either a market-directed or a command-directed economy. The structure is similar except for the role of government. The basic structure consists of three *participants* (consumers, business firms, and government), two *markets* (resource markets and product markets), and three *flows* (goods and services, resources, and money). This structure is shown in Figure 2-1.

The first participant group, consumers, need a vast amount of goods and services. Instead of producing these goods and services themselves, consumers obtain them by going to product markets and exchanging their money for the goods and services they want. But where do the consumers get their money? They get their money by going to resource markets and exchanging their resources (labor, land, and capital) for income (wages, rent, interest).

In the meantime the participant group known as business firms are seeking money income, which they obtain by offering goods and services to the product markets. To produce these goods and services, they first go to the resource markets and buy the proper mix of productive resources.

Thus the marketing system consists of a flow of resources being turned into a flow of goods and services, and a flow of money expenditures being turned into a flow of money income. Another important flow (not shown in Figure 2-1) is the

Figure 2-1
Structure of a National Marketing System

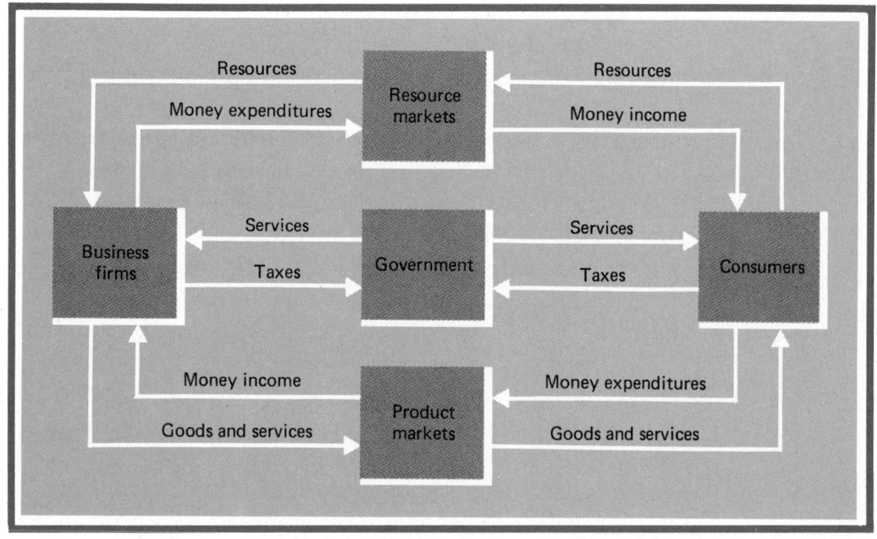

flow of information and communications, which facilitates the exchange processes.

The third participant in the national marketing system is government. In a market-directed economy, government's major role is to provide certain services to consumers and business firms and to finance these services by collecting taxes from these participants. The theory of the system is that consumers are free to buy what they want and business firms are free to sell what they want. Prices on the resource and product markets move up and down with changes in demand and supply. If prices are too high, goods do not sell, inventories pile up, and workers are laid off. This is a signal to business firms to reduce or transfer their resources to other industries. Conversely, if consumers are buying the goods in substantial quantities, this is a signal that further resources could well be transferred into this industry. The whole system is driven by consumers voting on which goods they want and what prices they will pay. The government's tasks are mainly (1) providing consumer information, education, and protection; (2) preventing anticompetitive behavior—such as price fixing—where one firm takes unfair advantage of other firms; and (3) producing certain goods and services that business firms are unable or unwilling to produce.

On the other hand, the government plays the major role in command-directed economies such as the USSR and mainland China. The government owns and operates the business firms, decides what to produce, and sets the prices in the factor and product markets. Consumers normally face a much smaller range of products and have more limited options with respect to the jobs they can take. The marketing system is less responsive to changing consumer needs because the government moves more slowly and is not necessarily willing to satisfy all classes of needs.

Participants and Forces in a National Marketing System

We will now take a closer look at the major participants and forces in a national marketing system. We should recognize that business firms play different roles in the system, there are various types of consumers, and there are various publics and forces that influence the system (see Figure 2-2).

The *task system* involves the major participants who play a role in supplying, exchanging, and consuming economic goods and services. One group of participants consists of resource suppliers, such as farmers, miners, timber producers, energy producers, workers, and financers. Their resources are purchased by a second group, manufacturers and processors, who convert these resources into food, wood products, machinery, metal, and other products. A third group consists of distributors and facilitators, who help bring these goods and services to their proper markets where a fourth group, consumers—such as households, schools, hospitals, and governments—proceed to purchase and consume them. Thus the task system consists of specialized organizations and individuals who are good at carrying out certain economic functions.

Although the basic direction of economic flow is shown as moving from left to right in Figure 2-2, it should be recognized that the actual flows are multidirectional. For example, manufacturers and processors sell some of their finished goods back to resource suppliers; thus International Harvester sells its farm equipment to farmers. Furthermore, distributors and facilitators also provide distribution services to resource suppliers selling to each other and to manufac-

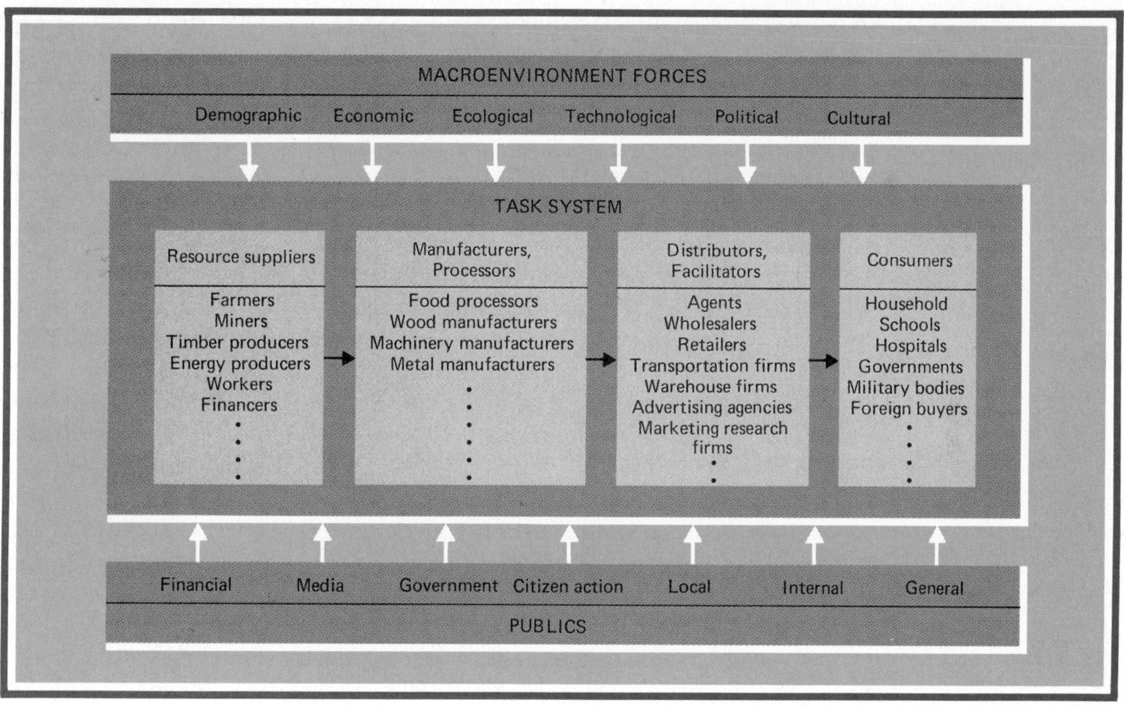

Figure 2-2 Major Participants and Forces in a National Economic System

turers, as well as distribution services to manufacturers selling to other manufacturers. Finally, consumers are not only consumers but also resource suppliers.

In addition to the participants in the task system, there is another set of participants, known as publics, who watch and influence the performance of the participants within the task system. A *public* is any group that has an actual or potential interest in or impact on other organizations. Banks, newspapers, government agencies, citizen action groups, and other publics are taking an increasing interest in evaluating and influencing the participants in the task system. We will discuss these publics' influence on marketing activity later in this chapter.

Finally, all of the participants are inescapably affected by major macroenvironment forces that roll like juggernauts, creating new threats and new opportunities. Every organization must find some way to not only monitor the changing demographic, economic, ecological, technological, political, and cultural forces but interpret them and respond to them. We will look at these macroenvironmental forces later in the chapter and discuss their marketing implications in depth in Chapter 7.

How to Research a National Marketing System

Although all modern economies share the general relationships shown in Figures 2-1 and 2-2, major differences in marketing practices and philosophies can be found from country to country. Marketers in one country cannot assume that they will find the same marketing practices in another country. Each country must be freshly researched in terms of its marketing structure and dynamics.

Who would have an interest in researching the marketing system of a particular country? Government officials in that country would want to examine and evaluate the national marketing system in order to improve its functioning. Domestic firms in that country would want to know how the marketing system operates in order to perform well in the marketplace. Foreign firms that are considering doing business in that country would want to know how its marketing system works. Finally, various international agencies that make loans or provide technical assistance would want to research the nation's marketing system.

As major new markets open in China, the Middle East, South America, and other parts of the world, companies looking for opportunities must have a systematic method for quickly and efficiently grasping the major features of the marketing system of any country. To illustrate, suppose the Pepsico Company wants to expand its soft-drink market penetration on the South American continent. It studies the various countries where it is not yet operating and identifies Bolivia, among other countries, as having a high sales potential for its soft drinks. This is based on a preliminary reading of the market size, purchasing power, soft-drink consumption, and particular competitors. Additional information would be needed, such as What are the major urban markets? What are the major channels of distribution? What are the normal markups given to middlemen? and What advertising media are available?

Table 2-1 outlines the major types of information needed to understand a national marketing system. To get further information, the marketing research department at Pepsico would obtain an overseas business report from the U.S.

Table 2-1
Information Requirements for Understanding a National Marketing System

OVERALL MARKET CHARACTERISTICS

A. Population
B. Geographical characteristics
C. Urban/rural characteristics
D. Income size, distribution, and growth
E. Consumption patterns
F. Cultural values
G. Government role and laws on marketing

MARKETING CHARACTERISTICS

A. Number of people engaged in sales and marketing
B. Major industries
   (1) Size distribution of firms (2) Employment
C. Channels of distribution
   (1) Wholesaling (number, size, types, operating characteristics) (2) Retailing (number, size, types, operating characteristics) (3) Other middlemen (4) Import channels (5) Export channels (6) Agricultural channels
D. Facilitating intermediaries
   (1) Transportation (roads, trucks, railroads, air, waterways) (2) Storage and warehousing (3) Communication (mail, telephone and telegraph, newspapers, radio, television, billboard) (4) Banking and credit (5) Marketing research agencies (6) Advertising agencies
E. Marketing mix
   (1) Product development (2) Pricing (3) Advertising and sales promotion (4) Sales force and sales management (5) Marketing research (6) Physical distribution

Department of Commerce describing that country. For example, a 1977 report entitled *Marketing in Bolivia* supplies valuable information about that country's marketing system, along with a bibliography listing additional sources of information. Some of the things Pepsico will learn about Bolivia are:

- Bolivia has 5.5 million people whose per capita income is among the lowest in South America. Only 31 percent of the population is urban and it is concentrated in a few large cities, such as La Paz, Cochabamba, and Santa Cruz.
- Bolivia depends mainly on imported products, the exceptions being alcoholic beverages and soft drinks, processed foods, shoes, television sets, plastics, and some clothing items.
- There are no chain-type retail stores nor large supermarket outlets. Retail stores are small in size and volume and are run as family businesses.
- The mountainous terrain of Bolivia has discouraged emphasis on highway travel; the highway system contains only 1,050 miles of paved roads.
- There are only ten advertising agencies in Bolivia. The principal advertising medium is the press (50 percent), followed by radio (25 percent), television (15 percent), and motion picture theaters, neon signs, billboards, and direct mail (10 percent).

EXHIBIT 2-1

JUAN LOPEZ'S LIFE IN LA PAZ, BOLIVIA

The city of La Paz, Bolivia, has a population of five hundred thousand, and over 80 percent of its residents are extremely poor. Juan Lopez's life is typical of that endured by many Bolivians. Juan wakes up in the morning and has a cup of hot coffee. At lunch, he usually has a little rice. At dinner, he may eat beans and codfish. This pattern of eating repeats itself in almost dreary monotony from day to day, not because it is Juan's preference or because he knows of no other foods, but because these foods are the only ones he can afford. Over 50 percent of Juan's budget goes to food.

How does Juan obtain his food? He buys most of it from Manuel Sunio, a small grocer, whose store is five minutes away from Juan's home. Manuel has been in the grocery business for five years, having opened his store after breaking away from a sugar plantation where he had worked most of his life. His store occupies only 400 square feet, and he lives in the back of it with his wife and two sons. The store carries basic staples such as rice, beans, coffee, and sugar. These basic foods are sold unpackaged and unbranded. Manuel scoops up an amount, weighs it on a hanging scale, and wraps it in a newspaper.

During a typical day, Manuel is visited by almost all of his customers, about thirty or forty persons. Shopping is a daily thing for a La Paz family, since they buy in small quantities (they lack storage space or enough money to buy in large quantities), need fresh bread (there are no preservatives to extend shelf life), and need milk daily (there are few refrigerators). They come in and chat with Manuel and with each other because grocery shopping is a social as well as an economic activity. Manuel often extends credit to his customers because their earnings fluctuate with the time of the year, being higher during the harvesting season.

Manuel's store is one of several small food stores in Juan's area. For his other food needs, such as bakery products, meat, fish, and candy, Juan shops at other specialized stores in the immediate neighborhood. Outside of food, Juan occasionally shops for tobacco, fabric, and hardware. His wife makes clothes for the family and acquires used clothing from charity sources. Juan's family owns no appliances because there is no electricity. As for furniture, Juan finds old crates and then hammers them into forms that will be useful as chairs, cabinets, and so on. The bed itself is simply a high pile of rags. Thus he meets his family's furniture needs not through the marketing system but through self-production.

Different groups in La Paz have different feelings toward the marketing system of La Paz. Juan feels that food prices are too high and that Manuel and other shopkeepers are to blame because of high markups. He thinks that Manuel's store is not very clean and that Manuel occasionally adulterates the quality of the coffee with cheap beans. Yet he doesn't switch stores, because the other shopkeepers are considered even worse in these respects. Also, he owes Manuel a lot of money.

Manuel, in turn, thinks that the wholesalers' prices are too high, especially for the amount of work they do. He thinks his own markups are reasonable because he lends so much credit and also has to cover the costs of spoilage and theft.

Government officials in La Paz think that there are too many small grocery stores, each operating inefficiently at a high cost. These stores do not believe in "price competition" but rather in "live and let live," resulting in high prices for consumers. Some officials would like to see a modern supermarket chain established in La Paz so that these small stores would have some competition. They think that consumers like Juan would flock to these new large clean stores, even if they are located farther away. The officials are concerned, of course, about the many bankruptcies and high unemployment that might result and the violent measures that the small shopkeepers might take against the new supermarkets. The officials also wish they had more confidence that people like Juan would actually patronize the new supermarkets. Otherwise these supermarkets would stand idle and the marketing reform would not result in lower prices to consumers.

This information will not be very encouraging to the Pepsico Company. However, Pepsico may decide to dig further by making some field trips to Bolivia and talking to knowledgeable business and government officials. It must also try to get a picture of Bolivian consumers and their needs and wants. The kind of life that a typical Bolivian leads is described in Exhibit 2-1. When Pepsico has enough information, it can decide whether it should enter its products in the Bolivian market. The key is the detailed study of the major characteristics of that nation's marketing system.

industry marketing systems

We can now shift our analysis of marketing systems from the national level to the industry level. Various participants, markets, and flows arise in each industry to facilitate the production, distribution, and consumption of its products. Wroe Alderson, one of the leading marketing scholars, saw the role of industries as that of transforming the heterogeneous raw materials found in nature into meaningful assortments that match the need patterns of consumers. "The whole economic process may be described as a series of transformations from meaningless to meaningful heterogeneity."[2]

The marketer's task in understanding an industry marketing system is to identify the major participants, markets, and flows that interact to produce the transformation of raw resources into finished goods and services. We will illustrate the marketing systems found in two different industries.

Magazines and Paperback Books Industry Marketing System

Publishers of magazines and paperbacks have the major task of distributing billions of dollars worth of magazines and paperbacks to the American public each year. Figure 2-3 shows the various distribution channels available to these publishers. We can use the term *distribution structure* to describe all available arrangements in an industry to get products from the producers to consumers.

Consider the distribution of magazines. Consumers get their copies of *Time, Business Week,* or *Sports Illustrated* in one of three ways. They can buy the magazine in a large retail outlet (e.g., supermarket, chain store, mass merchandiser), or buy it at a small retail outlet (e.g., neighborhood drugstore, newsstand), or receive it through the mail on a subscription basis. Large retailers obtain their magazine supply from one of the following: the publishers, the independent wholesalers, the national magazine distributors, or the national distributors who handle magazines and other items. Small retailers normally get their magazines from independent wholesalers or national magazine distributors. As for subscription sales, the publisher either handles this function directly or turns it over to subscription agents and pays a commission. Large magazine publishers normally run their own subscription operation and also sell directly to large retailers, whereas small magazine publishers have to work through independent middlemen to get their lesser-known magazines into circulation.

Figure 2-3
Distribution Channels for Magazines and Paperback Books

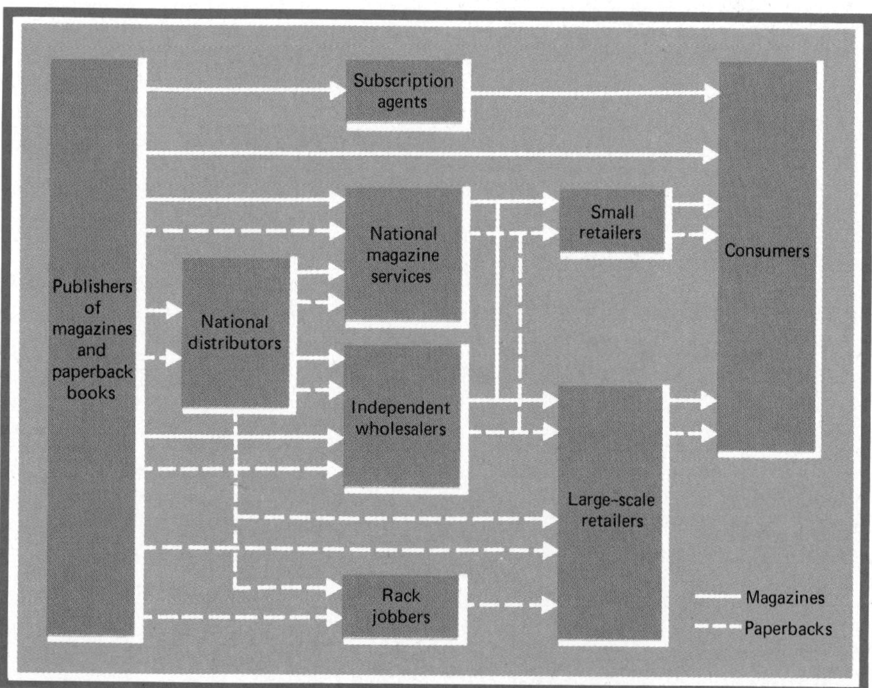

Source: Edwin H. Lewis, "Description and Comparison of Channels of Distribution," in *Handbooks of Modern Marketing,* ed. Victor P. Buell (New York: McGraw Hill Book Company, 1970), Section 4, p. 6.

Paperbacks are distributed in a similar way, with two differences. First, they are not normally sold through the mails because the cost of mail promotion and distribution is too great in relation to their price. Second, paperback publishers will often consign their titles to rack jobbers, who arrange for their distribution and display in large retail outlets. Rack jobbers handle the shelving, display, and rotation of titles, which would otherwise have to be handled by the retailers.

Paint Industry Marketing System

We will now illustrate the marketing system for a product that is sold to a great variety of end users, namely, paint. Figure 2-4 shows the major market participants involved in the distribution of paint. There are four major classes of end users: government and exports, contractors, the general public, and commercial and industrial users. In 1974 they collectively purchased 475 million gallons of paint. The manufacturers who produced this quantity of paint sold some of it directly to these various end users, some of it to wholesalers, and some of it to retailers. The wholesalers in turn sold most of their paint to retailers and the rest of it directly to final users. The retailers, of which there are several types, resold most of their paint to contractors and the general public.

This system makes it clear that one of the major tasks of marketing management is channel management. Marketing managers must identify, choose, and manage complex relations with a variety of other institutions whose services

Figure 2-4
Distribution Channels for Paint

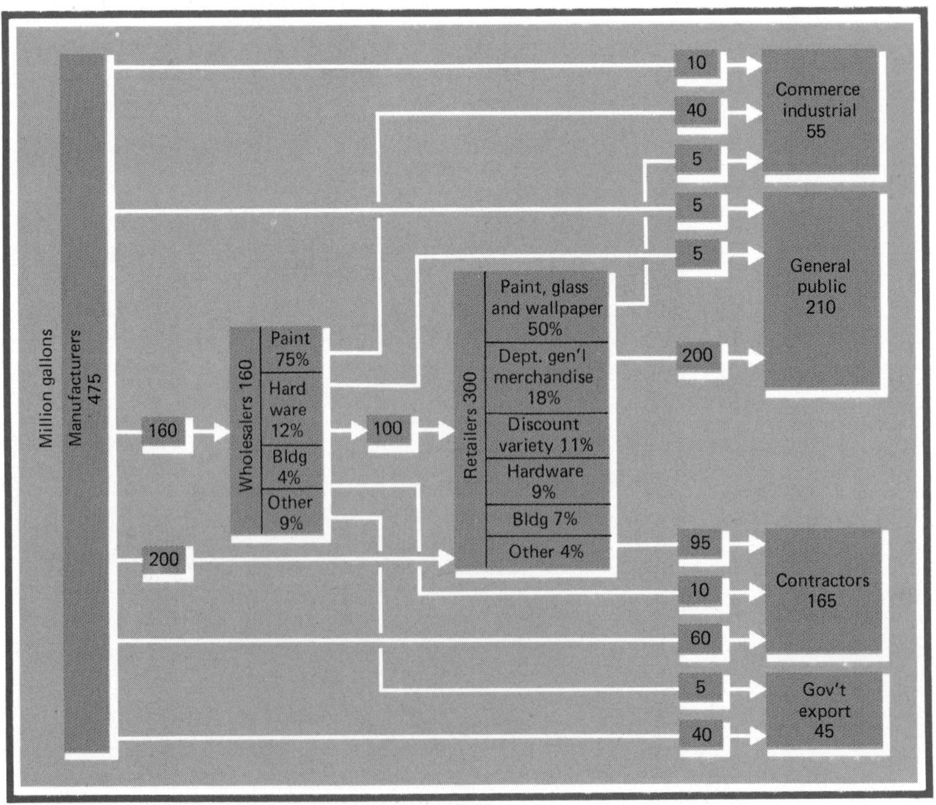

Source: Estimates by C. H. Kline & Co., 1978.

are needed and whose efficiency ultimately affects the producer's sales and profits.

company marketing systems

We are also able to define a marketing system from the company's point of view:

- A **company marketing system** is the set of major participants, markets, and forces that make up the company's marketing environment.

We can visualize the company as operating in a marketing environment made up of several levels of complexity. Six levels of the company's marketing environment are identified in Figure 2-5. At the center stands the company. Next to the company are various marketing channel firms that participate in the activities necessary to produce and distribute the company's products. Next are shown the markets that the company serves. Then there are the competitors who also offer goods and services of potential interest to the same markets. Both the company and its competitors operate under the watchful eye of multiple publics who have an interest in and a potential impact on their actions. Finally, all of the institutions and markets operate in a macroenvironment of major demographic, economic, ecological, political, technological, and cultural forces that have a significant and continuous impact on their performance.

We will now examine each level of the company's marketing environment. To illustrate these levels, we will discuss them in connection with the Schwinn Bicycle Company of Chicago, a major U.S. producer of bicycles.

The Company

At the center of any marketing system stands the company. We are concerned with the group within the company called marketing managers. At Schwinn there is a marketing department consisting of a vice-president of marketing, sales managers and a sales force, an advertising manager, a marketing research manager, a marketing planning executive, a pricing specialist, and some other marketing executives. Not every organization will have these marketing positions. Some organizations, especially nonprofit organizations, will not even have a marketing department or marketing managers. However, all organizations en-

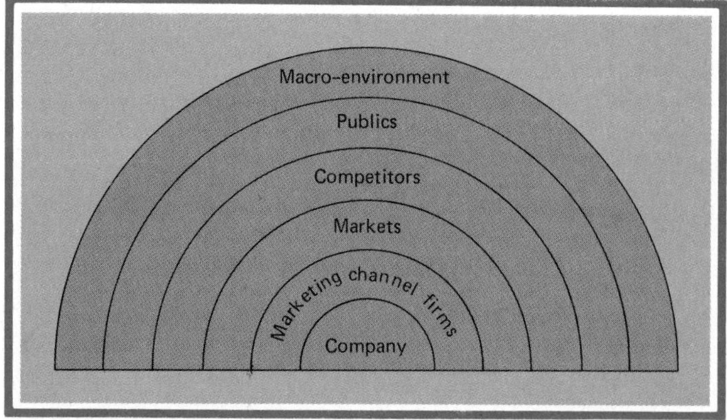

Figure 2-5 Levels in the Marketing Environment of a Company

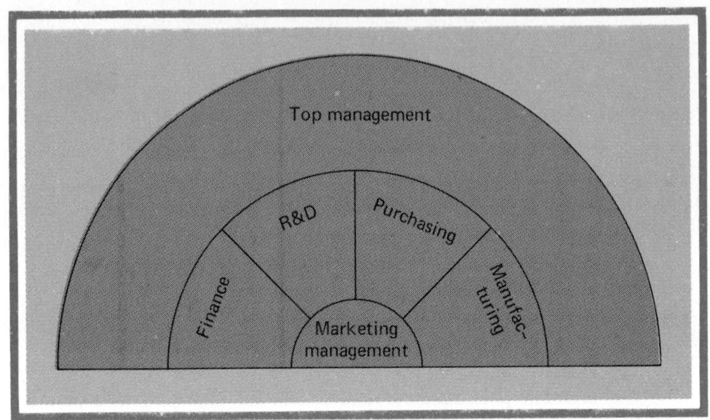

Figure 2-6
Company's Internal Environment

gage in marketing activities whether or not they are recognized as such or are carried out by people who are called marketing managers.

Now the marketing managers at Schwinn must base their marketing decisions not only on the forces operating in the external environment but also on the forces operating in the company's internal environment. The main forces in the company's internal environment are shown in Figure 2-6.

The first level of the company's internal environment that marketing management must consider is the other major departments of the company. All the major departments cooperate in developing the annual and long-range business plan. Marketing management supplies important inputs into the business-planning process and thereby provides an analysis that is often the starting point of the business-planning process. Throughout the planning process, however, marketing management works with and needs the thinking and support of the other departments.

Four major departments are shown in Figure 2-6. Financial management at Schwinn is concerned with the availability of funds to carry out the marketing plan, the efficient allocation of these funds to different products and marketing efforts, the likely rates of return that will be realized, and the level of risk in the sales forecast and marketing plan. Research and development management is concerned with the technical problems of designing safe and attractive bicycles and developing efficient methods of producing them. Purchasing is concerned with the availability and costs of obtaining needed supplies to produce the number of bicycles called for in the sales forecast. Finally, manufacturing is concerned with whether there will be sufficient production capacity and manpower, and with whether marketing has called for an inordinate number of models to be produced. Other departments not shown—such as accounting, personnel, and credit—also have to be contacted by marketing managers for their views and assistance.

A second level of the company's internal environment is top management. Top management at Schwinn includes the bicycle division general manager, the executive committee, the chief executive officer, the chairman of the board, and the board of directors. These higher levels of management set the company's mission, objectives, broad strategies, and policies. Marketing managers must make their decisions in the larger context defined by top management. Furthermore, their plans will be reviewed by these higher levels of management before they can be implemented.

Marketing management must also take into account the company's internal "culture" in developing its plans. Every organization has a culture molded by its history, leading personalities, and accomplishments. Culture describes the way in which the company's managers look upon the world and their mission. Many organizations have a traditional business culture, sticking to the "tried and true" ways of doing things and avoiding risk. Others have an innovative culture, always looking for new and better ways to perform their tasks. Some companies are dominated by a financial culture, others by a production culture, and still others by a sales culture. One of the greatest challenges to top management is to transform the existing culture of an organization into a marketing culture.

Marketing Channel Firms

No company can perform by itself all the activities involved in the production and distribution of its products and services to its final markets. It must work with other firms to get the job done. The major types of firms that it may work with are illustrated in Figure 2-7 and can be defined as follows:

1. **Suppliers** are business firms and individuals who supply resources needed by the producer to produce the particular good or service.
2. **Merchant middlemen** are business firms—such as wholesalers and retailers—that buy, take title to, and resell merchandise (often called *resellers*).
3. **Agent middlemen** are business firms—such as manufacturer's representatives and brokers—that are hired by producers and find buyers and negotiate sales but do not take title to the merchandise.
4. **Facilitators** are business firms—such as transportation companies, warehouses, banks, and insurance companies—that assist in the logistical and financial tasks of distribution but do not take title to goods or negotiate purchases or sales.
5. **Marketing firms** are business firms—such as advertising agencies, marketing research firms, and marketing consulting firms—that assist in targeting and promoting the sellers' products to the right markets.

We are now able to define *marketing channel:*

- A **marketing channel** is the set of all the firms and individuals that cooperate to produce, distribute, and consume the particular good or service of a particular

Figure 2-7
Marketing Channel Firms

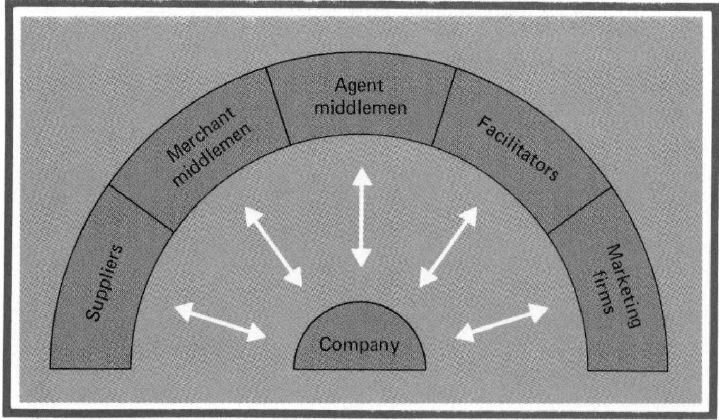

producer. Therefore a marketing channel consists of the five types of marketing channel firms listed earlier, plus the producer and the end user.

A distribution channel is a subset of the firms and individuals in a marketing channel:

- A **distribution channel** is the set of all the firms and individuals that take title, or assist in transferring title, to the particular good or service as it moves from the producer to the consumer. Thus a distribution channel includes primarily the merchant middlemen (because they take title) and the agent middlemen (because they assist in transferring title). It also includes the producer and the final consumers as starting and ending points. The distribution channel does not include suppliers, facilitators, and marketing firms.

We can illustrate the marketing channel in the case of Schwinn bicycles. To produce and distribute bicycles, Schwinn works with a host of firms that make up the marketing channel for its bicycles. These firms are shown in Figure 2-8.

First the Schwinn Company contracts with various suppliers for productive resources needed in bicycle manufacture, such as materials (oil, metal); components (tires, ball bearings, chains); energy (heat, light); manpower; and funds. Second, Schwinn uses some agents—here, manufacturer's representatives—to locate and place orders with resellers. Third, Schwinn also sells its bicycles directly to merchant middlemen (wholesalers and retailers). The particular agent and merchant middlemen used make up the distribution channel for Schwinn

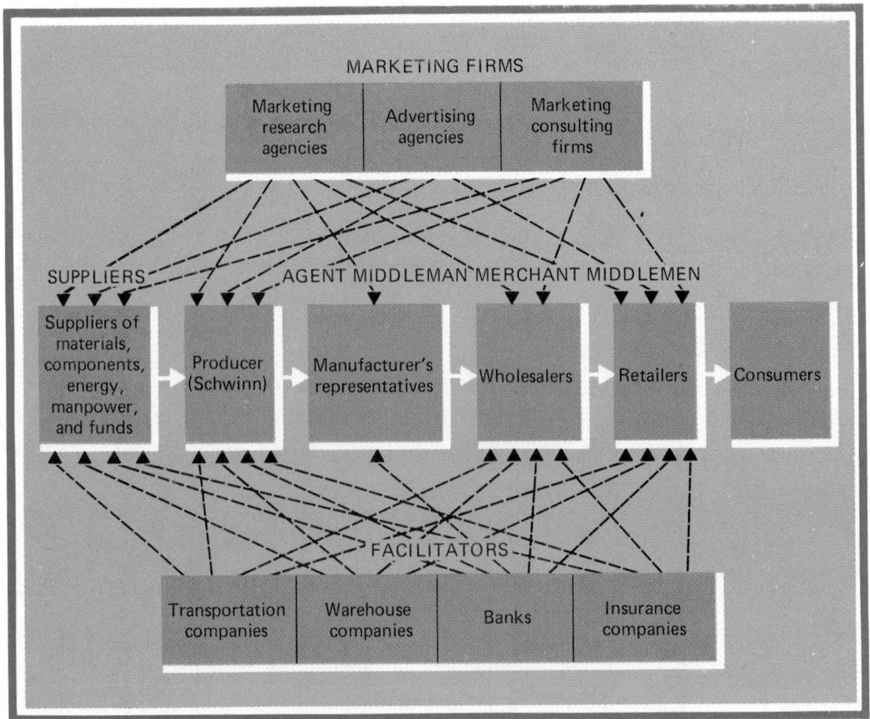

Figure 2-8
Types of Marketing Channel Firms

bicycles. Fourth, Schwinn hires the services of various facilitators (transportation companies, warehouse companies, banks, and insurance companies) to facilitate and finance the physical distribution of its bicycles to final markets. Fifth, Schwinn hires the services of various marketing firms (marketing research agencies, advertising agencies, and marketing consulting firms) to improve its marketing efficiency and effectiveness.

Schwinn always has the option of performing additional marketing activities internally instead of through other firms. It faces a number of "make-or-buy" decisions. Should Schwinn do its own marketing research or use a marketing research agency? Prepare its own advertising or use an advertising agency? Develop its own truck fleet or use a trucking firm? Sell directly to retailers or sell through wholesalers? The fact is that marketing intermediaries normally develop greater efficiency in carrying out these activities because of their broad experience and scale of operations. The company typically finds it cheaper to hire marketing intermediaries than to carry out these functions itself.

A glimpse of the reason for using marketing intermediaries can be given here, although more will be said about this in Chapter 14. Schwinn's bicycles will not have utility for the customer unless they are in the right form, in the right place, at the right time, and in the customer's possession. Thus the marketing task consists of creating the following utilities:

- *Form utility:* the utility created by making materials available in the right form. Thus an assembled bicycle has more form utility than a pile of wheels, chains, and handlebars.
- *Place utility:* the utility created by making something available for purchase in the right place. A Schwinn bicycle in the Minneapolis retail store has more utility for a Minneapolis buyer than the same bicycle in Schwinn's Chicago warehouse.
- *Time utility:* the utility created by making something available at the right time. Thus a Schwinn bicycle that can be delivered today has more utility than one that could not be delivered until six weeks from today.
- *Possession utility:* the utility created by taking ownership of a good. Thus a Schwinn bicycle owned by the consumer has more utility than one that is only on loan to the consumer.

To produce these utilities efficiently, Schwinn will find it more economical to work with other firms than to do the whole job itself. Let us ask why Schwinn does not sell its bicycles directly to consumers. There are two major reasons. First, Schwinn produces over a million bicycles annually, whereas each consumer buys only one or a few. There is a *discrepancy in the quantities* made by the producer and wanted by the consumer. It would be very costly for Schwinn to sell each bicycle individually. It would be better for Schwinn to sell dozens of bicycles at a time to middlemen who are equipped to sell smaller quantities of them in their individual trade areas. Second, Schwinn offers only one brand of bicycle, whereas the consumer might want to see and compare various brands. There is a *discrepancy of assortment* between Schwinn's assortment and the consumer's desired assortment. If all consumers insisted on buying bicycles from stores carrying several brands, Schwinn would be forced to sell to multibrand bicycle retailers. (Up to now, however, Schwinn has chiefly sold only through its own franchised dealers.) Altogether, certain discrepancies between the producer's capabilities and the market's requirements underlie the producer's interest in working with market intermediaries to reach and serve its target markets effectively.

Markets

The next level of the company's marketing environment consists of its actual and potential markets. The company can choose to operate in one or more of five basic types of markets. These markets are illustrated in Figure 2-9 and can be defined as follows:

1. *Consumer markets:* the set of individuals and households that buy products intended for personal consumption.
2. *Producer markets:* the set of organizations that buy products for the purpose of using them in the production process to make profits or achieve other objectives.
3. *Reseller markets:* the set of organizations that buy products in order to resell them at a profit.
4. *Government markets:* the set of government agencies that buy products for the purpose of producing public services, and/or transfer these products to others who need them.
5. *International markets:* the set of buyers found in other countries. This set includes foreign consumers, producers, resellers, and governments.

A company can choose to sell in any of the five types of markets. For example, Schwinn could consider selling its bicycles directly to consumers through factory or retail-owned outlets. It could sell its bicycles to producers who wished to use them in their operations to deliver goods or ride around the plant, and so on. It could sell bicycles to bicycle wholesalers and retailers, who in turn would resell them to consumer and producer markets. It could sell bicycles to government agencies. And it could sell bicycles to foreign consumers, producers, resellers, and governments. Each type of market has particular characteristics that call for careful study by the seller. (The buying characteristics of different markets are discussed in Chapters 8, 9, and 20.)

Each market is capable of further subdivision into *market segments.*

- A **market segment** is a subset of buyers who have similar needs and/or responses to marketing offers.

Figure 2-9
Basic Types of Markets

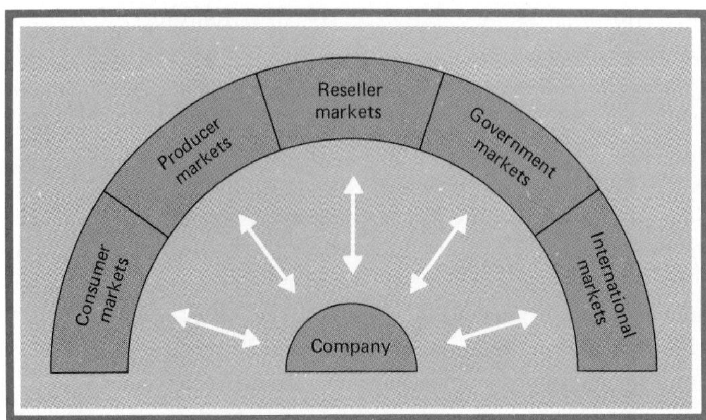

Thus the consumer market for bicycles can be segmented into the following subgroups: (1) consumers seeking an inexpensive bicycle, (2) consumers seeking a medium-quality bicycle, and (3) consumers seeking a fine bicycle.

A bicycle manufacturer that decides to design bicycles for the consumer market has to decide whether to sell in one, two, or all three market segments. Small bicycle manufacturers will normally specialize in one market segment so that they can do a good job in spite of limited resources. Suppose a small bicycle manufacturer decides to specialize in the fine-bicycle market segment. It will undertake a study of who buys fine bicycles, where they are located, their media habits, and the retailers they patronize. It will then design and produce a fine bicycle, make it available in the right retail outlets, and advertise it in the media read by fine-bicycle buyers. This small firm can, through concentrating its marketing attention on one market segment, create a high level of consumer satisfaction and loyalty in that market.

A large company such as Schwinn will normally choose to serve more than one market segment. However, it will not try to develop one bicycle design and one marketing program for the entire market. Instead, it will try to develop different bicycle lines and marketing programs for the distinct segments of the market it chooses to serve. We will say more about market segmentation in Chapter 10.

Competitors

The competitive environment constitutes still another level of the company marketing environment. The company must identify and monitor its competitors in order to gain and hold a profitable share of the market.

The competitive environment does not consist only of other companies or products but also of more basic things. Every company faces four major types of competitors in trying to serve its target markets. These competitors are illustrated in Figure 2-10 and can be defined as follows:

1. *Desire competitors:* other immediate desires that the consumer might want to satisfy.
2. *Generic competitors:* other basic ways in which the buyer can satisfy a particular desire.

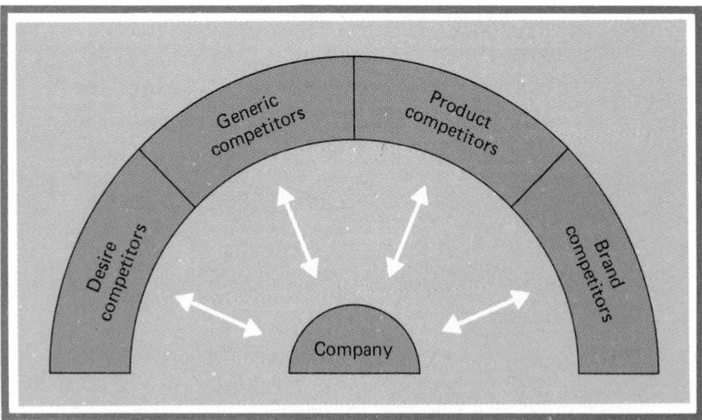

Figure 2-10
Types of Competitors

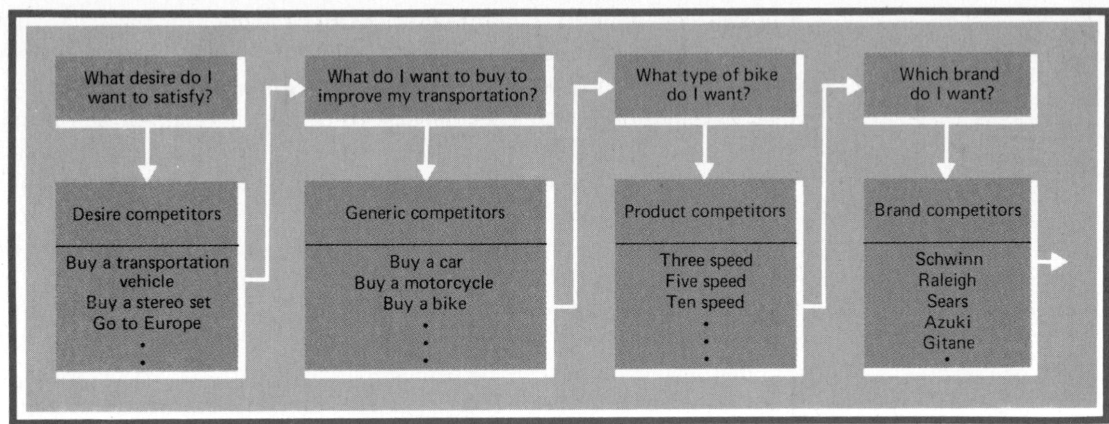

Figure 2-11 *Four Types of Competition*

3. *Product form competitors:* other product forms that can satisfy the buyer's particular desire.
4. *Brand competitors:* other brands of the same product that can satisfy the buyer's particular desire.

Let us discuss these four types of competitors in relation to the Schwinn Company. Schwinn's marketing vice-president would like to know who the major competitors are. The best way to do this is to research how people make bicycle-buying decisions. Suppose John Adams, a college freshman, is considering what to do with some discretionary income (see Figure 2-11). Several possibilities come to mind, including buying a transportation vehicle, buying a stereo set, and taking a trip to Europe. These are called *desire competitors* (because they represent immediate desires). Suppose he decides that he needs better transportation. His next question is, What do I want to buy to improve my transportation? Among the possibilities are buying a car, a motorcycle, or a bicycle. This is the set of *generic competitors.* If buying a bicycle turns out to be the most attractive alternative, John will next think about what type of bicycle to buy. This leads to a set of *product form competitors,* such as three-speed, five-speed, and ten-speed. John might tentatively decide on a ten-speed bicycle, in which case he will want to examine several *brand competitors,* such as Schwinn, Raleigh, Sears, Azuki, and Gitane.

In this way the marketing vice-president at Schwinn can determine all of the competitors standing in the way of selling more Schwinn bicycles. This information will help the manager spot opportunities to raise the attractiveness of Schwinn bicycles vis-à-vis the various desire, generic, product form, and brand competitors.

Publics

The company's marketing environment also involves various publics. We define *public* as follows:

- A **public** is any group that has an actual or potential interest in or impact on an organization's ability to achieve its objectives.

A public can facilitate or impede a company's ability to serve its markets. In general, a company can view any of its publics in one of three ways. A *welcome public* is a public that the company is interested in and that is interested in the company (e.g., donors). A *sought public* is one that the company is interested in but that does not take a strong interest in the company (e.g., mass media). An *unwelcome public* is one that the company shuns but that insists on taking an interest in the company (e.g., a citizens' action group).

The company has to market not only to its target customers but often to its major publics. Suppose the company wants some response from a particular public, such as its goodwill, favorable word of mouth, or donations of time or money. This calls for analyzing what the company could offer of value to the public in order to elicit the desired response. In other words, the company has to plan a benefit package that will build up the desired relationship with the target public.

The multitude of publics surrounding an organization can be classified into seven generic types (see Figure 2-12):

1. *Financial publics.* Financial publics include all the groups who take an interest in and might influence the organization's ability to obtain funds. Banks, investment houses, stock brokerage firms, and stockholders are the major financial publics. A company like Schwinn would seek to cultivate the goodwill of these groups by issuing annual reports, answering financial questions, and satisfying the financial community that its house is in order.
2. *Media publics.* Media publics include media companies that carry news, features, and editorial opinion: specifically, newspapers, magazines, and radio and television stations. A company like Schwinn is interested in obtaining as much favorable coverage and as little unfavorable coverage as possible. Getting more and better coverage from the press calls for understanding what the press is really interested in. The effective press relations manager knows most of the news editors and systematically develops a mutually beneficial relation with them. The manager offers interesting news items, informational material, and quick access to top management. In return, the media editors are more likely to give the company fair coverage.
3. *Government publics.* Management is increasingly finding it necessary to take government developments into account when it formulates marketing plans and policies on product safety, dealer rights and restraints, truth-in-advertising, and so on. For example, the Supreme Court has ruled against Schwinn because of the

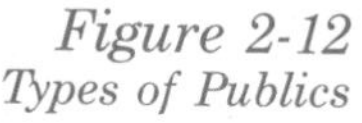

Figure 2-12
Types of Publics

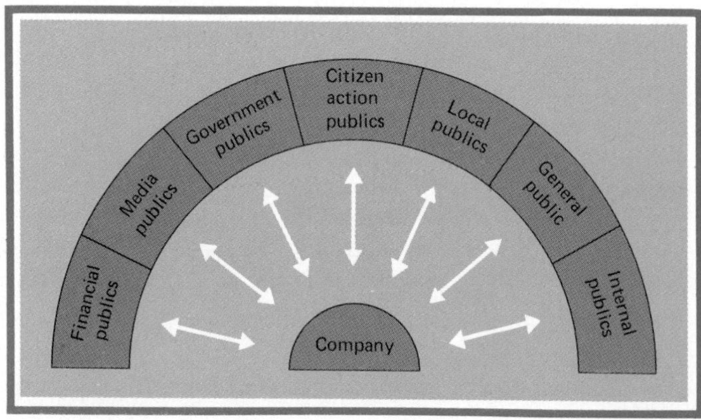

company's effort to restrain its franchised dealers from selling Schwinn bicycles to discount houses and nonfranchised dealers.[3] Managers at Schwinn and other companies have to make greater use of the company's lawyers for advice on what they can and cannot do. They are enlarging their government relations department to anticipate developments, see legislators, express concerns, and rally support. They are also joining with other organizations in trade associations to lobby for the common interests of their industry.

4. *Citizen action publics.* A company's marketing decisions are increasingly being affected by consumer organizations, environmental groups, minority groups, and other vocal public interest groups. For example, some parent groups are lobbying for greater safety features in bicycles. Bicycles are the nation's number-one hazardous product, based on the frequency and severity of injuries as reported by a group of hospitals.[4] Schwinn has the opportunity to achieve leadership in product safety design. The company also has a public affairs department, which stays in touch with consumer groups. And the company works through the bicycle manufacturers' trade association to search for constructive ways to deal with common industry problems.
5. *Local publics.* Every organization is physically located in one or more areas and comes into contact with local publics such as neighborhood residents, community organizations, and district officials. For example, people who live near a factory usually complain about noise, smoke, and parking. Companies usually appoint a

EXHIBIT 2-2

CITIZEN ACTION GROUP CALLS FOR BOYCOTT OF NESTLE PRODUCTS

Even the most venerable marketing companies can wake up one day and find one of their products under attack by a citizen action group who thinks the company is acting irresponsibly. In fact, the attacking group is likely to call for a boycott of all the company's products, even though only one is under criticism. The publicity resulting from such boycott efforts can damage the goodwill a company has taken years to build.

Nestlé was singled out as such a target in 1978. Nestlé, the Swiss-based multinational which manufactures such well-known products as Nestlé crunch bars, Taster's Choice coffee, Stouffer's frozen foods, also produces infant baby formula.

The citizen's group is accusing Nestlé of irresponsibly marketing infant milk formula to third-world mothers who the group claims do not understand the importance of sterilizing procedures to make the powdered formula safe. They further accuse Nestlé of underplaying the importance of breast feeding to the health of the baby. Nestlé's selling effort, according to the citizen's group INFACT (Infant Formula Action Coalition), is carried on by persons wearing nurse's uniforms who are not really nurses. Nestlé counterargues that the medical representatives are qualified nurses or midwives "who work closely with local government health authorities clinics on such topics as the importance of breast feeding, diet for mothers, and proper formula use."

INFACT has been working on the boycott for months by a mail campaign which urges "more people have to know" and asks for financial help in bringing the message to more people. The INFACT letter names all the brands owned by Nestlé. Nestlé claims that the boycott has had no economic impact. However, Nestlé is worried about the future effects of the boycott which could give Nestlé a bad name and damage future sales.

Source: Adapted from *Marketing News* (published by the American Marketing Association), March 23, 1979, pp. 1–2.

community relations officer whose job consists of keeping close to the community, attending meetings, answering questions, and making contributions to worthwhile causes. Instead of waiting for local issues to erupt, the company invests in the community to build a bank of goodwill.

6. *General public.* The company is ultimately concerned with the attitude of the general public toward its products and activities. The general public does not act in an organized way toward the company, as citizen action groups do. But the members of the general public have a certain image of the company and its standing as a corporate citizen, and this affects their patronage. To build a good image, a company like Schwinn will lend its officers to community fund drives and make substantial contributions to charity. It will set up systems to respond to consumer complaints. And it will use institutional advertising to describe what kind of company it is.
7. *Internal publics.* Every organization has internal publics as well as the external publics listed above. The internal publics include blue-collar workers, white-collar workers, volunteers, managers, and the company's board of directors. The larger the company, the more important it is to develop internal newsletters and other forms of communication to inform and motivate the internal publics. If employees feel good about the company, they will show a positive attitude toward the external publics. Every employee of the company is involved in public relations, from the chief officer who meets the general public, to the financial vice-president who addresses the financial community, to the field sales representative who calls on customers.

Macroenvironment

The company and its marketing channel members, customers, competitors, and publics all operate in a larger macroenvironment of forces that shape opportunities for and pose threats to the successful functioning of the company. These forces largely represent "uncontrollables" in the company's situation. In the short run, the company has to adapt through judicious choice of the "controllable" factors, such as the markets it elects to serve and its marketing programs. In the long run, the company, along with other companies, can have a formative influence on the macroenvironmental forces.

The macroenvironment consists of the six major forces shown in Figure 2-13. A bicycle company such as Schwinn would be well advised to monitor each macroenvironmental force to stay abreast of possible new opportunities as well as emerging threats. Consider the following:

Figure 2-13
Forces in the Macroenvironment

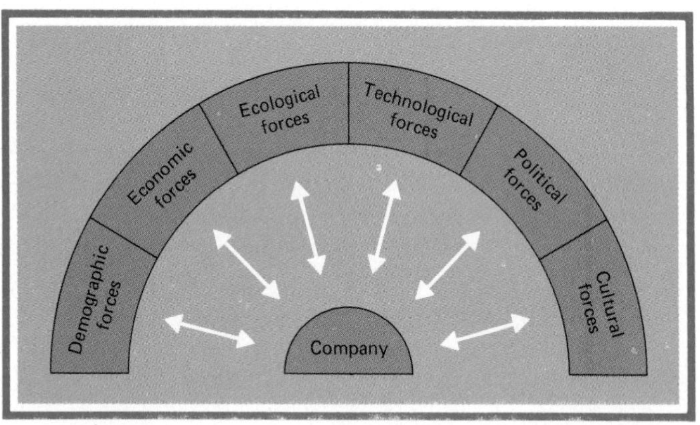

1. *Demographic forces.* This category covers all the main trends and developments in the size and character of the population, particularly birthrates, age distribution, geographical distribution, and marriage and divorce rates. Schwinn should pay particular attention to the implications of such factors as the aging population and the movement to the Sunbelt on the future demand for bicycles.
2. *Economic forces.* This category covers the major trends and developments in personal disposable income, discretionary income, the cost-of-living level, consumer savings and debt, and changing expenditure patterns. All of these will have an impact on the willingness and ability of consumers to buy bicycles, and on the type of bicycles they will buy. Bicycles are a discretionary item, and downward shifts in real income will substantially dampen demand.
3. *Ecological forces.* This category covers trends in the supply and cost of natural resources and energy, and problems of environmental deterioration and pollution control. In this case, ecological forces are favorable to bicycle demand. The high cost of gasoline and the polluting effects of automobiles will increase interest in bicycle transportation.
4. *Technological forces.* This category covers major developments in new products, materials, and processes that will have an impact on the industry. Schwinn will want to consider ways to use new metal and plastic materials, as well as the feasibility of adding a line of motorized bicycles (mopeds). Also it will want to watch for new technologies to bring down the cost of producing and assembling bicycles.
5. *Political forces.* This category covers major developments in legislation, government agency decisions and enforcement, and the impact of public interest groups on the industry. Schwinn will want to monitor legislation regarding product safety, occupational safety, truth-in-advertising, truth-in-credit, and other legal and political developments that may affect its marketing planning.
6. *Cultural forces.* This category covers major developments and shifts in cultural values and life styles as they would affect the particular industry and company. Schwinn will benefit from the growing national interest in physical exercise and outdoor activity.

We will examine these macroenvironmental forces in greater detail in Chapter 7 and point out the specific trends taking place and their implications for marketing decision making.

This concludes our discussion of the *structure* of marketing systems at the national, industry, and company levels. In the next chapter we will consider the *process* by which companies carry on their strategic planning and marketing decisions in an effort to maintain their viability in a rapidly changing marketplace.

summary

A marketer has to be skilled in analyzing marketing systems. A *marketing system* is the set of interacting participants, markets, and flows that are involved in an organized arena of exchange. Marketing systems exist at the national, industry, and company levels.

A *national marketing system* consists of consumers, business firms, product markets, resource markets, and government institutions and the flows of money, resources, and goods and services that interconnect them. In trying to understand the marketing system of a particular nation, one must examine the nation's characteristics and its major marketing institutions and practices.

An *industry marketing system* describes the participants, markets, and flows involved in moving the products of a particular industry to its final consumers. The industry marketing systems for magazines, paperbacks, and paint were described.

A *company marketing system* describes the set of interacting institutions, markets, and forces that make up the company's marketing environment. A company operates in a marketing environment consisting of six levels of complexity. The first level involves the company's internal environment—its several departments and management levels—as they affect marketing management's decision making. The second level consists of the marketing channel firms that cooperate to create marketing value for a marketplace: specifically the suppliers, agent middlemen, merchant middlemen, facilitators, and marketing firms. The third level consists of the major types of markets in which the company can sell: specifically the consumer, producer, reseller, government, and international markets. The fourth level consists of the four basic types of competitors facing any company offer: desire competitors, generic competitors, product form competitors, and brand competitors. The fifth level consists of all the publics that have an actual or potential interest in or impact on the organization's ability to achieve its objectives: financial, media, government, citizen action, and local, general, and internal publics. The sixth level consists of the major macroenvironmental forces impinging on the organization and its surrounding institutions: demographic, economic, ecological, technological, political, and cultural.

■ questions for discussion

1. What are the three major types of national marketing systems? Into which category do Saudi Arabia, Uganda, and Canada fall?
2. Who are the direct and indirect participants in the national marketing systems? Describe these participants in a decision to stimulate the development of solar energy.
3. Evaluate the Bolivian national marketing system.
4. Discuss the participants, markets, and flows for the brewery industry marketing system.
5. What is the first level in the company marketing system? Specifically, whom must the marketing manager take into consideration in making decisions at this level?
6. Describe the marketing channel firms that Procter & Gamble might use in marketing a new brand of laundry detergent.
7. Compare and contrast the consumer, producer, and reseller markets, using automobiles as an illustration.
8. Discuss the four types of competitors that someone planning to open a new pizza parlor near your campus must understand.

9. How do *publics* differ from *consumers*? Explain by using a specific example.
10. Comment on each of the relevant macroenvironmental factors that will have an impact on Exxon's marketing of gasoline.

references

1. From ROBERT AND LEONA RIENOW, *Moment in the Sun* (New York: Dial Press, 1967).
2. WROE ALDERSON, "The Analytical Framework for Marketing," *Proceedings—Conference of Marketing Teachers from Far Western States* (Berkeley: University of California Press, 1958).
3. U.S. v. Arnold Schwinn and Co. et al., 388 U.S. 365 (1967).
4. See "Dictating Product Safety," *Business Week,* May 18, 1974, p. 60. The list was prepared by the Consumer Product Safety Commission. The other hazardous products, in order of their degree of hazard, are stairs; nails, tacks, screws; football equipment; baseball equipment; basketball equipment; architectural glass; doors; tables; playground equipment; beds; chairs; chests, buffets, bookshelves; power lawn mowers; bathtubs and showers; and cleaning agents. (Autos, cigarettes, and some foods and drugs were excluded from the study.)

Cases

1 Ronco Teleproducts, Inc.

You've just scrambled an egg for breakfast, and now you have to wash out that messy bowl and rinse off the fork. What drudgery, you say. Wouldn't it be nice if chickens laid scrambled eggs?

That isn't in prospect yet. But Ronald M. Popeil has the next-best solution. "I know the trials and tribulations that go on in the kitchen," he says, "and it used to disturb me that any time someone wanted to scramble an egg, he had to make such a mess." So Mr. Popeil invented a battery-powered machine that scrambles eggs while they're still in the shell. Now Ronco Teleproducts Inc., of which Mr. Popeil is chairman, will gladly sell you the gadget . . . or, the machine. "It isn't just another gadget," Mr. Popeil insists.

Of course not. But it is one of the winners in this newspaper's Things-We-Could-Probably-Live-Without Contest. In our quest for serious new devices that are hard to take seriously, we also found shoes with built-in retractable roller skates, a cordless microphone that broadcasts your voice over any nearby FM radio, and an electric mousetrap. They all really exist, and the people who make and sell them point to a multitude of benefits.

Perfectly Blended Eggs

The Egg Scrambler, for instance, can come in handy at breakfast. It costs $7.77, and in essence it's a needle in a cup, mounted on an electric motor. You impale the egg—gently, of course—on the needle and press down until the motor starts. Then you count to five slowly, lift the egg off and break it into the pan. "Not only is there no mess," says Mr. Popeil, "but you get the perfectly blended egg."

Perfectly blended eggs, of course, banish forever that bane of breakfast—runny egg whites. Runny egg whites, Mr. Popeil explains, make French toast rubbery and scrambled eggs gooey. "I have solved the cleanup problem and the French-toast problem and the scrambled-egg problem," boasts the inventor.

Now, after breakfast, you're on your way to work, and suddenly mere walking isn't enough. But that's no problem if you're wearing Pop Wheels. All you have to do is lift up each foot, press a button, and you're on roller skates.

"Pop Wheels make so much sense," says Matthew F. Durda, president of American Pop Wheels Inc. "With Pop Wheels, you don't have to be O.J. Simpson to get around the airport fast."

Pop Wheels, which sell for about $40, originated in Switzerland, and found their way to Canada. Last year, Mr. Durda got the rights to market them in the U.S. Before that he sold used cars.

Mr. Durda's salesmanship shows as he discusses his new product. "It's almost like something out of a James Bond movie," he says. "The hinges come up and down like airplane landing wheels. You walk down the street, reach down and pop your wheels, and you're gone. The wheels are small, so it looks like you're floating on air."

Mr. Microphone Helps Out

When you get to work, you retract your landing gear, only to find that at your morning sales meeting the microphones have conked out.

But you're in luck. You're carrying Mr. Microphone, another brainchild of Mr. Popeil. Mr. Microphone is a $12.88 wireless device that lets you "broadcast" over any nearby FM radio set.

All you do is turn on Mr. Microphone, home in on the right frequency (somewhere between 88 and 102 on the dial), and you're in business. "If you use two radios, you broadcast in stereo," Mr. Popeil says. "This is perfect if you have to talk to a lot of people at a meeting. It isn't a toy."

Perhaps not, but Mr. Popeil admits that Mr. Microphone isn't strictly business either. "Lots of people would like to hear what their singing sounds like over the radio, and this lets them find out," he says. "People have a little ham in them, and you'd be surprised what they do when they get their hands on Mr. Microphone."

The electric mousetrap holds no surprises—except for mice. The trap is a tube-like device with a little hole in the end. If a mouse crawls in, attracted by a scented pellet, he sticks his head between two electrodes—and, zap.

For $14.99, the electric mousetrap doesn't do anything that a 39-cent wooden mousetrap won't do. But it has some advantages for the mouse and for you, asserts Joel DeWitt, vice president of Hall Industries Inc., which makes the device. "Our trap provides a humane, instantaneous death," he explains. "And when it's over, you can put your hand over your eyes and shake the mouse into the garbage can. You don't have to see the thing."

Mr. DeWitt adds, "Back in 1963, we were the first to introduce electric bug killers to consumers. It kind of follows that we'd be the first with electric mousetraps."

Source: Paul Ingrassia, "You Wouldn't Need Scrambler if Hens Laid Scrambled Eggs," *Wall Street Journal*, April 25, 1979.

Questions

1. Which product, the electric egg scrambler, Pop Wheels, Mr. Microphone, or the electric mousetrap has the greatest appeal for you? Which the least? Why?
2. What are your reactions to the marketing efforts for each of the products?
3. Select one of the above products and indicate:
   - whether you would use retail outlets to reach consumers and if so, what type(s) and why.
   - the general nature of your program to attract buyers.

2 U.S. Postal Service

Marie Jenkins, a newly arrived freshman at State University, needed a postage stamp to mail her first letter home. At a nearby chain drugstore she found a stamp machine but was dismayed when, in return for two quarters, she received only thirty-three cents' worth of stamps. Feeling that she had been cheated, she complained to the druggist. "That's the way it is," he said, and he suggested that she read the message posted on the machine. She left the store thinking how Mr. Whipple, her hometown druggist, pinched the Charmin and sold stamps over the counter at face value.

Later, Marie saw stamp machines offering various stamp values in several locations. These values and locations were as follows:

LOCATION	STAMP VALUES OFFERED BY AMOUNT PAID 25¢	50¢	$1.00
Chain drugstore	Four 3¢	Two 15¢ and one 3¢	Five 15¢
Motel	Four 3¢	Two 15¢ and one 3¢	Five 15¢
Bank	—	Three 15¢	—
Postal campus kiosk*	Face value	Face value	Face value
Post office	Face value	Face value	Face value

*Operated by U.S. Postal Service, unattended.

Ten days before her next check from home was due, Marie sat down to write to her family. Her mind drifted to what she now calls "The Great Stamp Machine Ripoff." As her thoughts floated through her mind, she asked herself, "Why do I let such a little thing get to me? My allowance is small but not that small. I guess it's the principle of the thing. It's not like expecting a 'free lunch,' which, according to my boyfriend, doesn't exist anyway." Coming back to reality, she stood up and shouted, "Phooey, why write anyway? I have no stamp and it takes too long. I'll just call home collect, even if I am asking for money."

Questions

1. What do you think of the druggist's reply to Marie? How would you have handled the situation?
2. How do you account for the price differences?
3. Should postage stamps be sold outside of post offices? Why or why not? If so, where, how, and at what prices?
4. A stamp machine operator proposed that the U.S. Post Office Department sell stamps at a discount to companies reselling at more convenient locations, thereby increasing the total sale of stamps. Evaluate this proposal.
5. What opportunities does the U.S. Post Office Department have to use a marketing approach in view of deteriorating services and increased private competition in the form of surface and air letter and parcel delivery systems, electronic message transfer systems, and data networks?

3 Great Waters of France, Inc.: Perrier

In less than two years the sales of Perrier sparkling mineral water from France skyrocketed from $1 million to $30 million per year in the United States. This phenomenal success in creating a new segment in the U.S. soft-drink market attracted numerous large and small competitors. The Perrier management is now faced with the problem of how to continue its meteoric rise, which surprised everyone, including the management.

Perrier's sales success is based upon a carefully planned and executed strategy, which involves a product sold at a premium price and backed with heavy advertising. Perrier is positioned as a healthful alternative to soft drinks or alcoholic beverages and as a product that is bought by affluent adults and those who try to be like them. A 23-ounce bottle now sells for 69¢–79¢, about 50 percent above the price of the average soft drink. Prior to the new mass-marketing thrust it sold for close to $1 in gourmet shops.

Perrier is a naturally carbonated spring water with smaller bubbles and a distinct flavor when compared with competing products, which are charged with machine-made carbon dioxide. The distinctively shaped green-tinted bottle, the equally distinctive label, the premium price, and the advertising all combine to play on snob appeal and build an elitist image. The new advertising included ads in high-fashion women's magazines and TV commercials narrated by Orson Welles. These commercials went to twenty-six major metropolitan markets and to an additional twenty-five metropolitan markets later on.

An essential part of the Perrier plan involved shifting distribution emphasis from gourmet shops to the soft-drink sections of supermarkets. Ironically here price competition runs rampant, shelf and special display space demands are severe, and costly promotions and trade allowances are essential.

In this environment, Perrier's elitist image is being given its most severe test. Some marketers believe that all of the elitist image-building efforts may not be able to offset the soft-drink section ambience and competitive behavior. They feel that it is only a matter of time until this highly visible item will be sold as a "price special" to draw customers.

Others contend that Perrier is a fad in this country and that its long life in France as a leading beverage will not be repeated in the United States.

Bruce Nevins, president of Great Waters of France, Inc., who developed his marketing abilities at Levi Strauss and Co., admits that Perrier's great growth was aided by Americans' rising concern with diet and health. He adds that Perrier is no more a fad than health is.

"Perrier Hopes to Bubble its Way into America's Goblets", *Advertising Age*, July 25, 1977; "French Bottler Tries to Replace US Pop with Natural Fizz", *Wall Street Journal*, April 12, 1978; "Perrier: The Astonishing Success of An Appeal to Affluent Adults", *Business Week*, January 22, 1979.

Questions

1. What reasons can be given for paying over one dollar per quart for water with gas from the bowels of the earth? Do they make sense? Need they make sense?
2. Is Perrier a fad? Is the Coors beer mystique a similar situation?
3. Is it likely that Perrier will become a price football? What steps should management take to preserve its image?
4. Where should Perrier be located in supermarkets?

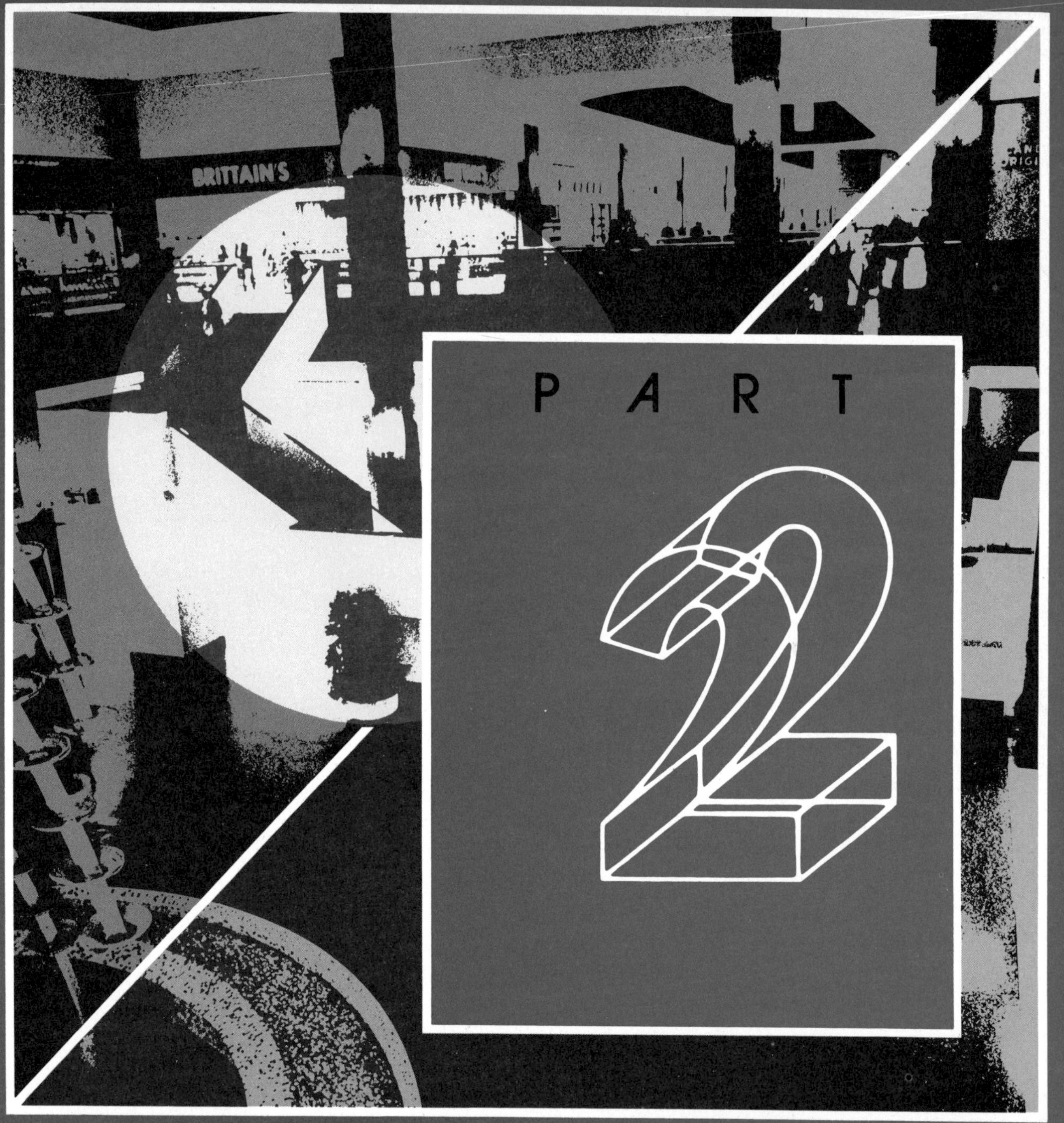

marketing's role in the company

STRATEGIC PLANNING AND THE MARKETING PROCESS

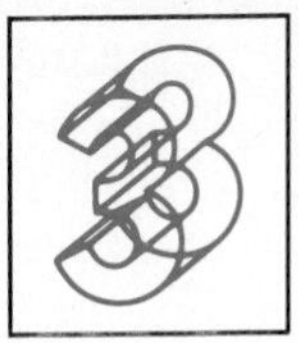

A few years ago, Olin Corp. was awash in aggressive marketing plans for goosedown sleeping bags, propane stoves, tents, and other camping products. At the same time, Olin was pushing industrial mainstays such as polyester film and polyvinyl chloride. But profits were still lackluster at best. Today, however, the $1.5 billion Stamford (Conn.) conglomerate has jettisoned all these products and is putting its capital into such areas as brass sheeting and hydrazine chemicals—products that fit in much better with its established corporate expertise. Reason: Olin has turned to a planning method that stresses overall corporate goals above individual product potentials.

The concept, known variously as strategy planning or strategy management, enables a company to spot—and capitalize on—its strengths in certain markets, and to sacrifice those market areas where growth is marginal. Although its cutthroat nature can make individual product managers unhappy at times, "it shows you how to drop your dogs and pick up stars," explains one veteran corporate planner.[1]

□We are now ready to look inside the company to examine the processes it uses to select markets, enter them profitably, and grow in these markets. In trying to cope with an ever-changing and challenging environment, modern companies use two key processes to build their future. The first is strategic planning, which enables top management to determine what businesses it wants to emphasize. The second is the marketing process, which enables the company to proceed in a systematic way to identify and turn specific opportunities into profitable businesses.

Companies will differ considerably in the degree to which they use strategic planning and the marketing process. The most outstanding companies use both. Many other companies fail to use one or both. As a result, it has been said that "there are three types of companies. Those who make things happen. Those who watch things happen. Those who wonder what happened."

We recognize at the outset that organizations do not have the same characteristics and objectives. This chapter (1) distinguishes major types of organizations that have strategic marketing problems, (2) analyzes the underlying requirements for successfully adapting any organization to its environment, (3) describes the major steps involved in company strategic planning, and (4) describes the major steps involved in carrying out the marketing process.

the age of organizations

Our society abounds in organizations that stand ready to serve every need, whether large or small, good or bad, elevated or prosaic. With little effort, Chicagoans can walk down Clark Street and instantly gratify their appetite for chicken, hamburger, or pizza—courtesy of Kentucky Fried Chicken, McDonald's, or Pizza Hut. If they are interested in buying something to wear, they can drive to the Old Orchard Shopping Center and rummage through racks of clothes at Marshall Field's, Baskin's, or Montgomery Ward's. Their desire for recreation or entertainment can be satisfied instantaneously—courtesy of the YMCA or the Biograph Theatre. If the weather is too cold, they can board a Boeing 747 at O'Hare Airport and reach the balmy shores of Miami three hours later—courtesy of Delta Airlines. All said, innumerable organizations stand ready to serve human needs by responding to them as business opportunities. The twentieth century is the age of organizations.

Organizations are so omnipresent that it is difficult to believe that life ever existed without them. Yet throughout most of human history, people have had to satisfy their needs through their own exertions. There was no fast-food outlet, health club, or local movie theatre available.

We define *organization* as follows:

- A **formal organization** is a social unit which is characterized by explicit goals, definite rules and regulations, a formal status structure and clear lines of communication and authority.[2]

Types of Organizations

Of the various ways to classify organizations in a society, we are primarily interested in whether the organization is privately or publicly owned and operated, and whether the organization is organized for profit or nonprofit purposes. These two distinctions lead to the four types of organizations shown in Figure 3-1.

Quadrant I of the figure shows private-for-profit firms and is called, at least

Figure 3-1
Four Types of Organizations

	Private	Public
Profit	I Private corporations Partnerships Sole proprietorships	II State-owned airlines State-owned telephone co.
Nonprofit	IV Private museums Private charities Private universities Private associations Private hospitals	III Government agencies Public schools Public hospitals

in the United States, the *first sector* because it has been entrusted with doing most of society's economic work—producing food, clothing, shelter, and so on.

Quadrants II and III make up the *second sector* (or public sector) and cover all the government organizations set up to carry on societal functions that normally yield no profit, have to be performed, and warrant public control. This includes such classic governmental functions as defense, public works, public education, and justice. Most of the public sector organizations are in Quadrant III. However, the government may also own and operate a few enterprises for profit (or at least cost recovery), as shown in Quadrant II.

Quadrant IV covers the remaining organizations in the society, those operated privately and not for profit. It is called the *third sector* (or nonprofit sector). Nonprofit organizations perform those societal functions that do not yield a profit, are desirable to perform, and need not be under public ownership. "Nonprofits" represent a *middle way* for meeting social needs, without resorting to the profit motive on the one hand or government bureaucracy on the other. The third sector contains tens of thousands of organizations, ranging from the Society for the Preservation and Encouragement of Barber Shop Quartet Singing in America to major foundations, colleges, hospitals, museums, charities, social agencies, and churches.

All of these organizations face the problem of survival. Private-for-profit firms survive by continuously adjusting their product lines and marketing programs to new opportunities in the marketplace. Government agencies and nonprofit firms survive to the extent that they continue to render valued services and maintain the support of constituencies. Every organization must know how to develop exchange values so that it can attract the resources required for its survival.

organization/environment adaptation

An organization's performance in the marketplace depends on the degree of creative alignment between the organization and its environment. The ideal organization examines its environment for opportunities, sets appropriate objectives, develops a strategy to achieve them, builds a framework to carry out these objectives, and designs management systems to support the organization's ability to carry out its strategy. This can be illustrated as follows:

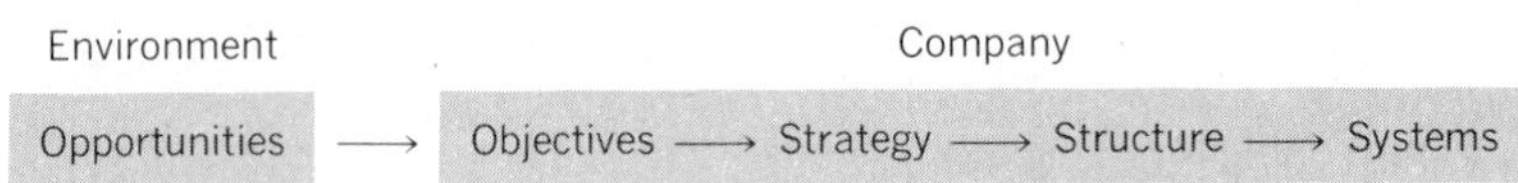

In practice, however, various problems can prevent this ideal from being realized. The main problem is that these various components alter at different rates, resulting in a lack of optimal alignment. Following is a typical company situation:

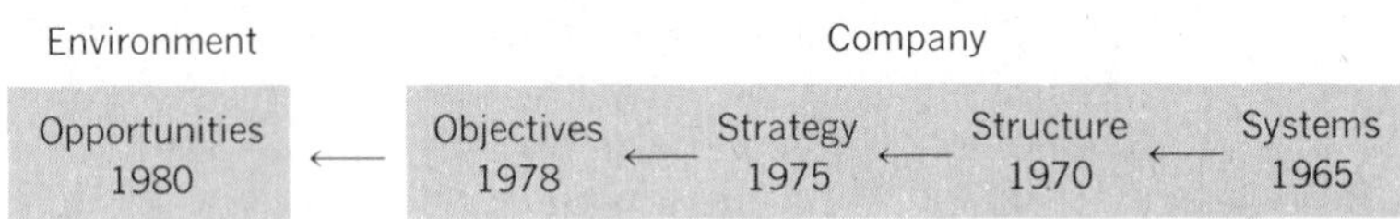

This says that the company is operating in a 1980 environment with objectives established in 1978, a strategy developed in 1975, an organizational structure developed in 1970, and management systems designed in 1965. In other words, the company's existing systems, structure, strategy, and objectives are dictating what opportunities it sees and pursues. Instead of modifying itself to take advantage of new opportunities, it looks only for opportunities that it can handle with its present setup. Consider the following example:

- The American Lung Association came into existence at the turn of the century to fight the dreaded disease of tuberculosis, which at that time was the major killer of Americans. Various chapters of the American Lung Association raised money to help the victims of tuberculosis by selling Christmas Seals to the general public. In the 1950s new miracle drugs were developed that effectively prevented the spread of tuberculosis, and for the first time, tuberculosis became a minor disease. Nevertheless, the organization continued to collect money for this disease while neglecting other lung diseases that were becoming more serious, such as lung cancer, emphysema, and asthma. Even in the 1970s, when the American Lung Association started to help the victims of these other diseases, it continued to raise money by selling Christmas Seals instead of considering new donor groups and new ways to raise money. In less than a decade its market share of all the money raised by major national health agencies has fallen from a high of 13 percent to a current level of 8 percent.

This is an example of highly nonadaptive behavior on the part of an organization. The organization runs an *efficient* machine, but not an *effective* machine. Peter Drucker made the observation long ago that it is more important to do the *right thing* than to do *things right.*

Of all the elements in the picture, the environment is the one that changes the fastest. Even bringing everything into alignment with this year's environment is not enough. A sophisticated corporation such as IBM or Xerox will attempt to forecast what its business environment will be in, say, 1985. Given this 1985 environmental forecast, it will set objectives that describe where it wants to be in 1985. It will then formulate a strategy to achieve these objectives by 1985. It will begin to alter the organization and its systems so that these will support the new strategy, rather than act as a drag on its fulfillment. This forward-looking thinking can be summarized as follows:

Environment		Company						
Opportunities 1985	→	Objectives 1985	→	Strategy 1985	→	Structure 1985	→	Systems 1985

Environmental Change

Although environments change, not all industries and companies are exposed to the same rate of environmental change. We can distinguish between different rates of change in a company's environment. Some companies operate in a fairly *stable environment* where the future is expected to be pretty much like the present. For example, ice-cream producers expect the consumption of ice cream to grow at roughly the population growth rate, and they plan accordingly. They foresee no major threats nor new opportunities in their environmental picture. Other companies operate in a *slowly evolving environment.* Watch manufacturers are witnessing new types of watches (digital, electronic) gradually replacing the older types of watches (spring, pinlever) in popularity, and they are able to adapt to these changes—if adapt they will—in an orderly way. Still other companies operate in a *turbulent environment,* in which major and unpredictable disturbances are the rule. Oil companies, for example, operate in an environment marked by sudden price changes, new oil discoveries, oil shortages, and new legislation and regulation. It seems that companies will increasingly find themselves operating in turbulent environments, and this will call for much more strategic flexibility.

Opportunity and Threat Analysis

In the face of a rapidly changing environment, companies need to operate an intelligence system that continually monitors major developments and trends in the environment. Company decision makers should be alerted to new developments as they occur. Each development should be assessed as to its implications for company planning and marketing decision making. Some trends and developments will represent threats to the company; others will represent opportunities; and still others will represent both. It is important that managers in charge of various divisions, products, and markets not only recognize the major threats and the major opportunities that surround their business but take steps to deal with them.

Suppose the various cigarette brand managers working at the Philip Morris Company are alerted to the following trends and developments affecting their business:

1. The U.S. surgeon general is asking Congress to pass a law requiring that every cigarette brand include a skull and crossbones on the front side of the package and the warning: "Scientific evidence shows that daily smoking shortens a person's life span by an average of seven years."
2. An increasing number of public places are prohibiting smoking or are setting up separate sections for smokers and nonsmokers.
3. A new insect is attacking tobacco-growing areas, leading to the possibility of smaller crops in the future and larger price increases if some means cannot be found to control it.
4. The research lab at Philip Morris is on the verge of discovering a way of turning lettuce leaves into benign tobacco. If successful, the new tobacco will be enjoyable and harmless.
5. Cigarette smoking is rapidly increasing in foreign markets, especially in developing nations.
6. Several groups are pressing for the legalization of marijuana so that it can be openly manufactured and sold through standard retail outlets.

Each of these items has implications for the cigarette business. The first three can be classified as environmental threats, which can be defined as follows:

- An **environmental threat** is a challenge posed by an unfavorable trend or specific disturbance in the environment which would lead, in the absence of purposeful marketing action, to the stagnation or demise of a company, product, or brand.

Figure 3-2
Threat and Opportunity Matrices

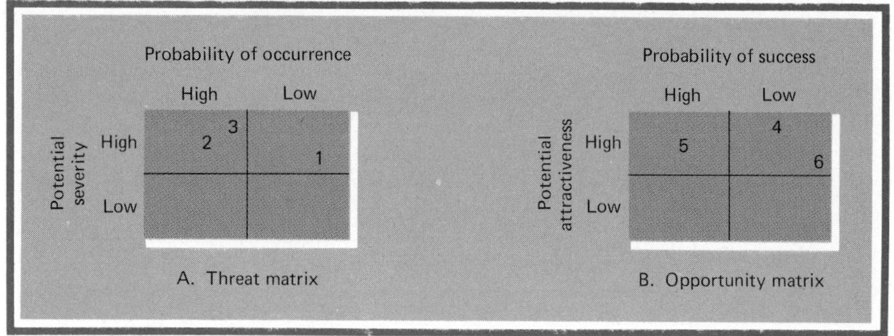

Not all threats warrant the same attention or concern. Managers should assess each threat according to two dimensions: (1) its potential severity as measured by the amount of money the company would lose if the threat materialized and (2) its probability of occurrence. The results of assessing the three threats listed above are shown in the threat matrix in Figure 3-2A. All three of these threats are high in their potential severity, and two of them have a high probability of occurring. Cigarette managers should concentrate on major threats (those in the high-severity–high-probability cell) and should have contingency plans ready in case they occur. These managers should also keep a close watch on threats in the southwest and northeast cells, although contingency plans are less necessary. They can, for all practical purposes, ignore threats in the southeast cell.

The last three trends and developments in the list can be classified as company marketing opportunities, which can be defined as follows:

- A **company marketing opportunity** is an attractive arena of relevant marketing action in which a particular company is likely to enjoy superior competitive advantages.

Not all opportunities, of course, are equally attractive. An opportunity can be assessed in terms of two basic dimensions: (1) its potential attractiveness as measured by the amount of profit it might yield to an average company and (2) the probability that this particular company will be able to outdo its competitors in carrying out this venture. The results of assessing the three opportunities are shown in the *opportunity matrix* in Figure 3-2B. These opportunities fall into two different cells according to the judgment of management. The managers will concentrate on opportunities falling in the northwest cell, will pay some attention to those in the southwest and northeast cells, and will pay little or no attention to opportunities falling in the southeast cell. Furthermore, management may want to dismiss certain financially attractive opportunities if they are unattractive on social grounds. The Philip Morris Company may want to pass up opportunities 5 and 6 because of their questionable moral or social character.

Considering the two matrices together, this business faces two major threats and one major opportunity. This makes it somewhat speculative: It is high on opportunity and high on risk. In fact, four outcomes are possible with this analysis. They are shown in the opportunity-threat matrix in Figure 3-3. An *ideal*

Figure 3-3
Opportunity-Threat Matrix

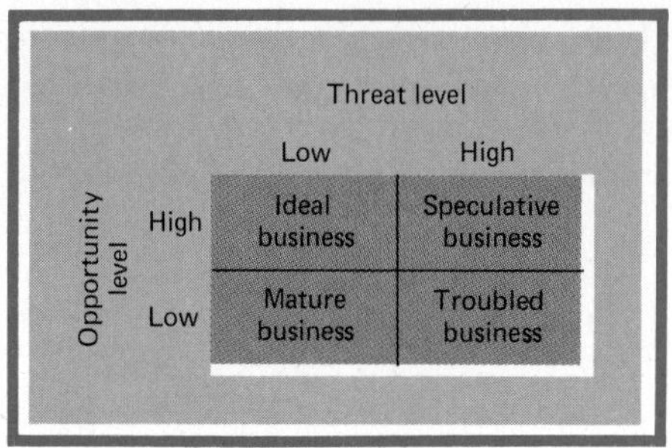

business is one that is high in major opportunities and low in or devoid of major threats. A *speculative business* is high in both major opportunities and threats. A *mature business* is low in both major opportunities and threats. Finally, a *troubled business* is low in opportunities and high in threats.

Organizational Response

Each business unit can seek to better its situation by moving toward its major opportunities and away from its major threats. With respect to opportunities, the firm must carefully appraise their quality. There is a whole profession of "futurologists" who conjure up wonderful products and services the public needs. Levitt has cautioned business executives to judge opportunities carefully:

> ▪ There can be a need, but no market; or a market, but no customer; or a customer, but no salesman. For instance, there is a great need for massive pollution control, but not really a market at present. And there is a market for new technology in education, but no customer really large enough to buy the products. Market forecasters who fail to understand these concepts have made spectacular miscalculations about the apparent opportunities in these and other fields, such as housing and leisure products.[3]

Even in pursuing a marketing opportunity, the firm can control its level of risk taking. The firm might make a *token investment* in marketing research and R & D just to keep up, without getting sidetracked from its main business. Or it might make a *moderate investment* in the hope of becoming one of the leaders. Or it might make a *substantial investment* in the hope of becoming the leader, although this may involve great risk to its present business.

In facing a major threat, the firm has three modes of adaptation available:

1. *Opposition.* The firm can try to fight, restrain, or reverse the unfavorable development. Thus Philip Morris can lobby for a law requiring all public establishments to permit customers to smoke if they wish.
2. *Modification.* The firm can try to reduce the threat's severity. Philip Morris can advocate separate smoking sections for smokers in public establishments as an alternative to a total ban on smoking.
3. *Relocation.* The firm can decide to shift gradually to another business in which it can produce more value. Philip Morris can decide to increase its market share of the beverage and food business and decrease its participation in the cigarette business. It has done this most successfully in buying and building up the Miller Brewing Company and the Seven-Up Company.[4]

In general, management has to pay attention to the key concepts of *market evolution* and *strategic fit.* All markets undergo evolutionary development marked by changing customer needs, technologies, competitors, channels, and laws. The firm should be looking out of a *strategic window* watching these changes and assessing the requirements for continued success in each market.[5] There is only a limited period when the fit between the requirements of a particular market and the firm's competencies is at an optimum. At these times the strategic window is open, and the firm should be investing in this market. In some subsequent period the firm will find that the evolutionary path of this market is such that it can no longer be effective and efficient in serving this market. It should then consider disinvesting and shifting its resources to areas of growing opportunity.

The major processes that a company uses to adapt to its environment are summarized in Figure 3-4. The company gathers information on broad macroeconomic forces, publics, competitors, marketing channels, markets, and target markets. This information plays an essential role within the company in carrying out two major adaptive processes, namely, the strategic-planning process and the marketing process.

The strategic-planning process takes place at the corporate and divisional levels. Top management sets the pace by defining the overall company mission, objectives and goals, growth strategy, and company portfolio plan. The same steps are repeated by the management in each division, since each division will have its own mission, objectives, strategy, and product portfolio.

The marketing process both supports the strategic-planning process and involves more detailed analysis and planning for specific marketing opportunities. The marketing process occurs at the level of the company's specific products and markets. It calls for marketing opportunity analysis, target market selection,

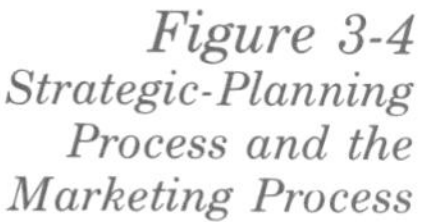

Figure 3-4
Strategic-Planning Process and the Marketing Process

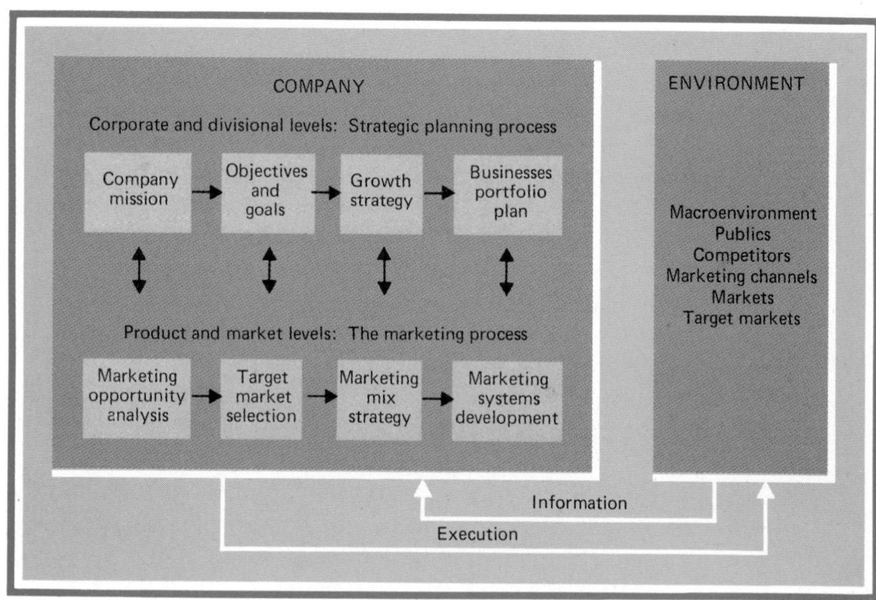

marketing mix strategy, and marketing management systems development. The decisions arrived at are executed in the environment, the results are fed back as new information, and further adaptive steps are taken.

strategic planning

This section examines the strategic-planning process. The next section focuses on the marketing process.

We define *strategic planning* as follows:

- **Strategic planning** is the managerial process of developing and maintaining a strategic fit between the organization and its changing marketing opportunities. It relies on developing a clear company mission, objectives and goals, a growth strategy, and product portfolio plans.

We will now discuss each component of the strategic-planning process.

Company Mission

An organization exists to accomplish something in the larger environment. Its specific purpose or mission is usually clear at the beginning. Over time, however, one or more things happen. Its mission may become unclear as the organization grows and develops new products and markets. Or the mission may remain clear but some managers may no longer be interested in it. Or the mission may remain clear but may lose its appropriateness because of new conditions in the environment.

When management senses that the organization is drifting, it is time to renew the search for purpose. It is time to ask the following questions:[6] *What is our business? Who is the customer? What is value to the customer? What will our business be? What should our business be?* These simple-sounding questions are among the most difficult the company will ever have to answer. Successful business firms continuously raise these questions and answer them thoughtfully and thoroughly.

More and more organizations are developing formal *mission statements* to answer these questions. A well-worked-out mission statement provides corporate personnel with a shared sense of opportunity, direction, significance, and achievement. The company mission statement acts as an "invisible hand" which guides widely scattered employees and enables them to work independently and yet collectively toward the realization of the organization's potentials.

Unfortunately, it is not easy to write an effective company mission statement. Some organizations will spend a year or two before they come up with a satisfactory statement about the purpose of their firm. In the process they will discover a lot about themselves and their latent opportunities.

An effective mission statement will be *market oriented, feasible, motivating,* and *specific.*

Market oriented. The mission statement should define the *business domain(s)* in which the organization will operate, in market-oriented terms if possible. Business domains can be defined in terms of *product class, technology, customer group, market need,* or some combination of these. Companies have traditionally defined their business domain in product terms such as "We manufacture slide rules" or in technological terms such as "We are a chemical-processing firm." Some years ago Theodore Levitt proposed that market definitions of a business are superior to product or technological definitions of a business.[7] His main argument was that products and technologies eventually become obsolete, whereas basic market needs generally endure forever. Thus a slide rule manufacturer will go out of business as soon as the electronic calculator is invented unless it defines itself in the business of meeting calculation needs, not making slide rules. A market-oriented mission statement calls for defining the business in terms of serving a particular customer group and/or meeting a particular type of market need.

Feasible. In developing a market-based definition of a business, management should steer between being too narrow and being too broad. A lead pencil manufacturer that says it is in the business of making communication equipment is stating its mission too broadly. A useful approach is to move from the current product to successively higher levels of abstraction and then decide on the most realistic level of abstraction for the company to consider. Figure 3-5 shows a prune company's options. A prune company can see itself as a dried fruit company, as a fruit company, or ultimately as a food company. Alternatively, it can see itself as a laxative company or ultimately as a pharmaceutical company. Each broadening step opens a vision of new opportunities but may also lead the company into unrealistic business ventures beyond its capabilities.

Motivating. A company mission statement should be inspirational and motivating. Employees would like to feel that their work is significant and that they are making a contribution to people's lives. If the Wrigley Company says that its mission is "to sell more gum," this is not very inspiring. If it says that its mission is "to make more money" or "to be the market leader," these are not very inspiring. Sales, profits, and market leadership should be the result of the company's successful pursuit of its mission, not the mission itself. The mission should be stated, if possible, as something to accomplish outside the firm.

Specific. Too many mission statements are written for public relations purposes and lack specific guidelines that will enable management to choose between alternative courses of action. The statement "We want to be the leading company in this industry producing the highest-quality products with the widest distribu-

Figure 3-5
Successive Expansions of Business Domains of a Prune Company

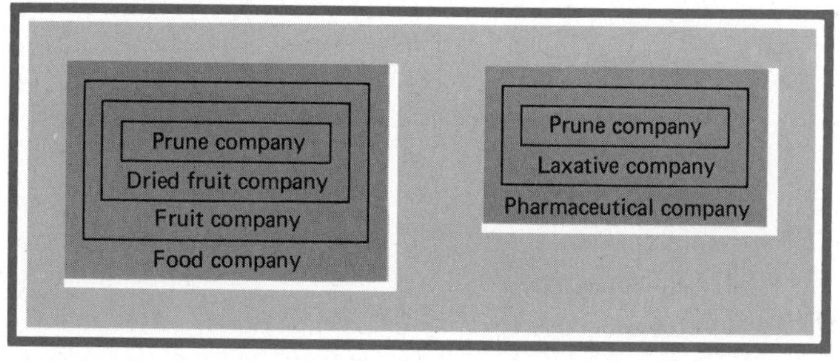

tion and service at the lowest possible prices" sounds good but fails to supply clear directions and guidelines. A mission statement should include major policies that the company plans to honor in the pursuit of its mission. Policies convey the value system of the company and the tone of its dealings with customers, suppliers, distributors, competition, and other market participants and publics.

The company's mission statement should serve it for many years. The company mission is not something that should be revised every few years in response to environmental changes or new unrelated opportunities. On the other hand, sometimes a company has to reconsider its mission if it no longer works or if it does not define an optimal course that the company can follow.

Company Objectives and Goals

The company's mission should be defined into a finer set of supporting objectives for each level of management. Each manager should know his or her objectives and be responsible for their accomplishment. This system is known as *management by objectives.*

As an illustration, the International Minerals and Chemical Corporation is in a number of businesses, among them the fertilizer business. The fertilizer division does not say that its mission is to produce fertilizer. Instead, it says that its mission is "to fight world hunger." This mission leads to a definite hierarchy of objectives (see Figure 3-6).[8] The mission to fight world hunger leads to the company objective of increasing agricultural productivity. Agricultural productivity in turn can be increased by researching new fertilizers that promise higher yields. But research is expensive and requires improved profits to plow back into research programs. So a major company objective becomes "profit improvement."

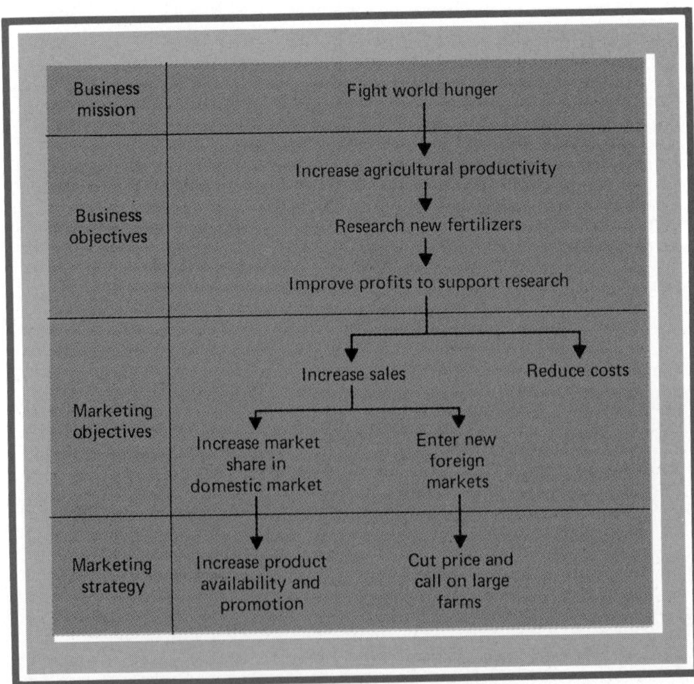

Figure 3-6 Hierarchy of Objectives for the International Minerals and Chemical Corporation, Fertilizer Division

Now profits can be improved by increasing the sales of current products, reducing current costs, or both. Sales can be increased by increasing the company's market share in the domestic market and entering new foreign markets. These two objectives are adopted by the marketing department as its current marketing objectives.

The next step is to develop marketing strategies to support these marketing objectives. To increase its domestic market share, the company will increase its product's availability and promotion. To enter new foreign markets, the company will cut prices and concentrate on large farms. These are the broad marketing strategies.

Each marketing strategy will be spelled out in greater detail for different marketing specialists within the marketing department (not shown in Figure 3-6). For example, increasing the product's availability will be given not only to the sales force as an objective for which they have to find a sales strategy but also to the advertising department as an objective for which they have to find an advertising strategy. The increased sales objective will also be turned into manufacturing objectives, financial objectives, and personnel objectives for these respective departments. In this way the mission of the firm becomes translated into a specific set of objectives for the current period.

To determine whether the department was successful, all the objectives have to be turned into specific quantitative *goals*. The objective "increase our market share" is not as satisfactory as "increase our market share to 15 percent by the end of the second year." Managers use the term *goals* to describe an objective that has been made highly specific with respect to *magnitude* and *time*. Turning the objectives into goals facilitates the process of management planning and control.

Company Growth Strategy

Among the various objectives that companies adopt, growth is one of the most common. Companies want to grow in sales, profits, and other dimensions. To accomplish this, companies have to select a target growth rate and formulate a strategy for achieving it.

Growth comes about in two ways. It is achieved through managing current products for growth and adding new products to fill the remaining growth gap. This is shown in Figure 3-7 for a hypothetical company with three product lines, A, B, and C. Product line A produces about 60 percent of the company's current profits, B about 30 percent, and C the remaining 10 percent. Looking ahead, the company expects A's earnings to decline, B's earnings to grow and then decline, and C's earnings to grow. By the sixth year, C will be contributing most of the profit, followed by B and A. The three product lines, however, will not in total earn enough to sustain the company's desired profit-growth rate. The figure shows a profit gap that must be filled in one of two ways: (1) improving the performance of the current product lines or (2) adding new product lines.

We will now examine a particular company to determine how it can systematically search for growth opportunities with its current products and possible new products.

- Modern Publishing Company (name disguised) publishes a leading health magazine that has a monthly circulation of three hundred thousand copies. The company's

Figure 3-7
Projected Profit Growth from Current Products

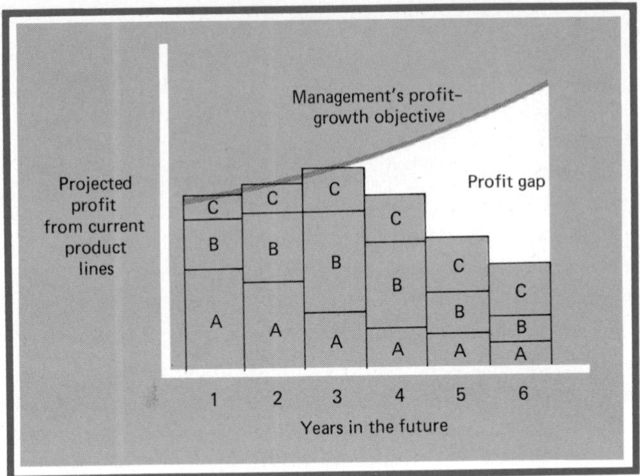

marketing environment is changing rapidly in terms of consumer interests, new competitors, and rising publishing costs. It is attempting to formulate a systematic plan for company growth during the 1980s.

A growth strategy can be generated by a company by moving through three levels of analysis. The first level identifies those opportunities available to the company in its current sphere of operations (*intensive growth opportunities*). The second level identifies those opportunities available through integration with other parts of this marketing channel system (*integrative growth opportunities*). The third level identifies those opportunities lying outside the current marketing channel system (*diversification growth opportunities*). Table 3-1 lists the specific possibilities found in each broad opportunity class.

Intensive growth. Intensive growth makes sense if a company has not fully exploited the opportunities in its current products and markets. Ansoff has proposed a useful device for generating ideas for intensive growth opportunities, a *product/market expansion matrix*.[9] This matrix, shown in Figure 3-8, focuses on three major types of intensive growth opportunities:

1. **Market penetration.** *Market penetration consists of the company's seeking increased sales for its current products in its current markets through more aggressive marketing effort.* This includes three possibilities:
   a. Modern can encourage current subscribers to increase their *purchase quantity* by giving gift subscriptions to friends.

Table 3-1
Major Classes of Growth Opportunities

I. INTENSIVE GROWTH	II. INTEGRATIVE GROWTH	III. DIVERSIFICATION GROWTH
A. Market Penetration B. Market Development C. Product Development	A. Backward Integration B. Forward Integration C. Horizontal Integration	A. Concentric Diversification B. Horizontal Diversification C. Conglomerate Diversification

Figure 3-8
Product/Market Expansion Matrix

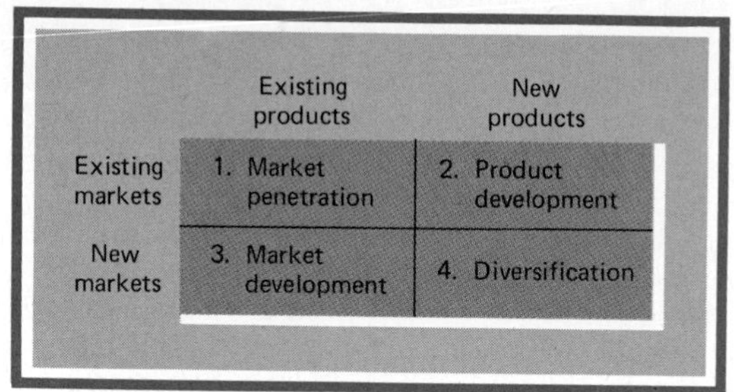

b. Modern can try to *attract away competitors' customers* by offering lower subscription rates or promoting its magazine as being superior to other health magazines.
c. Modern can try to *convert new prospects* who do not now read health magazines but who have the same profile as current readers.

2. **Market development.** *Market development consists of the company's seeking increased sales by taking its current products into new markets.* This includes three possibilities:
   a. Modern can distribute its magazine in *new geographical markets*—regional, national, or international—where it has not been available.
   b. Modern can try to make the magazine attractive to new types of individual readers by developing new features that appeal to these segments.
   c. Modern can try to sell its magazine to new types of institutional subscribers, such as hospitals, physicians' offices, and health clubs.
3. **Product development.** *Product development consists of the company's seeking increased sales by developing new or improved products for its current markets.* This includes three possibilities:
   a. Modern can develop one or more new health magazines that will appeal to the present readers of its health magazine.
   b. Modern can create different *regional versions* of its health magazine to increase its appeal.
   c. Modern can develop an abbreviated cassette edition of its monthly magazine as an alternative for certain markets that prefer listening to reading.

Integrative growth. Integrative growth makes sense if a company's basic industry has a strong growth outlook and/or the company can increase its profitability, efficiency, or control by moving backward, forward, or horizontally with the industry. Three possibilities can be defined as follows:

1. **Backward integration.** *Backward integration consists of a company's seeking ownership or increased control of its supply systems.* Modern might consider buying a paper supply company or a printing company to increase its control over supplies.
2. **Forward integration.** *Forward integration consists of a company's seeking ownership or increased control of its distribution systems.* Modern might see an advantage in buying some magazine wholesaler businesses or subscription agencies.
3. **Horizontal integration.** *Horizontal integration consists of a company's seeking ownership or increased control of some of its competitors.* Modern might consider acquiring other health magazines or health magazine publishing companies.

Diversification growth. Diversification growth makes sense if a company's marketing channel system does not show much additional opportunity for growth or profit, or if the opportunities outside the present marketing system are superior. Diversification does not mean that the company will take up any opportunity that comes along. The company would attempt to identify fields that make use of its distinctive competences or help it overcome a particular problem. There are three broad types of diversification moves:

1. **Concentric diversification.** *Concentric diversification consists of the company's seeking to add new products that have technological and/or marketing synergies with the existing product line; these products will normally appeal to new classes of customers.* Modern, for example, might consider starting a paperback division to take advantage of its network of magazine distributors.
2. **Horizontal diversification.** *Horizontal diversification consists of the company's seeking to add new products that could appeal to its current customers though technologically unrelated to its current product line.* For example, Modern might decide to open up a series of health clubs in the hope that readers of its health magazine would become club members.
3. **Conglomerate diversification.** *Conglomerate diversification consists of the company's seeking to add new products that have no relationship to the company's current technology, products, or markets; these products will normally appeal to new classes of customers.* Modern might want to enter new business areas, such as real estate, hotel management, and fast-food service.

Thus we see that a company can systematically identify growth opportunities through application of a marketing systems framework, looking first at current product/market opportunities, then at opportunities in other parts of the marketing channel system, and finally at relevant opportunities outside the system.

Company Portfolio Plan

After management examines the company's various growth opportunities, it is in a better position to make decisions with respect to its current product lines. Management must evaluate all of the company's current businesses so that it can decide which to build, maintain, phase down, or phase out. Its job is to keep refreshing the company's portfolio of businesses by withdrawing from poorer businesses and adding promising new ones.

Management's first step is to identify the key businesses making up the company. These can be called the strategic business units (SBUs). An SBU ideally has the following characteristics: (1) it is a single business; (2) it has a distinct mission; (3) it has its own competitors; (4) it has a responsible manager; (5) it controls certain resources; (6) it can benefit from strategic planning; and (7) it can be planned independently of the other businesses. An SBU can be one or more company divisions, a product line within a division, or sometimes a single product or brand.

The next step calls for management to rate all the SBUs in a way that would reveal how much resource support each SBU deserves. The two best-known evaluation schemes are those of the Boston Consulting Group and the General Electric Company.

Boston Consulting Group approach. The Boston Consulting Group (BCG), a leading management consulting firm, advises a company to review all of its SBUs and classify them in the growth-share matrix illustrated in Figure 3-9. The growth-share matrix consists of two important business indicators. The vertical

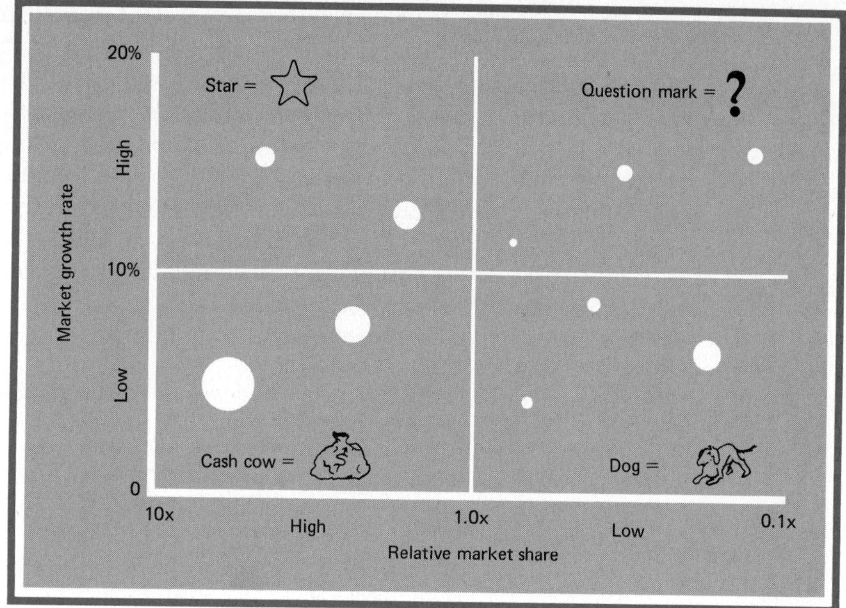

Figure 3-9
The BCG Growth-Share Matrix

indicator, *market growth rate,* refers to the annual growth rate of the market in which the product is located. In the figure the market growth rate goes from a low of 0 percent to a high of 20 percent, although a larger range could be shown. Market growth is arbitrarily divided into high and low growth by a 10 percent growth line.

The horizontal indicator, *relative market share,* refers to an SBU's market share relative to that of the industry's largest competitor. Thus a relative market share of 0.1 means that the company's SBU stands at 10 percent of the leader's share; and 10 means that the company's SBU is the leader and has ten times the share of the next-strongest company in the market. Relative market share is divided into high and low share, using 1.0 as the dividing line. Relative market share is drawn in log scale.

By dividing the growth-share matrix in the way indicated, four types of SBUs can be distinguished:

- *Stars.* Stars are high-growth, high-share SBUs. They are often cash-using SBUs because cash is necessary to finance their rapid growth. Eventually their growth will slow down, and they will then turn into cash cows and become major cash generators supporting other SBUs.
- *Cash cows.* Cash cows are low-growth, high-share SBUs. They produce a lot of cash that the company uses to meet its bills and support other SBUs that are cash using.
- *Question marks.* Question marks (also called "problem children" or "wildcats") are low-share SBUs in high-growth markets. They require a lot of cash to maintain their share, let alone increase it. Management has to think hard about whether to spend more to build these question marks into leaders. If it decides not to, the question marks will have to be phased down or phased out.
- *Dogs.* Dogs (also called "cash traps") are low-growth, low-share SBUs. They may generate enough cash to maintain themselves but do not promise to be a large source of cash.

The ten circles in the growth-share matrix represent the company's ten current SBUs. The company has two stars, two cash cows, three question marks, and three dogs. The areas of the circles are proportional to the SBU's dollar sales. This company is in fair shape, although not in good shape. Fortunately it has two good-sized cash cows whose cash throw-off helps finance the company's question marks, stars, and dogs. The company should consider taking some decisive action concerning its dogs and its question marks. The picture would be worse if the company had no stars, or had too many dogs, or had only one weak cash cow.

Having arrived at this picture, the task of company portfolio planning is to determine what role should be assigned to each of the company's SBUs in the future. Four alternative objectives can be pursued:

- *Build.* Here the objective is to increase the SBU's market share, even forgoing short-term earnings to achieve this objective. "Building" is especially appropriate for question marks, whose share has to grow if they are to become stars.
- *Hold.* Here the objective is to preserve the SBU's market share. This objective is especially appropriate for strong cash cows if they are to continue to yield a large positive cash flow.
- *Harvest.* Here the objective is to increase the SBU's short-term positive cash flow regardless of the long-term effect. This strategy is especially appropriate for weak cash cows whose future is dim and from whom more cash flow is needed. It can also be used with question marks and dogs.
- *Divest.* Here the objective is to sell or liquidate the business because resources can be better used elsewhere. This is especially appropriate not only for dogs but also for question marks that the company decides it cannot finance for growth.

As time passes, SBUs will change their position in the growth-share matrix. Each SBU has a life cycle (see Chapter 11). Many SBUs start out as question marks, move into the star category if they succeed, later become cash cows as market growth falls, and finally turn into dogs toward the end of their life cycle. This is why the company needs to continuously add new products and ventures in the hope that some of them will move up to star status and eventually become cash cows to help finance the other SBUs.[10]

General Electric approach. General Electric (GE) has gone beyond the BCG approach by introducing a more comprehensive portfolio planning tool called a *strategic business-planning grid* (see Figure 3-10). GE believes that in addition to market growth rate and relative market share, several factors have to be considered in evaluating an existing or prospective SBU. All of these factors can be combined under two major headings, industry attractiveness and business strength. The best businesses are obviously those that are in highly attractive industries and for which the particular company has high business strength.

In Figure 3-10 *industry attractiveness* is shown on the vertical axis. Industry attractiveness is a composite index made up of such factors as

- *Market size.* Large markets are more attractive than small markets.
- *Market growth rate.* High-growth markets are more attractive than low-growth markets.
- *Profit margin.* High-profit-margin industries are more attractive than low-profit-margin industries.

Figure 3-10
General Electric's Strategic Business-Planning Grid

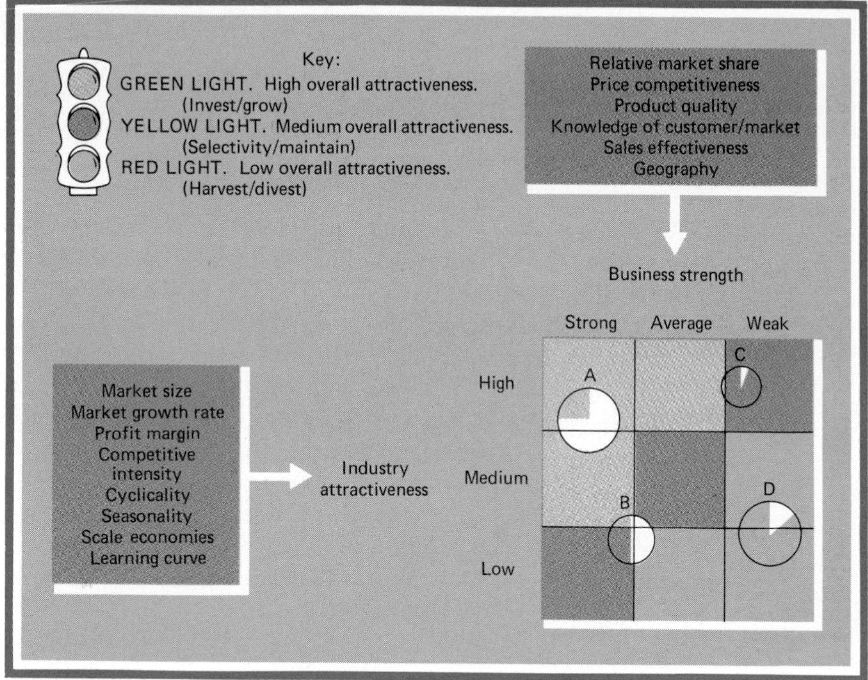

- *Competitive intensity.* Industries with many strong competitors are less attractive than industries with a few weak competitors.
- *Cyclicality.* Highly cyclical industries are less attractive than cyclically stable industries.
- *Seasonality.* Highly seasonal industries are less attractive than nonseasonal industries.
- *Scale economies.* Industries where unit costs fall with large plant size and distribution are more attractive than constant cost industries.
- *Learning curve.* Industries where unit costs fall as management accumulates experience in production and distribution are more attractive than industries where management has reached the limit of its learning.[11]

Each of these factors is represented by a scale (not shown). Each current and prospective industry is rated on all of the factors. The factors are given different weights, and a weighted average is taken to find the industry attractiveness score. For our purposes, an industry's attractiveness can be broadly described as high, medium, or low.

Business strength is shown on the horizontal axis. It is a composite index made up of such factors as

- *Relative market share.* The higher the company's relative market share, the greater its business strength.
- *Price competitiveness.* The higher the company's price competitiveness (that is, the lower its costs relative to those of its competitors), the greater its business strength.
- *Product quality.* The higher the company's product quality relative to that of its competitors, the greater its business strength.

- *Knowledge of customer/market.* The deeper the company's knowledge of customers and their needs and wants, the greater its business strength.
- *Sales effectiveness.* The greater the company's sales effectiveness, the greater its business strength.
- *Geography.* The greater the company's geographical presence and advantages in the market, the greater its business strength.

These factors are also scaled and weighted, and the company can figure out its business strength in any existing or prospective market. Its business strength can be broadly described as strong, average, or weak.

The grid is divided into three zones—green, yellow, and red. The green zone consists of the three cells at the upper left, indicating those industries that are favorable in industry attractiveness and SBU business strength and suggesting that the company has the green light to "invest and grow." The yellow zone consists of the diagonal cells stretching from the lower left to the upper right, indicating industries that are medium in overall attractiveness. The company usually decides to maintain the SBU's share rather than grow or reduce share. The red zone consists of the three cells at the lower right, indicating those industries that are low in overall attractiveness. Here the company gives serious consideration to harvesting or divesting.

The circles represent four current SBUs making up the company. The areas of the circles are proportional to the sizes of the industries in which these SBUs compete, while the pie slices within the circles represent each SBU's market share. Thus circle A represents a company SBU with a 75 percent market share in a good-sized industry that is highly attractive and in which the company has strong business strength. Circle B represents an SBU in which the company has a 50 percent market share but the industry is not very attractive. Circles C and D represent two other company SBUs in which the company has small market shares and not much business strength. Altogether, the company has to build A, maintain B, and make some basic decisions on what to do with C and D.

Management should also plot a grid showing projected positions of the SBUs if there is no change in strategies. By comparing the current and projected business grids, management can identify the major strategic issues and opportunities it faces.[12] This type of analysis led GE to sort its current mix of SBUs into five investment groups:[13]

1. *High-growth products deserving the highest investment support*—engineering plastics, medical systems, transportation
2. *Steady reinvestment products deserving high and steady investment*—major appliances, steam and gas turbines, lamps
3. *Support products deserving steady investment support*—meters, specialty transformers
4. *Selective pruning or rejuvenation products deserving reduced investment*
5. *Venture products deserving heavy R & D investment*—"10-ton aircraft engine," microwave ovens, man-made diamonds

Whether the BCG, GE, or some other analysis of the company's current portfolio of business is used, the main point is that the company must evaluate its SBUs as a basis for setting objectives and resource allocation priorities. The result of the analysis enables management to decide on the business objective for each SBU and on what resources it will be given. Then the task of the SBU's management and marketing personnel will be to figure out the best way to accomplish that objective. Marketing managers in certain businesses will find that their objective is not necessarily to build that business! This is somewhat contrary to their traditional mandate, which is to build sales. Their job may be to hold the existing volume in spite of fewer marketing dollars, or actually to reduce demand. Thus the generic task of marketing management is not to build demand but to manage demand. Marketing has to take its cue from the objective developed for the business in the course of strategic planning at the corporate level. Marketing contributes to the evaluation of the business's potential and where it stands in the matrix, but once the business's objective is set, marketing's task is to carry it out efficiently and profitably.

marketing process

We will now examine the other major process, the marketing process, which plays a key role in the company's ability to adapt creatively to its changing environment. We define *marketing process* as follows:

- The **marketing process** is the managerial process of identifying, analyzing, choosing, and exploiting marketing opportunities to fulfill the company's mission and objectives. More specifically, it consists of identifying and analyzing marketing opportunities, segmenting and selecting target markets, developing a competitive marketing mix strategy, and designing supporting marketing management systems for planning and control, information, and marketing personnel.

The steps in the marketing process are illustrated in the lower half of the company's box in Figure 3-4 and are discussed in the following sections.

Marketing Opportunity Analysis

The marketing process begins with the company's effort to find attractive opportunities. In this quest the marketing department plays a major role. Although new opportunities can be spotted by various persons in the company, marketers bear the major responsibility for generating, evaluating, and selecting attractive opportunities.

Marketers use several techniques to spot new opportunities. They make sure that various ideas arising in the firm flow to the marketing department where they can be evaluated. Marketers often conduct brainstorming sessions to develop new ideas. They make use of systematic techniques such as the product/market expansion matrix discussed earlier for locating growth opportunities. They watch a number of industries, which they rate on their attractiveness by using the GE approach mentioned earlier.

It is important to distinguish between *environmental opportunities* and *company opportunities*. There are attractive environmental opportunities available in any economy as long as there are unsatisfied needs. Currently there are great opportunities to develop new sources of energy, new food products, improved agricultural methods, improved forms of transportation, new forms of leisure, and improved teaching technology. There are opportunities in refuse disposal, low-cost legal services, containerization, prefab housing, water purification, day-care centers, and biomedical instruments. But none of these necessarily represent opportunities for any specific company. Fast-food restaurants are probably not an opportunity for U.S. Steel, nor are biomedical instruments an opportunity for Kentucky Fried Chicken.

To be successful, the company should be concerned with attractive environmental opportunities for which it has the required business strength. We call these *company opportunities.* The company must be able to bring to an attractive environmental opportunity more business strength than its potential competitors can. We make the following assumptions:

1. Every environmental opportunity has specific *success requirements.*
2. Each company has *distinctive competences,* that is, things that it can do especially well.
3. A company is likely to enjoy a *differential advantage* in an area of environmental opportunity if its distinctive competences outmatch those of its potential competition.

Suppose McDonald's, General Foods, and the American Tobacco Company all become interested in starting a national network of franchised day-care centers. Which firm would enjoy the greatest differential advantage? First we consider the success requirements. The success requirements would include (1) having a strong public image for trustworthiness, (2) having the ability to train and motivate people in a service business, and (3) having the technical ability to manage a franchising operation. Now McDonald's has distinctive competences in all three areas. General Foods has (1) a good corporate image but limited experience in (2) service businesses and (3) franchising. It acquired Burger Chef some years ago and later had to write it off at a corporate loss of $39 million. The American Tobacco Company raises mixed feelings in people who dislike cigarette smoking, and it also lacks experience in the other two areas. All things considered, it would appear that McDonald's would enjoy a major differential advantage in the operation of a successful national system of day-care centers.

The combination of attractive company marketing opportunities can be called the *company opportunity set.* Given these opportunities, the marketer's task is to evaluate each opportunity. Who would buy the product? How much would they pay? What would be the optimal features? How many units would be bought? Where are the buyers located? Who would the competition be? What distribution channels would be needed? The answers to these and other questions will lead to an estimate of the marketing opportunity's sales potential. Financial and manufacturing executives would add their estimates of costs. This information will enable the marketers to rank the opportunities and recommend those that should be selected for further development.

Target Market Selection

The second step of the marketing process is called target market selection. Suppose the company has spotted an especially attractive market. The issue becomes how to enter that market. Every market is filled with many more customer groups and customer needs than one company can normally serve, or serve in a competitively superior fashion. The task calls for market segmentation, that is, dividing the market into segments that differ in their requirements, buying responses, or other critical characteristics. Once a useful segmentation approach is developed, the company can consider which is the best part of the market to enter. The part of the market that the company decides to enter is called the *target market.*

- The **target market** is a well-defined set of customers whose needs the company plans to satisfy.

We will illustrate market segmentation and target market selection by using the following situation:

- A successful manufacturer of snow removal equipment is looking for a new product line. Management reviews several opportunities and finds the idea of manufacturing snowmobiles to be attractive in terms of market growth, sales potential, and company business strength. The marketing vice-president thoroughly investigates the structure of the snowmobile industry to determine whether the company could find a viable niche in this industry.

A useful approach to segmentation is to develop a *product/market grid.* Figure 3-11 illustrates a product/market grid for snowmobiles. The company can decide to manufacture any of three product types: gasoline, diesel, or electric. And it can design a snowmobile for any of three markets: consumer, industrial, or military. The marketing vice-president will proceed to estimate, for each of the nine product/market segments, its degree of market attractiveness and the company's degree of business strength. Suppose the segment that looks best is the "diesel-driven snowmobile for the industrial market segment" that is shaded in Figure 3-11.

Even this market segment may be larger than the company can serve, in which case *subsegmentation* is warranted. Figure 3-12 shows a subsegmentation of this market by customer use and customer size. Snowmobiles can be designed for use as delivery vehicles (i.e., used by business firms and the post office), as

Figure 3-11
Product/Market Grid for Snowmobiles

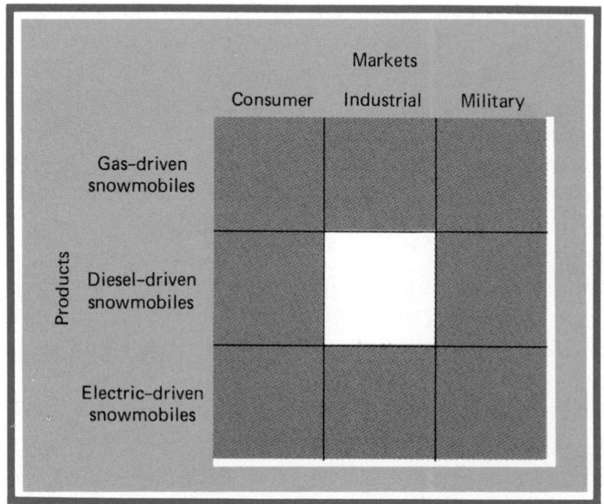

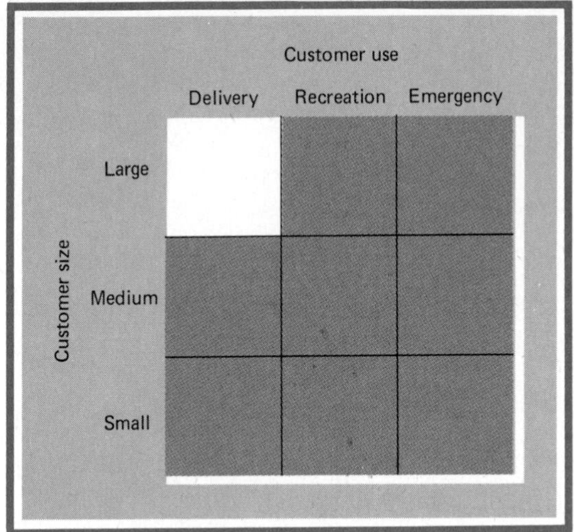

Figure 3-12
Subsegmentation by Customer Use and Customer Size

recreation vehicles (i.e., rented at resort hotel sites), or as emergency vehicles (i.e., used by hospitals and police forces). Their design will also be affected by whether the company will try to sell them to large, medium, or small customers. After evaluating the various subsegments, the marketing vice-president concludes that the "large customer, delivery segment" looks best. Thus management has arrived at a clear idea of its target market.

This target market may constitute the total ambition of the company in this market or may be viewed as a launching pad for later expansion to other market segments. Companies will usually consider any one of the five *market coverage strategies* shown in Figure 3-13:

1. *Product/market concentration* consists of the company's niching itself in only one part of the market, here making only diesel-driven snowmobiles for industrial buyers.
2. *Product specialization* consists of the company's deciding to produce only diesel-driven snowmobiles for all customer groups.
3. *Market specialization* consists of the company's deciding to make a variety of snowmobiles that serve the varied needs of a particular customer group, such as industrial buyers.
4. Selective specialization consists of the company's entering several product markets that have no relation to each other except that each provides an individually attractive opportunity.
5. *Full coverage* consists of the company's making a full range of snowmobiles to serve all the market segments.

Marketing Mix Strategy

The third step in the marketing process consists of developing a competitively effective marketing mix strategy for the target market. Marketing mix is one of the major concepts in modern marketing. We define it as follows:

- **Marketing mix** is the particular blend of controllable marketing variables that the firm uses to achieve its objective in the target market.

What variables make up a company's marketing mix? There are actually a

Figure 3-13
Five Patterns of Market Coverage (P = product, M = market)

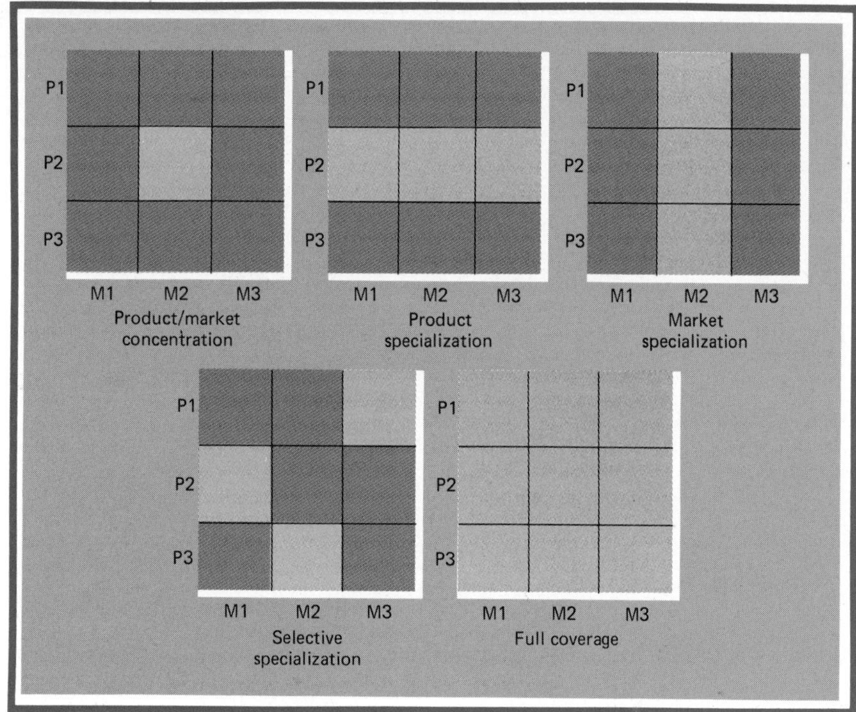

Source: Adapted from Derek F. Abell, *Defining the Business: The Starting Point of Strategic Planning* (Englewood Cliffs, N.J.: Prentice-Hall, 1980), Chap. 8 (forthcoming).

great number of marketing mix variables. Fortunately they can be classified into a few major groups. One of the most popular classifications has been proposed by McCarthy and is called the "four *P*'s": *product, price, place,* and *promotion.*[14] The particular marketing variables under each *P* are shown in Figure 3-14. The figure emphasizes that the marketing mix must be adapted to the target market.

How does the company choose the appropriate marketing mix for the target market? The answer is that the company must examine the wants of that market and the position of competitors, and it must make a decision on what it wants to competitively offer to that market. The company arrives at its marketing mix by deciding on the competitive position it wants to occupy in the target market.

We can illustrate competitive positioning by returning to the company that has decided to produce snowmobiles for business firms that will use them as delivery vehicles. Suppose this company learns through marketing research that business customers are primarily interested in two snowmobile attributes: size and speed. The company can ask prospective customers and dealers where they perceive competitors' snowmobiles to be located along these dimensions, and the results can be plotted in the *product space map* shown in Figure 3-15. Competitor A is seen as producing small/fast snowmobiles; B, medium-size/medium-speed snowmobiles; C, small-to-medium-size/slow snowmobiles; and D, large/slow snowmobiles. The areas of the circles are proportional to the competitors' sales.[15]

Given these competitor positions, what position should the new manufacturer seek? The company has two basic choices. One is to take a position next to

Figure 3-14
The Four P's of the Marketing Mix

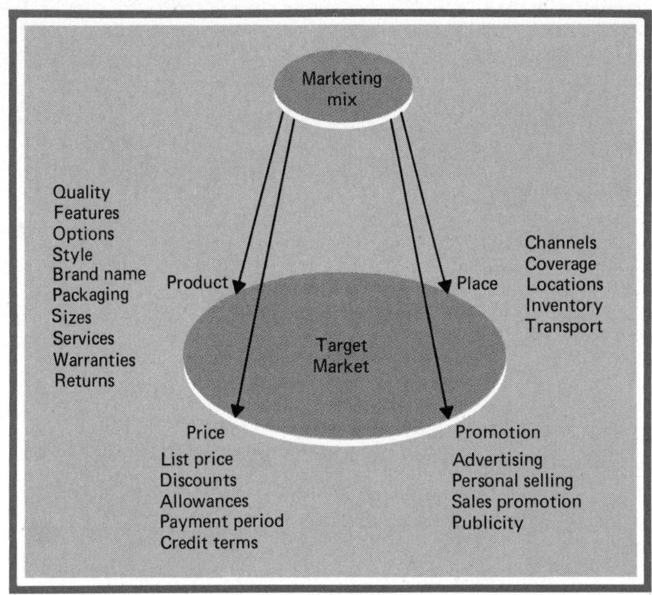

one of the existing competitors and fight to obtain the customers who want that type of snowmobile. The company might choose to do this if it feels that (1) it can build a better snowmobile of this type, (2) the market buying this type of snowmobile is large enough for two competitors, (3) it has more resources than the existing competitor, and/or (4) this position is the most consistent with the company's reputation and competence.

The other choice is to develop a snowmobile that is not currently offered to this market, such as a large/fast snowmobile (see empty northwest quadrant of Figure 3-15). The company would gain instant leadership in this part of the market, since competitors are not offering this type of snowmobile. But before making this decision, the company has to be sure that (1) it is technically feasible to build a large/fast snowmobile, (2) it is economically feasible to build a large/fast snowmobile at the planned price level, and (3) there are a sufficient number of buyers who would prefer a large/fast snowmobile to any other kind. If the answers are all positive, the firm has discovered a "hole" in the market and should quickly move to fill it.

Suppose, however, the company decides there is more profit potential and less risk in building a small/fast snowmobile to compete with competitor A. In this case the company would study A's snowmobile and other aspects of A's offer, seeking a way to differentiate its offer in the eyes of potential buyers. Instead of competitive positioning through *product/feature differentiation,* it might seek competitive positioning through *price/quality differentiation.* Suppose competitor A's snowmobile is of average quality and carries an average price. The company can offer a better-quality snowmobile than A's at a somewhat higher price, on the familiar argument "You pay more and get more." Or it can offer a better-quality snowmobile but charge the same as A on the argument "More quality for the same price." Or it can design an average-quality snowmobile and

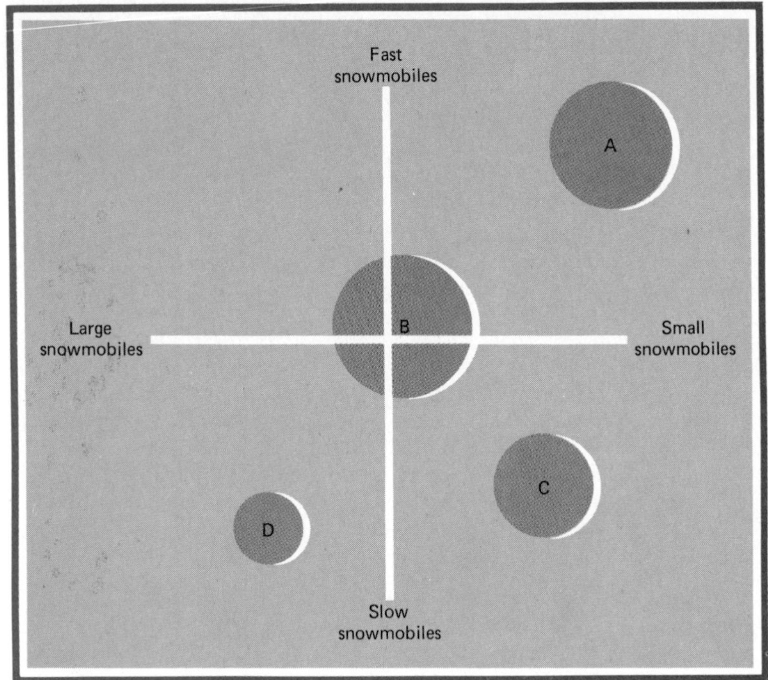

Figure 3-15
A Product Space Map Showing Perceived Offers of Four Competitors

charge less on the argument "Same quality for less money." Other price/quality strategies are also possible, and the company will have to choose its strategy carefully.

The company's decisions on the product's quality, features, price, advertising budget, marketing channels, and other marketing variables for this target market make up its *marketing mix*. The marketing mix is the means by which the company defines and supports the competitive position it seeks to occupy in the target market.

Marketing Management Systems Development

Once the company has chosen a target market and has defined its competitive position, it is ready to undertake *marketing management systems development.* Marketing cannot be carried out effectively unless certain management systems are created to support the marketing effort. The three principal systems needed by a company in managing its marketing effort can be described as follows:

1. *Marketing-planning and control system.* Every company should develop plans for the coming period covering its goals, strategies, marketing programs, and budgets. Companies vary considerably in how formally they do their planning, although most of them are moving toward increasingly formal planning. It is the author's position that a formal marketing-planning system is essential to achieving the maximum results sought in the marketplace. Formal marketing planning also requires the design of a marketing control system for checking on whether marketing goals are being achieved and what corrective actions, if any, are needed to improve marketing performance. (Chapter 4 discusses the nature and design of effective marketing-planning and control systems.)

2. *Marketing information system.* The job of effectively planning and controlling marketing effort calls for a great amount of continuous information about the macroenvironment, customers, marketing intermediaries, competitors, and other forces in the company's marketing environment. The gathering, processing, and dissemination of this information calls for the development of a marketing information system that is accurate, timely, and comprehensive. (Chapter 5 discusses the design and functioning of a marketing information system to support the company's marketing effort.)
3. *Marketing organization system.* The company must design an organization that is capable of effectively carrying out many and diverse marketing tasks. This includes a number of things. First, the company must design an organizational structure that leads to integrated, innovative, and responsible marketing planning and control. This usually means appointing a vice-president of marketing, who supervises several marketing executives and coordinates their reports. Second, each marketing job position—such as advertising manager, product manager, and sales manager—must be described in terms of the job's purpose, functions, tasks, and responsibilities. Third, the jobs must be filled by individuals who have adequate skills and motivation and the kind of personality that will enable them to do their marketing job effectively. (Chapter 6 discusses the major issues involved in developing an effective marketing organization.)

■ summary

Every organization must evolve a corporate strategy and marketing process if it is to survive and grow. The environment undergoes rapid change, and the organization must fit its objectives, strategy, structure, and systems into a viable relationship with the environment. The organization must continuously identify and evaluate marketing opportunities and threats and take the necessary actions.

Management is the entrepreneurial agent that interprets market needs and translates them into satisfactory products and services. To do this, management goes through a strategic-planning process and a marketing process. The strategic-planning process describes the steps taken at the corporate and divisional levels to develop long-run strategies for survival and growth. This provides the context for the marketing process, which describes the steps taken at the product and market levels to develop viable marketing positions and programs.

The strategic-planning process consists of defining the company mission, objectives and goals, a growth strategy, and portfolio plans. Developing a sound mission statement is a challenging undertaking. The mission statement must be market oriented, feasible, motivating, and specific if it is to serve its purpose of directing the firm to its best opportunities.

Strategic planning then calls for developing a set of objectives such as sales and market-share growth, profitability, and innovation to support the company mission. These objectives should be hierarchical, quantitative, realistic, and consistent.

To achieve growth, the company must identify market opportunities where it would enjoy a differential advantage over competitors. The company can generate relevant opportunities by considering intensive growth opportunities within its present product/market scope (such as market penetration, market development, and product development), integrative growth opportunities within its marketing channel system (such as backward, forward, and horizontal integration), and diversification growth opportunities outside its marketing channel system (such as concentric, horizontal, and conglomerate diversification).

Finally, strategic planning must define, for each strategic business unit (SBU) in the company's portfolio, whether it will be built, maintained, harvested, or terminated. As aids to doing this, companies can use either the BCG growth-share matrix or the GE strategic business-planning grid.

Within this context, the marketing process can be enacted. The first step consists of generating, evaluating, and recommending marketing opportunities. For any sound opportunity, the next step is to examine the product/market structure and identify the best target market. The third step is to decide on the best competitive position and marketing mix strategy for the company within that target market. The fourth step calls for designing three major marketing management systems—a planning and control system, an information system, and an organization system—for effectively carrying out the intended marketing effort.

EXHIBIT 3-1

SURVIVAL IS NOT THAT EASY

Nations (Assyria), species (dinosaurs), industries (horse carriages), and companies (Studebaker) have collapsed because they failed to meet environmental challenges with creative responses. History is filled with the names of specific products—Edsel, Corvair, *Collier's*—that, in spite of their momentous size, eventually became casualties.

No matter how large or well known an organization might be today, it is subject to customer erosion:

- Playboy, Incorporated, one of the most successful publishing companies in history, has watched its major magazine sales fall from a peak of 6.9 million copies in 1972 to 4.5 million in 1979.
- Kentucky Fried Chicken, one of the most successful fast-food franchisers in history, has experienced declining market share for the past several years.
- Pullman, Inc., the nation's oldest builder of railroad passenger cars, has decided to stop producing the Pullman car after 110 years of manufacture.
- Zenith, one of the most successful American television manufacturers, has watched its market share erode in recent years in the face of increasing competition from Japanese television manufacturers.
- Speaking of television, does anyone remember TV brands like Air King, DuMont, Emerson, Tele King, Hallicrafters, Capehart-Farnsworth, or some of the other hundred-odd brands available back in 1950?

questions for discussion

1. What are the four major types of organizations discussed in this chapter? Give an example of each.
2. Is the declining birthrate in the U.S. an environmental threat for Gerber? How has or how should the company respond?
3. Would you classify the college or university that you attend as a speculative, mature, or troubled organization? Why?
4. Why is strategic planning such an important process for organizations moving into the 1980s?
5. Develop a mission statement for Capitol Records. Also, discuss each of the essential characteristics of this statement for Capitol.
6. How do the major classes of growth opportunities differ? Into which class(es) would you place the following companies—McDonald's, IBM, and Tenneco?
7. Briefly describe the four types of strategic business units (SBUs) developed by the Boston Consulting Group. Classify Ford's current automobile models (i.e., Mustang II, Fiesta, Granada, LTD II, Fairmont, and Pinto) into each of the four categories. Defend your choices.
8. Relate the four major steps in the marketing process to a service of your choice.
9. It is argued that the success of L'eggs panty hose is due to the company's understanding of the marketing mix factors. Discuss the important marketing mix variables as they relate to L'eggs.
10. If managers do a good job of planning and control, they will be properly accomplishing the marketing management systems development step in the marketing process. Comment.

references

1. "Olin's Shift to Strategy," *Business Week,* March 27, 1978, p. 102. Reprinted by special permission, © 1978 by McGraw-Hill, Inc., all rights reserved.
2. The definition is based on the discussion in PETER BLAU AND RICHARD SCOTT, *Formal Organizations* (New York: Harper & Row, Pub., 1962), Chapter 1.
3. THEODORE LEVITT, "The New Markets—Think Before You Leap," *Harvard Business Review,* May-June 1969, pp. 53–67 (esp. pp. 53–54).
4. "Philip Morris: Turning 7 Up into the Miller of Soft Drinks," *Business Week,* April 2, 1979, pp. 66–67.
5. See DEREK F. ABELL, "Strategic Windows," *Journal of Marketing,* July 1978, pp. 21–26.
6. See PETER DRUCKER, *Management: Tasks, Responsibilities, Practices* (New York: Harper & Row, Pub., 1973), Chap. 7.
7. THEODORE LEVITT, "Marketing Myopia," *Harvard Business Review,* July-August 1960, pp. 45–56.
8. For a useful discussion of objectives setting, see CHARLES H. GRANGER, "The Hierarchy of Objectives," *Harvard Business Review,* May-June 1964, pp. 63–74.
9. H. IGOR ANSOFF, "Strategies for Diversification," *Harvard Business Review,* September-October 1957, pp. 113–24.

10. For additional reading, see CHARLES W. HOFER AND DAN SCHENDEL, *Strategy Formulation: Analytical Concepts* (St. Paul, Minn.: West Publishing, 1978), pp. 30–32; and GEORGE S. DAY, "Diagnosing the Product Portfolio," *Journal of Marketing,* April 1977, pp. 29–38.
11. The learning curve is very important to pricing and marketing strategy. See "Selling Business a Theory of Economics," *Business Week,* September 8, 1973, pp. 86–88.
12. For additional reading, see HOFER AND SCHENDEL, *Strategy Formulation,* pp. 32–34. Also see "General Electric's Stoplight Strategy for Planning," *Business Week,* April 28, 1975, p. 49.
13. "GE Growth Plans Outline by Jones," *Bridgeport Telegram,* November 8, 1974.
14. E. JEROME MCCARTHY, *Basic Marketing: A Managerial Approach,* 4th ed. (Homewood, Ill.: Richard D. Irwin, 1971), p. 44 (1st ed., 1960). Two alternative classifications are worth noting. Frey proposed that all marketing decision variables could be divided into two factors: (1) *the offering* (product, packaging, brand, price, and service), and (2) *methods and tools* (distribution channels, personal selling, advertising, sales promotion, and publicity). See ALBERT W. FREY, *Advertising,* 3rd ed. (New York: Ronald Press, 1961), p. 30. Lazer and Kelley proposed a three-factor classification: (1) *goods and service mix,* (2) *distribution mix,* and (3) *communications mix.* See WILLIAM LAZER AND EUGENE J. KELLEY, *Managerial Marketing: Perspectives and Viewpoints,* rev. ed. (Homewood, Ill.: Richard D. Irwin, 1962), p. 413.
15. These maps must be interpreted with care. Not all customers share the same perceptions. The map shows the average perception. Attention should also be paid to the scatter of perceptions.

THE MARKETING PLANNING AND CONTROL SYSTEM

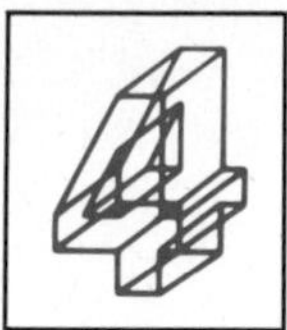

A major bank in Chicago operates a retail banking department and a commercial banking department. The commercial banking department's mission is to serve the varying financial needs of businesses in the Greater Chicago area and nation. The commercial department is divided into separate industry groups serving such industries as transportation, communication, utilities, and small manufacturers.

The bank's group serving the transportation industry deals with airlines, trucking firms, railroads, bus companies, and barge companies. For twenty years it was headed by a lending officer who was considered a successful manager. His group was able to increase the bank's outstanding loans to the transportation industry by 5 to 15 percent annually. He did not operate from a plan but instead encouraged his staff to spend a lot of time with transportation company executives and seize opportunities as they arose. When his department's performance occasionally slipped, he responded by putting pressure on his staff to go after business more aggressively.

The bank's management had been pleased with this executive's performance. After he retired, a younger man with an M.B.A. degree took over. He approached the job very differently. First he asked the bank's marketing department to conduct a study to determine the total amount of loans made by all banks in the area to transportation companies; the market shares, strategies, and interest charges of each major bank in the area competing for this business; and the major developments that would affect the financial needs of transportation companies in the future. Much useful information was obtained from this study. One of the major findings was that this bank was probably realizing less than 50 percent of its sales potential in this market. The new lending officer then proceeded to install a planning and control system, which called for setting goals, strategies, and action programs for different segments within the transportation lending market. Members of his staff were assigned specific segments to manage and had to develop goals, call plans, and controls that supported the department's plans. As a result of introducing the planning and control system, the new lending officer was able to double the bank's outstanding loans to the transportation industry in two years.

□ This example should make it clear that marketing planning and control is not practiced in every company. Every company, of course, is the scene of continuous decision making and problem-solving, activity but this should not be confused with marketing planning and control. The latter is a separate and higher-order activity which often rewards the company with improved sales and profit performance.

Here we will examine how organizations develop marketing-planning and control systems to serve their markets effectively. The relationship between marketing planning and control is shown in Figure 4-1 and constitutes a three-step process. The first step calls upon the company to plan its marketing effort, that is, to identify attractive target markets, develop effective marketing strategies, and develop detailed action programs. The second step involves the execution of the action programs in the marketing plan, both geographically and over time. The third step calls for marketing control activity to make sure that the objectives are being achieved. Marketing control requires the measuring of results, analyzing the causes of poor results, and taking corrective action. The corrective action consists of adjustments in the plan, its execution, or both.

The first part of this chapter will deal with marketing planning and the second part with marketing control.

marketing planning

Sooner or later all organizations ask themselves whether they need a business- and marketing-planning system, what shape it should take, and what should be done to make it work effectively. We will consider these questions in the following sections.

Benefits of Planning

Many companies operate without the benefit of a formal planning system, choosing to solve various problems as they arise. In the case of newer companies, their managers are so busy putting out various fires that they have no time for planning. In the case of mature companies, many managers argue that they have

Figure 4-1
The Marketing-Planning and Control System

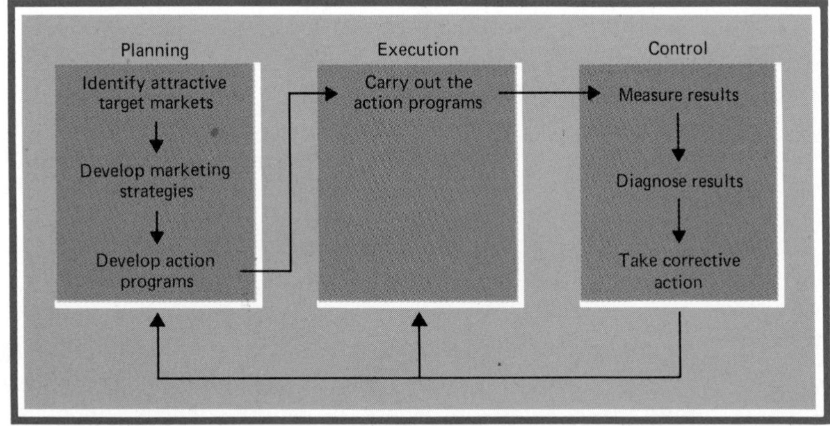

done well without formal planning and therefore it cannot be too important. They resist the idea of taking time to prepare a written document stating objectives, strategies, and action programs. Much preliminary work would be required before the document could be prepared, and the document itself would be too revealing of the condition of the business and the quality or lack of quality of the responsible officer's thinking. Many managers argue that their marketplace changes too fast for a plan to be useful or relevant and that it would end up collecting dust. And many managers also argue that planning becomes an annual ritual entered into halfheartedly by executives and wastes a lot of time. For these and other reasons, many companies have not yet introduced formal planning systems.

In spite of these objections, formal planning will yield a number of distinct benefits if sound procedures are used to guide the planning process. Melville Branch has listed the following major benefits of a formal planning system: (1) it encourages systematic thinking ahead by management; (2) it leads to a better coordination of company efforts; (3) it leads to the development of performance standards for control; (4) it causes the company to sharpen its guiding objectives and policies; (5) it results in better preparedness for sudden developments; (6) it brings about a more vivid sense in the participating executives of their interacting responsibilities.[1]

How Business Planning Evolves in Organizations

Rarely is an organization able to install an advanced business-planning system when it first decides to formalize its planning. Its business-planning system is likely to evolve through several stages—getting better, it is hoped, at each stage. Business-planning systems tend to move through four stages on their way to greater sophistication.

Unplanned stage. When businesses first become established, their managers are so busy hunting for funds, customers, equipment, and materials that they have little time for formal planning. Management is totally engrossed in the day-to-day operations required for survival. There is no planning staff and hardly any time to plan.

Budgeting system stage. Management eventually recognizes the desirability of installing a budgeting system to improve the planning of the company's cash flow. Management estimates total sales for the coming year and the expected costs and cash flows associated with this sales level. Each departmental manager prepares a budget for carrying out the department's work for the coming year. These budgets are financial and do not require the kind of attention that goes into real business planning. Budgets are not the same as plans.

Annual-planning stage. Management eventually recognizes the need to develop annual plans. It adopts one of three possible types of formal planning systems.

The first is *top-down planning,* so called because top management sets *goals* and *plans* for all the lower levels of management. This model is taken from military organizations where the generals prepare the plans and the troops carry them out. In commercial organizations this goes along with a Theory X view of employees, that is, they dislike work and responsibility and prefer to be directed.[2]

The second system is *bottom-up planning,* so called because the various units of the organization prepare their own goals and plans based on the best they think they can do, and they send them to upper management for approval. This style is based on Theory Y, that is, employees like work and responsibility and are more creative and committed if they participate in the planning and running of the enterprise.

Most companies use a third system known as *goals down—plans up planning.* Here top management takes a broad look at the company's opportunities and requirements and sets corporate goals for the year. The various units of the company are responsible for developing plans designed to help the company reach these goals. These plans, when approved by top management, become the official annual plan. A typical example is afforded by the Celanese Company:

- The annual planning process starts in late August, with top management receiving marketing research reports and sending out a guidance letter stating overall volume and profit goals. During September and October, product planning managers develop overall marketing plans in consultation with the field sales manager and the marketing vice president. In the middle of October, the marketing vice president reviews and approves the plans and submits them to the president for final approval. In the meantime, the field sales manager works with his regional sales managers and salesmen to develop field sales plans. Finally, in the fourth week in October, the controller prepares an operating budget; it goes, in early November, to top management for final approval. Thus, three months after the planning process started, a completed plan and budget are ready to be put into operation.[3]

Strategic-planning stage. In this stage the planning system of the company is elaborated in an effort to improve its overall effectiveness.

The major change is the addition of *long-range planning.* Management realizes that annual plans only make sense in the context of a long-range plan. In fact, the long-range plan should come first, and the annual plan should be a detailed version of the first year of the long-range plan. For example, managers at the American Hospital Supply Company prepare a strategic five-year plan early in the year and an annual operating plan later in the year. The five-year plan is reworked each year (called *rolling planning*) because the environment changes rapidly and requires an annual review of the long-run planning assumptions.

A further development is that the various plans begin to take on a more *strategic* character. When a company first turns to planning, the planning documents are very simple: They are long on statistics and specific tactical actions and short on strategy. One often looks in vain for a clear statement of strategy. In more advanced planning systems, the plan formats are constructed so as to require a section on strategy.

As the company gains experience with planning, an effort is made to *standardize the plan formats* so that higher management can compare the performance of similar units. It is important that the plans written for different comparable units, such as divisions, product lines, products, or brands, follow the same or a similar format to permit intelligent comparison by higher management.

As the planning culture takes hold in the company, further improvements are introduced. Marketing managers receive more training in the use of *financial analysis* and are required to justify their recommendations not in sales volume terms but in terms of contribution margin, cash flow, and rate of return on manageable assets. *Computer programs* are developed to help product managers examine the impact of alternative marketing plans and environmental assumptions on sales and profits.[4] The managers are eventually asked to develop *contingency plans* in addition to main plans showing how they would respond if specific major threats or opportunities were to arise. These and other developments mark the emergence of a true strategic-planning culture in the firm.

Steps in the Business- and Marketing-Planning Process

Business firms vary in the way they use the terms *business planning* and *marketing planning*. Some companies use the two terms interchangeably. Other companies say that they develop their marketing plan first and then their business plan. Still other companies say that they develop their business plan first and then their marketing plan.

The proper way to view the process of business and marketing planning is shown in Figure 4-2. The process starts with marketing executives playing the major role in attempting to describe the market, the sales, and the profits that the company could feasibly aim for, and the broad marketing strategies that might be pursued. At best, this can be called a *market analysis and forecast.* The marketing executives then work with the executives in charge of manufacturing, finance, personnel, and so on, to develop a *business plan,* which might involve revising the market analysis and forecast. Following the business plan's approval, the marketing department proceeds to develop a detailed plan called the *marketing plan,* which outlines the specific goals, strategies, programs, budgets, and controls that the various members of the marketing department will use to support the business plan. Other key executives will also develop versions of the business plan pertinent to their operation.

The following plans require strong marketing inputs:

1. *Product line plan.* A product line plan describes objectives, goals, strategies, and tactics for a specific product line. Each product line manager prepares this plan.
2. *Product plan.* A product plan describes objectives, goals, strategies, and tactics for a specific product or product category. Each product manager prepares this plan.
3. *Brand plan.* A brand plan describes objectives, goals, strategies, and tactics for a

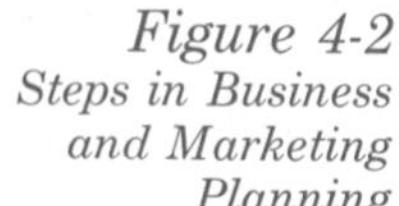
Figure 4-2
Steps in Business and Marketing Planning

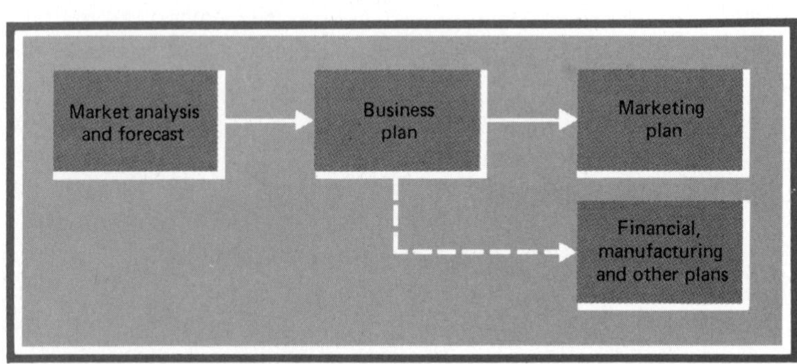

specific brand within the product category. Each brand manager prepa[...]
plan.

4. *Market plan.* A market plan is a plan for developing and serving a specific n[...] If the organization has market managers as well as product managers, the n[...] managers will prepare these plans.
5. *Product/market plan.* A product/market plan is a plan for marketing a specific product or product line of the company in a specific industrial or geographical market. An example would be a bank that markets its lending services to the transportation industry.

The Components of a Marketing Plan

How does a marketing plan look? Our discussion will focus on product or brand plans. A product or brand plan should contain the following major sections: *executive summary, situation analysis, objectives and goals, marketing strategy, action program,* and *budgets and controls* (see Figure 4-3).

Executive summary. The planning document should open with a short summary of the main goals and recommendations to be presented in the plan. Here is an abbreviated example:

- The 1980 Marketing Plan seeks to generate a significant increase in company sales and profits in comparison with the preceding year's achievements. The sales target is set at $80 million, which represents a planned 20 percent sales gain in comparison with last year. This increase is deemed to be attainable because of the improved economic, competitive, and distribution picture. The operating margin is forecast at $8 million, which represents a 25 percent increase in comparison with last year. To achieve these goals, the sales promotion budget will be $1.6 million, which represents 2 percent of projected sales. The advertising budget will be $2.4 million, which represents 3 percent of projected sales. . . . [More detail follows]

The executive summary permits higher management to quickly grasp the major thrust of each plan and then read further in search of the information that is most critical in evaluating the plan. To facilitate this, a table of contents should follow the executive summary.

Situation analysis. The first major section of the plan is the *situation analysis,* in which the manager describes the major features affecting his or her operation. The situation analysis comprises four subsections—background, normal forecast, opportunities and threats, and strengths and weaknesses.

Figure 4-3 *Contents of a Marketing Plan*

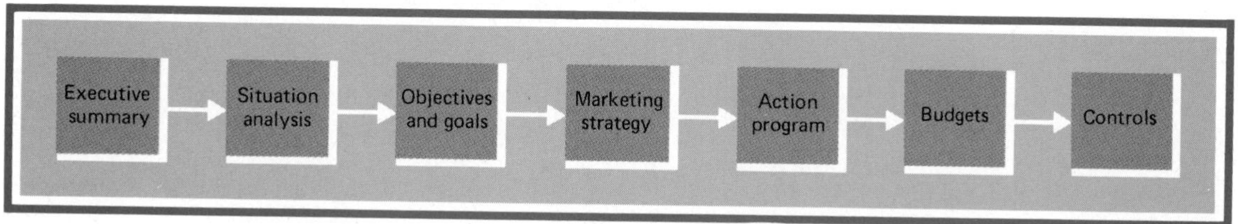

BACKGROUND

This section usually starts with a summary of key sales and profit data for the last several years. An example of five years of past data is shown in Table 4-1. Row 1 of the table shows that the market volume is growing at the rate of 200,000 units a year. Row 2 shows that the company's brand rose from a 6 percent share to a fairly stable 10 percent share. Row 3 shows that the product's price of $2 has been increasing recently. Row 4 shows that variable cost per unit originally declined but has been increasing recently. Row 5 shows that the gross contribution margin per unit—the difference between price (row 3) and unit variable cost (row 4)—first increased and then decreased in the most recent year. Rows 6 and 7 show sales volume in both units and dollars, and row 8 shows the total gross contribution margin. Row 9 shows a stable and then a rising level of overhead. Row 10 shows net contribution margin, that is, gross contribution margin less overhead. Rows 11 and 12 show advertising and distribution expenses, respectively. Finally, row 13 shows net operating profit after marketing expenses. The picture is one of growing sales, with profits, however, growing at a slower rate.

These data are followed by a description of noteworthy facts and trends relating to the market, distribution, and competition. The market section should describe market size and trends, major target market segments, and buyer behavior developments. The distribution section should describe the major trends occurring in marketing channels and physical distribution. The competition section should describe the major competitors and their market shares, strategies, and strengths and weaknesses. The factors underlying the most recent sales and profit results should be analyzed.

NORMAL FORECAST

The background section should be followed by a forecast of market size and company sales under "normal conditions," that is, assuming no major changes in the *marketing environment* or *marketing strategies*. This forecast could be

Table 4-1
Historical Product

VARIABLE	COLUMNS	1975	1976	1977	1978	1979
1. Market—total units		1,000,000	1,200,000	1,400,000	1,600,000	1,800,000
2. Share		.06	.08	.10	.10	.10
3. Price per unit $		2.00	2.00	2.00	2.20	2.40
4. Variable cost per unit $		1.20	1.10	1.10	1.30	1.55
5. Gross contribution margin per unit $	(3 − 4)	.80	.90	.90	.90	.85
6. Sales volume in units	(1 × 2)	60,000	96,000	140,000	160,000	180,000
7. Sales $	(3 × 6)	120,000	192,000	280,000	352,000	432,000
8. Gross contribution margin $	(5 × 6)	48,000	86,400	126,000	144,000	153,000
9. Overhead $		20,000	20,000	20,000	30,000	30,000
10. Net contribution margin $	(8 − 9)	28,000	66,400	106,000	114,000	123,000
11. Advertising $		8,000	12,000	15,000	18,000	20,000
12. Distribution $		4,000	8,000	15,000	15,000	20,000
13. Net operating profit $	(10 − 11 − 12)	16,000	46,400	76,000	81,000	83,000

obtained in a number of ways. The simplest method is straightforward extrapolation of past growth rates of market size and company sales. For example, the market volume in Table 4-1 for the coming year can be forecast at 2 million units, on the assumption that the 200,000 annual increase continues. Market share can be assumed to stay at 10 percent. Prices can be expected to rise by, say, twenty cents. Another method is to forecast the economy and other major variables affecting sales and then incorporate these estimates in a statistical demand equation to forecast sales (see Chapter 5, pp. 163–64). Still another method is to gather sales-force estimates of what they expect to sell next year. Most companies use two or more forecasting methods and take an average of the estimates.

The forecast would have to be revised if quite different environmental conditions are expected or strategies are planned. If the forecast does not satisfy higher management, the product or brand manager would have to consider new strategies and would hope to find one that promised a higher level of sales and profits.

OPPORTUNITIES AND THREATS

The normal forecast section should be followed by a section in which the manager identifies the main opportunities and threats in the external environment facing the business unit. Usually the manager is aware of a number of these but should be challenged to put them into words. Higher management can list and raise questions about threats and opportunities that are listed or missing.

Table 4-2A shows the opportunities and threats listed by a product line manager in charge of a company's line of television sets. The opportunities and threats describe *outside* factors facing the business unit. They are written so as to suggest some possible actions that might be warranted. The manager may be asked to rate the opportunities and threats for their potential impact and probability as an indicator of which deserve the most attention and planning.

STRENGTHS AND WEAKNESSES

In this section the manager lists the main internal strengths and weaknesses of the business unit. This is shown for the television product line in Table 4-2B. The list of strengths has implications for strategy formulation, while the list of weaknesses has implications for investments to correct weaknesses. Higher management can raise important questions about each business unit based on each manager's list of strengths and weaknesses.

Objectives and goals. The situation analysis points out where the business stands and where it might go. The next task is to develop a statement about where the business *should* go. Managers have to set specific objectives and goals that will be accepted by higher management.

Higher management typically defines the company's overall goals for the coming period. The top management of an electronics firm may state that it wants the company to achieve (1) a 15 percent growth in sales volume, (2) a pretax profit of 20 percent on sales, and (3) a pretax profit of 25 percent on investment. Within this context, each manager develops goals for his or her business unit that will support the company goals. Those business units enjoying strong market positions will be expected to adopt even more ambitious goals than

Table 4-2

A. Major Opportunities and Threats in the Television Business

Opportunities

1. There is a growing market for life-size home television. We should give some thought to entering this market and attempting to establish leadership.
2. Our dealer coverage in the South is thin, although consumer preference for our brand is high.
3. The federal government is getting ready to slap a quota on foreign television sets.

Threats

1. Many consumers are shifting to lower-priced brands. We may have to lower prices on our existing line or introduce some new lower-cost models.
2. The cost of cabinet wood is expected to jump 15 percent in the coming year. We may have to find new substitute exterior materials.
3. The federal government may pass a more stringent product safety law. This would necessitate some product redesign.

B. Strengths and Weaknesses of the Company

Strengths

1. Ninety-five percent of the consumers know our brand. This awareness level is the highest in the industry.
2. Forty percent of the consumers believe that our brand is the most reliable one in the industry. No one brand comes close to this.
3. Our dealers are the best trained in the industry in terms of knowledge and salesmanship.

Weaknesses

1. Our brand is considered high in price relative to other brands, and it loses the price-conscious buyer. Pricing strategy should be reevaluated.
2. The quality of the picture is no longer the best in the industry. We need to invest more in research and development.
3. Our advertising campaign is not particularly creative or exciting. We may want to consider switching advertising agencies.

the company goals. Those operating in difficult markets will adopt more modest goals. Top management wants to "stretch" each business unit to its maximum potential.

Assume that the manager of the television product line in this company sees the key need to be that of increasing the profitability of the line. Suppose the line's current return on investment (ROI) is 10 percent, and higher management wants the television line to yield 15 percent. This can be accomplished by (1) increasing the sales revenue, (2) decreasing the cost (or not increasing it by as much as the higher sales revenue), and (3) decreasing the investment (or not increasing it by as much as the increase in profit). Any or all of these can be adopted as objectives for the coming period.

The objectives that the manager decides to emphasize can be turned into goals, that is, they can be given magnitudes and target dates. The manager might propose the following goals for attaining a 15 percent ROI in the television line: (1) attain a 12 percent increase in sales revenue for the coming year, (2) increase the expense budget by 8 percent for the coming year, and (3) hold the investment level constant for the coming year.

Each of these goals will in turn be broken down into subgoals for the various operating units. For example, the overall sales goal will eventually be allocated to the sales units of the company, such as sales regions, sales districts, and, finally, individual salespersons. In this form they are called sales quotas and will be based on the past performance and estimated potential facing each sales unit.

Marketing strategy. In this section, management outlines a marketing strategy for attaining its objectives. This strategy describes the "game plan" by which the business unit hopes to "win." More specifically, we can define *marketing strategy* as follows:

- **Marketing strategy** is the fundamental marketing logic by which the business unit intends to achieve its marketing objectives. Marketing strategy consists of a coordinated set of decisions on (1) target markets, (2) marketing mix, and (3) marketing expenditure level.

We will now examine the three components of marketing strategy.

TARGET MARKETS

A sound marketing strategy calls for giving different degrees of emphasis to the various market segments making up the market. These segments differ in their preferences, responses to marketing effort, and profitability. They differ in the degree to which the particular company is able to produce market satisfaction. Instead of going after all the market segments with equal fervor, the company would be smart to allocate its effort and energy to those market segments it can serve best from a competitive point of view. Here is an example:

- The ABC management consulting firm (named disguised) was having difficulty maintaining its billings in a highly competitive consulting market. Various competitors were beginning to specialize in certain industries and were building superior reputations in these industries as consultants. ABC operated as a generalist firm and therefore was less in demand than consulting firms specializing in each industry. It became clear to ABC's management that its marketing strategy was ill defined with respect to target markets and that if it did not make some hard choices as to which industries it would concentrate on, it would really be lacking a marketing strategy.

MARKETING MIX

The company should attempt to develop a cost-effective marketing mix for each target market that it pursues. The marketing mix will consist of a particular set of levels of the four *P*'s: product, price, place, and promotion. A company faces many choices in selecting a marketing mix for a particular target market. Consider the following example:

- The Papermate Pen Company (owned by Gillette) recently developed a new ballpoint pen called the Eraser Mate. This is the first pen ever developed that uses erasable ink. People who prefer pens to pencils can now erase their writing. (However, people are cautioned against using the pen to write checks.) The company faced the task of devising a marketing mix strategy for this pen. It considered charging a price of $1.69 or $1.99; setting an advertising budget of $200,000 or $500,000 for the first year; and setting a retailer discount of 20 or 30 percent off the retailer price. Given these three marketing mix variables and the two levels of each, the company can choose any of eight marketing mixes ($2 \times 2 \times 2$). For example, one marketing mix would be "high price, high advertising, low retailer discount," and another would be "low price, high advertising, and high retailer discount." Each marketing mix has to be analyzed for its probable impact on sales and profits, along with its likelihood of attracting competition into the market. The problem of choosing a marketing mix is even more challenging when we begin to recognize additional marketing variables and possible levels of each.

Members of the marketing department will have differing opinions on the effectiveness of the various marketing variables. The sales manager would like to spend marketing funds on hiring more salespersons; the advertising manager would like to buy more ads; the product manager would like to improve product quality or packaging; and the marketing research manager would like to conduct a deeper study of the market. These differences in opinion are one of the reasons that marketing must be planned in a coordinated way.

MARKETING EXPENDITURE LEVEL

Marketing strategy also calls for deciding on the dollar level of marketing expenditures. Even if the marketing mix is optimal, the company may be spending too much or too little on marketing. Companies typically establish their marketing budget at some conventional percentage of the sales goal. For example, a perfume company might set its marketing budget at 35 percent of sales, and a fertilizer company at 15 percent of sales. Companies entering a new market have to spend a fairly high amount of marketing dollars in relation to anticipated sales in the hope of building their market share. Companies know that the more they spend on marketing, the higher their sales will be. What they need to know is the point where increased sales no longer bring increased profits, but actually cut into profits.

Action program. The marketing strategy must be turned into a set of specific actions for accomplishing the marketing goals. A useful approach is to make someone responsible for each strategy element. Suppose the marketing strategy calls for "developing a substantially improved advertising campaign." This task might be assigned to Scott Fitz, advertising manager. Fitz should list the various actions required to develop an improved advertising campaign, such as "Gather the names of three highly regarded advertising agencies," "Listen to competitive proposals," "Select the best agency," "Approve the final copy," and "Approve the media plan." Each activity is assigned to someone in the advertising department along with a completion date. This format would be repeated for each strategy element.

The overall action plan may take the form of a table, with the twelve months (or fifty-two weeks) of the year serving as columns and various marketing activities serving as rows. Dates can be entered indicating when various activities or expenditures will be started, reviewed, and completed. This action plan is subject to change during the year as new problems and opportunities arise, but it serves as a general implementation framework for tactics.

Budgets. The goals, strategies, and planned actions allow the manager to formulate a supporting budget statement for the operation. The budget statement is essentially a projected profit and loss statement. On the revenue side, it shows the forecast number of units that would be sold and the average net realized price. On the expense side, it shows the costs of production, physical distribution, and marketing, broken down into finer categories. The difference, or projected profit, is shown. Management reviews the budget and either approves it or modifies it before approving it. Once approved, the budget is the basis for material procurement, production scheduling, manpower planning, and marketing operations.

Controls. The last section of the plan deals with the controls that will be applied to monitor the plan's progress. Normally the goals and budgets are spelled out for each month or quarter. This means that higher management can review the results each period and spot those businesses that are not attaining their goals. The managers of these deficient businesses have to offer an explanation and indicate what actions they plan to take. (The marketing control system will be discussed in greater detail later in this chapter.)

Developing the Marketing Budget

We will now examine more closely the task of constructing a marketing budget to attain a given level of sales and profits. We will first illustrate a common marketing budget-setting approach and then describe certain improvements suggested by marketing resource allocation theory.

Target profit planning. Assume that John Smith is the ketchup product manager at the Heinz Company and that it is now time for him to prepare his annual plan. If he is like most managers, he will follow the procedure shown in Table 4-3, called *target profit planning.*

John Smith first estimates the total market for ketchup for the coming year. (We will consider only the household market here.) An estimate can be formed by applying the recent growth rate of the market (6 percent) to this year's market size (23.6 million cases). This forecasts a market size of 25 million cases for next year. He then forecasts Heinz's sales based on the assumption that its past

Table 4-3
A Target Profit-oriented Product Plan

1. *Forecast of total market* This year's total market (23,600,000 cases) × recent growth rate (6%)	25,000,000 cases
2. *Forecast of market share*	28%
3. *Forecast of sales volume* (1 × 2)	7,000,000 cases
4. *Price to distributor*	$4.45 per case
5. *Estimate of sales revenue* (3 × 4)	$31,150,000
6. *Estimate of variable costs* Tomatoes and spices ($0.50) + bottles and caps ($1.00) + labor ($1.10) + physical distribution ($0.15)	$2.75 per case
7. *Estimate of contribution margin to cover fixed costs, profits, and marketing* ([4 – 6] 3)	$11,900,000
8. *Estimate of fixed costs* Fixed charge $1 per case × 7 million cases	$7,000,000
9. *Estimate of contribution margin to cover profits and marketing* (7 – 8)	$4,900,000
10. *Estimate of target profit per case*	$1,900,000
11. *Amount available for marketing* (9 – 10)	$3,000,000
12. *Split of the marketing budget*	
Advertising	$2,000,000
Sales Promotion	$ 900,000
Marketing Research	$ 100,000

market share of 28 percent, will continue. Thus Heinz's sales are forecast to be 7 million cases.

Next he sets a distributor price of $4.45 per case for next year based mainly on expected increases in labor and material costs. Thus the planned sales revenue will be $31.15 million.

He then estimates next year's variable costs at $2.75 per case. This means that the contribution margin to cover fixed costs, profits, and marketing is $11.9 million. Suppose the company charges this brand with a fixed cost of $1 per case, or $7 million. This leaves a contribution margin of $4.9 million to cover profits and marketing.

At this step John Smith brings in the target profit goal. Suppose a profit level of $1.9 million will satisfy higher management. It is usually some increase, say 5 to 10 percent, over this year's profit. He then subtracts the target profit from what remains of the contribution margin to learn that $3 million is available for marketing.

The final step involves the product manager's splitting the marketing budget into its mix elements, such as advertising, sales promotion, and marketing research. The split is normally based on the preceding year's split and the way in which competitors are using their marketing budgets. He decides to spend two-thirds of the money on advertising, almost one-third on sales promotion, and the remainder on marketing research.

Although this method produces a workable marketing plan and budget, several improvements are possible:

1. The product manager estimated market size and market share by straightforward extrapolation of past trends. He should consider possible changes in the marketing environment that would lead to a different demand forecast.
2. The product manager assumed no change in his marketing strategy. But one of the reasons for planning is to consider alternative marketing strategies and their potential impact on company sales and profits. He should not estimate the company's market share until after he develops his marketing strategy.
3. The product manager set next year's price largely to cover expected cost increases rather than including consideration of demand and expected competitors' prices. Setting the price mainly on the basis of cost is not a market-oriented pricing method.
4. The product manager developed the marketing mix on "more-of-the-same" thinking rather than on hard rationales of how each marketing mix element would support the marketing objectives at this stage in the product's life cycle.
5. The product manager seems to be guided by the idea of finding a "satisficing" plan, one that produces satisfactory profits. Instead, he should try to find the optimal profit plan.

Profit optimization planning. We will now look at the theory of how to find the optimal profit plan. Profit optimization requires that the manager give explicit recognition to the relationship between sales volume and the various elements of the marketing mix. We will use the term *sales-response function* to describe the relationship between sales volume and one or more elements of the marketing mix.

- A **sales-response function** forecasts the likely sales volume during a specified time period associated with different possible levels of one or more marketing mix elements.

The best-known sales-response function is the demand function, illustrated in Figure 4-4A. This function shows that the lower the price, the higher the sales in any given period. In the illustration a price of $2 leads to sales of 6,000 units in that period, but a price of $1 would have led to sales of 10,000 units in that period. The illustrated demand curve is curvilinear, although other shapes are possible.

Suppose that the marketing variable is not price but total marketing dollars spent by the company on sales-force, advertising, and other marketing effort. In this case the sales-response function is likely to resemble Figure 4-4B. This function states that the more the company spends in a given period on marketing effort, the higher the sales are likely to be. The particular function is S-shaped, although other shapes are possible. The S-shaped function says that low levels of marketing expenditure are not likely to produce high levels of sales. The reason is that too few buyers will be reached, or reached effectively, by the company's message. Higher levels of marketing expenditure per period will produce much higher levels of sales. Very high expenditures per period, however, might not add more sales and would represent "marketing overkill."

The occurrence of eventually diminishing return to increases in marketing expenditures is plausible for the following reasons. First, there is an upper limit to the total potential demand for any particular product. The easier sales prospects are sold almost immediately; the more recalcitrant sales prospects remain. As the upper limit is approached, it becomes increasingly expensive to stimulate further sales. Second, as a company steps up its marketing effort, its competitors are likely to do the same, with the net result that each company experiences increasing sales resistance. And third, if sales were to increase at an increasing rate throughout, natural monopolies would result. A single firm would tend to take

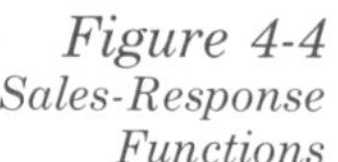

Figure 4-4
Sales-Response Functions

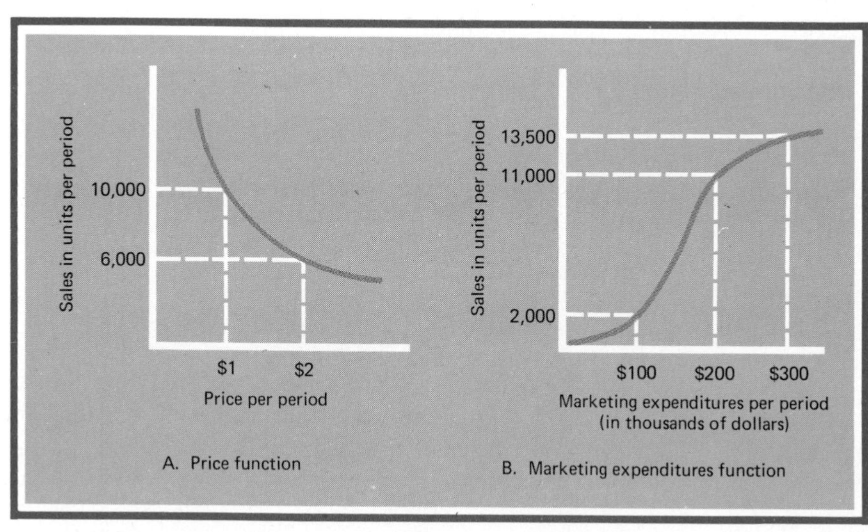

over in each industry because of the greater level of its marketing effort. Yet this is contrary to what we observe in industry.

How can marketing managers estimate the sales-response functions that apply to their business? Essentially, three methods are available. The first is the *statistical method,* where the manager gathers data on past sales and levels of marketing mix variables and estimates the sales-response functions through standard statistical estimation procedures.[5] The second is the *experimental method,* which calls for deliberately varying the marketing expenditure and mix levels in matched samples of geographical or other units and noting the resulting sales volume.[6] The third is the *judgmental method,* where experts are asked to make intelligent guesses about the needed magnitudes.[7]

Once the sales-response functions are estimated, how are they used in profit optimization? Graphically, we must introduce some further curves to find the point of optimal marketing expenditure. The analysis is shown in Figure 4-5. The key function that we start with is the sales-response function. It resembles the S-shaped sales-response function in the earlier Figure 4-4B except for two differences. First, sales response is expressed in terms of sales dollars instead of sales units so that we can find the profit-maximizing marketing expenditure. Second, the sales-response function is shown as starting above zero sales on the argument that some sales might take place even in the absence of marketing expenditures.

To find the optimal marketing expenditure, the marketing manager subtracts all nonmarketing costs from the *sales-response function* to derive the *gross-profit curve.* Next, marketing expenditures are drawn in such a way that a dollar on one axis is projected as a dollar on the other axis. This amounts to a 45° line when the axes are scaled in identical dollar intervals. The *marketing-expenditures curve* is then subtracted from the *gross-profit curve* to derive the *net-profit curve.* The net-profit curve shows positive net profits with marketing expenditures between M_L and M_U, which could be defined as the rational range of marketing expenditure. The net-profit curve reaches a maximum at M. Therefore the marketing expenditure that would maximize net profit is $\$M$.

Figure 4-5
Relationship between Sales Volume, Marketing Expenditures, and Profits

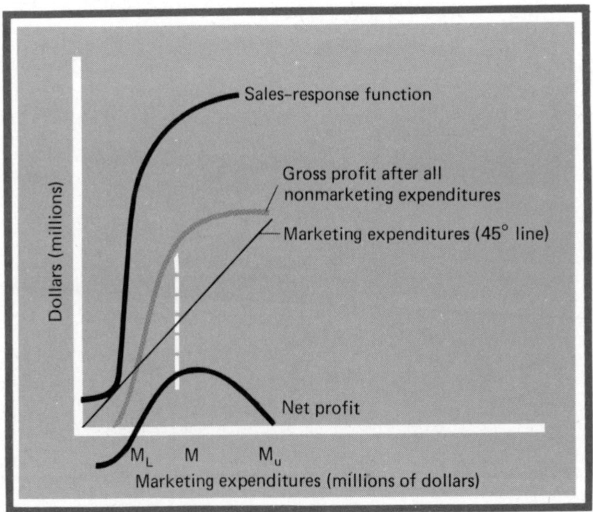

The graphical solution can alternatively be carried out numerically or algebraically; indeed it has to be if the sales volume is a function of more than one marketing mix variable. We will now present a numerical example of how this is done.

A NUMERICAL EXAMPLE

Ms. Sally Jones, a product manager, has been selling her product for some years by using a low-price, low-promotion strategy. The current price is $16, and $10,000 is being spent on advertising and another $10,000 on sales promotion. Sales are around 12,000 units, and profits are around $14,000. Higher management considers this unimpressive. Ms. Jones is anxious to find a better strategy to increase profits.

Her first step is to generate a set of alternative marketing mix strategies. She generates the eight strategies shown in the Price, Advertising, and Promotion columns of Table 4-4 (the first strategy is the current one). These strategies were formed by assuming a high and a low level of each of three marketing variables.

Her next step is to estimate the likely sales that would be attained with each alternative mix. Her sales estimates are shown in the last column of Table 4-4.

Her final step calls for determining which marketing mix maximizes profits, assuming the sales estimates are reliable. This calls for introducing a profit equation and inserting the different marketing mixes into this equation to see which maximizes profit.

Suppose fixed costs are $38,000 and unit variable costs are $10. Then expected profit can be computed for each marketing mix by using the profit equation:

Profit = Total revenue − Total cost

Profit = (Price × Quantity) − Total variable cost − Fixed cost − Marketing cost

Applying this to the first mix in Table 4-4, we get:

Profit = ($16 × 12,400) − ($10 × 12,400) − $38,000 − ($10,000 + $10,000)
= $16,400

At this point the product manager estimates the profit with each marketing mix shown in Table 4-4. The resulting profits are: #1($16,400), #2($13,000),

Table 4-4
Marketing Mixes and Estimated Sales

MARKETING MIX NO.	PRICE	ADVERTISING	PROMOTION	SALES
1.	$16	$10,000	$10,000	12,400
2.	16	10,000	50,000	18,500
3.	16	50,000	10,000	15,100
4.	16	50,000	50,000	22,600
5.	24	10,000	10,000	5,500
6.	24	10,000	50,000	8,200
7.	24	50,000	10,000	6,700
8.	24	50,000	50,000	10,000

#3(–$7,400), #4(–$2,400), #5($19,000), #6($16,800), #7(–4,200), and #8($2,000). Marketing mix #5, calling for a price of $24, advertising of $10,000, and promotion of $10,000, promises to yield the highest profits ($19,000).

This concludes our discussion of how marketing management can examine and discover the profit-optimizing marketing mix. This mix would be part of the larger marketing plan developed to achieve the company's objectives in the particular market it has chosen to serve. To be effective, the plan must be carefully executed, monitored, and revised when necessary. This brings us to the subject of marketing control.

marketing control

The purpose of marketing control is to maximize the probability that the company will achieve its short-run and long-run objectives in its target markets. Many surprises are likely to occur in the marketplace during the execution of the action programs, and these will call for continuous performance review and control. Various managers will have to exercise control responsibilities in addition to their planning and execution responsibilities.

Marketing control is far from being a single process. Three types of marketing control can be distinguished (see Table 4-5).

Annual plan control refers to the steps taken during the year to check ongoing performance against the plan, and the taking of corrective actions when necessary. *Profitability control* consists of efforts to determine the actual profitability of different products, territories, end-use markets, and trade channels.

Table 4-5
Types of Marketing Control

TYPE OF CONTROL	PRIME RESPONSIBILITY	PURPOSE OF CONTROL	APPROACHES
I. Annual plan control	Top management Middle management	To examine whether the planned results are being achieved	Sales analysis Market-share analysis Marketing expense-to-sales ratios Customer attitude tracking
II. Profitability control	Marketing controller	To examine where the company is making and losing money	Profitability by: Product Territory Market segment Trade channel Order size
III. Strategic control	Top management Marketing auditor	To examine whether the company is pursuing its best marketing opportunities and doing this efficiently	Marketing audit

Strategic control consists of a systematic examination and appraisal of the overall fit of the company to its marketing environment and opportunities. The following sections will deal with each form of marketing control.

Annual Plan Control

The purpose of annual plan control is to make sure that the company is achieving the sales, profits, and other goals that it established in its annual plan. This calls for the four steps shown in Figure 4-6. First, management must state well-defined goals in the annual plan for each month, quarter, or other period during the year. Second, management must have ways to continuously measure its performance and developments in the marketplace. Third, management must determine the underlying causes of any serious deviations in performance. Fourth, management must decide on the best corrective action to take to close the gaps between goals and performance. This may call for improving the ways in which the plan is being implemented, or even changing the goals.

This system is called *management by objectives*. Top management takes the initiative by developing the sales, profit, and other goals for the planning period. These goals are broken down into derived goals for successively lower levels of management. During the period, various managers receive reports that allow them to determine whether their subordinates are reaching their goals, and if not, to take the necessary corrective action.

What specific control tools are used by management to check on progress in reaching goals? The four main tools are sales analysis, market-share analysis, marketing expense-to-sales analysis, and customer attitude tracking.

Sales analysis. The first control tool used by managers is sales analysis. **Sales analysis** is the effort to measure and evaluate the actual sales being achieved in relation to the sales goals set for different managers. There are two specific tools in this connection.

Sales variance analysis is an attempt to determine the relative contribution of different factors to a gap in sales performance. Suppose the annual plan called for selling 4,000 widgets in the first quarter at $1 a widget, or $4,000. At quarter's end, only 3,000 widgets were sold at $0.80 a widget, or $2,400. The sales performance variance is −$1,600, or −40 percent of expected sales. The question arises, How much of this underperformance is due to the price decline and how much is due to the volume decline? The following calculation answers this question:

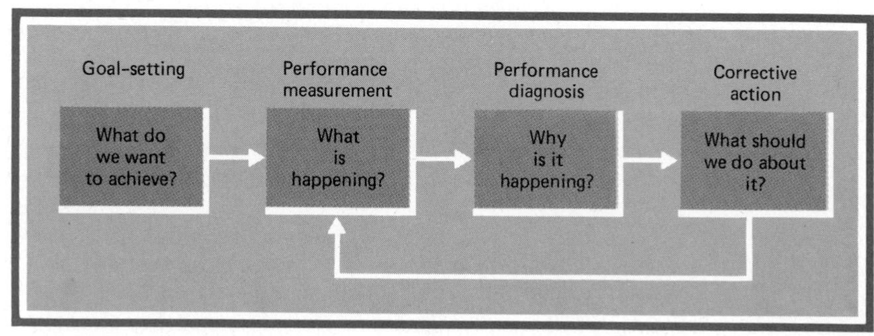

Figure 4-6
The Control Process

Variance due to price decline = ($1.00 − $0.80)(3,000)	= $ 600	37.5%
Variance due to volume decline = ($1.00)(4,000 − 3,000)	= $1,000	62.5%
	$1,600	100.0%

Accordingly, almost two-thirds of the sales variance is due to a failure to realize the volume target. Since this may be under more control normally than the price, the company should look closely into why its expected sales volume was not achieved.[8]

Micro-sales analysis may provide the answer. **Micro-sales analysis** is an attempt to determine the specific products, territories, and so forth, that failed to produce their expected share of sales. Suppose the company sells in three territories and expected sales were 1,500 units, 500 units, and 2,000 units, respectively, adding up to 4,000 widgets. The actual sales volume was 1,400 units, 525 units, and 1,075 units, respectively. Thus territory one showed a 7 percent shortfall in terms of expected sales; territory two, a 5 percent surplus; and territory three, a 46 percent shortfall! It is now clear that territory three is causing most of the trouble. The sales vice-president can check into territory three to see which, if any, of the following hypotheses explains the poor performance: (1) territory three's sales representative is loafing or has a personal problem; (2) a major competitor has entered this territory; (3) GNP is depressed in this territory.

Market-share analysis. A company's sales performance fails to reveal how well the company is doing in relation to its competitors. Suppose a company's sales increase. This could be due to a general improvement in the economy, in which all firms are participating. Or it could be due to improved marketing by this company in relation to its competitors. The normal way to remove the influence of the general environment is to track the company's market share. If the company's market share goes up, it is gaining on its competitors; if its market share goes down, it is probably losing out to its competitors.

Yet these conclusions from market-share analysis are subject to certain qualifications:[9]

- *The assumption that outside forces affect all companies in the same way is often not true.* The surgeon general's report on the harmful consequences of cigarette smoking caused total cigarette sales to falter but not equally for all companies. The companies that had established a reputation for a better filter were hit less hard.
- *The assumption that a company's performance should be judged against the average performance of all companies also is not always valid.* A company with greater than average opportunities should register a growing market share. If its market share remains constant, this may imply deficient rather than average management.
- *If a new firm enters the industry, then every existing firm's market share may fall (again, not necessarily equally).* Here is a case where a fall in the company's market share does not mean that the company is performing below the average of the industry.
- *Sometimes the decline in a company's market share is the result of a deliberate policy to improve profits.* Management, for example, may drop unprofitable customers or products, with resulting decline in market share.
- *Market share fluctuates for many reasons.* For example, the market share in a particular period can be affected by whether a large sale is made on the last day of

the period or at the beginning of the following period. A current shift in market share does not always have a significant marketing implication.

Marketing expense-to-sales analysis. Annual plan control also requires checking on marketing expenses in relation to sales to make sure that the company is not overspending to achieve its sales goals. The key ratio to watch is *marketing expense-to-sales.* In one company this ratio is normally 30 percent and is made up of five component expense-to-sales ratios: *sales force-to-sales* (15 percent); *advertising-to-sales* (5 percent); *sales promotion-to-sales* (6 percent); *marketing research-to-sales* (1 percent); and *sales administration-to-sales* (3 percent).

Management's job is to monitor the overall and component marketing expense ratios to detect whether any are getting out of control. These ratios will exhibit small random fluctuations that can well be ignored. Only fluctuations in excess of the normal range of variation are a cause for concern. The period-to-period fluctuations in each ratio can be charted on a *control chart* such as the one shown in Figure 4-7. This chart shows that the advertising expense-to-sales ratio normally fluctuates between 8 and 12 percent, say ninety-nine out of one hundred times. In the fifteenth period, however, the ratio exceeded the upper control limit. One of two opposing hypotheses can explain this occurrence:

- *Hypothesis A:* The company still has good control over sales, and this represents one of those rare chance events.
- *Hypothesis B:* The company has lost control over this cost as a result of some assignable cause.

If hypothesis A is accepted, no investigation is made to determine whether the environment has changed. The risk in doing this is that some real change has occurred and the company will fall behind. If hypothesis B is accepted, the environment is investigated at the risk that the investigation will uncover nothing and be a waste of time and effort.

The behavior of successive observations even within the control limits should also be watched for patterns that seem difficult to explain by chance. In Figure 4-7 it should be noted that the level of the expense-to-sales ratio rose

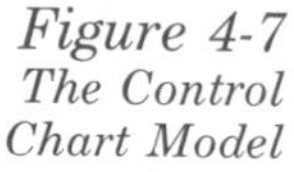
Figure 4-7
The Control Chart Model

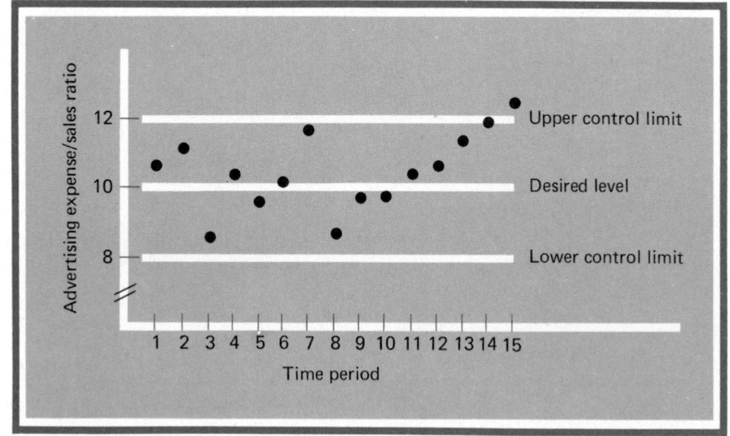

steadily from the ninth period onward. The probability of encountering a pattern of six successive increases in what should be a random and independent process is only one out of sixty-four.[10] This unusual pattern should have led to an investigation sometime before the fifteenth observation.

When an expense-to-sales ratio gets out of control, disaggregative data may be needed to track down the source of the problem. An *expense-to-sales deviation chart* can be used in this connection. Figure 4-8 shows the performances of different sales districts in terms of their quota attainment and expense attainment (in percentages). For example, district D has accomplished its quota nearly at the expected expense level. District B has exceeded its quota and its expenses are proportionately higher. The most troubling districts are in the second quadrant. For example, district J has accomplished less than 80 percent of its quota and its expenses are disproportionately high. The next step is to prepare a similar chart for each deviant district that shows sales representatives' standings on percentage of quota attainment and expense attainment. Within district J, for example, it may turn out that the poor performance is associated with a few sales representatives.

Customer attitude tracking. The preceding annual plan control measures are largely quantitative. Alert companies also set up systems to track the attitudes of customers, dealers, and other marketing system participants as they are occurring. The assumption is that attitude change occurs first; this attitude change leads to purchasing behavior change; and then management eventually sees this in sales reports. By monitoring current customer attitudes toward the company and its products, management can take much earlier action.

Figure 4-8
Comparison of Expense and Revenue Deviations by District

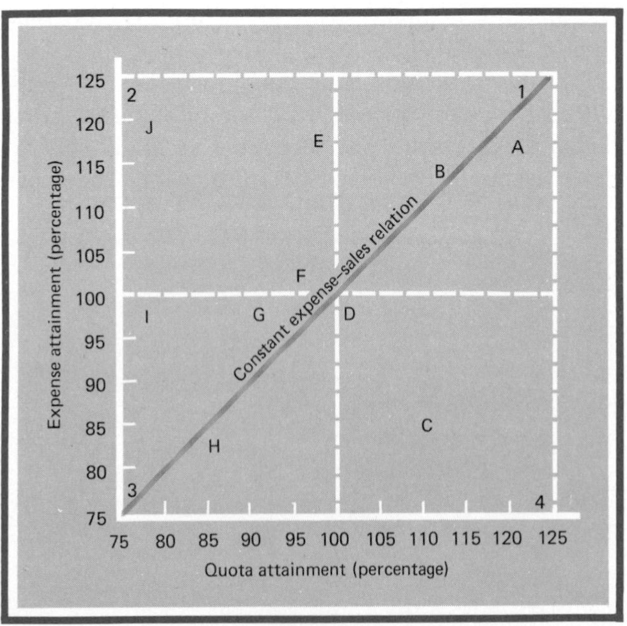

Source: Adapted from D. M. Phelps and J. H. Westing, *Marketing Management*, 3/e. (Homewood, Ill.: Richard D. Irwin, Inc., 1968), p. 754. © 1968 by Richard D. Irwin, Inc.

Companies use the following major systems for tracking customer attitudes:

1. Complaint and suggestion systems. At a minimum, companies should record, analyze, and respond to any written or oral complaints that come in from customers. These complaints should be tabulated according to the type of complaint, and the more serious and frequent ones should be given early attention. Many retailers, such as hotels, restaurants, and banks, have gone further and provide suggestion cards to encourage customer feedback. Some companies have organized consumer affairs departments to handle and anticipate customer problems. The argument can be made that market-oriented companies should strive to maximize the opportunity for consumer complaints so that management can get a more complete picture of consumer reactions to their products and services.

2. Customer panels. Some companies have created panels consisting of a cross-section of customers who have agreed to communicate their attitudes periodically through phone calls or mail questionnaires coming from the company. These panels are thought to be more representative of the range of customer attitudes than customer complaint and suggestion systems.

3. Customer survey feedback systems. A customer survey feedback system consists of periodically administering standardized questionnaires to a random sample of customers. Questions may be asked about the friendliness of the staff, the quality of the service, and so on.[11]

Corrective action. Corrective action has already been mentioned several times in this chapter. When actual performance deviates too much from the annual plan goals, companies go through a well-known cycle of defensive maneuvers to correct the situation. Consider the following case:

- A large fertilizer producer found itself falling behind in its sales goals for the year. This was happening to its competitors as well, all of whom had built excess capacity. Some of the competitors were beginning to cut prices in order to achieve their planned sales volume.

In attempting to save and reverse the situation, this company was observed to go through a number of increasingly drastic steps:

1. *Production cutting.* The company found its inventories rising and proceeded to order cutbacks in production.
2. *Price cutting.* The company began to cut its prices selectively (higher discounts, freight allowances, and so on) to meet competition and retain its share of market.
3. *Increased pressure on sales force.* The company put more pressure on its sales force to meet their quotas. The sales representatives in turn started "beating down" doors, pressuring customers to buy more or buy before the end of the year.
4. *Fringe expenditure cutting.* The company proceeded to cut the budgets for personnel hiring and training, advertising, public relations, charities, and research and development.
5. *Manpower cuts.* The company began to lay off, retire, or fire personnel in various departments, particularly in staff services such as public relations, marketing research, and operations research.
6. *Bookkeeping adjustments.* The company undertook some fancy bookkeeping to

bring about a better picture of profits, including changing the depreciation base, recording purchases wherever possible as capital items rather than as expenses, selling some company assets for leaseback in order to increase cash resources, and recording sales to phantom buyers, revising them as returned merchandise in the following year.

7. *Investment cutting.* The company began to cut back on its investment in plant and equipment.
8. *Selling property.* The company started to consider selling some of its product lines or divisions to other companies.
9. *Selling the company.* The ultimate step this company considered was selling out or merging with another company that had good finances or some complementarities with this firm.

Profitability Control

Besides annual plan control, companies carry on periodic research to determine the actual profitability of their different products, territories, customer groups, trade channels, and order sizes. This task requires an ability to assign marketing and other costs to specific marketing entities and activities.

Methodology of marketing profitability analysis. Marketing profitability analysis is a tool for helping the marketing executive determine whether any current marketing activities should be eliminated, added, or altered in scale.[12] The starting point for marketing profitability analysis is the company's profit

EXHIBIT 4-1

A NEW MARKETING JOB POSITION—MARKETING CONTROLLERS!

Large companies such as General Foods, Du Pont, Johnson & Johnson, TWA, and American Cyanamid have established job positions known as *marketing controllers* to monitor marketing expenses and activities. Marketing controllers are trained in both finance and marketing and can perform a sophisticated financial analysis of past and contemplated marketing expenditures.

Marketing controllers carry out the following activities:

1. Maintain record of adherence to profit plans
2. Closely control media expense
3. Prepare brand managers' budgets
4. Advise on optimum timing for strategies
5. Measure the efficiency of promotions
6. Analyze media production costs
7. Evaluate customer and geographic profitability
8. Present sales-oriented financial reports
9. Assist direct accounts in optimizing purchasing and inventory policies
10. Educate the marketing area to financial implications of decisions

Source: Adapted from Sam R. Goodman, *Techniques of Profitability Analysis* (New York: John Wiley, 1970), pp. 17–18. Reprinted by permission of John Wiley & Sons, Inc.

Table 4-6A
A Simplified Profit and Loss Statement

Sales		$60,000
Cost of goods sold		39,000
Gross margin		$21,000
Expenses		
Salaries	$9,300	
Rent	3,000	
Supplies	3,500	
		15,800
Net profit		$5,200

and loss statement. A simplified profit and loss statement is shown in Table 4-6A. Profits are arrived at by subtracting cost of goods sold and other expenses from sales. The marketing executive's interest would be in developing analogous profit statements by functional marketing breakdowns, such as products, customers, or territories. To do this, the "natural" expense designations (such as salaries, rent, supplies) would have to be reclassified into "functional" expense designations. Consider the following example:

- The marketing vice-president of a lawn-mower firm wishes to determine the costs and profits of selling through three different types of retail channels: hardware stores, garden supply shops, and department stores. The company produces only one model of lawn mower. Its profit and loss statement is shown in Table 4-6A.

This marketing vice-president's task would involve the following steps:

Step 1: Identifying the functional expenses. Assume that the expenses listed in Table 4-6A are incurred to carry out the activities of selling the product, advertising the product, packing and delivering the product, and billing and collecting. The first task is to show how much of each natural expense was incurred in each of these activities.

Suppose that most of the salaries expense went to sales representatives and the rest went to an advertising manager, packing and delivery help, and an office accountant. Let the breakdown of the $9,300 be $5,100, $1,200, $1,400, and $1,600, respectively. Table 4-6B shows the allocation of the salary expense to these four activities.

Table 4-6B also shows the rent account of $3,000 as allocated to the four activities. Since the sales representatives work away from the office, none of the building's rent expense is assigned to the selling activity. Most of the floor space

Table 4-6B
Mapping Natural Expenses into Functional Expenses

NATURAL ACCOUNTS	TOTAL	SELLING	ADVERTISING	PACKING AND DELIVERY	BILLING AND COLLECTING
Salaries	$ 9,300	$5,100	$1,200	$1,400	$1,600
Rent	3,000	—	400	2,000	600
Supplies	3,500	400	1,500	1,400	200
	$15,800	$5,500	$3,100	$4,800	$2,400

and rental of equipment arises in connection with packing and delivery. A small portion of the floor space is taken up by the activities of the advertising manager and the office accountant.

Finally, the supplies account lumps together promotional materials, packing materials, fuel purchases for delivery, and home-office stationery. The $3,500 in this account should be reassigned to the functional uses made of the supplies. The result of this and the previous breakdowns is that the total expenses of $15,800 are reclassified from a natural basis into a functional activity basis.

Step 2: Assigning the functional expenses to the marketing entities. The next task is to determine how much of each activity has gone into serving each type of channel. Consider the selling effort. The selling effort devoted to each channel is approximated by the number of sales calls made in each channel. This is given in the Selling column of Table 4-6C. Altogether 275 sales calls were made during the period. Since the total selling expense amounted to $5,500 (see Table 4-6B), the selling expense per call averaged $20.

As for the advertising expense, Table 4-6C shows this allocated on the basis of the number of advertisements addressed to the different trade channels. Since there were 100 advertisements altogether, the advertising expense of $3,100 means that the average advertisement cost $31.

The basis chosen for allocating the packing and delivery expense was the number of orders placed by each type of channel; this same basis also was used for allocating the expense of billing and collections.

Step 3: Preparing a profit and loss statement for each marketing entity. It is now possible to prepare a profit and loss statement for each type of channel. The results are shown in Table 4-6D. Since hardware stores accounted for one-half of total sales ($30,000 out of $60,000), this channel is charged with half of the cost of goods sold ($19,500 out of $39,000). This leaves a gross margin from hardware stores of $10,500. From this must be deducted the proportions of the functional expenses that hardware stores consumed. According to Table 4-6C, hardware stores received 200 out of 275 total sales calls. At an imputed value of $20 a call, hardware stores have to be charged with $4,000 of the selling expense.

Table 4-6C
Bases for Allocating Functional Expenses to Channels

CHANNEL TYPE		SELLING	ADVERTISING	PACKING AND DELIVERY	BILLING AND COLLECTING
		NO. OF SALES CALLS IN PERIOD	NO. OF ADVERTISE-MENTS	NO. OF ORDERS PLACED IN PERIOD	NO. OF ORDERS PLACED IN PERIOD
Hardware		200	50	50	50
Garden supply		65	20	21	21
Department stores		10	30	9	9
		275	100	80	80
Functional expense	=	$5,500	$3,100	$4,800	$2,400
No. of units		275	100	80	80
	=	$20	$31	$60	$30

Table 4-6D
Profit and Loss Statements for Channels

	HARDWARE	GARDEN SUPPLY	DEPT. STORES	WHOLE COMPANY
Sales	$30,000	$10,000	$20,000	$60,000
Cost of goods sold	19,500	6,500	13,000	39,000
Gross margin	$10,500	$ 3,500	$ 7,000	$21,000
Expenses				
Selling ($20 per call)	$ 4,000	$ 1,300	$ 200	$ 5,500
Advertising ($31 per advertisement)	1,550	620	930	3,100
Packing and delivery ($60 per order)	3,000	1,260	540	4,800
Billing ($30 per order)	1,500	630	270	2,400
Total expenses	$10,050	$ 3,810	$ 1,940	$15,800
Net profit (or loss)	$ 450	$ (310)	$ 5,060	$ 5,200

Table 4-6C also shows that hardware stores were the target of 50 advertisements. At $31 an advertisement, the hardware stores are charged with $1,550 of the advertising activity. The same reasoning applies in computing the share of the other functional expenses to charge to hardware stores. The result is that hardware stores gave rise to $10,050 of the total expenses. Subtracting this from the gross margin, the profit from the activities of selling to hardware stores is small ($450).

The same analysis is repeated for the other channels. It turns out that the company is losing money in selling through garden supply shops and makes virtually all of its profits from sales to department stores. Clearly, gross sales through each channel are not a reliable indicator of the net profits being made in each channel.

Determining the best corrective action. The results of a marketing profitability analysis do not constitute an adequate information basis for deciding on corrective action. It would be naive to conclude that garden supply shops (and possibly hardware stores) should be dropped as channels in order to concentrate on department stores. Such information as the answers to the following questions would be needed first:

- To what extent do buyers buy on the basis of the type of retail outlet versus the brand? Would they seek out the brand in those channels that are not eliminated?
- What are the future market trends with respect to the importance of these three channels?
- Have marketing efforts and policies directed at the three channels been optimal?

On the basis of this and other information, marketing management will want to define its major alternatives:

- *Establish a special charge for handling smaller orders to encourage larger orders.* This move is based on the assumption that small orders are the ultimate cause of the relative unprofitability of dealing with garden supply shops and hardware stores.
- *Give more aid to garden supply shops and hardware stores.* This is based on the assumption that the managers of these stores could increase their sales with more training or promotional materials.

- *Reduce the number of sales calls and the amount of advertising going to garden supply shops and hardware stores.* This is based on the assumption that some of these costs can be saved without reducing proportionately the level of sales to these channels.
- *Do nothing.* This is based on the assumption that current marketing efforts are optimal and that either future marketing trends point to an imminent improvement in the profitability of the weaker channels or dropping any type of channel would reduce rather than improve profits because of repercussions on production costs or on demand.
- *Don't abandon any channel as a whole but only the weakest retail units in each channel.* This is based on the assumption that a more detailed cost study would reveal many profitable garden shops and hardware stores whose profits are concealed by the poor performance of other stores in these categories.

To evaluate these alternatives, each would have to be spelled out in greater detail. In general, marketing profitability analysis provides information on the relative profitability of different channels, products, territories, or other marketing entities. It does not imply that the best course of action is to drop the unprofitable marketing entities, nor does it actually measure the likely profit improvement if these marginal marketing entities are dropped.

Strategic Control

From time to time, companies must stand back and undertake a critical review of their overall marketing effectiveness. This goes beyond carrying out annual plan control and profitability control. Marketing is one of the major areas where rapid obsolescence of objectives, policies, strategies, and programs is a constant possibility. Because of the rapid changes in the marketing environment, each company should periodically reassess its overall approach to the marketplace. A major tool in this connection is the marketing audit.[13]

The marketing audit. Companies are increasingly turning to marketing audits to assess their marketing opportunities and operations. We define *marketing audit* as follows:

- A **marketing audit** is a *comprehensive, systematic, independent,* and *periodic* examination of a company's—or business unit's—marketing environment, objectives, strategies, and activities with a view to determining problem areas and opportunities and recommending a plan of action to improve the company's marketing performance.

Let us examine the marketing audit's four characteristics:

1. *Comprehensive.* The marketing audit covers all the major marketing issues in a business, not only one or a few marketing troublespots. The latter would be called a functional audit if it covered only the sales force, or pricing, or some other marketing activity.
2. *Systematic.* The marketing audit involves an orderly sequence of diagnostic steps covering the organization's marketing environment, internal marketing system, and specific marketing activities. The diagnosis is followed by a corrective action plan involving both short-run and long-run proposals to improve the organization's overall marketing effectiveness.

3. *Independent.* The marketing audit is normally conducted by an inside or outside party who is relatively independent of the marketing department, has obtained top-management's confidence, and has the needed objectivity.
4. *Periodic.* The marketing audit should normally be carried out periodically instead of only when there is a crisis. It promises benefits for the company that is seemingly successful, as well as the company that is in deep trouble.

The components of a marketing audit are outlined in Table 4-7. As indicated in the table, a comprehensive evaluation of a company's marketing situation would involve six major components. First, the marketing auditor would examine pertinent information about the current and future character of the *marketing environment* in which the company operates. The aim is to identify the major opportunities and threats facing the company. Second, the marketing auditor would take a look at the company's *marketing mission, objectives,* and *strategy* to see if they represent a sound adaptation of the firm to its best opportunities. Third, the marketing auditor would analyze whether the *marketing organization* is well adapted to carrying out the company's marketing objectives and strategy. Fourth, the marketing auditor would check on whether the company's major *marketing management systems* of information, planning, and control are adequate to support the company's marketing effort. Fifth, the marketing auditor would want to analyze the company's *marketing profitability,* particularly to learn where the company is making its profits and whether its marketing activities are being conducted in a cost-effective way. Sixth, the marketing auditor would examine one or more major *marketing functions*—product, price, distribution, sales force, and promotion—to see whether these functions are well managed.

Not all of these components need to be reviewed, or reviewed extensively, in a marketing audit. The purpose of the audit is to judge whether the company is performing optimally from a marketing point of view. The auditor will produce some short-run and long-run recommendations of actions that the company can take to improve its performance. It is up to management to consider these recommendations carefully and implement those that it feels will contribute to improved marketing performance. The marketing audit is not a marketing plan but rather an independent appraisal by an inside or outside auditor of the main problems and opportunities facing the company and what it can do about them.

■ summary

The marketing-planning and control system is one of three major systems supporting the company's operations in the marketplace. The system involves the three steps of planning, execution, and control. In this chapter we focused on planning and control.

Companies can be found operating planning systems with various degrees of sophistication—from simple budgeting systems, to annual-planning systems, to strategic-planning systems. Normally the planning process starts with a preliminary market analysis and forecast, which is used to build the business plan, which in turn is followed by the development of a detailed marketing plan to be imple-

Table 4-7
Components of a Marketing Audit

PART I. MARKETING ENVIRONMENT AUDIT

Macroenvironment

A. *Demographic*

1. What major demographic developments and trends will pose opportunities or threats for this company?
2. What actions has the company been taking in response to these developments and trends?

B. *Economic*

1. What major developments and trends in income, prices, savings, and credit will have an impact on the company?
2. What actions has the company been taking in response to these developments and trends?

C. *Ecological*

1. What is the outlook for the cost and availability of natural resources and energy needed by the company?
2. What concerns have been expressed about the company's role in pollution and conservation and what steps has the company taken?

D. *Technological*

1. What major changes are occurring in product technology? In process technology? What is the company's position in these technologies?
2. What major generic substitutes might replace this product?

E. *Political*

1. What laws now being proposed could affect marketing strategy and tactics?
2. What federal, state, and local agency actions should be watched? What is happening in the areas of pollution control, equal employment opportunity, product safety, advertising, price control, and so forth, that is relevant to marketing strategy?

F. *Cultural*

1. What attitude is the public taking toward business and toward products such as those produced by the company?
2. What changes now occurring in consumer and business life styles and values have a bearing on the company's marketing strategy?

Task Environment

A. *Markets*

1. What is happening to market size, growth, geographical distribution, and profits?
2. What are the major market segments? What are their expected rates of growth? Which are high-opportunity and low-opportunity segments?

B. *Customers*

1. How do current customers and prospects rate the company and its competitors, particularly with respect to reputation, product quality, service, sales force, and price?
2. How do different classes of customers make their buying decisions?
3. What are the evolving needs and satisfactions being sought by the buyers in this market?

C. *Competitors*

1. Who are the major competitors? What are the objectives and strategy of each major competitor? What are their strengths and weaknesses? What are the sizes and trends in market shares?
2. What trends can be foreseen in future competition and substitutes for this product?

D. *Distribution and Dealers*

1. What are the main trade channels bringing products to customers?
2. What are the efficiency levels and growth potentials of the different trade channels?

E. *Suppliers*

1. What is the outlook for the availability of different key resources used in production?
2. What trends are occurring among suppliers in their pattern of selling?

F. *Facilitators and Marketing Firms*

1. What is the outlook for the cost and availability of transportation services?
2. What is the outlook for the cost and availability of warehousing facilities?
3. What is the outlook for the cost and availability of financial resources?
4. How effectively is the advertising agency performing?

G. *Publics*

1. What publics (financial, media, government, citizen, local, general, and internal) represent particular opportunities or problems for the company?
2. What steps has the company taken to deal effectively with its key publics?

PART II. MARKETING STRATEGY AUDIT

A. *Business Mission*

1. Is the mission of the business clearly stated in market-oriented terms?
2. Is the mission feasible in terms of the business's opportunities and resources?

B. *Marketing Objectives and Goals*

1. Are the corporate objectives clearly stated and do they lead logically to the marketing objectives?
2. Are the marketing objectives stated in the form of clear goals to guide marketing planning and subsequent performance measurement?
3. Are the marketing objectives appropriate, given the company's competitive position, resources, and opportunities? Is the appropriate strategic objective to build, hold, harvest, or terminate this business?

C. *Strategy*

1. What is the core marketing strategy for achieving the objectives? Is it a sound marketing strategy?
2. Are enough resources (or too much resources) budgeted to accomplish the marketing objectives?
3. Are the marketing resources allocated optimally to prime market segments, territories, and products of the organization?
4. Are the marketing resources allocated optimally to the major elements of the marketing mix—i.e., product quality, service, sales force, advertising, promotion, and distribution?

PART III. MARKETING ORGANIZATION AUDIT

A. *Formal Structure*

1. Is there a high-level marketing officer with adequate authority and responsibility over those company activities that affect the customer's satisfaction?
2. Are the marketing responsibilities optimally structured along functional, product, end user, and territorial lines?

B. *Functional Efficiency*

1. Are there good communication and working relations between marketing and sales?
2. Is the product management system working effectively? Are the product managers able to plan profits or only sales volume?
3. Are there any groups in marketing that need more training, motivation, supervision, or evaluation?

C. *Interface Efficiency*

1. Are there any problems between marketing and manufacturing that need attention?
2. What about marketing and R & D?
3. What about marketing and financial management?
4. What about marketing and purchasing?

PART IV. MARKETING SYSTEMS AUDIT

A. *Marketing Information System*

1. Is the marketing intelligence system producing accurate, sufficient, and timely information about developments in the marketplace?
2. Is marketing research being adequately used by company decision makers?

B. *Marketing Planning System*

1. Is the marketing planning system well conceived and effective?
2. Is sales forecasting and market potential measurement soundly carried out?
3. Are sales quotas set on a proper basis?

C. *Marketing Control System*

1. Are the control procedures (monthly, quarterly, etc.) adequate to ensure that the annual plan objectives are being achieved?
2. Is provision made to analyze periodically the profitability of different products, markets, territories, and channels of distribution?
3. Is provision made to examine and validate periodically various marketing costs?

D. *New-Product Development System*

1. Is the company well organized to gather, generate, and screen new-product ideas?
2. Does the company do adequate concept research and business analysis before investing heavily in a new idea?
3. Does the company carry out adequate product and market testing before launching a new product?

PART V. MARKETING PRODUCTIVITY AUDIT

A. *Profitability Analysis*

1. What is the profitability of the company's different products, served markets, territories, and channels of distribution?
2. Should the company enter, expand, contract, or withdraw from any business segments and what would be the short- and long-run profit consequences?

B. *Cost-Effectiveness Analysis*

1. Do any marketing activities seem to have excessive costs? Can cost-reducing steps be taken?

PART VI. MARKETING FUNCTION AUDITS

A. *Products*

1. What are the product line objectives? Are these objectives sound? Is the current product line meeting these objectives?
2. Are there particular products that should be phased out?
3. Are there new products that are worth adding?
4. Are any products able to benefit from quality, feature, or style improvements?

B. *Price*

1. What are the pricing objectives, policies, strategies, and procedures? To what extent are prices set on sound cost, demand, and competitive criteria?
2. Do the customers see the company's prices as being in line or out of line with the perceived value of its offer?
3. Does the company use price promotions effectively?

C. *Distribution*

1. What are the distribution objectives and strategies?
2. Is there adequate market coverage and service?
3. Should the company consider changing its degree of reliance on distributors, sales reps, and direct selling?

D. *Advertising, Sales Promotion, and Publicity*

1. What are the organization's advertising objectives? Are they sound?
2. Is the right amount being spent on advertising? How is the budget determined?
3. Are the ad themes and copy effective? What do customers and the public think about the advertising?
4. Are the advertising media well chosen?
5. Is sales promotion used effectively?
6. Is there a well-conceived publicity program?

E. *Sales Force*

1. What are the organization's sales-force objectives?
2. Is the sales force large enough to accomplish the company's objectives?
3. Is the sales force organized along the proper principle(s) of specialization (territory, market, product)?
4. Does the sales force show high morale, ability, and effort? Are they sufficiently trained and incentivized?
5. Are the procedures adequate for setting quotas and evaluating performances?
6. How is the company's sales force perceived in relation to competitors' sales forces?

mented by the marketing department. The marketing plan contains the following sections: executive summary, situation analysis, objective and goals, marketing strategy, action program, budgets, and controls. The marketing strategy section of the plan defines the target markets, marketing mix, and marketing expenditure level that will be used to achieve the marketing objectives. The marketing budget section of the plan can be developed either by setting a target profit goal or by using sales-response functions to identify the profit-optimizing marketing plan.

Marketing control is the natural sequel to marketing planning. Companies need to exercise at least three types of marketing control.

Annual plan control is the task of monitoring the current marketing effort and results to make sure that the annual sales and profit goals will be achieved. The main tools are sales analysis, market-share analysis, marketing expense-to-sales analysis, and customer attitude tracking. If underperformance is detected, the company can implement a variety of corrective measures, including cutting production, changing prices, increasing sales-force pressure, and cutting fringe expenditures.

Profitability control is the task of determining the actual profitability of different marketing entities, such as the firm's products, territories, market segments, and trade channels. Marketing profitability analysis reveals the weaker marketing entities, although it does not indicate whether the weaker units should be bolstered or phased out.

Strategic control is the task of making sure that the company's marketing objectives, strategies, and systems are optimally adapted to the current and forecast marketing environment. It uses the tool known as the *marketing audit,* which is a comprehensive, systematic, independent, and periodic examination of the organization's marketing environment, objectives, strategies, and activities. The purpose of the marketing audit is to determine marketing opportunity and problem areas and recommend a short-run and long-run action plan to improve the organization's overall marketing effectiveness.

■ questions for discussion

1. Do most businesses historically begin their marketing planning by engaging in the strategic-planning process? If not, what usually happens?
2. A recently hired member of the marketing staff at Kellogg's was helping to put together the marketing plan for Rice Krispies. She asked, "Why is the executive summary needed?" How would you advise her?
3. Briefly discuss the aspects of the situation analysis stage that a marketing planner for Gallo Wine would have to consider.
4. What major decisions constitute the marketing strategy phase of the marketing plan? Why is it so essential that they be well coordinated?
5. The idea of having a marketing controller who is well versed in both marketing and finance was discussed in this chapter. Would this individual be helpful in the latter stages of marketing planning? Why?
6. A friend of yours is planning to open a discothèque. He realizes that marketing "control" is essential for success. How would you advise him on the options he has for exercising marketing control in his new venture?
7. What are the relative advantages and disadvantages of customer attitude tracking when compared with the other annual plan control approaches?
8. The heart of the strategic control process is the marketing audit. Briefly discuss the characteristics and purpose of this concept.
9. Marketing planning and marketing control are two sets of activities that are independent and unrelated. Comment.

■ references

1. MELVILLE C. BRANCH, *The Corporate Planning Process* (New York: American Management Association, 1962), pp. 48–49.
2. DOUGLAS MCGREGOR, *The Human Side of Enterprise* (New York: McGraw-Hill, 1960).
3. *The Development of Marketing Objectives and Plans: A Symposium* (New York: Conference Board, 1963), p. 38.
4. For an example, see the case "Concorn Kitchens," in *Marketing Management Casebook,* ed. Harper W. Boyd, Jr., and Robert T. Davis (Homewood, Ill.: Richard D. Irwin, 1971), pp. 125–36.

5. For examples of empirical studies using fitted sales-response functions, see DOYLE L. WEISS, "Determinants of Market Share," *Journal of Marketing Research,* August 1968, pp. 290–95; DONALD E. SEXTON, JR., "Estimating Marketing Policy Effects on Sales of a Frequently Purchased Product," *Journal of Marketing Research,* August 1970, pp. 338–47; and JEAN-JACQUES LAMBIN, "A Computer On-Line Marketing Mix Model," *Journal of Marketing Research,* May 1972, pp. 119–26.
6. See RUSSELL ACKOFF AND JAMES R. EMSHOFF, "Advertising Research at Anheuser-Busch," *Sloan Management Review,* Winter 1975, pp. 1–15.
7. See PHILIP KOTLER, "A Guide to Gathering Expert Estimates," *Business Horizons,* October 1970, pp. 79–87.
8. For further discussion, see JAMES M. HULBERT AND NORMAN E. TOY, "A Strategic Framework for Marketing Control," *Journal of Marketing,* April 1977, pp. 12–20.
9. See ALFRED R. OXENFELDT, "How to Use Market-Share Measurement," *Harvard Business Review,* January-February 1959, pp. 59–68.
10. There is a chance of one-half that any succeeding observation will be higher and the same chance that it will be lower (excluding the possibility that two successive values are identical). Therefore the probability of finding six successively higher values is given by $(1/2)^6 = 1/64$.
11. For an application to a hotel chain, see ARTHUR J. DALTAS, "Protecting Service Markets with Consumer Feedback," *Cornell Hotel and Restaurant Administration Quarterly,* May 1977, pp. 73–77.
12. For a basic text, see DONALD R. LONGMAN AND MICHAEL SCHIFF, *Practical Distribution Cost Analysis* (Homewood, Ill.: Richard D. Irwin, 1955).
13. For details, see PHILIP KOTLER, WILLIAM GREGOR, AND WILLIAM RODGERS, "The Marketing Audit Comes of Age," *Sloan Management Review,* Winter 1977, pp. 25–43. A preliminary marketing audit tool is described in PHILIP KOTLER, "From Sales Obsession to Marketing Effectiveness," *Harvard Business Review,* November-December 1977, pp. 67–75.

THE MARKETING INFORMATION SYSTEM

The country's largest athletic-shoe producer is Converse, a division of the Eltra Corporation. Converse makes two-thirds of all U.S. basketball shoes. But in the late 1970s, basketball shoes were not the hottest item. All the action was taking place in running shoes. Jogging became a crusade for 25 million Americans. And joggers were not satisfied in running in battered sneakers, old shorts, and a torn T-shirt. They were rushing out to buy jogging shoes carrying such brand names as Adidas, Puma, Tiger, Nike, Brooks, New Balance, and Etonic, in what had mushroomed into a $500 million industry.

What about Converse? Converse's management initially chose to stay on the sidelines. "We thought jogging would be more of a fad," confessed one of its executives. But somehow their **marketing intelligence** *was off. Sales continued to soar and Converse decided to offer a line of shoes to the market. They had to decide whether to develop shoes for the high end, low end, or both ends of the market. This required conducting* **marketing research** *to learn what joggers wanted in the way of shoes, how they judged shoes, and how they selected retail outlets and brands. It was also necessary to find out what each competitor was offering and to be alert to innovations in shoe material and style. For example, Nike had just introduced and touted a model called Tailwind "which rides on a cushion of polyurethane-encapsulated air chambers" and is "the next generation of footwear." Converse, on the basis of its research into the market's needs, designed dozens of possible models and proceeded to test them with joggers to see which were preferred. Ultimately, Converse introduced a lineup of nine models. Backing them with aggressive marketing budgets, Converse managed to capture a five percent share of the U.S. market. Frederick J. Huser, Converse's running-shoe marketing manager, now consults the sales information system daily to see what models are selling in what sizes in what parts of the country. His most important resource is information, and in his effort to build further market share, he needs all the information he can get to plot his marketing strategy.*[1]

□When we discussed marketing planning and control in the preceding chapter, we emphasized the form that these processes take. In this chapter we want to emphasize their substance, which is information. At every turn, marketing managers face the need for information. Marion Harper put it this way: "To manage a business well is to manage its future; and to manage the future is to manage information."[2]

The chapter is divided into four sections, which answer the following four questions:

- What is a marketing information system and how is it used?
- What is marketing research, how does it work, and how does it fit into a marketing information system?
- What information systems do companies use to measure current market demand?
- What information systems do companies use to forecast future market demand?

the concept of a marketing information system

During the nineteenth century, sellers were generally close to buyers and knew their wants firsthand. The owner of a general store knew his customers and their responses to things. A small manufacturer would personally visit prospective and current customers and gather their reactions. Marketing information was picked up just by being around people, observing them, and asking questions.

During the twentieth century, three developments have created a need for more and better marketing information:

1. *The transition from local to national marketing.* As a company's market area expanded, its managers had less firsthand experience with customers and had to rely on formal systems for gathering the needed information about the market.
2. *The transition from buyer needs to buyer wants.* As incomes increased, buyers became more demanding and selective in the goods they bought. Producers found it harder to predict how buyers would feel about different features, styles, and other attributes, and they therefore turned to formal systems for researching market preferences.
3. *The transition from price to nonprice competition.* As sellers increased their use of competitive weapons such as branding, product differentiation, advertising, and sales promotion, they required information on the effectiveness of these marketing tools. Not only markets but also the tools of marketing had to be researched.

Although the need for marketing information grew geometrically, the supply never seemed sufficient. In many companies today, marketers are still not satisfied with their marketing information. Their complaints include the following:

- There is not enough marketing information of the right kind.
- There is often much marketing information of the wrong kind.
- Marketing information is so dispersed throughout the company that usually a great effort must be made to locate simple facts.
- Important marketing information is sometimes suppressed by subordinates if they believe it will reflect unfavorably on their performance.
- Important information often arrives too late to be useful.
- Information often arrives in a form that leaves no idea of its accuracy, and there is no one to turn to for confirmation.

A growing number of companies are therefore taking a comprehensive look at the marketing information needs of their executives and are beginning to develop a more formal *marketing information system* (MIS) to meet these needs. A study of 193 major U.S. companies found that 77 percent either had installed or were in the process of installing an MIS.[3] Among the leaders in designing a marketing information system were AT&T, Pillsbury, American Airlines, General Electric, Coca-Cola, Johnson and Johnson, and RCA.

An MIS represents a formal effort to systematize the many information flows needed by marketing managers so that marketing information will be more available and useful to them. We define a *marketing information system* as follows:[4]

- A **marketing information system** is a continuing and interacting structure of people, equipment, and procedures designed to gather, sort, analyze, evaluate, and distribute pertinent, timely, and accurate information for use by marketing decision makers to improve their marketing planning, execution, and control.

The marketing information system's role and major subsystems are illustrated in Figure 5-1. The box at the left side of the figure shows the marketing environment that marketing managers must monitor—target markets, marketing channels, competitors, publics, and macroenvironmental forces. Developments and trends in the marketing environment are picked up in the company through one of four subsystems making up the marketing information system—the internal reports system, marketing intelligence system, marketing research system, and analytical marketing system. The information then flows to the appropriate marketing managers to help them in their marketing planning, execution, and control. The resulting actions then flow back to the marketing environment as marketing decisions and communications.

We will now take a closer look at the four major subsystems of the company's MIS.

Internal Reports System

Every company produces periodic internal reports which provide management with current data on sales, costs, inventories, cash flows, and accounts receivable and payable. In too many companies, these reports often come too late to satisfy marketing management. It does little good for a marketing manager in a lawnmower company to learn one month late that sales in Texas are falling sharply. Had the reports come in earlier, the manager could have found out what was happening and taken quick corrective action.

In this connection, the computer has been the major force for progress and has permitted companies to build first-rate internal reports systems. Here are three company examples of advanced systems:

- *General Mills.* The executives at General Mills receive their information daily. The zone, regional, and district sales managers in the Grocery Products Division start their day with a teletype report on orders and shipments in their area the day before. The report also contains progress percentages to compare with target percentages and last year's progress percentages.
- *Schenley.* Schenley's system allows its key executives to retrieve within seconds, via video-display desk consoles and printers, current and past sales and inventory

Figure 5-1
The Marketing Information System

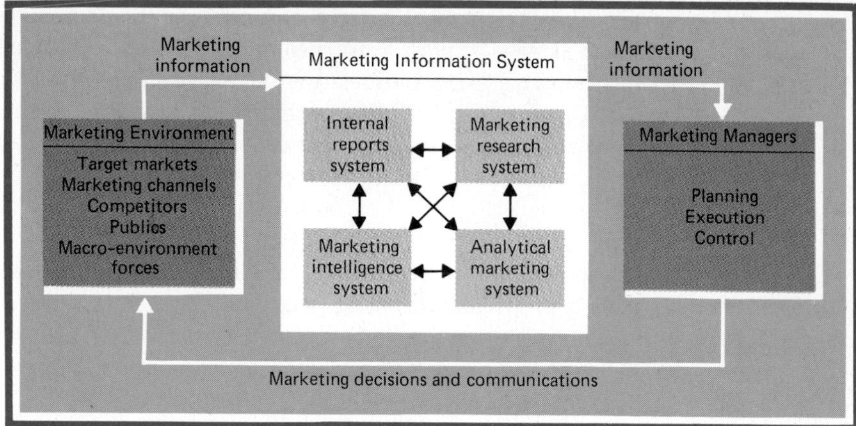

figures for any brand and package size for each of four hundred distributors. An executive can determine within seconds all areas where sales are lagging behind expectations.

- *Mead Paper*. Mead Paper's system permits its sales representatives in buyers' offices to obtain on-the-spot answers to customers' queries about paper availability. The sales representative dials Mead Paper's computer center. The computer determines whether paper is available at the nearest warehouse and when it can be shipped; if it is not in stock, the computer checks the inventory at other nearby warehouses until one is located. If the paper is nowhere in stock, the computer program goes through a production-scheduling routine to determine where and when the paper can be produced and shipped. The sales representative gets an answer in seconds, and this places him or her in an advantageous position in relation to competitors.

Any company that undertakes to improve its internal reports system should first research the managers who will use it. The goal is to design not the most elegant sytem but one that will meet the users' needs and abilities.[5] A useful set of questions is listed in Table 5-1. After getting this information, the company should design the marketing information system in a way that reconciles what executives would like to have, what executives really need, and what is economically feasible to offer. The information to be provided should be tied to the major decisions that the marketing managers make. For example, brand managers, in

Table 5-1
Questionnaire for Determining Marketing Information Needs

1. What types of decisions are you regularly called upon to make?
2. What types of information do you need to make these decisions?
3. What types of information do you regularly get?
4. What types of special studies do you periodically request?
5. What types of information would you like to get that you are not now getting?
6. What information would you want daily? Weekly? Monthly? Yearly?
7. What magazines and trade reports would you like to see routed to you on a regular basis?
8. What specific topics would you like to be kept informed of?
9. What types of data-analysis programs would you like to see made available?
10. What do you think would be the four most helpful improvements that could be made in the present marketing information system?

Source: Philip Kotler, "A Design for the Firm's Marketing Nerve Center," *Business Horizons*, Fall 1966, p. 70.

order to make informed decisions on how much to spend on advertising, should know the degree of target market awareness and knowledge of the company's brand, the advertising budgets and strategies of competitors, the relative effectiveness of advertising in the promotional mix, and so on. The MIS should be designed to provide these and other measures needed to make key marketing decisions.

Marketing Intelligence System

Whereas the internal reports system supplies executives with results data, the marketing intelligence system supplies executives with *happenings data.* We define *marketing intelligence system* as *the set of sources and procedures by which marketing executives obtain their everyday information about developments in the external marketing environment.*

Marketing executives carry on marketing intelligence mostly on their own by reading newspapers and trade publications, talking to various outsiders, and relying on subordinates. To the extent that their intelligence work is casual, important information will often be overlooked. Marketing managers may learn of a competitive move, a new customer need, or a dealer problem too late to make the best response.

A company can take some concrete steps to improve the quality of marketing intelligence received by its managers. First, the company should train and motivate the sales force to do a better job of spotting and reporting new developments. Sales representatives are the "eyes and ears" of the company and are in an excellent position to pick up advanced bits of information that would not appear in the usual internal reports on company sales activity. Yet they are also very busy and often fail to pass on significant information. The company must "sell" its sales force on their importance as intelligence gatherers and emphasize this in their sales bonuses. The sales force's intelligence responsibilities should be facilitated by designing sales call reports that are easy to fill out. Sales representatives should know which managers in their company should receive what information.

Second, the company should also motivate distributors, retailers, and other allies to pass along important intelligence. The company might also hire full-time specialists to gather marketing intelligence. Many companies send out comparison shoppers to learn how various brands are selling and how helpful retail sales personnel are. Interviewing customers and dealers to learn about new opportunities and problems is a legitimate intelligence activity. Much can be learned about competitors through such overt means as (1) pricing or purchasing competitors' products; (2) attending "open houses" and trade shows; (3) reading competitors' published reports and attending stockholders' meetings; (4) talking to competitors' former employees and present employees, dealers, distributors, suppliers, and freight agents; (5) hiring a clipping service; and (6) reading the *Wall Street Journal, New York Times,* and trade-association papers.

Third, many companies supplement their own intelligence work by purchasing information from outside specialists. The A. C. Nielsen Company sells bimonthly data (based on a sample of sixteen hundred stores) on brand shares, retail prices, percentage of stores stocking the item, and percentage of stock-out stores. The Market Research Corporation of America sells reports (based on the purchase diaries of a representative panel of seventy-five hundred households scattered throughout the country) on weekly movements of brand shares, sizes, prices, and deals. Clipping services may be hired to report on competitors' ads, advertising expenditures, and media mixes.

Fourth, the company can establish an office that is specifically responsible for improving the quality and circulation of marketing intelligence. The staff would perform a number of services. It would scan the major publications, abstract the relevant news, and disseminate it in newsletter form to the appropriate marketing managers. It would develop a master index so that all the past and current information could easily be stored and retrieved. The staff would also assist managers in evaluating the reliability of any piece of information. These and other services would greatly enhance the quality of the information available to marketing managers.

Marketing Research System

From time to time, marketing managers need to make a specific study of a situation so that they will have enough information to make an intelligent decision. Consider the following situations:

- Playboy, Inc., would like to find out more about the incomes, educational levels, and life styles of the current readers of its magazine, their reading preferences, and their attitudes toward some possible format changes in the magazine.
- Pacific Stereo operates a large chain of audio equipment stores in major American cities. The company has not yet opened any stores in medium-size cities such as Hartford, Connecticut, and El Paso, Texas. Management wants to undertake a major study to measure the market potential of these cities in order to select the best ones for entry.
- Barat College, located in Lake Forest, Illinois, is competing in a tough market to attract above-average women high-school graduates to the college. It needs to know such things as what percentage of its target market has heard of the college; what do they know; how did they hear about Barat; and how do they feel about going to Barat. This information would help it formulate an improved marketing communications program aimed at its target market.

In such situations, managers cannot simply wait for information to arrive in bits and pieces. Each situation calls for a formal project to gather the necessary information. Managers usually do not have the skills or the time needed to obtain the information themselves in an efficient way. There is a clear need for marketing research. We define *marketing research* as follows:

- **Marketing research** is the systematic design, collection, analysis, and reporting of data and findings relevant to a specific marketing situation facing the company.

To help meet the needs of their managers for marketing research information, many companies have established marketing research departments. Over 73 percent of all large companies have formal marketing research departments.[6] In small companies the marketing research department consists of one or two professional researchers, but in large companies it may consist of one or two dozen full-time employees. The marketing research manager normally reports to the marketing vice-president or marketing services manager. He or she performs

Table 5-2
Research Activities of 798 Companies

TYPE OF RESEARCH	PERCENT DOING
Advertising research:	
Motivation research	48
Copy research	49
Media research	61
Studies of ad effectiveness	67
Business economics and corporate research:	
Short-range forecasting (up to 1 year)	85
Long-range forecasting (over 1 year)	82
Studies of business trends	86
Pricing studies	81
Plant and warehouse location studies	71
Product mix studies	51
Acquisition studies	69
Export and international studies	51
MIS (management information system)	72
Operations research	60
Internal company employees	65
Corporate responsibility research:	
Consumers "right to know" studies	26
Ecological impact studies	33
Studies of legal constraints on advertising and promotion	51
Social values and policies studies	40
Product research:	
New-product acceptance and potential	84
Competitive-product studies	85
Testing of existing products	75
Packaging research—design or physical characteristics	60
Sales and market research:	
Measurement of market potentials	93
Market-share analysis	92
Determination of market characteristics	93
Sales analysis	89
Establishment of sales quotas, territories	75
Distribution channels studies	69
Test markets, store audits	54
Consumer-panel operations	50
Sales compensation studies	60
Promotional studies of premiums, coupons, sampling, deals, etc.	52

Source: Dik Warren Twedt, ed., *1978 Survey of Marketing Research* (Chicago: American Marketing Association, 1978), p. 41.

such roles as study director, administrator, internal company consultant, and advocate. The other marketing researchers in the department are usually specialized by skill, such as survey expert, statistician, behavioral scientist, or model builder.

The marketing research department usually gets a budget anywhere from 0.01 to 3.50 percent of company sales. Between one-half and three-quarters of this money is spent directly by the department, and the remainder is spent in buying the services of outside marketing research companies.

Bradford's Directory lists over 350 outside marketing research companies. These companies fall into three major categories:[7]

1. *Syndicated-service research firms.* These firms specialize in gathering continuous consumer and trade information, which they sell in the form of standardized

reports on a fee-subscription basis to all clients. Marketing management can purchase syndicated reports on television audiences from the A. C. Nielsen Company or the American Research Bureau (ARB); on radio audiences from the ARB; on magazine audiences from Simmons or the Target Group Index (TGI); on warehouse movements from the Selling Areas-Marketing, Inc. (SAMI); and on retail shelf audits from Nielsen. Nielsen, the largest of these firms, had estimated billings of $211 million in 1975.[8]

2. *Custom marketing research firms.* These firms can be hired to carry one-of-a-kind research projects to provide data needed by a particular client. They participate with the client in designing the study, and the report becomes the client's property. One of the leading custom marketing research firms is Market Facts, with annual billings of approximately $15 million.
3. *Specialty-line marketing research firms.* These firms provide specialized services to other marketing research firms and company marketing research departments. The best example is the field service firm, which sells field interviewing services to other firms.

Marketing researchers have been steadily expanding their activities and techniques. Table 5-2 lists thirty-three different marketing research activities carried on by 798 companies, and the percentage of companies involved in each activity. The ten most common activities are determination of market characteristics, measurement of market potentials, market-share analysis, sales analysis, studies of business trends, competitive-product studies, short-range forecasting, new-product acceptance and potential, long-range forecasting, and pricing studies. We will return to marketing research later in this chapter and describe the major steps in marketing research procedure.

EXHIBIT 5-1

THE DEVELOPMENT OF MARKETING RESEARCH

In 1879 the N. W. Ayer and Son advertising agency conducted a mail survey of state agricultural officials. This has been identified as perhaps the earliest formal marketing research study in the United States. It was not until 1911, however, that the Curtis Publishing Company established the first company marketing research department. A few years later, marketing research departments were established at Swift and Company and the U.S. Rubber Company.

The passage of time has been accompanied by a steady improvement in the tools for conducting marketing research. Marketing research technology has witnessed six phases:

1. *1880–1920—the industrial statistics phase.* During this period, census work became more important. Survey research was developed. Herman Hollerith of the Census Bureau invented the paper card with holes punched, leading to the mechanical tabulation of data.
2. *1920–40—the random sampling, questionnaire, and behavioral measurement development phase.* Market researchers learned how to sample populations efficiently and how to design better questionnaires.
3. *1940–50—the management awareness phase.* Company management became interested in using market research to help in marketing decision making rather than as a pure information-gathering activity. Market research changed its name to marketing research.

4. *1950–60—the experimentation phase.* Marketing researchers started applying experimental methods and more-scientific methodology to marketing questions.
5. *1960–70—the computer analysis and quantitative methods phase.* Marketing researchers turned their attention to building mathematical models of marketing decision situations and applying the computer to marketing information and decision analysis.
6. *1970 to date—the consumer theory development phase.* Marketing researchers improved their concepts and methods for qualitative research to explain and predict consumer behavior.

Sources: Gerald Zaltman and Philip C. Burger, *Marketing Research: Fundamentals and Dynamics* (Hinsdale, Ill: Dryden Press, 1975), pp. 4-6; Robert Bartels, *The History of Marketing Thought,* 2nd ed. (Columbus, Ohio: Grid, 1976), Chap. 9; and Jack J. Honomichl, "Since First Straw Vote in 1824, Research Grows," *Advertising Age,* April 19, 1975, pp. 106–9.

Analytical Marketing System

The analytical marketing system consists of a set of advanced techniques for analyzing marketing data and marketing problems. These techniques result in more findings and conclusions than can be obtained by only commonsense manipulation of the data. Large companies, such as Lever Brothers, General Electric, and RCA, tend to make extensive use of analytical marketing systems. Other companies, however, resist these approaches as being too technical or too academic.

An analytical marketing system contains two sets of tools known as the statistical bank and the model bank (see Figure 5-2). *The* **statistical bank** *is a collection of advanced statistical procedures for learning more about the relationships within a set of data and their statistical reliability.* These procedures allow management to go beyond the frequency distributions, means, and standard deviations in the data. Managers often want answers to such questions as

- What are the major variables affecting my sales and how important is each one?
- If I raised my price 10 percent and increased my advertising expenditures 20 percent, what would happen to sales?
- What are the most discriminating predictors of persons who are likely to buy my brand versus my competitor's brand?
- What are the best variables for segmenting my market and how many segments will be created?

Figure 5-2
Analytical Marketing System

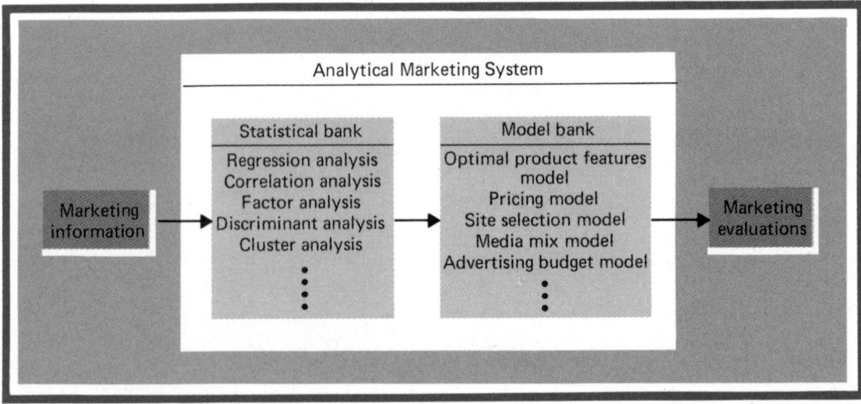

The statistical techniques themselves are somewhat technical, and the interested reader is advised to consult other sources.[9]

The **model bank** *is a collection of models that will help marketers develop better marketing decisions.* Each model consists of a set of interrelated variables that represent some real system, process, or outcome. These models can help answer the questions *what if* and *which is best.* In the last twenty years, marketing scientists have developed a great number of models to help marketing executives do a better job of pricing, designing sales territories and sales call plans, selecting sites for retail outlets, developing optimal advertising media mixes, developing optimal-size advertising budgets, and forecasting new-product sales. Here are examples of some models in current use:

- A new-product manager can sit down at a terminal, dial a new-product computer program called Sprinter III, and type in various estimates as they are called for by the computer, including the estimated size of the target group, recent product trial rates, repeat-purchase rates, the promotional budget, size of investment, target rate of return, product price, and gross profit margin. The computer will digest this information and print out a monthly forecast for the next few years of the total number of buyers, company market share, period profits, and discounted cumulative profits. The new-product manager can change various estimates to see their effect on sales and profits.[10]
- An advertising manager can dial a media-selection program called MEDIAC, type in information on the size of the advertising budget, the number and size of important market segments, media exposure and cost data, ad size and color data, sales seasonality, and other information, and the computer will recommend a media schedule that is calculated to achieve maximum exposure and sales impact in the customer segments.[11]
- A sales manager can dial a sales-redistricting program, type in data on the workload and/or sales potential of various counties, their distances from each other, and the number of desired sales territories. The computer will digest this information and assign various counties to make up new sales territories in such a way that (a) the sales territories are approximately equal in workload and/or sales potential, and (b) the sales territories are compact in shape, thus cutting down travel costs.[12]
- A marketing executive can dial a dealer site-location program, type in a proposed location and size for a new dealership in a large city, and receive a forecast of sales and market share for the new dealership, and the loss of sales to other dealerships.[13]

This concludes our review of the nature of a marketing information system and its main subsystems—internal reports, marketing intelligence, marketing research, and analytical marketing.

marketing research procedure

Almost every marketer will occasionally need marketing research. In a large consumer-packaged-goods company like Procter and Gamble, a brand manager will probably commission three or four marketing research studies annually. Marketing managers in smaller companies will undoubtedly order fewer marketing research studies. Administrators of nonprofit organizations are increasingly finding that they need marketing research, such as when a hospital wants to know whether people in its service area have a positive attitude toward the hospital, or when a college wants to determine what kind of image it has among high-school counselors, or when a political organization wants to find out what voters think of its candidate versus other candidates.

The challenge facing managers who need marketing research is to know enough about is potentialities and limitations so that they can get the right information at a reasonable cost and use it intelligently. If they know nothing about marketing research, they might allow the wrong information to be collected, or collected too expensively, or interpreted incorrectly. One protection against this is to work with only highly experienced and credible marketing researchers and agencies because it is in their interest to do a good job and produce information that leads to correct decisions. An equally important protection is that managers should know enough about marketing research procedure to assist in its planning and in the interpretation of results. This section will describe the five basic steps involved in good marketing research (see Figure 5-3). We will illustrate these steps in connection with the following situation:

- Some years ago Braniff Airlines was a relatively unknown air carrier flying in the southwestern part of the United States. The larger airlines it competed with were better known and were preferred by air travelers. Braniff had trouble filling its planes to capacity, and management was eager to find a way to "break into the big time." Braniff asked Mary Wells, president of Wells, Rich, Greene, one of the best-known advertising agencies in the country, to help it find a creative solution. Mary Wells accepted the assignment but did not turn it over to the copywriters at that point. She felt that much more had to be known about the air travel market before a creative solution could be found. The problem was assigned to the agency's marketing research department, which spent the next several weeks researching the market.

Research Objectives and Problem Definition

The first step in research is to define the research objectives. The objective may be to learn more about a market, or to find a practical idea for increasing the sales of a product or service, or to find data to support or refute a strongly held viewpoint. Defining the research objectives makes it easier to arrive at a useful definition of the problem. If the problem is stated vaguely, if the wrong problem is defined, or if the uses of the research are not made clear, then the research results may prove useless to the manager.

The marketing researchers working on the Braniff case defined the objective as one of finding a strategy to produce a permanent increase in the number of passengers flying Braniff. The problem of attracting more passengers was then divided into two subproblems. One was to attract away regular passengers from the other air carriers. The other was to increase the total number of passengers who flew along its routes. The researchers concentrated on the first problem, which was the challenge of building a preference for Braniff. The problem was

Figure 5-3
The Marketing Research Process

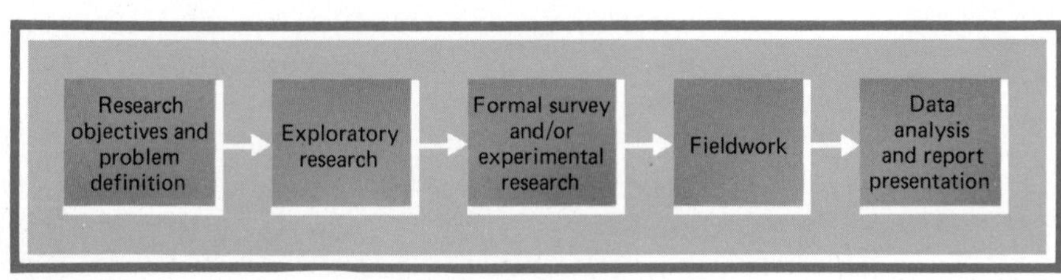

that people based their air carrier decision primarily on schedule convenience and air carrier size and reputation. Many other features, such as in-flight service and food, and baggage handling, did not differ much among carriers. The marketing researchers quickly realized that Braniff had to find something different that would attract national attention and allow it to stand out as an interesting airline.

Exploratory Research

Exploratory research calls for carrying out a number of informal procedures to learn more about the market before any final research is done. The major procedures at this stage include collecting secondary data, doing observational research, and conducting informal interviews with individuals and groups.

Secondary data research. In seeking information, a researcher can gather secondary data, primary data, or both. **Secondary data** *are those that already exist somewhere, having been collected for another purpose.* If the right secondary data exist, the researcher should prefer them because they can normally be obtained more quickly and less expensively. Otherwise the researcher has to gather **primary data,** *which consist of originally collected data for the specific purpose at hand.*

In looking for secondary data, the Braniff investigators can consult the following seven major sources of secondary data:[14]

1. *Internal company records.* The researchers should check Braniff's files for sales figures, passenger studies, and competitive and other relevant data.
2. *Government.* The federal government publishes more marketing data than any other source in the country. The Braniff researchers should especially consult U.S. Civil Aeronautics data on the characteristics of the air travel market.
3. *Trade, professional, and business associations.* The researchers should check with the Air Transport Association of America, which is the trade association of the major carriers. It operates a library that could contain some useful data. Other associations might also be consulted.
4. *Private business firms.* The researchers could see whether any useful data might be found in travel agencies, hotel chains, and other organizations interested in the air travel market.
5. *Marketing firms.* Marketing research firms, advertising agencies, and media firms (newspaper and magazine publishers, radio and TV broadcasters) may possess some useful past studies of the air travel market.
6. *Universities, research organizations, and foundations.* These organizations are often a good source of secondary data. For example, the Transportation Center at Northwestern University has published some original studies on the air travel market.
7. *Published sources.* Much marketing information can be found in books, journals, magazines, and newspapers. Among the marketing journals, marketers like to consult the *Journal of Marketing, Journal of Marketing Research,* and *Journal of Consumer Research.* Useful general business magazines include *Business Week, Fortune, Forbes, Harvard Business Review,* and *Sales & Marketing Management.* The Braniff researchers will also want to consult trade magazines such as *Aviation Weekly.* Newspapers such as the *Wall Street Journal* and the *New York Times* are very useful. Published sources make the library the most rewarding one-stop shopping center for secondary data.

If good ideas and findings come from secondary data, this is fine. However, the researcher must be careful to evaluate the secondary data, since they were collected for a variety of purposes and under a variety of conditions that may limit their usefulness. Marketing researchers should check these data for relevance, impartiality, validity, and reliability.

Observational research. Another exploratory research procedure involves personal observation in various situations. Braniff researchers, for example, might linger around airports or airline offices and listen to how travelers talk about the different carriers. The researchers might fly on competitors' equipment to observe the in-flight service. These and other observational steps might suggest some interesting new ideas for Braniff to consider.

Casual interviewing. The researchers can talk casually to various people—travelers, travel agents, stewardesses, and others—about flying and can obtain their impressions of the various airlines. They can do this by striking up a conversation, rather than acting as interviewers at this stage.

Focus group interviewing. One of the most useful exploratory research steps consists of *focus group interviewing.* From six to ten persons who are typical of the target market are invited to gather for a few hours to discuss a product, a service, an organization, or other marketing entity. A trained leader probes the group's feelings and behavior toward the entity, encouraging as much free discussion as possible. The comments are recorded and are subsequently examined by marketing executives for clues about the market's thinking. Several focus group interviews might be held to sample the thinking of different market segments. The findings do not have sampling validity but provide a basis for effective questionnaire construction for a subsequent formal survey of the market.[15]

Formal Survey Research

The role of exploratory research is to produce a much better understanding of the problem and what needs to be measured formally. At this stage, various hypotheses can be formed and tested.

- Suppose the Braniff researchers noticed through the exploratory research that many travelers repeatedly said that airplanes were rather dull looking. "Planes have no color," one respondent said. The researchers began to feel that Braniff, by introducing bold colors in the exterior and interior of its aircraft, would stand out from all the other airlines. The bold colors would extend to the seats, the walls, and even the stewardesses' outfits. But how would passengers feel about colors? What would they think about such an airline? What colors would they find most pleasing?

At this point the marketing researcher can proceed to design a survey research project, an experimental research project, or both. We will describe survey research in this section and experimental research in the next section.

Many managers take an overly simplistic view of survey work. They think that it consists of constructing a few obvious questions and finding an adequate number of people in the target market to answer them. The fact is that amateur research is liable to many errors. Designing a reliable survey is definitely the job for a professional marketing researcher. However, users of marketing research should know the fundamentals of developing the research instrument, the sampling plan, and the fieldwork.

Research instrument. The main research instrument is the questionnaire. The construction of a good questionnaire calls for considerable skill. Every questionnaire should be pretested on a pilot sample of persons before being used on a large scale. A professional marketing researcher can usually spot several errors in a casually prepared questionnaire (see Exhibit 5-2).

A common type of error occurs in the *types of questions asked:* the inclusion of questions that cannot be answered, or would not be answered, or need not be answered, and the omission of other questions that should be answered. Each

EXHIBIT 5-2

A "QUESTIONABLE" QUESTIONNAIRE

Suppose the following questionnaire had been prepared by a beer company brand manager who needed data quickly at a time when the company's marketing researcher was on vacation. How would you feel about each question?

1. What is your income to the nearest hundred dollars?
2. Are you a heavy or a light beer drinker?
3. Do you ever get drunk? Yes ( ) No ( )
4. How much beer did you drink in April of last year? In April of this year?
5. What TV programs did you watch a week ago Monday?
6. What other concoctions do you favor?
7. Do you think it is right to buy a foreign beer brand and put Americans out of work?

Comments:

1. People do not necessarily know their income to the nearest hundred dollars, nor do they want to reveal their income that closely. Furthermore, a questionnaire should never open with such a personal question.
2. What do "heavy" and "light" mean in consumption per week? Would anyone want to admit that he or she is a heavy drinker?
3. "Drunk" is a relative term. Besides, will people admit it? Furthermore, is yes or no the best way to allow a response to the question? Why is the question being asked in the first place?
4. Who can remember this?
5. Who can remember? The important thing is what programs does the person normally watch?
6. What is a "concoction"? Don't use big words on me.
7. Loaded question. How can one answer yes, given the bias?

question should be checked to determine whether it is necessary in terms of the research objectives. Questions that are merely interesting should be dropped because they lengthen the time required and try the respondent's patience.

The *form of questions* can make a substantial difference to the response. An *open-end question* is one that the respondent is free to answer in his or her own words. For example, "What is your opinion of Braniff Airlines?" A *closed-end question* is one in which the possible answers are supplied. The respondent may be asked to answer in one of two ways (*dichotomous questions*), to answer in one of several ways (*multiple-choice questions*), to place marks along a scale (*scaling questions*), and so forth. The choice between open-end and closed-end questions affects the thoughtfulness of responses, the costs of interviewing, and the quality of analysis.

The *choice of words* calls for considerable care. The researcher should strive for simple, direct, unambiguous, and unbiased wording. It is important that the questions be pretested on a sample of respondents before they are used on a wide scale.

Other dos and don'ts arise in connection with the *sequencing of questions* in the questionnaire. The lead questions should create interest, if possible. Open-end questions are usually better here. Difficult questions or personal questions should be used toward the end of the interview so that an emotional reaction will not affect subsequent answers or cause the respondent to break off the interview. To avoid confusing the respondent, the questions should be asked in as logical an order as possible. Classificatory data on the respondent are usually asked for last because they tend to be less interesting and are on the personal side.

Sampling plan. Research design also includes a sampling plan, which calls for four decisions:

1. *Sampling unit.* This answers the question, *Who is to be surveyed?* The proper sampling unit is not always obvious from the nature of the information sought. In the Braniff survey to find out who makes the air carrier choice, should the sampling unit be the businessperson, the businessperson's spouse, or secretary, or some combination of the three? Where the roles of instigators, influencers, deciders, users, and/or purchasers are not combined in the same person, the researcher must determine not only what information is needed but also who is most likely to have it.
2. *Sample size.* This answers the question, *How many people should be surveyed?* Large samples obviously give more reliable results than small samples. However, it is not necessary to sample the entire target market or even a substantial part of it to achieve satisfactory precision. Samples amounting to less than a fraction of 1 percent of a population can often provide good reliability, given a creditable sampling procedure.
3. *Sampling procedure.* This answers the question, *How should the respondents be chosen?* To obtain valid and reliable inferences about the target market, a random probability sample of the population should be drawn. Random sampling allows the calculation of confidence limits for sampling error. Thus one could conclude that "the chances are ninety-five in a hundred that the interval 'five to seven trips per year' contains the true number of trips taken annually by air travelers in the Southwest." But random sampling is almost always more costly than nonrandom sampling. Some marketing researchers feel that the extra expenditure for probability sampling could be put to better use. Specifically, more of the money of a fixed

research budget could be spent in designing better questionnaires and hiring better interviewers to reduce response and nonsampling errors, which can be just as fatal as sampling errors. This is a real issue, one that the marketing researcher and marketing executives must carefully weigh.

4. *Means of contact.* This answers the question, *How should the subjects be contacted?* The choices are telephone, mail, or personal interviews. *Telephone interviewing* is the best method for gathering information quickly. It permits the interviewer to clarify questions if they are not understood. The two main drawbacks of telephone interviewing are that only people with telephones can be interviewed, and only short, not too personal, interviews can be carried out. The *mail questionnaire* may be the best way to reach persons who would not give personal interviews or who might be biased by interviewers. On the other hand, mail questionnaires require simple and clearly worded questions, and the return rate is usually low and/or slow. *Personal interviewing* is the most versatile of the three methods. The interviewer can ask more questions and can supplement the interview with personal observations. Personal interviewing is the most expensive method and requires more technical and administrative planning and supervision.

Fieldwork. After the research design has been determined, the research department must supervise, or subcontract, the task of collecting the data. This phase is generally the most expensive and the most liable to error. Four major problems arise:

1. *Not present.* When the respondent is not at home or at work, the interviewer must either call back later or substitute another respondent.
2. *Refusal to cooperate.* After finding the designated individual, the interviewer must interest him or her in cooperating.
3. *Respondent bias.* The interviewer must encourage accurate and thoughtful answers.
4. *Interviewer bias.* Interviewers are capable of introducing a variety of biases into the interviewing process, through the mere fact of their age, sex, manner, or intonation. In addition, there is the problem of conscious interviewer bias or dishonesty.

Experimental Research

We have discussed research design in its most common form, that of designing a survey. An increasing number of market researchers are eager to go beyond measuring the opinions and intentions of a target market and are seeking to measure actual cause-and-effect relationships. For example, the Braniff researchers might like to know the answers to such questions as

- Would warm colors or cold colors in the airplane create more positive passenger feelings for Braniff?
- What would be the effect of competitively superior meals on repeat business?
- Which of these two types of advertising would have the greater effect on Braniff's sales: direct comparison advertising mentioning its competitors by name or advertising simply describing Braniff's good points?
- How much more business would be obtained if children were allowed to fly free when accompanying their parents?

Each of these questions could be answered by the survey method by asking people for their opinions. However, people may not give their true opinions or carry them out. Experimental research is more rigorous. Situations are created where the actual behavior of the target market can be observed and the causes determined.

Let us apply the experimental method to the first question. Suppose Braniff identifies three of its routes that are similar in major respects, and about 20 percent of the air travelers along each route say they prefer Braniff. Suppose Braniff now paints its aircraft flying the first route in warm colors, paints its aircraft flying the second route in cold colors, and does not change the colors of its aircraft flying the third route. If aircraft colors make no difference, at the end of a certain period of time we should still find about 20 percent of the air travelers along each route preferring Braniff. Suppose, however, that at the end of the experiment 30 percent of the air travelers along the first route prefer Braniff, 10 percent along the second route prefer Braniff, and 20 percent along the third route prefer Braniff. We would be inclined to conclude that warm colors increase passenger interest and satisfaction, whereas cold colors upset passengers. However, we must be sure that the sample size is adequate and that other hypotheses could not explain the same results. For example, if the airline crews on the warm-color planes began to feel better and act more friendly, then it might be their friendliness more than the colors that made the difference in passenger satisfaction. Maybe warm colors are not needed so much as hiring and training more friendly airline personnel.[16]

The experimental method is being increasingly recognized in marketing circles as the most rigorous and conclusive one to use if the proper controls can be exercised and the cost is reasonable. The method requires selecting matched groups of subjects, giving them different treatments, controlling extraneous

EXHIBIT 5-3

WHY DID PEOPLE RESIST BUYING INSTANT COFFEE?

One of the best examples of creative marketing research along experimental lines was conducted by Mason Haire to determine why housewives resisted buying instant coffee when it was first introduced. Housewives were heard to complain that it did not taste like real coffee. Yet in blindfold tests, many of these same housewives could not distinguish between a cup of instant coffee and a cup of real coffee. This indicated that much of their resistance was psychological. Haire decided to design two long shopping lists, the only difference being that regular coffee was on one list and instant coffee on the other. The housewives were asked to guess the social and personal characteristics of the woman whose shopping list they saw. The comments were pretty much the same with one significant difference: A higher proportion of the housewives whose list contained instant coffee described the subject as "lazy, a spendthrift, a poor wife, and failing to plan well for her family." These women obviously were imputing to the fictional housewife their own anxieties and negative images about the use of instant coffee. The instant-coffee company now knew the nature of the resistance and could develop a campaign to change the image of the housewife who serves instant coffee.

Source: See Mason Haire, "Projective Techniques in Marketing Research," *Journal of Marketing,* April 1950, pp. 649–56.

variables, and checking on whether observed differences are statistically significant. To the extent that the design and execution of the experiment eliminates alternative hypotheses that might explain the same results, the research and marketing managers can have confidence in the conclusions.[17]

Data Analysis and Report Presentation

The last step in survey research procedure is to extract pertinent information and findings from the data to present to management. The researcher tabulates the data and develops one-way and two-way frequency distributions. Averages and measures of dispersion are computed for the major variables. The researcher will attempt to apply some of the advanced statistical techniques and decision models in the analytical marketing system in the hope of discovering additional findings.

The researcher's purpose is not to overwhelm members of management with numbers and fancy statistical techniques—this will lose them. The researcher's purpose is to present major findings that are relevant and can resolve the major marketing decisions facing management that gave rise to the study. The study is useful when it reduces the amount of uncertainty facing the marketing executives (see Exhibit 5-4).

EXHIBIT 5-4

MARKETING MANAGERS AND MARKETING RESEARCHERS: A CLASH OF CULTURES?

One would think that marketing managers would flock to marketing researchers to find needed information. But the fact is otherwise. There are too many marketing managers who do not use marketing research, or use it too rarely. Is it that they would rather spend the money on selling and promotional effort than on knowing more about the market? Clearly, the more they know about the market, the better they can spend their money. Several factors operate to keep the relationship from becoming more productive:

- *Intellectual differences.* Intellectual differences in the mental styles of line managers and researchers often get in the way of productive relationships. All too often the marketing researcher's report seems too academic, complicated, and tentative, whereas the manager wants concreteness, simplicity, and certainty.
- *A narrow conception of marketing research.* Many executives see marketing research as only a fact-finding operation. The marketing researcher is supposed to design a questionnaire, choose a sample, carry out interviews, and report results, often without being given a careful definition of the problem or of the decision alternatives before management. As a result, some of the fact finding fails to be useful. This reinforces management's idea of the limited good that can come from marketing research.
- *Uneven caliber of marketing researchers.* Some companies view marketing research as little better than a clerical activity and reward it as such. In these cases, less-able individuals are attracted, and their weak training and deficient creativity are reflected in their output. The disappointing output reinforces management's prejudice against expecting too much from marketing research. Management continues to pay low salaries, perpetuating the basic difficulty.
- *Late results.* Marketing research that is carefully designed may take a long time to carry out. Often the report is ready after the decision has had to be made, or when the issue has become less salient to the executives.

- *Occasional erroneous findings by marketing research.* Many executives want conclusive information from marketing research, although usually marketing processes do not yield more than probabilistic findings. The problem is complicated by the low budgets often given to marketing researchers to get the information. Executives become disappointed and are apt to think that marketing research is not really worthwhile. Clearly, marketing managers and marketing researchers have to be educated about the other party's needs and capabilities.

measurement of market demand

Marketing research can be carried on for the many purposes shown in Table 5-2. Two important research activities will be examined in the remainder of this chapter. One is the recurrent need of marketing managers to measure current market demand for a given product. According to Table 5-2, 93 percent of all companies engage in the measurement of market potentials. The other research activity, which we will look at in the following section, involves market and sales forecasting, which is carried on by over 80 percent of all companies.

Key Concepts in Market Demand Measurement

Many different terms are used by businesspeople to describe market demand. Before getting to the question of how a manager can estimate market demand, we want to develop a uniform set of definitions for the following terms: *market demand, market forecast, market potential, company demand, company sales forecast,* and *company potential.*

Market demand. In evaluating marketing opportunities, the first step is to estimate *market demand,* which we define as follows:

- **Market demand** for a *product* is the *total volume* that would be *bought* by a defined *customer group* in a defined *geographical area* in a defined *time period* in a defined *marketing environment* under a defined *marketing program.*

There are eight elements in this definition.

PRODUCT

Market demand measurement requires a careful definition of the product class boundaries. A company that manufactures tin cans has to define whether its market consists of metal-can users or container users. This depends on the degree of substitutability between items in the smaller and larger product class.

TOTAL VOLUME

Market demand can be measured in terms of physical volume, dollar volume, or relative volume. The U.S. market demand for automobiles may be described as 10 million cars or $60 billion. The market demand for automobiles in Greater Chicago can be expressed as 3 percent of the nation's total demand.

BOUGHT

In measuring market demand, it is important to define whether "bought" means the volume ordered, shipped, paid for, received, or consumed. For example, a forecast of new housing for the next year usually means the number of units that will be ordered, not completed (called housing starts).

CUSTOMER GROUP

Market demand may be measured for the whole market or for any segment(s). Thus a steel producer may estimate the volume to be bought separately by the construction industry and by the transportation industry.

GEOGRAPHICAL AREA

Market demand should be measured with reference to well-defined geographical boundaries. A forecast of next year's passenger automobile sales will vary depending upon whether the boundaries are limited to the United States or include Canada and/or Mexico.

TIME PERIOD

Market demand should be measured with reference to a stated period of time. Thus market demand could indicate the next calendar year, the next five years, or the year A.D. 2000.

MARKETING ENVIRONMENT

Market demand is affected by a host of uncontrollable factors. Every forecast of demand should explicitly list the assumptions made about the demographic, economic, ecological, technological, political, and cultural environment.

MARKETING PROGRAM

Market demand is also affected by factors under the control of the sellers. Demand in most markets will show some elasticity with respect to industry price, promotion, product improvements, and distribution effort. Thus a market demand forecast requires assumptions about future industry prices, product features, and marketing expenditures.

The most important thing to realize about market demand is that it is not a single number, but a function. For this reason it is also called the *market demand function* or *market response function*. The functional nature of market demand is shown in Figure 5-4. In the two graphs in this figure, market demand is shown on the vertical axis, industry marketing expenditures on the horizontal axis. The market demand function in Figure 5-4A is shown as a curve that rises with higher levels of industry marketing expenditure. The curve is defined for a given marketing environment. It should be noted that the market demand function is *not* a picture of market demand *over time*. Rather, the curve shows alternative current forecasts of market demand associated with alternative possible levels of industry marketing effort in the current period.

The shape of the curve has to be determined for each market. The curve in the illustration has the familiar S shape, suggesting that market demand shows

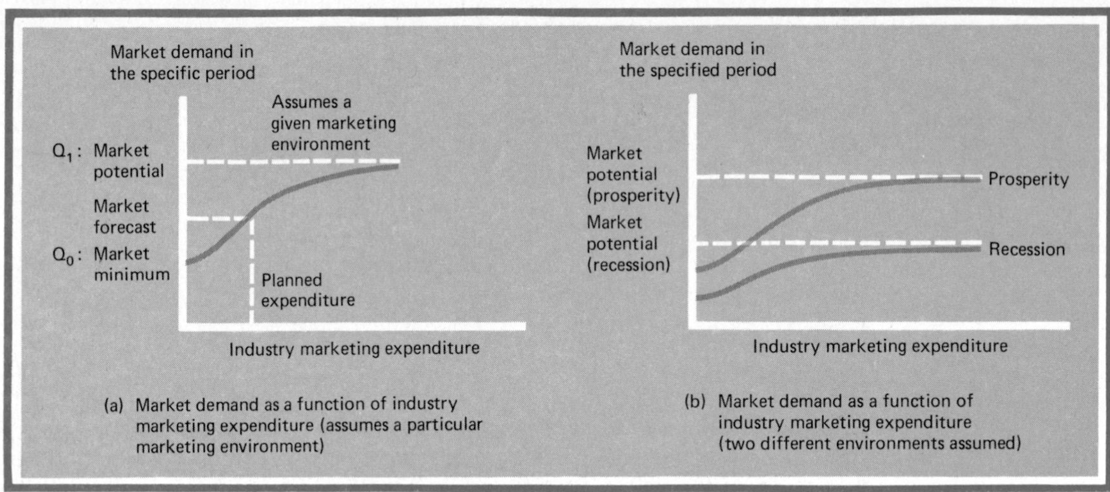

Figure 5-4 Market Demand

first increasing and then diminishing sales response to increased industry marketing expenditure. Some base sales, the *market minimum,* would take place without any demand-stimulating marketing expenditures by the industry. Positive marketing expenditures will yield increasing, then decreasing, returns. Still higher marketing expenditures would not stimulate much further demand, thus suggesting an upper limit to market demand, called the *market potential.*

The distance between the market minimum and the market potential shows the overall *marketing sensitivity of demand* in that industry. We can think of two extreme types of markets, the *expansible* and the *nonexpansible.* The total size of an expansible market, such as a market for a new product, is quite affected by the level of marketing expenditures. In terms of Figure 5-4A, the distance between Q_0 and Q_1 is relatively large. A nonexpansible market, illustrated by cigarettes or steel, is not much affected by the level of marketing expenditures; and the distance between Q_0 and Q_1 is relatively small. The firm selling in a nonexpansible market can take the market's size (the level of *primary demand*) for granted and concentrate its marketing resources on getting a desired market share (the level of *selective demand*).

Market forecast. Only one of the many possible levels of industry marketing expenditure will actually occur. The market demand corresponding to the planned expenditure is called the *market forecast.* The market forecast shows the expected market demand for the planned marketing expenditure and the given environment.

Market potential. The market forecast shows the expected market demand, not the highest possible market demand. For the latter, we have to visualize the level of market demand for a "very high" level of industry marketing expenditure, where further increases in marketing expenditure would have little effect in stimulating further demand. **Market potential** is the limit approached by market demand as industry marketing expenditure goes to infinity, for a given set of competitive prices and a given environment.

Market potential is always defined for a given set of competitive prices. If all prices went to zero, we could ask how many units the market would acquire of the free good. We would call this the *market capacity*. The market potential is always less than the market capacity.

The phrase "for the given environment" is also crucial in the concept of market potential. The market potential for automobiles is higher during prosperity than during a recession because market demand is income-elastic. The dependence of market potential on the environment is illustrated in Figure 5-4B.

Company demand. We are now ready to define *company demand*. **Company demand** is the company's sales resulting from its share of market demand. Company demand, like market demand, is a function—called the *company demand function* or *sales-response function*—and is subject to all the determinants of market demand *plus whatever influences company market share.*

But what influences company market share? The company's market share is influenced by the following: (1) the company's price in relation to competitors, (2) the company's total marketing expenditures in relation to competitors, (3) the company's marketing mix in relation to competitors, (4) the company's allocation of its funds to products and territories, (5) the company's efficiency in spending its marketing funds. Management scientists have built these factors into mathematical models of market-share determination to be used by companies to help set their marketing strategies.[18]

Company sales forecast. Company demand describes estimated company sales at alternative levels of company marketing expenditure and price. It remains for management to set its marketing decision variables. These variables will imply a particular level of sales: The **company sales forecast** is the expected level of company sales based on a chosen marketing plan and assumed marketing environment.

Too often the sequential relationship between the company sales forecast and the company marketing plan is confused. One frequently hears that the company should plan its marketing effort on the basis of its sales forecast. The forecast-to-plan sequence is valid if forecast sales are unaffected or minimally affected by company marketing expenditures. The sequence is not valid if market demand is expansible. The company sales forecast does not establish a basis for deciding on the amount and composition of marketing effort. Quite the contrary, the company sales forecast is the *result* of an assumed blueprint for marketing action. The sales forecast must be viewed as a dependent variable that is affected, among other things, by the planned marketing activity of the firm.

Two other concepts—sales quota and sales budget—are worth mentioning in relation to the company sales forecast. A **sales quota** is a sales goal set for a product line, company division, or sales representative. It is primarily a managerial tool for defining and stimulating sales effort. The sales quota set by management is arrived at through a joint consideration of the company sales forecast and the psychology of stimulating its achievement. The latter consideration generally leads to setting sales quotas that total to a slightly higher figure than the estimated sales forecast.

The other concept is a *sales budget.* A **sales budget** is a conservative estimate of the expected volume of sales and is used primarily for making current purchasing, production, and cash-flow decisions. The sales budget is arrived at through a joint consideration of the sales forecast and of the need to avoid excessive investment in case the forecast is not realized. The latter consideration generally leads to setting a sales budget slightly lower than the company sales forecast.

Company potential. Company sales potential is *the limit approached by company demand as company marketing expenditure increases in relation to competitors.* The absolute limit of company demand is, of course, the market potential. The two would be equal if the company achieved 100 percent of the market—that is, if the company became a monopolist. In most cases, company sales potential is less than market potential, even when company marketing expenditures increase considerably over those of competitors. The reason is that each competitor has a hard core of loyal buyers who are not very responsive to other companies' efforts to woo them away.

Methods of Estimating Current Demand

We are now ready to consider practical methods of estimating current demand. There are two types of current demand estimates in which a seller might be interested: *total market potential* and *territorial potential.* Total market potential is of interest whenever a seller is facing a decision to introduce a new product or drop an existing one. The seller wants to know whether the total size of the market is sufficient to justify the company's participation.

Total market potential. Total market potential is the maximum amount of sales (in units or dollars) that might be available to all the firms in an industry during a given period under a given level of industry marketing expenditures and given environmental conditions. A common way to estimate total market potential is as follows:

$$\tilde{Q} = n \times q \times p \tag{5-1}$$

where $\tilde{Q}$ = total market potential
n = number of buyers in the specific product/market under the given assumptions
q = quantity purchased by an average buyer
p = price of an average unit

Thus, if there were potentially 100 million buyers of phonograph records each year, and the average buyer bought six records a year, and the average price was \$5, then the total market potential for phonograph records would be approximately \$3 billion (= 100,000,000 × 6 × \$5).

A variation on formula (5-1) is known as the *chain ratio method.* It is based on the notion that it may be easier to estimate the separate components of a magnitude than the magnitude directly. Consider the following example:

- The U.S. Navy seeks to attract 112,000 new male recruits each year from American high schools. The question is whether this is a reasonable target in relation to the market potential. The market potential has been estimated by using the following chain ratio method:

Total number of male high-school students	10,000,000
Percentage who are militarily qualified (no physical, emotional, or mental handicaps)	× .50
Percentage of those qualified who are potentially interested in military service	× .15
Percentage of those qualified and interested in military service who consider the Navy the preferred service	× .30

This chain of numbers shows the market potential to be 225,000 recruits. Since this exceeds the target number of recruits sought, the U.S. Navy should not have much trouble meeting its target if it does a reasonable job of marketing the Navy. But many of the potential recruits are lost somehow. They are not contacted; their parents talk them out of military service; they hear negative things from friends; they form a bad impression of the Navy at the recruiting office. The result is that the Navy barely manages to recruit the target number it seeks.

Territorial potentials. Companies are concerned with selecting the best territories to sell in and allocating their marketing budget optimally among these territories. The basis for these decisions lies in estimating the market potential of different territories. Two major methods are available: the ***market-buildup method,*** which is used primarily by industrial-goods firms, and the ***index-of-buying-power method,*** which is used primarily by consumer-goods firms.

MARKET-BUILDUP METHOD

The market-buildup method calls for identifying all the potential buyers for the product in each market and adding up the estimated potential purchases of each. Consider the following example.

A manufacturer of mining instrumentation equipment has just developed an instrument for detecting the difference between "fool's gold" and real gold. Fool's gold is a form of iron ore that is often confused with metallic gold. By detecting it in advance, miners would not waste their time with deposits of fool's gold. The manufacturer intends to price the instrument at $1,000. He sees each mine as potentially buying one or more instruments, depending on the mine's size (as indicated by the number of miners). His problem consists of determining what the market potential is for this instrument in each mining state and whether it is worth hiring a sales representative to cover that state. He would want to place a sales representative in each state that has a market potential of over $300,000.

One of the states being considered is Colorado. To find the market potential for Colorado, the manufacturer should begin by consulting the Standard Industrial Classification (S.I.C.) developed by the U.S. Bureau of the Census. The S.I.C. classifies industries according to the *product produced* or *operation performed.* All industries fall into the ten major divisions shown in column 1 of Table 5-3. Each of these major industrial groups is assigned a two-digit code. Mining, for example, bears the code numbers 10 to 14. One form of mining, metal mining, bears the code number 10, as shown in column 2. Within metal mining are found further breakdowns into three-digit S.I.C. numbers, as shown in column 3. For

Table 5-3
The Standard Industrial Classification (S.I.C.)

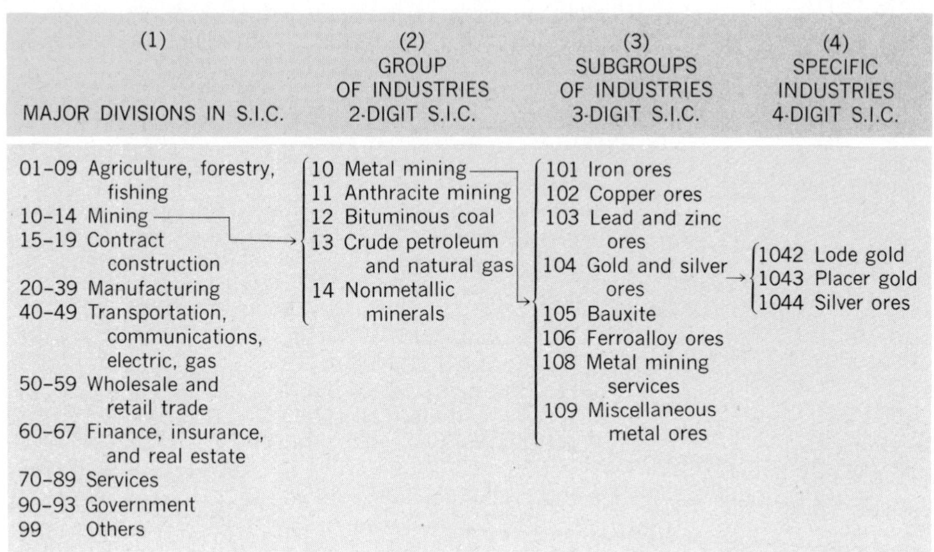

(1) MAJOR DIVISIONS IN S.I.C.	(2) GROUP OF INDUSTRIES 2-DIGIT S.I.C.	(3) SUBGROUPS OF INDUSTRIES 3-DIGIT S.I.C.	(4) SPECIFIC INDUSTRIES 4-DIGIT S.I.C.
01–09 Agriculture, forestry, fishing	10 Metal mining →	101 Iron ores	
10–14 Mining →	11 Anthracite mining	102 Copper ores	
15–19 Contract construction	12 Bituminous coal	103 Lead and zinc ores	
20–39 Manufacturing	13 Crude petroleum and natural gas	104 Gold and silver ores →	1042 Lode gold
40–49 Transportation, communications, electric, gas	14 Nonmetallic minerals	105 Bauxite	1043 Placer gold
50–59 Wholesale and retail trade		106 Ferroalloy ores	1044 Silver ores
60–67 Finance, insurance, and real estate		108 Metal mining services	
70–89 Services		109 Miscellaneous metal ores	
90–93 Government			
99 Others			

Source: *The Standard Industrial Classification Manual* (Washington, D.C.: U.S. Bureau of the Budget, 1967).

example, the gold and silver ores category is assigned the code number 104. Finally, gold and silver ores are subdivided into further groups in column 4, each being given a four-digit code number. Thus lode gold has the code number 1042. Our manufacturer is interested in mines that mine both lode deposits and placer deposits.

Next the manufacturer turns to the Census of Mining to determine how many gold-mining establishments there are in each state, their locations within the state, the number of employees, annual sales, and net worth. Using the data on Colorado, he prepares the market potential estimate shown in Figure 5-5. Column 1 of this figure classifies mines into three groups, depending on the number of employees. Column 2 shows the number of mines in each group.

Figure 5-5
Market-Buildup Method Using S.I.C.: Instrument Market Potential in Colorado

S.I.C.	(1) NUMBER OF EMPLOYEES	(2) NUMBER OF MINES	(3) POTENTIAL NUMBER OF INSTRUMENT SALES PER EMPLOYEE SIZE CLASS	(4) UNIT MARKET POTENTIAL (2 × 3)	(5) DOLLAR MARKET POTENTIAL × $1,000 PER INSTRUMENT
1042	Under 10	80	1	80	
(lode deposits)	10–50	50	2	100	
	Over 50	20	4	80	
		150		260	$260,000
1043	Under 10	40	1	40	
(placer deposits)	10–50	20	2	40	
	Over 50	10	3	30	
		70		110	110,000
					$370,000

Column 3 shows the potential number of instruments that might be purchased by mines in each size class. Column 4 shows the unit market potential and is found by multiplying columns 2 and 3. Finally, column 5 shows the dollar market potential, given that each instrument sells for $1,000. Colorado thus appears to have a dollar market potential of $370,000, which means that it would pay to hire one sales representative for the state of Colorado.

INDEX-OF-BUYING-POWER METHOD

Consumer goods companies also face the problem of estimating territorial market potentials. Consider the following example.

A shirt manufacturer, in looking for ways to expand sales, gets the idea of opening up a national system of franchised stores that would sell T-shirts. Each store would carry a wide selection of sizes and colors and would print an emblem chosen by the customer on each T-shirt at no extra charge. There would be hundreds of emblems from which to choose. The manufacturer estimates that total national sales could reach $100 million annually. He would be willing to sell a franchise in any town where the store might generate more than $60,000 sales a year. He would place advertisements in the *Wall Street Journal* to attract potential franchisees, examine their business qualifications, and make sure that the town had enough buying potential to warrant opening a store.

One of the first applications came from a recent philosophy graduate of the University of Illinois at Champaign. This person had inherited some money and wanted to buy a franchise. He seemed qualified in the light of having taken some marketing and business courses at the university. The manufacturer's main concern was whether a store in Champaign, Illinois, could gross enough sales to make the venture rewarding to both the franchisee and the manufacturer.

The manufacturer decides to evaluate the effective buying power of Champaign. Each year *Sales and Marketing Management* magazine publishes the *Survey of Buying Power.*[19] This survey estimates the buying power index for each region, state, and metropolitan area of the nation. The buying power index is based on three factors: the area's share of the nation's disposable personal income, retail sales, and population. The buying power index for a specific area is given by

$$B_i = .5y_i + .3r_i + .2p_i \qquad (5\text{-}2)$$

where

B_i = percentage of total national buying power found in area i
y_i = percentage of national disposable personal income originating in area i
r_i = percentage of national retail sales in area i
p_i = percentage of national population located in area i

The three coefficients in the formula reflect the relative weight given to the three factors. Thus disposable personal income is the most important factor in buying power, followed by retail sales, and then population.

Now the manufacturer looks up Champaign, Illinois, and finds that this market has .0764 percent of the nation's disposable personal income, .0900 percent of the nation's retail sales, and .0770 of the nation's population. The buying power index for Champaign is therefore

$$B = .5\,(.0764) + .3\,(.0900) + .2\,(.0770) = .0806$$

That is, .0806 percent of the nation's purchase of this manufacturer's T-shirts might be expected to take place in Champaign. Since the manufacturer is hoping to sell $100 million nationally each year, this amounts to selling $80,600 (= $100,000,000 × .000806) in Champaign. Since a successful store is one selling more than $60,000 annually, the manufacturer leans toward selling a franchise to this applicant.

The manufacturer has to recognize that the weights used in the buying power index are somewhat arbitrary. They apply mainly to consumer goods that are neither low-priced staples nor high-priced luxury goods. Other weights can be assigned if they are more appropriate. Furthermore, the manufacturer would want to adjust the market potential for additional factors, such as competitors' presence in that market, local promotional costs, seasonal factors, and local market idiosyncrasies. For example, since Champaign is a college town with a student population of over thirty thousand, this factor might make Champaign even more attractive than it first appeared.

market and sales forecasting

Having looked at ways to estimate current demand, we are now ready to examine the problem of forecasting future demand. Very few products or services lend themselves to easy forecasting. These cases generally involve a product whose absolute level or trend is fairly constant and a situation where competitive relations are nonexistent (public utilities) or stable (pure oligopolies). In most markets, market demand and especially company demand are not stable from one year to the next, and good forecasting becomes a key factor in company success. Poor forecasting can lead to overly large inventories, costly price markdowns, or lost sales due to being out of stock. The more unstable the demand, the more critical is forecast accuracy and the more elaborate is forecasting procedure. We will examine six major methods of forecasting demand in the following paragraphs.

Surveys of Buyer Intentions

Forecasting is the art of anticipating what buyers are likely to do under a given set of conditions. This suggests that a most useful source of information would be the buyers themselves. This is especially true if the buyers have clearly formulated intentions, will carry them out, and will describe them to interviewers.

In regard to *major consumer durables,* several research organizations regularly issue reports on consumer buying intentions. These organizations ask the following type of question to determine whether the consumer intends to buy, within a stated period, each of several different durables:

Do you intend to buy an automobile within the next six months?

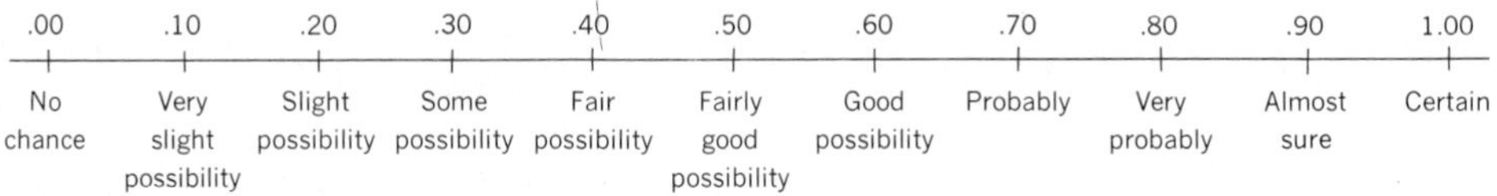

This is called a *purchase probability scale*. In addition, the various surveys inquire into the consumer's present and future personal finances, and expectations about the economy. The various bits of information are combined into a *consumer sentiment measure* (Survey Research Center of the University of Michigan) or a *consumer confidence measure* (Sindlinger and Company). Consumer durable-goods producers subscribe to these indices in the hope of learning in advance of major shifts in consumer buying intentions so that they can adjust their production and marketing plans accordingly.[20]

In the realm of *industrial buying*, intention surveys regarding plant, equipment, and materials have been carried out by various agencies. The two best-known capital-expenditures surveys are the one conducted by the U.S. Department of Commerce in collaboration with the Securities and Exchange Commission and the one conducted annually in the late fall by McGraw-Hill through its publication *Business Week*. Most of the estimates have been within a 10 percent error band of the actual outcomes.

Composites of Sales-Force Opinions

Where it is impractical to make direct buyer inquiries, the company may decide to ask its sales representatives for estimates. An example is the Pennwalt Corporation:[21]

- In August, the field sales personnel are provided with tabulating cards to prepare their sales forecasts for the coming year. Individual cards are prepared for each product sold to each major customer, showing the quantity shipped to the customer in the previous six months. Each card also provides space in which the field salesmen post their forecasts for the coming year. Additional tab cards are also supplied for those customers who were not sold in the current six-month period but who were customers in the prior year; and finally, blank cards are provided for submitting forecasts of sales to new customers. Salesmen fill in their forecasts (on the basis of current prices) using their own informed judgment; in some divisions, they are also in a position to substantiate their forecasts by obtaining purchase estimates from their customers.

Few companies use their sales force's estimates without some adjustments. In the first place, sales representatives are biased observers. They may be congenitally pessimistic or optimistic, or they may go to one extreme or another because of a recent sales setback or success. Furthermore, they are often unaware of larger economic developments and do not know whether their company's marketing plans will influence future sales in their territory. They may understate demand so that the company will set a low sales quota.[22] They may not have the time to prepare careful estimates or may not consider it worthwhile to do so.

Assuming these biasing tendencies can be countered, a number of benefits can be gained by involving the sales force in forecasting. First, because they are in closer contact with the customers, sales representatives may have more knowledge of or better insight into developing trends than any other single group. This is especially likely where the product is fairly technical and is subject to a changing technology. Second, because of their participation in the forecasting process, the sales representatives may have greater confidence in the derived sales quotas, and this may increase their incentive to achieve them. Finally, a "grass-roots" forecasting procedure results in estimates broken down by product, territory, customer, and sales representative.

Automobile companies gather estimates of sales directly from their dealers. These estimates are subject to the same strengths and weaknesses as sales-force estimates.

Firms sometimes resort to outside experts for estimates of future demand. This happens when a firm uses or buys general economic forecasts or special industry forecasts prepared outside the firm. This also happens when the firm invites a group of experts to estimate a probabilistic event, such as a successful new technology or a change in business conditions.

There are at least three ways to gather the judgments of a group of experts. These experts may meet as a committee and come up with a group estimate (*group discussion method*). They may supply their separate estimates to a project leader who merges them into a single estimate (*pooled individual estimates method*). They may supply individual estimates and assumptions that are reviewed by the project leader, revised, and followed by a second round of individual estimation, a third round, and so forth, until the assumptions and estimates converge (*Delphi method*). The third method is becoming increasingly popular for developing market and technological forecasts.[23]

Market-Test Method

In cases where buyers do not plan their purchases carefully or are very erratic in carrying out their intentions or where experts are not very good guessers, a more direct market test of likely behavior is desirable. A direct market test is especially desirable in forecasting the sales of a new product or the likely sales of an established product in a new channel of distribution or territory. Where a short-run forecast of likely buyer response is desired, a small-scale market test is usually an ideal answer. Market testing is discussed in Chapter 11.

Time-Series Analysis

As an alternative to costly surveys or market tests, some firms prepare their forecasts on the basis of a statistical-mathematical analysis of past data. The underlying logic is that past data are an expression of enduring causal relations that can be uncovered through quantitative analysis. They can be used to predict future sales. Thus forecasting becomes an exercise in adroit backcasting.

A time series of past sales of a product can be analyzed into four major temporal components.

The first component, *trend* (T), is the result of basic developments in population, capital formation, and technology. It is found by fitting a straight or gradually curved line through the time-series data. If the trend turns out to be statistically significant, then it becomes central in the preparation of a long-range forecast.

The second component, *cycle* (C), is seen in the wavelike movement of sales. Many sales are affected by swings in the level of general economic activity, which tends to be somewhat periodic. Isolation of the cyclical component can be useful in intermediate-range forecasting.

The third component, *season* (S), refers to a consistent pattern of sales movements within the year. The term "season" is used broadly to describe any recurrent hourly, weekly, monthly, or quarterly sales pattern. The seasonal component may be related to weather factors, holidays, and/or trade customs. The seasonal pattern provides the investigator with a norm for forecasting short-range sales.

The fourth component, *erratic events* (E), includes strikes, blizzards, fads, riots, fires, war scares, price wars, and other disturbances. These erratic components have the effect of obscuring the more systematic components, and the problem becomes one of starting with the original "noisy" time series and separating the underlying systematic forces from the erratic.

Classical time-series analysis involves procedures for decomposing the original sales series (Y) into the components, T, C, S, and E. Then these components can be recombined to produce the sales forecast for a future period. Here is an example:

- A medium-size insurance company sold 12,000 new ordinary life insurance policies this year. It would like to predict next year's December sales. The long-term trend shows a 5 percent sales growth rate per year. This alone suggests sales next year of 12,600 (= 12,000 × 1.05). However, a business recession is expected next year and will probably result in total sales achieving only 90 percent of the expected trend-adjusted sales. This means sales next year will more likely be 11,340 (= 12,600 × .90). If sales were the same each month, this would mean monthly sales of 945 (= 11,340 ÷ 12). However, December is an above-average month for insurance policy sales, with a seasonal index standing at 1.30. Therefore December sales may be as high as 12,285 (= 945 × 1.3). No erratic events, such as strikes or new insurance regulations, are expected. Therefore the best estimate of the number of new policies that will be sold next December is 12,285.

Statistical Demand Analysis

Time-series analysis treats past and future sales as a function of time, rather than of any real demand factors. Numerous real factors affect the sales of any product. **Statistical demand analysis** is a set of statistical procedures designed to discover the most important real factors affecting sales and their relative influence. The factors most commonly analyzed are prices, income, population, and promotion.

Statistical demand analysis consists of expressing sales (Q) as a dependent variable and trying to explain sales variation as a result of variation in a number of independent demand variables $X_1, X_2, \ldots, X_n$; that is,

$$Q = f(X_1, X_2, \ldots, X_n) \quad (5\text{-}3)$$

This says that the level of sales, Q, is a function of the levels of the independent factors $X_1, X_2, \ldots, X_n$. Using a technique called multiple-regression analysis, various equation forms can be statistically fitted to the data in the search for the best predicting factors and equation.[24]

As an illustration, a soft-drink company found that the per capita sales of soft drinks by state was well explained by[25]

$$Q = -145.5 + 6.46X_1 - 2.37X_2 \quad (5\text{-}4)$$

where X_1 = mean annual temperature of the state (farenheit)
X_2 = annual per capita income in the state (in hundreds)

For example, New Jersey had a mean annual temperature of 54 and an annual per capita income of 24 (in hundreds). Using (5-4), we would predict per capita soft-drink consumption in New Jersey to be

$$Q = -145.5 + 6.46\ (54) - 2.37\ (24) = 147$$

Actual per capita consumption was 143. To the extent that this equation predicted this well for other states, it would serve as a useful sales-forecasting tool. Marketing management would predict next year's temperature and per capita income for each state and use equation (5-3) to derive a sales forecast for each state.

Marketing researchers are constantly improving the available tools for producing sales forecasts. In fact, the whole area of marketing information systems is constantly being improved. Therefore marketers' demands for solid information on which to base their marketing decisions are being met by an encouraging increase in data and tools that will aid them in their marketing planning, execution, and control.

EXHIBIT 5-5

THE FUTURE OF MARKETING RESEARCH

Computers and electronic communication hardware are bringing about a quiet revolution in marketing research. Some research firms now conduct their interviewing from a centralized location using a combination of WATS lines, cathode-ray tubes (CRT), and data-entry terminals. Here is how it works. Professional telephone interviewers sit in separate booths and draw telephone numbers at random from somewhere in the nation. In dialing the person whose number has been selected, the interviewers use WATS lines, which means that the research firm has prepaid the telephone company so that it can make a certain large number of long-distance calls. When the phone is answered, the interviewer asks the person a set of questions, reading them from the cathode-ray tube. The interviewer types the respondent's answers right into the computer, using the data-entry terminal. This eliminates editing and coding, reduces the number of errors, and saves time.

Other research firms have set up interactive terminals in shopping centers. Persons willing to be interviewed sit down at a terminal, read the questions from the CRT, and type in their answers. Most respondents enjoy this form of "robot" interviewing.

Another major marketing research breakthrough is occurring in supermarkets with the advent of electronic cash registers, optical scanners, and the Universal Product Code. As a customer passes through the checkout line, his or her items are read by an optical scanner which records the brand, size, and price. These data enter a computer where they can be analyzed for the purposes of improved inventory control and marketing decision making. Supermarket managers and consumer goods manufacturers are able to measure the profitability of each brand and size and also the impact of different prices and promotions.

■ summary

In carrying out their responsibilities for marketing planning, execution, and control, marketing managers need a great deal of information. Too often, however, such information is not available, or comes too late, or cannot be trusted. An increasing number of companies have become aware of these information deficiencies and are taking concrete steps to improve their marketing information systems.

A well-designed marketing information system consists of four major subsystems. The first is the internal reports system, which provides current data on sales, costs, inventories, cash flows, and accounts receivable and payable. A number of companies have developed advanced computer-based internal reports systems to allow for speedier and more comprehensive information. The second is the marketing intelligence system, which supplies marketing executives with everyday information about developments in the external marketing environment. Here a better-trained sales force, special intelligence personnel, purchased data from syndicated sources, and an intelligence office can improve the marketing intelligence available to company executives. The third system is marketing research, which involves collecting special information that is relevant to a specific marketing problem facing the company. Approximately 73 percent of all large companies operate marketing research departments to help their executives obtain the information they need. The fourth system is the analytical marketing system, which consists of advanced statistical procedures and models to help develop more rigorous findings from information. A small but growing number of companies are building statistical and model banks to improve their analytical capabilities.

Marketing managers who need marketing research can work with professional marketing researchers to design the necessary study. Marketing research involves a five-step procedure consisting of research objectives and problem definition, exploratory research, formal survey and/or experimental research, fieldwork, and data analysis and report presentation.

One of the major tasks of marketing research is to estimate current market demand. A company should use a clear set of concepts for demand measurement and should especially note the distinction between *market demand* and *company demand,* and between *forecasts* and *potentials*. Current demand may be estimated for the market as a whole or for various territories. In the latter case, the market-buildup method is commonly used for industrial goods, and the index-of-buying-power method is commonly used for consumer goods.

For estimating future demand, the company may use one or any combination of at least six different forecasting methods: surveys of buyer intentions, sales-force estimates, expert opinions, market tests, time-series analysis, or statistical demand analysis. These methods vary in their appropriateness with the purpose of the forecast, the type of product, and the availability and reliability of data.

■ questions for discussion

1. How does a marketing information system differ from a marketing intelligence system?
2. What is the overriding objective of the marketing research system at Prentice-Hall?

3. Briefly describe the meaning of an analytical marketing system. Do you feel that a men's clothing store in a small town would use this type of system? Why?
4. Once the research objectives and the problem are defined, the researcher is then ready to begin the formal surveying of people. Comment.
5. Which type of research would be most appropriate in the following situations and why?
   a. Post cereals wants to investigate the effect that children have on the actual purchase of its products.
   b. Your college bookstore wants to gather some preliminary information as to how students feel about the merchandise and service provided by the bookstore.
   c. McDonald's is considering locating a new outlet in a fast-growing suburb.
   d. Gillette wants to test the effect of two new advertising themes for its Right Guard lime stick deodorant on sales in two cities.
6. The president of a campus organization to which you belong has asked you to conduct a marketing research project on why membership is declining. Discuss how you would apply the steps in the marketing research procedure to this project.
7. Relate the concepts of market potential and company demand to Miller Lite beer.
8. What are the two major methods of estimating current company demand? Which one do you think Levi Strauss should use?
9. Discuss two market and sales forecasting techniques that Wilson might use for a new line of tennis rackets.

references

1. Based on material found in "The Jogging-Shoe Race Heats Up," *Business Week,* April 9, 1979, pp. 124–25.
2. MARION HARPER, JR., "A New Profession to Aid Management," *Journal of Marketing,* January 1961, p. 1.
3. RICHARD H. BRIEN, "Marketing Information Systems: The State of the Art," *Combined 1972 Conference Proceedings* (Chicago: American Marketing Association, 1973), p. 20.
4. This definition is adapted from "Marketing Information Systems: An Introductory Overview," in *Readings in Marketing Information Systems,* ed. Samuel V. Smith, Richard H. Brien, and James E. Stafford (Boston: Houghton Mifflin, 1968), p. 7.
5. DONALD F. COX AND ROBERT E. GOOD, "How to Build a Marketing Information System," *Harvard Business Review,* May-June 1967, pp. 145–54.
6. Dik Warren Twedt, ed., *1978 Survey of Marketing Research* (Chicago: American Marketing Association, 1978).
7. ERNEST S. BRADFORD, *Bradford's Directory of Marketing Research Agencies and Management Consultants in the United States and the World,* 1973–1974, 15th ed. (Middlebury, Vt.: Bradford Co.).
8. JACK J. HONOMICHL, "Research Top Ten: Who They Are and What They Do," *Advertising Age,* July 15, 1974, pp. 24, 27.

9. See David A. Acker, ed., *Multivariate Analysis in Marketing: Theory and Applications* (Belmont, Calif.: Wadsworth, 1971).
10. Glen L. Urban, "SPRINTER Mod III: A Model for the Analysis of New Frequently Purchased Consumer Products," *Operations Research*, September-October 1970, pp. 805–54.
11. See J.D.C. Little and L. M. Lodish, "A Media Planning Calculus," *Operations Research*, January-February 1969, pp. 1–35.
12. See Sidney W. Hess, "Realignment of Sales and Service Districts," Working Paper (Philadelphia: Management Science Center, Wharton School, University of Pennsylvania, July 1968).
13. T. E. Hlavac, Jr., and J.D.C. Little, "A Geographic Model of an Automobile Market," Working Paper No. 186–66 (Cambridge: Massachusetts Institute of Technology, Alfred P. Sloan School of Management, 1966).
14. For an excellent annotated reference to major secondary sources of business and marketing data, see Thomas C. Kinnear and James R. Taylor, *Marketing Research: An Applied Approach* (New York, McGraw-Hill, 1979), pp. 128–31, 138–71.
15. See Keith K. Cox and others, "Applications of Focus Group Interviews in Marketing," *Journal of Marketing*, January 1976, pp. 77–80; and Bobby J. Calder, "Focus Groups and the Nature of Qualitative Marketing Research," *Journal of Marketing Research*, August 1977, pp. 353–64.
16. To conclude the story, Braniff decided to introduce different colors on different airplanes, calling for "the end of the plain plane." People at airports spotted Braniff's planes, the news media gave Braniff considerable publicity, and Braniff soon became one of the most-talked-about and best-recognized airlines. Braniff's market share increased substantially, thus achieving its objectives through a combination of effective marketing research, product redesign, and marketing communications.
17. For more reading on experimental research, see Seymour Banks, *Experimentation in Marketing* (New York: McGraw-Hill, 1965).
18. See Philip Kotler, *Marketing Decision Making: A Model Building Approach* (New York: Holt, Rinehart & Winston, 1971), esp. Chap. 4.
19. For a helpful exposition on using this survey, see "Putting the Four to Work," *Sales and Marketing Management*, October 28, 1974, pp. 13ff.
20. See "How Good Are Consumer Pollsters?" *Business Week*, November 9, 1969, pp. 108–10.
21. Adapted from *Forecasting Sales*, Business Policy Study No. 106 (New York: National Conference Board, 1963).
22. However, see Jacob Gonik, "Tie Salesmen's Bonuses to Their Forecasts," *Harvard Business Review*, May-June 1978, pp. 116–23.
23. See Normal Dalkey and Olaf Helmer, "An Experimental Application of the Delphi Method to the Use of Experts," *Management Science*, April 1963, pp. 458–67.
24. See William F. Massy's "Statistical Analysis of Relations between Variables," in *Multivariate Analysis in Marketing: Theory and Applications*, ed. David A. Acker (Belmont, Calif.: Wadsworth, 1971), pp. 5–35.
25. See "The DuPort Company," in *Marketing Research: Text and Cases* (3rd ed.), ed. Harper W. Boyd, Jr., and Ralph Westfall (Homewood, Ill.: Richard D. Irwin, 1972), pp. 576–81.

THE MARKETING ORGANIZATION

In the mid-1970s the world's largest corporation (in earnings and assets) made the decision, according to its Chairman John D. deButts, that it would "become a marketing company." Who would have believed that the American Telephone and Telegraph Company (AT&T) did not qualify as a marketing company? Ma Bell, as AT&T is affectionately called, had a large sales and service force, product managers, advertising managers, and marketing researchers. But somehow Ma Bell did not have a true marketing organization. There was no marketing leadership at the top. There was no marketing-planning system. Product development was not harnessed to the changing needs and wants of the marketplace.

The company's marketing backwardness contributed to its costly "Picturephone" fiasco in the 1960s. AT&T's top management had given its blessing to a multimillion-dollar program to develop a picture telephone that would enable callers to see each other on small screens while speaking. When the technical work was completed, Bell executives were so enamored with the technical wizardry that they launched the Picturephone in 1969 accompanied by predictions of annual sales of $1 billion by 1980. Unfortunately their enthusiasm was not matched by that of potential customers, who balked at paying more than $100 a month for the service. Virtually no buyers appeared, and Bell had to pull the product out of the test market after a couple of years. Its executives retreated to a corner, defeated by a marketplace they did not understand.

But the final blow to Ma Bell's marketing insularity came with the Supreme Court's famous Carterfone decision in 1968, which allowed Bell customers for the first time to buy non-Bell equipment and attach it to Bell service lines. Suddenly dozens of companies began to produce and sell terminal equipment at much lower prices to Bell's former customers. Bell's monopoly was broken, and now it had to learn how to do battle not only with regulators but with aggressive competitors.

How does a company reorganize overnight to become market-oriented? One of the first things it must do is go out and hire the best possible marketing talent. And where does it go to find the best marketing talent to run a high-technology company? Clearly, IBM has got to be one of the places to raid. So Ma Bell hired away IBM's Archie J. McGill, who at the age of thirty-three had been the youngest vice-president in IBM's history. McGill joined AT&T because he saw AT&T's attempt to

become a marketing company as "the greatest challenge in American business."

Since McGill and the other marketing whiz kids came aboard, things have not been the same at AT&T. The company created three executive vice-presidential posts to supervise business services, residential services, and network services, respectively. "Amazingly, it was the company's first substantial effort to structure itself along the lines of its major market segments." In a period of three years, the marketing department added over six hundred new managers, certainly the fastest company marketing buildup in history. Many of the new marketers are "market managers," and each of these managers has been put in charge of a business market, such as hotels, banks, and colleges, and is responsible for developing a marketing plan for that market. Others are product managers in charge of developing marketing plans for major services, such as WATS, international calling, and PBX switchboards. Ma Bell also runs a large, increasingly professional sales force, which is specialized by business market. And finally, the marketing department includes various functional marketing specialists carrying on marketing research, advertising, sales promotion, and other marketing functions. But all this might not be enough to change the traditional culture of the company, which is used to acting as a passively regulated company rather than a hard-hitting competitor. In order not to take any chances, Bell is putting fifteen thousand of its managers and supervisors through marketing training programs to "build a marketing culture" at Bell.[1]

□AT&T's story is dramatic, although not unique. Many organizations have had the experience of suddenly discovering the depth of their marketing weakness when their markets changed or tough competitors emerged. Today, sundry banks, hospitals, colleges, and other organizations are suddenly awakening to the need to understand their markets better and to install marketing organizations. Fortunately they do not have to add six hundred or sixty or even six new marketers in most cases. A college that is failing to attract a sufficient number of students may find the answer by adding only one savvy marketing thinker to its staff, someone who brings along a fresh perspective and new ideas.

Here we want to look at designs for the marketing organization. The marketing-planning and control system and the marketing information system only become effective when a marketing organization knows how to use them. This chapter answers the following questions:

- How do marketing departments evolve in the typical company?
- How should the marketing department be organized?
- What is the relationship between the marketing department and the other company departments?
- What steps are involved in producing a companywide marketing orientation?

the evolution of the marketing department

The modern marketing department is the product of a long evolution. From very humble beginnings, it has evolved through five stages. Companies can be found today in each of these stages.

Simple Sales Department (Stage One)

All companies start out with four simple functions. Someone must raise and manage capital (finance), produce the product or service (operations), sell it (sales), and keep the books (accounting). The selling function is headed by a sales manager or a sales vice-president, who basically manages a sales force and also does some selling. When the company needs some occasional marketing research or advertising, the sales vice-president also handles this because it supports the objective of obtaining more sales. Nevertheless, the sales vice-president is mainly interested in the sales force, and these other assignments are often handled halfheartedly. This stage is illustrated in Figure 6-1A.

Sales Department with Ancillary Functions (Stage Two)

As the company expands, it finds that it needs marketing research, advertising, and customer service on a more continuous and expert basis. The sales vice-president hires a few specialists to perform these functions. Instead of supervising each of these specialists, the sales vice-president may hire a marketing director to plan and control the nonselling functions (see Figure 6-1B).

Figure 6-1
Stages in the Evolution of the Marketing Department

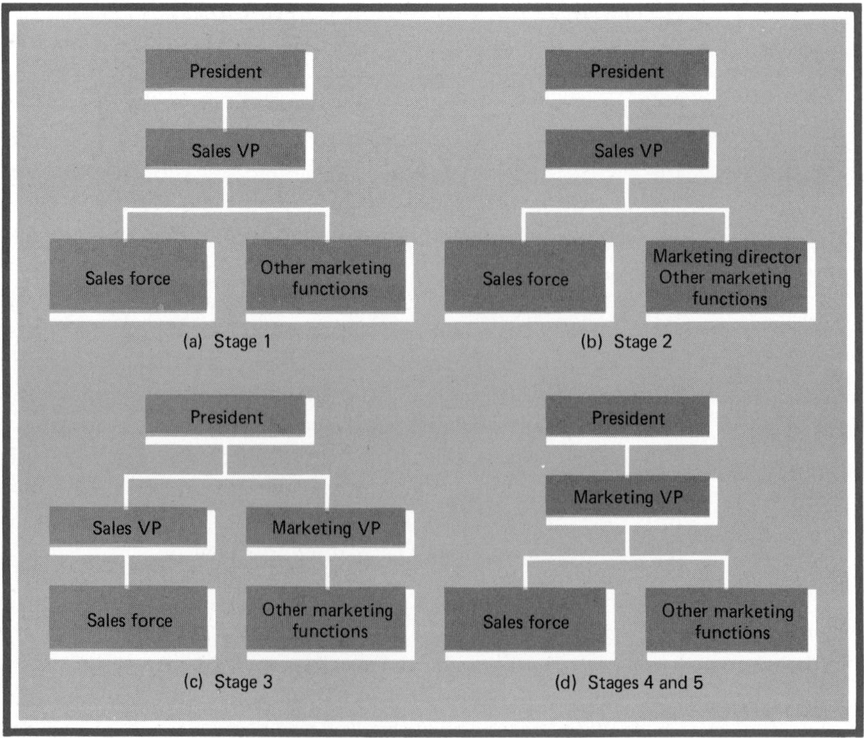

Separate Marketing Department (Stage Three)

The continued growth of the company inevitably increases the importance of other marketing functions—marketing research, new-product development, advertising and promotion, customer service—relative to sales-force activity. Nevertheless, the sales vice-president continues to give disproportionate time and attention to the sales force. The marketing director will argue that sales could be facilitated by more budget going into these other marketing activities. The company president or executive vice-president will eventually see the advantage of establishing a marketing department that is relatively independent of the sales vice-president (see Figure 6-1C). The marketing department will be headed by a marketing vice-president who will report, along with the sales vice-president, to the president or executive vice-president. At this stage, sales and marketing are seen as separate and equal functions in the organization that are supposed to work closely together.

Modern Marketing Department (Stage Four)

Although the sales vice-president and the marketing vice-president are supposed to work harmoniously together, their relationship is often characterized by rivalry and distrust. The sales vice-president sees a conspiracy to make the sales force less important in the marketing mix; and the marketing vice-president seeks to gain power over all the customer-impinging functions. The sales vice-president tends to be short-run oriented and preoccupied with achieving current sales. The marketing vice-president tends to be long-run oriented and preoccupied with planning the right products and marketing strategy to meet the customers' long-run needs.

At times it seems that the sales and the marketing people represent two different cultures in the organization. The salespeople usually have less education and are more practical and "streetwise," whereas the marketing people are younger, better educated, and less experienced in selling. Often the salespeople do not trust or believe the marketing people's findings. Some companies arrange for the marketing people to get more selling experience and even assign them a few customers to keep them close to the selling situation.

If there is too much conflict between sales and marketing, the company president may (1) eliminate the marketing vice-president's office and place marketing activities back under the sales vice-president, (2) instruct the executive vice-president to handle conflicts that arise, or (3) place the marketing vice-president in charge of everything, including the sales force. The last solution is eventually chosen in many companies and forms the basis of the modern marketing department, a department headed by a marketing vice-president with subordinates reporting from every marketing function, including sales management (see Figure 6-1D).

Modern Marketing Company (Stage Five)

A company can have a modern marketing department and yet not operate as a modern marketing company. Whether it is the latter depends upon how the officers of the company view the marketing function. If they view marketing as primarily a selling function, they are missing the point. The vice-president of marketing, no matter how well he or she runs the marketing department, meets frequent resistance from other vice-presidents in attempting to carry out a companywide customer orientation. The manufacturing vice-president holds to the logic of cost minimization and resents interrupting production schedules to please customers. The financial vice-president is not sure about the return from investments in marketing research, communication, and promotion and normally reacts to sales declines by recommending cuts in market development expenditures. Other departments also resist cooperating to produce satisfied customers. Ultimately the job may call for increasing the power and authority of the marketing vice-president over the other business functions. Only a few companies have attained the stature of true marketing companies.

ways of organizing the modern marketing department

An examination of modern marketing departments reveals numerous arrangements. All marketing organizations must somehow accommodate to four basic dimensions of marketing activity: *functions, geographical units, products,* and *end-use markets.*

Functional Organization

The most common form of marketing organization has various functional marketing specialists reporting to a marketing vice-president, who is in charge of coordinating all of their activities. Figure 6-2 shows five such specialists, who bear the titles of marketing administration manager, advertising and sales promotion manager, sales manager, marketing research manager, and new-products manager, respectively. Additional functional specialists might include a customer service manager, a marketing-planning manager, and a physical distribution manager.

The main advantage of a functional marketing organization is its administrative simplicity. On the other hand, this organizational form suffers from certain disadvantages as the company's product line or number of markets increases. First, there is inadequate detailed planning for specific products and markets, since no one is assigned full responsibility for any product or market. Products that are not favorites with various functional specialists tend to get neglected. Second, each functional group develops its own subgoals, which include trying to gain more budget and status vis-à-vis the other functions. The marketing vice-president has to constantly sift the claims of competing functional specialists and faces a difficult problem in coordination.

Figure 6-2
Functional Organization

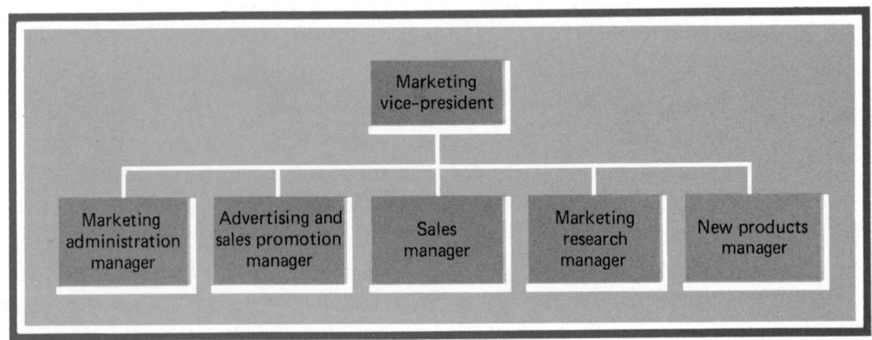

Figure 6-3
Geographical Organization

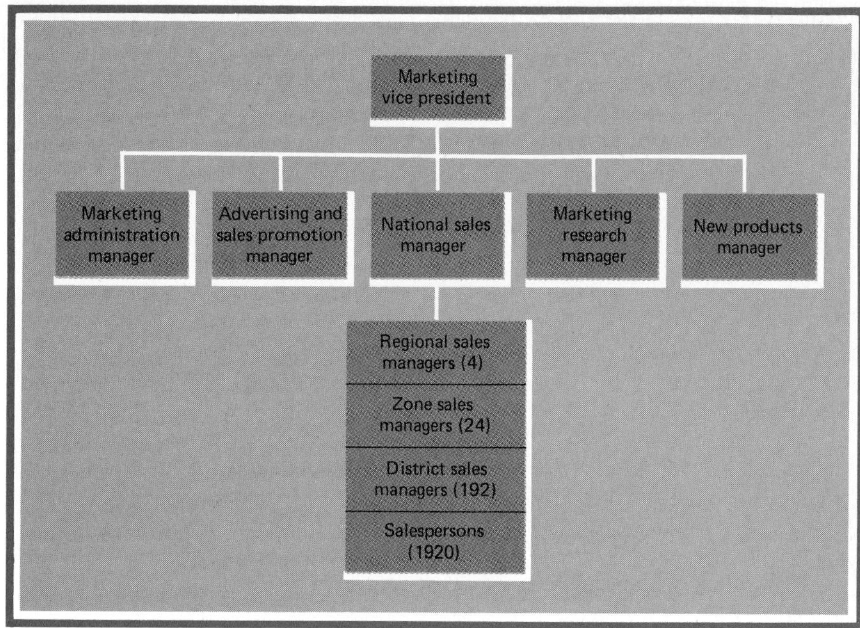

Geographical Organization

A company selling in a national market often organizes its sales force (and sometimes other functions) along geographical lines. Figure 6-3 shows 1 national sales manager, 4 regional sales managers, 24 zone sales managers, 192 district sales managers, and, finally, 1,920 salespersons. The span of control increases each step as we move from the national sales manager down toward the district sales managers. Shorter spans allow managers to give more time to subordinates and are warranted when the sales task is complex, the salespersons are highly paid, and the salesperson's impact on profits is substantial.

Product Management Organization

Companies producing a variety of products and/or brands often establish a product management organization (also called a brand management organization). The product management organization does not replace the functional management organization but serves as another layer of management. The product management organization is headed by a products manager who supervises several product group managers who in turn supervise product managers in charge of specific products (see Figure 6-4).

The decision to establish a product management organization is influenced by the extent of product heterogeneity and the sheer number of products. If the company product lines can benefit from specialized marketing programs, or if the sheer number of products is beyond the capacity of a functional marketing organization to handle, a product management organization is a natural recourse.

Product management first made its appearance in the Proctor and Gamble Company in 1927. A new company soap, Camay, was not doing well, and one of the young executives, Neil H. McElroy (later president of P&G), was assigned to give his exclusive attention to developing and promoting this product. This he did successfully, and the company soon afterward added other product managers.

Figure 6-4
Product Management Organization

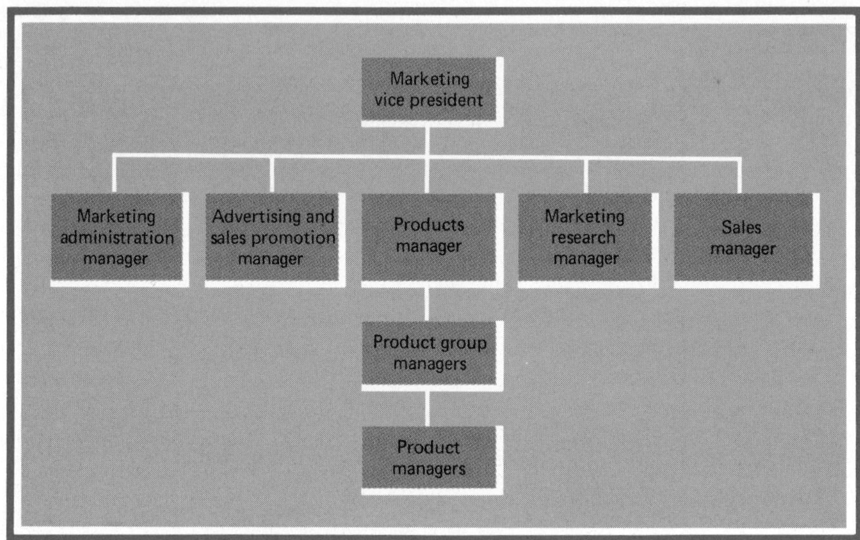

Since then a large number of firms, especially in the food, soap, toiletries, and chemical industries, have established product management organizations. General Foods, for example, uses a product management organization in its Post Division. There are separate product group managers in charge of cereals, pet food, and beverages. Within the cereal product group, there are separate product managers for nutritional cereals, children's presweetened cereals, family cereals, and miscellaneous cereals. In turn, the nutritional cereal product manager supervises brand managers.[2]

The product management organization creates a focal point of planning and responsibility for individual products. The product manager's role is to create product strategies and plans, see that they are implemented, monitor the results, and take corrective action. This responsibility breaks down into the following six tasks:

1. Developing a long-range and competitive strategy for the product
2. Preparing an annual marketing plan and sales forecast
3. Working with advertising and merchandising agencies to develop copy, programs, and campaigns
4. Stimulating interest in and support of the product among the sales force and distributors
5. Gathering continuous intelligence on the product's performance, customer and dealer attitudes, and new problems and opportunities
6. Initiating product improvements to meet changing market needs

These basic functions are common to both consumer and industrial product managers. Yet there are some important differences in their jobs and emphases.[3] Consumer product managers tend to manage fewer products than industrial product managers. They spend considerably more time dealing with advertising and sales promotion. They spend most of their time working with others in the company and various agencies, and little time in direct contact with customers. They tend to be younger and better educated. Industrial product managers, by contrast, think more carefully about the technical aspects of their product and possible improvements in design. They spend more time with laboratory and engineering personnel in the company. They work more closely with the sales force and key buyers. They tend to pay less attention to advertising, sales promotion, and promotional pricing. They emphasize rational product factors, not emotional ones.

The product management organization introduces several advantages in the management of the firm's marketing activity. First, the product manager can balance and harmonize the various functional marketing inputs needed by a product. Second, the product manager is in a position to react quickly to problems in the marketplace without involving several different people in lengthy meetings. Third, smaller brands, because they have a product champion, are not as neglected in this system as they tend to be in functional marketing organizations. Fourth, product management is an excellent training ground for promising young executives, for it involves them in almost every area of company operations (see Figure 6-5).

But a price is paid for these advantages. First, the product management organization introduces many sources of conflict and frustration that might not

Figure 6-5
The Product Manager's Interactions

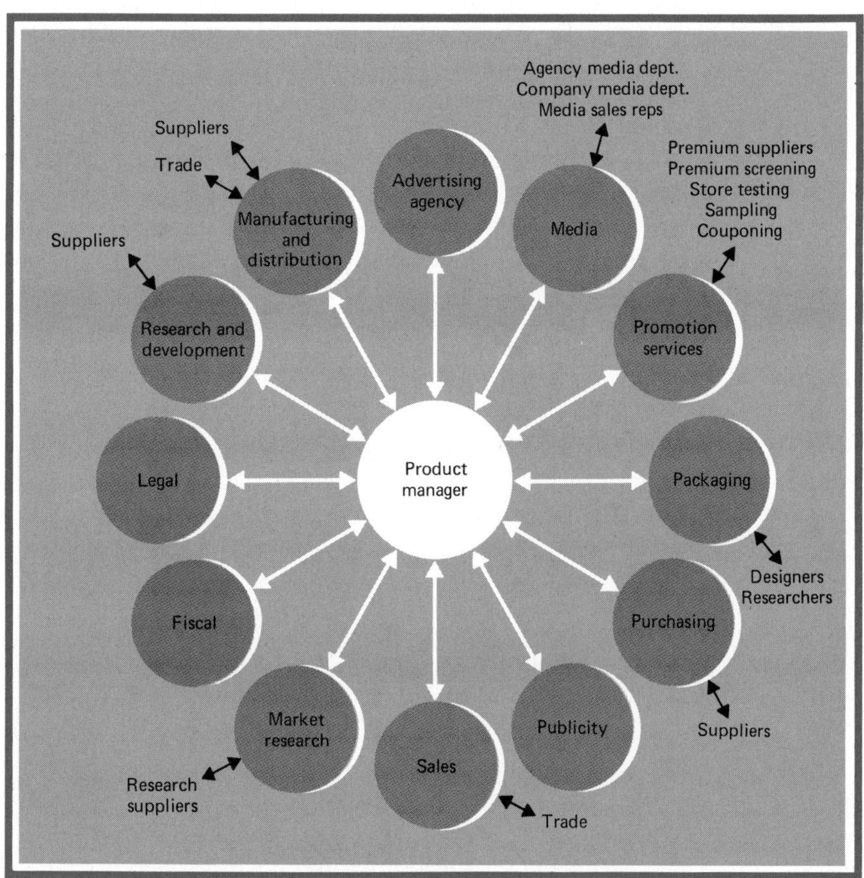

Adapted from "Product Managers: Just What do They Think?", *Printers Ink,* October 28, 1966, p. 15.

otherwise be present.[4] Product managers are typically not given enough authority to carry out their responsibilities effectively. They have to rely on their persuasive skills when seeking the cooperation of various resource managers. They spend so much time trying to get the support of advertising, sales, and manufacturing managers that they have little time for planning. They have been told by their superior that they are "mini-presidents," but they are often treated like low-level coordinators. They solicit the help of specialists but often do not follow their advice. Sometimes they are forced to go over the heads of others. They are bogged down by a great amount of paperwork. If such frustrations lead to a rapid turnover of product managers, it can damage the sound long-range planning of products.

Second, product managers become experts in their product but rarely have a chance to become experts in any of the functions for which they are responsible. They vacillate between posing as experts and being cowed by real experts. This is particularly unfortunate when the product basically depends on a specific type of expertise, such as advertising. In this case it would almost make more sense to put the product in the hands of an advertising specialist.

Third, the product management organization often turns out to be costlier than anticipated. Originally, one person is appointed to manage each major product. Soon thereafter, product managers are appointed to manage even minor products. Each product manager, usually overworked, pleads and gets an *assistant brand manager*. Later, both the product manager and the assistant brand manager, still overworked, persuade management to give them a *brand assistant*. Product managers who supervise the more important company products, in their frustration in having to coax time from advertising, packaging, and other specialists, next pressure to hire their own specialists. In one large brewery, the main brand manager has his own advertising department. With all these personnel, payroll costs climb. In the meantime the company continues to increase its number of functional specialists in copy, packaging, media, promotion, market surveys, statistical analysis, and so on. The company soon finds itself stuck with a costly superstructure of product management people and a superstructure of functional specialists.

When a company has a product management organization that breeds too much conflict or cost, it should think about possible improvements. Although P&G eventually managed to achieve a smooth-working product management organization, many of its imitators have not been as successful. Pearson and Wilson have suggested the following steps to make the product management system work better:[5]

1. *Clearly delineate the limits of the product manager's role and responsibility for the management of a product.* [Product managers are essentially proposers, not deciders.] . . .
2. *Build a strategy development and review process to provide an agreed-to framework for the product manager's operations.* [Too many companies allow product managers to get away with shallow marketing plans featuring a lot of statistics but little strategic rationale.] . . .
3. *Take into account areas of potential conflict between product managers and functional specialists when defining their respective roles.* [Clarify which decisions

are to be made by the product manager, which by the expert, and which will be shared.] . . .

4. *Set up a formal process that forces to the top all conflict-of-interest situations between product management and functional line management.* [Both parties might be expected to put all issues in writing and forward them to general management for settlement.] . . .
5. *Establish a system for measuring results that is consistent with the product manager's responsibilities.* [If product managers are to be held accountable for profit, they should be given more control over the factors that affect their operations' profitability.] . . .

The product manager position is undergoing several important changes. In many companies product managers are assuming greater responsibility for brand profitability. Cost inflation has resulted in companies' being less satisfied with the sheer volume they sell and more concerned with the profits they make. The product manager is becoming more of a profit center and must put a profit test to the various items in his or her line and to the various marketing expenditures. Some companies are even holding their product managers responsible for excessive costs of inventory and receivables.

Product managers are also working more closely with other managers in the company to find ways of securing scarce supplies, developing substitute ingredients, engineering product economies, smoothing production, and keeping total costs down. Another trend is that higher levels of marketing management are exercising greater control over brand managers —they now realize that there is a need for more coordinated planning of whole product lines rather than simply brands and that brand managers should be more responsive to consumerists' concerns with advertising truthfulness and product safety.[6]

Market Management Organization

Many companies will sell a product line to a highly diverse set of markets. For example, Smith Corona sells its electric typewriters to consumer, business, and government markets. U.S. Steel sells its steel to the railroad, construction, and public utility industries. Where the company sells to customers who fall into distinct user groups having different buying practices or product preferences, some market specialization is desirable in the marketing organization.

The general structure of a market management organization is similar to the product management organization shown earlier in Figure 6-4. Along with functional managers there is a *markets manager* who supervises several *market managers* (also called *market development managers, market specialists,* or *industry specialists*). Market managers are responsible for developing long-range and annual plans for the sales and profits in their markets. They have to draw resource help, such as marketing research or advertising, from the functional specialists in the organization. This system's strongest advantage is that the company is organized to monitor and focus on the needs of distinct customer groups.

An increasing number of companies are reorganizing their management structures along market lines. Hanan calls these *market-centered organizations* and argues that "the only way to ensure being market-oriented is to put a company's organizational structure together so that its major markets become the centers around which its divisions are built."[7] Xerox has converted from geographical selling to selling by industry. The Mead Company is clustering its marketing activities around home building and furnishing, education, and leisure markets.

Product Management/ Market Management Organization

Companies that produce multiple products that flow into multiple markets face a real dilemma. They could utilize a product management organization, which requires product managers to be familiar with highly divergent markets. Or they could utilize a market management organization, which means that market managers would have to be familiar with highly divergent products bought by their markets. Or they could install both product and market managers, that is, a product/market organization.

It would seem that a product management/market management organization would be desirable in a multiple-product, multiple-market company. The rub, however, is that this system is both costly and generates conflict. There is

EXHIBIT 6-1

THE HEINZ COMPANY MOVES TOWARD A MARKET MANAGEMENT SYSTEM

One of the most dramatic shifts to market centeredness has occurred at the Heinz Company. Before 1964 Heinz was primarily organized around a brand management system, with separate brand managers for soups, condiments, puddings, and so on. Each brand manager, such as the ketchup brand manager, was responsible for both grocery sales and institutional sales. Then, in 1964, Heinz created a separate marketing organization for institutional sales. Thus ketchup sales to institutions would be the responsibility of the institutional product managers rather than the brand managers. Recently Heinz split the marketing organization into three broad groups: groceries, commercial restaurants, and institutions. Each group contains further market specialists. For example, the institutional division contains separate market specialists for schools, colleges, hospitals, and prisons. The market manager positions are as follows:

GROCERIES	COMMERCIAL RESTAURANTS	INSTITUTIONS
Supermarkets Market Manager	Drug and Variety Stores Market Manager	Schools Market Manager
Wholesale Co-ops Market Manager	Drive-ins Market Manager	Colleges Market Manager
Wholesalers Market Manager	Coffee Shops Market Manager	Hospitals Market Manager
	Fine Restaurants Market Manager	Prisons Market Manager

the cost of supporting a three-dimensional *matrix organization* (i.e., two layers of program management in addition to one layer of resource management). There are also serious questions as to where authority and responsibility should reside. Here are two of the many dilemmas:

1. How should the sales force be organized? In the Du Pont example in Exhibit 6-2, should there be separate sales forces for rayon, nylon, and each of the other fibers? Or should the sales forces be organized according to men's wear, women's wear, and other markets? Or should the sales force not be specialized?
2. Who should set the prices for a particular product/market? In the Du Pont example, should the nylon product manager have final authority for setting nylon prices in all markets? What happens if the men's wear market manager feels that nylon will lose out in this market unless special price concessions are made on nylon?

Some companies are adopting a product/market organization, and others using this organization are having second thoughts. Most agree that only the

EXHIBIT 6-2

DU PONT USES A PRODUCT/MARKET MANAGEMENT SYSTEM

Du Pont's textile fibers division consists of both product managers and market managers:

		Market Managers			
		Men's wear	Women's wear	Home furnishings	Industrial markets
Product Managers	Rayon				
	Acetate				
	Nylon				
	Orlon				
	Dacron				

The product managers have the responsibility for planning the sales and profits of their respective fibers. These managers are primarily focused on short-run performance and uses of their fiber. Their job is to contact each market manager and ask for an estimate of how much material can be sold in each market. The market managers, on the other hand, have the responsibility for developing profitable markets for existing and potential Du Pont fibers. They take a long view of market needs and care more about evolving the right products for their market than pushing specific fibers. In preparing their market plan, they contact each product manager to learn about planned prices and availabilities of different materials. The final sales forecasts of the market managers and the product managers should add to the same grand total.

more important products and markets would justify separate managers. Some observers are not upset about the conflicts in this system on the argument that it provides the company with the benefit of both the short-run and the long-run view and the conflict is healthy.[8]

Corporate-Divisional Organization

As multiproduct companies grow, they have a tendency to turn their larger product groups into separate divisions. The larger divisions often set up their own marketing departments on the ground that this will give them more knowledgeable and controllable marketing resources. This poses the question as to what marketing services and activities should be retained at the corporate headquarters level.

Divisionalized companies have reached different answers to this question. Corporate marketing staffs seem to follow any of four models:[9]

1. *No corporate marketing.* Some companies do not have a corporate marketing staff. They do not see any useful function for marketing at the corporate level. Each division has its own marketing department.
2. *Minimal corporate marketing.* Some companies have a small corporate marketing staff that performs a few functions, primarily (a) assisting top management with overall opportunity evaluation, (b) providing divisions with consulting assistance on request, (c) helping divisions that are without marketing or that have weak marketing, and (d) attempting to promote the marketing concept to other departments in the company.
3. *Moderate corporate marketing.* Some companies have a corporate marketing staff that, in addition to the preceding activities, also provides various marketing services to the divisions. The corporate marketing staff might provide certain specialized *advertising services, sales promotion services,* and *sales administration services.*
4. *Strong corporate marketing.* Some companies have a corporate marketing staff that, in addition to the preceding activities, has the authority to participate strongly in the planning and control of divisional marketing activities.

marketing's relations with other departments

In principle, business functions should mesh harmoniously to achieve the overall objectives of the firm. In practice, however, departmental relations are often characterized by deep rivalries and misunderstandings that impede the realization of the company's objectives. Some interdepartmental conflict stems from differences of opinion as to what is in the best interests of the firm; some from real trade-offs between departmental well-being and company well-being; and some from unfortunate departmental stereotypes and prejudices.

The Question of Marketing's Importance in the Organization

There is much confusion about marketing's relative importance in the firm. In some firms it is just another function, no more or no less important than the other functions. All functions count in influencing corporate strategy, and none takes leadership. This view is illustrated in Figure 6-6A.

If the company faces slow growth—or even worse, a sales decline—the marketers start arguing for a larger budget in order to build market demand.

Figure 6-6
Evolving Views of Marketing's Role in the Company

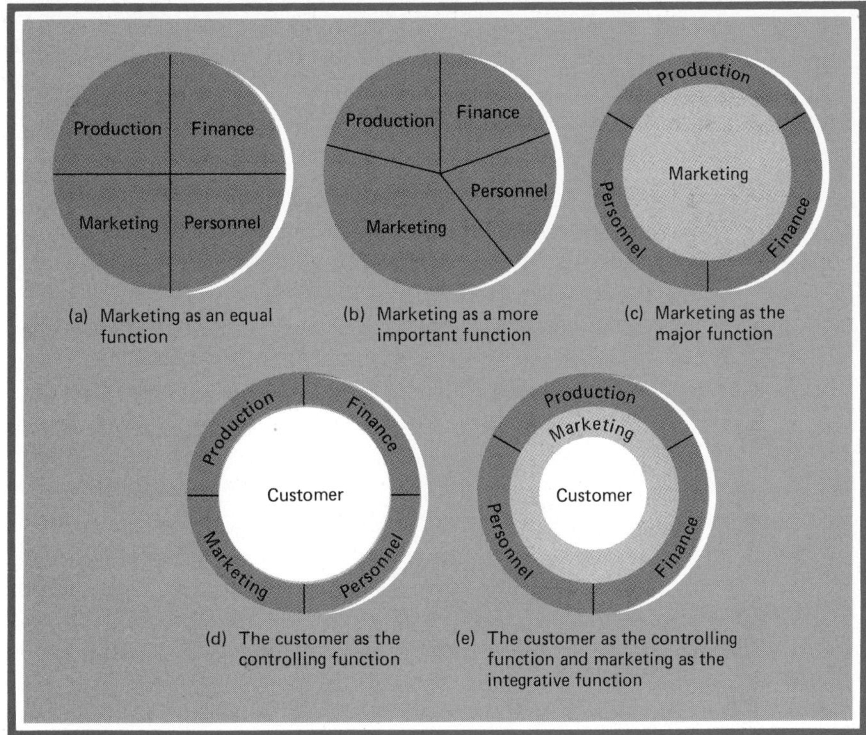

They claim that marketing is a more important function than the others (see Figure 6-6B).

Some marketers go further and say that marketing is the central function of the firm, not just a more important function. They quote Drucker's statement: "The aim of the business is to create customers." They say it is marketing's responsibility to define the company's mission, products, and markets and to direct all the other functions in the task of serving customers (see Figure 6-6C).

This view incenses the other department heads, who do not want to think of themselves as working for marketing. Enlightened marketers respond by putting the customer at the center of the company rather than having the marketing department at the center. They argue for a *customer orientation* in which all functions work together to sense, serve, and satisfy the customer (see Figure 6-6D).

Finally, some marketers say that marketing still needs to command a central position in the firm if customers' needs are to be correctly interpreted and efficiently satisfied (see Figure 6-6E). The marketer's argument for this concept of the corporation can be summarized as follows:

1. The assets of the firm have little value without the existence of customers.
2. The key task of the firm is therefore to create and hold customers.
3. Customers are attracted through promises and held through satisfaction.
4. Marketing's task is to define an appropriate promise to the customer and to ensure the delivery of satisfaction.

5. The actual satisfaction delivered to the customer is affected by the performance of the other departments.
6. Marketing needs influence or control over these other departments if customers are to be satisfied.

Types of Interdepartmental Conflict

In the typical organization each department has an impact on customer satisfaction through its own activities and decisions. Under the marketing concept, it is desirable to coordinate them because the satisfaction gained by the customer is a function of the *totality* of customer-impinging stimuli, not simply of the stimuli managed by the marketing department.

The marketing department is very willing to accept this responsibility and use its influence. The reason for appointing a marketing vice-president is twofold: (1) to bring about an integration and coordination of the formal marketing activities of the company, such as sales forecasting, marketing research, advertising, sales force, promotion, and customer service, and (2) to deal with the vice-presidents of finance, operations, and so on, on a regular basis so that they will develop a deeper appreciation of the value and benefits of a customer orientation. But there is little unanimity on how much influence and authority marketing should have over other departments to bring about coordinated marketing.

Other departments resent having to bend their efforts to the will of the marketing department. Just as marketing stresses the customer's point of view, other departments wish to stress the importance of their tasks. Inevitably, departments and individuals define company problems and goals in terms slanted by self-interest. The reason is that each deals continuously with problems in a local portion of the overall system. The major departmental differences in point of view—or organizational conflicts—between marketing and other departments are summarized in Table 6-1. We will briefly describe the typical concerns of each department.

R & D. The R & D manager is interested in making new discoveries and expects marketing people to be able to find markets for them. This executive focuses attention on functional product features and tends to overlook the market's psychology of buying.

Engineering. The product engineer is interested in designing a product that meets engineering standards of simplicity and economy. This executive tends to concentrate on these attributes at the expense of those that would increase the product's marketability.

Purchasing. The purchasing agent's main concern is to keep down the costs of acquiring the company's required inputs. This executive's material and design recommendations often conflict with qualities that marketing would like to build into the product.

Manufacturing. The production officer is interested in keeping down manufacturing costs. But manufacturing economies are achieved in ways often incompatible with the goal of high customer satisfaction.

Table 6-1
Summary of Organizational Conflicts between Marketing and Other Departments

DEPARTMENT	THEIR EMPHASIS	MARKETING'S EMPHASIS
R & D	Basic research	Applied research
	Intrinsic quality	Perceived quality
	Functional features	Sales features
Engineering	Long design lead time	Short design lead time
	Few models	Many models
	Standard components	Custom components
Purchasing	Narrow product line	Broad product line
	Standard parts	Nonstandard parts
	Price of material	Quality of material
	Economical lot sizes	Large lot sizes to avoid stockouts
	Purchasing at infrequent intervals	Immediate purchasing for customer needs
Manufacturing	Long production lead time	Short production lead time
	Long runs with few models	Short runs with many models
	No model changes	Frequent model changes
	Standard orders	Custom orders
	Ease of fabrication	Aesthetic appearance
	Average quality control	Tight quality control
Inventory	Fast-moving items, narrow product line	Broad product line
	Economical level of stock	High level of stock
Finance	Strict rationales for spending	Intuitive arguments for spending
	Hard and fast budgets	Flexible budgets to meet changing needs
	Pricing to cover costs	Pricing to further market development
Accounting	Standard transactions	Special terms and discounts
	Few reports	Many reports
Credit	Full financial disclosures by customers	Minimum credit examination of customers
	Low credit risks	Medium credit risks
	Tough credit terms	Easy credit terms
	Tough collection procedures	Easy collection procedures

Inventory. The executive responsible for inventory management wants to keep down inventory costs. This executive is typically more concerned with holding down carrying costs than with the less-tangible costs of stockout.

Finance. The financial officer likes to keep a tight rein on company expenditures and wants to see profit on each transaction. This often conflicts with the need to take initial losses in order to develop loyal customers.

Accounting. The accountant's natural interest is in keeping down the costs of the company's reporting operation. Therefore this executive is apt to resent nonstandard marketing transactions and to resist requests by the marketing department for a multitude of sales and cost analyses.

Credit. The credit officer looks on the bad debt as a blot on his or her own performance. To minimize credit losses this executive tends to set higher standards for customer credit than seems reasonable to the salesperson who is working so hard to find customers.

It is no wonder that many departments resent the marketing concept. Marketing, in trying to mobilize the company's resources to develop customer satisfaction, often causes other departments to do a poorer job *in their terms.* Requests and pressures by the marketing department can increase product design and material purchasing costs, disrupt production schedules, increase accounting costs, and create budget headaches.

strategies for building a companywide marketing orientation

Only a handful of American companies—such as P&G, IBM, Caterpillar—are truly marketing-oriented. A much larger number of companies are sales-oriented, which they confuse with being marketing-oriented. At some point in the company's history, something happens to create a disturbing awareness of the company's lack of a true marketing orientation. Among the most common triggering circumstances are the following:

1. *Sales decline.* The company starts experiencing falling sales and the need to improve its marketing research, advertising, and sales promotion. In the newspaper business, for example, newspaper circulation is falling. Publishers are beginning to realize that they know very little about why people read newspapers. These publishers are commissioning consumer research and are redesigning the format so that their newspapers will be more contemporary, relevant, and interesting.
2. *Slow growth.* The company's growth may slow down and lead the company to search for new markets. It then recognizes the need for marketing know-how if it is to successfully identify, evaluate, select, and enter new markets. Dow Chemical had to acquire sophisticated brand management talent when it decided to develop food-wrapping products for the consumer market.
3. *Changing buying patterns.* The company may find that its customers' tastes and preferences are changing. During the 1960s American automobile manufacturers failed to understand why people who had always bought American cars were switching to small foreign-made cars like the Volkswagen and Toyota. After losing about 20 percent of the car market, American automobile manufacturers began to recognize the need to replace their sales orientation with a marketing orientation.
4. *Increased competition.* The company may suddenly find its market invaded by a sophisticated marketer and may be forced to improve its marketing to meet the challenge. This happened recently to the American Hospital Supply Corporation (AHS). One of its divisions is the market leader in supplying nonwoven disposable surgical gowns to hospitals. When P&G entered the market with a softer disposable gown, AHS realized that it was facing a sophisticated competitor. AHS is now in the process of thoroughly building up its marketing strength.
5. *Increasing sales expenditures.* The company may find that its expenditures on advertising, sales promotion, marketing research, and customer service are increasing without rhyme or reason. When this happens, the company may decide to reorganize and consolidate its marketing functions.

When any of these circumstances occur, top management's problem is how to convert the company from a traditional sales company to a modern marketing company. The issue is how to get all of the departments to think "customer." A companywide customer orientation has been expressed in many different ways:

- We're not the boss; the consumer is. What the consumer wants, the consumer gets.
- Under the marketing concept, the customer is at the top of the organization chart.
- A company should prefer a franchise over a market to a franchise over a plant.
- Look at the company through the customer's eyes.
- Instead of trying to market what is easiest for us to make, we must find out much more about what the consumer is willing to buy. In other words, we must apply our creativeness more intelligently to *people,* and their wants and needs, than to *products.*[10]

To acquire a modern marketing orientation, the company must consider the following.

Presidential Leadership

The company president's enthusiasm for marketing is a prerequisite to establishing a modern marketing company. The company president must understand the difference between marketing and sales, believe that marketing is the key to company growth and prosperity, and build marketing into presidential speeches and decisions.

Marketing Task Force and Outside Marketing Consultant

The president should appoint a marketing task force to develop a strategy for bringing modern marketing into the company. This task force should examine the need for marketing, set objectives, and anticipate problems in introducing it. The marketing task force would probably benefit from including an experienced outside marketing consultant to offer guidance and assistance.

A Corporate Marketing Department

A key step consists of establishing a corporate marketing department and hiring a capable and experienced marketing vice-president. The company should hire marketing talent away from leading marketing companies and should also hire recent graduates who have an MBA degree in marketing.

In-House Marketing Seminars

The new corporate marketing department should develop a program of in-house marketing seminars for top corporate management, divisional general managers, marketing and sales personnel, manufacturing personnel, R & D personnel, and so on. The seminars should start with the higher levels of management and move to lower levels. The aim of the marketing seminars is to bring about changes in the marketing knowledge, attitudes, and behavior of various executive groups.

Promotion of Market-Oriented Executives

The company should favor market-oriented individuals in selecting new division managers. A large public accounting firm that is currently trying to become market-oriented is giving preference to market-oriented rather than financially oriented individuals in promoting staff members to managing partners.

Installation of a Modern Marketing-Planning System

An excellent way to train an organization to think marketing is to install a modern market-oriented planning system. Managers will start their planning with market opportunity considerations and formulate marketing strategies to capitalize on these opportunities. Other departments will do their planning around these marketing strategies and forecasts.

EXHIBIT 6-3

BANKS LEARN THEIR MARKETING SLOWLY

Thirty years ago most banks neither understood nor practiced marketing. Bankers simply assumed that customers needed them. In the mid-1950s, however, competition increased to the point where some banks aggressively turned to marketing, though still not quite understanding it. Marketing has evolved through five stages in the banking industry:

1. *Marketing is advertising, sales promotion, and publicity.* At first the banks thought marketing simply amounted to the use of some advertising, sales promotion, and publicity to attract new customers.
2. *Marketing is smiling and a friendly atmosphere.* Banks then realized that keeping the new customers required a pleasant manner and an attractive environment.
3. *Marketing is innovation.* Then some banks realized that marketing consists of developing new services to meet new needs and wants. The marketing department would research customer needs, design new services, and develop plans for marketing them.
4. *Marketing is positioning.* Many banks soon found themselves going after the same customers and looking very much alike. A few banks started to concentrate on certain target markets in order to develop a distinct position in the market.
5. *Marketing is analysis, planning, and control.* Banks are currently realizing that effective marketing requires certain organizational forms and advanced systems of marketing analysis, planning, and control.

Not only banks but other institutions that turn to marketing seem to go through a period of "slow learning" before they fully grasp the revolutionary character of marketing.

The job of implementing a marketing orientation throughout the company is an uphill and never-ending battle. The purpose is not to resolve every issue in favor of the customer, no matter what the cost; but rather to remind others that customers are the foundation of the company's business.[11]

summary

The modern marketing department evolved through several stages to reach its contemporary form. It started as a simple sales department consisting of only a sales force. Later the sales department took on some ancillary functions, such as advertising and marketing research. As the ancillary functions grew in importance, many companies created a marketing department separate from the sales department to manage these other marketing activities. But the heads of sales and marketing often disagreed on company marketing policy, and eventually the two departments were merged into a modern marketing department headed by the marketing vice-president. A modern marketing department, however, does not automatically create a modern marketing company unless the other officers accept a customer orientation as the hub of the enterprise.

Modern marketing departments are organized in a number of ways. The most common form is the functional marketing organization in which the various marketing functions are headed by separate managers who report to the marketing vice-president. Another common form is the product management organization in which major products are the responsibility of product managers who work with the various functional specialists in the company to develop and achieve their plans for the product. Another, less common, form is the market management organization in which major markets are the responsibility of market managers who work with the various functional specialists to develop and achieve their plans for the market. Some large companies use a product management/market management organization, which combines both systems of management. Finally, multidivision companies normally develop a corporate marketing staff and separate marketing department for each division.

Marketing must work smoothly with the other functions in a company. In its pursuit of the customer's interests, marketing frequently comes into conflict with R & D, engineering, purchasing, manufacturing, inventory, finance, accounting, credit, and other functions that stress a cost minimization logic. These conflicts can be reduced when the company president commits the company to a customer orientation and when the marketing vice-president learns to work effectively with the other officers. Acquiring a modern marketing orientation requires presidential support, a marketing task force, outside marketing-consulting help, the establishment of a corporate marketing department, in-house marketing seminars, new marketing personnel, promotion of market-oriented executives, and a market-oriented marketing-planning system.

■ questions for discussion

1. Discuss how the marketing department probably evolved in the Chrysler Corporation.
2. What are the major advantages and disadvantages to organizing by function, geography, or end-use markets?
3. Discuss the pros and cons of instituting the product management organization for International Harvester's line of farm equipment (i.e., tractors, combines, implements such as plows and harrows.)
4. How does the product management/market management organization differ from the corporate-divisional organization?
5. Marketing is the most important function in any firm. Comment.
6. What do you think would be the area of strongest interdepartmental conflict with marketing in the following organizations? (a) Dow Chemical, (b) Catalina (swimwear), (c) Continental Bank of Illinois, and (d) Mars (candy company).
7. If a local museum was experiencing declining attendance, what strategies for building a marketing orientation would you suggest that the museum implement?

■ references

1. For further details on the marketing revolution at AT&T, see BRO UTTAL, "Selling Is No Longer Mickey Mouse at A.T.&T.," *Fortune,* July 17, 1978, pp. 98–104; and "Behind AT&T's Change at the Top," *Business Week,* November 6, 1978, pp. 115–39.
2. For details, see "General Food Corporation: Post Division," in *Organization Strategy: A Marketing Approach,* ed. E. Raymond Corey and Steven H. Star (Boston: Division of Research, Graduate School of Business Administration, Harvard University, 1971), pp. 201–30.
3. See ELMER E. WATERS, "Industrial Product Manager . . . Consumer Brand Manager: A Study in Contrast," *Industrial Marketing,* January 1969, pp. 45–49.
4. See DAVID J. LUCK, "Interfaces of a Product Manager," *Journal of Marketing,* October 1969, pp. 32–36.
5. ANDRALL E. PEARSON AND THOMAS W. WILSON, JR., *Making Your Organization Work* (New York: Association of National Advertisers, 1967), pp. 8–13.
6. For further reading, see RICHARD M. CLEWETT and STANLEY F. STASCH, "Shifting Role of the Product Manager," *Harvard Business Review,* January-February 1975, pp. 65–73; VICTOR P. BUELL, "The Changing Role of the Product Manager in Consumer Goods Companies," *Journal of Marketing,* July 1973, pp. 3–11; "The Brand Manager: No Longer King," *Business Week,* June 9, 1973; and JOSEPH A. MOREIN, "Shift from Brand to Product Line Marketing," *Harvard Business Review,* September-October 1975, pp. 56–64.
7. MARK HANAN, "Reorganize Your Company around Its Markets," *Harvard Business Review,* November-December 1974, pp. 63-74.
8. See B. CHARLES AMES, "Dilemma of Product/Market Management," *Harvard Business Review,* March-April 1971, pp. 66–74.
9. See WATSON SNYDER, JR., AND FRANK B. GRAY, *The Corporate Marketing Staff: Its Role and Effectiveness in Multi-Division Companies* (Cambridge, Mass.: Marketing Science Institute, April 1971).
10. This last quote is from CHARLES G. MORTIMER, "The Creative Factor in Marketing," Fifteenth Annual Parlin Memorial Lecture (Philadelphia Chapter, American Marketing Association, May 13, 1959).
11. For further discussion see EDWARD S. MCKAY, *The Marketing Mystique* (New York: American Management Association, 1972), pp. 22–30.

Cases

4 The Maytag Company

They still make them like they used to at The Maytag Co. in Newton, Iowa. But it doesn't seem to matter as much to washing machine buyers, and that may soon matter a great deal to Maytag. The Iowa manufacturer is holding on to its traditional share of the market—around 15% for washers; and its profit margin—11.5% last year—is almost twice the industry average. But the way the home-laundry business has been shaping up lately, Maytag may be caught in a long-term trend that could jeopardize its position as a successful independent in a business dominated by giant companies.

Maytag's problem is that, despite the fact that its products are, to cite the company's slogan, "built to last longer," they also cost more than competitors' machines, roughly $100 more. And that's apparently getting to be too much more for many people. While Maytag has picked up only a percentage point or so in market share since 1973, Whirlpool Corp., the biggest washermaker—including Sears, Roebuck & Co.'s house brands—increased its share by six percentage points in the same period, to nearly 45% of the total market.

In 1977, with the upturn of the home-building industry, automatic laundry equipment shipments by the industry climbed 11%. But Maytag's revenues were up only 8.8% to $299 million, and its net went up only 4.2%. Meanwhile, Whirlpool's net from appliance sales jumped 25% to 30% last year. Then, in this year's first quarter, a time of rising shipments for the industry, Maytag reported a 6.5% drop in sales (to $76 million) and a nearly 20% drop in earnings (to 57 cents a share).

Don't weep yet for Maytag. It earned better than 25% on stockholders' equity last year—and this without any debt leverage at all. But Maytag's very profitability, depending as it does on a premium-priced product, makes the company somewhat vulnerable. For one thing, since it doesn't sell to the big catalog chains, it lacks the aggressive marketing support of a company like Sears.

Then, too, real estate contractors usually don't look for the longest-lasting product on the market when they make purchases for acres of tract housing. They look for price. So do most first-time home buyers. Maytag is in the least likely position to benefit from further growth in the housing industry.

That means the company has to rely on the replacement market much more than others in the industry for its sales growth. And that's where its problems are going to be most acute. (It has been running those television spots featuring the Maytag repairman who has had nothing much to do for more than ten years.) That extra $100 or so that Maytag asks from consumers may still be worth it in terms of lower service costs, but the competitors may be catching up in quality. "The quality gap that existed five or ten years ago doesn't exist anymore," says Arnold P. Consdorf, editor of *Appliance Manufacturer*, a trade publication. "Model for model, I really don't see much difference as far as premium quality goes." Ned Davis, the appliance industry analyst at Mitchell, Hutchins, Inc., feels that strong new housing sales don't explain the whole difference in recent growth rates between Whirlpool and Maytag: "The critical thing is that the rationale to run out and buy a Maytag has declined." And a majority of dealers in a small sampling interviewed by *Forbes* agreed, citing consumer resistance to Maytag's higher price, despite a *Consumer Reports* comparison published last fall that still rates it as the washer that requires the fewest repairs and saves energy.

Out in Newton they don't seem terribly upset by the prospect before them. "The quality of all appliances has improved," Daniel J. Krumm, Maytag's affable president, concedes, but, he claims, "we have kept our edge." That remains to be seen. Meanwhile, however, Maytag's quality image hasn't rubbed off in the principal field it has chosen for diversification: dishwashers. The giant in that field is an obscure private company called Design & Manufacturing, Inc. that makes dishwashers for Sears and other major retailers and dominates the market with a 45% slice of the pie. Worse yet, somebody else—Hobart Corp.'s KitchenAid—has already beaten Maytag to the high-quality, high-price niche, vying with General Electric for the number-two spot with around 19% of the business. Maytag's market share in dishwashers has ambled between 4% and 6% since the start of a company-wide $50-million capital investment program that began in 1973, although it's been making dishwashers since 1966. "We might as well be selling the Jones dishwasher," Krumm admits.

In laundry machines, its basic business, Maytag does have alternatives. "We could vastly increase our sales if we made lower-quality machines, but how long could we make the premium one?" says Krumm, 51, who has been with Maytag for 25 years. They could, of course, also cut their prices closer to the levels of competitors in the washing machine segment of the market and probably boost volume substantially. That fat margin would certainly allow for it. But could it still earn 25% on its capital and continue to command a relatively high (11) price/earnings ratio?

There's no question that Maytag could finance pretty much anything it chose to do to work itself out of its still-profitable dilemma. It doesn't have a nickel of long-term debt on its books and no short-term either, and its $164 million in assets include over 20% in cash and equivalents. But it will probably have to make a major move soon. The simple, straightforward formula that has worked so well for so many years looks like it may no longer be valid.

Questions

1. What is Maytag's marketing strategy for its laundry equipment?
2. Why has it been so successful?
3. Should Maytag use the same strategy for its dishwashers, considering the widely held view that the Hobart Corporation's KitchenAid is already the premium product in the field? What would you recommend? Why?
4. In which of the following directions should Maytag attempt to grow:
   a. New-product types—e.g., stoves, refrigerators?
   b. New markets—e.g., builder, institutional, international?
   c. New channels—e.g., sell to Sears, Montgomery Ward, K-Mart?
   d. Develop a cheaper line of products? If so, should they be sold under the Maytag name or some other brand name?

5 The Pillsbury Company: Totino's Pizza

Frozen pizzas are hot. In fact, frozen pizzas are so hot that, after 15 years of continuous growth and after having reached sales in the United States of over half a billion dollars in 1977, their annual growth in dollars continues at an incredible 20 per cent.

Among the top three companies contending for supremacy in this enormous pie is Totino's, a subsidiary of the Pillsbury Company, Minneapolis, Minn. Advancing in a market of such limitless possibilities is like exploring an unknown, virgin rain forest. If you want to get out of the jungle alive you had better have more than one string to your bow. Totino's believes it has found that something extra to give it an edge.

A crisp crust pizza with some quite revolutionary features is Totino's new contribution to the frozen pizza marketplace. The company is so crust-confident that it is mounting the largest advertising campaign in its history this fall to boost the new product.

The object of Totino's confidence might best be described as an uneven, crusty layer of rounded hills puffed out as air bubbles from the surface. The crust is said to be crispy when bitten into, with a breadlike texture. It was invented by Totino's own Rose Totino.

"Today, for every 10 consumers who buy frozen pizza," said Rose, "three do not repeat. The repeat purchase pattern for all frozen pizza is just 67.1 per cent. Crust is the big reason. Consumers tell us that too many frozen pizzas have a crust like cardboard. And they won't buy it if they don't like the crust."

"But they love my new crisp crust. Tests show the repeat purchase intent soars after trial. It sells more pizza to more shoppers more often."

The new crust pizza products, which began shipment across the nation on September 5, were preceded by extensive consumer testing which, reports the company, indicated success for the products. Brokers to whom the products have been introduced are all reported to have welcomed it.

Totino's is pitching its new crust pizzas against the pizzerias. Its purpose is to broaden the frozen market, seeking to convince food store owners that the product can do what the owners dream about—lure buyers away from fast-food pizzerias and back into the store.

Headlining the state of pizza products with the new, crisp crust, and the only variety being introduced nationally at this time, is Totino's "Classic" brand pizza. This 20-ounce pizza comes in three varieties: a combination pizza with sausage, pepperoni, mozzarella, cheddar and Romano cheeses, and red and green peppers; sausage and mushroom (20.75 ounces); and pepperoni and mushroom varieties, each including mozzarella, cheddar, and Romano cheese and the red and green peppers. The addition of mushrooms to the latter two varieties is a first use of this ingredient for Totino's. The Classic brand name will be used only on the new, crisp crust product.

Under its "Party" pizza brand Totino's is introducing in six selected markets five varieties of an approximately 12-ounce pizza, all featuring the new crust. These are the kind of meal-on-a-crust pizzas that have been found to be so popular in the Middle West. The varieties are Canadian bacon, hamburger, sausage, pepperoni and cheese. Initial markets are Des Moines, Iowa; Omaha, Nebraska; Kansas City, Missouri; Denver, Colorado; Salt Lake City, Utah; Chicago, Illinois. Premiering in 8 selected markets are three varieties of new "Extra!" brand pizza, approximately 15 ounces each and also featuring the new crisp crust. Varieties are sausage, pepperoni, and a combination pizza. These and the Classic pizzas feature windows on their boxes to reveal the transparent inner wrapper.

Promotion will be headlined in appropriate markets by a television ad campaign, with accompanying color ads in local newspapers. A 60-second TV ad promotes the Classic and Extra! brands, while there are individual 20-second ads for the Classic and Extra! products. All of this begins early this month, as the transported product reaches retailer shelves.

Cents-off coupons will be featured in the newspaper advertisements. Party pizzas will carry in-pack coupons redeemable in Classic product, while Extra! brand pizzas will carry coupons redeemable on a second purchase of the product.

All of the new crust variety pizzas will be handled through normal distributor channels. Suggested retail prices are $2.49 to $2.59 for the Classic varieties, $1.69 to $1.79 for Extra!, and $1.09 to $1.19 for Party.

Source: "Totino's Heralds Unique Pizza Crust with Biggest Promotion Campaign," *Quick Frozen Foods*. October 1978. Reprinted by permission from *Quick Frozen Foods*. Copyright 1978.

Appendix: Additional Industry Information

1. Frozen pizza sales amounted to about $500 million in 1978 compared with pizzeria sales of almost $5 billion—about ten times more than grocery pizza sales. While frozen pizza represents about 30 percent of all pizza consumed, over 70 percent of all pizza, including pizzeria pizza, is eaten at home.
2. Pizza is popular because it is considered a balanced meal, provides good sensory experience, and is a finger food and fun to eat. Among frozen foods, pizza's growth rate is exceeded only by poultry's. It is less sensitive to recessionary/inflationary conditions than other frozen foods.
3. Regional taste differences are wide, and the variety makes it difficult for fast-food chains to customize, which makes it easier for small regional pizza chains to survive. Pizza is more fragmented and less chain-dominated than the hamburger segment of the fast-food chain business. Regional taste differences were also a reason why, until recently, the frozen pizza industry was highly fragmented—no strong national brands.
4. Frozen pizza categories and trade estimates of shares and growth rates for a recent year are:

	% OF TOTAL	GROWTH RATE
Single serve	17	−6
Regular	54	+8
Mid-size	8	−13
Deluxe	21	+47

5. The popularity of pizza crosses market segments. *Chain Institutions Magazine* found that in a recent year over 48 percent of the service operations surveyed reported that pizza is a "good seller" when it is on the menu. They included full-service restaurants, fast-food restaurants, hotels/motels, hospitals/nursing homes, schools, colleges/universities, and employee feeding facilities.
6. The high growth rate of frozen pizza sales has attracted a number of large food processors, including Pillsbury (Totino's), Quaker Oats (Celeste), American

Home Products (Chef Boy-ar-dee), Nestlé (Stouffer's), General Mills (Saluto), and H. J. Heinz (La Pizzeria). The major independents are Jeno's, Tony's, and John's. Jeno's and Totino's are the market leaders, with market shares of about 19 percent each. Celeste and Tony's have about 8–9 percent each, and the others each have about 5 percent or less.

7. Major consumer goods companies are strongly entrenched in non-Totino's marketing areas. Local brands have strong positions in many of the same areas. The geographic areas in which Totino's pizzas are marketed account for about 75 percent of the nation's frozen pizza business. Totino's has a very strong brand position in those areas. It is particularly strong in the deluxe and party (regular) categories.
8. Frozen food brokers are commonly used to sell the product. Jeno's is said to be the only firm with its own warehouse delivery system.
9. Trade deals are a major marketing tool for the industry. They are designed to encourage low-price promotions by the retailer to the consumer. The warfare for market share keeps prices low and cuts potentially high margins. In the trade, it is said that no one is making a lot of money yet from frozen pizzas.

Source for Appendix: Based on materials presented by Mr. George Masko, V.P. The Pillsbury Company to the Marketing Policy Class at Northwestern's J. L. Kellogg Graduate School of Management, February, 1979.

Questions

1. What are the major marketing threats and opportunities for Totino's pizza?
2. Should Totino's consider pizzerias, regional frozen pizza firms, and national food processors with pizza products of equal importance as competitors? If so, why? If not, which is the most important? The least important?
3. What are Totino's competitive advantages and how can they be used effectively?
4. What factors may limit (a) the rate of growth of frozen pizza sales and (b) Totino's rate of growth and profitability?
5. As the marketing manager for Totino's, what additional information do you feel you would need to develop for
   a. Next year's marketing plan for Totino's in general terms?
   b. A three-year marketing plan?

6 Hanes Corporation: From L'eggs to Faces

Hanes Corp. plowed along for 57 years as a none-too-sparkling apparel producer until 1971, when it introduced L'eggs, a distinctively packaged line of women's pantyhose. The product rapidly propelled the company's sales and earnings upward and made Hanes the dominant force in the $1.2 billion women's hosiery market. This week, banking on the marketing and distribution expertise it gained from the L'eggs venture, Hanes will begin a foray into a market that is wholly new to it: the $1.6 billion cosmetics business.

In some 700 supermarkets and 300 drug and discount stores in Kansas City and Cincinnati, display racks will blossom with an 80-item line of Hanes's cosmetics, called L'aura.[1] If the tests prove successful, Hanes will probably push the line into other markets by early next year. The cosmetics line, Hanes hopes, will give the company the same kind of boost that it got from L'eggs in 1971. Revenues that year were $176 million; they hit $372 million last year. And earnings are up more than fivefold since 1971, reaching $18.6 million last year.

The new venture takes Hanes into a segment of a crowded and ferociously competitive market. But the segment it has picked out—sales in supermarkets and discount drug stores—is one that giants of the cosmetics business, such as Revlon, Avon Products, and Chesebrough-Pond's, have yet to enter to any significant degree. Up to now two brands have been dominant in this market: Maybelline (a product of Schering-Plough Corp.) and Cover Girl (a Noxell Corp. product).

Hanes figures that a marketing and distribution strategy borrowed from its L'eggs venture will win it a substantial share of the market. Among the key elements in that strategy:

- The cosmetics will be sold from open displays, appealing to the impulse shopper. The displays are being built by New York City's Howard Display, Inc., which created the award-winning L'eggs displays. And Hanes is pushing to have them placed near checkout counters, just as it has done with its L'eggs displays.
- The packaging will be distinct from any other cosmetics on supermarket shelves, just as the packaging for L'eggs set that product apart from the competition. Each cosmetics item will be packaged in a burgundy-colored box with small plastic windows; supermarket competitors usually use plastic-blister packaging.
- Hanes's own sales force will keep the displays in proper shape and will replenish stocks. Bypassing the middleman and serving retailers directly in this fashion proved to be a major element in L'eggs' success, and Hanes is counting on the approach to work with L'aura.

But until Hanes begins a blitz of heavy TV and print advertising for the new line in Kansas City and Cincinnati toward the end of August, the company is being very cautious in talking about its new product. President Robert E. Elberson has said only: "This is one of the few times that a company has introduced an entire line of cosmetics at once. Usually one or two products are introduced and line extensions follow."

Behind the caution lies Elberson's disappointment with an earlier effort to transfer the L'eggs marketing concept to selling socks and men's underwear. That effort, begun two years ago, has not reached far beyond the initial test markets in half a dozen cities, and although Hanes has not scrapped the product lines, they are not expected to move into the national marketplace any time soon. One problem, Hanes found, was that competition from such widely known brands as Fruit of the Loom was deeply entrenched. And in order to carry a full range of colors

[1]The name *L'aura* was changed to *L'erin* at the request of Richardson-Merrell Co., which was already using it.

and sizes, the company had to use much larger display racks than it needs for L'eggs or L'aura.

Each L'aura display rack takes up 4 sq. ft., which is a lot for today's crowded supermarkets to relinquish without fairly sure profits in sight. But Harry P. Knabb, manager of purchasing and package development for L'eggs New Ventures Div., says that stores in the two test markets are cooperating and "early indications are favorable." Larry Day, director of general merchandising for Great Atlantic & Pacific Tea Co. in the Kansas City area, adds: "All of our 30 stores in this area will carry the line. The products are attractively packaged, and I'm optimistic." The test market retailers will get a 40% markup on the cosmetics.

Tough competition. It will probably cost Hanes heavily to establish an image for its new line and to take a slice out of the competition. When it started selling L'eggs in 1971, leadership in the hosiery business was conspicuously absent: Hundreds of companies sold some 600 different brands of stockings and pantyhose, and consumers generally saw their products as being all alike. Hanes's product, with its unique egg-shaped container, easily stood out and won the customer's attention.

Cosmetics, though, already has imaginative market leaders working hard to maintain the customer's loyalty. "Hanes will have to convince the consumer that its products are different," says Frank LeCates, an analyst at Donaldson, Lufkin & Jenrette Securities Corp., "and to do this it will have to pull its products through with heavy and expensive advertising." Hanes, maintaining its low profile before the test marketing of its new line begins, in keeping mum on its ad spending plans for its new cosmetics. But the company is no slouch when it comes to spending for advertising. Last year its ad budget was more than $27.1 million—only a shade behind the $29.7 spent by Revlon, a company almost three times its size.

Source: "A Hosiery Giant Jumps from L'eggs to Faces," Reprinted from the August 22 issue of *Business Week* by special permission,

Questions

1. What basic characteristics of the strategy are responsible for the phenomenal success of L'eggs?
2. Indicate the reasons why workingwomen shopping in supermarkets (a) would be and (b) would not be inclined to buy the following products: women's panty hose, cosmetics, men's socks, or men's underwear.
3. Indicate the reason why supermarkets (a) would be and (b) would not be inclined to offer the following products for sale: women's panty hose, cosmetics, men's socks, or men's underwear.
4. What modifications in the L'eggs strategy, if any, would you suggest for use with L'erin cosmetics?

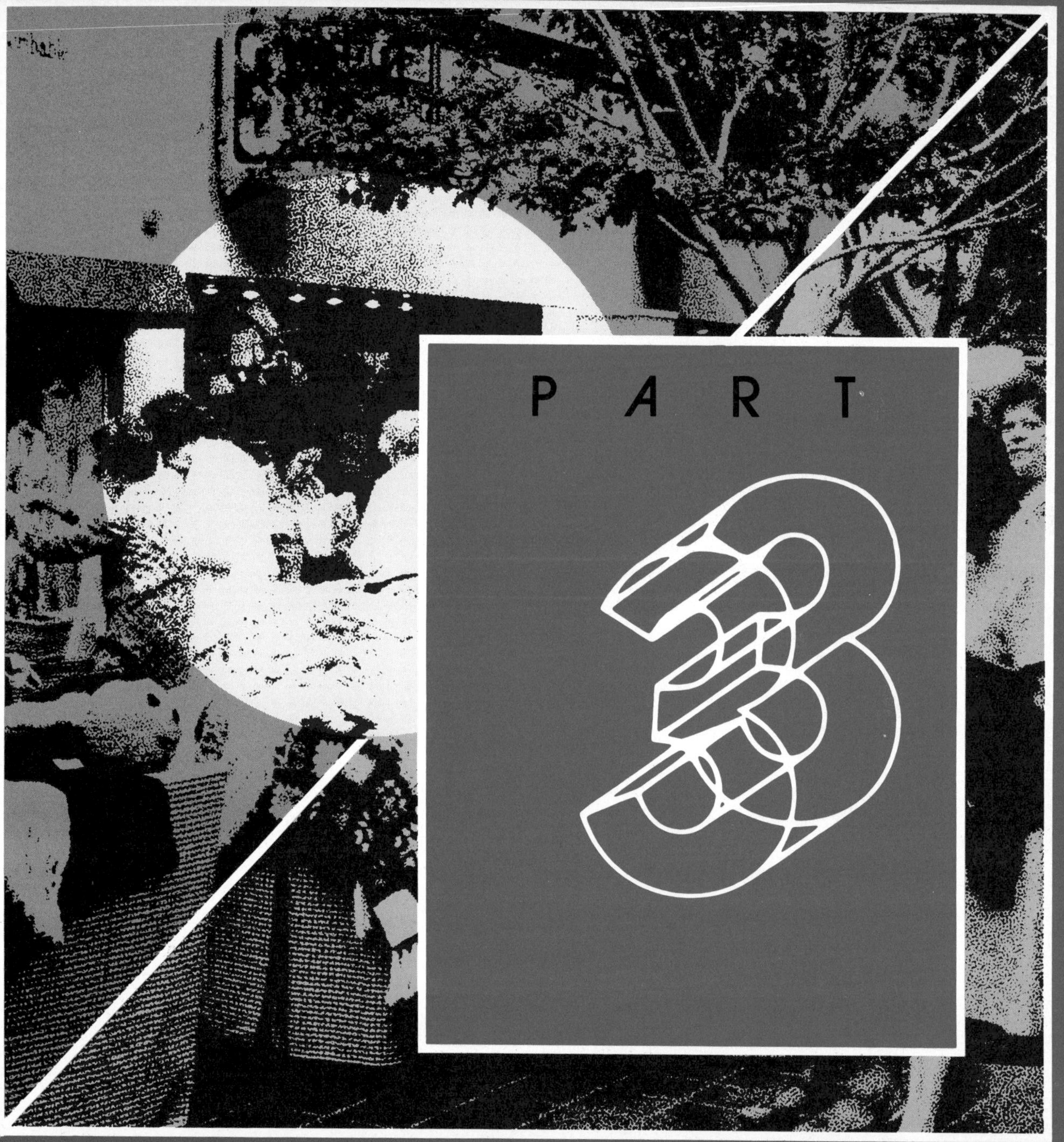

target market analysis

THE MARKETING ENVIRONMENT

The Wilson Sporting Goods Company isn't smiling much today, at least not its tennis division. As the market leader with an estimated 35 percent of the tennis racket and tennis ball market, is isn't happy about the decline in tennis racket sales from a peak of 9 million units in 1975 to about 7 million units in 1979. Many retailers are now complaining about carrying an inventory glut of new frames, imports, and lower-priced rackets.

The big question is whether this is a temporary dip or a permanent decline in a sports craze that attracted as many as 34 million Americans in the mid-1970s. The sports environment is tricky to predict. Other sports have shown booms and busts in the past. Bowling peaked in the early 1960s, snowmobiles in 1971, and skiing in 1973. The sequel is familiar in all cases: New producers are attracted to the rapidly expanding industry in its boom phase, new plants are built, overcapacity develops, prices are cut drastically, and marginal competitors are forced out before the industry stabilizes to a lower and more normal level of operation.

What's causing the slowdown? In part, many persons who joined the tennis bandwagon found they couldn't play well and they have been dropping out. Fewer new players are coming in because they are being attracted to racquetball and jogging, which are currently hot sports. (Fortunately, Wilson enjoys a good position in racquetball, with an annual sales growth of 30 percent.) Some potential new players are scared off by the price of rackets and balls, and many current players are finding that tennis club membership fees that range from $300 to $600 for a season are too high. The changing age distribution has something to do with it because the young adult group, which is the source of most of the new players, is growing at a much slower rate than in the early 1970s.

Tennis equipment manufacturers don't plan to sit back and take it on the chin. The sport is basically sound and feeds into the growing national interest in physical exercise and health. Exciting tennis personalities playing championship matches can be watched by millions of TV viewers. Tennis fans can live out tennis life styles at luxurious tennis clubs and ranches in many scenic parts of the country.

From time to time, the industry is able to stimulate a fresh wave of replacement racket buying as a result of technological breakthroughs. This happened with the introduction of metal rackets to replace wooden rackets in the early 1970s and is now happening with the development of oversized rackets. The Prince racket, which measures

112 square inches compared with the normal 70 square inches, was pooh-poohed when introduced in 1976. However, it caught on with players who tried it and is now racking up sales of over one hundred thousand units a year. The oversized racket carries a higher price tag and is attracting a host of imitators.

So Wilson has to watch the tennis marketing environment with great care. The environment seems to call the shots and Wilson has to take the swings.[1]

□Marketing planning begins with the company analyzing its marketing environment. The marketing environment is in continual flux, spinning off new opportunities and new threats. Instead of changing in a slow and predictable way, the environment is capable of causing major surprises and shocks. Which oil companies in 1971 would have predicted the end of cheap energy in the following years? How many managers at Gerber Foods foresaw the end of the "baby boom"? Which auto companies foresaw the tremendous impact Ralph Nader and consumers would have on their business decisions? Drucker has called this an *Age of Discontinuity,*[2] and Toffler has described it as *Future Shock.*[3]

The key to an organization's success is its ability to spot and adapt to changes in the marketing environment. Every company needs to establish an environmental monitoring system that continually tracks the changing environment. A major company such as General Electric employs over one hundred professionals to monitor the marketing environment (see Exhibit 7-1). Smaller companies have to settle for simply being alert and occasionally using an outside consultant to assess its marketing environment objectively.

In this chapter we focus on the *macroenvironment, which is the totality of major institutions and forces that are external and potentially relevant to the firm.* The macroenvironment can be factored into six major components: demographic, economic, ecological, technological, political, and cultural. We will examine the current trends occurring in each component of the macroenvironment and consider their implications for company marketing strategy.

EXHIBIT 7-1

ENVIRONMENTAL FORECASTING AT GENERAL ELECTRIC

General Electric operates one of the most sophisticated environmental forecasting departments of any major company. The company has abandoned the extrapolation methods of the past and instead views the future as probabilistic. In January of each year, the forecasters prepare three different scenarios of the environment:

- —A benchmark scenario,
- —A "best of all possible worlds" scenario, and
- —A "worst of all possible worlds" scenario.

Each scenario is a self-contained picture of relevant trends, events, and discontinuities that are selected for their occurrence probability and their potential impact on the business. For example, the forecasters see a substantially different consumer market in the 1980s with a different age distribution, birthrate, consumer life styles, and attitudes toward business. To GE, forecasting is the business of managing uncertainty through anticipating possible scenarios and preparing contingency plans.

Source: See Ian H. Wilson, William R. George, and Paul J. Soloman, "Strategic Planning for Marketers," *Business Horizons*, December 1978, pp. 65-73.

demographic environment

The demographic environment is of major interest to marketers because people make up markets. Seven major demographic trends are reviewed below.

Worldwide Explosive Population Growth

Perhaps the major fact about the world population is its "explosive" growth:

- In 1970 the population totaled 3.6 billion and the rate of growth was 2.1 percent per year. The doubling time at this growth rate is 33 years. Thus, not only has the population been growing exponentially, but the rate of growth has also been growing.[4]

The world population explosion has been a major concern of many governments and groups throughout the world. Two factors underlie this concern. First, the earth's resources may not be able to support this much human life, particularly at levels of living that represent the aspiration of most people. And second, the rate of population growth is not equal everywhere but is highest in the countries and communities that can least afford it.

The rate of increase of the world's population has great importance for business. A growing population means growing human needs. It means growing markets if there is sufficient purchasing power. On the other hand, if there is insufficient purchasing power, it means recession and vigorous attacks against business institutions.

Slowdown in U.S. Birthrate

The "baby boom" in the United States has been replaced by a "birth dearth." The U.S. population stood at 216.8 million on July 1, 1977.[5] The birthrate dipped below the "replacement rate" of 2.0 children per family to a record low of 1.8 in 1977. The preschool population declined 11.2 percent between 1970 and 1977. Among the factors contributing to smaller families are (1) the desire to improve personal living standards, (2) the increasing desire of women to work outside the home, (3) improved technology and knowledge of birth control, and (4) the increasing concern about the future of civilization on this planet.

The declining birthrate is a threat to some industries, a boon to others. It has created sleepless nights for executives in such businesses as children's toys, clothes, furniture, and food. For many years the Gerber Company advertised "Babies are our business—our *only* business" but quietly dropped this slogan some time ago. The company now sells life insurance to older folks, using the theme "Gerber now babies the over-50's." Johnson and Johnson has responded by successfully persuading adults to use the company's baby powder, baby oil, and baby hair shampoo. Meanwhile industries such as hotels, airlines, and restaurants have benefited from the fact that young couples have more leisure time and income.

Aging of U.S. Population

Recent generations have benefited from a substantial decline in the death rate. Average life expectancy is now 72.5 years and may reach 74.0 years by the year 2000. This, coupled with the declining birthrate, has meant an aging U.S. population. The median age in the United States is now 30 and is forecast to reach 35 by the year 2000.[6]

Different age groups, of course, will increase at different rates. The number of children and teenagers will increase by only 2 percent in the 1980–90 decade, foretelling a possible weakening in influence of America's youth culture. The decline forebodes a slowdown in the sales growth of motorcycles, baseball and football equipment, denim clothing, records, and colleges.

The 20–34 age group will undergo a modest increase of only 3 percent in this decade. Marketers who sell to this group—furniture makers, vacation planners, tennis and ski equipment manufacturers—will have to market more usage of these products to this group, since the number of users will not increase substantially.

The 35–49 age group will undergo the greatest increase of all age groups in the coming decade, namely, 37 percent. Members of this group are well established in their work life and are a major market for large homes, new automobiles, clothing, and educational expenses for their children.

The 50–64 age group will shrink by 1 percent in this decade. These "empty-nesters" whose children have left home will find themselves with more time and income on their hands. This group is a major market for eating out, travel, expensive clothes, and golf and other forms of recreation.

The over-65 age group will show the second largest increase in the coming decade, up by 20 percent. This group foretells a burgeoning demand for retirement homes and communities, campers, quieter forms of recreation (fishing, golf), single-portion food packaging, and medical goods and services (medicine, eyeglasses, canes, hearing aids, and convalescent homes). This group also means a slowing down in the adoption of new cultural ideas, more conservative politics, and new rights demanded by senior citizens to protect their standard of living.

The Changing American Family

The American ideal of the two-children, two-car suburban family has been losing some of its luster. There will be fewer families forming and surviving, and they will show a different orientation. Here are the major forces at work:

1. *Later marriage.* Although 96 percent of all Americans will marry, the average age of couples marrying for the first time has been rising over the years and now stands at 23.8 years for males and 21.3 years for females. This will slow down the sales of engagement and wedding rings, bridal outfits, and life insurance.
2. *Fewer children.* Couples with no children under 18 now make up 47 percent of all families. The newly married are also delaying childbearing longer. Of those families that have children, the mean number of children is 1.8, down from 3.5 in 1955.

3. *Higher divorce rate.* The United States has the world's highest divorce rate, with about 38 percent of the marriages ending in divorce. This has created over a million single-parent families and the need for additional housing units. About 79 percent of those divorced remarry, leading to the phenomenon of the "blended" family. Currently about 72.2 percent of all males are married and 66.2 percent of all females.
4. *More working wives.* Today more than 40 percent of all married women with school-age children hold some kind of job. There is less stigma attached to working, a greater number of job opportunities, and new freedom resulting from birth-control acceptance. Women who work constitute a market for better clothing, day-nursery services, home-cleaning services, and more frozen dinners. The growing number of workingwomen means less viewing of television soap operas and less reading of domestic women's magazines. Their incomes contribute 40 percent of the household's income and influence the purchase of higher-quality goods and services. Marketers of such things as tires, automobiles, insurance, and travel service have found it necessary to change their advertising messages and media selections so as to reach the increasingly significant workingwomen's market.[7]

The Rise of Nonfamily Households

An important development is the rapid rise in the number of *nonfamily households.* These households take several forms, each constituting a different market segment with special needs:

1. *Single-adult households.* Many young adults leave home earlier and move into their own apartments. In addition, many divorced and widowed people live alone. Altogether, more that 15.5 million people live alone and account for 21 percent of all the households. The SSWD group (single, separated, widowed, divorced) need smaller apartments; inexpensive and smaller appliances, furniture, and furnishings; and food that is packaged in smaller sizes. Their car preferences are different in that they buy half of all Mustangs and other small specialty cars, and only 8 percent of the large cars.[8] Singles are a market for various services that supply opportunities for singles to meet each other, such as singles bars, tours, and cruises.
2. *Two-person cohabitor households.* There may be as many as 3 million to 6 million unmarried people living together today, primarily heterosexual couples but homosexual couples as well. Since their arrangements are more temporary, they are a market for inexpensive or rental furniture and furnishings.
3. *Group households.* Group households can be found consisting of three or more persons of the same or opposite sex sharing expenses by living together. This is a frequently found pattern among college students and also occurs among certain secular and religious groups who live in communes.

Marketers should consider the special needs and buying habits of nonfamily households, since their numbers are growing more rapidly than those of family households.

Geographical Shifts in Population

Americans are a mobile people, with approximately one out of five, or 42 million Americans, moving each year. Among the major mobility trends are the following:

1. *Movement of people to the Sunbelt states.* Over the next decade the West will experience a population growth of 17 percent, and the South will experience a growth of 14 percent. Major cities in the North, on the other hand, have been experiencing a decline in population between 1970 and 1976 (New York, 4.7 percent; Pittsburgh, 4.1 percent; Jersey City, 5.8 percent; and Newark, 3.2 percent). These

regional population shifts are of special interest to marketers because of marked differences in regional expenditure patterns and consumer behavior. Consumers in the West, for example, spend relatively less on food and relatively more on automobiles than their counterparts in the Northeast. The exodus to the Sunbelt will lessen the demand for warm clothing and home heating equipment and increase the demand for air conditioning.

2. *Movement from rural to urban areas.* This movement has been going on for over a century. In 1880 approximately 70 percent of the nation's population lived in rural areas; at the present time approximately 70 percent live in urban areas. Cities tend to be characterized by a faster pace of living, more commuting, typically higher incomes, and a greater variety of goods and services than can be found in the small towns and rural areas that dot America. The largest cities, such as New York, Chicago, and San Francisco, account for most of the sales of expensive furs, perfumes, luggage, and works of art; and these cities support the opera, ballet, and other forms of "high culture." Recently, however, there has been a slight shift of population back to rural areas.

3. *Movement from the city to the suburbs.* Many persons have moved far away from their places of work, owing largely to the development of automobiles, major highways, and rapid rail and bus transit. Cities have become surrounded by suburbs, and these suburbs in turn by "exurbs." The U.S. Census Bureau has created a separate population classification for sprawling urban concentrations, called Standard Metropolitan Statistical Areas (SMSA).[9] Over 75 percent of the nation's entire population (and 95 percent of the nation's urban population) are estimated to live in the 277 recognized Standard Metropolitan Statistical Areas, and it is the SMSAs rather than the cities proper that constitute the primary market focus of firms. Firms normally distinguish between the city and the suburban segments of the metropolitan areas. About 60 percent of the total metropolitan population now live in suburbs. Suburban areas are frequently marked by a style of living different from that in the cities. Suburbs tend to be characterized by casual, outdoor living, greater neighbor interaction, higher incomes, and younger families. Suburban dwellers are the source of much of the demand for station wagons, home workshop equipment, garden furniture, lawn and gardening tools and supplies, and outdoor cooking equipment. Retailers have recognized the importance of convenience and have brought their goods out to the suburbs through the development of branch department stores and suburban shopping centers.

   At the same time, marketers should recognize a recent countermovement back to the central city, especially in cities where urban renewal has been successful. Young adults as well as older adults whose children have grown up are attracted by the superior cultural and recreational opportunities and less interested in suburban commuting and gardening. This means strong opportunities for new high-rise apartment construction and new retail outlets with the central city.

A Better-educated Populace

The number of Americans who have attended or graduated from college will reach 44 million by 1985, or 19 percent of the population. This will present both opportunities and challenges to marketers. A greater number of better-educated, white-collar workers will mean increased affluence and demand for quality products, books, upscale magazines, and travel. It will also mean a decline in television viewing because the better-educated consumers tend to watch TV less than does the population at large.

These demographic trends are highly reliable for the short and intermediate run. There is little excuse for a company's being suddenly surprised by a demo-

Table 7-1 The Changing Population Mix and Which Industries Are Likely to Profit

INDUSTRY	BABY BOOM GENERATION MATURES	MORE ELDERLY PERSONS	MORE WORKING WOMEN	SMALLER FAMILY UNITS
Airlines	Many will have more money for travel as they get older. ✔✔✔	They have the time to travel but inflation may rob them of the means. ✔	Second Income allows more families to take trips; more single women have money. ✔✔✔	More disposable income per member; more economical to fly than drive. ✔✔
Apparel	Will spend more on clothes as they age; shift from casual to higher quality. ✔✔✔	Older people spend less on clothing.	Career women need more clothing and have the money to buy it. ✔✔✔	A shift toward higher-quality, higher-margin merchandise. ✔✔
Cosmetics	This group is moving through prime cosmetic-usage years. ✔✔✔	Elderly women often spend less on cosmetics.	Career women use more cosmetics, and can better afford them. ✔✔✔	More income, more divorced women, more single women. ✔✔
Electronics (Consumer)	Rising incomes provide means to buy better-quality stereos, TVs, etc. ✔✔	Little demand from this group; often forced to make do with older products.	Can buy more and higher-priced merchandise. ✔✔	More income per capita; electronic entertainment replaces family activities. ✔✔
Machinery (Agricultural)	No significant effect.	No significant effect.	No significant effect.	Need for mechanized equipment as substitute for manual labor. ✔
Pollution control	No significant effect.	Driving less; will lessen demand for exhaust control equipment. ✔	Slightly increased use of packaging materials adds to waste problems. ✔	Slightly increased use of packaging materials adds to waste problems. ✔
Health care	Little effect.	Largest consumers of health care products and services. ✔✔✔	Working women are having fewer children.	No significant effect.
Home furnishings	Will want to improve home environments. ✔✔✔	Very small factor in this market.	With two paychecks, can afford better furnishings. ✔✔	More households, all needing basic furnishings. ✔✔
Leisure time	With rising incomes, they will spend more on travel and recreation. ✔✔✔	Has most leisure time of all; if inflation abates, will be heavier spenders. ✔	Single or married, they have money to spend on leisure activities. ✔✔✔	More money per person, and with fewer children, more time for leisure. ✔✔✔
Restaurants	This large group will have more money to eat out. ✔✔✔	The elderly tend to eat out less.	Little time or energy to cook at home. ✔✔✔	Smaller families visit restaurants more frequently. ✔✔✔
Retailing	As affluence increases, group will trade up in merchandise purchases. ✔✔✔	Very price conscious.	Likely to spend more on high-margin merchandise. ✔✔✔	High demand stemming from more disposable income per capita. ✔✔✔
Textiles	Likely to expand wardrobes and spend heavily on home furnishings. ✔✔	The elderly buy less clothing and home furnishings.	Good for both apparel and furnishings. ✔✔✔	A shift toward higher-priced fabrics. ✔

✔✔✔Very positive ✔✔Positive ✔Mildly positive □Neutral □Negative

Source: *Chicago Tribune,* April 8, 1979, Section 5, p. 1.

graphic development. The alert firm can list the major demographic trends, spell out their implications for the particular industry, and classify these implications as running from very positive to very negative. This is done in Table 7-1 for twelve major industries. In the case of airlines, for example, each population trend is expected to have a positive sales and profit impact.

economic environment

Markets require not only people but purchasing power. Total purchasing power is a function of current income, prices, savings, and credit availability. Marketers should be aware of four main trends in the economic environment.

Slowdown in Real Income Growth

In 1976 American per capita income stood at $6,393 and median household income stood at $12,686. Although money income per capita keeps rising, there has been little or no growth in real income per capita for the last several years. Real income per capita has been hurt by (1) an inflation rate exceeding the money income growth rate, (2) an unemployment rate between 6 and 8 percent, and (3) an increase in the tax burden. These developments have reduced *disposable personal income,* which is the amount people have left after taxes. Furthermore, many people have found their *discretionary income* reduced, which is the amount they have left after paying for their basic food, clothing, shelter, insurance, and other necessaries. Reductions in discretionary income hurt sellers of discretionary goods and services, such as automobiles, large appliances, and vacations. On the positive side, however, there has been a rise in two-earner families, which has increased average family income.

In response to the real income decline, many Americans have turned to more cautious buying. A survey by *Better Homes and Gardens* indicated that 72 percent of the respondents were buying more "store brands" and fewer "national brands" to save money.[10] Many companies have introduced economy versions of their products and have turned to price appeals in their advertising messages. As for durable goods, some consumers have postponed their purchase of these items and other consumers have made a purchase out of fear that prices will be 10 percent higher next year. Many families have begun to feel that a large home, two cars, foreign travel, and private higher education are now beyond their reach.

Marketers should also pay attention to income differences as well as average income trends. Income distribution in the United States is still pronouncedly skewed. At the top are *upper-class consumers,* whose expenditure patterns have not been affected by current economic events and who are a major market for luxury goods (Rolls Royces starting at $49,000) and services (round-the-world cruises starting at $10,000). There is a comfortable *middle class* that exercises some expenditure restraint but is able to afford expensive clothes, minor antiques, and a small boat or second home. The *working class* must stick closer to the basics of food, clothing, and shelter and must husband its resources and try hard to save. Finally, there is the *underclass* (persons on welfare) and *retirees,* who have to count their pennies carefully when making purchases of even the most basic kind.

Income levels and growth rates also vary regionally. They are affected by the level of local economic activity and employment, the rate of in- and out-migration, and union wage scales. Marketers have to take geographical income differences into account in planning their marketing programs.

Continued Inflationary Pressure

A high rate of inflation continues to push up the prices of homes, furniture, medical care, and food. Inflation leads consumers to search for opportunities to save money, including buying cheaper brands in large economy sizes, buying from less-expensive retail outlets, performing more of their own services, and bartering services with others.

Changing Savings and Debt Patterns

Consumer expenditures are also affected by consumer savings and debt patterns. Eighty-four percent of American spending units hold some liquid assets, the median amount being $800. Americans hold their savings in the form of bank savings accounts, bonds and stocks, real estate, insurance, and other assets. These savings are a major source of financing major durable purchases.

Consumers can also increase their purchases through borrowing. Consumer credit has been a major contributor to the rapid growth of the American economy, enabling people to buy more than their current income and savings permitted, thus creating more jobs and still more income and more demand. In 1978, outstanding consumer credit (including home mortgages) stood at $1 trillion, or $4,600 for every man, woman, and child in America. The cost of credit, however, is also high (with interest rates between 10 and 20 percent), and consumers are spending around twenty-one cents of every dollar they earn to pay off existing debts. This retards the further growth of housing and other durable-goods markets that are heavily dependent on credit.

Changing Consumer Expenditure Patterns

As people's incomes change, marketers can expect pronounced shifts in the relative demand for different categories of goods and services. The particular types of shifts were stated as early as 1875 by the German statistician Ernst Engel, who compared the budgets of individual working-class families. Engel observed that while rising family income tended to be accompanied by increased spending in all categories, *the percentage spent on food tended to decline, the percentage spent on housing and household operations tended to remain constant, and the percentage spent on other categories (clothing, transportation, recreation, health, and education) and savings tended to increase.* These "laws" have generally been validated in subsequent budget studies. At the same time, a company involved in a particular product category will want to look more closely at how expenditures in this product category vary with income. For example, a higher income may not lead to buying more food but may lead to buying higher-quality food, thus causing food expenditures to remain constant for a while. But, in general, as incomes rise, people will spend a higher proportion of their incomes on major durables, luxury goods, and services.

Changes in such major economic variables as money income, cost of living, interest rates, and savings and borrowing patterns have an immediate impact on the marketplace. Some industries are particularly income-sensitive, and companies in these industries would be well advised to invest in sophisticated economic-forecasting information systems. Businesses do not have to be wiped out by a downturn in economic activity. With adequate forewarning, they can take the necessary steps to tighten their sales and ride out the economic storm.

ecological environment

The 1960s witnessed a growing public concern over whether the natural environment was being irreparably damaged by the industrial activities of modern nations. Kenneth Boulding pointed out that the planet earth was like a spaceship in danger of running out of fuel if it failed to recycle its materials. The Meadowses and others, in *The Limits to Growth,* raised concern about the adequacy of future natural resources to sustain economic growth. Rachel Carson, in *The Silent Spring,* pointed out the environmental damage to water, earth, and air caused by industrial activity of certain kinds. These warnings led to the formation of various watchdog groups such as the Sierra Club and Friends of the Earth, as well as concerned legislators who have proposed various measures to regulate the impact of industrial activity on the natural environment.

Marketers should be aware of the challenges and opportunities created by four trends in the ecological environment.

Impending Shortages of Certain Raw Materials

The earth's materials fall into three groups: the infinite, the finite renewable, and the finite nonrenewable. *Infinite resources,* such as water and air, pose no immediate problem, although some groups argue that there is too high a level of pollution. Environmental groups have lobbied for the banning of aerosol cans because of their potential damage to the ozone layer of air, and they have fought against the pollution of water bodies such as Lake Erie and various streams by unregulated industrial wastes.

Finite renewable resources, such as forests and food, pose no immediate problem, but perhaps a longer-run problem. Companies in the forestry business are now required to reforest timberlands in order to protect the soil and to ensure a sufficient level of wood supply to meet future demand. Food supply can be a major problem in that the amount of arable land is relatively fixed and urban areas are constantly expanding to absorb farmland.

Finite nonrenewable resources, such as oil, coal, and various minerals, do pose a serious problem:

- . . . it would appear at present that the quantities of platinum, gold, zinc, and lead are not sufficient to meet demands . . . silver, tin, and uranium may be in short supply even at higher prices by the turn of the century. By the year 2050, several more minerals may be exhausted if the current rate of consumption continues.[11]

The marketing implications are many. Firms that rely on these minerals face substantial cost increases, even if the materials remain available. They may not find it easy to pass these cost increases on to the consumer. There is a need to find substitute minerals. Firms engaged in research and development and exploration have an incredible opportunity to develop valuable new sources and materials.

Increased Cost of Energy One finite nonrenewable resource, oil, has created the most serious problem for future economic growth. The major industrial economies of the world are heavily dependent on oil, and until substitute forms of energy can be developed on a practical basis, oil will continue to dominate the world political and economic picture. The shortage of oil and its price manipulation have created a frantic search for alternative forms of energy. Coal is once again popular, and companies are searching for practical schemes to harness solar, nuclear, wind, and other forms of energy. In the solar energy field alone, hundreds of firms are putting out first-generation products to harness solar energy for heating homes and other uses.[12] Other firms are searching for ways to make a practical electric automobile, with a potential prize of billions going to the winner.

Increased Levels of Pollution Some portion of modern industrial activity will inevitably damage the quality of the natural environment. One has only to think of the disposal of chemical and nuclear wastes, the dangerous mercury levels in the ocean, the quantity of DDT and other chemical pollutants in the soil and food supply, and the littering of the environment with nonbiodegradable bottles, plastics, and other packaging materials.

The public concern constitutes a marketing opportunity in two ways. First, it creates a large market for pollution control solutions such as scrubbers and recycling centers. Second, it creates a major marketing opportunity for finding alternative ways to produce and package goods that do not cause environmental damage.[13]

Increasing Government Intervention in Natural Resource Management The growing concern with the deteriorating quality of the natural environment has led various government agencies to take an active role in regulating and enforcing conservation and pollution control behavior. Ironically, the effort to protect the environment often runs counter to the attempt to increase employment and economic growth, such as when business is forced to buy expensive pollution cleanup equipment instead of investing in capital-producing goods. From time to time, conservation politics takes a back seat to economic growth politics. Marketing management must be alert to regulatory developments and to the opportunities that open up with the effort to protect the natural environment.

Marketing management will have to pay increasing attention to the ecological environment, both in terms of obtaining needed resources and in terms of avoiding damage to the natural environment. Business can expect to face increasing controls from both government and pressure groups. Instead of opposing all forms of regulation, business should try to find societally acceptable solutions to the material and energy problems facing the nation.

technological environment

The most dramatic force shaping people's destiny is technology. Technology has released such wonders as penicillin, open-heart surgery, and the birth-control pill. It has released such horrors as the hydrogen bomb, nerve gas, and the submachine gun. It has released such mixed blessings as the automobile, television set, and white bread. Depending upon whether one is more enthralled with the wonders or the horrors determines one's attitude toward technology.

Every new technology may potentially spawn a major industry. One has only to think of transistors, xerography, computers, and antibiotics. These industries not only create but destroy. Transistors hurt the vacuum-tube industry and xerography hurt the carbon-paper business. The auto hurt the railroads and television hurt the movies. Schumpeter saw technology as a force for "creative destruction." Every enterprise must watch what is new in the environment, for this might eventually destroy it. If it has the imagination, the new might save it. It is discouraging that most phonograph companies did not enter the radio field, wagon manufacturers did not enter the automobile business, and steam locomotive companies did not enter the diesel locomotive business.

The growth rate of the economy is intimately tied to how many *major* new technologies will be discovered in the coming years. Unfortunately, technological discoveries do not arise evenly through time—the railroad industry created a lot of investment and then there was a dearth until the auto industry emerged; later radio created a lot of investment and then there was a dearth until television appeared. In the absence of major innovations that open up great markets and opportunities, an economy can stagnate.

In the meantime there are sure to be small innovations filling the gaps. Freeze-dried coffee probably made no one happier and antiperspirant deodorants probably made no one wiser, but they meet certain daily needs in an improved manner.

New technology creates some major long-run consequences that are not always foreseeable. The contraceptive pill, for example, led to smaller families, more working wives, and larger discretionary incomes—resulting in higher expenditures on vacation travel, among other things. Little did the airlines foresee that the pill would increase their traffic. The pill also led to the enlargement of the average size of brassieres, something that the women's lingerie industry had missed entirely.

Following are some of the main trends in technology that the marketer should watch.

Accelerating Pace of Technological Change

Most of the technological products we take for granted today were not available even one hundred years ago. Abraham Lincoln did not know of automobiles, airplanes, phonographs, radio, or the electric light. Woodrow Wilson did not know of television, aerosol cans, home freezers, automatic dishwashers, room air conditioners, antibiotics, or electronic computers. Franklin Delano Roosevelt did not know of xerography, synthetic detergents, tape recorders, birth-control pills, or earth satellites. And in 1963 John Kennedy did not know of the following.

RECENT INNOVATIONS		
Rotary engines	Videotape machines for home use	Four-channel stereo
Fuel-injection engines	Trash compactors	Water beds
Electronic pocket calculators	Microwave ovens	Noncholesterol egg substitutes
Felt-tipped and nylon-tipped pens	Freeze-dried coffee	Sugar substitutes
Digital wristwatches	Polaroid movie cameras	

People have usually greeted new ideas with skepticism. Even well-qualified experts have sometimes called them impossible. Consider the following major forecasting blunders:

- *The Automobile* "The ordinary 'horseless carriage' is at present a luxury for the wealthy; and although its price will probably fall in the future, it will never, of course, come into as common use as the bicycle."
  Literary Digest, October 14, 1899
- *Commercial Television* "While theoretically and technically television may be feasible, commercially and financially I consider it an impossibility, a development of which we need waste little time dreaming."
  Lee DeForest, 1926
- *Moon Landing* "Landing and moving around the moon offers so many serious problems for human beings that it may take science another 200 years to lick them."
  Science Digest, August 1948

Alvin Toffler, in his book *Future Shock,* sees quite the opposite, namely, an *accelerative thrust* in the successful invention, exploitation, and diffusion of new technologies.[14] More ideas are being worked on; the time lag between idea and successful implementation is falling rapidly; and the time between introduction and peak production is shortening considerably. He sees technology as feeding on itself. As someone has observed, 90 percent of all the scientists who ever lived are now alive.

Unlimited Innovational Opportunities

There seems to be no dearth of ideas for needed new products and services, only a temporary delay in bringing them to a state of technical fruition.[15] Among the most important things that scientists are working on today are the following.

NEEDED INNOVATIONS		
Practical solar energy	Home computer systems	Happiness pills
Cancer cures	Lung and liver pills	Chemical control of mental illness
Electric cars	Household robots to do cleaning and cooking	Electronic anesthetic for pain killing
Desalinization of seawater	Nonfattening, tasty, nutritious foods	Totally safe and effective contraceptive

In addition, scientists are also working on more-far-out fantasy products, including the following.

FANTASY INNOVATIONS		
Small flying cars	Three-dimensional television	Space colonies
Single-person rocket belts	Commercial space shuttle	Human clones

The challenge in each case is not only technical but commercial, namely, to command the marketing skills to present new technological products to target markets in a highly attractive and affordable manner.

EXHIBIT 7-2

THE HOME OF THE FUTURE

Ring . . . "Oh, hello, Madge," said Blanche as her Picturephone screen came into focus. "Would you hold on for one moment while I instruct the computer not to let my French gourmet dinner overcook? You know how temperamental these gourmet dishes are if you let them cook more than five minutes." As Blanche attends to her dinner, Madge types a few code words into her computer terminal and receives her facsimile newspaper, with the lead story describing a giant transparent bubble being put over Minneapolis to keep the city at 68° all year around. Blanche returns. "Say, Blanche, did you see that marvelous movie on three-dimensional TV last night?" "No, I didn't, but I preprogrammed my computer to have it videotaped before I left in my new electric car for an evening out on the town."

Is this the future? Where home entertainment, cooking, and news reports are controlled by mini-computers in the home? Not exactly. As a matter of fact, the dialogue of Madge and Blanche only scratches the surface of the home of the future.

Many envision a day when the home computer will act as a central control device for functional as well as entertainment purposes in the home. For example, the computer will act as a monitor and control for efficient air conditioning and heating, dishwashing, security control, and personal budget management. It will direct a home robot to carry out cleaning activities.

In the entertainment domain, the computer will provide a basis for developing computer "art" and "music" along with an expansive array of games to be played. It will also serve as a learning center for children and adults alike and allow home access to any document in the public library.

What is the marketing challenge posed by the home computer? Marketers will have to learn how to market a whole new life style centered on an extremely automated, electronically-assisted environment. As all chores are handled and pleasures provided by the flick of a switch, people will have an increased appetite for new experiences. The day of marketing "experiences" rather than products will have arrived.

Source: Adapted from an unpublished term paper by Rob Philiotis, with his permission.

High R & D Budgets

One of the fastest-growing budgets in this generation has been the nation's research and development budget. In 1976, R & D expenditures exceeded $37 billion, or almost 2.3 percent of the gross national product (GNP).

The federal government is the largest supplier of R & D funds, and industry is the largest user. Almost 90 percent of the funds go to applied R & D. The remainder is spent on basic research, almost half of which takes place in colleges and universities.

The five industries spending the most on R & D are aircraft and missiles, electrical equipment and communication, chemicals and allied products, machinery, and motor vehicles and other transportation. The least R & D spending is found in such industries as lumber, wood products, furniture, textiles, apparel, and paper and allied products. Industries at the top range spend between 5 and 10 percent of their sales dollar on R & D, and those in the lowest range spend less than 1 percent of their sales dollar. A recent study showed a high correlation between R & D expenditures and company profitability. Six companies—Merck, AT&T, Dow, Eastman Kodak, IBM, and Lilly—averaged 5.7 percent in their R & D expenditures-to-sales ratio, and their profitability averaged 15.3 percent of sales. At the other end were Boeing, Chrysler, Goodyear, McDonnell-Douglas, Signal Companies, and United Technologies, which averaged an R & D investment of only 3.5 percent of sales and were much less profitable companies.[16]

Most of today's research is carried out by scientific teams working in research laboratories rather than by lone independent inventors of the breed of Thomas Edison, Samuel Morse, or Alexander Graham Bell. Managing scientific personnel poses major challenges. These people are professionals who resent too much cost control. Many of them are more interested in solving scientific problems than in coming up with marketable products. Yet companies are making some progress in convincing their scientific personnel that there is a need for a stronger marketing orientation.

Concentration on Minor Improvements Rather Than Major Discoveries

Tight money in recent years has led many companies to concentrate on pursuing minor product improvements rather than gambling on major innovations. In the past, such companies as Du Pont, Bell Laboratories, and Pfizer would invest heavily to make major breakthroughs and were successful in many cases. Even these companies seem to be pursuing more modest goals today. Most companies are content to put their money into improving such things as antiperspirant deodorants, automobile styles, and soft-drink flavors. Some part of every R & D budget is spent simply to match or copy competitors' products rather than to strive to surpass them.

Increased Regulation of Technological Change

Technological change is encountering more regulation and opposition than ever before. As products become more complex, the public needs to be assured of their safety. Government agencies have responded by expanding their powers to investigate and ban new products that might be directly harmful or have questionable side effects. Thus the Federal Food and Drug Administration has issued elaborate regulations governing the scientific testing of new drugs, resulting in (1) much higher research costs, (2) lengthening the time between idea and introduction from five to about nine years, and (3) driving much drug research to other parts of the world where regulations are less stringent. Safety and health regulations have substantially increased in other areas, such as food, automobiles, clothing, electrical appliances, and construction. Marketers must be aware of these regulations and take them seriously when proposing, developing, and launching new products.

Technological change is also meeting opposition from those who see large-scale technology as threatening to destroy nature, privacy, simplicity, and even the human race. These individuals have opposed the construction of new nuclear plants, high-rise buildings, and recreational facilities in national parks. They have clamored for *technological assessment* of new technologies before permitting them to be commercialized in this society.

Marketers must understand the technological environment and the nuances of technology. They must be able to envision how technology can be connected up with human needs. They must work closely with R & D people to encourage more market-oriented research. They must be alert to possible negative aspects of any innovation that might harm the users and bring about distrust and opposition.

political environment

Developments in the political environment are increasingly affecting decisions on the marketing of goods and services. *Political system* is a broad term covering the rules and institutions by which a nation is governed. It consists of an interacting set of *laws, government agencies,* and *pressure groups* that influence and constrain the conduct of various organizations and individuals in the society.

We will now examine the main political trends and their implications for marketing management.

Increasing Amount of Legislation Regulating Business

In the United States and several other countries, the basic political model is that of *liberal democracy.* Consumers and business firms are free to pursue their self-interest except where this pursuit is clearly harmful to others or to the larger society. Government is to play a minor role, limiting itself to those activities that cannot be carried on by other groups, namely (1) war and defense, (2) public works (roads, public monuments), (3) public services (fire, police, schools, justice), and (4) regulation to maintain competition and protect public health. Over the years the government sector has steadily increased its power and is now the major employer in the United States, accounting for 19 percent of the nonagricultural labor force and spending approximately 21 percent of the gross national product. Its growth has been abetted by the demands of pressure groups to receive favors or protection. While many nations have gone over to a socialist model of society with government owning and operating major industries, U.S. citizens prefer to view government as a regulator, not an initiator, of economic activity.

Legislation affecting business has steadily increased over the years, partly in reaction to the growing complexity of technology and business practices. The legislation seeks to accomplish any of three purposes. *The first is to protect companies from each other.* Business executives all praise competition in the abstract but try to neutralize it when it touches them. If threatened, they show their teeth:

- ReaLemon Foods, a subsidiary of Borden, held approximately 90 percent of the reconstituted lemon juice market until 1970. Fearing antitrust action, ReaLemon began to allow companies on the West Coast and in the Chicago area to make inroads. By 1972, however, a Chicago competitor, Golden Crown Citrus Corporation, had captured a share that ReaLemon considered too large. ReaLemon went on the offensive and in 1974, the Federal Trade Commission filed a complaint charging ReaLemon with predatory pricing and sales tactics.[17]

So laws are passed to define and prevent unfair competition. These laws are enforced by the Federal Trade Commission and the Antitrust Division of the attorney general's office. Sometimes, unfortunately, the laws end up protecting the inefficient rather than promoting the efficient. Some students of business regulation go so far as to charge that "judges and the Federal Trade Commission have remade the law into a body of rules of which a large portion impair competition and the ability of the economy to operate efficiently."[18] But, by and large, regulations are needed to keep executives fearful about overstepping the line in trying to neutralize or harm competitors. It is difficult to imagine that the economy would be more efficient if competition were not supervised by some regulatory agencies.

The second purpose of government regulation is to protect consumers from business firms. A few firms are ready to adulterate their products, mislead through their advertising, deceive through their packaging, and bait through their prices. Unfair consumer practices must be defined and agencies established to protect consumers. Many business executives see purple with each new consumer law, and yet a few have said that "consumerism may be the best thing that has happened . . . in the past 20 years."[19]

The third purpose of government regulation is to protect the larger interests of society against unbridled business behavior. Gross national product might be rising, and yet the quality of life might be deteriorating. Most firms are not charged with the social costs of their production or products. Their prices are artificially low and their sales artificially high until agencies such as the Environmental Protection Agency shift the social costs back to these firms and their customers. As the environment continues to deteriorate, new laws and their enforcement will continue or increase. Business executives have to watch these developments in planning their products and marketing systems.

The marketing executive cannot plan intelligently without a good working knowledge of the major laws and regulations that exist to protect competition, consumers, and the larger interests of society. The laws are numerous. The main federal laws affecting marketing are listed in Table 7-2. The earlier laws dealt mainly with protecting competition, and the later laws with protecting consumers. Marketing executives should know these federal laws and, particularly, the evolving courts' interpretations.[20] And they should know which state and local laws affect their local marketing activity.

More Vigorous Government Agency Enforcement

To enforce the laws, Congress has established a number of important federal regulatory agencies such as the Federal Trade Commission, the Food and Drug Administration, the Interstate Commerce Commission, the Federal Communications Commission, the Federal Power Commission, the Civil Aeronautics Board, the Consumer Products Safety Commission, the Environmental Protection Agency, and the Office of Consumer Affairs. These agencies can have a major impact on a company's marketing decisions and results. Consider the following example:

- In 1973 the rotary-engine Mazda was experiencing a new high in sales. People were impressed by its smooth ride, low repair costs, and reduced air pollution. Then the Environmental Protection Agency issued a disturbing report in late 1973 in which

Table 7-2
Milestone U.S. Legislation Affecting Marketing

SHERMAN ANTITRUST ACT (1890)

Prohibited (a) "monopolies or attempts to monopolize" and (b) "contracts, combinations, or conspiracies in restraint of trade" in interstate and foreign commerce.

FEDERAL FOOD AND DRUG ACT (1906)

Forbade the manufacture, sale, or transport of adulterated or fraudulently labeled foods and drugs in interstate commerce. Supplanted by the Food, Drug, and Cosmetic Act, 1938; amended by Food Additives Amendment in 1958 and the Kefauver-Harris Amendment in 1962. The 1962 amendments dealt with pretesting of drugs for safety and effectiveness and labeling of drugs by generic name.

MEAT INSPECTION ACT (1906)

Provided for the enforcement of sanitary regulations in meat-packing establishments, and for federal inspection of all companies selling meats in interstate commerce.

FEDERAL TRADE COMMISSION ACT (1914)

Established the commission, a body of specialists with broad powers to investigate and to issue cease and desist orders to enforce Section 5, which declared that "unfair methods of competition in commerce are unlawful." (Amended by Wheeler-Lea Act, 1938, which added the phrase "and unfair or deceptive acts or practices.")

CLAYTON ACT (1914)

Supplemented the Sherman Act by prohibiting certain specific practices (certain types of price discrimination, tying clauses and exclusive dealing, intercorporate stockholdings, and interlocking directorates) "where the effect . . . may be to substantially lessen competition or tend to create a monopoly in any line of commerce." Provided that violating corporate officials could be held individually responsible; exempted labor and agricultural organizations from its provisions.

ROBINSON-PATMAN ACT (1936)

Amended the Clayton Act. Added the phrase "to injure, destroy, or prevent competition." Defined price discrimination as unlawful (subject to certain defenses) and provided the FTC with the right to establish limits on quantity discounts, to forbid brokerage allowances except to independent brokers, and to prohibit promotional allowances or the furnishing of services or facilities except where made available to all "on proportionately equal terms."

MILLER-TYDINGS ACT (1937)

Amended the Sherman Act to exempt interstate fair-trade (price fixing) agreements from antitrust prosecution. (The McGuire Act, 1952, reinstated the legality of the nonsigner clause.)

ANTIMERGER ACT (1950)

Amended Section 7 of the Clayton Act by broadening the power to prevent intercorporate acquisitions where the acquisition may have a substantially adverse effect on competition.

AUTOMOBILE INFORMATION DISCLOSURE ACT (1958)

Prohibited car dealers from inflating the factory price of new cars.

NATIONAL TRAFFIC AND SAFETY ACT (1966)

Provided for the creation of compulsory safety standards for automobiles and tires.

FAIR PACKAGING AND LABELING ACT (1966)

Provided for the regulation of the packaging and labeling of consumer goods. Required manufacturers to state what the package contains, who made it, and how much it contains. Permitted industries' voluntary adoption of uniform packaging standards.

Table 7-2 (continued)

CHILD PROTECTION ACT (1966)
Banned sale of hazardous toys and articles. Amended in 1969 to include articles that pose electrical, mechanical, or thermal hazards.
FEDERAL CIGARETTE LABELING AND ADVERTISING ACT (1967)
Required that cigarette packages contain the statement "Warning: The Surgeon General Has Determined That Cigarette Smoking Is Dangerous to Your Health."
TRUTH-IN-LENDING ACT (1968)
Required lenders to state the true costs of a credit transaction, outlawed the use of actual or threatened violence in collecting loans, and restricted the amount of garnishments. Established a National Commission on Consumer Finance.
NATIONAL ENVIRONMENTAL POLICY ACT (1969)
Established a national policy on the environment and provided for the establishment of the Council on Environmental Quality. The Environmental Protection Agency was established by "Reorganization Plan No. 3 of 1970."
FAIR CREDIT REPORTING ACT (1970)
Ensured that a consumer's credit report would contain only accurate, relevant, and recent information and would be confidential unless requested for an appropriate reason by a proper party.
CONSUMER PRODUCT SAFETY ACT (1972)
Established the Consumer Product Safety Commission and authorized it to set safety standards for consumer products as well as exact penalties for failure to uphold the standards.
CONSUMER GOODS PRICING ACT (1975)
Prohibited the use of price maintenance agreements among manufacturers and resellers in interstate commerce.
MAGNUSON-MOSS WARRANTY/FTC IMPROVEMENT ACT (1975)
Authorized the FTC to determine rules concerning consumer warranties and provided for consumer access to means of redress, such as the "class action" suit. Also expanded FTC regulatory powers over unfair or deceptive acts or practices.

it stated that Mazda's fuel consumption was such that it was achieving only 11 miles per gallon in city driving. Mazda executives objected, claiming the figure should be 17 to 21 miles per gallon, but the charge stuck in the public's mind. Mazda sales declined 39 percent in the first five months of 1974.

These agencies are required to operate with objectivity and fairness in enforcing the law. They are allowed some discretion in establishing new rules and regulations to govern certain types of industry practices. From time to time, they come into head-on conflict with business in what seem to be overzealous and capricious actions on the agency's part. The agencies are dominated by lawyers and economists, both of whom often lack a practical sense of how business and marketing works. In recent years, however, the Federal Trade Commission and some of the agencies have added marketing personnel to achieve a better understanding of the issues they are judging.

EXHIBIT 7-3

THE FTC VS. THE BREAKFAST CEREAL INDUSTRY

The adversarial and costly nature of business regulation is well illustrated in the long-drawn-out suit by the Federal Trade Commission (FTC) against the four leading ready-to-eat breakfast cereal companies, Kellogg, General Mills, General Foods, and Quaker Oats. In 1972, the Federal Trade Commission charged these firms with practicing a *shared monopoly*. This is a new untested legal concept which, if upheld in the courts, would allow the FTC to attack other oligopolistic industries such as automobiles, steel, and oil. The charge was that the Big Four of this industry (1) do not compete on a price basis, (2) enjoy monopoly level profits, and (3) make it tough for other firms to enter this industry because of their large advertising budgets and their grip on shelf space through their brand proliferation. While the Big Four were not charged with any explicit price conspiracy, it was suggested that they tacitly agreed not to compete on price but on promotion. Since the case began in 1972, the FTC staff working on the case has turned over several times, and both sides have spent tens of millions of dollars prosecuting and defending the case, with very little progress. Recently, a court ordered the FTC to release Quaker Oats from the suit on the grounds that its market share (10 percent) was too small to be charged with "shared monopoly," after Quaker Oats had spent millions of dollars defending itself. Cases like this tend to go on even after the original issues vanish, simply because the sides will fight to the end. Business firms complain that they are the ultimate victims because government agencies do not have to (1) show a profit and (2) are less accountable to others for their actions.

Source: See "Too Many Cereals for the FTC," *Business Week*, March 20, 1978, pp. 116, 171.

Growth of Public Interest Groups

The third major political development is the rapid growth in recent years of public interest groups lobbying for increased consumer protection and business regulation. The most successful of these is Ralph Nader's *Public Citizen* group, which watchdogs the consumers' interest. Nader, more than any other single individual, has lifted consumerism into a major social force, first with his successful attack on auto safety (resulting in the passage of the National Traffic and Motor Vehicle Safety Act of 1962), and then through further investigations into meat processing (resulting in the passage of the Wholesome Meat Act of 1967), truth-in-lending, auto repairs, insurance, and X-ray equipment. In addition to Nader's, there are hundreds of other consumer interest groups—private and governmental—operating at the national, state, and local levels. Other groups that affect marketing decision making include groups seeking to protect the environment (Sierra Club, Environmental Defense) or to advance the "rights" of women, blacks, senior citizens, and so on.

Various developments—new laws, more active enforcement, growing pressure groups—have severely constrained marketer freedom. Marketers have increasingly had to clear their planned moves with the company's legal and public relations departments. The private marketing transaction has gradually moved into the public domain, and marketers can no longer follow the simple credo of meeting consumer wants. Salancik and Upah put it this way:

- There is some evidence that the consumer may not be king, nor even queen. The consumer is but a voice, one among many. Consider how General Motors makes its cars today. Vital features of the motor are designed by the United States government; the exhaust system is redesigned by certain state governments; the production materials used are dictated by suppliers who control scarce material resources. For other products, other groups and organizations may get involved. Thus, insurance companies directly or indirectly affect the design of smoke detectors; scientific groups affect the design of spray products by condemning aerosols; minority activist groups affect the design of dolls by requesting representative figures. Legal departments also can be expected to increase their importance in firms, affecting not only product design and promotion but also marketing strategies. At a minimum, marketing managers will spend less time with their research departments asking "What does the consumer want" and more and more time with their production and legal people asking "What can the consumer have."[21]

cultural environment

Another major component of the macroenvironment is the cultural system. People grow up in a particular society that shapes their basic beliefs, values, and norms. They absorb, almost unconsciously, a world view that defines their relationship to themselves, others, institutions, society-at-large, nature, and the cosmos. The following cultural characteristics can affect marketing decision making.

Core Cultural Values Have High Persistence

People in a given society hold many beliefs and values, not all of which are equally important. Those that are most central can be called core beliefs and values.

The set of core beliefs and values in a society have a high degree of persistence. For example, most Americans believe in work, getting married, giving to charity, and being honest. These beliefs shape and color more specific attitudes and behaviors found in everyday life. Core beliefs and values are passed on from parents to children and are reinforced by the major institutions of society—schools, churches, business, and government.

People also hold secondary beliefs and values that are more open to change in the wake of new social forces. Believing in the institution of marriage is a core belief; believing that people ought to get married early is a secondary belief. Debates about whether cultural change is slow or fast in this society often fail to distinguish between core and secondary beliefs and values.

Marketers who would like to change core beliefs and values would be wise not to try. Suppose a women's clothing designer wants to sell women on the idea of going topless. This designer would be attacking a core value held by both men and women. The same designer, however, may have success in selling women on wearing shorter skirts or lower necklines because this does less violence to their core beliefs.

Each Culture Consists of Subcultures

A society is made up of people who share the same core beliefs and values. Yet there are always certain groups of deviants, such as criminals or anarchists. Furthermore, there can be much variation in the secondary beliefs and values that people hold, giving rise to *subcultures.* For example, immigrants, the super-rich, and the intelligentsia, because they have had different life experiences and face different issues, will exhibit different systems of beliefs and values. This will be reflected in different patterns of consumer wants and behavior.

One also finds intergenerational differences in culture stemming from differences in life experiences. In a modern American family, the grandparents are conservative in their tastes and careful in their expenditures; the parents work and play hard and purchase many things on credit; their eighteen-year-old son might show little interest in either work or consumption. Recently a ten-year-old boy was told by his mother to behave more like his fourteen-year-old brother, to which he retorted: "Mom, he's from a different generation."

Secondary Cultural Values Undergo Shifts through Time

Although core cultural values are fairly persistent, there are always cultural events taking place that are worth monitoring. Consider the impact that such culture heroes as the "hippies," the Beatles, and Elvis Presley, as well as *Playboy* magazine, have on young people's hairstyles, clothing, and sexual norms. Cultural swings are always taking place, as indicated in the somewhat tongue-in-cheek version in Table 7-3.

The measurement and forecasting of cultural change is still highly speculative. Occasionally some major corporations, marketing research firms, and futures research firms issue reports that summarize cultural trends. One of the best known of these is the Monitor series put out by the Yankelovich marketing research firm. Monitor tracks forty-one different cultural values, such as "anti-bigness," "mysticism," "living for today," "away from possessions," and "sensuousness," describing the percentage who share the attitude as well as the percentage who are anti-trend. For example, the percentage of people who place a strong value on "physical fitness and well being" has been going up steadily over the years (35 percent currently), with the main support group being people under thirty, especially young women and the upscale, and people living in the West. About 16 percent of the population, however, is anti-trend.

A distinction should be drawn between describing the *dominant value system* and describing *trends in the value system.* Most people in this society see themselves as "happy, home-loving, clean, and square" (the dominant value system), and there is a slight trend toward less-conventional behavior (e.g., open marriage, cohabitation). But the less-conventional behavior is never practiced by more than a small percentage of the population, despite the distorted coverage of the news media. Thus major producers will want to cater to dominant value groups, and minor producers might see less-conventional groups as a market niche opportunity.

The major cultural values and value shifts in people's relationship to themselves, others, institutions, society, nature, and the cosmos can be summarized as follows.

Table 7-3
Four Decades of Cultural Change

	'50s	'60s	'70s	'80s
Chic Diseases:	Ulcers	Gonorrhea	Tennis elbow	Bed sores
Drugs of Choice:	Alcohol	Marijuana	Cocaine	Alcohol
What'll It Be:	7-and-7's	Harvey Wallbangers	White wine or orange juice	Aqua Velva
Sex Symbols Female Div:	Marilyn Monroe	Sophia Loren	Farrah Fawcett Majors	Bianca Jagger
Danger— Men at Work:	Lawyer	Communal farmer	Rock promoter	Stockbroker
Danger— Women at Work:	Homemaker	Executive	Lawyer	Communal farmer
Hair Today:	Crewcut	Waist-length	Frizz	The bald spot
Hair Tomorrow:	Ponytail	Waist-length	Frizz	The Mohawk
You Were What You Ate:	Steak and potatoes	Granola and sprouts	Cold soup and crepes	Instant Breakfast Baco Bits
Dancing:	The Lindy	The Frug	The Hustle	The Slump
The Family:	Swiss Family Robinson	The Manson Family	The Osmond Family	The Test Tube Family
Sporting Propositions:	Baseball	Football	Running	Limping
Salvation:	Psychoanalysis	LSD	est	YMCA

Source: Octavio Diaz, "Fickle Fads," *Miami Herald,* October 8, 1978.

People's relation to themselves. People vary in how much emphasis they put on gratifying their own needs versus serving others. More people focus on self-fulfillment today, seeking to do the things they want to do rather than follow conventions or please other people. Some are *pleasure-seekers,* wanting to have fun, change, and escape from the humdrum. Others are pursuing *self-realization* by joining therapeutic or religious groups.

The marketing implications of this trend toward self-fulfillment are many. People seek self-expression through the product, brand, and service choices they make. They are more willing to buy their "dream cars" and take "dream vacations." They will spend more time in the wilderness, in health activities (jogging, tennis, yoga), and in introspection and will be interested in arts and crafts. The leisure industry (camping, boating, arts and crafts, sports) has a good growth outlook as a result of this search for self-fulfillment.

People's relation to others. People choose to live their lives with different degrees of sociability, from the hermit who completely avoids others to the gregarious person who only feels happy and alive in the company of others. One trend seems to be a desire for more *open and easy relationships* with others. People want to be able to say things on their mind without causing offense. They want to "tell it like it is."

For marketers, this means several things. People may prefer that products such as furniture be more casual and less formal and pretentious. They may want packaging to provide more complete and honest information. They may want advertising messages to be more realistic. They may want salespersons to be more honest and helpful.

People's relation to institutions. People vary in how they feel about major institutions such as corporations, government agencies, trade unions, universities, and hospitals. Most people accept these institutions, although there are always groups that are highly critical of particular institutions, whether business, government, labor, or others. By and large, people are willing to work in the major institutions and rely on them to carry out society's work. The trend that is occurring is a *decline in institutional loyalty.* People are inclined to give a little less to these institutions and trust them a little less. The work ethic has gradually been eroding.

The marketing implications of this decline in institutional loyalty are several. Companies will be challenged to find new ways to build consumer confidence in themselves and their products. They will have to review their advertising communications to make sure that their messages do not raise the question, Can you trust this company? They will have to review their various interactions with the public to make sure that they are coming across as "good guys." More companies are turning to *social audits*[22] and to enlightened *public relations*[23] to maintain a positive relationship with their publics.

People's relation to society. People vary in their attitudes toward the society in which they live, from patriots who defend it, to reformers who want to change it, to discontents who want to leave it. There is a trend toward *declining patriotism* and stronger criticism and cynicism as to where the country is going.

People's orientation to their society will influence their consumption patterns, levels of savings, and attitudes toward the marketplace.

People's relation to nature. People vary in their relation to nature. Some feel subjugated by it, others are in harmony with it, and still others seek mastery over it. One of the major long-term trends in Western society has been people's growing mastery over nature through technology. Along with this has been the attitude that nature is bountiful and that nature's riches are infinite. More recently there has been a growing awareness of nature's fragility and a desire to preserve its magnificence. People are becoming aware that nature can be destroyed or spoiled by human activities.

Consumers are increasingly participating in such activities as camping, hiking, boating, and fishing. Business is responding by producing a large assortment of hiking boots, tenting equipment, and other gear for nature enthusiasts. Tour operators are packaging more tours to wilderness areas in Alaska and northern Finland. Food producers have found growing markets for "natural" products such as 100 percent natural cereal, natural ice cream, and health foods. Marketing communicators are using beautiful natural backgrounds in advertising many of their products.

People's relation to the universe. People vary in their belief system about the origin of the universe and their place in it. Most Americans are monotheistic, although their religious conviction and practice has been waning through the years. Church attendance has been falling steadily, with the exception of certain evangelical movements reaching out to bring people back into organized religion. Some of the religious impulse has not been lost but has been translated into a growing interest in Eastern religions, mysticism, and the occult. More Americans than ever are studying yoga, zen, and transcendental meditation.

The marketing implications are several. As people lose their religious orientation, they increase their efforts to enjoy their one life on earth as fully as possible. Their interest centers on earthly possessions and experience. Secularization and materialism go hand in hand. "Enjoy yourself" becomes the dominant theme, and people gravitate to those goods and services that offer them fun and pleasure in this life. In the meantime, religious institutions face a continuing decline in membership and support, and they turn to marketers for help in reworking their appeals to compete against the secular attractions of modern society.

In summary, cultural values are showing the following long-run trends:

Other-centeredness	⟶	Self-fulfillment
Postponed gratification	⟶	Immediate gratification
Hard work	⟶	The easy life
Formal relationships	⟶	Informal, open relationships
Religious orientation	⟶	Secular orientation

■ summary

Those who plan and manage products operate within a complex and rapidly changing marketing macroenvironment, which the firm must continuously monitor and adapt to if it is to survive and prosper. The macroenvironment consists of the totality of major institutions and forces that are external and potentially relevant to the firm. The macroenvironment can be factored into six components: the demographic, economic, ecological, technological, political, and cultural environments.

The demographic environment is characterized by a worldwide explosive population growth, a slowdown in the U.S. birthrate, the aging of the U.S. population, a changing American family, the rise of nonfamily households, geographical shifts in population, and a better-educated populace. The economic environment shows a slowdown in real income growth, continued inflationary pressure, changing savings and debt patterns, and changing consumption expenditure patterns. The natural environment is marked by impending shortages of certain raw materials, increased cost of energy, increased levels of pollution, and increasing government intervention in natural resource management. The technological environment exhibits an accelerating pace of technological change, unlimited innovational opportunities, high R & D budgets, concentration on minor improvements rather than major discoveries, and increased regulation of technological change. The political environment shows an increasing amount of legislation regulating business, more vigorous government agency enforcement, and the growth of public interest groups. Finally, the cultural environment shows long-run trends toward self-fulfillment, immediate gratification, the easy life, informal and open relationships, and a more secular orientation.

■ questions for discussion

1. Discuss how changes in the demographic environment are likely to affect the following marketers in the next twenty years—(a) Mattel, (b) Holiday Inns located in the Midwest, (c) retirement communities, (d) marriage counselors.
2. It is the year 2000 A.D. The price of gasoline is $4 per gallon, the price of hamburger is $6 per pound, the average home costs $200,000, and the annual rate of inflation has been 10 percent for the last twenty years. Given this economic information, what might you speculate the market size or potential for luxury products would be?
3. It has been stated that "technology will solve our ecological problems and marketing need not worry about them." Respond to this statement.
4. What major factors are currently inhibiting significant technological innovations in the United States? Do you think this situation will change soon?
5. The political environment has become increasingly volatile in recent years. How have Ralph Nader, the FTC, and the actions of Congress affected marketing decision making in recent years?
6. What current cultural values do you see having the strongest long-run impact on marketing in the U.S.?
7. Discuss in some depth how the six macroenvironmental forces discussed in this chapter may affect the marketing of Coca-Cola in 1990.

■ references

1. This was written by the author based on information in George Lazarus, "Bloom off Tennis Boom, Devotees Still Trading Up," *Chicago Tribune,* April 8, 1979, Sec. 5, p. 6.
2. Peter Drucker, *Age of Discontinuity* (New York: Harper & Row, Pub., 1969).
3. See Alvin Toffler, *Future Shock* (New York: Bantam, 1970), p. 28.
4. Donella H. Meadows, Dennis L. Meadows, Jorgen Randers, and William W. Behrens III, *The Limits to Growth* (New York: New American Library, 1972), p. 41.
5. Most of the statistical data in this chapter, unless otherwise indicated, can be found in the *Statistical Abstract of the United States, 1977.*
6. See "The Graying of America," *Newsweek,* February 28, 1977, pp. 50–65.
7. See Ellen Graham, "Advertisers Take Aim at a Neglected Market: The Working Woman," *Wall Street Journal,* July 5, 1977, p. 1.

   See June Kronholz, "A Living-Alone Trend Affects Housing, Cars, and Other Industries," *Wall Street Journal,* November 16, 1977, p. 1.
9. An SMSA consists of a county or group of contiguous counties with a total population of at least 100,000 and a central city with a minimum population of

50,000 (or two closely located cities with a combined population of 50,000). The government has identified 277 SMSAs, and they account for almost three-fourths of the nation's population.

10. Reported in "Private Brands Seek Growth in Faltering Economy," *Grey Matter,* June 1974, p. 1.
11. *First Annual Report of the Council on Environmental Quality* (Washington D.C.: Government Printing Office, 1970), p. 158.
12. See "The Coming Boom in Solar Energy," *Business Week,* October 9, 1978, pp. 88–104.
13. See KARL E. HENION II, *Ecological Marketing* (Columbus, Ohio: Grid, 1976).
14. TOFFLER, *Future Shock,* pp. 25–30.
15. For an excellent and comprehensive list of future possible products, see DENNIS GABOR, *Innovations: Scientific, Technological, and Social* (London: Oxford University Press, 1970).
16. "Corporate Growth, R & D, and the Gap Between," *Technology Review,* March-April 1978, p. 39.
17. DENNIS D. FISHER, "ReaLemon Sales Tactics Hit," *Chicago Sun-Times,* July 4, 1974.
18. See YALE BROZEN, "Antitrust Out of Hand," *Conference Board Record,* March 1974, pp. 14-19.
19. LEO GREENLAND, "Advertisers Must Stop Conning Consumers," *Harvard Business Review,* July-August 1974, p. 18.
20. For recent cases, see G. DAVID HUGHES, "Antitrust Caveat for the Marketing Planner," *Harvard Business Review,* March-April 1978, pp. 40ff.; and RAY O. WERNER, "The 'New' Supreme Court and the Marketing Environment, 1975–1977," *Journal of Marketing,* April 1978, pp. 56–62.
21. These are extracts from GERALD R. SALANCIK AND GREGORY D. UPAH, "Directions for Interorganizational Marketing" (Unpublished paper, School of Commerce, University of Illinois, Champaign, August 1978).
22. See RAYMOND A. BAUER AND DAN H. FENN, JR., "What Is a Corporate Social Audit?" *Harvard Business Review,* January-February 1973, pp. 37–48.
23. LEONARD L. BERRY AND JAMES S. HENSEL, "Public Relations: Opportunities in the New Society," *Arizona Business,* August-September 1973, pp. 14–21.

CONSUMER MARKETS AND BUYING BEHAVIOR

The giant Du Pont Company of Wilmington, Delaware, was sure that it had a winner in its new Corfam "leather" for men's and women's shoes. Du Pont had been searching for a leather substitute since the 1930s, knowing that leather would one day be in short supply. In 1955 the company's scientists successfully synthesized a material called Corfam that had the necessary properties for a shoe material: permeability, strength, flexibility, and durability. A pilot plant was set up in 1958 to produce the new material for consumer evaluation. In 1959, following enthusiastic consumer response, Du Pont built a larger plant which came on stream in 1961. Du Pont's total investment was $25 million.

The company selected seventeen top women's shoemakers and fifteen top men's shoemakers who agreed to buy the material from Du Pont and incorporate it in attractive shoe models. Du Pont set a high price for Corfam because it felt that Corfam offered certain superior quality over leather, such as greater ease of care and durability. The material would be used in high-priced shoes to give consumers confidence in its quality, and Du Pont would consider penetrating the lower-priced shoe market at a later date.

The manufacturers' shoes featuring Corfam were launched at the 1963 National Shoe Fair, and many shoe retailers placed orders. Du Pont created a merchandising team to visit retail shoe stores to train salesmen how to sell them. Du Pont created point-of-sale material, window displays, and national advertising of Corfam at an initial cost of $2 million.

Du Pont was highly pleased with the results. One million pairs of Corfam shoes were bought by consumers in 1964; 5 million in 1965; and 15 million in 1966. But in 1967, Corfam shoe sales began to slip. What happened?

There was a disturbingly low rate of Corfam shoe rebuying by former purchasers. Du Pont had not done a sufficient job of analyzing the consumer shoe market and consumer shoe-buying behavior to catch a number of nuances in time. For example:

1. *Corfam shoes were promoted as having high durability and ease of care. But high-priced shoe buyers were not primarily motivated by these factors in their choice of shoes.*
2. *Corfam shoes were promoted as having the same "breathing" as leather. But many Corfam shoe buyers found the shoes unusually warm.*
3. *Corfam was promoted as a material that did not stretch so that its fit*

would be right the first time. But many consumers bought a tight-fitting size thinking that it would stretch.

4. ***Consumers chose shoes for their style, not material. They never achieved enough of an interest in Corfam to ask the retailer if they could see the Corfam shoes.***
5. ***Corfam might have gone over much better had it been used in domestic low-priced shoes. High-quality shoe buyers were increasingly shifting their purchases to imported high-styled leather shoes from Italy and elsewhere.***

By 1971 Du Pont found the situation desperate and decided to stop its production of Corfam material for shoes. It incurred a loss of $100 million in one of the most expensive product failures in history.[1]

□This example highlights how careful marketers have to be in analyzing consumer markets. The best assumption to make is that consumers' buying behavior is never simple. Consumers often turn down what appears to be a winning offer. If they do not vote for a product, the product is dead. The new plant and equipment might as well have been built on quick sand. Du Pont found this out. So did Ford when it launched the famous (or infamous) Edsel, losing a cool $350 million in the process.[2] And so did Brown-Forman Distillers Corporation when consumers decided not to drink its new Frost 8/80, a "dry, white" whisky, which it thought would be a smashing success.[3]

The market is the sovereign force in the economy and therefore has to be the starting point in company planning. A company must begin its thinking not with its products but with customer groups and customer needs. What the company finds out about the market affects and determines its product development, pricing, distribution channels, advertising messages and media, and other elements of the marketing mix.

What Is a Market?

At the outset we should clarify how the term *market* is being used. The term has acquired many usages over the years.

1. In one of the earliest usages a market consisted of a *physical place* where buyers and sellers gathered to exchange goods and services. Medieval towns had market squares where sellers brought their goods and buyers shopped for goods. Most American cities at one time had well-known sections called markets where owners of goods set up carts and buyers came from all over the city to look for bargains. Today, transactions occur all over the city in what are called shopping areas rather than markets.
2. To an economist, a market describes all the buyers and sellers involved in actual or potential transactions with respect to some good or service. Thus the soft-drink market consists of major sellers such as Coca-Cola, Pepsi-Cola, and Seven-Up and all the consumers who buy soft drinks. The economist is interested in describing and evaluating the *structure, conduct,* and *performance* of the market.
3. To a marketer, a market is *the set of all actual and potential buyers of a product.* Thus the marketer limits *market* to mean the buyer side of the economist's

definition of a market, with the seller side being called the industry or competition. The marketer wants to know several things about the market, such as its size, purchasing power, needs, and preferences.

We will adopt the last definition of *market.* The definition hinges on the definition of the term *buyer. A buyer is anyone who might conceivably buy a given product.* This means a person or an organization who (1) might have a latent interest in the product and (2) the means to acquire it. A buyer is someone who is potentially "willing and able to buy."

Let us apply this to the market for microwave ovens. The market consists of both individual households and organizations such as restaurants. Focusing on households, not all will be in the market. Some consumers have no interest—their kitchens are too small; they feel that these machines are too complex; they fear that they are dangerous. And among interested consumers, many are unwilling to pay $400 or more for this appliance.

This means that the size of a market at a given time is a function of existing parameters such as consumer beliefs and product prices. A seller can expand the size of a market by recognizing its dependence on these parameters. A manufacturer of microwave ovens can sponsor an educational campaign to convince consumers that microwave ovens are safe. Or the manufacturer might lower its prices below $400, which will expand the number of consumers who can afford it.

The job of a marketer is to know the market. To understand a specific market, one needs a working knowledge of the operating characteristics of four generic types of markets: *consumer market, producer market, reseller market,* and *government market.* These markets are distinguished on the basis of the buyers' role and motives rather than the characteristics of the purchased product. Consumers are individuals and households buying for personal use. Producers are individuals and organizations buying for the purpose of producing. Resellers are individuals and organizations buying for the purpose of reselling. Governments are governmental units buying for the purpose of carrying out governmental functions.

Because markets are complex, we need a common framework for grasping the character of a market. The marketer can develop a good understanding of any market by asking the following five questions: (1) Who is in the market? (*Buying population*) (2) What buying decisions do buyers make? (*Buying decisions*) (3) Who participates in the buying process? (*Buying participants*) (4) What are the major influences on the buyers? (*Buying influences*) (5) How do the buyers make their buying decisions? (*Buying process*)

We will examine these questions for consumer markets in this chapter and for organizational markets in the next chapter.

who is in the consumer market? *(buying population)*

The *consumer market* consists of *all the individuals and households who buy or acquire goods and services for personal consumption.* Our discussion will focus on the American consumer market. In 1976 the American consumer market consisted of 217 million persons who annually consume about $1.1 trillion worth of products and services—the equivalent of $5,080 worth for every man, woman, and child. Each year this market grows by another 1.5 million persons and another $100 billion, representing one of the most lucrative consumer markets in the world.[4]

Consumers vary tremendously as to their ages, incomes, educational levels, mobility patterns, and tastes. Marketers have found it worthwhile to distinguish different consumer groups and develop products and services tailored to their needs. If a market segment is large enough, some companies may set up special marketing programs to serve this market. Here are two examples of special consumer groups.

- *Black consumers.* Constituting an important group in the United States are the 25 million black Americans with an aggregate personal income of almost $100 billion. Blacks are especially good consumers—out of proportion to their numbers—of such products as cooked cereals, syrup, soft drinks, alcoholic beverages, clothing, shoes, and canned luncheon meats. Studies show that blacks usually favor the more popular brands within a product category and tend to be brand loyal consumers. All this means that certain marketers would find it worthwhile to apply differentiated marketing effort in reaching black Americans. This could take the form of additional expenditures put into black advertising vehicles such as *Ebony* and *Jet,* making more use of blacks in commercials, and even developing distinctive products (i.e., black cosmetics), packaging, or appeals for the black market. At the same time the marketer should recognize that the black market contains several consumer subsegments that may require different marketing approaches.[5]
- *Young adult consumers.* This market consists of 29 million persons between the ages of 18 and 24. The young adult market can be divided into three subgroups: college students, young singles, and young marrieds. Young adults spend disproportionately on books, records, stereo equipment, cameras, fashion clothing, hair driers, and many personal-care and grooming products. They are generally low in brand loyalty and high in new-product interests. Marketers find young adults an attractive market for several reasons: (1) they are receptive to trying new products; (2) they are more oriented toward spending than saving, and (3) they will be buying products for a longer time.[6]

Other consumer submarkets—elderly consumers,[7] women consumers,[8] Spanish-American consumers[9]—could be similarly researched to see if tailored products and marketing programs would make competitive sense.

The 217 million American consumers buy an incredible variety of goods and services. These goods and services can be classified in different ways to throw light on their marketing characteristics (see Chapter 12, pp. 369–73). Here we will concentrate on trying to understand consumer behavior.

what buying decisions do consumers make? *(buying decisions)*

We are now ready to consider what buying decisions consumers make. At first glance, the consumer appears to make a simple "to-buy or not-to-buy" decision. On closer scrutiny, the consumer really goes through an elaborate decision process involving many decisions along the way. The marketer can ill afford to look at only the final decision to buy. All the decisions, from the decision to seek information to the decision on style, method of payment, and other aspects of the purchase, must be studied to see where the marketer could have leverage on the final buying decision.

Three Classes of Buying Situations

The number of subdecisions involved in buying anything varies with the complexity of the product and buying situation. There are great differences between buying toothpaste, a tennis racket, an expensive camera, and a new car. Howard and Sheth have suggested that consumer buying can be viewed as problem-solving activity and have distinguished three classes of buying situations.[10]

Routinized response behavior. The simplest type of buying behavior occurs in the purchase of low-cost, frequently purchased items. Buyers have very few decisions to make—they are well acquainted with the product class, know the major brands, and have fairly clear preference among the brands. They do not always buy the same brand because the choice can be influenced by stockouts, special deals, and a wish for variety. But, in general, buyers' operations are routinized, and they are not likely to give much thought, search, or time to the purchase. The goods in this class are often called *low-involvement goods.*

The marketer's task in this situation is twofold. With respect to current customers, the marketer should provide positive reinforcement. The brand's quality, stock level, and value must be maintained. With respect to noncustomers, the marketer must break their normal buying habits by cues that call attention to the brand and its value in relation to the buyers' preferred brands. These cues include new features or benefits, point-of-purchase displays, price specials, and premiums.

Limited problem solving. Buying is more complex when buyers confront an unfamiliar brand in a familiar product class that requires information before making a purchase choice. For example, persons thinking about buying a new tennis racket may hear about a new oversized brand called the Prince. They may ask questions and look at ads to learn more about the new brand concept before choosing. This is described as limited problem solving because buyers are fully aware of the product class and the qualities they want but are not familiar with all the brands and their features.

The marketer recognizes that consumers are trying to reduce risk through information gathering. The marketer must design a communication program that will increase the buyer's brand comprehension and confidence.

Extensive problem solving. Buying reaches its greatest complexity when buyers face an unfamiliar product class and do not know what criteria to use. For example, a man may become interested in buying a citizen-band transceiver for the first time. He has heard brand names such as Cobra, Panasonic, and Midland but lacks clear brand concepts. He does not even know what product-class attributes to consider in choosing a good citizen-band transceiver. He is in a state of extensive problem solving.

The marketer of products in this class must understand the information-gathering and evaluation activities of prospective buyers. The marketer's task is to facilitate the buyer's learning of the attributes of the product class, their relative importance, and the high standing of the brand on the more important attributes.

Major Subdecisions Involved in the Buying Decision

We are now ready to examine the various subdecisions involved in a particular buying decision. We will consider the following case:

- Betty Smith is a married college graduate who works as a brand manager in a leading consumer-packaged-goods company. She is currently interested in finding a new leisure time activity that will offer some contrast to her working day. This need has led her through a process that culminated in the purchase of a Nikon camera. Betty was asked to reconstruct the decisions she made that ultimately led to the purchase of the camera. The decision steps are shown in Figure 8-1.

The buying process started with Betty feeling a need for some new activity. She tried to clarify the nature of her need and decided that she wanted some new form of self-expression (*need-class decision*). She considered various alternatives and decided that photography would be fun to try (*generic-class decision*). In considering the different classes of photographic equipment, she concluded that she wanted a camera (*product-class decision*). She decided that a complex 35-mm camera would be best (*product-form decision*). Among the brands she saw, Nikon gave her the most confidence (*brand decision*). She decided to go to dealer 2, who was reputed to run the best camera shop in town (*vendor decision*). She also thought of suggesting that her girlfriend buy a camera and take up photography but dropped the idea (*quantity decision*). She decided to buy the camera on the

Figure 8-1 *Consumer Buying Decisions for a Camera*

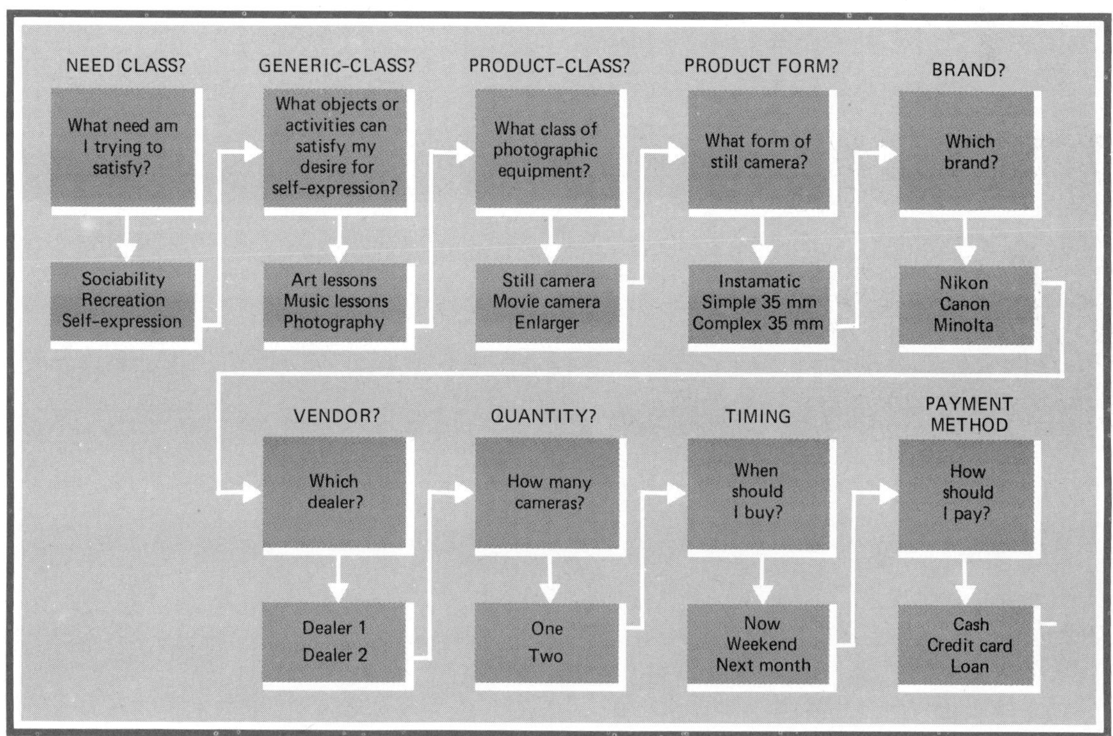

weekend (*timing decision*). And, finally, she decided to pay for it using her credit card (*payment-method decision*).

This mapping of the consumer's subdecisions provides a lot of clues for the camera marketer. Let us return to Figure 8-1. Each box contains a decision facing the consumer and a set of alternative solutions called an *evoked set.*[11] *An evoked set is the set of alternatives that the buyer might or did consider at that stage of the decision process.* Marketers have a strong interest in the size and contents of the evoked set at each decision point. The Nikon company would not have sold a camera to Betty Smith if she had not moved through the decision chain: Self-expression → Photography → Cameras. Thus, in selling cameras, the Nikon Company could gain from promoting the value of self-expression, and the role of cameras in photographic self-expression. If Betty had followed a different chain, neither Nikon nor any other camera manufacturer would have made a sale.

Given that Betty became interested in a camera, Nikon needed to be one of the brands included in her brand evoked set. If Betty had not heard of or been told about Nikon, Nikon would not have made the sale. Therefore we start with the concept of the *total set* representing all the brands of cameras that are available to this consumer (i.e., sold in the local area), whether or not the buyer knows about them (see Figure 8-2).[12] The total set can be divided into the consumer's *awareness set* (those brands that she recalls) and the *unawareness set.* We can see that Nikon is one of four brands in Betty's awareness set. Of these brands, three meet her buying criteria and they constitute her *consideration set;* the other is relegated to an *infeasible set.* As she gets information or gives thought to these brands, two of the brands remain strong choices and constitute her *choice set,* the other being relegated to a *nonchoice set.* She carefully evaluates the brands in the choice set and then makes her final decision, in this case choosing a Nikon camera.

The company's task is to work hard to get its brand included in the buyer's awareness set and to remain in the successive consideration and choice sets. The marketer must research the other brands that are likely to be included and the

Figure 8-2
Successive Sets Involved in Consumer Decision Making

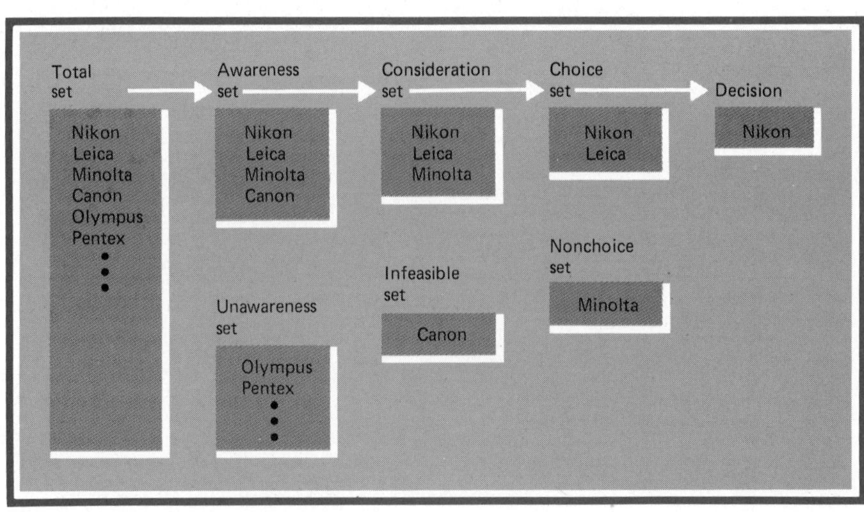

criteria used by the buyer as she moves to successively smaller sets in making her decision.

who participates in the consumer buying process? (*buying participants*)

In consumer marketing there is a strong temptation to identify the *buyer* (also called the *customer* or *decision-making unit*) and focus most of the effort on influencing that buyer. For some products, this seems logical because their purchase is relatively simple and involves primarily one participant in the decision-making process. Thus men are normally the decision-making unit for pipe tobacco, and women are the decision-making unit for panty hose, with little influence coming from the other. On the other hand, the decision-making unit for a family automobile or vacation is likely to consist of husband, wife, and older children. In these cases the marketer must take steps to identify the other participants in the buying process and the roles they play.

Let us look more closely at the problem of identifying the buying participants, namely, all of those who have exerted some direct influence on a buying decision. Suppose the Plaza Hotel in New York City is anxious to attract more wedding parties to its facilities. Its promotion program will be more efficient if it can identify the major buying participants and select the messages and media that would be most effective with these participants. The most frequent participants in the hotel wedding selection decision are the bride and groom, the bride and groom's families, friends of the families, friends of the bride and groom, and the wedding consultants.

The next thing to note is that these participants can play up to five different roles in the buying process:

1. *Initiator.* The initiator is the person who first suggests or thinks of the idea of buying the particular product or service.
2. *Influencer.* An influencer is a person whose views or advice carries some weight in making the final decision.
3. *Decider.* The decider is a person who ultimately determines any part of or the entire buying decision: whether to buy, what to buy, how to buy, when to buy, or where to buy.
4. *Buyer.* The buyer is the person who makes the actual purchase.
5. *User.* The user is the person(s) who consumes or uses the product or service.

For example, the bride's girlfriend may have initiated the question of where the wedding party would be held. Afterward the bride may have consulted several persons to obtain their opinions. The actual decision may be made jointly by the bride and groom, with the bride being slightly dominant. The bride and her mother might act as the buyer by signing the contract with the hotel. The users consist of the bride and groom and their entire wedding party.

The hotel should therefore identify and sort out the roles played by the different decision participants in selecting a hotel. The hotel will want to direct most of its publicity at the deciders. If brides do most of the deciding, then the hotel will want to research the typical criteria used by brides in selecting hotels.

A bride may be particularly interested in the elegance of the ballroom and the quality of the food. The bride's father may be particularly interested in the cost. Knowing who are the main buying participants and what attributes they look at most helps the marketer in fine tuning the marketing program.

what are the major influences on consumer buyers?

(buying influences)

A multitude of influences come into play in shaping the buying behavior of the various participants in a buying decision. Returning to the earlier illustration of Betty Smith's purchase of a camera, we can sort the various influences on her decision into four major groups. There are influences associated with the *buyer* (here Betty Smith), the *product*, the *seller*, and the *situation*:

1. *Buyer characteristics.* We would first need to know several things about Betty Smith to understand how she came to buy a Nikon camera. The various things could be grouped into *cultural, social, personal,* and *psychological* characteristics (see Figure 8-3), and will be discussed in the next section.
2. *Product characteristics.* Various product characteristics will influence the buying decision. Betty Smith will pay attention to the Nikon's features, styling, quality, price, and backup services in making her decision. The marketer has control over these product attributes and can design them in such a way that they will maximize the product's appeal to the target market.
3. *Seller characteristics.* Various seller characteristics will influence the buying outcome. In this case Betty Smith will form an opinion about the manufacturer, Nikon, and the retail outlet, say the ABC Camera Company. Betty will have a certain image of Nikon's reliability and service as a manufacturer. Betty will also form an impression of the retailer's knowledgeability, friendliness, and service. Thus the manufacturer and the retailer will want to consider the seller characteristics that make a difference to whether Betty buys the camera.
4. *Situational characteristics.* Various situational factors also influence the buying decision. One such factor is the *time pressure* felt by Betty Smith to make a decision. Under great time pressure, she might make the decision with less information and rely more on the salesperson than she would if she had more time to investigate. Other factors include the time of year, the weather, chance meetings with friends who have opinions about cameras, the current economic outlook, and so on.

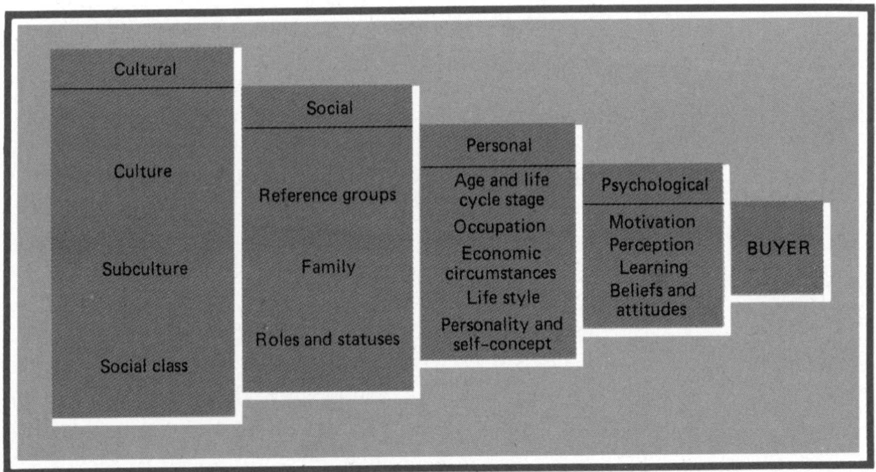

Figure 8-3 *Buyer Characteristics Influencing Consumer Buying Behavior*

All four components of the buying situation—the buyer, product, seller, and situation—interact to produce the buying outcome. We will have much to say about the product, seller, and situation in the following chapters. Here we will concentrate on the buyer characteristics shown in Figure 8-3. We want to understand how the buyer's cultural, social, personal, and psychological characteristics influence the buying outcome.

Cultural Characteristics

The broadest influence on the buyer consists of the buyer's cultural characteristics, particularly the buyer's culture, subculture, and social class. We will look at the role played by each of these.

Culture. Culture is the most fundamental determinant of a person's wants and behavior.[13] Whereas the behavior of lower creatures is largely governed by instinct, human behavior is largely learned. The child growing up in a society learns a basic set of values, perceptions, preferences, and behaviors through a process of socialization involving the family and other key institutions.

Betty Smith's knowledge and interest in cameras is a function of being raised in a modern society where camera technology and a whole set of consumer learnings and values have developed. Betty is able to consider a camera because she knows what cameras are; she knows how to read instructions on how to operate cameras; and her society has accepted the idea of women photographers. In another culture, say a remote backward tribe in central Australia, a camera would mean nothing. It would simply be a curiosity. International marketers know that cultures are at different stages of development and interest with respect to buying cameras and other objects and have to consider this in choosing target markets and preparing marketing programs.

Subculture. Each culture contains smaller groups or subcultures, and each of these provides more specific identification and socialization for its members. Four types of subcultures can be distinguished. *Nationality groups* such as the Irish, Polish, Italians, and Puerto Ricans are found within large communities and exhibit distinct ethnic tastes and proclivities. *Religious groups* such as the Catholics, Mormons, Presbyterians, and Jews represent subcultures with specific cultural preferences and taboos. *Racial groups* such as the blacks and orientals have distinct cultural styles and attitudes. *Geographical areas* such as the Deep South, California, and New England are distinct subcultures with characteristic life styles.

Betty Smith's interest in various goods will obviously be influenced by her nationality, religion, race, and geographical background. This would most likely be true of her food preferences and might also influence her clothing choices, recreations, and career aspirations. Her subculture identifications may or may not have played a prominent role in her wanting to buy a camera and choosing a Nikon. We can imagine that subcultures attach different meanings to picture taking, and this could have influenced her interest.

Social class. Virtually all human societies exhibit social stratification. Stratification may take the form of a caste system where the members of different castes are reared for certain roles and cannot change their caste membership.

More frequently, stratification takes the form of social classes. *Social classes are relatively homogeneous and enduring divisions in a society which are hierarchically ordered and whose members share similar values, interests, and behavior.* Social scientists have identified the six social classes shown in Table 8-1.

Social classes have several characteristics: (1) persons within a given social class tend to behave more alike; (2) persons are ranked as occupying inferior or superior positions according to their social class; (3) social class is not indicated

Table 8-1
Characteristics of Six Major American Social Classes

1. *UPPER UPPERS* (LESS THAN 1 PERCENT). Upper uppers are the social elite who live on inherited wealth and have a well-known family background. They give large sums to charity, run the debutante balls, maintain more than one home, and send their children to the finest schools. They are a market for jewelry, antiques, homes, and vacations. They often buy and dress conservatively, not being interested in ostentation. While small as a group, they serve as a reference group for others to the extent that their consumption decisions trickle down and are imitated by the other social classes.

2. *LOWER UPPERS* (ABOUT 2 PERCENT). Lower uppers are persons who have earned high income or wealth through exceptional ability in the professions or business. They usually come from the middle class. They tend to be active in social and civic affairs and seek to buy the symbols of status for themselves and their children, such as expensive homes, schools, yachts, swimming pools, and automobiles. They include the *nouveaux riches*, whose pattern of conspicuous consumption is designed to impress those below them. The ambition of lower uppers is to be accepted in the upper-upper stratum, which is more likely to be achieved by their children than themselves.

3. *UPPER MIDDLES* (12 PERCENT). Upper middles possess neither family status nor unusual wealth. They are primarily concerned with "career." They have attained positions as professionals, independent businesspersons, and corporate managers. They believe in education and want their children to develop professional or administrative skills so that they will not drop into a lower stratum. Members of this class like to deal in ideas and "high culture." They are joiners and highly civic-minded. They are the quality market for good homes, clothes, furniture, and appliances. They seek to run a gracious home entertaining friends and clients.

4. *LOWER MIDDLES* (30 PERCENT). Lower middles consist of primarily white-collar workers (office workers, small-business owners), "gray collars" (mailmen, firemen), and "aristocrat blue collars" (plumbers, factory foremen). They are concerned with "respectability." They exhibit conscientious work habits and adhere to culturally defined norms and standards, including going to church and obeying the law. The home is important, and lower middles like to keep it neat and "pretty." They buy conventional home furnishings and do a lot of their own work around the home. They prefer clothes that are neat and clean rather than high-styled.

5. *UPPER LOWERS* (35 PERCENT). Upper lowers are the largest social class segment, the blue-collar working class of skilled and semiskilled factory workers. While they seek respectability, their main drive is security, "protecting what they have." The working-class husband has a strong "all-male" self-image, being a sports enthusiast, outdoorsman, and heavy smoker and beer drinker. The working-class wife spends most of her time in the house cooking, cleaning, and caring for her children. She sees being the mother of her children as her main vocation, and she has little time for organizations and social activity.

6. *LOWER LOWERS* (20 PERCENT). Lower lowers are at the bottom of society and consist of poorly educated, unskilled laborers. They are often out of work and on some form of public assistance. Their housing is typically substandard and located in slum areas. They often reject middle-class standards of morality and behavior. They buy more impulsively. They often do not evaluate quality, and they pay too much for products and buy on credit. They are a large market for food, television sets, and used automobiles.

Source: Adapted from James F. Engel, Roger D. Blackwell, and David T. Kollat, *Consumer Behavior*, 3rd ed. (New York: Holt, Rinehart & Winston, 1978), pp. 127–28.

by any single variable but is measured as a weighted function of one's occupation, income, wealth, education, value orientation, and so on; and (4) social class is continuous rather than discrete, with individuals able to move into a higher social class or drop into a lower one.

Social classes show distinct product and brand preferences in such areas as clothing, home furnishings, leisure activity, and automobiles. As a result, marketers of certain goods will want to focus their effort on only one or a few social classes. A manufacturer of fine traditional furniture such as Baker will specialize in designing furniture for higher-social-class consumers, whereas the Kroehler Company will design most of its furniture for the working class. The target social class will suggest the type of retailing to use. Certain stores are perceived as appealing to the higher social classes, others to the lower social classes. The social classes differ in their media exposure, with higher-social-class consumers tending to have greater exposure to magazines and newspapers. When lower-class consumers read magazines, they tend to be romance and movie magazines. The social classes differ in their television program preferences, with the higher-social-class members preferring current events and drama and the lower-social-class members preferring soap operas and quiz shows. There are also pronounced language differences between the social classes. Thus the advertiser, who is normally middle class, has to be skillful in composing words and dialogues that ring true to the target social class.

In the case of Betty Smith, we would guess that she comes from a higher-social-class background. She is a college graduate and is undertaking the purchase of an expensive camera, which requires some skill in operating. She may harbor the idea of becoming a professional photographer, another sign of higher-class aspirations.

Social Characteristics

A consumer's behavior is influenced not only by broad cultural factors but also by social factors, such as the consumer's reference groups, family, and social roles and statuses.

Reference groups. Reference groups are all those groups that influence a person's attitudes, opinions, and values. Some are *primary groups* (also called face-to-face groups, such as family, close friends, neighbors, and fellow workers), and others are *secondary groups* (fraternal organizations, professional associations). People are also influenced by groups in which they are not members, called *aspirational groups* (such as sports heroes and movie stars).

A person is significantly influenced by his or her reference groups in at least three ways. These reference groups expose the person to possible new behaviors and life styles. They also influence the person's attitudes and self-concept because he or she normally desires to "fit in." And they create pressures for conformity that may affect the person's actual product and brand choices.

A company would like to know whether a consumer's decisions to purchase its product and brand are importantly influenced by reference groups, and if so, which reference groups. With regard to some products, such as soap and canned peaches, the buyer normally makes choices without any reference group influence. Betty Smith's friends are not a factor in her decision to buy soap or the brand of soap she buys. To the extent that product or brand choice is not subject to reference group influence, the seller's marketing communications should stress the product's attributes, price, and quality, or other differential advantages.

There are other products where reference group influence tends to be a strong factor in product and/or brand choice.[14] Reference group influence tends to be strong when the product is visible and conspicuous to other people whom the buyer respects. Betty Smith's decision to buy a camera and her brand choice may be strongly influenced by some of her reference groups. Friends who belong to a photography club may have a strong influence on her decision to buy a good camera and on the brand she chooses. At the same time, another reference group, such as her girlfriends, probably have no influence on either decision. The more cohesive the reference group, the more effective its communication process and the higher the person esteems it, the more influential it will be in shaping the person's product and brand choices.

If sellers sense that certain reference groups have a high impact on consumer behavior, their task is to figure out how to reach the group opinion leaders. At one time, sellers thought that *opinion leaders* were primarily community social leaders whom the mass market imitated because of "snob appeal." Today it is recognized that opinion leaders are found in all strata of society and that a specific person may be an opinion leader in certain product areas and an opinion follower in other areas. The marketer tries to reach the opinion leaders by identifying certain personal characteristics associated with opinion leadership, determining the media read by opinion leaders, and developing messages that are likely to be picked up by opinion leaders.

Family. Among the buying participants who most directly influence individual buying decisions are members of the buyer's family. Actually, we can distinguish between two families in every person's life. The *family of orientation* consists of one's parents. From his or her parents a person acquires a mental set involving not only religion, politics, and economics but also personal ambition, self-worth, and love. Even if the buyer no longer interacts very much with his or her parents, the parents' influence on the unconscious behavior of the buyer can be significant. In countries where parents continue to live with their children, their influence can be crucial.

Even more important as an influence on everyday buying behavior is one's *family of procreation*. The family is the most important consumer-buying organization in society, and it has been researched extensively.[15] Marketers are interested in the roles and relative influence of the husband, wife, and children in the purchase of a large variety of products and services.

Husband-wife involvement varies widely by product category. The wife has traditionally been the main purchasing agent for the family, especially in the areas of food, sundries, and staple clothing items. This is changing with the increased number of working wives and the willingness of husbands to do more of the family purchasing. Marketers of staple products would therefore be making a mistake to continue to think of women as the main or only purchasers of their products.

In the case of more expensive and less frequently purchased products and services, husbands and wives engage in more joint decision making. The issue that arises is which member has the greater influence on the decision to purchase a particular product or service. Either the husband is more dominant, or the wife, or they have equal influence (the last is called syncretic). The following products and services fall under each:

- *Husband-dominant*: life insurance, automobiles, television
- *Wife-dominant*: washing machines, carpeting, non-living-room furniture, kitchenware
- *Syncretic*: living-room furniture, vacation, housing, outside entertainment

At the same time, the dominance of a family member varies for different subdecisions within a product category. For example, Davis found that the decision of "when to buy an automobile" was influenced primarily by the husband in 68 percent of the cases, primarily by the wife in 3 percent of the cases, and equally in 29 percent of the cases.[16] On the other hand, the decision of "what color of automobile to buy" was influenced primarily by the husband in 25 percent of the cases, by the wife in 25 percent of the cases, and equally in 50 percent of the cases. An automobile company would take these varying decision roles into account in designing and promoting its cars.

In the case of Betty Smith buying a camera, her husband will play an influencer role. He will have an opinion about her buying a camera and the kind of camera to buy. At the same time, she will be the primary decider, purchaser, and user.

Roles and statuses. A person participates in many groups throughout his or her life—family, other reference groups, organizations, and institutions. The specific position that a person has in each group can be defined in terms of *role* and *status*. For example, with her parents, Betty Smith plays the role of *daughter;* in her family, she plays the role of *wife;* in her company, she plays the role of *brand manager*. A *role* consists of a set of activities that the individual is supposed to perform according to the definition and expectations of the individual and the persons around him or her. Each of Betty's roles will influence some of her buying behavior.

Each role has a *status* attached to it, which reflects the general esteem accorded to that role in society or in the eyes of the immediate group. The role of brand manager has more status in this society than the role of daughter. As a brand manager, Betty will buy the kind of clothing that reflects her role and status.

Personal Characteristics

A buyer's decisions are also influenced by personal outward characteristics, notably the buyer's age and life-cycle stage, occupation, economic circumstances, life style, and personality and self-concept. We will examine these personal characteristics in the following paragraphs.

Age and life-cycle stage. There is no question that the goods and services that people buy change over their lifetime. The type of food that people eat changes from baby food in the early years, to most foods in the growing and mature years, to special diets and food taboos in the later years. People's taste in clothes, furniture, and recreation is also age-related.

Not only does age affect one's buying decisions, it also affects one's marital status, presence or absence of children, and their ages. Marketers have combined these factors into the concept of the *family life cycle*. Nine stages of the family life cycle have been distinguished. They are listed in Table 8-2, along with the financial situation and typical product interests of each group. Marketers are increasingly defining their target markets in life-cycle-stage terms and are developing appropriate products and marketing plans.

Some recent work is now attempting to identify *psychological life-cycle stages*. Adults will experience certain *passages* or *transformations* as they go through life.[17] Thus Betty Smith may move from being a satisfied brand manager and wife to being an unsatisfied person searching for a new way to fulfill herself. This may have contributed to her currently strong interest in photography. Marketers should therefore pay more attention to the changing needs of adults for goods and services that might be associated with these adult passages.

Occupation. A person's occupation will lead to certain needs and wants for goods and services. A blue-collar worker will buy work clothes, work shoes, lunch boxes, and bowling recreation. A company president will buy expensive blue serge

Table 8-2 An Overview of the Life Cycle and Buying Behavior

STAGE IN LIFE CYCLE	BUYING OR BEHAVIORAL PATTERN
1. *Bachelor stage:* Young single people not living at home	Few financial burdens. Fashion opinion leaders. Recreation-oriented. Buy: basic kitchen equipment, basic furniture, cars, equipment for the mating game, vacations.
2. *Newly married couples:* Young, no children	Better off financially than they will be in near future. Highest purchase rate and highest average purchase of durables. Buy: cars, refrigerators, stoves, sensible and durable furniture, vacations.
3. *Full nest I:* Youngest child under six	Home purchasing at peak. Liquid assets low. Dissatisfied with financial position and amount of money saved. Interested in new products. Like advertised products. Buy: washers, dryers, TV, baby food, chest rubs and cough medicines, vitamins, dolls, wagons, sleds, skates.
4. *Full nest II:* Youngest child six or over	Financial position better. Some wives work. Less influenced by advertising. Buy larger-sized packages, multiple-unit deals. Buy: many foods, cleaning materials, bicycles, music lessons, pianos.
5. *Full nest III:* Older married couples with dependent children	Financial position still better. More wives work. Some children get jobs. Hard to influence with advertising. High average purchase of durables. Buy: new, more tasteful furniture, auto travel, nonnecessary appliances, boats, dental services, magazines.
6. *Empty nest I:* Older married couples, no children living with them, head in labor force	Home ownership at peak. Most satisfied with financial position and money saved. Interested in travel, recreation, self-education. Make gifts and contributions. Not interested in new products. Buy: vacations, luxuries, home improvements.
7. *Empty nest II:* Older married couples, no children living at home, head retired	Drastic cut in income. Keep home. Buy: medical appliances, medical-care products that aid health, sleep, and digestion.
8. *Solitary survivor, in labor force*	Income still good but likely to sell home.
9. *Solitary survivor, retired*	Same medical and product needs as other retired group; drastic cut in income. Special need for attention, affection, and security.

Source: William D. Wells and George Gubar, "Life Cycle Concept in Marketing Research," *Journal of Marketing Research,* November 1966, pp. 355–63, here p. 362.

suits, air travel, country club membership, and a large sailboat. In general, marketers can study whether certain occupational groups will have an above-average interest in the company's products and services. The company can even choose to specialize in producing the products and services needed by a particular occupational group.

Economic circumstances. A person's economic circumstances will greatly affect the goods and services he or she considers and buys. People's economic circumstances consist of their *spendable income* (its level, stability, and time pattern), *savings and assets* (including the percentage that is liquid), *borrowing power,* and *attitude toward spending versus saving.* Thus Betty Smith can only consider buying an expensive Nikon if she has enough spendable income, savings, or borrowing power and she places a higher importance on spending than saving. Marketers of various income-sensitive goods and services pay continuous attention to trends in personal income, savings, and interest rates. If economic indicators predict a worsening economic climate, marketers can take positive steps to redesign, reposition, and reprice their product, reduce their production and inventories, and do other things to protect their financial solvency.

Life style. A person's buying behavior is also affected by his or her chosen life style. People coming from the same subculture, social class, and even occupational group may lead quite different life styles. Betty Smith, for example, can choose to live like a capable homemaker, a career woman, or a free spirit. As it turns out, she plays several roles and her way of reconciling them becomes her life style. If she gravitates toward becoming a professional photographer, this has further life-style implications, such as keeping odd hours and doing a considerable amount of traveling.

Marketers believe that a person's product and brand choices are a key indicator of his or her life style. The following male is very real to us as a result of knowing his consumer preferences:

- He's a bachelor . . . lives in one of those modern high-rise apartments and the rooms are brightly colored. He has modern, expensive furniture, but not Danish modern. He buys his clothes at Brooks Brothers. He owns a good hi-fi. He skis. He has a sailboat. He eats Limburger and any other prestige cheese with his beer. He likes and cooks a lot of steak and would have filet mignon for company. His liquor cabinet has Jack Daniels bourbon, Beefeater gin, and a good Scotch.[18]

The implications of the life-style concept are well stated by Boyd and Levy:

- Marketing is a process of providing customers with parts of a potential mosaic from which they, as artists of their own life styles, can pick and choose to develop the composition that for the time seems the best. The marketer who thinks about his products in this way will seek to understand their potential settings and relationships to other parts of consumer life styles, and thereby to increase the number of ways they fit meaningfully into the pattern.[19]

Personality and self-concept. Another characteristic influencing a person's buying behavior is personality. Personality describes the person's distinguishing character traits, attitudes, and habits. Each person has a distinct personality marked by his or her degree of extroversion versus introversion, creativity versus conventionality, activeness versus passiveness, and so on. Suppose Betty Smith is extroverted, creative, and active. This would explain to some extent her interest in photography. It would also imply that she would be active in searching for a camera, talking to people, asking them questions, and buying when it felt right.

Marketers of various products search for potential personality traits that their target market might reveal. For example, a beer company might discover that heavy beer drinkers are more outgoing, aggressive, and dogmatic. It might decide to develop a brand image for its beer that would appeal to this type of person. The likely step is to feature in its ads a real person who has these traits so that heavy beer drinkers can identify and feel that this is their brand. While personality variables have not shown up that strongly in all product areas, some companies have been able to use personality segmentation to advantage.[20]

Many marketers use a related concept to personality—a person's *self-concept* (also called self-image). All of us carry around a complex mental picture of ourselves. For example, Betty may see herself as extroverted, creative, and active. To that extent, she would favor a camera that projects the same qualities. If the Nikon is promoted as a camera for extroverted, creative, and active persons, then its brand image would match her self-image. The implication is that marketers should develop brand images that match the self-image of the target group in the market.

The theory, however, is not that simple. What if Betty's *actual self-concept* (how she views herself) differs from her *ideal self-concept* (how she would like to view herself) and from her *others-self-concept* (how she thinks others see her). Which of her selves will she try to satisfy with the choice of a camera? Some marketers feel that buyers' choices will correspond more to their actual self-concept, other marketers favor the ideal self-concept, and still other marketers favor the others-self-concept. As a result, self-concept theory has had a mixed record of success in predicting consumer responses to brand images.[21]

Psychological Characteristics

A person's buying choices are also influenced by four major psychological processes—motivation, perception, learning, and beliefs and attitudes. We will explore the role played by these psychological processes in the following paragraphs.

Motivation. We saw that Betty Smith became interested in buying a camera. Why? What was she really seeking? What needs was she trying to satisfy?

A person will have all kinds of needs at any point in time. Some needs are *biogenic*. They arise from physiological states of tension such as might be caused by the need for food, drink, sex, and bodily comfort. Other needs are *psychogenic*. They arise from psychological states of tension such as the need for recognition, response, or variety of experience. Most of these needs will not be intense enough to motivate the person to act at a given point in time. A need becomes a motive when it is aroused to a sufficient level of intensity. A *motive* (or drive) is a stimulated need which is sufficiently pressing to direct the person toward the goal of satisfying the need. After the need is satisfied, the person's tension is discharged and he or she returns to a state of equilibrium.

Psychologists have proposed various theories of human motivation. Three of the most popular are the theories of Sigmund Freud, Abraham Maslow, and Frederick Herzberg. Each has interesting implications for consumer marketing.

FREUD'S THEORY OF MOTIVATION

Freud asserts that people are not likely to be conscious of the real motives guiding their behavior because these motives have been shaped in early childhood and are often repressed from their own consciousness. Children enter the world with strong self-gratification drives. Very quickly and painfully they learn that instant need gratification is not possible. Repeated frustration leads the child to perfect more subtle means for gratification.

The child's psyche grows more complex as the child grows older. One part, the *id,* remains the reservoir of strong drives and urges. Another part, the *ego,* becomes the child's conscious center for planning to obtain satisfactions. A third part, the *superego,* causes the instinctive drives to be channeled into socially approved outlets to avoid the pain of guilt or shame.

The guilt or shame a person feels about some urges, especially sexual urges, leads to their repression. Through such defense mechanisms as rationalization and sublimation, these urges are denied or are transformed into socially acceptable behavior. Yet these urges are never eliminated or under perfect control; they emerge in dreams, in slips of the tongue, in neurotic and obsessional behavior, or ultimately in mental breakdowns when the ego can no longer maintain the delicate balance between the impulsive power of the id and the oppressive power of the superego.

Human behavior, therefore, is never simple. A person does not fully understand his or her motivational wellsprings, nor are they obvious to a casual observer. If Betty is about to purchase an expensive camera, she may describe her motive as wanting a hobby or career. At a deeper level, she may be purchasing the camera to impress others with her creative talent. At a still deeper level, she may be buying the camera to feel young and independent again.

An important marketing implication of Freudian motivation theory is that buyers are motivated by *psychological* as well as *functional* product concerns. When Betty looks at a camera, she will not only process information about the camera's performance but also react to other cues. The camera's shape, size, weight, material, color, and case are all capable of triggering certain emotions. A rugged-looking camera can arouse Betty's feelings about being independent, which she can either handle or try to avoid. The manufacturer, in designing the camera's features, should be aware of the impact of visual and tactile elements in triggering consumer emotions that can stimulate or inhibit purchase.

The leading exponent of Freudian motivation theory in marketing is Ernest Dichter, who for over two decades has been interpreting buying situations and product choices in terms of underlying unconscious motives. Dichter calls his approach *motivational research,* and it consists of "in-depth interviews" with a few dozen target buyers to uncover their deeper motives triggered by the product. Various "projective techniques" are used to throw the ego off guard—techniques such as word association, sentence completion, picture interpretation, and role playing.[22]

Motivation researchers have produced some interesting and occasionally bizarre hypotheses as to what may be in the buyer's mind regarding certain purchases. They have suggested that

- Consumers resist prunes because they are wrinkled-looking and remind people of old age.
- Men smoke cigars as an adult version of thumbsucking. They like their cigars to have a strong odor in order to prove their masculinity.
- Women prefer vegetable shortening to animal fats because the latter arouse a sense of guilt over killing animals.
- A woman is very serious when baking a cake because unconsciously she is going through the symbolic act of giving birth. She dislikes easy-to-use cake mixes because the easy life evokes a sense of guilt.

MASLOW'S THEORY OF MOTIVATION

Abraham Maslow's interest lay in identifying the relationship of various human needs to each other. His theory of motivation can be stated as follows:[23]

1. A person has many needs. In the order of importance, they are *physiological* needs, *safety* needs, *social* needs, *esteem* needs, and *self-actualization* needs.
2. A person will try to satisfy the more important needs first.
3. When a person succeeds in satisfying an important need, it will cease being a motivator for the present time, and he or she will be motivated to satisfy the next-most-important need.

For example, a starving man (need 1) will not take an interest in the latest doing in the art world (need 5), nor even in how he is seen or esteemed by others (need 3 or 4), nor even in whether he is breathing clean air (need 2). But as each important need is satisfied, the next-most-important need will come into play.

What light does Maslow's theory throw on Betty Smith's interest in buying a camera? We can guess that Betty has satisfied her physiological, safety, and social needs; in which case, they are not motivators of her interest in cameras. We can consider the possibility that her camera interest comes from a strong need for more esteem from others. If this need is satisfied, we would guess that her camera interest is meeting her need for self-actualization. She wants to actualize her potential as a creative person and express herself through photography.

HERZBERG'S THEORY OF MOTIVATION

Frederick Herzberg is also interested in the role that different needs play in a person's motivation.[24] He has developed a "two-factor theory" of motivation, which distinguishes between *dissatisfiers* (factors that cause dissatisfaction) and *satisfiers* (factors that cause satisfaction). For example, if the Nikon camera did not come with a warranty, this would be a dissatisfier. Betty would like a product warranty. At the same time, the presence of a product warranty would not act as a satisfier or motivator of her purchase, since it is not a source of intrinsic satisfaction with the Nikon camera. The Nikon camera's capacity to shoot scenes at one thousandth of a second would be a satisfier. Faster camera speeds would increase Betty's ability to enjoy the camera and photography.

The marketing implications of this theory of motivation are twofold. First, sellers should do their best to eliminate dissatisfiers from affecting the buyer—dissatisfiers such as insufficient printed information on how the camera is operated, an arrogant salesperson, and a poorly designed carrying case. While these things will not sell the camera, they might easily unsell the camera. Second, the manufacturer should carefully identify the major satisfiers or motivators of purchase in the camera market and be sure to include them. These factors will make the major difference as to which camera brand the customer buys.

Perception. A motivated person is ready to act. How the motivated person decides to act is influenced by his or her perception of the situation. Two people in the same motivated state and objective situation may act quite differently because they perceive the situation differently. Betty Smith might see a fast-talking camera salesperson as aggressive and insincere. Another camera buyer might see the same salesperson as intelligent and helpful.

Why do people have different perceptions of the same situation? We start with the notion that all of us apprehend a stimulus object through *sensations*, that is, flows of information through one or more of our five senses: sight, hearing, smell, touch, and taste. However, each of us attends, organizes, and interprets this sensory information in an individual way. In fact, *perception* can be defined as "the process by which an individual selects, organizes, and interprets information inputs to create a meaningful picture of the world."[25] Perception depends not only on (1) the character of the physical stimuli but also on (2) the relation of the stimuli to the surrounding field (the Gestalt idea) and on (3) conditions within the individual.

People can have quite different perceptions of the same stimulus object or situation because of three perceptual processes: selective exposure, selective distortion, and selective retention.

SELECTIVE EXPOSURE

People are exposed to a tremendous amount of stimuli every moment of their lives. Even limiting this to commercial stimuli, the average person may be exposed to over fifteen hundred ads a day. It is impossible for a person to attend to all of these stimuli. Most of the stimuli will be screened out. The real challenge is to explain which stimuli people will notice. People will be selectively exposed to certain stimuli:

1. People are more likely to notice stimuli that bear on a current felt need of theirs. Betty Smith will notice all kinds of ads about cameras because she is motivated to buy one; she will probably not notice ads about stereophonic equipment.
2. People are more likely to notice stimuli that they anticipate. Betty Smith is more likely to notice cameras in the camera store than a line of radios also carried by the store, because she did not expect the store to carry radios.
3. People are more likely to notice stimuli whose change level is large in relation to the normal size of the stimuli. Betty Smith is more likely to notice an ad offering $100 off the list price of a Nikon than one offering $5 off the list price of a Nikon.[26]

Selective exposure means that marketers have to work especially hard to gain the attention of consumers in the marketplace. Their messages will be lost on most people who are not in the market for the product. Even people who are in the market may not notice the message unless it stands out from the surrounding sea of stimuli. Ads that are larger in size, or use four colors where most ads are black and white, or are novel and provide contrast are more likely to be noticed.

SELECTIVE DISTORTION

Even stimuli that consumers note do not necessarily come across in the intended way. Each person has an organized mind-set and attempts to fit incoming stimuli into preexisting modes of thinking. *Selective distortion* is the name given to the tendency of people to twist information into personal meanings. Thus Betty Smith may hear the salesperson mention some good and bad points about a competing camera brand. Since she already has a strong leaning toward Nikon, she is likely to distort the points she hears in order to conclude that Nikon is the better camera. People tend to interpret information in a way that will support rather than challenge their preconceptions.

SELECTIVE RETENTION

People will forget much that they learn. They will tend to retain information that supports their attitudes and beliefs. Because of selective retention, Betty is likely to remember good points mentioned about the Nikon and forget good points mentioned about competing cameras. She remembers Nikon's good points because she "rehearses" them more whenever she thinks about her decision to buy a camera.

These three perceptual factors—selective exposure, distortion, and retention—mean that marketers have to work hard to break through very strong perceptual filters. This explains why marketers have to buy so much message repetition, and why they place such an emphasis on message dramatization.

Learning. When people act, they experience direct and indirect effects which influence their future behavior. *Learning* is the name given to changes in an individual's behavior arising from experience. Most behavior is learned. The exception is behavior based on instinctive responses, growth, or temporary physiological states of the organism, such as hunger or fatigue.

Learning theorists hold that a person's learning is produced through the interplay of drives, stimuli, cues, responses, and reinforcement.

We saw that Betty Smith has a drive toward self-actualization. A *drive* is defined as a strong internal stimulus impelling action. Her drive becomes a *motive* when it is directed toward a particular drive-reducing *stimulus object*, in this case a camera. Betty's response to the idea of buying a camera is conditioned by the surrounding configuration of cues. *Cues* are minor stimuli that determine when, where, and how the person responds. Her husband's opinion on buying a camera, the economic outlook, and the season of the year are all cues that may affect her *response* to the impulse to buy a camera.

Suppose Betty buys the camera. If the experience is *rewarding,* the probability is that she will use the camera more and more. Her response to cameras will be reinforced.

Later on, Betty may also want to buy a tape recorder and may experience cues similar to those that existed when she bought a camera. If she responds in the same way to these cues and buys the tape recorder and is satisfied, this reinforces her response to similar stimuli and drives in the future. We say that she *generalizes* her response to similar stimuli.

A countertendency to generalization is *discrimination.* When Betty has the opportunity to use two similar cameras on a trial basis and finds one more rewarding, her ability to discriminate between fairly similar cue configurations in the future improves. Discrimination means she has learned to recognize differences in sets of stimuli and can adjust her responses accordingly.

The practical import of learning theory for marketers is that they can build up demand for a product by associating it with strong drives, using motivating cues, and providing positive reinforcement. A new company can enter the market by appealing to the same drives as competitors and providing similar cue configurations because buyers are more likely to transfer loyalty to similar brands than to dissimilar brands (generalization). Or it may aim its brand to appeal to a different set of strong drives and offer cue inducements to switch.

Beliefs and attitudes. Through the learning process, people acquire their beliefs and attitudes. These in turn influence their buying behavior.

A *belief* is a *descriptive thought that a person holds about something.* Betty Smith may believe that a Nikon takes great pictures, stands up well under rugged usage, and costs $550. These beliefs may be based on real knowledge, opinion, or faith. They may or may not carry an emotional charge. For example, Betty Smith's belief that a Nikon camera is black may or may not matter to her decision.

Manufacturers, of course, are very interested in the beliefs that people carry in their heads about their products and services. These beliefs make up product and brand images, and people's behavior will partly be a function of their beliefs. If some of the beliefs are wrong and inhibit purchase, the manufacturer would want to launch a campaign to correct these beliefs.

An *attitude* describes a person's *enduring favorable or unfavorable cognitive evaluations, emotional feelings, and action tendencies toward some object or idea.*[27] People have attitudes regarding almost everything: religion, politics, clothes, music, food, and so on. Attitudes put them into a frame of mind of liking or disliking things, moving toward or moving away from them. Thus Betty Smith may hold such attitudes as "Buy the best," "The Japanese make the best products in the world," and "Creativity and self-expression are among the most important things in life." The Nikon camera is therefore salient to Betty because it fits well into her preexisting attitudes. A company would benefit greatly from researching the various attitudes people have that might bear on its product.

Attitudes function in people's lives to enable them to have a fairly consistent behavior toward similar classes of objects. People do not have to interpret and react to everything in a fresh way. Attitudes economize on energy and thought. For this very reason, attitudes are very difficult to change. A person's various attitudes have settled into a consistent pattern, and to change one may require painful adjustments in many other attitudes.

Thus a company would be well advised to try to fit its products into existing attitudes, rather than to try to change people's attitudes. There are exceptions, of course, where the greater cost of trying to change attitudes might pay off.

- Honda entered the U.S. motorcycle market facing a major decision. It could either sell its motorcycles to a small market of people already interested in motorcycles or try to increase the number of people who would be interested in motorcycles. The latter would be more expensive because many people had negative attitudes about motorcycles and motorcycle riders. They associated motorcyclists with negative elements such as knives, black leather jackets, and crime. Honda took the second course and launched a major campaign based on the theme "You meet the nicest people on a Honda." Its campaign worked and many people adopted a new attitude toward motorcycling.

We are now in a position to appreciate the incredible complexity involved in the act of someone buying something. The person's choice is the result of the complex interplay of cultural, social, personal, and psychological factors. Many of these factors are beyond the influence of the marketer. However, they are useful in identifying those buyers who might be more interested in the product than others. Other factors are subject to marketer influence and clue the marketer on how to develop certain product, price, place, and promotion elements for optimum impact on the marketplace.

how do consumers make their buying decisions? *(buying process)*

We are now ready to examine the actual stages the buyer passes through to reach a buying decision and outcome. Although we will focus on one person, we should realize that there may be a changing set of buying participants in the different stages with different types of influence on the buyer. In addition, there will be other influential factors on the person's buying behavior coming in at each stage. The purpose of distinguishing different stages in the buying process is to identify what marketers can do to facilitate and influence favorable buying outcomes.

The model in Figure 8-4 shows the consumer as passing through five stages: *problem recognition, information search, information evaluation, purchase decision,* and *postpurchase behavior.* This model emphasizes that the buying process starts long before the actual purchase and has consequences long after the purchase. It encourages the marketer to focus on the buying process rather than the purchase decision.[28]

Problem Recognition

The buying process starts with the buyer recognizing a problem or need. The buyer senses a difference between his or her actual state and a desired state. The need can be triggered by internal or external stimuli. In the former case, one of the person's normal needs—hunger, thirst, sex—rises to a threshold level and becomes a drive. From previous experience, the person has learned how to cope

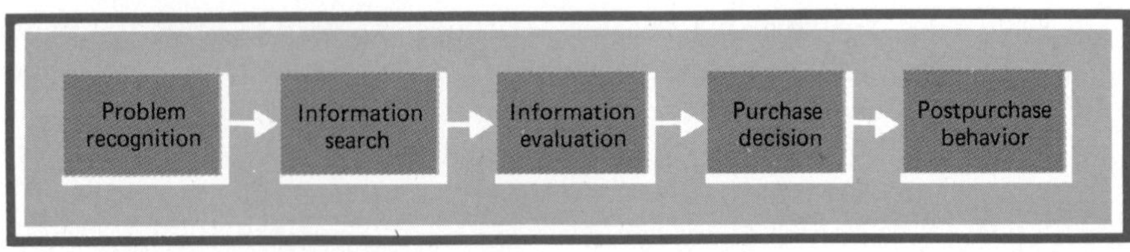

Figure 8-4
Five-Stage Model of the Consumer Buying Process

with this drive and is motivated toward a class of objects that he or she knows will satisfy this drive.

Or a need can be aroused by an external stimulus. A woman passes a bakery and the sight of freshly baked bread stimulates her hunger; she admires a neighbor's new car; or she watches a television commercial for a Jamaican vacation. All of these can lead her to recognize a problem or need.

The challenge to the marketer at this stage is to determine the circumstances usually triggering consumer problem recognition. The marketer should research consumers to find out (a) what kinds of felt needs or problems arose, (b) what brought them about, and (c) how they led to this particular product. Betty Smith might answer that she felt a need for a new hobby; this happened when her "busy season" at work slowed down; and she was led to think of cameras as a result of a friend's talking to her about photography. By gathering such information, the marketer will have a chance to identify the more frequent stimuli that give rise to interest in the product category. The marketer can then develop marketing plans that capitalize on these stimuli.

Information Search

An aroused consumer may or may not search for more information. If the consumer's drive is strong and a well-defined gratification object is near at hand, the consumer is likely to buy it then. If not, the consumer's need may simply be stored in memory. The consumer may undertake no further search, some further search, or very active search for information bearing on the need.

Assuming that the consumer undertakes some search, we distinguish between two levels. The milder search state is called *heightened attention.* Here Betty Smith simply becomes more receptive to information about cameras. She pays attention to ads about cameras, notices cameras that are used by friends, and listens more to camera conversation.

Or Betty may go into *active information search,* where she will look for reading material, phone friends, and engage in other search activities to gather product information. How much search she undertakes depends upon the strength of her drive, the amount of information she initially has, the ease of obtaining additional information, the value she places on additional information, and the satisfaction she gets from search. Normally the amount of consumer search activity increases as the consumer moves from decision situations of limited problem solving to extensive problem solving.

Of key interest to the marketer are the major information sources that the consumer will turn to and the relative influence each will have on the subsequent purchase decision. *Consumer information sources* fall into four groups:

- *Personal sources* (family, friends, neighbors, acquaintances)
- *Commercial sources* (advertising, salespersons, dealers, packaging, displays)
- *Public sources* (mass media, consumer rating organizations)
- *Experiential sources* (handling, examining, using the product)

The relative influence of these information sources varies with the product category and the consumer's personal characteristics. Generally speaking, the consumer receives the most information exposure about a product from commercial sources, that is, marketer-dominated sources. On the other hand, the most effective exposures tend to come from personal sources. Each type of source may perform a somewhat different function in influencing the buying decision. Commercial information normally performs an *informing* function, and personal sources perform a *legitimizing* or an *evaluation* function. For example, physicians normally learn of new drugs from commercial sources but turn to other doctors for evaluation information.

The marketer will find it worthwhile to study the consumers' information sources whenever (1) a substantial percentage of the target market engages in active search and (2) the target market shows some stable patterns of using the respective information sources. Identifying the information sources and their respective roles and importance calls for interviewing consumers and asking them how they happened to hear about the product, what sources of information they turned to, and what influence each source of information had. The marketer can use the findings to plan effective marketing communications and stimulate favorable word of mouth.

Information Evaluation

The incoming information helps the consumer clarify and evaluate the alternatives in the evoked set. The marketer needs to know how the consumer processes the incoming information to arrive at product judgments. Unfortunately there is no simple and single information evaluation process used by all consumers, or even by one consumer in all buying situations. There are several consumer evaluation processes.

Certain basic concepts help in understanding consumer evaluation processes. The first concept is that of *product attributes*. We assume that each consumer sees a given product as a bundle of attributes. The consumer perceives the product in terms of where it stands on these attributes. The attributes of normal interest to buyers in some familiar product classes are:

- *Cameras:* picture sharpness, camera speeds, range, camera size, ruggedness, price
- *Hotels:* location, cleanliness, atmosphere, cost
- *Mouthwash:* color, effectiveness, kills germs, price, taste/flavor
- *Brassieres:* comfort, fit, life, price, style
- *Lipstick:* color, container, creaminess, prestige factor, taste/flavor
- *Tires:* safety, tread life, ride quality, price

While the above attributes are of normal interest, individual consumers will vary as to which they consider relevant. The market for a product can often be segmented according to the attributes that have primary interest to different customer groups.

Second, the consumer is likely to attach different *importance weights* to the relevant attributes. A distinction can be drawn between the importance of an attribute and its salience.[29] Salient attributes are those that come to the consumer's mind when he or she is asked to think of a product's attributes. The marketer must not conclude that these are necessarily the most important attributes. Some of them may be salient because the consumer has just been exposed to a commercial message mentioning them or has had a problem involving them, hence making these attributes "top-of-the-mind." Furthermore, in the class of nonsalient attributes may be some that the consumer forgot but whose importance would be recognized when they are mentioned. Marketers should be more concerned with attribute importance than attribute salience.

Third, the consumer is likely to develop a set of *brand beliefs* about where each brand stands on each attribute. The set of beliefs held about a particular brand is known as the *brand image.* The consumer's beliefs or perceptions may be at variance with the true attributes due to his or her particular experience and the effect of selective perception, selective distortion, and selective retention.

Fourth, the consumer is assumed to have a *utility function* for each attribute. The utility function describes how the consumer expects product satisfaction to vary with alternative levels of each attribute. For example, Betty Smith may expect her satisfaction from a camera to increase with the speed of its lens; to peak with a medium-weight camera as opposed to a very light or heavy one; to be higher for a 35-mm camera than for a 135-mm camera. If we combine the attribute levels where the utilities are highest, they make up Betty's ideal camera. The camera would also be her preferred camera if it were available and affordable.

Fifth, the consumer arrives at attitudes (judgments, preferences) toward the brand alternatives through some *evaluation procedure.* Consumers have been found to apply different evaluation procedures to make a choice among multiattribute objects.[30]

To illustrate consumer evaluation procedures, let us leave Betty Smith and turn to Bob Carr, who is trying to choose a college:

- Bob Carr is a high-school senior who has applied to and been accepted at four colleges. He is trying to decide which one to attend. He is primarily interested in the following college attributes: academic quality, social life, location, and cost. His beliefs about the standings of each college on each attribute are shown in Table 8-3. Which college is he likely to choose?

Marketers have observed the following alternative evaluation procedures that consumers use to develop preferences within a set of objects:

1. *Conjunctive model.* Here the consumer sets minimum attribute levels that he will consider and drops those objects that fall short on any attribute. Bob Carr might decide that he will only consider colleges with an academic quality greater than 7 *and* a social life greater than 8. Only college B will satisfy him in this case.

Table 8-3
A High-School Student's Beliefs about Four Colleges

COLLEGE	Attribute			
	ACADEMIC QUALITY	SOCIAL LIFE	LOCATION	TUITION
A	10	8	6	4
B	8	9	8	3
C	6	8	7	5
D	4	3	10	8

Note: Ten represents the highest desirable score on that attribute. In the case of tuition, a high number means a low tuition, which makes the college more desirable.

2. *Disjunctive model.* Here the consumer will consider objects that meet at least one minimum attribute level. Bob might decide that he will only consider colleges with an academic quality greater than 7 *or* a social life greater than 8. Here colleges A or B will remain in the consideration set.
3. *Lexicographic model.* Here the consumer will rank the attributes in order of importance. He will compare the objects on the first ranked attribute and choose the superior one. If two objects are tied, he repeats the process with the second attribute. Bob might decide that academic quality is the most important attribute. In this case, he will choose college A.
4. *Expectancy-value model.*[31] Here the consumer assigns importance weights to the attributes and chooses the object that maximizes the expectancy value. Suppose Bob assigns the following importance weights to the four respective attributes: .4, .3, .2, and .1. That is, Bob assigns 40 percent of the importance to the college's academic quality, 30 percent to its social life, 20 percent to its location, and 10 percent to its tuition cost. To find the expectancy value for each college, these weights are multiplied by the beliefs about that college. This would lead to the following expectancy values:

$$\begin{aligned}
\text{College A} &= .4(10) + .3(8) + .2(6) + .1(4) = 8.0\\
\text{College B} &= .4(8) + .3(9) + .2(8) + .1(3) = 7.8\\
\text{College C} &= .4(6) + .3(8) + .2(7) + .1(5) = 6.7\\
\text{College D} &= .4(4) + .3(3) + .2(10) + .1(8) = 5.3
\end{aligned}$$

   We would therefore predict that Bob, given his weights, will favor college A.
5. *Ideal object model.* Here the consumer decides on the ideal level of each attribute. Suppose Bob would most prefer a college with the levels of 9, 9, 10, and 4 on the respective attributes. The further a college is from these levels, the more Bob would dislike it. According to this information, Bob would prefer colleges B, A, C, and D in this order.
6. *Determinance model.* Here the consumer ignores attributes that may be important but pretty much at the same level for all objects. Suppose the four colleges all have excellent athletic programs. In spite of the fact that Bob may attach high importance to the athletic program, it will have no determinance on his college choice, since all colleges in his set are equal on this attribute. Determinant attributes are those that are both important and highly variable in the class of objects.[32]

Marketers can gain useful insights by interviewing a sample of buyers to find out how most of them form their evaluations in that product class. Suppose the marketer discovers that most of the buyers form their preferences by comparing actual objects with their ideal object. Suppose college A, which would be the second choice of students like Bob Carr (according to the ideal object model), wants to strengthen its chances of attracting this consumer segment. It can consider at least six alternative strategies:[33]

1. *Modifying the object.* The college could alter its attributes to bring it closer to this segment's ideal college. For example, college A could improve the social life so that it gets a higher rating. This is called *real repositioning.*
2. *Altering beliefs about the object.* The college could try to alter students' perceptions of where it actually stands on key attributes. Thus Bob Carr may believe that the tuition is higher than it actually is, and marketing communications can be used to correct this. This is called *psychological repositioning.*
3. *Altering beliefs about the competitors' brands.* The college could try to alter

students' perceptions of where a leading competitor stands on different attributes. This is called *competitive depositioning.*

4. *Altering the attribute importance weights.* The college could try to persuade students to attach more importance to those attributes that the college happens to excel in. For example, college A can attempt to persuade students that academic quality is the most important aspect of any college.
5. *Calling attention to neglected attributes.* The college could try to convince students that they should pay attention to an attribute that they are normally unaware of or indifferent to. If college A is located near a skiing area, it might tout skiing as a fringe benefit of attending college.
6. *Shifting the ideal product.* The college could try to persuade students to change their ideal levels for one or more attributes. College A might try to convince students that a location in a cold climate (rated at 6) is ideal, since they can get more studying done.

Purchase Decision

The evaluation stage leads the consumer to form a ranked set of preferences among the alternative objects in the evoked set. Normally the consumer will move toward the purchase of the most preferred object. He or she will form a purchase intention. However, at least three factors may intervene between forming a purchase intention and making a purchase decision. These factors are shown in Figure 8-5.[34]

The first is the *attitudes of others.* Suppose Bob Carr prefers college B but his father prefers college A. As a result, Bob's "purchase probability" for college A will be somewhat reduced. The extent to which the attitude of another buying participant will reduce one's preferred alternative depends upon two things: (1) the intensity of the other person's negative attitude toward the consumer's preferred alternative and (2) the consumer's motivation to comply with the other person's wishes.[35] The more intense the other person's negativism, and the closer the other person is to the consumer, the more the consumer will revise downward his or her purchase intention.

Purchase intention is also influenced by *anticipated situational factors.* The consumer forms a purchase intention on the basis of such factors as expected family income, expected total cost of the product, and expected benefits from the product.

Figure 8-5
Steps between Information Evaluation and a Purchase Decision

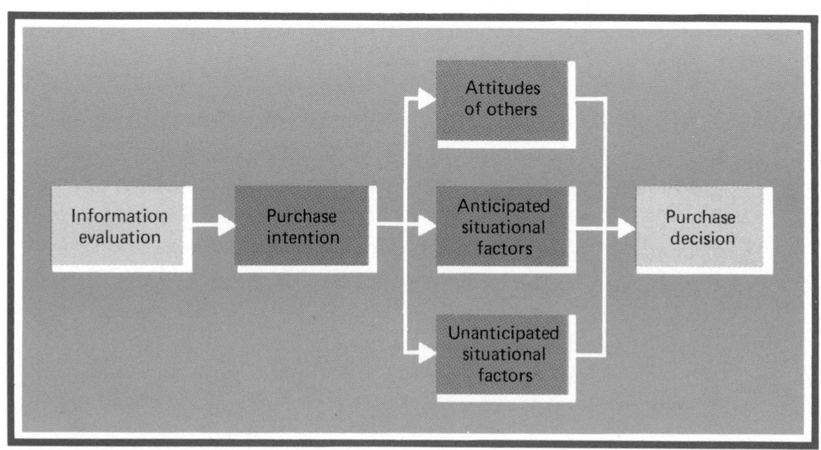

When the consumer is about to act, *unanticipated situational factors* may erupt to prevent the carrying out of the purchase intention. Bob Carr may learn that he cannot get a college loan to attend college A. He may not like the looks of the campus when he visits it. He may be turned off by some of the students or professors he meets. Marketers believe that unanticipated factors in the *critical contact situation* can have a great influence on the final decision.

Thus preferences and even purchase intentions are not completely reliable predictors of actual buying behavior. They give direction to purchase behavior but fail to include a number of additional factors that may intervene.

The decision of an individual to modify, postpone, or avoid a purchase decision is heavily influenced by *perceived risk.* Marketers have devoted a lot of effort to understand buying behavior as *risk taking.*[36] Consumers cannot be certain about the performance and psychosocial consequences of their purchase decision. This produces anxiety. The amount of perceived risk varies with the amount of money at stake, the amount of attribute uncertainty, and the amount of consumer self-confidence. A consumer develops certain routines for reducing risk, such as decision avoidance, information gathering from friends, and preference for national brand names and warranties. The marketer must understand the factors that provoke a feeling of risk in the consumer and attempt to provide information and support that will help reduce this risk.

Postpurchase Behavior

After purchasing and trying the product, the consumer will experience some level of satisfaction or dissatisfaction. Based on this, the consumer will engage in postpurchase actions that will have implications for the marketer. Here we want to look at the marketing implications of postpurchase satisfaction and postpurchase actions.

Postpurchase satisfaction. What determines whether the buyer is highly satisfied, somewhat satisfied, somewhat unsatisfied, or highly unsatisfied with a purchase? There are two major theories about this.

One theory, called the *expectations-performance theory,* holds that a consumer's satisfaction is a function of the consumer's product *expectations* and the product's *perceived performance.*[37] If the product matches expectations, the consumer is satisfied; if it exceeds them, the consumer is highly satisfied; if it falls short, the consumer is dissatisfied.

Consumers form their expectations on the basis of messages and claims sent out by the seller and other communication sources. If the seller makes exaggerated claims for the product, consumers who buy the product will experience *disconfirmed expectations,* which lead to dissatisfaction. Thus if college A fails to perform as Bob Carr was led to expect, Bob will revise downward his attitude toward college A and may drop out, transfer, or bad-mouth the college. On the other hand, if the college meets his expectations, he will tend to be a satisfied student.

The larger the gap between expectations and performance, the greater the consumer's dissatisfaction. Here the consumer's coping style also comes in. Some consumers will tend to magnify the gap when the product is not perfect, and they will be highly dissatisfied. Other consumers will tend to minimize the gap and will feel less dissatisfied.[38]

This theory suggests that the seller should make product claims that faithfully represent the product's likely performance so that buyers experience satisfaction. Some sellers might even understate performance levels so that consumers would experience higher-than-expected satisfaction with the product.

The other theory of postpurchase satisfaction is called the *cognitive dissonance theory.* It holds that almost every purchase is likely to lead to some postpurchase discomfort, and the issues are how much discomfort and what will the consumer do about it. As stated by Festinger and Bramel:

- When a person chooses between two or more alternatives, discomfort or dissonance will almost inevitably arise because of the person's knowledge that while the decision he has made has certain advantages, it also has some disadvantages. That dissonance arises after almost every decision, and further, that the individual will invariably take steps to reduce this dissonance.[39]

The amount of dissonance will be a function of the following factors:

1. The more attractive the rejected alternative, the greater will be the magnitude of the dissonance.
2. The more important the decision, the stronger will be the dissonance.
3. The intensity of dissonance becomes greater as the number of negative characteristics increases.
4. As the number of rejected alternatives increases, the greater will be the dissonance.
5. The greater the perceived similarity of alternatives (cognitive overlap), the greater the dissonance.
6. The more recent the decision between alternatives, the greater will be the magnitude of dissonance because of the phenomenon of forgetting.
7. A decision that violates a strongly held attitude produces greater dissonance than a decision that rebuts a weaker belief.[40]

Under this theory, we can expect Bob Carr to feel some postpurchase dissonance about his college choice. Problems with professors, other students, housing, or athletics are likely to stir doubts in his mind as to whether he made the right choice. He will undertake certain actions to reduce this dissonance.

Postpurchase actions. The consumer's satisfaction or dissatisfaction with the purchase choice will feed back on subsequent behavior. If the consumer is satisfied, then he or she will exhibit a higher probability of purchasing the product on the next occasion. The satisfied consumer will also tend to say good things about the product to others. According to marketers: "Our best advertisement is a satisfied customer."

A dissatisfied consumer will of course respond differently. The dissatified consumer will seek ways to reduce the dissonance because of a drive in the human organism "to establish internal harmony, consistency, or congruity among his opinions, knowledge, and values."[41] Dissonant consumers will resort to one of two courses of action. They may try to reduce the dissonance by *abandoning or returning* the product, or they may try to reduce the dissonance seeking information that might *confirm* its high value (or avoiding information that might disconfirm its high value). In the case of Bob Carr, he might withdraw from the college or, alternatively, he might seek information that would lead him to feel better about the college.

Marketers can take positive steps to help buyers feel good about their choices. Automobile companies often send a cordial letter to new car owners congratulating them on having selected such a fine car. They place ads showing satisfied owners buying their new car.[42] They solicit customer suggestions for improvements and list the location of available services. They write instruction booklets that are dissonance-reducing. They send owners a magazine that contains articles describing the pleasures of owning the new car. Postpurchase communications to buyers have been shown to result in fewer product returns and order cancellations.[43]

Thus we see that understanding the consumer buying process is the foundation of successful marketing. By understanding how buyers go through the stages of problem recognition, information search, information evaluation, the purchase decision, and postpurchase behavior, the marketer can pick up many clues as to how to meet the buyer's needs. By understanding the various participants in the buying process and the major influences on their buying behavior, the marketer can develop an efficient marketing program to support an attractive offer to the target market.

■ summary

Markets have to be understood before marketing can be planned. A *market* is the set of all the individuals and organizations who are actual or potential buyers of a product or service. To understand a market, we ask five questions: (1) Who is in the market? (2) What buying decisions do buyers make? (3) Who participates in the buying process? (4) What are the major influences on the buyers? and (5) How do the buyers make their buying decisions? In this chapter we examined these questions for consumer markets.

The consumer market buys goods and services for personal use and consumption. It is the ultimate market for which economic activities are organized. The market itself consists of many submarkets, such as black consumers, young adult consumers, and elderly consumers.

The consumer buying decision is made up of many subdecisions. The buyer decides on the need class, generic class, product class, product form, brand, vendor, quantity, timing, and method of payment. The number of conscious decisions made by the consumer depends upon whether the purchase situation is one of routinized response behavior, limited problem solving, or extensive problem solving.

Buying decisions are typically influenced by other participants, who play such roles as initiator, influencer, decider, buyer, and user. The marketer's job is to identify the other buying participants, their buying criteria, and their level of influence on the buyer. The marketing program should be designed to appeal to and reach the other key participants as well as the buyer.

The many factors influencing the buying participants can be grouped into buyer characteristics, product characteristics, seller characteristics, and situational characteristics. Of these, we examined most closely the buyer characteristics. The buyer's behavior is influenced by four major variables: cultural (culture, subculture, and social class), social (reference groups, family, and roles and statuses), personal (age and life-cycle stage, occupation, economic circumstances, life style, and personality and self-concept), and psychological (motivation, perception, learning, and beliefs and attitudes). All of these provide clues as to how to reach and serve the buyer more effectively.

In buying anything, the buyer goes through problem recognition, information search, information evaluation, purchase decision, and postpurchase behavior. The marketer's job is to understand the buyer's behavior at each stage and what influences are operating. This understanding allows the marketer to develop a significant and effective marketing program for the target market.

■ questions for discussion

1. Using the definitions of a market adopted in this text, are you part of the market for a single-family home? Why?
2. Who makes up the consumer market for Monet jewelry?
3. Explain which of the three classes of buying situations would probably apply to the purchase decision for (a) a European vacation, (b) a six-pack of beer, (c) a new suit, and (d) a museum to attend.
4. Apply the five different roles in the decision process to your decision regarding college.
5. Discuss the influence of cultural characteristics (culture, subculture, and social class) on the patronage of department stores.
6. Which of the social characteristics have the greatest effect on an individual's record album purchases?
7. Based on recent demographic trends, are there any stages of a family life cycle that are not included in Table 8-2? Discuss the marketing implications.
8. The self-concept is synonymous with personality. Discuss.
9. What level of Maslow's hierarchy of needs are marketers of the following products primarily attempting to satisfy? (a) smoke detectors, (b) Bell Telephone long-distance dialing, (c) Seagram's VO, (d) life insurance, and (e) transcendental meditation.
10. Attitudes are a central concept to understanding an individual's consumer behavior. Why?
11. Relate the stages of the consumer buying process to your latest purchase of a pair of shoes.
12. Why is the postpurchase behavior stage included in the model of the buying process?

references

1. This was prepared by the author based on material in "The $100-million Object Lesson," *Fortune,* January 1971; and "The End of Corfam," *Wall Street Journal,* March 17, 1971, p. 1.
2. See Exhibit 11-1, pages 333–34.
3. FREDERICK C. KLEIN, "How a New Product Was Brought to Market Only to Flop Miserably," *Wall Street Journal,* January 5, 1973, pp. 1, 19.
4. *Statistical Abstract of the United States,* 1977.
5. See KEVIN A. WALL, "New Market: Among Blacks, the Haves Are Now Overtaking the Have-Nots," *Advertising Age,* February 11, 1974, pp. 35-36; MARY JANE SCHLINGER AND JOSEPH T. PLUMMER, "Advertising in Black and White," *Journal of Marketing Research,* May 1972, pp. 149–53; and RAYMOND A. BAUER AND SCOTT M. CUNNINGHAM, "The Negro Market," *Journal of Advertising Research,* April 1970, pp. 3–12.
6. See MELVIN HELITZER AND CARL HEYEL, *The Youth Market* (New York: Media Books, 1970), p. 58; and GEORGE W. SCHIELE, "How to Reach the Young Consumer," *Harvard Business Review,* March-April 1974, pp. 77–86.
7. See "The Graying of America," *Newsweek,* February 28, 1977, pp. 50–65.
8. See RENA BARTOS, "What Every Marketer Should Know about Women," *Harvard Business Review,* May-June 1978, pp. 73–85.
9. See A. H. KIZILBASH AND E. T. GARMAN, "Grocery Retailing in Spanish Neighborhoods," *Journal of Retailing,* Winter 1975–76, pp. 15–22ff.
10. JOHN A. HOWARD AND JAGDISH N. SHETH, *The Theory of Buyer Behavior* (New York: John Wiley, 1969), pp. 27–28.
11. Ibid., p. 26.
12. See CHEM L. NARAYANA AND ROM J. MARKIN, "Consumer Behavior and Product Performance: An Alternative Conceptualization," *Journal of Marketing,* October 1975, pp. 1–6.
13. See the earlier discussion in Chapter 7.
14. See FRANCIS S. BOURNE, *Group Influence in Marketing and Public Relations,* Foundation for Research on Human Behavior (Ann Arbor, Mich.: The Foundation, 1956).
15. See HARRY L. DAVIS, "Decision Making within the Household," *Journal of Consumer Research,* March 1976, pp. 241–60; HARRY L. DAVIS AND BENNY P. RIGAUX, "Perception of Marital Roles in Decision Processes," *Journal of Consumer Research,* June 1974, pp. 51–60; and HARRY L. DAVIS, "Dimensions of Marital Roles in Consumer Decision-Making," *Journal of Marketing Research,* May 1970, pp. 168–77.
16. See DAVIS, "Dimensions of Marital Roles."
17. GAIL SHEEHY, *Passages: Predictable Crises in Adult Life* (New York: Dutton, 1974); and ROGER GOULD, *Transformations* (New York: Simon & Schuster, 1978).
18. SIDNEY J. LEVY, "Symbolism and Life Style," in *Toward Scientific Marketing,* ed. Stephen A. Greyser (Chicago: American Marketing Association, 1964), pp. 140–50.
19. HARPER W. BOYD, JR., and SIDNEY J. LEVY, *Promotion: A Behavioral View* (Englewood Cliffs, N.J.: Prentice-Hall, 1967), p. 38.
20. See Chapter 10, p. 301.
21. For more reading, see EDWARD L. GRUBB AND HARRISON L. GRATHWOHL, "Consumer Self-Concept, Symbolism, and Market Behavior: A Theoretical Approach," *Journal of Marketing,* October 1967, pp. 22–27; IRA J. DOLICH, "Congruence Relationships between Self-Images and Product Brands," *Journal of Marketing Re-*

search, February 1969, pp. 40–47; and E. LAIRD LANDON, JR., "The Differential Role of Self-Concept and Ideal Self-Concept in Consumer Purchase Behavior," *Journal of Consumer Research,* September 1974, pp. 44–51.

22. See ERNEST DICHTER, *Handbook of Consumer Motivations* (New York: McGraw-Hill, 1964).

23. ABRAHAM H. MASLOW, *Motivation and Personality* (New York: Harper & Row, Pub., 1954, pp. 80–106.

24. See FREDERICK HERZBERG, *Work and the Nature of Man* (Cleveland: William Collins Publishers, 1966); and ROBERT J. HOUSE AND L. WIDGOR, "Herzberg's Dual-Factor Theory of Job Satisfaction and Motivation: A Review of the Empirical Evidence and a Criticism," *Personnel Psychology,* 20 (1967), 369–80.

25. BERNARD BERELSON AND GARY A. STEINER, *Human Behavior: An Inventory of Scientific Findings* (New York: Harcourt Brace Jovanovich, 1964), p. 88.

26. This relationship is known as Weber's law and is one of the main laws in psychophysics. See Chapter 12, p. 367.

27. See DAVID KRECH, RICHARD S. CRUTCHFIELD, and EGERTON L. BALLACHEY, *Individual in Society* (New York: McGraw-Hill, 1962), Chap. 2.

28. Several models of the consumer buying process have been developed by marketing scholars. The most prominent models are those of JOHN A. HOWARD AND JAGDISH N. SHETH, *The Theory of Buyer Behavior* (New York: John Wiley, 1969); FRANCESCO M. NICOSIA, *Consumer Decision Processes* (Englewood Cliffs, N.J.: Prentice-Hall, 1966); and JAMES F. ENGEL, ROGER D. BLACKWELL, AND DAVID T. KOLLAT, *Consumer Behavior,* 3rd ed. (New York: Holt, Rinehart & Winston, 1978).

29. JAMES H. MYERS AND MARK I. ALPERT, "Semantic Confusion in Attitude Research: Salience vs. Importance vs. Determinance," in *Advances in Consumer Research* (Proceedings of the Seventh Annual Conference of the Association of Consumer Research, October 1976), IV, 106–10.

30. See PAUL E. GREEN AND YORAM WIND, *Multiattribute Decisions in Marketing: A Measurement Approach* (Hinsdale, Ill.: Dryden Press, 1973), Chap. 2.

31. For an excellent review of this model, see WILLIAM L. WILKIE AND EDGAR A. PESSEMIER, "Issues in Marketing's Use of Multi-Attribute Attitude Models," *Journal of Marketing Research,* November 1973, pp. 428–41.

32. See JAMES H. MYERS AND MARK I. ALPERT, "Determinant Buying Attitudes: Meaning and Measurement," *Journal of Marketing,* October 1968, pp. 13–20.

33. See HARPER W. BOYD, JR., MICHAEL L. RAY, AND EDWARD C. STRONG, "An Attitudinal Framework for Advertising Strategy," *Journal of Marketing,* April 1972, pp. 27–33.

34. See JAGDISH N. SHETH, "An Investigation of Relationships among Evaluative Beliefs, Affect, Behavioral Intention, and Behavior," in *Consumer Behavior: Theory and Application,* ed. John U. Farley, John A. Howard, and L. Winston Ring (Boston: Allyn & Bacon, 1974), pp. 89–114.

35. See MARTIN FISHBEIN, "Attitude and Prediction of Behavior," in *Readings in Attitude Theory and Measurement,* ed. Martin Fishbein (New York: John Wiley, 1967), pp. 477–92.

36. See RAYMOND A. BAUER, "Consumer Behavior as Risk Taking" in *Risk Taking and Information Handling in Consumer Behavior,* ed. Donald F. Cox (Boston: Division of Research, Harvard Business School, 1967); and JAMES W. TAYLOR, "The Role of Risk in Consumer Behavior," *Journal of Marketing,* April 1974, pp. 54–60.

37. See JOHN E. SWAN AND LINDA JONES COMBS, "Product Performance and Consumer Satisfaction: A New Concept," *Journal of Marketing Research,* April 1976, pp. 25–33.

38. See Rolph E. Anderson, "Consumer Dissatisfaction: The Effect of Disconfirmed Expectancy on Perceived Product Performance," *Journal of Marketing Research,* February 1973, pp. 38–44.

39. Leon Festinger and Dana Bramel, "The Reactions of Humans to Cognitive Dissonance," in *Experimental Foundations of Clinical Psychology,* ed. Arthur J. Bachrach (New York: Basic Books, 1962), pp. 251–62.

40. Rom J. Markin, Jr., *Consumer Behavior: A Cognitive Orientation* (New York: Macmillan, 1974), pp. 145–47.

41. Leon Festinger, *A Theory of Cognitive Dissonance* (Stanford, Calif.: Stanford University Press, 1957), p. 260.

42. Research shows that new car owners read significantly more advertisements about the car they just purchased than they do about other cars. See D. Ehrlich, I. Guttman, P. Schonback, and J. Mills, "Post-Decision Exposure to Relevant Information," *Journal of Abnormal and Social Psychology,* January 1957, pp. 98-102.

43. See James H. Donnelly, Jr., and John M. Ivancevich, "Post-Purchase Reinforcement and Back-Out Behavior," *Journal of Marketing Research,* August 1970, pp. 399–400.

ORGANIZATIONAL MARKETS AND BUYING BEHAVIOR

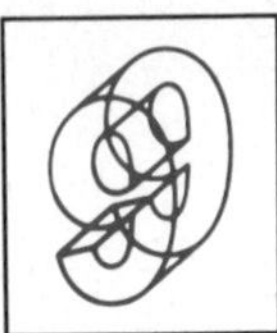

Colleges not only have to teach their students but feed them. Not wanting a student riot on their hands over bad food or high prices, many colleges pay close attention to this problem. They have two options. Colleges can set up their own food service operations by hiring their own staff, buying food daily, and carrying out the cleanup operations. Or they can contract for the services of a food service company. Today over 3,100 schools and colleges across the nation have opted for the latter. They have engaged the services of one of the more than 150 food service companies that stand ready to develop menus, cook, and clean up for the college market.

Choosing the right food service company, however, is not easy for colleges. Recently, the University of California's Irvine campus awarded a contract to Greyhound Corporation's Food Management, Inc., for a low bid of $2.46 per student per day. They were subsequently notified by Greyhound that it was canceling the contract by invoking a 90-day cancellation clause, saying that its costs had risen to more than $3 a day. The Irvine campus subsequently awarded the contract to the Saga Corporation for $3.13 per student.

Involved in the selection of the Food Service Company may be the college's purchasing department, some student representatives, the business manager, and sometimes even the college president. They are seeking a contract that will provide students with so many food choices, second and third helpings, and a reasonable amount of meat in relation to poultry or pasta, all at a cost not to exceed so many dollars per student. They examine each major food service company's reputation for food quality, service, and reliability before making a choice. On the other hand, the food service companies, who want the contract, are becoming more demanding. They are attempting to shift away from fixed-fee contracts to contracts with escalator clauses. Sometimes they underbid the other bidders, get the contract, and subsequently attempt to raise the price or sometimes cut the quality of the food or service under the pressure of spiraling costs.

The more progressive institutional contract feeders keep searching for new ways to lower their costs in order to be low bidders. The largest institutional feeder, ARA Food Services Company, has developed a computerized food purchasing, production, and service system that includes portion control and predicts how students will choose from a multiple-choice menu. Saga Corporation is running a waste education campaign directed at students who leave much of the food on their plates.[1]

□This example shows some of the things involved in organizations selling goods and services to other organizations. These sellers, called *industrial marketers,* must do their best to understand the buying organization's needs, resources, policies, and buying procedures. They must take into account several considerations not normally found in marketing directly to consumers.

1. Organizations buy goods and services for the purpose of making profits, reducing costs, serving their internal clienteles' needs, and meeting social and legal obligations.
2. More persons tend to formally participate in organizational buying decisions than in consumer buying decisions. The decision participants usually have different organizational responsibilities and apply different criteria to the purchase decision.
3. The buyers must heed formal policies, constraints, and requirements established by their organizations.
4. The buying instruments, such as request for quotations, proposals, and purchase contracts, add another dimension not found in consumer buying.

Organizations make up a vast market for a multitude of goods and services such as raw materials, manufactured parts, installations, accessory equipment, supplies, and business services. (The classification of industrial products is discussed in Chapter 12, pp. 372–73.) Sellers who specialize wholly or partly in selling their products to other organizations need to understand organizational buying behavior. Webster and Wind define *organizational buying* as "the decision-making process by which formal organizations establish the need for purchased products and services, and identify, evaluate, and choose among alternative brands and suppliers."[2]

the producer market

Who Is in the Producer Market? (Buying Population)

The **producer market** (also called the industrial or business market) consists of *all the individuals and organizations who acquire goods and services that enter into the production of other products or services that are sold, rented, or supplied to others.* The major types of industries making up the producer market are (1) agriculture, forestry, and fisheries; (2) mining; (3) manufacturing; (4) construction; (5) transportation; (6) communication; (7) public utilities; (8) banking, finance, and insurance; and (9) services. There are over 14 million different industrial units and each is a market for specific types of goods and services. They employ over 87 million workers, generate an annual national income of over $1 trillion, and constitute a buying market for the goods of most firms.

More dollars are involved in sales to industrial buyers than to consumers. To bring a simple pair of shoes into existence, hide dealers (mainly meat packers) must sell the hides to tanners, who sell the leather to shoe manufacturers, who sell the shoes to wholesalers, who in turn sell the shoes to retailers. Each party in the chain of production and distribution pays more than the previous party. The transactions based on one pair of finished shoes selling for $30 may have been $4 (hide dealer to tanner), $5 (tanner to shoe manufacturer), $20 (shoe manufacturer to wholesaler), and $24 (wholesaler to retailer), making a total of $53, whereas the transaction to the consumer involved but $30. We can appreciate why there is more industrial marketing going on than consumer marketing.

Industrial markets have certain characteristics that contrast sharply with consumer markets. These characteristics are described in the following paragraphs.

Fewer buyers. The industrial marketer normally deals with far fewer buyers than does the consumer marketer. Goodyear Tire Company's fate in the industrial market depends entirely on its getting an order from one of four auto companies: General Motors, Ford, Chrysler, or American Motors. But when Goodyear sells to consumers, it has a potential market of 70 million American automobile owners.

Larger buyers. Even in industrial markets consisting of many firms, a few of them normally account for most of the purchasing. In such industries as motor vehicles, telephone and telegraph, cigarettes, aircraft engines and engine parts, and organic fibers, the top four manufacturers account for over 70 percent of total production.

Geographically concentrated buyers. More than half of the nation's producers are concentrated in the seven states of New York, California, Pennsylvania, Illinois, Ohio, New Jersey, and Michigan. Particular manufacturing industries, such as petroleum, rubber, and steel, show even greater geographic concentration. Most agricultural output comes from a relatively small number of states; and specific commodities, such as tobacco and citrus fruit, are grown in even fewer states. This geographical concentration of producers helps to reduce the costs of selling to them. Industrial marketers will want to watch any pronounced tendencies toward or away from further geographic concentration.

Derived demand. The demand for industrial goods is ultimately derived from the demand for consumer goods. Thus animal hides are purchased because consumers buy shoes, purses, and other leather goods. If the demand for these consumer goods slackens, so will the demand for all the industrial goods entering into their production.

Inelastic demand. The total demand for industrial goods and services is not much affected by price changes. Shoe manufacturers are not going to buy much more leather if the price of leather falls unless (1) leather is a major cost in shoe manufacture, (2) the manufacturers will cut their prices of leather shoes drastically, and (3) shoe buyers will buy more shoes. Nor are shoe manufacturers going to buy much less leather if the price of leather rises unless they can (1) find ways to economize on the amount of leather used in shoes or (2) find leather substitutes. Demand is especially inelastic in the short run because producers cannot make many changes in their production methods. Demand is also inelastic for industrial goods that represent a small percentage of the item's total cost. For example, an increase in the industry price of metal eyelets for shoes will barely affect the demand level. At the same time, producers will use price to decide which supplier to buy from, although it will have less effect on the amount bought.

Fluctuating demand. The demand for industrial goods and services tends to be much more volatile than for consumer goods and services. This is especially true of major installations of plant and equipment. Swings in these goods in turn accelerate the swings in raw materials such as metals and other minerals. Thus a small change in consumer demand can lead to a large increase in industrial demand—economists refer to this as the *accelerator principle.* Sometimes a rise (fall) of only 10 percent in consumer demand can cause as much as a 200 percent rise (fall) in industrial demand in the next period. This phenomenon has led many industrial marketers to diversify their product lines to achieve some cyclical balance.

Professional purchasing. Industrial goods are purchased by trained professionals who spend their lives learning how to buy better. Consumers, on the other hand, are much less trained in the art of careful buying. The more complex the industrial purchase, the more likely that several persons will participate in the formal decision-making process. Buying committees made up of technical experts and top management are common in the purchase of major goods. This means that industrial marketers have to rely heavily on well-trained sales representatives to deal with the well-trained buyers. Although advertising, sales promotion, and publicity also play an important role in the industrial promotional mix, personal selling acts as the main tool in producing sales.

Miscellaneous characteristics. Here are a few additional characteristics that tend to distinguish industrial buying from consumer buying:

1. *Direct purchasing.* Industrial buyers more often buy directly from the producers rather than through middlemen, whereas consumers most often buy from middlemen. This is especially true of items that are technically complex and expensive.
2. *Reciprocity.* Industrial buyers often select suppliers who also buy from them, a practice known as reciprocity. An example of reciprocity would be a paper manufacturer who decides to buy needed chemicals from a chemical company that is buying a considerable amount of its paper. Reciprocity is a dangerous game to play. The practice is forbidden by both the Federal Trade Commission and the Justice Department's antitrust division. The reason is that it shuts out competition in an unfair manner. A buyer can still choose a supplier that it also sells something to, but it should be able to show that it is getting competitive prices, quality, and service from that supplier.[3]
3. *Leasing.* Industrial buyers are increasingly turning to equipment leasing instead of outright purchase. This happens with computers, shoe machinery, packaging equipment, heavy construction equipment, delivery trucks, machine tools, and sales-force automobiles. The lessee gains a number of advantages, such as having more available capital, getting the seller's latest products, receiving better servicing, and gaining some tax advantages. The lessor often ends up with a larger net income and the chance to get its goods into markets that might not have been able to afford outright purchase.[4]

This concludes our review of the major characteristics that distinguish industrial buying from consumer buying.

What Buying Decisions Do Producers Make? (Buying Decisions)

The industrial buyer, like the consumer buyer, does not make a single decision but rather a whole set of decisions in making a purchase. The number of decisions made depends on the type of buying situation. The major types of buying situations are described in the following paragraphs.

Major types of buying situations. Robinson and others distinguish among three types of buying situations called *buyclasses.*[5] They are analogous to the three consumer buying situations discussed in Chapter 8, which we called routinized response behavior, limited problem solving, and extensive problem solving.

STRAIGHT REBUY

The straight rebuy describes the simplest buying situation where the buying organization reorders something without any modifications. It is usually handled on a routine basis by the purchasing department. The buyer chooses from suppliers already on its "list," giving much weight to its past buying experience with the various suppliers. The "in" suppliers make an effort to keep up product and service quality. They often propose automatic reordering systems so that the purchasing agent will save time on reordering from them. The "out" suppliers attempt to offer something new or create some dissatisfaction so that the buyer will reconsider the buying assumptions. Out-suppliers will attempt to get their foot in the door with a small order and then try to enlarge their "purchase share" over time.

MODIFIED REBUY

The modified rebuy describes a situation where the buyer is seeking to modify product specifications, prices, other terms, or suppliers, in connection with something it purchases. Somehow the purchasing executive thinks he or she can do better. The modified rebuy usually expands the number of decision participants. The in-suppliers get nervous and have to put their best foot forward to protect the account. The out-suppliers see it as an opportunity to make a "better offer" to gain some new business.

NEW TASK

The new task faces a company buying a product or service for the first time. The greater the cost and/or risk, the larger the number of decision participants and the greater their information seeking. The new-task situation is the marketer's greatest opportunity and challenge. The marketer must plan to reach as many key buying influences as possible and provide information and assistance in helping them resolve their problem, hopefully in favor of the marketer's product. Because of the complicated selling involved in the new task, many companies use a specialized sales force, called a *missionary sales force,* to carry out this task.

Major subdecisions involved in the buying decision. The number of decisions involved in a particular buying project varies with the type of buying situation, being the fewest in the case of a straight rebuy and the most numerous in the new-task situation. In the new-task situation, the buying center will have to determine (1) product specifications, (2) price limits, (3) delivery terms and times, (4) service terms, (5) payment terms, (6) order quantities, (7) acceptable suppliers, and (8) the selected supplier. Different decision participants will influence each decision, and the order in which the decisions will be made will vary.

The marketer's task is to anticipate the full range of decisions facing the buyer and offer an attractive and convenient total solution if possible. Suppose, for example, that the buyer wants to build a fertilizer plant. At one extreme, the buyer can make all the separate decisions and hire its own architects, engineers, contractors, legal staff, and so on. At the other extreme, the buyer can hire one company that will put together the whole package. The second is called a *turnkey operation* because all the buyer has to do is turn the key when the plant is ready to start operating. The underlying idea is that the marketer should try to sell a system, not just a single component, because buyers find this more convenient and attractive. *Systems selling* is a key industrial marketing strategy for winning and holding accounts.[6]

Who Participates in the Producer Buying Process? (Buying Participants)

Who does the buying of the hundreds of billions of dollars of products and services needed by the industrial market? Buying organizations vary tremendously, from small firms with one or a few purchasing executives to huge corporations with large purchasing departments headed by a vice-president of purchasing. In some cases the purchasing executives make the entire decision as to product specifications and supplier, in other cases they are responsible for supplier selection only, and in still other cases they make neither decision but simply place the order. They typically make the decisions regarding smaller items and carry out the wishes of others regarding major capital items.

Webster and Wind call the decision-making unit of a buying organization the *buying center,* defined as "all those individuals and groups who participate in the purchasing decision-making process, who share some common goals and the risks arising from the decisions."[7]

The buying center includes all members of the organization who play any of five roles in the purchase decision process:[8]

1. *Users.* Users are the members of the organization who will use the product or service. In many cases the users initiate the buying project and play an important role in defining the purchase specifications.
2. *Influencers.* Influencers are those members inside and outside of the organization who directly or indirectly influence the buying decision. They often help define specifications and also provide information for evaluating alternatives. Technical personnel are particularly important as influencers.
3. *Buyers.* Buyers are organizational members with formal authority for selecting the supplier and arranging the terms of purchase. Buyers may help shape product specifications, but they play their major role in selecting vendors and negotiating within the purchase constraints. In more complex purchases, the buyers might include high-level officers of the company participating in the negotiations.
4. *Deciders.* Deciders are organizational members who have either formal or informal power to select or approve the final suppliers. In the routine buying of standard items, the buyers are often the deciders. In more complex buying, the officers of the company are often the deciders.
5. *Gatekeepers.* Gatekeepers are members of the organization who control the flow of information to others. For example, purchasing agents often have authority to

prevent salespersons from seeing users or deciders. Other gatekeepers include technical personnel and even switchboard operators. The main impact of gatekeepers is to influence the inflow of information on buying alternatives.

Within any organization, the buying center will vary in size and composition for different classes of products. More decision participants will be involved in buying a computer, for example, than in buying paper clips. The challenge to the industrial marketer is to figure out: Who are the major decision participants? In what decisions do they exercise influence? What is their relative degree of influence? and What evaluation criteria does each decision participant use?

Consider the following example:

- The American Hospital Supply Corporation is one of several competitors selling nonwoven disposable surgical gowns to hospitals. Its first task is to identify those persons in a hospital who normally participate in the buying decisions for surgical gowns. The decision participants turn out to be (1) the vice-president of purchasing, (2) the operating room administrator, and (3) the surgeons. Each party plays a different role. The hospital's vice-president of purchasing analyzes whether the hospital should buy disposable gowns or reusable gowns. If the analysis shows that it is less expensive to buy reusable gowns and relaunder them, then the suppliers of disposable gowns are closed out of this market. If the findings favor buying disposable gowns, then the operating room administrator is responsible for comparing various competitors' products and prices and making a choice. This administrator considers such qualities as the gown's absorbency, antiseptic quality, design, and cost and normally buys the brand that meets the functional requirements at the lowest cost. Finally, surgeons influence the decision retroactively by reporting their satisfaction or lack of satisfaction with the particular brand. The surgeons consider the gown's style and comfort.

Since a buying center may include anywhere from one to a dozen persons, the industrial marketer may not have the time or resources to reach them all. Smaller companies try to determine the *key buying influences* and concentrate their limited advertising and personal selling resources on them. Larger companies go for *multilevel in-depth selling* to reach as many decision participants as possible. Their salespeople virtually "live" with the customer when it is a major account with recurrent sales.

What Are the Major Influences on Producer Buyers? (Buying Influences)

Industrial buyers are subject to many influences when they make their buying decisions. The marketer must understand these influences. Some marketers assume that the most important influences are rational. They view the organization as behaving in the manner of a rational buyer pursuing economic objectives in an efficient way. The organization is seen as making its decisions in favor of the supplier who offers the minimum price, or offers the best product, or buys things from the company in return (i.e., reciprocity), or is the most ready to accommodate. This view implies that industrial marketers should primarily concentrate on offering strong economic benefits to buyers.

Other marketers emphasize the role of personal motives in the buying process, such as buyers who respond to personal favors (self-aggrandizement), or to attention (ego-enhancement), or to personal risk containment (risk avoiders). A study of buyers in ten large companies concluded that

- . . . corporate decision-makers remain human after they enter the office. They respond to "image"; they buy from companies to which they feel "close"; they favor suppliers who show them respect and personal consideration, and who do extra things "for them"; they "over-react" to real or imagined slights, tending to reject companies which fail to respond or delay in submitting requested bids.[9]

This suggests that industrial marketers should concentrate on the human and social factors in the buying situation and that they could overcome offer deficiencies by being more manipulative of emotional and interpersonal factors.

Industrial buyers actually respond to both rational and personal factors. Where there is substantial similarity in what suppliers offer in the way of products, price, and service, industrial buyers have little basis for rational choice. Since they can meet organizational goals with any one of a number of suppliers, buyers can bring in personal factors. On the other hand, where competing products differ substantially, industrial buyers are more accountable for their choice and pay more attention to objective factors. Short-run personal gain becomes less motivating than the long-run gain that comes from serving their organization well.

Webster and Wind have proposed that the various influences on industrial buyers be classified into four main groups: environmental, organizational, interpersonal, and individual.[10] Figure 9-1 shows the main influences in each group that industrial marketers should focus on in trying to understand the buying situation.

Environmental factors. Industrial buyers are heavily influenced by their company's current and expected environment. Of particular interest are economic factors, such as changes in the level of primary demand, the economic outlook, and the cost of money. As the level of economic risk or uncertainty rises, industrial buyers cease making new investments in plant and equipment and refrain from adding raw materials to their inventories. There is little that the industrial marketer can do to stimulate purchases except cut prices to a level where the buyers are willing to take some risk.

Figure 9-1
Major Factors Influencing Industrial Buying Behavior

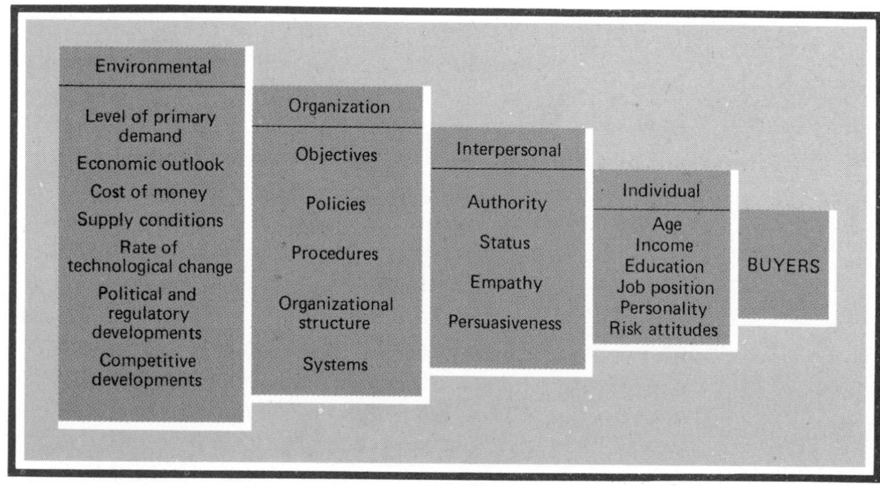

An environmental factor of increasing importance is imminent shortages in key materials. Companies are showing a greater willingness to buy and hold larger inventories of scarce materials. They are willing to sign long-term contracts to guarantee the supply of these materials. Du Pont, Ford, Chrysler, and several other major companies have established *supply planning* as a major responsibility of their purchasing executives.[11]

Industrial buyers also watch technological, political, and competitive developments in the environment. It is the job of the industrial marketer to monitor the same factors, determine how they will affect the buyer, and prepare to turn these problems into opportunities.

Organizational factors. Each buying organization has its own objectives, policies, procedures, organizational structure, and systems. It is the job of the marketer to know these as well as possible. Such questions arise as How many people will be involved in the buying decision? Who will they be? What are their evaluative criteria? and What are the company's policies and constraints on the buyers? Suppliers are limited in how much they can find out and must work patiently at trying to accumulate information.

The industrial marketer should be aware of the following organizational developments occurring in the purchasing area.

1. *Purchasing department upgrading.* Purchasing departments have typically occupied a low position in the management hierarchy, in spite of often being responsible for managing more than half of the typical organization's costs. The recent combination of inflation and shortages has led many companies to upgrade their purchasing departments. Several large corporations have elevated the heads of purchasing to vice-presidential levels. Caterpillar and some other companies have combined several functions—such as purchasing, inventory control, production scheduling, and traffic—into a high-level function called material management. Many companies are looking for top talent, hiring MBAs, and offering higher compensation. This means that industrial marketers must correspondingly upgrade their sales personnel to match the caliber of the new buyers.

2. *Centralized purchasing.* In multidivisional companies, much purchasing is carried out by the separate divisions because of their differing needs. But in recent years there has been a tendency toward recentralization of the purchasing function. Headquarters is identifying those materials that are purchased by several divisions and is buying them centrally. This gives the buyer more purchasing clout. The individual plants can buy from another source if they can get a better deal, but in general, centralized purchasing produces substantial savings for the company.[12] For the industrial marketer, this development means dealing with fewer and higher-level buyers. Instead of the seller's regional sales forces dealing separately with the various plants of the buyer, the seller may have to deal with the buyer as a national account that is handled through a national account sales force. National account selling is more complex and demands a more sophisticated sales force and marketing effort.

3. *Long-term contracts.* More industrial buyers are seeking long-term contracts with suppliers as opposed to placing single-purchase orders for a

definite amount and date of delivery. These contracts call for much more skillful negotiation, and buyers are adding negotiating specialists to their staffs. Industrial marketers, in turn, will have to add skilled negotiators to their staffs.

4. *Purchasing performance evaluation.* Some buying organizations are setting up incentive systems to reward purchasing managers for especially good performance, in much the same way that sales personnel receive bonuses for especially good performance. These systems will lead purchasing managers to further increase their drive to seek the best terms.

Interpersonal factors. Industrial buying takes place within a context of interpersonal influences that go beyond the formal organizational characteristics. The buying center usually includes several participants with different statuses, authority, empathy, and persuasiveness. The industrial marketer is not likely to know what kind of group dynamics will take place during the buying process, although whatever information he or she can find out about the personalities involved would be useful.

Individual factors. Each buying participant brings into the buying situation personal motivations, perceptions, and preferences, as influenced by the participant's age, income, education, professional identification, personality, and attitudes toward risk. Buyers definitely have different buying styles. Some of the younger, higher-educated buyers are "computer freaks" and make rigorous analyses of competitive proposals before making a supplier choice. Other buyers are "tough guys" from the "old school" and play off the sellers, as indicated in the following report:

> ▪ . . . A good example of a cagey buyer is [the] vice president in charge of purchasing for Rheingold's big New York brewery. . . . Using the leverage of hundreds of millions of cans a year, like many other buyers, he takes punitive action when one company slips in quality or fails to deliver. "At one point American started talking about a price rise," he recalls, "Continental kept its mouth shut. . . . American never did put the price rise into effect, but anyway, I punished them for talking about it." For a three-month period he cut the percentage of cans he bought from American.[13]

The point is that industrial marketers must know their customers and must adapt their tactics not only to known environmental, organizational, and interpersonal factors but also to the quirks of individuals involved in the buying process.

How Do Producers Make Their Buying Decisions? (Buying Process)

We now come to the issue of how industrial buyers move through the buying process (also called procurement process). We could describe the industrial buying process as consisting of the same five stages as the consumer buying process—problem recognition, information search, information evaluation, purchase decision, and postpurchase behavior. However, there are certain features of industrial buying methodology that call for a more elaborate model. Robinson and others have proposed eight stages of the industrial buying process called *buyphases.*[14] They are: *problem recognition, general need description, product specification, supplier search, proposal solicitation, supplier selection, order routine specification,* and *performance review.* The buyphases are described below.

Problem recognition. The buying process has its beginnings when someone in the company recognizes a problem or need that can be met by acquiring a good or a service. Problem recognition can occur as a result of internal or external stimuli. Internally, the most common events leading to problem recognition are the following:

- The company decides to launch a new product and needs new equipment and materials to produce this product.
- A machine breaks down and requires replacement or new parts.
- Some purchased material turns out to be unsatisfactory, and this raises the question of finding another supplier.
- A purchasing manager senses an opportunity to obtain better prices or quality.

Externally, the buyer may be exposed to some new ideas at a trade show, or see an ad, or receive a visit from a sales representative who offers a better product or a lower price. Industrial marketers cannot sit back and wait for buyers to phone them. When they have a superior offer, they develop promotions and make calls on buyers. Often they help buyers recognize a latent need. For example, sales representatives of Bell Telephone will often visit companies to show them how they can save money in the long run by switching to more sophisticated telephone equipment.

General need description. Having recognized a need, the buyer proceeds to determine the general characteristics and quantity of the needed item. For standard items, this is not much of a problem. For more complex items, the buyer will work with others in the company—engineers, users, and so on—to define the general characteristics they are seeking. They will want to rank the importance of reliability, durability, price, and other attributes desired in the item.

The industrial marketer can be of assistance to the buying company in this phase. Often the buyer is not sure of the value of different characteristics. An alert seller can help the buyer define the company's needs.

Product specification. Here the buying organization proceeds to develop the technical specifications for the item. A *value analysis* engineering team will be put to work on the problem. *Value analysis,* which General Electric pioneered in the late forties, is *an approach to cost reduction in which components are carefully studied to determine if they can be redesigned or standardized or made by cheaper methods of production.* The team will carefully examine the high-cost components in a given product—usually 20 percent of the parts will constitute about 80 percent of the costs. The team will then decide on the product specifications and spell them out in the clearest and most technically accurate manner possible. In this way the buyer, who may be unsure, can be protected against making an error. Furthermore, accurately written specifications will allow the buyer to legally refuse to accept merchandise that only roughly approximates the intended items.

Supplier search. The buyer now proceeds to identify the most appropriate vendors. The buyer can turn to trade directories, or do a computer search, or phone other companies for their recommendations. Some of the vendors will be dropped from consideration because they are not large enough to supply the needed quantity, or they have a poor credit standing, or they have a poor reputation for delivery and service. The buyer will end up with a small list of qualified suppliers. The newer the buying task, and the more complex and expensive the item, the greater the amount of time spent in searching for and qualifying suppliers. The selling company's job is to make sure that it is listed in major directories and is well known and well thought of by opinion leaders.

Proposal solicitation. In this stage the buyer will invite qualified suppliers to submit proposals. Some suppliers will only send a catalog or a sales representative. Where the item is complex or expensive, the buyer will require detailed written proposals from each potential supplier. These proposals will be reviewed and the weaker ones dropped. The buyer may request formal presentations by the remaining suppliers. All this implies that industrial marketers must be skillful in researching, writing, and presenting proposals. Their proposals should be marketing documents, not just technical documents. Their oral presentations should inspire confidence in a way that goes beyond the quality of the written proposals. They should portray the capabilities and resources of the company and position it so that it stands out from the competition.

Supplier selection. In this stage the members of the buying center will review the proposals and move toward supplier selection. They will consider not only the formal competence of the various suppliers to make the specified item but also their ability to deliver the item on time and provide necessary services. The buying center will often draw up a list of the desired supplier attributes and their relative importance. In selecting a chemical supplier, a buying center listed the following attributes in order of importance:

1. Technical support services
2. Prompt delivery
3. Quick response to customer needs
4. Product quality
5. Supplier reputation
6. Product price
7. Complete product line
8. Sales representatives' caliber
9. Extension of credit
10. Personal relationships
11. Literature and manuals

The members of the buying center will then rate the candidate suppliers against these attributes and will identify the most attractive suppliers. They may use a supplier evaluation model similar to one of the consumer evaluation models described earlier in Chapter 8, pp. 255–56.

The buyers may attempt to negotiate with the favored suppliers for still better prices and terms before making the final selections. In the end, they may select a single supplier or a few suppliers. Many buyers prefer multiple sources of supply so that they will not be totally dependent on one supplier in case something goes wrong and they will be able to watch the prices and performance of the suppliers as a check-and-balance system. The buyer will normally place most of the order with one supplier, and less with the other suppliers. For example, a buyer using three suppliers may buy 60 percent of the needed quantity from the prime supplier and 30 and 10 percent, respectively, from the two other suppliers. The prime supplier will make an effort to protect its prime position, while the others will try to expand their supplier share. Out-suppliers in the meantime will attempt to get a foot in the door by making an especially good price offer and hoping thereafter to work their way up to being a more major supplier.

Order routine specification. The buyer now writes the final order with the chosen supplier(s) listing the technical specifications, the quantity needed, the expected time of delivery, return policies, warranties, and so on. In the case of MRO items (maintenance, repair, and operating items), buyers are increasingly moving toward favoring *blanket contracts* rather than writing *periodic purchase orders.* Writing a new purchase order each time stock is needed is expensive. Nor does the buyer want to write fewer and large purchase orders because this means carrying more inventory. A blanket contract establishes a long-term relationship where the supplier promises to resupply the buyer as needed on agreed price terms over a specified period of time. The stock is held by the seller; hence the name "stockless purchase plan." The buyer's computer automatically prints out or teletypes an order to the seller when stock is needed. Blanket contracting tends to lead to more single-source buying and the buying of more items from that single source. This locks the supplier in tighter with the buyer and makes it difficult for out-suppliers to break in, unless the buyer experiences strong dissatisfaction with the supplier.[15]

Performance review. In this stage the buyer reviews the results of dealing with the particular supplier(s). Instead of waiting to hear from user groups as to their satisfaction with the purchased items, the buyer may contact them and request a rating of satisfaction with various aspects of the order. The performance review may lead the buyer to continue, modify, or drop the relationship with the seller. The seller's job is to monitor the same variables used by the buyer to make sure that the seller's company is delivering the expected satisfaction to the buyer.

We have described the buying stages that would operate in a new-task buying situation. In the modified rebuy or straight rebuy situation, some of these stages would be compressed or bypassed. Each stage represents a narrowing by the buyer of the number of supplier alternatives, with the clear implication that sellers should try to become part of the buyer's buying process as early as possible.

The eight-stage buyphase model represents the essential steps of the industrial buying process, although in any real situation, further steps and idiosyncrasies can occur. The industrial marketer therefore has to model each situation more specifically. Each buying situation involves a particular flow of work, and this *buyflow* can provide many clues to the marketer. A buyflow map for the purchase of a tests stand for automotive engines is shown in Figure 9-2. The map shows five different company personnel (represented by desk symbols) who were involved in this buying decision process at one time or another. Two suppliers also were involved, as well as other outside influences (shown in the

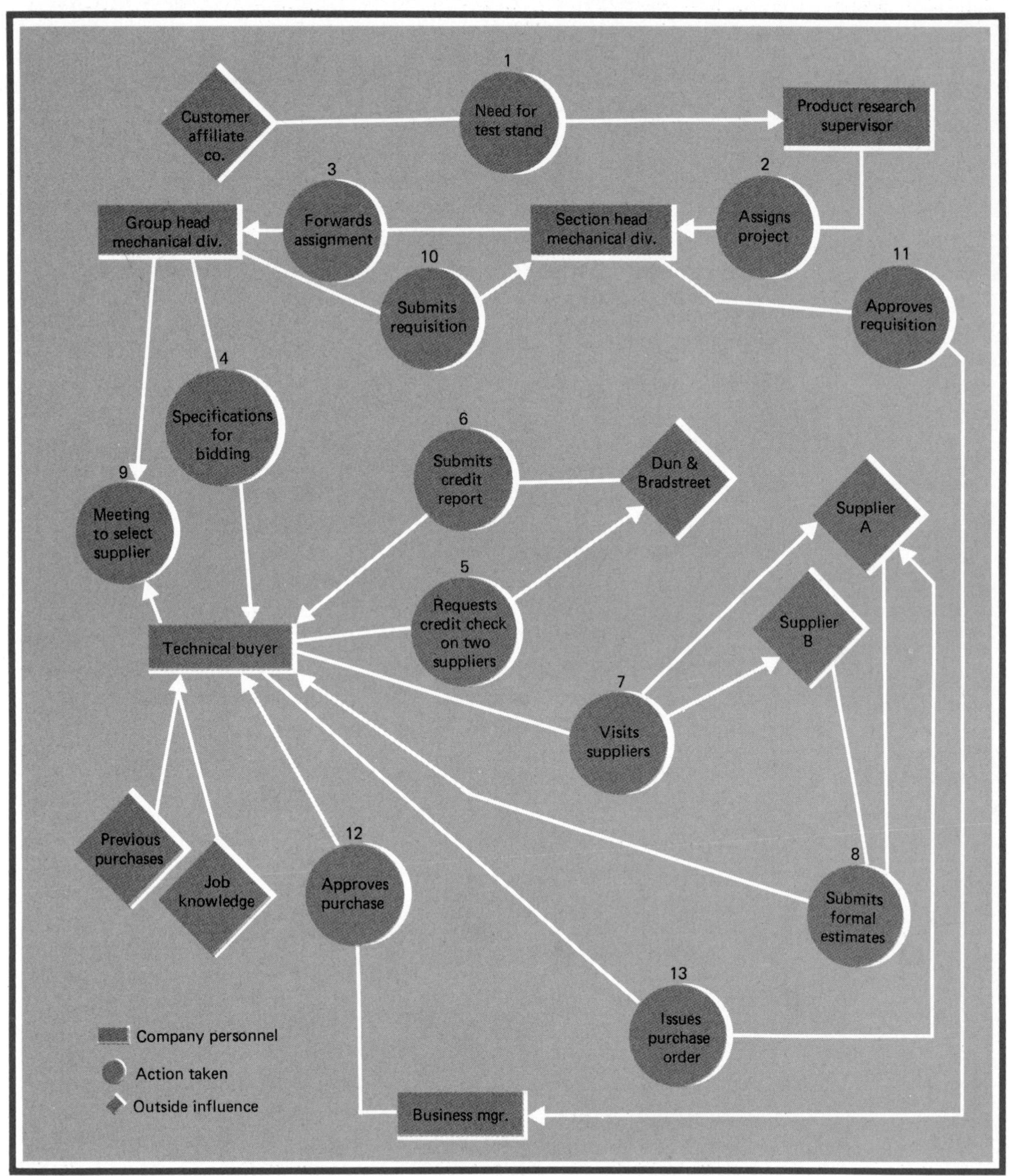

Figure 9-2 *Map of Company Purchase of Test Stand for Automotive Engines*

Source: Murray Harding, "Who Really Makes the Purchasing Decision?" *Industrial Marketing,* September 1966, p. 77.

diamond-shaped figures). Finally, thirteen different events (shown as circles) led to the placing of the order ultimately with one of the suppliers.

Thus we see that marketing to industrial buyers is a challenging area. The key step is to know the customer's needs and buying patterns. Using this knowledge, the industrial marketer can proceed to design an effective marketing plan for selling and servicing the customer.

the reseller market

Who Is in the Reseller Market? (Buying Population)

The **reseller market** consists of *all the individuals and organizations who acquire goods for the purpose of reselling or renting them to others at a profit.* Instead of producing form utility, the reseller market produces time, place, and possession utility. The reseller market includes over 276,000 wholesaling firms employing 4,216,000 persons, and 1,665,000 retailing firms employing 11,961,000 persons; both sectors account for over 16 percent of the national income. Resellers are more geographically dispersed than producers but more concentrated than consumers.

Resellers purchase (1) goods for resale and (2) goods and services for conducting their operations. The latter are bought by resellers in their role as "producers," so we shall confine the discussion here to the goods they purchase for resale.

Resellers handle a vast variety of products for resale, indeed everything produced except the few classes of goods that producers choose to sell directly to final customers. The excluded class includes heavy or complex machinery, customized products, and products sold on a direct-mail or a door-to-door basis. With these exceptions, most products are sold to the final buyer through one or more selling intermediaries.

What Buying Decisions Do Resellers Make (Buying Decisions)

Resellers have to make three major types of decisions: (1) what assortment to carry, (2) what vendors to buy from, and (3) what prices and terms to negotiate. Of these, the assortment decision is the key. The assortment represents the combination of products and services that the reseller will offer to the market, and it positions the reseller in the marketplace. Wholesalers and retailers can choose one of four assortment strategies:

1. *Exclusive assortment:* representing the line of only one manufacturer
2. *Deep assortment:* representing a given homogeneous product family in depth, drawing on many producers' outputs
3. *Broad assortment:* representing a wide range of product lines that still fall within the natural coverage of the reseller's type of business
4. *Scrambled assortment:* representing many unrelated product families

Thus a camera store can decide to sell only Kodak cameras (exclusive assortment), many brands of cameras (deep assortment), cameras, tape recorders, radios, and stereophonic equipment (broad assortment), or the last plus stoves and refrigerators (scrambled assortment). The assortment the reseller ultimately chooses will influence its customer mix, marketing mix, and supplier mix.

The buying decisions facing resellers vary with the type of buying situation. Three buying situations can be distinguished.

The new-item situation describes the case where the reseller has been offered a new item. Here the reseller will give a "yes-no" answer, depending on how good the item looks. This differs from the new-task situation faced by producers who have to definitely purchase the needed item from someone.

The *best-vendor situation* faces the reseller who knows what is needed but must determine the best supplier. This occurs in two situations: (1) when the reseller can carry only a subset of the available brands offered because of space constraints; (2) when the reseller wants to sponsor a private brand and is seeking a willing and qualified producer. Resellers such as Sears and the A&P sell a substantial number of items under their own name; therefore much of their buying operation consists of vendor selection.

The *better-terms situation* arises when the reseller wants to obtain a better set of terms from current suppliers. The buyer is not eager to change the supplier but does want more advantageous treatment. Legally sellers are prevented, under the Robinson-Patman Act, from giving different terms to different resellers in the same reseller class unless these reflect corresponding cost differences, distress sales, or a few other special conditions. Nevertheless, individual resellers and classes of resellers (discounters, mass merchandisers) do press their suppliers for preferential treatment, and this can take many forms, such as more supplier services, easier credit terms, and higher volume discounts.

Who Participates in the Reseller Buying Process? (Buying Participants)

Who does the deciding and buying for wholesale and retail organizations? In small "mom and pop" firms, the merchandise selection and buying functions may be carried out by the owner or other persons who also carry out other functions in the firm. In large firms, buying is a specialist function and often a full-time job. It is carried out in different ways by department stores, supermarkets, drug wholesalers, and so on, and differences can even be found within each type of distributive enterprise.

Much of the flavor of reseller buying practices can be sensed by examining the particular case of supermarket chains and the respective roles played by corporate-headquarter buyers, storewide buying committees, and the individual store managers. In the corporate headquarters of a supermarket chain will be found specialist buyers (sometimes called merchandise managers) for different product lines carried by the supermarket. These buyers have the responsibility for developing brand assortments and listening to presentations by salespersons offering new brands. In some chains these buyers have great latitude with respect to accepting or rejecting new items. In many chains, however, their latitude is limited to screening "obvious rejects" (and sometimes "obvious accepts"); otherwise they must bring most of the new-item proposals to the chain's buying committee at one of the weekly meetings.

There is some evidence that buying committees serve a "checking" function rather than an actual decision-making function. Borden found that the buyer's recommendation is highly important and influential to the committee decision.[16] The buyer decides what to communicate to the committee, thus exerting considerable influence on the decision. Buying committees exert some important indirect effects on product evaluations and decisions. By serving as a "buffer" between buyers and salespersons, committees provide buyers with an excuse for rejecting a seller's proposition.

Even if an item is accepted by a chain-store buying committee, it will not necessarily appear in a large number of the chain's outlets. According to one supermarket chain executive: "No matter what the sales representatives sell or buyers buy, the person who has the greatest influence on the final sale of the new item is the store manager." In the nation's chain and independent supermarkets, two-thirds of the new items accepted at the warehouse are ordered on the individual store manager's own decision, and only one-third represent forced distribution.[17]

This picture of the reseller organization's buying procedure for new items points to the formidable problem faced by the producers of new items. Industry offers the nation's supermarkets between 150 and 250 new items each week, of which store space does not permit more than 10 percent to be accepted.

Several studies have attempted to rank the major criteria used by buyers, buying committees, and store managers. A. C. Nielsen Company conducted a study in which store managers were asked to rank on a three-point scale—with three being the highest—the importance of different elements in influencing their decision to accept a new item.[18] The final ranking showed:

Evidence of consumer acceptance	2.5
Advertising/promotion	2.2
Introductory terms and allowances	2.0
Why item was developed	1.9
Merchandising recommendations	1.8

The first three items are reported to be the most important criteria in other studies also.[19] They suggest that sellers stand the best chance when they can report strong evidence of consumer acceptance, present a well-designed and extensive introductory advertising and sales promotion plan, and provide incentives to the retailer.

These respective roles of chain buyers, chain buying committee, and store manager characterize, with some variation, the buying organizations of other distributive enterprises. Large department stores or chains rely on buyers for merchandise lines, and usually they have a lot of authority and latitude. They may report to buying committees. The buyers are aided by assistant buyers, who carry out preliminary search as well as clerical tasks involved in ordering. The buyers may perform other functions such as demand forecasting, stock control, and merchandising. Individual store managers or their staff usually have some freedom with respect to which goods to order and display prominently.

What Are the Major Influences on Reseller Buyers? (Buying Influences)

Resellers are influenced by the same set of factors—environmental, organizational, interpersonal, and individual—that were shown in Figure 9-1 as influencing industrial buyers. The seller has to note these influences and develop strategies that help the resellers make money or reduce their costs.

The role of the individual buyer's buying style should be taken into account. Dickinson has distinguished the following buyer types in reseller organizations:

1. *Loyal buyer.* This type remains loyal to a resource, or group of resources, year after year, for reasons other than that he obtains the best deal.
2. *Opportunistic buyer.* This type selects mainly from a preselected list of those vendors who will further his long-term interests. Within his preselected list, he will pursue the best arrangement possible.
3. *Best-deal buyer.* This type looks for and selects the best deal available to him in the market at a given point in time.
4. *Creative buyer.* This type tries not to accept the marketing mixes offered by any of the vendors. He attempts to sell his offers to the market. This may or may not involve a change in the physical product.
5. *Advertising buyer.* This type attempts primarily to obtain advertising money; advertising money must be a part of every deal and are the prime target of each negotiation.
6. *The chiseler.* This type of buyer constantly negotiates extra concessions in price at the time of the offering. He tends to accept the vendor offer carrying the greatest discount from the price he feels that other accounts might pay.
7. *Nuts-and-bolts buyer.* This buyer selects merchandise that is the best constructed, assuming that the merchandise policies of the vendor are acceptable within a very broad range. He is more interested in the thread count than in the number that will sell.[20]

How Do Resellers Make Their Buying Decisions? (Buying Process)

For new items, reseller buyers conduct a buying process consisting of approximately the same steps as those described for the industrial buyer. We will therefore not repeat these steps here. For more standard items, the buying process is largely a matter of reordering goods when the inventory levels get low. This may be done by writing new purchase orders or may be accomplished automatically by computer inventory control systems. The orders will be placed with the same suppliers as long as their terms, goods, and services are satisfactory. Buyers will try to renegotiate prices from time to time as their margins erode due to rising operating costs. In many retail lines the profit margin on sales is so low (for example, 1 to 2 percent in supermarkets) that a sudden decline in demand or rise in operating costs will drive profits into the red.

The buying procedures used by resellers are becoming more sophisticated over time. Buyers are mastering the principles of demand forecasting, merchandise selection, stock control, space allocation, and display. They are learning to measure return on a profit-per-cubic-foot basis rather than only on a product-by-product basis.[21] Major changes in purchasing operations are being made possible by advances in computers and telecommunications. Computers are finding increased application in keeping current inventory figures, computing economic order quantities, preparing purchasing orders, developing requests for vendor quotations or expediting of orders, and generating printouts of dollars spent on vendors and products. Through telecommunications, the buyer can feed prepunched cards describing items and quantities needed into a transmitter which is linked to the supplier's receiving equipment. The supplier's equipment prepares cards or tapes, which become the input for mechanized preparation of shipping tickets, invoices, and other documents. Many resellers have moved over to stockless purchasing of reorder items, which means that the suppliers are responsible for carrying the inventory and delivering goods on short notice.

All this means that sellers are facing increasingly sophisticated buyers and buying systems in reseller organizations. They need to understand the resellers' changing requirements and to develop competitively attractive offers and services that fit the buyers' evaluative criteria in choosing suppliers.

the government market

Who Is in the Government Market? (Buying Population)

The **government market** consists of *governmental units of all types—federal, state, and local—who purchase or rent goods for carrying out the main functions of government.* In 1976 governmental units purchased $365 billion of products and services, or 21 percent of the gross national product, making it the nation's largest customer. The federal government accounts for approximately 60 percent of the total spent by government at all levels.

Athough substantial government purchasing takes place in Washington, D.C., state capitals, and major cities, it takes place also in every county and village. The federal government operates an elaborate set of geographically dispersed buying information offices. Local products and services may be bought by local government offices, army posts, and so on.

What Buying Decisions Do Government Buyers Make? (Buying Decisions)

Government buying is premised on a fundamental objective that differs from that found in the other sectors of the economy. Government does not pursue a personal consumption or a profit-making objective; rather, it buys a level and mix of products and services that it or the voters establish as necessary or desirable for the maintenance of the society.

The result is that government agencies buy an amazing range of products and services. They buy bombers, sculpture, chalkboards, furniture, toiletries, clothing, materials-handling equipment, fire engines, mobile equipment, and fuel. In 1975 the governmental units spent approximately $95 billion for education, $87 billion for defense, $39 billion for public welfare, $35 billion for health and hospitals, $23 billion for highways, $16 billion for natural resources, and smaller sums for postal service, space research, and housing and urban renewal. The mix of expenditures varied considerably with the particular type of governmental unit, with defense looming large in the federal budget (34 percent) and education looming large in the state and local budgets (38 percent). No wonder the government market represents a tremendous market for any producer or reseller.

Each good that the government decides to buy requires further decisions on how much to buy, where to buy it, how much to pay, and what other services to require. These decisions are made, in principle, on the basis of trying to minimize *taxpayer cost.* In normal circumstances, government buyers will favor the lowest-cost bidders that can meet the stated specifications.

Who Participates in the Government Buying Process? (Buying Participants)

Who in the government does the buying of the $365 billion of goods and services? Government buying organizations are found at the federal, state, and local levels. The federal level is the largest, and its buying units can be subclassified into the civilian and military sectors. The *federal civilian buying* establishment consists of seven categories: departments (Commerce), administration (General Services Administration), agencies (Federal Aviation Agency), boards (Railroad Retirement Board), commissions (Federal Communications Commission), the executive office (Bureau of the Budget), and miscellaneous (Tennessee Valley Authority). "No single federal agency contracts for all the government's requirements and no single buyer in any agency purchases all that agency's needs for any single item of supplies, equipment or services."[22] Many agencies control a substantial percentage of their own buying, particularly for industrial products and specialized equipment. At the same time, the General Services Administration plays a main role in attempting to centralize the procurement of the items most commonly used by the civilian section (office furniture and equipment, vehicles, fuels, and so on) and to promote standardized buying procedures for the other agencies. It acts in the capacity of a wholesaler on its own account, and as a reseller and an agent middleman for other government agencies.

Federal military buying is carried out by the Defense Department largely through the Defense Supply Agency and the three military departments of the Army, Navy, and Air Force. The Defense Supply Agency was set up in 1961 to procure and distribute supplies used in common by all military services in an effort to reduce costly duplication (thus it is the equivalent of the General Services Administration in the military sector). It operates six supply centers, which specialize in construction, electronics, fuel, personnel support, industrial, and general supplies. The trend has been toward "single managers" for major product classifications. Each individual service branch procures equipment and supplies in line with its own mission; for example, the Army Department operates special branches for acquiring its own material, vehicles, medical supplies and services, and weaponry.

State and local buying agencies include school districts, highway departments, hospitals, housing agencies, and many others.

What Are the Major Influences on Government Buyers? (Buying Influences)

Like other organizational buyers, government buyers are influenced by environmental, organizational, interpersonal, and individual factors. Perhaps the unique thing about government buying is that it is monitored carefully by outside publics. One outside watchdog is Congress, and certain congressmen have made a career out of exposing instances of government extravagance and waste. Another watchdog is the Bureau of the Budget, which checks on government spending and seeks to constantly improve public spending efficiency. In addition, there are many private watchdog groups who watch different agencies to see how they spend the public's money.

As a result of making spending decisions subject to public review, government organizations tend to be involved in much more paper work than is considered necessary in private industry. Elaborate forms must be filled out and must carry several signatures before purchases are approved. The level of bureaucracy is higher, and marketers have to either find ways to "cut the red tape" or live with it.

Another influence on government buying is the growing role of noneconomic criteria to guide vendor selection. The new criteria come out of government reform programs and call for favoring depressed business firms or areas, small business firms, and business firms that do not practice racial, sex, or age discrimination. Sellers should keep these factors in mind when deciding whether to go after a particular government business.

How Do Government Buyers Make Their Buying Decisions? (Buying Process)

Government buying practices appear complex to the uninitiated supplier because of the many agencies and procedures that characterize the government market. Yet most of this can be mastered in a short time, and the government is generally helpful in diffusing information about its buying needs and procedures. In fact, government is often as anxious to attract new suppliers as the suppliers are to find customers. For example, the Small Business Administration prints a useful booklet "U.S. Government Purchasing, Specifications, and Sales Directory" listing thousands of items most frequently purchased by government and cross-referenced by the agencies most frequently using them. The Government Printing Office prints "Commerce Business Daily," which lists current proposed defense procurements estimated to exceed $10,000 and civilian agency procurements expected to exceed $5,000, as well as information about recent contract awards that can provide leads to subcontracting markets. The General Services Administration operates Business Service Centers in several major cities, whose staff is set up to provide a complete education on the way it and other agencies buy and the steps that the supplier should follow. Various trade magazines and associations provide information on how to reach schools, hospitals, highway departments, and other government agencies.

Government buying procedures can be classified into two major types: the *open bid* and the *negotiated contract.* In both cases the emphasis is on competitive procurement. Open-bid buying means that the government procuring office invites bids from qualified suppliers for carefully described items, generally awarding a contract to the lowest bidder. Specifically, the interested supplier fills out an application requesting to be placed on the bidders' lists. The supplier receives mailings of "invitations for bids," which carefully specify the item and quantity needed. The specifications include a description of the materials, dimensions, quality, reliability, and packing and crating requirements, as well as the terms of the contract that will be awarded to the successful bidder. The supplier firm must carefully consider whether it can meet the specifications and likes the terms. For commodities and standard items, such as fuel or school supplies, the specifications are not a hurdle. However, specifications may constitute a hurdle for nonstandard items, although the government unit is barred from issuing such narrow specifications that only one existing seller can meet them. Furthermore, the government procurement office is usually—but not always—required to award the contract to the lowest bidder on a winner-take-all basis. In some cases allowance can be made for the supplier's superior product or reputation for completing contracts. A more recent development is to ask for bids, particularly on equipment, to cover its life-cycle maintenance as well as initial price. The award will go to the firm submitting the lowest life-cycle bid, rather than bid for the original equipment only. This practice was started by the Defense Department when it realized that it might spend up to ten times the original purchase price to own and operate the equipment.

In negotiated-contract buying, the agency works with one or a few companies and directly negotiates a contract with one of them covering the project and terms. This occurs primarily in connection with complex projects, often involving major research and development cost and risk and/or where there is little effective competition. Contracts can have countless variations, such as *cost-plus pricing, fixed-pricing,* and *fixed price-and-incentive* (the supplier earns more if costs are reduced). Contract performance is open to review and renegotiation if the supplier's profits appear excessive.

Government contracts won by large companies give rise to substantial subcontracting opportunities, as much as 50 percent, for small companies. Thus government purchasing activity in turn creates derived demand in the producer market. Subcontracting firms, however, must go after this business with a willingness to place performance bonds with the prime contractor, thereby assuming some of the risk.

By and large, many companies that have served the government have not manifested much of a marketing orientation—for a number of reasons. Total government spending is determined by elected officials rather than by marketing effort to develop this market. The government's procurement policies have emphasized price, leading the suppliers to invest all their effort in a technological orientation to bring their costs down. Where the product's characteristics are carefully specified, product differentiation is not a marketing factor. Nor is advertising and personal selling of much consequence in winning bids on an open-bid basis.

More companies are now establishing marketing departments to guide government-directed marketing effort. These companies realize that it is necessary to coordinate bids and prepare them more scientifically, to propose projects to meet government needs rather than just to respond to government initiatives, to gather competitive intelligence, and to prepare better communication programs to describe the company's competence.

■ summary

The organizational market consists of all the organizations that buy goods for purposes of further production, or resale, or distribution to others. Organizations are a market for raw and manufactured materials and parts, installations, and accessory equipment, as well as supplies and services.

Producer organizations buy goods and services for the purpose of increasing sales, cutting costs, or meeting social and legal requirements. Compared with consumer buyers, the producer market consists of fewer buyers, larger buyers, and more geographically concentrated buyers; the demand is derived, relatively inelastic, and more fluctuating; and the purchasing is more professional. Industrial buyers have to make a number of decisions that vary with the type of buying situation or buyclass. Buyclasses comprise three types: straight rebuys, modified rebuys, and new tasks. The decision-making unit of a buying organization, the buying center, consists of individuals who play any of five roles: users, influencers, buyers, deciders, and gatekeepers. The industrial marketer needs to know: Who are the major decision participants? In what decisions do they exercise influence? What is their relative degree of influence? and What evaluation criteria does each decision participant use? The industrial marketer also needs to understand the major environmental, organizational, interpersonal, and individual influences operating in the buying process. The buying process itself consists of eight stages called buyphases: problem recognition, general need description, product specification, supplier search, proposal solicitation, supplier selection, order routine specification, and performance review. As industrial buyers become more sophisticated, industrial marketers must upgrade their own marketing capabilities.

The reseller market consists of individuals and organizations who acquire and resell goods produced by others. Resellers have to decide on their assortment, suppliers, prices, and terms. They face three types of buying situations: new items, new vendors, and new terms. In small wholesale and retail organizations, buying may be carried on by one or a few individuals; in larger organizations, by a whole purchasing department. In a modern supermarket chain, the major decision participants include headquarters buyers, storewide buying committees, and individual store managers. With new items, the buyers go through a buying process similar to the one shown for industrial buyers; and with standard items, the buying process consists of routines for reordering and renegotiating contracts.

The government market is a vast one that annually purchases $365 billion of products and services—for the pursuit of defense, education, public welfare, and other public needs. Government buying practices are highly specialized and specified, with open bidding and/or negotiated contracts characterizing most of the buying. Government buyers operate under the watchful eye of Congress, the Bureau of the Budget, and several private watchdog groups. Hence they tend to fill out more forms, obtain more signatures, and move more slowly in placing orders.

■ questions for discussion

1. It has been argued that a college of business administration is an industrial marketer. What characteristics of an industrial market does the demand for students (i.e., industrial products) exhibit?
2. Into which of the major types of buying situations would you classify the following? (a) United Airline's purchase of an additional DC-10, (b) Caterpillar's purchase of diesel engine parts, (c) Pacific Power and Electric's purchase of solar energy panels.
3. How would the participants in the producer buying process differ between a small machine tool shop and U.S. Steel?
4. Discuss the major environmental factors that would influence Greyhound's purchase of buses.
5. Apply the buyphases to an industrial product with which you are familiar.
6. How do the two major types of resellers differ in the way they make their buying decisions?

7. The government market is not a significant one for most products. Comment.
8. How do the buying influences on the government buyer differ from those on the producer or reseller buyer?

■ references

1. Some of this information is drawn from "The College Caterers Are Dropping Out," *Business Week,* April 23, 1979, pp. 36–37.
2. FREDERICK E. WEBSTER, JR., AND YORAM WIND, *Organizational Buying Behavior* (Englewood Cliffs, N.J.: Prentice-Hall, 1972), p. 2.
3. See REED MOYER, "Reciprocity: Retrospect and Prospect," *Journal of Marketing,* October 1970, pp. 47–54.
4. See LEONARD J. BERRY AND KENNETH E. MARICLE, "Consumption without Ownership: Marketing Opportunity for Today and Tomorrow," *MSU Business Topics,* Spring 1973, pp. 33–41.
5. PATRICK J. ROBINSON, CHARLES W. FARIS, AND YORAM WIND, *Industrial Buying and Creative Marketing* (Boston: Allyn and Bacon, 1967.)
6. See Chapter 12, p. 393, footnote 6.
7. WEBSTER AND WIND, *Organizational Buying Behavior,* p. 6.
8. Ibid., pp. 78–80.
9. See MURRAY HARDING, "Who Really Makes the Purchasing Decision?" *Industrial Marketing,* September 1966, p. 76. This point of view is further developed in ERNEST DICHTER, "Industrial Buying Is Based on Same "Only Human" Emotional Factors That Motivate Consumer Market's Housewife," *Industrial Marketing,* February 1973, pp. 14–16.
10. WEBSTER AND WIND, *Organizational Buying Behavior,* pp. 33–37.
11. See "The Purchasing Agent Gains More Clout," *Business Week,* January 13, 1975, pp. 62–63.
12. Ibid.
13. WALTER GUZZARDI, JR., "The Fight for 9/10 of a Cent," *Fortune,* April 1961, p. 152.
14. ROBINSON, FARIS, AND WIND, *Industrial Buying.*
15. See LEONARD GROENEVELD, "The Implications of Blanket Contracting for Industrial Purchasing and Marketing," *Journal of Purchasing,* November 1972, pp. 51–58; and H. LEE MATHEWS, DAVID T. WILSON, AND KLAUS BACKHAUS, "Selling to the Computer Assisted Buyer," *Industrial Marketing Management,* 6 (1977), 307–15.
16. NEIL H. BORDEN, JR., *Acceptance of New Food Products by Supermarkets* (Boston: Division of Research, Graduate School of Business Administration, Harvard University, 1968).
17. ROBERT W. MUELLER AND FRANKLIN H. GRAF, "New Items in the Food Industry, Their Problems and Opportunities" (Special report to the Annual Convention of the Supermarket Institute, Cleveland, May 20, 1968), p. 2.
18. Ibid, p. 5.
19. "Merchandising New Items at Retail: The Payoff at Point of Purchase," *Progressive Grocer,* June 1968; and BORDEN, *Acceptance of New Food Products,* p. 203. Also see DAVID B. MONTGOMERY, *New Product Distribution: An Analysis of Supermarket Buyer Decisions* (Cambridge, Mass.: Marketing Science Institute, March, 1973).

Montgomery found the two most important variables to be company reputation and the perceived newness of the product.

20. Roger A. Dickinson, *Buyer Decision Making* (Berkeley, Calif.: Institute of Business and Economic Research, 1967), pp. 14–17.
21. See Robert D. Buzzell, *Product Profitability Measurement and Merchandising Decisions* (Boston: Harvard University Press, 1965).
22. Stanley E. Cohen, "Looking in the U.S. Government Market," *Industrial Marketing,* September 1964, pp. 129–38.

MARKET SEGMENTATION AND TARGETING

Peugeot-Citroen is the eighth largest automobile manufacturer in the world and the forty-ninth largest company in the world, with $7 billion in assets. A French company, Peugeot-Citroen spent $400 million in the early 1970s developing its new Peugeot 604SL. The car was unveiled at the 1975 Autoshow in France and was an immediate success. France and several other European countries adopted it as the official state car.

The U.S. market at the time accounted for only 1 percent of Peugeot's worldwide sales, particularly of its 504 series. The company hoped that by introducing the new 604SL in the United States, the U.S. market would ultimately account for 10 percent of its worldwide sales.

But who would the American customer be? At a price tag of over $13,000, most Americans would not be interested. Identifying the best prospects and promoting the car to them would be a challenge. The best prospects appeared to be present owners of luxury cars, such as the Mercedes, BMW, Volvo, Jaguar, and Seville. Research indicated that the target customers would be upper income, college educated, and mostly professional, managerial, and entrepreneurial. This elite group of consumers accounted for only 0.7 percent of all new-car sales and 4.8 percent of total industry imports. Finding them was "going to be like trying to pick the chips out of chocolate chip ice cream," according to researcher Louis Van Leeuwen.

The Peugeot also needed a theme that would distinguish it from the other luxury cars in its class. "We tried to separate Peugeot from domestic cars and distinguished its appeal from the safety thrust of Volvo, the macho-oriented BMW, and economy pitches of other companies." The company chose to emphasize the engineering quality of the 604SL, referring to the forty-six thousand separate quality control checks and the road testing of every vehicle, feeling that the target customers were more interested in performance than style. The company decided that the target customers most likely to consider a 604 were the owners of, in decreasing order of importance, a Volvo, Mercedes, BMW, Jaguar, or Seville.

After identifying the target market, the company proceeded to make a number of marketing-planning decisions. It knew that its main dealer thrust would be in cities with concentrated affluent populations, such as New York, Boston, Chicago, San Francisco, and Los Angeles. It also knew that it needed to find cost-effective media that would efficiently reach audiences who were in the 35–64 age group, had a median

income of $50,000, were college educated, and were in the professional/managerial/entrepreneurial class.

How well did the company segment the market and pick its targets? New buyers of the 604s were asked what cars they had considered. The answers that came back were: Mercedes, 42 percent; BMW, 37 percent; Seville, 24 percent; and Volvo, 9 percent. Seven months after the 604 was introduced, it captured a 6.3 percent share of the luxury car market. It had found the needle in the haystack.[1]

□ An organization that decides to operate in the automobile or any other market soon recognizes that it cannot serve and appeal to all buyers. The buyers may be too numerous, widely scattered, and varied in their buying requirements and buying practices. Different competitors will be in the best position to serve particular segments of the market. Each company, instead of competing everywhere, should identify the most attractive parts of the market that it could serve effectively.

Sellers have not always adhered to this philosophy. In deciding how to operate in a market, sellers have gone through three stages:

- *Mass marketing.* Mass marketing is a style of marketing where the seller mass-produces and mass-distributes one product and attempts to attract all kinds of buyers. Thus at one time Coca-Cola produced only one drink for the whole market, hoping it would become everyone's favorite drink. The argument for mass marketing is that it should lead to the lowest costs and prices and therefore create the largest potential market. The mass marketer pays little or no attention to differences in demand.
- *Product-differentiated marketing.* Product differentiation is a style of marketing where the seller produces two or more products designed to look different from each other and competitors' products. The products may exhibit different features, styles, quality, sizes, and so on. Thus today Coca-Cola produces many different-flavored soft drinks in many sizes and types of containers. They are not designed to meet differing needs of specific groups in the market but rather to offer variety to buyers.
- *Target marketing.* Target marketing is a style of marketing where the seller distinguishes between different groups (segments) making up the market, chooses one or more of these segments to focus on, and develops products and marketing mixes tailored to meet the needs of each target market. For example, Coca-Cola developed Tab specifically to meet the needs of the group of soft-drink consumers who want to keep their weight down.

Companies can be found today practicing each style of marketing. However, there is a strong movement away from mass marketing and product-differentiated marketing toward target marketing. At least three benefits can be identified for target marketing:

1. *Sellers are in a better position to spot market opportunities.* They are able to notice market segments whose needs are not being fully met by current product offers.

Figure 10-1
Steps in Market Segmentation and Target Marketing

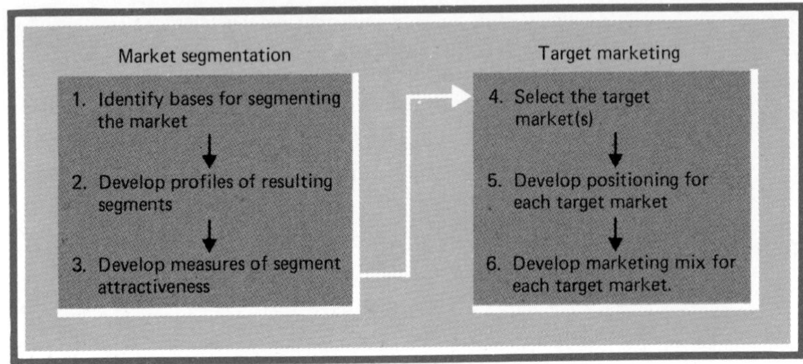

2. *Sellers can make finer adjustments of their product to match the desires of the market.* They are able to interview members of the target market and get a good picture of their specific needs and desires.
3. *Sellers can make finer adjustments of their prices, distribution channels, and promotional mix.* Instead of trying to draw in all potential buyers with a "shotgun" approach, sellers can create separate marketing programs aimed at each target market (called a "rifle" approach).

Target marketing comprises two major steps (see Figure 10-1). The first is **market segmentation,** the *act of dividing a market into distinct and meaningful groups of buyers who might merit separate products and/or marketing mixes.* Market segmentation requires that the company identify different bases for segmenting the market, develop profiles of the resulting market segments, and develop measures of each segment's attractiveness. The second step is **target marketing,** the *act of selecting one or more of the market segments and developing a positioning and market mix strategy for each.* This chapter will describe the major concepts and tools involved in market segmentation and target marketing.

market segmentation

Markets consist of buyers, and buyers are likely to differ in one or more respects. They may differ in their desires, resources, geographical locations, buying attitudes, buying practices, and so on. Any of these variables can be used to segment a market. We will first illustrate the general approach to segmenting a market.

The General Approach to Segmenting a Market

Figure 10-2A shows a market consisting of six buyers before it is segmented. The maximum number of segments that a market can contain is the total number of buyers making up that market. Each buyer is potentially a separate market because of unique needs and desires. Ideally, a seller might study each buyer in order to tailor the best marketing program to that buyer's needs. Where there are only a few major customers, this is done to some extent. For example, the major airframe producers such as Boeing and McDonnell-Douglas face only a few buyers and treat them as separate markets. This ultimate degree of market segmentation is illustrated in Figure 10-2B.

Most sellers, however, will not find it worthwhile to "customize" their

Figure 10-2
Different Approaches to Market Segmentation

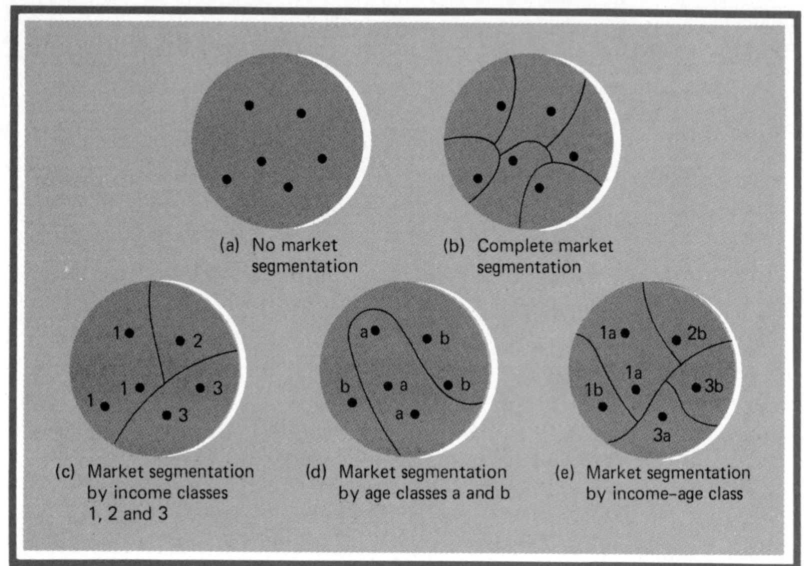

product to satisfy each buyer's specific wants. Instead, the seller identifies broad classes of buyers who differ in their product requirements and/or marketing responses. For example, the seller may discover that income groups differ in their product requirements and marketing responses. In Figure 10-2C, a number (1, 2, or 3) is used to identify each buyer's income class. Lines are drawn around buyers in the same income class. Segmentation by income class results in three segments, the most numerous segment being income class 1 in the illustration.

On the other hand, the seller may find pronounced differences in buyer behavior between younger and older buyers. In Figure 10-2D the same individuals are shown, but a letter (*a* or *b*) is used to indicate the buyer's age class. Segmentation of the market by age class results in two segments, both equally numerous.

It may turn out that income and age both count heavily in differentiating the buyer's behavior toward the product. The seller may find it desirable to partition the market according to those joint characteristics. In terms of the illustration, the market can be broken into the following six segments: 1*a*, 1*b*, 2*a*, 2*b*, 3*a*, and 3*b*. Figure 10-2E shows that segment 1*a* contains two buyers, segment 2*a* contains no buyers (a null segment), and each of the other segments contains one buyer. In general, as the market is segmented on the basis of a larger set of joint characteristics, the seller achieves finer precision, but at the price of multiplying the number of segments and thinning out the populations in the segments. If the seller segmented the market using all conceivable characteristics, the market would again look like Figure 10-2B, where each buyer would be a separate segment.

In the preceding illustration, the market was segmented by income and age. This resulted in different *demographic segments*. Suppose, instead, buyers are asked how much they want of each of two product attributes (say, *bitterness* and *lightness* in beer). This results in identifying different *preference segments* in the market. Three different patterns can emerge:

Figure 10-3
Basic Market Preference Patterns

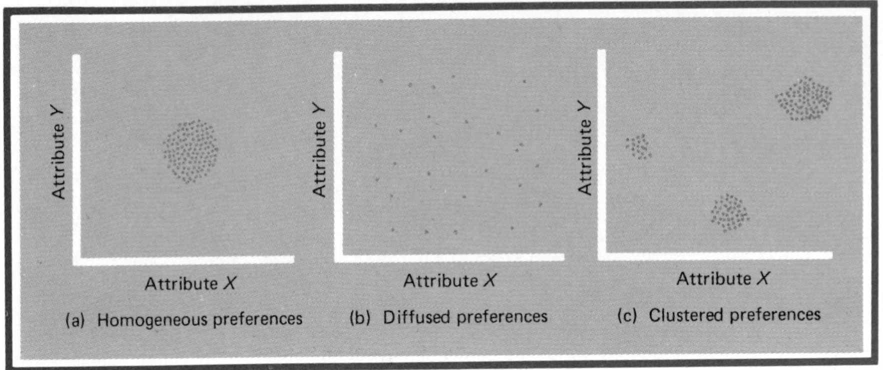

1. *Homogeneous preferences.* Figure 10-3A reveals a market where all the consumers have roughly the same preference. The market shows no *natural segments,* at least as far as the two attributes are concerned. We would predict that sellers would all go after the same customers and would offer highly similar products.
2. *Diffused preferences.* At the other extreme, consumer preferences may be scattered fairly evenly throughout the space with no concentration (Figure 10-3B). We would predict that sellers would seek footholds in different parts of the market and would offer products that would satisfy those customers.
3. *Clustered preferences.* An intermediate possibility is the appearance of distinct preference clusters called *natural market segments* (Figure 10-3C). We would predict that each seller would seek leadership in a particular market segment by designing products and marketing programs that would appeal to that segment.

Thus we find that segmentation procedures could indicate the existence of natural market segments, or could be used to construct artificial market segments, or could reveal the lack of any market segments. We will now examine specific variables that can be used in segmenting consumer markets.

Bases for Segmenting Consumer Markets

There is no one way, or right way, to segment a market. A market can be segmented in a number of ways by introducing different variables and seeing which reveal the best market opportunities. Sometimes the marketer merely has to try out the various segmentation variables, singly and in combination, before hitting on an insightful way to view the market structure. Here we will review the major geographic, demographic, psychographic, and behavioristic variables used in segmenting consumer markets (see Table 10-1).

Geographic segmentation. In geographic segmentation, the market is divided into different geographical entities, such as nations, states, regions, counties, cities, or neighborhoods, based on the notion that consumer needs or responses vary geographically. The company decides to (1) operate in one or a few parts of the country as a specialist in meeting consumer needs or (2) operate broadly but pay attention to variations in geographic needs and preferences. For example, General Foods' Maxwell House ground coffee is sold nationally but is flavored regionally. People in the West prefer a stronger coffee than people in the East.

Companies also distinguish their geographical markets according to market potential and other bases. Beatrice Foods sorts the various markets for its

Table 10-1
Major Segmentation Variables for Consumer Markets

VARIABLES	TYPICAL BREAKDOWNS
Geographic	
Region	Pacific, Mountain, West North Central, West South Central, East North Central, East South Central, South Atlantic, Middle Atlantic, New England
County size	A, B, C, D
City or SMSA size	Under 5,000, 5,000–19,999, 20,000–49,999, 50,000–99,999, 100,000–249,999, 250,000–499,999, 500,000–999,999, 1,000,000–3,999,999, 4,000,000 or over
Density	Urban, suburban, rural
Climate	Northern, southern
Demographic	
Age	Under 6, 6–11, 12–19, 20–34, 35–49, 50–64, 65+
Sex	Male, female
Family size	1–2, 3–4, 5+
Family life cycle	Young, single; young, married, no children; young, married, youngest child under six; young, married, youngest child six or over; older, married, with children; older, married, no children under 18; older, single; other
Income	Under $3,000, $3,000–$5,000, $5,000–$7,000, $7,000–$10,000, $10,000–$15,000, $15,000–$25,000, $25,000 and over
Occupation	Professional and technical; managers, officials, and proprietors; clerical, sales; craftsmen, foremen; operatives; farmers; retired; students; housewives; unemployed
Education	Grade school or less; some high school; graduated high school; some college; graduated college
Religion	Catholic, Protestant, Jewish, other
Race	White, black, oriental
Nationality	American, British, French, German, Scandinavian, Italian, Latin American, Middle Eastern, Japanese
Psychographic	
Social class	Lower lowers, upper lowers, lower middles, upper middles, lower uppers, upper uppers
Life style	Straights, swingers, longhairs
Personality	Compulsive, gregarious, authoritarian, ambitious
Behavioristic	
Purchase occasion	Regular occasion, special occasion
Benefits sought	Economy, convenience, prestige
User status	Nonuser, ex-user, potential user, first-time user, regular user
Usage rate	Light user, medium user, heavy user
Loyalty status	None; medium; strong; absolute
Readiness stage	Unaware, aware, informed, interested, desirous, intending to buy
Marketing-factor sensitivity	Quality, price, service, advertising, sales promotion

Dannon yogurt brand into three groups, based on the number of years since the brand was introduced. These groups consist of *embryonic markets* (one to five years), *growth markets* (six to ten years), and *mature markets* (eleven or more years). Dannon allocates different resources and uses different marketing strategies in these three groups of markets.

Demographic segmentation. In demographic segmentation, the market is divided into different groups on the basis of demographic variables such as age, sex, family size, family life cycle, income, occupation, education, religion, race, and nationality. Demographic variables have long been the most popular bases for distinguishing customer groups. One reason is that consumer wants, preferences, and usage rates are often highly associated with demographic variables. Another is that demographic variables are easier to measure than most other types of variables. Even when the target market is described in nondemographic terms (say, a personality type), the link back to demographic characteristics is necessary in order to know the size of the target market and how to reach it efficiently.

Here we will illustrate how certain demographic variables have been applied creatively to market segmentation.

AGE AND LIFE-CYCLE STAGE

Consumer wants and capacities change with age. Even children who are six months old differ from children who are three months old in their consumption potential. Alabe Products, a toy manufacturer, realized this and designed twelve different toys to be used by babies sequentially as they move from the age of three months to one year. Crib Jiminy is to be used when babies begin to reach for things, Talky Rattle when they first grasp things, and so on.[2] This segmentation strategy means that parents and gift givers can more easily find the appropriate toy by simply considering the baby's age.

Recently the same strategy was used successfully by General Foods, only this time for dog food. Research shows that many dog owners think of their dog as a family member whose food needs change as the dog gets older. So General Foods formulated four types of canned dog food for different stages of the dog's life cycle: Cycle 1 for puppies, Cycle 2 for young dogs, Cycle 3 for overweight dogs, and Cycle 4 for older dogs. General Foods, which hitherto had had a weak share of the canned dog food market, managed to grab a large share through this creative segmentation strategy.[3]

Nevertheless, age and life cycle can be tricky variables. For example, the Ford Motor Company used buyers' age in developing its target market for its Mustang automobile; the car was designed to appeal to young people who wanted an inexpensive sporty automobile. Ford found, to its surprise, that the car was being purchased by all age groups. It then realized that its target market was not the chronologically young but those who were psychologically young.

SEX

Sex segmentation has been a longstanding practice in such product and service categories as clothing, hairdressing, cosmetics, and magazines. From time to time, marketers of other products and services will notice an opportunity for sex segmentation. An excellent example is the cigarette market. Most cigarette brands are smoked by men and women alike. Increasingly, however, feminine brands like Eve and Virginia Slims have been introduced accompanied by appropriate flavor, packaging, and advertising cues to reinforce the image of the target market. Today it is as unlikely to see men smoking Eve as it is to see women smoking Marlboros. Another industry that is beginning to recognize the potential for sex segmentation is the automobile industry. In the past, cars were designed to appeal to both male and female family members. With more working-women and women car owners, however, some manufacturers are studying the opportunity to design "feminine" cars to meet the preferences of women drivers.

INCOME

Income segmentation is another longstanding practice in such product and service categories as automobiles, boats, clothing, cosmetics, and travel. Other industries occasionally recognize its possibilities. For example, Suntory, the Japanese liquor company, has introduced a scotch selling for $75 to attract the people who want the very best.

At the same time, income can sometimes incorrectly predict who will buy certain products. One would think that working-class families would buy Chevrolets and managerial-class families would buy Cadillacs. Yet many Chevrolets are bought by middle-income families (often as a second car), and some Cadillacs are bought by working-class families (such as high-paid plumbers and carpenters). Members of the working class were among the first purchasers of expensive color television sets; it was cheaper for them to buy these sets than go out to movies and restaurants. Coleman suggested that a distinction should be drawn between the "underprivileged" segments and the "overprivileged" segments of each social class.[4] The cheapest, most economical cars are not bought by the really poor, but rather by "those who think of themselves as poor relative to their status aspirations and to their needs for a certain level of clothing, furniture, and housing which they could not afford if they bought a more expensive car." On the other hand, medium-priced and expensive cars tend to be purchased by the overprivileged segments of each social class.

MULTIVARIABLE SEGMENTATION

Very often an organization will segment a market by combining two or more variables. The Charles Home for the Blind (name disguised) serves the needs of partially and totally blind persons for care, psychological counseling, and vocational training. However, it is not able to serve all types of blind people because of limited facilities and because blind people's needs differ and other institutions can more easily handle some of these needs. A multiple segmentation of blind persons is shown in Figure 10-4, where they are distinguished according to age, sex, and

Figure 10-4
Segmentation of Blind Persons by Three Demographic Variables

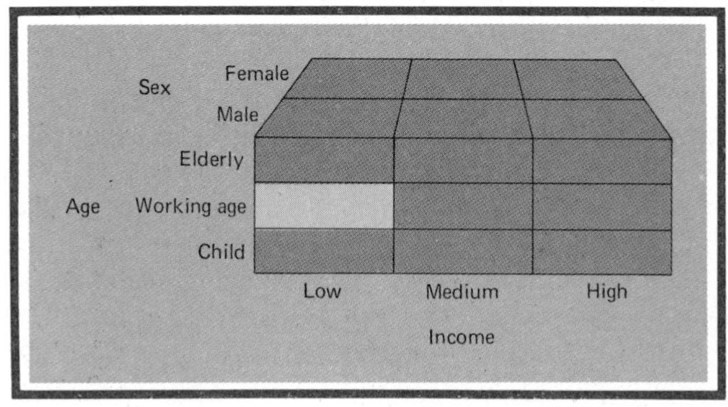

income. The Charles Home has decided to concentrate on serving low-income males of working age. It feels that it can do the best job for these persons and has created special programs to meet their needs.

Psychographic segmentation. In psychographic segmentation, buyers are divided into different groups on the basis of their social class, life style, or personality characteristics. People within the same demographic group can exhibit very different psychographic profiles. The fact that demographics do not necessarily reveal anything about attitudes and living styles has led to psychographic segmentation.

SOCIAL CLASS

We described the six American social classes in Chapter 8, p. 240, and showed that social class has a strong influence on the person's preferences in cars, clothes, home furnishings, leisure activities, reading habits, retailers, and so on. Many consumer companies design products and/or services for specific social classes, building in those features that are clearly appealing to the target social class.

LIFE STYLE

Life-style segmentation is the attempt to distinguish groups exhibiting different life styles. Every person has a life style and there are a limited number of life styles. Researchers have found that they can identify life styles by interviewing people about their *activities, interests,* and *opinions* and then clustering them into groups sharing common activities, interests, and opinions. Using this approach, the Chicago-based advertising agency of Needham, Harper and Steers has identified ten major life-style types and the percentage of the population in each life-style group:[5]

- Ben, the self-made businessman (17%)
- Scott, the successful professional (21%)
- Dale, the devoted family man (17%)
- Fred, the frustrated factory worker (19%)
- Herman, the retiring homebody (26%)
- Cathy, the contented housewife (18%)
- Candice, the chic suburbanite (20%)
- Eleanor, the elegant socialite (17%)
- Mildred, the militant mother (20%)
- Thelma, the old-fashioned traditionalist (25%)

Each of these types is characterized by specific activities, interests, and opinions, as well as product preferences and media preferences.

This general life-style information is used in the following way. In preparing a marketing strategy for a product, the marketers will attempt to determine which life-style groups are likely to find the product most appealing. For example, Candice would be the prime candidate for yogurt. Knowing this, it is possible to develop advertising copy and media mixes more exactly. The advertising copywriter just imagines Candice's life style and develops a commercial about yogurt with which she can connect.

Some researchers are less convinced that these general life-style types are useful and prefer more product-specific life-style studies. Ruth Ziff has studied life styles that emerge in the purchase of drug items, personal items, household items, and food items.[6] In the case of drug items, for example, she has identified the following four product class life styles (percentage of each shown in parentheses):

- *Realists* (35 percent) are not health fatalists, nor excessively concerned with protection or germs. They view remedies positively, want something that is convenient and works, and do not feel the need for a doctor-recommended medicine.
- *Authority seekers* (31 percent) are doctor-and-prescription oriented, are neither fatalists nor stoics concerning health, but they prefer the stamp of authority on what they do take.
- *Skeptics* (23 percent) have a low health concern, are least likely to resort to medication, and are highly skeptical of cold remedies.
- *Hypochondriacs* (11 percent) have a high health concern, regard themselves as prone to any bug going around, and tend to take medication at the first symptom. They do not look for strength in what they take, but need some mild authority reassurance.[7]

Drug firms would be the most effective in marketing their products to hypochondriacs and the least effective in marketing their products to skeptics. If each of the above life-style groups exhibits distinct demographic characteristics and media preferences, drug companies can increase their efficiency in reaching target markets.

PERSONALITY

Marketers have also used personality variables to segment markets. They try to endow their products with *brand personalities* (brand image, brand concept) designed to appeal to corresponding *consumer personalities* (self-images, self-concepts). In the late fifties, Fords and Chevrolets were promoted as having different personalities. Ford buyers were thought to be "independent, impulsive, masculine, alert to change, and self-confident, while Chevrolet owners are conservative, thrifty, prestige-conscious, less masculine, and seeking to avoid extremes."[8] Evans investigated whether this was true by subjecting Ford and Chevrolet owners to the Edwards Personal Preference test, which measured needs for achievement, dominance, change, aggression, and so on. Except for a slightly higher score on dominance, Ford owners did not score significantly differently from Chevrolet owners, and Evans concluded that "the distributions of scores for all needs overlap to such an extent that [personality] discrimination is virtually impossible." Work subsequent to Evans on a wide variety of products and brands has occasionally turned up personality differences but more often has not. Westfall found some evidence of personality differences between the owners of convertibles and nonconvertibles, the former appearing to be more active, impulsive, and sociable.[9] Gottlieb found compulsive people to be heavier users of aspirin.[10] Tucker and Painter found some statistically significant but weak personality correlations for nine products in their study.[11]

Behavioristic segmentation. In behavioristic segmentation (also called product-related segmentation), buyers are divided into groups on the basis of their knowledge, attitude, use, or response to an actual product or its attributes. Many marketers believe that behavioristic variables are the best starting point for constructing effective market segments.

PURCHASE OCCASION

Buyers can be distinguished according to occasions when they purchase a product. For example, air travelers include those whose flying relates to business, vacation, or family. An airline can decide to specialize in serving people for whom one of these occasions dominates. Thus charter airlines serve people for whom a vacation is the occasion for flying. Other airlines might specialize in serving people for whom business is the occasion for flying.

Occasion segmentation is often used by firms seeking to build up product category usage. For example, orange juice is most commonly consumed at breakfast. An orange juice company can try to promote drinking orange juice as part of the evening meal. Certain national holidays—Mother's Day and Father's Day for example—were promoted indirectly to increase the sales of such products as candy and flowers. The Curtis Candy Company was primarily responsible for starting the "trick-or-treat" custom at Halloween, with every home ready to dispense candy to eager little callers knocking at its door.

BENEFITS SOUGHT

Buyers can be segmented according to the particular benefit(s) that they are seeking through the purchase of the product. Yankelovich applied benefit segmentation to the purchase of watches. He found that "approximately 23 percent of the buyers bought for lowest price, another 46 percent bought for durability and general product quality, and 31 percent bought watches as symbols of some important occasion."[12] The better-known watch companies at the time were focusing almost exclusively on the third segment by producing expensive watches, stressing prestige, and selling through jewelry stores. Then the U.S. Time Company came along and decided to focus on the first two segments by creating Timex watches and selling them through mass merchandisers. This segmentation strategy led to its becoming the world's largest watch company.

In using benefit segmentation, the task is to determine the major benefits that people might be looking for in the product class, the kinds of people who might be looking for each benefit, and the existing brands that come close to delivering each benefit. Researchers are increasingly using "perceptual mapping" to accomplish this. Perceptual mapping involves interviewing consumers with special questions and applying advanced statistical techniques to the data. A perceptual mapping of the sports car market is illustrated in Figure 10-5. Various benefits sought by sports car buyers are shown in quotation marks; various sports cars are shown in small polygons; and various stereotyped owners are shown underlined. Note the Corvette and Jaguar sports cars in the upper right of the figure. They are close to the benefit "high top speed" and to the stereotyped car owners "amateur racer" and "rally enthusiast." Also note the benefits "prestigious" and "beautiful lines" in the upper left. None of the studied sports cars quite fits these descriptions, which means that there is an opportunity to design an even more "prestigious" and "beautiful lines" car than those studied. Also look at

Figure 10-5
A Perceptual Map of Sports Car Benefits, Cars, and Stereotyped Owners

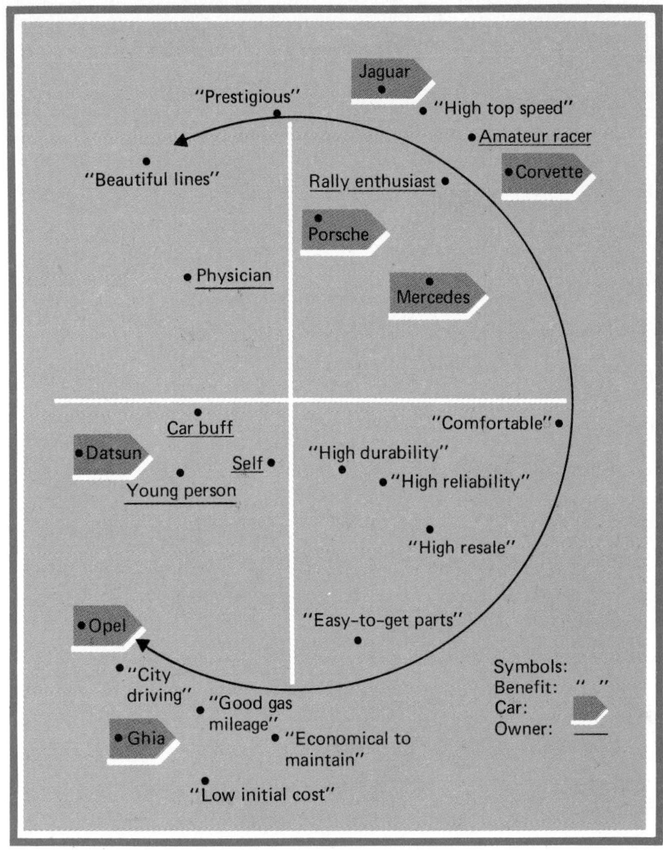

Source: Modified from Paul Green, "A Multidimensional Model of Product Features Association," *Journal of Business Research,* April 1974, p. 113.

the Opel and the Ghia in the lower left. Their benefits are "city driving," "good gas mileage," "economical to maintain" and "low initial cost." No particular stereotyped owner is shown. Note also the cluster of benefits at the lower right called "high durability," "high reliability," and "high resale," and the surprising absence of an existing sports car matching those benefits. This might be another opportunity for a sports car manufacturer.

One of the most successful benefit segmentations was reported by Haley, who studied the toothpaste market (see Table 10-2). Haley's research uncovered four benefit segments: those seeking economy, protection, cosmetic, and taste benefits. Each benefit-seeking group had a heavy representation of a particular demographic, behavioristic, and psychographic group. For example, decay prevention seekers consisted of a higher number of large families, heavy toothpaste users, and people with conservative life styles. The table also shows that certain brands were well positioned in each benefit segment.

A toothpaste company can use these results to clarify which benefit segment it is appealing to, its characteristics, and the major competitive brands. The same company can also search for a new benefit that is not currently being served (such as "better breath") and launch a brand dedicated to delivering this benefit.

Table 10-2
Benefit Segmentation of the Toothpaste Market

BENEFIT SEGMENTS	DEMOGRAPHICS	BEHAVIORISTICS	PSYCHOGRAPHICS	FAVORED BRANDS
Economy (low price)	Men	Heavy users	High autonomy, value oriented	Brands on sale
Medicinal (decay prevention)	Large families	Heavy users	Hypochondriac, conservative	Crest
Cosmetic (bright teeth)	Teens, young adults	Smokers	High sociability, active	Macleans, Ultra Brite
Taste (good tasting)	Children	Spearmint lovers	High self-involvement, hedonistic	Colgate, Aim

Source: Adapted from Russell J. Haley, "Benefit Segmentation: A Decision Oriented Research Tool," *Journal of Marketing,* July 1963, pp. 30–35.

USER STATUS

Many markets can be segmented into nonusers, ex-users, potential users, first-time users, and regular users of a product. High-market-share companies such as Kodak (in the film market) are particularly interested in going after potential users, whereas a small film competitor will concentrate on trying to attract regular users to its brand. Potential users and regular users require different kinds of communication and marketing efforts.

In the social marketing area, agencies such as antidrug agencies pay close attention to user status. They direct most of their effort at young people who might be potential users and try to immunize them from an interest in hard drugs. They sponsor rehabilitation programs to help regular users who want to quit their habit. They utilize ex-users to lend credibility to various programs.

USAGE RATE

Many markets can be segmented into light-, medium-, and heavy-user groups of the product (called volume segmentation). Heavy users may constitute only a small percentage of the numerical size of the market but a major percentage of the unit volume consumed. Some consumer-panel data on usage rates for popular consumer products are shown in Figure 10-6. Using beer as an example, the chart shows that 68 percent of the panel members did not drink beer. The 32 percent who did were ranked from low to high in their usage rates. The lower 16 percent were classified as light users and accounted for only 12 percent of total beer consumption. The heavy half accounted for 88 percent of the total consumption—that is, for over seven times as much consumption as the light users. Clearly a beer company would prefer to attract one heavy user to its brand rather than several light users. Most beer companies target the heavy beer drinker, using appeals such as Schaefer's "One beer to have when you're having more than one."

The hope is that the heavy users of a product have certain common demographics, personal characteristics, and media habits. In the case of heavy beer drinkers, their profile shows that more of them are members of the working class when compared with light beer drinkers and that they are between the ages of 25 and 50 (instead of under 25 and over 50), watched television more than three and one-half hours per day (instead of under two hours), and preferred to watch

Figure 10-6
Annual Purchase Concentration in Several Product Categories

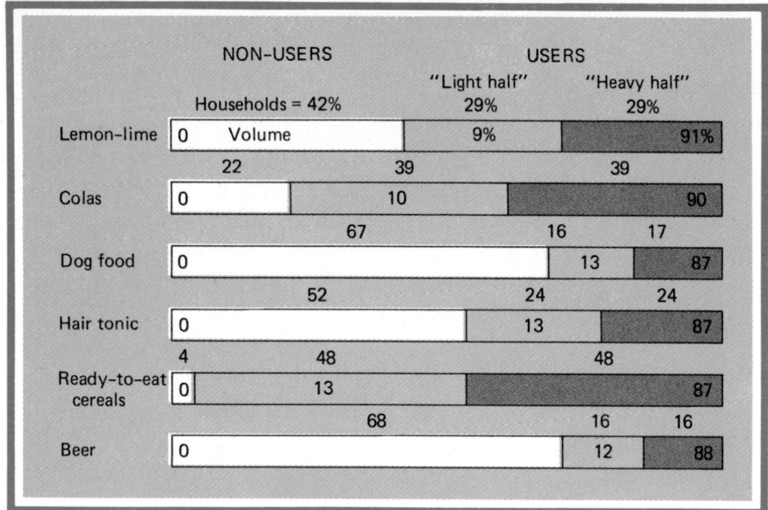

Source: Dik Warren Twedt, "How Important to Marketing Strategy Is the 'Heavy User?'" *Journal of Marketing,* January 1964, p. 72.

sports programs.[13] Profiles like this are obviously helpful to the marketer in developing pricing, message, and media strategies.

In the area of social marketing campaigns, agencies often face a heavy-user dilemma. The heavy users are often the most resistant to the selling proposition. A family-planning agency, for example, would normally target its marketing effort to those families who would have the most children; but these families are also the most resistant to birth control messages. The National Safety Council should target its marketing effort primarily to the unsafe drivers; but these drivers are also the most resistant to safe-driving appeals. The agencies must consider whether to use their limited budget to go after a few heavy users who are highly resistant or many light users who are less resistant.

LOYALTY STATUS

A market can also be segmented according to loyalty patterns of consumers. Consumers can be loyal to brands (Schlitz), stores (Sears), and other entities. We will deal here with brand loyalty. Suppose there is a market with five brands: A, B, C, D, and E. Buyers can be divided into four groups according to their loyalty status:[14]

- *Hard-core loyals.* Those consumers who buy only one brand all the time. Thus a buying pattern over six periods of A,A,A,A,A,A would represent a consumer with undivided loyalty to brand A.
- *Soft-core loyals.* Those consumers who show a loyalty to two or three brands. The buying pattern A,A,B,B,A,B would represent a consumer with a divided loyalty between brands A and B.
- *Shifting loyals.* Those consumers who are moving from favoring one brand to favoring another. The buying pattern A,A,A,B,B,B would suggest a consumer who is shifting brand loyalty from A to B.

- *Switchers.* Those consumers who buy a number of brands and show no loyalty to any. The buying pattern A,C,E,B,D,B would suggest a nonloyal consumer who is either *deal-prone* (responds to the brand on sale) or *variety-prone* (wants something different).

Each market is made up of different degrees of the four types of buyers. A brand-loyal market is one with a high percentage of the buyers showing hard-core brand loyalty. Thus the toothpaste market and the beer market seem to be fairly high brand-loyal markets. Companies selling in a brand-loyal market have a hard time gaining more market share, and companies trying to enter such a market have a hard time getting in.

A company can learn a great deal by analyzing loyalty patterns in its market. First it should study the demographic and psychographic characteristics of its own hard-core loyals. Thus, if the hard core loyals using Colgate toothpaste are more middle class, have larger size families, and are more health conscious, this specifically defines the target market for Colgate.

By studying its soft-core loyals, the company can determine which brands are most competitive with its own. If many Colgate buyers also buy Crest, Colgate can attempt to develop improved positioning against Crest, even possibly using direct comparison advertising.

By looking at those customers who are shifting out of its brand, the company can learn about marketing deficits that it needs to correct. As for nonloyals, the company attracts them (if it wants to) by putting its brand on sale or providing other special trial incentives.

In classifying consumers, the company has to be aware that what appear to be brand-loyal purchase patterns in some cases may reflect *habit, indifference,* a *low price,* or the *nonavailability* of other brands. The concept of brand loyalty has some ambiguities and must be used with care.

STAGES OF BUYER READINESS

At any specific time, there is a distribution of people in various stages of readiness toward buying the product. Some members of the potential market are unaware of the product; some are aware; some are informed; some are interested; some are desirous; and some intend to buy. The particular distribution of people over stages of readiness makes a big difference in designing the marketing program. Suppose a health agency wants to attract women to take an annual Pap test to detect cervical cancer. At the beginning, most of the potential market is unaware of the concept. The marketing effort should go into high-reach advertising and publicity using a simple message. If successful, more of the market will be aware of the Pap test and the advertising should be changed to dramatize the benefits of taking an annual examination and the risks of not taking it, so as to move more people into a stage of desire. Facilities should also be readied for handling the large number of women who may be motivated to take the examination. In general, the marketing program must be adjusted to the changing distribution of buyer readiness.

MARKETING FACTORS

Markets can often be segmented into groups responsive to different marketing factors such as price and price deals, product quality, and service. This information can help the company in allocating its marketing resources.[15] The marketing variables are usually proxies for particular benefits sought by buyers. A company that specializes in a certain marketing factor will build up hard-core loyals seeking that factor or benefit. Thus Avon, which sells cosmetics on a door-to-door basis, appeals to women who like personal attention and service.

Bases for Segmenting Industrial Markets

In segmenting industrial markets, we can use some of the variables used in consumer market segmentation and add a few new ones. Industrial buyers can be segmented geographically and by several behavioristic variables: benefits sought, user status, usage rate, loyalty status, readiness stage, and marketing factor sensitivity. Rather than reviewing these, however, we will look at some other variables.

The most common way to segment industrial markets is by *end users*. Different end users often seek different benefits and can be approached with different marketing mixes. This can be illustrated for the transistor market:

- The market for transistors consists of three industrial submarkets: military, industrial, and commercial.

  The military buyer attaches the utmost importance to the producer's quality standards and the adequacy of plant facilities. Firms selling transistors to the military market must make a considerable investment in R & D, use sales representatives who know military buying procedures, and specialize in limited-line products.

  Industrial buyers, such as computer manufacturers, look for high quality and good service. Price itself is not a critical matter unless it becomes exorbitant. In this market, transistor manufacturers must make a modest investment in R & D, use sales representatives who have technical knowledge concerning the product, and offer a broad line.

  Commercial buyers, such as pocket-radio manufacturers, buy their components largely on price and delivery. Transistor manufacturers selling in this market need little or no R & D effort, use high-pressure sales representatives who are relatively nontechnical, and offer the most common lines that can be mass-produced.

Customer size is another key segmentation variable. Many companies have found it useful to set up separate systems for dealing with major and minor customers. For example, Steelcase, a major manufacturer of office furniture, divides its customers into two groups:

- *Major accounts.* Accounts such as IBM, Prudential, and Standard Oil are singled out and handled by national account managers who work in conjunction with field district managers.
- *Dealer accounts.* Smaller accounts are handled through field sales personnel working with dealers who are franchised to sell Steelcase products.

Most industrial companies do not stop at single variable segmentation but define their target market opportunities by applying a succession of segmentation variables. This is illustrated in Figure 10-7 for an aluminum company:[16]

- The aluminum company first undertook *macrosegmentation* consisting of three steps.[17] It looked at which end-use market to serve: automobile, residential, or

Figure 10-7
Three-Step Segmentation of the Aluminum Market

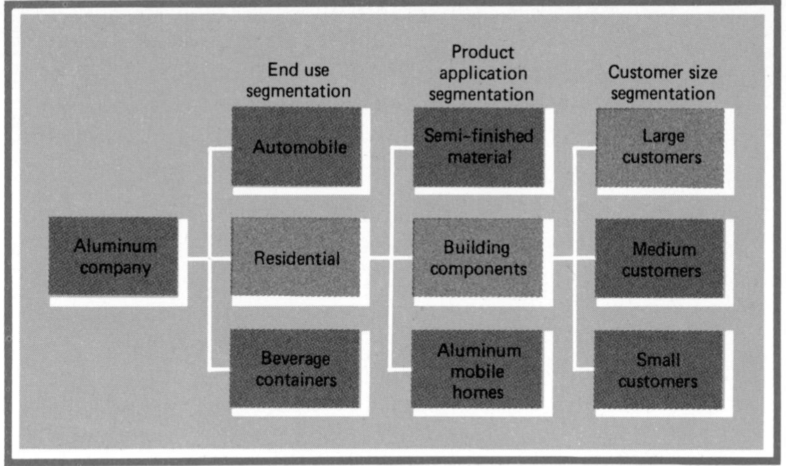

Source: Based on an example in E. Raymond Corey, "Key Options in Market Selection and Product Planning," *Harvard Business Review*, September-October 1975, pp. 119–28.

beverage containers. Choosing the residential market, it determined the most attractive product application: semifinished material, building components, or aluminum mobile homes. Deciding to specialize in producing building components, it next determined the best customer size to serve, and this turned out to be large customers.

The second stage consisted of forming microsegments within the macrosegment of large customers buying building components. The company realized that large customers fell into three groups—those who bought on price, service, and quality. Because the aluminum company had a high service profile, it decided to concentrate on the service-motivated microsegment of the market.

Requirements for Effective Segmentation

Clearly, there are many ways to segment a market. Not all resulting segments are effective from a marketing point of view. The buyers of table salt, for example, could be subdivided into blond and brunette customers. But hair color is not relevant to the purchase of salt. In fact, salt buyers may not be segmentable. If all salt buyers wanted to buy the same amount of salt each month, believed all salt was the same, and wanted to pay the same price, this market would be minimally segmentable from a marketing point of view.

To be useful, market segments must exhibit the following characteristics:

- The first is *measurability,* the degree to which the size and purchasing power of the resulting segments can readily be measured. Certain segmentation variables are difficult to measure. An illustration would be the size of the segment of teen-age smokers who smoke primarily to rebel against their parents.
- The second is *accessibility,* the degree to which the resulting segments can be effectively reached and served. Suppose a perfume company finds that heavy users of its brand are single women who are out late at night and frequent bars. Unless this groups lives or shops at certain places and watches certain media, there is no way to reach them efficiently.
- The third is *substantiality,* the degree to which the resulting segments are large and/or profitable enough to be worth pursuing. A segment should be the largest possible homogeneous group of buyers that it pays to go after with a specially

designed marketing program. Segmental marketing is expensive, as we shall see. It would not pay, for example, for an automobile manufacturer to develop a line of cars designed for persons who are less than five feet tall.

Evaluating the Attractiveness of Different Market Segments

Given a set of market segments that have the characteristics of measurability, accessibility, and substantiality, the marketer's next task is to evaluate the attractiveness of each market segment.

A useful analytical approach is illustrated in Figure 10-8.[18] The market is one of the mechanical line of a steel-fabricating company. Stage 1 shows a segmentation of this market, using as two variables the customer-prospect mix and the product-service mix. The customer-prospect mix consists of contractors in the electrical, general, and plumbing line, respectively. The product-service mix consist of three products sold to these contractors: pipe hangers, concrete inserts, and electrical supports. Nine cells result from this joint segmentation of the market. Each cell represents a distinct submarket, or product-market segment. A dollar figure is placed in each cell, representing the company's sales in that submarket.

Relative company sales in the nine submarkets provide no indication of their relative profit potential as segments. The latter depends upon market demand, company costs, and competitive trends in each submarket. Stages 2 and 3 show how a particular product submarket, the general-contractor market for concrete inserts, can be analyzed in depth.

Stage 2 appraises present and future sales in the selected submarket. The vertical axis accommodates estimates of industry sales, company sales, and company market share. The horizontal axis is used to project future sales in these categories and market share. The company sold in this submarket last year $200,000 worth of goods, or one-fourth of total estimated industry sales. Looking ahead, the company expects industry sales in this submarket to rise by 6 percent and its own sales to rise by 15 percent.

Stage 3 probes deeper into the marketing thinking behind the sales forecasts of Stage 2. The horizontal axis shows the promotional mix that the company is using or plans to use to stimulate the sales of concrete inserts to general contractors. The vertical axis shows the distribution mix that the company is using or plans to use to move concrete inserts into the hands of general contractors. The actual promotion-distribution mix could be detailed by placing budget figures in the relevant cells. The company will use all three types of distribution and rely mainly on personal selling and field service for stimulating sales to general contractors.

By carrying out this analysis, the seller is led to think systematically about each segment as a distinct opportunity. The analysis of the profit potential of each segment will help the seller decide on the appropriate target markets to serve.

target marketing

Market segmentation reveals the market segment opportunities facing the firm. At this point the firm has to decide between three broad market selection strategies (see Figure 10-9):

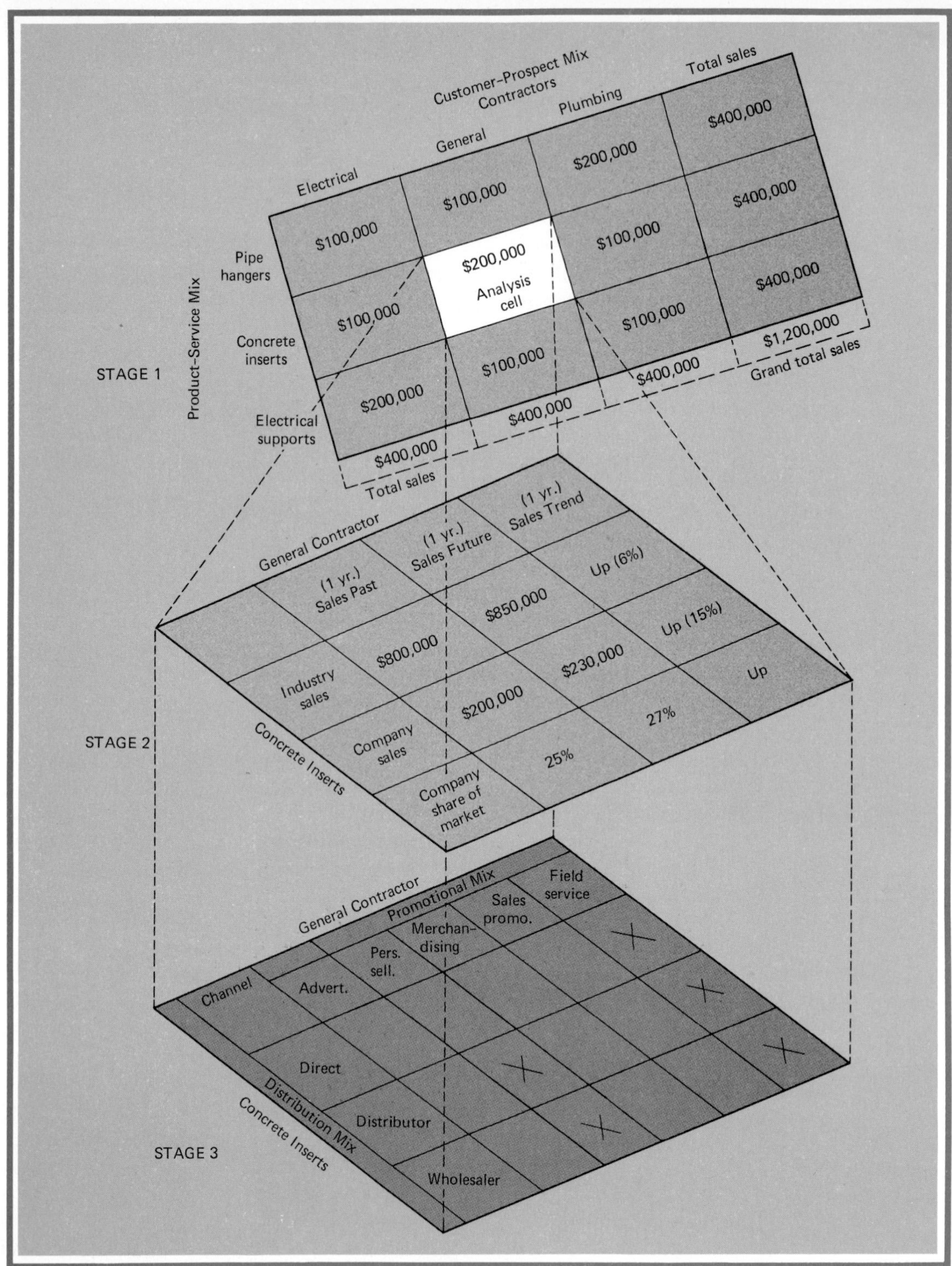

Figure 10-8 Analyzing the Worth of Different Market Segments for Steel-Fabricated Products

Source: From an unpublished paper by Rhett W. Butler (Northwestern University, 1964).

Figure 10-9
Three Alternative Market Selection Strategies

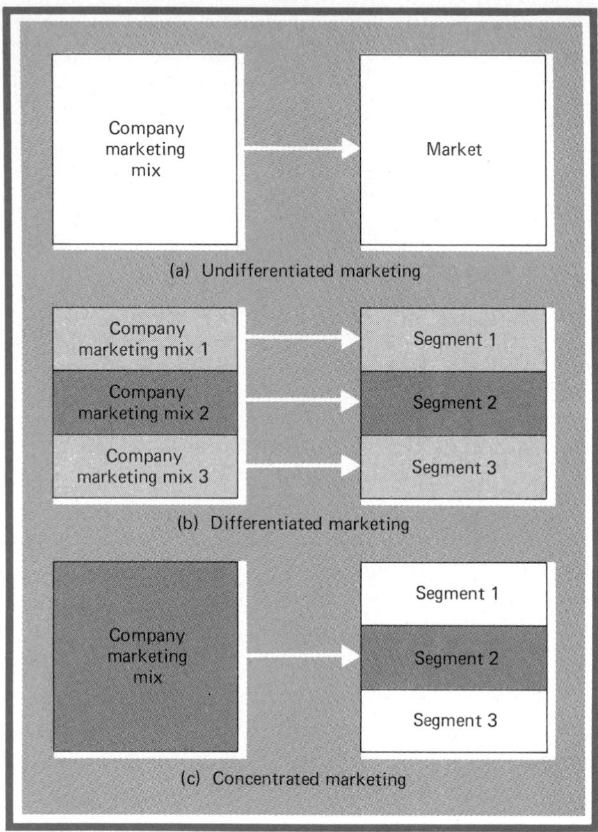

1. *Undifferentiated marketing.* The firm might decide to go after the whole market with one offer and marketing mix, trying to attract as many customers as possible (this is another name for mass marketing).
2. *Differentiated marketing.* The firm might decide to go after several market segments, developing an effective offer and marketing mix for each.
3. *Concentrated marketing.* The firm might decide to go after one market segment and develop the ideal offer and marketing mix.

Here we will describe the logic and merits of each of these strategies.

Undifferentiated Marketing

In undifferentiated marketing,[19] the firm chooses not to recognize the different market segments making up the market. It treats the market as an aggregate, focusing on what is common in the needs of people rather than on what is different. It tries to design a product and a marketing program that will appeal to the broadest number of buyers. It relies on mass channels, mass advertising media, and universal themes. It aims to endow the product with a superior image in people's minds. An excellent example of undifferentiated marketing is the Hershey Company's earlier production of only one chocolate candy bar to suit all.

Undifferentiated marketing is primarily defended on the grounds of cost economies. It is thought to be "the marketing counterpart to standardization and mass production in manufacturing."[20] The fact that the product line is kept narrow minimizes production, inventory, and transportation costs. The undifferentiated advertising program enables the firm to enjoy media discounts through large usage. The absence of segmental marketing research and planning lowers the costs of marketing research and product management. On the whole, undifferentiated marketing results in keeping down several costs of doing business.

Nevertheless, an increasing number of marketers have expressed strong doubts about the effectiveness of this strategy. Gardner and Levy, for example, admitted that "some brands have very skillfully built up reputations of being suitable for a wide variety of people" but added:

> ▪ In most areas audience groupings will differ, if only because there are deviants who refuse to consume the same way other people do. . . . It is not easy for a brand to appeal to stable lower middle-class people and at the same time to be interesting to sophisticated, intellectual upper middle-class buyers. . . . It is rarely possible for a product or brand to be all things to all people.[21]

The firm practicing undifferentiated marketing typically develops a product and marketing program aimed at the largest segment of the market. When several firms in the industry do this, the result is intense competition for the largest segment(s) and undersatisfaction of the smaller ones. Thus the American auto industry for a long time produced only large automobiles. The "majority fallacy," as this has been called by Kuehn and Day, describes the fact that the larger segments may be less profitable because they attract disproportionately heavy competition.[22] The recognition of this fallacy has led many firms to reevaluate the opportunities latent in pursuing smaller segments of the market.

Differentiated Marketing

Under differentiated marketing, a firm decides to operate in two or more segments of the market but designs separate product and/or marketing programs for each. Thus General Motors tries to produce a car for every "purse, purpose, and personality." By offering product and marketing variations, it hopes to attain higher sales and a deeper position within each market segment. It hopes that a deep position in several segments will strengthen the customers' overall identification of the company with the product field. Furthermore, it hopes for greater loyalty and repeat purchasing because the firm's offerings have been bent to the customer's desire rather than the other way around.

In recent years an increasing number of firms have moved toward a strategy of differentiated marketing. This is reflected in trends toward multiple product offerings and multiple trade channels and media. Here is an excellent example of differentiated marketing:[23]

> ▪ Edison Brothers operates nine hundred shoe stores that fall into four different chain categories, each appealing to a different market segment. Chandler's sells higher-priced shoes. Baker's sells moderate-priced shoes. Burt's sells shoes for budget shoppers, and Wild Pair is oriented to the shopper who wants very stylized shoes. Within three blocks on State Street in Chicago are found Burt's, Chandler's, and Baker's. Putting the stores near each other does not hurt them because they are aimed at different segments of the women's shoe market. This strategy has made Edison Brothers the country's largest retailer of women's shoes.

The net effect of differentiated marketing is to create more total sales than undifferentiated marketing. "It is ordinarily demonstrable that total sales may be increased with a more diversified product line sold through more diversified channels."[24] However, it also tends to be true that differentiated marketing increases the costs of doing business. The following costs are likely to be higher:

- *Product modification costs.* Modifying a product to meet different market segment requirements usually involves some R & D, engineering, and/or special tooling costs.
- *Production costs.* Generally speaking, it is more expensive to produce, say, ten units of ten different products than one hundred units of one product. This is especially true the longer the production setup time for each product and the smaller the sales volume of each product. On the other hand, if each model is sold in sufficiently large volume, the higher costs of setup time may be quite small per unit.
- *Administrative costs.* Under differentiated marketing, the company has to develop separate marketing plans for the separate segments of the market. This requires extra marketing research, forecasting, sales analysis, promotion, planning, and channel management.
- *Inventory costs.* It is generally more costly to manage inventories of differentiated products than an inventory of only one product. The extra costs arise because more records must be kept and more auditing must be done. Furthermore, each product must be carried at a level that reflects basic demand plus a safety factor to cover unexpected variations in demand. The sum of the safety stocks for several products will exceed the safety stock required for one product. Thus carrying differentiated products leads to increased inventory costs.
- *Promotion costs.* Differentiated marketing involves trying to reach different segments of the market through advertising media most appropriate to each case. This leads to lower usage rates of individual media and the consequent forfeiture of quantity discounts. Furthermore, since each segment may require separate creative advertising planning, promotion costs are increased.

Since differentiated marketing leads to higher sales and higher costs, nothing can be said in advance regarding the optimality of this strategy. Some firms are finding, in fact, that they have overdifferentiated their market offers. They would like to manage fewer brands, with each appealing to a broader customer group. Called "reverse line extension" or "broadening the base," they seek a larger volume for each brand. Johnson and Johnson, for example, managed to attract adults to use its baby shampoo. Blue Nun was launched as a white wine equally good for meat and fish courses.

Concentrated Marketing

Both differentiated marketing and undifferentiated marketing imply that the firm goes after the whole market. However, many firms see a third possibility, one that is especially appealing when the company's resources are limited. Instead of going after a small share of a large market, the firm goes after a large share of one or a few submarkets. Put another way, instead of spreading itself thin in many parts of the market, it concentrates its forces to gain a good market position in a few areas.

Many examples of concentrated marketing can be cited. Volkswagen has concentrated on the small-car market; Hewlett-Packard on the high-priced calculator market; and Richard D. Irwin on the economics and business texts market. Through concentrated marketing the firm achieves a strong market position in the particular segments it serves, owing to its greater knowledge of the segments' needs and the special reputation it acquires. Furthermore, it enjoys many operating economies because of specialization in production, distribution, and promotion. If the segment of the market is well chosen, the firm can earn high rates of return on its investment.

At the same time, concentrated marketing involves higher than normal risks. The particular market segment can suddenly turn sour; for example, when young women suddenly stopped buying sportswear and turned to knit dresses one year, it caused Bobbie Brooks's earnings to go deeply into the red. Or a competitor may decide to enter the same segment. For these reasons, many companies prefer to diversify in several market segments.

Choosing among Market Selection Strategies

Particular characteristics of the seller, the product, and the market serve to constrain and narrow the actual choice of a market selection strategy.[25]

The first factor is *company resources.* Where the firm's resources are too limited to permit complete coverage of the market, its only realistic choice is concentrated marketing.

The second factor is *product homogeneity.* Undifferentiated marketing is more suited for homogeneous products such as grapefruit or steel. Products that are capable of great variation, such as cameras and automobiles, are more naturally suited to differentiation or concentration.

The third factor is *product stage in the life cycle.* When a firm introduces a new product into the marketplace it usually finds it practical to introduce one or, at the most, a few product versions. The firm's interest is to develop primary demand, and undifferentiated marketing seems the suitable strategy; or it might concentrate on a particular segment. In the mature stage of the product life cycle, firms tend to pursue a strategy of differentiated marketing.

The fourth factor is *market homogeneity.* If buyers have the same tastes, buy the same amounts per periods, and react in the same way to marketing stimuli, a strategy of undifferentiated marketing is appropriate.

The fifth factor is *competitive marketing strategies.* When competitors are practicing active segmentation, it is difficult for a firm to compete through undifferentiated marketing. Conversely, when competitors are practicing undifferentiated marketing, a firm can gain by practicing active segmentation if some of the other factors favor it.

■ summary

Sellers can take three different approaches to a market. *Mass marketing* is the decision to mass-produce and mass-distribute one product and attempt to attract all kinds of buyers. *Product differentiation* is the decision to produce two or more products differentiated in terms of style, features, quality, sizes, and so on, so as to offer variety to the market and distinguish the seller's products from competitors' products. *Target marketing* is the decision to distinguish the different groups that make up a market and to develop appropriate products and marketing mixes for each target market. Sellers today are moving away from mass marketing and product differentiation toward target marketing, because the latter is more helpful in spotting market opportunities and developing more effective products and marketing mixes.

The key step in target marketing is *market segmentation*, which is the act of dividing a market into distinct and meaningful groups of buyers who might merit separate products and/or marketing mixes. The investigator tries different variables to see which reveal the best segmentation opportunities. For consumer marketing, the major segmentation variables are broadly classified as geographic, demographic, psychographic, and behavioristic. Industrial markets can be segmented by such variables as end use, customer size, geographical location, and product application. The effectiveness of the segmentation exercise depends upon arriving at segments that are measurable, accessible, and substantial. The resulting segments can subsequently be evaluated for their profit potential and other measures of attractiveness.

The seller then has to choose a market selection strategy, either ignoring segment differences (undifferentiated marketing), developing different products and marketing programs for each segment (differentiated marketing), or going after only one or a few segments (concentrated marketing). No particular strategy is superior in all circumstances. Much depends on company resources, product homogeneity, product stage in the life cycle, market homogeneity, and competitive marketing strategies.

■ questions for discussion

1. What three stages do sellers move through in their approach to a market? Relate these to the Ford Motor Company.
2. After the market segmentation process is completed, the organization should begin developing the marketing mix factors. Comment.
3. Besides age and sex, what other demographic segmentation variables are used by the brewery industry? Explain. Also, identify major benefit segments in the beer market.
4. Discuss the life style or cycle segments you will be in between now and the year 2000.
5. If you were a manager of a mass transit company, how would you use benefit segmentation to appeal to potential riders?
6. Give specific examples of marketers who have been successful in segmenting their markets on each of the following bases: low price; high quality; and service.
7. In what ways do you think that IBM has segmented its market?
8. Has Wendy's International hamburger chain met the requirements for effective segmentation? Why?

9. Differentiated marketing is always the best approach to target marketing. Comment.
10. If Levi's were considering adding a new line of women's skirts for casual wear, how would it go about the market segmentation and target marketing process?

references

1. This was written by the author and adapted from LOUIS VAN LEEUWEN, "The Launch of the 604: A Case History in Car Market Segmentation," in *Marketing Expansion in a Shrinking World,* ed. Betsy Gelb (Chicago: American Marketing Association 1978 Business Proceedings, 1978), pp. 120–22.
2. "Can the Baby Toy Market Be Segmented 12 Ways?" *Business Week,* February 14, 1977, p. 62.
3. "Dog Food Concept Turns into a Scrap," *Business Week,* April 19, 1976, pp. 137–38.
4. RICHARD P. COLEMAN, "The Significance of Social Stratification in Selling," in *Marketing: A Maturing Discipline,* ed. Martin L. Bell (Chicago: American Marketing Association, 1961), pp. 171–84.
5. See PETER W. BERNSTEIN, "Psychographics Is Still an Issue on Madison Avenue," *Fortune,* January 16, 1978, pp. 78–84. Other life-style classifications have been developed. The firm of Yankelovich, Skelly and White breaks the market into six life-style segments, and the firm of Leo Burnett has identified nineteen life styles.
6. RUTH ZIFF, "Psychographics for Market Segmentation," *Journal of Advertising Research,* April 1971, pp. 3–9.
7. Ibid., p. 6.
8. Quoted in FRANKLIN B. EVANS, "Psychological and Objective Factors in the Prediction of Brand Choice; Ford versus Chevrolet," *Journal of Business,* October 1959, pp. 340–69.
9. RALPH WESTFALL, "Psychological Factors in Predicting Product Choice," *Journal of Marketing,* April 1962, pp. 34–40.
10. MAURICE J. GOTTLIEB, "Segmentation by Personality Types," in *Advancing Marketing Efficiency,* ed. Lynn H. Stockman (Chicago: American Marketing Association, 1959), p. 154.
11. W. T. TUCKER AND JOHN J. PAINTER, "Personality and Product Use," *Journal of Applied Psychology,* October 1961, pp. 325–29.
12. See DANIEL YANKELOVICH, "New Criteria for Market Segmentation," *Harvard Business Review,* March-April 1964, pp. 83–90, here p. 85.
13. FRANK M. BASS, DOUGLAS J. TIGERT, AND RONALD T. LONSDALE, "Market Segmentation: Group versus Individual Behavior," *Journal of Marketing Research,* August 1968, p. 276.
14. This classification was adapted from GEORGE H. BROWN, "Brand Loyalty—Fact or Fiction?" *Advertising Age,* June 1952–January 1953, a series.
15. See RONALD FRANK, WILLIAM MASSY, AND YORAM WIND, *Market Segmentation* (Englewood Cliffs, N.J.: Prentice-Hall, 1972), Part IV.
16. The illustration is from E. RAYMOND COREY, "Key Options in Market Selection and Product Planning," *Harvard Business Review,* September-October 1975, pp. 119–28.
17. WIND AND CARDOZO suggest that industrial segmentation should proceed by first developing macrosegments and then microsegments. See YORAM WIND AND RICHARD CARDOZO, "Industrial Market Segmentation," *Industrial Marketing Management,* 3 (1974), 153–66.

18. The general approach is described in WILLIAM J. CRISSY AND FRANK H. MOSSMAN, "Matrix Models for Marketing Planning: An Update and Expansion" *MSU Business Topics,* Autumn 1977, pp. 17–26. The example was developed elsewhere.

19. See WENDELL R. SMITH, "Product Differentiation and Market Segmentation as Alternative Marketing Strategies," *Journal of Marketing,* July 1956, pp. 3–8; and ALAN A. ROBERTS, "Applying the Strategy of Market Segmentation," *Business Horizons,* Fall 1961, pp. 65–72.

20. SMITH, "Product Differentiation," p. 4.

21. BURLEIGH GARDNER AND SIDNEY LEVY, "The Product and the Brand," *Harvard Business Review,* March-April 1955, p. 37.

22. ALFRED A. KUEHN AND RALPH L. DAY, "Strategy of Product Quality," *Harvard Business Review,* November-December 1962, pp. 101–2.

23. NATALIE MCKELVY, "Shoes Make Edison Brothers a Big Name," *Chicago Tribune,* February 23, 1979, Sec. 5, p. 9.

24. ROBERTS, "Applying the Strategy of Market Segmentation," p. 66.

25. R. WILLIAM KOTRBA, "The Strategy Selection Chart," *Journal of Marketing,* July 1966, pp. 22–25.

Cases

7 Fotomat Corporation

Fotomat Corporation operates a chain of thirty-four hundred drive-thru kiosks, located in high-traffic areas, marketing film and camera accessories and providing photofinishing services. The company was founded in 1968 and at that time did not offer photofinishing. The service was added in 1972, and in 1979 it accounted for 82 percent of its $197 million in revenues. Fotomat has about 9.5 percent of the photofinishing market, which is a distant second to Kodak at over 80 percent. In addition to its kiosks, Fotomat owns and operates twelve processing plants. The company plans to expand its operations at the rate of four hundred to five hundred kiosks per year.

Fotomat has encountered major problems in recent years. Increasing costs and competition, and changing markets, have lowered its sales per outlet and reduced profit margins. As a result, Fotomat has explored different products to supplement sales at the kiosks. These attempts include pantyhose, key making, shoe repair, instant printing, and, most recently, videotapes.

In the early years the company found its strength in convenience, reliability, speedy service, and a guarantee. Fotomat offers to replace for free any film that does not turn out properly—even if due to customer negligence. The company focused on the "instamatic" photographer, who is not as concerned with picture quality as with speed and convenience in getting back his prints or slides. This, however, was becoming a problem because of the rapidly increasing importance of the Polaroid and Kodak instant cameras. The increasing popularity of 35-mm cameras, which are used by a class of customer not attracted to Fotomat, further limited sales potential.

Fotomat's management now faces the challenge of how to meet the market changes and increased competition in order to increase profitability and ensure future viability.

When Fotomat was founded in 1968, Kodak had well over 90 percent of the market. How could Fotomat hope to compete with a firm that manufactures cameras, film, processing chemicals, and supplies and provides processing, printing, and enlarging services? Richard Irwin, Fotomat president, answered this question as follows:

- By building a better mousetrap. The key to this business is that it is a service-oriented industry and you have to offer people convenience. So we locate our kiosks where people can trade with us easily, and on a drive-thru basis. We put out kiosks near high traffic areas like shopping centers and offer quality service. We do not necessarily try to be lowest priced. (*Commercial and Financial Chronicle, June 6, 1975*)

In 1978 revenues totaled $197 million, 82 percent of which came from film processing and 18 percent from the sale of merchandise. From these sales, Fotomat generated profits of approximately $10 million. However, recent developments have signaled some distressing signs on the horizon.

Fotomat is not the only company that has learned that giant Kodak could be forced to concede some of its share in the processing market. Competition has arrived in many forms. There are increasing numbers of local and regional processors, as well as new kiosk chains following Fotomat's lead. Supermarkets, drugstores, and discount chains have recently made major investments in photofinishing services. "Minilabs" have made it possible for one-day, on-the-spot, film-processing services to be offered by many stores.

The rash of new competitors makes it difficult for Fotomat to peddle its wares in front of a store that quite possibly can process film faster and cheaper and can provide the customer with one-stop shopping. Direct-mail processing (e.g., Sunday supplements) firms have increased convenience to the photofinishing consumer and have captured market share also.

Competition is not the only change in the market with which Fotomat is confronted. Forty-five percent of all cameras sold in 1978 were instants (Polaroid type). This camera requires no film-processing service. Conventional camera sales grew at about 10 percent, most of which were 35-mm units. Thirty-five millimeter now accounts for 33 percent of all photofinishing volume, is forecast to rise to 50 percent in two to three years, and to 80–90 percent in ten years. Thirty-five-millimeter camera owners are a dramatically increasing market that presents Fotomat with an image problem. These consumers are more quality conscious and less concerned with convenience. Again, quoting Mr. Irwin:

- We've emphasized instamatic finishing for so long in our advertising and marketing that the guy taking 35 mm pictures doesn't think of using our service. (*Forbes*, February 5, 1979)

Each kiosk is staffed by part-time "Fotomates," usually housewives or high-school students who are paid the minimum wage. The company favors this system, since the labor costs are low and part-time help is difficult to unionize. But here, Fotomat has fallen victim to rising minimum wage requirements that have recently increased labor costs and cut into profit margins. Prime kiosk locations are becoming scarce, as is part-time labor in urban areas. Competitive price cutting is common, and sales per kiosk have been falling in recent years. All this translates into lower profit margins for Fotomat.

The company has tried to introduce many products to supplement and boost kiosk sales. Each attempt has proved to be less than promising, prompting one astute observer to quip, "The only common thread throughout the product line is desperation." Fotomat is constrained in its product line due to the small size and drive-thru nature of its kiosks, and further by its special-segment photography image.

The company is now gearing up at another attempt, hoping that this new product—videotapes—will prove to be compatible. Fotomat will offer three services in regard to the videotape market: (1) the transferring of home movies onto videotape cassettes; (2) the sale of blank tapes; and (3) the rental of tapes. The rental units will contain movies, golf and tennis lessons, and other prerecorded material.

In summary, Fotomat has realized that the consumer and competitive markets are changing. The company's task at this point is to somehow restructure operations and product offerings to meet these changes. One observer feels that the strategic constraint is the kiosk concept itself and that possibly Fotomat's future growth and profitability lie in more conventional retail stores.

Source: This case was based upon materials developed by Kurt Coughenour, John Cummings, and Mark Perrin drawing from a number of sources, including "Fotomat Focuses on Videotape," *Business Week*, January 29, 1979.

Questions

1. What is your feeling concerning a Fotomat kiosk as a place to have film processed? To purchase film? To purchase a camera or photographic equipment?
2. What product—services should Fotomat offer in the kiosk to make them more profitable?
3. What changes other than in products and services sold, should Fotomat consider in an effort to increase profitability? For example: changes in hours? Location? Promotion?
4. Should Fotomat open regular retail stores to sell cameras, other photograph equipment, and accessories?

8 Henry F. Ortlieb Brewing Company

An affable, well-dressed man walked into a restaurant here one evening recently and ordered a bottle of Ortlieb's beer, a local brand. "I'm sorry," the waitress said. "We don't have any Ortlieb's."

"Then give me a bottle of birch beer," replied Joseph Ortlieb, owner of Henry F. Ortlieb Brewing Co., a small concern that has been making beer in Philadelphia since 1869. Mr. Ortlieb says that when dinner arrived, he swallowed his pride and "ordered a draft of Miller's."

As this incident suggests, life is sometimes frustrating for a small brewer, especially when giant national competitors, such as Anheuser-Busch Inc. and Miller Brewing Co., and large regional brewers have successfully established themselves in his own backyard. And the disappointments range, of course, beyond not being able to buy a bottle of his own beer. They include such far more serious setbacks as the loss of customers to slick, well-financed national and regional advertising campaigns.

"When you're an ant in a battle of elephants," one small brewer says, "you're going to get stomped on." "The years are numbered for small plants," says another, J. M. Magenau Jr., who closed his ailing Erie, Pa., brewery in March after deciding he couldn't match the big companies' costly advertising programs.

Ferment in the Industry

Joe Ortlieb agrees that "we don't have the dollars like they (the big brewers) do." But he would rather fight than fold. And he is doing so with some success. Henry F. Ortlieb Brewing returned to profitability last year after sustaining losses from 1973 through 1976. And in May of this year the company's total production rose sharply, to 44,000 barrels from 31,300 a year earlier. The 49-year-old Mr. Ortlieb is jubilant about that figure—"more beer, I think, than we ever put out before," he says.

But no one denies that these are less than heady times for small breweries. Since 1960, about 125 of them have perished. Today, although there are still 45 brewing companies in business in this country, the industry is controlled by a handful of giants.

In 1960, total production of the five industry leaders at that time represented about 33% of all U.S. beer shipments. By 1968, that figure had increased to about 47%, and by last year, the figure for the current top five had risen to more than 70%. Some analysts believe that the battle for dominance may now be between the big two—Anheuser-Busch and the Miller Brewing unit of Philip Morris Inc.—as they slug it out with national advertising campaigns, new products and increased capacity.

What Ortlieb Faces

In this area, Ortlieb faces competition from four of the top five national brands—the two leaders plus No. 3 Jos. Schlitz Brewing Co. and No. 4 Pabst Brewing Co. (Adolph Coors Co., ranked in fifth place, doesn't compete here.) In addition, Ortlieb battles for the hearts and throats of Philadelphians with two of the country's biggest regional brewers—F. & M. Schaefer Corp., which leads in sales in Philadelphia, and C. Schmidt & Sons Inc. Two other firms—Carling National Breweries Inc. and Genesee Brewing Co.—are also strong here.

Tiny Henry F. Ortlieb is at the bottom of the barrel. "Ortlieb is small enough in volume that they don't appear in any of our charts," a major beer distributor here says.

Still, Joe Ortlieb says that "things look good for us." His sales of 331,000 barrels last year may be tiny compared with Anheuser-Busch's national total of 36.6 million, but they represent a 2.7% rise for Ortlieb. And in the first five months of this year, Ortlieb's output rose to 164,000 barrels, up 25.8% from a year earlier.

Indeed, Mr. Ortlieb, a grandson of founder Trupert Ortlieb, has been moving with confidence since he became sole owner of the company two years ago. Mr. Ortlieb, whose title is president, has assembled a new management team, including a brewmaster recruited from Rheingold Breweries Inc. and a new sales manager from Schmidt & Sons, Philadelphia's other, and much larger, brewery. He also has begun modernizing and expanding his aging plant, the newest section of which was built in 1948.

"Willingness to Take Chances"

Beyond that, Mr. Ortlieb has begun a modest advertising campaign to remind Philadelphians that his little brewery is still afloat. He has also computerized the company's financial operations and added a new product, McSorley's ale.

"Joe seems willing to take chances," says Ross Heuer, editor of Brewers Digest, a trade journal. "There are probably a dozen small breweries that are resisting (the trend), and Ortlieb is one of the primary examples."

One factor that enables Ortlieb to resist is its loyal following in this area, at least among older quaffers. Charlie Lawn, a 55-year-old Philadelphia cab driver, says he has been drinking Ortlieb's for 30 years and doesn't intend to switch. A beer distributor here asserts that in Philadelphia's working-class neighborhoods, "there are pockets where Ortlieb's is so strong, nobody else can sell."

Mr. Ortlieb says that "people are amazing. The brand loyalty they've developed is just outstanding." Ortlieb's traditionally has been a strong seller within "the shadow of the smokestack," he says. His advertising, he adds, plays up the fact that "we're a local beer hoping for local support."

Joe Ortlieb is much involved in that advertising campaign. He stars in his own radio and television commercials, and in one TV spot, acknowledging that Ortlieb can be a difficult name to remember, he encouraged people to ask for "Joe's beer." Mr. Heuer, the Brewers Digest editor, calls Mr. Ortlieb's advertising "very imaginative" and adds that "the public knows he's a working brewery president—he's not an ivory-tower man."

Mr. Ortlieb spent a record $250,000 on advertising last year. This year he will spend about 25% less, he says, conceding that he can't compete with "the tremendous advertising that's carried on by the national breweries," such as Anheuser-Busch (its major brand is Budweiser) and Miller. Their advertising "just inundates the consumer," he says.

As a result of that advertising, beer distributors and retailers here say young drinkers prefer the national or regional brands to Ortlieb's hometown brew. Regular customers tend to be "the old-time drinkers who have been drinking Ortlieb's for 30 years," says Carmen Shick, manager of a local distributor.

So, believing the older drinker to be more price-conscious, Ortlieb retails a case of its standard canned beer for about $5.75, underpricing most major national brands by $1.20 to $1.40 a case. At the same time, Ortlieb is aiming its ad campaign at a "younger group," the men in their late 20s to late 40s, who drink the most beer, says Haven Babb, an account executive at Schaefer Advertising Inc., a King of Prussia, Pa., agency that handles Mr. Ortlieb's advertising.

As for the under-25 drinker, Mr. Ortlieb sees him as "fickle," faddishly hopping from one highly promoted brand to another. However, the small brewer isn't forsaking that market, either. Last fall it acquired highly regarded McSorley's ale. "We think this will lead us to the youth market," Mr. Ortlieb says. He plans to test-market McSorley's along the south Jersey shore because "You get a lot of kids down there in the summer."

The Fight with Schaefer

Despite the local loyalty, the advertising campaign and Mr. Ortlieb's personal involvement, Ortlieb's share of the market has declined over the years. Joseph Farrell, the company's sales manager, says the firm's share of beer sales in Philadelphia County has shrunk to about 11% from an estimated 15% to 16% five years ago. It has fallen even more in suburban regions, declining to an estimated 2% in one nearby county, he adds. Moreover, while the company's overall beer sales rose last year, its mainstay Ortlieb brand, on the skids for several years, slipped another 13%, to 152,587 barrels, Mr. Farrell says.

But the sales manager insists that Ortlieb's major brand will rebound this year. One reason is that Ortlieb hopes to siphon business away from Schaefer, the New York-based regional brewer that is No. 1 in the Philadelphia market. Mr. Farrell believes that Schaefer, an old foe that invaded Ortlieb territory in the mid-1960s, isn't competing as aggressively as it once did.

The contrast between the two companies could hardly be sharper. Schaefer's two breweries produced 4.6 million barrels of beer last year—14 times more than Ortlieb did at its only plant. Schaefer regards its Lehigh Valley plant, about 60 miles northwest of here, as "the most efficient" in the East.

The little Ortlieb brewery, actually a collection of old brick buildings dating back to the 19th Century, is in a deteriorated industrial section of Philadelphia. The plant's annual capacity is 500,000 barrels, and until recently it could operate at only 70% of capacity.

Still, the Ortlieb people assert that their old plant produces a better beer. At Schaefer, William J. Schoen, president, says that Ortlieb makes "a good product" but that the two brewers produce different types of beer.

Sprucing Up the Plant

Mr. Ortlieb has been sprucing up his plant ever since he bought out his relatives in early 1976. Antiquated wood tubs, which were used to grow yeast (a plant that causes fermentation), have been replaced with shiny metal tanks. In the brewhouse, "we've started to automate," says Joseph Johnston, the spirited brewmaster who came from Rheingold. Beer production has increased, Mr. Ortlieb says, and "we waste less water."

Ortlieb officials report that the company has spent $800,000 on capital projects in the past two years and may spend an additional $1 million this year. "We're now making plans for a five-year program, all departments, to increase capacity by at least 25%," Mr. Johnston says.

He adds that Mr. Ortlieb frequently participates in the daily tasting sessions at which the brewmaster and his assistants sample beer that has been aged from six to eight weeks. If the clarity, odor and taste are deemed satisfactory, the brews are packaged the next day. "Beer tasting is an art," says Mr. Ortlieb, taking a mouthful of one of his brands.

He describes the main Ortlieb brand as having a "more full-bodied flavor" and as being a maltier, heavier brew with a slightly darker color than the national premium brands. "We decided to give our beer a different character than Bud or Schlitz," he explains, although the industry trend is away from heavier beers.

Is this difference an advantage to Ortlieb? "I'm not really sure," Mr. Ortlieb says. "Sometimes I think it might help us. Sometimes I think it might hurt us."

Low-Calorie Beers

Aware that the big brewers have successfully marketed low-calorie beers, Ortlieb has its own light beer "on the drawing board," the official says, adding that it may be introduced this year. Mr. Ortlieb says he previously tried to develop a beer with an extremely low calorie content (about a calorie per ounce, against regular beer's 12 or so per ounce). But the experimental brew had a "terrible" taste, and "I wouldn't dare sell it," he says.

Joe Ortlieb knows what his customers want. Because he often visits local taverns, "his marketing research is mostly firsthand," says Mr. Heuer, the Brewers Digest editor. When his company does something that Ortlieb consumers either like or dislike, Joe Ortlieb "will hear it directly from the man at the bar," Mr. Heuer adds.

Mr. Ortlieb is a shirt-sleeve executive who has worked at the brewery since his college days, beginning in the warehouse, where he loaded trucks. He studied business at Bucknell University in Lewisburg, Pa., and brewing at the United States Brewers Academy in Mount Vernon, N.Y. As head of the company, he has impressed subordinates as a hard worker who often spends Saturdays at the plant.

And that's the image he is trying to put across to the public, says Mr. Babb, the advertising man. "He's asking you to give (his product) a try because he's put his whole life into the brewery," Mr. Babb says.

Mr. Ortlieb is determined that his effort won't be in vain, despite the demise of so many other small beer firms. Jesting grimly, Mr. Ortlieb says that if enough others go down the drain, "someday I'll be the 10th-largest brewery in the nation."

Source: John L. Moore, "Squeezed by Nationals, A Local Brewery Keeps Its Head Above Water," *Wall Street Journal*, July 10, 1978.

Questions

1. Does Ortlieb Brewing Company have a market niche? If so, what is it and what is happening to it?
2. What could Ortlieb do to improve his *marketing* efforts?
3. What could Ortlieb do to improve his marketing *management* efforts?
4. Evaluate Joe Ortlieb's marketing research and marketing intelligence system.
5. How should Ortlieb react to a proposal that he join a group of small non-competing breweries which would permit the use of selected common brand names on locally brewed beer to permit joint advertising or at least wider recognition for the jointly used brand names?

9 American Cyanamid Company

The American Cyanamid Company is a diversified, multinational company involved in the research, development, manufacturing, and marketing of more than twenty-five hundred products. The company has operating divisions in agricultural, pharmaceutical, specialty chemical, and consumer products. Cyanamid perceives itself primarily as a research and development company with a strong ability to develop a basic chemical product and turn it into a family of diversified products.

One of Cyanamid's many products is its Cyalume® lightstick. First marketed in 1971, this chemiluminescent light was the result of ten years of research at American Cyanamid. The Cyalume lightstick is a clear, wand-shaped plastic tube, six inches in length, containing two liquid chemical components. One liquid is held in an inner glass vial apart from the other, which is contained only by the plastic tube. The chemicals react and produce excited molecules that give off a visible yellow-green light.

Since the device utilizes a chemiluminescence process, it produces no heat and does not require any form of ignition to operate. As a result, the device can be activated and used under water, as well as in other situations where battery or electrical power is not available, or where a spark from conventional lighting devices might be dangerous. For example, the lightstick is safe for illuminating the scenes of mining or industrial accidents where explosive concentrations of gases or fumes may be present.

Each lightstick is a self-contained unit capable of producing light for an eight-hour time duration. However, only the first three hours of this light output are considered to be useful working light. The product is dependable, with a shelf life of at least two years when stored under normal conditions. In addition, the product is safe—both of the chemical liquids contained within the tube are nontoxic and require no special measures in the case of contact with the skin or eyes. In summary, it is flameless, cool, waterproof, windproof, lightweight, compact, non-corrosive, and nontoxic.

The lightstick, however, does have some limitations. The intensity of the light produced by the lightstick is low and shines in all directions. The light cannot be confined to a narrow beam for projection in specific directions, such as that produced by a flashlight. Light cannot be shut off once activated, and it is affected by temperature. Maximum light is emitted at temperatures ranging from 70° to 80°F. At temperatures below 32°F., there is a very substantial reduction in light emission. The lightstick is also sensitive to humidity. It is wrapped in an airtight outer foil wrapper. Should the wrapper be punctured and the lightstick not used within a few days, the light emission will be reduced. If it is left in the damaged wrapper for a longer period of time, it is possible for it to be totally deactivated.

The chemiluminescence technology used in the Cyalume lightstick is unique and is protected by several U.S. patents held by the American Cyanamid Company. The patents are effective for a number of years, and a new generation of patents is a strong possibility. The product has been approved or accepted by the U.S. Bureau of Mines, the Federal Aviation Administration, the U.S. Navy, and the General Services Administration for special use as a marker or for lighting work areas.

After several years of production and distribution of the lightstick by the Organic Chemicals Division to the industrial and military users, sales increased significantly. The OCD has in the past avoided selling to novelty users, fearing that such displays would detract from more serious uses of the product, especially those of an emergency nature.

Corporate management believed there was a large untapped potential in both the consumer and the industrial/military markets. Both divisions were requested to prepare independent reports recommending the major markets for the product and general approaches by which they could be reached at a profit. The memorandum included the following statements:

- I want your suggestions as to what markets look promising and strategies we should adopt if we go into these markets. I do not expect you to provide any quantitative data in your report—especially with respect to the strategies you suggest we use in entering these markets. Thus, your reports will be essentially qualitative in nature. You are to present your reports at our next executive meeting with the understanding that once we, as a group, are agreed on what general strategies we have to adopt if we are to have any reasonable chance of being successful, that you and your staffs will be assigned the responsibility of detailing the precise strategies to be employed and the expenditures required. Following this we will meet and decide whether such an investment is feasible and desirable.

These reports were to be rough in the sense that specific data were not required. Essentially, they were to be reports that would take the planners through the planning process in a quick and rough way to get the "feel" of the problem and give corporate management ideas as a basis for further thought. Special attention was to be given to how the product would be used, why it would be selected over other modes, who would buy it, where it would be bought, and how important price would be.

Source: Condensed from a case prepared by Mr. Willard Moran, V.P. Consumer Products, American Cyanamid Company.

Questions

1. What four or five major questions would you pose to guide your preparation of a report on either the consumer or industrial market?
2. Diagram a market planning process you might use in drawing up a rough plan for the chemical light. (See diagrams in text.)
3. What opportunities for the chemical light exist in the consumer market?
4. How should the emergency segment be reached in retail stores? Placement? Communications?
5. List as many specific uses as possible of the light stick in industry, government and other not-for-profit organizations. Use an outline, a series of lists or some other basis for classifying your ideas.

PART 4

marketing mix strategy

CHAPTER 11

NEW-PRODUCT DEVELOPMENT AND PRODUCT LIFE-CYCLE STRATEGIES

After World War II, Brunswick Corporation, the market leader in bowling and billiard equipment, was searching for an appropriate field into which it could expand. The company looked for a field in which it could use its expertise in the fabrication of large wooden objects for nonretail markets. The market that was finally selected was the school furniture industry.

To discover what could be done within this industry, Brunswick went to educators and conducted three hundred interviews. Many educators expressed great dissatisfaction with the heavy rigid furniture bolted to the floor in the typical classroom. Using this information, Brunswick decided to develop a line of light, flexible, movable classroom furniture. This furniture would facilitate team teaching, small-group learning, and the use of classroom television.

The initial step in the development process was a series of sketch drawings. These sketches were shown to educators and school officials to obtain their reactions. Some educators thought that the chairs looked too flimsy, and others raised questions about the orthopedics of the chair. This led to a series of revised sketches. Then Brunswick produced a set of handmade prototypes that were tested in the company's offices.

A final prototype was then selected, and a limited number of chairs were produced for further testing. In these tests educators and children were exposed to the chairs to see how they would be used and would withstand various kinds of maltreatment. Children were placed in a room with the chairs and photographed as they used the chairs with and without supervision. On a larger scale, model classrooms were constructed using the full Brunswick furniture line. These classrooms served as places to observe the use of the chairs as well as provide a selling tool for displaying the furniture to educators.

When it was decided that the furniture met the educators' needs and would survive the abuse of the children, Brunswick introduced the chair at the annual National Education Association convention. It sold out the entire first year's production capacity before the end of the convention.

This was not, however, the end of product development or testing. As reports of field usage were fed back to Brunswick, the chair was modified to cope with unforeseen problems. For example, in California it became a craze among the high-school students to peel the desk arm away from the chair. The chair was redesigned to prevent this problem.

There were also internal inputs for chair development and testing. In this case many of the changes were initiated by manufacturing for cost cutting. The wooden chair gave way to the fiberglass models as new structural designs were adapted. The cost per chair was cut from $18 to $5.

Brunswick enjoyed great success for several years with its new school furniture. However, manufacturers who had been more strongly entrenched in the school furniture market began to copy this furniture. Soon Brunswick was being outdistanced by its competitors. Brunswick's school furniture sales passed through the classic product life cycle of introduction, growth, maturity, and decline. Some years later Brunswick sold its school furniture division.

□ A company has to be good at developing new products. It also has to be good at managing them in the face of changing tastes, technologies, and competition. Every product appears to go through a life cycle.

Figure 11-1 illustrates the hypothetical course of sales and profits over the life of a product. During product development, the company accumulates increasing costs. After the product is launched, its sales pass through an introduction period, then through a period of strong growth, followed by maturity, and eventually by decline. Meanwhile its profits go from negative to positive, peak in the growth or mature sales stages, and then decline.

The existence of a product life cycle means that the firm faces two major challenges. The first is to find new products to replace those that are in a declining stage of their life cycle (the problem of *new-product development*). The second is to know how to manage existing products optimally in each stage of their product life cycle (the problem of *life-cycle strategies*). Some companies concentrate mostly on developing and launching new products, sometimes to the detriment of skillfully managing their existing products. Other companies put

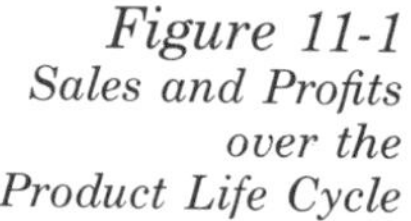

Figure 11-1
Sales and Profits over the Product Life Cycle

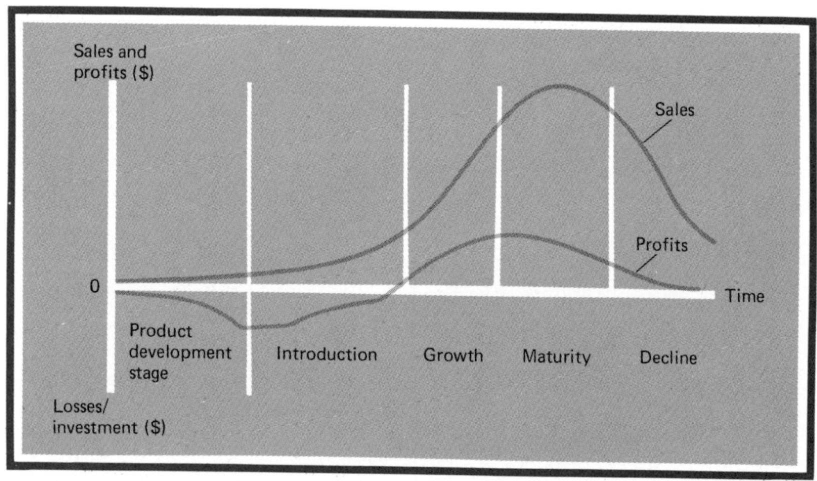

most of their effort into current product management and fail to provide enough new products on which to base their future. Somehow companies must try to strike a balance between these two extremes.

This chapter first looks at the problem of developing new products and then discusses the problem of managing them successfully over their life cycle.

new-product development strategy

Under modern conditions of competition, it is risky for a company to rely only on its existing products. Customers want and expect a stream of new and improved products. Competition will do its best to meet these desires. A company program that includes searching for new products is a necessity.

The company can obtain new products in two basic ways. It can obtain them through *acquisition* by buying a whole company, or buying a patent, or buying a license to produce someone else's product. Or it can go the route of *new-product development* by setting up its own research and development department. We will concentrate on new-product development. By "new products" we mean *original products, product improvements, product modifications,* and *new brands* that the firm brings into existence through its own R & D efforts. We will also be concerned with whether the consumer sees the items as "new," although this will not be our primary focus.

Innovation can be very risky. Ford lost an estimated $350 million on its ill-fated Edsel (see Exhibit 11-1). Du Pont lost an estimated $100 million on its synthetic leather called Corfam; Xerox's venture into computers was a disaster; and the French Concorde aircraft will probably never recover its investment. Here are a number of consumer-packaged-goods products that were launched by well-known companies but failed:

- Red Kettle soup (Campbell)
- Knorr soup (Best)
- Cue toothpaste (Colgate)
- Flavored ketchups (Hunt)
- Babyscott diapers (Scott)
- Nine Flags men's cologne (Gillette)
- Vim tablet detergent (Lever)
- Post dried fruit cereal (General Foods)
- Gablinger's beer (Rheingold)
- Resolve analgesic (Bristol-Myers)
- Mennen E deodorant (Mennen)
- Reef mouthwash (Warner-Lambert)

Various estimates of the new-product failure rate have been made, putting it anywhere from 20 to 80 percent. One of the more careful studies indicated at the time that the new-product failure rate was 40 percent for consumer products, 20 percent for industrial products, and 18 percent for services.[1] The failure rate for new consumer products is especially alarming.

In the future, successful new-product development may even be more difficult to achieve, for several reasons:

- *Shortage of important new-product ideas.* Some scientists think there is a shortage of important new technologies of the magnitude of the automobile, television, computers, xerography, and wonder drugs.
- *Fragmented markets.* Keen competition is leading to increasingly fragmented

markets. Companies have to aim new products at smaller market segments rather than the mass market, and this means lower sales and profits.

- *Growing social and governmental constraints.* New products have to increasingly satisfy public criteria such as consumer safety and ecological compatibility. Government requirements have slowed down the rate of innovation in the drug industry and have considerably complicated product design and advertising decisions in such industries as industrial equipment, chemicals, automobiles, and toys.
- *Costliness of new-product development process.* A company typically has to develop a great number of new-product ideas in order to finish with a few good ones. Booz, Allen and Hamilton studied this question in regard to fifty-one companies and summarized its findings in the form of a decay curve of new-product ideas (see Figure 11-2). Of every fifty-eight odd ideas, about twelve pass the initial screening test, which shows them to be compatible with company objectives and resources. Of these, some seven remain after a thorough evaluation of their profit potential. About three survive the product development stage, two survive the test-marketing stage, and only one is commercially successful. Thus, about fifty-eight new ideas must be generated to find one good one. This one successful idea must be priced at a profitable enough level to cover all the money lost by the company in researching fifty-seven other ideas that failed.
- *Capital shortage.* The high cost of new-product development is no longer affordable by many companies because of the high cost of money. Therefore many companies tend to emphasize product modification and imitation rather than true innovation.
- *Shorter life spans of successful products.* Even when a new product turns out to be a commercial success, rivals are so quick to follow suit that the new product is typically fated for only a short happy life. The race to be first on the market sometimes assumes grotesque proportions. Alberto-Culver was so eager to beat a new Procter and Gamble shampoo to the market that it devised a name and filmed a TV commercial before it had even developed its own product.

EXHIBIT 11-1

THE COSTLIEST NEW-PRODUCT FAILURE IN HISTORY: FORD'S EDSEL

The costliest new-product failure in history may have been Ford's Edsel automobile, introduced in 1957. In the early fifties the Ford Motor Company began to feel the need for adding a new automobile to its product line. At that time, Fords and Chevrolets each had 25 percent of the auto market. But there was a difference. Chevrolet car owners, when they became more prosperous, moved up to the Buick-Oldsmobile-Pontiac class. Owners of Fords, as they moved to higher-status cars, switched over to General Motors' Buicks, Oldsmobiles, and Pontiacs. They simply did not find Ford's intermediate-price Mercury appealing and could not afford the more elegant Lincoln.

The problem facing Ford was to develop a new attractive intermediate-price car for Ford and Chevrolet owners who wanted to move to a higher-status level. Ford conducted extensive marketing research in the mid-1950s indicating that the middle class was growing and would be buying more and better cars. Ford studied car owner demographics, desires, and preferences and finally set about designing a car that would meet a market demand as well as meet Ford's need for a full product line. The car's design was kept top secret, although Ford ran a lot of publicity to excite the public about the coming of a new and unique car. Ford also decided, at a tremendous cost, to establish a separate dealer system for Edsel. Edsel was to be sold by Edsel dealers exclusively. The company also worked feverishly to find a captivating name for the new car—over six thousand possibilities were considered. Ford hired poetess Marianne Moore to dream up names, and she proposed such names as Bullet Cloisonne, Mongoose Civique, and Andante Con Motor. Ignoring the research and the literary suggestions, the car was named Edsel in honor of Henry Ford's only son.

The car was launched with great fanfare on September 4, 1957. On that day sixty-five hundred cars were purchased or ordered. That day belonged to Edsel, but it was the only such day. Although over 2 million people went to look at the car in showrooms, few bought it. By January 1958 the exclusive dealerships had been discontinued and Ford had created a new Mercury-Edsel-Lincoln Division. In November 1959 the production of the Edsel was discontinued.

What happened in the planning of the Edsel that hurt it so badly? Some of the fault lies with Ford's execution of the Edsel idea, rather than the idea itself. First, many consumers did not find the car attractively designed. The front of the car carried vertical lines and the back carried horizontal lines, suggesting that two design teams went to work on separate ends of the car. Furthermore, the front grill was peculiar looking and became the butt of many Freudian jokes. Second, Ford's advertising strategy was to make the Edsel sound like a most advanced and innovative car. However, consumers did not see it this way when they examined it or test drove it. It seemed like another medium-priced car. Ford got itself into trouble by overpromising. Third, and a very serious jolt to the Edsel's acceptance, was Ford's hurry to get the car on the road and exposed to potential buyers. In its rush to produce, quality control was careless and the first Edsels were poorly made. The car received bad word of mouth from some owners and journalists.

But the strongest blow came from the outside. The car was introduced in 1957 just as the economy began to move into a major recession. People began to look for cheaper means of transportation and to turn in great numbers to the Volkswagen and the American Motors Rambler. There was a strong reaction against chrome and flashy cars like the Edsel. Yet there had been nothing in the research data collected a few years earlier to forecast these changes in the economy and cultural values. The Edsel was a victim of poor timing, and it cost the company $350 million.

Sources: William H. Reynolds, "The Edsel Ten Years Later," *Business Horizons,* Fall 1967, pp. 39–46; and John Brooks, *The Fate of the Edsel and Other Business Adventures* (New York: Hayes and Row, 1963).

Figure 11-2
Decay Curve of New-Product Ideas (51 Companies)

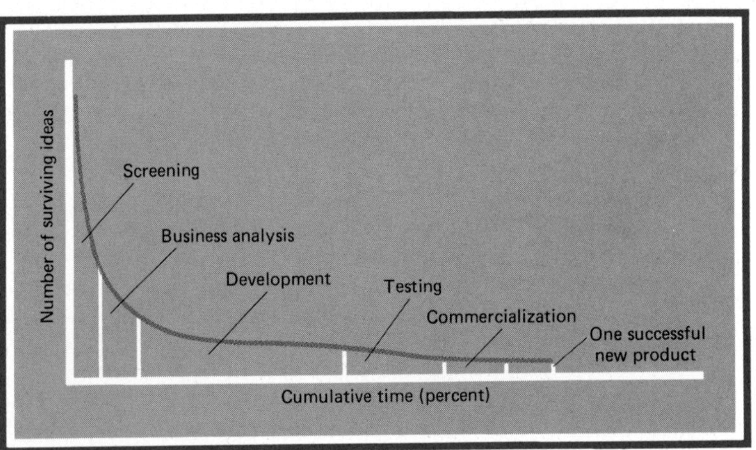

Source: Redrawn from *Management of New Products,* 4th ed. (New York: Booz, Allen & Hamilton, 1968), p. 9.

Thus management faces a dilemma: It should develop new products, and yet the odds weigh heavily against their success. The answer lies in knowing why new products fail and designing a new-product development process that reduces the most common risks of failure.

Why do many new products fail? There are a number of reasons. Too often a high-level executive pushes a favorite idea through in spite of insufficient or even negative marketing research findings. Or the idea is good, but the market size is overestimated. Or the actual product is not designed as well as it should be. Or it is incorrectly positioned in the market, not advertised effectively, or overpriced. Sometimes the costs of product development are higher than expected, or the competitors respond with more ammunition than expected.

To prevent these errors, the company must improve its organizational arrangements for handling the new-product development process. The major organizational arrangements are described in Table 11-1. The new development process itself consists of the eight steps shown in Figure 11-3. We are now ready to examine these steps.

Idea Generation

The first stage in the new-product development process is the generation of new-product ideas. The search should be systematic rather than haphazard. Otherwise the company will find scores of ideas, most of which will not be

Table 11-1
Ways Companies Organize for New-Product Development

1. *PRODUCT MANAGERS.* Many companies leave new-product development up to their product managers. In practice, this system has several faults. The product managers are usually too busy managing their product lines to give much thought to new products other than brand modifications or extensions; they also lack the specific skills and knowledge needed to successfully develop new products.

2. *NEW-PRODUCT MANAGERS.* General Foods and Johnson and Johnson have new-product managers who report to group product managers. This position adds professionalization to the new-product function; on the other hand, new-product managers tend to think in terms of product modifications and line extensions limited to their product market.

3. *NEW-PRODUCT COMMITTEES.* Most companies have a high-level management committee charged with reviewing new-product proposals. Consisting of representatives from marketing, manufacturing, finance, engineering, and other departments, its function is not development or coordination so much as it is the reviewing and approving of new-product plans.

4. *NEW-PRODUCT DEPARTMENTS.* Large companies often establish a new-product department headed by an executive who is given substantial authority and access to top management. The department's major responsibilities include generating and screening new ideas, directing and coordinating research and development work, and carrying out field testing and precommercialization work.

5. *NEW-PRODUCT VENTURE TEAMS.* Dow, Westinghouse, Monsanto, and General Mills assign major new-product development work to venture teams. A venture team is a group specifically brought together from various operating departments and charged with the responsibility of bringing a specific product to market or a specific new business into being.

Sources: This relies on information in *Organization for New-Product Development* (New York: Conference Board, 1966); and David S. Hopkins, *Options in New-Product Organization* (New York: Conference Board, 1974).

Figure 11-3
Major Stages in New-Product Development

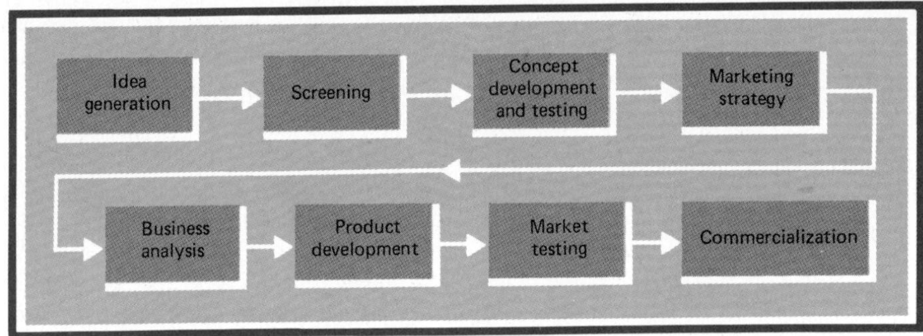

appropriate to its type of business. In one company a new product came all the way up to final approval after a cost of more than a million dollars only to be killed by members of top management, who decided they did not want to get into that type of business.

Top management can avoid this by carefully defining its business domains, objectives, and strategies for the new-product development program. Its business domains should state what business areas the company wants to emphasize and how far afield it will go. The objectives should state what the company wants to accomplish with its new products, whether it is high cash flow, market-share domination, or some other objective. The strategy should state the relative effort that should be devoted to developing original products, modifying existing products, and imitating competitors' products.

In looking for new-product ideas, there are many excellent sources. Customers, according to the marketing concept, are a logical starting point in the search for new-product ideas. Their needs and wants can be monitored through direct customer surveys, projective tests, focused group discussions, and the letters and complaints they send in. Scientists are another source insofar as they may discover or identify new materials or features that could lead to original products or product improvements. Companies should also watch competitors' products to see which ones are attracting customers. The company's sales force and dealers are another good source of ideas because they are in daily contact with customers. Other idea sources are inventors, patent attorneys, university and commercial laboratories, industrial consultants, management consultants, advertising agencies, marketing research firms, trade associations, and industrial publications.

Whatever the source of the idea, at least one of four general processes is responsible for producing it—inspiration, serendipity, customer request, or formal creativity techniques. Other than maintaining as creative an atmosphere as possible and being alert to the occasional lucky accident, companies have little control over the first two processes. Moreover, they seldom have significant input into what a customer might request, though a perceptive salesperson might sometimes work with a customer to help clarify needs the manufacturer can satisfy. Companies, however, can train their executives to use certain "creativity techniques." There are dozens of such techniques, three of which are described on the following page.[2]

1. *Customer problem analysis.* This calls for interviewing customers and asking them to name problems they have with the product. Thus the owners of movie projectors might respond by saying that they would like to be able to speed up their movie projectors when they come to boring stretches of film. This then becomes an idea for a new-product feature that a movie projector manufacturer can adopt.
2. *Product modification analysis.* Here the investigator looks at the various attributes of the product and thinks about opportunities to modify, magnify, minify, substitute, rearrange, reverse, or combine one or more features.[3] The same movie projector manufacturer can consider making a very small projector, or substituting a new material for an old material, or developing a new rewinding device.

EXHIBIT 11-2

WILD NEW IDEAS—KEEP THEM COMING

There is usually no dearth of wild ideas. Take Burt Shulman, who works for IBM and in his spare time has invented a number of things: a gadget that blows smoke away from the noses of people who use soldering guns; an alarm-clock radio that senses when it is going to snow or rain and wakens the sleeper earlier than usual; a tiny machine designed to help improve the circulation of desk-bound executives by continuously moving their feet up and down; a device that permits motorists to breathe fresh air when they are caught in traffic jams; ultrasonic tweezers for the permanent removal of ingrown hairs; and most recently a jogging machine strapped on the jogger's back to help the jogger run at twenty miles an hour. None of these, unfortunately, have been commercial successes.

Occasionally a wild idea does work. A leader in the wild-idea department is a contact lens for chickens! A contact lens for chickens is no joke but a money-saving device that could revolutionize chicken farming in the United States. There were 470.8 million chickens in 1978, and 80 percent of these birds were on 3 percent of the U.S. chicken farms having more than ten thousand birds per farm. Raising chickens for egg production is big business, and a device that saves chickens from pecking each other to death and makes them concentrate on eating and producing eggs is a new product with a large market to serve. The comb of a chicken and the way it holds its head are the signals of the pecking order, and if the chicken cannot see the cues to the pecking order, the cannibalism among the chickens is greatly reduced. When the bird wears a contact lens, its perception is reduced to twelve inches and its visual accuracy is reduced also so that it cannot recognize the comb of another chicken. The lens also helps to solve the problem of the most submissive birds' having a hard time getting to the feeding trough and therefore producing less because they eat less. This way the birds eat the same amount and are more productive. Since chicken farms already have to spend money debeaking birds in order to avoid cannibalism and debeaking often creates trauma, the expense of putting lenses in chickens would not differ considerably from money already spent by the farmer to avoid cannibalism among the birds.

Who knows what will be next? A contraceptive pet food to keep down the cat population? Don't laugh. The Carnation Company of Los Angeles is working on it.

Sources: Prepared by the author. "Burt Shulman" is described in Richard Severs, ". . . or Jogger Huff Puffing: It's a Gas," *Chicago Tribune*, January 7, 1979. "Contact lens for chickens" is adapted from Darral G. Clarke, "Optical Distortion, Inc.," in *Problems in Marketing*, ed. Steven H. Star and others (New York: McGraw-Hill, 1977), pp. 538–50.

3. *Brainstorming.* Here a group of six to ten people (who may or may not be company personnel) are given a specific problem, such as "think of new ways to show movies in the home." A few days later they meet to generate ideas. The rules governing brainstorming sessions are fourfold: (1) criticism is prohibited; (2) freewheeling is welcomed; (3) quantity is wanted; and (4) the group seeks to combine and improve ideas suggested. The participants agree not to criticize any ideas until after the idea generation stage.[4]

Idea Screening

The purpose of idea generation is to create a number of good ideas. The main purpose of all the succeeding stages is to *reduce* the number of ideas. The first idea-pruning stage is screening.

In the screening stage, the company must seek to avoid two types of errors. A *DROP-error* occurs when the company dismisses an otherwise good idea because of a lack of vision of its potentialities. Some companies still shudder when they think of some of the ideas they dismissed:

- Xerox saw the novel promise of Chester Carlson's copying machine; IBM and Eastman Kodak did not see it at all. RCA was able to envision the innovative opportunity of radio; the Victor Talking Machine Company could not. Henry Ford recognized the promise of the automobile; yet only General Motors realized the need to segment the automobile market into price and performance categories, with a model for every classification, if the promise was to be fully achieved. Marshall Field understood the unique market development possibilities of installment buying; Endicott Johnson did not, calling it "the vilest system yet devised to create trouble." And so it has gone.[5]

If a company makes too many DROP-errors, its standards are obviously too conservative.

A *GO-error* occurs when the company lets a poor idea proceed to development and commercialization. We can distinguish at least three types of product failures that ensue. An *absolute product failure* loses money and its sales do not cover variable costs; a *partial product failure* loses money but its sales cover all the variable costs and some of the fixed costs; and a *relative product failure* yields a profit that is less than the company's normal rate of return.

The job of screening is to spot and drop poor ideas as early as possible. The rationale is that product development costs rise substantially at each successive stage of the process. When products reach later stages, management often feels that so much has been invested in developing the product that it ought to be launched in the hope of recouping some of the investment. But this is letting good money chase bad money, and the real solution is to not let poor product ideas get this far.

Most companies require their executives to write up each new-product idea on a standard form that can be reviewed by a new-product committee. At this stage the ideas are rough, and the form simply requires a description of the product, the target market, competition, and some rough guesses as to market size, product price, development time and costs, manufacturing costs, and level of return.

Even if the idea looks good, the question arises, Is the idea appropriate for the particular company? That is, Does it mesh well with the company's objec-

Table 11-2
Product-Idea Rating Device

PRODUCT SUCCESS REQUIREMENTS	(A) RELATIVE WEIGHT	(B) COMPANY COMPETENCE LEVEL											
		.0	.1	.2	.3	.4	.5	.6	.7	.8	.9	1.0	RATING (A × B)
Company personality and goodwill	.20							√					.120
Marketing	.20										√		.180
Research and development	.20								√				.140
Personnel	.15							√					.090
Finance	.10										√		.090
Production	.05									√			.040
Location and facilities	.05				√								.015
Purchasing and supplies	.05										√		.045
Total	1.00												.720*

Adapted with modifications from Barry M. Richman. "A Rating Scale for Product Innovation," *Business Horizons,* Summer 1962, pp. 37–44.

* Rating scale: .00–.40 poor; .41–.75 fair; .76–1.00 good. Present minimum acceptance rate: .70.

tives, strategies, and resources? Table 11-2 shows a common type of rating form for this question. The first column lists factors required for successful launching of the product in the marketplace. In the next column, management assigns weights to these factors according to their importance. Thus management believes marketing competence will be very important (.20), and purchasing and supplies competence will be of minor importance (.05). The next task is to rate the company's degree of competence on each factor on a scale from .0 to 1.0. Here management feels that its marketing competence is very high (.9) and its location and facilities competence is low (.3). The final step is to multiply the relative importance of the success requirements by the corresponding levels of company competence to obtain a single overall rating of the company's fitness to carry this product successfully into the market. Thus, if marketing is an important success requirement, and this company is very good at marketing, this will increase the overall rating of the product idea. In the example the product idea scored .72, which, in the company's experience, places it at the high end of the "fair idea" level.[6]

The checklist serves as a means of promoting systematic evaluation and discussion of the product idea among members of management—it is not designed to make the important decision for them.

Concept Development and Testing

Those ideas that survive screening must undergo further development into full product concepts. It is important to distinguish between a product idea, a product concept, and a product image. A *product idea* is a possible product, described in objective and functional terms, that the company can see itself offering to the market. A *product concept* is a particular subjective consumer meaning that the company tries to build into the product idea. A *product image* is the particular subjective picture that consumers actually acquire of the product.

Concept development. Assume that an automobile manufacturer develops the technology that enables an electric car to travel up to fifty miles an hour and go one hundred miles before needing to be recharged. The manufacturer estimates that the electric car's operating costs would be about half of those of a conventional car.

This is a product idea. Customers, however, do not buy product ideas; they buy a product concept. The marketer's task is to develop this product idea into some alternative product concepts, evaluate their relative appeal to customers, and choose the best one.

Among the product concepts that might be created for the electric car are:

- Concept 1. An inexpensive subcompact designed as a second family car to be used by the homemaker for short shopping trips, and so forth. The car is styled in such a way that it is easy to enter, load groceries in, and transport children in.
- Concept 2. A medium-cost, intermediate-size car designed as an all-purpose family car.
- Concept 3. A medium-cost sporty compact appealing mainly to young people.
- Concept 4. An inexpensive subcompact designed to appeal to the conscientious citizen who wants basic transportation, low fuel cost, and low ecological pollution.

Concept testing. Concept testing calls for taking these concepts to an appropriate group of target consumers and getting their reactions. The concepts may be presented symbolically or physically. At this stage a word and/or picture description suffices, although the reliability of a concept test increases, the more concrete and physical the stimulus. The consumers are presented with an elaborated version of each concept. Here is concept 1:

- An efficient, fun-to-drive, electric-powered car in the subcompact class that seats four. Great for shopping trips and visits to friends. Costs half as much to operate as similar gasoline-driven cars. Goes up to fifty miles an hour and does not need to be recharged for one hundred miles. Priced at $4,000.

Consumers will be asked to react to this concept with questions similar to those shown in Table 11-3. The consumers' responses will enable the company to determine which of several alternative concepts has the strongest appeal. For example, the last question in Table 11-3 goes after the consumer's *intention-to-buy* and usually reads: "Would you *definitely, probably, probably not, definitely not* buy this product?" Suppose 10 percent of the consumers said "definitely" and another 5 percent said "probably." The company would project these figures to

Table 11-3
Major Questions in a Concept Test for an Electric Car

1. Is the concept of an electric car clear to you?
2. What do you see as distinct benefits of an electric car compared with a conventional car?
3. Do you find the claims about the electric car's performance believable?
4. Would an electric car meet a real need of yours?
5. What improvements can you suggest in various features of the electric car?
6. Who would be involved in a possible purchase decision and who would use the car?
7. What do you think the price of the electric car should be?
8. Would you prefer an electric car to a conventional car? For what uses?
9. Would you buy an electric car? (Definitely, probably, probably not, definitely not.)

the corresponding population size of this target group to estimate whether the sales volume would be sufficient. Even then, the estimate is at best tentative because people do not always carry out their stated intentions.

Marketing Strategy Development

Suppose the first-listed concept for the electric car tests our best. The next step calls for developing a preliminary concept of the marketing strategy for introducing this electric car into the market. This is necessary in order that the full product and marketing concept can be evaluated from a business point of view in the next stage.

The marketing strategy statement consists of three parts. The first part describes the size, structure, and behavior of the target market, the intended positioning of the new product in this market, and the sales, market share, and profit goals being sought in the first few years. Thus:

- The target market is households who need a second car for short shopping trips and visits to friends. The car will be positioned as more economical to buy and operate, and more fun to drive, than cars currently available to this market. The company will aim to sell five hundred thousand cars in the first year, at a loss not exceeding $3 million. The second year will aim for sales of seven hundred thousand cars with a planned profit of $5 million.

The second part of the marketing strategy statement outlines the product's intended price, distribution strategy, and marketing budget for the first year:

- The electric car will be offered in three colors and will have optional air-conditioning and power-drive features. It will sell at a retail price of $4,000, with 15 percent off the list price to dealers. Dealers who sell over ten cars per month will get an additional discount of 5 percent on each car sold that month. An advertising budget of $6 million will be split 50:50. Advertising copy will emphasize the car's economy and fun. During the first year, $100,000 will be spent on marketing research to monitor who is buying the car and their satisfaction levels.

The third part of the marketing strategy statement describes the intended long-run sales and profit goals and marketing mix strategy over time:

- The company intends to ultimately capture 6 percent of the total auto market and realize an after-tax return on investment of 15 percent. To achieve this, product quality will start high and be further improved over time through technical research. Price will be raised in the second and third years if competition permits. The total advertising budget will be boosted each year by about 10 percent. Marketing research will be reduced to $60,000 per year after the first year.

Business Analysis

Once management has developed a satisfactory product concept and marketing strategy, it is in a position to do a hardheaded analysis of the business attractiveness of the proposal. Management must review the future sales, costs, and profit estimates to determine whether they satisfy the company's objectives. If they do, the product concept can be moved to the product development stage.

Estimating sales. The key to whether a product should be developed is whether its sales will be high enough to return a satisfactory profit to the firm.

One can obtain some helpful bench marks by carefully examining the sales history of similar products and surveying market opinion. At the very least, management should have estimates of minimum and maximum sales to provide some indication of the risk involved.

Sales forecasting methods were described in Chapter 5 (pp. 160–64). In predicting the future sales of a product, much depends on whether it is a one-time purchased product, an infrequently purchased product, or a frequently purchased product.

Figure 11-4A illustrates the product life-cycle sales that can be expected for one-time purchased products. Sales rise at the beginning, peak, and later approach zero as the number of potential buyers are exhausted. If new buyers keep entering the market, the curve will not quite go down to zero.

Infrequently purchased products are exemplified by many durable goods, such as automobiles, toasters, and industrial equipment. These goods exhibit replacement cycles, dictated either by their physical wearing out or their obsolescence associated with changing styles, features, and tastes.[7] Sales forecasting for this category of products consists of separately estimating first-time sales and replacement sales (see Figure 11-4B).

Frequently purchased products, such as consumer and industrial nondurables, have product life-cycle sales resembling Figure 11-4C. The number of first-time buyers initially increases and then decreases as there are fewer left (assuming a fixed population). Repeat-purchase sales occur soon, providing that the product satisfies some fraction of people who become steady customers. The sales curve eventually falls to a plateau level representing a level of steady repeat-purchase volume; by this time the product is no longer in the class of new products.

Estimating costs and profits. After preparing a long-range sales forecast, management can proceed to estimate the expected costs and profits of this venture over the same period of time. The costs are gathered through discussions with R & D, manufacturing, accounting, and finance offices. The planned marketing costs listed in the marketing strategy statement are included in the analysis. The marketer estimates the expected sales and net profits for a number

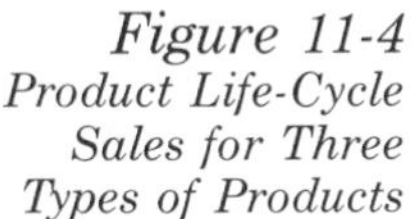

Figure 11-4
Product Life-Cycle Sales for Three Types of Products

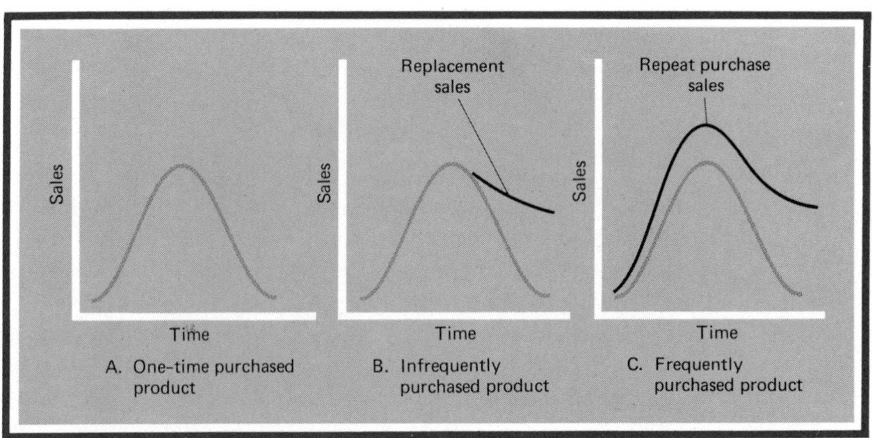

of years out. The next step is to calculate the financial attractiveness of the proposal. This can be done using techniques such as breakeven analysis, payout period analysis, or rate-of-return analysis, which are described in standard finance textbooks.

Product Development

If the product concept scores high in the business analysis, it can be turned over to the R & D department and/or the engineering department to be developed into a physical product. Up to now it has existed only as a word description, a drawing, or a very crude mock-up. This step calls for a large jump in investment, which dwarfs the idea-evaluation costs incurred in the earlier stages. Much time and many dollars go into trying to develop a technically feasible product. This stage will provide an answer as to whether the product idea can be translated into a technically and commercially feasible product. If not, the company's accumulated investment will be lost except for any useful byproduct information gained in the process.

The R & D department will undertake the developing of one or more physical versions of the defined product concept. It succeeds if it finds a prototype that satisfies the following criteria: (1) the prototype is seen by consumers as successfully embodying the key attributes described in the product concept statement; (2) the prototype performs safely under normal use and conditions; (3) the prototype can be produced for the budgeted manufacturing costs.

The work of developing a successful product prototype can take days, weeks, months, or even years. The R & D people must not only know how to design the required functional characteristics but also know how to convey the psychological aspects of the product concept through *physical cues.* In the case of the electric car, they may want to convey the idea that it is a well-built and safe car. This calls for designing the car to look rugged. Management must investigate how consumers inspect a car to decide how well built it is. One common practice consists of slamming a car door to listen to its "sound." If the car does not have "solid-sounding" doors, then consumers will think that it is not well built.

When the prototypes are ready, they must be put through a series of rigorous functional and consumer tests. The *functional tests* are conducted under laboratory and field conditions to make sure that the product performs safely and effectively. The new car must start well; its tires must not fall off; it must be able to maneuver corners without overturning. *Consumer testing* involves bringing a sample of consumers in to test drive the prototype and rate their reactions to the overall car and each of its attributes.

Market Testing

After management is satisfied with the prototype's functional performance and the consumers' initial response, it will arrange for the manufacture of a certain volume to be used in further market testing. *Market testing* is the stage where the product and marketing program are introduced into more authentic consumer settings to learn how consumers and dealers react to handling, using, and repurchasing the product, and how large the market is.

The amount of market testing is influenced by the amount of *investment cost* and *risk* on the one hand, and the *time pressure* and *research cost* on the other. Products involving a substantial investment and risk deserve to be market tested so as not to make a mistake; the cost of the market tests will be an insignificant percentage of the cost of the project itself.

Methods of market testing vary with the type of product (see Table 11-4). For example, companies testing frequently purchased consumer packaged goods will want to estimate four components of sales, namely, *trial, first repeat, adoption,* and *frequency of purchase.* From these, total sales can be forecast.[8] The

Table 11-4
Methods of Market Testing

CONSUMER PACKAGED GOODS

Sales wave research. Here a sample of consumers are given the new product to try at no cost in their homes. They are then reoffered the product or competitive brands as many as three to five times (sales waves) at a reduced cost, with the company noting each time how many consumers selected their product again and what comments they reported about satisfaction.

Simulated store technique. Here a sample of consumers are invited to a brief screening of some television commercials. One of the commercials advertises the new product, but it is not singled out for attention. The consumers are given a small amount of money and are invited into a store where they may use the money to buy any items or keep the money. The company notes how many consumers buy the new product and competing brands. This provides a measure of trial and the commercial's effectiveness against competing commercials. The consumers reconvene and are asked the reasons for their purchase or nonpurchase. Some weeks later they are reinterviewed by phone to determine product attitudes, usage, satisfaction, and repurchase intention, as well as being offered an opportunity to repurchase any products.

Controlled test marketing. Several research firms have arranged a controlled panel of stores which have agreed to carry new products for a certain fee. The company with the new product specifies the number of stores and geographical locations it wants. The research firm takes responsibility for delivering the product to the participating stores and controlling shelf location, number of facings, displays and point-of-purchase promotions, and pricing according to prespecified plans. Sales results can be tracked to determine the impact of various factors on demand.

Test markets. Test markets are the ultimate form of testing a new consumer product in a situation resembling the one that would be faced in a full-scale launching of the product. The company locates a small number of representative test cities in which the company's sales force will try to sell the trade on carrying the product and giving it good shelf exposure. The company will put on a full advertising and promotion program in these markets similar to the one that would be used in national marketing. Test marketing is undertaken to achieve a more reliable forecast of future sales and to pretest alternative marketing plans.

INDUSTRIAL DURABLE GOODS

Product-use tests. The manufacturer selects a small group of potential customers who agree to use the new product for a limited period. The manufacturer's technical people observe how the customers' workers use the product. This clues the manufacturer about customer training and servicing requirements. After the test, the customer is given an opportunity to express purchase intent and other reactions.

Trade shows. Trade shows draw a large number of buyers who view new exhibits in a few concentrated days. The manufacturer can see how much interest buyers show in the new product, how they react to various features and terms, and how many orders or purchase intentions they indicate.

Distribution and dealer display rooms. The new industrial product can also be tested in *distributor and dealer display rooms,* where it may stand next to the manufacturer's other products and possibly competitors' products. This method yields preference and pricing information in the normal selling atmosphere for the product.

Controlled or test marketing. Some manufacturers will produce a limited supply of the product and give it to the sales force to sell in a limited set of geographical areas that will be given promotional support, printed catalog sheets, and so on.

Sources: For methods of testing consumer products, see Edward M. Tauber, "Forecasting Sales Prior to Test Market," *Journal of Marketing,* January 1977, pp. 80–84. For methods of testing industrial products, see Morgan B. MacDonald, Jr., *Appraising the Market for New Industrial Products* (New York: Conference Board, 1967), Chap. 2.

company hopes to find all of these at high levels. Too often, however, it will find many consumers trying the product but not rebuying it, showing a lack of product satisfaction. Or it might find high first-time repurchase but little repeat purchase after that. Or it might find high adoption but low frequency of purchase (as in the case of many gourmet frozen foods) because the buyers have decided to use the product only on special occasions.

Commercialization

Market testing presumably gives management enough information to make a final decision about whether to launch the new product. If the company goes ahead with commercialization, it will face its largest costs to date. The company will have to build or rent a full-scale manufacturing facility. And it may have to spend, in the case of a new consumer packaged good, between $10 million and $20 million for advertising and sales promotion alone in the first year.

In deciding to launch the new product, the company must make four basic decisions. Let us see how these decisions would apply to an electric car.

When (timing). The first decision concerns whether it is the right time to introduce the new product. If the electric car will cannibalize another car made by the company, its introduction might be delayed until the other car's stock is drawn down through normal sales.[9] If the electric car can still be improved, the company may prefer to miss the selling season in order to come out with a better car in the following year. If the company decides to go ahead, it should time its introduction for the right season.

Where (geographical strategy). The next decision is whether the company should launch the new product in a *single locality,* a *region,* a *set of regions,* the *national market,* or the *international market.* Few companies have the confidence, capital, and capacity to put new products into full national distribution from the start. Instead they will develop a *planned market rollout* over time. Small companies, in particular, will select an attractive city and put on a blitz campaign to win a share. They will spread out to other cities as they gain a foothold. Large companies will generally introduce their product into a whole region and then move on to the next region. A few companies with large national distribution networks, such as auto companies, will launch their new models in the national market unless there are production shortages.

To whom (target market prospects). Within the rollout markets, the company must target its distribution and promotion to the best prospect groups. Presumably the company has already profiled the prime prospects on the basis of data gathered in the market testing or earlier stages. Prime prospects for a new consumer product would ideally have four characteristics:[10] (1) they would be early adopters of the product; (2) they would be heavy users of the product; (3) they would be looked upon as opinion leaders and give the product good word of mouth and influence others to buy it; (4) they could be reached at a low cost.

How (introductory marketing strategy). The final step is to develop the marketing strategy for introducing the new product into the rollout markets. It calls for allocating the marketing budget among the marketing mix elements and sequencing the various activities. Thus the electric car's launch might be preceded by a major publicity campaign several weeks before the car arrives in the showrooms, then by a major advertising campaign once it arrives in the showrooms, and then by offers of gifts to draw more people to the showrooms. In other words, the company will prepare and execute a rollout marketing plan for each of its rollout markets.

In making these various commercialization decisions, the management should be guided by the useful findings in the field known as innovation diffusion and adoption theory (see Table 11-5). These findings clearly point out the high risks involved in new-product development and the careful planning that is needed. In the case of the electric car, it turns out that the Ford Motor Company has made the largest investment among the big auto makers but has become pessimistic about early market acceptance. Ford has been endeavoring to perfect a sodium-sulfur battery with a twenty-year life. Until this happens and it can produce a car up to the market's standard, it would rather wait than have another Edsel on its hands.

Table 11-5
Major Findings in Innovation Diffusion and Adoption

In launching a new product, a firm should be guided by researchers' major findings in the field of innovation diffusion and adoption theory. These findings can be as follows.

STAGES OF ADOPTION. Individual consumers go through a series of stages of acceptance in the process of adopting a new product. The stages are *awareness, interest, evaluation, trial,* and *adoption.* Thus the manufacturer of a new electric car must think about what can be done to efficiently move people through each stage. For example, if people have awareness and interest but are not coming into a dealer's showrooms, the manufacturer must develop promotional incentives to attract people into the showrooms.

CONSUMER ADOPTER TYPES. People differ markedly in their penchant for trying new products. There are *innovators* (the first 2.5 percent of the individuals to adopt a new product), *early adopters* (the next 13.5 percent), *early majority* (the next 34 percent), *late majority* (the next 34 percent), and *laggards* (the last 16 percent). The electric car manufacturer should try to identify the characteristics of people who are likely to be early adopters, such as having a high income and being active in the community, and should then focus its promotion on this group.

ROLE OF PERSONAL INFLUENCE. Personal influence plays a large role in the adoption of new products. The statements of other people about a new product carry heavy weight with a prospect, especially if the product is risky or costly. The electric car manufacturer will want to research what opinion leaders and early buyers say to others about the new electric car and to correct any product features that give rise to complaints as soon as possible. The manufacturer may also want to use a "testimonial advertising" approach in which some attractive sources assure other people that the electric car is reliable and fun to drive.

INNOVATION CHARACTERISTICS. Certain characteristics of the innovation strongly affect the rate of adoption. The main ones are the innovation's *relative advantage* over other products, its *compatibility* with the person's life style, its *complexity,* its *divisibility* into small trial units, and its *communicability.* Thus an electric car will be more appealing to the extent that it saves buyers a lot of money, fits their life style, is simple to operate, can be test driven, and is easy to understand.

Source: These and other ideas are elaborated in Everett M. Rogers and F. Floyd Shoemaker, *Communication of Innovations* (New York: Free Press, 1971).

product life-cycle strategies

Once a new product is launched, management crosses its fingers and hopes that the product will enjoy a long and happy life. While under no illusion that the product will last forever, it wants the product to return a decent profit, considering all the effort and risk that went into it. Management hopes that its "question mark" will become a "star" and expects that it will eventually settle into being a "cash cow." When it becomes a "dog," this will be the time to drop it.

Portfolio theory, which we reviewed in Chapter 3 (pp. 80–85), has "product life-cycle theory" (PLC) as one of its major underpinnings. The life cycle of a typical product exhibits an S-shaped sales curve marked by four distinct stages in addition to the product development stage (see Figure 11-1):

1. *Introduction* is a period of slow sales growth as the product is introduced in the market. The profit curve in Figure 11-1 shows profits as being almost nonexistent in this stage because of the heavy expenses of product introduction.
2. *Growth* is a period of rapid market acceptance and substantial profit improvement.
3. *Maturity* is a period of a slowdown in sales growth because the product has achieved acceptance by most of the potential buyers. Profits peak in this period and start to decline because of increased marketing outlays to sustain the product's position against competition.
4. *Decline* is the period when sales show a strong downward drift and profits erode.

Not all products pass through the idealized S-shaped product life cycle shown in Figure 11-1. Some products show a rapid growth from the very beginning, thus skipping the slow sales period implied by the introductory stage. Other products, instead of going through a rapid-growth stage, go directly from introduction to maturity. Some products move from maturity to a second point of rapid growth. Cox studied the life cycles of 754 ethical-drug products and found six different product life-cycle patterns.[11] The most typical form was a "cycle-recycle" pattern (see Figure 11-5A). Cox explained the second "hump" in sales as being caused by a traditional promotional push in the decline stage. Some investigators have reported a "scalloped" pattern (see Figure 11-5B), which represents a succession of life cycles for this product based on the discovery of new product characteristics, new uses, or new market. The history of nylon's sales

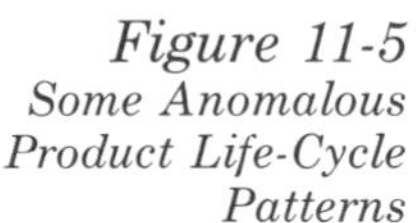

Figure 11-5
Some Anomalous Product Life-Cycle Patterns

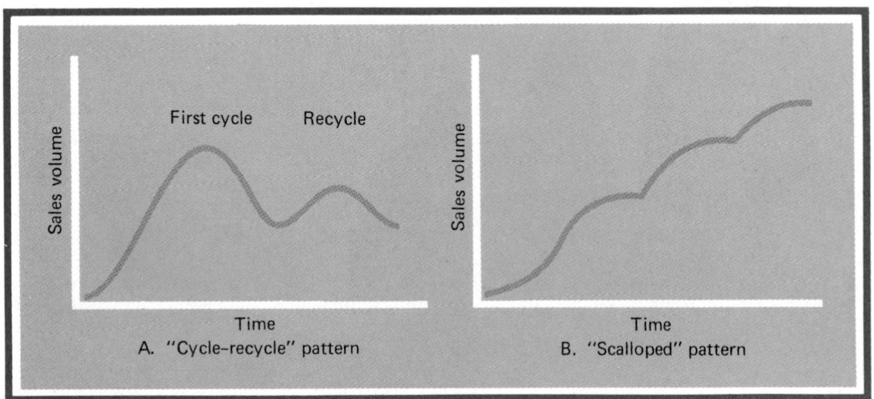

shows a scalloped pattern because of the many new uses—parachutes, hosiery, shirts, carpeting—discovered over time.

The PLC concept should be defined with respect to whether the product is a product class (gasoline-powered automobiles), a product form ("convertible top" automobiles), or a brand (Mustang). The PLC concept has a different degree of applicability in these three cases. *Product classes* have the longest life cycles. The sales of many product classes can be expected to continue in the mature stage for an indefinite duration, since they are highly population related (cars, perfume, refrigerators, and steel). *Product forms,* on the other hand, tend to exhibit the standard PLC histories more faithfully than do product classes. Product forms such as the "dial telephone" and "cream deodorants" seem to pass through a regular history of introduction, rapid growth, maturity, and decline. As for *brands,* a brand's sales history can be erratic because changing competitive strategies and tactics can produce substantial ups and downs in sales and market shares, even to the extent of causing a mature brand to suddenly exhibit another period of rapid growth. The life-cycle histories of several well-known car brands are shown in Figure 11-6.

The PLC concept can also be applied to what are known as styles, fashions, and fads. Their special life-cycle features are described in Exhibit 11-3.

The PLC concept is useful mainly as a framework for developing effective marketing strategies in different stages of the product life cycle. We now turn to the major stages and consider the appropriate marketing strategies.

Introduction Stage

The introduction stage takes place when the new product is first made available for general purchase in the marketplace. The introduction into one or more markets takes time, and sales growth is apt to be slow. Such well-known products as instant coffee, frozen orange juice, and powdered coffee creamers lingered for

Figure 11-6
Product Life Curves for Selected Automobiles

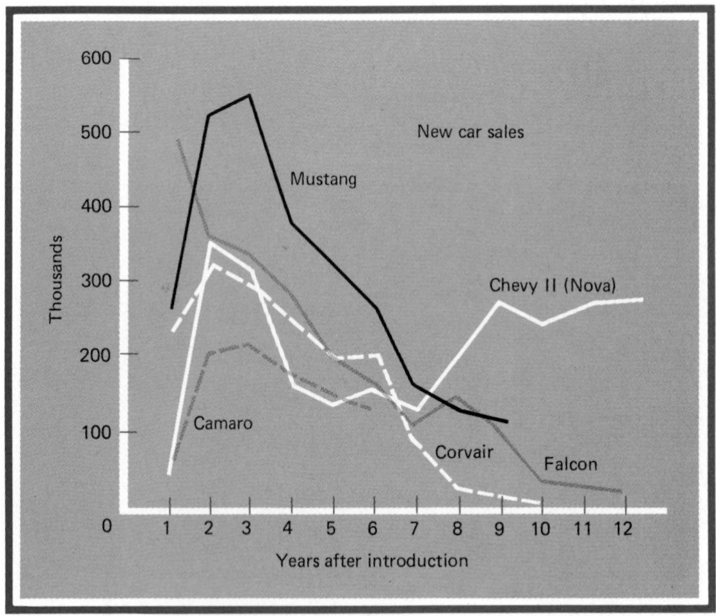

EXHIBIT 11-3

STYLE, FASHION, AND FAD CYCLES

In product markets where style and fashion are influential, cycles can also be observed, and it is important that marketers understand and try to predict them.

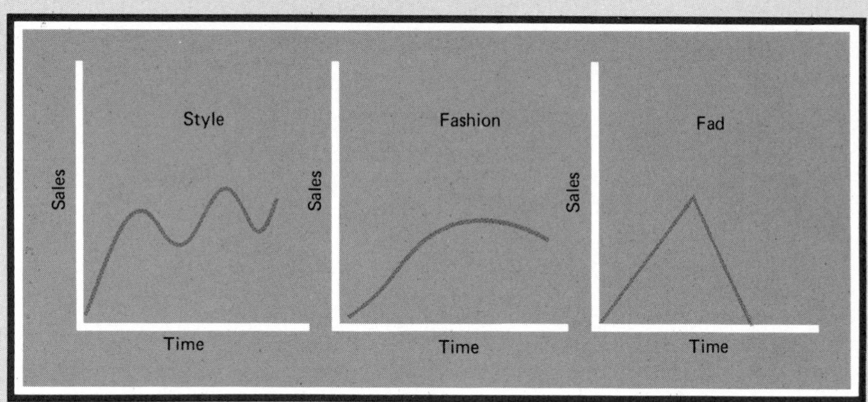

A *style* is a basic and distinctive mode of expression appearing in a field of human endeavor. For example, there are styles in homes (colonial, ranch, Cape Cod), clothing (formal, casual, funky), and art (realistic, surrealistic, abstract). Once a style is invented, it may last for generations, coming in and out of vogue. A style exhibits a cycle showing several lives of renewed interest.

A *fashion* is a currently accepted or popular style in a given field. For example, jeans are a fashion in today's clothing, and disco is a fashion in today's dance. Fashions tend to pass through four stages. In the *distinctiveness* stage, some consumers take an interest in something new to set themselves apart from other consumers. The products may be custom-made or produced in small quantities by some manufacturers. In the *emulation* stage, other consumers take an interest out of a desire to emulate the fashion leaders, and additional manufacturers begin to produce larger quantities of the product. In the *mass fashion* stage, the fashion has become extremely popular and manufacturers have geared up for mass production. Finally, in the *decline* stage, consumers start moving toward other incipient fashions that are beginning to catch their eye.

Thus fashions tend to grow slowly, remain popular for a while, and decline slowly. The length of a fashion cycle is hard to predict. Wasson believes that fashions come to an end because they represent an inherent purchase compromise such that the consumer starts looking for missing attributes after a while. For example, as automobiles get shorter, they get less comfortable, and then a growing number of buyers start wanting longer cars. Furthermore, too many consumers adopt the fashion, thus turning others away. Reynolds suggests that the length of a particular fashion cycle depends on the extent to which the fashion meets a genuine need, is consistent with other trends in the society, as well as societal norms and values, and does not meet technological limits as it develops. Robinson, however, sees fashions as living out inexorable cycles regardless of economic, functional, or technological changes in society.

Fads are particular fashions that come quickly into the public eye, are adopted with great zeal, peak early, and decline very fast. Their acceptance cycle is short, and they tend to attract only a limited following. They often have a novel or capricious aspect, as when people start buying "pet rocks" or run naked and "streak." Fads appeal to people who are searching for excitement or who want a way to distinguish themselves from others or have something to talk about to others. Fads do not survive because they normally do not satisfy a strong need or do not satisfy it well. It is difficult to predict whether something will only be a fad, and if so, how long it will last—a few days, weeks, or months. The amount of media attention it receives, along with other factors, will influence its duration.

Sources: Prepared by the author from various sources including Chester R. Wasson, "How Predictable Are Fashion and Other Product Life Cycles?" *Journal of Marketing,* July 1968, pp. 36–43; William H. Reynolds, "Cars and Clothing: Understanding Fashion Trends," *Journal of Marketing,* July 1968, pp. 44–49; and Dwight E. Robinson, "Style Changes: Cyclical, Inexorable, and Foreseeable," *Harvard Business Review,* November-December 1975, pp. 121–31.

many years before they entered a stage of rapid growth. Buzzell identified four causes for the slow growth of many processed food products: (1) delays in the expansion of production capacity; (2) technical problems ("working out the bugs"); (3) delays in making the product available to customers, especially in obtaining adequate distribution through retail outlets; (4) customer reluctance to change established behavior patterns.[12] In the case of expensive new products, sales growth is retarded by additional factors, such as the small number of buyers who are attuned to innovations and the high cost of the product.

In the introductory stage, profits are negative or low because of the low sales and heavy distribution and promotion expenses. Much money is needed to attract distributors and "fill the pipelines." Promotional expenditures are at their highest ratio to sales "because of the need for a high level of promotional effort to (1) inform potential consumers of the new and unknown product, (2) induce trial of the product, and (3) secure distribution in retail outlets."[13]

There are only a few competitors and they produce basic versions of the product, since the market is not ready for product refinements. The firms direct their selling effort to those buyers who are the readiest to buy, usually higher-income groups. Prices tend to be on the high side because "(1) costs are high due to relatively low output rates, (2) technological problems in production may have not yet been fully mastered, and (3) high margins are required to support the heavy promotional expenditures which are necessary to achieve growth."[14]

Growth Stage

If the new product satisfies the market, sales will start climbing substantially. The early adopters will continue their purchasing and a large number of conventional consumers will begin to follow their lead, especially if there is favorable word of mouth. New competitors will enter the market attracted by the opportunities for large-scale production and profit. They will introduce new-product features, and this will expand the market. The increase in the number of competitors leads to an increase in the number of distribution outlets, and factory sales jump just to fill the pipelines.

Prices tend to remain where they are or fall only slightly during this period, insofar as demand is managing to increase quite rapidly. Companies maintain their promotional expenditures at the same or at a slightly raised level to meet competition and continue educating the market. Sales rise much faster, causing a decline in the promotion-sales ratio.

Profit margins peak during this stage as promotion costs are spread over a larger volume and unit manufacturing costs fall faster than price declines due to the "experience curve" effect.[15] During this stage the firm tries to sustain rapid market growth as long as possible. This is accomplished in several ways:

1. The firm undertakes to improve product quality and add new-product features and models.
2. It vigorously searches out new market segments to enter.
3. It keeps its eyes open to new distribution channels to gain additional product exposure.
4. It shifts some advertising copy from building product awareness to trying to bring about product conviction and purchase.
5. It decides when the time is right to lower prices to attract the next layer of price-sensitive buyers into the market.

The firm that aggressively pursues any or all of these market-expanding strategies will increase its competitive position. But this comes at additional cost. The firm in the growth stage faces a trade-off between high market share and high current profit. By spending a lot of money on product improvement, promotion, and distribution, it can capture a dominant position; but it forgoes maximum current profit in the hope, presumably, of making up for this in the next stage.

Maturity Stage

At some point a product's rate of sales growth will slow down, and the product will enter a stage of relative maturity. This stage normally lasts much longer than the previous stages, and it poses some of the most formidable challenges to marketing management. *Most products are in the maturity stage of the life cycle, and therefore most of marketing management deals with the mature product.*

The beginning of a slowdown in the rate of sales growth has the effect of producing overcapacity in the industry. This overcapacity leads to intensified competition. Competitors engage more frequently in markdowns and off-list pricing. There is a strong increase in promotional budgets, in the form of trade and consumer deals. Other firms increase their research and development budgets to find better versions of the product. These steps, to the extent that they do not stimulate adequate sales increases, mean some profit erosion. Some of the weaker competitors start dropping out. The industry eventually consists of a set of well-entrenched competitors whose basic orientation is toward gaining competitive advantage.

The product manager of a mature product should not be content to simply defend its current position. A good offense will provide the best defense of this product. The company should consider the three possible strategies of market, product, and marketing mix modification.

Market modification. Here the product manager looks for opportunities to find new buyers for the product. First the manager looks for *new markets and market* *segments* that have not yet tried the product. Next the manager looks for ways to stimulate *increased usage* among present customers. Then the manager may want to consider *repositioning* the brand to appeal to a larger or faster-growing part of the market.

Product modification. A product manager can also try to change product characteristics—such as product quality, features, or style—in order to attract new users and more usage.

A strategy of *quality improvement* aims at increasing the functional performance of the product—such aspects as its durability, reliability, speed, and taste. This strategy is effective to the extent that (1) the product is capable of quality improvement, (2) buyers believe the claims about improved quality, and (3) a sufficient number of buyers are highly responsive to improved quality.

A strategy of *feature improvement* aims at adding new features that expand the product's versatility, safety, or convenience. Stewart outlines five advantages flowing from a strategy of feature improvement:

1. The development of new functional features is one of the most effective means of building a company image of progressiveness and leadership.
2. Functional features are an extremely flexible competitive tool becase they can be adapted quickly, dropped quickly, and often can be made optional at very little expense.
3. Functional features allow the company to gain the intense preference of preselected market segments.
4. Functional features often bring the innovating company free publicity.
5. Functional features generate a great amount of sales-force and distributors' enthusiasm.[16]

A strategy of *style improvement* aims at increasing the aesthetic appeal of the product. The periodic introduction of new-car models is an example of style competition rather than quality or feature competition.

Marketing mix modification. The product manager should consider the possibility of stimulating sales through altering one or more elements of the marketing mix. One tactic is to cut *prices* in order to attract new triers and competitors' customers. Another is to develop a more effective *advertising* campaign that attracts consumers' attention and interest. A more direct way to attract other brand users is through aggressive promotion—trade deals, cents-off, gifts, and contests. The company can also consider moving into higher-volume *market channels,* particularly discount channels, if these channels are in a growth stage. The company can also offer new or improved service to the buyer as a patronage-building step.

Decline Stage

Most product forms and brands eventually enter a stage of sales decline. The decline may be slow, as in the case of oatmeal cereal; or rapid, as in the case of the Edsel automobile. Sales may plunge to zero and the product may be withdrawn from the market, or they may petrify at a low level and continue for many years at that level.

Sales decline for a number of reasons. Technical advances may give birth to new-product classes and forms, which become effective substitutes. Changes in fashion or tastes lead to buyer erosion. The lower costs of imported products hurt the domestic producers. All of these have the effect of intensifying overcapacity and price competition, leading to a serious erosion of profits.

As sales and profits decline, a number of firms withdraw from the market in order to invest their resources in more profitable areas. Those remaining in the industry tend to reduce the number of product offerings. They withdraw from smaller market segments and marginal trade channels. The promotion budget is reduced. The price may also be reduced to halt the decline in demand.

Unless strong retention reasons exist, carrying a weak product is very costly to the firm. The cost of sustaining a weak product is not just the amount of uncovered overhead and profit. No financial accounting can adequately convey all the hidden costs: The weak product tends to consume a disproportionate amount of management's time; it often requires frequent price and inventory adjustment; it generally involves short production runs in spite of expensive setup times; it requires both advertising and sales-force attention that might better be diverted to making the "healthy" products more profitable; its very unfitness can cause customer misgivings and cast a shadow on the company's image. The biggest cost imposed by carrying weak products may well lie in the future. By not being eliminated at the proper time, these products delay the aggressive search for replacement products; they create a lopsided product mix, long on "yesterday's breadwinners" and short on "tomorrow's breadwinners"; they depress current profitability and weaken the company's foothold on the future.

A company faces a number of tasks and decisions to ensure the effective handling of its aging products.

Identifying the weak products. The first task is to establish a system that will identify those products that are in a declining stage. Six steps are involved:

1. A product review committee is appointed with the responsibility for developing a system for periodically reviewing weak products in the company's mix. This committee includes representatives from marketing, manufacturing, and the controller's office.
2. This committee meets and develops a set of objectives and procedures for reviewing weak products.
3. The controller's office fills out data for each product showing trends in market size, market share, prices, costs, and profits.
4. This information is run against a computer program that identifies the most dubious products. The criteria include the number of years of sales decline, market-share trends, gross profit margin, and return on investment.
5. Products put on the dubious list are then reported to those managers responsible for them. The managers fill out forms showing where they think sales and profits on dubious products will go with no change in the current marketing program and with their recommended changes in the current program.
6. The product review committee examines the product rating form for each dubious product and makes a recommendation to leave it alone, or to modify its marketing strategy, or to drop it.[17]

Determining marketing strategies. In the face of declining sales, some firms will abandon the market earlier than others. The firms that remain enjoy a temporary increase in sales as they pick up the customers of the withdrawing firms. Thus any particular firm faces the issue of whether it should be the one to stay in the market until the end. For example, Procter and Gamble decided to remain in the declining liquid-soap business until the end and made good profits as the others withdrew.

If it decides to stay in the market, the firm faces further strategic choices. The firm could adopt a *continuation strategy,* in which case it continues its past marketing strategy: same market segments, channels, pricing, and promotion. Or the firm could follow a *concentration strategy,* in which case it concentrates its resources only in the strongest markets and channels while phasing out its efforts elsewhere. Finally, it could follow a *harvesting strategy,* in which case it sharply reduces its expenses to increase its current profits, knowing that this will accelerate the rate of sales decline and ultimate demise of the product. In some situations the hard-core loyalty may remain strong enough to allow marketing the product at a greatly reduced level of promotion, and at the old or even a higher price, both of which mean good profits. An interesting example is afforded by Ipana toothpaste:

- Ipana toothpaste was marketed by Bristol-Myers until 1968, when it was abandoned in favor of promoting new brands. In early 1969, two Minnesota businessmen picked up the Ipana name, concocted a new formula, but packaged the product in tubes similar to those used by the former marketer. With no promotion, the petrified demand for Ipana turned out to be $250,000 in the first seven months of operation.[18]

Table 11-6
Product Life Cycle: Characteristics and Responses

	INTRODUCTION	GROWTH	MATURITY	DECLINE
CHARACTERISTICS				
SALES	Low	Fast growth	Slow growth	Decline
PROFITS	Negligible	Peak levels	Declining	Low or zero
CASH FLOW	Negative	Moderate	High	Low
CUSTOMERS	Innovative	Mass market	Mass market	Laggards
COMPETITORS	Few	Growing	Many rivals	Declining number
RESPONSES				
STRATEGIC FOCUS	Expand market	Market penetration	Defend share	Productivity
MKTG. EXPENDITURES	High	High (declining %)	Falling	Low
MKTG. EMPHASIS	Product awareness	Brand preference	Brand loyalty	Selective
DISTRIBUTION	Patchy	Intensive	Intensive	Selective
PRICE	High	Lower	Lowest	Rising
PRODUCT	Basic	Improved	Differentiated	Rationalized

Source: Peter Doyle, "The Realities of the Product Life Cycle," *Quarterly Review of Marketing,* Summer 1976, p. 5.

The drop decision. When a product has been singled out for elimination, the firm faces some further decisions. First, it has the option of selling or transferring the product to someone else or dropping it completely. Second, it has to decide whether the product should be dropped quickly or slowly. Third, it has to decide on the level of parts inventory and service to maintain to cover existing units.

The key characteristics of each of the four stages of the product life cycle are summarized in Table 11-6. In addition, the table summarizes the type of responses typically made by business organizations in each stage.[19]

■ summary

More and more organizations are recognizing the advantages of developing new products and services. Their current offerings are facing shortening life spans and must be replaced by newer products.

New-product development, however, can lead to costly failures. The risks of innovation are as great as the rewards. A large percentage of new products fail in the marketplace, and a still larger percentage have to be dropped before commercialization. The key to successful innovation lies in developing better organizational arrangements for handling new-product ideas and developing sound research and decision procedures at each stage of the new-product development process.

The new-product development process consists of eight stages: idea generation, idea screening, concept development and testing, marketing strategy and development, business analysis, product development, market testing, and commercialization. The purpose of each successive stage is to decide whether the idea should be further developed or dropped. The company seeks decision criteria for each stage that minimize the chances of poor ideas moving forward and good ideas being rejected. The last stage, commercialization, involves the introduction of the products that have passed the previous tests; it is benefited by marketing planning and strategy based on an understanding of the consumer-adoption process.

Every new product that is launched enters a product life cycle marked by a changing set of problems and opportunities. The sales history of the typical product is commonly thought to follow an S-shaped curve made up of four stages. The *introduction* stage is marked by slow growth and minimal profits as the product is pushed into distribution. If successful, the product enters a *growth* stage marked by rapid sales growth and increasing profits. During this stage the company attempts to improve the product, enter new market segments and distribution channels, and reduce its prices slightly. There follows a *maturity* stage in which sales growth slows down and profits stabilize. The company seeks innovative strategies to renew sales growth, including market, product, and marketing mix modification. Finally, the product enters a stage of *decline* in which little can be done to halt the deterioration of sales and profits. The company's task during this period is to identify the truly declining products, develop for each one a strategy of continuation, concentration, or harvesting, and finally phase out the product in a way that minimizes the hardship to company profits, employees, and customers.

questions for discussion

1. Discuss what you believe to be the two most important reasons why successful new-product development may be even more difficult in the future.
2. The guiding principle in the idea generation stage is to limit the number of new-product ideas that are proposed. Comment.
3. At what stage in the new-product development process is the consumer first contacted? Explain briefly.
4. Once the marketing strategy development stage is completed, the firm then begins actual product development. Comment.
5. What type of market testing would you suggest for the following new products? (a) Clairol hair-care product, (b) American Motors line of trucks, and (c) Samsonite plastic suitcases.
6. Is the first stage in the product life cycle just an extension of the final stage in the new-product development process?
7. Discuss the role and importance of promotional expenditures in each stage of the product life cycle.
8. Which one of the strategies discussed in the maturity stage did the following companies utilize? (a) Arm and Hammer baking soda, (b) State Farm insurance, (c) Ford Mustang.
9. There is nothing the manager can do once a product reaches the decline stage. Comment.

references

1. David S. Hopkins and Earl L. Bailey, "New Product Pressures," *Conference Board Record,* June 1971, pp. 16–24.
2. For a useful discussion of creativity techniques, see Sidney J. Parnes and Harold F. Harding, eds., *Source Book for Creative Thinking* (New York: Scribner's, 1962), p. 255.
3. See Alex F. Osborn, *Applied Imagination,* 3rd ed. (New York: Scribner's, 1963), pp. 286–87.
4. Ibid. p. 156.
5. Mark Hanan, "Corporate Growth through Venture Management," *Harvard Business Review,* January-February 1969, p. 44.
6. Refinements of this technique can be found in John T. O'Meara, Jr., "Selecting Profitable Products," *Harvard Business Review,* January-February 1961, pp. 83–89; and John S. Harris, "New Product Profile Chart," *Chemical and Engineering News,* April 1969, pp. 110–18.
7. The physical life expectancies (in years) of some major appliances are: freezer, 20.4; refrigerator, 15.2; electric range, 12.1; color TV, 12.0; and automatic washing machine, 10.8. See M. D. Ruffin, and K. J. Tippett, "Service Life Expectancy of Household Appliances: New Estimates from the USDA," *Home Economics Research Journal,* 3 (1975), 159–70.
8. See Edward M. Tauber, "Forecasting Sales Prior to Test Market," *Journal of Marketing,* January 1977, pp. 80–84. Also see Robert Blattberg and John

Golanty, "Tracker: An Early Test Market Forecasting and Diagnostic Model for New Product Planning," *Journal of Marketing Research,* May 1978, pp. 192–202.

9. See Roger A. Kerin, Michael G. Harvey, and James T. Rothe, "Cannibalism and New Product Development," *Business Horizons,* October 1978, pp. 25–31.
10. Philip Kotler and Gerald Zaltman, "Targeting Prospects for a New Product," *Journal of Advertising Research,* February 1976, pp. 7–20.
11. William E. Cox, Jr., "Product Life Cycles as Marketing Models," *Journal of Business,* October 1967, pp. 375–84.
12. Robert D. Buzzell, "Competitive Behavior and the Product Life Cycle," in *New Ideas for Successful Marketing,* ed. John S. Wright and Jac L. Goldstucker (Chicago: American Marketing Association, 1966), pp. 46–68, here p. 51.
13. Ibid., p. 51.
14. Ibid., p. 52.
15. The experience curve describes the rate at which costs fall as a function of accumulated production experience. See "Selling Business a Theory of Economics," *Business Week,* September 8, 1973, pp. 86–88.
16. John B. Stewart, "Functional Features in Product Strategy," *Harvard Business Review,* March-April 1959, pp. 65–78.
17. This system is spelled out in detail in the author's "Phasing Out Weak Products," *Harvard Business Review,* March-April 1965, pp. 107–118. Also see Paul W. Hamelman and Edward M. Mazze, "Improving Product Abandonment Decisions," *Journal of Marketing,* April 1972, pp. 20–26.
18. "Abandoned Trademark Turns a Tidy Profit for Two Minnesotans," *Wall Street Journal,* October 27, 1969, p. 1.
19. For further reading on the product life-cycle concept, see Theodore Levitt, "Exploit the Product Life Cycle," *Harvard Business Review,* November-December 1965, pp. 81–94; and Nariman K. Dhalla and Sonia Yuspeh, "Forget the Product Life Cycle Concept!" *Harvard Business Review,* January-February 1976, pp. 102–12.

PRODUCT, BRANDING, PACKAGING, AND SERVICE STRATEGY

When is a lipstick more than a lipstick? When an Avon lady sits in your living room and sells it to you. The world's largest seller of cosmetics, whose 1976 sales were well over one billion dollars, knows that when the customer buys lipstick, she is buying much more than lip color. No doubt a crucial element of Avon's success is a high-quality product. But why buy Avon and not Revlon, which also makes a high-quality product?

The Avon lady is one of the reasons. The Avon lady's call brings to the buyer a bundle of benefits: convenience, a break from routine, conversation, personal attention, help on how to look better, and even a friend. Avon's product is all of these things, and no other major cosmetics firm makes a similar offer.

Avon markets its wares through an army of 680,000 Avon representatives who call on over 85 million households in the U.S. and 17 other countries. The majority of the reps are married women with families who work part time to supplement their husband's incomes. They sell their products to other homemakers whose needs they understand. Suburban housewives in the upper-, lower- and middle-income brackets are the majority of Avon's customers.

Avon maintains strong morale among its sales force through sales training, sales meetings to demonstrate new products, and internal promotions such as prizes and contests. The sales force is organized into five levels. A general manager oversees two regional managers. Each regional manager supervises eight divisional managers, each of whom supervises 18 district managers. A district manager is responsible for recruiting, training, and supervising approximately 150 Avon representatives.

The typical Avon representative works 15 hours a week and earns about $1,400 a year, before expenses, on about $3,500 of sales. She gets a commission varying between 25 and 40 percent and also receives a flat fee of $7.50 for each new Avon representative she recruits. There is a great turnover of salespeople because many Avon representatives work only until they can accumulate enough cash to make some major purchases.

Avon's product line is highly diversified—thirteen hundred products, including jewelry and household items. If a customer says that she already uses Revlon lipstick, the representative can turn to jewelry or household items and make a sale. Another very strong support for purchase is the Avon money-back guarantee, which offers a full refund if the customer is not satisfied with the product.

Avon also supplies its salespeople with a handsome color catalog. The customer can browse this catalog, which lists a few hundred products. The company also runs specials throughout the year to stimulate sales and reduce inventories.

One of the most interesting features of the Avon product is the packaging. The packaging of the product is so important that one-third of Avon's items are repackaged every year. The packages are attractive and often double as reusable containers such as mugs or salt and pepper shakers. Many Avon containers have become collector's items.

Avon's salespeople provide continuous feedback to Avon's management about the satisfaction or complaints or needs of their customers. And when Avon tests new products, these products are first tested in clinics with Avon's own representatives.

Clearly a lipstick is more than a lipstick when Avon sells it.

□ Avon's exceptional success in the rough-and-tumble cosmetics world is based on developing an original and attractive product concept for its target market. Avon is not just selling cosmetics, but an augmented product that has won a worldwide market following. Marketers do not believe that "a product is a product is a product." Constructing the product concept is the most important first step in marketing mix planning.

When we examine "product," the first *P* of the marketing mix, we find that it is a complex multidimensional concept (see Figure 12-1). The offer of an organization to a target market consists of a *product mix* that is made up of product lines. Each *product line* contains product items. Each *product item* is a *physical product* plus *branding* plus *packaging* plus *services*. The organization has to make decisions and develop strategies for all of these components of product. The six components of product are discussed in the following sections of this chapter.

product mix decisions

Every organization has a product mix. We define *product mix* as follows:[1]

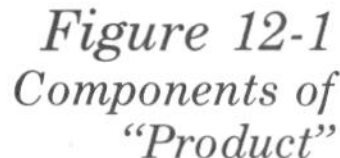

Figure 12-1
Components of "Product"

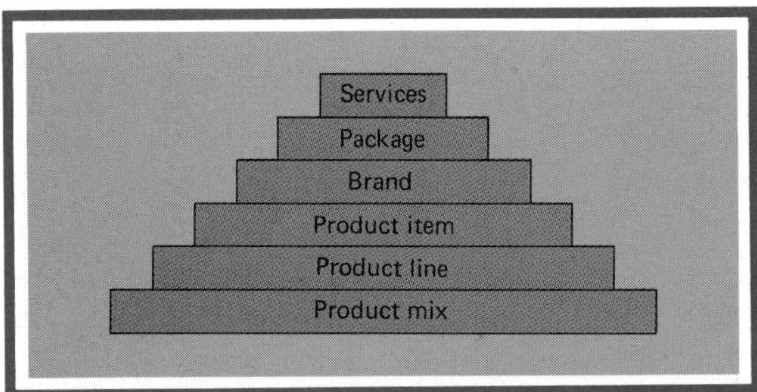

- **Product mix** (also called *product assortment*): the set of all product lines and items that a particular seller offers for sale to buyers.

This definition in turn requires defining *product lines* and *product items:*

- **Product line:** a group of products within a product mix that are closely related, either because they function in a similar manner, are sold to the same customer groups, are marketed through the same types of outlets, or fall within given price ranges.
- **Product item:** a distinct unit within a product line that is distinguishable by size, price, appearance, or some other attribute. The item is sometimes called a stock-keeping unit, product variant, or subvariant.

Avon's product mix consists of three major product lines: cosmetics, jewelry, and household items. Each of these product lines consists of several sublines: for example, cosmetics breaks down into lipstick, rouge, powder, and so on. Each line and subline has many individual items.

Altogether, Avon's product mix includes 1,300 items. A large supermarket handles as many as 10,000 items; a typical K-Mart stocks 15,000 items; and General Electric manufactures as many as 250,000 items.

A company's product mix can be described as having a certain width, depth, and consistency. These concepts are illustrated in Table 12-1 in connection with selected Procter and Gamble consumer products.

The width of P&G's product mix refers to how many different product lines are carried by the company. If P&G only carried the five lines shown, then its product mix width would be five. (In fact, P&G produces many additional lines, including mouthwashes, toilet tissue, disposable diapers, and so on.)

The depth (also called length) of P&G's product mix refers to the number of items or brands in total. If Table 12-1 represented P&G's entire product mix, its depth would be eighteen. We can also talk about the depth of an average product line at P&G. This is obtained by dividing the total depth (here 18) by the number of lines (here 5), or 3.6. That is, the average product line at P&G consists of 3.6 brands.

The consistency of the product mix refers to how closely related the various product lines are in end use, production requirements, distribution channels or in some other way. P&G's product lines are consistent insofar as they are consumer

Table 12-1
Product Mix Width and Product Line Depth Shown for Procter and Gamble Products

← Product mix width →

↑ Product line depth ↓

DETERGENTS	SOAP	SHAMPOO	TOOTHPASTE	POTATO CHIPS
Bold Bonus Cheer Dash Duz Gain Oxydol Tide	Camay Ivory Lava Safeguard Zest	Head & Shoulders Prell	Crest Gleam II	Pringles

goods and they go through the same distribution channels, namely, food stores. The lines are less consistent insofar as they present quite different benefits to buyers.

All three dimensions of the product mix have marketing strategy implications. By increasing the width of the product mix, the company can try to capitalize on its good reputation and skills in present markets. By increasing the depth of its product mix, the company can try to attract the patronage of buyers of widely differing tastes and needs. By increasing the consistency of its product mix, the company can try to acquire an unparalleled reputation in a particular area of endeavor.

product line decisions

Each product line of a company needs a marketing strategy. Many companies assign a specific person to manage each line and develop a marketing plan. This product line manager will have to make a number of tough decisions. Before making these decisions, he or she will analyze the sales, profits, and competition facing each item in the line.

The various items in a product line normally contribute different amounts to sales and profits. A frequently heard statement is that the top 20 percent of the items contribute 80 percent of the profits (known as the 20-80 rule). A product line manager should examine the percentage of total sales and profits contributed by each item in the line.

A product line with five items is illustrated in Figure 12-2. The first item contributes 50 percent of the product line's sales and 30 percent of its profits. The first two items contribute 80 percent of the product line's sales and 60 percent of its profits. If these two items were hit hard by a competitor, the product line's sales and profitability would decline drastically. These items must be carefully monitored and defended. On the other hand, the last product item only contributes 5 percent of the product line's sales and profits. The manager should think about dropping this slow seller from the line.

Figure 12-2
Product Item Contributions to a Product Line's Total Sales and Profits

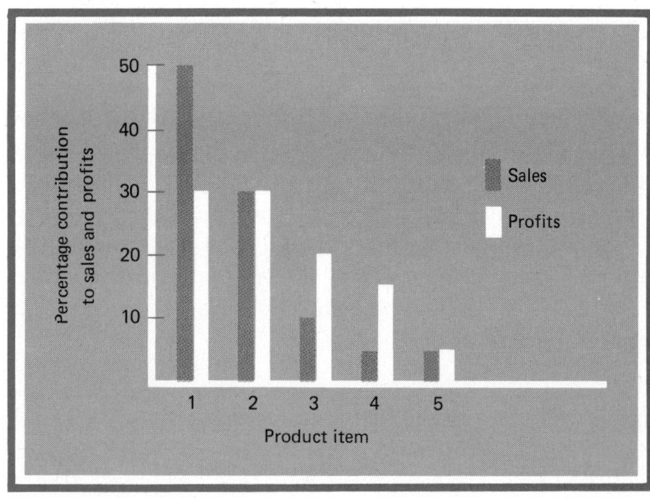

Figure 12-3
Product Map for a Paper Product Line

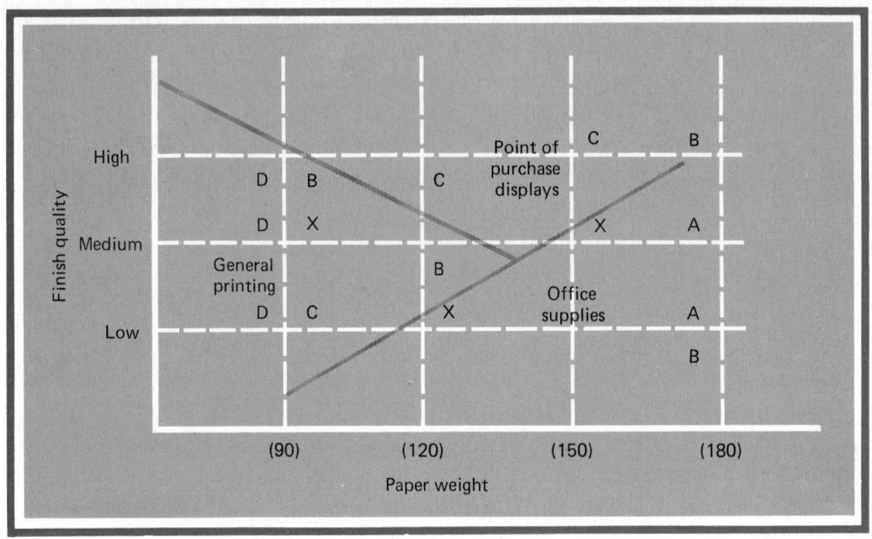

Source: Benson P. Shapiro, Industrial Product Policy: Managing the Existing Product Line (Cambridge, Mass: Marketing Science Institute, September 1977), p. 101.

The manager should also review how the product line is positioned against competitors' product lines. Consider a paper company with a product line consisting of paperboard.[2] Two of the major attributes of paperboard are the paper weight and the finish quality. Paper weights are usually offered at standard levels of 90, 120, 150, and 180. Finish quality is offered at three standard levels. The product map in Figure 12-3 shows the location of the various items in the product lines of four competitors, A, B, C, and D, as well as company X. For example, competitor A offers two product items in the extra-high-weight class with variable finish quality.

This product mapping of the product line is useful for designing marketing strategy. It shows which competitors' items are competing with each of company X's items. For example, company X's 90-weight/medium-quality paper competes with competitor D's paper. On the other hand, its 150-weight/medium-quality paper has no direct competitor. The map reveals locations for possible new-product items. For example, no manufacturer offers a 150-weight/low-quality paper.

Another benefit of the product map is that it is possible to identify market segments and even specific customers according to their paper-buying preferences. Figure 12-3 shows the types of paper, by weight and quality, preferred by the general printing industry, the point-of-purchase display industry, and the office supply industry, respectively. The map shows that company X is well positioned to serve the needs of the general printing industry, but on the borderline of serving the other two industries, unless it brings out more paper types that meet their needs.

Product Line Length

A major issue facing product line managers is what should be the length of the product line. The line is too short if the manager can increase profits by adding items; the line is too long if the manager can increase profits by dropping items.

The question of the optimal length of the product line goes back to the company's objectives. Companies that want to be positioned as full-line companies and/or are seeking high market share and market growth will tend to have longer lines. They are less concerned when some items fail to contribute an adequate amount of profit. Companies that are keen on high profitability, on the other hand, will carry shorter lines consisting of "cherry-picked" items.

Product lines have a strong tendency to lengthen over time, in an almost unplanned fashion. Several forces are at work:[3]

1. Excess manufacturing capacity puts pressure on the product line manager to dream up new items.
2. New items are easy to design because they are variations on the existing items.
3. Sales personnel and distributors put pressure on the product line manager for a more complete product line to satisfy their customers.
4. The product line manager sees opportunities for additional product items in specific products and markets.

As a result, the product line manager gradually adds items to the product line in the search for more volume and profits. But as items are added, the following costs go up: (1) designing and engineering costs, (2) inventory-carrying costs, (3) manufacturing changeover costs, (4) order-processing costs, (5) transportation costs, and (6) promotional costs to introduce the new items.

Eventually something happens to call a halt to the mushrooming of the product line. Manufacturing capacity may be in short supply and top management may refuse to let the line grow any further. Or the controller may raise questions about the line's profitability and a study may be undertaken to determine how to improve margins. In the latter case the study will show a large number of money-losing items, and they will be pruned from the line in one major effort to increase profitability. This pattern of gradual line growth followed by sudden line retrenchment will repeat itself many times, resulting in an undulating "life-cycle" pattern.

In managing a product line, management must make the following decisions: (1) Should the line be stretched? (2) Should the line be filled? (3) Should the line be modernized? and (4) Which item(s) in the line should be featured? These decisions are discussed in the following paragraphs.

Line-Stretching Decision

Every company product line stretches over a certain range of the total range offered by the industry as a whole. For example, Lincoln automobiles are located in the high range of the automobile market, Granadas in the middle range, and Pintos in the low range. *Line stretching* is the act of lengthening the company's product line beyond its current range. We will examine three types of line-stretching decisions: a downward stretch, an upward stretch, and a two-way stretch.

Downward stretch. Many companies establish themselves initially at the high end of a market and subsequently add products to the lower end. Beech Aircraft has historically produced expensive private aircraft, whereas Piper has designed less-expensive and smaller private planes. A few years ago Piper decided to design some larger planes. Beech responded by designing some smaller planes. A company may decide to stretch toward the lower end of the market for any of the following reasons:

1. The company is attacked at the high end and decides to counter-attack by invading the low end.
2. The company finds that slower growth is taking place at the high end and decides to stretch its product line downward.
3. The company originally entered the high end in order to establish an image of quality and intended all the time to roll downward.
4. The company adds a low-end unit to fill a hole that would otherwise attract a new competitor.

In making a downward stretch, the company faces some risks. First, the new low-end item might "cannibalize" higher-end items, leaving the company worse off. Consider the following:[4]

- Ford introduced the small-size Falcon in 1959 to attract economy-car buyers. But many of its buyers were those who would have bought the standard-size Ford. In effect, Ford reduced its own profit margin by failing to design its car for a really different segment than standard Ford buyers.

Second, the low-end item might provoke competitors to counteract by moving into the higher end. Third, the company's dealers may not be willing or able to handle the lower-end products.

Upward stretch. Companies that are positioned at the low end of the market may want to enter the higher end of the market for either of the following reasons:

1. The company may be attracted by a faster growth rate or higher margins at the upper end of the market.
2. The company may want to position itself as a full-line manufacturer.

An upward stretch decision is accompanied by several risks. The higher-end competitors may not only be well entrenched but the move may tempt them to enter the lower end of the market. Prospective customers may not believe that the company has the wherewithal to produce quality products for the higher end of the market. Finally, the company's sales representatives and distributors may not have the talent or training to serve the higher end of the market, thus requiring intensive training or new sales reps and distributors.

Two-way stretch. Companies that are strongly positioned in the midrange of a market may decide to go after market dominance by stretching their line in both directions. Texas Instruments' strategy in the electronic hand calculator market provides an excellent illustration of a two-way stretch. Before Texas Instruments (TI) entered this market, the market was dominated primarily by Bowmar at the low-price/low-quality end and Hewlett-Packard at the high-price/high-quality end (see Figure 12-4). TI introduced its first calculators in the medium-price/medium-quality end of the market. Gradually it added more machines at

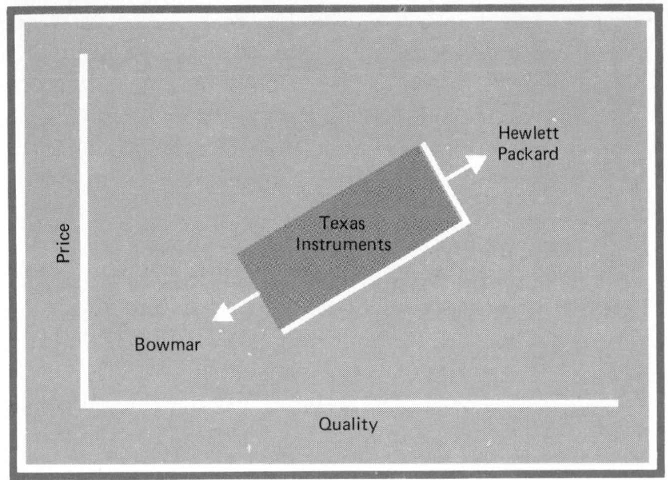

Figure 12-4
Two-Way Product Line Stretch Illustrated in the Hand Calculator Market

each end. It offered better calculators at the same price as, or at lower prices than Bowmar, ultimately destroying it; and it designed high-quality calculators selling at a much lower price than Hewlett-Packard calculators, taking away a good share of HP's sales at the higher end. This two-way stretch won TI the indisputable leadership position in the hand calculator market.

Line-Filling Decision

A product line can also be lengthened by adding more items within the present range of the line. There are five main motives for line filling: (1) reaching for incremental profits, (2) trying to satisfy dealers who complain about lost sales because of missing items in the line, (3) trying to utilize excess capacity during slow times, (4) trying to be the leading full-line house, and (5) trying to keep the competitors from finding holes and getting in.

Line filling can be overdone, resulting in cannibalization and customer confusion. The company should strive to make each item differentiable in the consumer's mind. Each item should possess a *just noticeable difference.* According to Weber's law, customers are more attuned to relative than to absolute differences.[5] They will perceive the difference between boards two and three feet long and boards twenty and thirty feet long, but not boards twenty-nine and thirty feet long. The company should make sure that product item differences within its line are at least as large as just noticeable differences.

Line Modernization Decision

In some cases the product line is adequate in length but needs to be modernized. For example, a company's line of machine tools may have a 1920s look and lose out to better-styled competitors' lines.

When a company recognizes that its line needs modernization, the issue is whether to overhaul the line piecemeal or in one fell swoop. A piecemeal approach allows the company to test how customers and dealers feel about the new style before committing the whole line to that style. Furthermore, piecemeal modernization poses less of a drain on the company's cash flow. A major disadvantage of piecemeal modernization is that it allows competitors to see what the company is doing and gives them breathing time to redesign their own line.

Line-Featuring Decision

The product line manager typically selects one or a few items for special featuring to draw attention to the line. Sometimes managers promote items ("promotional models") at the low end of the line to serve as "traffic builders." Thus Sears will announce a special low-priced sewing machine to bring people into the sewing machine department. Recently Rolls Royce announced an economy model selling for only $49,000—in contrast to its high-end model selling for $108,000—to bring people into its showrooms. Once the customers arrive, some salespeople will try to influence them to buy at the higher end of the line.

At other times, managers will feature a high-end item to give the product line "class." Stetson promotes a man's hat selling for $150, which few people buy but which acts as a "flagship" to enhance the whole line.

There are other decisions facing product line managers in addition to those mentioned. The product line managers have to set prices on the various items in the line (see Chapter 13, pp. 416–17). They have to be good at pruning weaker items in the product line (see Chapter 11, pp. 353–55). And they have to be skilled in planning and managing each individual product in the line. We now turn to the marketing of the individual product item.

product item decisions

A pair of skis, a haircut, a nightclub act featuring Woody Allen, and a vacation in Hawaii are all examples of individual product items, or products for short. We define *product* as follows:

- A **product** is anything that can be offered to a market for attention, acquisition, use, or consumption that might satisfy a need. It includes physical objects, services, persons, places, organizations, and ideas. Other names for a product would be *the offer, value package,* or *benefit bundle.*

Core, Tangible, and Augmented Product

In developing a product to offer to a market, the product planner should distinguish three levels of the concept of a product. At the most fundamental level is the *core product,* which answers the question, What is the buyer really buying? Every product is really the packaging of a problem-solving service. The woman purchasing lipstick from Avon is not simply buying lip color; she is buying hope. Avon's competitor, Charles Revson of Revlon, Inc., recognized this early: "In the factory, we make cosmetics; in the store we sell hope." Theodore Levitt pointed out that "purchasing agents do not buy quarter-inch drills; they buy quarter-inch holes." And supersalesman Elmer Wheeler would say: "Don't sell the steak—sell the sizzle." The marketer's job is to uncover the need hiding under every product and to sell *benefits,* not *features.* The core product stands at the center of the total product, as illustrated in Figure 12-5.

The product planner has to make the core product tangible to the buyer. At this level, it is called the *tangible product.* Lipsticks, computers, educational seminars, political candidates, are all tangible products. If it is a physical object, it may have up to five characteristics: a *quality level, features, styling,* a *brand name,* and *packaging.* If it is a service, it may have some or all of these characteristics in an analogous manner.

Figure 12-5
Three Levels of Product

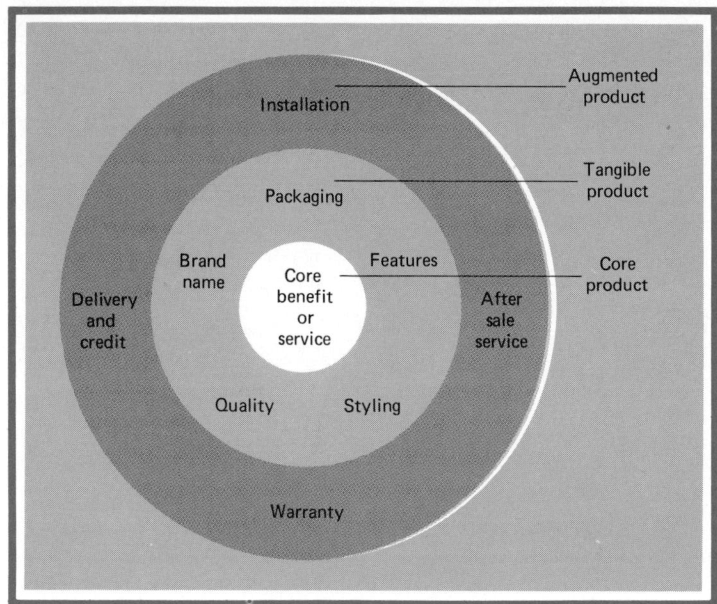

Finally, the product planner has to decide on additional services and benefits that will be offered along with the tangible product. They make up the *augmented product.* We saw how Avon's augmented product—personal attention, delivery, money-back guarantee, and so on—has been a key factor in Avon's success. IBM is another super example of a company whose success is traceable to its skillful augmentation of its tangible product—the computer. While the other computer companies were busy telling potential buyers about the features of their computers, IBM recognized that the customer was actually interested in buying solutions, not hardware. What customers wanted was instruction, canned software programs, programming services, quick repairs, guarantees, and so on. IBM sold a system, not just a computer.[6]

The augmented product notion leads the seller to look at the buyer's total *consumption system:* "The way a purchaser of a product performs the total task of whatever it is that he or she is trying to accomplish when using the product."[7] Doing this, the seller should be able to recognize many opportunities for augmenting its product offer in a competitively effective way. According to Levitt:

- The *new competition* is not between what companies produce in their factories, but between *what they add to their factory output in the form of packaging, services, advertising, customer advice, financing, delivery arrangements, warehousing, and other things that people value.*[8]

The firm that develops the right augmented product will thrive on this competition.

Classification of Goods

In trying to develop marketing strategies for individual products, marketers have looked at product characteristics and have classified products in ways that would

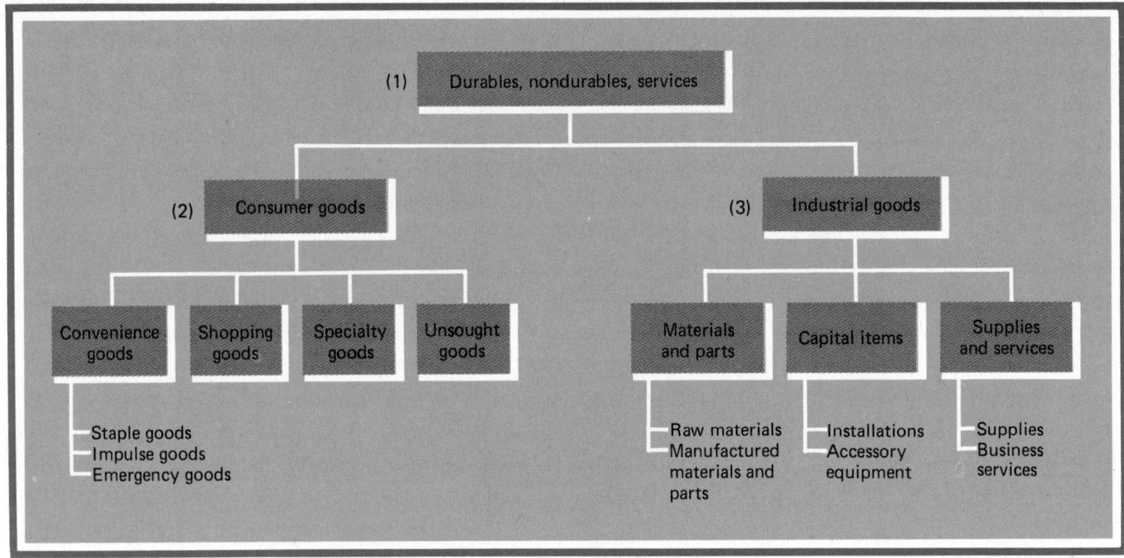

Figure 12-6 *A Comprehensive Classification of Goods*

suggest appropriate strategies. A comprehensive classification of goods is shown in Figure 12-6. We will discuss the three major breakdowns shown in the figure.

Durable goods, nondurable goods, and services. Marketers have suggested that marketing strategies would have some relation to the durability and tangibility of a good. On this basis, three types of products can be distinguished:[9]

- **Nondurable goods.** *Nondurable goods are tangible goods that normally are consumed in one or a few uses.* Examples would include beer and soap. Since these goods are consumed fast and purchased frequently, the appropriate strategy is to make them available in many locations, charge only a small markup, and use a lot of advertising to induce trial and provide postpurchase reinforcement.
- **Durable goods.** *Durable goods are tangible goods that normally survive many uses.* Examples would include refrigerators and clothing. Durable products are likely to need more personal selling and service, command a higher margin, and require more seller guarantees.
- **Services.** *Services are activities, benefits, or satisfactions that are offered for sale.* Examples would include haircuts and repairs. Services are intangible, inseparable, variable, and perishable. As a result, they are likely to require more quality control, supplier credibility, and adaptability. Because of the growing importance of services in our society, their marketing will be examined in Chapter 20, pp. 623–30.

Consumer goods. Consumers buy a vast number of goods. A useful way to classify these goods is on the basis of *consumer shopping habits* because they have implications for marketing strategy. We can distinguish among convenience, shopping, specialty, and unsought goods.[10]

- **Convenience goods.** *Convenience goods are those consumer's goods that the customer usually purchases frequently, immediately, and with the minimum of effort in comparison and buying.* Examples would include tobacco products, soap, and newspapers.

Convenience goods can be further subdivided into staples, impulse goods, and emergency goods. *Staples* are goods purchased on a regular basis, and brand loyalty is a factor that helps the customer choose quickly. For example, for one buyer the routinely purchased soft drink is Coke, the aspirin is Bayer, the cracker is Ritz. The *impulse good* is purchased without any planning or search effort. Therefore the good has to be available in many places because once the current need is satisfied, the consumer does not normally look for the product. Thus candy bars and magazines are placed next to cash register checkouts because shoppers may not have thought of buying them. The *emergency good* is purchased when a need is urgent—umbrellas during a rainstorm, boots and shovels during the first winter snowstorm. Manufacturers of emergency goods will try to place them in many outlets so they will not lose the sale when the customer needs these goods.

- **Shopping goods.** *Shopping goods are goods that the customer, in the process of selection and purchase, characteristically compares on such bases as suitability, quality, price, and style.* Examples would include furniture, clothing, used cars, and major appliances.

Shopping goods can be divided into homogeneous goods and heterogeneous goods. The buyer sees homogeneous shopping goods as being essentially similar in quality but different enough in price to justify shopping comparisons. Thus consumers might shop for the best buy in a washing machine or a toaster, assuming that the various brands are essentially similar. Therefore the seller has to be prepared to "talk price" to the buyer. But in shopping for clothing, furniture, and more heterogeneous goods, other qualities of the product may be more important to the consumer than the price. If the buyer wants a pin-striped suit, the cut, fit, and look are likely to be more important than small price differences. The seller of heterogeneous shopping goods must therefore carry a good assortment to satisfy individual tastes and must have well-trained sales personnel who can meet the customer's need for information and advice.

- **Specialty goods.** *Specialty goods are goods with unique characteristics and/or brand identification for which a significant group of buyers are habitually willing to make a special purchasing effort.*

Examples would include specific brands and types of fancy goods, cars, hi-fi components, photographic equipment, and men's suits. For example, a Mercedes would be a specialty good to those buyers who want it and are willing to travel to the only Mercedes dealer, who might be miles away. Specialty goods do not involve the buyer's making shopping comparisons; the buyer only invests shopping time to reach the outlets carrying these goods. The seller of a specialty good does not necessarily have to be established in a convenient location; however, it is important that prospective buyers receive information as to this location.

- **Unsought goods.** *Unsought goods are goods the consumer either does not know about or knows about but does not have an interest in purchasing.* New products such as smoke detectors and food processors are unsought goods until the consumer is made aware of them through advertising. The classic examples of known but unsought goods are life insurance, cemetery plots, gravestones, and encyclopedias.

By their very nature, unsought goods require a lot of marketing effort in the form of advertising and personal selling. Some of the most important modern techniques in personal selling have developed out of the challenge of selling unsought goods.

Industrial goods. The industrial market buys a vast variety of goods and services. An effective industrial-goods classification would suggest appropriate marketing strategies in the industrial market. It is not too useful to classify industrial goods according to the *shopping habits of the producers,* as we did in consumer-goods classification, because producers do not shop in the same sense. More often suppliers seek them out. Industrial goods are more usefully classified in terms of *how they enter the production process and their relative costliness.* We can distinguish between materials and parts, capital items, and supplies and services.

- **Materials and parts.** *Materials and parts are those industrial goods that enter the manufacturer's product completely.* They fall into two classes: raw materials and manufactured materials and parts.

Raw materials are exemplified by *farm products* (e.g., wheat, cotton, livestock, fruits and vegetables) and *natural products* (e.g., fish, lumber, crude petroleum, iron ore). Each is marketed somewhat differently. *Farm products* are supplied by many small producers and require the development of marketing intermediaries to provide assembly, grading, storage, transportation, and selling services. The supply of farm products is somewhat expandable in the long run, but not in the short run. Farm products' perishable and seasonal nature gives rise to special marketing practices. Their homogeneity results in relatively little advertising and promotional activity.

Natural products are highly limited in supply. They usually have great bulk and low unit value and require substantial transportation to move them from producer to user. There are fewer and larger producers, who tend to market them directly to industrial users. Because of user dependency of these materials, long-term supply contracts are common. The homogeneity of natural materials limits the amount of demand creation activity. Price is the major factor in supplier selection.

Manufactured materials and parts are exemplified by *component materials* (e.g., iron, yarn, cement, wires) and *component parts* (e.g., small motors, tires, castings). *Component materials* are usually fabricated further—for example, pig iron going into steel and yarn being woven into cloth. The standardized nature of component materials usually means that price and vendor reliability are the most important purchase factors. *Component parts* enter the finished product completely with no further change in form, as when small motors are put into vacuum cleaners and tires are added on automobiles. Most manufactured materials and parts are sold directly by their producers to industrial users, with orders often placed a year or more in advance. Price and service are the major marketing considerations, and branding and advertising tend to be unimportant.

- **Capital items** *Capital items are those industrial goods that enter the finished product partly.* They include two groups: installations and accessory equipment.

Installations consist of *buildings* (e.g., factories and offices) and *fixed equipment* (e.g., generators, drill presses, computers, elevators). Installations represent major purchases and determine the scale of operation of the firm. They are usually sold directly by the producer to the industrial user, with the typical sale being large and preceded by a long negotiation period. A top-notch sales force is needed, which often includes sales engineers. The sellers have to be willing to design to specification and to supply postsale services. Advertising is used but is much less important than personal selling.

Accessory equipment comprises *portable factory equipment and tools* (e.g., hand tools, lift trucks) and *office equipment* (e.g., typewriters, desks). These types of equipment do not become part of the finished product, nor do they influence the scale of production. They simply aid in the production process. They have a shorter life than installations but a longer life than operating supplies. Although some manufacturers of accessory equipment may sell direct, more often they use middlemen because the market is geographically dispersed, the buyers are numerous, and the orders are small. Quality, features, price, and service are major considerations in vendor selection. The sales force tends to be more important than advertising, although the latter can be used effectively.

- **Supplies and Services** *Supplies and services are items that do not enter the finished product at all.* Supplies are of two kinds: *operating supplies* (e.g., lubricants, coal, typing paper, pencils) and maintenance and repair items (paint, nails, brooms).

Supplies are the equivalent of convenience goods in the industrial field because they are usually purchased with a minimum effort on a straight rebuy basis. They are normally marketed through intermediaries because of the great number of customers, their geographical dispersion, and the low unit value of these goods. Price and service are important considerations because supplies are quite standardized and brand insistence is not high.

Business services include *maintenance and repair services* (e.g., window cleaning, typewriter repair) and *business advisory services* (e.g., legal, management consulting, advertising). Maintenance and repair services are usually supplied under contract. Maintenance services are often provided by small producers, and repair services are often available from the manufacturers of the original equipment. Business advisory services are normally new task-buying situations, and the industrial buyer will choose the business service supplier on the basis of the supplier's reputation and personnel.

The preceding discussion of product classifications makes it clear that a product's characteristics will have a major influence on the marketing strategy. At the same time, marketing strategy will also depend on such factors as the product's stage of the life cycle, the number of competitors, the degree of market segmentation, and the condition of the economy.

brand decisions

In developing a marketing strategy for individual products, the seller has to confront the issue of branding. Branding can add value to a product and is therefore an intimate aspect of product strategy.

First, we should become familiar with the language of branding. Here are some key definitions:[11]

- **Brand:** a name, term, sign, symbol, or design, or a combination of them which is intended to identify the goods or services of one seller or group of sellers and to differentiate them from those of competitors.
- **Brand name:** that part of a brand which can be vocalized—the utterable. Examples are Avon, Chevrolet, Disneyland, American Express, and UCLA.
- **Brand mark:** that part of a brand which can be recognized but is not utterable, such as a symbol, design, or distinctive coloring or lettering. Examples are the Playboy bunny and the Metro-Goldwyn-Mayer lion.
- **Trademark:** a brand or part of a brand that is given legal protection because it is capable of exclusive appropriation. A trademark protects the seller's exclusive rights to use the brand name and/or brand mark.
- **Copyright:** the exclusive legal right to reproduce, publish, and sell the matter and form of a literary, musical, or artistic work.

Branding poses a number of challenging decisions to the marketer. The key decisions are described in Figure 12-7 and are discussed in the following paragraphs.

Branding Decision

The first decision is whether the company or its dealers should even put a brand name on specific products. Historically, most products went unbranded. Producers and middlemen sold their goods directly out of barrels, bins, and cases, without any supplier identification. The earliest signs of branding were in the efforts of medieval guilds to require craftsmen to put trade marks on their products to protect the tradesmen and to protect the consumer against inferior quality by allowing producers to be traced. In the high arts, too, branding began with great artists and not-so-great artists signing their names to their works.

In the United States the earliest brand promoters were the patent medicine manufacturers. But branding's real growth occurred after the Civil War with the growth of national firms and national advertising media. Some of the early brands are still with us, such as Borden's Condensed Milk, Quaker Oats, Vaseline, and Ivory Soap.

The growth of brand names has been so dramatic that today, in the United States, hardly anything is sold unbranded. Salt is packaged in distinctive manufacturers' containers, oranges are stamped with growers' names, common nuts and bolts are packaged in cellophane with a distributor's label, and various parts of an automobile—spark plugs, tires, filters—bear visible brand names different from the name of the automobile. Even chicken has recently been branded successfully:[12]

- Frank Perdue of Perdue Farms, Salisbury, Maryland, has converted a basic agricultural product into a brand-name purchase. Consumers in New York, New Jersey, Pennsylvania, Connecticut, Massachusetts, and elsewhere on the East

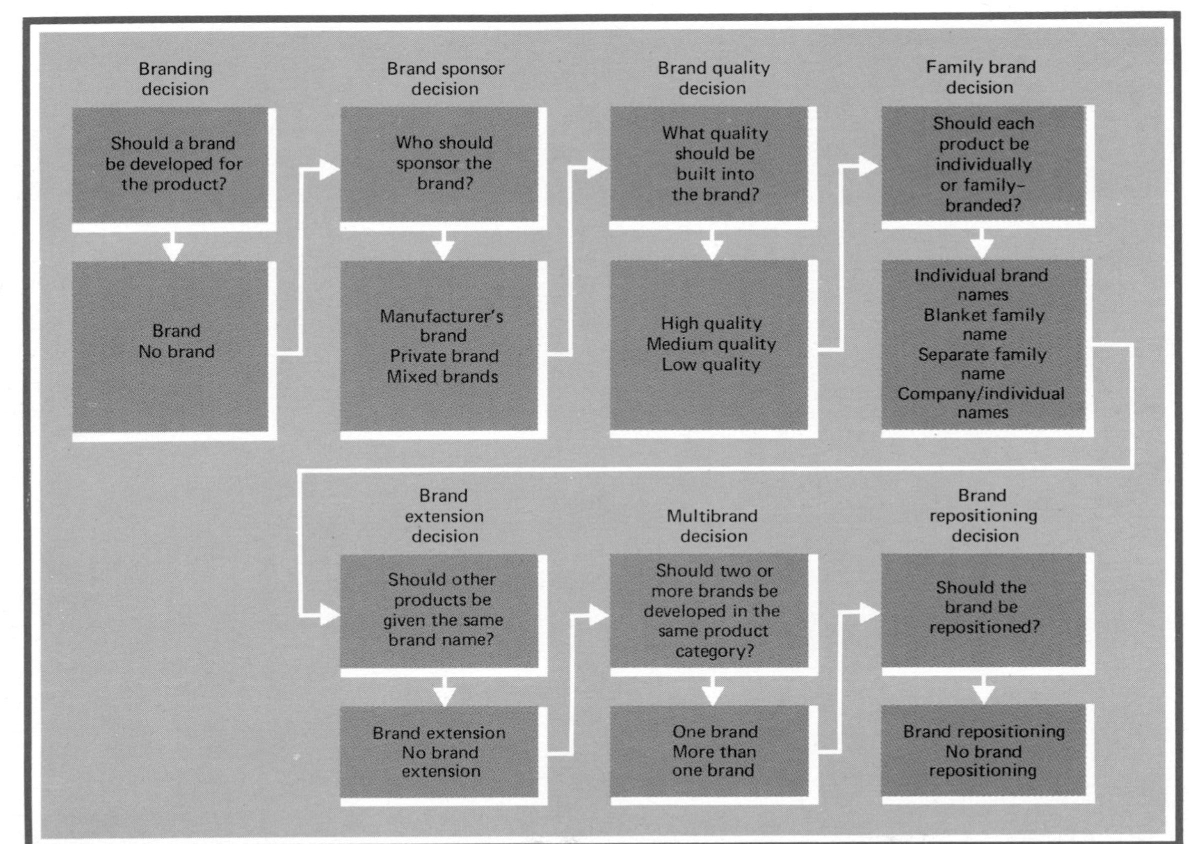

Figure 12-7 *An Overview of Branding Decisions*

Coast ask for a Perdue-brand chicken. Perdue spends about $1 million annually on television and radio advertising where he gets on the air describing the merits of the chickens that he sells. The theme is "It takes a tough man to make a tender chicken," and he offers a money-back guarantee to dissatisfied customers.

At the same time, there has been some indication of a return to "no branding" of certain staple consumer goods and pharmaceuticals. These "generics" are packaged plainly with no manufacturer identification (see Exhibit 12-1). The obvious intent of generics is to bring down the cost to the consumer by saving on packaging and advertising. Thus the issue of branding versus no branding is very much alive today.

This raises the question of why have branding in the first place. Who benefits? How do they benefit? At what cost? We have to look at branding from the buyer's viewpoint, the seller's viewpoint, and society's viewpoint.

Buyer's viewpoint. It is commonly thought that branding is an invention of sellers to serve primarily their own interests. The truth is that buyers in most cases want branding because it is an important information source and creates a number of buyer benefits.

First, a brand tells the buyer something about the product's quality. Suppose a buyer goes shopping for a television set and sees several different sets, none of them carrying brand names. The buyer could tell very little about the quality and reliability of the different sets. However, if they carried such names as Zenith, Sony, Sears, and Sanyo, they would conjure up different images of the probable quality and reliability of the various sets. In the Soviet Union, where television sets are produced in different factories and not branded, Soviet consumers look for identification marks on the set indicating which factories they came from because the factories have different reputations for reliability. The Soviet consumer would welcome branding as a way to determine the quality of different products.

Second, brand names contribute to increased shopping efficiency. Imagine the homemaker going into a supermarket and finding thousands of unlabeled products. The homemaker would probably want to physically touch, taste, or smell many of the products to be sure of their quality, which could vary from week to week. If the homemaker asked another member of the family to do the shopping, she would have to communicate the quality desired in each product. It is far more efficient to communicate in brand names than in general product descriptions.

Third, brand names help call consumers' attention to new products that might benefit them. They become the basis upon which a whole story can be built about the new product and its special qualities.

Seller's viewpoint. But why should sellers resort to branding when it clearly involves a cost—packaging, labeling, legal protection—and a risk if the product should prove unsatisfying to the user? It turns out that branding gives the seller several advantages.

First, the seller's brand name makes it easier for the seller to handle orders and track down problems. Thus Anheuser-Busch receives an order from a retailer for a hundred cases of Michelob eight-ounce beer instead of an order for "some of your better beer." Furthermore, the seller finds it easier to trace the order if it is misshipped or to find out why the beer was rancid if consumers complain.

Second, the seller's brand name and trademark give it legal protection when there are unique product features, which would otherwise be easy to copy if the product went unbranded.

Third, branding gives the seller the opportunity to attract a loyal set of customers whose regular purchases give it more sales stability and long-run profit. This is accomplished by supporting the brand with good product quality and promotion. The degree to which the brand name works to give the seller more profit depends on the seller's success in moving customers through the states of *brand recognition, brand preference,* and ultimately *brand insistence.*

Society's viewpoint. The question arises as to whether branding benefits the society as a whole, and how much branding is necessary or desirable in particular product categories. Those who favor branding offer the following arguments:

1. Branding leads to higher and more consistent product quality. A brand essentially makes a promise to consumers about delivering certain satisfactions. The seller cannot easily tamper with the brand's quality or be careless about quality control because the consumers have developed certain expectations. Branding also makes it advantageous for some sellers to go after the high-quality end of the market.
2. Branding increases the rate of innovation in society. Without branding, producers would not have an incentive to look for new features that could be protected against imitating competitors. Branding gives producers an incentive to seek distinctive product features, and this results in much more product variety and choice for consumers.
3. Branding increases shopper efficiency, since it provides much more information about the product and where to buy it.

Others criticize branding as going too far in this society. Their criticisms include the following:

1. Branding leads to false and unnecessary differentiation of goods, especially in homogeneous product categories.
2. Branding leads to higher consumer prices, since the brands have to be supported by a lot of advertising, packaging, and other costs which are ultimately passed on to consumers.
3. Branding increases the status consciousness of people who buy certain brands to "impress" other people.

Overall, it is probably safe to say that branding adds net value to consumers and society *and* it can be overdone in some categories and lead to higher costs. The societal issues posed by branding will be examined in Chapter 21, pp. 650–51.

Brand Sponsor Decision

After the branding decision has been made, the manufacturer has three options with respect to brand sponsorship. The product may be launched as a *manufacturer's brand* (also called a national brand) where the manufacturer is recognized as the producer of the product. Or the manufacturer may sell the product in bulk to middlemen who put on a *private brand* (also called middlemen brand, dis-

EXHIBIT 12-1

A FOOD CHAIN ADDS A GENERIC LINE OF ITEMS

In late 1978 Dominick's Finer Foods, a large Chicago-based supermarket chain, introduced a forty-item "generic" line. Generics are unbranded, plainly packaged, less-expensive versions of common products purchased in supermarkets, such as spaghetti, paper towels, and peaches. They offer standard quality at a price that may be as much as 30 percent lower than that of nationally advertised brands and 15 percent lower than that of private labels.

A year earlier the Jewel Food Stores, another large Chicago-based chain, had introduced a forty-item generic line, which has now been expanded to 140 generics and accounts for approximately 4 percent of Jewel's sales. Jewel's success with generics apparently forced Dominick's hand.

How far generics will penetrate the U.S. shopper's breadbasket is still an open question. Their initial push occurred in Europe where the large French food chain, Carrefour, introduced them in 1976, and where they now account for 40 percent of the chain's total volume. While no one expects the same penetration in the United States, more than ten thousand out of thirty-five thousand U.S. stores are now carrying generic items.

There is no doubt that the price savings of generics have pocketbook appeal to American consumers in this age of high inflation. A Nielsen survey indicated that 59 percent of shoppers are aware of generic products, and 44 percent have purchased them at least once. Four out of five shoppers believe that the lower prices result from the reduced advertising expenditures and the simple packaging. Only one out of five shoppers believes that the lower cost is related to lower quality. Yet lower quality is one of the major factors. For example, the paper towels may be less absorbent and the detergent may lack perfume. Yet consumers are impressed by the savings, and generics such as peanut butter, preserves, canned vegetables, and tomato products have especially won their acceptance.

What is the appeal of generics to the retailers? Generics could be seen as cutting into their profits on higher-priced brands. But in many cases retailers have reported their profit rate as being the same or higher for generics, in spite of their lower prices. Furthermore, many chains have added generics as a way of luring customers and in the hope that these customers will also buy more expensive products once they are in the store.

The real group threatened by generics consists of the national brand companies, not so much in connection with their strong brands as with their weaker brands. Why pay 30 percent more for a branded item when its quality is not noticeably different from that of its generic cousin?

Sources: Prepared by the author from miscellaneous sources, including "Generic Groceries Keep Adding Market Share," *Marketing News,* February 23, 1979, p. 16; George Lazarus, "Generic Label Carving Place on Grocery Shelf," *Chicago Tribune,* May 9, 1979, Business section.

tributor brand, or dealer brand). Or the manufacturer may decide to produce some output under its own name and some output that is sold under private labels. For example, Kellogg's, International Harvester, and IBM produce virtually all of their output under their own brand names. Warwick Electronics produces virtually all of its output under various distributors' names. Whirlpool produces output both under its own name and under distributors' names.

Manufacturers' brands tend to dominate the American scene. Consider such well-known brands as Campbell's soup and Heinz ketchup. In recent times, however, large retailers and wholesalers have turned to developing their own brands. In the tire market, the private-label tires of Sears and J. C. Penney are as well known today as are the manufacturers' brands of Goodyear, Goodrich, and Firestone. Sears as a retailer has created several brand names that command brand preference and even brand insistence—over 90 percent of Sears's products are sold under its own labels. The A&P has created different grade private labels for its canned goods, and they account for over 25 percent of its sales. More and more department stores, service stations, clothiers, drugstores, and appliance dealers are responding to these advantages by launching their own brands.

Why do middlemen bother with sponsoring their own brands? They have to hunt down qualified suppliers to make sure that they deliver the specified quality. They have to order in fairly large quantities, tie up their capital in inventories, and be exposed to the risks of fire, theft, obsolescence, and deterioration. They have to do some promotion of the private label; in fact, Sears spent $83 million on major media promotion in 1975. They have to take the chance that if their private-label product is not good, the customer will develop a negative image about their other products.

In spite of these possible disadvantages, middlemen are turning to private brands because they can make money on them. They can often find manufacturers who have excess capacity and will produce the private label at a low cost. Other costs, such as advertising and physical distribution, may also be low. This means that the private brander is able to charge a lower price and often make a higher profit margin. Furthermore, the private brander may be able to develop brand preference or brand insistence, and this will draw traffic into its stores for brands that other retailers cannot duplicate.

The competition between manufacturers' and middlemen's brands is called *the battle of the brands.* In this confrontation, middlemen have many advantages. Retail shelf space is scarce, and many manufacturers, especially newer and smaller ones, cannot introduce products into distribution under their own name. Middlemen take special care to maintain the quality of their brands, thus building consumers' confidence. Many buyers know that the private-label brand is often manufactured by one of the larger manufacturers anyway. Middlemen's brands are often priced lower than comparable manufacturers' brands, thus appealing to budget-conscious shoppers, especially in times of inflation. Middlemen give more prominent display to their own brands and make sure they are better stocked. For these and other reasons, the former dominance of the manufacturers' brands is weakening. Indeed, some marketing commentators predict that middlemen's brands will eventually knock out all but the strongest manufacturers' brands.

Manufacturers of national brands are in a very trying situation. Their instinct is to spend a lot of money on consumer-directed advertising and promotion to maintain strong brand preference. Their price has to be somewhat higher to cover this promotion. At the same time, the mass distributors exert considerable pressure on them to put more of their promotional money toward trade allowances and deals if they want adequate shelf space. Once manufacturers start giving in, they have less to spend on consumer promotion and their brand leadership starts slipping. This is the national brand manufacturers' dilemma.[13]

Brand Quality Decision

In developing a brand, the manufacturer has to establish the brand's quality level and other attributes that will support the brand's targeted position in the marketplace. Quality is one of the major positioning tools of the marketer. *Quality* stands for *the rated ability of the brand to perform its functions.* It is an overall measure reflecting the product's durability, reliability, precision, ease of operation and repair, and other valued attributes. Some of these attributes can be measured objectively. From a marketing point of view, quality should be measured in terms of buyers' perceptions of quality.

Most brands are established initially at one of four quality levels: low, average, high, and superior. In one study investigators found that profitability rose with brand quality (see the curve in Figure 12-8A).[14] This suggests that a company should aim at delivering high quality. Superior quality increases profitability only slightly over high quality, whereas inferior quality hurts profitability substantially. At the same time, if all competitors tried to deliver high quality, this would not be as effective. Quality must be chosen with a target market segment in mind.

Another issue is how a company should manage brand quality through time. The three options are illustrated in Figure 12-8B. The first option, where the manufacturer invests in continuous research and development to improve the product, usually produces the highest return and market share. Procter and Gamble is a major practitioner of product improvement strategy, which, combined with the high initial product quality, helps explain its leading position in many markets. The second option is to maintain product quality. Many companies leave their quality unaltered after its initial formulation unless glaring faults or opportunities occur. The third option is to reduce product quality through time. A few companies will adulterate their products quite deliberately as a way to increase profits, at least in the short run.

Figure 12-8
Brand Quality Strategies and Profitability

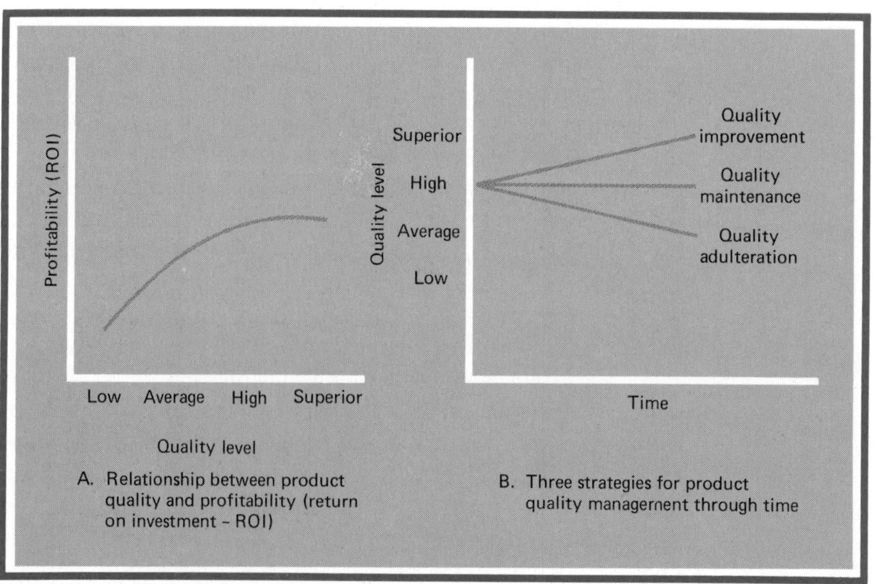

Family Brand Decision

Manufacturers who choose to produce most of their output under their own name still face several choices. At least four brand-name strategies can be distinguished:

1. *Individual brand names.* This policy is followed by such companies as Procter and Gamble (Tide, Bold, Dash, Cheer, Gain, Oxydol, Duz) and Genesco, Inc. (Jarman, Mademoiselle, Johnson & Murphy, and Cover Girl).
2. *A blanket family name for all products.* This policy is followed by such companies as Heinz and General Electric.
3. *Separate family names for all products.* This policy is followed by Sears (Kenmore for appliances, Kerrybrook for women's clothing, and Homart for major home installations).
4. *Company trade name combined with individual product names.* This policy is followed by Kellogg's (Kellogg's Rice Krispies and Kellogg's Raisin Bran).

What are the advantages of an individual brand-names strategy? A major advantage is that the company does not tie its reputation to the product's acceptance. If the product fails, it is not a bad mark for the manufacturer. Or if the new product is of lower quality, the company does not dilute its reputation.

The opposite policy, that of using a blanket family name for all products, also has some advantages. The cost of introducing the product will be less, because there is no need for "name" research, or for expensive advertising to create brand-name recognition and preference. Furthermore, sales will be strong if the manufacturer's name is good. Thus Campbell's is able to introduce new soups under its brand name with extreme simplicity and instant response.

Where a company produces or sells quite different types of products, it may not be appropriate to use one blanket family name. Thus Swift and Company, in producing both hams and fertilizers, developed separate family names (Premium and Vigoro). When Mead Johnson developed a diet supplement for *gaining* weight, it created a new family name, Nutriment, to avoid confusion with its family brand for weight-*reducing* products, Metrecal. Companies will often invent different family brand names for different quality lines within the same product class. Thus A&P sells a primary, secondary, and tertiary set of brands—Ann Page, Sultana, and Iona, respectively.

Finally, some manufacturers will want to associate their company name along with an individual brand for each product. In these cases the company name legitimizes, and the individual name individualizes, the new product. Thus the Quaker Oats in *Quaker Oats Cap'n Crunch* allows the new product to benefit from the company's reputation in the breakfast-cereal field and Cap'n Crunch allows room to individualize and dramatize the product.

The brand name chosen should not be a casual afterthought but an integral reinforcer of the product concept. Among the desirable qualities for a brand name are: (1) *It should suggest something about the product's benefits.* Examples: Coldspot, Beautyrest, Craftsman, Accutron; (2) *It should suggest product qualities such as action, color, or whatever.* Examples: Duz, Sunkist, Spic and Span, Firebird. (3) *It should be easy to pronounce, recognize, and remember.* Short names help. Examples: Tide, Crest. (4) *It should be distinctive.* Examples: Mustang, Kodak.

Some marketing research firms have developed elaborate name-research procedures including *association tests* (what images come to mind), *learning tests* (how easily is the name pronounced), *memory tests* (how well is the name remembered), and *preference tests* (which names are preferred).

The goal of many firms is to build a unique brand name that will eventually become identified with the generic product. Such brand names as Frigidaire, Kleenex, Levis, Jello, Scotch tape, and Fiberglas have succeeded in this way. However, their very success has threatened some of the companies with the loss of exclusive rights to the name. Cellophane and shredded wheat are now names in the common domain.

Brand Extension Decision

A brand extension strategy is any effort to use a successful brand name to launch product modifications or additional products. After Quaker Oats' success with Cap'n Crunch dry breakfast cereal, it used the brand name and cartoon character to launch a line of ice-cream bars, T-shirts, and other products. Brand extension has also been used by Armour's Dial soap to cover a variety of new products that could not easily find distribution without the strength of the Dial name. In general, brand extension saves the manufacturer the high cost of promoting new names and confers instant brand quality on the new product. At the same time, if the new product fails to satisfy consumers, it might hurt consumers' attitudes toward the other products carrying the same name.[15]

Multibrand Decision

In a multibrand strategy, a seller develops two or more brands that compete with each other. The technique was pioneered by P&G when it introduced Cheer detergent as a competitor for its already successful Tide. Although Tide's sales dropped slightly, the combined sales of Cheer and Tide were higher. P&G now produces at least eight different detergent brands.

There are several reasons why manufacturers turn to multibrand strategy. First, there is the severe battle for shelf space in the nation's supermarkets. Each brand that the distributors accept gets some allocation of shelf space. Second, few consumers are so loyal to a brand that they will not try another. The only way to capture the "brand switchers" is to offer several brands. Third, creating new brands develops excitement and efficiency within the manufacturer's organization. Companies such as General Motors and P&G see their individual managers competing to outperform each other. Fourth, a multibrand strategy enables the company to take advantage of different market segments. Consumers respond to various benefits and appeals, and even marginal differences between brands can win a large following.[16]

Brand Repositioning Decision

However well a brand is initially positioned in a market, a number of circumstances may call for repositioning thinking: (1) a competitor may have placed its brand next to the company's brand, thus cutting into its market share in that segment; (2) customer preferences may have shifted, leaving the company's brand less in the center of a preference cluster; and (3) new customer preference clusters may have formed that represent attractive opportunities.

Figure 12-9
Distribution of Perceptions and Preferences in the Beer Market

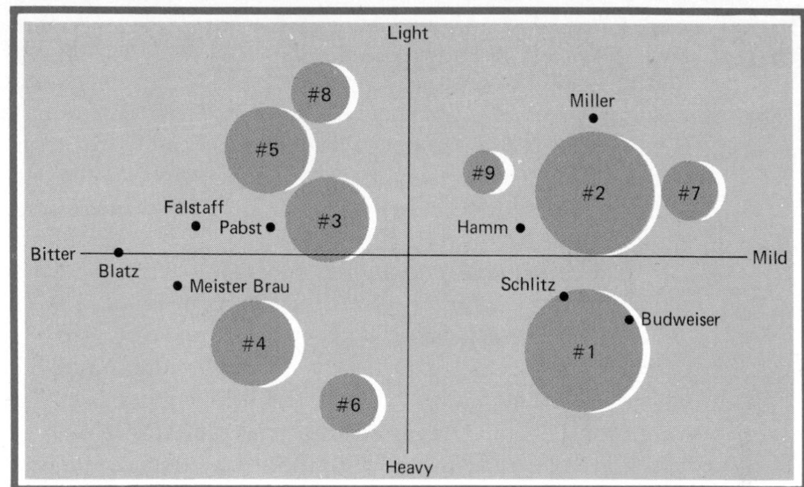

The problem and method of analysis for considering repositioning alternatives for a brand can be illustrated in connection with Hamm's position in the beer market. Figure 12-9 shows the distribution of beer brand perceptions and taste preferences on two attributes: lightness and mildness. The dots represent the perceived positions of the various brands, and the circles represent preference clusters. The larger circles represent more-intense densities of preference. This information would reveal that Hamm no longer meets the preferences of any distinct segment.

To remedy this, Hamm's task is to identify the best preference cluster in which to reposition Hamm. Preference cluster #1 would not be a good choice because Schlitz and Budweiser are well entrenched. Preference cluster #2 seems like a good choice because of its size and the presence of only one competitor, Miller. Preference cluster #9 would be another possibility, although it is relatively small. Hamm can also think about a long-shot repositioning toward the supercluster #3, #5, and #8 or the supercluster #4 and #6.

Management must weigh two factors in making its choice. The first is the *cost* of shifting the brand to that segment. The cost includes changing the product's qualities, packaging, advertising, and so on. In general, the repositioning cost *rises* with the repositioning distance. The more radical the brand image change that is contemplated, the greater the investment required to alter people's images. Hamm would need more money to reposition its brand in segment #8 than segment #2. It might be better for Hamm to create a new brand for segment #8 than to reposition its present brand.

The other factor is the *revenue* that would be earned by the brand in the new position. The revenue depends upon (1) the number of consumers in the preference segment, (2) their average purchase rate, (3) the number and strength of competitors already in that segment or intending to enter it, and (4) the price normally charged for brands selling to that segment.

packaging decisions

In the case of many physical products that are offered to the market, the marketer has to confront the issue of packaging. Packaging can vary from a very minor element (e.g., inexpensive hardware items) to a major marketing element (e.g., cosmetics). Some packages—such as the Coke bottle and the L'eggs container—are world famous. Many marketers have called packaging a fifth *P*, along with price, product, place, and promotion. Most marketers, however, treat packaging as another aspect of product.

We can define *packaging* and the *activities involved in designing and producing the container or wrapper for a product.* The container or wrapper is called the *package*. The package may include up to three levels of material. The *primary package* is the product's immediate container. Thus the bottle holding Old Spice After-Shave Lotion is the primary package. The *secondary package* refers to additional layers of material that protect the primary package and which are discarded when the product is about to be used. The cardboard box containing the bottle of after-shave lotion is a secondary package and provides additional protection and promotion opportunity. The *shipping packaging* refers to further packaging necessary for storage, identification, or transportation. Thus the corrugated boxes carrying six dozen boxes of Old Spice After-Shave Lotion are shipping packaging. Finally, *labeling* is part of the language of packaging and refers to any printed information appearing on or with the packaging that describes the product.

Packages go all the way back to the dawn of history. Primitive peoples had to carry wild berries and other fruit from the forests to caves, and they used animal skin and grass baskets as containers. Earthenware was developed eight thousand years ago in China and was shaped into a variety of containers for holding solid and liquid objects. Glass appeared in ancient Egypt and became a major container for liquids. By the Middle Ages packaging materials included leather, cloth, wood, stone, earthenware, and glass. For centuries, packaging's main role was to hold, protect, and transport goods.

In more recent times, packaging has taken on the additional role of a potent marketing tool. Well-designed packaging can create *convenience value* for the consumer and act as an effective promotional medium for the producer. Various factors have contributed to the potency of packaging as a marketing tool:

1. *Self-service.* An increasing number of products are sold on a self-service basis as a result of the growth of supermarkets and discount houses. The package must now perform many of the sales tasks. It must attract attention, describe the product's features, give the consumer confidence, and make a favorable overall impression.
2. *Consumer affluence.* The rise in consumer affluence has meant that consumers are willing to pay a little more for the convenience, appearance, dependability, and prestige of better packages.
3. *Company and brand image.* Companies are recognizing the power of well-designed packages to contribute to instant consumer recognition of the company or brand. There is hardly a film buyer who does not immediately recognize the familiar yellow packaging of Kodak film.
4. *Innovational opportunity.* Innovative packaging can bring about large benefits to consumers and profits to producers. Uneeda Biscuit's innovation in 1899 of a new type of stay-fresh unit package (paperboard, inner paper wrap, and paper overwrap)

was a great success in keeping crackers in much better condition for a longer period of time than the old cracker boxes, bins, and barrels could. Kraft's development of processed cheese in tins helped extend cheese's shelf life and earned Kraft a reputation for reliability. The first companies to put their soft drinks in pop-top cans and their sprays in aerosol cans attracted many new customers. Today plastic cooking bags are an area of innovational opportunity.

Developing the package for a new product requires a large number of decisions. The first task is to establish the *packaging concept.* The packaging concept is a definition of what the package should basically *be* or *do* for the particular product. Should the main function(s) of the package be to offer superior product protection, introduce a novel dispensing method, suggest certain qualities about the product or the company, or something else?

- General Foods developed a new dog-food product in the form of meatlike patties. Management decided that the unique and palatable appearance of these patties demanded the maximum visibility. Visibility was defined as the basic packaging concept, and management considered alternatives in this light. It finally narrowed down the choice to a tray with a film covering.[17]

A host of further decisions must be made on the component elements of package design—*size, shape, materials, color, text,* and *brand mark.* Decisions must be made between much text or little text, between cellophane and other transparent films, a plastic or a laminate tray, and so on. Each packaging element must be harmonized with the other packaging elements; size suggests certain things about materials, materials suggest certain things about colors, and so forth. The packaging elements also must be guided by decisions on pricing, advertising, and other marketing elements.

After the packaging is designed, it must be put through a number of tests. *Engineering tests* are conducted to ensure that the package stands up under normal conditions; *visual tests,* to ensure that the script is legible and the colors harmonious; *dealer tests,* to ensure that dealers find the packages attractive and easy to handle; and *consumer tests,* to ensure favorable consumer response.

In spite of these precautions, a packaging design occasionally gets through with some basic flaw that is discovered belatedly:

- Sizzl-Spray, a pressurized can of barbecue sauce developed by Heublein, . . . had a potential packaging disaster that was discovered in the market tests. . . . "We thought we had a good can, but fortunately we first test marketed the product in stores in Texas and California. It appears as soon as the cans got warm they began to explode. Because we hadn't gotten into national distribution, our loss was only $150,000 instead of a couple of million."[18]

It should be clear why developing the packaging for a new product may cost a few hundred thousand dollars and take from a few months to a year to put into final form. The importance of packaging cannot be overemphasized, considering the several functions it performs in consumer attraction and satisfaction. Companies, at the same time, must pay attention to the growing societal concerns about packaging and make decisions that serve society's interests as well as immediate customer and company objectives (see Exhibit 12-2).

EXHIBIT 12-2

PACKAGING AND PUBLIC POLICY

Packaging is attracting growing public interest, and marketers who make packaging decisions must be conscious of societal concerns that will affect their packaging decisions. The following four issues should be noted.

1. *Fair packaging and labeling.* The public has traditionally been concerned with packaging and labeling that might be false and misleading. The Federal Trade Commission Act of 1914 held that false, misleading, or deceptive labels or packages would be considered unfair competition. Consumers have also been concerned with the confusing sizes and shapes of packages, which make price comparisons difficult. In response, Congress passed the Fair Packaging and Labeling Act in 1967, which established mandatory labeling requirements, encouraged the adoption of additional voluntary industry-wide packaging standards, and empowered federal agencies to set packaging regulations in specific industries. The Food and Drug Administration has required processed-food producers to include *nutritional labeling* clearly stating the amounts of protein, fat, carbohydrates, and calories contained in the contents of the package, as well as vitamin and mineral content expressed as a percentage of the recommended daily allowance. Consumerists are actively lobbying for additional labeling legislation to require *open dating* (to describe the freshness of the product), *unit pricing* (to describe the cost of the item in some standard measurement unit), *grade labeling* (to rate the A, B, C quality level of certain consumer goods), and *percentage labeling* (to describe the percentage of each important ingredient).
2. *Excessive cost.* Critics have called packaging excessive in many cases, charging that it raises prices. They point to secondary "throwaway" packaging and raise the question of its value to the consumer. They point to the fact that the package sometimes costs more than the contents; for example, Evian moisturizer consists of five ounces of natural spring water packaged in an aerosol spray selling for $5.50. Marketers retort that critics do not understand all the functions being performed by the package and that marketers as well as anyone want to keep packaging costs down.
3. *Scarce resource.* The growing concern over shortages of paper, aluminum, and other materials raises the question of whether industry should try harder to reduce its packaging. For example, the growth of nonreturnable glass containers has resulted in using up to seventeen times as much glass as with returnable containers. The throwaway bottle is also an energy waster, which can be ill afforded in this time of energy shortages. Some states have passed laws prohibiting or taxing nonreturnable containers.
4. *Pollution.* As much as 40 percent of the total solid waste in this country is made up of package material. Many packages end up in the form of broken bottles and bent cans littering the streets and countryside. All of this packaging creates a major problem in solid waste disposal that is a huge consumer of labor and energy.

All of these questionable aspects of packaging have mobilized public action and interest in new laws that might further affect marketing decision making in the packaging area. Marketers must be equally concerned and must attempt to create ecological packaging when they develop packaging concepts for their products.

service decisions

A company's offer to the marketplace usually includes some service component. The service component can be a minor or a major part of the total offer. In fact, the offer can range from a pure good on the one hand to a pure service on the other. Four categories of offer can be distinguished:

1. *A pure tangible good.* Here the offer consists primarily of a tangible good such as soap, toothpaste, or salt. No explicit services accompany the product.
2. *A tangible good with accompanying services.* Here the offer consists of a tangible good accompanied by one or more services to enhance its consumer appeal. For example, an automobile manufacturer sells an automobile that is accompanied by a warranty, service and maintenance instructions, and so on. Levitt observes that "the more technologically sophisticated the generic product (e.g., cars and computers), the more dependent are its sales on the quality and availability of its accompanying customer services (e.g., display rooms, delivery, repairs and maintenance, application aids, operator training, installation advice, warranty fulfillment). In this sense, General Motors is probably more service intensive than manufacturing intensive. Without its services, its sales would shrivel."[19]
3. *A major service with accompanying minor goods and services.* Here the offer consists of a major service along with some additional services and/or supporting goods. For example, airline passengers are essentially buying transportation service. They arrive at their destinations without anything tangible to show for their expenditure. However, the trip includes some tangibles, such as food and drinks, a plane ticket stub, and an airline magazine. The service requires a capital-intensive good called an airplane for its realization, but the primary item is a service.
4. *A pure service.* Here the offer consists primarily of a service. Examples include psychotherapy and massages. The client of a psychoanalyst receives a pure service, with the only tangible element in the service situation consisting of an office and a couch.

Thus the company's product can be a good or a service, and additional services might be included. Here we shall focus on customer services accompanying the main offer. Services are discussed further in Chapter 20, pp. 623–30. The marketer faces three decisions with respect to customer service: (1) What elements of customer service should be included in the customer services mix? (2) What level of service should be offered? and (3) In what forms should the services be provided?

The Service Elements Decision

The marketer's first task is to survey customers to identify the main service elements in the industry and their relative importance. For example, Canadian buyers of industrial equipment ranked thirteen service elements in the following order of importance: (1) delivery reliability, (2) prompt quotation, (3) technical advice, (4) discounts, (5) after-sales service, (6) sales representation, (7) ease of contact, (8) replacement guarantee, (9) wide range of manufacturer, (10) pattern design, (11) credit, (12) test facilities, and (13) machining facilities.[20] These importance rankings suggest that the seller should at least match competition on delivery reliability, prompt quotation, technical advice, and other elements deemed most important by the customers.

But the issue of which service elements to emphasize is more subtle than this. A customer service element can be highly important and yet not be a determinant of customer preference if all the suppliers are perceived to be equal on this attribute. Consider the following example:

- The Monsanto Company was seeking a way to improve its customer services mix. Purchasing agents were asked to rate Monsanto, Du Pont, and Union Carbide on several attributes. All three companies, it turned out, were seen by customers as offering high delivery reliability and having good sales representatives. However, none were viewed as rendering sufficient technical service. Monsanto then carried out a study to determine how important technical service is to chemical buyers, and found out it had high importance. Monsanto then hired and trained additional technical people and launched a campaign describing itself as the leader in technical service. This discovery gave Monsanto an opportunity to develop a valued difference in the minds of buyers.

The Service Level Decision

Customers not only expect important service elements to be included in the product offer, but they also want the right amount and quality of service. If bank customers face lengthy waits in line or confront frowning bank tellers, they will be inclined to switch their business to another bank.

Companies must maintain a constant check on their own and competitors' service levels in relation to customers' expectations. The company can monitor service deficiencies through a number of devices: *comparison shopping, periodic customer surveys, suggestion boxes,* and *complaint-handling systems.* The task is not to *minimize* complaining behavior but to *maximize* it so that the company can really know how it is doing and the disappointed customers can obtain satisfaction.

A useful device is to periodically survey a sample of customers to find out how they feel about each service element. Figure 12-10A shows how fourteen service elements (attributes) of an automobile dealer's service department were rated by customers as to importance and performance. The importance of a service element was rated on a four-point scale of "extremely important," "important," "slightly important," and "not important." The dealer's performance was rated on a four-point scale of "excellent," "good," "fair," and "poor." For example, the first service element, "Job done right the first time," received a mean importance rating of 3.83 and a mean performance rating of 2.63, indicating that customers felt it was highly important, although not being performed that well by this service department. The ratings of the fourteen elements are displayed in Figure 12-10B. The figure is divided into four sections. Quadrant A shows the important service elements that are not being offered at the desired performance levels; they include elements 1, 2, and 9. The dealer should concentrate on improving the service department's performance on these elements. Quadrant B shows important service elements where the department is performing well; its job is to maintain the high performance. Quadrant C shows minor service elements that are being delivered in a mediocre way, but which do not need any attention since they are not very important. Quadrant D shows that a minor service element, "Send out maintenance notices," is being performed in an excellent manner, a case of possible "overkill." This classification of service elements according to their importance and performance provides marketers with guidelines as to where they should concentrate their effort.

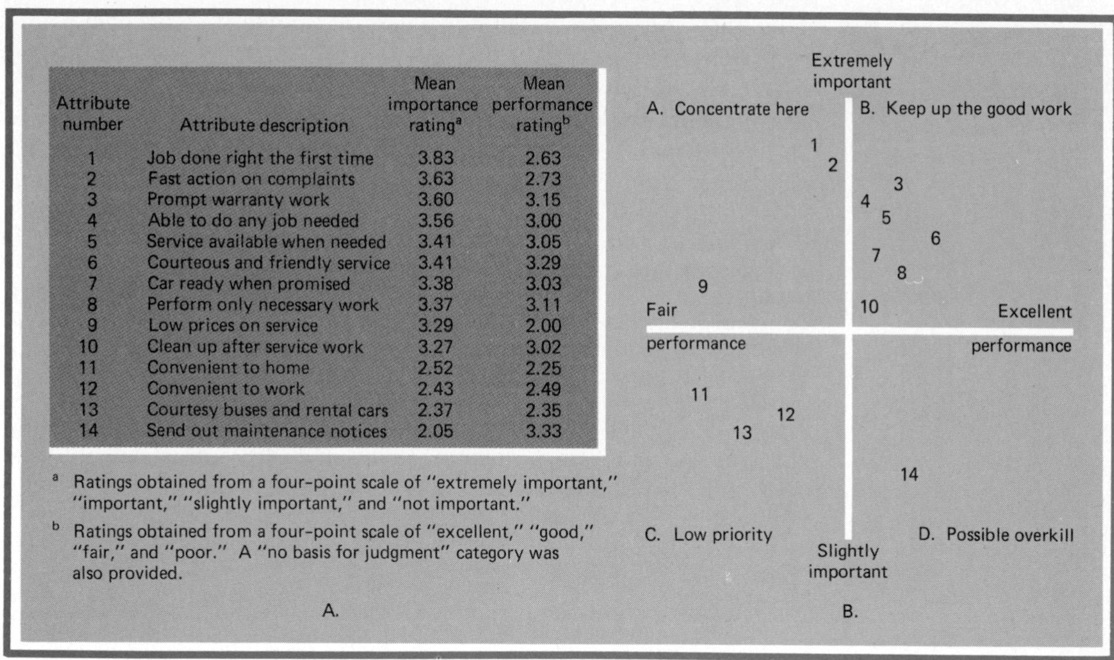

Attribute number	Attribute description	Mean importance rating[a]	Mean performance rating[b]
1	Job done right the first time	3.83	2.63
2	Fast action on complaints	3.63	2.73
3	Prompt warranty work	3.60	3.15
4	Able to do any job needed	3.56	3.00
5	Service available when needed	3.41	3.05
6	Courteous and friendly service	3.41	3.29
7	Car ready when promised	3.38	3.03
8	Perform only necessary work	3.37	3.11
9	Low prices on service	3.29	2.00
10	Clean up after service work	3.27	3.02
11	Convenient to home	2.52	2.25
12	Convenient to work	2.43	2.49
13	Courtesy buses and rental cars	2.37	2.35
14	Send out maintenance notices	2.05	3.33

[a] Ratings obtained from a four-point scale of "extremely important," "important," "slightly important," and "not important."

[b] Ratings obtained from a four-point scale of "excellent," "good," "fair," and "poor." A "no basis for judgment" category was also provided.

A.

Figure 12-10 *Importance and Performance Ratings for Automobile Dealer's Service Department*

Source: John A. Martilla and John C. James, "Importance-Performance Analysis," *Journal of Marketing,* January 1977, pp. 77–79.

The Service Form Decision

Marketers must also decide on the forms in which to offer various service elements. First there is the question of how to price the service element. Consider, for example, what Zenith should do in connection with offering repair services on its television sets. Zenith has three pricing options:

1. It could offer free television repair service for a year with the sale of its set.
2. It could offer the customer an option to buy a service contract.
3. It could decide not to offer any repair service, leaving this to independent television repair specialists.

Second there is the question of how the repair service should be provided. Zenith has three choices:

1. It could hire and train its own service repair people and locate them throughout the country.
2. It could make arrangements with distributors and dealers to provide the repair services.
3. It could leave it to independent companies to provide the necessary repair services.

For each such service element, various options exist as to how it could be provided to customers. The company's decision depends very much on customers' preferences as well as competitors' strategies.

The Customer Service Department

Given the importance of customer service as a competitive weapon, companies would do well to consider developing a strong customer service department reporting to the vice-president of marketing. Customer service departments are found in many companies, although their scope and authority vary widely. Ideally, these departments should integrate and be responsible for a number of customer services, including the following:[21]

1. *Complaints and adjustments.* The company should establish procedures for facilitating and handling complaints. Whirlpool and some other companies have set up hot lines to facilitate consumer complaining. By keeping statistics on the types of complaints, the customer service department can recognize and press for changes in product design, quality control, high-pressure selling, and so on. It is much less expensive to preserve the goodwill of existing customers than to attract new customers or woo back lost customers.
2. *Credit service.* The company should offer customers a number of options in financing their purchase, including installment credit contracts, open-book credit, loans, and leasing options. The costs of extending credit are usually more than made up by the gross profit on the additional sales and the reduced cost of marketing expenditures to overcome the customers' objection of not having enough money.
3. *Maintenance service.* The company should make provision for supplying customers with a parts and service system that is effective, speedy, and reasonable in cost. While maintenance service is often run by the production department, marketing should monitor customers' satisfaction with this service.
4. *Technical service.* The company should make sure that customers who buy complex materials and equipment are provided with technical services such as custom design work, installation, customer training, applications research, and process improvement research.
5. *Information service.* The company should consider setting up an information unit that is responsible for answering customer inquiries and disseminating information on new products, features, processes, expected price changes, order backlog status, and new company policies. The information can be disseminated through company newsletters and selectively to specific customers.

All of the preceding services should be coordinated and used as tools in creating customer satisfaction and loyalty.

Thus we see that product strategy is a multidimensional and complex subject calling for decisions on product mix, product line strategy, and branding, packaging, and service strategy. These decisions must be made not only with a full understanding of consumer wants and competitors' strategies but also with increasing attention to the growing public policy affecting product decisions (see Exhibit 12-3).

■ summary

Product is the first and most important element of the marketing mix. Product strategy calls for making coordinated decisions on the product mix, product lines, individual product items, brands, packaging, and services.

Product mix describes the set of products offered to customers by a particular seller. The product mix can be described as having a certain width, depth, and

EXHIBIT 12-3

PRODUCT DECISIONS AND PUBLIC POLICY

Marketing managers must make their product decisions in the context of various laws and regulations designed to protect the public. The main areas of product concern are as follows.

Product additions and deletions. Decisions to add products, particularly through acquisitions, may be prevented under the Antimerger Act if the effect threatens to lessen competition. Decisions to drop old products must be made with an awareness that the firm has legal obligations, written or implied, to its suppliers, dealers, and customers who have a stake in the discontinued product.

Patent protection. The firm must heed the U.S. patent laws in developing new products. The firm is prevented from designing a product that is "illegally similar" to another company's established product. A recent example is Polaroid's suit trying to prevent Kodak from selling its new instant picture camera on the grounds that it infringes on Polaroid's instant camera patents.

Product quality and safety. Manufacturers of foods, drugs, cosmetics, and certain fibers must comply with specific laws regarding product quality and safety. The Federal Food, Drug, and Cosmetic Act protects consumers from unsafe and adulterated food, drugs, and cosmetics. Various acts provide for the inspection of sanitary conditions in the meat and poultry processing industries. Safety legislation has been passed to regulate fabrics, chemical substances, automobiles, toys, and drugs and poisons. The Consumer Product Safety Act of 1972 established a Consumer Product Safety Commission, which has the authority to ban or seize imminently hazardous products and set severe penalties for violation of the law. If consumers have been injured by a product that has been defectively designed, they can sue manufacturers or dealers. *Product liability suits* are now occurring at the rate of over one million per year, with awards running as high as $500,000. This has resulted in a substantial increase in *product recalls.* General Motors spent $3.5 million on postage alone when it had to notify 6.5 million car owners of defective motor mounts.

Product warranties. Many manufacturers offer written product warranties to convince customers of their product's quality. But these warranties are often subject to certain qualifications and written in a language that the average consumer does not understand. Too often, consumers learn that they are not entitled to services, repairs, and replacements that seem to be implied. To protect consumers, Congress passed the Magnuson-Moss Warranty–Federal Trade Commission Improvement Act in 1975. The act requires that full warranties meet certain minimum standards, including repair "within a reasonable time and without charge" or a replacement or full refund if the product does not work "after a reasonable number of attempts" at repair. Otherwise the company must make it clear that it is offering only a limited warranty. The law has led several manufacturers to switch from full to limited warranties and others to drop warranties altogether as a marketing tool.

Sources: Howard C. Sorenson, "Products Liability: The Consumer's Revolt," *Best's Review,* September 1974, p. 48; "Managing the Product Recall," *Business Week,* January 1975, pp. 46–48; Roger A. Kerin and Michael Harvey, "Contingency Planning for Product Recall," *MSU Business Topics,* Summer 1975, pp. 5–12; and "The Guesswork on Warranties," *Business Week,* July 14, 1975, p. 51.

consistency. All three dimensions of the product mix can be used for strategic positioning.

Each product line in the product mix requires its own strategy. Management should first examine the current items in the line in terms of their relative sales and profit contribution, and how they are positioned against competitors' items. Based on these findings, management can consider various line decisions. *Line stretching* involves the question of whether a particular line should be extended downward, upward, or both ways. *Line filling* raises the question of whether additional items should be added within the present range of the line. *Line modernization* raises the question of whether the line needs a new look, and whether the new look should be installed piecemeal or all at once. *Line featuring* raises the question as to which end of the line should be featured in promoting the line.

Each product item offered to customers can be looked at on three levels. The *core product* is the essential service that the buyer is really buying. The *tangible product* is the features, styling, quality, brand name, and packaging that constitute the tangible product. The *augmented product* is the tangible product plus the various services accompanying it, such as warranty, installation, service maintenance, and free delivery.

Companies also have to develop brand policies for the product items in their lines. They must decide whether to brand at all, whether to do manufacturing or private branding, what quality they should build into the brand, whether to use family brand names or individual brand names, whether to extend the brand name to new products, whether to put out several competing brands, and whether to reposition any of the brands.

Physical products require packaging decisions that create benefits such as protection, economy, convenience, and promotion. Marketers have to develop a packaging concept and test it functionally and psychologically to make sure it achieves the desired objectives and is compatible with public policy.

Finally, companies have to develop a set of customer services that are desired by customers and effective against competitors. The company has to decide on the most important service elements to consider, the level at which each element should be offered, and the form in which each element should be provided. The service mix can be coordinated by a customer service department that is responsible for complaints and adjustments, credit, maintenance, technical service, and information service.

■ questions for discussion

1. Relate the concepts of product mix, product line, and product item to General Motors.
2. Ektelon, the manufacturer of racquetball racquets, has a wide product line. Comment.
3. Discuss the core, tangible, and augmented product for your favorite brand of perfume or after-shave lotion.
4. What distinguishes a durable good from a nondurable good? Give an example of each.

5. In how many retail outlets must each type of consumer goods (i.e., convenience, shopping, specialty, and unsought) be distributed in a particular geographic area? Explain why.
6. Industrial goods always become part of the finished product. Comment.
7. Who benefits from the use of brand names? Explain briefly.
8. National brands are always of higher quality than private brands. Comment.
9. Two of the most expensive and widely discussed brand-name changes in recent years have been ENCO (*Esso*) to *Exxon* and *Bank Americard* to *Visa*. Why do you think these companies went to this expense?
10. What three factors have contributed to packaging importance as a strategic tool for marketers? Provide a specific company example for each factor.
11. Describe some of the service decisions that the following marketeers must make. (a) women's dress shop, (b) savings and loan, and (c) sporting goods store.
12. If the Arrow shirt company were planning to develop a customer service department, what services should the company text.

references

1. This and the following two definitions are (with some modifications) taken from *Marketing Definitions: A Glossary of Marketing Terms,* compiled by the Committee on Definitions of the American Marketing Association (Chicago: American Marketing Association, 1960).
2. See BENSON P. SHAPIRO, *Industrial Product Policy: Managing the Existing Product Line* (Cambridge, Mass.: Marketing Science Institute, September 1977), pp. 3–5, 98–101. Also see BARBARA B. JACKSON and BENSON P. SHAPIRO, "New Way to Make Product Line Decisions," *Harvard Business Review,* May-June 1979, pp. 139–49.
3. See the discussion in SHAPIRO, *Industrial Product Policy,* pp. 9–10.
4. MARK HANAN, *Market Segmentation* (New York: American Management Association, 1968), pp. 24–26.
5. See STEUART HENDERSON BRITT, "How Weber's Law Can Be Applied to Marketing," *Business Horizons,* February 1975, pp. 21–29.
6. Systems selling really originated as systems buying, to describe government practices in buying major weapons and communication systems. Instead of purchasing and putting all the components together, the government would solicit bids from prime contractors who would be willing to assemble the package or system. The winning prime contractor would then buy or bid for the subcomponents. Sellers have increasingly recognized that buyers like to purchase in this way and have responded with augmented product offerings.
7. See HARPER W. BOYD, JR., AND SIDNEY J. LEVY, "New Dimensions in Consumer Analysis," *Harvard Business Review,* November-December 1963, pp. 129–40.
8. THEODORE LEVITT, *The Marketing Mode* (New York: McGraw-Hill, 1969), p. 2.
9. The three definitions can be found in *Marketing Definitions.*
10. The first three definitions that follow can be found in *Marketing Definitions.* For further readings on this classification of goods, see RICHARD H. HOLTON, "The Distinction between Convenience Goods, Shopping Goods, and Specialty Goods,"

Journal of Marketing, July 1958, pp. 53–56; LOUIS P. BUCKLIN, "Retail Strategy and the Classification of Consumer Goods," *Journal of Marketing,* January 1963, pp. 50–55; LEO V. ASPINWALL, "The Characteristics of Goods Theory," in *Managerial Marketing: Perspectives and Viewpoints* (rev. ed.), ed. William Lazer and Eugene J. Kelley (Homewood, Ill.: Richard D. Irwin, 1962), pp. 633–43; and GORDON E. MIRACLE, "Product Characteristics and Marketing Strategy," *Journal of Marketing,* January 1965, pp. 18–24.

11. The first four definitions can be found in *Marketing Definitions.*
12. See BILL PAUL, "It Isn't Chicken Feed to Put Your Brand on 78 Million Birds," *Wall Street Journal,* May 13, 1974, p. 1.
13. See E. B. WEISS, "Private Label?" *Advertising Age,* September 30, 1974, pp. 27ff. For an excellent example of decision theory applied to a national bakery facing this dilemma, see ROBERT D. BUZZELL AND CHARLES C. SLATER, "Decision Theory and Marketing Management," *Journal of Marketing,* July 1962, pp. 7–16.
14. SIDNEY SCHOEFFLER, ROBERT D. BUZZELL, AND DONALD F. HEANY, "Impact of Strategic Planning on Profit Performance," *Harvard Business Review,* March-April 1974, pp. 137–45.
15. See THEODORE R. GAMBLE, "Brand Extension," in *Plotting Marketing Strategy,* ed. Lee Adler (New York: Simon & Schuster, 1967), pp. 170–71.
16. See ROBERT W. YOUNG, "Multibrand Entries," in Adler, *Plotting Marketing Strategy,* pp. 143–64.
17. "General Foods–Post Division (B)," Case M-102, Harvard Business School, 1964.
18. "Product Tryouts: Sales Tests in Selected Cities Help Trim Risks of National Marketing," *Wall Street Journal,* August 10, 1962, p. 1.
19. THEODORE LEVITT, "Production-Line Approach to Service," *Harvard Business Review,* September-October 1972, pp. 41–42.
20. PETER G. BANTING, "Customer Service in Industrial Marketing: A Comparative Study," *European Journal of Marketing,* 10, No. 3 (1976), 140.
21. SEE RALPH S. ALEXANDER AND THOMAS L. BERG, *Dynamic Management in Marketing* (Homewood, Ill.: Richard D. Irwin, 1965), pp. 419–28.

PRICING STRATEGY

The Easy Rider Motor Company manufactures a recreational vehicle—specifically a truck camper—called the Free Spirit, which it sells through franchised dealers at a retail price of $12,000. The dealers have been pressuring the company to add a second recreational vehicle to the line at the higher end. In response, the company has designed the High Rise and is about to set its price to dealers and customers. Here are the major facts:

1. The company has enough plant capacity to produce up to five hundred units per year of the new model. Any more than this would require investing in new plant capacity.
2. The fixed costs of producing the High Rise are estimated at $500,000. The direct costs are estimated at $10,000 per unit.
3. There is one major competitor producing a high-quality recreational vehicle, which is retailing for $14,000. The competitor charges its dealers $11,200, which is a 20 percent dealer discount off the list price. The company estimates that the competitor's profit margin is approximately $1,400 per unit. The competitor sells about six hundred units per year.
4. The company would like its High Rise to sell at retail for at least $2,200 more than its Free Spirit.
5. The company displayed the High Rise at the latest retail trade show, and over two-thirds of the visitors reported that the High Rise seemed better designed than the competitor's model.

With this information, what dealer and retail price should the Easy Rider Motor Company establish for the High Rise? If the company is cost oriented, it could simply start with the fact that each unit costs $10,000 to manufacture and add a markup for the profit it wants per unit. If the company wants $1,400 gross profit per unit, the dealers would pay $11,400 and in turn mark it up for the profit they want per unit. The fault with this approach is that it ignores the competitor's price and the consumers' perceived value of the High Rise.

A market-oriented approach would start with where potential buyers see the value of the High Rise. For example, if market testing indicates that potential buyers think that the High Rise is worth at least $500 more than the competitor's truck camper, then the company might consider a retail price of $14,500. It might decide to offer its dealers a 22 percent dealer discount to motivate them at a higher level than the competitor's dealers, which means that dealers would pay $11,310 and the company would make a gross profit of $1,310 per unit.

The company will also want to consider other pricing alternatives. The High Rise's retail price might be set at $14,499 instead of $14,500

because odd pricing makes the price sound a little lower. Or the High Rise might be priced at the competitor's price of $14,000 so that the companies are left to fight for market share on the basis of nonprice competition. Or the company might price the High Rise below the competitor's price to grab for a higher market share. However, this violates the wish to price the High Rise at $2,200 or more than the Free Spirit; also, it could lead to a higher volume of orders than the company could fill, and this would require increased investment. On the other hand, the company might want to consider pricing the High Rise higher than $14,500 to suggest a real Cadillac (called prestige pricing).

The Easy Rider Motor Company's pricing problem is even more complicated. The company can produce the High Rise with optional features (better heating, lighting, bedding, and so on) and will have to figure out a price structure for the different options. Price will also depend on the size of the planned promotion budget because this will make a difference in the company's ability to convince the market to pay a high price. The High Rise could cannibalize some of the sales of the Free Spirit, depending on how close their prices are. Or conversely, the High Rise could increase the sales of the Free Spirit, since the dealers will be able to attract more traffic with the longer product line.[1]

□ Many considerations must be taken into account in attempting to set a price on a product. Price will be a major direct determinant of demand and a major influence on the setting of the other marketing mix variables. If the Easy Rider Motor Company sets a high price on its new High Rise recreation vehicle, it must also build in high product quality and plan an expensive promotion program.

All profit organizations and many nonprofit organizations face the task of setting a price on their products or services. Price goes by many names:

- Price is all around us. You pay *rent* for your apartment, *tuition* for your education, and a *fee* to your physician or dentist. The airline, railway, taxi, and bus companies charge you a *fare;* the local utilities call their price a *rate;* and the local bank charges you *interest* for the money you borrow. The price for driving your car on Florida's Sunshine Parkway is a *toll,* and the company that insures your car charges you a *premium.* The guest lecturer charges an *honorarium* to tell you about a government official who took a *bribe* to help a shady character steal *dues* collected by a trade association. Clubs or societies to which you belong may make a special *assessment* to pay unusual expenses. A lawyer you use regularly may ask for a *retainer* to cover his services. The "price" of an executive is a *salary,* the price of a salesperson may be a *commission,* and the price of a worker is a *wage.* Finally, although economists would disagree, many of us feel that *income taxes* are the price we pay for the privilege of making money![2]

Historically, sellers considered price to be one of the key influences on buyer choice behavior. In the 1950s and 1960s, however, nonprice factors became relatively more important. Table 13-1 shows how marketing managers ranked

Table 13-1
Comparison of 1964 and 1975 Rankings of Marketing Activities

MARKETING ACTIVITY	1975 RANK ORDER OF IMPORTANCE	1964 RANK ORDER OF IMPORTANCE
Pricing	1	6
Customer services	2	5
Sales personnel management	3	3
Product research and development	4	1
Marketing cost budgeting and control	5	9
Physical distribution	6	11
Market research	7	2
Marketing organization structure	8	7
Advertising and sales promotion planning	9	4
Distribution channel control	10	8
Extending customer credit	11	10
Public relations	12	12

Sources: Robert A. Robicheaux, "How Important Is Pricing in Competitive Strategy?" in *Proceedings: Southern Marketing Association,* ed. Henry W. Nash and Donald P. Robin, January 1976, pp. 55–57. Robicheaux conducted the 1975 study. The 1964 study was conducted by Jon G. Udell, "How Important Is Pricing in Competitive Strategy?" *Journal of Marketing,* January 1964, pp. 44–48.

twelve marketing activities in 1964. Pricing was not named among the five most important factors in marketing success. But in 1975, because of worldwide inflation, many marketers believed that price was the most important element in the marketing mix.

Price is the only element in the marketing mix that creates sales revenues; the other elements are costs. In spite of the importance of setting the right price, most companies do not handle pricing well. The most common mistakes can be summarized as follows: pricing is too cost oriented in that companies fail to take sufficient account of demand intensity and customer psychology; price is not revised enough to capitalize on changed conditions in the marketplace; price is too often set independently of the rest of the marketing mix rather than as an intrinsic element of market-positioning strategy; and price is not varied enough for different product items and market segments.

The pricing function is handled in a variety of ways in different companies. In small companies, pricing is often a decision of top management rather than the marketing or sales department. In large companies, price determination is typically in the hands of divisional and product line managers. Even here, top management sets the general pricing objectives and policies and often has to approve the prices proposed by lower levels of management. In industries where pricing is a key factor (aerospace, railroads, oil companies), companies will often establish a separate pricing department to set prices or assist others in the determination of appropriate prices. Depending on the situation, this department reports to either the marketing department or top management. Others who exert an influence on pricing include sales managers, production planners and managers, and finance specialists and accountants.

In this chapter we will consider the following major pricing problems: (1) What price should be set on a product for the first time? (2) When should a company initiate a change in price? (3) How should a company respond to a competitor's change in price? and (4) How should prices be set on several interrelated items in a product line?

setting price

Pricing is a problem when a company develops new or different products, when it sells existing products to new middlemen or customers, and when it regularly enters bids on new contract work. The setting of price is rarely a simple matter. It is only simple in a *price-taking* market, that is, a market where each seller must charge the going price. As conditions approach perfect competition (i.e., homogeneous product, high information, and high mobility of resources), such as is found in several raw material markets, suppliers pretty much have to charge the same as their competitors. If they charge more (without offering any extra services), no one will buy; and there is no reason to charge less as long as buyers are paying the going price.

Most markets, however, do not meet the conditions of perfect competition and call for *price making.* The pricing decision can be very complex, as we saw in the case of Easy Rider Motor Company. Marketing executives need to follow a methodology that brings in all the major considerations. A pricing methodology is shown in Figure 13-1 and is discussed in the following paragraphs.

Target Market Objectives

Before a price can be set, management has to clarify the target market(s) for the product and the company's marketing objectives. Thus the Easy Rider Motor Company has to decide on whether its target market is young people with modest incomes, full-nest families with high incomes, or retirees with declining incomes. This will make a difference in setting the price as well as in designing the recreational vehicle and promoting it.

The company also has to decide on its marketing objectives in that market. The following alternative objectives are the most common.

Current profit maximization. Economists have worked out a simple yet elegant model for pricing to maximize current profits. The model assumes that the firm can estimate the *demand level* and therefore the *total revenue* at each possible price. Furthermore, it can estimate its *total cost* at each possible price. The firm then locates the price that produces the greatest difference between total revenue and total cost, that is, the highest total profit. This is the optimal price (see Exhibit 13-1).

Market-share leadership. An increasing number of companies believe that long-run profitability is associated with achieving a dominant market share. Texas Instruments and other companies will set out to achieve a high market share by setting prices as low as possible (called *market penetration pricing*).

Figure 13-1
Methodology for Setting Prices

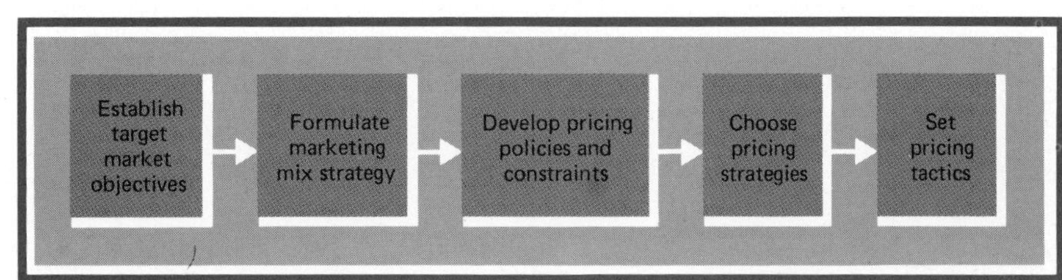

EXHIBIT 13-1

FINDING THE OPTIMAL PRICE

The Supersound Company is preparing to introduce a new tape recorder into the market to be priced somewhere between $100 and $200. It first estimates the *demand function,* that is, the estimated quantity (Q) that would be purchased this year at various prices (P) that might be charged. The demand equation is

$$Q = 1{,}000 - 4P$$

This equation illustrates the "law of demand," that is, less will be bought at higher prices. If price, say, is $100, demand will be 600 units; if price is raised to $200, demand will be 200 units.

It next estimates the *cost function,* which describes the estimated total cost (C) for alternative quantities per period (Q) that might be produced. Suppose the *cost equation* is

$$C = 6{,}000 + 50Q$$

Here $6,000 represents the fixed cost of production (salaries, overhead, etc.), and $50 represents the cost per unit (labor, material, etc.). Thus it will cost the company $26,000 to produce 400 units.

Then it estimates *total revenue* (R), which is the price times the quantity sold—that is,

$$R = PQ = (1{,}000 - 4P) = 1{,}000P - 4P^2$$

Finally it estimates *total profits* (Z) as the difference between total revenue and total cost—that is,

$$\begin{aligned} Z &= R - C \\ Z &= (1{,}000P - 4P^2) - (6{,}000 + 50Q) \\ Z &= 1{,}000P - 4P^2 - 6{,}000 - 50(1{,}000 - 4P) \\ Z &= 1{,}000P - 4P^2 - 6{,}000 - 50{,}000 + 200P \\ Z &= -56{,}000 + 1{,}200P - 4P^2 \end{aligned}$$

Total profits turn out to be a second-degree function of price. It is a hatlike figure (a parabola), and profits reach their highest point, $34,000, at a price of $150. No other price would yield a higher profit.

The economist's model has value in showing the role played by the demand and cost function in setting price. But it also has several limitations in practice: (1) it assumes that the other marketing mix variables are held constant, when in fact they would have to be adjusted for different price settings; (2) it assumes that competitors do not change their prices, when in fact they will react with different prices to different price settings of the company; (3) it ignores the reaction of other parties in the marketing system—government, suppliers, dealers, and so on—to various prices that might be charged; and (4) it assumes that the demand and cost functions can be reliably estimated, when in fact great difficulties exist.

They will build high plant capacity to produce a high volume, set the price at or below that of competitors to win a large market share, and keep bringing their price down as their costs fall. They may lose money for the first few years but will make it up later when they dominate the market and have the lowest costs.

Any of several conditions might favor setting a low price:[3] (1) the market appears to be highly price-sensitive, and therefore a low price will stimulate more rapid market growth; (2) the unit costs of production and distribution fall with accumulated production experience; or (3) a low price would discourage actual and potential competition.

Market skimming. Firms may want to take advantage of the fact that some buyers are willing to pay a much higher price than others because the product has high current value to them. These firms will set a high initial price to yield a high profit margin per unit sold, although this will mean fewer units sold.

Market skimming makes sense under the following conditions: (1) a sufficient number of buyers have a high current demand; (2) the unit production and distribution costs of producing a smaller volume are not so much higher that they cancel the advantage of charging what some of the traffic will bear; (3) the high initial price will not attract more competitors; (4) the high price creates an impression of a superior product.

As time passes, the firm will lower its price to draw in the more price-elastic segments of the market. Du Pont is a prime practitioner of market skimming, particularly on new patent-protected discoveries such as cellophane and nylon. It will charge a high initial price and only lower it gradually to bring in new price-sensitive segments. Polaroid is another practitioner. It will introduce an expensive version of a new camera and gradually introduce lower-priced models in a bid for the mass market.

Product quality leadership. A company might adopt the objective of being the product quality leader in the market. This normally calls for charging a high price to cover the high product quality and high cost of research to improve the product.

Marketing Mix Strategy

Management must now develop a marketing mix strategy that will help it achieve its marketing objectives. For example, if the Easy Rider Motor Company adopts a product quality leadership objective, this will normally call for high product quality, a high price, and high promotion. The appropriate marketing mix, however, is not always so straightforward, and trade-offs will exist between the various marketing variables. Consider, for example, the various combinations that are possible with any two elements of the marketing mix, such as price and product quality. Suppose each can be set independently at a high, medium, or low level. Figure 13-2 shows nine resulting marketing mix strategies. Sometimes more than one marketing mix can support a given marketing objective. The Easy Rider Motor Company can pursue product quality leadership by using in principle any of the three strategies in the first row. The difference is that lower prices will normally bring about more market share, along with product quality leadership. The main point is that price cannot be set independently of the question of overall marketing mix strategy.

Figure 13-2
Nine Marketing Mix Strategies on Price/Quality

Product quality	Price: High	Price: Medium	Price: Low
High	1. Premium strategy	2. Penetration strategy	3. Superbargain strategy
Medium	4. Overpricing strategy	5. Average-quality strategy	6. Bargain strategy
Low	7. Hit-and-run strategy	8. Shoddy-goods strategy	9. Cheap-goods strategy

Pricing Policies and Constraints

Management must scrutinize the contemplated price and other elements of the marketing mix for their compatibility with company policies and external constraints. Many companies have pricing policies that define such things as the price image that the company wants, its position on price discounts, and its philosophy of meeting competitors' prices. Any price being considered must be compatible with the price policies of the company.

In determining prices, the decision maker has to consider the possible reactions of various parties affected by the pricing decision: distributors, competitors, suppliers, government, and company executives. See Exhibit 13–2.

Pricing Strategy

Pricing strategy is the task of defining the initial price range and planned price movement through time that the company will use to achieve its marketing objectives in the target market. In developing its pricing strategy, the management must look ahead and anticipate the expected movements of *cost, demand,* and *competition* over time and how price should be adapted to them. Although all three elements should always be considered, many pricing strategies in practice lean heavily on one of the three elements. As a result, various pricing strategies have been described as being heavily cost oriented, demand oriented, or competition oriented. We will now explore these strategies.

Cost-oriented pricing strategies. Many firms set product prices largely on the basis of product costs. Typically, all costs are included, including an arbitrary allocation of overhead made on the basis of the expected sales level.

MARKUP PRICING

The most elementary examples of cost-oriented pricing are markup pricing and cost-plus pricing. In both cases price is determined by adding some fixed percentage to the unit cost. Markup pricing is most commonly found in the retail trades where the retailer adds predetermined but different markups to various goods. Cost-plus pricing is most often used to describe the pricing of jobs that are nonroutine and difficult to "cost" in advance, such as construction and military-weapon development.

Markups vary considerably among different goods. Some common markups on the retail price in department stores are 20 percent for tobacco goods, 28 percent for cameras, 34 percent for books, 41 percent for dresses, 46 percent for costume jewelry, and 50 percent for millinery.[4] In the retail grocery industry, items like coffee, canned milk, and sugar tend to have low average markups, while items like frozen foods, jellies, and some canned products have high average markups. In addition, quite a lot of dispersion is found around the averages. Within the frozen-foods category, for example, one study showed that the markups on retail price ranged from a low of 13 percent to a high of 53 percent.[5]

Many hypotheses have been advanced to explain the variations in markups within selected product groups. Preston conducted a study to determine how much of the markup variance within common grocery-product groups could be explained by differences in unit costs, turnover, and manufacturers' versus private brands. The principal finding was that over 40 percent of the variation remained unexplained in most product categories and was probably due to erratic decisions, random factors, and frequently better adaptations to the current market than could be provided by these factors.[6]

EXHIBIT 13-2

PRICE DECISIONS AND PUBLIC POLICY

Pricing is a major marketing decision area where knowledge of the law is essential. Management must avoid price fixing (except for resale price maintenance), price discrimination, charging less than the minimum legal price, raising prices unduly, or advertising deceptive prices.

Price fixing. Sellers must set prices without talking to competitors about their prices. Otherwise price collusion will be suspected. Price fixing is illegal *per se*, that is, the government is not interested in the reasons why the firms engaged in price fixing. The only exception to the rule occurs in a few cases where price agreements are carried out under the supervision of a government agency, as in many local milk industry agreements, in the regulated transportation industries, and in fruit and vegetable cooperatives.

Resale price maintenance. A seller can require a dealer to charge a fixed price for its product. If the dealer refuses to charge the suggested price and continues to discount, the seller can simply refuse to do business with this dealer. Simple refusal of this kind is not a violation of the Sherman Antitrust Act. But the seller must be careful not to add other behaviors to this refusal because these other behaviors could be enough to create a violation of the law. For example, the dealer must not punish the retailer by shipping late or denying the retailer advertising allowances.

Price discrimination. The Robinson-Patman Act was passed to ensure that sellers would offer the same price terms to a given level of trade. For example, every retailer is entitled to the same price terms whether the retailer is Sears or the local bicycle shop. However, price discrimination is allowed if the seller can prove its costs are different when selling to different retailers; for example, that it costs less to sell a large volume of bicycles to Sears than to sell a few bicycles to a local dealer. Or the seller can discriminate in its pricing if the seller manufactures different qualities of the same product for different retailers. The burden is on the seller to prove that these differences exist and that the price differences are proportional. Price differentials may also be used by marketing managers to "meet competition" in "good faith," providing the firm is trying to meet competitors at its own level of competition and that the price discrimination is temporary, localized, and defensive rather than offensive.

Minimum pricing. A seller is not allowed to sell below cost for a long period with the intention to destroy competition. Wholesalers and retailers in over half the states face laws requiring a minimum percentage markup over their cost of merchandise plus transportation. Called Unfair Trade Practices, they are designed to protect small merchants from larger merchants who might otherwise be able to sell items below cost to attract customers.

Price increases. Companies are free to increase their prices to any level the market will bear, except in times of price controls. The major exception to the freedom of pricing is regulated public utilities. Since utilities have a monopoly power in their own areas, their price schedules are regulated in the public interest. The government has used informal influence from time to time to discourage major industry price hikes because of inflationary concerns.

Deceptive pricing. Deceptive pricing is a more common problem in the sale of consumer goods than business goods, because consumers typically possess less information and buying acumen. In 1958 the Automobile Information Disclosure Act was passed, requiring auto manufacturers to affix on the windshield of each new automobile a statement giving the manufacturer's suggested retail price, the prices of optional equipment, and the dealer's transportation charges. In the same year, the FTC issued its *Guides against Deceptive Pricing,* warning sellers not to claim a price reduction unless it is a saving from the usual retail price, not to advertise "factory" or "wholesale" prices unless this is true, not to advertise comparable value prices on imperfect goods, and so forth.

Does the use of a rigid customary markup over cost make logical sense in the pricing of products? Generally, no. Any model that ignores current demand elasticity in setting prices is not likely to lead, except by chance, to the achievement of maximum profits, in either the short or the long run. As demand elasticity changes, as it is likely to do seasonally, cyclically, or over the product life cycle, the optimal markup will also change.

Still, markup pricing remains popular for a number of reasons. First, there is generally less uncertainty about costs than about demand. By pinning the price to unit costs, sellers simplify their own pricing task considerably; they do not have to make frequent adjustments as demand conditions change. Second, where all firms in the industry use this pricing approach, their prices are likely to be similar if their costs and markups are similar. Price competition is therefore minimized, which it would not be if firms paid attention to demand variations when they priced. Third, there is the feeling that cost-markup pricing is fairer to both buyers and sellers. Sellers do not take advantage of buyers when the latter's demand becomes acute; yet the sellers earn a fair return on their investment.

TARGET PRICING

Another cost-oriented pricing approach is that of *target pricing,* in which the firm tries to determine the price that would give it a specified target rate of return on its total costs at an estimated standard volume. Target pricing has been most closely associated with General Motors, which prices its automobiles so as to achieve a long-run average rate of return of 15 to 20 percent on its investment. This pricing approach is also closely associated with the pricing policies of public utilities, which have a large investment and, in view of their monopoly position, are constrained by regulatory commissions to seek a fair rate of return on their costs.

Target pricing can be illustrated in terms of the breakeven chart in Figure 13-3. Management's first task is to estimate its total costs at various levels of output. The total-cost curve is shown rising at a constant rate until capacity is approached. Management's next task is to estimate the percentage of capacity at which it is likely to operate in the coming period. Suppose the company expects to operate at 80 percent of capacity. This means that it expects to sell eight hundred thousand units if its capacity is one million units. The total cost of producing this volume, according to Figure 13-3, is $10 million. Management's third task is to specify a target rate of return. If the company aspires to a 20 percent profit over costs, then it would like absolute profits of $2 million. Therefore one point on its total-revenue curve will have to be $12 million at a volume of 80 percent of capacity. Another point on the total-revenue curve will be $0 at a volume of zero percent of capacity. The rest of the total-revenue curve can be drawn between these two points.

Where does price come in? The slope of the total-revenue curve is price. In this example, the slope is $15 per unit. Thus if the company charges $15 per unit and manages to sell eight hundred thousand units, it will attain the target rate of return of 20 percent, or $2 million.

Target pricing, however, has a major conceptual flaw. The company used an estimate of sales volume to derive the price, but price is a factor that influences sales volume! A price of $15 may be too high or too low to move eight hundred thousand units. What is missing is a demand function, showing how many units the firm could expect to sell at different prices. With an estimate of the demand curve and with the requirement to earn 20 percent on costs, the firm could solve for those prices and volumes that would be compatible. In this way the firm would avoid setting a price that failed to generate the estimated level of output.

Figure 13-3
Breakeven Chart for Determining Target Price

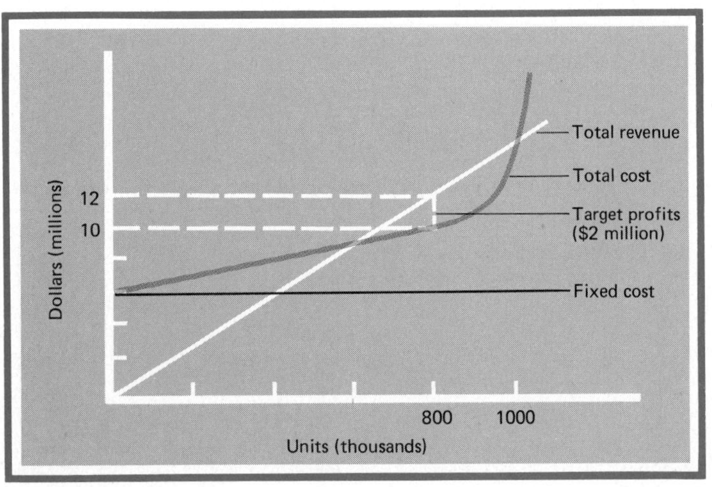

Demand-oriented pricing strategies. Demand-oriented pricing calls for setting a price based on consumer perceptions and demand intensity, rather than on cost.

PERCEIVED-VALUE PRICING

An increasing number of companies are basing their price on the product's *perceived value.* They see the buyers' perception of value, not the seller's level of cost, as the key to pricing. They use the nonprice variables in the marketing mix to build up perceived value in the minds of the buyers. Price is then set to capture the perceived value.

Perceived-value pricing is in line with modern market-positioning thinking. A company develops a product for a particular target market with a particular market positioning in mind with respect to price, quality, and service. Thus it makes an initial decision on offer value and price. Then the company estimates the volume it can sell at this price. This suggests the needed plant capacity, investment, and unit costs. Management then figures out whether the product will yield a satisfactory profit at the chosen price and cost. If the answer is yes, the company goes ahead with product development. Otherwise, the company drops the idea.

The key to perceived-value pricing is to make an accurate determination of the market's perception of the relative value of the company's offer versus

EXHIBIT 13-3

HOW CATERPILLAR USES PERCEIVED-VALUE PRICING

Caterpillar uses perceived value to set prices on its construction equipment. It might price a tractor at $24,000, although a similar competitor's tractor might be priced at $20,000. And Caterpillar will get more sales than the competitor! When a prospective customer asks a Caterpillar dealer why he should pay $4,000 more for the Caterpillar tractor, the dealer answers:

$20,000 would be the tractor's price if it were equivalent to the competitor's tractor
$3,000 is the price premium for superior durability
$2,000 is the price premium for superior reliability
$2,000 is the price premium for superior service
$1,000 is the price premium for the longer warranty on parts

$28,000 is the price to cover the value package
$4,000 discount

$24,000 final price

This stunned customer learns that although he is being asked to pay a $4,000 premium for the Caterpillar tractor, he is in fact getting a $4,000 discount! He ends up choosing the Caterpillar tractor because he is convinced that the lifetime operating costs of the Caterpillar tractor will be smaller.

competitors' offers. Sellers with an inflated view of the value of their offer may be overpricing their product. Other sellers may underestimate the perceived value and charge less than they could. Market research has to be carried out to establish the market's perceptions.[7]

DEMAND DIFFERENTIAL PRICING

Another form of demand-oriented pricing is demand differential pricing (also called *price discrimination*), in which a product or service is sold at two or more prices that do not reflect a proportional difference in marginal costs. Price discrimination takes various forms:

1. *Customer basis.* Here different customers pay different amounts for the same product or service. One car buyer pays the full list price, and another car buyer bargains and pays a lower price.
2. *Product-form basis.* Here different versions of the product are priced differently but not proportionately to their respective marginal costs. An electric dishwasher with a $5 formica top might be priced at $260, and the same dishwasher with a $10 wooden top might be priced at $280.
3. *Place basis.* Here different locations are priced differently, even though there is no difference in the marginal cost of offering the locations. A theatre varies its seat prices because of the different intensities of demand for the various locations.
4. *Time basis.* Here different prices are charged seasonally, by the day, and even by the hour. Public utilities typically vary their prices to commercial users by time of day and weekend versus weekday.

For price discrimination to work, certain conditions must exist.[8] First, the market must be segmentable, and the segments must show different intensities of demand. Second, there should be no chance that the members of the segment paying the lower price could turn around and resell the product to the segment paying the higher price. Third, there should be little chance that competitors will undersell the firm in the segment being charged the higher price. Fourth, the cost

EXHIBIT 13-4

AIRLINES MOVE TO DEMAND DIFFERENTIAL PRICING

The passengers on a plane bound from Cleveland to Miami may be paying as many as eleven different fares for the same flight. It depends on whether each passenger investigated the fare opportunities before buying. Those who checked carefully are benefiting from the heated-up competition between Eastern, United, and three other airlines flying this route. Many of the fares are aimed at segments of the market. The eleven possible fares are (1) $218 for first class, (2) $168 for standard economy class, (3) $136 for night coach, (4) $134 for weekend excursion, (5) $130 for Job Corps volunteers, (6) $128 for midweek excursion, (7) $118 for group-excursion tour, (8) $112 for military personnel, (9) $112 for youth fares, (10) $103 for weekend fares, and (11) $95 for the new part charter.

of segmenting and policing the market should not exceed the extra revenue derived from price discrimination. Fifth, the practice should not breed customer resentment and turning away.

Competition-oriented pricing strategies. When a company sets its prices chiefly on the basis of what its competitors are charging, its pricing strategy can be described as competition oriented. It is not necessary to charge the same price as the competition. The competition-oriented pricing firm may seek to keep its prices lower or higher than the competition by a certain percentage. The distinguishing characteristic is that it does *not* seek to maintain a rigid relation between its price and its own costs or demand. Its own costs or demand may change, but the firm maintains its price because competitors maintain their prices. Conversely, the same firm will change its prices when competitors change theirs, even if its own costs or demand have not altered.

GOING-RATE PRICING

The most popular type of competition-oriented pricing is where a firm tries to keep its price at the average level charged by the industry. Called *going-rate pricing,* it is popular for several reasons. Where costs are difficult to measure, it is felt that the going price represents the collective wisdom of the industry concerning the price that would yield a fair return. It is also felt that conforming to a going price would be least disruptive of industry harmony. The difficulty of knowing how buyers and competitors would react to price differentials is still another reason for this pricing.

Going-rate pricing primarily characterizes pricing practice in homogeneous product markets, although the market structure itself may vary from pure competition to pure oligopoly. The firm selling a homogeneous product in a highly competitive market has actually very little choice but to set the going price. In *pure oligopoly,* where a few large firms dominate the industry, the firm also tends to charge the same price as the competition, although for different reasons. Since there are only a few firms, each firm is quite aware of the others' prices, and so are the buyers. The slightest price difference would attract business to the lower-price firm. The individual oligopolist's demand curve has a kink in it at the level of the present prices. The demand curve tends to be elastic above the kink because other firms are not likely to follow a raise in prices; the demand curve tends to be inelastic below the kink because other firms are likely to follow a price cut. An oligopolist can gain little by raising its price when demand is elastic or lowering its price when demand is inelastic.

In markets characterized by *product differentiation,* the individual firm has more latitude in its price decision. Product and service differences desensitize the buyer to existing price differentials. Firms try to establish themselves in a pricing zone with respect to their competitors, assuming the role of a high-price, medium-price, or low-price firm. Their product and marketing program are made compatible with this chosen pricing zone, or vice versa. They respond to competitive changes in price to maintain their pricing zone.

SEALED-BID PRICING

Competitive-oriented pricing also dominates in those situations where firms compete for jobs on the basis of bids, such as original equipment manufacture and defense contract work. The bid is the firm's offer price, and it is a prime example of pricing based on expectations of how competitors will price rather than on a rigid relation based on the firm's own costs or demand. The objective of the firm in the bidding situation is to get the contract, and this means that it hopes to set its price lower than that set by any of the other bidding firms.

Yet the firm does not ordinarily set its price below a certain level. Even when it is anxious to get a contract in order to keep the plant busy, it cannot quote a price below marginal cost without worsening its position. On the other hand, as it raises its price above marginal cost, it increases its potential profit but reduces its chance of getting the contract.

The net effect of the two opposite pulls can be described in terms of the *expected profit* of the particular bid. Suppose a bid of $9,500 would yield a high chance of getting the contract, say .81, but only a low profit, say $100. The expected profit with this bid is therefore $81. If the firm bid $11,000, its profit would be $1,600, but its chance of getting the contract might be reduced, say to .01. The expected profit would be only $16. Table 13-2 shows these and some other bids and the corresponding expected profits.

One logical bidding criterion would be to state the bid that would maximize the expected profit. According to Table 13-2, the best bid would be $10,000, for which the expected profit is $216.

The use of the expected-profit criterion makes sense for the large firm that makes many bids and is not dependent on winning any particular contract. In playing the odds, it should achieve maximum profits in the long run. The firm that bids only occasionally and/or may need a particular contract badly will probably not find it advantageous to use the expected-profit criterion. The criterion, for example, does not distinguish between a $1,000 profit with a .10 probability and a $125 profit with an .80 probability. Yet the firm that wants to keep production going is likely to prefer the second contract to the first. In other words, the dollar value of expected profits may not reflect the utility value.

Pricing Tactics

Management ultimately has to establish specific prices within the context of the chosen pricing strategy. Two categories of pricing tactics are of particular interest, namely, psychological pricing and discount pricing. These are examined in the following paragraphs.

Psychological pricing tactics. The final price set on a product must take the psychology of the buyer into account. Four different pricing psychologies can be distinguished.[9]

Table 13-2
Effect of Different Bids on Expected Profit

COMPANY'S BID	COMPANY'S PROFIT	PROBABILITY OF GETTING AWARD WITH THIS BID (ASSUMED)	EXPECTED PROFIT
$ 9,500	$ 100	.81	$ 81
10,000	600	.36	216
10,500	1,100	.09	99
11,000	1,600	.01	16

ODD-EVEN PRICING

Many sellers believe that buyers favor odd prices over even prices. Instead of pricing a stereo amplifier at $300, the seller will price it at $299.95 or $295. Presumably the customer sees this as a $200 price rather than a $300 price, or sees it as a discount from the full price. This type of pricing has become customary, and newspaper ads are dominated with prices ending in odd numbers. Some psychologists have gone further and have argued that each digit has symbolic and visual qualities that should be considered in pricing. Thus 8 is symmetrical and should be used for a soothing effect, and 7 is angular and should be used when a jarring effect is desired.

PRICE LINING

Many sellers believe that buyers are not sensitive to small differences in price but only to large differences in price. The sellers will establish a limited number of prices for selected lines of merchandise. Thus a men's clothing store carries men's suits selling at three price levels: $150, $220, and $310. The customers will associate low-, average-, and high-quality suits with the three price "points." Even if the three prices are moderately changed, men will continue to buy suits at the price point they are used to. They are not sensitive to small changes in these price points.

PRESTIGE PRICING

Buyers often take price to be a sign of product quality, especially for products that they cannot easily evaluate. Bayer aspirin, although the highest-priced aspirin, continues to outsell lower-priced brands, indicating that people take its price to be a sign of higher quality. A woman who is shown two fur coats with different prices will almost always assume that the higher-priced coat has higher quality. Thus price has symbolic connotations that the seller must consider. At the same time, if the price is set too high, it can strain the buyer's credibility and create distrust of the retailer.

PROMOTIONAL PRICING

Buyers love to respond to special or low prices that indicate they are receiving a bargain. Supermarkets and department stores will often price a few of their products below their normal markup or even below cost. These are called *loss leaders* and are used to attract customers to the store in the hope that they will buy other things at normal markups. Sellers will also use *special-event pricing* in conjunction with sales seasons and special situations to draw in more customers. Thus linens are sold at especially low prices every January following the Christmas season as a means of attracting shopping-weary customers into the stores. Another promotional-pricing technique is *psychological discounting,* where the seller puts an artificially high price on a product and offers it at substantial savings; for example, "Was $359, Is $299." Illegitimate discount tactics are fought by the Federal Trade Commission and the Better Business Bureau. On the other hand, discounts from normal prices at which products were selling are a legitimate form of promotional pricing.

Discount pricing tactics. Pricing tactics call for establishing a *list price* (the official price) and a set of *discounts and allowances* that might be offered to dealers and customers as special incentives. The major forms of discounts and allowances are described below.

CASH DISCOUNTS

A cash discount is an offer of a price reduction to buyers who pay their bill promptly. A typical example would be "2/10, net 30," which means that payment is due within thirty days but the buyer can deduct 2 percent from the cost by paying the bill within ten days. The standard discount must be granted to all buyers on a nondiscriminatory basis. Such discounts have become customary in many industries and serve the purpose of improving the seller's liquidity and reducing credit collection costs and bad debts.

QUANTITY DISCOUNTS

A quantity discount is an offer of a price reduction to buyers who buy larger volumes. A typical example would be "$10 per unit for less than 100 units; $9 per unit for 100 or more units." Quantity discounts must be offered to all customers and are not supposed to exceed the cost savings to the seller associated with selling in large quantities. These savings include reduced expenses of selling, inventory, and transportation. They may be offered on a noncumulative basis (on each order placed) or a cumulative basis (on the number of units ordered over a given period). Discounts are an incentive to the buyer to buy more from a given seller rather than buying from multiple sources.

FUNCTIONAL DISCOUNTS

Also called trade discounts, functional discounts are payments to channel members for performing marketing functions required by the seller, such as selling, storing, and record keeping. A typical example would be when a manufacturer quotes a retail list price of $100 and discounts of 40 and 10 percent. The retailer's cost will be $60 ($100 minus 40 percent) and the wholesaler will pay $54 ($60 minus 10 percent). Manufacturers may offer different functional discounts to different trade channels because of the varying services they must perform, but manufacturers must offer the same functional discounts within each trade channel.

SEASONAL DISCOUNTS

A seasonal discount is an offer of a price reduction to buyers who buy merchandise or services out of season. Seasonal discounts allow the seller to maintain steadier production during the year. Ski manufacturers will offer seasonal discounts to retailers in the spring and summer in order to stimulate earlier ordering and keep their production going. Hotels, motels, and airlines will offer seasonal discounts in their slower selling periods.

ALLOWANCES

Allowances are other types of reductions from the list price. For example, trade-in allowances are price reductions granted for turning in an old item when buying a new one. Trade-in allowances are most common in the automobile industry and are also found in some other durable-goods categories. *Promotional allowances* are payments or price reductions to reward dealers for participating in advertising and sales-support programs.

This completes our review of a methodology for setting prices. The methodology requires establishing marketing objectives for the target market, formulating the broad marketing mix strategy, developing pricing policies and constraints, choosing pricing strategies, and setting pricing tactics. After setting the price, changes occurring in the environment will require the seller to consider altering the price. We now turn to this problem.

initiating price changes

Circumstances will often lead the seller to investigate the merits of initiating a price cut or increase. We will examine these two moves and also consider how to estimate the likely reactions of various parties, particularly buyers and competitors, to these moves.

Initiating Price Cuts

Several circumstances may lead a firm to consider cutting its price, even though this may threaten industrial harmony and provoke a price war. One circumstance is *excess capacity.* Here the firm needs additional business and presumably has failed to generate it through increased sales effort, product improvement, and other normal means of sales expansion. In the late 1970s various companies began to break ranks with "follow-the-leader pricing" and turned to "flexible pricing" to gain as much business as they could.[10]

Another circumstance is *falling market share* in the face of vigorous price competition. Several American industries—such as automobiles, consumer electronics, cameras, watches, and steel—have been losing market share, particularly to Japanese competitors whose high-quality goods carry lower prices than American products. This has led Zenith, General Motors, and others to take more aggressive pricing action. General Motors, for example, has begun to price by geography and has cut its subcompact car prices by 10 percent on the West Coast, where Japanese competition is strongest.

Still another circumstance provoking price cutting is a *drive for dominance through lower costs.* Either the aggressive pricer starts with lower costs than its competitors or it initiates price cuts in the hope of gaining market share which would lead to falling costs through larger volume.

Initiating Price Increases

Many companies have had to raise prices in recent years. They do this even though the price increases will be resented not only by customers and dealers but also by the company's own sales force. A successful price increase can increase profits considerably. For example, if the company's profit margin is 3 percent of sales, a 1 percent price increase will increase profits by 33 percent if sales volume is unaffected.

A major circumstance calling for upward price revision is the persistent worldwide *cost inflation.*[11] Rising costs unmatched by productivity gains squeeze profit margins and lead companies to regular rounds of price hikes. Prices are often raised by more than the cost increases in anticipation of further inflation or government price controls. Companies hesitate to make price commitments in long-term contracts for fear that cost inflation will erode their profit margins. Companies have become adept at inflation pricing through such measures as[12] (1) adopting delayed quotation pricing, (2) writing escalator clauses into contracts, (3) unbundling goods and services and pricing them separately, (4) reducing cash and quantity discounts and off-list pricing by sales force, (5) increasing minimum acceptance order sizes, (6) putting more sales power behind higher marginal products and markets, and (7) reducing product quality, features, or service.

The other major circumstance leading to price increases is *overdemand.* When a company cannot supply all of its customers, it can either raise its price or use allocation quotas, or both. Prices may be raised relatively invisibly by dropping discounts and adding higher-priced units to the line. Or prices may be pushed up boldly.

In passing price increases on to customers, the company should not act as a ruthless price gouger. The price increases should be accompanied by a well-thought-out communication program in which the customers are told why the prices are being increased, and how they might economize. The company's sales force should make regular calls on the customers and attempt to help them solve their problems.

Buyers' Reactions to Price Changes

Whether the price is to be moved up or down, the action is sure to affect buyers, competitors, distributors, and suppliers, and it may interest government as well. Here we will look at buyers' reactions.

Price elasticity of demand. The traditional analysis of buyers' reactions to price change utilizes the concept of *price elasticity of demand.* This is given by:

$$\text{Price elasticity of demand} = \frac{\text{\% change in quantity demanded}}{\text{\% change in price}}$$

A price elasticity of -1 means that sales rise (fall) by the same percentage as price falls (rises). In this case, total revenue is unaffected. A price elasticity greater than -1 means that sales rise (fall) by more than price falls (rises) in percentage terms; in this case, total revenue rises. A price elasticity less than -1 means that sales rise (fall) by less than price falls (rises) in percentage terms; in this case, total revenue falls.

Price elasticity of demand gives precision to the question of whether the firm's price is too high or too low. From the point of view of maximizing *revenue,* price is too high if demand is elastic and too low if demand is inelastic. Whether this is also true of maximizing *profits* depends on the behavior of costs.

Perceptual factors in buyers' response. Perceptual factors constitute an important intervening variable. Customers will not always put the most straightforward interpretation on a price change when it occurs.[13] A price reduction, which would normally attract more buyers, could mean other things to the buyers:[14] (1) the item is about to be superseded by a later model; (2) the item has some fault and is not selling well; (3) the firm is in financial trouble and may not stay in business to supply future parts; (4) the price will come down even further and it pays to wait; or (5) the quality has been reduced.

A price increase, which would normally deter sales, may carry a variety of different meanings to the buyers: (1) the item is very "hot" and may be unobtainable unless it is bought soon; (2) the item represents an unusually good value; or (3) the seller is greedy and is charging what the traffic will bear.

Competitors' Reactions to Price Changes

A firm contemplating a price change has to worry about competitors' as well as customers' reactions. Competitors' reactions are particularly important where the number of firms is small, the product offering is homogeneous, and the buyers are discriminating and informed.

How can the firm estimate the likely reactions of its competitors? Let us assume that the firm faces only one large competitor. The likely behavior of this competitor can be approached from two quite different starting points. One is to assume that the competitor has a set policy for reacting to price changes. The other is to assume that the competitor treats each price change as posing a fresh challenge and reacts according to self-interest at the time.

The problem is complicated because the competitor is capable of putting different interpretations on the company's price change. The competitor may take it to mean that (1) the company is trying to steal the market; (2) the company is not doing well and is trying to improve its sales; or (3) the company is hoping that the whole industry will reduce its prices in the interests of stimulating total demand.

When there is more than one competitor, the company must estimate each competitor's likely reaction. If all competitors behave alike, this amounts to analyzing only a typical competitor. If the competitors cannot be expected to react uniformly because of critical differences in size, market shares, or policies, then separate analyses are necessary. If it appears that a few competitors will match the price change, there is good reason to expect the rest will also match it.

responding to price changes

Let us reverse the previous question and ask how a firm should respond to a price change initiated by a competitor. The firm should first consider the following: (1) Why did the competitor change the price? Is it to steal the market, to utilize excess capacity, to meet changing cost conditions, or to evoke a calculated industry-wide price change to take advantage of total demand? (2) Is the competitor intending to make the price change temporary or permanent? (3) What will happen to the company's market share and profits if it ignores the price change? Are the other companies going to ignore the price change? and (4) What is the competitor's (and other firms') response likely to be to each possible reaction?

The best response requires an analysis of the particular situation. The company under attack has to consider the product's stage in the life cycle, its importance in the company's portfolio, the intentions and resources of the

Figure 13-4
Decision Program for Meeting a Competitor's Price Cut

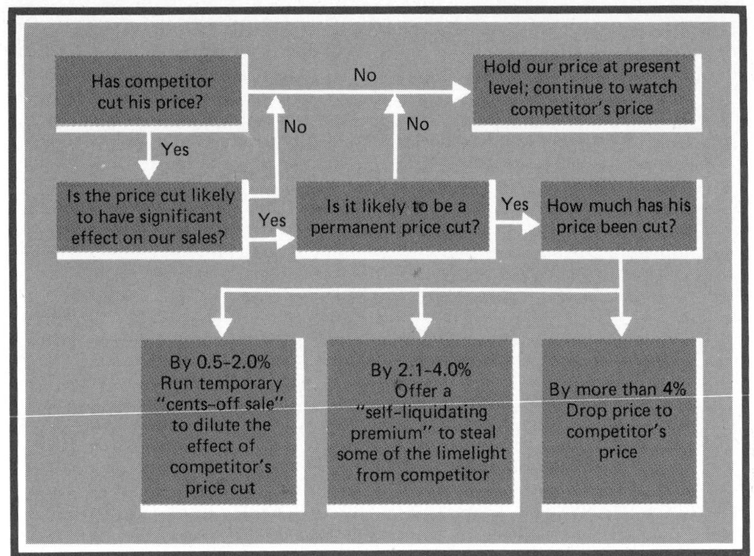

SOURCE: Redrawn, with permission, from an unpublished paper by Raymond J. Trapp, Northwestern University, 1964.

competitor, the price sensitivity versus value sensitivity of the market, the behavior of costs with volume, and the company's alternative opportunities.

An extended analysis of company alternatives is not always feasible at the time of a price change. The competitor who initiated the price change may have spent considerable time in preparing for this decision, but the company may have to react decisively within hours or days. About the only way to place such a decision on a sure footing is to anticipate the possible occurrence of price changes and to prepare an advanced program to guide managers' responses. An example of such a program to meet a possible price cut is shown in Figure 13-4. Reaction programs for meeting price changes are likely to find their greatest application in industries where price changes occur with some frequency and where it is important to react quickly. Examples could be found in the meat-packing, lumber, and oil industries.[15]

EXHIBIT 13-5

HOW HEUBLEIN, INC., PROTECTED ITS SMIRNOFF VODKA BRAND AGAINST A PRICE CUTTER THROUGH STRATEGIC PRICING

Heublein, Inc., produces Smirnoff vodka, the leading brand of vodka, with 23 percent of the American vodka market. In the 1960s it was attacked by another brand, Wolfschmidt, priced at one dollar less a bottle and claiming to be of the same quality. Heublein saw a real danger of customers switching to Wolfschmidt. Heublein considered the following possible reactions:

1. Lower the price of Smirnoff by one dollar or less to hold on to market share. This would reduce Smirnoff's profits.

2. Maintain the price of Smirnoff but increase advertising and promotion expenditures. This would reduce Smirnoff's profits.
3. Maintain the price of Smirnoff and let its market share fall. This would reduce Smirnoff's profits.

It seemed that Heublein faced a no-win situation.

At this point a fourth strategy suddenly occurred to management, and it was brilliant. Heublein *raised* the price of Smirnoff by one dollar! It introduced a new brand, Relska, to compete with Wolfschmidt at this price. And it introduced still another brand, Popov, at a lower price than Wolfschmidt. This strategy positioned Smirnoff as the elite brand and positioned Wolfschmidt as just another ordinary brand. Heublein's moves resulted in an increase in its total profits.

pricing the product line

The logic of setting or changing a price on an individual product has to be modified when the product is a member of a product line. In the latter case the quest is for a set of mutual prices that maximizes the profits of the line. This quest is made difficult because various company products are interrelated in demand and/or cost and are subject to different degrees of competition. We will consider two different situations.

The first situation has to do with a product line that consists of main products and satellite products. The satellite products take two forms. The first consists of *related optional products*. Here the buyer of the main product is free to buy none, one, or more optional products. The automobile customer can order such options as electric window controls, defoggers, and light dimmers. The restaurant customer can order or skip liquor in addition to the main course. The seller's task is to decide on prices for the related optional items. If the prices are too high, customers will either forgo purchase of the options or switch to other sellers who price these options lower. Management can choose between pricing these options high in order to serve as an independent profit source and pricing them low in order to act as a traffic builder. Many restaurants choose to price their liquor high and their food low. The food revenue covers the cost of the food and operating the restaurant, and the liquor produces the profit. Other restaurants will price their liquor low and food high to draw in a crowd that likes to drink.

The other type of satellite product is a *captive product* (or *after-market product*). Examples are razor blades, camera film, and copier supplies. Manufacturers of the main products (razors, cameras, and copiers) often price them low in order to stimulate purchase and then make their profit through a high markup on the supplies. Thus Kodak prices its cameras low because it makes its money on the film. Those camera makers who do not sell film have to price their cameras higher than Kodak in order to make the same overall profit.

The other interesting line-pricing situation arises in connection with *by-products*. In the production of processed meats, petroleum products, and other chemicals, there will often be byproducts. If the byproducts have no value and in some cases a cost of disposal, this will have to be considered in pricing the main product. The manufacturer will normally have a strong incentive to develop value either by finding a market for the product in its raw state or by processing it into a valued product where the processing cost is less than its value. The manufacturer should be willing to accept any price for the byproduct that covers more than its cost of processing and delivery, since this will contribute to profit or enable the seller to reduce the price of the main product to make it more competitive in the market.

■ summary

In spite of the increased role of nonprice factors in the modern marketing process, price remains an important element and is especially challenging in certain situations.

In setting an original price on a product, the company should follow a pricing methodology consisting of five steps. First, the company should carefully identify the target market and establish its marketing objective, such as current profit maximization, market-share leadership, market skimming, or product quality leadership. Second, the company should develop a broad idea of the appropriate marketing mix. Third, the company should consider the contemplated price in relation to the company's established pricing policies and the attitudes of important publics such as distributors, competitors, suppliers, government, and company executives. Fourth, the company should select a pricing strategy in the light of its possible orientation to cost (markup pricing, target pricing), demand (perceived-value pricing, differential demand pricing), or competition (going-rate pricing, sealed bidding). Fifth, the company should consider determining the price by paying attention to psychological pricing tactics (odd-even pricing, price lining, prestige pricing, and promotional pricing) and to discount pricing tactics (cash, quantity, functional, and seasonal discounts and allowances).

When a firm considers changing its price, it must carefully consider customers' and competitors' reactions. The probable reaction of customers is described in the price elasticity of demand. Competitors' reactions must be anticipated on the assumption either that they flow from a set reaction policy or that they flow from a fresh appraisal of the challenge each time. The firm initiating the price change must also consider the probable reactions of suppliers, middlemen, and government.

The firm that faces a competitor's price change must try to understand the competitor's intent and the likely duration of the change. If swiftness of reaction is desirable, the firm should preplan its reactions to different possible pricing developments.

Pricing is complicated when various products in a line have important demand and/or cost interrelationships. Then the objective is to develop a set of mutual prices that maximize the profits on the whole line.

questions for discussion

1. In setting prices it is essential only to establish target market objectives. Comment.
2. Do the following companies practice market penetration or market skimming in pricing their products? (a) McDonald's, (b) Curtis Mathes television sets, and (c) Bic Corporation. Why?
3. Relate the essential parties in developing pricing policies and constraints to Adidas's decision to price a new line of shoes.
4. What are the major types of cost-oriented pricing strategies? Provide a company example of each.
5. Which of the psychological pricing tactics do you think the following marketers utilize? (a) Hart Schaffner and Marx, (b) Safeway, and (c) K-Mart, and (d) Kinney Shoes.
6. Discuss two major discount pricing tactics that Head Skis might employ in dealing with the retail outlets that carry its products.
7. In recent years the majority of price changes made by marketers have been price increases. Why?
8. If a company is to respond accurately to price changes, it must thoroughly understand its competitors. Comment.
9. Public policy makers are charged with overseeing what three major pricing issues?

references

1. This example, developed by the author, is derived from an example found in DAVID J. SCHWARTZ, *Marketing Today: A Basic Approach,* 2nd ed. (New York: Harcourt Brace Jovanovich, 1977), pp. 542–44.
2. Ibid., p. 520.
3. See JOEL DEAN, *Managerial Economics* (Englewood Cliffs, N.J.: Prentice-Hall, 1951), pp. 420ff.
4. *Departmental Merchandising and Operating Results of 1965* (New York: National Retail Merchants Association, 1965).
5. See LEE E. PRESTON, *Profits, Competition, and Rules of Thumb in Retail Food Pricing* (Berkeley: University of California Institute of Business and Economic Research, 1963), p. 31.
6. Ibid., pp. 29–40.
7. See DANIEL A. NIMER, "Pricing the Profitable Sale Has a Lot to Do with Perception," *Sales Management,* May 19, 1975, pp. 13–14.
8. See GEORGE STIGLER, *The Theory of Price,* rev. ed. (New York: Macmillan, 1952), pp. 215ff.
9. For further discussion, see EDWARD R. HAWKINS, "Price Policies and Theory," *Journal of Marketing,* January 1954, pp. 233–40.
10. See "Flexible Pricing," *Business Week,* December 12, 1977, pp. 78–88.
11. See "Pricing Strategy in an Inflation Economy," *Business Week,* April 6, 1974, pp. 43–49.

12. Norman H. Fuss, Jr., "How to Raise Prices—Judiciously—to Meet Today's Conditions," *Harvard Business Review,* May-June 1975, pp. 10ff.

13. For an excellent review, see Kent B. Monroe, "Buyers' Subjective Perceptions of Price," *Journal of Marketing Research,* February 1973, pp. 70–80.

14. See Alfred R. Oxenfeldt, *Pricing for Marketing Executives* (San Francisco: Wadsworth, 1961), p. 28.

15. See, for example, William M. Morgenroth, "A Method for Understanding Price Determinants," *Journal of Marketing Research,* August 1964, pp. 17–26.

MARKETING CHANNEL AND PHYSICAL-DISTRIBUTION STRATEGY

Freightliner Corporation, a manufacturer of heavy-duty motor trucks, is like a new babe coming out of the woods. With a 7.7 percent share of the over-26,000-lb. diesel truck market, Freightliner is aiming at building up its dealership system and marketing programs in an aggressive move to take away business from the other majors, led by International Harvester (25.4 percent market share), Mack (16.8 percent), Ford (14.8 percent), Paccar (14.0 percent), and General Motors (11.7 percent).

Whereas its competitors have well-established dealership systems, Freightliner has to build one almost from scratch. After World War II the company started to build trucks to meet the special needs of Consolidated Freightways, Inc., a major trucker. In the fifties it began to sell its trucks to other buyers under a marketing agreement with White Motor Corporation. White's dealers handled both White trucks and Freightliner trucks, selling about an equal number of each. In 1975 Freightliner moved to marketing independence and ended its agreement with the White Motor Company. Now it had to stand on its own and build a whole new national dealership system.

Freightliner's management had to answer a lot of questions. Should the company set up only independent dealerships or also operate company-owned branches? For example, International Harvester sells its trucks through two thousand dealers and 184 company-owned branches. Should Freightliner establish exclusive dealerships carrying only its own trucks or dealerships carrying one or more additional truck lines? Should Freightliner work with dealers carrying light-duty trucks and recreational vehicles? Sometimes these arrangements are unsatisfactory because the dealers' sales force is not well trained in selling these vastly different types of vehicles to quite different types of customers. Should the new dealerships be located in major cities, small cities, or suburbs? What should new dealers pay for the franchise and how much capital should they have? To what extent should Freightliner finance the dealers' land, building, equipment, inventory, and receivables? What service policies should be required from the dealers? Should Freightliner's territory managers both sell and train dealers or should these functions be handled by a sales group and dealer training group, respectively?

Freightliner has already made many of these decisions. It decided against operating any company-owned branches because independent dealers find them threatening. Freightliner also decided to build

separate selling and training sales forces. In training the dealers, Freightliner wants them to know how to adjust their sales presentations to fleet versus owner-operator customers. Fleet customers seek economy in choosing trucks, while owner-operators often look for status symbols and comfort—lots of chrome and costly extras that sometimes push a $40,000 truck into the $60,000 price class. Freightliner is definitely customizing its trucks for the higher-price end of the market, putting it into keen competition with Peterbilt and Kenworth trucks produced by Paccar, Inc. Its advertising program, costing $1.75 million, will promote its trucks as efficient machines from the business standpoint. In this highly competitive market, Freightliner has to determine how it can stand out. Its trucks have to be great, and its advertising and pricing have to be effective. But the key to its success will be its ability to find, train, and motivate exceptional dealers with a will to win.[1]

□Marketing-channel decisions are among the most critical decisions faced by management. *The channels chosen for the company's products intimately affect every other marketing decision.* The firm's pricing decisions depend upon whether it seeks large and high-quality dealers or medium-size and medium-quality dealers. The firm's sales-force decisions depend upon how much selling and training the dealers will need. In addition, the channel decisions *involve the firm in relatively long term commitments to other firms.* When a truck manufacturer signs up independent dealers, it cannot easily replace them with company-owned branches if conditions change. Therefore management must choose its channels carefully with an eye on tomorrow's likely selling environment as well as today's.

In this chapter we will examine the following issues: (1) What is the nature of marketing channels and what trends are taking place? (2) What are the major decisions facing marketers with respect to designing, managing, and modifying their channels? (3) What role do physical-distribution decisions play in attracting and satisfying customers? In the following chapter we will shift our focus and examine marketing issues and decisions from the perspective of retailers and wholesalers.

the nature of marketing channels

Every producer seeks to link the marketing institutions that will help it best accomplish its objectives. This set of marketing institutions is called a *distribution channel.* In Chapter 2 (p. 47), we defined *distribution channel* as *the set of all the firms and individuals that take title, or assist in transferring title, to the particular good or service as it moves from the producer to the consumer.* We also distinguished between four groups: *merchant middlemen, agent middlemen, facilitators,* and *marketing firms* (see p. 47). Further classifications and definitions of middlemen will be given in Chapter 15.

Why Are Marketing Intermediaries Used?

Why is the producer generally willing to delegate some of the selling job to intermediaries? The delegation usually means the relinquishment of some control over how and to whom the products are sold. The producer appears to be placing the firm's destiny in the hands of intermediaries.

Since producers are free in principle to sell directly to final customers, there must be certain advantages or necessities for using middlemen. Some of the major factors are described below.

Many producers lack the financial resources to embark on a program of direct marketing. For example, General Motors' new automobiles are marketed by over eighteen thousand independent dealers; even General Motors would be hard pressed to raise the cash to buy out its dealers.

Direct marketing would require many producers to become middlemen for the complementary products of other producers in order to achieve mass distributional efficiency. For example, the Wm. Wrigley Jr. Company would not find it practical to establish small retail gum shops throughout the country or to sell gum door to door or by mail order. It would have to tie gum in with the sale of many other small products and end up in the drugstore and foodstore business. It is much easier for Wrigley to work through the existing and extensive network of privately owned distribution institutions.

Those producers who have the required capital to develop their own channels can often earn a greater return by increasing their investment in other parts of their business. If a company is earning a 20 percent rate of return on its manufacturing operation and foresees only a 5 percent rate of return on investing in direct marketing, it would not make sense to put money in direct marketing.

The use of middlemen largely boils down to their superior efficiency in making goods widely available and accessible to target markets. Marketing intermediaries, through their contacts, experience, specialization, and scale of operation, offer the firm more than it can usually achieve on its own.

From the point of view of the economic system, the basic role of marketing channels is to transform the heterogeneous supplies found in nature into meaningful goods assortments desired by people:

- The materials which are useful to man occur in nature in heterogeneous mixtures which might be called conglomerations since these mixtures have only random relationship to human needs and activities. The collection of goods in the possession of a household or an individual also constitutes a heterogeneous supply, but it might be called an assortment since it is related to anticipated patterns of future behavior. The whole economic process may be described as a series of transformations from meaningless to meaningful heterogeneity.[2]

Alderson has summarized this as follows: "The goal of marketing is the matching of segments of supply and demand."[3]

Figure 14-1 shows just one source of the economies effected by the use of middlemen. Part A shows three producers using direct marketing to reach each of three customers. This system requires nine different contacts. Part B shows the three producers working through one distributor, who in turn contacts the three customers. This system requires only six contacts. In this way the use of middlemen reduces the amount of work that must be done.

Figure 14-1
How a Distributor Effects An Economy of Effort

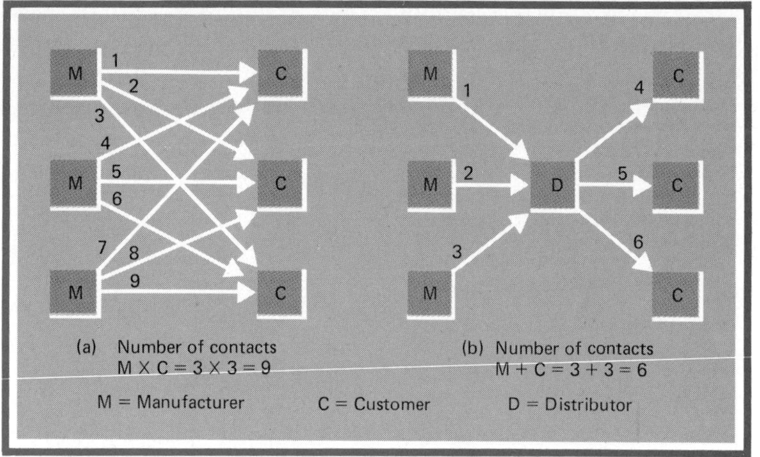

Marketing-Channel Functions

A marketing channel is essentially a method of organizing the work that has to be done to move goods from producers to consumers. The purpose of the work is to overcome various gaps that separate the goods and services from those who would use them. The work of middlemen is designed to create *form, time, place,* and *possession utilities.* The following major marketing-channel *functions* or tasks are involved in this work:[4]

1. *Research*—the gathering of information necessary for planning and facilitating exchange.
2. *Promotion*—the development and dissemination of persuasive communications about the offer.
3. *Contact*—the searching out and communicating with prospective buyers.
4. *Matching*—the shaping and fitting of the offer to the buyer's requirements. This includes such activities as manufacturing, grading, assembling, and packaging.
5. *Negotiation*—the attempt to reach final agreement on price and other terms of the offer so that transfer of ownership or possession can be effected.
6. *Physical distribution*—the transporting and storing of the goods.
7. *Financing*—the acquisition and dispersal of funds to cover the costs of the channel work.
8. *Risk taking*—the assumption of risks in connection with carrying out the channel work.

The first five functions deal primarily with consummating transactions; the last three deal with facilitating transactions.

It is not a question of *whether* these functions must be performed—they must be—but rather *who* is to perform them. All of the functions have three things in common: They use up scarce resources, they can often be performed better through specialization, and they are shiftable. To the extent that the manufacturer performs them, its costs go up and its prices have to be higher. When some of these tasks are delegated to middlemen, the producer's costs and prices are lower, but the middlemen must add a charge to cover the use of scarce resources. The issue of who should perform various channel tasks is largely one of relative efficiency and effectiveness.

Marketing functions, then, are more basic than the institutions that at any given time appear to perform them. Changes in channel institutions largely reflect the discovery of more efficient ways to combine or separate economic functions that must be carried out to provide useful assortments of goods to target customers.

Number of Channel Levels

Marketing channels can be characterized according to the number of channel levels. Each middleman that performs some work to bring the product and its title closer to the point of consumption constitutes a *channel level.* Since both the producer and the ultimate consumer perform some work, they are part of every channel. We will use the number of *intermediary levels* to designate the *length* of a channel. Figure 14-2 illustrates several marketing channels of different lengths.

A *zero-level channel* (also called a *direct marketing channel*) consists of a manufacturer selling directly to a consumer. Avon's sales representatives sell cosmetics directly to homemakers on a door-to-door basis; IBM's sales representatives sell computer equipment directly to user firms; and Bell Apple Orchard invites the public to pick their own apples at a flat price per bushel.

A *one-level channel* contains one selling intermediary. In consumer markets this intermediary is typically a retailer; in industrial markets it is often a sales agent or a broker.

A *two-level channel* contains two intermediaries. In consumer markets they are typically a wholesaler and a retailer; in industrial markets they may be a sales agent and a wholesaler.

A *three-level channel* contains three intermediaries. For example, in the meat-packing industry a jobber usually intervenes between the wholesalers and the retailers. The jobber buys from wholesalers and sells to the smaller retailers, who generally are not serviced by the large wholesalers.

Higher-level marketing channels are also found, but with less frequency. From the producer's point of view the problem of control increases with the

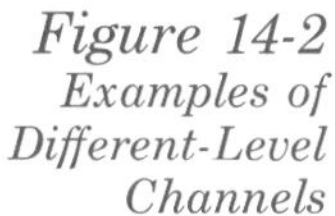

Figure 14-2
Examples of Different-Level Channels

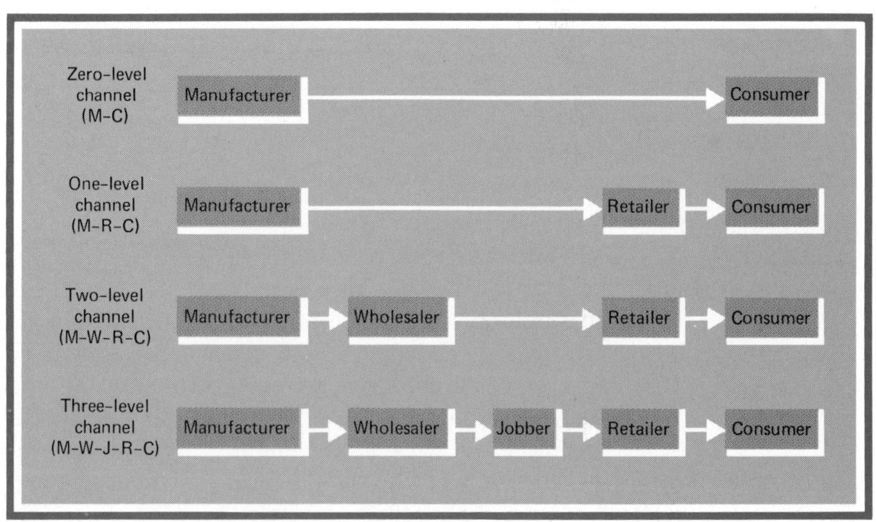

number of levels, even though the manufacturer typically deals only with the adjacent level.

Types of Channel Flows

The various institutions that make up a marketing channel are connected by several types of flows. The most important are the physical flow, title flow, payment flow, information flow, and promotion flow. These are illustrated in Figure 14-3 for the marketing of forklift trucks.

The *physical flow* describes the actual movement of physical products from raw materials to final customers. In the case of a forklift-truck manufacturer, such as Allis-Chalmers or Clark Equipment, raw materials, subassemblies, parts, and engines flow from suppliers via transportation companies (transporters) to the manufacturer's warehouses and plants. The finished trucks are warehoused and are later shipped to dealers in response to their orders. The dealers in turn sell and ship them to customers. Large orders may be supplied directly from the company warehouses or even from the plant itself. At each stage of movement, one or more modes of shipment may be used, including railroads, trucks, and airfreight.

The *title flow* describes the actual passage of title (of ownership) from one marketing institution to another. In the case of forklift trucks, title to the raw materials and components passes from the suppliers to the manufacturer. Title to the finished trucks passes from the manufacturer to the dealers and then to the customers. If the dealers only held the trucks on *consignment,* they would not be included in the diagram.

The *payment flow* shows customers paying their bills through banks and other financial institutions to the dealers, the dealers remitting payment to the manufacturer (less the commission), and the manufacturer making payments to the various suppliers. There will also be payments made to transporters and independent warehouses (not shown in the figure).

The *information flow* describes how information is exchanged among the institutions in the marketing channel. A two-way information exchange takes place between each successive stage in the channel, and there are several information flows between nonadjacent institutions.

Finally, the *promotion flow* describes directed flows of influence (advertising, personal selling, sales promotion and publicity) from one party to other parties in the system. Suppliers promote their name and products to the manufacturer. They may also promote their name and products to final customers in the hope of influencing the manufacturer to prefer products embodying their parts or materials. A promotion flow is also directed by the manufacturer to dealers (trade promotion) and final customers (end-user promotion).

If all of these flows were superimposed on one diagram, they would emphasize the tremendous complexity of even simple marketing channels. This complexity goes even further, once we start distinguishing among different types of retailers, wholesalers, and others (see Chapter 15).

Channels in the Service Sector

The concept of marketing channels is not limited to the distribution of physical goods. Producers of services and ideas also face the problem of making their output *available* and *accessible* to target populations. Current talk about

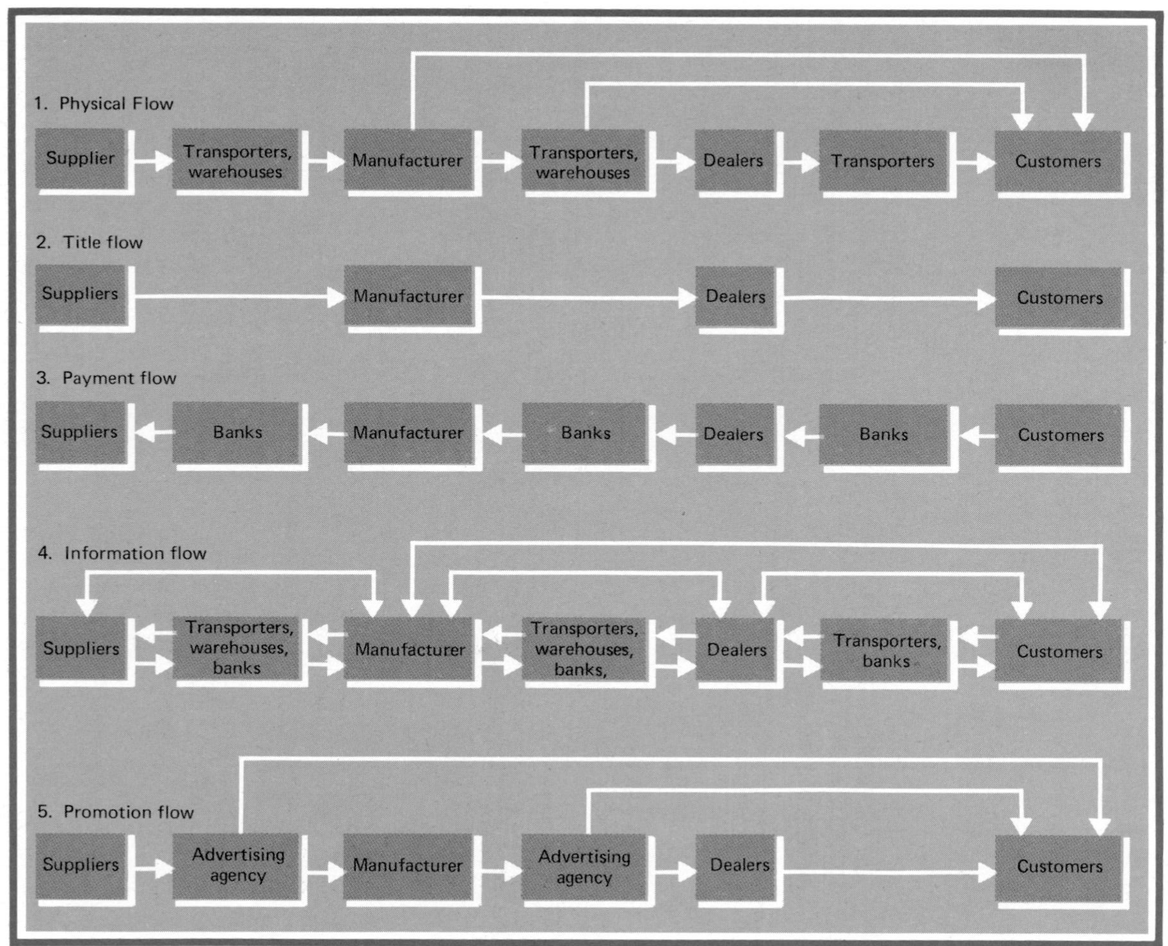

Figure 14-3 *Five Different Marketing Flows in the Marketing Channel for Forklift Trucks*

"educational dissemination systems" and "health delivery systems" is simply another way of describing marketing channels that distribute services in the nonprofit sector. The producers' problem is one of developing and locating a set of agencies and facilities to provide services to a spatially distributed population:

- Hospitals must be located in geographic space to serve the people with complete medical care, and we must build schools close to the children who have to learn. Fire stations must be located to give rapid access to potential conflagrations, and voting booths must be placed so that people can cast their ballots without expending unreasonable amounts of time, effort or money to reach the polling stations. Many of our states face the problem of locating branch campuses to serve a burgeoning and increasingly well educated population. In the cities we must create and locate playgrounds for the children. Many overpopulated countries must assign birth control clinics to reach the people with contraceptive and family planning information.[5]

Channels of distribution are also used in "person" marketing. Before 1940 seven different channels were available to a professional comedian seeking an audience: vaudeville houses, special events, nightclubs, radio, movies, carnivals, and theaters. In the 1950s television emerged as a strong channel and vaudeville disappeared. Politicians also must find cost-effective channels—mass media, rallies, coffee hours—for distributing their ideas to the voters.

Channels are normally thought to describe routes for the forward movement of products. Increasingly there is talk about the development of *backward channels.* According to Zikmund and Stanton:

- The recycling of solid wastes is a major ecological goal. Although recycling is technologically feasible, reversing the flow of materials in the channel of distribution—marketing trash through a "backward" channel—presents a challenge. Existing backward channels are primitive, and financial incentives are inadequate. The consumer must be motivated to undergo a role change and become a producer—the initiating force in the reverse distribution process.[6]

The authors go on to identify several types of middlemen that can play a role in the "backward channel," including (1) manufacturers' redemption centers, (2) "Clean-up Days" community groups, (3) traditional middlemen such as soft-drink middlemen, (4) trash-collection specialists, (5) recycling centers, (6) modernized "rag and junk men," (7) trash-recycling brokers, and (8) central-processing warehousing.

Growth of Vertical Marketing Systems

One of the most significant channel developments in recent years has been the emergence of *vertical marketing systems* to challenge and supplant *conventional marketing channels.* Conventional channels are "highly fragmented networks in which loosely aligned manufacturers, wholesalers, and retailers have bargained with each other at arm's length, negotiated aggressively over terms of sale, and otherwise behaved autonomously." By contrast, *vertical marketing systems* (VMSs) are "professionally managed and centrally programmed networks, pre-engineered to achieve operating economies and maximum market impact."[7] Vertical marketing systems offer effective competition to conventional marketing channels because they achieve impressive scale economies through their size, bargaining power, and elimination of duplicated services. In fact, they have emerged in the consumer-goods sector of American economy as the preferred mode of distribution, serving as much as 64 percent of the total market.

Corporate VMS. Three types of vertical marketing systems are shown in Figure 14-4. A *corporate vertical marketing system* has as its distinguishing characteristic the combining of successive stages of production and distribution under a single ownership. As examples:

- . . . Sherwin-Williams currently owns and operates over 2,000 retail outlets . . . Sears reportedly obtains 50 percent of its throughput from manufacturing facilities in which it has an equity interest. . . . Holiday Inns is evolving into a self-supply network that includes a carpet mill, a furniture manufacturing plant, and numerous captive redistribution facilities. In short, these and other organizations are massive, vertically integrated systems. To describe them as "retailers," "manufacturers," or "motel operators" oversimplifies their operating complexities and ignores the realities of the marketplace.[8]

Contractual VMS. A *contractual vertical marketing system* consists of independent firms at different levels of production and distribution integrating their programs on a contractual basis to obtain more economies and/or sales impact than they could achieve alone. Contractual VMSs have expanded the most in recent years and constitute one of the most significant developments in the economy. There are three major types of contractual VMSs.

Figure 14-4
Conventional and Vertical Marketing Channels

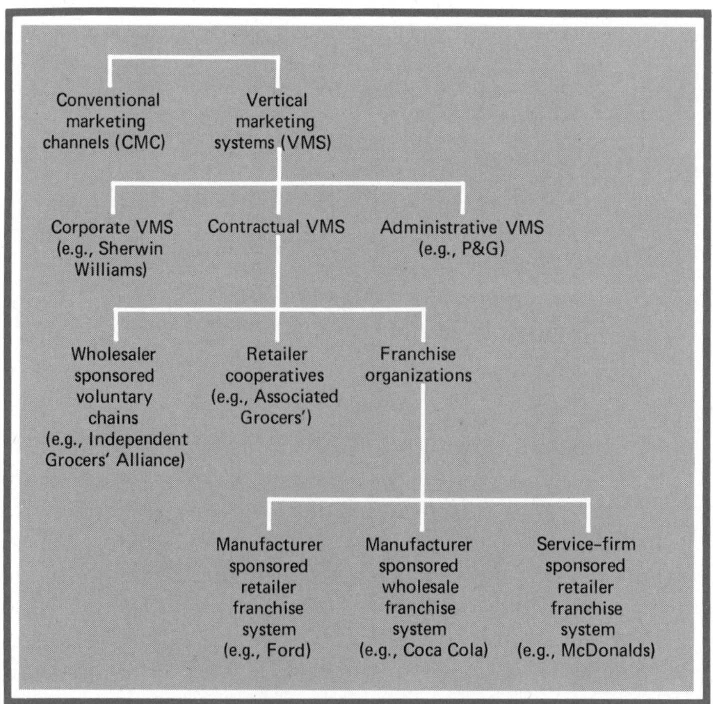

WHOLESALER-SPONSORED VOLUNTARY CHAINS

These originated when wholesalers attempted to save the independent retailers they served from the competition of large chain organizations. The wholesaler develops a program in which independent retailers join together to standardize their practices and/or to achieve buying economies that enable them as a group to withstand the inroads of the chains.

RETAILER COOPERATIVES

These arose through the efforts of groups of retailers to defend themselves against the corporate chains. The retailers organize a new business entity to carry on wholesaling and possibly production. Members are expected to concentrate their purchases through the retailer co-op and plan their advertising jointly. Profits are passed back to members in the form of patronage refunds. Nonmember retailers may also be allowed to buy through the co-op but do not receive patronage refunds.

FRANCHISE ORGANIZATIONS

Here several successive stages in the production-distribution process are linked under an agreement with one channel member called the franchiser. Franchising has been the fastest-growing and most interesting retailing development in recent years. Although the basic idea is an old one, some forms of franchising are quite new. Three forms of franchises can be distinguished.

The first is the *manufacturer-sponsored retailer franchise system,* exemplified by the automobile industry. A car manufacturer such as Ford licenses dealers to sell its cars, the dealers being independent businesspeople who agree to meet various conditions of sales and service.

The second is the *manufacturer-sponsored wholesaler franchise system,* which is found in the soft-drink industry. Coca-Cola, for example, licenses bottlers (wholesalers) in various markets who buy its syrup concentrate and then carbonate, bottle, and sell it to retailers in local markets.

The third is the *service-firm-sponsored retailer franchise system.* Here a service firm organizes a whole system for bringing its service efficiently to consumers. Examples are found in the auto rental business (Hertz, Avis), fast-food service business (McDonald's, Burger King), and motel business (Howard Johnson, Ramada Inn). This type of franchising system is discussed further in Chapter 15, pp. 477–78.

Administered VMS. An *administered vertical marketing system,* by contrast, achieves coordination of successive stages of production and distribution not through common ownership but through the size and power of one of the parties within the system. Thus manufacturers of a dominant brand are able to secure strong trade cooperation and suppport from resellers. Such companies as General Electric, Procter and Gamble, Kraftco, and Campbell Soup are able to command unusual cooperation from their resellers and retailers in connection with displays, shelf space, promotions, and price policies.

Many independents, if they have not joined VMSs, have become specialty-store operators, serving special segments of the market that are not available or attractive to the mass merchandisers. Thus there is a polarization in retailing, with large vertical marketing organizations on the one hand and specialty independent stores on the other. This development creates a problem for independent manufacturers. They are strongly aligned with independent middlemen whom they cannot easily give up. At the same time, they must eventually realign themselves with the high-growth vertical marketing systems. The manufacturers will probably have to accept less-attractive terms from these large buying organizations. Vertical marketing systems can always decide to bypass large manufacturers and set up their own manufacturing. *The new competition in retailing is no longer between independent business units but rather between whole systems of centrally programmed networks (corporate, administered, and contractual) competing against each other to achieve the best economies and customer response.*

Growth of Horizontal Marketing Systems

Another significant development is the readiness of two or more companies to form alliances to jointly exploit an emerging marketing opportunity. None of these companies is able to amass the capital, know-how, production, or marketing facilities to venture alone; or it prefers not to because of the high risk; or it sees a substantial synergy in the proposed relationship. The companies may set up temporary or permanent arrangements to work with each other, or to create another entity owned by the parents. Such developments in horizontal marketing systems have been described by Adler as *symbiotic marketing.*[9] For example, Dr. Pepper, in its effort to break into new markets, lacked bottlers for its soft drink and decided instead to license Coca-Cola bottlers to bottle Dr. Pepper. And we saw earlier that Freightliner as a truck producer entered a marketing agreement with the White Motor Company so that it could use the latter's dealers to sell Freightliner trucks.

Growth of Multichannel Marketing Systems

Companies are increasingly adopting multichannel systems to reach the same or different markets. For example, the John Smythe Company, a Chicago-based furniture retailer, sells a full line of furniture through its company-owned conventional furniture stores as well as through its Homemakers Division, which operates furniture warehouse showrooms. Furniture shoppers can spot many similar items in both types of outlets, usually finding lower prices at the latter. As another example, J. C. Penney operates department stores, mass-merchandising stores (called The Treasury), and specialty stores. Tillman has labeled large retailing stores with diversified retailing channels "merchandising conglomerates" or "conglomerchants" and has defined them as "a multiline merchandising empire under central ownership, usually combining several styles of retailing with behind-the-scenes integration of some distribution and management functions."[10]

A growing number of companies are operating multichannels that serve two different customer levels. This is called *dual distribution* and can be a source of many conflicts for the sponsoring company.[11] For example, General Electric sells large home appliances through independent dealers (department stores, discount houses, catalog retailers) and also directly to large tract builders. The independent dealers would like General Electric to get out of the business of selling to tract builders, thus competing with the retailers. General Electric defends its position by pointing out that builders and retailers are different classes of customers.

Roles of Individual Firms in a Channel

Our discussion of vertical, horizontal, and multichannel marketing systems underscores the dynamic and changing nature of channels. Each firm in an industry has to define its relationship to the dominant channel type. McCammon has distinguished five types of relationships:[12]

1. *Insiders* are the members of the dominant channel who enjoy continuous access to preferred sources of supply and high respect in the industry. They have an interest in perpetuating the existing channel arrangements and are the main enforcers of the industry code.
2. *Strivers* are those firms who are seeking to become insiders but have not yet arrived. They have less continuous access to preferred sources of supply, which can handicap them in periods of short supply. They adhere to the industry code because of their desire to become insiders.
3. *Complementors* neither are nor seek to be part of the dominant channel. They perform functions not normally performed by others in the channel, or serve smaller segments of the market, or handle smaller quantities of merchandise. They usually benefit from the present system and tend to respect the industry code.
4. *Transients,* like the complementors, are outside the dominant channel and do not seek membership. They go in and out of the market or move around as opportunities arise, but they are really members of another channel. They have short-run expectations and little incentive to adhere to the industry code.
5. *Outside innovators* are the real challengers and disrupters of the dominant channels. They come with an entirely new system for carrying out the marketing work of the channel; if successful, they cause major channel realignments. They are companies like McDonald's, Avon, and Holiday Inn, who doggedly develop a new system to challenge the old.

Another important role is that of *channel captain.* The channel captain is the dominant member of a particular channel, the one who organized it and leads it. For example, General Motors is the channel captain of a system consisting of a huge number of suppliers, dealers, and facilitators. The channel captain is not always a manufacturer, as the examples of McDonald's and Sears indicate. Some channels do not have an acknowledged captain in that the various firms do not even recognize that they are acting as part of a system.

Channel Cooperation, Conflict, and Competition

It should be clear that within and between marketing channels there are different degrees of cooperation, conflict, and competition.

Channel cooperation is usually the dominant theme among members of the same channel. The channel represents a coalition of dissimilar firms that have banded together for mutual advantage. Manufacturers, wholesalers, and retailers complement each other's needs, and their partnership normally produces greater profits for each participant than could have been secured by trying to carry out individually all of the channel's work. The need for channel cooperation is a natural extension of the marketing concept in that firms are trying to effectively sense, serve, and satisfy the needs of the target market.

Channel conflict, nevertheless, also tends to occur within each channel system. *Horizontal channel conflict* refers to conflict between firms at the same level of the channel. Some Ford car dealers in Chicago may complain about other Ford dealers in the city being too aggressive in their pricing and advertising and stealing sales from them. Some Pizza Inn franchisees may complain about other Pizza Inn franchisees cheating on the ingredients, maintaining poor service, and hurting the overall Pizza Inn image. In cases of horizontal channel conflict, the responsibility lies with the *channel captain* to set clear and enforceable policies, to see that information about intralevel channel conflict flows upward to management, and to take quick and definitive action to reduce or control this type of conflict, which, if left unchecked, could hurt the channel's image and cohesiveness.

Vertical channel conflict is even more common and refers to conflicts of interest between different levels of the same channel. For example, General Motors came into conflict with its dealers some years ago in trying to enforce policies on service, pricing, and advertising. And Coca-Cola came into conflict with its bottlers who agreed to bottle Dr. Pepper. Some amount of vertical channel conflict is healthy, and the problem is not one of eliminating it but of managing it better. The channel captain should attempt to develop *superordinate goals* for the system from which everyone would gain. Superordinate goals would include trying to minimize the total cost of moving the product through the system, improving information flows within the system, and cooperating to increase consumer acceptance of the product. Also, *administrative mechanisms* should be developed that increase participation and trust, and help to resolve conflicts, such as dealer and distributor councils and various conciliation, mediation, and arbitration mechanisms.[13]

Channel competition is another phenomenon of channel relations and describes the normal competition between firms and systems trying to serve the same target markets. *Horizontal channel competition* occurs between firms at the same channel level competing for sales in the same target market. Thus various appliance retailers such as department stores, discount stores, and catalog houses all compete for the consumer's appliance dollar. This competition is healthy and should result in consumers' enjoying a wider range of choice in the way of products, prices, and services. *Channel system competition* describes the competition between different whole systems serving a given target market. For example, are food consumers better served by conventional marketing channels, corporate chains, wholesale-sponsored voluntary chains, retailer-cooperatives, or food franchise systems? While each system will have some loyal followers, the share of the different systems in the total food business will shift over time in favor of those systems that are best able to meet changing consumer needs.

channel-design decisions

We will now look at channel decision problems from the producer's point of view. In Chapter 15, we will examine channel management decisions facing resellers.

In selecting channels of distribution, producers have to struggle with what is ideal and what is available. In the typical case a new firm starts as a local or regional operation selling to a limited market. Since it has limited capital, it usually utilizes existing middlemen. The number of middlemen in any local market is apt to be limited: a few manufacturer's sales agents, a few wholesalers, an established set of retailers, a few trucking companies, and a few warehouses. Deciding on the best channels may not be a problem. The problem may be to convince one or a few available middlemen to handle the line.

If the new firm is successful, it may branch out to new markets. Again, the producer will tend to work through the existing intermediaries, although this may mean using different types of marketing channels in different areas. In the smaller markets the firm may sell directly to the retailers; in the larger markets it may work only through distributors. In rural areas it may work with general-goods merchants; in urban areas, with limited-line merchants. In one part of the country it may grant exclusive franchises because the merchants are accustomed to work this way; in another, it may sell through any and all outlets willing to handle the merchandise. Thus the producer's channel system evolves in response to local opportunities and conditions, as well as other factors.

Identifying the Major Channel Alternatives

Let us assume that a company has defined its target market and desired positioning. It should next attempt to identify its major channel alternatives. A channel alternative is described by three elements: (1) the *types of business intermediaries,* (2) the *number of intermediaries,* and (3) the *terms and mutual responsibilities* of the producer and intermediaries.

Types of intermediaries. The firm should first identify the types of intermediaries available to carry on its channel work. Consider the following example:

- A manufacturer of test equipment for public utilities developed an audio device for detecting poor mechanical connections in any machinery with moving parts. The company executives felt that this product would have a market in all industries where electric, combustion, or steam engines were either used or manufactured. This meant such industries as aviation, automobile, railroad, food canning, construction, and oil. The existing sales force was small, and the problem was how to reach these diverse industries effectively. The following channel alternatives came out of management discussion:

1. *Company sales force.* Expand the company's direct sales force. Assign sales representatives to territories and give them responsibility for contacting purchasing agents in the relevant industries. Or specialize the company sales force by end-use industries.
2. *Manufacturer's agency.* Hire manufacturer's agencies operating in different regions or end-use industries to sell the new test equipment.
3. *Industrial distributors.*[14] Find distributors in the different regions and/or end-use industries who will buy and carry the new line. Give them exclusive distribution, adequate margins, product training, and promotional support.

Not only do conventional channel arrangements suggest themselves, but sometimes more innovative possibilities. This happened when the Conn Organ Company decided to merchandise organs through department and discount stores, thus drawing more attention to organs than they had ever enjoyed in the small music stores where they had always been merchandised. A daring new channel was exploited when a group decided to merchandise books through the mails in the now famous Book-of-the-Month Club. Other sellers, perceiving the success of the Book-of-the-Month Club, developed Record-of-the-Month clubs, Candy-of-the-Month clubs, and dozens of others.

Sometimes a company is forced to choose, or invent, a channel other than the one it prefers, because of the difficulty or cost of breaking into the preferred channel. The decision sometimes turns out extremely well. For example, the U.S. Time Company originally tried to enlist regular jewelry stores to carry its inexpensive Timex watches. But most jewelers refused to carry them. This forced the company to look for other channels, and it managed to get its watches into mass-merchandise outlets. This turned out to be a great decision because of the rapid growth of mass merchandising.

Number of intermediaries. The number of intermediaries to use at each stage is influenced by the degree of *market exposure* sought by the company. Three degrees of market exposure can be distinguished.

INTENSIVE DISTRIBUTION

Producers of convenience goods and common raw materials generally seek *intensive distribution*—that is, the stocking of their product in as many outlets as possible. The dominant factor in the marketing of these goods is their place utility. The producers of cigarettes, for example, try to enlist every possible retail outlet and device to create maximum brand exposure and convenience. This policy has culminated in the use of over one million outlets, which is about as intensive as distribution can get.

EXCLUSIVE DISTRIBUTION

Some producers deliberately limit the number of intermediaries handling their products. The extreme form of this is *exclusive distribution,* the policy of granting a limited number of dealers the exclusive right to distribute the company's products in their respective territories; it often goes along with *exclusive dealing,* where the manufacturer requires the dealers not to carry competing lines. This is found at the retail level with respect to the distribution of new automobiles, some major appliances, and some brands of women's apparel. Through granting exclusive distribution, the manufacturer hopes to gain a more aggressive selling effort and be able to exercise more direct controls over intermediaries' policies on prices, promotion, credit, and various services. Exclusive distribution also tends to enhance the image of the product and allow higher markups.

SELECTIVE DISTRIBUTION

Between intensive and exclusive distribution stands an intermediate arrangement called *selective distribution.* Selective distribution involves the use of more than one but less than all of the intermediaries who are willing to carry a particular product. It is used both by established companies with good reputations and by new companies seeking to obtain distributors by promising them selective distribution. The company does not have to dissipate its efforts over a lot of outlets, many of which would be marginal. It can develop a good working understanding with the selected intermediaries and expect a better than average selling effort. Selective distribution enables the producer to gain adequate market coverage with more control and less cost than intensive distribution.

Terms and responsibilities of channel members. The producer must determine the mix of conditions and responsibilities to be assumed by different channel members. The main elements in the "trade-relations mix" are the *price policies,* the *conditions of sale,* the *territorial rights,* and the *specific services to be performed by each party.*

Price policy is one of the major elements in the trade-relations mix. The producer usually establishes a list price and then allows discounts from it to various types of middlemen and possibly for various quantities purchased. In developing the schedule of discounts, the producer must proceed carefully because middlemen have strong feelings about the discounts they and others are entitled to.

Conditions of sale refer to the payment terms and to producer guarantees. Most producers grant cash discounts to their distributors for early payment. Producers may also extend certain guarantees to distributors regarding defective merchandise or price declines. The offer of a guarantee against price declines may be necessary to induce distributors to buy in large quantities rather than on an as-needed basis.

Distributors' territorial rights are another element in the trade-relations mix. Distributors want to know where the producer intends to enfranchise other distributors. They would also like to receive full credit for all sales taking place in their territory, whether or not these sales were stimulated through their personal efforts.

Mutual services and responsibilities must be carefully spelled out, especially in franchised- and exclusive-agency channels. For example, the Howard Johnson Company provides the restaurant leaseholders with the building, promotional support, a record-keeping system, training, and general administrative and technical assistance. In turn, the leaseholders are supposed to meet company standards regarding physical facilities, cooperate with new promotional programs, furnish requested information, and buy specified food products.

Evaluating the Major Channel Alternatives

Suppose a producer has identified several major channel alternatives for reaching the market and wants to decide which would best satisfy the long-run objectives of the firm. Each alternative should be rated against *economic, control,* and *adaptive* criteria. Consider the following situation:

- A Memphis furniture manufacturer wishes to contact and sell to a large number of retailers on the West Coast. The manufacturer is deciding between using a *direct sales force* and using a *manufacturer's sales agency.* Specifically:

  1. One alternative is to hire ten company sales representatives who would operate out of a sales office in San Francisco. They would be paid a base salary with the opportunity for further earnings through a commission plan.

  2. The other alternative is to use a San Francisco-based manufacturer's sales agency that has developed extensive contacts with retailers. The agency has thirty sales representatives who would receive a commission on the goods sold.

Economic criteria. Each channel alternative will produce a different level of sales and costs. The first issue is whether more sales will be produced through a company sales force or a sales agency. Most marketing managers believe that a company sales force will sell more. Company sales representatives concentrate entirely on the company's products; they are better trained to sell the company's products; they are more aggressive because their future depends on the company; they are more successful because customers prefer to deal directly with the company.

But these are abstract arguments. It is possible that the sales agency could produce as many sales as, or more sales than, a company sales force. First, the producer is considering hiring ten new company sales representatives versus using thirty agency sales representatives. The sheer difference in the size of the sales force would lead to more sales through the agency. Second, the agency's sales force may be just as aggressive as a direct sales force. This depends on how much commission the line offers them in relation to the other lines they represent. Third, some customers may prefer dealing with agents who represent a large number of manufacturers rather than dealing with salespersons from one company. Fourth, one of the chief assets of the agency is the extensive contacts built up over the years, which a company sales force would have to cultivate from scratch.

The next step calls for estimating the costs associated with selling different volumes under each system. They are shown in Figure 14-5. The fixed costs of engaging a sales agency are lower than those of establishing a company sales office. On the other hand, costs rise faster with additional sales through a sales agency because sales agents get a larger fixed percentage of sales than company salespeople who are only on part commission.

Looking at the chart, there is one sales level (S_B) at which selling costs would be the same for the two channels. The sales agency would constitute a superior channel at any volume of sales below S_B, and the company sales branch would constitute a superior channel at any volume higher than S_B. This analysis accords with common observations of the circumstances under which the two channels are used. Sales agents tend to be engaged by smaller firms, or by larger firms in their smaller territories, because in both cases the sales volume is too low to justify a company sales force.

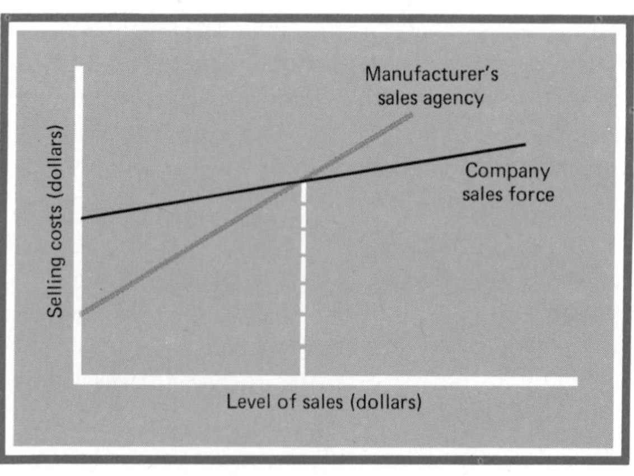

Figure 14-5
Breakeven Cost Chart for the Choice Between a Company Sales Force and a Manufacturer's Sales Agency

Control criteria. The evaluation must now be broadened by a consideration of the control aspects of the two channel alternatives. The use of sales agents can give rise to a number of control problems. The central fact is that the manufacturer's sales agency is an independent business interested in maximizing its own profits. The agent may not cooperate with the client's agent in an adjacent territory. The agent concentrates calls on the customers that are most important to the agency in terms of the total assortment of goods rather than on the customers who are most important to the client. The agent's sales force may not take the time to master the technical details concerning the client's product or use the client's promotion materials carefully.

Adaptive criteria. Each channel alternative involves some duration of commitment and loss of flexibility. A manufacturer who decides to use a sales agency may have to offer a five-year contract; during this period, other means of selling, such as direct mail, may become more efficient, but the manufacturer is not free to drop the sales agency. A channel alternative involving a long commitment should show evidence of being greatly superior on economic or control grounds in order to be considered.

channel-management decisions

After a company has determined its basic channel design, individual middlemen must be *selected, motivated,* and *evaluated.*

Selecting Channel Members

Producers differ in their ability to recruit qualified middlemen for the proposed channel operation. Some producers have no trouble finding specific business establishments to join the channel. Their proposal attracts more than enough middlemen either because of the high prestige of the firm or because the specific product or line appears to be a good moneymaker. For example, Ford was able to attract twelve hundred new dealers for its ill-fated Edsel. In some cases the promise of exclusive or selective distribution will influence a sufficient number of middlemen to join the channel. The main problem for the producer who can attract enough middlemen is one of selection. The producer must decide on what middlemen characteristics provide the best indication of their competence.

At the other extreme are producers who have to work hard to line up the desired number of qualified middlemen. When Polaroid started, it could not get photographic equipment stores to carry its new cameras and was forced to go to mass-merchandising outlets. Often small producers of new food products find it difficult to get shelf space in food outlets.

Whether producers find it easy or difficult to recruit middlemen, they should determine what characteristics distinguish the better middlemen from the poorer ones. They will want to evaluate the middlemen's number of years in business, the other lines carried, growth and profit record, solvency, cooperativeness, and reputation. If the middlemen are sales agents, producers will also want to evaluate the number and character of other lines carried and the size and quality of the sales force. If the middleman is a department store being considered for exclusive distribution, the producer will want to evaluate the store's location, future growth potential, and type of clientele.

Motivating Channel Members

Middlemen must be motivated to do their best job. The factors and terms that lead them to join the channel provide some of the motivation, but these must be supplemented by continuous supervision and encouragement from the producer. The producer must sell not only through the middlemen but to them.

The job of stimulating channel members to top performance must start with the manufacturer's attempting to understand the needs and wants of the particular middlemen. According to McVey, the middleman is often criticized by manufacturers "for failure to stress a given brand, or for the poor quality of his salesman's product knowledge, his disuse of supplier's advertising materials, his neglect of certain customers (who may be good prospects for individual items but not for the assortment), and even for his unrefined systems of record keeping, in which brand designations may be lost."[15] However, what are shortcomings from the manufacturer's point of view may be quite justifiable from the middleman's point of view. McVey listed the following four propositions to help understand middlemen:

> ▪ The middleman is not a hired link in a chain forged by a manufacturer, but rather an independent market. . . . After some experimentation, he settles upon a method of operation, performing those functions he deems inescapable in the light of his own objectives, forming policies for himself wherever he has freedom to do so. . . .
>
> [The middleman often acts] primarily as a purchasing agent for his customers, and only secondarily as a selling agent for his suppliers. . . . He is interested in selling any product which these customers desire to buy from him. . . .
>
> The middleman attempts to weld all of his offerings into a family of items which he can sell in combination, as a packaged assortment, to individual customers. His selling efforts are directed primarily at obtaining orders for the assortment, rather than for individual items. . . .
>
> Unless given incentive to do so, middlemen will not maintain separate sales records by brands sold. . . . Information that could be used in product development, pricing, packaging, or promotion-planning is buried in nonstandard records of middlemen, and sometimes purposely secreted from suppliers.[16]

These propositions serve as a provocative departure from otherwise stereotyped thinking about the performance of middlemen. The first step in motivating others is to see the situation from their viewpoint.

Producers vary in their level of sophistication with respect to handling distributor relations. We can distinguish between three approaches: *cooperation, partnership,* and *distribution programming.*[17]

Most producers see the problem of motivation as one of figuring out ways to gain *cooperation* from independent and sometimes difficult middlemen who "aren't loyal" or "are lazy." They will use the carrot-and-stick approach. They will dream up positive motivators such as higher margins, special deals, premiums, cooperative advertising allowances, display allowances, and sales contests. If these do not work, they will apply negative sanctions such as threatening to reduce the margins, slow down service, or terminate the relationship. The basic problem with this approach is that the producer has not really studied the needs, problems, strengths, and weaknesses of the distributors. Instead, the producer puts together a miscellaneous set of devices that are based on crude stimulus-response thinking. McCammon notes that many programs developed by the manufacturer "consist of hastily improvised trade deals, uninspired dealer contests, and unexamined discount structures . . . this traditional attitude toward distributor programming is a luxury that can no longer be easily afforded."[18]

More sophisticated companies try to forge a long-term *partnership* with their distributors. This calls for the manufacturer's developing a clear sense of what it wants from its distributors and what its distributors can expect from the manufacturer in terms of market coverage, product availability, market development, account solicitation, technical advice and services, and market information. The manufacturer seeks an agreement from its distributors on these policies and may set up compensation based on their adhering to these policies.

Distribution programming is still a further stage in the possible relation between manufacturers and their distributors. McCammon defines this as building a planned, professionally managed, vertical marketing system that incorporates the needs of both the manufacturer and the distributors.[19] The manufacturer sets up a special department within the marketing department called distributor relations planning, and its job is to identify the distributors' needs and build up the programmed merchandising and other programs to help each distributor operate as optimally as possible. This department and the distributors jointly plan the merchandising goals, inventory levels, space and visual merchandising plans, sales-training requirements, and advertising and promotion plans. The aim is to convert the distributors from thinking that they make their money primarily on the buying side (through an adversary relation with the supplier) to seeing that they make their money on the selling side by being part of a sophisticated vertical marketing system.

Evaluating Channel Members

The producer must periodically evaluate middlemen's performance against certain standards such as sales quota attainment, average inventory levels, customer delivery time, treatment of damaged and lost goods, cooperation in company promotional and training programs, and middleman services owed to the customer.

The producer typically issues sales quotas to define current performance expectations. The producer might list the sales of various middlemen after each sales period and send the rankings out. This device is intended to motivate middlemen at the bottom of the list to do better for the sake of self-respect (and continuing the relationship) and middlemen at the top to maintain their performance out of pride. A more useful measure is to compare each middleman's sales performance with performance in the preceding period. The average percentage of improvement for the group can be used as a norm. Another useful measure is to compare each middleman's performance with assigned quotas based on an analysis of the sales potential in the respective territories. After each sales period, middlemen are ranked according to the ratio of their actual sales to their sales potential. Diagnostic and motivational effort can then be focused on the underachievers.

channel-modification decisions

Every so often the market channel requires modification to meet new conditions in the marketplace. This fact struck a large manufacturer of major household appliances who had been marketing exclusively through franchised dealers. A

EXHIBIT 14-1

DISTRIBUTION DECISIONS AND PUBLIC POLICY

By and large, manufacturers are free under the law to develop whatever channel arrangements suit them. In fact, much of the force of the law affecting channels is to make sure that manufacturers are not stopped from using channels as the result of the exclusionary tactics of others. But this places them under obligation to proceed cautiously in their own possible use of exclusionary tactics. Most of the law is concerned with mutual rights and duties of the manufacturer and channel members once they have formed a relationship.

Exclusive dealing. Many manufacturers and wholesalers like to develop exclusive channels for their products. The policy is called "exclusive distribution" when the seller enfranchises only certain outlets to carry its products. It is called "exclusive dealing" when the seller requires these outlets to agree to handle only its products, or conversely, not to handle competitors' products. Both parties tend to draw benefits from exclusive dealing, the seller enjoying a more dependable and enthusiastic set of outlets without having to invest capital in them, and the distributors gaining a steady source of supply and seller support. However, the result of exclusive dealing is that other manufacturers are excluded from selling to these dealers. This has brought exclusive-dealing contracts under the purview of the Clayton Act, although such contracts are not illegal per se. They are legal as long as they do not substantially lessen competition, or tend to create a monopoly, and both partners enter into the agreement voluntarily.

Exclusive territorial distributorships. Exclusive dealing often includes exclusive territorial agreements. The seller may agree not to sell to other distributors in the area, and/or the buyer may agree to confine sales to its own territory. The first practice is fairly normal under franchise systems, being regarded as a way to promote increased dealer enthusiasm and dealer investment in the area. The seller is under no legal compulsion to establish more outlets than it wishes. The second practice, where the manufacturer tries to restrain each dealer to sell only in its own territory, has become a major legal issue.

Tying agreements. Manufacturers with a brand in strong demand occasionally sell it to dealers on condition they take some or all of the rest of the line. In the latter case, this practice is called "full-line forcing." Such tying arrangements are not illegal per se, but they do run afoul of the Clayton Act if they tend to lessen competition substantially. Buyers are prevented from exercising their free choice among competing suppliers of these other goods.

Dealers' rights. Sellers are largely free to select their dealers, but their right to terminate dealerships is somewhat qualified. In general, sellers can drop dealers "for cause." But they cannot drop dealers, for example, if the latter refuse to cooperate in a dubious legal arrangement, such as exclusive-dealing or tying arrangements.

relative loss in market share made the producer take stock of several distributional developments that had taken place since the original channel was designed, such as (1) an increasing share of major brand appliances were being merchandised through discount houses; (2) an increasing share of major appliances were being sold on a private-brand basis through large department stores; (3) a new market was developing in the form of volume purchases by tract home builders who preferred to deal directly with the manufacturers; (4) door-to-door and direct-mail solicitation of orders was being undertaken by some dealers and competitors; (5) the only strong independent dealers were those in small towns, and rural families were increasingly making their purchases in large cities. These and other developments in the ever-changing distribution scene led this manufacturer to undertake a major review of possible channel modifications.

Three different levels of channel modification are distinguished in the following paragraphs.

Adding or Dropping Individual Channel Members

The decision to add or drop a particular middleman usually requires a straightforward economic analysis. The question is, What would the firm's profits look like with and without this middleman? The analysis could be complex if the decision would have repercussions on the rest of the system. An automobile manufacturer's decision to grant another dealer franchise in a city will require taking into account not only that dealer's probable sales but the possible losses or gains in the sales of the manufacturer's other dealers.

Adding or Dropping Particular Marketing Channels

Sometimes a producer contemplates adding or dropping a marketing channel. For example, International Harvester might find that in using the same dealers to sell heavy trucks, light trucks, and recreational vehicles, its recreational vehicles suffer from neglect. That is, the dealers prefer to spend their energy selling trucks to fleet owners rather than selling single recreational vehicles to consumers. To improve the sale of its recreational vehicles, International Harvester would then consider establishing a new marketing channel, namely, recreational vehicle dealerships.

Modifying the Whole Channel

The most difficult channel modification decision involves revising the company's overall system of distribution. For example, an automobile manufacturer may consider replacing independent dealers with company-owned dealerships; a soft-drink manufacturer may consider replacing local franchised bottlers with centralized bottling and direct sales. These decisions must be made at the top-management level. They would not only change the channels but necessitate revising most of the marketing mix and policies to which the firm is accustomed. Such decisions have so many ramifications that any quantitative modeling of the problem can only be a first approximation.

physical-distribution decisions

Up to now, we have examined how companies select channels of distribution to carry their products to the final markets. We have not examined, however, the physical side of distribution, that is, how companies arrange for the efficient storing, handling, and moving of goods so that they will be at the place needed at the time needed. Customer attraction and satisfaction is deeply affected by the seller's physical-distribution capabilities. Here we will examine the nature, objectives, systems, and organizational aspects of physical distribution.

Nature of Physical Distribution

Physical distribution comprises the tasks involved in planning and implementing the physical flows of materials and final goods from points of origin to points of use or consumption to meet the needs of customers at a profit. The main elements of the physical-distribution mix are shown in Figure 14-6. Transportation is the major cost of physical distribution, followed by warehousing, inventory carrying, receiving and shipping, packaging, administration, and order processing. Management is becoming increasingly concerned about the total cost of physical distribution, which amounts to 13.6 percent of sales for manufacturing companies and 25.6 percent for reseller companies.[20] Authorities hold that substantial savings can be effected in the physical-distribution area, which has been described as "the last frontier for cost economies"[21] and "the economy's dark continent."[22] Physical-distribution decisions, when uncoordinated, result in profit suboptimization. Not enough use is being made of modern decision tools for blending economic levels of inventories, efficient modes of shipment, and sound plant, warehouse, and store locations.

Physical distribution, of course, is a potent tool in the demand-creation process. Companies can attract additional customers by offering better service or by cutting prices through reducing physical-distribution costs. Companies can lose customers when they fail to make their goods available on time. For example, in the summer of 1976 Kodak made the mistake of launching its national advertising campaign for its new instant camera before it had delivered enough cameras to the stores. Many customers went to buy the new camera and were told that it was not available, so they bought a Polaroid instead.

Traditional physical-distribution thinking starts with goods at the plant and tries to find low-cost solutions to get them to customers. Marketers have

Figure 14-6
Cost of Physical-Distribution Elements as a Percent of Total Physical-Distribution Cost

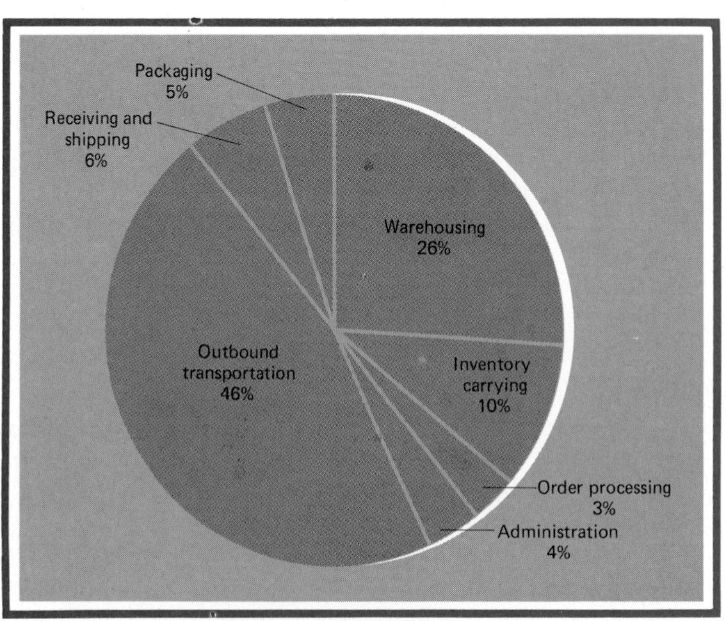

Source: Based on B. J. LaLonde and P. H. Zinszer, *Customer Service: Meaning and Measurement* (Chicago: National Council of Physical Distribution Management, 1976).

argued for *market logistics* thinking that starts with market considerations and works backward. Here is an example of how a market logistics viewpoint led to a creative physical distribution breakthrough:

- In Germany, consumers typically purchase soft drinks by the bottle. A soft-drink manufacturer, looking for an advantage, decided to design and test a six-pack. The manufacturer tested the idea with consumers, who responded positively to the convenience aspect of carrying bottles home in a six-pack. The retailers also responded positively because the bottles could be loaded faster on the shelves and could lead to more bottles being purchased per occasion. The manufacturer designed the six-packs to fit on the shelf in a way that maximized utilization of the shelf space. Then it designed cases and pallets that would bring these six-packs efficiently to the store's receiving rooms. The plant operations were redesigned to produce the new bottles and six-packs. The purchasing department let out bids for the new needed materials. Once implemented, this new way of packaging soft drinks was an instant hit with consumers, and the manufacturer's market share increased substantially.

The Physical-Distribution Objective

Many companies state their physical-distribution objective as *getting the right goods to the right places at the right time for the least cost.* Unfortunately, this provides little actual guidance. No physical-distribution system can simultaneously maximize customer service and minimize distribution cost. Maximum customer service implies such policies as large inventories, premium transportation, and many warehouses, all of which raise distribution cost. Minimum distribution cost implies such policies as slow and cheap transportation, low stocks, and few warehouses.

A company cannot achieve physical-distribution efficiency by letting physical-distribution managers simply keep down their own costs. Various physical-distribution costs interact, often in an inverse way:

- The traffic manager favors rail shipment over air shipment whenever possible. This reduces the company's freight bill. However, because the railroads are slower, this ties up company capital longer, delays customer payment, and may cause customers to buy from competitors offering more rapid service.

  The shipping department uses cheap containers to minimize shipping costs. This leads to a high damage rate of goods in transit and the loss of customer goodwill.

  The inventory manager favors holding low inventories to reduce total inventory cost. However, this results in many stockouts, backorders, accompanying paperwork, special production runs, and high-cost fast-freight shipments.

The import is that since physical-distribution activities are highly interrelated, decisions must be made on a total system basis.

The starting point for designing the physical-distribution system is to study what the customers want in the way of service and what the competitors are offering. Customers are interested in several things: (1) on-time delivery, (2) the supplier's willingness to meet the customer's emergency merchandise needs, (3) the care with which merchandise is delivered in good condition, (4) the supplier's readiness to take back defective goods and resupply them quickly, and (5) the supplier's willingness to carry inventory for the customer.

The company has to research the relative importance of the various services to the target customers. For example, service repair time is very important to buyers of copying equipment. Xerox has acknowledged this by developing a service delivery standard that is able "to put a disabled machine anywhere in the continental United States back into operation within three hours after receiving the service request." This is accomplished by running a separate division consisting of twelve thousand service personnel and parts managers.

The company must also look at competitors' service standards in setting its own. It will normally want to offer at least the same level of service as competitors. But the objective is to make profits, not necessarily maximize sales. The company has to look at the costs of providing different levels of service. Some companies will decide to offer less service but will charge a lower price and bear lower physical-distribution costs. Other companies will decide to offer more service than competitors and will charge a premium price to cover their higher service costs.

In the end the company will have to establish physical-distribution objectives to guide its physical-distribution system planning. For example, Coca-Cola wants "to put Coke within an arm's length of desire," and this has clear system design implications. Companies go further and define service standards for each service factor. One appliance manufacturer has established the following service standards: (1) to deliver at least 95 percent of the dealer's orders within seven days of order receipt, (2) to fill the dealer's orders with 99 percent accuracy, (3) to answer dealer inquiries on order status within three hours, and (4) to ensure that damage to merchandise in transit does not exceed one percent.

Given a set of physical-distribution objectives, the company is ready to design a physical-distribution system that will minimize the cost of achieving these objectives. The major decision issues are: (1) How should orders be handled? (*order processing*) (2) Where should stocks be located? (*warehousing*) (3) How much stock should be kept on hand? (*inventory*) and (4) How should goods be shipped? (*transportation*) We will now examine these four major elements and their implication for marketing.

Order Processing

Physical distribution starts with the receipt of a customer order. Sales representatives, dealers, and customers dispatch orders to the firm. The order department prepares multicopy invoices and dispatches them to various departments. Items that are out of stock are back-ordered. Items that are shipped are accompanied by shipping and billing documents that are also multicopied and go to various departments.

The company has a strong interest in carrying out these steps as quickly and accurately as possible. Sales representatives are supposed to send in their orders every evening, in some cases to phone them in when they are obtained. The order department should process these quickly. The warehouse should send the goods out as soon as possible. And bills should go out as soon as possible. The computer should be harnessed to expedite the order-shipping-billing cycle.

Industrial engineering studies of how sales orders flow through the company may help to shorten this cycle substantially. Some of the key questions are: What happens after the receipt of a customer purchase order? How long does the customer credit check take? What procedures are used to check inventory and how long does this take? How soon does manufacturing hear of new stock requirements? How long does it take for sales executives to learn of current sales?

Ringer and Howell reported a study of one company's order routine, which resulted in cutting down the elapsed time between the receipt and issuance of an order from sixty-two hours to thirty hours without any change in costs.[23] General Electric operates a computer-oriented system which, upon receipt of a customer's order, checks the customer's credit standing and whether and where the items are in stock. If the answers are positive, the computer system issues an order to ship, bills the customer, updates the inventory records, sends a production order for new stock, and relays the message back to the sales representative that the customer's order is on its way, all in less than fifteen seconds.

Warehousing

Every company must make provision for stocking its goods at various locations while they wait to be sold. A storage function is necessary because production and consumption cycles rarely match. Many agricultural commodities are produced continuously, although demand may be seasonal. The storage function overcomes discrepancies in timing and in quantities desired.

The company must determine the number of stocking locations to maintain. With more stocking locations, it can deliver goods to customers more quickly. This is favored by the marketers. However, warehousing costs go up with the number of locations that have to be managed. The number of stocking locations must be chosen with an eye to balancing customer delivery service and distribution costs.

Some of the company's stock will be kept at or near the plant, and the rest will be located in major warehouses throughout the country. The company may own some warehouses (*private warehouses*) and rent space in *public warehouses*. Companies have more control in owned warehouses, but at the same time they tie up their capital and face some inflexibility should desirable storage locations change. Public warehouses, on the other hand, charge only for the space being rented and provide additional services as desired, such as inspecting goods, packaging them, shipping them to customers, invoicing customers, and even providing desk space and telephone service for company salespeople. In using public warehouses, companies have a wide choice of locations and warehouse types, including those that specialize in cold storage, commodities only, and so on.

The *storage warehouse* is designed to store goods for moderate to long periods of time. Companies also use *distribution warehouses* (sometimes called *distribution centers*), which receive goods from many company plants on a daily basis, assemble them, and move them out to customers as soon as possible. The alternative would have required each plant to send less than carload quantities to each customer as orders come in, which would be very costly.

The older multistoried warehouses with the slow elevators and inefficient materials-handling arrangements are receiving competition from newer single-storied *automated warehouses* with advanced materials-handling sytems under the control of a central computer. In operating these automated warehouses costing \$10–\$20 million each, only a few employees are necessary. The computer reads store orders and directs lift trucks and electric hoists to gather goods, move them to loading docks, and issue invoices. These warehouses have reduced worker injuries, labor costs, and pilferage and breakage and have improved inventory control.

Inventory

Inventory levels represent another major type of physical-distribution decision affecting customer attraction and satisfaction. The marketer would like the company to carry enough stock to fill all customer orders immediately. However, it is not cost-effective for a company to carry this much inventory. *Inventory cost increases at an increasing rate as the customer service level approaches 100 percent.* The company would have to know whether sales and profits would increase enough to justify a higher investment in inventories.

Inventory decision making is a two-step decision process calling for knowing when to order, and how much to order. As inventory is drawn down, management must decide when a new order should be placed. The stock level when this is desirable is called the *order* (or *reorder*) *point.* An order point of 20 would mean that when the supply of an item falls to 20 units, it should be reordered.

The determination of the order point depends upon the order lead time, the usage rate, and the service standard. The higher these are, the higher the order point. Furthermore, if the order lead time and customer usage rate are variable, the order point would have to be higher by an amount of *safety stock.* The final order point is set on the basis of balancing the risks of stockouts against the costs of overstock.

The other decision is how much to order. The larger the quantity ordered, the less often an order has to be placed.

Much depends on determining order-processing costs versus inventory carrying costs. Order-processing costs for a manufacturer consist of *setup costs* and *running costs* for the item. If setup costs are very low, the manufacturer can produce the item often and the cost per item is pretty constant and equal to the running costs. However, if setup costs are high, the manufacturer can reduce the average cost per unit by producing a long run and carrying more inventory.

Order-processing costs must be compared with *inventory carrying costs.* The larger the average stock carried, the higher the inventory carrying costs. These carrying costs include (1) storage charges, (2) cost of capital, (3) taxes and insurance, and (4) depreciation and obsolescence. Inventory carrying costs may run as high as 30 percent of the inventory value. This means that marketing managers who want their companies to carry larger inventories must be able to convince top management that the higher inventories will yield additional sales with an incremental gross profit that would more than cover the incremental inventory carrying costs.

The optimal order quantity can be determined by observing how order-processing costs and inventory carrying costs sum up at different possible order levels. Figure 14-7 shows that the order-processing cost per unit decreases with the number of units ordered, because the order costs are spread over more units. Inventory carrying charges per unit increase with the number of units ordered, because each unit remains longer in inventory. The two cost curves are summed vertically into a total-cost curve. The lowest point on the total-cost curve is projected down on the horizontal axis to find the optimal order quantity Q^*.

Figure 14-7
Determining Optimal Order Quantity

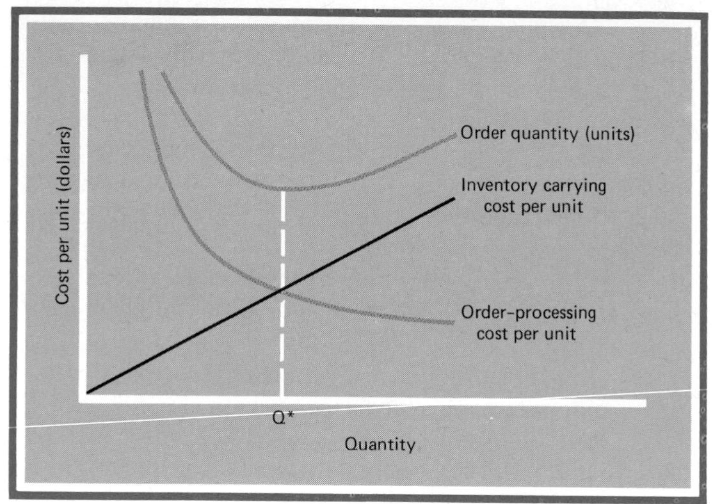

Transportation

Marketers take an interest in their company's transportation decisions. The company's choice of transportation carriers will affect the price of its products, its on-time delivery performance, and the condition of the goods when they arrive. These things will affect customers' interest in buying from this company and customers' postpurchase satisfaction.

In shipping goods from its plants to its warehouses, or from its warehouses to dealers or customers, the company can choose among five major transportation modes: *rail, water, truck, pipeline,* and *air*. The characteristics of each transportation mode are summarized in Table 14-1 and are discussed briefly in the following paragraphs.

Rail. In spite of a shrinking share of total transportation, railroads remain the nation's largest transportation carrier, accounting for 33 percent of the nation's total revenue ton-miles. Railroads are one of the most cost-effective modes of transportation for shipping carload quantities of bulk products—coal, sand,

Table 14-1
Characteristics of Major Transportation Modes

TRANSPORTATION MODE	1975 REVENUE TON-MILES (BILLIONS)	PERCENTAGE OF TOTAL	TYPICAL SHIPPED PRODUCTS
Rail	752.8	33.0%	Farm products, minerals, sand, chemicals, autos
Water	568.8	25.0%	Oil, grain, sand, gravel, metallic ores, coal
Truck	488.0	21.0%	Clothing, books, computers, paper goods
Pipeline	488.0	21.0%	Petroleum, coal, chemicals
Air	4.0	00.2%	Technical instruments, perishable food

Source for the "1975 Revenue Ton-Miles" column is the U.S. Department of Transportation, Office of Public Affairs, *Transportation USA* (Washington, D.C., Fall 1976), p. 3.

minerals, farm and forest products—over long land distances. The rate costs for shipping merchandise by rail are quite complex. The shipper's lowest rate comes from shipping carload rather than less-than-carload quantities. Manufacturers will often get together and combine shipments to common destinations to take advantage of lower rates. To meet its competition, especially the truckers, railroads have attempted to increase customer-oriented services. They have designed new kinds of equipment to handle categories of merchandise more efficiently, provided flatcars to permit the carrying of truck trailers by rail (piggyback), and provided in-transit services such as diversion of shipped goods to other destinations en route and processing of goods en route.

Water. A substantial amount of goods move by ships and barges on coastal and inland waterways. This means of transportation is very low in cost for shipping bulky, low-value, nonperishable products such as sand, coal, grain, oil, and metallic ores. On the other hand, water transportation is the slowest transportation mode and is dependent on climatic conditions.

Truck. Motor trucks have steadily increased their share of transportation and now account for 21 percent of total revenue ton-miles. They account for the largest portion of intracity as opposed to intercity transportation. Trucks are a highly flexible means of transportation in their route opportunities and time schedules. They can move merchandise door to door, thus saving shippers the need to transfer the goods from truck to rail and back again at a loss of time and risk of theft or damage. Trucks are an efficient mode of transportation for short hauls of high-value merchandise. Their rates are competitive with railway rates in many cases, and trucks can usually offer faster service.

Pipeline. Pipelines are a specialized means of shipping petroleum, coal, and chemicals from sources to markets. Pipeline shipment of petroleum products is less expensive than rail shipment, although more expensive than waterway shipment. Most pipelines are used by their owners to ship their own products, although they are technically available for use by any shipper.

Air. Air carriers transport less than one percent of the nation's goods but are becoming increasingly important as a transportation mode. Although airfreight rates are considerably higher than rail or truck freight rates, airfreight is an ideal transportation mode where speed is essential and/or distant markets have to be reached. Among the products frequently shipped by airfreight are high perishables (e.g., fresh fish, cut flowers) and high-value, low-bulk items (e.g., technical instruments, jewelry). Companies that use airfreight find that this reduces their required inventory levels, number of warehouses, and costs of packaging.

In choosing a transportation mode for a particular product, shippers may consider as many as six different criteria. Table 14-2 ranks the various transportation modes according to these criteria. Thus if a shipper is trying to achieve speed, the table shows that air and truck are the prime contenders for consideration. If the goal is low cost, then water and pipeline are the prime contenders,

Table 14-2 Transportation Modes Ranked According to Major Shipper Criteria (1 = highest rank)

	SPEED (DOOR-TO-DOOR DELIVERY TIME)	FREQUENCY (SCHEDULED SHIPMENTS PER DAY)	DEPENDABILITY (MEETING SCHEDULES ON TIME)	CAPABILITY (ABILITY TO HANDLE VARIOUS PRODUCTS)	AVAILABILITY (NO. OF GEOGRAPHIC POINTS SERVED)	COST (PER TON-MILE)
Rail	3	4	3	2	2	3
Water	4	5	4	1	4	1
Truck	2	2	2	3	1	4
Pipeline	5	1	1	5	5	2
Air	1	3	5	4	3	5

Source: Adapted from James L. Heskett, Robert J. Ivie, and Nicholas A. Glaskowsky, *Business Logistics* (New York: Ronald Press, 1964), pp. 71ff.

providing they can be used for the specific products. It should be noted that trucks appear to embody the most advantages, and this explains their rapid growth.

In addition to using single modes of transportation, the shipper will often combine two or more modes, thanks largely to containerization. *Containerization* means putting the goods in boxes or trailers that can easily be transferred between two or more modes of transportation. *Piggyback* describes the use of rail and trucks; *fishyback,* water and trucks; *trainship,* water and rail; and *airtruck,* air and trucks. Each coordinated mode of transportation offers specific advantages to the shipper. For example, piggyback is cheaper than trucking alone and yet provides flexibility and convenience.

In deciding on transportation modes, shippers can choose between private, contract, and common carriers. If the shipper decides to own its own truck or air fleet, the shipper becomes a *private carrier.* A *contract carrier* in an independent organization that sells transportation services to others on a contract basis. A *common carrier* provides services between predetermined points on a schedule basis and is available to all shippers at standard rates.

Decisions about transportation must take into account the complex trade-offs between various transportation modes and between the transportation mode chosen and its implications for other distribution elements such as warehousing and inventory. As the relative costs of different transportation modes change over time, companies need to reanalyze their options in the search for optimal physical-distribution arrangements.

Organizational Responsibility for Physical Distribution

By now it should be clear that decisions on warehousing, inventory, and transportation require the highest degree of coordination. A growing number of companies have set up a permanent committee composed of managers responsible for different physical-distribution activities; this committee meets periodically to develop policies for improving overall distribution efficiency. Other companies have centralized their physical-distribution activities under a vice-president of physical distribution. In some cases this person reports to the vice-president of marketing, and in other cases he or she is independent of marketing.

The location of the department within the company is a secondary concern. The important thing is the company's recognition that it needs to coordinate its physical-distribution and marketing activities in order to achieve high market impact at a reasonable cost.

summary

Marketing-channel decisions are among the most complex and challenging decisions facing the firm. Each channel system has a different potential for creating sales and generating costs. Once a particular marketing channel is chosen, the firm must usually adhere to it for a substantial period. The chosen channel will significantly affect and be affected by the rest of the marketing mix.

Each firm usually confronts a number of alternative ways to reach the market. They vary from direct selling to using one, two, three, or more intermediary channel levels. The firms making up the marketing channel are connected in different ways by physical, title, payment, information, and promotion flows. Marketing channels are not static but are characterized by continuous and sometimes dramatic change. Three of the most significant trends are the growth of vertical, horizontal, and multichannel marketing systems. These trends have important implications for channel cooperation, conflict, and competition.

Channel design calls for identifying the major channel alternatives in terms of the types of intermediaries, the number of intermediaries, and the channel terms and responsibilities. Each channel alternative has to be evaluated according to economic, control, and adaptive criteria.

Channel management calls for selecting particular middlemen and motivating them with a cost-effective trade-relations mix. Individual channel members must be periodically evaluated against their own past sales and other channel members' sales.

Channel modification at the individual member level, particular channel level, or whole channel level will be required from time to time as the environment changes.

Just as the marketing concept is receiving increasing recognition, a growing number of business firms are beginning to heed the physical-distribution concept. Physical distribution is an area of high potential cost savings, improved customer satisfaction, and competitive effectiveness. When order processors, warehouse planners, inventory managers, and transportation managers make decisions only within their own framework, they affect each other's costs and demand-creation capacity but do not take them into consideration. The physical-distribution concept calls for treating all these decisions within a unified framework. Then the important task becomes that of designing physical-distribution arrangements that minimize the total cost of providing a given customer service.

questions for discussion

1. Why are marketing intermediaries used? Explain by using a concrete example.
2. What major channel functions are labeled facilitating functions? Discuss these in relation to the sale of milk.

3. How many channel levels are commonly used by the following companies? (a) Sears, (b) Fuller Brush, and (c) A&P.
4. Channels of distribution do not differ for services and physical products. Comment.
5. Distinguish among the three major types of vertical marketing systems. Give an example of each.
6. There is no way to alleviate channel conflict. Comment.
7. Which of the following products would be intensively, exclusively, and selectively distributed and why? (a) Rolex watches, (b) Volkswagen automobiles, (c) Gillette blades, (d) Estée Lauder perfume.
8. After the channel design is determined, what three activities must the marketers undertake? Explain each briefly.
9. How do physical distribution decisions differ from channel decisions? What is the overriding objective of physical distribution?
10. In what ways has the computer facilitated physical distribution?
11. Which mode of transportation would probably be used to distribute the following products? (a) beer, (b) expensive jewelry, (c) natural gas, and (d) farm machinery.

■ references

1. This was written by the author based on "Going It Alone in Heavy Trucks," *Business Week,* June 13, 1977, pp. 56, 60, 63, and 65, and other sources.
2. WROE ALDERSON, "The Analytical Framework for Marketing," *Proceedings—Conference of Marketing Teachers from Far Western States* (Berkeley: University of California Press, 1958).
3. WROE ALDERSON, *Marketing Behavior and Executive Action: A Functionalist Approach to Marketing Theory* (Homewood, Ill.: Richard D. Irwin, 1957), p. 199.
4. This is the author's list. For other lists, see EDMUND D. MCGARRY, "Some Functions of Marketing Reconsidered," in *Theory in Marketing,* ed. REAVIS COX AND WROE ALDERSON (Homewood, Ill.: Richard D. Irwin, 1950), pp. 269–73; and LOUIS P. BUCKLIN, *A Theory of Distribution Channel Structure* (Berkeley: Institute of Business and Economic Research, University of California, 1966), pp. 10–11.
5. RONALD ABLER, JOHN S. ADAMS, AND PETER GOULD, *Spatial Organization: The Geographer's View of the World* (Englewood Cliffs, N.J.: Prentice-Hall, 1971), pp. 531–32.
6. WILLIAM G. ZIKMUND AND WILLIAM J. STANTON, "Recycling Solid Wastes: A Channels-of-Distribution Problem," *Journal of Marketing,* July 1971, p. 34.
7. BERT C. MCCAMMON, JR., "Perspectives for Distribution Programming," in *Vertical Marketing Systems,* ed. Louis P. Bucklin (Glenview, Ill.: Scott, Foresman, 1970), pp. 32–51.
8. Ibid., p. 45.
9. LEE ADLER, "Symbiotic Marketing," *Harvard Business Review,* November-December 1966, pp. 59–71.
10. ROLLIE TILLMAN, "Rise of the Conglomerchant," *Harvard Business Review,* November-December 1971, pp. 44–51.

11. See ROBERT E. WEIGAND, "Fit Products and Channels to Your Markets," *Harvard Business Review,* January-February 1977, pp. 95–105.

12. BERT C. MCCAMMON, JR., "Alternative Explanations of Institutional Change and Channel Evolution," in *Toward Scientific Marketing,* ed. Stephen A. Greyser (Chicago: American Marketing Association, 1963), pp. 477–90.

13. For an excellent summary of interorganizational conflict and power in marketing channels, see LOUIS W. STERN AND ADEL I. EL-ANSARY, *Marketing Channels* (Englewood Cliffs, N.J.: Prentice-Hall, 1977), Chap. 7.

14. For further reading on industrial distributors, see FREDERICK E. WEBSTER, JR., "The Role of the Industrial Distributor," *Journal of Marketing,* July 1976, pp. 10–16.

15. PHILLIP MCVEY, "Are Channels of Distribution What the Textbooks Say?" *Journal of Marketing,* January 1960, pp. 61–64.

16. Ibid.

17. See BERT ROSENBLOOM, *Marketing Channels: A Management View* (Hinsdale, Ill.: Dryden Press, 1978), pp. 192–203.

18. MCCAMMON, "Perspectives for Distribution Programming," p. 32.

19. Ibid., p. 43.

20. B. J. LALONDE AND P. H. ZINSZER, *Customer Service: Meaning and Measurement* (Chicago: National Council of Physical Distribution Management, 1976).

21. DONALD D. PARKER, "Improved Efficiency and Reduced Cost in Marketing," *Journal of Marketing,* April 1962, pp. 15–21.

22. PETER DRUCKER, "The Economy's Dark Continent," *Fortune,* April 1962, pp. 103ff.

23. JURGEN F. RINGER AND CHARLES D. HOWELL, "The Industrial Engineer and Marketing," in *Industrial Engineering Handbook,* (2nd ed.), ed. Harold Bright Maynard (New York: McGraw-Hill, 1963) pp. 10, 102–3.

RETAILING AND WHOLESALING STRATEGY

So retailers still face the urgent question: What will make consumers keep pouring into the nation's stores to part with their money? For some answers, store managers across the country increasingly are studying the phenomenal success of Federated Department Stores and especially its crown jewel, Bloomingdale's. Not every store, of course, can emulate Bloomingdale's specific techniques: ice cream made from Himalayan mangoes might not sell as well in the suburbs of Spokane as it does on Manhattan's East Side—especially not at $1.75 a pint. But any store can follow Bloomingdale's essential formula: first, know your customer, his age, affluence, customs, habits, tastes. Then set out to woo him with distinctive merchandise, flashy displays, and a general aura of showmanship, all calculated to make shopping an adventure—in fact, fun.

Headquarters has allowed Bloomingdale's full rein to exploit what it has long seen as its major market: young, affluent, fashion-conscious, traveled, professional people. They are attuned less to refrigerators and washing machines ("Bloomies" sells neither), more to clothes of fashion and quality, stereo equipment and wacky gadgetry for the compact Manhattan society of small apartments, crowded schedules and casual relationships. These consumers, to Bloomingdale's profit, go for such baubles as yogurt makers, $30 peanut-butter-making machines, "male chauvinist pig" neckties (30,000 sold so far) and even "Pet Rocks" that, at $4 each, roll over and play dead, sleep and stay in place—all on command. This market, Bloomingdale's has learned, enjoys tasting but does not stand still long enough to savor. It thrives on variety and excitement.

Thus Bloomingdale's does not merely display merchandise; it showcases it, turning the store into an adult Disneyland. Last week it was belts. In the men's store, hundreds of belts—leather, wool, seersucker, macramé, metal—bedeck rack upon rack. . . .

On any given day, Dr. Spock may be glimpsed there selecting towels, Walter Matthau trying on suits. Jacqueline Kennedy Onassis recently passed through to order presents to be sent to Caroline in London. Singer Diana Ross outfits herself and her children there—by long distance from California. Basketball Star Earl Monroe may drop in to pick up some after-shave lotion—and, he says, to "see how people with money act."

Behind the glitter lies a cooly calculated merchandising strategy. The flashy goods are a kind of patina on a store that also stocks many basic items: the customer—not necessarily young or particularly

fashionable—who is willing to settle for a $15 lamp can find one, but is more likely to come in to look at the latest in $250 lamps. So Bloomingdale's seeks to make itself a trendsetter, sensing the farthest-out ideas its market is ready for (or might be persuaded to accept), then moving in with appropriate goods and heavy promotion.

The method is not unique. All stores promote themselves, but Bloomingdale's does it louder, more frequently, and in unusual ways. . . . In the past seven years, Bloomingdale's Manhattan store alone has increased sales by more than 50%, to about $160 million. Bloomingdale's gets $350 of sales this year out of each square foot of floor space—about four times the average for all U.S. department stores.[1]

□ Bloomingdale's has what all retailers want—a magic that keeps customers coming back again and again. It has learned how to put drama into the ordinary act of shopping. It is a master at merchandising excitement to its target customers.

Not all customers want it. Many want to walk into a store, find good-quality merchandise at low prices, get helpful service, and get out again as fast as they can. Stores that succeed with this group of customers are the ones that have learned how to achieve operating efficiency and turn it into low prices. Sears, for example, earned its place as the world's largest retailer (responsible for one percent of the U.S. gross national product) by giving good value to its customers backed by a money-return guarantee and a sophisticated buying and merchandising operation behind the scenes.

One thing retailers have learned over the years, whether they sell to a class market or a mass market, is that they are operating in an environment of accelerating change. The successful retailing formulas of yesterday may not work today, and most probably will not work tomorrow. Where is W. T. Grant (one of the nation's oldest and largest variety chain stores) today? In bankruptcy. Where is Food Fair (the country's eighth-largest supermarket chain)? In bankruptcy court. And whatever happened to the great A&P? "Formerly considered a colossal near-monopoly, nemesis of small competitors, and trustbuster target, A&P has come to look like a mangy, toothless old lion."[2] And what about the great Montgomery Ward (the nation's fourth-largest general merchandise chain)? It is perpetually searching for a turnaround strategy to retrieve its former glory.

During the 1970s Sears painfully discovered the risks of a changing environment. Its strategies for each decade since its founding in 1886 were right on target, and it took over the number-one spot from the older Montgomery Ward's in the 1940s. Sears bet on economic growth in the postwar period, and Ward's bet on economic stagnation. Sears won the bet. It opened hundreds of new stores in the suburbs, renovated its old stores, and added new and nontraditional lines, such as insurance, savings banks, and paintings. It prospered through the early 1970s when it decided to change its strategy from expansion to upgrading. It would pursue affluent consumers by adding higher-quality lines and even designer merchandise. But its timing was bad. The boom turned into a bust, and Sears customers were in no mood to pay higher prices. They turned in increasing numbers to K-Marts and other discount merchandisers. Sears did not succeed in attracting the more discriminating buyers, and it began to lose many of its price-minded customers to competitors. In 1974 it experienced its first profit slump in thirteen years, a 24.8 percent decline. After its retailing profits peaked in 1976 at $441.2 million, they fell to $363.9 million for 1977 and $330.7 million for 1978. The question is, What should Sears be doing in the 1980s? And, indeed, is there a winning strategy for Sears in the 1980s?[3]

Modern retailers have to be alert to the signs of change and be prepared to shift their strategy—not too early and not too late. But even a decision to shift is not easy to implement. The large retailer is a prisoner of its own policies, which its managers have become accustomed to as the "conventional wisdom." And it is a prisoner of its public image, which consumers retain in their minds long after the store's reality has changed.

At the other end of the retailing spectrum is the small "mom and pop" store, the cauldron of new enterprise. Small retailers are important for several reasons: (1) they often create new forms of retailing which the large stores later copy; (2) they offer greater convenience to consumers because they are everywhere; (3) they often are more adaptable and give more personal service; and (4) they offer a chance for people to be their own boss and shape their own destiny.

At the same time, many persons who start small businesses are unprepared to run them. They think that all they need is a happy disposition and a warm smile. They lack technical skills and expertise. As many as 75 percent of new small retailers fail within five years. Both large and small enterprise are vulnerable to the winds of change.

In this chapter we focus on the institutions that make up the retailing and wholesaling sectors of the economy. We will take the viewpoint of managers of these institutions and examine how they act and respond to marketing initiatives by consumers and manufacturers. In the two main sections, *retailing* and *wholesaling,* we will ask similar questions: (1) What is the nature and importance of retailing (wholesaling)? (2) What are the major types of retailers (wholesalers)? (3) What marketing decisions do retailers (wholesalers) make? and (4) What is retailing's (wholesaling's) future?

retailing

Nature and Importance of Retailing

What is retailing? We all know that Sears is a retailer, but is this also true of an Avon lady knocking at a door, a contractor phoning a family about his services, a doctor seeing patients, a hotel offering a special priced weekend? Yes, they are all retailers. We define *retailing* as follows: *Retailing includes all the activities involved in selling goods or services directly to final consumers for their personal, nonbusiness use.* Any institution that does this—whether it be a manufacturer, a wholesaler, or a retail store—is doing retailing. It does not matter *how* the goods or services are sold (by person, mail, telephone, or vending machine) or *where* they are sold (in a store, on the street, or in the consumer's home). On the other hand, a *retailer* or *retail store* is any business enterprise whose sales volume primarily comes from retailing.

Retailing is one of the major industries in the United States. Retail stores constitute approximately 18 percent of all businesses in the United States, outnumbering manufacturing and wholesaling establishments by more than seven to one, and representing the third-largest source of employment in the nation, with over 13 million employees. The industry is composed of over 1.5 million single-unit establishments and over 34,000 multiunit organizations, and it generated a total of approximately $704 billion in sales in 1977.

Who are the nation's largest retailers? The ten largest ones and their sales in billions in 1976 were Sears Roebuck ($14.9), Safeway Stores ($10.4), K-Mart ($8.5), J. C. Penney ($8.4), A&P ($6.5), Kroger ($6.1), Montgomery Ward ($5.3), F. W. Woolworth ($5.2), Federated Department Stores ($4.4), and Lucky Stores ($3.5).[4] Thus we see that the largest retailers are primarily general merchandise department store chains and supermarket chains.

Types of Retailers

The millions of retailing units in this country come in all sizes and shapes. There is no one principle for classifying them, because new retailing forms keep emerging and combining the features of different pure retailing types. For example, a modern K-Mart store combines the principles of the supermarket and the discount store. While distribution functions cannot be eliminated, they can be combined in different ways to give rise to different institutional forms. All major retail innovations in the twentieth century have relied on creating new mixes of distribution functions to attain a strategic position in the marketplace.

One of the major distribution functions in retailing is "service." Retailing is positioned at the end of the "bulk-breaking" process, typically catering to a very large number of individual consumers each of whom generates only a small, heterogeneous purchase mix at a time. Retailing is therefore basically labor-intensive, and the amount of service occasioned by each sale affects its overall operating cost structure. Labor costs account for 50–60 percent of sales for a full-service retailer. Hence the price savings that usually accompanies self-service is likely to more than compensate consumers for serving themselves, especially for products such as groceries or everyday household goods where sales assistance is of little or no consequence.

Since there are a variety of customers with different service preferences and a variety of products with different service requirements, successful businesses may coexist with different levels of customer service. Table 15-1 distinguishes four levels of service and the retailing institutions typically employing them.

Self-service retailing in this country achieved its major growth in the 1930s as a result of depressed economic conditions. It has become institutionalized in the economy and is used by customers in all walks of life, especially for obtaining convenience goods and to some extent shopping goods. Self-service is the cornerstone of all discount operations. Many customers are willing to carry out their own "locate-compare-select" process in order to save money. At the next level is

Table 15-1
Classification of Retailers Based on the Amount of Customer Service

	DECREASING SERVICES	⟶		INCREASING SERVICES
	Self-service	**Self-selection**	**Limited-service**	**Full-service**
attributes	Very few services Price appeal Staple goods Convenience goods	Restricted services Price appeal Staple goods Convenience goods	Small variety of services Shopping goods	Wide variety of services Fashion merchandise Specialty merchandise
examples	Warehouse retailing Grocery stores Discount stores Mail-order retailing Automatic vending	Discount retailing Variety stores Mail-order retailing	Door-to-door sales Department stores Telephone sales Variety stores	Specialty stores Department stores

Source: Adapted from Larry D. Redinbaugh, *Retailing Management: A Planning Approach* (New York: McGraw-Hill, 1976), p. 12.

self-selection retailing, in which a salesperson is available for assistance if desired. Customers complete their transactions not by standing in a queue at the checkout counter but by finding salespeople and paying for the item, as in variety stores. The operating expenses of self-selection institutions are somewhat higher than those of self-service operations because of the additional staff requirements. In *limited-service retailing,* best exemplified by mass department store chains such as Sears, the quality of sales assistance is somewhat higher because these stores carry more shopping goods and customers need more information. The stores also offer services such as credit and merchandise return not found in the previous two forms of retailing, and hence their operating costs tend to be higher. Finally, in *full-service retailing,* exemplified by the class department stores, customers are greeted by salespeople who are ready to personally assist in every phase of the locate-compare-select process. This type of store is valued by customers who like to be "waited on" and like to develop personal relationships with store personnel. The high staffing cost, along with the fact that these stores normally carry specialty goods and slower-moving items (fashions, jewelry, cameras) and offer liberal merchandise return policies, various credit plans, free delivery, home servicing of durables, and customer facilities such as lounges and restaurants, results in high-cost retailing. Thus it is not surprising that full-service retailing has been on the decline for several decades.

Other schemes for classifying retailer types have also been proposed. Two of these schemes are shown in Figure 15-1. Gist has developed a margin-turnover classification that distinguishes retailer types according to the margins and volumes they pursue (see Figure 15-1A). A discount store, for example, works on the principle of setting low margins to draw in a large number of customers. Other combinations of profitable retailing are also possible, except a low-margin–low-turnover policy. Tigert has suggested that retailers can be classified according to assortment width and store size (see Figure 15-1B). Thus a furniture showroom warehouse is a very large store featuring a very narrow product line. Various other stores can be located in this grid.

In describing the many types of retailers, we will use the five principles of classification shown in Table 15-2: *product line sold, relative price emphasis, nature of business premises, control of outlets,* and *type of store cluster.*

Figure 15-1
Alternative Classification Schemes for Types of Retailers

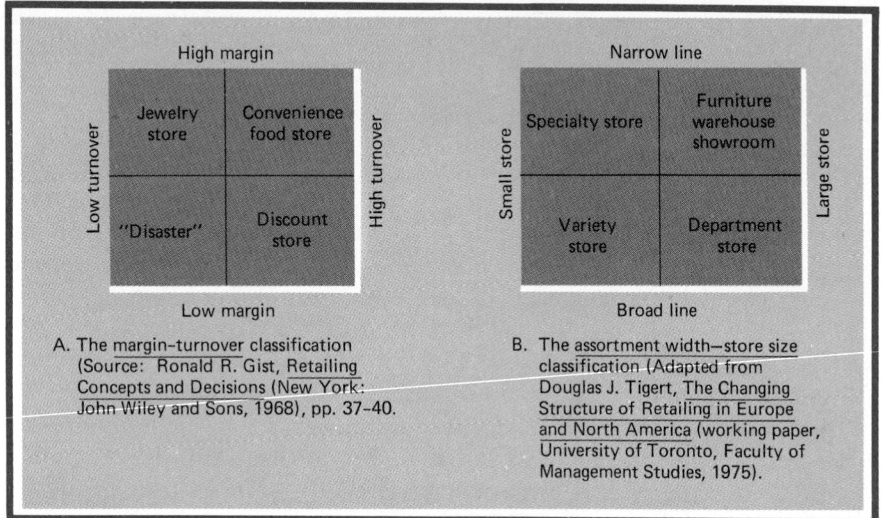

Product line sold. The first basis for classifying retailing institutions is according to the product line sold. Thus one finds grocery stores, liquor stores, furniture stores, and so on. More broadly, we can look at the length and depth of the product assortment and distinguish some major store types. Among the most important ones are the specialty store, department store, supermarket, convenience store, and superstore.

SPECIALTY STORE

A specialty store carries a narrow product line with a deep assortment within that line. Examples of specialty retailers are apparel stores, sporting goods stores, furniture stores, florists, and bookstores. Specialty stores can be subclassified by the degree of narrowness in their product line. A clothing store would be a *single-line store;* a men's clothing store would be a *limited-line store;* and a men's custom shirt store would be a *superspecialty store.* Some analysts contend that superspecialty stores will grow the fastest in the future to take advantage of increasing opportunities for market segmentation, market targeting, and prod-

Table 15-2
Types of Major Retail Outlets

PRODUCT LINE SOLD	RELATIVE PRICE EMPHASIS	NATURE OF BUSINESS PREMISES	CONTROL OF OUTLETS	TYPE OF STORE CLUSTER
Speciality store Department store Supermarket Convenience store Combination store, superstore, and hypermarche Service business	Discount store Warehouse store Catalog showroom	Mail and telephone order retailing Automatic vending Buying service Door-to-door retailing	Corporate chain Voluntary chain and retailer cooperative Consumer cooperative Franchise organization Conglomerchant	Central business district Regional shopping center Community shopping center Neighborhood shopping center

uct specialization. Some of the successful current examples are Athlete's Foot (sport shoes only), Tall Men (tall men's clothing), The Gap (primarily jeans), and Calculators, Inc. (primarily calculators).

The strong growth of specialty stores in recent years is tied to the boom of shopping centers, which typically have one or two anchor department stores and numerous specialty stores, the latter occupying 60–70 percent of the total shopping space. Although most specialty stores are independently owned, currently chain specialty stores are showing the strongest growth. The most successful chain specialty stores are based on well-worked-out retailing concepts that zero in on the needs of specific target markets. A good example is The Limited, a women's fashion clothing store chain. The Limited specializes in high-fashion clothes for the woman who is eighteen to thirty-five years old and is willing to pay a little more to get just the right look. The merchandise is presented in coordinated outfits, the employees are fashionably dressed and of the same age as the target market, and the store has a very contemporary atmosphere. Having defined its target market carefully, The Limited is able to achieve a number of advantages. It can study the fashion interests of eighteen- to thirty-five-year-old women; it can pretest new fashion ideas; it can build a unique image; it can aim its advertising carefully; and it can locate in shopping centers that are in areas with the right demographics.

DEPARTMENT STORE

A department store carries several product lines, typically clothing, home furnishings, and household goods, where each line is operated as a separate department managed by specialist buyers or merchandisers. Examples of well-known department stores are Bloomingdale's (New York), Marshall Field (Chicago), and Filene's (Boston).

There is some disagreement as to how the department store came about. Some writers believe that it grew out of the general store (because it carries several product lines); others believe that it grew out of the dry goods store (because many department store founders first ran dry goods stores). The Bon Marché, established in Paris in 1852, is widely considered to be the first department store.[5] It introduced four innovative principles: (1) low markups and rapid turnover, (2) marking and displaying the prices of merchandise, (3) encouraging customers to just look around without any pressure or obligation to purchase, and (4) a liberal complaints policy. Several other stores followed, with Whiteley's in Britain (1870s) being the first to gain the reputation for carrying "everything from a pin to an elephant," and Lewis (1870s) being the first to set up branches and employ the concept of central buying. In America the earliest department stores included Jordan Marsh, Macy's, Wanamaker's, and Stewart's. These stores created a concept of enjoyment shopping by being housed in huge impressive buildings in fashionable central locations with exciting displays and reputations for introducing new products. This was a far cry from going into the specialty stores of the time, which had little on display and where customers were discouraged from just looking around.

With the growth of cities, department stores developed as a major retailing institution in the downtown areas, with several stores clustering to give shoppers easy access to more than one department store. *Specialty department stores* also emerged, carrying only clothing, shoes, cosmetics, gift items, and luggage; examples are Saks Fifth Avenue and I. Magnin.

In the post–World War II period, department stores experienced a relative decline in their share of total retailing and in their profitability. Many observers believe that these stores are in the declining stage of the *retail life cycle*. The major factors responsible for their relative decline are (1) the increased competition among department stores, which has led to a "trading-up" and has escalated their operating and overhead costs to about 35 percent of sales; (2) the increased competition coming from other types of retailers, particularly discount houses, specialty store chains, and warehouse retailers; and (3) the heavy traffic, the poor parking, and the deterioration of central cities along with the rapid growth of the suburbs, which have made downtown shopping less appealing.

The result has been the closing of some department stores and amalgamation of others. Recently the department stores have been waging a "comeback" war, which is taking several forms. Many have opened branches in suburban shopping centers where the population growth is taking place and the parking is better. Others have added "bargain basements" to meet the discount threat. Still others are pouring money into remodeling their stores, including "going boutique." Some are experimenting with mail-order and telephone shopping. Others, like Dayton-Hudson, have diversified into other store types, such as discount and specialty stores, thus becoming "conglo-merchants" (see p. 478). Some department stores are retrenching on the number of employees, product lines, and customer services such as delivery and credit, but this strategy seems destined to remove one of their major appeals compared with their competitors, namely, better service. To survive, department stores are struggling to find a way to increase their thinning profit margins.

SUPERMARKET

A supermarket is a relatively large, low-cost, low-margin, high-volume, self-service operation "designed to serve the consumer's total needs for food, laundry, and household maintenance products."[6] A supermarket store can be independently owned, although most supermarket stores are operated by supermarket chains, the largest ones (in billions of 1975 dollars) being Safeway ($9.7), A&P ($6.5), Kroger ($5.3), Lucky ($3.1), Winn-Dixie ($3.0), and Jewel ($2.8).

The origin of the supermarket can be traced to two sources: John Hartford's introduction of the cash-and-carry Great Atlantic & Pacific Tea Company (A&P) food stores in 1912; and Clarence Saunders's Piggly-Wiggly stores, which introduced, around 1916, the principles of self-service, customer turnstiles, and checkout counters. However, supermarkets did not really become popular until the 1930s. Michael "King" Kullen is credited with starting the first successful supermarket, a self-service, cash-and-carry grocery operation on a large-scale basis (namely, 6,000 square feet of selling space as opposed to the 800 square feet in conventional stores at the time). Kullen anticipated that such a store would deliver sufficient volume to operate profitably with a gross margin of 9–10 percent of sales, which was half that of food stores at the time. He opened his first store in August 1930 in Jamaica, New York, and it was an immediate success. Within two years three hundred supermarkets had opened, and by 1939 there were approximately five thousand, accounting for 20 percent of total grocery sales. Today there are over thirty-seven thousand supermarkets in operation, and they account for 76 percent of total grocery sales.

What caused the major takeoff of the supermarket in the 1930s? There were several factors. The Great Depression forced *price-conscious behavior* on consumers and simultaneously allowed operators to obtain merchandise at low prices from distressed sources, as well as occupy large buildings at low rentals. The *mass ownership of automobiles* made distance less important and increased weekly shopping, thus reducing the need for small neighborhood stores. The *advances in refrigeration technology* meant that supermarkets and consumers could both store perishables longer. Developments in *packaging technology* meant that food products could be marketed in storable consumer-size packages (cans and boxes) rather than distributor-size containers (barrels and crates), and this stimulated preselling through branding and advertising that reduced the number of salesclerks needed in the store. Finally, the *integration of grocery, meat, and produce departments* made one-stop shopping feasible and attracted customers from considerable distances, thus giving stores the volume they needed for successful supermarket operations.

Over the years, supermarkets have moved in several directions to further build their sales volume. First, they have opened *larger stores,* with today's selling space occupying approximately 18,000 square feet as opposed to 11,700 square feet in the mid-1950s. The result has been that most of the chains now operate larger but fewer stores. Second, supermarkets have increased *the number and variety of items* they carry. A typical supermarket handled three thousand items in 1946, and this has increased to around eight thousand. The most significant increase has been in the number of nonfood items carried—items such as nonprescription drugs, beauty aids, housewares, magazines, books, toys—which now account for 8 percent of total supermarket sales. This "scrambled merchandising" is continuing, and many supermarkets are moving into prescriptions, appliances, records, sporting goods, hardware, garden supplies, and even cameras, in a further effort to find some high-margin lines to improve profitability. Third, supermarkets have typically *upgraded their facilities* through more expensive locations, larger parking facilities, carefully planned decor and architecture, longer store hours and Sunday openings, and a wide variety of customer services such as check cashing, restrooms, and background music. Fourth, the increasing competition for customers has led supermarkets into *promotional competition* taking the form of heavy advertising, trading stamps, and games of chance. And fifth, supermarkets have moved very heavily into *private brands* as a means of reducing their dependence on national brands and increasing their profit margins.

Most of these changes have increased the supermarkets' operating costs and vulnerability to innovative competition. Supermarkets are now getting an operating profit of about 1 percent on their sales and 10 percent on their net worth. Some supermarket chains are in particularly bad shape, notably the ailing giant, A&P. Suffering from years of inbred and undynamic management, A&P had too many small and unprofitable stores which it was unwilling to shut down or redesign. Its stores lacked a quality image, and many units were poorly managed and maintained. They lacked the space to carry nonfood items, which were higher margined. In the early 1970s management launched its ill-fated WEO ("Where

Economy Originates") campaign where it strove for a superdiscount image and slashed prices, and allowed its brand-name goods to become scarce and many of its stores to become dirty. This resulted in customers' leaving in droves. A&P then launched a new campaign called "Pride and Price" where the chain sought to improve its quality image. Management closed many of the small and weaker stores, opened several new large ones, and budgeted half a billion dollars for redesigning stores and retraining employees. So far this strategy has not managed to produce a dramatic turnaround for the ailing chain.[8]

Supermarkets have been hit hard by a number of innovative competitors (see Figure 15-2). The supermarket is typecast today as a large store selling its merchandise at a medium-price level. It is increasingly being challenged by other store types that meet better-defined customer needs with respect to preferred product assortments and price levels. The entire food market is becoming more refined and segmented and is no longer likely to be dominated by one major type of food retailer. One of the major challenges to supermarkets in recent years has been the growth of fast-food outlets (McDonald's, Kentucky Fried Chicken), with the result that Americans are now spending nearly 40 percent of their total food budgets outside of food stores.

Supermarkets have taken several steps to try to restore their sales volume and profitability. They have increased the number of their private brands (including generics), added more high-margined nonfood items, added "takeout" delicatessens and bakery departments, and started new types of stores, particularly combination stores and discount stores. While being essentially mass merchandisers, several chains are seeking to define the social-class target market better and are now designing their stores to serve specific social classes.

An interesting recent development is the spread of "supermarketing" to many other types of business, particularly in the drug, home improvement, toy, and sporting goods fields. The supermarket concept, according to McCammon, involves (1) self-service and self-selection displays; (2) centralization of customer services, usually at the checkout counter; (3) large-scale physical facilities; (4) a strong price emphasis; and (5) a broad assortment and wide variety of merchan-

Figure 15-2
Basic Store Types in Food Retailing

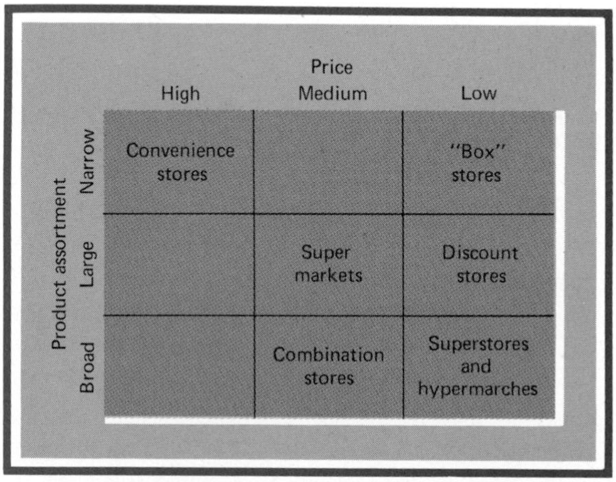

Product assortment	Price: High	Price: Medium	Price: Low
Narrow	Convenience stores		"Box" stores
Large		Super markets	Discount stores
Broad		Combination stores	Superstores and hypermarches

Source: Developed from Fred C. Allvine, "The Supermarket Challenged: New Competitive Strategies Needed," *Business Horizons,* October 1968, p. 65.

dise to facilitate multiple item purchases.[9] These principles, for example, are applied by Standard Brands in the home improvement retailing field and Walgreen's in the drug retailing field.

CONVENIENCE STORE

Convenience food stores are relatively small. They are located near residential areas, are open for long hours (twenty-four hours in some cases) and seven days a week, and carry a limited line of high-turnover convenience products. Examples are Seven-Elevens and White Hen Pantries. Their long hours and their use by consumers mainly for "fill-in" purchases make them relatively high price operations. Yet they presumably fill an important consumer need, and people seem willing to pay for the convenience. The number of such stores increased from approximately 2,000 in 1957 to 27,500 in 1977.[10]

Convenience food retailing has recently been extended to the food-gasoline store, such as is run by Arco and some other major gasoline chains. The customer drives up, and while the car is being serviced, he or she enters a tiny store carrying about one hundred convenience items—bread, milk, cigarettes, coffee, and soft drinks, buys a few, and charges the purchase with his or her oil credit card.

COMBINATION STORE, SUPERSTORE, AND HYPERMARCHE

At the other end of the spectrum from the convenience food stores are three types of stores that are larger than the conventional supermarket. The first of these is the *combination store,* which represents primarily a diversification of the food store into the growing drug and prescription field. Combination food and drug stores average 55,000 square feet of selling space. Three basic designs are used. The one followed by the Kroger chain is to locate its supermarkets and its Super X discount drugstores side by side. The major advantage is managerial—each store can be run as a distinct operation requiring little departure from regular practices. The Jewel Company prefers a single store with the drugs on one side and the foods on the other, offering easier access and convenience to the consumer and probably generating more sales "synergy" than the side by side. Borman's in Detroit has used an integrated design with the drugs sandwiched between the foods—the idea being to influence more cross-shopping and to generate even greater sales "synergy."

The *superstore* tends to be larger than the conventional supermarket (30,000 instead of 18,000 square feet of selling space) and aims at meeting the consumers' total needs for routinely purchased items: food products, beauty aids, personal-care products, alcoholic beverages and tobacco, housewares and hardwares, some clothing such as panty hose, magazines and books, garden products, stationery, and sewing items. In addition, the superstore offers services such as laundry, dry cleaning, shoe repair, check cashing and bill paying, and bargain lunch counters.[11] The superstores' primary attraction for the investor is the 5–6 percent higher prices over conventional supermarkets which they can charge for the wider assortment. Many leading chains have recently moved toward the superstore concept. For example, Kroger developed plans to build 114 superstores averaging 30,000 square feet of selling space.

The *hypermarche* is even larger than the superstore, ranging between 80,000 and 220,000 square feet. The hypermarche combines supermarket, discount, and warehouse retailing principles. Its product assortment goes beyond routinely purchased goods and includes furniture, heavy and light appliances, clothing items, and many other things. The hypermarche uses a price discount appeal in contrast to the normal pricing by superstores. It also operates on warehouse principles. Many products come prepacked in wire "baskets" direct from manufacturers, and these are stacked on five-tier metal racks to a height of twelve to fifteen feet. The restocking is done by forklift trucks, which move through the wide aisles during selling hours. The basic approach is one of bulk display and minimum handling by store personnel, with discounts offered to customers who carry heavy appliances out of the store themselves. The original hypermarche was opened by Carrefour in a suburb of Paris in 1963, and it was an immediate success. The real boom occurred in the late 1960s and early 1970s, particularly in France and Germany where a few hundred of them now operate. Some hypermarches were opened in Canada but did not meet with much success due to the overdevelopment of supermarkets in Canada. American chains are proceeding cautiously, preferring to open superstores instead, although a few operations such as J. C. Penney's The Treasury and the Jewel's Grand Bazaar have adopted some of the hypermarche's operating principles.

SERVICE BUSINESS

Here we want to briefly mention those business enterprises whose "product line" is *service* rather than products. Service retailers include hotels and motels, banks, airlines, colleges, hospitals, movie theatres, tennis clubs and bowling alleys, restaurants, repair services, and various personal service businesses such as barber and beauty shops, dry cleaners, and funeral homes. Service retailers in the United States are growing at a faster rate than product retailers at this stage in the evolution of the American economy. Each service industry has its own drama. Banks are looking for new ways to distribute their services efficiently, including the use of automatic tellers and eventually the use of a telephone system for paying bills. Health maintenance organizations (HMOs) promise to revolutionize the way consumers get and pay for their health services. The amusement industry has spawned Disneyworld and a host of imitators designed to turn fantasies into realities. Groups such as Transcendental Meditation, est, and Silva Mind Control have applied franchise and chain organization principles to mass-distribute personal growth services. And H&R Block has built a franchised network of accountants and tax specialists ready to help consumers pay as little as possible to Uncle Sam. We will say more about the nature of services marketing in Chapter 20 (pp. 423–30).

Relative price emphasis. Another way to distinguish retail forms is according to their price image and pricing policy. Most stores are middle-of-the-road pricers offering normal levels of customer service. Some stores offer shoppers higher-quality goods and/or more customer service, along with higher prices. An example would be Gucci's, which justifies its high prices by saying, "You will remember the goods long after the prices are forgotten." Still another group, discount stores, have specialized in selling goods for less than their normal prices (called off-list pricing); this is made possible by running lower-cost, lower-service operations. Discount stores will be examined here, along with two offshoots, warehouse stores and catalog showrooms.

DISCOUNT STORE

A discount store sells standard merchandise at lower prices than conventional merchants by accepting lower margins and working on higher volume. The mere use of discount pricing and specials from time to time does not make a discount store. Nor does the selling of cheap and inferior goods at low prices. A true discount store exhibits five elements: (1) the store regularly sells its merchandise at prices substantially lower than those prevailing in high-margin, low-turnover outlets; (2) the store emphasizes national brands, so that low price does not suggest inferior quality; (3) the store operates on a self-service, minimum-facilities basis; (4) the location tends to be in a low-rent area drawing customers from relatively long distances; and (5) the fixtures are spartan and functional.[12] In 1975 there were an estimated 6,387 discount department stores, with almost $33 billion in sales.[13]

Discount retailing has a long history, having been practiced, for example, by Alexander's and Mays, well-known New York discount houses. But the real explosion of discount retailing took place in the late 1940s when it moved from soft goods (clothing, toiletries) to hard goods (refrigerators, appliances, washing machines, dishwashers, air conditioners, furnishings, sporting goods). The early postwar discounters—firms such as Masters, Korvette, and Two Guys—were successful for a number of reasons. Many hard goods after the war achieved high levels of standardization and reliability, making their preselling possible and diminishing the need for in-store salesmanship. Furthermore a vast new group of price-conscious but affluent consumers emerged. The early discount stores operated from almost warehouse facilities in low-rent but heavily traveled districts, slashing services, advertising widely, and carrying a reasonable width and depth of branded products. They were able to operate with expenses of 12–18 percent of sales compared with 30–40 percent for the department and specialty stores. By 1960, discount stores accounted for one-third of all sales of household appliances, and the average stockturn was fourteen per year compared with four for a conventional department store.

In recent years, intense competition among discount houses, and between discount houses and department stores, has led many discount retailers to trade up. They have improved their decor, added new lines such as wearing apparel, added more services such as check cashing and easy returns, and opened new branches in suburban shopping centers, all of this leading to higher costs and forcing them to charge higher prices. Furthermore the department stores often cut their prices to avoid losing sales to the discounters, with the distinction between these two types of stores progressively blurring. Several major discount chains folded in the 1970s as a result of rising costs and losing their price edge.

Today's most successful general merchandise discount chain is K-Mart, with its 1,208 stores dotting the country. The parent company, S. S. Kresge Company, opened the first K-Mart in 1962 to replace its withering five-and-dime variety stores. K-Mart has been the nation's fastest-growing retailer (20 percent growth per year in sales and profits). It passed J. C. Penney in 1976 to become the nation's second-largest retailer (with $8.3 billion sales), moving to close the gap with first-place Sears ($14.3 billion). K-Mart's success is based on sticking to discount traditions: Decor is minimal, the sales staff is sparse, and consumers wander about a huge one-story building to find what they want, put their selections into shopping carts, and wheel them to checkout counters. Shoppers can choose among fifteen thousand specific items and are treated to many national brands rather than the "seconds" and "irregulars" featured by other discount stores. K-Mart's stores are built free-standing rather than within shopping centers and also are leased rather than owned, thus allowing K-Mart to spend more on merchandising.[14]

Discount retailing has moved beyond general merchandise into special merchandise forms, such as discount sporting goods stores and discount stereo equipment stores. Discount food retailing has been among the most interesting developments. In 1956 the Shop-Rite supermarket food chain dropped its trading stamps and launched a bold discount strategy. Economies were generated by operating fewer hours, reducing nonessential services, and having "everyday low prices," which eliminated the necessity for re-marking hundreds of prices every week. Its stores were larger than conventional supermarkets, offered wider assortments, and were located more centrally in larger trade areas with ready accessibility. Its greater efficiency permitted prices that were approximately 4 percent below those of conventional supermarkets, and the chain met with great success.

One of the most recent developments in discount food retailing is the "box" food stores. Pioneered by Aldi Discount Food, more than two hundred of these stores were operating nationally in early 1978. They are almost warehouse operations. Services are slashed to the barest minimum, with customers paying cash and bringing their own bags. Aldi stores carry about 450 high-turnover items; none are perishable, thus eliminating the need for costly refrigeration. Prices are posted on signs rather than on merchandise, thus saving marking costs. These box stores represent still another innovative way to segment the market and meet a set of underserved consumer needs.

WAREHOUSE STORE

A warehouse store is a no-frill, discount, reduced-service operation which seeks to move high volume at low prices. In its broad form, it includes hypermarches on the one hand and box food discount stores on the other. One of its most interesting forms is the *furniture showroom warehouse.* Conventional furniture stores have used warehouse sales for years to clear out old stock from time to time, but it took two brothers, Ralph and Leon Levitz, to refine the idea into a new merchandising concept. The Levitz brothers got the idea in 1953, and by 1977 they had built sixty-one furniture warehouse showrooms. Shoppers enter a football-field-size warehouse located in a suburban low-rent area. They pass through the warehouse section where they see a fantastic amount of inventory piled in neat tiers: approximately fifty-two thousand items worth about $2 million. They enter the showroom section of the warehouse containing approximately two hundred room settings in which the furniture is attractively displayed. Customers make their selections from floor samples and place them with salespeople. By the time the customer pays for the purchase, leaves, and drives to the loading entrance, the merchandise is ready. If heavy goods are purchased, they can be delivered in a few days (compared with the many weeks of delay with conventional furniture stores) or loaded on the customer's vehicle at a savings of many dollars.

The whole operation is targeted to buyers of medium-priced brand-name furniture who are seeking discount prices, usually 10–20 percent less than the prices charged by conventional outlets, and immediate availability. The shoppers enjoy the wide brand selection and low prices, but on the other hand they often complain about the limited customer service. Levitz stores have attracted a number of competitors, notably the Wickes Corporation, and units started by some of the major department store chains who have been most hurt by the emergence of the furniture showroom warehouse. The profit picture on these furniture warehouse showrooms is mixed because they are saddled with high inventory expenses, have to spend a lot on promotion to attract sufficient traffic into their out-of-the-way free-standing stores, and often face too many competitors located in the same markets.[15]

CATALOG SHOWROOM

A catalog showroom applies catalog and discounting principles to a wide selection of high-markup, fast-moving, brand-name goods. These include jewelry, power tools, luggage, cameras, and photographic equipment. These stores emerged in the late 1960s and have become one of retailing's hottest new forms, even posing a threat to the traditional discounter who has moved too much into improved decor, more service, and higher markups. Catalog showroom sales in 1978 totaled $5.65 billion, a jump from the $750 million ten years earlier. The industry is dominated by publicly owned companies such as Best Products Co., Service Merchandise, and Modern Merchandising. Currently there are about seventeen hundred catalog showrooms in the country operated by 470 companies.[16]

The catalog showrooms issue four-color catalogs, often five hundred pages long, and supplement them with smaller seasonal editions. They are available in the showroom and are also mailed to past buyers. Each item's list price and discount price are shown. The customer can order an item over the phone and pay delivery charges or drive to the showroom, examine a sample firsthand, and buy it out of stock. In this way, catalog showrooms differ from the traditional catalog merchandising of Sears and Ward's, whose catalogs are primarily vehicles for "in-home" shopping, where discounts do not exist, and whose customers have to wait for days or weeks before they receive the merchandise.

The customer who buys at the catalog showroom has to put up with certain inconveniences, such as driving some distance, standing in line to see a particular item (many are locked in enclosed cases), waiting for the item to be supplied from the back room, and finding little after-service if there are problems. However, the rapid growth of catalog showrooms indicates that customers are eager for the savings and willing to put up with less service. Catalog showrooms make their money by carrying primarily national brands in nonfashion goods categories, leasing stores in low-rent areas, doing with one-third fewer salespeople, minimizing opportunities for shoplifting by their case display, and operating largely on a cash basis.

Nature of business premises. Although the overwhelming majority of goods and services are sold through stores, the share of *nonstore retailing* has been growing much faster than store retailing. In 1977, nonstore retailing amounted to \$75 billion, or 12 percent of all consumer purchases. Some observers foresee that by the end of this century as much as a third of all general merchandise retailing will be done through nonstore channels.[17] Others go further and predict *robot retailing* where consumers can order their goods using home computers and receive or pick them up, without stepping into stores.[18] Here we will examine the major forms of nonstore retailing: mail-and-telephone-order retailing, vending machines, buying services, and door-to-door selling and in-house parties.

MAIL-AND-TELEPHONE-ORDER RETAILING

Mail-and-telephone-order retailing covers any selling that involves using the mail or telephone or get orders and/or using them to facilitate delivery of the goods. Mail order itself is as old as the mail system. Although it originated in the *mailed order* of a customer to a manufacturer or merchant, it took the form, after the Civil War, of merchants' attempting to stimulate customer orders by sending out catalogs, primarily to farmers living in rural areas where the variety of goods was limited. A. Montgomery Ward, established in 1872 in Chicago (in a hayloft over a stable), is popularly considered its major innovator and was followed fourteen years later by Sears and Roebuck. By 1918 these two concerns conducted giant catalog mail-order businesses, and there were a total of some twenty-five hundred other mail-order houses. In the 1930s and 1940s, however, many retailers discontinued their mail-order operations as the chain stores opened branches in smaller towns and brought more merchandise to their inhabitants, and as the number of automobiles and good roads increased. But today, far from being in a state of decline, the mail-and-telephone-order business is undergoing a resurgence.

Mail-and-telephone-order retailing today takes one of several forms.

1. *Mail-order catalog.* Here the seller mails a catalog to a select list of customers and makes the catalog available on its premises, either at no charge or at a nominal charge. This approach is used by *general merchandise* mail-order houses carrying a full line of merchandise, such as Sears and Ward's. Sears is the industry giant, with \$3 billion in catalog operations, and it sends out 300 million catalogs annually.[19] For years J. C. Penney's avoided mail order because it wanted to get customers into its stores, but it finally took the step in the 1950s and today is number two, selling over a billion dollars' worth of merchandise. These giant merchandisers also operate catalog counters in their stores and catalog offices in small communities where customers can go and examine the catalogs and place orders. The order is shipped from central warehouses to these catalog desks, and upon its arrival, the customer is phoned and is asked to pick it up. Recently, specialty department stores, such as Neiman-Marcus, Saks Fifth Avenue, and Bloomingdale's, have begun sending catalogs in a move to cultivate an upper-middle-class market in high-priced, often exotic, merchandise such as "his and her" bathrobes, designer jewelry, and gourmet foods. Several major corporations have also acquired or developed mail-order divisions. Xerox offers children's books; Avon sells women's apparel; W. R. Grace sells cheese; American

Airlines offers luggage; General Foods offers needlework kits; and General Mills sells sports shirts.[20]

2. *Direct response.* Here the direct marketer runs an ad in a newspaper, in a magazine, or on radio or television describing some product, and the customer can write or phone for it. The direct marketer chooses those media that maximize the number of orders for a given amount of advertising dollars. This strategy is best suited to specialty retailers dealing in a specific product market, such as phonograph records and tapes, books, and small appliances.

3. *Direct mail.* Here the direct marketer sends single mail pieces—letters, fliers, and foldouts—to prospects whose names are on special mailing lists of high-potential buyers of that product category. The mailing lists are purchased from mailing-list brokerage houses. Direct mail, called "junk mail" by its critics, has proved very successful in promoting books, magazine subscriptions, and insurance and is increasingly being used to sell novelty items, clothing apparel, and even gourmet foods. The major charities use direct mail to raise $21.4 billion, or over 80 percent of their total contributions.[21]

4. *Telephone selling.* Direct marketers are increasingly using the telephone to sell everything from home repair services to newspaper subscriptions to zoo memberships. Some telephone marketers have developed computerized phoning systems where households are dialed automatically and computerized messages presented. Telephone selling has incurred the opposition of several groups, who are proposing laws to ban or limit it.

Several factors have contributed to the recent increase in mail-and-telephone-order selling. The movement of women into the work force has substantially cut down the shopping time available to them. Other factors have made shopping less pleasant: the gasoline shortage and the spiraling costs of driving; traffic congestion and parking headaches; shoppers retreating to the suburbs and averse to visiting crime-plagued urban shopping areas; and a lack of sales help and having to queue at checkout counters. In addition, many chain stores have dropped slower-moving specialty items, thus creating an opportunity for direct marketers to promote these items. Finally, the development of "toll-free" phone numbers and the willingness of some firms to accept telephone orders at night or on Sundays has boosted this form of retailing.

AUTOMATIC VENDING

Automatic vending (also called automatic merchandising or robot retailing) through coin-operated machines has been a major post–World War II growth area, with total sales soaring to over $7 billion by 1972 (1.5 percent of total retail trade). The concept of automatic vending is not new, and one study cites a 215 B.C. book describing an Egyptian coin-actuated device for selling sacrificial water.[22] In the 1880s the Tutti-Frutti Company began installing chewing-gum machines at train stations. But today's machines have come a long way and have benefited from the space-age and computer technology. The new machines have licked the problem of requiring prices that conform to common coinage denominations, and the newest machines incorporate bill-changers that can discriminate between bills of different denominations, dispense merchandise, and return the proper change. Equally significant is the considerable variety of merchandise to which auto-vend has been successfully applied. Although the bulk of sales are still generated by impulse goods with very high convenience value (such as cigarettes, soft drinks, candy, newspapers, and hot beverages), a variety of other products (such as hosiery, cosmetics, food snacks, hot soups and food, paperbacks, record albums, film, T-shirts, insurance policies, shoeshines, and even fishing worms) are being successfully vended.

Vending machines are found everywhere—in the larger retail stores and in gasoline stations, cafeterias, and even railway dining cars. They are usually owned by a company that leases space in favorable locations and services the machines. According to National Automatic Merchandising Association estimates, over seven thousand machine operators in the United States operate more than 6 million machines.

To customers, vending machines offer the advantages of twenty-four-hour selling, self-service, and less damaged merchandise. At the same time, automatic vending is a relatively expensive channel, and prices of vended merchandise are often 15 to 50 percent higher. Vendor costs tend to be high because of frequent restocking at widely scattered locations, frequent machine breakdowns, and the high pilferage rate in certain locations. For the customer, the biggest irritations are malfunctioning, machine breakdowns and out-of-stocks, and the fact that merchandise cannot be returned.

Basically, automatic vending is still most feasible only for small, fairly standardized, low-unit-value, convenience items of well-known presold brands. In nonmerchandise fields, however, there have been some extensive developments. Vending machines supplying entertainment services—pinball machines, slot machines, and juke boxes—are now being followed by the new electronic computer games. A highly specialized area in which very rapid development is taking place is banking services. The *automatic teller* has revolutionized common bank transactions by allowing customers fully automated, twenty-four-hour service on checking, savings, withdrawals, and transfer of funds from one account to another. Automatic tellers are being set up not only on bank premises but also in shopping malls and office buildings.

It has been prophesied that automatic vending will eventually develop into the fully *automated store.* This would be a store or department where all the items are purchased by coin, with one attendant or no attendants present. Several experiments in automated stores were conducted by department stores in the late 1950s and early 1960s without much success. A totally different concept in automated store retailing was tested in Europe in the late 1960s. Such stores display only samples on the shelves. Next to each sample is a slot into which the customer inserts a key, given to him or her on entrance, which electronically registers the purchase. The order is assembled and ready for pickup in the short time required for checkout. Computer control and telecommunications are central to the system. For all practical purposes, however, the fully automated store has been a matter of research and anticipation only. It has not had much impact on any major field of retailing. Only in one field has it been a resounding success—the coin-operated, automated laundry store. It appears that the future of automation in retailing may just bypass the fully automated store, and the really revolutionary developments will come in "in-home" shopping through interactive telecommunication systems and highly automated order-processing, billing, and warehouse facilities.

BUYING SERVICE

A buying service is a storeless retailer serving specific clienteles—usually the employees of large organizations such as schools, hospitals, unions, and government agencies. The organization's members become members of the buying service, and they are entitled to buy from a selective list of retailers who have agreed to give discounts to members of the buying service. Thus a customer seeking a video recording machine would get a form from the buying service, take it to an approved retailer, and buy the appliance at a discount. The retailer would then pay a small fee to the buying service. United Buying Service is a current example of a successful buying service that offers its nine hundred thousand members the opportunity to buy merchandise at "cost plus 8 percent."

DOOR-TO-DOOR RETAILING

This old form of selling—which started centuries ago with itinerant peddlers—has burgeoned into a $6 billion industry, with over six hundred companies selling either *door to door,* or *office to office,* or at *home sales parties.* One of the pioneers, the Fuller Brush Company, still employs about ten thousand salespeople to sell its brushes, combs, brooms, and other products. Other pioneers include vacuum cleaner companies like Electrolux and bible-selling companies like the Southwestern Company of Nashville. Encyclopedia companies have used door-to-door selling for years, with World Book emerging as a leader by enlisting and training schoolteachers to sell its encyclopedias part time. Door-to-door selling improved its image considerably with Avon's entry into the industry, with its concept of the homemakers' friend and beauty consultant—the Avon lady. Its army of 995,000 representatives produced over $1.6 billion in sales in 1978, making it the world's largest cosmetics firm and the number one door-to-door marketer, several times larger than the next two leading door-to-door marketers, Electrolux and Tupperware. Tupperware helped popularize the home sales parties method of selling, in which several friends and neighbors are invited to a party in someone's home where Tupperware is available for purchase. Tupperware handles about 140 different products and works through fifty thousand independent dealers.[23]

Door-to-door selling's resurgence indicates that it meets the needs of people for the convenience and personal attention that is part of at-home buying. The prices of the items are not low, since door-to-door selling is expensive (the salespersons get a 20 to 50 percent commission), and there are the costs of soliciting and managing the sales force across widely dispersed geographic areas. The future of door-to-door retailing through personal calls made by salespeople is uncertain. With a majority of American households today consisting of single-person or two-person families (with both members working full time), the likelihood of finding anyone home during the day is rapidly diminishing. And with the new interactive telecommunication technologies expected to proliferate in the 1980s, the door-to-door salesperson may very well be replaced by a home computer.

Control of outlets. Retailing institutions are also classified according to their form of ownership. About 90 percent of all retail stores are independents, and they account for two-thirds of all retail sales. Several other forms—the corporate chain, voluntary chain and retailer cooperative, consumer cooperative, franchise organization, and conglomerchant—represent alternative ownership forms.

CORPORATE CHAIN

The chain store represents one of the most important retail developments of the twentieth century. The idea of one merchant or company owning and operating several stores is in itself not new: The Fuggers of Augsburg had branches in scores of European cities in the 1400s, and the Mitsui chain was operating in Japan in the 1600s. One of the earliest chains in America was the Great Atlantic & Pacific Tea Company (A&P), which started with one store in 1859 importing tea direct from the Orient and had expanded to twenty-five stores by 1869. Another was Woolworth's, which initiated the low-price, high-volume principle in the variety merchandise market and felt that a number of stores were necessary to make the variety store a success. However, the growth of chains in America was not very impressive until the first two decades of the twentieth century.

Gist has defined **chain store** as *two or more outlets that are commonly owned and controlled, sell similar lines of merchandise, have central buying and merchandising, and may use a similar architectural motif.*[24] Each characteristic deserves comment. The U.S. Bureau of the Census actually classifies chains in seven categories ranging from the two-to-three unit class to the over-one hundred unit class. Scholars are not in agreement as to how few units make up a chain. Common ownership and control is the unique feature of the corporate chain that distinguishes it from similar appearing forms such as voluntary chains and franchise organizations. A corporate chain unit sells similar lines of merchandise; this distinguishes it from a merchandising conglomerate which combines several corporate chains under common-owner ownership. Central buying and merchandising means that headquarters plays a key role in deciding on the chain's product assortment, placing bulk orders for the goods to get quantity discounts, distributing the goods to the individual store units, and establishing pricing, promotion, and other standardizing merchandising policies for the units. Finally, chains often develop a similar architectural motif to increase their unit's visibility and identifiability in the public eye.

Corporate chain organizations have appeared in all types of retail operations: supermarkets, discount, variety, speciality, and department stores. In terms of product line, the corporate chain (when defined as having eleven or more units) are strongest department stores (89% of the total sales volume of 1975), variety stores (81%), food stores (56%), shoe stores (44%), drug stores (39%), tire, battery accessory stores (25%), and women's apparel (25%).

The success of the corporate chain is based on their ability to achieve a price advantage over independents by moving toward a high volume and lower margins. Chains achieve their efficiency in several ways. First, their sheer size allows them to buy in huge quantities to take maximum advantage of quantity discounts and lower transportation costs. At one time they were accused of rustling better prices from manufacturers beyond the normal quantity discounts, but this was effectively stopped by the Robinson-Patman legislation (1936). Most authorities now question whether the chains' lower prices were totally founded on their bulk purchasing power. Second, chains were able to develop superior operational capabilities by hiring superior managers and developing specialized management practices in the areas of sales forecasting, inventory control, pricing, and promotion. Third, the chains achieved a true integration of wholesaling and retailing functions, whereas the independent retailers were always dealing with many different wholesalers. Fourth, the chains were able to achieve promotional economies by buying advertising that benefited all of their stores and whose cost was spread over a very large volume. And fifth, the chains permitted their units some degree of decentralized authority to meet variations in consumer preferences and competition in local markets. Probably the major threat to a chain's success consists of maintaining too much centralization and inflexibility in a rapidly changing environment.

VOLUNTARY CHAIN AND RETAILER COOPERATIVE

The *corporate chains* were so successful that they produced two reactions. The first was to inspire the passage of antichain legislation in the 1930s at the state level (fair-trade laws) and the federal level (Robinson-Patman Act). Most of these laws sought to prevent the chains from competing with independents through charging lower prices achieved through their centralized buying power. Second, the chains engendered a competitive survival response in the independents, who began to form two major types of associations: the *voluntary chain* (a wholesaler-sponsored group of independents engaged in bulk buying and common merchandising) and a *retailer cooperative* (a cooperative agreement between independent retailers who set up a central buying organization). The voluntaries and cooperatives were described earlier in Chapter 14, p. 431. These organizations gained the needed merchandising economies and programs and were soon able to meet the price challenge of the corporate chains. The point has been reached where the operations of corporate chains, voluntary chains, and retailer cooperatives are so similar that the major difference is chiefly the question of ownership.

CONSUMER COOPERATIVE

A consumer cooperative (or co-op) is any retail firm that is owned by its customers. Consumer co-ops are started by the residents of a community when they feel that local retailers are not serving them well, either charging too high prices or providing poor-quality products. The residents contribute money to start their own store, and they vote on its policies and elect a group to manage it. The store may set its prices low or, alternatively, set normal prices, but the members receive a patronage dividend based on the individual level of their purchases. A number of the most successful cooperatives are ideological and several are found in college communities. Although there are now a few thousand consumer cooperatives in the United States, they have never become an important force in distribution. The opposite is true in some European countries, especially the Scandinavian countries and Switzerland. A striking example is Migros in Switzerland, a consumer cooperative that accounts for 11 percent of the entire Swiss retail volume! Migros was founded in 1925 by Gottlieb Duttweiler as a corporate chain in the grocery business dedicated to challenging entrenched high-markup competitors in the grocery field. He was so successful that in 1946 he decided to turn Migros into a customer cooperative by selling one share of stock to each of his eighty-five thousand registered customers. Today Migros is a huge federation of 440 branch stores, 74 specialty stores, and numerous other enterprises essentially owned by its customers.

FRANCHISE ORGANIZATION

A franchise organization is a contractual association between a franchiser (who may be a manufacturer, wholesaler, or service organization) and franchisees (who are independent businesspeople who buy the right to own and operate one or more units in the franchise system). The main distinction between franchise organizations and the other contractual systems (voluntary chains and retailer cooperatives) is that franchise organizations are normally based on some unique product or service, or method of doing business, or trade name, goodwill, or patent, that the franchiser has developed.

Two other distinctions can be drawn. The compensation the franchiser receives can take on a complex form and can include (1) an initial fee, (2) a royalty on gross sales, (3) rental and lease fees (on equipment and fixtures supplied by the franchiser), (4) a share of the profits, and (5) sometimes a regular license fee. In a few cases franchisers have also charged management consulting fees, but usually such services are an integral part of the services the franchisee is entitled to as part of the package deal, since one of the most important objectives of the sponsor is to ensure a minimum quality of operation and service at the franchisee level. For example, McDonald's charges an initial fee of $150,000 for a franchise and receives a 3.0 percent royalty fee and a rental charge of 8.5 percent of the franchisee's volume. It also requires its new franchisees to go to Hamburger University for three weeks to "learn the ropes."

The other distinction is that there are usually very specific obligations relating to the terms on which the franchised "product" can be used or dispensed. McDonald's had required that all franchisees' equipment and many of its supplies must be obtained from it or its authorized suppliers. But this type of requirement has been challenged in the courts, and a federal court ruling has held that this clause must be dropped from franchising contracts. Franchisees can buy from whatever sources they wish as long as they meet strict quality standards.

In 1976 there were approximately 450,000 franchise outlets, with sales of $195 billion. Their heaviest concentration, according to the number of units, is in gasoline service stations (45.7 percent), automobile and truck dealers (8.5 percent), and fast-food restaurants (7.3 percent). In the group of fast-food retailers, which has had the most dramatic growth in recent years, the leaders in market share as of 1974 were McDonald's (19.8 percent), Kentucky Fried Chicken (11.7 percent), International Dairy Queen (6.0 percent), and Burger King (4.8 percent). McDonald's is the clear leader. But McDonald's, along with several other fast-food franchisers, is currently facing difficult times and will be hard pressed to maintain its momentum. Challenging these franchisers is the high inflation in labor costs (due to higher minimum wages) and food costs, forcing them to raise their prices to the customers. The high cost of gasoline and gasoline shortages are likely to reduce the amount of travel and hurt sales. Finally, new competitors are always arising, and some of their customers will be lost to the glamour of the latest new hamburger, pizza, or taco. What are their responses? Some of the franchisers have plans for opening reduced-size units in smaller towns; here they would find less competition. Others are moving into new institutional settings such as large factories, office buildings, colleges, and even hospitals. Others are experimenting with new products that they hope will appeal to the public and be profitable to the firms.

CONGLOMERCHANT

Conglomerchants (also called merchandising conglomerates) are free-form corporations that combine several diversified retailing lines and forms under central ownership, along with some integration of their distribution and management functions.[25] Major conglomerchants include Federated Department Stores, Allied Stores, Dayton Hudson, and J. C. Penney. One of the most profitable of the diversified retailers is the Melville Corporation, which operates the Thom McAn, Miles, and Vanguard shoe chains; Chess King, a string of 326 young men's fashion stores; Foxmoor, a women's junior apparel store; Clothes Ben, a chain of discount women's apparel stores; CVS, a chain of health and beauty aid stores; and Marshall, Inc., a regional chain that carries all kinds of name-brand clothing.[26]

In the 1980s, diversified retailing is likely to grow stronger and be adopted by more of the corporate chains. Whereas in the 1970s they concentrated on deepening their major business line, in the 1980s they will be looking for new types of retail businesses to launch. The major question will be whether diversified retailing produces management systems and economies that can make their separate retail lines more successful.

Type of store cluster. Another principle for retail classification is whether consumers face a single isolated store or one of several types of clustered stores. Most stores today cluster together in shopping districts, both because of zoning ordinances and to offer aggregate convenience, namely, one-stop shopping. Just as supermarkets and department stores save consumers time and energy in finding what they need, so do clustered stores. The four main types are the central business district, the regional shopping center, the community shopping center, and the neighborhood shopping center.

CENTRAL BUSINESS DISTRICT

Until the 1950s central business districts were the dominant form of retail cluster. Every large town and city had a central business district in which were located the department stores, specialty stores, banks, and major movie houses. And smaller business districts would be found in neighborhood and outlying areas. Then in the 1950s people began their great migration to the suburbs and gave rise to an explosive development of suburban shopping centers to serve their needs. Suburbanites reduced their shopping in the central business district, wishing to avoid the heavy traffic, expensive parking, and deteriorating urban scene. The abandonment of these central business districts accelerated the rate of urban blight and forced centrally located merchants to open branches in the growing suburban shopping centers, as well as make a major effort to revitalize the downtown area by building shopping malls and underground parking, and renovating their stores. Some central business districts have made a comeback, but others are in a state of slow and possibly irreversible decline.

REGIONAL SHOPPING CENTER

A *shopping center* is defined as "a group of commercial establishments planned, developed, owned, and managed as a unit related in location, size, and type of shop to the trade area that it services, and providing on-site parking in definite relationship to the types and sizes of stores it contains."[27] Of these, the regional shopping center is the most dramatic and competitive with the central business district and neighborhood shopping areas.

A regional shopping center is like a mini-downtown and contains from forty to over one hundred stores. To be profitable, it must serve a population of from one hundred thousand to one million customers who live within thirty minutes' driving time. In its early form, the regional shopping center often contained two strong department stores at either end of a mall and a balanced set of specialty stores between the anchor stores. This arrangement encouraged comparison shopping because the specialty stores typically carried goods that competed with the lines carried by the department stores. Thus a customer wishing to buy jeans could comparison-shop at Sears and Roebuck, Lord and Taylor, Just Jeans, The Gap, and The County Seat. Regional shopping centers have become more elaborate over the years, with all the stores being located in an enclosed mall, many malls having two stories, and many centers having three or four large department stores in one complex. Good design encourages freely moving traffic where all the stores can get exposure.

COMMUNITY SHOPPING CENTER

A community shopping center contains fifteen to fifty retail stores serving between twenty thousand and one hundred thousand residents, where 90 percent live within one and one-half miles of the center. One primary store is normally found, usually a branch of a department store or a variety store. The shopping center is also likely to include a supermarket, convenience goods stores, and professional offices—and sometimes a bank. The primary store will usually be located at the corner of the L in the case of L-shaped shopping centers and in the center in the case of line-shaped shopping centers. The stores nearest to the primary store normally sell shopping goods, and the other stores normally sell convenience goods.

NEIGHBORHOOD SHOPPING CENTER

The largest number of shopping centers consists of those that service neighborhoods. Neighborhood shopping centers contain five to fifteen stores and serve a population of less than twenty thousand residents. Customers walk to these centers or drive no more than five minutes. These are convenience shopping centers with the supermarket as the principal tenant and several service establishments, such as a dry cleaner, self-service laundry, shoe repair store, and a beauty shop. In contrast to the larger shopping centers, this is usually an unplanned strip of stores.

Shopping centers now account for approximately one-third of all retail sales, but they may be reaching their saturation point. Sales per square foot are dropping and vacancy rates are climbing; some bankruptcies have occurred. Shopping center developers are responding by planning to build smaller shopping centers in the 400,000-square-foot range, in medium-sized and smaller cities, and in primarily the fastest-growing areas of the nation, such as the Southwest.[28] Meanwhile, some people predict a quite different scene in shopping centers within the next decade: "Although you will still be able to find shopping centers in 1985, you may not be able to recognize them. They will be smaller, fewer in number, and their occupants will be dramatically different. Doctors, lawyers, dentists, clinics, contractors, churches, counselling centers, local government offices—and even the public library—will have found a place among the few surviving retail tenants."[29]

Retailer Marketing Decisions

Having looked at the various types of retailers, we will now examine the major types of marketing decisions made by retailers, specifically decisions in the areas of target market, product assortment and services, price, promotion, and place.

Target market decision. The first and most important decision facing a retailer consists of determining who is the target market. Until the target market is defined in demographic and psychographic terms, the retailer cannot make precise decisions on product assortment, store decor, advertising messages and media, price levels, and so on. Some stores are able to define quite narrow groups as their target market: A certain fashionable women's apparel store in downtown Palm Springs, California, knows that its primary market is upper-income women, primarily between thirty and fifty-five years of age, living within thirty minutes' driving time from the store. We saw earlier that Bloomingdale's in Manhattan is very clear about its target market group. However, too many retailers, both large and small, have not clarified their target market or are trying to satisfy some incompatible target markets, satisfying none of them well. Even Sears, which serves so many different people, must develop a better definition of which groups it will make its major target customers so that it can achieve more precision in its product assortment, prices, locations, and promotion with these groups.

A retailer should periodically carry out marketing research to make sure that it is delivering the expected satisfactions to its target market. Consider a store that seeks to attract discriminating shoppers, but unfortunately the store's image among such shoppers is the one shown by the solid line in Figure 15-3. The store's image is not appealing to its target market, and it has the choice of either going after a mass market or redesigning itself into a "classier store." Suppose it does the latter. Some time later a sample of its customers are interviewed for their perception of the store. The current image is now the one shown by the dashed line in Figure 15-3. The store has succeeded in bringing about a congruence between its target market and the store's image.

Product assortment and services decision. The modern retailer has to make decisions on three major "product" variables in retailing: product assortment, services mix, and store atmosphere.

The *product assortment* chosen by the retailer must match the shopping

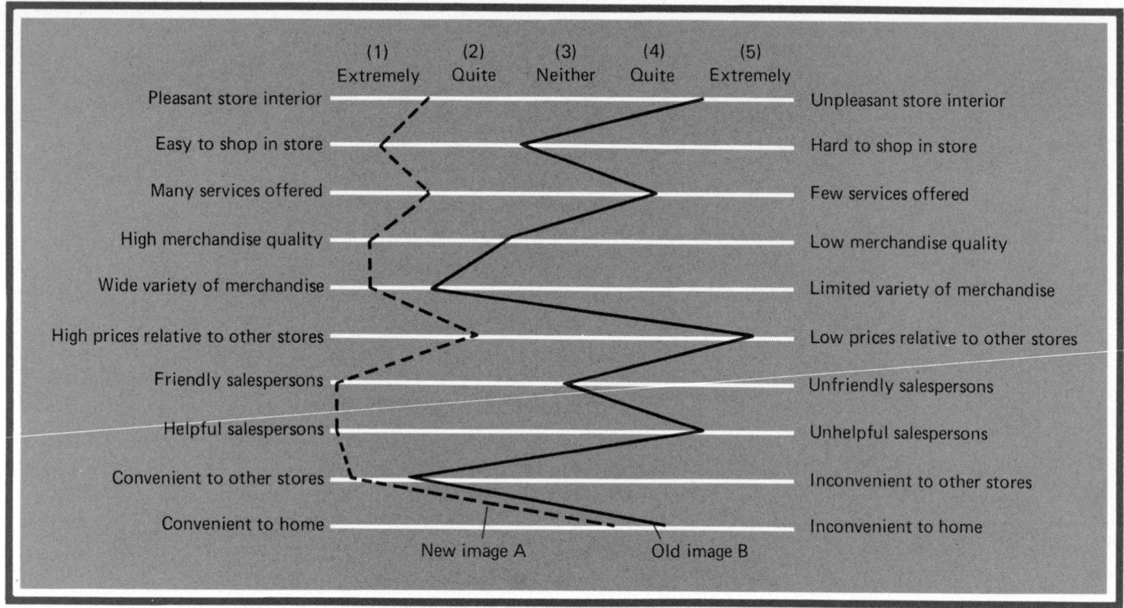

Figure 15-3 A Comparison between the Old and New Image of a Store Seeking to Appeal to a Class Market

Source: Adapted from David W. Cravens, Gerald E. Hills, and Robert B. Woodruff, *Marketing Decision Making: Concepts and Strategy* (Homewood, Ill.: Richard D. Irwin, 1976), p. 234.

expectations of the target market. In fact, it becomes a key element in the competitive battle among similar retailers. The retailer has to decide on product assortment *width* (narrow or wide) and *depth* (shallow or deep). Thus in the restaurant business, a restaurant can offer a narrow and shallow assortment (small lunch counters), a narrow and deep assortment (delicatessen), a wide and shallow assortment (cafeteria), or a wide and deep assortment (large restaurants). Another product assortment dimension is the quality of the goods. The customer is interested in the range of choice but is even more interested in the quality of the product.

Retailers also must make decisions on the *mix of services* they will provide their customers. The old "mom and pop" grocery stores offered home delivery, credit, and conversation to their customers, services that today's modern supermarkets have completely eliminated. Table 15-3 lists some of the major services that full-service retailers can offer. The service mix is one of the key tools of nonprice competition for differentiating one store from another.

The *store's atmospherics* is a third element in its product arsenal to differentiate itself from competition. Every store has a physical layout that makes it hard or easy to move around. Every store has a "feel"; one store is dirty, another is charming, a third is palatial, a fourth is somber. The store must embody a planned atmosphere that suits the target market and leans them toward purchase. A funeral parlor should be quiet, somber, and peaceful, and a discothèque should be bright, loud, and vibrating; the two should not be confused. The atmosphere is designed by creative people who know how to combine visual, aural, olfactory, and tactile stimuli to achieve the desired effect.[30]

Table 15-3
Typical Retail Services

Prepurchase services	Postpurchase services	Ancillary services
1. Accepting telephone orders	1. Delivery	1. Check cashing
2. Accepting mail orders (or purchases)	2. Regular wrapping (or bagging)	2. General information
3. Advertising	3. Gift wrapping	3. Free parking
4. Window display	4. Adjustments	4. Restaurants
5. Interior display	5. Returns	5. Repairs
6. Fitting rooms	6. Alterations	6. Interior decorating
7. Shopping hours	7. Tailoring	7. Credit
8. Fashion shows	8. Installations	8. Rest rooms
9. Trade-ins	9. Engraving	9. Baby attendant service
	10. COD delivery	

Source: Carl M. Larson, Robert E. Weigand, and John S. Wright, *Basic Retailing* (Englewood Cliffs, N.J.: Prentice-Hall, 1976), p. 364.

Place decision. The retailers' choice of locations is a key competitive factor in target market and reflecting the quality of goods they carry, the services they offer, and the type of price image they want. The cost of merchandise is the base for their pricing, and their ability to buy intelligently is a key ingredient in successful retailing. Retailers can often make as much money through smart buying as through smart selling. Beyond this, they must price carefully in a number of other ways. Low markups can be set on some items so they can work as *traffic builders* or *loss leaders,* in the hope that customers will buy additional items that bear a higher markup once they are in the store. In addition, retail management has to be adept in its use of markdowns on slower-moving merchandise. Shoe retailers, for example, expect to sell 50 percent of their shoes at the normal markup, 25 percent at a 40 percent markup, and the remaining 25 percent at cost. Their initial pricing anticipates these expected markdowns.

Promotion decision. Retailers use the normal promotional tools—advertising, personal selling, sales promotion, and publicity—to reach consumers. Advertising is a major tool, and retailer advertising can be found in newspapers, in magazines, on the radio, and on television. The advertising is occasionally supplemented by hand-delivered circulars and direct-mail pieces. Personal selling requires careful training of the salespeople in how to greet customers, meet their needs, and handle their doubts and complaints. Sales promotion may take the form of in-store demonstrations, trading stamps, grand prizes, and visiting celebrities. Publicity is always available to retailers who have something interesting to say. Consider the range of promotional styles available to three different art galleries that opened in Chicago:

- The (Seaberg-Isthmus Gallery) edged quietly into the local art world last month with a model of promotional-making-with-words, when a simple and informative letter announced (its opening). . . . Our second example is Origin, which received a lurid public-relations blast that embarrassed the young artist (Matt) and is enough to scare off the very people he would like to see in his studio-gallery. Somehow the hard sell and art mix poorly. . . . Our third example is a prime instance of non-sell. With no name but the address, 1017 W. Armitage, the workshop of Julian Frederick Harr has a tidy gallery up front (and) behind is a cluttered, chip-and-shaving sculptor's studio . . . In the long run, Harr, quietly building his people-traps, is better off than Matt, who will have to live down his own well-intentioned publicity. But the Seaberg-Isthmus soft sell is by far the most effective.[31]

Place decision. The retailers' choice of locations is a key competitive factor in their ability to attract customers. For example, customers primarily choose the banks that are nearest to them. Department store chains, oil companies, and fast-food franchisers are particularly careful in making their location decisions and in using advanced methods of site selection and evaluation.

The Future of Retailing

Retailing is one of the most dynamic and challenging areas of the economy. Today's retailer, looking ahead to tomorrow, has to take into account the fol-

EXHIBIT 15-1

THE GREAT RETAILERS

Managers in six different retail industries were asked to cite the person who had done the most for his industry in the last fifty years. Here are this half century's great retailers:

- Man-of-the-Half-Century in the *General Merchandise/Department Store* field: the late *James Cash Penney*. ". . . among his contributions are the first profit-sharing programs. He was a pioneer respondent to consumerism before it was recognized by that name; not only a believer in but an ardent practitioner of the Golden Rule."
- Man-of-the-Half-Century in the *Food Service* field: *Ray A. Kroc*, chairman of the McDonald's Corp. ". . . for bringing to the restaurant industry the most advanced concepts of franchising and for the application of the most advanced marketing and operational techniques to the food service industry."
- Man-of-the-Half-Century in the *Supermarket* field: *Sidney R. Rabb*, chairman of the Stop & Shop Co. ". . . reorganized the Super Market Institute into the kind of organization it is today. An industry leader in innovative merchandising and operations' techniques; renowned for introducing modern personnel relations concepts in the food field."
- Man-of-the-Half-Century in the *Discount Department Store* field: *Harry B. Cunningham*, honorary chairman of the S. S. Kresge Co. ". . . was the driving force behind the founding of K mart, which not only revolutionized his own company but set a model for industry leadership."
- Man-of-the-Half-Century in the *Chain Drug* field: the late *Charles R. Walgreen, Sr.* ". . . the pioneer who envisioned a chain drug industry when there was none, then built his chain into that industry's leading retailer."
- Man-of-the-Half-Century in the *Home Improvement Center* field: *John A. Walker*, executive vice president of Lowe's Companies, Inc. ". . . he introduced sophisticated marketing concepts to the lumberyard field, thereby creating a new retail apparatus, the modern home improvement center."

Source: "The Man of the Half-Century Awards," *Chain Store Age*, September 1975, pp. 76–77.

lowing major trends: (1) the slowdown in population growth and economic growth; (2) the rapidly increasing cost of capital, labor, and energy; (3) the changing consumer life styles, shopping patterns, and attitudes toward shopping; (4) the emergence of new technologies such as computerized checkout, electronic shopping, and more automatic vending; (5) the growing strength of major retailers in the total retail picture; and (6) the rise of consumerism and environmentalism and the increase in government regulations affecting retailing. Clearly, these trends are going to call for more *professional management* in retailing that goes beyond good merchandising skills. Top management will have to be skilled in designing and implementing profit performance systems. The key need will be to find ways to increase *retail productivity.*

The search for more productivity in the 1980s will favor the development of retailing forms that keep costs down. Many retailing innovations have come about in the past as solutions to problems of high-cost, high-price retailing. They have been explained by the *wheel of retailing* hypothesis.[32] According to this hypothesis, many new types of retailing institutions begin as low-status, low-margin, low-price operations. They become effective competitors of more conventional outlets, which have grown "fat" over the years. Their success gradually leads them to upgrade their facilities and offer additional services. This increases their costs and forces price increases until they finally resemble the conventional outlets that they displaced. They, in turn, become vulnerable to still newer types of low-cost, low-margin operations. This hypothesis appears to explain the original success and later troubles of department stores, supermarkets, and, more recently, discount houses. On the other hand, it does not explain the growth of suburban shopping centers and automatic vending, both of which started out as high-margin and high-cost operations.

Nevertheless, one can be sure that new retailing forms will emerge to meet new needs:

- A soft-drink manufacturer that sells private-brand colas, ginger ales, and so on, opened a chain of soft-drink stores for the take-home market at substantial savings. American Bakeries started Hippopotamus Food Store outlets that feature large institutional-sized packages at a 10 to 30 percent savings. One of the large New York banks recently instituted "house-call loans" where it will qualify a customer over the phone and then deliver the money in person. Adelphi University in Garden City, New York, developed a "commuter train classroom" in which executives who commute daily between Long Island and Manhattan can get their M.B.A.'s by sitting in on fifty-minute classes held in specially reserved cars on the commuter train. Marketers are continually seeking new ways to distribute their products and service.

The longevity of the new forms, however, is likely to be less than that of the previous great forms such as the department store and the supermarket. Table 15-4 lists the life-cycle characteristics of some major retailing institutions and indicates that the more recent ones are reaching their maturity much faster.[33]

Table 15-4
Life-Cycles of Retail Institutions

RETAIL INSTITUTIONS	EARLY GROWTH	MATURITY	APPROXIMATE TIME REQUIRED TO REACH MATURITY
Department stores	Mid-1860s	Mid-1960s	100 years
Variety stores	Early 1900s	Early 1960s	60 years
Supermarkets	Mid-1930s	Mid-1960s	30 years
Discount department stores	Mid-1950s	Mid-1970s	20 years
Fast-food service outlets	Early 1960s	Mid-1970s	15 years
Home improvement centers	Mid-1960s	Late 1970s	15 years
Furniture warehouse showrooms	Late 1960s	Late 1970s	10 years
Catalog showrooms	Late 1960s	Late 1970s	10 years

Source: From Bert C. McCammon, Jr., "The Future of Catalog Showrooms: Growth and Its Challenges to Management," Marketing Science Institute working paper (1973), p. 3.

wholesaling

Nature and Importance of Wholesaling

What is wholesaling? *Wholesaling* includes *all activities involved in selling goods or services to those who are buying for purposes of resale or business use.* Thus any sales and accompanying activities undertaken by one person or firm to sell to another person or firm where the buying is not for personal use can be referred to as wholesaling. A retail bakery that occasionally sells pastry to local hotels is engaging in wholesaling, not retailing, at that point. In this chapter the term *wholesalers* will be confined to those persons and firms that are primarily engaged in wholesaling activity. This excludes manufacturers and farmers, for example, because they are primarily engaged in production, and it excludes retailers.

A number of major differences can be noted between wholesalers and retailers. First, wholesalers deal with customers who buy something for resale or use in production, whereas retailers are selling to customers who are buying for personal consumption. This explains why wholesalers normally locate in less-accessible and less-attractive quarters where rents are lower. They also tend not to be promotion minded because they are dealing with hardheaded buyers buying for the purpose of making money or saving money. Second, wholesale transactions are usually larger than retail transactions, and wholesalers usually cover a larger trade area than retailers. As a result, many wholesalers have to become much more involved with sophisticated materials-handling systems and information systems. Third, the government deals with wholesalers and retailers in different ways regarding legal regulations and taxes.

Why are wholesalers used at all in the economic system? Conceivably, manufacturers could bypass them and sell directly to retailers or to final consumers. The answer lies in several efficiencies that wholesalers bring about. First, small manufacturers with limited financial resources cannot afford to develop direct-selling organizations. Second, even manufacturers with sufficient capital may prefer to use it primarily to expand production rather than carry out expensive distribution. Third, manufacturers recognize that wholesalers are typically more efficient than they themselves could be because of the wholesalers' scale of operation in distribution, their wider number of retail contacts, and their specialized skills. Fourth, manufacturers of single or limited lines find that retailers who carry many lines prefer to buy assortments from a wholesaler rather than deal directly with every single manufacturer.

Thus retailers, manufacturers, and other businesses are drawn to using wholesalers for a number of reasons, although when these reasons are less important, the wholesalers may be bypassed. Wholesalers are used because they are able to efficiently perform one or more valued functions, such as:

1. *Selling and promoting.* Wholesalers provide a sales force enabling manufacturers to reach many small customers at a relatively low cost. The wholesaler has more contacts and is often more trusted by the buyer than is the distant manufacturer. In addition to personal and telephone selling, wholesalers also mail out catalogs and promotional fliers and brochures.
2. *Buying and assortment building.* Wholesalers are able to select items, buy them, and build assortments needed by their customers, thus saving the customers considerable work.
3. *Bulk-breaking.* Wholesalers provide customers with savings through their ability to buy in carload lots and then sell smaller quantities adapted to the customers' varying needs.
4. *Warehousing.* Wholesalers provide a warehousing service, holding inventory until goods are ordered, thereby reducing the inventory costs and risks to both their suppliers and their customers.
5. *Transportation.* Wholesalers can provide quicker delivery to buyers because they are closer.
6. *Financing.* Wholesalers finance their customers by granting credit, and they finance their suppliers by ordering early and paying their bills on time.
7. *Risk bearing.* Wholesalers absorb some of the total risk in the channel by taking title and being responsible for theft, damage, spoilage, and obsolescence.
8. *Market information.* Wholesalers supply useful information to their suppliers and customers regarding competitors' activities, new products, imminent price developments, and so on.
9. *Management services and counseling.* Wholesalers often help retailers improve their operations by training their salesclerks, helping with stores' layouts and displays, and setting up systems for accounting and inventory control.

Thus we see that wholesalers are used because of their ability to perform one or more valued functions for manufacturers, retailers, and other business establishments. A number of major economic developments have contributed to wholesaling's growth over the years, including (1) the growth of mass production in large factories located away from the principal users of the output; (2) the growth of production in advance of orders rather than in response to specific orders; (3) an increase in the number of levels of intermediate producers and users; and (4) the increasing need for adapting products to the needs of intermediate and final users in terms of quantities, packages, and forms.[34]

Types of Wholesalers

In the last *Census of Business, Wholesale Trade* (1972), there were 370,000 wholesaling establishments in the United States, with a total annual sales volume of $728.5 billion. These wholesalers differ considerably in whether they take title to goods, the number and type of functions they perform, their method of operation, their size, and the range and kinds of goods they handle. This makes their classification somewhat difficult. We will rely mainly on the criteria of title ownership and type of operation and use a classification tied to the *Census of Business* data. Wholesalers can be classified into four major groups (see Table 15-5). *Merchant wholesalers* take title to the goods. In 1972 they accounted for \$354 billion, or almost half the total wholesale sales volume of \$728 billion.[35] *Brokers and agents* do not take title to the goods. They accounted for \$86 billion, or 12 percent of the total wholesale sales volume. *Manufacturers' sales branches and offices* are manufacturers' wholesaling operations. They accounted for \$256 billion, or about 35 percent of total wholesale sales volume. *Miscellaneous wholesalers* accounted for the remaining \$32 billion.

Merchant wholesalers. Merchant wholesalers are independently owned businesses that take title to the merchandise they handle. In different trades they may be called jobbers, distributors, or mill supply houses. They are the largest single group of wholesalers, accounting for roughly 50 percent of all wholesaling (in sales volume and in number of establishments). Merchant wholesalers can be

Table 15-5
Classification of Wholesalers

MERCHANT WHOLESALERS
Full-service wholesalers
Wholesale merchants (general merchandise, general line, specialty line)
Industrial distributors
Limited-service wholesalers
Cash-and-carry wholesalers
Truck wholesalers
Drop shippers
Rack jobbers
Producers' cooperatives
Mail-order wholesalers
AGENTS AND BROKERS
Brokers
Agents (manufacturer's agents, selling agents, purchasing agents, commission merchants)
MANUFACTURERS' AND RETAILERS' BRANCHES AND OFFICES
Sales branches and offices
Purchasing offices
MISCELLANEOUS WHOLESALERS
Agricultural assemblers
Petroleum bulk plants and terminals
Auction companies

subclassified into two broad types: full-service wholesalers and limited-service wholesalers.

FULL-SERVICE WHOLESALERS

Full-service wholesalers provide such services as carrying stock, using a sales force, offering credit, making deliveries, and providing management assistance. They include two types: wholesale merchants and industrial distributors.

WHOLESALE MERCHANTS. Wholesale merchants sell primarily to retailers and provide a full range of services. They vary mainly in the width of the product line they carry. *General merchandise wholesalers* carry several merchandise lines to meet the needs of both general merchandise retailers and single-line retailers. *General-line wholesalers* carry one or two lines of merchandise in a greater depth of assortment. Major examples are hardware wholesalers, drug wholesalers, and clothing wholesalers. *Specialty wholesalers* specialize in carrying only part of a line in great depth. Examples are health food wholesalers, seafood wholesalers, and automotive item wholesalers. They offer customers the advantage of more choice and greater product knowledge.

INDUSTRIAL DISTRIBUTORS. Industrial distributors are merchant wholesalers who sell to manufacturers rather than to retailers. They provide several services, such as carrying stock, offering credit, and providing delivery. They may carry a broad range of merchandise (often called a mill supply house), a general line, or a specialty line. Industrial distributors may concentrate on such lines as MRO items (maintenance, repair, and operating supplies), OEM items (original equipment supplies such as ball bearings, motors), or equipment (such as hand and power tools, and fork trucks). There are about twelve thousand industrial distributors in the United States, and their sales were approximately $23.5 billion in 1974.

LIMITED-SERVICE WHOLESALERS

Limited-service wholesalers offer fewer services to their suppliers and customers. There are several types of limited-service wholesalers.

CASH-AND-CARRY WHOLESALERS. Cash-and-carry wholesalers have a limited line of fast-moving goods and sell to small retailers for cash. Besides not providing credit, they normally do not deliver. A small fish store retailer, for example, normally drives every workday at dawn to a cash-and-carry fish wholesaler and buys several crates of fish, pays on the spot, and drives his merchandise back to his store and unloads it.

TRUCK WHOLESALERS. Truck wholesalers (also called truck jobbers) perform a selling and delivery function primarily. They carry a limited line of semiperishable merchandise (such as milk, bread, snack foods), which they sell for cash as they make their rounds of supermarkets, small groceries, hospitals, restaurants, factory cafeterias, and hotels.

DROP SHIPPERS. Drop shippers are usually found in bulk industries such as coal, lumber, and heavy equipment. They do not carry inventory or handle the product. Once an order is placed with them, they find a manufacturer, who ships the merchandise directly to the customer on the agreed terms and time of delivery. The drop shipper assumes title and risk during the period from the acceptance of the order to its delivery to the customer. Because drop shippers do not carry inventory, their costs are lower and the savings are realized by their customers.

RACK JOBBERS. Rack jobbers serve primarily grocery and drug retailers, mostly in the area of nonfood items. These retailers do not want to be bothered with ordering and maintaining displays of hundreds of nonfood items. The rack jobbers send out delivery trucks to stores, and the delivery person sets up toys, paperbacks, hardware items, health and beauty aids, and so on. They price goods, keep them fresh, set up point-of-purchase displays, and keep inventory records. Rack jobbers sell on consignment, which means that they retain title to the goods and bill the retailers only for the goods sold to consumers. Thus they provide such services as delivery, shelving, inventory carrying, and financing. They do little promotion because the products they carry are branded and are often highly advertised.

PRODUCERS' COOPERATIVES. Producers' cooperatives are owned by farmer-members and assemble farm produce to sell in local markets. Any profits they make are normally distributed to their members at the end of the year. They often attempt to improve product quality and promote a co-op brand name, such as Sun Maid raisins, Sunkist oranges, or Diamond walnuts.

MAIL-ORDER WHOLESALERS. Mail-order wholesalers send catalogs to retail, industrial, and institutional customers featuring jewelry, cosmetics, specialty foods, and other small items. Their main customers are businesses in small outlying areas. No sales force is maintained to call on customers. The orders are filled and sent by mail, truck, or other efficient means of transportation.

Agents and brokers. Agents and brokers differ from merchant wholesalers in two ways: They do not take title to goods, and they tend to perform even fewer functions than limited-service merchant wholesalers. Their main function is to facilitate buying and selling, and for this they will earn a commission of anywhere from 2 to 6 percent of the selling price. Like merchant wholesalers, they generally specialize by product line or customer types. They account for 12 percent of the total wholesale volume.

BROKERS

Brokers perform very few functions, the chief one being to bring buyers and sellers together. They seek out buyers or sellers and assist in negotiation. They are paid by the party who sought their services. They do not carry any inventory, get involved in any financing, or assume any risk. The most familiar examples are food brokers, real-estate brokers, insurance brokers, and security brokers.

AGENTS

Agents represent either buyers or sellers on a more permanent basis. There are several types.

Manufacturer's agents (also called manufacturer's representatives) are more numerous than any other type of agent wholesaler. They represent two or more manufacturers of complementary lines. They enter into a formal written agreement with each manufacturer covering pricing policy, territorial areas, order-handling procedure, delivery service and warranties, and commission rates. Presumably they are knowledgeable about each manufacturer's product line and use their extensive knowledge of customers and customer preferences in their area to sell the manufacturer's product. Manufacturer's agents are used in such lines as apparel, furniture, and electrical goods. Most manufacturer's agents are small businesses, with only a few employees who are skilled salespeople. They are hired by small manufacturers who cannot afford to maintain their own field sales force and by large manufacturers who want to use agents to open new territories or to represent them in territories that cannot support a full-time salesperson.

Selling agents are given contractual authority to sell the entire output of a manufacturer. The manufacturer either is not interested in getting involved in selling or feels unqualified. The selling agent serves as a sales department and has significant influence over prices, terms, and conditions of sale. The selling agent normally has no territorial limitations. Selling agents are found in such product areas as textiles, industrial machinery and equipment, coal and coke, chemicals, and metals.

Purchasing agents generally have a long-term relationship with buyers and make purchases for them, often receiving, inspecting, warehousing, and shipping the merchandise to the ultimate buyers. One type consists of *resident buyers* in major apparel markets, who look for suitable lines of apparel that can be carried by small retailers located in small cities. They are knowledgeable and provide helpful market information to clients as well as obtaining the best goods and prices available.

Commission merchants (or houses) are agents who take physical possession of products and negotiate sales. They are normally not employed on a long-term basis. They are used most often in agricultural marketing by farmers who cannot or do not want to sell their own output and do not belong to producers' cooperatives. A commission merchant might take a truckload of commodities to a central market, sell it for the best possible price, deduct a commission and expenses, and remit the balance to the producer.

Manufacturers' and retailers' branches and offices. The third major type of wholesaling consists of wholesaling operations conducted by sellers or buyers themselves rather than through independent wholesalers. There are two types.

SALES BRANCHES AND OFFICES

Manufacturers often set up their own sales branches and offices to obtain better control of inventory and improved selling and promotion. *Sales branches* carry inventory and represent an alternative to using merchant wholesalers. They are found in such industries as lumber and automotive equipment and parts. *Sales offices* do not carry any inventory and represent an alternative to using outside agents and brokers. They are most noticeable in dry goods and notion industries. Sales branches and offices are often much larger than the corresponding wholesalers and agents would be. They account for about 13 percent of all wholesale establishments and 35 percent of all wholesale volume.

PURCHASING OFFICES

Many retailers set up purchasing offices in major market centers such as New

York and Chicago. These purchasing offices perform a role similar to that of brokers or agents but are part of the buyer's organization.

Miscellaneous. A few specialized types of wholesalers are found in certain sectors of the economy.

AGRICULTURAL ASSEMBLERS

Agricultural assemblers collect farm products from farmers and build them into larger lots for shipment to food processors, bakers, and government. By taking advantage of carload or truckload rates and differences in area market prices, the assembler makes a profit.

PETROLEUM BULK PLANTS AND TERMINALS

Petroleum bulk plants and terminals specialize in selling and delivering petroleum products to filling stations, other retailers, and organizational users. Many are owned by major petroleum producers (in which case they are a manufacturer's sales branch), and others are owned by independent businesspeople (in which case they are a merchant wholesaler).

AUCTION COMPANIES

Auction houses are important in certain industries where buyers want to see and inspect goods prior to purchase, such as in the tobacco and livestock markets. The buyers come together and bid against each other until one bidder is left. This bidder gets the products if the bid is over a predetermined minimum.

Wholesaler Marketing Decisions

Wholesalers must make decisions on their target market product assortment and service, pricing, promotion, and place.

Target market decision. Wholesalers, like retailers, have to develop a better definition of their target market and not try to serve everyone. They can choose a target group of customers according to size criteria (e.g., only large retailers), type of customer (e.g., convenience food stores only), need for service (e.g., customers who need credit), or other criteria. Within the target group, they can identify the more profitable customers and seek to design stronger offers and build better relationships with them. They can propose automatic reordering systems, set up management training and advisory systems, and even move to sponsoring a voluntary chain. They can discourage the less-profitable customers by requiring larger orders or placing extra charges on smaller orders.

Product assortment and services decision. The wholesalers' "product" is the assortment that they carry. The wholesaler is subject to great pressure to carry a full line and have sufficient stock for immediate delivery. But this can kill profits. Wholesalers today are reexamining how many lines to carry and are increasingly settling for 80–90 percent coverage rather than 100 percent. They are increasingly studying the profits of the different lines and carrying only the more profitable ones. Many wholesalers are grouping their items on an ABC basis, with *A* standing for the more profitable items and *C* for the least profitable. Inventory-carrying levels are varied for the three groups, and the wholesaler is devoting more time to selling the more profitable items.

As for services, wholesalers have to reexamine which services count most in building strong customer relationships and which ones are frills and should be dropped or charged for. The key is not simply matching the services provided by competitors but finding a distinct mix of services valued by their customers.

Pricing decision. Conventional wholesaling pricing calls for marking up the cost of goods by a conventional percentage, say 20 percent, that will cover the wholesaler's various expenses. Expenses may run an average of 17 percent of the gross margin, leaving a profit margin of approximately 3 percent. In grocery wholesaling the average profit margin is often less than 2 percent. Wholesalers have to experiment with new approaches to pricing. At times they may find it profitable to cut their margin on some lines in order to win important new customers. They should also consider asking the supplier for a special price break that can be turned into an opportunity to increase the supplier's sales. Wholesalers have to become good at pricing systems contracts so that customers will be satisfied and will become more loyal to the particular wholesaler.

Promotion decision Most wholesalers are not promotion minded, either for themselves or for their suppliers. Their use of trade advertising, sales promotion, publicity, and personal selling is largely haphazard. Personal selling is particularly behind the times in that wholesalers still see selling as a single salesperson talking to a single customer instead of a team effort to sell, build, and service major accounts. As for nonpersonal promotion, wholesalers would benefit from adopting some of the image-making techniques used by retailers. They need to develop an overall promotional strategy. They also need to make greater use of supplier promotion materials and programs in ways that will be to their advantage.

Place decision. Wholesalers typically locate in low-rent, low-tax areas and put little money into their physical setting and offices. Often the materials-handling systems and order-processing systems lag behind the available technologies. To meet the challenge of rising costs, progressive wholesalers have been making time and motion studies of materials-handling procedures. The ultimate development is the automated warehouse where the orders are key punched on tabulating cards, which are then fed into a computer. The items are picked up by mechanical devices and conveyed on a belt to the shipping platform where they are assembled. This type of mechanization is progressing rapidly, and so is the mechanization of many office activities. Many wholesalers are turning to electronic data processing to carry out such functions as accounting, billing, inventory control, and forecasting, and they are alert to other technological developments that save office costs.

The Future of Wholesaling

Changes in wholesaling have been less dramatic than changes in retailing, but they are no less important. In the nineteenth century, wholesalers held the dominant position in marketing channels. Most manufacturers were quite small, and they were dependent on major wholesalers for the distribution of their product to the many small retailers who dotted the land. The wholesaler's power began to diminish in the twentieth century as manufacturers became larger and as giant chains and franchise systems appeared in retailing. Large manufacturers sought ways to sell direct to the major retailers, and the major retailers sought ways to buy direct from the manufacturers. The opportunity to go direct, even though not used most of the time, increased the power of the manufacturers and retailers relative to that of the wholesalers and forced the latter to find new ways of being efficient. During the 1920s, some thought that the majority of wholesalers were doomed by the growth of chain operations. Wholesalers declined in relative importance from 1929 on and did not regain their former relative position until as late as 1954. Absolute wholesale sales volume has continued to grow, but in relative terms wholesalers have just been holding their own.

Manufacturers always have the option of bypassing wholesalers, or replacing an inefficient wholesaler with a more dynamic one. The major complaints that manufacturers make about wholesalers are as follows: (1) they do not aggressively promote the manufacturer's product line, acting more like order takers; (2) they do not carry enough inventory and therefore fail to fill customers' orders fast enough; (3) they do not supply the manufacturer with up-to-date market and competitive information; (4) they do not attract high-caliber managers and bring down their own costs; and (5) they charge too much for their services.

These complaints are justified in many cases. Many wholesalers have not adapted or responded well to the rapidly changing world. According to Lopata:

- Technological advances, product line proliferation, changing retail structures, and social adjustments are only a few of the real problems that complicate the wholesaler's life. Each improved product passing through the wholesale level generates a new demand for investments in warehouse space, market analysis, and sales training, and for myriad adjustments in the wholesaler's information systems. Each major retailing shift designed to satisfy customer needs obliges him to adjust his selling patterns, to review his customer service levels, to study product assortments, and to revise his strategies.[36]

The progressive wholesalers are those who are willing to change their ways too meet the challenges of chain organizations, discount houses, and rising labor costs. They are adapting their services more to the needs of target customers and finding cost-reducing methods of transacting business.

■ summary

Retailing and wholesaling have spawned many kinds of institutions to meet the various needs of customers and to accommodate to the various characteristics of products. A glimpse of the drama and challenge of these two sectors has been presented in this chapter.

Retailing includes all the activities involved in selling goods or services directly to final consumers for their personal, nonbusiness use. Retailing is one of the major industries in the United States, employing over 13 million people and taking the form of over 1.5 million single-unit establishments and thirty-four thousand multiunit organizations. Retailers can be classified in several ways: according to the product line sold (specialty stores, department stores, supermarkets, convenience stores, combination stores, superstores, hypermarches, and service businesses); according to the relative emphasis placed on price (discount stores, warehouse stores, and catalog showrooms); according to the nature of the business premises (mail-and-telephone-order retailing, automatic vending, buying services, and door-to-door retailing); according to who controls the outlets (corporate chains, voluntary chains and retailer cooperatives, consumer cooperatives, franchise organizations, and conglomerchants); and according to the type of store cluster (central business districts, regional shopping centers, community shopping centers, and neighborhood shopping centers). The various retailers make basic marketing decisions on their target market, product assortment and services, pricing, promotion, and place. The future of retailing will be extremely challenging and will require improved professional management and solutions to increased retail productivity.

Wholesaling includes all the activities involved in selling goods or services to those who are buying for the purpose of resale or for business use. Wholesalers are absolutely necessary in the economic system to help manufacturers deliver their products efficiently to the many retailers and industrial users across the nation. Wholesalers can perform many functions, including selling, buying and assortment building, bulk-breaking, warehousing, transporting, financing, risk bearing, supplying market information, and providing management services and counseling. Wholesalers fall into four groups. Merchant wholesalers take possession of the goods. They can be subclassified as full-service wholesalers (wholesale merchants, industrial distributors) and limited-service wholesalers (cash-and-carry wholesalers, truck wholesalers, drop shippers, rack jobbers, producers' cooperatives, and mail-order wholesalers). Agents and brokers do not take possession of the goods but are paid a commission for facilitating buying and selling. Manufacturers' and retailers' branches and offices are wholesaling operations conducted by nonwholesalers to bypass the wholesalers. Miscellaneous wholesalers include agricultural assemblers, petroleum bulk plants and terminals, and auction companies. Wholesaling is just holding its own in the economy. Progressive wholesalers are adapting their services more to the needs of target customers and are seeking cost-reducing methods of transacting business.

■ questions for discussion

1. What is the major difference between retailers and wholesalers? Explain by using an example of each.
2. Compare and contrast the two types of retail stores classified according to the product line sold that market clothing.
3. Briefly discuss the types of retailers that sell food products. How has retailing in this area changed in the last twenty years?
4. Analyze the major differences between a warehouse store and a catalog showroom. What factors contributed to their growth?

5. Door-to-door retailing will decline in the 1980s. Comment.
6. If friends of yours were planning to open a card shop, which type of store cluster would you recommend that they select? Why?
7. Is there a difference between the approach taken in retailer marketing decisions and that taken in product marketing decisions? Explain.
8. The major distinction between merchant wholesalers and agents/brokers is that the former offer more services to the buyer. Comment.
9. Would a small manufacturer of lawn and garden tools seek a manufacterer's agent or a selling agent to handle the merchandise? Why?
10. Why, do you think, has the promotion area of marketing strategy been traditionally weak for wholesalers?

references

1. "Leading toward a Green Christmas," *Time,* December 1, 1975, pp. 74–80.
2. JOHN DENNIS MCDONALD, *The Game of Business* (New York: Doubleday, 1975), p. 102.
3. For more details, see PHYLLIS BERMAN, "Too Big for Miracles," *Forbes,* June 15, 1977, pp. 26–29.
4. *Fortune,* July 1977, pp. 168–69.
5. ERNEST SAMHABER, *Merchants Make History,* (New York, Harper & Row, Pub., 1964), pp. 345–48.
6. The quoted part of the definition is from WALTER J. SALMON, ROBERT D. BUZZELL, STANTON G. CORT, AND MICHAEL R. PEARCE, *The Super-Store—Strategic Implications for the Seventies* (Cambridge, Mass.: Marketing Science Institute, 1972), p. 83.
7. See "Supermarkets Eye the Sunbelt," *Business Week,* September 27, 1976, p. 61.
8. See "A&P Mystification," *Time,* October 13, 1975, pp. 63–64.
9. See BERT MCCAMMON, "High Performance Marketing Strategies," unpublished paper.
10. See "Convenience Stores: A $7.4 Billion Mushroom," *Business Week,* March 21, 1977, pp. 61–64.
11. SALMON and others, *Super-Store,* p. 4.
12. RONALD R. GIST, *Retailing Concepts and Decisions* (New York: John Wiley, 1968), pp. 45–46. The list of elements is slightly modified from Gist.
13. *Statistical Abstract of the United States,* 1976, p. 800.
14. See "The Hot Discounter," *Newsweek,* April 25, 1977, pp. 69–70.
15. See JONATHAN N. GOODRICH AND JO ANN HOFFMAN, "Warehouse Retailing: The Trend of the Future?" *Business Horizons,* April 1979, pp. 45–50.
16. "Catalog Showroom Hot Retailer," *Chicago Tribune,* December 6, 1978, Sec. 4, p. 12.
17. LEO BOGART, "The Future in Retailing," *Harvard Business Review,* November-December 1973, p. 26.
18. BELDEN MENKUS, "Remote Retailing a Reality by 1985?" *Chain Store Age Executive,* September 1975, p. 42.
19. "Millions by Mail," *Forbes,* March 15, 1976, p. 82.
20. See RITA REIF, "Mail Order: Old Road to New Sales," *New York Times,* August 24, 1975, Sec. 3, p. 1.

21. For an excellent text on direct-mail techniques, see BOB STONE, *Successful Direct Marketing Methods* (Chicago: Crain Books, 1975).

22. G. R. SCHREIBER, *A Concise History of Vending in the U.S.A.* (Chicago: Vend, 1961), p. 9.

23. See "How the 'New Sell' is Raking in Billions," *U.S. News and World Report,* May 8, 1978, pp. 74–75.

24. See RONALD R. GIST, *Marketing and Society: Text and Cases,* 2nd ed. (Hinsdale, Ill.: Dryden Press, 1974), p. 334.

25. See ROLLIE TILLMAN, "Rise of the Conglomerchant," *Harvard Business Review,* November-December 1971, pp. 44–51.

26. See PHYLLIS BERMAN,, "Melville Corp.: Discounting with a Difference," *Forbes,* April 16, 1979, pp. 93–94.

27. This is the definition of the Urban Land Institute and can be found in ROGER A. DICKINSON, *Retail Management: A Channels Approach* (Belmont, Calif.: Wadsworth, 1974), p. 9.

28. DAVID ELSNER, "Shopping Center Boom Appears to Be Fading Due to Overbuilding," *Wall Street Journal,* September 7, 1976, p. 1.

29. MENKUS, "Remote Retailing," p. 42.

30. For more discussion, see PHILIP KOTLER, "Atmospherics as a Marketing Tool," *Journal of Retailing,* Winter 1973–74, pp. 48–64.

31. HAROLD HAYDON, "Galleries: A Little Push Is Better Than Too Much or No Promotion at All," *Chicago Sun-Times,* October 30, 1970, p. 55.

32. For additional articles on the future of retailing, see WILLIAM R. DAVIDSON, ALBERT D. BATES, AND STEPHEN J. BASS, "The Retail Life Cycle," *Harvard Business Review,* November-December 1976, pp. 89–96; ALBERT D. BATES, "The Troubled Future of Retailing," *Business Horizons,* August 1976, pp. 22–28; and MALCOLM P. MCNAIR AND ELEANOR G. MAY, "The Next Revolution of the Retailing Wheel," *Harvard Business Review,* September-October 1978, pp. 81–91.

33. MALCOLM P. MCNAIR, "Significant Trends and Developments in the Postwar Period," in *Competitive Distribution in a Free, High-Level Economy and Its Implications for the University,* ed. A. B. Smith (Pittsburgh: University of Pittsburgh Press, 1958), pp. 1–25. Also see the critical discussion by STANLEY C. HOLLANDER, "The Wheel of Retailing," *Journal of Marketing,* July 1960, pp. 37–42. For other theories of retail change, see RONALD R. GIST, *Retailing Concepts and Decisions* (New York: John Wiley, 1968), Chap. 4.

34. DAVID A. REVZAN, *Wholesaling in Marketing Organization* (New York: John Wiley, 1961), pp. 10–11.

35. See *U.S. Census of Business, Wholesale Trade,* 1972.

36. RICHARD S. LOPATA, "Faster Pace in Wholesaling," *Harvard Business Review,* July-August 1969, p. 131.

MARKETING COMMUNICATIONS STRATEGY

Pizza Inn is a large franchised specialty-food restaurant system with over five hundred outlets grossing over $50 million annually. Pizza Inn's management is anxious to train its franchisees to see that everything they do communicates something to customers. At a recent sales meeting, management told the franchisees that they make impressions of four kinds. Impressions of the first kind are as follows:

Advertising. **Television, radio, outdoor, and newspaper advertisements all provide important impressions of Pizza Inn. Generic television and radio commercials are designed to encourage the consumer to "feel" a certain way about Pizza Inn. Your store is presented as a neighborhood family restaurant where people can enjoy a popular meal in clean, comfortable surroundings at a reasonable price. The invitation is open and friendly.**

Radio and Newspaper Support Promotions. **This kind of impression tells consumers they can expect extra value from Pizza Inn whether it's a Tuesday Night Special or an inexpensive T-shirt for the kids. In a secondary way, it also tells them you're willing to do something extra to get their business.**

Exterior Store Appearance. **The impression made by the store exterior also affects the consumer. Does it look neat? Is the sign doing its job? Does it look as if there is adequate parking and easy access?**

Community Involvement. **Little League. Chamber of Commerce. Lions. Rotary. If your business really is a neighborhood restaurant, these kinds of organizations provide a means to prove it. Your active involvement brings you one step closer to the consumer than just being a member of the chain-restaurant set. It's another impression that matters.**

You win. If all the first impressions were positive, consumers might get in their car and head your way. It's the second set of impressions that help determine if you will ever see them again:

Interior Store Appearance. **The layout should minimize confusion on where to sit and how to order. Is it neat? Are the tables cleared? They haven't ordered, so they can still walk out the door.**

Store Ambience. **Lighting. Temperature. Noise level. Smell—like food or an antiseptic? Are customers distributed to maximize service? Does your customer feel lonely, crowded, or comfortable?**

Personnel Appearance. ***Clean, neat uniforms. Acceptable grooming. A smile should be part of the uniform.***

Personnel Attitude. ***A genuine and friendly "Hello!" goes a long way. Promptness and attentiveness score high. A little concern about how the customer is doing is as meaningful a marketing tool as advertising.***

Menu Presentation. ***Is it easy to read? Is it easy to figure out and order from?***

Menu Selection. ***Is there something for everyone? Is everything on the menu available? Does every waitress or waiter know the menu well enough to answer questions or make suggestions?***

All these impressions, and we're not even to the food yet. But in the back of the customer's mind, a decision about coming back is already beginning to form. Let's move on to the third set of impressions:

Food Service. ***The pizza or sandwiches arrive at the table. Are they hot? Are the drinks cold? Is the salad bar freshly stocked and attractively laid out? Do they meet expectations? Will the waitress stop back in a few minutes and ask how everything is? If the waitress compliments the food, exhibits a pride in it, the customer's reaction is generally positive.***

Food Value. ***Here comes the check. If the customer is happy, the check reasonable, the family full and smiling—most of the battle is won. A big "thank you" from the waitress, and an invitation to return, really means something. The value is attached to the whole dining experience, as well as to the food.***

If all these impressions have been positive, you probably are in for a return visit from your new customers. But your competition is still talking to them, and you must continue to impress them. The fourth set of impressions are:

Advertising. ***The same advertising now has an added dimension to the customer. Now, it's reinforcement. It's a reminder. And it has a continuing promotional impact.***

Exterior Store Appearance. ***It's always there as the customer drives by, a constant reminder of one experience, an enticement for the next. Is it still neat?***

Community Involvement. ***The continuing exposure of the Pizza Inn owner or manager on a community level is a meaningful way to keep return business coming through the door. Loyalty to community is generally repaid in kind.***[1]

□Modern marketing calls for more than developing a good product, pricing it attractively, and making it readily accessible to target customers. The company must also manage its impressions in the marketplace. Its products, employees,

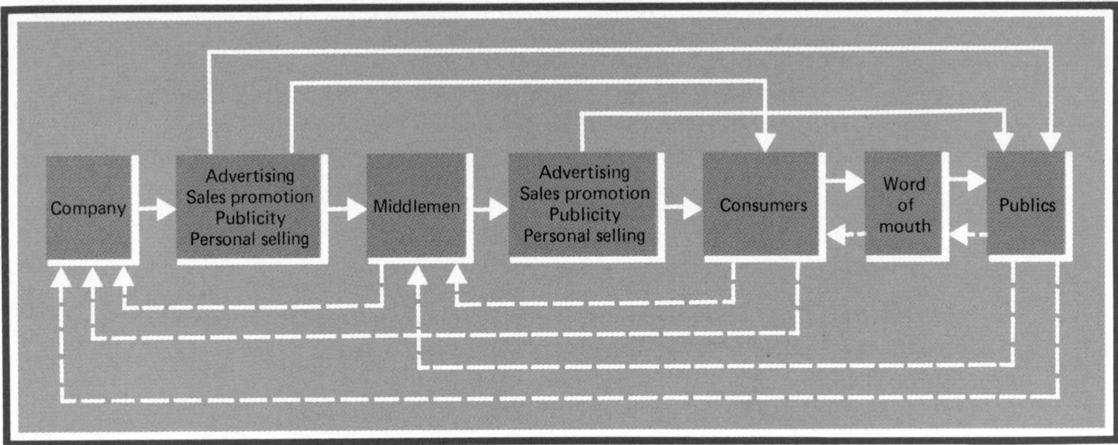

Figure 16-1 *The Marketing Communications System*

and actions will communicate something. What is communicated must not be left to chance. Every company is inevitably drawn into the role of a communicator and promoter.

Companies have responded by training their sales personnel to communicate friendliness and knowledge. They hire advertising agencies to develop effective ads; sales promotion specialists to build high incentive sales programs; and public relations firms to create image-building campaigns. They spend increasingly large sums on communications and promotion. For most companies the question is not whether to promote, but how much to spend and in what ways.

The modern company manages a complex marketing communications system (see Figure 16-1). The company uses its communications mix—advertising, sales promotion, publicity, and personal selling—to reach middlemen, consumers, and various publics. Its middlemen also develop a communications mix to reach consumers and various publics. Consumers engage in word-of-mouth communication with each other and with other publics. Meanwhile each group issues communication feedback to every other group.

The four major tools in the marketing communications mix are

- *Advertising:* any paid form of nonpersonal presentation and promotion of ideas, goods, or services by an identified sponsor
- *Sales promotion:* short-term incentives to encourage purchase or sale of a product or service
- *Publicity:* nonpersonal stimulation of demand for a product, service, or business unit by planting commercially significant news about it in a published medium or obtaining favorable presentation of it upon radio, television, or stage that is not paid for by the sponsor.
- *Personal selling:* oral presentation in a conversation with one or more prospective purchasers for the purpose of making sales[2]

Within each category are found specific *promotools* such as sales presentation, point-of-purchase displays, specialty advertising, trade shows, fairs, demonstrations, catalogs, literature, press kits, posters, contests, premiums, coupons, and trading stamps. At the same time we should recognize that communication goes beyond these specific communication tools. The product's styling, its price, the package's shape and color, the salesperson's manner and dress and so on, all communicate something to the buyers. The whole marketing mix, not just the promotional mix, must be orchestrated for maximum communication impact.

This chapter examines two major questions: What are the major steps in developing effective communications? How should the promotional mix be determined? Chapter 17 will examine the strategic use of the mass-communication tools of advertising, sales promotion, and publicity. Chapter 18 will focus on personal communications strategy through the sales force.

steps in developing effective communication

Marketers need to understand how to use communication. Communication by one party to another involves the eight elements shown in Figure 16-2. Two of these elements (in rectangles) represent the major parties in a communication—*sender* and *receiver*. Two others (in diamonds) represent the major communication tools—*message* and *media*. The remaining four (in ovals) represent major communications functions—*encoding, decoding, response,* and *feedback*. These elements can be defined as follows:

- *Sender:* the party sending the message to another party (also called the *source* or *communicator*)
- *Encoding:* the process of putting thought into symbolic form
- *Message:* the set of symbols that the sender transmits
- *Media:* the paths through which the message moves from sender to receiver
- *Decoding:* the process by which the receiver assigns meaning to the symbols transmitted by the sender
- *Receiver:* the party receiving the message sent by another party (also called the *audience* or *destination*)
- *Response:* the set of reactions that the receiver has after being exposed to the message
- *Feedback:* the part of the receiver's response that the receiver communicates back to the sender

The model underscores the key factors in effective communication. Senders must know what audiences they want to reach and what responses they want.

Figure 16-2
Elements in the Communication Process

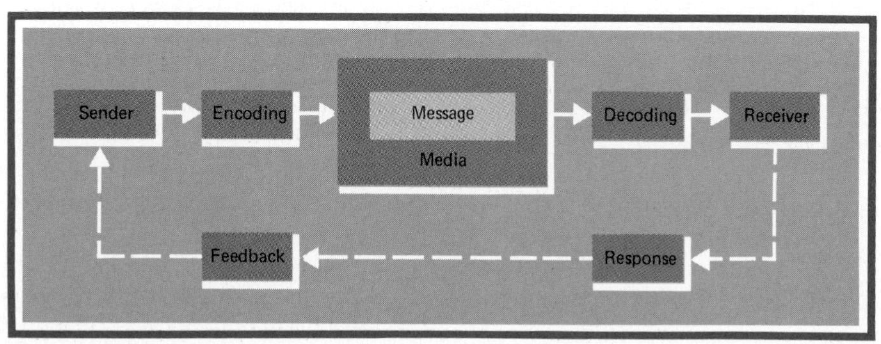

They must be skillful in encoding messages that take into account how the target audience tends to decode messages. They must transmit the message over efficient media that reach the target audience. They must develop feedback channels so that they can know the audience's response to the message.

We will examine the elements in the communication model mainly in terms of the *planning flow* (from target audience back to the communicator). The marketing communicator must make the following decisions: (1) identify the target audience, (2) clarify the response sought, (3) choose a message, (4) choose the media, (5) select source attributes, and (6) collect feedback.

Identifying the Target Audience

A marketing communicator must start with a clear target audience in mind. The audience may be potential buyers of the company's products, current users, deciders, or influencers. The audience may be individuals, groups, particular publics, or the general public. The target audience will critically influence the communicator's decisions on *what* is to be said, *how* it is to be said, *when* it is to be said, *where* it is to be said, and *who* is to say it.

Clarifying the Response Sought

Once the target audience is identified, the marketing communicator must define the target response that is sought. The ultimate response, of course, is purchase behavior. But purchase behavior is the end result of a long process of consumer decision making. The marketing communicator needs to know in which state the target audience stands at the present time and to which state it should be moved.

Any member of the target audience may be in one of six buyer *readiness states* with respect to the product or organization. These states—*awareness, knowledge, liking, preference, conviction,* or *purchase*—are described in the following paragraphs.

Awareness. The first thing to establish is how aware the target audience is of the product or organization. The audience may be completely unaware of the entity, know only its name, or know one or two things about it. If most of the target audience is unaware, the communicator's task is to build awareness, perhaps even just name recognition. This calls for simple messages repeating the name. Even then, building awareness takes time. Suppose a small private Iowa college called Pottsville sought applicants from Nebraska but had no name recognition in Nebraska. And suppose there were thirty thousand graduating high-school seniors in Nebraska who might potentially be interested in Pottsville College. The college might set the objective of making 70 percent of these students aware of Pottsville's name within one year.

Knowledge. The target audience may be aware of the entity but may not know much about it. In this case the communicator's goal will be to effectively transmit some key information about the entity. Thus Pottsville College may want its target audience to know that it is a private four-year college in Eastern Iowa that has distinguished programs in ornithology and thanatology. After waging a campaign, it can sample the target audience members to measure whether they have little, some, or much knowledge of Pottsville College, and the content of their knowledge. The particular set of beliefs that make up the audience's picture of an entity is called the *image*. Organizations must periodically assess their public images as a basis for developing communication objectives. (See Chapter 20, pp. 631–34.).

Liking. If the target audience members know the entity, the next question is, How do they feel about it? We can imagine a scale covering *dislike very much, dislike somewhat, indifferent, like somewhat, like very much.* If the audience holds an unfavorable view of Pottsville College, the communicator has to find out why and then develop a communications campaign to build up favorable feeling. If the unfavorable view is rooted in real inadequacies of the college, then a communications campaign would not do the job. The task would require first improving the college and then communicating its quality. Good public relations call for "good deeds followed by good words."

Preference. The target audience may like the entity but may not prefer it over others. It is one of several acceptable entities. In this case the communicator's job is to build the consumers' preference for the entity. The communicator will have to tout its quality, value, performance, and other attributes. The communicator can check on the success of the campaign by subsequently surveying the members of the audience to see if their preference for the entity is stronger.

Conviction. A target audience may prefer a particular entity but may not develop a conviction about buying it. Thus some high-school seniors may prefer Pottsville to other colleges but may not be sure they want to go to college. The communicator's job is to build conviction that going to college is the right thing to do. Building conviction that one should buy a particular entity is a challenging communications task.

Purchase. A member of the target audience may have conviction but may not quite get around to making the purchase. He or she may be waiting for additional information, may plan to act later, and so on. A communicator in this situation must lead the consumer to take the final step, which is called "closing the sale." Among action-producing devices are offering the entity at a low price if bought now, offering a premium, offering an opportunity to try it on a limited basis, or indicating that the entity will soon be unavailable.

The six states simplify to three stages known as the *cognitive,* (awareness, knowledge), *affective* (liking, preference, conviction), and *behavioral* (purchase). The communicator normally assumes that buyers pass through these stages in succession on the way to purchase. In this case the communicator's task is to identify the stage that most of the target audience is in and develop a communication message or campaign that will move them to the next stage. It would be nice if one message could move the audience through all three stages, but this rarely happens. Most communicators try to find a cost-effective communication approach to moving the target audience one stage at a time. The critical thing is to know where the audience is and what the next feasible stage is.

Some marketing scholars have challenged the idea that a consumer passes through *cognition* to *affect* to *behavior* in this order. Ray has suggested that some consumers pass from *cognition* to *behavior* to *affect.*[3] An example would be a student who has heard of Pottsville, enrolls there without much feeling, and afterward develops a strong liking for (or dislike of) the place. Ray has also suggested that sometimes consumers pass from *behavior* to *affect* to *cognition.* Thus a student may sign up for a course that he or she knows nothing about except that friends are taking it, develop a favorable feeling, and finally begin to understand the subject. Each version of the sequence has different implications for the role and influence of communications on behavior.

Choosing a Message

Having defined the response being sought from the target audience, the communicator can move on to developing a message or creative strategy. An ideal message is one that would manage to get *attention,* hold *interest,* arouse *desire,* and obtain *action* (known as the AIDA model). In practice, few messages will take the consumer all the way from awareness through purchase, but nevertheless the AIDA framework suggests some desirable qualities.

Formulating the message will require solving three problems: what to say (*message content*), how to say it logically (*message structure*), and how to say it symbolically (*message format*).

Message content. The communicator has to figure out what to say to the target audience that will produce the desired response. This has been called the *appeal, theme, idea,* or *unique selling proposition.* It amounts to formulating some kind of benefit, motivator, identification, or reason why the audience should think or do something.

Three types of appeals can be distinguished. *Rational appeals* aim at serving the audience's self-interest. They attempt to show that the product will yield the expected functional benefits. Examples would be messages demonstrating a product's quality, economy, value, or performance.

Emotional appeals are designed to stir up some negative or positive emotion that will motivate product purchase. Communicators have worked with fear, guilt, and shame appeals, especially in connection with getting people to start doing things they should (e.g., brushing their teeth, having an annual health checkup) or stop doing things they shouldn't (e.g., smoking, overimbibing, drug abuse, overeating). Advertisers have found that fear appeals work up to a point, but if there is too much fear the audience will ignore the message.[4] Communicators have also used positive emotional appeals such as love, humor, pride, and joy. Evidence has not established that a humorous message, for example, is necessarily more effective than a straight version of the same message.[5]

Moral appeals are directed to the audience's sense of what is right and proper. They are often used in messages exhorting people to support such social causes as a cleaner environment, better race relations, equal rights for women, and aiding the disadvantaged. An example is the March of Dimes appeal: "God made you whole. Give to help those He didn't." Moral appeals are less often used in connection with everyday products.

Message structure. A message's effectiveness also depends on its structure. The three major issues in message structure are conclusion drawing, one- versus two-sided arguments, and order of presentation.

Conclusion drawing raises the question of whether the communicator should draw a definite conclusion or leave it to the audience to decide. Drawing a conclusion is normally more effective, except when (1) the communicator is seen as untrustworthy, (2) the issue is very simple or personal, and (3) the audience is highly intelligent.[6] Conclusion drawing seems best suited to complex or specialized products where a single and clear use is intended.

One- or two-sided arguments raise the question of whether the communicator should only praise the product or also acknowledge some of its shortcomings. Intuitively, it would appear that the best effect is gained by a one-sided presentation—this is the predominant approach in sales presentations, political contests, and child rearing. Yet the answer is not so clear-cut. The major conclusions are that (1) one-sided messages tend to work best with audiences who are favorably disposed to the communicator's position, whereas two-sided arguments tend to work best with audiences who are opposed; (2) two-sided messages tend to be more effective with better-educated audiences; and (3) two-sided messages tend to be more effective with audiences who are likely to be exposed to counterpropaganda.[7]

Order of presentation raises the question of whether communicators should present their strongest arguments first or last. Presenting the strongest arguments first has the advantage of establishing attention and interest. This may be especially important in newspapers and other media where the audience does not attend to all of the message. However, it means an anticlimactic presentation. If a captive audience is involved, as in a sales presentation or conference, then a climactic presentation may be more effective. In a two-sided message, the issue is whether to present the positive argument first (primacy effect) or last (recency effect). If the audience is initially opposed, it would appear that the communicator would be smarter to start with the other side's argument. This will tend to disarm the audience and allow the speaker to conclude with the strongest argument.

Message format. The communicator must be able to convey the message in an effective format. If the message is to be carried in a print ad, the communicator has to develop the elements of headline, copy, illustration, and color. Advertisers are adept at using such attention-getting devices as *novelty and contrast, arresting pictures and headlines, distinctive formats, message size and position,* and *color, shape, and movement.*[8] If the message is to be carried over the radio, the communicator has to carefully choose words, voice qualities (speech rate, rhythm, pitch, articulation), and vocalizations (pauses, sighs, yawns). The "sound" of an announcer promoting a used automobile has to be different from one promoting a soft, comfortable bed mattress. If the message is to be carried on television or given in person, then all of these elements plus body language (nonverbal clues) have to be planned. Presenters have to pay attention to their facial expressions, gestures, dress, posture, and hair style. If the message is carried by the product or its packaging, the communicator has to pay attention to texture, scent, color, size, and shape.

- It is well known that color plays an important communication role in food preferences. When housewives sampled four cups of coffee that had been placed next to brown, blue, red, and yellow containers (all the coffee was identical, although this was unknown to the housewives), 75 percent felt that the coffee next to the brown container tasted too strong; nearly 85 percent judged the coffee next to the red container to be the richest; nearly everyone felt that the coffee next to the blue container was mild and the coffee next to the yellow container was weak.

Choosing Media

The communicator can now turn to the selection of efficient media or channels of communication. Channels of communication are of two broad types, *personal* and *nonpersonal.*

Personal communication. Personal channels are of three types. *Advocate channels* consist of company representatives directly contacting buyers in the target market. *Expert channels* consist of independent persons with expertise (consultants, authorities) making statements to target buyers. *Social channels* consist of neighbors, friends, family members, and associates who may communicate with target buyers. This last channel is also known as *word-of-mouth influence,* and it is the most persuasive in many product areas.

Personal influence in general tends to be most telling for products that are expensive or risky. Buyers will go beyond mass-media sources to seek the opinions of knowledgeable people. Personal influence also is telling for products that are highly social and visible.

Companies can take several steps to stimulate personal influence channels to work on their behalf. They can (1) identify individuals or companies that are influential and devote extra effort to them; (2) create opinion leaders out of certain persons, by supplying them with the product on attractive terms or selecting them as company representatives; (3) work through community influentials such as disc jockeys, class presidents, and presidents of women's organizations; (4) let the advertising feature testimonials by influentials as part of the content; and (5) develop advertising that is high in "conversation value."[9]

Nonpersonal communication. Nonpersonal channels carry influence without involving direct contact. Three types of nonpersonal channels can be distinguished. *Mass and selective media* consist of newspapers, magazines, radio, television, and billboards. Mass media are aimed at large, often undifferentiated, audiences; selective media are aimed at specialized audiences. *Atmospheres* are environments designed to create or reinforce the buyer's leanings toward purchase or consumption of the product. Thus dentists, lawyers, and boutiques each design their places of work to communicate confidence and other things that might be valued by the clients.[10] *Events* are occurrences designed to communicate particular messages to target audiences. Public relations departments often arrange events such as news conferences or grand openings to achieve specific communication effects on an audience.

Although personal communication is often more effective than mass communication, mass media may be the major way to stimulate personal communication. Mass communications affect personal attitudes and behavior through a *two-step flow-of-communication process.* "Ideas often flow from radio and print to opinion leaders and from these to the less active sections of the population."[11]

This two-step communication flow has several significant implications.

First, it says that mass media's influence on mass opinion is not as direct, powerful, and automatic as supposed. It is mediated by *opinion leaders,* persons who are members of primary groups and whose opinions tend to be sought out in one or more areas. Opinion leaders are more exposed to mass media than are the people they influence. They are the carriers of the messages to people who are less exposed to media, thus extending the influence of the mass media; or they may carry altered or no messages, thus acting as *gatekeepers.*

Second, this challenges the notion that persons are influenced in their consumption styles primarily by a "trickle-down" effect from the higher-status classes. Since people primarily interact with others in their own social class, they pick up their fashion and other ideas in this way—from people like themselves who are opinion leaders.

A third implication is that the mass communicator may accomplish message dissemination more efficiently by using a lower advertising budget and directing it specifically at opinion leaders, letting them carry the message to others. Thus a pharmaceutical firm may direct new drug promotion to influential doctors.

Selecting Source Attributes

A communicator's effect on an audience is also influenced by how the audience perceives the communicator. Marketers have known for years that messages delivered by highly credible sources will be more persuasive. Pharmaceutical companies will arrange for doctors to testify about their products' benefits because doctors have high credibility. Antidrug crusaders will use former drug addicts to warn high-school students against drugs because ex-addicts have higher credibility than teachers. Other marketers will hire well-known personalities such as newscasters or athletes to deliver their messages.

But what factors underlie source credibility? The three factors most often identified are expertise, trustworthiness, and likability.[12] *Expertise* is the degree to which the communicator is perceived to possess the necessary authority for what is being claimed. Doctors, scientists, and professors rank high on expertise where their advocacy pertains to their field of specialization. *Trustworthiness* is related to how objective and honest the source is perceived to be. Friends are perceived to be more trustworthy than strangers or salespeople. *Likability* is related to how attractive the source is to the audience. Qualities such as candor, humor, and naturalness tend to make a source more likable. The most highly credible source, then, would be a person who scored high on all three dimensions.

Collecting Feedback

After the message has been disseminated, the communicator must research its effects on the target audience. This generally involves surveying target audience members and asking them whether they recognize or recall the message; how many times they recall seeing it; what points they recall; how they felt about the message; and their previous and current attitudes toward the product and company. Ultimately the communicator would like to collect behavioral measures of audience response, such as how many people bought the product, liked it, and talked to others about it.

An example of feedback measurement is shown in Figure 16-3. In the figure, 80 percent of the total market are aware of brand A, 60 percent have tried it, and

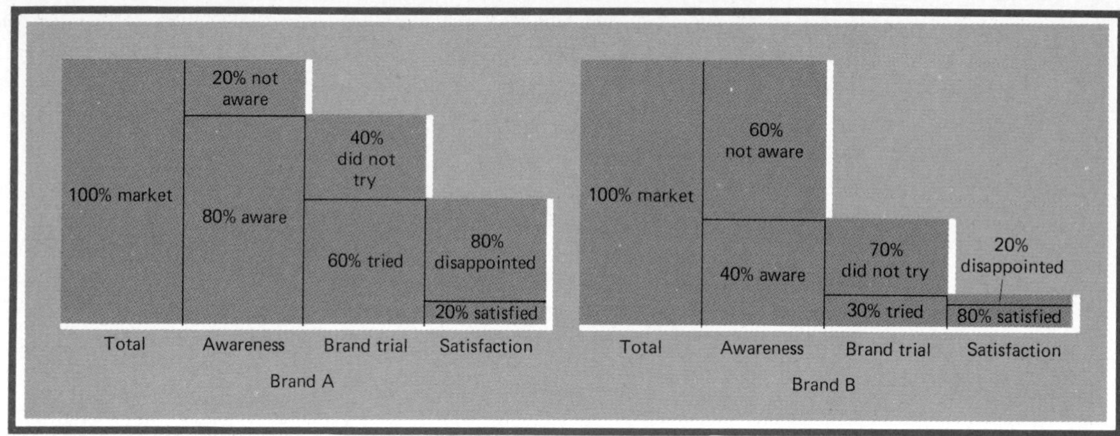

Figure 16-3 *Current Consumer States for Two Brands*

20 percent of those who have tried it are satisfied. This indicates that the communication program is effective in creating awareness but the product fails to meet the expectations. On the other hand, only 40 percent of the total market are aware of brand B, only 30 percent have tried it, and 80 percent of those who have tried it are satisfied. In this case the communication program needs to be strengthened to take advantage of the brand's satisfaction-generating power.

setting promotional budget and mix

We have looked at the steps involved in planning a specific communication directed at a specific target audience. But how does the company decide on (1) the total promotion budget and (2) its division among the major promotional tools? We turn now to these questions.

Establishing the Total Promotional Budget

One of the most serious marketing questions facing company management is how much to spend on promotion. Management finds it far easier to make budget decisions on plant, equipment, and supplies. In the case of promotion, management feels it is a big guessing game. Many years ago John Wanamaker, the department store magnate, said: "I know that half of my advertising is wasted. Unfortunately, I don't know which half."

One thing is clear. Industries, and companies within industries, differ considerably in how much they spend on promotion. Total promotional spending may amount to 30–50 percent of total sales in the cosmetics industry and only 15–20 percent in the industrial machinery industry. Within an industry, low- and high-spending companies will be found. Philip Morris, for example, is a high spender. When it acquired the Miller Brewing Company, and later the Seven-Up Company, it substantially increased total promotional spending. The additional promotional spending at Miller's brought it from a meager 4 percent market share to a 19 percent market share within a few years.

How do companies decide on their total promotional budget? The most common approach is to set the budget as a *percent of sales,* either this year's sales or next year's projected sales. The percentage chosen is one that management feels can be afforded and is reasonable in relation to what competitors are spending. This approach, however, begs the question of whether the company is overspending or underspending. Unless it has some way to determine the relation between total promotional expenditures and sales, it is flying blind. The company should seriously consider cutting its promotion percentage when it has few new products or things to say, and it should raise its promotion percentage in the opposite circumstances.

Companies can also be found that base their promotional budget on *competitors'* expenditures. They may eye some competitor and decide to spend more, less, or the same. They often choose to spend the same on the theory that this will neutralize the competitor's impact. But they should really spend more or spend less depending on their objective and the relative potency of the other elements in their marketing mix.

Other companies prefer to build their promotion budget by setting communication *objectives and tasks.* Their communication objectives suggest the communication tasks that must be carried out. The costs of these tasks are added, and the total promotion budget becomes the sum of the separate required costs.

The overall answer to how much weight promotion should receive in the total marketing mix (as opposed to product improvement, lower prices, more services, and so on) depends on where the company's products are in their life cycle, whether the products are essentially commodities or are highly differentiable, whether the products are routinely needed or have to be "sold," and other considerations. In theory, the total promotional budget should be established where the marginal profit from the last promotional dollar just equals the marginal profit from the last dollar in the best nonpromotional use. Implementing this principle, however, is another thing.

Establishing the Promotional Mix

Companies also have to decide how to split their total promotional budget among the main promotional elements. The most striking fact about the various promotional tools is their internal substitutability and their substitutability with other marketng mix elements. It is possible to achieve a given sales level by increasing advertising expenditures, personal selling, or sales promotion. It is also possible to achieve the same sales level by product improvement, lower prices, or additional customer services. This substitutability explains why marketing departments are increasingly trying to achieve administrative coordination of all of the tools of communication and marketing.

The theory of choosing the optimal promotional mix is as follows. Suppose management is about to split the promotional budget between advertising and sales promotion. Figure 16-4A shows that there are an infinite number of promotional mixes of these two elements. Every point on the A–S plane is a possible promotional mix. If the company has a fixed total budget, say K, it can spend all the money on advertising or on sales promotion or on any of the mixes in between

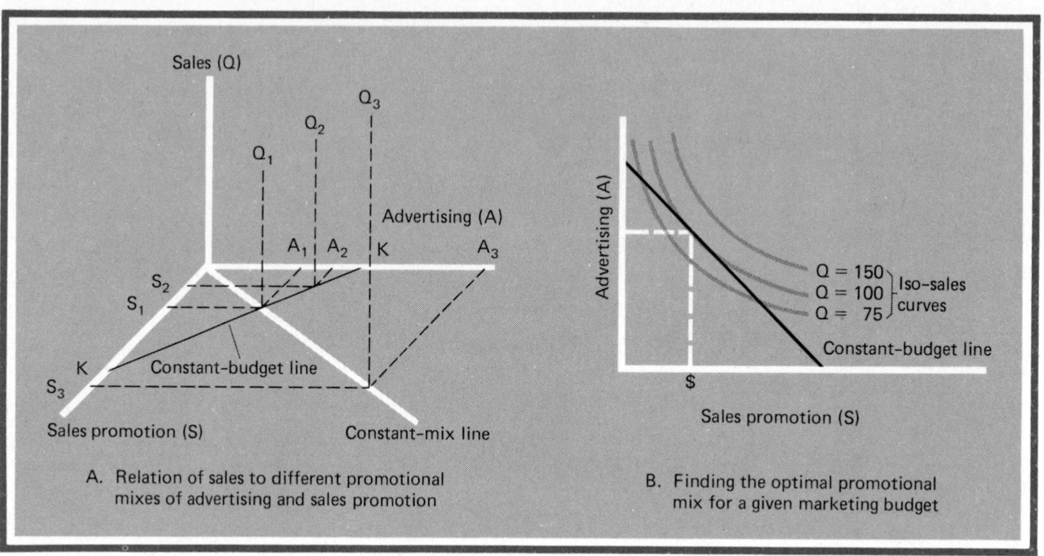

Figure 16-4 *The Sales Function Associated with Two Marketing Mix Elements*

shown on the *constant-budget line.* If, on the other hand, the company wants a particular split between advertising and sales promotion, it can settle for any mix shown on the *constant-mix line* up to its budget.

Associated with every possible marketing mix is a resulting sales level. Three sales levels are shown in Figure 16-4A. The marketing mix (A_1S_1)—calling for a small budget and a rough equality between advertising and promotion—is expected to produce sales of Q_1. The marketing mix (A_2S_2) involves the same budget with more expenditure on advertising than promotion; this is expected to produce slightly higher sales, Q_2. The mix (A_3S_3) calls for a larger budget but a relatively equal splitting between advertising and promotion, and with a sales estimate of Q_3.

For a given marketing budget, the money should be divided among the promotional tools in a way that gives the same marginal profit on the last dollar spent on each tool. A geometrical version of the solution is shown in Figure 16-4B. Here we are looking down at the A–S plane shown in Figure 16-4A. A constant-budget line is shown, indicating all the alternative promotional mixes that could be achieved with this budget. The curved lines are called *iso-sales curves.* An iso-sales curve shows the different mixes of advertising and personal selling that would produce a given level of sales. It is a projection into the A–S plane of the set of points resulting from horizontal slicing of the sales function shown in Figure 16-4A at a given level of sales. Figure 16-4B shows iso-sales curves for three different sales levels: 75, 100, and 150 units. Given the budget line, it is not possible to attain sales of more than 100 units. The optimum promotional mix is shown at the point of tangency between the budget line and the last-touching iso-sales curve about it. Consequently the promotional mix (A^*S^*), which calls for somewhat more advertising than promotion, is the sales-maximizing (and in this case profit-maximizing) promotional mix.

Again, the challenge is one of implementing the theory in practice. Man-

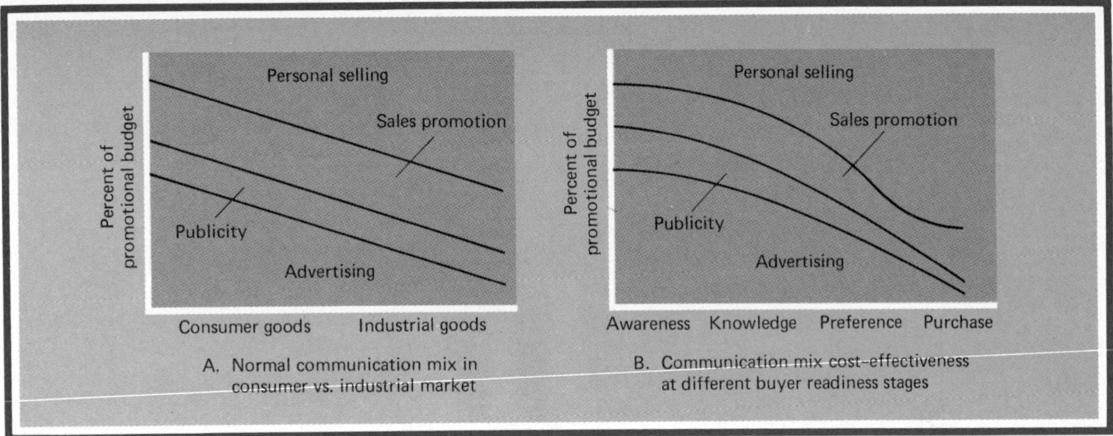

Figure 16-5 *Communication Mix as a Function of Type of Product and Buyer Readiness Stage*

agement must be able to estimate the amount of sales that would be produced by different combinations of promotional mix elements. Certain factors have a major influence on which promotional elements will have the most impact. These factors are reviewed below.

Type of product. Historically there has been a considerable difference in the communication mix used by consumer and industrial marketers. The mix differences are illustrated in Figure 16-5A. Advertising is widely felt to be the most important promotional tool in consumer marketing, and personal selling the most important promotional tool in industrial marketing. Sales promotion is considered to have an equal, though smaller, importance in both markets. And publicity is considered to have an even smaller, but equal, importance in both markets.

This view leads some marketers to act as if advertising were unimportant in industrial marketing and as if personal selling were unimportant in consumer marketing. These conclusions would be erroneous. While sales calls will normally have more impact than advertising in industrial-marketing situations, advertising can perform such useful functions as awareness building, comprehension building, efficient reminding, development of prospect leads, legitimation, and product reassurance. The importance of advertising in industrial marketing was classically captured in the McGraw-Hill ad shown in Figure 16-6. Advertising could have prevented most of the statements the buyer made in that ad. Morrill has shown, in the case of commodity marketing, that the combination of advertising with personal selling increased the sales-per-call by 23 percent over what they had been with no advertising. The total promotional cost as percent of sales was reduced by 20 percent.[13] Levitt's research has shown that advertising can play an important role in industrial marketing. (See Exhibit 16-1.)

Conversely, personal selling can make a strong contribution in consumer-goods marketing. It is not simply the case that "salesmen put products on shelves and advertising takes them off." Well-trained consumer-goods salespeople can sign up more dealers to carry the brand, influence them to devote more shelf space to the brand, and encourage them to cooperate in special promotions.

Figure 16-6
Advertising Has a Role to Play in Industrial Selling

Push or pull strategy. Companies vary in their preference for a push or pull strategy. A *push strategy* calls for using the sales force and trade promotion to push the product through the channels. The manufacturer pushes the product into the wholesalers' hands, and the wholesalers push the product on to the retailers' shelves, and it is hoped that the retailers have sufficient incentive to push the product on to the consumers. A *pull strategy* calls for spending a lot of money on advertising and consumer promotion aimed at the final consumer to build up demand for the product. If effective, consumers will go to their retailers and ask for the product, thus pulling it through the system. The retailers, upon hearing that the company is planning to spend lots of money to build demand, are likely to agree to carry the product even though at a lower margin. Companies differ in their predilection for push or pull. Lever Brothers relies more heavily on push, and Procter and Gamble on pull. Avon concentrates on personal selling (its advertising is only 1.5 percent of sales), whereas Revlon spends heavily on advertising (about 7.0 percent of sales). In selling vacuum cleaners, Electrolux spends heavily on a door-to-door sales force while Hoover relies more on advertising. This strategy choice clearly influences the funds spent on the different promotional tools.

Buyer readiness stage. Promotional tools differ in their cost-effectiveness in producing different customer responses. Figure 16-5B shows the general findings that have emerged from a number of studies.[14] Advertising, followed by sales promotion and publicity, are the most cost-effective tools in building buyer awareness, more than "cold calls" from sales representatives. Advertising is

EXHIBIT
16-1

ROLE OF CORPORATE ADVERTISING IN INDUSTRIAL MARKETING

A study conducted by Theodore Levitt sought to determine the relative roles of the company's reputation (built mainly by advertising) and the company's sales presentation (personal selling) in producing industrial sales. The experiment consisted of showing various groups of purchasing agents different filmed sales presentations of a new, but fictitious, technical product for use as an ingredient in making paint. The variables were the quality of the presentation and whether the salesperson represented a well-known company, a less-known but creditable company, or an unknown company. The reactions and ratings of the purchasing-agent groups were collected after the films and then again five weeks later. The findings were as follows:

1. A company's generalized reputation has a positive influence on sales prospects in improving the chances of (a) getting a favorable first hearing and (b) getting an early adoption of the product. Therefore, to the extent that corporate advertising can build up the company's reputation (other factors also shape its reputation), this will help the company's sales representatives.
2. Sales representatives from well-known companies have an edge in getting the sale, provided that their sales presentation is up to the expected standard. If, however, a sales representative from a lesser-known company makes a highly effective sales presentation, this can overcome the disadvantage. To this extent, smaller companies may find it better to use their limited funds in selecting and training better sales representatives rather than in advertising.
3. Company reputations tend to have the most effect where the product is complex, the risk is high, and the purchasing agent is less professionally trained.

Source: Theodore Levitt, *Industrial Purchasing Behavior: A Study in Communications Effects* (Boston: Division of Research, Harvard Business School, 1965).

highly cost-effective in producing knowledge, with personal selling coming in second. Buyer preference is influenced most by personal selling followed by advertising. Finally, buyer purchase is primarily influenced by sales calls, with an assist from sales promotion. Thus the buyer readiness stage is an important factor in formulating the promotional mix.

Product life-cycle stage. The different promotional elements perform with varying degrees of effectiveness at different stages of the product life cycle. In the introduction stage, advertising and publicity are cost-effective in producing high awareness, and sales promotion is useful in promoting early trial. Personal selling is relatively expensive, although it must be used to get the trade to carry the product.

In the growth stage, advertising and publicity continue to be potent, but sales promotion can be reduced because incentives for trial are less needed.

In the mature stage, sales promotion tends to increase relative to advertising. Buyers know the brands and need only a reminder level of advertising unless there are some new things worth saying about the product.

In the decline stage, advertising is cut down to a reminder level, publicity is eliminated, and salespeople give the product only minimal attention. Sales promotion, however, might continue strong.

Size of the total promotional budget. The size of the organization's promotional budget affects which promotional tools will be emphasized. Small organizations with low budgets cannot hope to spend much on television advertising or other expensive advertising media. They will rely on such things as publicity, direct mail, and personal selling. Nonprofit organizations in particular will rely heavily on "volunteers" as their promotional arm.

Responsibility for Marketing Communications Planning

Members of the marketing department hold different opinions as to how much to spend on the various promotional tools. The sales manager finds it hard to understand how the company could get more value by spending $80,000 to buy a single exposure of a thirty-second television commercial than by hiring three additional sales representatives for a whole year. The public relations manager feels that the company can gain by transferring some of the advertising budget to publicity.

Historically, companies left these decisions to different people. No one was given the responsibility for thinking through the roles of the various promotional tools and coordinating the company's promotional mix. Today, companies are moving toward the concept of *integrated communications.* This concept calls for (1) developing a corporate position, such as marketing communications director, who has overall responsibility for the company's persuasive communication efforts; (2) working out a philosophy of the role and the extent to which the different promotools are to be used; (3) keeping track of all promotional investments by product, promotool, stage of product life cycle, and observed effect, as a basis for improving subsequent effective use of each tool; and (4) coordinating the promotional inputs when major campaigns take place.

Coordinating the promotional activities promises to achieve more consistency in the company's *meaning* to its buyers and publics. It places a responsibility in someone's hand—where none existed before—to unify and manage the company's image as it comes through the thousand activities the company carries on. It leads to the determination of a total marketing communications strategy aimed at showing how the company can help customers solve their problems.

■ summary

Marketing communications is one of the four major elements of the company's marketing mix. The instruments of marketing communications—advertising, sales promotion, publicity, and personal selling—have separate and overlapping capabilities, and their effective coordination requires careful definition of communication objectives.

In preparing specific marketing communications, the communicator has to understand the eight elements of any communication process: sender, receiver, encoding, decoding, message, media, response, and feedback. The communicator's first task is to identify the target audience members and their characteristics. Next, the communicator has to define the sought response, whether it is awareness, knowledge, liking, preference, conviction, or purchase. Then a message must be constructed containing an effective content, structure, and format. Then media must be selected, both for personal communication and nonpersonal communication. The message must be delivered by someone with good source credibility, that is, someone who scores high on expertise, trustworthiness, and likability. Finally, the communicator must monitor how much of the market becomes aware and tries the product and is satisfied in the process.

The company has to decide how much to spend for total promotion. The most popular approaches are to set the promotional budget as a percent of sales, or to base it on competitors' expenditures, or to base it on an analysis and costing of the communication objectives and tasks.

The company also has to split the promotional budget among the major promotional tools. If management knew the sales associated with different promotional mixes, it chould choose the optimal promotional mix. In practice, companies are influenced in their promotional mix by the type of product, whether they prefer a push or pull strategy, the buyer's readiness stage, the product life-cycle stage, and the size of the total promotional budget. The interactions of the different promotional activities require organizational coordination for maximum impact.

■ questions for discussion

1. Apply the four major tools in the marketing communication mix to a professional sports team.
2. What two communication parties are used in any marketing communication? Discuss how they relate to McDonald's.
3. How would the six buyer readiness states relate to your last purchase of beer or a soft drink?
4. Which type of message content is used by the following marketers? (a) Bell Telephone Company, (b) Datsun, (c) American Lung Association, and (d) General Electric.
5. What major types of communication channels can an organization utilize? When should each be used?
6. State whether the following individuals are credible sources for marketing communication: (a) Reggie Jackson, (b) Neil Armstrong, and (c) Dorothy Hamill. Why?
7. How might a company set its promotional budget? Discuss the advantages of each approach.
8. The type of product being marketed has no relationship to the communication mix employed by the marketer. Comment.
9. Who should have responsibility for marketing communications planning? Why?

references

1. This has been adapted with a few changes from a brochure of Pizza Inn, with permission.
2. These definitions, with the exception of the one for sales promotion, are from *Marketing Definitions: A Glossary of Marketing Terms* (Chicago: American Marketing Association, 1960). The AMA definition of *sales promotion* covered, in addition to incentives, such marketing media as displays, shows and exhibitions, and demonstrations that can better be classified as forms of advertising, personal selling, or publicity. Some marketing scholars have also suggested adding *packaging* as a fifth element of the promotion mix, although others classify it as a product element.
3. MICHAEL L. RAY, *Marketing Communication and the Hierarchy-of-Effects* (Cambridge, Mass.: Marketing Science Institute, November 1973).
4. MICHAEL L. RAY AND WILLIAM L. WILKIE, "Fear: The Potential of an Appeal Neglected by Marketing," *Journal of Marketing,* January 1970, pp. 55–56; and BRIAN STERNTHAL AND C. SAMUEL CRAIG, "Fear Appeals: Revisited and Revised," *Journal of Consumer Research,* December 1974, pp. 22–34.
5. See BRIAN STERNTHAL AND C. SAMUEL CRAIG, "Humor in Advertising," *Journal of Marketing,* October 1973, pp. 12–18.
6. CARL I. HOVLAND AND WALLACE MANDELL, "An Experimental Comparison of Conclusion-Drawing by the Communication and by the Audience," *Journal of Abnormal and Social Psychology,* July 1952, pp. 581–88.
7. See C. I. HOVLAND, A. A. LUMSDAINE, AND F. D. SHEFFIELD, *Experiments on Mass Communication* (Princeton, N.J.: Princeton University Press, 1948), Vol. III, Chap. 8.
8. For a discussion of these devices, see JAMES F. ENGEL, ROGER D. BLACKWELL, AND DAVID T. KOLLAT, *Consumer Behavior,* 3rd ed. (Hinsdale, Ill.: Dryden Press, 1978), pp. 346–48.
9. These and other points are discussed in THOMAS S. ROBERTSON, *Innovative Behavior and Communication* (New York: Holt, Rinehart & Winston, 1971), Chap. 9.
10. See PHILIP KOTLER, "Atmospherics as a Marketing Tool," *Journal of Retailing,* Winter 1973–74, pp. 48–64.
11. P. F. LAZARSFELD, B. BERELSON, AND H. GAUDET, *The People's Choice,* 2nd ed. (New York: Columbia University Press, 1948), p. 151.
12. See JOHN C. MAHONEY, "Attitude Measurement and Formation" (Paper presented at the American Marketing Association Test Market Design and Measurement Workshop, Chicago, April 21, 1966).
13. *How Advertising Works in Today's Marketplace: The Morrill Study* (New York: McGraw-Hill, 1971), p. 4.
14. "What IBM Found about Ways to Influence Selling," *Business Week,* December 5, 1959, pp. 69–70; and HAROLD C. CASH AND WILLIAM J. CRISSY, "Comparison of Advertising and Selling," in *The Psychology of Selling* (Flushing, N.Y.: Personnel Development Associates, 1965), Vol. 12.

ADVERTISING, SALES PROMOTION, AND PUBLICITY STRATEGY

It is with good reason that Revlon has been called "the master" of fragrance and cosmetic marketing. The company created Charlie in 1973, and in no time it became the nation's leading fragrance. Charlie had been created in response to what Revlon saw as "a joyous genre of exciting, adventuresome, rule-breaking, world-shaking young women who shape their own lives and carve out their own careers with style and class." Charlie shows a pants-suited, short-haired girl hurriedly striding down a crowded sidewalk. To match the image projected by Charlie, Revlon chose a relatively "crisp" scent, a mixed floral with green amber undertones (see Figure 17-1).

Charlie was really the beginning of a revolution in fragrance to meet changing life styles in the early 1970s resulting in changing patterns of fragrance use. With Charlie, Revlon helped reverse the trend from expensive classical French perfumes for evenings to affordable American scents for everyday use. Charlie came on the scene at a reasonable price ($6 for 3½ oz. cologne spray), emphasized in copy that "fragrance isn't serious," and portrayed its models wearing fragrance not only for dates but on the job and while motorcycling or flying a kite in Central Park.

Charlie, which began life as a short fragrance line, has been expanded by Revlon to include not only more fragrance products but a complete makeup and skin-care line as well. A men's fragrance, Chaz, was also spun off from Charlie but has been noticeably less successful.

In 1975 Revlon spent $3.8 million in consumer media for its fragrances, using print, radio, network, and spot TV. Revlon also puts a great deal of emphasis on creating excitement with the retailers. With the advent of Charlie, Revlon launched a joint coordinated merchandising/promotional effort called Retail Partners. The program recognizes that sales can be accelerated through point-of-sale technology jointly prepared by store and manufacturer specialists. Co-op ads and in-store demonstrations had become jaded techniques, expected by retailers and consumers alike. Revlon wanted to use visual materials and special events to create an atmosphere for its products that would set them apart from competitors. Several times a year Revlon mails lavish retailer kits on Charlie with more than a dozen photographs and flowery prose. Retailers are encouraged to adapt these kits to their own displays by asking Revlon for blowups of certain photos to be used in store windows or for miniatures.

Charlie's success can be attributed to advertising, scent, packaging, trade promotion, and publicity. In 1974, just one year after giving birth

Figure 17-1
Ad Expressing a Life Style

to its fabulously successful Charlie fragrance, Revlon decided to introduce another line of life-style fragrance products, using the same marketing approach. Revlon launched Jontue in September 1975. Within one year Charlie's younger sister was among the nation's top seven fragrances.[1]

□ Most of the new fragrances launched by the cosmetics industry each year fail, not because their scents are weak, but because they come on the market without any distinction, drama, or excitement. Clearly the woman is not buying a scent but a fantasy. This is not to say that the Charlie image would have sold any scent; but even with a good scent, something extra is needed, that which we call positioning of the product in the consumer's mind.[2] To create Charlie, Revlon had to skillfully use the mass-promotion techniques of advertising, sales promotion, and publicity. These techniques are examined in this chapter.

advertising

Advertising consists of *nonpersonal forms of communication conducted through paid media under clear sponsorship.* This major form of marketing communication ran up a bill of over $38 billion in 1977. It is a tool by no means restricted to commercial firms. Advertising is used by museums, fund raisers, and various social action organizations to bring messages about themselves and their causes to various target publics. In fact, the twenty-fourth-largest advertising spender is a nonprofit organization—the U.S. government.

Within the commercial sector, the top one hundred national advertisers account for as much as one-fifth of all national advertising.[3] Table 17-1 lists the ten top advertisers in 1977. Procter & Gamble is the top spender, accounting

Table 17-1 *The Top 10 National Advertisers in 1977*

RANK	COMPANY	TOTAL ADVERTISING IN MILLIONS	TOTAL SALES IN MILLIONS	ADVERTISING AS A PERCENT OF SALES	MEDIA PERCENTAGE OF ADVERTISING BUDGET			
					TV	RADIO	MAGAZINE	NEWSPAPER
1	Procter & Gamble Co.	$460	8,100	5.7	92.7	0.1	5.7	1.5
2	General Motors Co.	312	54,961	0.5	49.9	8.0	18.7	20.2
3	General Foods Corp.	300	35,380	5.6	85.2	0.7	11.5	2.5
4	Sears Roebuck & Co.	290	17,224	1.7	68.7	3.5	27.8	—
5	K-Mart	210	9,941	2.1	74.3	7.7	18.0	—
6	Bristol-Myers	203	2,191	9.3	81.2	2.7	14.2	1.8
7	Warner-Lambert Co.	201	2,543	7.9	91.7	5.7	0.9	1.0
8	Ford Motor Co.	184	37,841	0.4	59.8	5.4	15.8	17.1
9	Philip Morris Inc.	184	5,202	3.5	25.1	1.4	28.7	31.6
10	American Home Products	171	1,972	8.7	91.6	3.2	3.8	1.4

Source: *Advertising Age,* August 28, 1978, pp. 30, 32.
The dollar magnitudes in the first column apply to measured and unmeasured media. The percentages in the last four columns apply to measured media only. Some of these percentages do not add up to 100 percent because some minor media are left out.

for $460 million, which amounts to 5.7 percent of its total sales of over $8 billion. The other major spenders are found in the auto, food, retailing, drug, and tobacco industries. Advertising as a percent of sales is lowest in the automobile industry and highest in the drug industry. Not shown is the Noxell Corporation, which spent 24.2 percent of its sales on advertising, and Block Drugs Company, which spent 22.8 percent. The highest-percentage spenders are found in drugs and cosmetics (between 10 and 20 percent), gum and candy (12 percent), and soaps (between 6 and 12 percent).

Table 17-1 also shows how the leading advertising spenders allocated their budgets to various media. Television received the lion's share of the advertising budget in almost all cases. The two auto companies, however, bought a more balanced mix of media. The table shows that companies within the same industry—Sears and K-Mart, Bristol-Myers and Warner-Lambert, and General Motors and Ford—varied in their ideas of the optimal percentage to spend on the various media.

Advertising comes in many forms and has many uses: It involves magazine and newspaper space; radio and television; outdoor displays (posters, signs, skywriting); direct mail; novelties (matchboxes, blotters, calendars); cards (car, bus); catalogs; directories; and circulars. It can be used for such diverse purposes as long-term buildup of the organization's image (*institutional advertising*), long-term buildup of a particular brand (*brand advertising*), information dissemination about a sale, service, or event (*classified advertising*), announcement of a special sale (*sale advertising*), and advocacy of a particular cause (*advocacy advertising*).

Because of the many forms and uses of advertising, it is difficult to make all-embracing generalizations about its distinctive qualities as a component of the promotional mix. Yet the following qualities can be noted:[4]

1. *Public presentation.* Advertising, unlike personal selling, is a highly public mode of communication. Its public nature confers a kind of legitimacy to the product and

also suggests a standardized offering. Because many persons receive the same message, buyers know that their motives for purchasing the product will be publicly understood.

2. *Pervasiveness.* Advertising is a pervasive medium that permits the seller to repeat a message many times. It also allows the buyer to receive and compare the messages of various competitors. Large-scale advertising by a seller says something positive about the seller's size, popularity, and success.
3. *Amplified expressiveness.* Advertising provides opportunities for dramatizing the company and its products through the artful use of print, sound, and color. Sometimes the tool's very success at expressiveness may, however, dilute or distract from the message.
4. *Impersonality.* Advertising, in spite of being public, pervasive, and expressive, cannot be as compelling as a company sales representative. The audience does not feel obligated to pay attention or respond. Advertising is only able to carry on a monologue, not a dialogue, with the audience.

Advertising's roots go back to early history (see Exhibit 17-1). Although it is now thought of as primarily a marketing tool used in private enterprise economies, it can be found in virtually all the countries of the world, including socialist countries (see Exhibit 17-2) and developing nations. Evidently the modern economies find advertising to be a cost-effective way to disseminate messages, whether it be to build brand preference for a drink such as Coke in over 150 countries of the world or to motivate a developing nation's people to drink milk or practice birth control.

EXHIBIT 17-1

HISTORICAL MILESTONES IN ADVERTISING

Advertising is not a new activity of modern industrialism but an ancient practice that goes back to the very beginnings of recorded history. The diggings of archaeologists in the countries rimming the Mediterranean Sea have turned up evidence of the use of *signs* to announce various events and offers. The Romans painted walls to announce forthcoming gladiatorial contests and the Phoenicians painted murals on prominent rocks along trade routes extolling the wares they sold, a precursor of modern outdoor advertising. In Pompeii, a wall has been found praising a politician and asking for the people's votes.

Another early form of advertising was the use of *town criers.* In Greece during the Golden Age, town criers were paid to circulate through the streets of Athens announcing the sale of slaves, cattle, and other goods, as well as making public announcements. An early "singing commercial" used in ancient Athens went as follows: "For eyes that are shining, for cheeks like the dawn/ For beauty that lasts after girlhood is gone/ For prices in reason, the woman who knows/ Will buy her cosmetics of Aesclyptos." These town criers were the forerunners of radio as an advertising medium and the car loudspeakers used by modern political candidates.

The third early form of advertising was the *mark* placed by artisans on their individual goods, such as pottery. As the reputation of a particular artisan spread through word of mouth, buyers began to look for his distinctive mark just as trademarks and brand names are used today. They would pay a premium: For example, Osnabrück linen was carefully controlled for quality and commanded a price 20 percent higher than that of other Westphalian linens. As production became more centralized and markets became more distant, the mark or identifying name took on more significance.

The turning point, however, in the history of advertising was 1450, the year Gutenberg invented the printing press. No longer did advertisers have to produce extra copies of a sign by hand. The first-known printed advertisement in the English language appeared in 1478.

Starting in 1622, an important new medium gave advertising a substantial forward push, namely, the first English newspaper, *The Weekly Newes*. Later Joseph Addison and Richard Steele published the *Tatler* and became devotees of advertising. Addison included this advice to copy writers: "The great art in writing advertising is the finding out the proper method to catch the reader, without which a good thing may pass unobserved, or be lost among commissions of bankrupts." The September 14, 1710, issue of the *Tatler* contained competitive ads for razor strops and patent medicine attempting to convince the readers of the products' superiority over competing products.

Advertising had its greatest growth in the United States rather than England. Benjamin Franklin is often called the father of American advertising because his *Gazette*, first published in 1729, attained the largest circulation and advertising volume of any paper in colonial America. Several factors contributed to America's becoming the cradle of advertising. First, American industry led in the mechanization of production, which created surpluses and the need to convince consumers to buy more. Second, the development of a fine network of waterways, highways, and roads made the transportation of goods and advertising media to the countryside feasible. Third, the establishment in 1813 of compulsory public education led to the decline of illiteracy and the growth of newspapers and magazines. The invention of radio and, later, television created two more amazing media for the dissemination of advertising.

Sources: Written by the author based on information presented in John S. Wright, Daniel S. Warner, Willis L. Winter, Jr., and Sherilyn K. Zeigler, *Advertising*, 4th ed. (New York: McGraw-Hill, 1977), pp. 10–17, and other sources.

EXHIBIT 17-2

ADVERTISING IN THE SOVIET UNION

Who ever would have thought that more than one hundred advertising agencies would be plying their trade today in the Soviet Union? Certainly not Marx! According to traditional Marxist-Leninist doctrine, advertising is a tool of capitalistic exploitation. It siphons off the surplus value belonging to underpaid workers and puts it in the hands of overpaid white-collar workers who are nonproductively employed writing jingles.

Yet there has been an impressive growth of advertising agencies in the Soviet Union. The initial argument was that these agencies exist to develop advertising to support Soviet goods in export markets where it is necessary to compete against Western and other nations. But many advertisements also appear in print and broadcast media reaching Russian consumers. Another rationale was established at the 1957 Prague Conference of Advertising Workers of Socialist Countries, which made three points as to how advertising was to be used: (1) to educate people's tastes, develop their requirements, and thus actively form demand; (2) to help the consumer by providing information about the most rational means of consumption; and (3) to help to raise the culture of trade. Furthermore, Soviet advertising is to be ideological, truthful, concrete, and functional. The Soviets claim that their advertising does not indulge in devices used in the West. Their ads will not use celebrities—only experts will be used to promote a product. They will not use mood advertising. They will not create brand differentiation when none exists.

Experts think that the main use of Soviet advertising is to help industry move products that come into excess supply where the Soviets do not want to do the logical thing, cut prices.

To handle advertising, four different organizational arrangements can be used. In small companies, advertising is the responsibility of a single person in the sales department, who might handle other functions as well and occasionally work with an advertising agency. Large companies tend to set up a separate advertising department, whose head reports to the vice-president of marketing. In some cases the advertising department will be small in that it will rely primarily on a hired advertising agency to create, test, and place advertising. The advertising department's job is to develop the total budget, approve agency ads and campaigns, and handle direct-mail advertising, dealer displays, and other forms of advertising not ordinarily performed by the agency. In other cases, especially in retail organizations, the advertising department will be large and will perform all the tasks without the help of an advertising agency. Advertising agencies, however, have several advantages and have become an important part of the American advertising scene (see Exhibit 17-3).

EXHIBIT 17-3

WHAT IS AN ADVERTISING AGENCY AND HOW DOES IT WORK?

Madison Avenue, USA, is a phrase familiar to most Americans, and it describes an actual avenue in New York City where a number of major advertising agencies are headquartered with their approximately thirty thousand agency people. But most of the nation's six thousand agencies are found outside New York, and there are few cities that do not have at least one agency, even if it is a one-person shop. The seven largest U.S. agencies in terms of world billings are J. Walter Thompson, Young & Rubicam, McCann-Erickson, Leo Burnett, Ogilvy and Mather, BBDO, and Ted Bates. The world's largest advertising agency, however, is not found in the United States but in Japan, and its name is Dentsu.

Advertising agencies first appeared in the last half of the nineteenth century in the form of salespeople and brokers who worked for various media and received a commission for selling advertising space to companies. As the competition among the media for advertising business grew, the salespeople began to attract customers by helping them compose and prepare their advertisements. Eventually this tie with the advertisers strengthened to the point where today the agencies are closer to the advertisers than to the media.

An advertising agency today is an independent company that provides advertising services and sometimes general marketing services to its clients. There are several reasons why even a company that has a strong advertising department may want to use an advertising agency. Most significantly, agencies are able to employ specialists in the technical preparation and placement of advertising, and these specialists often can perform the necessary tasks better and more efficiently than the firm's own staff. Also, an agency brings an outside perspective to bear on the company's problems, as well as a broad range of experience from working with a diverse set of clients and situations. Another advantage is that because of the way in which agencies are often paid for their work, use of an agency may cost a firm next to nothing. In addition, since a firm is free to cancel its business with an agency at any time, an agency has more of an incentive to perform effectively and efficiently than does a permanent advertising department.

An advertising agency is typically organized around four departments: *creative*, which handles the development and production of ads; *media*, which selects media and places ads in them; *research*, which determines audience characteristics and wants; and *business*, which handles the public relations and business activities of the agency. Each account is supervised by an account executive, and personnel in each department are assigned to work on several accounts. Some of the larger agencies are able to assign departmental personnel to only one account, and these persons become experts on the product being promoted.

New business is sometimes attracted to an agency because of its reputation or size. Generally, however, a limited number of agencies are invited to compete for a firm's account by developing and presenting a "mini-ad-campaign" for the product. Each agency makes a private presentation, and the firm then selects one agency to handle its advertising.

Compensation to ad agencies has primarily been in the form of commissions, although some has been in the form of fees. Typically, an agency receives a commission of 15 percent of the cost of the media time or space it purchases for its client. Thus an advertising agency may buy $60,000 of magazine space for a client. The magazine bills the advertising agency for $51,000 ($60,000 less 15 percent), and the agency turns around and bills the client for the full $60,000, keeping for itself the $9,000 commission. If the client bought the space directly from the magazine, it would have to pay the full $60,000 because these commissions are only offered to accredited advertising agencies.

This is obviously a holdover practice from the days when the agencies were working for the media, and there has been a growing dissatisfaction with it on the part of both advertisers and agencies. Large advertisers complain that they pay more for the same services that are being offered smaller ones simply because they place more advertising. All advertisers are uncomfortable with the fact that the incentives might drive agencies away from low-cost media and short advertising campaigns. Agencies are unhappy because they often find it necessary to perform extra services for an account without receiving additional compensation. Today there is a growing trend toward compensation on either a straight fee basis or by a combination of commission and fee.

Other trends have also buffeted the advertising agency industry in recent years. Full-service advertising agencies are encountering increasing competition from limited-service advertising agencies specializing in only media buying, or advertising writing, or advertising production. Economic trends have increased the power of the business managers in agencies, who are demanding more profit-mindedness from the creative staff. Some advertisers have also begun to form their own *in-house* agencies, thus pulling some longstanding accounts away from agencies. Finally, the Federal Trade Commission and other public policy makers have recently expressed the opinion that agencies must share equal responsibility with the client for deceptive advertising, which would make them liable for financial penalties or the cost of corrective ads. These trends will effect some changes in the industry in future years, but advertising agencies provide a highly demanded service and can be expected to endure.

Major Decisions in Advertising

In developing an advertising campaign, marketing managment must make five important decisions. These decisions are shown in Figure 17-2 and are examined in the following sections.

Objectives Setting

Before an advertising budget and program can be developed, advertising objectives must be set. These objectives must flow from prior decision making on the target market, market positioning, and marketing mix. The marketing mix strategy defines the job that advertising has in the total marketing plan.

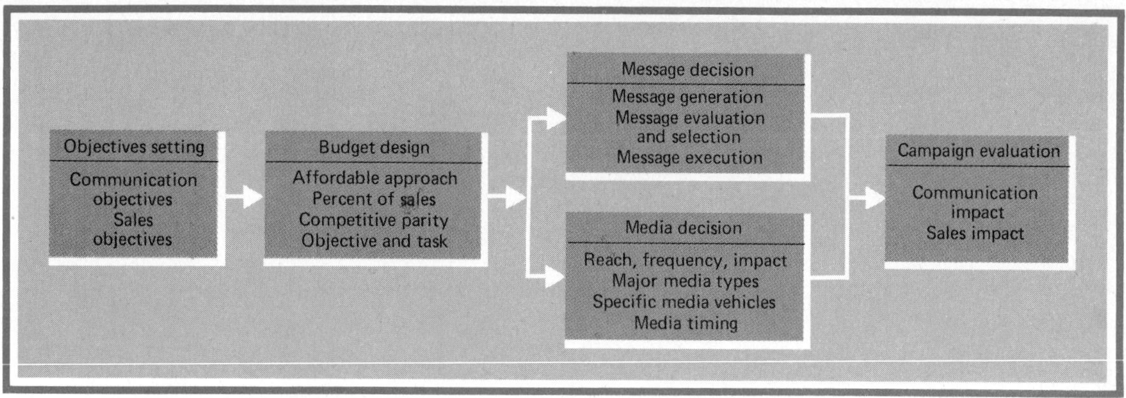

Figure 17-2 *Major Decisions in Advertising Management*

At the same time, there are many specific communication and sales objectives that can be assigned to advertising. Colley has distinguished fifty-two possible advertising objectives in his *Defining Advertising Goals for Measured Advertising Results.*[5] He outlines a method called DAGMAR (after the book's title) for turning advertising objectives into specific measurable goals. An *advertising goal* is a specific communication task, to be accomplished among a defined audience, in a given period of time. DAGMAR outlines a specific approach to measuring whether advertising goals have been achieved.

The various possible advertising objectives can be sorted into whether their aim is to inform, persuade, or remind. The *inform* category includes such advertising objectives as telling the market about a new product, suggesting new uses for a product, informing the market of a price change, explaining how the product works, describing various available services, correcting false impressions, reducing consumers' fears, and building a company image. This category includes *pioneering advertising,* which seeks to build *primary demand,* that is, demand for a product category. It informs the target market about what the product is, what it does, and where it is available. It does not emphasize the brand name or compare brands. Thus advertising sponsored by the yogurt industry to inform consumers about the food's nutritional benefits and many uses would be pioneering advertising.

The *persuade* category includes such advertising objectives as building brand preference, encouraging switching to the advertiser's brand, trying to change the customer's perception of the importance of different product attributes, persuading the customer to purchase now, and persuading the customer to receive a sales call. This category includes *competitive advertising,* whose purpose is to build *selective demand,* that is, demand for a particular brand. Competitive advertising attempts to promote a brand's uses, features, and benefits that may not be available from the other brands. For example, the Chivas Regal ad in Figure 17-3 attempts to persuade the audience that Chivas Regal delivers status like no other brand of Scotch. The ad seeks to build a "very best" position for Chivas Regal in the consumer's mind by associating it with "very best" examples of other products. Some competitive advertising has moved into the category of *comparison advertising,* which seeks to establish the superiority

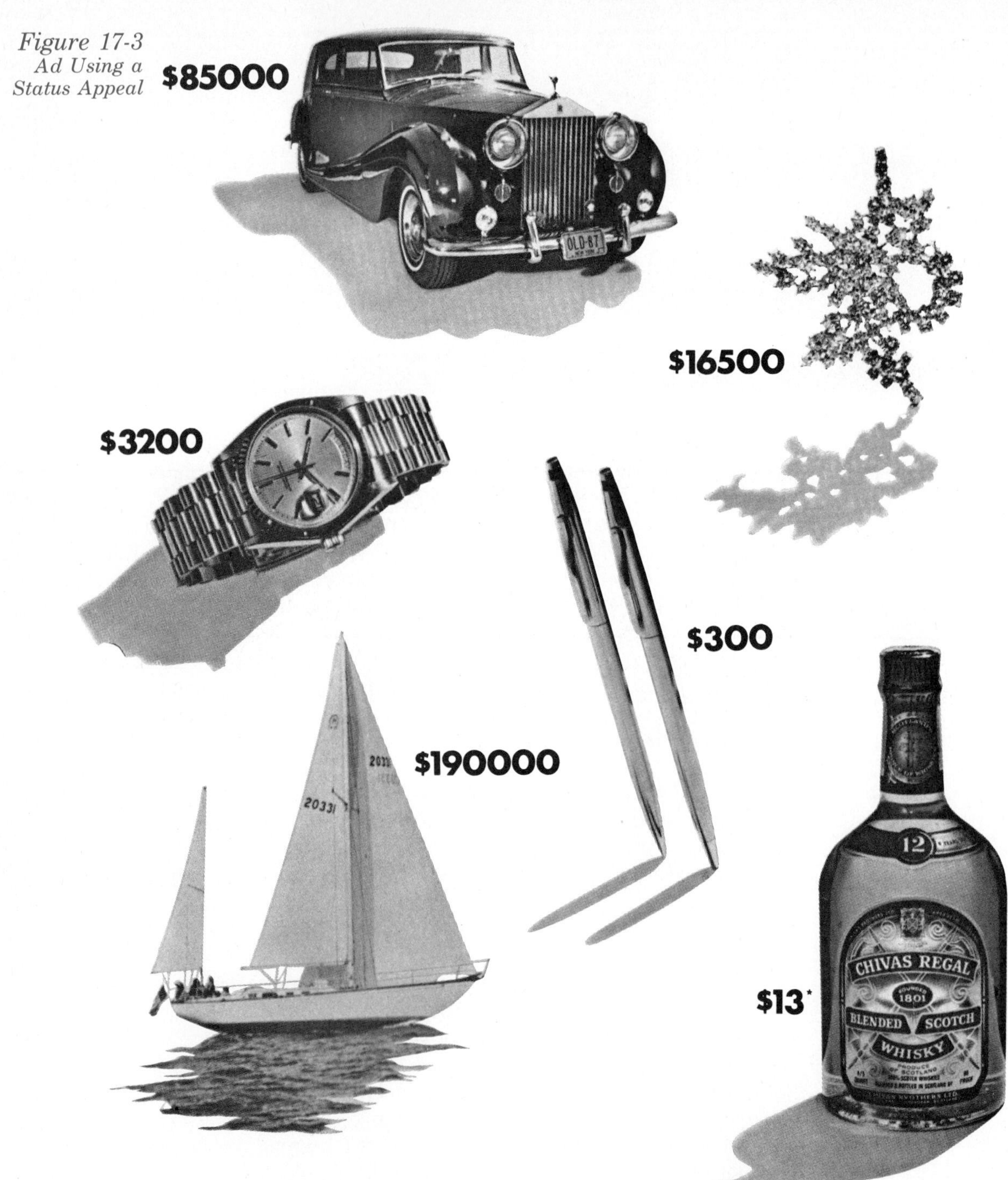

Figure 17-3
Ad Using a Status Appeal

of one brand along one or more product characteristics through specific comparison with one or more other brands in the product class.[6] An example is the Volvo ad shown in Figure 17-4, which seeks to position the Volvo as a more sensible car than those that are longer or shorter, and it illustrates and mentions three other brands by name. Comparison advertising is increasingly being used by advertisers of deodorants, toothpastes, tires, and automobiles.

The *remind* category includes such advertising objectives as reminding consumers that the product may be needed in the near future, reminding them where to buy it, keeping it in their minds during off seasons, and maintaining its top-of-the-mind awareness. This category includes *reinforcement advertising,* which seeks to assure current users that they have made the right choice. Automobile companies' ads will often depict satisfied customers enjoying some special feature of the make they bought.

Budget Decision

After setting the advertising objective, the company has to establish advertising budgets for individual products and overall advertising. The company wants to spend the least needed to attain the communicaton and sales goals. This is difficult to determine. Four of the most common methods used to arrive at advertising budgets are described below.

Affordable method. Many companies set the advertising budget on the basis of what they think the company can afford. One advertising executive explained this method as follows: "Why it's simple. First, I go upstairs to the controller and ask how much they can afford to give us this year. He says a million and a half. Later, the boss comes to me and asks how much we should spend, and I say 'Oh, about a million and a half.' Then we have an advertising appropriation."[7]

Setting budgets in this manner in tantamount to saying that the relationship between advertising expenditure and sales results is at best tenuous. If the company has sufficient funds, it should spend them on advertising as a form of insurance.

The basic weakness of the affordable approach is that it leads to a fluctuating advertising budget, which makes it difficult to plan for long-range market development.

Percentage-of-sales method. Many companies set their advertising expenditures at a specified percentage of sales (either current or anticipated) or of the sales price. A railroad company executive said: "We set our appropriation for each year on December 1 of the preceding year. On that date we add our passenger revenue for the next month, and then take 2% of the total for our advertising appropriation for the new year."[8] Automobile companies typically budget a fixed percentage for advertising based on the planned price for each car, and oil companies tend to set the appropriation at some fraction of a cent for each gallon of gasoline sold under their own label.

A number of advantages are claimed for this method. First, the percentage-of-sales method means that advertising expenditures are likely to vary with what the company can "afford." This pleases the more financial-minded members of top management who feel that expenses of all types should bear a close

Figure 17-4
Ad Using a Brand Comparison Appeal

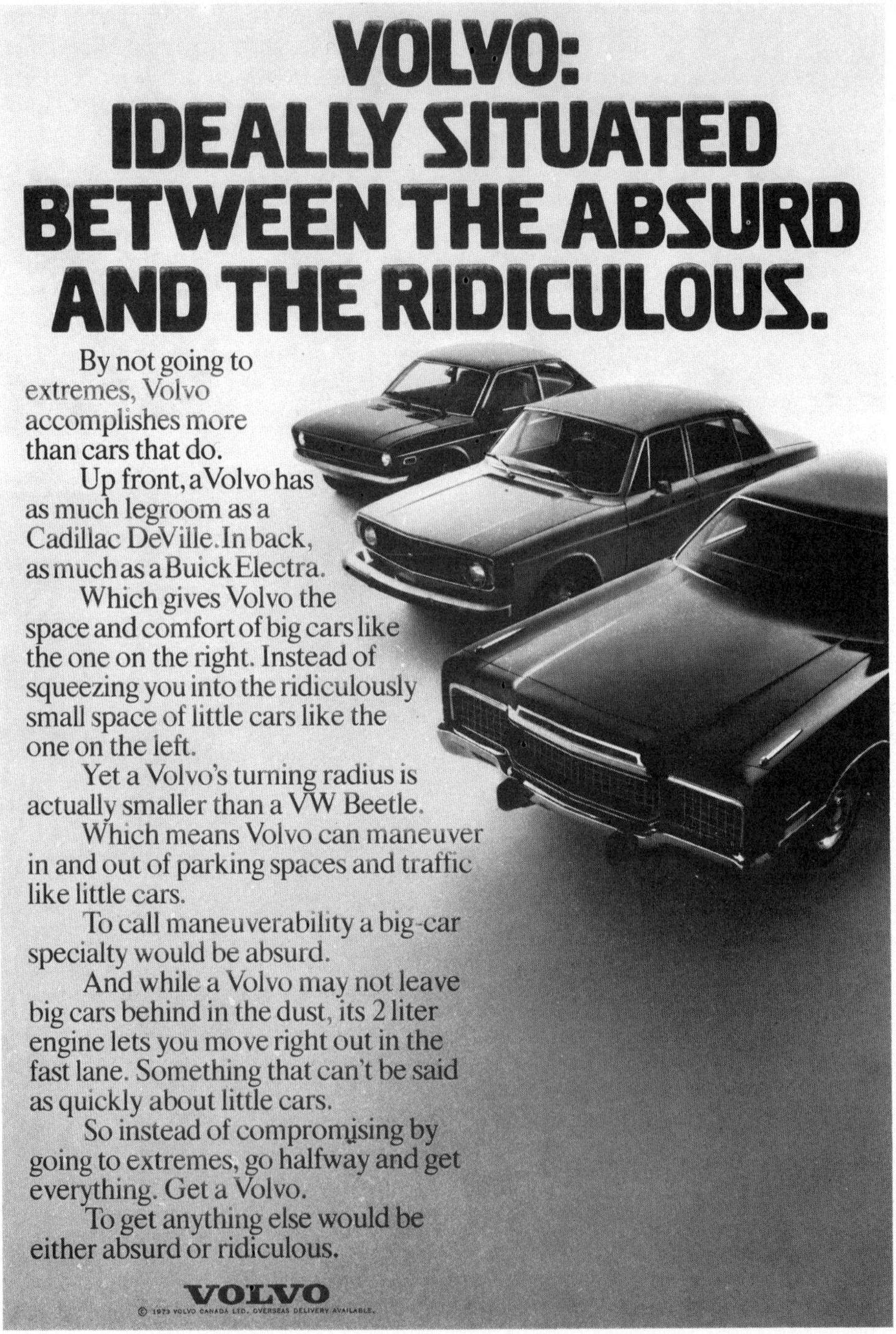
VOLVO: IDEALLY SITUATED BETWEEN THE ABSURD AND THE RIDICULOUS.
By not going to extremes, Volvo accomplishes more than cars that do.
Up front, a Volvo has as much legroom as a Cadillac DeVille. In back, as much as a Buick Electra.
Which gives Volvo the space and comfort of big cars like the one on the right. Instead of squeezing you into the ridiculously small space of little cars like the one on the left.
Yet a Volvo's turning radius is actually smaller than a VW Beetle.
Which means Volvo can maneuver in and out of parking spaces and traffic like little cars.
To call maneuverability a big-car specialty would be absurd.
And while a Volvo may not leave big cars behind in the dust, its 2 liter engine lets you move right out in the fast lane. Something that can't be said as quickly about little cars.
So instead of compromising by going to extremes, go halfway and get everything. Get a Volvo.
To get anything else would be either absurd or ridiculous.
VOLVO
© 1973 VOLVO CANADA LTD. OVERSEAS DELIVERY AVAILABLE.

relationship to the movement of corporate sales over the business cycle. Second, this method encourages management to think in terms of the relationship between advertising cost, selling price, and profit per unit. Third, this method encourages competitive stability to the extent that competing firms spend approximately the same percentage of their sales on advertising.

In spite of these advantages, the percentage-of-sales method has little to justify it. It uses circular reasoning in viewing sales as the cause of advertising rather than as the result. It leads to an appropriation set by the availability of funds rather than by the opportunities. It discourages experimentation with countercyclical advertising or aggressive spending. The dependence of the advertising budget on year-to-year fluctuations in sales militates against the planning of long-range advertising programs. The method does not provide a logical basis for the choice of a specific percentage, except what has been done in the past, or what competitors are doing, or what the costs will be. Finally, it does not encourage the constructive development of advertising appropriations on a product-by-product and territory-by-territory basis but instead suggests that all allocations be made at the same percentage of sales.

Competitive-parity method. Some companies set their advertising budgets specifically to match competitors' outlays—that is, to maintain competitive parity. This thinking is illustrated by the executive who asked a trade source: "Do you have any figures which other companies in the builders' specialties field have used which would indicate what proportion of gross sales should be given over to advertising?"[9]

Two arguments are advanced for this method. One is that competitors' expenditures represent the collective wisdom of the industry. The other is that maintaining a competitive parity helps to prevent advertising wars.

Neither of these arguments is valid. There are no a priori grounds for believing that competition is using more logical methods for determining outlays. Advertising reputations, resources, opportunities, and objectives are likely to differ so much among companies that their budgets are hardly a guide for another firm to follow. Furthermore, there is no evidence that appropriations based on the pursuit of competitive parity do in fact stabilize industry advertising expenditures.

Knowing what competition is spending on advertising is undoubtedly useful information. But it is one thing to know this and another to follow it blindly.

Objective-and-task method. The objective-and-task method calls upon advertisers to develop their budget by (1) defining their advertising objectives as specifically as possible, (2) determining the tasks that must be performed to achieve these objectives, and (3) estimating the costs of performing these tasks. The sum of these costs is the proposed advertising budget.

Ule developed an example to show how the objective-and-task method can be used by a new filter-tip cigarette, Sputniks (name fictitious), to establish the necessary advertising budget.[10] The steps are as follows:

1. *Establish the market-share goal.* The advertiser wants 8 percent of the market. There are 50 million cigarette smokers, which means the company wants to attract 4 million regular Sputnik smokers.

2. *Determine the percent of the market that should be reached by Sputnik advertising.* The advertiser hopes to reach 80 percent (40 million smokers) with his advertising.
3. *Determine the percent of aware smokers that should be persuaded to try the brand.* The advertiser would be pleased if 25 percent of aware smokers, or 10 million smokers, tried Sputnik. This is because he estimates that 40 percent of all triers, or 4 million persons, would become loyal users. This is the market goal.
4. *Determine the number of advertising impressions per one percent trial rate.* The advertiser estimates that 40 advertising impressions (exposures) for every one percent of the population would bring about a 25 percent trial rate.
5. *Determine the number of gross rating points that would have to be purchased.* A gross rating point is one exposure to one percent of the target population. Since the company wants to achieve 40 exposures to 80 percent of the population, it will want to buy 3,200 gross rating points.
6. *Determine the necessary advertising budget on the basis of the average cost of buying a gross rating point.* To expose one percent of the target population to one impression costs an average of $3,277. Therefore 3,200 gross rating points would cost $10,486,400 (= $3,277 × 3,200) in the introductory year.

This method has the advantage of requiring management to spell out its assumptions about the relationship between dollars spent, exposure levels, trial rates, and regular usage. Its major limitation is that the market-share goal is established at the beginning on the basis of what management wants, rather than as a result derived from a profit-maximizing approach to sales.

Other decision models. Advertising researchers have recently proposed more advanced models for setting the advertising budget. These models call for estimating the *advertising sales-response function* showing the relationship between different possible levels of advertising expenditure and resulting sales (see Chapter 4, pp. 110–11). For example, Vidale and Wolfe estimated this function through a statistical analysis of past data on advertising and sales for a range of products.[11] John Little recommended the use of advertising experiments in different markets to discover the impact of varying levels of advertising expenditure on sales.[12] Ackoff and Emshoff used experimental procedures in the case of Budweiser beer and were able to show the Anheuser-Busch Company how it could substantially increase its market share without increasing its ad budget.[13] We expect to see the further use of mathematical models to arrive at sound advertising budgets.

Message Decision

Given the advertising goals and budget, management has to develop a creative strategy. Advertisers and their agencies go through three steps: message generation, message evaluation and selection, and message execution.

Message generation. Message generation involves the developing of a number of alternative messages that will help the product achieve its desired positioning in the market.

Creative people use different methods to generate ideas for effective advertising messages. Many creative people proceed *inductively.* To gather ideas, they talk to consumers, dealers, experts, and competitors. The Schlitz campaign "When you are out of Schlitz you are out of beer" came about because the advertising agency executive overheard a customer at a bar say this to the bartender when the latter said he was out of Schlitz.

Today there is increasing interest in *deductive* frameworks for generating advertising messages. Maloney proposed one possible framework (see Table 17-2). He suggested that buyers may be expecting any of four types of reward from a product: *rational, sensory, social,* or *ego-satisfaction.*[14] And they may visualize these rewards from *results-of-use experience, product-in-use experience,* or *incidental-to-use experience.* Crossing the four types of rewards with the three types of experience generates twelve types of advertising messages.

Message evaluation and selection. The task of selecting the best message out of a large number of possibilities calls for evaluation criteria. Twedt has suggested that contending messages be rated on three scales: *desirability, exclusiveness,* and *believability.*[15] He believes that the communication potency of a message is the product of the three factors because if any of the three has a low rating, the message's communication potency will be greatly reduced.

The message must first say something desirable or interesting about the product. This is not enough, however, since many brands will be making the same claim. Therefore the message must also say something exclusive or distinctive that does not apply to every brand in the product category. Finally, the message must be believable or provable. By asking consumers to rate different messages on desirability, exclusiveness, and believability, these messages can be evaluated for their communication potency.

For example, the March of Dimes was searching for an advertising theme to raise money for its fight against birth defects.[16] A brainstorming session led to over twenty possible messages. A group of young parents were asked to rate each message for interest, distinctiveness, and believability, assigning up to 100 points for each. For example, the message "Five hundred thousand unborn babies die each year from birth defects" scored 70, 60, and 80 on interest, distinctiveness, and believability, while "Your next baby could be born with a birth defect" scored

Table 17-2 Examples of Twelve Types of Appeals

TYPES OF POTENTIALLY REWARDING EXPERIENCE WITH A PRODUCT	POTENTIAL TYPE OF REWARD			
	RATIONAL	SENSORY	SOCIAL	EGO-SATISFACTION
Results-of-Use Experience	1. Get clothes cleaner	2. Settles stomach upset completely	3. When you care enough to serve the best	4. For the skin you deserve to have
Produce-in-Use Experience	5. The flour that needs no sifting	6. Real gusto in a great light beer	7. A deodorant to guarantee social acceptance	8. The shoe for the young executive
Incidental-to-Use Experience	9. The plastic pack keeps the cigarette fresh	10. The portable television that's lighter in weight, easier to lift	11. The furniture that identifies the home of modern people	12. Stereo for the man with discriminating taste

Source: Adapted from John C. Maloney, "Marketing Decisions and Attitude Research," in *Effective Marketing Coordination,* ed. George L. Baker, Jr. (Chicago: American Marketing Association, 1961).

58, 50, and 70. The first message outperforms the second and would be preferred for advertising purposes.

Message execution. The impact of message depends not only upon what is said but also upon how it is said. In fact, message execution can be decisive for those products that are essentially the same, such as detergents, cigarettes, coffee, and beer. The advertiser has to put the message across in a way that will win the target audience's attention and interest.

To guide the development of message execution, the advertiser usually prepares a *copy strategy statement* describing the objective, content, support, and tone of the desired ad. Here is a copy strategy statement for a Pillsbury product called 1869 Brand Biscuits:

- The *objective* of the advertising is to convince biscuit users that now, for the first time, they can buy a canned biscuit that's as good as homemade—Pillsbury's 1869 Brand Biscuits. The *content* consists of emphasizing the following product characteristics of the 1869 Brand Biscuits: (1) they look like homemade biscuits, (2) they have the same texture as homemade biscuits, and (3) they taste like homemade biscuits. *Support* for the "good as homemade" promise will be twofold: (1) 1869 Brand Biscuits are made from a special kind of flour (soft wheat flour) used traditionally to make homemade biscuits but never before used in making canned biscuits, and (2) the use of traditional American biscuit recipes. The *tone* of the advertising will be a news announcement, yet tempered by a warm, reflective mood emanating from a look back at traditional American baking quality.

It is the task of the creative people to find a *style,* a *tone, words,* and *format factors* that make for effective message execution.

Any message can be put across in different *execution styles,* such as

1. *Slice-of-life.* This shows one or more persons using the product in a normal setting. A family might be shown at the dinner table expressing satisfaction with a new brand of biscuits.
2. *Life style.* This emphasizes how a product fits in with a life style. The ad for a certain brand of Scotch shows a handsome middle-aged man holding a glass of Scotch in one hand and steering his yacht with the other.
3. *Fantasy.* This creates a fantasy around the product or its use. Revlon's ad for its Jontue fragrance features a barefoot woman wearing a chiffon dress and shows her coming out of an old French barn, crossing a meadow, and confronting a handsome young man on a white steed, who carries her away.
4. *Mood or image.* This builds an evocative mood or image around the product, such as beauty, love, or serenity. No claim is made about the product except through suggestion. Many cigarette ads, such as those for Salem and Newport cigarettes, create moods.
5. *Musical.* This shows one or more persons or cartoon characters singing a song or jingle involving the product. Many cola ads have used this format.
6. *Personality symbol.* This creates a character that represents or personifies the product. The character might be *animated* (Green Giant, Cap'n Crunch, Mr. Clean) or *real* (Marlboro man, Morris the Cat).
7. *Technical expertise.* This shows the care that the company exercises and the experience it has had in selecting the ingredients for this product or in manufacturing the product. Thus Hills Brothers shows one of its buyers carefully selecting the coffee beans, and Italian Swiss Colony emphasizes the many years of experience the company has had in winemaking.

8. *Scientific evidence.* This presents survey or scientific evidence that the brand is preferred to or outperforms one or more other brands. For years, Crest toothpaste has featured scientific evidence to convince toothpaste buyers of the superior anticavity-fighting properties of Crest.
9. *Testimonial evidence.* This features a highly credible or likable source endorsing the product. It could be a celebrity like O. J. Simpson (Hertz Rent-a-Cars) or ordinary people saying how much they like the product.

The communicator must also choose an effective *tone* for the ad. Procter & Gamble advertising, for example, is consistently positive in its tone: Its ads say something superlatively positive about the product in the clearest possible way. Humor is avoided so as not to take attention away from the message. On the other hand, Volkswagen's ads for its famous "Beetle" automobile typically took on a humorous and self-deprecating tone ("the Ugly Bug").

Words that are memorable and attention-getting must be found. This is nowhere more apparent than in the development of headlines and slogans to lead the reader into an ad. There are six basic types of headlines: *news* ("New Boom and More Inflation Ahead . . . and What You Can Do about It"); *question* ("Have You Had It Lately?"); *narrative* ("They Laughed When I Sat Down at the Piano, but When I Started to Play!"); *command* ("Don't Buy Until You Try All Three"); *1-2-3 ways* ("12 Ways to Save on Your Income Tax"); and *how-what-why* ("Why They Can't Stop Buying").[17] Look at the care that airlines have lavished on finding the right way to describe their airline as safe without explicitly mentioning safety as an issue: "The Friendly Skies of United" (United); "The Wings of Man" (Eastern); and "The World's Most Experienced Airline" (Pan American).

Format elements such as ad size, color, and illustration can make a difference in an ad's impact, as well as its cost. A minor rearrangement or alteration of mechanical elements within the advertisement can improve its attention-gaining power by several points. Larger-size ads gain more attention, though not necessarily by as much as their difference in cost. The use of four-color illustrations instead of black and white increases ad effectiveness and also ad cost.

Media Decision

The advertiser's next task is to find efficient advertising media to carry the advertising message. The steps are (1) deciding on reach, frequency, and impact; (2) choosing among major media types; (3) selecting specific media vehicles; and (4) deciding on media timing.

Deciding on reach, frequency, and impact. Before selecting media, the advertiser must determine the desired reach, frequency, and impact needed to achieve the advertising objectives:

1. *Reach.* The advertiser must decide on how many persons in the target audience should be exposed to the ad campaign during the specified period of time. For example, the advertiser might seek to reach 70 percent of the target audience during the first year.
2. *Frequency.* The advertiser must also decide on how many times the average person in the target audience should be exposed to the message within the specified time period. For example, the advertiser might seek an average exposure frequency of

three. Krugman has argued that fewer than three exposures to a message may be insufficient to have an effect, and more than three exposures may be wasteful.[18]

3. *Impact.* The advertiser must also decide on the quality of impact that the exposure should have. Messages on television typically have more impact than messages on radio because television stimulates sight and sound, not just sound. Within a media form such as magazines, the same message in one magazine (say, *Playboy*) may deliver more credibility than in another (say, *Police Gazette*). For example, the advertiser may seek a quality exposure of 1.5 where 1.0 is the value of an exposure in an average medium.

Now suppose the advertiser's product might appeal to a market of 1 million consumers. The goal is to reach 700,000 consumers (= 1,000,000 × .7). Since the average consumer will receive three exposures, 2,100,000 exposures (= 700,000 × 3) must be bought. Since high-impact exposures of 1.5 are desired, a rated number of exposures of 3,150,000 (= 2,100,000 × 1.5) must be bought. If a thousand exposures of this impact cost $10, the advertising budget will have to be $31,500 (=3,150 × $10). In general, the more reach, frequency, and impact the advertiser seeks, the higher the advertising budget will have to be.

Choosing among major media types. The media planner has to examine the major media types for their capacity to deliver reach, frequency, and impact. Profiles of the major advertising media are shown in Table 17-3. The major media types, in order of their advertising volume, are *newspapers, television, direct mail, radio, magazines,* and *outdoor.* Each medium has certain advantages and limitations. Professional media planners make their choice among these major media types by considering several variables, the most important ones being

1. *Target audience media habits.* For example, radio and television are the most effective media for reaching teen-agers.
2. *Product.* A product like women's dresses might be shown to advantage in color magazines, and Polaroid cameras might best be demonstrated on television. Media types have different potentialities for demonstration, visualization, explanation, believability, and color.
3. *Message.* A message announcing a major sale tomorrow will require radio or newspapers. A message containing a great deal of technical data might require specialized magazines or mailings.
4. *Cost.* Television is very expensive, and newspaper advertising is inexpensive. What counts, of course, is the cost-per-thousand exposures rather than the total cost.

Assumptions about media impact and cost must be reexamined at regular intervals. For a long time, television enjoyed the supreme position in the media mix, and magazines and other media were neglected. Then media researchers began to notice television's reduced effectiveness due to increased clutter. Advertisers have been beaming shorter and more numerous commercials at the television audience, resulting in poorer attention and impact. Furthermore, television advertising costs have been rising faster than other media costs. Several companies have found that a combination of print ads and television commercials often does a better job than television commercials alone. This illustrates how advertisers must periodically reevaluate different media to determine what they are getting for their money.

Table 17-3
Profiles of Major Media Types

MEDIUM	VOLUME IN BILLIONS (1978)	EXAMPLE OF COST (1977)	ADVANTAGES	LIMITATIONS
Newspapers	$11.1	$9,975 one page, weekday *Chicago Tribune*	Flexibility; timeliness; good local market coverage; broad acceptance; high believability	Short life; poor reproduction quality; small "pass-along" audience
Television	$7.6	$2,700 for thirty seconds of prime time in Chicago	Combines sight, sound, and motion; appealing to the senses; high attention; high reach	High absolute cost; high clutter; fleeting exposure; less audience selectivity
Direct mail	$5.3	$950 for the names and addresses of 19,000 veterinarians	Audience selectivity; flexibility; no ad competition within the same medium: personalization	Relatively high cost; "junk mail" image
Radio	$2.6	$179 for one minute of prime time in Chicago	Mass use; high geographic and demographic selectivity; low cost	Audio presentation only; lower attention than television; nonstandardized rate structures; fleeting exposure
Magazines	$2.2	$30,915 one page, four color in *Newsweek*	High geographic and demographic selectivity; credibility and prestige; high-quality reproduction; long life; good pass-along readership	Long ad purchase lead time; some waste circulation; no guarantee of position
Outdoor	$0.4	$824 prime billboard cost per month in Chicago	Flexibility; high repeat exposure; low cost; low competition	No audience selectivity; creative limitations

Note: The volume in billions in column 2 is from *Advertising Age,* January 8, 1979, p. S-8. Miscellaneous media add another $9 billion, making the total $38.2.

On the basis of these characteristics, the media planner has to decide on how to allocate the given budget to the major media types. For example, a firm launching a new biscuit mix may decide to allocate $3 million to daytime network television, $2 million to women's magazines, and $1 million to daily newspapers in twenty major markets.

Selecting specific media vehicles. The next step is to choose the specific media vehicles within each media type that would produce the desired response in the most cost-effective way. Consider the category of women's magazines, for example, which includes *Cosmopolitan, Family Circle, Ladies' Home Journal, McCall's, Ms, Playgirl, Redbook, Seventeen,* and *Women's Day.* The media planner turns to several volumes put out by Standard Rate and Data that provide circulation and costs for different ad sizes, color options, ad positions, and quantities of insertions. Beyond this, the media planner evaluates the different magazines on qualitative characteristics such as credibility, prestige, geographical editioning, occupational editioning, reproduction quality, editorial climate, lead time, and psychological impact. The media planner makes a final judgment as to which specific vehicles will deliver the best reach, frequency, and impact for the money.

THE COST-PER-THOUSAND CRITERION

Media planners calculate the *cost per thousand persons* reached by a particular vehicle. If a full-page, four-color advertisement in *Newsweek* costs $30,000 and *Newsweek's* estimated readership is 6 million persons, then the cost of reaching each one thousand persons is $5. The same advertisement in *Business Week* may cost $18,000 but reach only 2 million persons, at a cost per thousand of $9. The media planner would rank the various magazines according to cost per thousand and would initially favor those magazines with the lowest cost per thousand.

The cost-per-thousand criterion provides a crude starting measure of a media vehicle's exposure value. Several adjustments have to be applied to this initial measure. First, the measure should be adjusted for *audience quality.* For a baby lotion advertisement, a magazine read by one million young mothers would have an exposure value of one million, but if read by one million old men would have a zero exposure value. Second, the exposure value should be adjusted for the *audience attention probability.* Readers of *Vogue,* for example, pay more attention to ads than readers of *Newsweek.* Third, the exposure value should be adjusted for the *editorial quality* (prestige and believability) that one magazine might have over another.

Media planners are increasingly using more sophisticated measures of media effectiveness and employing them in mathematical models for arriving at the best media mix. Many advertising agencies use a computer program to select the initial media, and then make further improvements based on subjective factors that could not have been put into the model.[19]

Deciding on media timing. The advertiser has to decide how to schedule the purchased advertising over the year (macroscheduling) and within shorter segments of time (microscheduling).

MACROSCHEDULING

Here the challenge is to strategically schedule the advertising expenditures over the year in response to such factors as the seasonal pattern of industry sales and expected competitive plans or developments. Suppose industry sales of a particular product peak in December and wane in March. Any individual seller in this market has three broad options. The firm can vary its advertising expenditures to follow the seasonal pattern; it can vary its advertising expenditures to oppose the seasonal pattern; or it can hold its expenditures constant throughout the year. The vast majority of firms tend to pursue a policy of seasonal rather than constant or counterseasonal advertising. Even here, the firm faces options. It has to decide whether its advertising expenditures should lead or coincide with seasonal sales. It also has to decide whether its advertising expenditures should be more intense, proportional, or less intense than the seasonal amplitude of sales.

MICROSCHEDULING

Here the challenge is to allocate the purchased advertising over a short period of time to obtain the maximum impact. Suppose the advertiser wants to schedule thirty spot radio announcements within the month of September and is trying to choose the particular times.

One way to classify the multitude of possibilities is shown in Figure 17-5. The left side of the figure shows that advertising messages for the month can be concentrated in a small part of the month ("burst" advertising), dispersed continuously throughout the month, or dispersed intermittently throughout the month. The top side of the figure shows that advertising messages can be beamed with a level frequency, a rising frequency, a falling frequency, or an alternating frequency. The advertiser's problem is to decide which of these twelve general patterns would be the most effective distribution plan for the messages.

The most effective pattern depends upon the advertising communication objectives in relation to the nature of the product, target customers, distribution channels, and other marketing factors. Consider the following cases:

- A *retailer* wants to announce a preseason sale of skiing equipment. She recognizes that only certain people will be interested in the message. Furthermore she recognizes that the target buyers only need to hear the message once or twice to know whether they are interested. Her objective is to maximize the *reach* of the message, not the *repetition*. She decides to concentrate the messages of the days of

Figure 17-5
Classification of Advertising Timing Patterns

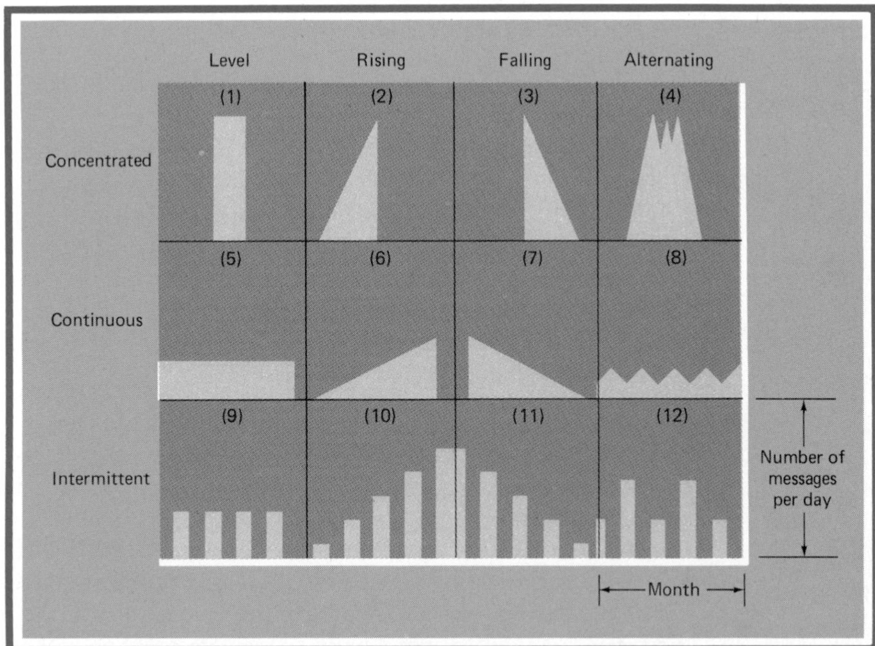

the sale at a level rate, but varying the time of day to avoid the same audiences. She uses pattern (1).

A *muffler manufacturer-distributor* wants to keep his name before the public. Yet he does not want his advertising to be too continuous because only 3 to 5 percent of the cars on the road need a new muffler at any given time. He has therefore chosen to use intermittent advertising. Furthermore, he recognizes that Fridays are paydays for many potential buyers, and this would influence their interest in replacing a worn-out muffler. So he sponsors a few messages on a midweek day and more messages on Friday. He uses pattern (12).

The timing pattern should take into account three general factors. *Buyer turnover* expresses the rate at which new buyers appear in the market; the higher this rate, the more continuous the advertising ought to be to reach these new buyers. *Purchase frequency* is the number of times during the period that the buyer buys the product; the higher the purchase frequency, the more continuous the advertising ought to be to keep the brand on the buyer's mind. The *forgetting rate* is the rate at which the buyer forgets the brand in the absence of stimuli; the higher the forgetting rate, the more continuous the advertising ought to be to keep the brand in the buyer's mind.

In launching a product, advertisers must make a choice between ad continuity and ad pulsing. *Continuity* is achieved by scheduling exposures evenly within a given time period. *Pulsing* (or flighting) refers to scheduling exposures unevenly over the same time period. Thus fifty-two exposures could be scheduled continuously at one a week throughout the year, or flighted in several concentrated bursts. Those who favor pulsing feel that (1) the audience will learn the message more thoroughly and (2) money could be saved. Anheuser-Busch's research indicated that Budweiser could suspend advertising in a particular market and experience no adverse sales effect for at least a year and a half.[20] At that point, the company could introduce a six-month burst of advertising and restore the previous growth rate. This analysis led it to adopt a pulsing advertising strategy.

When the decisions are made on the media vehicles and their timing, they should be displayed in a chart to give a bird's-eye view of the total media schedule. According to the sample media schedule shown in Figure 17-6, "As the World Turns" will be used each weekday except for the summer months; "Hollywood Squares" will be used three times a week throughout the year; *Family Circle* will be used at the beginning of each month except for the summer months; and the *Reader's Digest* will be used every month.

Campaign Evaluation

The planned advertising campaign should be evaluated before, during, and after its launch. Researchers have developed several techniques to measure the communication and sales effects of advertising.

Communication-effect research. Communication-effect research seeks to discover whether the advertising is achieving the intended communication effects. There are various ways to evaluate the communication effectiveness of, say, an individual ad. Called *copy testing,* it can occur before an ad is put into actual media and after it has been printed or broadcast. The purpose of *ad pretesting* is

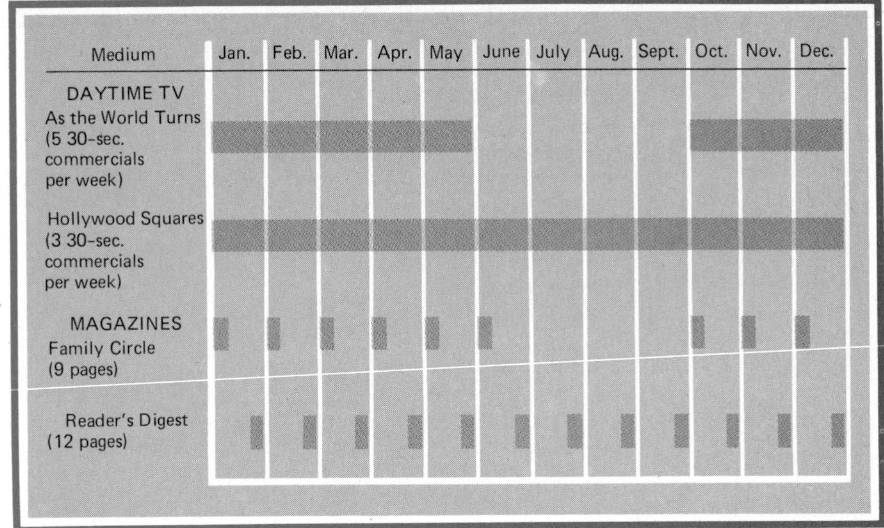

Figure 17-6
A Sample Media Schedule

Source: S. Watson Dunn and Arnold M. Barban, *Advertising: Its Role in Modern Marketing,* 4th ed. (Hinsdale, Ill.: Dryden Press, 1978), p. 523.

to make improvements in the advertising copy to the fullest extent possible prior to its release. There are three major methods of ad pretesting:

1. *Direct ratings.* Here a panel of target consumers or advertising experts examine alternative ads and fill out rating questionnaires. Sometimes a single question is raised, such as "Which of these ads do you think would influence you most to buy the product?" Or a more elaborate form consisting of several rating scales may be used, calling for a rating of the ad's attention strength, read-through strength, cognitive strength, affective strength, and behavioral strength. The underlying theory is that an effective ad must score high on all of these properties if it is ultimately to stimulate buying action. Too often ads are evaluated only on their attention- or comprehension-creating abilities. At the same time, it must be appreciated that direct rating methods are less reliable than harder evidence of an ad's actual impact on target consumers. Direct rating scales help primarily to screen out poor ads rather than identify great ads.
2. *Portfolio tests.* Here respondents are given a dummy portfolio of ads and are told to take as much time as they want to read them. After putting them down, the respondents are asked to recall the ads they saw—unaided or aided by the interviewer—and to play back as much as they can about each ad. The results are taken to indicate an ad's ability to stand out and its intended message to be understood.
3. *Laboratory tests.* Some researchers assess the potential effect of an ad through measuring physiological reactions—heart beat, blood pressure, pupil dilation, perspiration—through such equipment as galvanometers, tachistoscopes, size-distance tunnels, and pupil dilation measuring equipment. These physiological tests at best measure the attention-getting power of an ad rather than any impact it has on beliefs, attitudes, or intentions.

There are two popular *ad posttesting* methods, the purpose of which is to assess the actual communication impact of the ad after it has appeared in media:

1. *Recall tests.* Recall tests involve finding persons who are regular users of the media vehicle and asking them to recall advertisers and products contained in the issue

under study. They are asked to recall or play back eveything they can remember. The administrator may or may not aid them in their recall. Recall scores are prepared on the basis of their responses and are used to indicate the power of the ad to be noticed and retained.

2. *Recognition tests.* Recognition tests call for sampling the readers of a given issue of, say, a magazine, asking them to point out what they recognize as having seen and/or read. For each ad, three different Starch readership scores (named after Daniel Starch, who provides the leading service) are prepared from the recognition data: (a) *noted,* the percentage of readers of the magazine who say they have previously seen the advertisement in the particular magazine; (b) *seen/associated,* the percentage of readers who say they have seen or read any part of the ad that clearly indicates the names of the product or service of the advertiser; and (c) *read most,* the percentage of readers who not only looked at the advertisement but say that they read more than half of the total written material in the ad. The Starch organization also furnishes *adnorms,* that is, the average scores for each product class for the year, and separately for men and women for each magazine, to enable advertisers to evaluate their ads in relation to competitors' ads.

Sales-effect research. Communication-effect advertising research undoubtedly helps advertisers improve the quality of message content and presentation, but it reveals little as to how much sales may be affected, if at all. What sales conclusion can the advertiser draw in learning that its recent campaign has increased brand awareness by 20 percent and brand preference by 10 percent? What has the advertiser learned about the sales productivity of its advertising dollar and therefore how much to spend?

The sales effect of advertising will generally be more difficult to measure than the communication effect. The reason is that sales are influenced by many factors besides advertising, such as the product's features, price, and availability and competitors' actions. The fewer or more controllable these other factors, the easier it is to measure advertising's impact on sales. Advertising sales effectiveness is easiest to measure in mail-order situations and hardest to measure in brand or corporate-image-building advertising. Efforts to measure the sales impact of advertising usually follow one of two approaches.

The *historical approach* involves the researcher in fitting past company sales to past company advertising expenditures on a current or lagged basis using advanced statistical techniques. For example, Montgomery and Silk examined the impact of three sales techniques—direct mail, samples and literature, and journal advertising—on the sales of a pharmaceutical firm.[21] Their statistical results indicated that the firm was overdoing direct mail and underspending on journal advertising in allocating its advertising funds.

Other researchers use *experimental design* to measure the sales impact of advertising. Du Pont, for example, was one of the earliest companies to design an experiment to measure the effects of varying levels of advertising expenditure on sales. In the case of Du Pont paint, management thought that the advertising budget was too low.[22] It divided fifty-six sales territories into high, average, and low market-share territories. Within each group Du Pont spent the normal amount for advertising in one-third of the group; in another third, two and one-half times the normal amount; and in the remaining third, four times the normal amount. At the end of the experimental period, Du Pont was able to estimate how much extra sales were created by higher levels of advertising

EXHIBIT 17-4

ADVERTISING DECISIONS AND PUBLIC POLICY

The company must develop its advertising program so that it does not invite charges of deception or discrimination. Here are the major issues.

False advertising. Advertisers must avoid making false claims, such as citing a fabricated scientific study or asserting that a product cures something that it does not cure. Advertisers must also avoid false demonstrations, such as using plexiglass instead of sandpaper in a commercial to demonstrate that a razor blade can shave sandpaper.

Deceptive advertising. Advertisers must avoid creating ads that have the capacity to deceive, even though no one may be deceived. Thus a floor wax cannot be advertised as giving six-months' protection unless this is under typical conditions, and a diet bread cannot be advertised as having fewer calories if the only reason is that the slices are thinner. The problem is one of distinguishing between deception in advertising and puffery, which is more normal.

Bait-and-switch advertising. Bait-and-switch advertising, where the seller attracts buyers' interest on false pretenses, comes under FTC surveillance. For example, the seller offers or advertises an exceptionally good buy such as a $59 sewing machine and then finds some excuse for not selling the advertised item but selling something else. This includes refusing to sell the product, disparaging its features, demonstrating a defective product, or imposing unreasonable delivery dates or service terms.

Promotional allowances and services. In planning its advertising program, the company must be sure to make promotional allowances and services available to all customers on proportionately equal terms.

expenditure. Du Pont found that higher levels of advertising expenditure led to increased sales at a diminishing rate; and that the sales response was less pronounced in the areas where Du Pont had a higher market share.

Advertising clearly involves major sums of money that can easily be misspent by companies that fail to take the proper steps of defining the advertising objectives; making careful budget, message, and media decisions; and evaluating the campaign results. Advertising is also an area of considerable public attention and scrutiny, stemming from its power to influence life styles and opinions. In recent years, advertising has been subjected to increasing regulation designed to ensure that it performs responsibly. If advertisers are to be effective in their use of advertising, they must be aware of public policy developments affecting advertising. (See Exhibit 17-4.)

sales promotion

Sales promotion comprises a wide variety of tactical promotional tools of a short-term incentive nature designed to stimulate earlier and/or stronger target market response. These tools can be subclassified into tools for *consumer promotion* (e.g., samples, coupons, money-refund offers, prices-off, premiums, contests, trading stamps, demonstrations), *trade promotion* (e.g., buying allowances, free goods, merchandise allowances, cooperative advertising, push money, dealer sales contests), and *sales-force promotion* (e.g., bonuses, contests, sales rallies).

Although sales promotion tools are a motley collection, they have two distinctive qualities:

1. *Insistent presence.* Many sales promotion tools have an attention-getting, sometimes urgent, quality that can break through habits of buyer inertia toward a particular product. They tell the buyers of a chance that they won't have again to get something special. This appeals to a broad spectrum of buyers, although particularly to the economy-minded, with the disadvantage that this type of buyer tends to be less loyal to any particular brand in the long run.
2. *Product demeaning.* Some of these tools suggest that the seller is anxious for the sale. If they are used too frequently or carelessly, they may lead buyers to wonder whether the brand is desirable or reasonably priced.

Sales promotion tools are used by a large variety of organizations, including manufacturers, distributors, retailers, trade associations, and various nonprofit institutions. As examples of the last, churches sponsor bingo games, theatre parties, testimonial dinners, and raffles.

Sales promotion activities have grown rapidly in recent years. Between 1969 and 1976, sales promotion expenditures increased at an average rate of 9.4 percent per year compared with 5.4 percent for advertising and were estimated at over $30 billion in 1976.[23] Furthermore, sales promotion expenditures are expected to continue to grow faster than advertising expenditures.

Various factors have contributed to the rapid growth of sales promotion, particularly in consumer markets.[24] Internal factors include the following: (1) promotion has become more acceptable to top management as an effective means to stimulate sales; (2) more product managers are qualified to use sales promotion tools; and (3) product managers are under greater pressure to obtain quick sales response. External factors include the following: (1) the number of brands has increased; (2) competitors have become more promotion-minded; (3) inflation and recession have made consumers more deal-oriented; (4) trade pressure for more manufacturers' deals has grown; and (5) there is a belief that advertising efficiency has declined due to costs, media clutter, and government control.

No single purpose can be advanced for sales promotion tools, since they are so varied in form. A free sample stimulates consumer trial, while a free management advisory service cements a long-term relationship with a retailer. Overall, sales promotion techniques make three contributions to exchange relationships: (1) *communication*—they gain attention and usually provide information that will, it is hoped, lead to trying the product; (2) *incentive*—they incorporate some concession, inducement, or contribution that is designed to represent value to the receiver; and (3) *invitation*—they include a distinct invitation to engage in the transaction now.

Incentive promotions are adopted by sellers to attract nonbrand users to try the brand and/or to reward brand-loyal users for their loyalty. Since both types of buyers will buy during the promotion period, both purposes are served, although the primary purpose is usually to attract nonbrand users to the brand. The nonbrand users are of two types, those who are loyal to other brands and those who tend to be brand switchers. Incentive promotions primarily attract the brand switchers because the brand-loyal users of other brands do not always notice or act on the promotion. Since brand switchers are what they are, sales promotions are unlikely to turn them into brand-loyal users. Incentive promotions used in markets of high brand similarity produce a high sales response in the short run but little permanent gain. In markets of high brand dissimilarity, incentive promotions are more likely to alter market shares permanently.

Sellers usually think of sales promotion as an activity designed to break down brand loyalty, and advertising as an activity designed to build up brand loyalty. Therefore an important issue for marketing managers is how to divide the budget between promotion and advertising. Companies can be found dividing their funds in a ratio of anywhere from 20:80 to 80:20 on sales promotion and advertising, respectively. This ratio has been rising over the past several years in response to the consumers' heightened sensitivity to price. Management should resist letting this ratio get too high. When a brand is on deal too much of the time, the dealing dilutes the brand image. The consumer begins to think of it as a cheap brand. No one knows when this happens, but probably there is risk in putting a well-known brand on deal more than 30 percent of the time. In fact, dominant brands should use dealing infrequently, since most of it only gives a subsidy to current users.

Prentice has suggested that sales promotion tools can be divided into two groups, those that are "consumer franchise building" and those that are not.[25] The former impart a selling message along with the deal, as in the instances of free samples, coupons when they include a selling message, and premiums when they are related to the product. Sales promotion tools that are not consumer franchise building include price-off packs, consumer premiums not related to a product, contests and sweepstakes, consumer refund offers, and trade allowances. Sellers are urged to use consumer franchise-building promotions whenever possible because they enlarge the consumers' understanding of the brand.

Ultimately, sales promotion seems most effective when used in conjunction with advertising. "In one study, point-of-purchase displays related to current TV commercials were found to produce 15 percent more sales than similar displays not related to such advertising. In another, a heavy sampling approach along with TV advertising proved more successful than either TV alone or TV with coupons in introducing a product."[26]

Major Decisions in Sales Promotion

A company that is considering sales promotion must (1) establish the sales promotion objectives, (2) select the sales promotion tools, (3) develop the sales promotion program, (4) pretest the sales promotion program, (5) implement and control the sales promotion program, and (6) evaluate the sales promotion results.

Establishing the Sales Promotion Objectives

Sales promotion objectives are derived from basic *marketing communication objectives,* which in turn are derived from more basic *marketing objectives* developed for the product. Within this context, the specific objectives set for sales promotion will vary with the type of target market. For *consumers,* objectives include encouraging more usage and purchase of larger-size units by users, building trial among nonusers, and attracting trial by other brand users. For *retailers,* objectives include inducing retailer stocking of new items or larger volume, encouraging off-season buying, encouraging stocking of related items, offsetting competitive promotions, building brand loyalty of retailer, and gaining entry into new retail outlets. For the *sales force,* objectives include encouraging support of a new product or model, encouraging more prospecting, and stimulating sales in off-season.

Selecting the Sales Promotion Tools

A wide range of sales promotion tools are available to accomplish the various objectives. The selection decision must take into account the type of market, sales promotion objectives, competitive conditions, and cost-effectiveness of each tool. The main tools are described below.

Samples, coupons, price packs, premiums, and trading stamps. These techniques make up the bulk of consumer promotions and account for more sales promotion dollars than any other set of sales promotion tools. The first of these, *samples,* are offers of a free sample or trial of a product to consumers.[27] The sample might be delivered door to door, received in the mail, picked up in a store, found attached to another product, or featured in an advertising offer. Sampling is the most effective and most expensive way to introduce a new product. For example, Lever Brothers had so much confidence in the superiority of its new mouthwash called Signal that it decided to distribute a free sample to two out of three American households at a cost of $15 million in 1978. The samples are typically offered in "trial-size" containers rather than in regular sizes. A recent trend is for manufacturers to introduce these trial-size containers into stores to be sold at a low price. These, of course, are not technically samples.

Coupons are certificates that entitle the bearer to a stated saving on the purchase of a specific product. Over 40 billion coupons were distributed in 1976, with an average value of fourteen cents each. Coupons can be mailed, enclosed in other products, or inserted in ads. They are a good way to stimulate sales of a mature brand as well as induce early trial of a new brand. P&G's plan for breaking into the Pittsburgh market in 1977 with its Folger brand of coffee included a mailed thirty-five-cent discount coupon on a one-pound can and a coupon-in-can worth ten cents, in addition to extensive area television and a strong discount to retailers. Coupon redemption rates vary, depending on the value of the coupon and the way it is distributed, being highest when carried in newspapers (40 percent), in/on packs (30 percent), in magazines (14 percent), and by direct mail (11 percent).[28]

Price packs (also called cents-off deals) are offers to consumers of a certain amount of money off the regular price of a product, flagged on the label or package. The price pack may take the form of a *reduced-price pack,* which is single packages sold at a reduced price; a *multiple pack,* which is two or more packages sold at a reduced price (such as two for the price of one); or a *banded pack,* which is two related products banded together (such as a toothbrush and toothpaste). Price packs are very effective in stimulating short-term sales, even more so than coupons.

Premiums are items of merchandise that are offered at a relatively low cost or free as an incentive or bonus to purchasers of a particular product. A *with-pack premium* accompanies the product inside (in-pack) or outside (on-pack) the package. The package itself, if a *reusable container,* may serve as a premium. A *free-in-the-mail premium* is an item that the company will mail to consumers who send in a request for it together with a proof of purchase, such as a boxtop. A *self-liquidating premium* is an item that the company will sell at well below its normal retail price to consumers who request it; it is called self-liquidating because the company usually recovers the cost of the sales promotion. In March 1975 the Continental Illinois National Bank and Trust Company of Chicago offered a calculator for $8.95 to anyone depositing $300 in a new or previously held savings account. In the first two weeks alone, the premium attracted thirty-five hundred new savings accounts, well paying for itself. A recent trend is for manufacturers to offer consumers all kinds of premiums bearing the company's name. The Budweiser fan can order T-shirts, hot-air balloons, and hundreds of other items with Bud's name on them.[29]

Trading stamps are a special type of premium in which consumers receive stamps from retailers in making purchases and can redeem them for merchandise through premium catalogs or stamp redemption centers. These stamps are used by grocery stores, gasoline stations, department stores, and so on. The first merchants who adopt them usually attract new business and force the other merchants to adopt them defensively. Eventually they become a burden to everyone and some merchants start dropping them and offer lower prices instead. Their popularity fluctuates over the years.[30]

Point-of-purchase displays and demonstrations. Called POP, this sales promotion technique covers displays and demonstrations that take place at the point of purchase or sale, that is, next to the merchandise. Thus a large five-foot-high cardboard display figure of Cap'n Crunch carrying hundreds of Cap'n Crunch cereal boxes and located near the store's entrance is an example. Unfortunately, many retailers do not like to handle the thousands of displays, signs, and posters that they receive from manufacturers each year, even when the manufacturer's sales force offers to set them up. The retailers' space is too limited and they receive too many, thus leading to a negative attitude. Manufacturers are responding by creating better-quality POP materials and tying them in with television or print messages for reinforcement. The elaborate L'eggs panty hose display is one of the most creative in the history of POP materials and a major factor in the success of this brand.[31]

Trade promotion. Manufacturers have worked out a number of techniques for securing the cooperation of wholesalers and retailers. These middlemen require some benefit, usually reflected in profit or personal gain. Manufacturers may offer a *buying allowance,* which is a short-term offer of cents-off on each case purchased during a stated period of time. The purpose is to encourage dealers to buy an item or quantity that they might not buy otherwise. It is often used to introduce a new product and compensate buyers for the trouble of adding it to their stock. The buyers can use the buying allowance for immediate profit, advertising, or price redemptions. They may receive the buying allowance as a check ("bill-back") or as a deduction from the face of the invoice ("off-invoice").

Or manufacturers may offer a *merchandise allowance,* which is a short-term contractual agreement to compensate the dealer for featuring the manufacturer's products. An *advertising allowance* compensates dealers for featuring the manufacturer's product in their newspaper ads, radio programs, or handbills. A *display allowance* compensates them for carrying or building special displays of the product. The compensation is made upon "proof of performance."

Or manufacturers may offer *free goods,* which are extra cases of merchandise offered to middlemen who buy a certain quantity. Another technique is to offer *push money* (also called premium money, PMs, or spiff), which is cash or gifts to dealers or their sales force to push the manufacturer's goods. For example, a manufacturer may offer a dealer's salespersons a PM of $10 for each appliance sold. Many retailers do not like push money, and it can also be expensive for manufacturers because they pay on all of their sales, whether the salespersons pushed their products or not.

Manufacturers also make use of *specialty advertising,* which consists of gift items that carry the company's name and help to reinforce a relationship between the manufacturer and middlemen. Advertising specialties include pens, pencils, calendars, paperweights, matchbooks, memo pads, ashtrays, yardsticks, and many other items. These specialties are either mailed to the middlemen or delivered in person by sales representatives. They generally succeed in enhancing the manufacturer's image in the middlemen's minds.[32]

Business conventions and trade shows. Industry trade associations organize annual or more frequent conventions for their members and typically sponsor a trade show at the same time. Those who sell to this particular industry are invited to participate in the trade show to display and demonstrate their products to association members. Over fifty-six hundred trade shows take place every year, drawing approximately 80 million people. The vendors who participate in the trade show expect several benefits, including developing new sales leads, maintaining customer contact, introducing new products, meeting new customers, and selling more to present customers.[33]

Contests, sweepstakes, and games. These devices present to consumers, dealers, or sales forces an opportunity to win something—such as cash prizes, trips, or goods—as a result of luck or extra effort. In the consumer area, a *contest* calls for consumers to submit an entry—a jingle, estimate, suggestion—to be examined by a panel of judges who will select the best entries. A *sweepstake* calls for consumers to merely submit their names to be included in a drawing of prize winners. A *game* calls for consumers to receive something every time they make a purchase—such as bingo numbers, missing letters—which may or may not help them win a prize. On the other hand, *sales contests* describe contests aimed at dealers or the sales force that take the form of a competition to induce them to redouble their sales efforts over a stated period, with prizes going to the top performers.

Developing the Sales Promotion Program

A sales promotion program involves more than selecting one or more promotions. The marketer must make some additional decisions to define the full promotion program. The main decisions are size of incentive, conditions for participation, distribution vehicle for promotion, duration of promotion, timing of promotion, and overall budget for promotion.

Size of incentive. The marketer has to determine the most cost-effective size of the incentive. A certain minimum incentive size will be necessary if the promotion is to be successful. Beyond this, a higher incentive level will produce more sales response, but at a diminishing rate. Some of the large consumer-packaged-goods firms have a sales promotion manager who keeps records on the effectiveness of different promotions used throughout the company and who correlates their incentive value with the sales response in order to gain insight into the sales-response function. As a result, the sales promotion manager can recommend incentive levels with a degree of expertise that would not normally be possessed by individual brand managers who only carry out one or two promotions a year.

Conditions for participation. Incentives may be made available to everyone or to select groups. For example, a premium may be made available to only those who turn in boxtops or other evidence of previous consumption. Sweepstakes may be limited to certain states and not made available to families of company personnel, or persons under a certain age. By carefully choosing conditions for participation, the seller can selectively discourage those who are unlikely to become regular users of the product. On the other hand, if the conditions are too restrictive, only the most loyal or deal-prone consumers will participate.

Distribution vehicle for promotion. The marketer must decide how to promote and distribute the promotion program to the target audience. Suppose the promotion is a fifteen-cents-off coupon. Such a coupon could be distributed in the package, store, mail, or advertising media. Each distribution method involves a different level of reach and cost. For example, in-pack coupons primarily reach current users, whereas mailed coupons can be directed at nonbrand users, although at a greater cost.

Duration of promotion. If sales promotions are offered for too short a period, many prospects will not be able to take advantage, since they may not be repurchasing at the time or may be too busy with other things. If the promotion runs for too long a period, the customers may begin to view this as a long-term price concession and the deal will lose some of its "act now" force and also raise questions about the brand's real quality. According to one researcher, the optimal frequency is about three weeks per quarter, and optimal duration is the length of the average purchase cycle.[34]

Timing of promotion. A schedule of sales promotion will usually be constructed by brand managers. This schedule has to be approved by sales and divisional management in terms of total divisional marketing strategy. The schedule is a planning instrument and requires careful coordination of production, sales, and distribution. At the same time, some unplanned promotions will also be needed and require preparation on short notice.

Total sales promotion budget. The total budget for sales promotion can be developed in two ways. It can be built from the ground up, where the marketer decides on various promotions to use during the year and estimates the cost of each. The cost of a particular promotion consists of the *administrative cost* (printing, mailing, and promoting), the *incentive cost* (cost of premium or cents-off, including rate of redemption), and the *expected number of units* that will be sold on deal. In the case of a coupon deal, the cost would take into account the fact that only a fraction of the consumers will redeem the coupons. In the case of an in-pack premium, the cost must include the costs of procurement and packaging of the premium offset by any price increase on the package.

The more common way to arrive at a total sales promotion budget is to use a conventional percentage of the total budget for advertising and sales promotion. For example, toiletries may get a sales promotion budget of 20–40 percent of the total promotion budget, whereas packaged goods may get as much as 30–60 percent. These percentages vary substantially for different brands in different markets and are influenced by the product life-cycle stage and competitors' expenditures on sales promotion.

Organizations with multiple brands should ensure that brand budgets are coordinated in order to gain economies from sales promotion activities. Although not all sales promotion activities can be preplanned, coordination gives cost-saving advantages such as single mailings of multiple coupons to consumers.

Strang, in his study of seventeen leading U.S. consumer-goods manufacturers and advertising agencies, found three major planning inadequacies in sales promotion: (1) lack of consideration of cost-effectiveness; (2) use of simplistic decision rules, such as extensions of last year's spending, percentage of expected sales, maintenance of a fixed ratio to advertising, and the "left-over approach"; and (3) advertising and promotional budgets being prepared independently.[35]

Pretesting the Sales Promotion Program

Sales promotion pretests should be conducted whenever possible to determine if the tools are appropriate, the size of the incentive is optimal, and the method of presentation is effective. A survey by the Premium Advertisers Association indicated that fewer than 42 percent of premium offerers ever tested the premiums' effectiveness.[36] Yet promotions can usually be tested quickly and inexpensively. Groups of consumers can be asked to rate or rank different possible deals according to their preference. Or trial tests can be run in limited geographical areas.

Implementing and Controlling the Sales Promotion Program

Effective control of sales promotions requires that specific goals and implementation plans for individual promotions be established. Program implementation must cover two critical time factors, lead time and sell-off time. *Lead time* is the time necessary to bring the program up to the point of announcing the deal. *Sell-off time* begins at the date of release and ends when approximately 90 to 95 percent of the deal merchandise is in the hands of consumers, which may take one to several months, depending on the deal duration.

Evaluating the Sales Promotion Results

Evaluation is a crucial requirement for improving any program. Yet, according to Strang, "evaluation of promotion programs receives . . . little attention. Even where an attempt is made to evaluate a promotion, it is likely to be superficial. . . . Evaluation in terms of profitability is even less common."[37]

Manufacturers can use any of four methods to measure sales promotion effectiveness: sales performance movement, analysis of consumer panel data, consumer surveys, and experimental studies.

The most common consumer promotion evaluation technique consists of comparing *sales performance movement* before, during, and after a promotion. Suppose a company has a 6 percent market share in the prepromotion period, which jumps to 10 percent during the promotion, falls to 5 percent immediately after the promotion, and rises to 7 percent after some time. In this case the promotion evidently attracted new triers as well as more purchasing from existing customers. They loaded up on the goods, and after the promotion, sales fell as consumers worked down their inventories. The long-run rise to 7 percent indicates, however, that the company gained some new users. In other cases the brand's share may return to the prepromotion level, with the result that the promotion only altered the time pattern of demand rather than the total demand.

Consumer panel data could be used to examine the kinds of people who responded to the promotion and what they switched to after the promotion. A consumer panel data study by Dodson, Tybout, and Sternthal found that deals generally enhance brand switching, the rate depending on the type of deal. Media-distributed coupons induce substantial switching, cents-off deals induce somewhat less switching, and package coupons hardly affect brand switching. Furthermore, consumers generally return to their preferred brands after the deal.[38]

If more information is needed, *consumer surveys* can be conducted to learn how many recall the promotion, what they thought of it, how many took advantage of it, and how it affected their subsequent brand choice behavior.

Sales promotions can also be evaluated through carefully arranged *experiments* that vary such attributes as incentive value, duration, and distribution media. Some large companies test alternative strategies in selected market areas with each of their national promotions.

Thus we see that sales promotion can play an important role in the total promotion mix. Although it is used on an ad hoc and residual basis by many firms, it can be used more systematically and effectively by defining the sales promotion objectives, selecting the appropriate tools, constructing the sales promotion program, pretesting it, implementing and controlling it, and evaluating the results.

publicity

Another major marketing communications tool is publicity. *Publicity* has been defined as the activity of "securing editorial space, as divorced from paid space, in all media read, viewed, or heard by a company's customers or prospects, for the specific purpose of assisting in the meeting of sales goals."[39] To the extent that an organization can create events and news around a marketable entity, it is using publicity. And the results can sometimes be spectacular. Consider the case of the diet drink Metrecal:

- Almost overnight, Metrecal became part of the American tribal customs, fashions and language. The signs were everywhere. Drugstores served Metrecal across soda fountains. Newspapers printed Metrecal-inspired cartoons. Fashionable luncheon clubs served Metrecal cocktails. Steve Allen and a probate judge in Charleston, South Carolina, wrote songs about Metrecal. Don Wilson, the announcer, danced "The Metrecal Bounce" on television. Overweight football players in Chicago ate at "the Metrecal table."[40]

What kinds of entities can be publicized? Almost anything. Publicity is used to promote various brands, products, persons, places, ideas, activities, organizations, and even nations. For example, trade associations have used publicity to rebuild interest in such products as eggs, milk, and potatoes. Publicity is commonly used to launch new products and brands, as well as to rekindle interest in mature brands. Organizations with low visibility have used publicity to draw more attention, while organizations with poor public images have used publicity to describe positive things they have done. Nations have employed publicity to attract more tourists, foreign investment, or international support.

The appeal of publicity is based on its three distinctive qualities:

1. *High credibility.* News stories and features seem to most readers to be authentic, media-originated reports. They have a higher degree of credibility than if they were to come across as being sponsored by a seller.
2. *Off guard.* Publicity can reach many potential buyers who otherwise avoid salespeople and advertisements. The reason is that the message is packaged in a way that gets to the buyers as news rather than as a sales-directed communication.
3. *Dramatization.* Publicity has, like advertising, a potential for dramatizing a company or product.

Publicity is part of a larger concept, that of public relations. Today's public relations practitioners perform the following functions:[41]

1. *Press relations.* The aim of press relations is to place newsworthy information into the news media to attract attention to a person, product, or service.
2. *Product publicity.* Product publicity involves various efforts to publicize through news media and other means specific products and happenings related to products.
3. *Corporate communications.* This activity covers internal and external communications to draw attention to and promote understanding of the institution.
4. *Lobbying.* Lobbying refers to the effort to deal with legislators and government officials to defeat unwanted legislation and regulation and/or to promote wanted legislation and regulation.
5. *Counseling.* Counseling is the provision of general advice to the company about what is happening in the society and what the company might do in the way of changing its ways or improving its communications.

Since publicity is part of public relations, those skilled in publicity are usually found not in the company's marketing department but in its public relations department. The public relations department is typically located at corporate headquarters rather than in the various divisions; and its staff is so busy dealing with various publics—stockholders, employees, legislators, city officials—that publicity to support product marketing objectives may be neglected. One frequent solution is to establish a publicity unit within the marketing department.

Publicity is often described as a marketing stepchild because it is relatively underutilized in relation to the real contribution it can make. Publicity has in many cases created a memorable impact on public awareness that advertising

EXHIBIT 17-5

THE ENTERTAINMENT INDUSTRY PERFECTS ITS "HYPE" TECHNIQUES

In the entertainment world, a "hype" is a shot in the public's arm to make sure that a movie, record, or performer "takes." The entertainment industry keeps evolving new techniques to perfect its marketing of new products. Here are some techniques currently being used by the movie industry.

The work in promoting Paramount Pictures' *Saturday Night Fever* began months before its scheduled release. Robert Stigwood, the producer, started the promotion by issuing the motion picture's sound track to the music marketplace six weeks prior to the film's release. Dominated by the "disco"-style music of the Bee Gees, a British group, the records and tapes generated high-volume sales and received saturation radio airplay. Consequently, when the film opened, the market literally queued up at the box office. Additionally, Stigwood capitalized on Americans' fascination with celebrities by engineering a prime-time television "special" on the night of the Hollywood premiere of *Saturday Night Fever* to build up the film's star, John Travolta. The film's success was phenomenal. Stigwood's achievement stemmed not only from his ability to recognize a musical trend ("disco") or a talented new performer (John Travolta) but from his sophisticated understanding of how to orchestrate the mass media of film, music, radio, and television to create a crescendo of market excitement for his new product.

Another successful hype was given to *Close Encounters,* which cost $13 million to produce and $7 million to promote. Much of it was spent on a new technique of TV advertising called *roadblock* where, on the same night, ninety-second commercials are aired simultaneously on all three networks, guaranteeing that most TV viewers will hear about the movie before it opens around the country. The promoters sought to create a major public event, all the time keeping the plot a secret and emphasizing the credibility of unidentified flying objects (UFOs). The advent of the film was accompanied by a proliferation of supplementary promotions including UFO T-shirts, sleeping bags, comic books, and posters.

The low-budget film *Vanishing Wilderness* was promoted by its producer, Arthur Dubs, with a new technique called *four walling,* which reverses the traditional approach to promoting movies. Movies are normally booked in one or two theatres in various cities around the country in the hope that they will get good critical reviews, in which case ads will be prepared incorporating the critics' comments as the film is moved into several major theatres ("red-carpet exhibition") and later into neighborhood theatres ("showcase exhibition"). Dubs reversed this by going to one city at a time and renting every available low-rent theatre and then launching an advertising blitz designed to pull in as many people as possible in a one- or two-week period before the film moved to another town. Four walling works best with low-budget films with a G or GP rating in towns where low-cost theatres are available for rent. The movie is rolled out from small markets to larger ones to benefit from the test marketing of different advertising techniques as experience is gained.

alone could not have accomplished, or accomplished at the same low cost. The company does not pay for the space or time in the media. It does pay for the staff time used to develop the stories and induce the media to use them, but this is minimal. If the company has a real story to tell, it could be picked up by all the news media and be worth millions of dollars in equivalent advertising. Furthermore, it would be more credible as news than if it were delivered as advertising.

What kinds of factors indicate that publicity would have a high potential in the total promotional mix? Here are the main ones:

1. *Newsworthiness.* Products that can support interesting stories that news editors will accept are the best candidates for publicity.
2. *Stimulus for sales force and dealers.* Publicity can be useful in boosting the enthusiasm of the sales force and dealers when it might be lacking. For example, news stories appearing about a new product before it is launched will help the sales force gain a hearing from retailers.
3. *Need for credibility.* Publicity introduces an element of credibility by virtue of communicating the message in an editorial context. Credibility is needed by new products as well as mature products that the market has questioned.
4. *Small budget.* Publicity, while it is not without cost, tends to be low in cost for producing exposures in comparison with direct-mail and media advertising. The smaller the company's marketing communications budget, the stronger the case for using imaginative publicity to neutralize the advantage of a competitor who has more money to spend on advertising.

Major Decisions in Publicity

In considering when and how to use product publicity, management should (1) establish the publicity objectives, (2) choose the publicity messages and vehicles, and (3) evaluate the publicity results.

Establishing the Publicity Objectives

The first task is to set specific objectives for the publicity. As an example, the Wine Growers of California hired the public relations firm of Daniel J. Edelman, Inc., in 1966 to create a publicity program to support two major marketing objectives: (1) convince Americans that wine drinking is a pleasurable part of good living and (2) improve the image and market share of California wines among all wines. To contribute to these marketing objectives, the following publicity objectives were established: (1) develop magazine stories about wine and get them placed in top magazines (*Time, House Beautiful*) and in newspapers (food columns, feature sections); (2) develop stories about wine's many health values and direct them to the medical profession; and (3) develop special programs for the young adult market, college market, governmental bodies, and various ethnic communities. Then these objectives were translated into specific goals for audience-response variables so that results could be evaluated at the end of the publicity campaign.

Choosing the Publicity Messages and Vehicles

The publicist next sets about determining whether there are any interesting stories to tell about the product. As an example, suppose a college with a low visibility adopts the objective of achieving more public recognition. The publicist will review the college's various components to see whether any natural stories exist. Do any faculty members have unusual backgrounds or are any working on unusual projects? Are any new and unusual courses being taught? Are any exceptional students with unusual backgrounds enrolled? Are any interesting events taking place on campus? Is there a story about the architecture, history, or aspirations of the college? Usually a search along these lines will uncover hundreds of stories that can be fed to the press with the effect of creating much more public recognition of the college. Ideally, the stories chosen should symbolize the kind of college this college wants to be. The stories should support its desired market positioning.

If the number of good stories is insufficient, the publicist then dreams up newsworthy events that the college could sponsor. Here the publicist gets into *creating news* rather than *finding news.* The ideas include hosting major academic conventions, featuring well-known speakers, and developing news conferences. Each event is an opportunity to develop a multitude of stories directed to relevant media vehicles and audiences.

Event creation is a particularly important skill in publicizing fund-raising drives for nonprofit organizations. Fund-raisers have developed a large repertoire of special events, including *anniversary celebrations, art exhibits, auctions, benefit evenings, bingo games, book sales, cake sales, contests, dances, dinners, fairs, fashion shows, parties in unusual places, phonothons, rummage sales, tours,* and *walkathons.* No sooner does one type of event get created, such as a walkathon, than competitors spawn new versions such as readathons, bikeathons, and jogathons.

A publicist is able to find or create stories on behalf of even mundane products. Some years ago the Potato Board, an association of more than fifteen thousand U.S. potato growers, decided to finance a publicity campaign to encourage more potato consumption.[42] A national attitude and usage study indicated that many consumers perceived potatoes as too fattening, not nutritious enough, and not a good source of vitamins and minerals. These attitudes were being disseminated by various opinion leaders, such as food editors, diet advocates, and doctors. Actually, potatoes have far fewer calories than most people imagine, and they contain several important vitamins and minerals. The Potato Board decided to develop separate publicity programs for each major audience: consumers, doctors and dieticians, nutritionists, home economists, and food editors. The consumer program called for generating many stories about the potato for network television and national women's magazines, developing and distributing *The Potato Lover's Diet Cookbook,* and placing articles and recipes in food editors' columns. The food editors' program consisted of organizing food editor seminars conducted by nutrition experts, and a tour of major markets by a leading diet authority who talked with food editors.

Publicity can also be highly effective in brand promotion. One of the top brands of cat food is Star-Kist Foods' 9-Lives. Its brand image revolves around one of the most famous felines in the world, Morris the Cat. The advertising agency of Leo Burnett, which created Morris for its ads, wanted to make him more of a living, breathing, real-life feline to whom cat owners and cat lovers could relate. It hired a public relations firm, which then proposed and carried out the following ideas: (1) launch a Morris "Look-Alike" contest in nine major markets, with Morris being booked for personal appearances and extensive stories appearing about the search for a look-alike; (2) write a book called *Morris, An*

Intimate Biography, describing the adventures of this famous feline; (3) establish a coveted award called "The Morris," a bronze statuette given to the owners of award-winning cats selected at local cat shows; (4) sponsor an "Adopt-a-Cat Month," with Morris as the official "spokescat" for the month, urging people to adopt stray cats as Morris once was; and (5) distribute a booklet called "The Morris Method" on cat care. All of these publicity steps strengthened the brand's market share in the cat food market.

Implementing the Publicity Plan

Implementing publicity requires a great deal of care. Take the matter of placing stories in the media. A great story is easy to place, no matter who does the placing. But most stories are less than great and may not get past busy editors. One of the chief assets of publicists is the personal relationships they have established with media editors. Publicists are often ex-journalists who know a number of the media editors and know what they want. Media editors want interesting, well-written stories and easy access to sources of further information. Publicists look at media editors as a market to satisfy so that these editors will in turn be inclined to use their stories.

Publicity also requires extra care when it involves staging special events such as testimonial dinners, news conferences, and national contests. Publicists need a good head for detail and also for coming up with quick solutions when things go wrong.

Evaluating the Publicity Results

The most difficult thing about measuring publicity's contribution is that it is typically used with other marketing communication tools and its contribution is hard to separate. If it is used before the other tools come into action, as often happens in launching a new product, its contribution is easier to evaluate.

Publicity is designed with certain audience-response objectives in mind, and these objectives form the basis of what is measured. The major response measures are exposures, awareness/comprehension/attitude change, and sales.

The easiest and most common measure of publicity effectiveness is the number of *exposures* created in the media. Most publicists supply the client with a "clippings book" showing all the media that carried news about the product and a summary statement such as the following:

- Media coverage included 3,500 column inches of news and photographs in 350 publications with a combined circulation of 79.4 million; 2,500 minutes of air time on 290 radio stations and an estimated audience of 65 million; and 660 minutes of air time on 160 television stations with an estimated audience of 91 million. If this time and space had been purchased at advertising rates, it would have amounted to $1,047,000.[43]

The purpose of citing the equivalent advertising cost is to make a case for publicity's cost-effectiveness, since the total publicity effort must have cost less than $1,047,000. Furthermore, publicity usually creates more reading and believing than ads.

Still, this exposure measure is not very satisfying. There is no indication of how many people actually read, saw, or heard the message, and what they thought afterward. Furthermore, there is no information on the net audience reached, since publications have overlapping readership.

A better measure calls for finding out what change in product *awareness/comprehension/attitude* occurred as a result of the publicity campaign (after allowing for the impact of other promotional tools). This requires the use of survey methodology to measure the before-after levels of these variables. The Potato Board carried out this type of evaluation and learned, for example, that the number of people who agreed with the statement "Potatoes are rich in vitamins and minerals" went from 36 percent before the campaign to 67 percent after the campaign, a significant improvement in product comprehension.

Sales and profit impact is the most satisfactory measure if obtainable. For example, 9-Lives sales had increased 43 percent at the end of the "Morris the Cat" publicity campaign. However, advertising and sales promotion had been stepped up, and their contribution had to be allowed for in estimating publicity's net contribution.

Publicity tends to be relatively underutilized in marketing campaigns. Sometimes it takes a publicity genius to remind us of its great potential. (See Exhibit 17-6.)

EXHIBIT 17-6

A PUBLICITY AND PROMOTION GENIUS—BILL VEECK

From time to time individuals appear who seem to have a creative genius for promoting particular products, services, places, persons, organizations, or ideas. They can dream up more publicity ideas and create more sales impact than any amount of conventional marketing planning. P. T. Barnum had this genius when promoting the circus.

The all-time showman in promoting a sport, namely, baseball, is Bill Veeck, part owner of the Chicago White Sox. Veeck loves baseball and has done ingenious things to draw in the crowds. The key to his thinking is that the spectator is coming to be entertained and not just to watch the game.

Veeck's various publicity and promotion ideas include the following: (1) proclaiming a "Bat Day" where the kids take home a bat from the White Sox team carrying a Coca-Cola endorsement and paid for largely by the Coca-Cola Company; (2) instituting a "Same Name Day" when people having a certain last name, say, Smith, get into the park free; (3) deciding that tickets could be promotional devices and putting the pictures of White Sox players on the backs of tickets, thus making them "collectibles"; (4) letting fans know that if it rains, they will get free plastic rain capes; (5) having a huge bell-and-whistle system built that would blast off and be heard for blocks whenever a White Sox player hit a home run; (6) hiring a midget to play on the White Sox team—the midget was almost always walked to first base because of the difficulty of striking him out; and (7) establishing an annual trophy award to go to the most outstanding performer on the White Sox team and in the first year awarding it to Nancy Faust, the organist. Ms. Faust was honored by the Chicago Symphony Orchestra, whose members were dressed in formal attire and played "Take Me Out to the Ballgame" in the ballfield while fans accompanied the orchestra with any musical instruments they cared to bring along.

Sources: This was prepared by the author from several sources, including Bill Veeck and Ed Linn, *The Hustler's Handbook* (New York: Putnam's, 1965) Chap. 1.

summary

Three of the four major tools of promotion are advertising, sales promotion, and publicity. They are mass-marketing tools as opposed to personal selling, which targets one or a few buyers at most.

Advertising—the use of paid media by a seller to communicate persuasive information about its products, services, or organization—is a potent promotional tool. American marketers spend over $38 billion annually on advertising and it takes many forms (national, regional, local; consumer, industrial, retail; product, brand, institutional; and so on). Advertising decision making is a five-step process consisting of objectives setting, budget decision, message decision, media decision, and campaign evaluation. Advertisers should establish clear goals as to whether advertising is supposed to inform, persuade, or remind buyers. The advertising budget can be established on the basis of what is affordable, as a percentage-of-sales, on the basis of competitors' expenditures, or on the basis of objectives and tasks. The message decision calls for generating messages, evaluating and selecting among them, and executing them effectively. The media decision calls for a number of steps: defining the reach, frequency, and impact goals; choosing among major media types; selecting specific media vehicles; and scheduling the media over the year and in shorter time periods. Finally, campaign evaluation calls for a continuous effort researching the communication and sales effects of advertising programs before, during, and after they are run.

Sales promotion covers a wide variety of short-term incentive tools—such as coupons, premiums, contests, and buying allowances—designed to stimulate consumer markets, the trade, and the organization's own sales force. Sales promotion expenditures have been growing at a faster rate than advertising in recent times. The effective use of sales promotion calls for the following steps: establishing the sales promotion objectives; selecting the sales promotion tools; developing, pretesting, implementing and controlling the sales promotion program; and evaluating the sales promotion results.

Publicity—which is the securing of free editorial space or time—tends to be the least utilized of the major marketing communication tools, although it has great potential for building awareness and preference in the marketplace. Three main steps are involved in publicity work: establishing the publicity objectives; choosing the publicity messages and vehicles; and evaluating the publicity results.

questions for discussion

1. What kind of organizational arrangements can be used for advertising? Give an example of each.
2. The major objective of advertising is to inform. Comment.
3. If Procter and Gamble were introducing a new brand of shampoo, what method would the company use to set the advertising budget? Why?
4. Explain the major aspects of the message decision and relate them to a specific product.
5. Which media would the following organizations utilize for their advertising? (a) your college is trying to raise funds from alumni and parents for a new

business building; (b) J. C. Penney wants to promote its Labor Day sale nationally; (c) General Mills is going to advertise a new type of Betty Crocker cake mix; (d) a local blood bank wants to attract more donors; (e) a small restaurant is promoting a new luncheon menu; and (f) an automobile dealership wants to publicize its convenient location.

6. If advertisers a, c, d, and f in question 5 wanted to evaluate their campaigns, how would you suggest that they do it?
7. Sales promotion tools are only effective when used for consumer promotion. Comment.
8. Which sales promotion tools are most widely utilized for supermarket products? Why?
9. How might Del Monte evaluate whether its national sales promotion campaign was successful?
10. What distinguishes publicity from all other forms of promotion?
11. Discuss how you would develop a publicity campaign for the American Cancer Society or Wheaties.

■ references

1. This is extracted with some adaptations from KAREN BOIKO, "Jontue: Revlon Does It Again—But Differently," *Product Marketing,* March 1977, pp. 26–30, with permission.
2. See JACK TROUT AND AL RIES, "The Positioning Era Cometh," *Advertising Age,* April 24, 1972; "Positioning Cuts through Chaos in Market Place," *Advertising Age,* May 1, 1972; and "How to Position Your Product," *Advertising Age,* May 8, 1972.
3. Statistical information in this chapter on advertising's size and composition draws on the special issue of *Advertising Age* on the one hundred leading national advertisers, August 28, 1978, esp. p. 29.
4. See SIDNEY J. LEVY, *Promotional Behavior* (Glenview, Ill.: Scott, Foresman, 1971), Chap. 4.
5. See RUSSELL H. COLLEY, *Defining Advertising Goals for Measured Advertising Results* (New York: Association of National Advertisers, 1961).
6. See WILLIAM L. WILKE AND PAUL W. FARRIS, "Comparison Advertising: Problem and Potential," *Journal of Marketing,* October 1975, pp. 7–15.
7. Quoted in DANIEL SELIGMAN, "How Much for Advertising?" *Fortune,* December 1956, p. 123.
8. ALBERT WESLEY FREY, *How Many Dollars for Advertising?* (New York: Ronald Press, 1955), p. 65.
9. Ibid., p. 49.
10. G. MAXWELL ULE, "A Media Plan for 'Sputnik' Cigarettes," *How to Plan Media Strategy* (American Association of Advertising Agencies, 1957 Regional Convention), pp. 41–52.
11. M. I. VIDALE AND H. B. WOLFE, "An Operations-Research Study of Sales Response to Advertising," *Operations Research,* June 1957, pp. 370–81.
12. JOHN D. C. LITTLE, "A Model of Adaptive Control of Promotional Spending," *Operations Research,* November 1966, pp. 1075–97.
13. See RUSSELL L. ACKOFF AND JAMES R. EMSHOFF, "Advertising Research at Anheuser-Busch, Inc. (1963-68)," *Sloan Management Review,* Winter 1975, pp. 1-15.

14. JOHN C. MALONEY, "Marketing Decisions and Attitude Research," in *Effective Marketing Coordination,* ed. George L. Baker, Jr. (Chicago: American Marketing Association, 1961), pp. 595-618.

15. DIK WARREN TWEDT, "How to Plan New Products, Improve Old Ones, and Create Better Advertising," *Journal of Marketing,* January 1969, pp. 53–57.

16. See WILLIAM A. MINDAK AND H. MALCOLM BYBEE, "Marketing's Application to Fund Raising," *Journal of Marketing,* July 1971, pp. 13–18.

17. See "Powerful Headlines Uncover Basic Wants," *Marketing Insights,* May 19, 1969, pp. 16–17.

18. See HERBERT E. KRUGMAN, "What Makes Advertising Effective?" *Harvard Business Review,* March-April 1975, pp. 96–103, here p. 98.

19. See DENNIS H. GENSCH, "Computer Models in Advertising Media Selection," *Journal of Marketing Research,* November 1968, pp. 414–24.

20. PHILIP H. DOUGHERTY, "Bud 'Pulses' the Market," *New York Times,* February 18, 1975, p. 40.

21. DAVID B. MONTGOMERY AND ALVIN J. SILK, "Estimating Dynamic Effects of Market Communications Expenditures," *Management Science,* June 1972, pp. 485–501.

22. See ROBERT D. BUZZELL, "E. I. Du Pont de Nemours & Co.: Measurement of Effects of Advertising," in his *Mathematical Models and Marketing Management* (Boston: Division of Research, Graduate School of Business Administration, Harvard University, 1964), pp. 157–79.

23. ROGER A. STRANG, "Sales Promotion—Fast Growth, Faulty Management," *Harvard Business Review,* July-August 1976, pp. 115–24, here pp. 116–17.

24. Ibid., pp. 116–19.

25. See ROGER A. STRANG, ROBERT M. PRENTICE, AND ALDEN G. CLAYTON, *The Relationship between Advertising and Promotion in Brand Strategy* (Cambridge, Mass.: Marketing Science Institute, 1975), Chap. 5.

26. STRANG, "Sales Promotion," p. 124.

27. Most of the definitions in this section have been adapted from JOHN F. LUICK AND WILLIAM LEE SIEGLER, *Sales Promotion and Modern Merchandising* (New York: McGraw-Hill, 1968).

28. See LESTER A. NEIDELL, "Alternative Couponing Methods and Buying Patterns," *Southern Journal of Business,* January 1971, pp. 33–43.

29. For further reading, see CARL-MAGNUS SEIPEL, "Premiums—Forgotten by Theory," *Journal of Marketing,* April 1971, pp. 26-34.

30. See FRED C. ALLVINE, "The Future for Trading Stamps and Games," *Journal of Marketing,* January 1969, pp. 45–52.

31. "Our L'eggs Fit Your Legs," *Business Week,* March 27, 1972.

32. See WALTER A. GAW, *Specialty Advertising* (Chicago: Specialty Advertising Association, 1970).

33. See SUZETTE CAVANAUGH, "Setting Objectives and Evaluating the Effectiveness of Trade Show Exhibits," *Journal of Marketing,* October 1976, pp. 100–105.

34. ARTHUR STERN, "Measuring the Effectiveness of Package Goods Promotion Strategies" (Paper presented to the Association of National Advertisers, Glen Cove, February 1978).

35. STRANG, "Sales Promotion," p. 119.

36. RUSSELL D. BOWMAN, "Merchandising and Promotion Grow Big in Marketing World," *Advertising Age,* December 1974, p. 21.

37. STRANG, "Sales Promotion," p. 120.

38. JOE A. DODSON, ALICE M. TYBOUT, AND BRIAN STERNTHAL, "Impact of Deals and Deal Retraction on Brand Switching," *Journal of Marketing Research,* February 1978, p. 79.

39. GEORGE BLACK, *Planned Industrial Publicity* (Chicago: Putnam Publishing, 1952), p. 3.

40. PETER WYDEN, *The Overweight Society* (New York: Morrow, 1965), p. 50.

41. Adapted from SCOTT M. CUTLIP AND ALLEN H. CENTER, *Effective Public Relations,* 3rd ed. (Englewood Cliffs, N.J.: Prentice-Hall, 1964), pp. 10–14.

42. For details, see JOSEPH M. COOGLE, JR., "Media, Advertising, and Public Relations," in *Review of Marketing 1978,* ed. Gerald Zaltman and Thomas V. Bonoma (Chicago: American Marketing Association, 1978), pp. 481–84.

43. ARTHUR M. MERIMS, "Marketing's Stepchild: Product Publicity," *Harvard Business Review,* November-December 1972, pp. 111–12.

PERSONAL SELLING AND SALES MANAGEMENT STRATEGY

At the age of 29, Kim Kelley is already something of a legend around Honeywell Inc. "He's the one who cried when he made his sale, isn't he?" a fellow Honeywell salesman asks with a chuckle.

Indeed he is. Kim stood there in his customer's office last June and bawled like a baby. And for good reason. Kim had just shaken hands on an $8.1 million computer sale to the state of Illinois. He had gambled his whole career on making that sale. He had spent three years laying the groundwork for it, and for three solid months he had been working six days a week, often 14 hours a day, competing against salesmen from four other computer companies.

It was a make-or-break situation for Kim Kelley, and, standing there with tears of joy and relief streaming down his cheeks, he knew he had it made. A bright future with Honeywell was assured, and he had just made an $80,000 commission—more money than he had earned in all four of his previous years with the company.

. . . Such is the life of the "big-ticket" salesman who pursues multimillion-dollar contracts while others sell in bits and drabs. Lured by fat commissions (1% of the equipment's total value in Honeywell's case), they devote months to delicate planning and months more to the heat of battle, all to make one big sale.

He was sent to Springfield in 1970 and told to keep four or five big sales simmering but to put only one at a time "on the front burner." Kim wasted little time picking his target, the state government, the biggest potential customer in his region. His long-range strategy was to devote at least half his time to pursuing the state, and to use the balance to scratch out small sales elsewhere to meet his annual quota of $500,000 worth of new equipment.

For three years, he patiently made daily rounds of key state offices, pausing a few minutes in each one to drop off technical documents or just to chat. He pursued the bureaucrats further at after-hours hangouts like the American Legion hall. "People don't buy products, they buy relationships," Kim believes.

Toward the end of 1972, the Illinois Secretary of State asked for bids for a massive new computer system. Five manufacturers responded: Honeywell, Burroughs, Univac division of Sperry Rand, Control Data and International Business Machines.

In the ensuing three-month scramble, Control Data was eliminated because of "high cost," according to Noel Sexton, head of a technical committee assigned by the state to evaluate the bids. IBM was never in strong contention, says Hank Malkus, who was then division administrator in the secretary's office. "IBM doesn't tailor its equipment to a customer's need. They just say, 'Here's our equipment, you make your system fit it,'" Mr. Malkus contends.

That made the contest a three-horse race between Honeywell, Burroughs and Univac. "The equipment was close," says Patrick Halperin, executive assistant to the secretary of state. "But the staff felt far more comfortable with Honeywell because they felt Kim had been more thorough in his marketing."

Indeed he was. Kim dealt solely with the committee. "Some of the other vendors put more emphasis on selling to the front office and tried to play on previous friendships," Mr. Sexton recalls.

Kim fed the committee information, not persuasion. "When we asked to see customers," says Mr. Malkus, "Kim just gave us a list of Honeywell users and said, choose." Univac, on the other hand, annoyed committee members by discouraging them from interviewing users.

Kim flew in Honeywell experts and top marketing officials from Boston, Minneapolis, Phoenix and Chicago to answer technical questions on engineering, financing, installation and service. "He showed the ability of his firm to cooperate," says Mr. Halperin.

"Incredible attention to detail" helped, too, Kim thinks. The committee was asking for new bits of information daily—things like how much air conditioning his equipment would need. Kim answered every question within two days, always hand-delivering replies to each committee member. "That gave me five minutes more selling time with each one," he explains.

When Hank Malkus gruffly ordered him down to the state capitol last June, Kim knew it was "decision day," but he didn't know who had won. Minutes later, Mr. Malkus was grinning, his secretary was hugging Kim, and Kim was crying.[1]

□ Every organization has one or more persons like Kim Kelley who have responsibility for contacting and selling to prospects and customers. We call this group the sales force. Sales forces are found not only in most business organizations but in nonprofit organizations as well. College recruiters represent a sales-force arm of the college seeking to sell prospective students on coming to that college. Churches form membership committees who are responsible for attracting new members. The U.S. Agricultural Extension Service consists of agricultural specialists who try to educate and sell farmers on using the latest technology. Hospitals, museums, and other organizations use a staff of fund-raisers to contact prospective donors and sell them on supporting the organization.

The traditional term used to describe the persons in the sales force is *salesmen*. However, this term is becoming obsolete because of the increasing number of women who are taking on sales responsibilities. We will use the terms *sales representatives* and *salespersons,* although *salesmen* will occasionally be used where appropriate. Many other terms have come into use to describe people who work in sales, including *account executive, sales consultant, field representative, manufacturer's representative, agent, service representative,* and *marketing representative.*

There are probably more stereotypes about sales representatives than about any other group. "Salesman" is likely to conjure up an image of Arthur Miller's pitiable Willy Loman in *Death of a Salesman* or Meredith Willson's cigar-smoking, back-slapping, joke-telling Harold Hill in *The Music Man*—a glib, boisterous character always ready with a glad hand and a racy story. Sales representatives are typically pictured as loving sociability—in spite of some recent evidence that many sales representatives actually dislike it. They are criticized for aggressively foisting goods on people—in spite of the fact that buyers often search out sales representatives.

Actually the term *sales representative* covers a broad range of positions in our economy, within which the differences are often greater than the similarities. McMurry devised the following classification of sales positions:

1. Positions where the salesperson's job is predominantly to deliver the product, e.g., milk, bread, fuel, oil.
2. Positions where the salesperson is predominantly an inside order-taker, e.g., the haberdashery salesperson standing behind the counter.
3. Positions where the salesperson is also predominantly an order-taker but works in the field, as the packing house, soap, or spice salesperson does.
4. Positions where the salesperson is not expected or permitted to take an order but is called on only to build good will or to educate the actual or potential user . . . the distiller's "missionary person" or the medical "detailer" representing an ethical pharmaceutical house.
5. Positions where the major emphasis is placed on technical knowledge, e.g., the engineering salesperson who is primarily a consultant to the "client" companies.
6. Positions which demand the creative sale of tangible products like vacuum cleaners, refrigerators, siding, and encyclopedias.
7. Positions requiring the creative sale of intangibles, such as insurance, advertising services, or education.[2]

The positions move along a spectrum ranging from the least to the most creative types of selling. The earlier jobs call primarily for maintaining accounts and taking orders, while the latter require hunting down prospects and creating new sales. Most of the discussion here will deal with the more creative types of selling.

Personal selling is the most effective tool at certain stages of the buying process, particularly in building up buyers' preference, conviction, and action. The reason is that personal selling, when compared with advertising, has three distinctive qualities:[3]

1. *Personal confrontation.* Personal selling involves an alive, immediate, and interactive relationship between two or more persons. Each party is able to observe each other's needs and characteristics at close hand and make immediate adjustments.

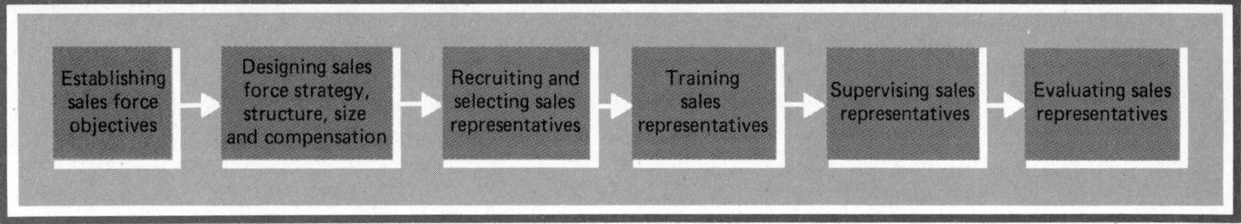

Figure 18-1 Major Steps in Sales-Force Management

2. *Cultivation.* Personal selling permits all kinds of relationships to spring up, ranging from a matter-of-fact selling relationship to a deep personal friendship. In most cases the sales representative must use art to woo the buyer. The sales representative will at times be tempted to put on pressure or to dissemble to get an order but will normally keep the customer's long-run interests at heart.
3. *Response.* Personal selling makes the buyer feel under some obligation for having listened to the sales talk or using up the sales representative's time. The buyer has a greater need to attend and respond, even if the response is a polite "thank you."

These distinctive qualities come at a cost. Personal selling happens to be the company's most expensive contact and communication tool, costing companies an average of $50 a sales call in 1978.[4] In 1977, American firms spent over $100 billion on personal selling compared with $38 billion on advertising. They spent it on an army of over 5.4 million Americans who are engaged in sales work.

We now turn to the major decisions facing company management in building and managing an effective sales force as part of the total marketing mix. These steps are shown in Figure 18-1 and are examined in the following sections.

EXHIBIT 18-1

MILESTONES IN THE HISTORY OF SELLING AND SALESMANSHIP

Robert Louis Stevenson observed that "everyone lives by selling something." Selling is one of the world's oldest professions. Paul Hermann described the discovery of a Bronze Age (circa 1000 B.C.) traveling salesman's sample case: ". . . a solid wooden box, 26 inches in length, containing in specially hollowed compartments various types of axe, sword blades, buttons, . . . etc." Early sellers and traders, though, were not always held in high esteem. The Roman word for *salesman* meant "cheater," and Mercury, the god of cunning and barter, was regarded as the patron deity of merchants and traders.

The buying and selling of commodities flourished over the centuries and became institutionalized in market towns. In time, itinerant peddlers began to carry goods to people in their homes and thus served those who were unable to get to the market towns.

The first salesmen in the United States were *Yankee peddlers (pack peddlers)* who, beginning in the late 1700s, carried such things as clothing, spices, household wares, and notions in backpacks from distribution and manufacturing centers in the East Coast colonies to settlers in the western frontier regions. The pack peddlers would also trade with the Indians, receiving furs in exchange for knives, beads, and ornaments. Many of the traders came to be regarded as shrewd, unprincipled tricksters who would not think twice about putting sand in the sugar, dust in the pepper, and chicory in the coffee. They often sold colored sugar water as "medicine" guaranteed to cure all possible ills.

In the early 1800s some of the peddlers began to use horse-drawn wagons and to stock heavier goods such as furniture, clocks, dishes, weapons, and ammunition. Some of these *wagon peddlers* settled down in frontier villages and opened the first *general stores* and *trading posts.*

It became customary for some of the larger retailers to travel once or twice a year to the nearest major city to replenish their stocks. Eventually wholesalers and manufacturers began to employ *greeters,* or *drummers,* who would seek out retailers in their hotels and invite them to visit the particular displays of their respective employers. The drummers began to employ increasingly insistent techniques to attract attention to their firms, such as meeting incoming trains and ships and even riding out a distance to meet incoming merchants so as to beat their competitors to the draw. In time this pursuit of one-upmanship led drummers to travel all the way to their customers' places of business, and these early traveling salesmen became an important part of the U.S. marketing system in the late 1800s. Prior to 1860 there were fewer than one thousand traveling salesmen, many of whom were primarily credit investigators who collected credit data, collected on past-due accounts, and only secondarily took orders for goods. By 1870 the number of traveling salesmen had increased to about seven thousand, by 1880 it was twenty-eight thousand, and by 1900 it was just under ninety-three thousand.

One of the first businessmen to develop modern selling and sales management techniques was John Henry Patterson (1844–1922), widely regarded as the father of modern salesmanship. At the age of forty Patterson bought controlling interest in a company that manufactured one of the earliest cash registers and which later became known as the National Cash Register Company (NCR). He built this small, barely surviving firm into the market leader of the cash register industry, controlling at one time 90 percent of the market. The key to his success was professionalizing the sales management function. He would ask his best salesmen to demonstrate their sales approaches to the others. The best sales approach would be written down and printed in a "Sales Primer" and distributed to all NCR salesmen to be followed to the letter. This was the beginning of the *canned sales approach.* In addition, Patterson assigned his salesmen exclusive territories and sales quotas to stretch their effort. His company held frequent sales meetings that served the double purpose of sales training and play. In between sales meetings, he sent his salesmen regular communications on how to sell. One of the young men whom Patterson trained was Thomas J. Watson, who later founded IBM. Patterson had shown other companies the way to turn their sales forces into effective instruments for growth and profit.

Sources: Written by the author based on various sources, including Paul Hermann, *Conquest by Man* (New York: Harper & Row, Pub., 1954), p. 38; Frederic Russell, Frank Beach, and Richard Buskirk, *Textbook of Salesmanship* (New York: McGraw-Hill, 1969), pp. 8–10; Bertrand Canfield, *Salesmanship: Practices and Principles* (New York: McGraw-Hill, 1950), p. 6; and Thomas and Marva Belden, *The Lengthening Shadow* (Boston: Little, Brown, 1962), p. 44.

establishing sales-force objectives

The sales force is part of the marketing mix and, as such, is capable of achieving certain marketing objectives better than other tools in the marketing mix. Companies have described their sales-force objectives in different ways. For example, IBM wants its sales representatives to be responsible for "selling, installing, and upgrading" customer computer equipment; AT&T wants its sales representatives to be responsible for "developing, selling, and protecting" accounts. It turns out that sales representatives are expected to perform as many as six tasks for their company:

1. *Prospecting.* Sales representatives are expected to find and cultivate new customers.
2. *Communicating.* Sales representatives are supposed to be skillful in communicating information about the company's products and services to existing and potential customers.
3. *Selling.* Sales representatives are expected to be effective in the art of "salesmanship"—approaching, presenting, answering objections, and closing sales.
4. *Servicing.* Sales representatives must provide various services to the customers—consulting on their problems, rendering technical assistance, arranging financing, and expediting delivery.
5. *Information gathering.* Sales representatives are expected to carry out some market research and intelligence work and supply sales reports on their customer calls.
6. *Allocating.* Sales representatives are expected to evaluate customer profitability and advise the company on allocating scarce products to their customers in times of product shortages.

Companies become more specific and often spell out norms for how much time should go into each activity. Dixon describes one company that advises its sales representatives to spend 80 percent of their time with current customers and 20 percent of their time with prospects; and 85 percent of their time selling the established products and 15 percent of their time selling the new products.[5] If norms are not established, sales representatives will tend to spend most of their time selling established products to current accounts and neglect other important market development activities.

As companies become more market-oriented, they require their sales forces to carry out more marketing tasks. The traditional view is that salespeople produce the targeted sales volume and the company worries about profits. Their training should primarily consist of learning the art of salesmanship. The newer view is that salespeople are supposed to produce customer satisfaction and company profit. They should be skilled in analyzing sales data, measuring market potential, gathering market intelligence, and developing marketing strategies and plans. The sales representatives need analytical marketing skills, and this becomes especially critical at the higher levels of sales management. Marketers believe that a marketing-oriented rather than a sales-oriented sales force will be more effective in the long run.

designing sales-force strategy

Once the company establishes its sales-force objectives, it is ready to face questions of sales-force strategy, structure, size, and compensation.

Sales-Force Strategy

Sales-force strategy is developed by the company through an understanding of the customer buying process and how the company can best position itself against competitors pursuing the same business. The first thing to clarify is the type of selling situation that must be handled by the sales force. Five types of selling situations can be distinguished:

1. *Sales representative to buyer.* Here a single sales representative talks to a single prospect or customer in person or over the phone.
2. *Sales representative to buyer group.* Here a sales representative appears before a buying committee to make a sales presentation about a specific product.
3. *Sales team to buyer group.* Here a sales team (such as a company officer, a sales representative, and a sales engineer) makes a sales presentation to a buying group.
4. *Conference selling.* Here the sales representative brings resource people from the company to meet with one or more buyers to discuss problems and mutual opportunities.
5. *Seminar selling.* Here a company team of technical people conducts an educational seminar for a technical group in a customer company about recent state-of-the-art developments. The aim is to enhance customer knowledge and loyalty rather than to make a specific sale.

Thus the sales representative does not necessarily handle the whole selling job and may serve as a "matchmaker" bringing together company and customer personnel. The sales representative may act as the "account manager" who initiates and facilitates interactions between various people in the buying and selling organizations. Selling is increasingly becoming a matter of teamwork, requiring the support of other personnel, such as (1) *top management,* which is increasingly becoming involved in the sales process, especially when *national accounts*[6] or *major sales*[7] are at stake; (2) *technical people,* who often work with the sales representatives to supply technical information needed by the customer before, during, or after the purchase of the product; (3) *customer service representatives,* who provide installation, maintenance, and other services to the customer; and (4) an *office staff* consisting of sales analysts, order expediters, and secretarial personnel.

Once the company clarifies the type of selling it must perform, it can use either a direct or a contractual sales force. A *direct* (or *company*) *sales force* consists of full- or part-time paid employees who work exclusively for the company. This sales-force category includes *inside sales personnel,* who conduct their business from their offices using the telephone and receiving visits from prospective buyers, and *field sales personnel,* who travel and visit customers. A *contractual sales force* consists of manufacturer's reps, sales agents, or brokers, who are paid a commission on the sales they obtain.

Sales-Force Structure

Part of sales-force strategy is how to structure the company's sales force to have maximum impact on the market. This is relatively simple if the company sells only one product line to one end-using industry with customers found in many locations. The answer would be a territorial-structured sales force. If the company sells many different products to many types of customers, it might have to develop product-structured or customer-structured sales forces. These alternative sales-force structures are discussed in the following paragraphs.

Territorial-structured sales force. In the simplest sales organization each sales representative is given an exclusive territory in which to represent the company's full line. This sales structure has a number of advantages. First, it results in a clear definition of the salesperson's responsibilities. As the only salesperson working the territory, he or she bears the credit or blame for area sales to the extent that personal selling effort makes a difference. This tends to encourage a high level of effort, especially when management is able to gauge fairly accurately the area's sales potential. Second, responsibility for a definite territory increases the sales representative's incentive to cultivate local business and personal ties. These ties tend to improve the quality of the sales representative's selling effectiveness and personal life. Third, travel expenses are likely to be relatively small, since each sales representative's travel takes place within the bounds of a small geographical territory.

Along with this structure goes a hierarchy of sales management positions. Several territories will be supervised by a district sales manager, the several districts will be supervised by a regional sales manager, and the several regions will be supervised by a national sales manager or sales vice-president. Each higher-level sales manager takes on increasing marketing and administrative work in relation to the time available for selling. In fact, sales managers are paid for their management skills rather than their selling skills. The new sales trainee, in looking ahead at the career path, can hope to eventually become a sales representative, then a district manager, and depending on his or her ability and motivation, a promotion into the higher levels of sales or general management.

The territorial form of sales organization works quite well in companies that have a relatively homogeneous set of products and customers. But these same companies, as their products and markets become diversified, find this form increasingly less effective. At the heart of the problem is the fact that the sales representative, to be effective, must know the company's products and markets. But there is a clear limit to how much knowledge a sales representative can acquire about different types of products and customers.

Product-structured sales force. The importance of sales representatives' knowing their products, together with the development of product divisions and management, has led many companies to structure their sales force along product lines. Specialization of the sales force by product is particularly warranted where the products are technically complex, highly unrelated, and/or very numerous.

The mere existence of different company products, however, is not a sufficient argument for specializing the sales force by product. A major drawback may exist if the company's separate product lines are bought by many of the same customers. For example, the American Hospital Supply Corporation has several product divisions, each with its own sales force. It is conceivable that as many as seven different sales representatives from the American Hospital Supply Corporation could call on the same hospital on the same day. This means that company sales personnel travel over the same routes, and each uses up valuable time waiting in the outer office to see the customer's purchasing agents. These extra costs must be weighed against the benefits that may result from the higher level of customer service and more knowledgeable product representation.

Customer-structured sales force. Companies often specialize their sales forces along customer lines. Separate sales forces may be set up for different industries, for major versus regular accounts, and for current versus new-business development. The most obvious advantage of customer specialization is that each sales force can become more knowledgeable about specific customer needs. At one time General Electric's sales representatives specialized in certain products (fan motors, switches, and so forth), but it later changed to specialization in markets, such as the air-conditioning market and auto market, because this is how customers saw the problem of fan motors, switches, and so forth. A customer-specialized sales force can sometimes also reduce total sales-force costs. A large pump manufacturer at one time used a single sales force of highly trained sales engineers to sell to both original equipment manufacturers (who needed to deal with technical representatives) and jobbers (who did not need to deal with technical representatives). Later the company split its sales force and staffed the one selling to jobbers with less highly trained sales representatives.

The major disadvantage of customer-structured sales forces arises if the various types of customers are scattered evenly throughout the country. This means an overlapping coverage of territories, which is always more expensive.

Complex sales-force structures. When a company sells a wide variety of products to many types of customers over a broad geographical area, it often combines several principles of sales-force structure. Sales representatives may be specialized by territory-product, territory-customer, product-customer, or ultimately by territory-product-customer. A sales representative may then be responsible to one or more line managers and/or one or more staff managers.

Sales-Force Size

Once the company clarifies its sales-force strategy and structure, it is ready to consider the question of sales-force size. Sales representatives are among the most productive and expensive assets in a company. Increasing their number will increase both sales and costs.

Most companies use the *workload approach* to establish the size of their sales force.[8] This method consists of the following steps:

1. Customers are grouped into size classes according to their annual sales volume.
2. The desirable call frequencies (number of sales calls on an account per year) are established for each class. They reflect how much call intensity the company seeks in relation to competitors.
3. The number of accounts in each size class is multiplied by the corresponding call frequency to arrive at the total workload for the country, in sales calls per year.
4. The average number of calls a sales representative can make per year is determined.
5. The number of sales representatives needed is determined by dividing the total annual calls required by the average annual calls made by a sales representative.

Suppose the company estimates that there are one thousand A accounts and two thousand B accounts in the nation; and A accounts require thirty-six calls a year and B accounts twelve calls a year. This means the company needs a sales force that can make sixty thousand sales calls a year. Suppose the average sales representative can make one thousand calls a year. The company would need sixty full-time sales representatives.

Sales-Force Compensation

To attract the desired number of sales representatives, the company has to develop an attractive compensation plan. Sales representatives and management tend to seek different, and often conflicting, objectives, which—it is hoped—are reconciled by the plan. Sales representatives would like a plan that provides income regularity, reward for above-average performance, and fair payment for experience and longevity. On the other hand, an ideal compensation plan from management's point of view would emphasize control, economy, and simplicity. Management is obviously hard pressed to reconcile all these objectives in one plan. Plans with good control features are generally not simple. Management objectives, such as economy, will conflict with sales representatives' objectives, such as financial security. In the light of these conflicting objectives, it is understandable why compensation plans exhibit a tremendous variety, not only among industries but among companies within the same industry.

Management must determine the level and components of an effective compensation plan. The *level of compensation* must bear some relation to the "going market price" for the type of sales job and abilities required. For example, the average earnings of the experienced salesperson in 1977 amounted to $24,500.[9] If the market price for sales manpower is well defined, the individual firm has little choice but to pay the going rate. To pay less would not bring forth the desired quantity or quality of applicants, and to pay more would be unnecessary. More often, however, the market price for sales manpower is not well defined. For one thing, company plans vary in the importance of fixed and variable salary elements, fringe benefits, and expense allowances. And data on the average take-home pay of sales representatives working for competitive firms can be misleading because of significant variations in the average seniority and ability levels of the competitors' sales force. Published comparisons of industry-by-industry sales-force compensation levels are infrequent and generally lack sufficient detail.

The company must also determine the *components of compensation*—a fixed amount, a variable amount, expenses, and fringe benefits. The *fixed amount,* which might be salary or a drawing account, is intended to satisfy the sales representatives' need for some stability of income. The *variable amount,* which might be commissions, bonus, or profit sharing, is intended to stimulate and reward greater effort. *Expense allowances* are intended to enable the sales representatives to undertake selling efforts that are considered necessary or desirable. And *fringe benefits,* such as paid vacations, sickness or accident benefits, pensions, and life insurance, are intended to provide security and job satisfaction.

Top sales management must decide which elements should be in the compensation plan and their relative importance. A popular rule seems to favor making about 70 percent of the salesperson's total income fixed and allocating the remaining 30 percent among the other elements. But the variations around this average are so pronounced that it can hardly serve as a sufficient guide in planning. For example, fixed compensation should have more emphasis in jobs with a high ratio of nonselling duties to selling duties and in jobs where the selling task is technically complex. Variable compensation should have more emphasis in jobs where sales are cyclical and/or depend on the personal initiative of the sales representative.

Fixed and variable compensation taken alone give rise to three basic types of sales-force compensation plans—straight salary, straight commission, and combination salary and commission. In one study, 28 percent of the companies paid straight salary, 21 percent paid straight commission, and 51 percent paid salary plus commission.[10]

recruiting and selecting sales representatives

Having established the strategy, structure, size, and compensation of the sales force, the company has to move to recruiting and selecting, training, supervising, and evaluating sales representatives. Various strategies and policies guide these decisions.

Importance of Careful Selection

At the heart of a successful sales-force operation is the selection of effective sales representatives. The performance levels of an average and a top sales representative are quite different. A survey of over five hundred companies revealed that 27 percent of the sales force brought in over 52 percent of the sales.[11] Beyond the differences in sales productivity are the great wastes in hiring the wrong persons. Of the sixteen thousand sales representatives who were hired by the surveyed companies, only 68.5 percent still worked for the company at the end of the year, and only 50.0 percent were expected to remain throughout the following year. The cost of recruiting, training, and supervising an individual salesperson for one year was estimated at the time at $8,730. As a result, the surveyed companies were expected to lose around $70 million, or half their investment. This loss would be much larger in today's dollars.

The financial loss due to turnover is only part of the total cost. The new sales representative who remains with the company receives a direct income averaging around half of the direct selling outlay. If he or she receives $14,000 a year, another $14,000 may go into fringe benefits, expenses for travel and entertainment, supervision, office space, supplies, and secretarial assistance. Consequently the new sales representative should be capable of creating sales on which the gross margin at least covers the selling expenses of $28,000. If this margin were 10 percent, for example, he or she would have to sell at least $280,000 of product to constitute a breakeven resource for the company.

What Makes a Good Sales Representative?

Selecting a good sales representative would not be a problem if one knew exactly what to look for. If ideal sales representatives are outgoing, aggressive, and energetic, it would not be too difficult to check for these characteristics in applicants. But a review of the most successful sales representatives in any company is likely to reveal that many are introverted, mild mannered, and far from energetic. The successful group will also include men and women who are tall and short, articulate and inarticulate, well groomed and slovenly.

Nevertheless, the search for the magic combination of traits that spells sure-fire sales ability continues unabated. The number of lists that have been drawn up is countless. Most of them recite the same qualities. McMurry wrote: "It is my conviction that the possessor of an *effective* sales personality is a *habitual 'wooer,' an individual who has a compulsive need to win and hold the affection of others*. . . . His wooing, however, is not based on a sincere desire for love because, in my opinion, he is convinced at heart that no one will ever love him. Therefore, his wooing is primarily exploitative . . . his relationships tend to be transient, superficial and evanescent."[12] McMurry went on to list five additional traits of the super salesperson: a high level of energy, abounding self-confidence, a chronic hunger for money, a well-established habit of industry, and a state of mind that regards each objection, resistance, or obstacle as a challenge.[13]

Mayer and Greenberg offered one of the shortest lists of traits exhibited by effective sales representatives.[14] Their seven years of fieldwork led them to conclude that the effective salesperson has at least two basic qualities: (1) *empathy,* the ability to feel as the customer does; and (2) *ego drive,* a strong personal need to make the sale. Using these two traits, they were able to make fairly good predictions of the subsequent performance of applicants for sales positions in three different industries.

It may be true that certain basic traits may make a person effective in any line of selling. From the viewpoint of a particular company, however, these basic traits are rarely enough. Each selling job is characterized by a unique set of duties and challenges. One has only to think about selling insurance, computers, and automobiles to realize the different educational, intellectual, and personality requirements that would be sought in the respective sales representatives.

How can a company determine the characteristics that its prospective sales representatives should "ideally" possess? The particular duties of the job suggest some of the characteristics to look for in applicants. Is there a lot of paper work? Does the job call for much travel? Will the salesperson confront a high proportion of refusals? In addition, the traits of the company's most successful sales representatives suggest additional qualities to look for. Some companies compare the traits of their best sales representatives with those of their poorest sales representatives to see which characteristics differentiate the two groups.

Recruitment Procedures

After management develops general criteria for new sales personnel, it must try to attract a sufficient number of applicants. The recruiting is turned over to the personnel department, which seeks applicants by various means, including soliciting names from current sales representatives, using employment agencies, placing job ads, and contacting college students. As for college students, companies have not found it easy to sell them on selling. A survey of one thousand male students in 123 colleges indicated that only one in seventeen college students showed an interest in selling.[15] The reluctant ones gave such reasons as "Selling is a job and not a profession," "It calls for deceit if the person wants to succeed," and "There is insecurity and too much travel." To counter these objections company recruiters emphasized starting salaries, income opportunities, and the fact that one-fourth of the presidents of large U.S. corporations started out in marketing and sales.

Applicant-Rating Procedures

Recruitment procedures, if successful, will attract more applicants than the company needs, and the company's task will consist of selecting the best applicants. The selection procedures can vary from a single informal interview to prolonged testing and interviewing, not only of the applicant but of the applicant's family.

An increasing number of companies are giving formal tests to applicants for sales positions. Although test scores are only one information element in a set that includes personal characteristics, references, past employment history, and interviewer reactions, they are weighed quite heavily by some companies, such as IBM, Prudential, Procter & Gamble, and Gillette. Gillette claims that the use of tests has resulted in a 42 percent reduction in turnover and that test scores have correlated well with the subsequent progress of new sales representatives in the sales organization.

The choice of an appropriate battery of tests is not simple. Standard tests are available to measure intelligence, interests, personality, interpersonal skills, and sales aptitude. There are also tailor-made tests for special selling situations. These tests vary considerably in reliability and validity. Furthermore, many of them are vulnerable to manipulation by the applicant. A person can fake a lower IQ or spot red-herring questions, such as "Do you prefer golf or reading?" Whyte laid down the following rules for the job applicant who takes company psychological tests: (1) give the most conventional answer; (2) show that you like things as they are; (3) indicate that you never worry; and (4) deny any taste for books or music.[16]

training sales representatives

Not too long ago many companies sent their new sales representatives out into the field almost immediately after hiring them. The sales representative would be supplied with a pack of samples, order books, and instructions to sell west of the Mississippi. Training programs were considered luxuries. A training program meant large outlays for instructors, materials, and space; the payment of a base salary to a person who was not yet selling; and lost opportunities because he or she was not in the field.

A new sales representative can now expect to spend from a few weeks to many months in the limbo state known as training. The median training period in weeks is twenty-eight in industrial products companies, twelve in service companies, and four in consumer products companies.[17] In some companies, such as steel or data-processing companies, the new sales representative is not on his or her own for two years!

IBM expects its sales representatives to spend 15 percent of their time each year in additional training. The annual sales-training bill for a major U.S. corporation can run into millions of dollars. Several factors have convinced sales management that extended training may add more value than cost. The sales representative of today is selling to more cost-conscious and value-conscious buyers. Furthermore, he or she is selling a host of products, often loosely related, and sometimes technically complex. More reports are expected of this person. The company wants to be represented by a mature and knowledgeable sales representative.

The purpose of the training is to create the following knowledge, skills, and attitudes in the sales force:

1. *The sales representative should know the company and identify with it.* Most companies devote the first part of the training program to describing the history and objectives of the company, the organizational setup and lines of authority, the

names of the chief officers, the company's financial structure and facilities, and the company's chief products and sales volume.

2. *The sales representative should know the company's products.* The sales trainee is shown how the products are produced and how they function in various uses.
3. *The sales representative should know customers' and competitors' characteristics.* The sales representative is introduced to the different types of customers and their needs, buying motives, and buying habits. He or she learns about the company's and competitors' strategies and policies.
4. *The sales representative should learn how to make effective sales presentations.* The sales representative is trained in the basic principles of salesmanship. Part of the training time is used to develop the sales representative's personality and interpersonal skills. In addition, the company outlines the major sales arguments for each product, and some go so far as to provide a sales script.
5. *The sales representative should be introduced to field procedures and responsibilities.* The sales representative should know how to divide time between active accounts and potential accounts; how to use the expense account, prepare reports, and route effectively.

Principles of Salesmanship

One of the major objectives of sales-training programs is to train company sales personnel in the art of selling. The sales-training industry today involves expenditures of hundreds of millions of dollars in training programs, books, cassettes, and other materials. Almost a million copies of books on selling are purchased every year, bearing such provocative titles as *How to Outsell the Born Salesman, How to Sell Anything to Anybody, The Power of Enthusiastic Selling, How Power Selling Brought Me Success in 6 Hours, Where Do You Go from No. 1,* and *1000 Ways a Salesman Can Increase His Sales.* One of the most enduring books is Dale Carnegie's *How to Win Friends and Influence People.*

All of the sales-training approaches are designed to convert a salesperson from being a passive *order taker* to a more active *order getter. Order takers* operate on the following assumptions: (1) customers are aware of their own needs; (2) they cannot be influenced or would resent any attempt at influence; and (3) they prefer salespersons who are courteous and self-effacing. An example of an order-taking mentality would be a Fuller brush salesman who knocks on dozens of doors each day, simply asking if the consumer needs any brushes.

In training salespersons to be *order getters* there are two basic approaches, a sales-oriented approach and a customer-oriented approach. The first one trains the salesperson to be adept in the use of *high-pressure selling techniques,* such as those used in selling encyclopedias or automobiles. The techniques include overstating the product's merits, criticizing competitive products, using a slick canned presentation, selling yourself, and offering some concession to get the order on the spot. The assumptions behind this form of selling are that (1) the customers are not likely to buy except under pressure; (2) they are influenced by a slick presentation and ingratiating manners; and (3) they will not regret the transaction after signing the order, or if they do, it doesn't matter.

The other approach attempts to train sales personnel in *customer problem solving.* Here the salesperson studies the customer's needs and wants and proposes profitable solutions. An example would be a sales representative who examines a customer's situation and proposes a plan that would make or save the customer money. Thus the salesperson does what is good for the customer, not

EXHIBIT 18-2

HOW WELL TRAINED ARE SALES REPS?

A vice-president of a major food company spent one week watching fifty sales presentations to a busy buyer for a major supermarket chain. Here are some of his reactions:

- I watched a soap company representative come in to the buyer. He had three separate new promotional deals to talk about with six different dates. He had *nothing* in writing. . . . After the salesman left, the buyer looked at me and said, "It will take me 15 minutes to get this straightened out."

  I watched another salesman walk in to the buyer and say, "Well, I was in the area, and I want you to know that we have a great new promotion coming up next week." The buyer said, "That's fine. What is it?" He said, "I don't know. . . . I'm coming in next week to tell you about it." The buyer asked him what he was doing there today. He said, "Well, I was in the area."

  Another salesman came (and) said, "Well, it's time for us to write that order now . . . getting ready for the summer business." The buyer said, "Well, fine, George, how much did I buy last year in total?" The salesman looked a little dumfounded and said, "Well, I'll be damned if I know. . . ."

  The majority of salesmen were ill-prepared, unable to answer basic questions, uncertain as to what they wanted to accomplish during the call. They did not think of the call as a studied, professional presentation. They didn't have a real idea of the busy retailer's *needs and wants*.

Source: From an address given by Donald R. Keough at the Twenty-seventh Annual Conference of the Super-Market Institute in Chicago, April 26–29, 1964.

what is immediately good for the salesperson. The assumptions behind this approach are that (1) customers have latent needs that constitute opportunities for the sales representative; (2) they appreciate good suggestions; and (3) they will be loyal to sales representatives who have their long-term interests at heart. Certainly the problem solver is a more compatible image for the salesperson under the marketing concept than the hard seller or order taker.

Most sales-training programs view the selling process as consisting of a set of steps that the salesperson has to carry out, each involving certain skills. These steps are shown in Figure 18-2 and are discussed on the following page.[18]

Figure 18-2 Major Steps in Effective Selling

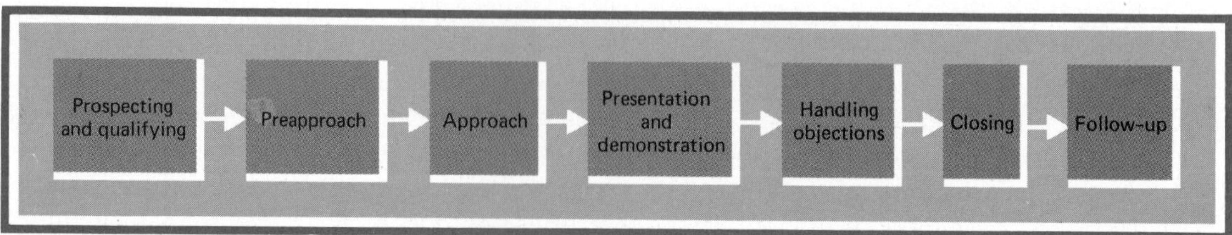

Prospecting and qualifying. The first step in the sales process is to identify prospects. Although the company can supply leads, the sales representatives also need skill in developing their own leads. Leads can be developed in the following ways: (1) asking current satisfied customers for the names of other potential buyers; (2) cultivating other referral sources, such as suppliers, dealers, noncompeting sales representatives, bankers, and trade association executives; (3) joining organizations where there is a high probability of meeting or learning about new prospects; (4) engaging in speaking and writing activities that are likely to increase the salesperson's visibility; (5) examining various data sources (newspapers, directories) in search of names; (6) using the telephone and mail to track down leads; and (7) dropping in unannounced on various offices (cold canvassing).

Sales representatives also need to know how to screen the leads to avoid wasting valuable time on poor leads. Prospects can be qualified by examining their financial ability, volume of business, special requirements, location, and likelihood of continuous business. The salesperson should phone or write to prospects to see if they are worth pursuing further.

Preapproach. This step involves the salesperson in learning as much as possible about the prospect company (what it needs, who is involved in the purchase decision) and its buyers (their personal characteristics and buying styles). The salesperson can consult standard sources (such as *Moody's, Standard and Poor, Dun and Bradstreet*), acquaintances, and others to learn about the company. The salesperson should determine *call objectives,* which might be to qualify the prospect, or gather information, or make an immediate sale. Another task is to decide on the best *approach,* which might be a personal visit (possibly with a respected intermediary), a phone call, or a letter. The best *timing* should be thought out because many prospects are especially busy at certain times of the year. Finally, the salesperson should give some thought to an *overall strategy* to use in the approach step.

Approach. This step involves the salesperson in knowing how to meet and greet the buyer to get the relationship off to a good start. It consists of how the salesperson looks, the opening lines, and the follow-up remarks. The salesperson's looks include his or her appearance, manner, and mannerisms. The salesperson is encouraged to wear clothes similar to what buyers usually wear, such as open shirts and no ties in Texas; show courtesy and attention to the buyer; and avoid distracting mannerisms, such as pacing the floor or staring at the customer. The opening line should be positive and pleasant, such as "Mr. Smith, I am Bill Jones from the ABC Company. My company and I appreciate your willingness to see me. I will do my best to make this visit profitable and worthwhile for you and your company." This might be followed by some light talk to further the acquaintance, some key questions, or the showing of a display or sample to attract the buyer's attention and curiosity.

Presentation and demonstration. After getting acquainted and "sizing up" the buyer, the salesperson attempts to tell the company "story" to the buyer, showing how the product will make or save money for the buyer. The salesperson covers the *features* of the product but concentrates on selling the *benefits*. The aim is to demonstrate the want-satisfying characteristics of the company and its products. The salesperson will follow the AIDA formula in presenting the product: get *attention,* hold *interest,* arouse *desire,* and obtain *action.*

Companies use three different styles of sales presentation. The oldest is the *canned approach,* which is a memorized sales talk covering the main points deemed important by management. It is based on stimulus-response thinking, that is, the buyer is passive and can be moved to purchase by the use of the right stimulus words, pictures, terms, and actions. Thus an encyclopedia salesperson might describe the encyclopedia as "a once-in-a-lifetime buying opportunity" and show some beautiful four-color pages of sports pictures, hoping that these will trigger an irresistible desire for the encyclopedia on the part of the buyer. Canned presentations are used primarily in door-to-door and telephone cold canvassing and have been pretty much abandoned by other companies in favor of more flexible approaches.

The *formulated approach* is also based on stimulus-response thinking but attempts to identify early the buyer's needs and buying style and then use a formulated approach to this type of buyer. In this approach the salesperson does some presenting at the beginning and attempts to draw the buyer into the discussion in a way that will indicate the buyer's needs and attitudes. As these are picked up, the salesperson moves into a formulated presentation that is appropriate to that buyer and shows how the product will satisfy that buyer's needs. It is not canned but follows a general plan.

The *need-satisfaction approach* does not start with a prepared presentation designed to sell the customer but rather a search for the customer's real needs. The customer is encouraged to do most of the talking so that the salesperson can grasp the customer's real needs and respond accordingly. The need-satisfaction approach calls for good listening and problem-solving skills. This approach is well described by an IBM sales representative: "I get inside the business of my key accounts. I uncover their key problems. I prescribe solutions for them, using my company's systems and even, at times, components from other suppliers. I prove beforehand that my systems will save money or make money for my accounts. Then I work with the account to install the system and make it prove out."[19]

Sales presentations can be improved considerably with various demonstration aids, such as booklets, flip charts, slides, movies, and actual product samples. To the extent that the buyer can participate by seeing or handling the product, he or she will better remember its features and possibilities.

Handling objections. Customers will almost always pose objections during the presentation or when asked to place an order. Their sales resistance could take a psychological or a logical form. Psychological resistance includes (1) resistance to interference, (2) preference for established habits, (3) apathy, (4) reluctance to giving up something, (5) unpleasant associations with the other person, (6) tendency to resist domination, (7) predetermined ideas, (8) dislike of making decisions, and (9) neurotic attitude toward money.[20] Logical resistance might consist of objections to the price, delivery schedule, or certain products or company characteristics. To handle these objections, the salesperson uses such techniques as maintaining a positive approach, trying to have the buyer clarify and define the objections, questioning the buyer in such a way that the buyer has to answer his or her own objections, denying the validity of the objections, and turning the objection into a reason for buying. The salesperson needs training in the broader skills of negotiation, of which handling objections is a part.[21]

Closing. In this step the salesperson attempts to close the sale. Some salespeople never get to this stage, or they do not do it well. They lack confidence in themselves or their company or product, or feel guilty about asking for the order, or do not recognize the right psychological moment to close the sale. Salespersons have to be trained in recognizing specific closing signals from the buyer, including physical actions, statements or comments, and questions signaling a possible readiness to close. Salespersons can then use one of several closing techniques. They can ask the prospect for the order, recapitulate the points of agreement, offer to help the secretary write up the order, ask whether the buyer wants A or B, get the buyer to make minor choices such as the color or size, or indicate what the buyer will lose if the order is not placed now. The salesperson may offer the buyer specific inducements to close, such as a special price, an extra quantity at no charge, or a gift.

Follow-up. This last step is necessary if the salesperson wants to ensure customer satisfaction and repeat business. Immediately after closing, the salesperson should attempt to complete any necessary details on delivery time, purchase terms, and other matters. The salesperson should also consider scheduling a follow-up call when the initial order is received to make sure there is proper installation, instruction, and servicing. This visit is designed to detect any problems, to assure the buyer of the salesperson's interest and service, and to reduce any cognitive dissonance that might have arisen.

supervising sales representatives

The new sales representative is given more than a territory, a compensation package, and training—he or she is given supervision. Supervision is the fate of everyone who works for someone else. It is the expression of the employers' natural and continuous interest in the activities of their agents. Through supervision, employers hope to direct and motivate the sales force to do a better job.

Directing Sales Representatives

Companies differ in the extent to which they try to prescribe what their sales representatives should be doing. Much depends upon the nature of the selling job. Sales representatives who are paid mostly on commission and who are expected to hunt down their own prospects are generally left on their own. Those who are salaried and must cover a definite set of accounts are likely to receive substantial supervision.

A major purpose of supervision is to help the sales representatives use their *time* effectively and efficiently. The effective use of time means that the sales representatives make sound decisions on which customers and prospects to spend the time on in the first place. The efficient use of time means that the sales representatives are able to plan their call time so as to maximize the ratio of selling to nonselling time.

Developing customer targets and call norms. Most companies classify their customers into account types, such as A, B, and C, reflecting the sales volume, profit potential, and growth potential of the different accounts. They establish a certain desired number of calls per period that their sales force should make to each account type. Thus A accounts may receive nine calls a year; B, six calls; and C, three calls. The exact levels that are set depend upon competitive call norms and expected account profitability.

The real issue is how much sales volume could be expected from a particular account as a function of the annual number of calls made to that account. Magee described an experiment where sales representatives were asked to vary their call pattern in a particular way to determine what effect this would have on sales.[22] The experiment called first for sorting accounts into major classes. Each account class was then randomly split into three sets. The respective sales representatives were asked, for a specified period of time, to spend less than five hours a month with accounts in the first set, five to nine hours a month with those in the second set, and more than nine hours a month with those in the third set. The results demonstrated that additional call time increases sales volume, leaving only the question of whether the magnitude of sales increase was sufficient to justify the additional cost.

EXHIBIT 18-3

HOW EFFICIENTLY DO COMPANIES MANAGE THEIR SALES FORCE?

There is much evidence of inefficiency in the way companies manage their sales force. A survey of 257 Fortune "500" companies revealed the following:

- 54% have not conducted an organized study of sales representatives' use of time, even though most respondents felt that time utilization represents an area for improvement.
- 25% do not have a system for classifying accounts according to potential.
- 30% do not use call schedules for their sales force.
- 51% do not determine the number of calls it is economical to make on an account.
- 83% do not determine an approximate duration for each call.
- 51% do not use a planned sales presentation.
- 24% do not set sales objectives for accounts.
- 72% do not set profit objectives for accounts.
- 19% do not use a call report system.
- 63% do not use a prescribed routing pattern in covering territories.
- 77% do not use the computer to assist in time and territorial management.

Source: Robert Vizza, "Managing Time and Territories for Maximum Sales Success," *Sales Management,* July 15, 1971, pp. 31–36.

Developing prospect targets and call norms. Companies like to specify how much time their sales force should spend prospecting for new accounts. For example, Spector Freight wants its sales representatives to spend 25 percent of their time prospecting, and to stop calling on a prospect after three unsuccessful calls.

There are various reasons why many companies try to set up a minimum requirement for the canvassing of new accounts. If left alone, many sales representatives will spend most of their time in the offices of current customers. Current customers are better-known quantities. The sales representatives can depend upon them for some business, whereas a prospect may never deliver any business or deliver it only after many months of effort. Unless the sales representatives receive a bonus for opening new accounts, they may avoid new-account development. Some companies rely on a salaried missionary sales force to open new accounts.

Using sales time efficiently. Sales representatives should know how to schedule planned sales calls and use their time efficiently. One tool is the preparation of an *annual call schedule* showing which customers and prospects to call on in which months, and which activities to carry out. The activities include such things as participating in trade shows, attending sales meetings, and carrying out marketing research projects.

The other tool is *time-and-duty analysis* to determine how to use sales call time more efficiently. The sales representative's time is spent in the following ways:

- *Travel.* Travel time is the time spent in travel between rising in the morning and arriving at a lodging in the evening. In some jobs it can amount to as much as 50 percent of total time. Travel time can be cut down by substituting faster for slower means of transportation—recognizing, however, that this will increase costs. More companies are encouraging air travel (commercial or private plane) for their sales force in order to increase their ratio of selling to total time.
- *Food and breaks.* Some portion of the sales force's workday is spent in eating and in taking breaks. If this involves dining with a customer, it will be classified as selling time, otherwise as food and breaks.
- *Waiting.* Waiting consists of time spent in the outer office of the buyer. This is dead time unless the sales representative uses it to plan or to fill out reports.
- *Selling.* Selling is the time spent with the buyer in person or on the phone. It breaks down into "social talk" (the time spent discussing other things) and "selling talk" (the time spent discussing the company and its products).
- *Administration.* This is a miscellaneous category consisting of the time spent in report writing and billing, attending sales meetings, and talking to others in the company about production, delivery, billing, sales performance, and other matters.

No wonder actual selling time may in some companies amount to as little as 15 percent of total working time! If it could be raised from 15 percent to 20 percent, this would be a 33 percent improvement. Companies are constantly seeking ways to help their sales representatives use their time more efficiently. This takes the form of training them in the effective use of the telephone ("phone power"), simplifying the record-keeping forms and requirements, using the computer to develop call and routing plans, and supplying them with marketing research reports on the customer.

Motivating Sales Representatives

A small percentage of sales representatives in any sales force can be expected to do their best without any special prompting from management. To them, selling is the most fascinating job in the world. They are ambitious and self-starters. But the majority of sales representatives on nearly every sales force require personal encouragement and special incentives to work at their best level. This is especially true of creative field selling for the following reasons:

1. *The nature of the job.* The selling job is one of frequent frustration. Sales representatives usually work alone; their hours are irregular; and they are often away from home. They confront aggressive, competing sales representatives; they have an inferior status relative to the buyer; they often do not have the authority to do what is necessary to win an account; they lose large orders that they have worked hard to obtain.
2. *Human nature.* Most people operate below capacity in the absence of some special incentive. They will not "kill themselves" without some prospect of financial gain or social recognition.
3. *Personal problems.* The sales representative, like everyone else, is occasionally preoccupied with personal problems, such as sickness in the family, marital discord, or debt.

Management can affect the morale and performance of the sales force through its organizational climate, sales quotas, and positive incentives.

Organizational climate. Organizational climate describes the feeling that the sales representatives get from their company regarding their opportunities, value, and rewards for a good performance. Some companies treat their sales representatives as if they were of minor importance. Other companies treat their sales representatives as the prime movers and allow unlimited opportunity for income and promotion. The company's attitude toward its sales representatives acts as a self-fulfilling prophecy. If they are held in low opinion, there is much turnover and poor performance; if they are held in high opinion, there is little turnover and high performance.

The quality of personal treatment from the sales representative's immediate superior is an important aspect of the organizational climate. An effective sales manager keeps in touch with the members of the sales force through regular correspondence and phone calls, personal visits in the field, and evaluation sessions in the home office. At different times the sales manager is the sales representative's boss, companion, coach, and confessor.

Sales quotas. Many companies set sales quotas for their sales representatives specifying what they should sell during the year and by product. Their compensation is often, though not always, related to their degree of quota fulfillment.

Sales quotas are developed each year in the process of developing the annual marketing plan. The company first decides on a sales forecast that is reasonably achievable. This becomes the basis of planning production, work-force size, and financial requirements. Then management establishes sales quotas for all of its regions and territories which typically add up to more than the sales forecast. Sales quotas are set higher than the sales forecast in order to stretch the sales managers and salespeople to their best effort. If they fail to make their quotas, the company nevertheless may make its sales forecast.

Each field sales manager takes the assigned quota and divides it up among the sales representatives. Actually, there are three schools of thought on quota setting. The *high-quota school* sets quotas that are above what most sales representatives will achieve but that are possible for all. Its adherents are of the opinion that high quotas spur extra effort. The *modest-quota school* sets quotas that a majority of the sales force can achieve. Its adherents feel that the sales force will accept the quotas as fair, attain them, and gain confidence from attaining them. Finally, the *variable-quota school* thinks that individual differences among sales representatives warrant high quotas for some, modest quotas for others. According to Heckert:

> ▪ Actual experience with sales quotas, as with all standards, will reveal that sales representatives react to them somewhat differently, particularly at first. Some are stimulated to their highest efficiency, others are discouraged. Some sales executives place considerable emphasis upon this human element in setting their quotas. In general, however, good men will in the long run respond favorably to intelligently devised quotas, particularly when compensation is fairly adjusted to performance.[23]

Positive incentives. Companies use a number of positive motivators to stimulate sales-force effort. Periodic *sales meetings* provide a social occasion, a break from routine, a chance to meet and talk with "company brass," and a chance to air feelings and to identify with a larger group. Companies also sponsor *sales contests* when they want to spur the sales force to make a special selling effort above what would be normally expected. Other motivators include honors and awards, profit-sharing plans, and vacations with pay.

evaluating sales representatives

We have been describing the *feedforward* aspects of sales supervision—the efforts of management (1) to communicate what the sales representatives should be doing and (2) to motivate them to do it. But good feedforward requires good feedback. And good feedback means getting regular information from and about sales representatives to evaluate their performance.

Sources of Information

Management obtains information about its sales representatives through a number of channels. Probably the most important source of information is the sales representative's periodic reports. Additional information is obtained through personal observation, customers' letters and complaints, and conversations with other sales representatives.

A distinction can be drawn between sales reports that represent *plans for future activities* and those that represent *write-ups of completed activities.* The best example of the former is the *salesperson's work plan,* which most sales representatives are required to submit for a specified future period, usually a week or a month in advance. The plan describes the calls they will make and the routing they will use. This report serves the purposes of encouraging the sales force to plan and schedule their activities, informing management of their whereabouts, and providing a basis for comparing their plans with their accomplishments. Sales representatives can be evaluated on their ability to "plan their work and work their plan." Occasionally, management contacts individual sales representatives after receiving their plans to suggest improvements.

Companies moving toward annual marketing planning in depth are beginning to require their sales representatives to draft an annual *territory marketing plan* in which they outline their program for developing new accounts and increasing business from existing accounts. The formats vary considerably, some asking for general ideas on territory development and others asking for detailed volume and profit estimates. This type of report casts sales representatives into the role of market managers and profit centers. The plans are studied by their sales managers and become the bases for rendering constructive suggestions to sales representatives and developing branch sales objectives and estimates for higher-level management.

Several reports are used by sales representatives to write up their completed activities and accomplishments. Perhaps the best known is the *call report* in which the salesperson records pertinent aspects of his or her dealings with a customer, including competitive brands used, best time for calling, degree and type of resistance, and future account promise. Call reports serve the objectives of keeping sales management informed of the salesperson's activities, indicating the status of the customers' accounts, and providing information that might be useful in subsequent calls. Sales representatives also report *expenses* incurred in the performance of selling duties, for which they are partly or wholly reimbursed. The objective from management's standpoint is primarily to exercise control over the type and amount of expenses and secondarily to have the requisite expense data for income-tax purposes. It is also hoped that the sales representatives will exercise more care in incurring expenses when they must report them in some detail. Additional types of reports that some companies require from their sales representatives include a report on new business secured or potential new business, a report on lost business, and a report on local business and economic conditions.

These various reports supply the raw data from which sales management can extract key indicators of sales performance. The key indicators they watch are (1) average number of sales calls per salesperson per day, (2) average sales call time per contact, (3) average revenue per sales call, (4) average cost per sales call, (5) entertainment cost per sales call, (6) percentage of orders per hundred sales calls, (7) number of new customers per period, (8) number of lost customers per period, and (9) sales-force cost as a percentage of total sales. An analysis of these statistics will raise useful questions, such as: Are sales representatives making too few calls per day? Are they spending too much time per call? Are they spending too much on entertainment? Are they closing enough orders per hundred calls? Are they producing enough new customers and holding on to the old customers?

Formal Evaluation of Performance

The sales force's reports along with other reports from the field and the manager's personal observations supply the raw materials for formally evaluating members of the sales force. Formal evaluation procedures lead to at least three benefits. First, they lead management to develop specific and uniform standards for judging sales performance. Second, they lead management to draw together all its information and impressions about individual sales representatives and make more systematic, point-by-point evaluations. And third, they tend to have a constructive effect on the performance of sales representatives. The constructive effect comes about because the sales representatives know that they will have to sit down one morning with the sales manager and explain certain facets of their routing or sales call decisions or their failure to secure or maintain certain accounts.

Salesperson-to-salesperson comparisons. One type of evaluation frequently made is to compare and rank the sales performance of the various sales representatives. Such comparisons, however, can be misleading. Relative sales performances are meaningful only if there are no variations from territory to territory in the market potential, workload, degree of competition, company promotional effort, and so forth. Furthermore, sales are not the best denominator of achievement. Management should be more interested in how much each sales representative contributed to net profits. And this cannot be known until the sales representatives' sales mix and sales expenses are examined. A possible ranking criterion would be the sales representative's *ratio of actual contribution to company net profits to potential contribution to company net profits.* A ratio of 1.00 would mean that the sales representative delivered the potential sales in his or her territory. The lower a sales representative's ratio, the more supervision and counseling he or she needs.

Current-to-past-sales comparisons. A second common type of evaluation is to compare a sales representative's current performance with his or her past performance. This should provide a more direct indication of progress. An example is shown in Table 18-1.

The sales manager can learn many things about John Smith from the information in this table. One of the first things to note is that Smith's total sales increased every year (line 3). This does not necessarily mean that Smith is doing a better job. The product breakdown shows that he has been able to push further the sales of product B than product A (lines 1 and 2). According to his quotas for the two products (lines 4 and 5), his success in increasing sales of product B may be at the expense of product A. According to gross profits (lines 6 and 7), the company earns about twice as much on A as B as a ratio to sales. The picture begins to emerge that Smith may be pushing the higher-volume, lower-margin product at the expense of the more profitable product. In fact, although he increased total sales by $1,100 between 1978 and 1979 (line 3), the gross profits on his total sales actually decreased by $580 (line 8).

Sales expense (line 9) shows a steady increase, although total expense as a percentage of total sales seems to be under control (line 10). The upward trend in Smith's total dollar expense does not seem to be explained by any increase in the number of calls (line 11), although it may be related in part to his success in acquiring new customers (line 14). However, there is a possibility that in prospecting for new customers, he is neglecting present customers, as indicated by an upward trend in the annual number of lost customers (line 15).

Table 18-1
Form for Evaluating Sales Representative's Performance

	Territory: Midland		Sales Representative:	John Smith
	1976	1977	1978	1979
1. Net sales product A	$251,300	$253,200	$270,000	$263,100
2. Net sales product B	$423,200	$439,200	$553,900	$561,900
3. Net sales total	$674,500	$692,400	$823,900	$825,000
4. Percent of quota product A	95.6	92.0	88.0	84.7
5. Percent of quota product B	120.4	122.3	134.9	130.8
6. Gross profits product A	$ 50,260	$ 50,640	$ 54,000	$ 52,620
7. Gross profits product B	$ 42,320	$ 43,920	$ 55,390	$ 56,190
8. Gross profits total	$ 92,580	$ 94,560	$109,390	$108,810
9. Sales expense	$ 10,200	$ 11,100	$ 11,600	$ 13,200
10. Sales expense to total sales (%)	1.5	1.6	1.4	1.6
11. Number of calls	1,675	1,700	1,680	1,660
12. Cost per call	$ 6.09	$ 6.53	$ 6.90	$ 7.95
13. Average number of customers	320	324	328	334
14. Number of new customers	13	14	15	20
15. Number of lost customers	8	10	11	14
16. Average sales per customer	$ 2,108	$ 2,137	$ 2,512	$ 2,470
17. Average gross profit per customer	$ 289	$ 292	$ 334	$ 326

The last two lines show the level and trend in Smith's sales per customer and the gross profits on his sales per customer. These figures become more meaningful when they are compared with overall company averages. For example, if John Smith's average gross profit per customer is lower than the company's average, he may be concentrating on the wrong customers or may not be spending enough time with each customer. Looking back at his annual number of calls (line 11), it may be that Smith is making fewer annual calls than the average salesperson. If distances in his territory are not much different, this may mean he is not putting in a full workday, he is poor at planning his routing or minimizing his waiting, or he spends too much time with certain accounts.

Qualitative evaluation of sales representatives. The evaluation usually extends to the salesperson's knowledge of the company, products, customers, competitors, territory, and responsibilities. Personality characteristics can be rated, such as general manner, appearance, speech, and temperament. The sales manager can also consider any problems in motivation or compliance. Since an almost endless number of qualitative factors might be included, each company must decide what would be most useful to know. It also should communicate these criteria to the sales representatives so that they are aware of how their performance is judged and can make an effort to improve it.

EXHIBIT
18-4

PERSONAL SELLING AND PUBLIC POLICY

Sales representatives must follow the rules of "fair competition" in trying to obtain orders. Certain activities have been declared illegal or are heavily regulated. For example, sales representatives are to refrain from getting business by offering bribes to buyers, purchasing agents, or other influence sources. It is illegal for them to procure technical or trade secrets of competitors through espionage or bribery. They must be careful not to disparage competitors or their products by suggesting things that are not true. They must not sell used items as new or mislead the customer about the buying advantages. They must inform customers of their rights, such as the seventy-two-hour "cooling-off" period in which customers can return the merchandise and receive their money back. They must not discriminate against buyers on the basis of their race, sex, or creed.

Source: Adapted from Ovid Riso, ed., *The Dartnell Sales Manager's Handbook*, 11th ed. (Chicago: Dartnell Corporation, 1968), pp. 320–22.

summary

Most companies utilize sales representatives, and many companies assign them the pivotal role in the creation of sales. The high cost of this resource calls for an effective process of sales management consisting of six steps: establishing sales-force objectives; designing sales-force strategy, structure, size, and compensation; recruiting and selecting; training; supervising; and evaluating.

As an element of the marketing mix, the sales force is capable of achieving certain marketing objectives effectively. The company has to decide on the proper mix of sales activities for the sales force, drawn from the following: prospecting, communicating, selling and servicing, information gathering, and allocating. Under the marketing concept, the sales force is expected to acquire skills in marketing analysis and planning in addition to the traditional selling skills.

Given the sales-force objectives, sales-force strategy answers the questions of what type of selling would be most effective (solo selling, team selling, etc.), what type of sales-force structure would work best (territorial, product, or customer-structured), how large the sales force should be, and how the sales force should be compensated in terms of pay level and pay components such as salary, commission, bonus, expenses, and fringe benefits.

Sales representatives must be recruited and selected on the basis of scientific procedures to hold down the high costs of hiring the wrong persons. Sales-training programs are becoming more elaborate and are designed to familiarize the salesperson with the company's history, its products and policies, the characteristics of the market and competitors, and the art of selling. The art of selling involves training salespeople in a seven-step sales process: prospecting and qualifying, preapproach, approach, presentation and demonstration, handling objections, closing, and follow-up. The salesperson needs supervision and continuous encouragement because he or she must make many decisions and is subject to many frustrations. Periodically, the salesperson's performance must be formally evaluated to help him or her do a better job.

questions for discussion

1. How does personal selling differ from advertising?
2. Relate the six tasks of selling to an automobile sales representative.
3. In what alternative ways can a sales force be structured? Relate each to a specific company that sells industrial products.
4. A combination of straight salary and commission is probably the best way to compensate a sales force. Comment.
5. What two personal qualities do you think are most important to a successful sales representative? Why?
6. You have just been hired by the World Book Encyclopedia Company to be a salesperson for the summer. Discuss how you would progress through the steps in effective selling.
7. What are the major tasks that those who supervise sales representatives must undertake?
8. How would your manager in question 6 go about evaluating your selling job for World Book at the end of the summer?

references

1. Excerpts are from THOMAS EHRICH, "To Computer Salesmen, the "Big-Ticket" Deal Is the One to Look For," *Wall Street Journal,* January 22, 1974, p. 1.
2. ROBERT N. MCMURRY, "The Mystique of Super-Salesmanship," *Harvard Business Review,* March-April 1961, p. 114.
3. See SIDNEY J. LEVY, *Promotional Behavior* (Glenview, Ill.: Scott, Foresman, 1971), pp. 65–69.
4. JOHN STEINBRINK, *Compensation of Salesmen: Dartnell's 19th Biennial Survey* (Chicago: Dartnell Corporation, 1978).
5. See WILLIAM R. DIXON, "Redetermining the Size of the Sales Force: A Case Study," in *Changing Perspectives in Marketing Management,* ed. Martin R. Warshaw (Ann Arbor: University of Michigan, Michigan Business Reports, 1962) No. 37, p. 58.
6. ROGER M. PEGRAM, *Selling and Servicing the National Account* (New York: Conference Board, 1972).
7. WILLIAM H. KAVEN, *Managing the Major Sale* New York: American Management Association, 1971); and BENSON P. SHAPIRO AND RONALD S. POSNER, "Making the Major Sale," *Harvard Business Review,* March-April 1976, pp. 68–78.
8. WALTER J. TALLEY, "How to Design Sales Territories," *Journal of Marketing,* January 1961, pp. 7–13.
9. JOHN P. STEINBRINK, "How to Pay Your Sales Force," *Harvard Business Review,* July-August 1978, pp. 111–22.
10. Ibid.

11. The survey was conducted by the Sales Executives Club of New York and was reported in *Business Week,* February 1, 1964, p. 52.
12. McMurry, "Mystique of Super-Salesmanship," p. 117.
13. Ibid., p. 118.
14. David Mayer and Herbert M. Greenberg, "What Makes a Good Salesman?" *Harvard Business Review,* July-August 1964, pp. 119–25.
15. "Youth Continues to Snub Selling," *Sales Management,* January 15, 1965, p. 69. Also see Donald L. Thompson, "Stereotype of the Salesman," *Harvard Business Review,* January-February 1972, p. 21.
16. William H. Whyte, Jr., *The Organization Man* (New York: Simon & Schuster, 1956), pp. 405–10.
17. "Double-Digit Hikes in 1974 Sales Training Costs," *Sales and Marketing Management,* January 6, 1975, p. 54.
18. Some of the following discussion is based on W.J.E. Crissy, William H. Cunningham, and Isabella C. M. Cunningham, *Selling: The Personal Force in Marketing* (New York: John Wiley, 1977), pp. 119–29.
19. Mark Hanan, "Join the Systems Sell and You Can't Be Beat," *Sales and Marketing Management,* August 21, 1972, p. 44. Also see Mark Hanan, James Cribbin, and Herman Heiser, *Consultative Selling* (New York: American Management Association, 1970).
20. Crissy, Cunningham, and Cunningham, *Selling,* pp. 289–94.
21. See Gerald I. Nierenberg, *The Art of Negotiation* (New York: Hawthorn, 1968); and Chester L. Karrass, *The Negotiating Game* (Cleveland: World Publishing, 1970).
22. See John F. Magee, "Determining the Optimum Allocation of Expenditures for Promotional Effort with Operations Research Methods," in *The Frontiers of Marketing Thought and Science,* ed. Frank M. Bass (Chicago: American Marketing Association, 1958), pp. 140–56.
23. J. B. Heckert, *Business Budgeting and Control* (New York: Ronald Press, 1946), p. 138.

Cases

10 King-Cola Corp.

Watch out, Pepsi and Coke, you've got some new competition.

Sure, the two soft drink giants have faced young rivals before, but none quite like King-Cola Corp., which is announcing its debut today.

For one thing, King-Cola isn't made up of a bunch of fresh-faced kids. The company's chairman and founder will be 83 years old next month. Its vice chairman and manufacturing expert is 68. Another vice chairman is 72.

They aren't inexperienced either. King-Cola's top brass have seen first-hand how the folk in Atlanta and Purchase, N.Y. have become No. 1 and No. 2 in the cola business. Consider the resumes of some of King-Cola's new officers:

—Walter S. Mack, chairman. He was the first president of Pepsi-Cola Co., the forerunner of today's PepsiCo Inc., and a man credited with several of its famous marketing ploys.

—Thomas Elmezzi, vice chairman and 43 year veteran of Pepsi. He's one of the fewer than two dozen people in the company's history to have been privy to the closely guarded recipe for Pepsi Cola.

—Richard D. Harvey, board member. He spent 28 years at Coca-Cola Co. and claims to have been its first brand manager. He has also been marketing director for Coke's U.S. division and a corporate vice president, management development.

Their aim is to become nothing less than the leader of the $11.5 billion U.S. soft drink business. "No reason why we shouldn't be," says the confident and energetic Mr. Mack, sitting in his partially furnished Park Avenue office. Above him are photos of himself and Franklin D. Roosevelt, Hubert H. Humphrey and Lyndon B. Johnson.

"The two leading brands of cola are muscle-bound with their old methods of franchising," Mr. Mack adds. "It ties them up."

Game Plan

Mr. Mack figures to beat his larger rivals by taking advantage of their decades-old franchise system, which gives bottlers perpetual rights to soft drink bottling and distribution in their respective areas. Both Coke and Pepsi have hundreds of bottlers, who deliver their products to the door of every supermarket, gas station, and convenience store in their areas.

That's an expensive way of distributing products, most food marketers agree. Less costly is distribution through supermarket warehouses and food brokers, which deliver a variety of goods in each truckload.

Mr. Mack says he's the one to modernize soft drink distribution, although others have also tried unsuccessfully to unseat Coke and Pepsi. By delivering King-Cola to warehouses, Mr. Mack estimates that he can cut his distribution costs to a nickel per case of 24 cans. Each can holds 12 ounces.

Shipping those same cases directly to store doors cost about $1 each, he says.

The payoff for cola drinkers will be a less costly beverage. King-Cola will retail for between $1.09 and $1.19 a six-pack. Coke and Pepsi sell for about $1.59 to $1.79.

King-Cola is currently trying to sign up 29 U.S. licensees, who will operate "kingdom" ("I like to play with words,"says Mr. Mack.) for the bottling and distribution of the cola, which doesn't taste too different from other colas currently on the market, according to an informal lunchroom taste-test at this newspaper. (Mr. Mack, naturally, says the brand is superior and lacks the aftertaste of other soft drinks.)

A Kingdom for a License

The license for each Kingdom will run about $1 million or $2 million. Mr. Mack claims he has no shortage of interested takers, including one from Jordon who has plunked down $500,000 for an option on a Mideast kingdom. Stockholders aren't being solicited.

King-Cola's chief says he expects his product to be in stores early next year and selling as much as 50 million cases in the first year. That would give King-Cola at least a 1% share of the market.

"If you can arrange for Coke and Pepsi to sue me, we might double that," says Mr. Mack. "I don't expect them to sit back. They'll do everything they can to compete with us."

A lawsuit from the industry giants would be great publicity, he figures, but Mr. Mack isn't counting on his competitors to make his name for him. King-Cola has hired Wells, Rich, Greene, Inc., a well-known ad agency, for that.

So far, though, neither Coke nor Pepsi has shown any ill-will toward King-Cola. A Coke spokesman hadn't any comment on the latest competitor. At Pepsi, where a company biography lists Mr. Mack as the originator of the familiar red, white, and blue Pepsi logo and as the overseer of the first soft drink can and a famous Pepsi jingle ("Pepsi-Cola hits the spot, 12 full ounces, that's a lot"), they're wishing him well.

"We welcome competition," says a Pepsi spokesman. "It helps build the market."

Bill Abrams, "Pepsi, Coke Veterans Launch King-Cola, Plan Soda Pop War," *Wall Street Journal,* Thursday, Sept. 14, 1978. Reproduced by permission of Wall Street Journal,

Questions

1. Is there a market for King-Cola? Who would be likely to buy King-Cola? Why? Where? For what occasions?
2. Is the distribution plan sound from the point of view of a prospective licensee? The King-Cola Corporation?
3. According to the June 25, 1979, issue of *Advertising Age,* Canada Dry has announced that it has formed a subsidiary to market a new 99 percent caffeine-free cola, Spur Cola. It is to be sold at a lower price than Coca-Cola or Pepsi-Cola. It is claimed that lower costs achieved by distribution to supermarket warehouses rather than to retail stores will make this possible. What impact will these developments have on the success of King-Cola? What response, if any, should King-Cola make?
4. What threats are posed by potential actions of environmentalists? Could King-Cola effectively respond to such threats? How would these responses affect the company's hoped-for competitive advantage?
5. Should King-Cola seek private-label contracts either as a temporary or as a permanent measure?

11 Loctite Corporation

Loctite is a highly profitable and rapidly growing manufacturer and marketer of adhesives and sealants, and related specialty chemicals, with annual sales of more than $100 million. The company's growth has been in the "wonder glues," specifically in the anaerobic type, which *cures quickly in absence of air,* and the "crazy glues" (cyanoacrylates), which *cure instantly upon exposure to moisture,* which is present in trace amounts on surfaces to be bonded. In the industrial market this product sells for over $60 per pound, which contains roughly thirty thousand drops and is generally applied a few drops at a time. Consumer packages are much smaller, containing about one-tenth of an ounce and selling for up to $2 per tube, or about $20 or more per ounce.

The company's phenomenal success in the industrial market has attracted competitors, including some large and aggressive ones, such as Esmark and the 3M Company. Competitive anaerobic and cyanoacrylate products are being marketed in most countries where the company conducts business. The company has substantial patent protection on its anaerobics in the United States and, to a lesser extent, in a number of foreign countries. Nearly all competitive anaerobic sealants and adhesives are sold at lower prices than the company's products and, in some instances, at substantially lower prices. Although the company has selectively reduced prices to meet competition from time to time, it believes that attention to technical service and customer needs has generally enabled it to maintain its market position without significant price reductions.

The company plans to intensify its "application engineering" approach, which helped it overtake Eastman Kodak in the more competitive "crazy glue," or cyanoacrylates, market. This approach casts well-trained, technical service personnel as customer problem solvers using Loctite's products, often especially formulated for the customer's application.

The Company has actively extended its marketing activities into the automotive aftermarket and the consumer market. Increased activity in the automotive aftermarket has resulted principally from the acquisition of the Permatex Company, and in the consumer market from the acquisition of the Woodhill Chemical Sales Corporation. The U.S. business of these two acquired subsidiaries was consolidated to form the company's Woodhill-Permatex Group.

The company has three principal user markets for its products: the industrial market, the consumer market, and the automotive aftermarket. The company reaches user markets through its three marketing organizations: the Industrial Products Group, the Woodhill-Permatex Group, and the International Group. Each marketing organization has the responsibility for developing marketing strategies and techniques for its area of operation within the framework of overall corporate marketing plans.

The Industrial Products Group principally services industrial customers in the United States and Canada. The Woodhill-Permatex Group services the domestic consumer market and automotive aftermarkets. The International Group is responsible for servicing all markets for the company's products throughout the remainder of the world and conducts its principal activities throughout the European continent, in some Middle and Far Eastern countries, and in Latin America.

In the Industrial Products Group, approximately 60 percent of sales are made through independent distributors, some of which sell adhesives and sealants made by others, and the remainder of sales are made directly to end-users. The company provides close and continued contact with its distributors and major end-users to provide technical assistance and support for the use of its products. In the United States and Canada, sales are made through approximately 120 technically trained district managers, salesmen, and representatives, and through approximately 2,800 independent industrial distributors.

The Woodhill-Permatex Group services nonindustrial markets in the United States. The group markets its line of automotive repair products under the Permatex trademark through an estimated twenty-five thousand automotive and related warehouse distributors and jobbers. The company employs approximately thirty salesmen and manufacturer's representatives to familiarize auto parts and supply dealers with these products. The group also markets the company's consumer products, primarily to the hardware, automotive, and building supply channels under the Duro/Woodhill, Super-Glue, and other trademarks. These sealant, adhesive, and related chemical specialty repair products are sold through an estimated eighty thousand outlets in the United States.

In the International Group, most sales are made through a network of national distributors, some of which are wholly or partly owned by the company. The company supports these distributors with marketing and technical assistance from its regional headquarters in Paris and Hong Kong, as well as from Newington, Connecticut.

This case is based primarily on the 1978 Loctite Corporation's annual report and form 10-K filed with the SEC by the company.

Questions

1. How can Loctite, a small company in the chemical-processing industry, hope to compete with multibillion-dollar firms?
2. How may each of these basic types of adhesives be used? Think of adhesives as "chemical fasteners" versus nails, screws, and bolts as "mechanical fasteners." List as many uses as possible.
3. How would you plan the market targets for Loctite in view of the many product applications in almost every industry, business, and home?
4. What changes do you feel should be made in Loctite's marketing activities in the industrial market? The consumer market?

12 Texas Instruments, Inc.: Learning Aid Products

Texas Instruments' drive into consumer markets has been expanded beyond hand-held calculators in the past five years by the introduction of five new hand-held learning aid products (LAPs) at relatively low prices. The Little Professor, Dataman, and First Watch have numerical memories and displays. The first two teach math, and the third teaches how to tell time. The Spelling B and Speak & Spell teach how to spell, and they have both numerical and alphabetical memories and displays. Speak & Spell is further distinguished by its voice capability.

Although they differ significantly in both form and function from other TI consumer products (calculators and watches) and are in the introductory stage of the product life cycle, the marketing strategy that has been pursued to date is virtually identical to that employed for the company's more mature products. Their educational value suggests that they could be marketed to schools as a supplementary learning aid. Only a limited effort has been made to develop either the educational or the entertainment markets. As with any new-product introduction, TI is faced with assessing market potential and familiarizing potential customers with a previously unheard-of product. These problems are particularly acute in this case because the products were developed as an outgrowth of technological innovation rather than in response to consumer needs.

The company is at the point where it must decide what strategies and action programs it should use to ensure successful participation in the market for small electronic learning aid products.

TI's Consumer Products Group's direct sales force sells LAPs as well as calculators and digital watches to major retail chains. Smaller stores either place their orders directly with TI or purchase through distributors. In 1978 advertising amounted to about $1 million and was confined to the four weeks following Thanksgiving. The sole advertising medium used was television (prime and fringe time), with very heavy exposure. The company uses some trade magazine advertising, but the program is not extensive. Cooperative advertising is offered to retailers on an accrual basis, with a specified percentage of total purchases available to dealers for co-op advertising purposes.

TI achieved its dominant position in hand-held calculator sales by using a low-margin, high-volume strategy. Relatively low prices were established in the anticipation that large production volumes, coupled with accumulated experience in manufacturing and marketing, would result in a series of unit cost decreases which would in turn permit still lower prices.

The learning aids began in 1972 when TI, along with such firms as Bowmar, National Semiconductor, and Commodore, packaged inexpensive calculators with game books. By 1975 National Semiconductor had introduced the Quiz Kid, an owl-shaped, hand-held machine in which the user inputted simple math problems, and what he or she believed to be the correct answer. The device then indicated with a green or a red light whether the answer was correct or incorrect.

TI's Little Professor, introduced in 1976, was further refined one year later with the introduction of Dataman. These machines were distinguished by the preprogramming of specific math problems within each machine's memory. The Dataman extended the capability of the Little Professor by adding game-playing capabilities and a fluorescent "stadium scoreboard" display for correct answers.

In 1978 Spelling B and Speak & Spell were introduced. These products are noteworthy for their alphabetic capabilities. Speak & Spell uses TI's new voice synthesizer technology. It contains 230 of the most commonly misspelled words in order of difficulty. It asks you to spell a word which it clearly pronounces. When you finish spelling, you press a button, and if you were right it says, "That is correct, now spell *treasure*." If you had misspelled the word, it would have said, "Wrong, try again," and you would have had another chance. If you missed again, the unit would have said, "The correct spelling is T-R-E-A-S-U-R-E." The unit also automatically displays the number of right and wrong answers at the end of a block of ten words. Speak & Spell can be used as a pronounciation guide and as the basis for a number of games, and it will accept additional small memory cartridges that raise the spelling difficulty. The new technology involved holds enormous potential, since voice-command control will eventually be an important aspect of life. In 1978 the retail price for Speak & Spell, a truly sophisticated learning aid, was only $49.50. Spelling B, which has no voice capability, sold for $30.

The speech synthesis chip, which has brought such wide attention to Speak & Spell, is a far more advanced (and compact) version of the circuit and chip systems that have been used for almost two decades in commercial and industrial "talking machines," such as in banking systems and disconnected/new-number messages by telephone companies. The memory capability of Speak & Spell is more than twice that of any previous portable voice memory system. The speech synthesis capability of Speak & Spell was almost universally hailed as a major innovation and, as a result, has received a great deal of attention.

Several future uses have been proposed for voice synthesis chips, including not only warning systems in airplanes and automobiles to replace "idiot lights" but also foreign language education and electronic games (such as chess and backgammon).

An example of the potential is the electronic dictionary, already being offered by at least two firms. It can translate as many as fifteen hundred English words and phrases into a foreign language, such as French, German, Spanish, Russian, and Japanese. Languages can be changed by switching cartridges or cassettes, available at $25 to $50 each. Both the Lexicon and the Craig are pocket-size and sell for about $200.

Based upon the article "Electronic Gadgets That Can Talk, Spell, May Open New Path for Consumer Goods," *Wall Street Journal*, June 12, 1978; and materials developed by Leonard J. Feldman, Ernest M. Koneck, Jr., and Melinda A. Stimson.

Questions

1. What markets exist for learning aid products of the TI type? Who are the buyers? Why would they buy? How and where?
2. What priority would you assign the different markets in a marketing plan for TI?
3. What are your recommendations regarding pricing, distribution channels, and marketing communications?

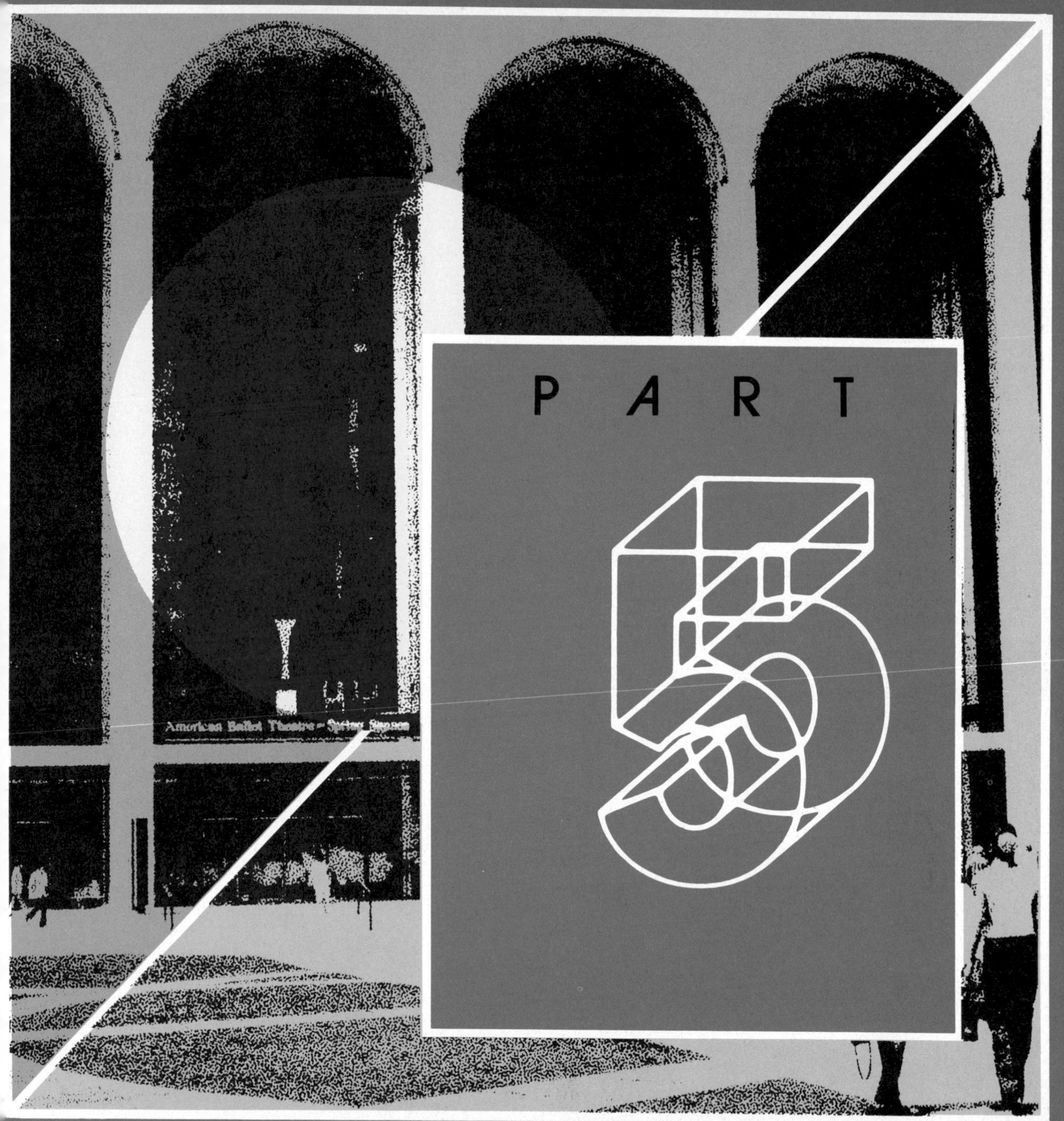

marketing's role in society

INTERNATIONAL MARKETING

Levi Strauss & Company is well known throughout the world as the maker of the famous tight-fitting blue jeans, a product it has been making since 1850. Its jeans conjure up the image of the Old American West as well as the new American consciousness that holds to the value of simplicity, ruggedness, frugality. Teen-agers around the world have adopted the blue jean as their uniform. Jeans are a prized article in the Soviet Union and other countries where their sale is limited or actively discouraged.

Levi Strauss, whose headquarters are in San Francisco, started to sell its jeans abroad more as an afterthought than anything else. Its huge U.S. market was too big for the company to need further markets. Yet orders started coming in from abroad, and Levi Strauss set up some casual exporting arrangements. The demand continued to grow, and although total export sales are still only a small percentage of Levi Strauss's total sales, the absolute dollar volume is large and the rate of growth is high.

Levi Strauss's export business is handled through an International Division headed by an international director who reports directly to the president. The company operates a warehouse in Antwerp, Belgium, which stocks all the fast-moving items and delivers them to any European market within two or three days. The job of selling jeans and other Levi Strauss products has been handed over to distributors, one for each major European country. Each distributor is responsible for local warehousing and reselling to retailers. A distributor is free to select and develop retail accounts, subject to certain broad company policies aiming at a uniform resale price among retail accounts, and certain promotion policies. The distributors are billed for all merchandise shipped to them.

Levi Strauss is now considering whether it should step up its international operations. Worldwide demand for jeans continues strong, and aggressive competitors such as Blue Bell (Wrangler brand) are moving into Europe fast, not to mention the emergence of European competitors with their own factories in Europe. Those in Levi Strauss who are expansion-minded are urging bold steps to further penetrate the European market. They want to start production in several European countries to replace export. They also want to replace foreign distributors with company-owned sales branches out of which Levi Strauss salespeople would work and sell directly to retailers. By "Europeanizing," the company would be able to spot many more market opportunities and even make inroads into other clothing, such as the lederhosen worn in the German countries.

More conservative executives at Levi Strauss have reservations. They can imagine a sudden repudiation of blue jeans by European teenagers and young adults, possibly in a sudden wave of anti-Americanism or as a result of new fashion interest. They see this step as diverting cash from further development of the American market, which is now taking new turns. For example, designer jeans bearing such names as Calvin Klein, Sassoon, and Vanderbilt have experienced a rapid takeoff.

Levi Strauss's managers have a lot to ponder regarding the company's future role in the world market. Are they facing a golden opportunity or a dangerous snare?

□Mixed feelings about expanding abroad when the U.S. domestic market is so large have been a factor keeping Levi Strauss and many other American companies from taking an aggressive world posture. Most American firms prefer domestic marketing to foreign marketing. Domestic marketing is generally simpler and safer. Managers do not have to learn another language, deal with a different currency, face political and legal uncertainties, or adapt the product to a different set of needs and expectations.

There are mainly two factors that might draw American companies into international marketing. First, they might be *pushed* into it by a weakening of marketing opportunities at home. The growth of GNP may slow down, or government may become increasingly antibusiness, or the tax burden may become too heavy. It is also possible that the government might push business into expanding abroad in order to earn more foreign exchange and reduce the U.S. trade deficit.[1] Second, American companies might be *pulled* into foreign trade by growing opportunities for their product in other countries. Without abandoning the domestic market, they might find other markets an attractive place to make a profit even after allowing for the extra costs and encumbrances they might face in operating abroad.

At the present time, American exports account for only 6 percent of the U.S. gross national product. This still makes the United States the world's largest exporting nation in absolute dollars. Other countries have less of a choice about their level of involvement in world trade. Countries like the United Kingdom, Belgium, the Netherlands, and New Zealand have to sell more than half their output abroad in order to have high employment and be able to pay for imported goods. International marketing is second nature to the companies in these countries.

Some companies here and abroad have gone into world marketing on such a large scale that they can be called *multinational companies.* Among American companies selling more than 50 percent of their output abroad are Hoover (67.9 percent), Mobil Oil (67.6 percent), Otis Elevator (58.8 percent), CPC International (54.4 percent), Standard Oil of California (54.4 percent), Gulf Oil (54.1 percent), and Pfizer (51.9 percent).[2] Such companies as IBM, Caterpillar, Chrysler, Coca-Cola, Dow Chemical, and Xerox earn more than half of their profits abroad, and their foreign operations appear to be growing faster than their domestic operations. These American companies face formidable multinational competitors such as Royal Dutch/Shell, British Petroleum, Unilever, Philips, Volkswagenwerk, Nippon Steel, Siemens, Toyota Motor, and Nestlé.

In the same way that some American companies have been aggressively expanding abroad, many foreign companies have entered the American market in the pursuit of riches. Their names and brands have become household words, such as Sony, Honda, Datsun, Nestlé, Perrier, Norelco, Mercedes Benz, and Volkswagen, with many Americans showing a preference for these brands over domestic brands. There are many other favored products that appear to be produced by American firms but are really owned by foreign multinationals. This group includes Bantam Books, Baskin-Robbins Ice Cream, Capitol Records, Kiwi Shoe Polish, Lipton Tea, and Saks Fifth Avenue. America is also attracting huge foreign investments in tourist and real estate ventures, notably Japanese purchases of land in Hawaii, Kuwait's development of a resort island off the South Carolina coast, and Arab purchases of Manhattan office buildings—and one offer by a Saudi Arabian sheik to buy the Alamo for his son.

As international competition intensifies, American companies have to increase their sophistication in handling international marketing operations. Some of America's most successful marketers have fumbled when they went abroad. Kentucky Fried Chicken opened eleven outlets in Hong Kong, but they all failed within two years. Apparently Hong Kong citizens found it too messy to eat chicken with their hands. McDonald's located its first European outlet in a suburb of Amsterdam, but sales were disappointing. McDonald's missed the fact that most Europeans live in the central city and are less mobile.

One may ask the question whether international marketing really involves any new principles that have not been examined in our previous discussion of effective marketing management. Obviously the principles of setting marketing objectives, choosing target markets, developing marketing positionings and marketing mixes, and carrying out marketing control apply. The principles are not new, but the differences between nations may be so great that the international marketer must master special environmental factors and institutions and be prepared to drop some of the most basic assumptions about how people respond to marketing stimuli.

We now turn to the basic decisions that a company faces in considering international marketing. The six major steps are shown in Figure 19-1 and are examined in the following sections.

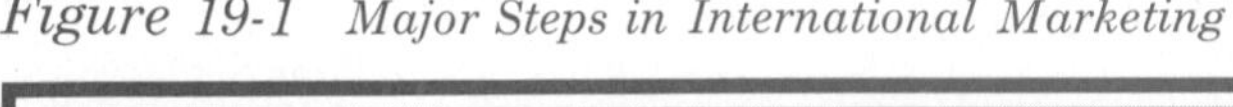

Figure 19-1 Major Steps in International Marketing

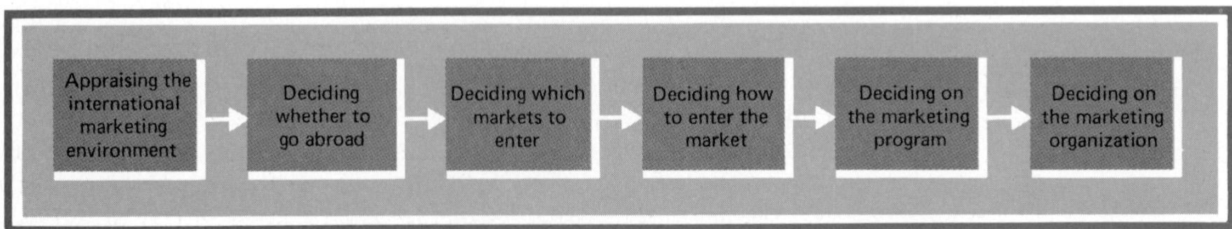

appraising the international marketing environment

Before deciding to sell abroad, a company will have to learn many new things. The company will have to acquire a thorough understanding of the international marketing environment. The international marketing environment has undergone significant changes since 1945, creating both new opportunities and new problems. The most significant changes are[3]: (1) the internationalization of the world economy reflected in the rapid growth of world trade and investment; (2) the gradual erosion of the dominant position of the United States and its attendant problems of an unfavorable balance of trade and a falling value of the dollar in world markets; (3) the rising economic power of Japan in world markets; (4) the establishment of a working international financial system offering improved currency convertibility; (5) the shift in world income since 1973 to the oil-producing countries; (6) the increasing trade barriers put up to protect domestic markets against foreign competition; and (7) the gradual opening up of major new markets, namely China, the USSR, and the Arab countries.

The International Trade System

The American company looking abroad must start with an appreciation of the international framework for world trade and finance. In attempting to sell to another country, the American firm will face various trade restrictions. The most common trade restriction is the *tariff,* which is a tax levied by the foreign government against designated imported products. The tariff is normally based on the goods' weight, volume, or value. The tariff may be designed to raise revenue (revenue tariff) or to protect domestic firms (protective tariff). The exporter may also face a *quota,* which sets limits on the amount of goods that the importing country will accept in certain product categories. The purpose of the quota is to conserve on foreign exchange and protect local industry and employment. An *embargo* is the ultimate form of quota in that imports in prescribed categories are totally banned. Trade is also discouraged by *exchange control,* which regulates the amount of available foreign exchange and its exchange rate against other currencies. The American company may also confront a set of *nontariff barriers,* such as foreign government discrimination against American company bids, and product standards that discriminate against American product features. For example, the Dutch government bars tractors that run faster than ten miles an hour, which means that most American-made tractors are barred.

At the same time, certain forces in the international economy seek to liberalize and foster trade between nations, or at least between some nations. The General Agreement on Tariffs and Trade (GATT) is an international accord that has reduced the overall level of tariffs throughout the world on six different occasions. In addition, certain countries have formed *economic communities,* the most important of which is the European Economic Community (EEC, or more popularly known as the Common Market). The EEC's members are the major Western European nations, and they are striving to reduce tariffs within the community, reduce prices, and expand employment and investment. EEC has taken the form of a *customs union,* which is a *free trade area* (no tariffs facing the members) that imposes a uniform tariff for trade with nonmember nations. The next move would be toward a true *common market* or *economic union* in which all members would operate under the same trade policies, as is the case within the United States. Since the EEC, other economic communities have been formed, notably the Latin American Free Trade Association (LAFTA), the Central American Common Market (CACM), and the Council for Mutual Economic Assistance (CMEA) (East European countries).

Each nation within the international community has unique features that must be grasped. A nation's readiness for different products and services, and its general attractiveness as a market to foreign firms, depend on its economic, political-legal, cultural, and business environment.

Economic Environment

In considering possible export markets, the international marketer must study each country's economy. Two economic characteristics in particular reflect the country's attractiveness as an export market.

The first is the country's *industrial structure.* The country's industrial structure shapes its goods and service requirements, income levels, employment levels, and so on. Four types of industrial structure can be distinguished:

1. *Subsistence economies.* In a subsistence economy the vast majority of people are engaged in simple agriculture. They consume most of their output and barter the rest for simple goods and services. For obvious reasons, they offer few opportunities for exporters.
2. *Raw-material exporting economies.* These economies are rich in one or more natural resources but poor in other respects. Much of their revenue comes from exporting these resources. Examples are Chile (tin and copper), Congo (rubber), and Saudi Arabia (oil). These countries are good markets for extractive equipment, tools and supplies, materials-handling equipment, and trucks. Depending on the number of foreign residents and wealthy native rulers and landholders, they are also a market for Western-style commodities and luxury goods.
3. *Industrializing economies.* In an industrializing economy, manufacturing is beginning to play a role of some importance, probably accounting for somewhere between 10 and 20 percent of the country's gross national product. Examples include Egypt, the Philippines, India, and Brazil. As manufacturing increases, the country relies more on imports of textile raw materials, steel, and heavy machinery, and less on imports of finished textiles, paper products, and automobiles. The industrialization tends to create a new rich class and a small but growing middle class, both demanding new types of goods, some of which can be satisfied only by imports.
4. *Industrial economies.* Industrial economies have built up their industrial base to the extent that they become exporters of manufactured goods and investment funds. They trade manufactured goods among themselves and also export them to other types of economies in exchange for raw materials and semifinished goods. The large and varied manufacturing activities of these industrial nations and their sizable middle class make them rich markets for all sorts of goods.

The second economic characteristic is the country's *income distribution.* Income distribution is related to a country's industrial structure but is also affected by the political system. The international marketer can distinguish countries with five different types of income distribution patterns: (1) very low family incomes, (2) mostly low family incomes, (3) very low, very high family incomes, (4) low, medium, high family incomes, and (5) mostly medium family incomes. Consider the market for Lamborghinis, an automobile costing more than $30,000. The market would be very small in countries with type (1) or (2) income patterns. The largest single market for Lamborghinis turns out to be Portugal (income pattern 3), the poorest country in Europe but one with enough wealthy status-conscious families to be able to afford them.

Political-Legal Environment

Nations differ greatly in the favorableness of their political-legal environment for imports and foreign investment. At least four factors should be considered by the marketer who is evaluating whether to do business in a particular country.

Attitudes toward international buying. Some nations are very receptive, indeed encouraging, to foreign firms, and others are very hostile. As an example of the former, Mexico for a number of years has been attracting foreign investment by offering investment incentives, site-location services, and a stable currency. On the other hand, India has required the exporter to deal with import quotas, blocked currencies, stipulations that a high percentage of the management team be nationals, and so on. IBM and Coca-Cola made a decision to leave India because of all the "hassles."

Political stability. One must consider not only the host country's present political climate but also its future stability. Governments change hands, sometimes quite violently. Even without a change in government, a regime may decide to respond to new popular feelings. At worst, the foreign company's property may be expropriated; or its currency holdings may be blocked; or import quotas or new duties may be imposed. Where political instability is high, international marketers may still find it profitable to do business with the host country, but the situation will affect their mode of entry. They will favor export marketing to direct foreign investment. They will keep their foreign stocks low. They will convert their currency rapidly. As a result, the people in the host country end up paying higher prices, have fewer jobs, and get less-satisfactory products.[4]

Monetary regulations. Sellers want to realize profits in a currency of value to them. In the best situation, the importer can pay either in the seller's currency or in hard world currencies. Short of this, sellers might accept a blocked currency if they can buy other goods in that country that they need or goods that they can sell elsewhere for a needed currency. In the worst case they have to take their money out of the host country in the form of relatively unmarketable products that they can sell elsewhere only at a loss. Besides currency restrictions, a fluctuating exchange rate also leads to unusual risks for the exporter.

Government bureaucracy. A fourth factor is the extent to which the host government runs an efficient system for assisting foreign companies: efficient customs-handling procedures, market information, and other factors conducive to doing business. Perhaps the most common shock to American and other business executives is the extent to which various impediments to trade exist, all of which disappear if a suitable payment (bribe) is made to some official(s).

Cultural Environment

Perhaps the most difficult aspect of international markets is the consumer buying preferences and patterns, which are full of surprises:

- The average Frenchman uses almost twice as many cosmetics and beauty aids as does his wife.
- The Germans and the French eat more packaged, branded spaghetti than the Italians.
- Italian children like to eat a bar of chocolate between two slices of bread as a snack.
- Women in Tanzania will not give their children eggs for fear of making them bald or impotent.

And industrial buying styles vary tremendously:

- South Americans are accustomed to talking business in close physical proximity with other persons—in fact, almost nose to nose. The American business executive retreats, but the South American pursues. And both end up being offended.
- In face-to-face communication Japanese business executives rarely say no to an American business executive. Americans are frustrated and don't know where they stand. Also, Americans tend to come to the point quickly and directly in business dealings. Japanese business executives tend to find this offensive.
- In France, wholesalers just don't care to promote a product. They simply ask their retailers what they want today, and they deliver it. If an American company builds its strategy around the French wholesaler, it is almost always bound to fail.

Each country (and even regional groups within each country) has cultural traditions, preferences, and taboos that must be carefully studied by the marketer.[5]

deciding whether to go abroad

Companies initially get involved in international marketing in one of two ways. In some cases someone—a domestic exporter, a foreign importer, a foreign government—solicits the company to sell abroad. In other cases the company starts to think on its own about going abroad. It might face over capacity or simply see better marketing opportunities in other countries than at home.

Before going abroad, the company should try to define its *international marketing objectives and policies.* First, it should decide *what proportion of foreign to total sales* it will ultimately seek. Most companies will start small when they venture abroad. Some will plan to stay small, seeing foreign operations as a small part of their business. Other companies will have more grandiose international expansion plans, seeing foreign business as ultimately equal to or even more important than their domestic business.

Second, the company must choose between marketing in a *few countries* and marketing in *many countries.* A company with a fixed budget for international expansion has a choice of entering only a few foreign markets and developing them well (*market concentration*) or entering several markets, each on a smaller scale (*market proliferation*). The Bulova Watch Company, for example, made the latter choice and expanded into over one hundred countries in the late 1960s and early 1970s. It spread itself too thin, made profits in only two countries, and lost around $40 million.

Third, the company must decide on the *types of countries* it wants to market in. The types of countries that are attractive will depend on the product, geographical factors, income and population, political climate, and numerous other factors. The seller may have a predilection for certain country groups or parts of the world.

deciding which markets to enter

After developing a list of possible export markets, the company will have to find some procedure for screening and ranking them. Consider the following example:

- CMC's market research in the computer field revealed that England, France, West Germany, and Italy offer us significant markets. England, France, and Germany are about equal-size markets, while Italy represents about two thirds the potential of any one of those countries. . . . Taking everything into consideration, we decided to set up first in England because its market for our products is as large as any and its language and laws are similar to ours. England is different enough to get your feet wet, yet similar enough to the familiar U.S. business environment so that you do not get in over your head.[6]

The market choice seems relatively simple and straightforward. Yet one can question whether the reason given for selecting England—the compatibility of its language and culture—should have been given this prominence. Normally the candidate countries should be ranked on several criteria, such as (1) market size, (2) market growth, (3) cost of doing business, (4) competitive advantage, and (5) risk level.

The core of the ranking procedure is to try to determine the probable rate of return on investment in each market. Five steps are involved:[7]

1. *Estimate of current market potential.* The first step is to estimate current market potential in each candidate market. This *marketing research task* calls for using existing published data supplemented by primary data collection through company surveys and studies of various kinds. The U.S. Department of Commerce and several large banks are increasing the amount of information available about foreign markets.
2. *Forecast of future market potential.* The firm also needs a forecast of future market potential. This is complicated because the market analyst is usually insufficiently versed in the economic, political, cultural, and business currents of another country. Many foreign countries do not show the stability of government, currency, or law that permits reliable forecasting.
3. *Forecast of sales potential.* Estimating the company's sales potential requires forecasting its probable market share. The normal difficulties of forecasting market shares are compounded in a foreign marketing environment. The foreign company will find itself competing with other foreign companies as well as with home-country firms. It has to estimate how the buyers will feel about the relative merits of its product, selling methods, and company. Even if the buyers are impartial, their government may put up barriers in the form of quotas, tariffs, taxes, specifications, or even outright boycotts.
4. *Forecast of costs and profits.* Costs will depend on the company's contemplated entry strategy. If it resorts to exporting or licensing, its costs will be spelled out in the contracts. If it decides to locate manufacturing facilities abroad, its cost estimation will require an understanding of local labor conditions, taxes, trade

practices, and stipulations regarding the hiring of nationals as key employees. After estimating future costs, the company subtracts them from estimated company sales to find company profits for each year of the planning horizon.

5. *Estimate of rate of return on investment.* The forecast income stream must be related to the investment stream to derive an implicit rate of return. The estimated rate of return should be high enough to cover (1) the company's normal target return on its investment and (2) the risk and uncertainty of marketing in that country. The risk premium has to cover not only the chance that the basic estimates of sales and costs may be wrong but also the chance that unanticipated monetary changes (devaluation, blocked currency) and political changes (future discrimination against foreign business firms, or even expropriation) may occur.

deciding how to enter the market

Once a company decides that a particular foreign market represents an attractive opportunity, its task is to determine the best mode of entering that market. Here it has three major entry strategies: *exporting* (home production and selling abroad), *joint venturing* (joining with foreign companies in some way), and *direct investment* abroad.[8] Each succeeding strategy tends to involve more commitment, risk, and possible profits. The three types of market entry strategies are shown in Figure 19-2, along with the various options under each.

Export

The simplest way for a company to get involved in a foreign market is through export. It can get involved in export on two levels. *Occasional exporting* is a passive level of involvement where the company may export surpluses from time to time and sell goods to resident buyers representing foreign companies. *Active exporting* takes place when the company makes a commitment to expand exports to a particular market. In either case the company continues to produce all of its goods in the home country. It may or may not modify them for the export market. Exporting involves the least change in the company's product lines, organization, investments, or company mission.

Figure 19-2
Alternative Market Entry Strategies

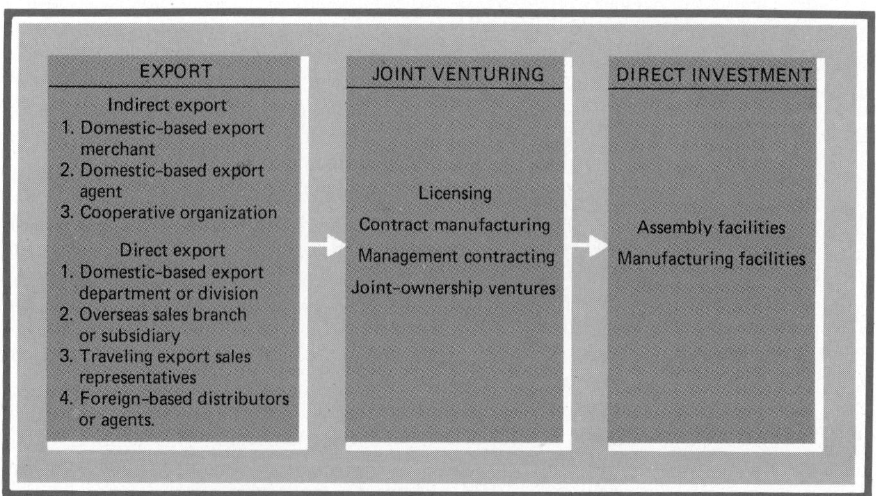

A company can decide to export its product in two broad ways. It can hire independent international marketing middlemen (indirect export), or it can assume direct responsibility for selling to the foreign buyers or importers (direct export).

Indirect export. Indirect export is the more popular of the two for the firm that is just beginning its exporting activity. First, it involves less investment. The firm does not have to develop an overseas sales force or a set of contacts. Second, it involves less risk. International-marketing middlemen presumably bring know-how and services to the relationship, and the seller will normally make fewer mistakes.

Three types of domestic middlemen arrangements are available to the exporting company:

1. *Domestic-based export merchant.* This middleman buys the manufacturer's product and sells it abroad on its own account. The exporting company simply makes its sales to the export merchant.
2. *Domestic-based export agent.* In this case the company retains some of the chores and all of the risk, because the agent simply agrees to seek foreign buyers for a commission. Within the agent class there are several variants: *export buying agents* reside in the manufacturer's country, represent foreign buyers, place orders with the manufacturer, take care of shipments, and make payment; *brokers* exist to find buyers, are paid a commission, and do not handle the products; and *manufacturer's export agents* represent several exporters whose interests are noncompeting and carry out selling and other services.
3. *Cooperative organization.* A cooperative organization carries on exporting activities on behalf of several producers and is partly under the administrative control of the producers. This form is often used by producers of primary products—fruits, nuts, and so on—for foreign sales. Another form consists of piggyback arrangements between two or more domestic manufacturers trying to develop a complementary product line for a foreign market.

Direct export. Sellers who are approached by foreign buyers will most likely undertake direct export instead of paying service charges to middlemen. So will larger sellers or those whose market has grown to sufficient size to justify undertaking their own export activity. The investment and risk are somewhat greater, but so is the potential return.

Here, too, there are several ways in which the company can carry on direct exporting activity:

1. *Domestic-based export department or division.* This consists of an export sales manager with some clerical assistants. They carry on the actual selling and draw on regular company departments for marketing assistance in such areas as advertising, credit, and logistics. It might evolve into a self-contained export department or sales subsidiary carrying out all the activities involved in export, and possibly be operated as a profit center.
2. *Overseas sales branch or subsidiary.* This may be established in addition to, or instead of, a domestic export department. An overseas sales branch allows the manufacturer to achieve greater presence and program control in the foreign market. The sales branch handles sales distribution, and it may handle warehousing and promotion as well. It often serves as a display center and customer service center.

3. *Traveling export sales representatives.* The company can decide to have one or more home-based sales representatives travel abroad at certain times to take orders or find business.
4. *Foreign-based distributors or agents.* Foreign-based distributors would buy and own the goods; foreign-based agents would sell the goods on behalf of the company. They may be given exclusive rights to represent the manufacturer in that country or only general rights.

Joint Venturing

A second broad method of entering a foreign market is to join with nationals in the foreign country to set up production and marketing facilities. Joint venturing differs from exporting in that a partnership is formed that leads to some production facilities abroad, and it differs from direct investment in that an association is formed with someone in that country. Four types of joint venture can be distinguished.

Licensing. Licensing represents a comparatively simple way for a manufacturer to become involved in international marketing. The licensor enters an agreement with a licensee in the foreign market, offering the right to use a manufacturing process, trademark, patent, trade secret, or other item of value for a fee or royalty. The licensor gains entry into the market at little risk; the licensee gains production expertise, or a well-known product or name, without having to start from scratch. Gerber introduced its baby foods in the Japanese market through a licensing arrangement. It did not have the staff to develop and operate its own production facility, nor did it want to risk the capital loss if the Japanese were not receptive to its products. Coca-Cola has carried out its international marketing activities by licensing bottlers around the world—or, more technically, *franchising* bottlers, because it supplies the syrup needed to produce the product.

Licensing has potential disadvantages in that the firm has less control over the licensee than if it had set up its own production facilities. Furthermore, if the licensee is very successful, the firm has forgone these profits, and if and when the contract ends, it may find it has set up a competitor. To avoid these dangers the licensor must establish a mutual advantage in working together, and a key to doing this is to remain innovative so that the licensee continues to depend on the licensor.

Contract manufacturing. Instead of licensing a foreign company to manufacture and market its products, the firm may wish to retain the marketing responsibility. But it may not be ready to invest in its own foreign production facilities. Under these conditions, an excellent option is to contract with local manufacturers to produce the product. Sears has used this method in opening up department stores in other countries, as in Mexico and Spain. Sears enters into contracts with qualified local manufacturers to produce many of the products it sells.

Contract manufacturing has the drawback of less control over the manufacturing process and the loss of potential profits on manufacturing. On the other hand, it offers the company a chance to get started faster, with less risk, and with the opportunity to possibly form a partnership or buy out the local manufacturer later.

Management contracting. Here the domestic firm agrees to supply the management know-how to a foreign company that is willing to supply the capital. Thus the domestic firm is really exporting management services rather than its own products. This arrangement is used by the Hilton hotel system in undertaking to manage hotels throughout the world.

Management contracting is a low-risk method of getting into a foreign market, and it starts yielding income right from the beginning. The arrangement is especially attractive if the contracting firm is given an option to purchase some share in the managed company within a stated period. On the other hand, the arrangement is not sensible if the company can put its scarce management talent to better uses or if there are greater profits to be made by undertaking the whole venture. Management contracting prevents the company from setting up its own operations for a period of time.

Joint-ownership ventures. An increasingly popular arrangement consists of foreign investors' joining with local investors to create a local business in which they share joint ownership and control. The foreign investor may buy an interest in a local company, a local company may buy an interest in an existing operation of a foreign company, or the two parties may form a new business venture.

From the point of view of the foreign investor, a joint venture may be necessary or desirable for economic or political reasons. Economically, the firm may find it lacks the financial, physical, or managerial resources to undertake the venture alone. Or the foreign government may require joint ownership with local companies as a condition for entry.

Joint ownership can have certain drawbacks for the foreign firm. The partners may disagree over investment, marketing, or other policies. Whereas many American firms like to reinvest earnings for growth, local firms often like to pay out these earnings. Whereas American firms tend to accord a large role to marketing, local investors may see marketing as simply selling. If the American firm has only a minority interest, then its views are overruled in these disagreements. Furthermore, joint venturing can hamper the plans of a multinational company seeking to carry out specific manufacturing and marketing policies on a worldwide basis. The agreement may also make it difficult for the foreign firm to enter other markets where its partner already operates.

Direct Investment

The ultimate form of involvement in a foreign market is investment in foreign-based assembly or manufacturing facilities. Companies just starting out in the market would be well advised to avoid this scale of participation at the outset. However, as experience is gained through export channels, and if the foreign market appears large enough, foreign production facilities offer distinct advantages. The company may secure these advantages partially through licensing or joint-ownership ventures, but if it wants full control (and profits), it may give serious consideration to direct investment.

The advantages of direct investment are several. First, the firm may secure real cost economies in the form of cheaper labor or raw materials, foreign government investment incentives, freight savings, and so on. Second, the firm will gain a better image in the host country because it demonstrates its concern with that country's future. Third, the firm develops a deeper relationship with government, customers, local suppliers, and distributors, enabling it to make a better adaptation of its products to the local marketing environment. Fourth, the firm retains full control over the investment and therefore can develop manufacturing and marketing policies that serve its long-term international objectives.

The main disadvantage is that the firm has exposed a large investment to certain risks, such as blocked or devalued currencies, worsening markets, or expropriation. In some cases, however, the firm has no choice but to accept these risks if it wants to operate effectively in the host country.

deciding on the marketing program

Companies that operate in one or more foreign markets must decide how much, if at all, to adapt their marketing mix to local conditions. Here we will examine their product, promotion, price, and distribution options.

Product

Keegan distinguished five possible strategies involving the adaptation of product and promotion to a foreign market (see Figure 19-3).[9] Here we will focus on the three product options, ignoring what the company does with promotion.

The first strategy, *straight extension,* means introducing the product in the foreign market without any change. Top management says to its marketing people: "Take the product as it is and find customers for it." The first step, however, should be to determine whether the foreign consumers use that product. Deodorant usage among men ranges from 80 percent in the United States to 55 percent in Sweden, 28 percent in Italy, to 8 percent in the Philippines. Many Spaniards do not use such common products as butter and cheese.

Straight extension has been used successfully by Coca-Cola to introduce its soft drinks everywhere in the world, but it has failed for some other producers. General Foods introduced its standard powdered Jell-O in the British market only to find that British consumers prefer the solid-wafer or cake form. Campbell Soup lost an estimated $30 million in introducing its familiar red-and-white-label condensed soups in England and failing to explain that consumers should add

Figure 19-3
Five International Product and Promotion Strategies

Promotion \ Product	Don't change product	Adapt product	Develop new product
Don't change promotion	1. Straight extension	3. Product adaptation	5. Product invention
Adapt promotion	2. Communication adaptation	4. Dual adaptation	

water; the consumers saw the small-size cans and thought they were expensive. Straight extension is a tempting strategy because it involves no additional R & D expense, manufacturing retooling, or promotional modification. But it can be costly in the long run.

The second strategy, *product adaptation,* involves altering the product to meet local conditions or preferences. Thus Heinz varies its baby-food products: In Australia it sells a baby food made from strained lamb brains; and in the Netherlands, a baby food made from strained brown beans. General Foods blends different coffees for the British (who drink their coffee with milk), the French (who drink their coffee black), and Latin Americans (who want a chicory taste).

The third strategy, *product invention,* calls for creating something new. This can take two forms. *Backward invention* is the reintroducing of earlier product forms that happen to be well adapted to the needs of that country. The National Cash Register Company reintroduced its crank-operated cash register that could sell at half the cost of a modern cash register and sold substantial numbers in the Orient, Latin America, and Spain. This illustrates the existence of *international product life cycles* where countries stand at different stages of readiness to accept a particular product.[10] *Forward invention* is creating a brand new product to meet a need in another country. For example, there is an enormous need in less-developed countries for low-cost high-protein foods. Companies such as Pillsbury, Swift, and Monsanto are researching the food needs of these countries, formulating new foods, and developing mass-communication programs to gain product trial and acceptance. Product invention would appear to be the costliest of all strategies, but the payoffs to the successful firm also appear to be the greatest.

Promotion

Companies face two options with respect to their promotion strategy abroad. They can either use the same promotion strategy used in the home market or change it for each local market.

Consider message, for example. Many multinational companies favor using a highly standardized advertising theme and approach in order to create worldwide impact.[11] A classic case is Exxon's use of the "Put a tiger in your tank" theme for several years in its worldwide advertising; this gave the company international recognition. The theme may be carried out literally everywhere or subject to minor adaptations for local conditions. The latter is more common because of variations in cultural norms and taboos. For example, the colors in the American print ad might have to be modified to avoid taboo colors in other countries. Purple is associated with death in most of Latin America; white is a mourning color in Japan; and green is associated with jungle sickness in Malaysia. Even names may have to be modified. In Germany, *mist* means "manure" and *scotch* (scotch tape) means "schmuck"; in Spain, Chevrolet's *Nova* translates as *no va,* which means "it doesn't go"! In Sweden, Helene Curtis had to rename its Every Night Shampoo to Every Day because Swedes wash their hair in the morning.

Other companies will let their international divisions and subsidiaries develop an ad from scratch, feeling that the optimum appeal should be found for each market. For example, the Schwinn Bicycle Company may use a pleasure appeal to sell its bicycles in the United States and a safety appeal to sell its bicycles in Scandinavia.

In the case of media, much more international adaptation is normally required. The company will find that media availabilities differ considerably from country to country. For example, commercial television time in Germany is available for about an hour each evening, and marketers must buy time months in advance. In Sweden, commercial TV time is nonexistent. Commercial radio is nonexistent in France and Scandinavia. Magazines are a major medium in Italy and a minor one in Austria. Newspapers are national in the United Kingdom and local in Spain.

Price

Manufacturers often price their products lower for the foreign market than for the domestic market. This may occur for a number of reasons. The foreign market may be one of low incomes, and a low price is necessary if the goods are to sell. Or the manufacturer may use a low price to build market share against domestic and other foreign competitors. Or the manufacturer may simply want to dump excess goods that have no market at home. If the manufacturer charges less in the foreign market than in the home market, this is called *dumping.* The Zenith Company accused some Japanese television manufacturers of dumping their TV sets on the U.S. market at the cost of many domestic production jobs. If the U.S. Customs Bureau finds that dumping has occurred, it can levy a special tax called a dumping tariff.

Manufacturers do not have much control over the retail prices charged by the foreign middlemen who carry their products. Many foreign middlemen prefer high markups, even though this means selling fewer units. They also like to buy on credit and this increases the manufacturer's cost and risk.

Distribution Channels

The international company must take a *whole-channel* view of the problem of getting its products to the final users or consumers. It must see the channel of distribution as an integrated whole, from the manufacturer on one end to the final user or buyer on the other end.[12] Figure 19-4 shows the three major links between the seller and ultimate buyer. The first link, *seller's headquarters organization,* supervises the channels and is part of the channel itself. The second link, *channels between nations,* does the job of getting the products to the overseas markets. The third link, *channels within nations,* is extremely pertinent. Too many American manufacturers think of their channels as ending with the

Figure 19-4
Whole-Channel Concept for International Marketing

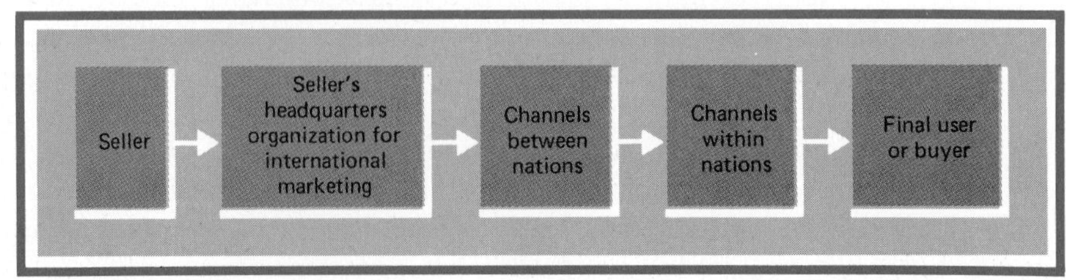

channels between nations, and they fail to observe what happens to their product once it arrives in the foreign market. If the channels within the foreign market are weak or inefficient, then the target customers fail to achieve satisfaction and the company fails to achieve its international objectives.

With respect to consumer goods, within-country channels of distribution vary considerably from country to country. There are striking differences in the *number and type of middlemen* serving each foreign market. To get soap into Japan, Procter & Gamble has to work through probably the most complicated distribution system in the world. It must sell to a *general wholesaler* who sells to a *basic product specialty wholesaler* who sells to a *specialty wholesaler* who sells to a *regional wholesaler* who sells to a *local wholesaler* who finally sells to *retailers*. All of these distribution levels may result in a doubling or tripling of the price to the Japanese consumer over the price to the importer.[13] The distribution system would be different in each country.[14] If P&G takes its soap to tropical Africa, the company sells to an *import wholesaler* who sells to a *mammy* who sells to a *petty mammy* who sells the soap *door to door*.

Another important difference is the *size and character of retail units* abroad. Whereas large-scale retail chains dominate the U.S. scene, most foreign retailing is in the hands of many small independent retailers. In India, hundreds of thousands of retailers operate tiny shops or sell in open markets. Their markups are high, but the real price is often brought down through much price haggling. Large-scale retail chains such as supermarkets could conceivably bring down prices, but they are difficult to start because of many economic and cultural resistances.[15] People's incomes are low, and they consequently prefer to shop daily for small amounts rather than weekly for large amounts. They do not have the storage and refrigeration space to keep food for several days. Packaging is not well developed because it would add too much to the cost. Consumers like to see and handle the food and often distrust packaged food. These and other factors have kept large-scale retailing from spreading rapidly in developing countries.

With respect to industrial goods, within-country channels in advanced countries resemble those found in the United States. In the less-developed countries, importers are strong and foreign companies must leave their fate in the importers' hands. If companies seek their own distributors, they must carefully sort out the good ones from the poor ones. Often the company has to offer exclusive distribution to a local distributor, and its success in this market is tied up with how well it has chosen its distributor.

Thus companies have to decide how standardized their marketing programs should be. In favor of standardization is the lower cost of developing uniform products and marketing programs. Against standardization is the greater adaptation of the company's products and marketing programs to local needs. Each company must decide. Beecham tries to make its advertising program uniform: It likes to use a successful campaign everywhere. Nestlé, on the other hand, will vary its advertising program in different countries. A recent survey of twenty-seven leading multinationals in consumer-packaged-goods industries reached the following conclusion: "To the successful multinational, it is not really important whether marketing programs are internationally standardized or differentiated;

the important thing is that the *process* through which these programs are developed is standardized. At the heart of this process is the annual marketing planning system they use."[16]

deciding on the marketing organization

Companies manage their international marketing activities in different ways. The different organizational arrangements often parallel their degree of involvement in international marketing.

Export Department

A firm normally gets started in international marketing by responding to a few orders that come in fortuitously. At first it simply ships out the goods. If its international sales expand, the company usually organizes an export department consisting of a sales manager and a few clerical assistants. As sales increase further, the staff of the export department is expanded to include various marketing services so that it can go after business more aggressively and not depend on the domestic staff. If the firm moves beyond exports into a program of joint ventures or direct investment, the export department will no longer serve these purposes.

International Division

Many companies eventually become involved in a number of different international markets and ventures. A company may export to one country, license to another, have a joint-ownership venture in a third, and own a subsidiary in a fourth, and it may eventually create an international division or subsidiary with responsibility for all of its international activity. The international division is headed by an international division president, who sets goals and budgets and is given total responsibility for the company's growth in the international market.

International divisions are organized in a variety of ways. Usually the international division's corporate staff consists of functional specialists in marketing, manufacturing, research, finance, planning, and personnel. This staff will plan for, and provide services to, various operating units. The operating units may be organized according to one or more of three principles. First, the operating units may be *geographical organizations.* For example, reporting to the international division president may be vice-presidents for different areas such as North America, Latin America, Europe, Africa, and the Far East. The area vice-presidents are responsible for a sales force, sales branches, distributors, and licensees in their respective areas. Or the operating units may be *product-group organizations,* with a vice-president responsible for worldwide sales of each product group. The vice-presidents may draw on corporate staff area specialists for expertise on different areas. Finally, the operating units may be *international subsidiaries,* each headed by a president. The various subsidiary presidents report to the president of the international division.

A major disadvantage of the international division concept is that the corporation's top management may think of it as just another division and never really get involved enough to fully appreciate and plan for global marketing. Top management may not give the division the attention it deserves, and in difficult times may cut its budget.

Multinational Organization

Several firms have passed beyond the international division organization and have become a truly multinational organization. They stop thinking of themselves as national marketers who venture abroad and start thinking of themselves as global marketers. This means the top corporate management and staff are involved in the worldwide planning of manufacturing facilities, marketing policies, financial flows, and logistical systems. The various operating units around the world report directly to the chief executive or executive committee, not to the head of an international division. The company trains its executives in worldwide operations, not just domestic *or* international. Management talent is recruited from many countries; components and supplies are purchased where they can be obtained at the least cost; and investments are made where the anticipated returns are greatest.

Major companies will undoubtedly have to go multinational in the 1980s if they are going to grow. As foreign companies continue to invade the home market with some success, home companies will have to move aggressively into those international markets that are best suited to the company's distinctive products and competencies. They will have to evolve from *ethnocentric* companies where they treat their foreign operations as secondary to their domestic operations, to *geocentric* companies where they view the entire world as a single market.[17]

■ summary

Companies are drawn into international marketing for a variety of reasons. Sometimes they are pushed in by inadequate or poor opportunities in the home market, and sometimes they are pulled in by superior opportunities abroad. International competition is becoming fiercer and, given the risks, companies need a systematic way to make their international-marketing decisions.

The first step is to appraise the international-marketing environment, particularly the international trade system. In considering a particular foreign market, its economic, political-legal, and cultural characteristics must be assessed. Second, the decision to go abroad must be considered in terms of what proportion of foreign to total sales the company will seek, whether it will do business in a few or many countries, and what types of countries it would want to market in. The third step is to decide which particular markets to enter, and this calls for making a hard evaluation of the probable rate of return on investment against the level of risk. Fourth, the company has to decide how to enter each attractive market, whether it should be through export, joint venturing, or direct investment. Many companies start as exporters, move to joint venturing, and finally undertake direct investment as their overseas business expands. Companies must next decide on the extent to which their products, promotion, price, and distribution should be adapted to individual foreign markets. Finally, the company must develop an effective organization for pursuing international marketing. Most firms start with an export department and graduate to an international division. A few pass this stage and move to a multinational organization, which means that worldwide marketing is planned and managed by the top officers of the corporation.

questions for discussion

1. In appraising the international marketing environment, the economic environment of the country is the most important consideration for the firm. Comment.
2. Discuss the relevant aspects of the political-legal environment that might affect K-Mart's decision to open retail outlets in Italy.
3. What steps are involved in deciding which markets to enter? Relate these steps to a consumer product example.
4. Briefly discuss the three major strategies that a firm might use to enter a foreign market.
5. How does licensing differ from the other joint venture possibilities?
6. What product strategy possibilities might Hershey's consider in marketing its chocolate bars in South American countries?
7. The price of products sold in foreign markets is usually lower than in the domestic market. Why?
8. Which type of international marketing organization would you suggest for the following companies? (a) Huffy bicycles is planning to sell three models in the Far East; (b) a small manufacturer of toys is going to market its products in Europe; and (c) Dodge is contemplating selling its full line of cars and trucks in Kuwait.

references

1. See "The Reluctant Exporter," *Business Week,* April 10, 1978, pp. 54–66.
2. *Fortune,* November 1974, p. 175.
3. See WARREN J. KEEGAN, "Multinational Product Planning: New Myths and Old Realities," in *Multinational Product Management* (Cambridge: Marketing Science Institute, 1976), pp. 1–8.
4. For a system of rating the political stability of different nations, see F. T. HANER, "Rating Investment Risks Abroad," *Business Horizons,* April 1979, pp. 18–23.
5. For further examples, see DAVID A. RICKS, MARILYN Y. C. FU, AND JEFFERY S. ARPAN, *International Business Blunders* (Columbus, Ohio: Grid, 1974).
6. JAMES K. SWEENEY, "A Small Company Enters the European Market," *Harvard Business Review,* September-October 1970, pp. 127–28.
7. See DAVID S. R. LEIGHTON, "Deciding When to Enter International Markets," in *Handbook of Modern Marketing,* ed. Victor P. Buell (New York: McGraw-Hill, 1970), Sec. 20, pp. 23–28.
8. The discussion of entry strategies in this section is based on the discussion in GORDON E. MIRACLE AND GERALD S. ALBAUM, *International Marketing Management* (Homewood, Ill.: Richard D. Irwin, 1970), Chaps. 14–16.
9. WARREN J. KEEGAN, "Multinational Product Planning: Strategic Alternatives," *Journal of Marketing,* January 1969, pp. 58–62.
10. LOUIS T. WELLS, JR., "A Product Life Cycle for International Trade?" *Journal of Marketing,* July 1968, pp. 1–6.
11. RALPH Z. SORENSON AND ULRICH E. WIECHMANN, "How Multinationals View Marketing Standardization," *Harvard Business Review,* May-June 1975, pp. 38–54.

12. See MIRACLE AND ALBAUM, *International Marketing Management,* pp. 317–19.
13. See WILLIAM D. HARTLEY, "How Not to Do It: Cumbersome Japanese Distribution System Stumps U.S. Concerns," *Wall Street Journal,* March 2, 1972, pp. 1, 8.
14. For a description of the distribution systems in selected countries, see WADINAMBIARATCHI, "Channels of Distribution in Developing Economies," *Business Quarterly,* Winter 1965, pp. 74–82.
15. However, see ARIEH GOLDMAN, "Outreach of Consumers and the Modernization of Urban Food Retailing in Developing Countries," *Journal of Marketing,* October 1974, pp. 8–16.
16. SORENSON AND WIECHMANN, "How Multinationals View Marketing Standardization."
17. See YORAM WIND, SUSAN P. DOUGLAS, AND HOWARD V. PERLMUTTER, "Guidelines for Developing International Marketing Strategies," *Journal of Marketing,* April 1973, pp. 14–23.

MARKETING OF SERVICES, ORGANIZATIONS, PERSONS, PLACES, AND IDEAS

Recently the Evanston Hospital, a major five-hundred-bed hospital serving the north shore area of Chicago, appointed Dr. John McLaren as its first vice-president of marketing, possibly the first time a person was ever appointed to this position in any hospital in the world. Hospitals have had vice-presidents of development and public relations, but this appointment raised a number of eyebrows both inside and outside the hospital. Why should a hospital need any marketing?

Before 1970, if hospitals had any problem, it was too many patients. There were bed shortages, and many prospective patients and their physicians had to queue up. The situation turned around drastically in the 1970s, and hospitals found themselves with falling patient admissions and falling patient-days. Given their high fixed costs and their rising labor costs, their declining patient census could spell the difference between being in the black and being in the red.

Hospitals began to scramble for ways to get a larger share of the available patients. Since most patients go to the hospital chosen by their physicians, the key market target was the physician. Every hospital began to ask itself how it could attract more of the "high-yield" physicians to its staff, and how it could influence them to assign more of their patients to its own rooms instead of other hospitals' rooms. The key seemed to be in knowing what physicians want from a hospital affiliation—things like good equipment to work with, good colleagues and nursing staffs, a good hospital image, good parking, and even some ego benefits such as prima donna treatment.

The more hospitals looked into the problem, the more complex the marketing challenges appeared. A hospital had to understand exactly what its community's health needs consisted of, what image the community had of the different hospitals, how its own patients felt about the hospital's service and care, what impression its physical facility made, and so on. Furthermore, hospitals began to realize that they could no longer be full-service hospitals offering every kind of medical service. This led to too much community duplication of equipment and services and underutilized capacity. Hospitals began to pick and choose medical services—heart, pediatrics, burn treatment, psychiatry—in which to specialize.

Meanwhile some hospitals seemed to go overboard in making a pitch for patients. Sunrise Hospital in Las Vegas ran a large advertisement featuring the picture of a ship with the following caption: "Introducing the Sunrise Cruise. Win a Once-in-a-Lifetime Cruise Simply by

Entering Sunrise Hospital on Any Friday or Saturday: Recuperative Mediterranean Cruise for Two." St. Luke's Hospital in Phoenix introduced nightly bingo games for all patients (except cardiac cases), producing immense patient interest as well as a net annual profit of $60,000. A Philadelphia hospital, in competing for maternity patients, made a practice of serving a candlelight dinner (with steak and champagne) for the parents of a newborn child on the evening before their departure.

Then what is Dr. John McLaren's job going to be at the Evanston Hospital? Anything but simple. His responsibility will be to promote particular hospital services (services marketing), the hospital itself (organization), marketing some of its key physicians (person marketing), Evanston as a place (place marketing), and ideas on how people can get well and stay well (idea marketing).

□ Marketing as a discipline developed initially in connection with selling physical products such as toothpaste, cars, steel, and equipment. In talking about marketing, there is a tendency to emphasize physical goods because they are more tangible and familiar. This product focus causes people to overlook the many other types of entities that are subject to marketing analysis, planning, and control. The purpose of this chapter is to examine the increasing applications of marketing concepts to entities other than physical goods, namely, services, organizations, persons, places, and ideas.

services marketing

One of the major developments in post–World War II America has been the phenomenal growth of service industries—from about 35 percent of GNP to almost 50 percent of GNP. Furthermore, approximately 66 percent of the nongovernmental labor force is engaged in service industries, and this percentage is expected to rise as the United States increasingly moves into a postindustrial society. In contrast, the United Kingdom has approximately 50 percent of its work force employed in the service sector, followed by France (46 percent), Germany (41 percent), and Italy (35 percent). As a result of rising affluence, more leisure, and the growing complexity of products that require servicing, the United States has become the world's first service economy.

Service industries are quite varied. The entire government sector, with its courts, employment services, hospitals, loan agencies, military services, police and fire departments, post office, regulatory agencies, and schools, is in the service business. The private nonprofit sector, with its art groups and museums, charities, churches, colleges, foundations, and hospitals, is in the service business. A good part of the business sector, with its airlines, banks, computer service bureaus, hotels, insurance companies, law firms, management consulting firms, medical practices, motion picture companies, plumbing repair companies, and real estate firms, is in the service business.

Not only are there traditional industries in the service business but new types of service firms keep popping up all the time:

- For a fee, there are now companies that will balance your budget, baby-sit your philodendron, wake you up in the morning, drive you to work, or find you a new home, job, car, wife, clairvoyant, cat feeder, or gypsy violinist. Or perhaps you want to rent a garden tractor? A few cattle? Some original paintings? Or maybe some hippies to decorate your next cocktail party? If it is business services you need, other companies will plan your conventions and sales meetings, design your products, handle your data processing, or supply temporary secretaries or even executives.[1]

Nature and Characteristics of a Service

We define a *service* as follows:

- A **service** is any activity or benefit that one party can offer to another that is essentially intangible and does not result in the ownership of anything. Its production may or may not be tied to a physical product.

Thus renting a hotel room, depositing money in a bank, traveling on an airplane, visiting a psychiatrist, having a haircut, having a car repaired, watching a professional sport, seeing a movie, having clothes cleaned in a dry-cleaning establishment, getting advice from a lawyer—all involve buying a service.

Services have a number of characteristics that must be considered when designing service-marketing programs.

Intangibility. Sales are intangible, that is, they cannot be seen, tasted, felt, heard, or smelled before they are bought. Thus the woman getting a "face lift" cannot see the result before the purchase, and the patient walking into a psychiatrist's office cannot know the content or value of the service in advance. Under the circumstances, purchase requires having faith in the service provider.

Service providers can do certain things to improve the client's confidence. First, they can try to increase the service's tangibility by a number of devices. A plastic surgeon can make a drawing or a clay model showing the changes the operation will make in the patient's appearance. Second, service providers can place more emphasis on the benefits of the service rather than just describing its features. Thus a college admissions officer can talk to prospective students about the great jobs its alumni have found instead of only describing life on the campus. Third, service providers can put brand names on their service to increase confidence, such as Magikist cleaning, United Airlines' Red Carpet service, and Transcendental Meditation. And fourth, service providers can use a highly regarded celebrity to personalize and create confidence in the service, as Hertz has done with its O. J. Simpson ads.

Inseparability. A service is inseparable from the source that renders it. Its very act of being created requires the source, whether a person or a machine, to be present. In other words, production and consumption occur simultaneously with the service. This is in contrast to a product that exists whether or not its source is present. Consider going to a Rolling Stones rock concert. The entertainment value is inseparable from the performer. It is not the same service if an announcer tells the audience that Mick Jagger of the Rolling Stones is indisposed and therefore his record will be played instead, or that Donny and Marie Osmond will substitute. What this means is that the number of people who can buy this particular service—watching Mick Jagger perform live—is limited to the amount of time that Mick Jagger wants to give concerts, until such time as means are found to clone him. Thus strong consumer preferences can considerably limit the scale of operation of the service firm.

Several strategies exist for getting around this limitation. The service provider can learn to work with larger groups. We have seen psychotherapists move from one-on-one therapy to small-group therapy to groups of over three hundred people in a large hotel ballroom getting "therapized." Or the service provider can learn to work faster—the psychotherapist can spend thirty minutes with each patient instead of fifty minutes and thus see more patients. Or the service organization can train more competent service providers and build up client confidence in them, as H & R Block has done with its national network of trained tax consultants.

Variability. The same service can be highly variable, depending not only on *who* is providing it but *when* it is being provided. A heart transplant operation performed by Dr. Christiaan Barnard is likely to be of higher quality than the same operation performed by a recently graduated M.D. And Dr. Barnard's service quality can vary depending on his energy and mental set at the time of the operation. Purchasers of services are aware of their high variability and engage in normal risk-reducing behavior by talking to others and trying to select the best provider.

Service firms can take two steps to ensure high and consistent quality in their service offers. The first step consists of developing a good personnel selection and training program. Airlines, banks, and hotels spend substantial sums of money to train their personnel to provide uniform and courteous service. One is supposed to find, for example, the same friendly and helpful personnel in every Marriott Hotel. This is not without creating some "role strain," since the personnel are under cross-pressure to be friendly and at the same time to work fast. The second step consists of developing adequate customer satisfaction monitoring systems. The main tools for this are suggestion and complaint systems, customer surveys, and comparison shopping.[2]

Perishability. Services cannot be stored. Although a car can be kept in inventory until it is sold, the revenue from an unoccupied airplane seat on a particular flight is lost forever. The reason many doctors charge patients for missed appointments is that the service value only existed at that point when the patient did not show up. The perishability of services is not a problem when demand is steady, because it is easy to staff the services in advance. When demand fluctuates considerably, service firms have difficult problems. For example, public transportation companies have to use much more equipment because of peak demand during rush hours than they would if public transportation needs were smooth during the day.

Service organizations have several means available to try to produce a better match between demand and service capacity. Sasser has described several strategies for managing demand and supply.[3] On the demand side:

1. *Differential pricing* can be used to shift some demand from peak to off-peak periods. Examples include low early-evening movie prices and special weekend prices for car rentals.
2. *Nonpeak demand can be developed,* as when McDonald's opened its Eggs McMuffin breakfast program and hotels developed their mini-vacation weekend.
3. *Complementary services* can be developed during peak time to provide alternatives to waiting customers, such as cocktail lounges to sit in while waiting for a table and automatic tellers in banks.
4. *Reservation systems* are a way to presell service and know how much is needed, and airlines, hotels, and physicians employ them extensively.

On the supply side:

1. *Part-time employees* can be used to serve peak demand, as when colleges add part-time teachers when enrollment goes up and restaurants call in part-time waitresses when needed.
2. *Peak-time efficiency routines* can be introduced, such as employees' performing only essential tasks during peak periods, or paramedics added to help physicians.
3. *Increased consumer participation* in the tasks can be used, as when consumers fill out their own medical records or bag their own groceries.
4. *Shared services* can be developed, as when several hospitals agree to limit and share medical equipment purchases.
5. *Facilities with built-in expansion possibilities* can be developed, as when an amusement park buys surrounding land in case it is needed for later expansion.

Classification of Services

Services can be classified in several ways. First, to what extent is the service *people-based* or *equipment-based?* Thus a psychiatrist needs a minimum of equipment, perhaps a couch, whereas a pilot needs an expensive piece of equipment called an airplane. In people-based services, we can distinguish between those involving professionals (accounting, management consulting), skilled labor (plumbing, car repair) and unskilled labor (janitorial service, lawn care). In equipment-based services, we can distinguish between those involving automated equipment (automated car washes, vending machines), equipment operated by relatively unskilled labor (taxis, motion picture theatres), and equipment operated by skilled labor (airplanes, computers).[4] Even within a specific service industry, different service providers vary in the amount of equipment they use—contrast James Taylor with his single guitar and the Rolling Stones with their tons of audio equipment. Sometimes the accompanying equipment adds value to the service (stereo amplification), and sometimes it exists to reduce the amount of labor needed (automated car washes).

Second, to what degree is the *client's presence* necessary to the service? Thus brain surgery involves the client's presence, but a car repair does not. To the extent that the client must be present, the service provider has to be considerate of his or her needs. Thus beauty shop operators will invest in their shop's decor, play background music, and engage in conversation if the client desires it.

Third, what about the *client's purchase motive?* Does the service meet a *personal* need (personal services) or a *business* need (business services)? For example, physicians will price physical examinations differently, depending upon whether they are serving private patients or providing a prepaid service to the employees of a particular company. Service providers can develop different service offers and marketing programs for personal service versus business service target markets.

Fourth, what about the *service provider's motives* (*profit* or *nonprofit*) and *form* (*private* or *public*)? These two characteristics, when crossed, produce four quite different types of service organizations, those shown earlier in Chapter 3, Figure 3-1, page 67. Clearly the marketing programs of, say, a private investor hospital will differ from those of a private charity hospital or a Veterans Administration hospital.

The Extent and Importance of Marketing in the Service Sector

Service firms typically lag behind manufacturing firms in their development and use of marketing. George and Barksdale surveyed four hundred service and manufacturing firms and concluded that

- in comparison to manufacturing firms, service firms appear to be: (1) generally less likely to have marketing mix activities carried out in the marketing department, (2) less likely to perform analysis in the offering area, (3) more likely to handle their advertising internally rather than go to outside agencies, (4) less likely to have an overall sales plan, (5) less likely to develop sales training programs, (6) less likely to use marketing research firms and marketing consultants, and (7) less likely to spend as much on marketing when expressed as a percentage of gross sales.[5]

Why have service firms neglected marketing? Several reasons can be given. Many service businesses are small (shoe repair, barbershops) and do not use management techniques such as marketing, which they think would be expensive or irrelevant. There are also service businesses (law and accounting firms) that are antagonistic to the idea of marketing, believing that it is unprofessional to apply any marketing planning to their services and even prohibiting it in their code of ethics. Other service businesses (colleges, hospitals) had so much demand for years that they had no need for marketing until recently.

Today, as competition intensifies, as costs rise, as productivity stagnates, and as service quality deteriorates, an increasing number of service firms are taking an interest in marketing. They can profit by studying the few service industries that have already moved into marketing. Airlines were one of the first service industries to formally study their customers and competition and take positive steps to make the travelers' trips easier and more pleasant. They first had to build people's confidence in air travel and then try to outperform each other in preflight, inflight, and postflight services to win customer loyalty. Banks represent a service industry that moved from hostility to active use of marketing in a relatively short period of time. At first they saw marketing mainly as promotion and friendliness, but they have now moved toward setting up marketing organization, information, planning, and control systems.[6] One of their strategies was to hire away marketers from General Foods, P&G, and other top marketing companies to bring in marketing sophistication as soon as possible, although this was not without some tension between financial and marketing types.[7] Many banks have now redesigned their "atmospheres" so that they are more like living rooms than mausoleums, expanded their service hours, increased the number of service products, and so on. As for other service industries, such as stock brokerage, insurance, and lodging, the marketing concept has come in unevenly, with some leaders taking major marketing steps (Merrill Lynch, Hyatt Regency) and most other firms lagging behind.

As competition becomes keener, more marketing sophistication will be needed in service marketing. One of the main agents of change will be product marketers who decide to move into service industries because they see that this is where the economy is moving. Sears moved into services marketing years ago and owns Allstate, the nation's largest stock casualty insurance company. Allstate in turn owns Allstate Savings and Loan Association, the eleventh largest S & L in California; and Sears runs concessions in its stores for income tax counseling and car rentals. Xerox Corporation operates a major business in sales management training (Xerox Learning), and Gerber Products has moved into nursery schools and insurance.

One of the main needs in services marketing is to find ways to increase productivity. Since the service business is highly labor-intensive, costs have been accelerating, as exemplified by the soaring costs of hospital services. Many people incorrectly assume that little can be done to increase productivity in service businesses. There are five approaches to improving service-firm productivity. The first is to have service providers work harder or more skillfully for the same pay. Working harder is not a likely solution, but working more skillfully can occur through better selection and training procedures. The second is to increase the quantity of service by surrendering some quality. Thus it is possible for doctors to give less time to each patient and for hospitals to increase the patients-to-nurse ratio. The third is to add capital-intensive equipment to increase service delivery capabilities. Levitt has recommended that management adopt a "manufacturing attitude" toward the production of services as represented by the assembly-line principles that McDonald's applied to fast-food retailing, culminating in the "technological hamburger."[8] Commercial dishwashing, jumbo jets, multiple-unit motion picture theatres—all represent technological solutions to expanded service. The fourth is to reduce or obsolete the need for a service by inventing a product solution, the way television substituted for outside entertainment, the wash-and-wear shirt reduced the need for the commercial laundry, and penicillin reduced the need for tuberculosis sanitariums. And the fifth is to design a more effective service that eliminates or reduces the need for a less effective service. Thus promoting nonsmoking clinics and physical exercise like jogging may reduce the need for more expensive curative medical services later on. Also, hiring paralegal workers replaces the need for using more expensive legal professionals.

Marketing Mix Decisions for Service Firms

Almost everything we said earlier in this book about marketing mix decisions applies to service firms as well as product firms. To illustrate this we will examine one industry, the college industry, and consider its product, price, place, and promotion opportunities.

Product planning is a challenging area for a service organization. A college consists of a set of schools, departments, and courses. The college needs certain star programs to attract top students to its campus (a fine music school), and it needs some cash cows (the business school) to pay for some of its question marks (philosophy) and dogs (foreign languages). Colleges have to be hardheaded about whether to keep an expensive, but optional, program. New York University's faculty split down the middle over whether to retain its School of Social Work in the face of it high cost and falling enrollment. Beyond developing a balanced portfolio of course offerings, college administrators need skill in developing, testing, and launching new programs. When De Paul University decided to develop a new bachelor's degree program for adults, its planners spent months studying adults' educational desires and competitive programs in order to develop a competitively viable program. They designed its features (open to persons over twenty-four years of age, pass-fail, learning contract, and credit for past experience), decided upon its name (School of New Learning), tested this in the market, and launched it when it was "a sure thing." Another aspect of product planning calls for developing customer feedback systems (teacher evaluation forms, complaint systems) so that the college can be sure it is rendering a quality product. One other product-planning step is to see whether credit exchange programs can be formed with other colleges to amplify the offer that the college can offer to prospective students.

Service industries must be more imaginative in their *pricing*. Many of them set their prices as a straightforward markup over cost (auto service dealers), and others charge what the traffic will bear (physicians). Yet there are many other ways of pricing that might meet the financial needs of the service provider and/or the clients. Colleges, for example, charge essentially the same tuition for all students. They do not consider the varying cost or demand for different programs. One can imagine a college pricing each course differently (as a function of its costs, competition, and demand). One can also imagine paying professors for the number of students who enroll, stay enrolled, and express high satisfaction with the course. Colleges could offer a discount to students who paid their four years of tuition in advance, and they could adjust loan repayment plans to the student's relative success in the job market. One can imagine the college offering quantity discounts for large community groups that enroll in its evening programs. Although some of these ideas are not feasible, they suggest the many creative pricing approaches available to a service industry.

Service providers have several options with respect to *service delivery systems,* although this is not always fully appreciated. Many people think that because services are intangible, inseparable, and perishable, the concept of middlemen and physical distribution activities is not relevant to services. Consider, however, the services involved in a college. The major service delivery system for educational services is campus classrooms occupied by teachers and students. The college hires service providers called teachers, who deliver the service to students face to face. But there are several additional options available. An expansion-minded college can offer extension courses in outlying communities. It can do what Adelphi College did—teach a college course on a commuter railroad car every morning and evening. It can develop correspondence courses and educational cassettes and films. The next step would be to open permanent branches in other locations within the state, much like the Bank of America's branch banks in California. Then the next step would be to open branches in different parts of the country and the world, much like a McDonald franchise system, offering consistent quality mass-produced education. Finally, it might get into the "holographic" transmission of teaching services:

- Imagine a "celebrity" biology teacher entering a holography studio at 8:45 A.M. At 9:00, he starts teaching and his three-dimensional image is transmitted simultaneously into 50 college classrooms, some of which may be thousands of miles away. Students in these classrooms see him, in three-dimensional full color, waving his hands, pacing the floor, furrowing his brow. In this manner, one gifted teacher instead of 50 average teachers presents the course, thereby providing better instruction with enormous cost savings . . . there would be phone hookups in each of the 50 classrooms to permit students to raise questions directly with the "holographic" professor.[9]

Finally, service organizations have many opportunities to use *promotion* in connection with their business. Promotion can be used to build interest in the service, to differentiate the firm's offer from competitors' offers, and to build the organization's overall image. Service organizations can make extensive use of publicity, personal selling, advertising, and even sales promotion. Colleges, for example, rely heavily on their public relations staff to obtain local and even national publicity. The public relations staff hunts for news items and also creates newsworthy events to increase the college's visibility and favorable image in the minds of different college publics. Personal selling is used extensively in the admissions and fund-raising offices. Admissions officers travel to target high schools to promote their college and are increasingly using movies and film strips to communicate the intangible qualities of their college in a more tangible way. On campus, they interview and entertain high-school seniors, sometimes for an entire weekend. In the fund-raising area, the college's development staff identifies wealthy alumni and potential donors, as well as foundations, government agencies, and business firms whose support might be cultivated. Like true salespeople, they study their prospects and approach them with well-thought-out propositions designed to create donor interest and conviction. As for advertising, colleges have traditionally distributed catalogs and brochures and are increasingly using direct mail as a means of reaching, informing, and influencing their target markets. These materials are now using better graphics and, as mentioned earlier, one college—Barat College of Lake Forest, Illinois—went further and described its good and bad points in true consumerist fashion. Colleges have traditionally run newspaper ads (especially for evening courses and programs), and many colleges are now using magazines, local radio stations, and, in a few cases, television. Drake College placed a billboard ad near O'Hare Field in Chicago showing a beautiful coed and indicating that Drake was only forty minutes away (by air) from Chicago. Finally, sales promotion has been put to some use (or misuse) by some colleges, such as those that distribute free frisbees advertising their college name on the beaches of Fort Lauderdale or release scholarship balloons on high-school campuses. However, no college has as yet offered free typewriters, trading stamps, money-back guarantees, or finder's fees in the effort to fill its classrooms in the face of a declining college student population. Thus we see that a service industry—in this case, colleges—uses many different kinds of promotional tools.

organization marketing

We will use the term *organization marketing* to describe *those activities undertaken to create, maintain, or alter attitudes and/or behavior of target audiences toward particular organizations.* Thus we do not mean the normal marketing activities undertaken to sell the organization's products and services but rather those undertaken to "sell" the organization itself. Organization marketing has traditionally been the responsibility of the public relations department. This is evident from the following widely used definition of *public relations:*

- Public relations is the management function which evaluates public attitudes, identifies the policies and procedures of an individual or an organization with the public interest, and plans and executes a program of action to earn public understanding and acceptance.[10]

It can be argued that public relations is essentially marketing management shifted from a product/service to an organization.[11] Many of the same skills are needed: knowledge of audience needs, desires, and psychology; skill at communication; an ability to design and execute programs aimed at influence. The recognition of the similarities, or at least complementarities, between marketing and public relations has led several companies to combine both functions under single control. An example is the appointment at General Electric of a vice-president of marketing and public affairs who "will be responsible for all corporate activities in advertising, public affairs, and public relations. He will also handle corporate marketing, including research and personnel development."

The general methodology of organization marketing consists of three steps: (1) assessing the current image of the organization, (2) determining a desirable image for the organization, and (3) developing a marketing plan for bringing about the desired image.

Image Assessment

No fruitful image work can be done with an organization until research is conducted to determine how the organization is seen by its various key publics. The *set of beliefs that a person or group holds of an object* is called its *image.* The organization might be quite pleased with its measured image and simply want to do the work necessary to maintain it. Or the organization might discover that it has some serious image problems, in which case its interest lies in correcting and improving its image.

Image assessment calls for developing a survey instrument to measure the organization's image among its major publics. One part of the survey will establish the visibility-favorability position of the organization's image, and the other part will measure the content of the organization's image.

Figure 20-1A shows the results of measuring the visibility-favorability images of five management consulting firms. The two management consulting firms in quadrant I are in the best position. Firm 1 in particular is highly visible and enjoys the highest repute. Firm 3 in quadrant II also has high repute but is less well known. Its marketing need is to increase its visibility so that more people will know how good it is. Firm 4 in quadrant III is less well regarded than the preceding firms, but fortunately not many people know about it. This firm should maintain a low profile and introduce improvements in its management consulting practice designed to attract more approval. If effective, firm 4 will move to quadrant II, from which it can then seek more publicity. Finally, firm 5 in quadrant IV is in the worst situation in that it is seen as a poor service provider

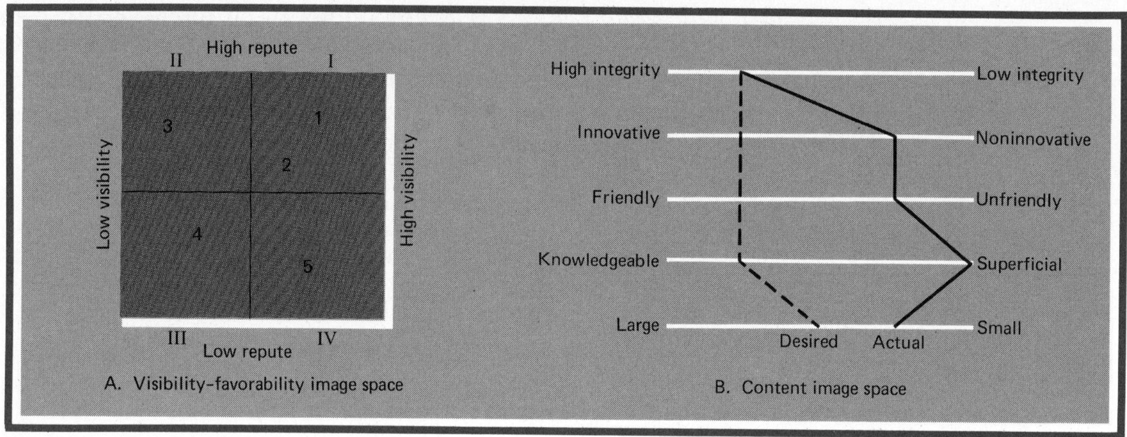

Figure 20-1 *Image Assessment Tools*

and everyone knows about this. This is sometimes called the "Amtrak syndrome." The firm's best course of action is to try to reduce its visibility (which would move it to quadrant III) and then plan to move successively to quadrants II and I. Of course this would take several years—if the firm ever accomplished it at all. Thus it should be clear that a firm's initial position in the visibility-favorability space defines the basic type of strategy it should pursue.

The second part of the image study is designed to reveal the content of the organization's image. One of the major tools for measuring the content of an image is the *semantic differential.*[12] The semantic differential involves identifying a set of appropriate object attributes and stating each attribute in bipolar terms. Respondents are asked to place a mark on each scale according to their impression of the degree to which the object possesses that attribute. The image researcher then averages the responses on each scale and represents this by a point. The points of the various scales are connected vertically, forming an image profile of the object.

Suppose firm 4 in Figure 20-1A finds its image profile to be that shown by the solid line in Figure 20-1B. Firm 4 is regarded as being high in integrity but not particularly innovative, friendly, knowledgeable, or large. The firm will either be surprised to learn this or recognize its validity. In either case the firm knows that these image weaknesses handicap its growth and profitability.

The firm should recognize that its "average" image as shown in Figure 20-1 (A and B) is probably not its image among every key public and even within each key public. The organization's image should be separately examined for each key public, and where it is acceptable, little marketing effort need be directed toward that public. The image consistency should also be examined within each key public. The firm may want its image to be highly specific or may prefer it to be somewhat varied.

Image Choice

The next step calls for the organization to identify the image that it would like to have. It must be realistic and not aim for the "impossible." Let us assume that management consulting firm 4 decides that a feasible and desirable image to aim for is that shown by the dashed line in Figure 20-1B. The firm is pleased with its integrity standing but would like to be seen as more innovative, friendly, and knowledgeable, as well as larger. It might place different weights on each image component so that it can concentrate on improving the more important components. It might even seek to cultivate somewhat different images among different publics, as long as they were broadly consistent.

Image Planning and Control

At this point firm 4 has to develop a marketing plan that will eventually shift its actual image toward the desired one. Suppose that it wants to put most of the planning weight on increasing its reputation as a knowledgeable firm. If the firm really lacks knowledgeable consultants, then the key step is to hire better consultants. If the firm has highly knowledgeable consultants but they are not very visible, then its task is to give them more exposure. In this case its knowledgeable consultants should be encouraged to join business and trade associations, give speeches, write articles, develop public seminars on "hot" new topics, and sponsor awards that draw favorable attention to the firm and suggest their interest in advancing knowledge in the management consulting industry.[13]

From time to time the firm must resurvey its publics to see whether its activities have succeeded in improving its image. The job cannot be accomplished overnight because of the limitation of funds and the "stickiness" of public images. But if the firm is making no progress, it should be concerned that either its substance or its image communications are deficient.

We have illustrated the methodology of organization marketing using the example of a management consulting firm. Here are additional examples of organizations' taking concrete steps to improve their image among key publics.

- *Police department.* Police departments are often criticized by community groups. They have responded in a number of ways. "Officer Friendly" programs are launched in which police officers visit schools, appear on television, and try in other ways to improve their image. One city provided new uniforms (blazers) for the police so that they would appear less formidable. Various police-department administrators are beginning to talk about the use of *market research* (what does the public want from us), more *advertising* (like the ad in New York City: "Leave your keys in cars . . . it helps thieves"), and better *distribution* (where to locate police services in relation to crime rates).
- *Church marketing.* Churches have a longstanding interest in the problem of developing and maintaining believers. Missionary and evangelic work represents this tradition in its pure form. At certain points in history, religious enthusiasm for conversion reached unusual proportions, as in the Inquisition. Today the methods of attracting and maintaining members are more subtle. A book entitled *Successful Church Publicity* discusses the various problems of church marketing under such topics as "publicizing the right message," "slanting publicity toward prospects," "word-of-mouth publicity," "direct mail campaigns," "outdoor signs," "chimes and sound systems."[14] The Billy Graham organization is probably the most sophisticated evangelic organization in its use of modern campaign concepts, involving words, music, and celebrities, all harmonized and crescendoed to create an outburst of religious feeling.
- *American Cancer Society.* The American Cancer Society competes with other medical charitable organizations in seeking to win the goodwill and support of the

public. In its brochure directed to local units, it attempts to educate the volunteer and professional chapters on the handling of newspapers, pictures, company publications, radio and television, movies, special events, controversial arguments, and so on. Under special events, for example: "Dramatic special events attract attention to the American Cancer Society. They bring color, excitement, and glamour to the program. Well planned, they will get excellent coverage in newspapers, on radio and TV, and in newsreels. . . . A Lights-on Drive, a one-afternoon or one-night House-to-House program have such dramatic appeal that they stir excitement and enthusiasm . . . keep in mind the value of bursts of sound such as fire sirens sounding, loudspeaker trucks, fife and drum corps. . . . A most useful special event is the ringing of church bells to add a solemn, dedicated note to the launching of a drive or education project. This should be organized on a Division or community basis, and the church bell ringing may be the signal to begin a House-to-House canvass. Rehearsals of bell ringing, community leaders tugging at ropes, offer good picture possibilities."[15]

person marketing

In addition to products, services, and organizations, persons are also marketed. *Person marketing* consists of *activities undertaken to create, maintain, or alter attitudes and/or behavior toward particular persons.* The three most common types of person marketing are celebrity marketing, political candidate marketing, and personal marketing.

Celebrity Marketing

Celebrity marketing has a long history going back to the Caesars; in recent times it has been most conspicuously associated with the buildup of Hollywood stars and entertainers. Hollywood actors and actresses would hire *press agents* to promote their stardom. For a retainer, the press agent would manage to get frequent mentions and pictures of the star in the mass media and also schedule the star's appearance in highly visible locations and conventions. At one point in his career, Bing Crosby owed 60 percent of every dollar he made to other people, including a personal manager, business manager, road manager, lawyer, and record company. One of the great promoters was the late Brian Epstein, who adroitly managed the Beatles' rise to stardom and in the process received a larger share of the money than any Beatle. Today celebrities are promoted not by single press agents but by entire organizations. One day Bucky Dent of the Yankees phoned the William Morris Agency and asked Lee Salomon to take over his public life.[16] They proceeded to line him up to visit children's hospitals, Little Leagues, and conventions; to co-host "A.M. New York" and appear on the Merv Griffin show; to have posters made and marketed; to make a commercial for a car manufacturer; and to get spreads in *Playboy* and other magazines.

Celebrity marketers cannot work miracles; much depends on the talent and personality of the star. And if the star is a born promoter, there is no limit. Elton John is said to have made the most money in the history of the music business, more than the Beatles or Elvis Presley. Besides selling over 42 million albums, his concerts are always filled. Elton wears one of over two hundred pairs of glasses, pounds the piano with his feet, bats tennis balls into the crowd, and hires actors to wander around the stage dressed as Frankenstein or Queen Elizabeth. Whether these are his ideas or those of his manager, he is able to carry them off.

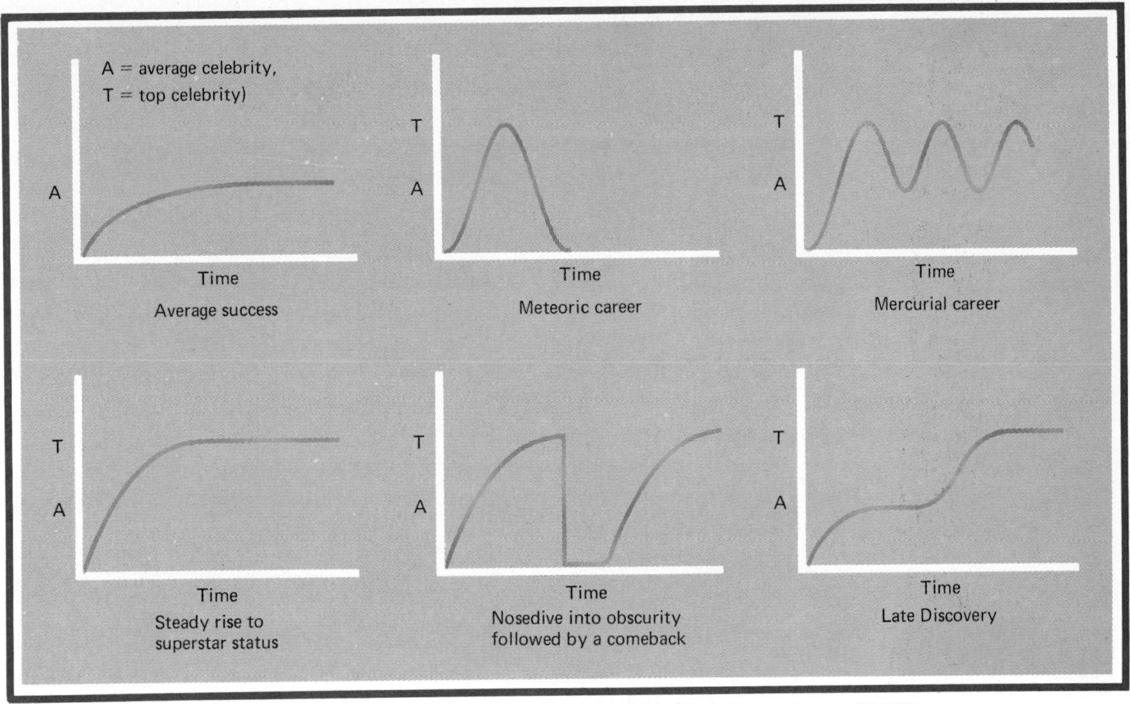

Source: Charles Seton, "The Marketing of a Free Lance Fashion Photographer" (unpublished student paper, January 20, 1978).

Figure 20-2 Celebrity Career Life Cycles

Celebrity marketers all recognize that celebrity life cycles are quite varied and often limited (see Figure 20-2). The head of marketing for Polygram, a major international record conglomerate, likens a performer's career to a crate of strawberries that must be packaged, brought to the market, and sold before they spoil and become worthless. Mike Gormley, national publicity director for Mercury Records, describes a typical meeting: "We get together every six weeks. We'll go down our sales figures. If we decide a group is getting 'no action'—meaning no airplay or sales—we'll drop them. If promotion doesn't get results, you don't just throw away more money."[17] Some "has-been" celebrities, such as Eddie Fisher, will try to relaunch, but they find that it is a long road back to the top.[18]

Political Candidate Marketing

Political candidate marketing has become a major industry and area of specialization. Every few years the public is treated to an endless number of campaigns attempting to put various candidates for local, state, and national offices in the best light. In the 1972 presidential election year, the various candidates for all offices managed to spend over $400 million in less than two months on their campaigns. The money was spent on media advertising, direct mail and telephone, and in other ways.

Political campaigns have increasingly been compared to marketing campaigns in which the candidate goes into the voter market and uses modern marketing techniques, particularly marketing research and commercial advertising, to maximize voter "purchase." The marketing analogy is more than coincidental. The very essence of a candidate's interface with the voters is a marketing one, not only in recent times but far back into the past. Candidates seeking to win elections cannot avoid marketing themselves. The only question is how to do it effectively.

Interest in the marketing aspects of elections has been stimulated to a large extent by the spectacular growth in *political advertising*. There has also been a substantial growth of *scientific opinion polling* (i.e., marketing research), *computer analysis of voting patterns* (i.e., sales analysis), and *professional campaign management firms* (i.e., marketing organizations). The subtleties of the marketing approach go beyond the rising expenditure levels and the use of certain information and planning approaches. They are delineated in a series of popular books, such as White's *The Making of the President 1960* and McGinness's *The Selling of the President 1968*.[19] In a quieter way, several scholarly works have also noted the marketing character of political elections.[20]

It would be a gross mistake to think that election campaigns have taken on a marketing character only in recent years. *Campaigning has always had a marketing character*. Prior to the new methodology, candidates sought office through the handshake, baby-kissing, teas, and speechmaking. They still use these methods. *The "new methodology" is not the introduction of marketing methods into politics but rather an increased sophistication and acceleration of their use.* According to Glick:

> ▪ The personal handshake, the local fund-raising dinner, the neighborhood tea, the rally, the precinct captain and the car pool to the polls are still very much with us . . . the new campaign has provided a carefully coordinated strategic framework within which the traditional activities are carried out in keeping with a Master Plan. It centers on a shift from the candidate-controlled, loosely knit, often haphazard "play-it-by-ear" approach to that of a precise, centralized "team" strategy for winning or keeping office. Its hallmarks include the formal strategic blueprint, the coordinated use of specialized propaganda skills, and a more subtle approach to opinion measurement and manipulation. And, though there is a world of difference between selling a candidate and merchandising soap or razor blades, some of the attributes of commercial advertising have been grafted onto the political process.[21]

Political candidates seeking election start with *marketing research* to identify and understand the major market segments and the major issues of concern to each segment. They and their advisers then develop a *candidate concept* consisting of a political philosophy, choice of issues and positions, a personal style, and a case describing the candidate's background and qualifications. The next step calls for developing a *communication and distribution strategy* involving the use of mass and selective media, scheduled personal appearances, and the assistance of volunteers and party workers. Through the use of these marketing tools, the candidate is prepared to wage a good fight for votes, with the ultimate outcome determined by the voters.[22]

Personal Marketing

Personal marketing encompasses the efforts of individuals to create certain impressions about themselves in the minds of others. Erving Goffman considers impression management a ubiquitous human trait,[23] and Erich Fromm observes that "in order to have success it is not sufficient to have the skill and equipment for performing a given task but that one must be able to 'put across' one's personality in competition with many others."[24] Gilbert and Sullivan gave this advice: "If you wish in the world to advance, / Your merits you're bound to enhance, / You must stir it and stump it, and blow your trumpet, / Or, trust me, you haven't a chance."

Personal marketing takes on higher-than-normal importance during job interviewing, public appearances, and marriage courtship. Many books have been written advising job seekers (whether they be college students, college professors, or seasoned executives) on how to write better résumés and conduct better interviews. Gootnick, for example, provides the following advice:

1. *Pre-interview:* arrive a little earlier to get into the right frame of mind; if you will be late, phone the interviewer; look businesslike.
2. *Interview opening:* use the interviewer's name and apply a firm handshake; flow with the small talk and be relaxed.
3. *Interview development:* start developing why you are interested in the job and your qualifications.
4. *Interview closing:* summarize your key credentials, express enthusiasm, express appreciation, and ask what the next step will be.
5. *Post-interview:* record the key points about the company on paper and evaluate your own success on appearance, oral communications skill, and social skill. Send a "thank you" letter in about five days expressing appreciation and reiterating your key qualifications.[25]

Clearly, the whole framework resembles that of a sales presentation.

Company recruiters were surveyed as to the importance of different job candidate attributes and ranked them as follows: personality and leadership potential; motivation and clear-cut goals; maturity and previous business or military experience; communication skills; analytical ability; reputation of the school; and grades.[26] Among the things that most hurt in an interview are poor appearance; inability to express oneself; poor listening skills; lack of common courtesy; lack of preparation for interview; lack of confidence, interest, and enthusiasm; conceit and overconfidence; being evasive, deceitful, and dishonest; high-pressure selling; and being long-winded or abrupt.[27]

The key point is that the job seeker must see the recruiting company as a buyer and must try to understand the buyer's motives and buying criteria. Then it is up to the job seeker to determine whether he or she has the qualifications and wants to use personal marketing to get the job. The objective is not to falsify one's true self, which would eventually catch up with the person on the job, but to project oneself in as favorable a light as possible, given what business firms look for in applicants. A person who cannot succeed in this is probably mismatched to a corporate business career in the first place.

Interestingly enough, at the same time that job seekers are marketing themselves, so is the recruiting company. A recruiter who is interested in a specific candidate will try to impress the candidate and position the company favorably against other companies. The recruiter will try as hard to understand the job seeker's choice criteria as the job seeker will try to understand the recruiter's choice criteria.[28] Thus while the job seeker is doing personal marketing, the company is doing organizational marketing.

- To help job seekers and ambitious executives, a cottage industry of "image doctors" has sprung up to give business pros advice about everything from what to wear to what to say and how to say it. For a sizeable fee, these consultants will lower the pitch of your voice, remove your accent, correct your "body language," modify your unacceptable behavior, eliminate your negative self-perceptions, select your wardrobe, restyle your hair, and teach you how to speak off the cuff or read a speech without putting your audience to sleep.[29]

The various personal image consultants, who take on both corporate and individual clients, consist of speech and public appearance trainers, dress consultants, and personal public relations consultants.[30]

place marketing

Place marketing involves *activities undertaken to create, maintain, or alter attitudes and/or behavior toward particular places.* Five types of place marketing can be distinguished.

Domicile Marketing

Domicile marketing involves the effort to develop and/or promote the sale or rental of single-family dwellings, apartments, and other types of housing units. Domicile marketing has traditionally relied on the classified want ad and the real estate agent. Advanced marketing practices have recently emerged in connection with condominium selling and the development of total communities.[31] Large builders attempt to research housing needs and develop housing products attuned to the price ranges and preferences of specific market segments. Some high-rise apartments have been built for the young set, others for the geriatric set, filled with the features, symbols, and services appropriate to each. Entire housing communities have been designed with specific life-cycle and/or life-style groups in mind.

Business Site Marketing

Business site marketing involves the effort to develop, sell, or rent business sites or properties such as plants, stores, offices, and warehouses. Larger developers have become quite sophisticated in researching business needs and responding with total real estate solutions, such as industrial parks, shopping centers, and new office buildings. Most states operate industrial development offices staffed with directors who identify and call on various companies and try to sell them on the advantages of locating new plants in their states. To increase their leads they spend large sums on advertising in major business publications, and they offer to fly prospects to the site when necessary. Various cities in trouble, such as New York City, Detroit, and Atlanta, have developed special task forces to work on the problem of refurbishing the city's image and drawing new business to the area. Foreign nations, such as Ireland, Greece, and Turkey, have also been eager marketers of their homeland as a potential location for business investment.

Land Investment Marketing

Land investment marketing involves efforts to develop and sell land for investment purposes. The buyers—corporations, doctors, small investors, speculators—plan to sell the land when it rises sufficiently in value. Land investment marketing has been instrumental in developing large parts of Florida and the Far West. Land developers have worked out elaborate marketing programs involving mass-media advertising and publicity, direct mail, personal sales calls, free dinner meetings, and even free flights to the site.

Vacation Marketing

Vacation marketing involves the effort to attract vacationers to various spas, resorts, cities, states, and even whole nations. The effort is carried on by travel agents, airlines, motor clubs, oil companies, hotels, motels, and various governmental units. The power of marketing to promote places was demonstrated in the career of the late Steve Hannagan: "He built monuments to his skill and the power of press-agentry in making the Memorial Day auto races at Indianapolis a national event and in making Miami Beach and Sun Valley into nationally known resorts."[32]

Vacation marketers have classified tourists into major types and have scrutinized their behavior in order to develop more targeted communication appeals.[33] Today almost every city and state in the nation is in the business of advertising and publicizing its tourist attractions. Miami Beach, Florida, is again trying to attract tourists and is using a number of measures, including considering making gambling legal in the city; and the Virgin Islands is trying to "repopularize" the islands after some bad tourist incidents. Some other places, however, are using marketing techniques just as strenuously to demarket themselves. Palm Beach, Florida, is letting its beach erode to discourage tourists; Oregon has put out some negative statements about its weather; Yosemite National Park is considering prohibiting snowmobiling, conventions, and private car usage; and several European countries, such as Finland and France, would just as well discourage tourists from vacationing in certain areas where they feel the ravages of mass tourism exceed the revenues.

Nation Marketing

Nations engage in continuous public relation activities to win a favorable image among the citizens of other countries. The day-to-day job is carried on by the information officers attached to embassies. One officer said his job was to "project the true image of his country."[34] Others describe this work as *propaganda,* which is defined as "the deliberate attempt by some individual or group to form, control, or alter the attitudes of other groups by the use of the instruments of communication, with the intention that in any given situation the reaction of those so influenced will be that desired by the propagandist."[35] Arthur E. Meyerhoff, the president of an advertising agency, observed: "We have not effectively applied our sales techniques to selling ourselves and our ideas to other countries . . . the job has never been given to the people who know how to do it. These are people who have popularized cornflakes and automobiles, and they are skilled in the art of persuasion, which is the basis for successful propaganda."[36]

idea marketing

One further application of marketing theory is to the marketing of "ideas." In the preceding paragraph Meyerhoff indicates that there is a need for marketing the idea of American democracy more effectively to other nations. In one sense, all marketing is the marketing of ideas, whether it be the idea of brushing one's teeth, the idea that Crest is the most effective decay preventer, or anything else. Here, however, idea marketing will be used to cover efforts to market ideas as such. We will further confine our discussion of the marketing of social ideas, such as are embodied in public health campaigns to reduce smoking, alcoholism, drug abuse, and overeating; environmental campaigns to promote wilderness protection, clean air, and resource conservation; and a myriad of other campaigns such as family planning, women's rights, and racial equality. This area has been called *social marketing,* and it is defined as follows:[37]

- Social marketing is the design, implementation, and control of programs seeking to increase the acceptability of a social idea, cause, or practice in a target groups(s). It utilizes market segmentation, consumer research, concept development, communications, facilitation, incentives, and exchange theory to maximize target group response.

Social marketing, in contrast to ordinary business marketing, has more of the characteristics of a change technology than a response technology. In trying to get smokers to stop smoking, social marketing seems to be based on the selling concept rather than the marketing concept. Yet the lesson of a consumer orientation is not lost on the social marketer. The social marketer tries to understand why smokers smoke, what pleasures they get, and what difficulties they have in trying to stop smoking. All of this is important in trying to formulate an effective marketing plan that will encourage people to give up smoking.

Social marketing can pursue different objectives such as: (1) produce *understanding* (knowing the nutritional value of different foods); (2) trigger a particular *one-time* action (participating in a mass immunization campaign); (3) attempt to *change behavior* (auto seat-belt campaign); (4) change a *basic belief* (convincing people to prefer socialism).

Social marketing calls for much more than public advertising. The Advertising Council of America has carried out dozens of campaigns for social objectives, including "Smokey the Bear," "Keep America Beautiful," "Join the Peace Corps," "Buy Bonds," and "Go to College." But the concept of social marketing is much broader. Many public advertising campaigns fail because of the tendency to assign advertising the primary if not the exclusive role in accomplishing social objectives. This ignores the marketing truism that a given marketing objective requires the coordination of the promotional mix with the goods and service mix and the distribution mix. Wiebe, in his study of four social campaigns, showed how their differential success was related to how closely they resembled the conditions of selling a normal product or service.[38] The great success of the Kate Smith radio marathon to sell bonds one evening was due, in Wiebe's opinion, to the presence of force (patriotism), direction (buy bonds), mechanism (banks, post offices, telephone orders), adequacy and compatibility (many centers to purchase the bonds), and distance (ease of purchase). These easily translate into factors such as product, price, place, and promotion. The other three social campaigns—recruiting Civil Defense volunteers, stimulating people to take steps to help juvenile delinquents, and arousing citizens against crime—met with much less success because of the lack or mishandling of product, price, place, or promotion variables.

Any organization with a cause can approach its task by developing a marketing plan. Thus social marketing can be said to take place if Procter & Gamble sponsors a campaign in a developing nation aimed at encouraging people to take better care of their teeth, or Coca-Cola sponsors a campaign calling upon people not to carelessly throw away their empty soft-drink containers in public places. Furthermore, the concepts and techniques making up social marketing are available to all sides of an issue. We cannot call it social marketing if we agree with the cause and propaganda if we disagree with it. Proabortion groups and antiabortion groups can both use social marketing.

The social marketer, in designing a social change strategy, goes through a normal marketing-planning process. The first step is to define the social change objective. Suppose the objective is "to reduce the number of teen-age smokers from 60 percent to 40 percent of the teen-age population within five years." The next step is to analyze the beliefs, attitudes, values, and behavior of the target group, here teen-agers, and to identify key segments of the target market who would respond to different marketing approaches. An analysis is also made of the major competitive forces that support teen-age smoking. This is followed by concept research, in which the social marketer generates and tests alternative concepts that might be effective in dissuading teen-agers from smoking (see Exhibit 20-1). The next step is channel analysis, in which the social marketer identifies and assesses the most effective communication and distribution approaches to the target market. This is followed by the formal development of a marketing plan and a marketing organization to carry it out. Finally, provision is made to monitor ongoing results and take corrective action when called for.

EXHIBIT 20-1

CAN SOCIAL MARKETING REDUCE CIGARETTE SMOKING?

The weight of scientific evidence demonstrates a link between cigarette smoking and such medical ailments as lung cancer, heart disease, and emphysema. Most cigarette smokers are aware of the bad effects of cigarette smoking. The problem is one of formulating and distributing solutions that will give them the means or will to reduce their cigarette dependence. The four *P*s suggest several possible types of solutions:

1. *Product*
   a. Require manufacturers to add a tart or bitter ingredient to the tobacco.
   b. Find a way to cut down further the tar and nicotine in cigarettes (for example, develop better filters).
   c. Find a new type of tobacco for cigarettes that tastes as good but does not have harmful ingredients (for example, lettuce leaf).
   d. Find or promote other products that will help people relieve their tensions, such as gum chewing or other oral pacifiers.
2. *Promotion*
   a. Increase fear of early death among smokers.
   b. Create guilt or shame among cigarette users.
   c. Strengthen some other goal of smokers that supersedes their satisfaction from smoking.
   d. Urge smokers to cut down the number of cigarettes they smoke or to smoke only the first half of the cigarette.

3. *Place*
   a. Make cigarettes harder to obtain conveniently.
   b. Make cigarettes unavailable.
   c. Make it easier for cigarette smokers to find places offering help, like anti-smoking clinics.
   d. Make it harder to find public places that allow cigarette smoking.
4. *Price*
   a. Raise substantially the price of a pack of cigarettes.
   b. Raise the cost of life and health insurance to smokers.
   c. Offer a monetary or nonmonetary reward to smokers each period they forgo smoking.

Antismoking campaigns appear to be worthwhile. However, social marketers should be aware of some unanticipated secondary consequences. People who stop smoking have a tendency to eat more and gain weight. Overweight is estimated to shorten people's lives by approximately fourteen years, whereas smoking is estimated to shorten people's lives by seven years. Liquor, interestingly enough, is estimated to shorten consumers' lives by four years. This might suggest that the social marketer should either leave the smoker alone or encourage the smoker to stop smoking and start drinking.

Social marketing is still too new to evaluate its effectiveness in comparison with other social change strategies. Social change itself is hard to produce with any strategy, let alone one that relies on voluntary response. The ideas of social marketing have been mainly applied in the areas of family planning,[39] environmental protection,[40] energy conservation, improved nutrition, auto driver safety, and public transportation, with some encouraging successes. More applications will have to take place before we can actually determine social marketing's potential as a social change strategy.

summary

Marketing, which was first developed in connection with products, has been broadened in recent years to cover other "marketable" entities, namely, services, organizations, persons, places, and ideas.

The United States is the world's first service economy in that a majority of its people are employed in service industries. *Services* can be defined as activities or benefits that one party can offer to another that are essentially intangible and do not result in the ownership of anything. Services are intangible, inseparable, variable, and perishable. Services can be classified according to whether they are people-based or equipment-based, whether the client's presence is necessary, whether the client is a consumer or business, and whether the service provider is a profit or nonprofit firm in the private or public sector. Service industries have lagged behind manufacturing firms in adopting and using marketing concepts. Yet rising costs and increased competition have forced service industries to search for new ways to increase their productivity. Marketing can make a contribution by calling for more systematic planning of service concepts and their pricing, distribution, and promotion.

Organizations can also be marketed. *Organization marketing* describes those activities undertaken to create, maintain, or alter attitudes and/or behavior of target audiences toward particular organizations. It calls for three steps: (1) assessing the organization's current image, (2) determining a desirable image, and (3) developing a marketing plan for bringing about the desired image.

Person marketing consists of activities undertaken to create, maintain, or alter attitudes and/or behavior toward particular persons. The three most common types are celebrity marketing, political candidate marketing, and personal marketing.

Place marketing involves activities undertaken to create, maintain, or alter attitudes and/or behavior toward particular places. The five most common types are domicile marketing, business site marketing, land investment marketing, vacation marketing, and nation marketing.

Idea marketing involves efforts to market ideas. In the case of social ideas it is called *social marketing* and consists of the design, implementation, and control of programs seeking to increase the acceptability of a social idea, cause, or practice in a target group. Social marketing goes further than public advertising in that it coordinates advertising with the other elements of the marketing mix. The social marketer proceeds by defining the social change objective, analyzing consumer attitudes and competitive forces, developing and testing alternative concepts, developing appropriate channels for the idea's communication and distribution, and, finally, monitoring the results. Social marketing has been applied in the areas of family planning, environmental protection, antismoking campaigns, and other public issues.

■ questions for discussion

1. Relate the four distinctive characteristics of services to a service that you have purchased recently.
2. Producers of services have historically been more marketing-oriented than producers of products. Comment.
3. Explain how the distribution channel is important to the following service marketers: (a) Coopers and Lybrand ("Big 8" accounting firm), (b) Paramount Pictures, (c) Joe's Repair Shop, and (d) the local repertory theater.
4. What is the primary purpose of the individual charged with organization marketing? Explain.
5. How would you apply "personal marketing" to your attempt to secure a job?
6. The only places that can effectively be marketed are those that people enjoy visiting. Comment.
7. What distinguishes social marketing from social advertising? Explain.

references

1. "Services Grow While the Quality Shrinks," *Business Week,* October 30, 1971, p. 50.
2. For a good discussion of quality control systems at the Marriott Hotel chain, see G. M. Hostage, "Quality Control in a Service Business," *Harvard Business Review,* July-August 1975, pp. 98–106.
3. See W. Earl Sasser, "Match Supply and Demand in Service Industries," *Harvard Business Review,* November-December 1976, pp. 133–40.
4. See Dan R. E. Thomas, "Strategy Is Different in Service Businesses," *Harvard Business Review,* July-August 1978, p. 161.
5. William R. George and Hiram C. Barksdale, "Marketing Activities in the Service Industries," *Journal of Marketing,* October 1974, p. 65.
6. See Daniel T. Carroll, "Ten Commandments for Bank Marketing," *Bankers Magazine,* Autumn 1970, pp. 74–80.
7. See G. Lynn Shostack, "Banks Sell Services—Not Things," *Bankers Magazine,* Winter 1977, pp. 40–45.
8. Theodore Levitt, "Product-Line Approach to Service," *Harvard Business Review,* September-October 1972 , pp. 41–52; also see his "The Industrialization of Service," *Harvard Business Review,* September-October 1976, pp. 63–74.
9. Philip Kotler, "Educational Packagers: A Modest Proposal," *Futurist,* August 1978, pp. 239–42.
10. *Public Relations News,* October 27, 1947.
11. For this argument, see Philip Kotler and William Mindak, "Marketing and Public Relations," *Journal of Marketing,* October 1978, pp. 13–20.
12. The semantic differential technique was originally presented in C. E. Osgood, C. J. Suci, and P. H. Tannenbaum, *The Measurement of Meaning* (Urbana, Ill.: University of Illinois Press, 1957). For a discussion of various image measurement techniques, see the author's *Marketing for Nonprofit Organizations* (Englewood Cliffs, N.J.: Prentice-Hall, 1975), pp. 131–37.
13. For additional ways to market the services of a professional services firm, see Philip Kotler and Richard A. Connor, Jr., "Marketing Professional Services," *Journal of Marketing,* January 1977, pp. 71–76.
14. Carl F. H. Henry, *Successful Church Publicity: A Guidebook for Christian Publicists* (Grand Rapids, Mich.: Zondervan Publishing House, 1943).
15. *Public Information Guide* (New York: American Cancer Society, 1965), p. 19.
16. Carol Oppenheim, "Bucky Dent: The Selling of a Sudden Superstar," *Chicago Tribune,* December 16, 1978, Sec. 2, p. 1.
17. "In the Groove at Mercury Records," *Chicago Daily News,* Panorama magazine, October 16, 1976.
18. John E. Cooney, "Eddie Fisher Discovers That Regaining Fame Is a Daunting Goal," *Wall Street Journal,* February 20, 1978, p. 1.
19. Theodore White, *The Making of the President 1960* (New York: Atheneum, 1961); and Joe McGinness, *The Selling of the President 1968* (New York: Trident Press, 1969).
20. See E. Glick, *The New Methodology* (Washington, D.C.: American Institute for Political Communication, 1967); and Dan Nimmo, *The Political Persuaders: The Techniques of Modern Election Campaigns* (Englewood Cliffs, N.J.: Prentice-Hall, 1970).
21. Glick, *New Methodology,* p. 1.
22. For an elaboration, see Kotler, *Marketing for Nonprofit Organizations,* Chap. 19, "Political Candidate Marketing," pp. 365–88.

23. Erving Goffman, *The Presentation of Self in Everyday Life* (New York: Doubleday Anchor Books, 1959), p. xi.
24. Erich Fromm, *Man for Himself* (New York: Holt, Rinehart and Winston, 1947), pp. 67–116.
25. David Gootnick, *Getting a Better Job* (New York: McGraw-Hill, 1978).
26. "Grading the Recruit," *MBA Magazine,* March 1974, p. 43.
27. Gootnick, *Getting a Better Job.*
28. Orlando Behling, George Labovitz, and Marion Gainer, "College Recruiting: A Theoretical Base," *Personnel Journal,* January 1968, pp. 13–19.
29. Jacqueline A. Thompson, "The Image Doctors: A Guide to the Personal Packaging Consultants," *MBA Magazine,* September 1977, p. 1.
30. For a list of firms, see ibid., pp. 24, 25, 28, 29.
31. For a description of the marketing of a "new town" in Texas called The Woodlands, see Betsy D. Gelb and Ben M. Enis, "Marketing a City of the Future," in *Marketing Is Everybody's Business* (Santa Monica, Calif.: Goodyear, 1977).
32. See Scott Cutlip and Allen H. Center, *Effective Public Relations,* 3rd ed. (Englewood Cliffs, N.J.: Prentice-Hall, 1964), p. 10.
33. See William D. Perreault, Donna K. Darden, and William R. Darden, "A Psychographic Classification of Vacation Life Styles," *Journal of Leisure Research,* 9, No. 3 (1977), 208–24.
34. Yair Aharoni, "How to Market a Country," *Columbia Journal of World Business,* Spring 1966, pp. 41–49.
35. Terence H. Qualter, *Propaganda and Psychological Warfare* (New York: Random House, 1962), p. 27.
36. Arthur E. Meyerhoff, *The Strategy of Persuasion: The Use of Advertising Skills in Fighting the Cold War* (New York: Berkley Publishing Corp., 1968), pp. 14–15.
37. See Philip Kotler and Gerald Zaltman, "Social Marketing: An Approach to Planned Social Change," *Journal of Marketing,* July 1971, pp. 3–12.
38. G. D. Wiebe, "Merchandising Commodities and Citizenship on Television," *Public Opinion Quarterly,* Winter 1951–52, pp. 679–91.
39. See Eduardo Roberto, *Strategic Decision-Making in a Social Program: The Case of Family-Planning Diffusion* (Lexington, Mass.: Lexington Books, 1975).
40. See Karl E. Henion II, *Ecological Marketing* (Columbus, Ohio: Grid, 1976).

MARKETING AND SOCIETY

Giant Foods Inc. is a leading supermarket chain in the Washington, D.C., area. In 1970 the company adopted, as a response to the growing consumer movement, a new concept of its business. The typical food chain is content to carry those food products that manufacturers want to sell and buyers want to buy, without making any judgments or offering consumers any advice. Giant, however, adopted a different view: "We are the customer's channel for food. We should strive to help the customer obtain the best value possible, not only in his pocketbook but also in his/her food intake. Our store should be an instrument to help the customer know how to buy good food value."

This consumer orientation has been implemented through a series of specific measures:

1. *The chain would not carry any "rip-off" foods.*
2. *The chain would try to carry low-, medium-, and high-priced versions of basic food to give the consumer a real choice.*
3. *The chain would occasionally point out that some food item is too expensive and that a substitute item would save the consumer money and give the same benefit.*
4. *The chain would post the prices of each brand clearly and in unit terms (pounds, pints, etc.) so that consumers could make price comparisons.*
5. *The chain would date perishable products so that consumers could gauge their freshness.*
6. *The chain would employ full-time home economists to answer consumer questions in the store about food values, recipes, and other problems.*
7. *The chain would provide easy means for consumers to register complaints.*
8. *The chain would appoint a well-known consumer advocate to its board of directors so that management would always be aware of the consumer's point of view.*

Through these measures, Giant moved from being a distributor acting in the sellers' interests to being an agent acting in the customer's interests. Did the consumer orientation pay? According to a spokesman for the company, "these actions have improved Giant's goodwill immeasurably and have earned the admiration of leaders of the consumer movement."

□Giant Foods is a company that is taking a responsible and creative approach to marketing. Responsible marketers seek to interpret buyer wants and creatively respond with appropriate products, priced to yield good value to the buyers and profit to the producer. The *marketing concept* is a philosophy of service and mutual gain. Its practice leads the economy by an invisible hand to satisfy the diverse and changing needs of millions of consumers.

Not all marketing conforms to this theory. Some individuals and companies engage in questionable marketing practices. In addition, certain private marketing transactions, seemingly innocent in themselves, have profound implications for the larger society. Consider the sale of cigarettes. Ordinarily, companies should be free to sell cigarettes, and smokers should be free to buy them. However, this transaction is tinged with public interest. First, the smoker may be shortening his or her own life. Second, this places a burden on the smoker's family, and on society-at-large. Third, other people in the presence of the smoker may have to inhale the smoke and may experience discomfort and harm. This is not to say that cigarettes should be banned. Rather, it shows that private transactions may involve profound questions of public policy.

The businessperson can easily brush aside public policy questions by pointing to the great wealth created in America by its mass-production and mass-consumption philosophy. Surely a few excesses, abuses, and wastes are a small price to pay for the cornucopia of material goods enjoyed in this country.

But this attitude is dangerous. If the public *feels* there are things wrong with marketing, it is folly to ignore these feelings. For reasons both of self-interest and of conscience, marketers should critically examine their role in society.

This chapter will consider the macroconsequences of micromarketing behavior. It will address the following questions: (1) What are the most frequent social criticisms leveled against private marketing activity? (2) What steps have private citizens taken to try to curb or correct alleged marketing ills? (3) What steps have legislators and government agencies taken to try to curb or correct alleged marketing ills? (4) What steps have enlightened companies taken to carry out socially responsible marketing? and (5) What principles might guide future public policy toward marketing?

social criticisms of marketing

The various social criticisms of marketing can be classified into those alleged to hurt individual consumers, society as a whole, and other business firms. We will examine the major criticisms in the following paragraphs.

Marketing's Impact on Individual Consumer Welfare

Critics have accused the American marketing system of harming consumers through (1) high prices, (2) deceptive practices, (3) high-pressure selling, (4) shoddy or unsafe products, (5) planned obsolescence, and (6) poor service to disadvantaged consumers.

High prices. Many critics charge that the American marketing system causes prices to be higher than they would be under more "sensible" arrangements. They point to three different factors.

HIGH COSTS OF DISTRIBUTION

A longstanding charge is that prices are inflated by greedy middlemen who mark up the price of products substantially beyond the value of their services. This criticism is an ancient one. Plato held that shopkeepers practiced the acquisitive rather than the productive arts and brought nothing new into existence. Aristotle condemned shopkeepers as making their profit at the expense of the buyer. These views persisted into the Middle Ages, with the Church placing various restrictions on middlemen freedom.

One of the most thorough contemporary studies of distribution costs appeared in 1939 in the book *Does Distribution Cost Too Much*?[1] It was undertaken after observing that selling and distribution costs rose from 19.8 percent of product costs in 1850 to 50.4 percent of product costs in 1920. The authors concluded that distribution did cost too much and pointed their finger at ". . . duplication of sales efforts, multiplicity of sales outlets, excessive services, multitudes of brands, and unnecessary advertising . . . misinformed buying on the part of consumers . . . and, among distributors themselves, lack of a proper knowledge of costs, too" great zeal for volume, poor management and planning, and unwise price policies.[2]

How do retailers answer these charges? They argue as follows: First, middlemen perform a lot of work that would otherwise have to be performed by the manufacturers or the consumers. Second, the rising markup covers the provision of improved services that consumers want: more convenience, larger stores and assortment, longer store hours, return privileges, and so on. Third, the costs of operating stores, such as personnel and utilities, keep rising and forcing retailers to raise their prices. And fourth, competition in much of retailing is so intense that margins are actually quite low. For example, supermarket chains are barely left with one percent profit on their sales after taxes.

HIGH ADVERTISING AND PROMOTION COSTS

Modern marketing is also accused of pushing up prices because of the heavy use of advertising and sales promotion. First, there are "commodity" products—gasoline, aspirin, coffee, sugar, flour, cigarettes—that are branded and heavily promoted by manufacturers to create psychological differentiation. For example, a dozen tablets of a well-known brand of aspirin sell for the same price as one hundred tablets of lesser-known brands. Critics feel that if "commodity" products were sold in bulk, their prices would be considerably lower. Second, there are slightly differentiated products—cosmetics, detergents, toiletries—where the costs of packaging and promotion can amount to 40 percent or more of the manufacturer's price to the retailer. Much of the packaging and promotion adds psychological rather than functional value to the product. Besides the manufacturer's promotion costs, many retailers undertake their own promotional efforts—advertising, trading stamps, games of chance, and so on—thereby adding several more cents to retail prices.

Businesspeople answer these charges of heavy promotion with the following observations: First, consumers are not interested only in the functional aspects of products. They buy concepts, such as products that make them feel affluent, beautiful, or special. The manufacturer's task is to develop concepts for the market that consumers are willing to pay for. Consumers usually have the option of buying pure functional versions of the product at a lower price. Second, branding exists to give confidence to buyers. A brand name signifies a certain quality, and consumers are willing to pay for well-known brands even if they cost a little more. Third, heavy advertising is necessary simply to inform the many potential buyers of the existence and merits of a brand. If consumers want to know what is available on the market, they must expect manufacturers to spend large sums of money on advertising. Fourth, heavy advertising and promotion is necessary for the individual enterprise because competitors are doing it. The individual enterprise would risk its survival if it did not match competitive expenditures at some level to gain and hold "share of mind." At the same time, companies are very cost conscious about promotion and try to spend their money wisely. And fifth, heavy sales promotion is necessary from time to time because goods are produced ahead of demand in a mass-production economy. Special incentives have to be offered to buyers to clear excess inventories.

EXCESSIVE MARKUPS

Critics charge that certain business sectors are particularly guilty of marking up goods excessively. They point to the drug industry where a pill costing five cents to manufacture may cost the consumer forty cents; they point to the pricing tactics of funeral homes who prey on the emotions of bereaved relatives;[3] they point to the high charges of television and auto repair people. The alleged exploitation is dramatized from time to time in books with such provocative titles as *The Poor Pay More, The Hucksters, The Permissible Lie, The Innocent Consumer vs. the Exploiters, The Thumb on the Scale or the Supermarket Shell Game,* and *100,000,000 Guinea Pigs.*

Businesspeople respond to these criticisms with the following observations: First, there are, unfortunately, some unscrupulous business owners who take advantage of consumers. They should be reported to better business bureaus and other agencies set up to protect consumers. Second, most business owners, on the other hand, deal fairly with consumers because they want their repeat business. And third, consumers often overlook the justification for high prices. For example, pharmaceutical markups cover not only the cost of purchasing, promotion, and distributing existing medicines but also the huge research and development costs spent in the search for new and improved medicines.

Deceptive practices. Businesspeople are often accused of engaging in deceptive practices—practices that mislead consumers into believing they will get more value than they actually do. Certain industries account for a disproportionate share of these complaints. Among the worst offenders are certain insurance companies (alleging that policies are "guaranteed renewable" or underwritten by the government), publishing companies (approaching subscribers under false pretenses), mail-order land-sales organizations (misrepresenting land tracts or improvement costs), home improvement contractors (using bait-and-switch tactics), automotive repair shops (advertising ultra-low repair prices and then "discovering" a necessary major repair), home freezer plans (falsely representing the savings), correspondence schools (overstating employment opportunities after course completion), vending machine companies (falsely guaranteeing top locations), studios offering dance instruction (signing up elderly people for lessons beyond their life expectancy), and companies selling medical devices (exaggerating therapeutic claims).

Three types of deceptive practices can be distinguished. *Deceptive pricing* includes such practices as advertising "factory" or "wholesale" prices falsely or advertising a large price reduction from list where the list was artificially high. *Deceptive promotion* includes such practices as overstating the product's attributes, misrepresenting the guarantees, falsely photographing the product's accomplishments, luring the customer to the store for a bargain that is out of stock or downgraded by the salesperson, and running rigged contests. *Deceptive packaging* includes such practices as exaggerating the apparent contents of a package through a subtle design, not filling the package to the top, advertising cents-off on the package when it is the normal price, and describing the size in misleading terms.

Deceptive practices in pricing, promotion, and packaging have given rise to legislative and administrative remedies. In 1938 the Wheeler-Lea Act gave the FTC clear power to regulate "unfair or deceptive acts or practices." Since that time the FTC has published several guidelines specifying those practices that will be considered deceptive. The toughest problem remains in the area of trying to distinguish between *puffery* and *deception* in advertising. As a case in point, Shell Oil advertised that Super Shell with platformate consistently gave more mileage than the same gasoline without platformate. Now this happened to be true, but what Shell did not say is that almost all gasoline sold for automobile use includes platformate. Its defense was that it had never claimed that platformate was an exclusive Shell feature. The FTC, on the other and, felt that the intent of the ad was to deceive, although the message was literally honest.

Defenders of advertising freedom offer three arguments: First, most businesspeople avoid deceptive practices because such practices would harm their businesses in the long run. Consumers would fail to get what they were promised and would patronize the more reliable entrepreneurs. Second, most consumers recognize advertising exaggeration and exercise a healthy skepticism when they buy. And third, advertising puffery is intrinsic to communicating a product concept, is practiced by all institutions in society, and actually makes life more interesting. According to Theodore Levitt:

- There is hardly a company that would not go down in ruin if it refused to provide fluff, because nobody will buy pure functionality. . . . Worse, it denies . . . man's honest needs and values. If religion must be architectured, packaged, lyricized, and musicized to attract and hold its audience, and if sex must be perfumed, powdered, sprayed, and shaped in order to command attention, it is ridiculous to deny the legitimacy of more modest, and similar, embellishments to the world of commerce. . . . Many of the so-called distortions of advertising, product design, and packaging may be viewed as a paradigm of the many responses that man makes to the conditions of survival in the environment. Without distortion, embellishment, and elaboration, life would be drab, dull, anguished, and at its existential worst. . . . I shall argue that embellishment and distortion are among advertising's legitimate and socially desirable purposes; and that illegitimacy in advertising consists only of falsification with larcenous intent.[4]

High-pressure selling. Another criticism is that salespeople in certain industries apply high-pressure selling techniques (hard sell) that are effective in inducing people to buy goods they had no thought of buying. It is often said that such goods as encyclopedias, insurance, real estate, and jewelry are sold, not bought. The salespeople in these industries are trained in delivering smooth canned talks to entice purchase. They work hard at selling because of sales contests promising big prizes to those who turn in the best performance. The following pep talk was given by a sales manager to his salespeople at a sales meeting:

> ▪ One thought this morning—high pressure . . . Everybody's afraid of the word! Been so easy selling last couple of years everybody's squeamish about doing any work. . . . Order takers, that's what we've become. . . . What's the answer? Pressure, brother, high pressure and lemme tell you the guys that don't wise up are going to get left behind, but fast.[5]

Businesspeople recognize that buyers can often be talked into buying things they did not start out wanting or needing. This is the reason for recent legislation requiring door-to-door salespeople to announce their purpose at the door—to sell the product. Buyers are also allowed a "three-day cooling-off period" in which they can cancel their contract after rethinking it. In addition, consumers can take their complaints to better business bureaus when they feel that undue selling pressure was applied.

Shoddy or unsafe products. Another criticism is that products often lack the quality they should have. One type of complaint is that products are not made well, or used to be made better. "If (the consumer) somehow escapes rattles, pings, loose buttons or missing knobs, there probably will be dents, mismatched sizes, static, fluttering, leaking or creaking."[6] Automobiles receive a disproportionate number of complaints. Consumers Union, an independent testing agency that publishes *Consumer Reports,* tested thirty-two cars and found something wrong with all of them. "Cars were delivered with rain leaks, fender dents, nonaligned windows, broken distributor caps, ignition locks that wouldn't lock."[7] Other products that are singled out include color television sets, various appliances, and clothing. While it cannot be proved that quality has deteriorated over the years—maybe instead consumers have become more sophisticated or choosier—many persons think that many products fall short on quality.

A second type of complaint concerns whether certain products deliver any benefit. Consumers got a shock on hearing that dry breakfast cereal may have little nutritional value. Robert B. Choate, a Washington nutritional specialist, told a Senate subcommittee: "In short, (the cereals) fatten but do little to prevent malnutrition. . . . The average cereal . . . fails as a complete meal even with milk added. . . . It is apparent . . . that we humans are viewed not as beings to be nourished, but as suckers to be sold . . . these comments gain importance when one understands the extent to which children demand foods huckstered to them on television."[8] Choate added that consumers could often get more nutrition by eating the cereal package than the contents.

A third type of complaint has to do with products' safety characteristics. For years Consumers Union has been reporting various hazards found in tested products—electrical dangers in appliances, carbon monoxide poisoning from room heaters, finger risks in lawn mowers, and faulty steering in automobiles.

Altogether, product quality has been a problem in certain industries for a number of reasons, including occasional manufacturer indifference, increased product complexity, poorly trained labor, and insufficient quality control.

EXHIBIT 21-1

A CONTRAST IN COMPANY RESPONSE TO UNSAFE PRODUCTS

This is the story of two companies, one that moved too slowly after its tire failures allegedly killed twenty-nine people and injured fifty, and another that moved swiftly when its toy killed two children.

Concern over the performance of the Firestone 500 radial tire was first indicated in 1976 when a Ralph Nader group started receiving consumer complaints. The National Highway Traffic Safety Administration (NHTSA) started its investigation after more than five hundred complaints had been received. Over fourteen thousand consumer complaints were compiled. Then Firestone sought an injunction against release of the NHTSA report. The Firestone Company waited until it was forced by the government to recall 13 million Firestone 500 radial tires.

Parker Brothers Toy Company, a subsidiary of General Mills, voluntarily recalled a spectacularly successful toy called Riviton, a kit consisting of plastic parts, rubber rivets, and a riveting tool. When Parker Brothers heard of the first death, it was assumed to be a freak accident never to be repeated. When the second death was caused by the same part of the toy, "the decision was very simple. Were we supposed to sit back and wait for death No. 3?" said Randolph Barton, president of Parker Brothers. In support of the swift responsible behavior exhibited by Parker Brothers, Susan King, chairman of the Consumer Product Safety Commission, stated that the company was "a model of social responsibility."

Sources: James Meteja, "Firestone Radials: A Punctured Image," *Chicago Tribune,* August 13, 1978, p. 1; and Charles W. Stevens, "One Producer Finds Recall Is Best Policy for Hazardous Toy," *Wall Street Journal,* March 2, 1979, p. 1.

On the other hand, several forces also lead manufacturers to have an interest in producing good quality: First, large manufacturers, as they add more products to their line, become increasingly concerned with their reputations. A customer who has had a bad or disappointing experience with one of their products may avoid buying any of their other products in the future. The concern with customer satisfaction is reinforced by the increased intensity and sophistication of competitors and the spread of the marketing concept. Second, large retailers are increasingly trying to develop their own name for quality, and they express this both in the national brands they select to sell and in their own private-label brands. And third, consumer groups are standing in the wings to point out poor-quality products and to penalize companies for unsafe products. No company wants bad publicity. For example, Ralph Nader's *Unsafe at Any Speed* exposed safety defects in General Motors' Corvair that led to the demise of this popular car. In addition to consumer groups, various laws and government agencies are mandated to protect the consumers against poor or unsafe products.

Planned obsolescence. Critics have charged that producers in certain industries cause their products to become obsolete before they actually need replacement. Three types of obsolescence can be distinguished.

Planned style obsolescence means a deliberate policy by manufacturers to change users' concepts of acceptable appearance to make them dissatisfied with their present goods. At different times, manufacturers of women's apparel, men's apparel, automobiles, furniture, and even homes have been accused of this. The annual style change of Detroit automobiles is considered a prime offender.

Planned functional obsolescence means a deliberate policy by manufacturers to "withhold fully developed attractive features whose present absence and subsequent introduction may be used to encourage an eariler replacement of the product. . . ."[9] Suppose the manufacturers of automobiles had a whole set of improvements—with respect to safety, pollution reduction, gasoline economy, handling—that they could introduce today but that they deliberately withheld.

Planned material obsolescence means that manufacturers deliberately choose materials and components that are subject to higher breakage, wear, rot, or corrosion. For example, many drapery manufacturers have switched to using a higher percentage of rayon in their drapes. They argue that rayon reduces the price of the drapes and has a better holding power. Critics suggest that substituting rayon will cause the drapes to fall apart after two cleanings instead of four.

Businesspeople answer these charges as follows: First, consumers like style changes. They get tired of their old goods. Women want a new look in fashion; men want a new-styled automobile. No one has to buy the new look. Obviously if enough people did not like it, it would not take over. Second, companies withhold new functional features when they are not adequately tested, when they add more cost to the product than consumers are willing to pay, and for other good reasons. They do this at the risk of having a competitor introduce the new feature and steal the market. Third, companies often substitute new materials in the effort to lower their own costs and consumer prices. They do not deliberately design their products to break down earlier because this would risk losing their customers to other brands. And fourth, much of so-called planned obsolescence is really the working out of dynamic competitive and technological forces in a free society, leading to ever-improving goods and services.

Poor service to the disadvantaged consumer. The American marketing system has been accused of poorly serving the interests of disadvantaged consumers. According to David Caplovitz in his *The Poor Pay More,* the urban poor often have to shop in smaller stores carrying inferior goods and charging higher prices.[10] In 1968 the chairman of the FTC, Paul Rand Dixon, reported a Washington, D.C., study confirming that

- the poor pay more—nearly twice as much—for appliances and furniture sold in Washington's low-income area stores. . . . On the average, goods purchased for $100 at wholesale sold for $255 in the low-income stores compared with $159 in the general market stores. . . . As might have been anticipated, installment credit is a major marketing factor in selling to the poor . . . some low-income market retailers imposed effective annual finance charges as high as 33 percent. . . .[11]

Ironically, the profits of the merchants were not unusually high:

- The findings of the economic study suggest that the marketing system for distribution of durable goods to low-income consumers is costly. Low income market retailers have markedly higher costs, partly because of high bad debt expenses, but to a greater extent because of higher selling, wage, and commission costs. These

> expenses reflect in part greater use of home demonstration selling, and expenses associated with the collection and processing of installment contracts. Thus, although their markups are often two or three times higher than general market retailers, on the average low-income market retailers do not make particularly high profits.[12]

Clearly, better marketing systems must be built in low-income areas, and low-income people must be protected against abuses. The FTC has increased its enforcement procedures against merchants who take advantage of the poor by advertising false values, selling old merchandise as new, or charging too much for credit. An effort is under way to make it harder for merchants to win court judgments and garnishments against low-income people who were wheedled into making their purchases. A more promising and powerful remedy may come in the form of incentives and possible subsidies to mass retailers to open up outlets in low-income areas.[13]

Marketing's Impact on Society-as-a-Whole

The American marketing system has also been accused of contributing to some social "bads" in American society—specifically, excessive materialism, false wants, insufficient social goods, cultural pollution, and excessive political power.

Excessive materialism. The American business system has been accused of creating a lopsided interest in material possessions. People tend to judge others by what they own rather than by what they are. People are not considered successful unless they own a suburban home, two cars, and the latest clothes and appliances.

Most people enter the materialistic race with great vigor. Only a few, however, win the big prizes. Many others drop out along the way. Some vigorously repudiate the system. The emphasis on material accumulation leaves many people unhappy or frustrated. According to the New Left: "We oppose the depersonalization that reduces human beings to the status of things. . . . Loneliness, estrangement, isolation describe the vast distance between man and man today. These dominant tendencies cannot be overcome by better personnel management, nor by improved gadgets, but only when a love of man overcomes the idolatrous worship of things by man."[14]

Some of this may be changing. Dominant value systems tend to breed countercultural groups and values. An increasing number of Americans are losing their drive for possessions, particularly (and ironically) among the more affluent. They are relaxing more, playing more, and learning to get along with less. "Small is beautiful" and "less is more" describe the developing ideology. More emphasis is being placed on cultivating close relationships and simple pleasures than on being "hooked on things."

False wants. This dominant cultural interest in things is not seen as a natural state of mind but rather as a state of mind created by Madison Avenue. Business hires Madison Avenue to stimulate people's desires for goods. Madison Avenue uses the mass media to create materialistic models of the good life. Conspicuous consumption on the part of some then proceeds to create invidious desires by others. People work harder to earn the necessary money. Their purchases increase the output and productive capacity of the Industrial State. In turn, the Industrial State makes greater use of Madison Avenue to stimulate desire for the industrial output. Thus people are seen as a manipulated link in the cycle between production and consumption. Wants come to depend on output. This is what Galbraith calls the "dependence effect." According to Galbraith:

- The control or management of demand is, in fact, a vast and rapidly growing industry in itself. It embraces a huge network of communications, a great array of merchandising and selling organizations, nearly the entire advertising industry, numerous ancillary research, training and other related services and much more. In everyday parlance this great machine, and the demanding and varied talents that it employs, are said to be engaged in selling goods. In less ambiguous language it means that it is engaged in the management of those who buy goods.[15]

And Marcuse:

- "False" (needs) are those which are superimposed upon the individual by particular social interests. Most of the prevailing needs to relax, to have fun, to behave and consume in accordance with the advertisements, to love and hate what others love and hate, belong to this category of false needs.[16]

These quotations probably exaggerate the power of business to synthesize and stimulate wants. It may be possible to brainwash some people in a prisoner-of-war camp or in a totalitarian society where all the means of persuasion are under state control and no counterpropaganda is permitted. Under normal social conditions, however, the individual is exposed to conflicting life styles and value systems through personal experience and the mass media. Some of the mass advertiser's intended effect is diminished by gatekeepers who screen out or change the messages before they reach large sections of society. In addition, persons have elaborate perceptual defenses against the mass media—selective attention, perception, distortion, and retention. The mass media are most effective when they appeal to existing needs rather than attempt to create new ones—which is hard to call manipulation. Furthermore, people tend to be information seekers with respect to the more consequential purchases, which makes them less reliant on single advocate sources. Even inconsequential purchases, which may be triggered off by advertising messages, lead to repeat purchase only if the product performance meets the expectations. Finally, the high failure rate of new products removes credence from the claim that companies, even the biggest and most sophisticated ones, are able to manage demand.

On a deeper level, our wants and values are influenced not only by marketers but also by family, peer groups, religion, ethnic background, and education. If Americans are highly materialistic, this value system arose out of basic socialization processes that go much deeper than the influence of business and mass media could alone produce.

Insufficient social goods. Business has been accused of overstimulating demand for private goods at the expense of public goods. In fact, as private goods increase, they require a proportionate complement of public services that is usually not forthcoming:

- An increase in the consumption of automobiles requires a facilitating supply of streets, highways, traffic control, and parking space. The protective services of the police and the highway patrols must also be available, as must those of the hospitals. Although the need for balance here is extraordinarily clear, our use of privately produced vehicles has, on occasion, got far out of line with the supply of the related public services. The result has been hideous road congestion, an annual massacre of impressive proportions, and chronic colitis in the cities.[17]

Thus private consumption leads to a "social imbalance" and "social costs" that neither the producers nor the consumers appear willing to pay for. Some way must be found to restore a social balance between private goods and public goods. Manufacturing firms could be required to bear the full social costs of their operations. In this way, they would build these costs into the price. Where buyers did not find the private goods worth the price, those firms would go out of existence and the resources would move to other uses that could support the sum of the private and social costs.

Cultural pollution. Critics charge the marketing system with creating *cultural pollution.* People's senses are constantly being assaulted by advertising noise. Serious programs are interrupted by commercials; serious printed matter is lost between pages of ads; magnificent landscapes are marred by billboards. These interruptions intrude sex, power, or status continuously into people's consciousness.

Yet it appears that the flood of advertising strikes people in different ways. In a study of consumer attitudes toward advertising, Bauer and Greyser found that advertising was a low-salience topic, something like the daily weather.[18] Although people occasionally complain about it, they are not too serious in their complaints. Only 15 percent of the 1,856 persons interviewed thought advertising needed change, and these tended to be the people who see a need for change in many institutions. The average respondent tended to "pay some attention" to about seventy-six ads in an average day and did not find more than 16 percent of them annoying or offensive. Some people thought that the best part of television programming was the ads!

Businesspeople usually answer the charges of commercial noise with these arguments: First, they hope that their ads largely reach only the target audience. But because of mass-communication channels, some ads are bound to reach people who have no interest in the product and are therefore left bored or irritated. People who buy magazines addressed to their own interests—such as *Vogue* or *Fortune*—rarely complain about the ads because they advertise products of interest. And second, the ads are responsible for making radio as well as television a free medium and for keeping down the costs of magazines and newspapers. Most people are happy to accept the commercials as a small price to pay.

Excessive political power. Another criticism against business is that it wields too much political power. There are "oil," "cigarette," and "auto" senators who stand ready and able to protect particular industries' interests against the public interest. Business is also accused of holding too much power over the mass media, neutralizing its freedom to report independently and objectively. As stated some years ago by one critic: "How can *Life, Post,* and *Reader's Digest* afford to tell the truth about the scandalously low nutritional value of most packaged foods . . . when these magazines are being subsidized by such advertisers as General Foods, Kellogg's, Nabisco, and General Mills? . . . The answer is *they cannot and do not.*"[19]

The various industries in America do attempt to promote and protect their interests. They have a right to representation in Congress and the mass media, although it is possible for their influence to become too extensive and controlling. Fortunately, many powerful business interests thought to be untouchable have been tamed in the public interest. Standard Oil was dismantled in 1911, and the meat-packing industry took a trouncing after the exposures of Upton Sinclair. Ralph Nader inspired legislation requiring the automobile industry to build more safety into its vehicles, and the Surgeon General's Report required cigarette companies to include a health warning on their packages. Business's control over the media is also changing as more sponsors share the tabs for major network shows and as the media themselves become more courageous in featuring editorial material designed to interest different segments of the market. This does not mean that the charge of excessive power in the hands of business is invalid, but that countervailing forces operate to check and offset these powerful interests.

Marketing's Impact on Other Businesses

Critics have also charged that many companies, in their zeal for profits, ride roughshod over other companies. Large firms are accused of taking over or ruining small firms, thus leading to less competition. Three types of problems are identified: anticompetitive mergers, artificial barriers to entry, and predatory competition.

Anticompetitive acquisition. A recurrent accusation against the business system is that many firms expand by acquiring other firms rather than by internally developing new and needed products. Within a certain time period, the nine leading ethical drug companies developed eight new businesses internally and acquired sixteen other businesses.[20] As another example, P&G acquired Clorox, the major producer of household liquid bleach.[21] But the Supreme Court ruled that P&G's acquisition would deprive the industry of potential competition not only from P&G, had it entered the market on its own, but also from smaller firms that might be discouraged from entering this market.

Acquisition is a complicated subject. Acquisitions can be beneficial to the society under the following circumstances: (1) when the acquiring company gains economies of scale leading to lower costs and lower prices; (2) when a well-managed company takes over a poorly managed company and improves its efficiency; and (3) when an industry that was fairly noncompetitive becomes competitive after this action takes place. And other acquisitions could be harmful, particularly when a vigorous young competitor is absorbed and fewer firms come to dominate the major share of the business.

Barriers to entry. Critics have charged that modern marketing practices often create substantial barriers to entry in certain industries. These barriers may be in the form of patents, substantial promotion requirements, tie-ups of suppliers or dealers, and so on.

The antitrust people recognize that some barriers to entry are associated with real economies of large-scale enterprise. Other barriers could be challenged both by existing law and by new legislation. For example, some critics have suggested putting a progressive tax on advertising expenditures to reduce the impact of selling costs as a particularly prevalent barrier to entry.

Predatory competition. In certain instances firms go after other firms with the intention of hurting or destroying them. Their attack may involve setting their prices below costs, threatening to cut off business with suppliers, or disparaging the competitor's products.

There are various laws to prevent predatory competition. The difficulty at times is to establish that the intent or action was really predatory. In the classic A&P case where this large retailer, enjoying various economies and volume discounts, was able to charge lower prices than smaller "mom and pop" grocery stores, there is a serious question whether this was predatory competition or the healthy competition of a more efficient retailing institution against the less efficient.[22]

citizen actions to regulate marketing

Since business has historically been seen as the real or alleged cause of many economic and social ills, it is not surprising that grass-roots movements have arisen from time to time to discipline business and call for legislative remedy. The two major antibusiness movements have been *consumerism* and *environmentalism.*

Consumerism

During this century American business firms have been the target of an organized consumer movement on three different occasions. The first consumer movement took place in the early 1900s and was fueled by such factors as rising prices, Upton Sinclair's exposés of conditions in the meat industry, and ethical drug scandals. The second consumer movement took place in the mid-1930s and was fueled by an upturn in consumer prices in the midst of the Depression and another drug scandal. The third movement began in the 1960s as a result of a complex set of developments. Consumers had become better educated; products had become increasingly complex and hazardous; discontent with American institutions was widespread; influential writings by John Kenneth Galbraith, Vance Packard, and Rachel Carson accused big business of wasteful and manipulative practices; in 1962 the presidential message of John F. Kennedy declared that consumers have the right to safety, to be informed, to choose, and to be heard. Congressional investigations of certain industries proved embarrassing; and finally Ralph Nader appeared on the scene to crystallize many of the issues.[23]

Since the early 1960s many private consumer organizations have emerged; several pieces of consumer legislation have been passed; and several state and local offices of consumer affairs have been created. Furthermore, the consumer movement has taken on an international character and has become very strong in Scandinavia and the Low Countries and is becoming increasingly popular in France, Germany, and Japan.

But what is this movement? Put simply, *consumerism is an organized movement of concerned citizens and government to enhance the rights and power of buyers in relation to sellers.* The traditional sellers' rights include

1. The right to introduce any product in any size and style, provided it is not hazardous to personal health or safety; or, if it is, to introduce it with the proper warnings and controls
2. The right to price the product at any level, provided there is no discrimination among similar classes of buyers
3. The right to spend any amount of money to promote the product, provided it is not defined as unfair competition
4. The right to formulate any product message, provided it is not misleading or dishonest in content or execution
5. The right to introduce any buying incentive schemes they wish

The traditional buyers' rights include

1. The right not to buy a product that is offered for sale
2. The right to expect the product to be safe
3. The right to expect the product to be what is claimed

Comparing these rights, many believe that the balance of power lies on the sellers' side. It is true that the buyer can refuse to buy any product. But it is generally felt that the buyer is really without sufficient information, education, and protection to make wise decisions in the face of highly sophisticated sellers. Consumer advocates therefore call for the following additional consumer rights:

4. The right to be adequately informed about the more important aspects of the product
5. The right to be protected against questionable products and marketing practices
6. The right to influence products and marketing practices in directions that will enhance the "quality of life"

Each of these proposed rights leads to a whole series of specific proposals by consumerists. The right to be informed includes such things as the right to know the true interest cost of a loan (*truth-in-lending*), the true cost per standard unit of competing brands (*unit pricing*), the basic ingredients in a product (*ingredient labeling*), the nutritional quality of foods (*nutritional labeling*), the freshness of products (*open dating*), and the true benefits of a product (*truth-in-advertising*).

The proposals related to additional *consumer protection* include the strengthening of consumers' position in cases of business fraud, the requiring of more safety to be designed into products, and the issuing of greater powers to existing government agencies.

The proposals relating to *quality-of-life* considerations include regulating the ingredients that go into certain products (detergents, gasoline) and packaging (soft-drink containers), reducing the level of advertising and promotional "noise," and creating consumer representation on company boards to introduce consumer welfare considerations in business decision making.

EXHIBIT 21-2

RALPH NADER—AMERICAN HERO?

Ralph Nader was a young lawyer when his sensational book, *Unsafe at Any Speed,* was published in 1965. This book meticulously documented that many auto deaths were due to faulty car design rather than faulty driving. General Motors tried to investigate Nader's private life, and when its sleuthing was exposed, he became an overnight hero of the consumerists and the American public. His articulateness and forcefulness led to the passage of the Auto Safety bill, which requires manufacturers to build more safety features into their cars. Since then, Nader and his raiders have researched and exposed unsafe conditions in the meat-packing industry, fishing industry, drug industry, and toy industry; in railroads and buses; and in routine dental X-rays—often resulting in new legislation.

Is Ralph Nader antibusiness? Not according to Ralph Nader. He sees his role as quite the opposite: "It's a disservice to view this as a threat to the private-enterprise economy or to big business. It's just the opposite. It is an attempt to preserve the free-enterprise economy by making the market work better; an attempt to preserve the democratic control of technology by giving government a role in the decision-making process as to how much or how little "safety" products must contain."

Environmentalism

Whereas consumerists focus on whether the marketing system is efficiently serving consumer needs and wants, environmentalists focus on the impact of modern marketing on the environment and the costs that are borne in serving these consumer needs and wants. In 1962 Rachel Carson's *Silent Spring* presented a documented criticism of pesticidal pollution of the environment.[24] It was no longer a matter of wasted resources but a matter of human survival. In 1970 the Ehrlichs coined the term "eco-catastrophe" to symbolize the harmful impact of certain American business practices on the environment.[25] And in 1972 the Meadowses and others published *The Limits to Growth,* which warned people, through the evidence of systems simulation, that the quality of life would eventually decline in the face of unchecked population growth, spreading pollution, and continued exploitation of natural resources.[26]

These concerns underpin the movement known as environmentalism. *Environmentalism is an organized movement of concerned citizens and government to protect and enhance people's living environment.* Environmentalists are concerned with strip mining, forest depletion, factory smoke, billboards, and litter; with the loss of recreational opportunity; and with the increase in health problems due to bad air, water, and chemically sprayed food.

Environmentalists are not against marketing and consumption; they simply want them to operate on more ecological principles. They do not think the goal of the marketing system should be the maximization of *consumption* or *consumer choice* or *consumer satisfaction* as such. The goal of the marketing system should be the maximization of *life quality.* And life quality means not only the quantity and quality of consumer goods and services but also the quality of the environment.

Environmentalists want environmental costs formally introduced into the decision making of producers and consumers. They favor the use of tax mechanisms and regulations to impose the true social costs of antienvironmental business and consumption activity. Requiring business to invest in antipollution devices, taxing nonreturnable bottles, banning high-phosphate detergents, and other measures are viewed as necessary to lead businesses and consumers to move in directions that are environmentally sound.

Environmentalists are in many ways more critical of marketing than are consumerists. They complain that there is too much wasteful packaging in the United States, whereas consumerists like the convenience offered by modern packaging. Environmentalists feel that mass advertising leads people to buy more than they need, whereas consumerists worry more about deception in advertising. Environmentalists dislike the proliferation of shopping centers, whereas consumerists welcome new stores and more competition.

Thus environmentalism is a more radical challenge to current marketing philosophy than consumerism. It does not accept the sacredness of consumer sovereignty and satisfaction. It rejects the marketing concept that calls for "finding needs and filling them" because the concept leaves out societal and ecological considerations. Environmentalists are ready to question consumer needs and wants and intervene to prevent environmental abuse. Consumption is not, in their minds, the be-all and end-all of human existence.

Environmentalism has hit certain industries hard. Steel companies and public utilities have been forced to invest billions of dollars in pollution-control equipment and costlier fuels. The auto industry has had to introduce expensive emission-control devices in cars. The soap industry has had to research and develop low-phosphate detergents. The packaging industry has been required to develop ways to reduce litter and increase biodegradability in its products. The gasoline industry has had to formulate new low-lead and no-lead gasolines. Naturally, these industries are inclined to resent environmental regulations, especially when formulated and imposed too rapidly to allow the companies to make the proper adjustments. These companies have had to absorb large costs and pass them on to buyers.

As for marketers, their life has become more complicated. They have to check more carefully into the ecological properties of the product and its packaging. They have to raise prices to cover environmental costs, knowing this will make the product harder to sell. Yet there is no turning back to the "cowboy" economy of the 1950s and 1960s when few managers worried about the effect of product and marketing decisions on the quality of the environment. It was partly that indifference that led to the growth of environmentalism in the first place.[27]

public actions to regulate marketing

Usually private citizen agitation against specific marketing practices will stimulate public policy debate and lead to legislative and judicial proposals. Some legislators will see these issues as important and will draft bills. The bills will be subjected to prolonged debate, many will be defeated in the process, others will be substantially modified and sometimes made "toothless," and a few will emerge in really workable form.

Figure 21-1
Major Marketing Decision Areas That May Be Called into Question under the Law

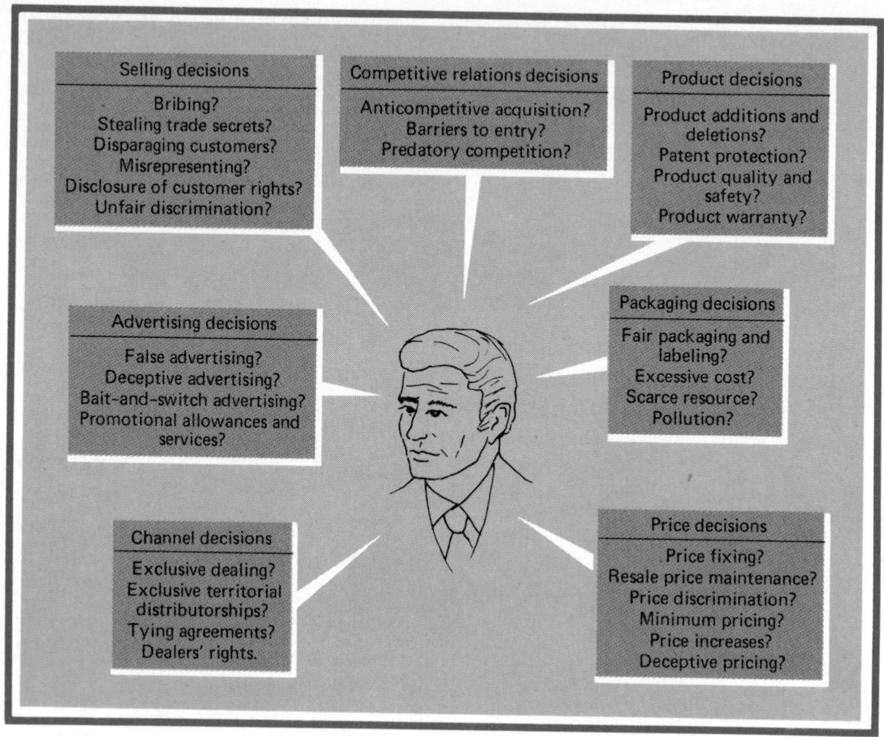

We listed many of the laws bearing on marketing in Chapter 7, pps. 219–20. The task is to translate these and other laws into understandings that marketing executives have as they make decisions in the areas of competitive relations, products, price, promotion, and channels of distribution. Figure 21-1 summarizes the major issues in each area facing members of management as they do their marketing planning. The specific dos and don'ts have already been reviewed in each of the appropriate chapters.

business actions toward socially responsible marketing

Initially, many companies actively opposed consumerism and environmentalism. They thought that many of the criticisms of the marketing system were either unjustified or unimportant. They resented the power of strong consumer leaders to point an accusing finger at their products and cause their sales to plummet. This happened when Ralph Nader called the Corvair automobile unsafe, when Robert Choate accused breakfast cereals of "empty calories," and when Herbert S. Denenberg published a list showing the wide variation in premiums different insurance companies were charging for the same protection. Businesses also resented consumer proposals that appeared to increase business costs more than helping the consumer. They felt that most consumers would not pay attention to unit pricing or ingredient labeling and that the doctrines of advertising substantiation, corrective advertising, and counteradvertising would stifle advertising creativity. They felt that the consumer was better off than ever, that large companies were very careful in developing safe products and promoting them

EXHIBIT 21-3

FUTURE GOVERNMENT REGULATORS MAY PUT HARDER QUESTIONS TO MARKETERS

The trend toward increased regulation of company marketing activity may lead to the specter of new government commissions being formed. Here is a scenario of the critical questions that new government commissions might put to businesspeople in the future.

A company developing a new product may have to get the approval of a *Federal Products Commission.* Commission members are likely to put the following questions to the company: (1) Is the new product sufficiently different from existing products? (2) Are the product differences, if any, of sufficient benefit to the buyers and society? (3) Is the product relatively safe and healthful for the user? (4) Is the new product designed for minimum ecological harm? (5) Is the production process minimally polluting?

A *Federal Advertising Commission* will want to approve all major ads. Commission members will raise the following questions: (1) Does the ad tell the truth about the product? (2) Does the ad use humanistic or base appeals? (3) Is the level of company or industry advertising expenditures excessive from a social point of view?

A *Federal Distribution Commission* would have the responsibility for protecting the retail environment in which products and services are sold. Commission members are likely to ask the following questions: (1) Is the new outlet necessary? (2) Is the outlet's location and design suitable? (3) Are the outlet's merchandising policies in the best interest of the consumers?

A *Federal Fair Price Commission* will try to make sure that the prices charged for goods and services are "fair" to the buyer. Commission members will ask the following questions: (1) Is the price clearly stated in a standard unit before the purchase is made? (2) Does the price yield an undue profit to the seller over a long period? (3) Does the price reflect all the social costs created by the product?

No one really wants to see these commissions established because they mean bureaucratic interference with the working of the free market. Yet the irony is that the questions are good ones that should properly be put to marketers, preferably by themselves. Indeed, to the extent that marketers manage to produce good products, advertising, and distribution and avoid excessive pricing, there will be less of a basis for a popular movement to create these commissions.

honestly, and that new consumer laws would only lead to new constraints and higher seller costs that would be passed on to the consumer in higher prices. Thus many companies opposed the consumer movement and lobbied vigorously against new legislation.

At the present time most companies have come around to accepting the new consumer rights in principle. They might oppose certain pieces of legislation on the ground that such measures are not the best way to solve a particular consumer problem. But they recognize the consumers' right to information and protection. Here we want to examine responsible and creative business responses to the changing marketing environment and marketing opportunities. We first examine a concept of enlightened marketing and then the issue of marketing ethics.

A Concept of Enlightened Marketing

A concept of enlightened marketing grows out of the concept of enlightened capitalism. Two centuries ago Adam Smith, in his *Wealth of Nations,* attempted to show that freedom of enterprise and private property would result in a dynamic and progressive economy. His basic postulate was that people will naturally pursue their self-interest and, if given the freedom to do this, they and the society will benefit. Through free enterprise, entrepreneurs will put their resources into the areas of highest profit opportunity. Profits are usually high where needs must be met. As resources move in, costs would be brought down through healthy competition. The system would be characterized by efficiency and flexibility. It would be guided by the "invisible hand" of the price system to produce needed goods without resort to government bureaucracy and direction.

This system can of course be abused by companies that do not follow the rules of proper business behavior. Companies that try to destroy competitors, raise barriers to entry, and gain the protection and favors of legislators are not competing fairly. Hence a concept of enlightened capitalism is needed in which businesspeople would recognize that their long-run interests would be best served by self-reliant and honest activity within the rules of the system. Enlightened marketing holds that the company's marketing should support the best long-run performance of the marketing system. Enlightened marketing, as such, embodies five principles.

Consumer-oriented marketing. The company should view and organize its marketing activities from the consumers' point of view. It should strive to effectively and efficiently sense, serve, and satisfy a defined set of needs of a defined group of customers. Consider the following example:

- Barat College, a women's college in Lake Forest, Illinois, recently published a college catalog that spelled out with great candor Barat College's strong and weak points. Among the weak points it shared with applicants were the following: "An exceptionally talented student musician or mathematician . . . might be advised to look further for a college with top faculty and facilities in that field. . . . The full range of advanced specialized courses offered in a university will be absent. . . . The library collection is average for a small college, but low in comparison with other high-quality institutions."

The effect of "telling it like it is" is to build confidence so that applicants will really know what they will find at Barat College, and to emphasize that Barat College will strive to improve its consumer value as rapidly as time and funds permit.

Innovative marketing. The company should continuously search for real product and marketing improvements. The company that overlooks new and better ways to do things will eventually find itself challenged by a company that has found a better way. One of the best examples of an innovative marketer is Procter & Gamble (P&G):

- P&G's approach to markets is to search for benefits that customers might be missing. In the case of Crest toothpaste, P&G spent years seeking a toothpaste that would be effective in reducing tooth decay, since most toothpastes either made no such claim or implied some effectiveness at fighting tooth decay without really being effective. Some time later P&G decided to enter the shampoo market and develop a benefit that many customers wanted but no brand provided, that of dandruff control. After years of research, it launched Head and Shoulders, which became an instant market leader. P&G then looked for a way to enter the paper products business. It noticed a real need on the part of new parents for a "disposable" diaper that would be low enough in price to replace the chores of handling and washing cloth diapers. After years of research, P&G was able to develop a very effective paper diaper at a cost that most families could afford. The product was named Pampers, and it immediately won and maintained market leadership in spite of many efforts to dethrone it.

Value marketing. The company should put most of its resources into value-building marketing investments. A number of things marketers do—one-shot sales promotions, minor packaging changes, advertising puffery—may work in the short run to raise sales but add less value to the consumer than real efforts to improve the product's features, convenience, availability, information, and so on. One of the best examples of a value-oriented marketer is Giant Foods, described at the beginning of this chapter. Also consider the following example:

- Kundenkreditbank is a large and profitable chain of consumer banks in Germany. Its chairman, Stefan Kaminsky, made the decision to target the bank to serve primarily working-class customers. He developed a careful misson statement for the bank. Instead of saying that the bank would engage in loans, deposits, checking, and safekeeping, or that it would meet consumers' financial needs, he adopted a consumer enhancement mission: The bank would help consumers increase their total assets so they could achieve a higher standard of living. This mission meant that Kaminsky's banks had to be ready to offer a high level of customer service and advice. This led to the notion that his own employees should be well trained and should be well acquainted with their customers. They should know their customers as well as lawyers or doctors know their clients or patients. It would not be amiss for a customer to phone the banker at home in the evening because of a pressing problem. Kaminsky decided that his branches should never have more than six employees. If a branch's size grows beyond the service ability of six employees, a new branch is opened nearby. When he hires the branch manager, Kaminsky says: "I want you to understand that you will be in this branch for thirty years. These employees are your family. You will be rewarded for good performance through salary increases and bonus participation in the income earned by your branch. The government shares in the income, the shareholders share in the income, and the employees share in the income. Even the customers will share." So the branch manager does not look forward to being rewarded by moving to headquarters. The result is that the branch manager digs deep roots in the community. The branch bank operates like a club. In one section of the bank is a table with consumer reports and cassettes to help consumers buy goods and brands more carefully. The bank's personnel do everything they can to help the customers increase their assets.

Sense-of-mission marketing. The company should define its mission in broad social terms rather than narrow product terms. When a company defines a social mission, company personnel feel better about the nature and importance of their work and have a clearer sense of direction. Consider the following statement of mission by the International Minerals and Chemical Corporation:

- We're not merely in the business of selling our brand of fertilizer. We have a sense of purpose, a sense of where we are going. The first function of corporate planning is to decide what kind of business the company is in. Our business is *agricultural productivity*. We are interested in anything that affects plant growth, now and in the future.[28]

Societal marketing. An enlightened company will make its marketing decision not only by considering the *consumers' wants* and the *company's requirements* but also by considering the *consumers' long-run interests* and the *society's long-run interests*. The company is aware that neglecting the last two considerations is a disservice to consumers and society.

Alert companies have recognized societal problems as the basis for opportunities. As stated by Drucker, consumerism is "the shame of the total marketing concept. It is essentially a mark of the failure of the concept. . . . Consumerism means that the consumer looks upon the manufacturer as somebody who is interested, but who really doesn't know what the consumer's realities are. . . . *Consumerism actually should be, must be, and I hope will be, the opportunity of marketing. This is what we in marketing have been waiting for.*"[29] (Italics added)

The aim of a societally oriented marketer is to design not only pleasing products but also salutary products. The distinction is made clear in Figure 21-2. Current products can be classified according to their degree of *immediate consumer satisfaction* and *long-run consumer benefit. Desirable products* are those that combine high immediate satisfaction and high long-run benefit, such as tasty, nutritious breakfast foods. *Pleasing products* are those that give high immediate satisfaction but may hurt consumer interests in the long run, such as cigarettes. *Salutary products* are those that have low appeal but are also highly beneficial to the consumer in the long run, such as low-phosphate detergents. Finally, *deficient products* are those that have neither immediate appeal nor salutary qualities, such as a bad-tasting patent medicine.

The company might as well forget about deficient products because too much work would be required to build in pleasing and salutary qualities. On the other hand, the company should invest its greatest effort in developing desirable products—e.g., new foods, textiles, appliances, and building materials—which combine intrinsic appeal and long-run benefit. The other two categories, pleasing and salutary products, also present a considerable challenge and opportunity to the company.

The challenge posed by pleasing products is that they sell extremely well but they ultimately hurt the consumer's interests. The product opportunity is

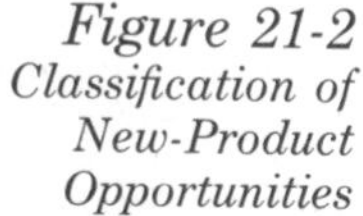
Figure 21-2
Classification of New-Product Opportunities

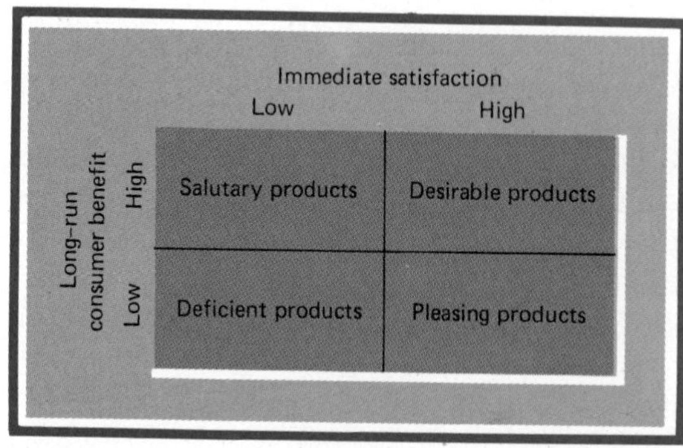

therefore to formulate some alteration of the product that adds salutary qualities without diminishing any or too many of the pleasing qualities. For example: (1) Sears developed and promoted a phosphate-free laundry detergent that became a big-selling brand; (2) Pepsi-Cola developed a one-way plastic soft-drink bottle that is biodegradable in solid waste treatment; and (3) American Oil and Mobil Oil developed and promoted no-lead and low-lead gasolines in response to the oil shortage. And the challenge posed by salutary products is to add some pleasing qualities so that they will become more desirable in the consumers' minds.

Marketing Ethics

Even with the best of intentions, marketers will face many moral dilemmas. The question of the best thing to do will often be unclear. Since not all executives will have the finest moral sensitivity, it is important that the company develop explicit corporate marketing policies. *Policies* are "broad, fixed guidelines that everyone in the organization must adhere to, and that are not subject to exception."[30] They cover distributor relations, advertising standards, customer service, pricing, product development, and general ethical standards.

Even the finest set of guidelines cannot anticipate or resolve all the ethically difficult situations confronting the marketer. Consider Howard Bowen's classic questions about the marketer's responsibilities:

- Should he conduct selling in ways that intrude on the privacy of people, for example, by door-to-door selling . . . ? Should he use methods involving ballyhoo, chances, prizes, hawking, and other tactics which are at least of doubtful good taste? Should he employ "high pressure" tactics in persuading people to buy? Should he try to hasten the obsolescence of goods by bringing out an endless succession of new models and new styles? Should he appeal to and attempt to strengthen the motives of materialism, invidious consumption, and "keeping up with the Joneses"?[31]

Table 21-1 lists fourteen ethically difficult situations that marketers could well face during their careers. If marketers decide in favor of the immediate sales-producing actions in all fourteen cases, their marketing behavior might well be described as immoral or amoral. On the other hand, if they refuse to go along with *any* of the actions, they might be ineffective as marketing managers and unhappy because of the constant moral tension. Obviously managers need a set of principles that will help them determine the moral gravity of each situation and how far they can go in good conscience.

All ethical philosophies deal with one or more of three characteristics of the *act.* They judge either the act itself (moral idealism), the actor's motives (intuitionism), or the act's consequences (utilitarianism).

Moral idealism is the most rigid in that it postulates certain acts to be bad under all (or most) circumstances. Moral idealism gives marketing managers the most definite answers to most of the questions raised in Table 21-1. They would refuse to hear private information or spy on competitors, deceive customers, and so on. As one executive put it, " I would refuse to do anything that I would be ashamed to admit to on national television." By refusing to let the ends justify the means, these executives would derive a greater feeling of correct conduct.

Table 21-1
Some Morally Difficult Situations in Marketing

1. You work for a cigarette company and up to now have not been convinced that cigarettes cause cancer. A recent report has come across your desk that clearly establishes the connection between cigarette smoking and cancer. What would you do?
2. Your R & D department has modernized one of your products. It is not really "new and improved," but you know that putting this statement on the package and in the advertising will increase sales. What would you do?
3. You have been asked to add a stripped-down model to the low end of your line that could be advertised to attract customers. The product won't be very good, but the sales representatives could be depended upon to persuade buyers to buy the higher-priced units. You are asked to give the green light for developing this stripped-down version. What would you do?
4. You are interviewing a former product manager who just left a competitor's company. You are thinking of hiring him. He would be more than happy to tell you all the competitor's plans for the coming year. What would you do?
5. One of your dealers in an important territory has had family troubles recently and is not producing the sales he used to. He was one of the company's top producers in the past. It is not clear how long it will take before his family trouble straightens out. In the meantime, many sales are being lost. There is a legal way to terminate the dealer's franchise and replace him. What would you do?
6. You have a chance to win a big account that will mean a lot to you and your company. The purchasing agent hinted that he would be influenced by a "gift." Your assistant recommends sending a fine color television set to his home. What would you do?
7. You have heard that a competitor has a new product feature that will make a big difference in sales. He will have a hospitality suite at the annual trade show and unveil this feature at a party thrown for his dealers. You can easily send a snooper to this meeting to learn what the new feature is. What would you do?
8. You are eager to win a big contract, and during sales negotiations you learn that the buyer is looking for a better job. You have no intention of hiring him, but if you hinted that you might, he would probably give you the order. What would you do?
9. You have to make a choice between three ad campaigns outlined by your agency for your new product. The first (A) is a soft-sell, honest informational campaign. The second (B) uses sex-loaded emotional appeals and exaggerates the product's benefits. The third (C) involves a noisy, irritating commercial that is sure to gain audience attention. Preliminary tests show that the commercials are effective in the following order: C, B, and A. What would you do?
10. You are a marketing vice-president working for a beer company, and you have learned that a particularly lucrative state is planning to raise the minimum legal drinking age from 18 to 21. You have been asked to join other breweries in lobbying against this bill and to make contributions. What would you do?
11. You want to interview a sample of customers about their reactions to a competitive product. It has been suggested that you invent an innocuous name like the Marketing Research Institute and interview people. What would you do?
12. You produce an antidandruff shampoo that is effective with one application. Your assistant says that the product would turn over faster if the instructions on the label recommended two applications. What would you do?
13. You are interviewing a capable woman applicant for a job as sales representative. She is better qualified than the men just interviewed. At the same time, you suspect that some of your current salesmen will react negatively to her hiring, and you also know that some important customers may be ruffled. What would you do?
14. You are a sales manager in an encyclopedia company. A common way for encyclopedia representatives to get into homes is to pretend they are taking a survey. After they finish the survey, they switch to their sales pitch. This technique seems to be very effective and is used by most of your competitors. What would you do?

Intuitionism is less rigid, leaving it up to individual managers to sense the moral gravity of the situation. If managers feel that their motives are good and that they are not out to hurt anyone, they are taking an intuitive approach to these morally difficult situations.

Utilitarianism is the most deliberative of the three systems, seeking to establish the moral locus not in the act or the motives but in the consequences. If the consequences of the act to the individual and society, both the good ones and the bad ones, represent a net increase in society's happiness, or at least not a net decrease, the act is right.

Ultimately each marketer must choose and work out a philosophy of proper behavior. Every moral system is predicated on some conception of the good life and the relation of one's welfare to that of others. Once the marketer works out a clear philosophy and set of principles, they will help cut through the many knotty questions posed by marketing and other human activities.

Marketing executives of the 1980's will find their job full of challenges. They will face abundant marketing opportunities opened up by technological advances in solar energy, home computers and robots, cable television, modern medicine, and new forms of transportation, recreation, and communication. At the same time, forces in the socioeconomic environment will increase the constraints under which marketing can be carried out. Those companies that are able to pioneer new values and practice societally responsible marketing will have a world to conquer.

EXHIBIT 21-4

CONSTRUCTIVE RESPONSES TO CONSUMERISM

In 1974 Professors Greyser and Diamond surveyed major companies to learn what steps they took to respond to consumerism. They found that 51 percent upgraded product quality and performance standards; 26 percent established industry product standards; 24 percent increased research commitments to better identify consumer wants and needs; 23 percent modified products for greater safety, ease of use, and repair; 22 percent made postsale follow-up calls on consumers; 20 percent supported industry self-regulation efforts; 19 percent made advertisements more informative; 16 percent developed owner's manuals on product use, care, and safety; 15 percent created new organizational positions to deal with consumer affairs; and 14 percent provided more informative product labeling.

In developing constructive consumer programs, a major issue is how to bring consumer influence from the outside into the company decision-making process. In addition to the usual steps of consumer surveys and suggestion and complaint systems, further positive steps can be taken. The Stop and Shop Companies in Boston appointed a *consumer advisory board* consisting of twenty-five women shoppers, who hold monthly meetings with the food chain's high-level managers. A large number of leading manufacturers have created a *consumer affairs unit* that handles customer inquiries and complaints, disseminates information to customers, deals with consumer interest groups, and acts as a consumer ombudsman. The consumer affairs unit also carries out a *consumer affairs audit* to determine how well the company is serving customers. It reports its findings to management for constructive response.

Sources: Stephen A. Greyser and Steven L. Diamond, "Business Is Adapting to Consumerism," *Harvard Business Review*, September-October 1974, p. 57; and E. Patrick McGuire, *The Consumer Affairs Department: Organization and Functions* (New York: Conference Board, 1973).

principles for future public policy toward marketing

Finally, we want to consider a set of principles that might guide the formulation of public policy toward marketing. Too often, various laws are passed to correct specific abuses without considering them in the context of a larger set of principles that the society wants to achieve through its marketing system. Here we will propose seven basic principles on which the marketing system and public policy might be modeled.

The Principle of Consumer and Producer Freedom

To the maximum extent possible, marketing decisions should be made by consumers and producers under relative freedom. There are three possible levels of *producer freedom* in a society.

The *first level* is where producers have no freedom to decide what to produce. The State prescribes or approves all products. The *second level* is where producers are free to produce whatever they think the market wants, with the exception of certain product categories for which they must gain approval. These exceptions usually include addicting drugs, dangerous medicines, pornography, explosives, and so on. The *third level* is where producers are free to produce anything the market will pay for.

Similarly, there are three possible levels of *consumer freedom.* The *first level* is where consumers have no freedom to decide what to consume. They must live in prescribed homes, eat prescribed food, wear prescribed clothing, and participate in prescribed rituals and recreations. The *second level* is where consumers are free to consume whatever is available, with the exception of certain product categories that are banned or require special permission. These exceptions include vice products, dangerous drugs, and so on. The *third level* is where consumers are free to buy and consume anything that the producers are willing to offer.

There is a tendency to find producer and consumer freedom at approximately the same level in different societies. Examples of *level one societies* are monasteries, kibbutzim, tribal groups, highly religious communities, and communist societies. Here production and consumption patterns are precisely determined. Citizen satisfaction is likely to be high because individuals have a limited concept of material and cultural alternatives, and the tensions of human choice are not present. The possibility of self-actualization is particularly unavailable.

Level two societies describe most modern industrial states that permit most things to be produced and consumed. These societies have active entrepreneurial classes seeking to learn what consumers want and responding with a large variety of goods and services to meet different needs and desires. When active producer competition is present, consumers generally enjoy a high degree of choice and satisfaction with the available products and services. Their greatest dissatisfaction is felt in two areas: (1) in product categories that are not available or restricted and (2) in social goods that are scarce relative to private goods.

Level three societies that impose hardly any restrictions on either production or consumption are rare, although certain societies have more freedom than others. Taking a normally restricted product category such as pornography, Spain is at level one, the United States is at level two, and Denmark is at level three. It is rare to find any nation at level three in all product categories.

This principle states that a high level of marketing freedom is important if a marketing system is to deliver a high level of life quality. People are able to achieve satisfaction in *their* terms rather than in terms defined by someone else. It leads to a closer matching of products to desires and therefore the chance of greater fulfillment. High freedom for producers and consumers is the cornerstone of a dynamic marketing system. But further propositions are necessary to implement this freedom and to prevent the social dysfunctions of absolute freedom.

The Principle of Curbing Potential Harm

The political system intervenes in producer or consumer freedom only if serious harm would occur in the absence of intervention. To the extent possible, transactions freely entered into by producers and consumers are their private business, not the concern of third parties. The exception to this is transactions that *harm or threaten to harm one or both of the parties or a third party.* The principle of transactional harm is widely recognized as grounds for government intervening in transactions. The major issue is whether there is real and sufficient actual or potential harm to justify the intervention. For this, it is necessary to distinguish five different levels of harm that might result from a private transaction.

The *no-harm situation* describes the case where neither the production nor the consumption of the product or service harms *producers, consumers, third parties,* or *society* in the *short or long run.* This will serve as the benchmark case. The more immediate the harm, the lower the level number.

Level one harm is where the production of the good is a source of short-run or long-run harm to those who produce it. Workers are hurt when they are subjected to noxious or dangerous processes or to abusively long hours. Child labor laws and factory safety laws have been passed to reduce the likelihood of harm to those engaged in production.

Level two harm is where the consumption or use of the good can cause immediate harm to the consumer because of either ignorance or intention. This type of harm justifies the banning or regulation of unsafe drugs, materials, toys, and so on. The amount of regulation varies with the potential severity, incidence, and imminence of the harm.

Level three harm is where the consumers are gratified by the product but harmed in the long run. Level three harm has been used to justify restriction or prohibition, for example, of pornographic materials or cigarettes. Thus it is argued that the consumer of pornographic material will suffer degradation of character or the smoker of cigarettes will lose his or her health. There is an implication that this may in turn cause others to suffer—family or other citizens—but the primary emphasis is on protecting the specific consumer from being harmed through ignorance or indifference. There is a serious question, however, of how far the State should be allowed to intervene in cases of level three harm. The possibilities range from simple advertisement of the danger (such as requiring cigarette manufacturers to include the following statement on their cigarette packages: "Warning: The surgeon general has determined that cigarette smoking is dangerous to your health"), to enforcing restricted consumption (restricted to certain groups like youngsters or restricted in amount available for consumption per period), to outright prohibition of consumption (such as the Eighteenth Amendment passed in 1919 prohibiting the manufacture, sale, or transportation of intoxicating liquors). The mood of the times is toward increased government responsibility for informing the public of the potential harm of the product.

Level four harm is where neither the producers nor the consumers are harmed in the short or long run as such, but adjacent third parties are harmed during or after production or consumption. Third parties that may be harmed are persons living or traveling near the place of production or consumption who may inhale the bad air, or be exposed to physical danger through high voltage or dangerous equipment, or be exposed to sights or sounds that may cause physical or mental pain. For example, there are growing proposals to limit smoking to certain areas of a public facility or pornography to certain areas of a city.

Level five harm is where neither the producers nor the consumers are harmed in the short or long run as such, but society is harmed in the long run. The major example of level five harm is environmental pollution caused by unregulated production or consumption. This pollution grows arithmetically or geometrically with industrial development and tends not to be regulated until a nation satisfies the basic needs of its people. Environmental pollution is viewed as a small price to pay for rapid economic development when per capita incomes are low. Many developing nations either have no laws regulating pollution or carefully avoid enforcing the laws so as not to discourage investment. In industrially advanced nations, the abundance of material goods and the growing scarcity of clean air, water, and nature are prompting regulation and enforcement to reduce this source of societal harm.

In examining the five levels of potential harm, levels one and two are almost universally recognized as justified areas of regulation by the State because they involve imminent and serious potential harm to the producers or consumers. Level three is coming under increasing regulation as reform organizations exert pressure on the State to regulate or at least inform users of the potential long-run harm from the use of certain products. Levels four and five are just beginning to be regulated in the more advanced countries. The society that is trying to maximize life quality will probably become more active in regulating levels three, four, and five harm where the long-run negative effects are substantial.

The Principle of Meeting Basic Needs

The marketing system should serve the needs of disadvantaged consumers as well as affluent consumers. In a free-enterprise system, producers produce goods for markets that are willing and able to buy. If certain groups lack purchasing power, they may go without essential goods, causing harm to their physical or psychological well-being.

The social imbalance of goods and services appears both in poor and in rich nations. Some groups in the population are able to obtain a great quantity of goods while other groups struggle to obtain the basic requisites of food, clothing, and shelter. Social services such as medical care and education are also ill distributed.

The two common solutions to the problem of unbalanced social output are the Russian solution and the Scandinavian solution. The Russian solution calls for a complete determination by the State of the mix of goods and services through the mechanism of central planning. The State attempts to supply goods in the order of their need priority, making sure that *everyone* has a basic level of food, clothing, shelter, medical care, and education. Beyond this, the State invests the surplus resources in the development of less "necessary" goods and services.

The Scandinavian solution calls for preserving the principle of producer and consumer freedom but using economic and political interventions to bring social output closer into line with need priorities. Through high and progressive income taxes, the surplus incomes of the rich are transferred to the poor through welfare payments and improved social services. The system eliminates persons at the extremes of incomes. Most people are in the middle enjoying basic amenities and looking forward to "higher goods and services" as something all inhabitants will progress toward rather than the few.

Many of the free nations of the world are moving toward the Scandinavian solution, although it is recognized that this creates in its wake greater government bureaucracy, some loss of freedom, and some loss of individual incentive.

The Principle of Economic Efficiency

The marketing system strives to supply goods and services efficiently and at low prices. Every society is characterized by scarce resources in relation to the population's needs and wants. The extent to which these needs and wants can be satisfied depends upon the efficiency with which the scarce resources are used. Inefficiency or waste exists if the society could produce the same output with fewer resources or more output with the same resources. The cost of the inefficiency is measured by the satisfaction that consumers would have enjoyed from the goods that were not produced because of the inefficiency.

Free economies and centrally planned economies use different principles to achieve efficiency. Free economies rely on active producer competition and informed buyers to make a market efficient. Competitors are assumed to be profit maximizers who develop products, prices, and marketing programs attuned to buyer needs and values and watch their costs carefully. Buyers are assumed to be utility maximizers who are aware of competitive products, prices, and qualities and choose carefully. The presence of active competition and well-informed buyers is assumed to keep quality high and prices low.

The centrally planned economy thinks of efficiency in terms of accurate forecasting of consumer and industry demand and the arrangement of production methods and capacities to mass-produce the required goods and services at low cost. There is a premium placed on production efficiency through group incentives and bonuses. There is less attention paid to consumer efficiency in terms of consumer information, waiting time, and assortment choice.

The Principle of Innovation

The marketing system encourages authentic innovation. An effective marketing system makes provision for continuous investment in both process and product innovation. Process innovation seeks to bring down the costs of production and distribution. Product innovation seeks to formulate new products to meet the ever-evolving consumer needs and desires.

Product innovation raises the issue of distinguishing between authentic and trivial innovation. Marketers tend to be concerned with the market's acceptance of new features and styles, not with whether the innovation represents a genuine contribution to human welfare. Much of what is called innovation is simply *imitation* of other brands with a slight difference to provide a talking point for the new brand. The consumer may confront ten brands in a product class that represents far less real product choice than implied by the number of brands. This disproportion between the number of brands and the number of really different products is known as the problem of *brand proliferation.* An effective marketing system is one that encourages real product innovation and differentiation to meet the preferences of different market segments. However, it relies mainly on exhortation and consumer education rather than interfering with the principle of maximum producer and consumer freedom.

The Principle of Consumer Education and Information

The marketing system invests heavily in consumer education and information as a primary means to increase long-run consumer satisfaction and welfare. The principle of economic efficiency requires that the society actively invest in consumer education and information. This is particularly important in technologically advanced nations where goods and brands are confusing because of their plentifulness and conflicting claims and therefore the consumer must have some way of evaluating product differences and making intelligent choices. As self-evident as this is, many modern nations provide woefully inadequate consumer education and information. In fact, four levels of "consumer investment" can be found.

Level one consumer investment is where there is little or no manufacturer information, government information, or private consumer organization information, and little or no consumer education. This level characterizes most economies at the start of their industrial development, and the situation is one of "buyer beware."

Level two consumer investment is where there is some manufacturer-supplied information in the form of branding and labeling, but little or no government or private information. Most of the manufacturer-supplied information is promotionally rather than educationally oriented. Consumer education is underdeveloped, taking the form of a few home economics courses poorly taught and lowly esteemed within the educational establishment.

Level three consumer investment is where there is more manufacturer information, some government publications directed at the consumers to help them recognize values in major product categories, and some private consumer organizations' ratings of products available to subscribers. Consumer education in the public schools is taught with more competence but still is a very brief part of the curriculum. This is generally the level of consumer investment found currently in the United States.

Level four consumer investment is where full manufacturer information is required by law (such as nutritional labeling and freshness dating in the case of foods) and more accurate manufacturer advertising resulting from vigorous enforcement of truth-in-advertising legislation. Private consumer organizations and the government are also active in disseminating product information and evaluations, as well as in leaning hard on manufacturers to provide better information and better products. Finally, the schools have consumer education programs that run for several years and train future citizens in the purchase of foods, drugs, automobiles, appliances, fabrics, insurance, banking service, and so on. This level of consumer investment is currently found in Sweden.

The Principle of Consumer Protection *The marketing system must supplement consumer education and information with consumer protection in certain product areas and market practice areas.* Consumer education and information cannot do the whole job of protecting consumers. Modern products are often so complex technologically that even trained consumers cannot buy them with confidence. Consumers will not be able to discern whether a color television set has too high a level of radiation, whether a new automobile is designed with adequate safety, and whether a new drug product is without dangerous side effects. Therefore it is necessary for a government agency to review and render a verdict on the safety levels of products in many product classes, notably foods, drugs, toys, appliances, fabrics, automobiles, and housing. The failure to pursue this actively would lead to an increase in the number of deaths and disability cases. Even well-intentioned producers often do not recognize product faults until they are pointed out to them.

Consumer protection also stretches to cover production and marketing activities that are environmentally destructive. Here the consumers may readily buy products and fail to understand the consequences that their consumption has not only on the quality of the land and water but on the kind of air they breathe. Consumer protection also covers the prevention of deceptive practices and certain high-pressure selling techniques in situations where the consumer acting alone would be defenseless.

The assumption behind these seven principles is that the goal of the marketing system is not to maximize producers' profits or total consumption or consumer choice, but rather to maximize life quality. That is, how well can the citizens of a society satisfy their basic material needs, experience a high availability of varied and good-quality products, enjoy their physical environment, and find satisfaction in their cultural environment? Since the marketing system has a major impact on the quality of life, it must be managed on principles consistent with improving the quality of life.

■ summary

A marketing system should function to sense, serve, and satisfy consumer needs and enhance the quality of consumers' lives. In endeavoring to meet consumer needs, businesspeople may take certain actions that are not to everyone's liking or benefit. The marketing system has frequently been criticized, and marketing executives should be fully aware of this.

Marketing's impact on consumer welfare has been criticized for high prices, deceptive practices, high-pressure selling, shoddy or unsafe products, planned obsolescence, and poor service to disadvantaged consumers. Marketing's impact on society has been criticized for excessive materialism, false wants, insufficient social goods, cultural pollution, and excessive political power. Marketing's impact on business competition has been criticized for anticompetitive acquisition, high barriers to entry, and predatory competition.

These felt abuses of the marketing system have given rise to various citizen action movements, the most important being consumerism and environmentalism. *Consumerism* is an organized social movement seeking to strengthen the rights and power of consumers vis-à-vis sellers. Resourceful marketers will recognize it as an opportunity to serve consumers better through providing more consumer information, education, and protection. *Environmentalism* is an organized social movement seeking to minimize the harm done by marketing practices to the environment and quality of life. It calls for intervening in consumer wants when their satisfaction would create too much environmental cost.

Citizen action has led to the passage of many new laws designed to protect consumers in the area of product safety, truth-in-packaging, truth-in-lending, and truth-in-advertising.

While many businesses initially opposed these social movements and laws, most of them now realize that there is a need for positive consumer information, education, and protection. Some companies have gone further and have pursued a policy of enlightened marketing based on the principles of consumer orientation, innovation, value creation, social mission, and societal orientation. In addition, these companies have formulated company policies and guidelines and have described ways in which their executives can deal with moral dilemmas.

Future public policy must be guided by a set of principles that will improve the marketing system's contribution to the quality of life. The set of principles calls for relative consumer and producer freedom, intervention only where there is potential harm, arrangements to adequately meet basic consumer needs, the practice of economic efficiency, emphasis on authentic innovation, and the provision of consumer education, information, and protection.

■ questions for discussion

1. Which two criticisms of marketing's impact on individual consumer welfare are the most legitimate? Briefly defend your position.
2. Those critics of marketing's impact on society are really condemning our American business system rather than just the area of marketing. Comment.
3. The Federal Trade Commission is proposing to restrict mergers between large (over $2 billion in sales) corporations. Which of the criticisms of marketing's impact on other businesses would this help to alleviate? Why?
4. How does consumerism differ from environmentalism? Which poses the greater threat to marketing? Explain.
5. Discuss the five principles of enlightened marketing.
6. Ethical issues facing marketing will decrease in the 1980s. Comment.
7. If you were the marketing manager at Dow Chemical Company, how would you deal with the principle of curbing potential harm with regard to water pollution?
8. How might the scarcity of natural resources including energy affect the principles of economic efficiency and innovation in the future?
9. What relationship exists between the principles of consumer education and information and consumer protection? Which will be the dominant one in the next ten years? Why?

■ references

1. Paul W. Stewart and J. Frederick Dewhurst with Louis Field, *Does Distribution Cost Too Much?* (New York: Twentieth Century Fund, 1939).
2. Ibid., p. 348.
3. Jessica Mitford, *The American Way of Death* (New York: Simon & Schuster, 1963).
4. Excerpts from Theodore Levitt, "The Morality(?) of Advertising," *Harvard Business Review,* July-August 1970, pp. 84–92.
5. "Confessions of a Diaper Salesman," *Fortune,* March 1949.
6. "Rattles, Pings, Dents, Leaks, Creaks—And Costs," *Newsweek,* November 25, 1968, p. 92.
7. Ibid.
8. "The Breakfast of Fatties?" *Chicago Today,* July 24, 1970.
9. Gerald B. Tallman, "Planned Obsolescence as a Marketing and Economic Policy," in *Advancing Marketing Efficiency,* ed. L. H. Stockman (Chicago: American Marketing Association, 1958), pp. 27–39.
10. David Caplovitz, *The Poor Pay More* (New York: Free Press, 1963).
11. A speech delivered at Vanderbilt University Law School, reported in *Marketing News,* August 1, 1968, pp. 11, 15.
12. Ibid.
13. For further reading, see Alan R. Andreasen, *The Disadvantaged Consumer* (New York: Free Press, 1975).
14. Mitchell Cohen and Dennis Hale, eds., *The New Student Left,* rev. ed. (Boston: Beacon Press, 1969), pp. 12–13.
15. John Kenneth Galbraith, *The New Industrial State* (Boston: Houghton Mifflin, 1967), p. 200.
16. Herbert Marcuse, *One Dimensional Man* (Boston: Beacon Press, 1964), pp. 4–5.
17. John Kenneth Galbraith, *The Affluent Society* (Boston: Houghton Mifflin, 1958), p. 255.
18. Raymond A. Bauer and Stephen A. Greyser, *Advertising in America: The Consumer View* (Boston: Graduate School of Business Administration, Harvard University, 1968).
19. From an advertisement for *Fact* magazine, which does not carry advertisements.
20. Mark Hanan, "Corporate Growth through Venture Management," *Harvard Business Review,* January-February 1969, p. 44.
21. FTC v. Procter & Gamble, 386 U.S. 568 (1967).
22. See Morris Adelman, "The A & P Case: A Study in Applied Economic Theory," *Quarterly Journal of Economics,* May 1949, p. 238.
23. For more details, see Philip Kotler, "What Consumerism Means for Marketers," *Harvard Business Review,* May-June 1972, pp. 48–57.
24. Rachel Carson, *Silent Spring* (Boston: Houghton Mifflin, 1962).
25. Paul R. Ehrlich and Ann H. Ehrlich, *Population, Resources, Environment: Issues in Human Ecology* (San Francisco: W. H. Freeman, 1970).
26. Donnella H. Meadows, Dennis L. Meadows, Jorgen Randers, and William W. Behrens III, *The Limits to Growth* (New York: Universe Books, 1972).
27. See Norman Kangun, "Environmental Problems and Marketing: Saint or Sinner?" in *Marketing Analysis for Societal Problems,* ed. Jagdish N. Sheth and Peter L. Wright (Urbana: University of Illinois, 1974).

28. Gordon O. Pehrson, quoted in "Flavored Algae from the Sea?" *Chicago Sun-Times,* February 3, 1965, p. 54.
29. Peter Drucker, "The Shame of Marketing," *Marketing/Communications,* August 1969, pp. 60, 64.
30. Earl L. Bailey, *Formulating the Company's Marketing Policies: A Survey* (New York: Conference Board, Experiences in Marketing Management, No. 19, 1968), p. 3.
31. Howard R. Bowen, *Social Responsibilities of the Businessman* (New York: Harper & Row, Pub., 1953), p. 215.

Cases

13 STP Corporation

The STP Corporation is a marketer of oil and gasoline additives and other branded packaged automotive consumer products in the United States and more than 130 other countries. After a period of rapid expansion involving major policy and ownership changes, there is need for critical audit of the corporation's activities, particularly its product lines and markets served.

STP markets a variety of branded consumer products that are bought by the owners of the more than 100 million autos in use today in the United States alone. It focuses on satisfying the needs of the rapidly developing population of do-it-yourself consumers. STP is in an ideal position to take advantage of the economic factors that have forced consumers to keep their cars longer and to maintain them personally.

STP Oil Treatment, the company's original product, remains the cornerstone of the product line. Over 40 million cans were sold last year, and this product continues to be the overwhelming favorite oil additive for motorists around the world.

In the United States STP markets products ranging from oil and gas additives and carburetor cleaner to a comprehensive line of oil, gas and air filters, PCV valves, and breather elements. It was the first company in the automotive after-market to introduce nationally a multigrade motor oil developed to extend oil drain intervals to fifteen thousand miles or one year (whichever comes first) under normal driving conditions for cars in good mechanical condition.

STP Double Oil Filters continue to help the sale of other products in the marketplace and are a stable profit contributor.

STP Gas Treatment was a significant factor in STP's growth, and the new easy-to-pour plastic packaging, coupled with the improved formula, should result in continued gains. Trade response has been favorable to the new space-age-shaped packaging.

Prior to its acquisition by Esmark, STP had been involved in ongoing discussions with the Federal Trade Commission with regard to certain of the company's advertising claims for *STP Oil Treatment.* Even earlier, *Consumer Reports* had published an unfavorable rating of the same product and the claims made. Some of the early advertising messages were delivered by Andy Granatelli, former chairman of STP. The FTC matter was settled in February 1978, and advertising for that product, which had been stopped temporarily, resumed.

STP extended its product line beyond the limitations of an automobile engine by introducing domestically and internationally *Son of a Gun!,* a multipurpose restorer and beautifier of leather, wood, vinyl, and rubber. It is a product that has uses for the home as well as for the automobile, and one that includes women as significant potential buyers. *Son of a Gun!,* like so many of STP's other successful products, has shown itself to be highly responsive to effective advertising and sales promotion activities.

STP has achieved exposure and visibility for its products and its distinctive red, white, and blue STP logo. Primary to this marketing posture is radio, television, and print advertising supplemented by point-of-sale promotions. Merchandising techniques include retailer utilization of a variety of effective display units, mobiles, and informative brochures. Beyond this is the visibility and excitement of STP's auto-racing activities, which range from participation in drag racing and Indy car races to sponsorship of six-time world stock car champion Richard Petty.

Products bearing the STP label are sold in more than 130 countries. Currently more than thirty STP-branded international items are in the product line, including such diverse items as all-purpose silicon spray lubricant, insect sprays, brake fluid, car wax, radiator cleaner and flush, multipurpose spray penetrant, and radiator treatment.

This dedication to an expanded product line has been accelerated. The international division plans to introduce more than a dozen new car-care products into the marketplace, along with a program to make package design more adaptable to different languages and cultures.

Some of the other products considered for possible addition to the product line are oils for boats, motorcycles, diesel engines, and machinery and an aerosal insecticide.

This case is based on the 1978 Esmark, Inc., annual report and form 10-K filed with the SEC by the company.

Questions

1. How do you account for the success of the STP Corporation?
2. What should be the company's market product line criteria? Evaluate each of the new products mentioned in the last paragraph, indicating whether they should be added to the line.
3. Indicate the reasons why STP Corporation should or should not use each of the following strategies:

- Low price
- Direct sale to retailers
- Advertising primarily in specialized magazines for car, boat, motorcycle buffs
- Company-owned and -operated distribution in foreign markets

4. What major environmental forces are likely to affect the future of the STP Corporation?
5. What differences, if any, exist between marketing STP products in the United States and marketing them in foreign countries? What changes should STP make in its marketing activities for the United States? For foreign markets?

14 John Drew, Attorney: Mass Merchandising of Legal Services

John Drew is a lawyer who owns and operates an independent legal clinic. Realizing the widespread need for low-cost legal services by middle-income Americans and encouraged by the success of his own clinic, he is looking for a way to make more money by greater involvement in this growing market.

High-volume, low-cost legal clinics are similar to dental and optical services found in some of the large retail chains. They rent use of space and pay for their own advertising. Some are storefront operations. Most offer only routine services, such as writing wills, handling divorces, probating wills, and handling real estate transactions and bankruptcy filings, which allow a streamlined low-cost operation. More complex matters may be handled at higher fees or referred to another law firm.

Among the several growth possibilities Drew is considering are the following:

1. Increase the billings of his present clinic by adding one or two lawyers and some paralegal personnel, also increase advertising expenditures and the availability of the service to regular clients by providing a toll-free 800 telephone number.
2. Establish a network for independent lawyers who currently serve or would like to serve the high-volume, low-cost legal services market. Such a network would result in lower costs and increased benefits from joint advertising and the centralization of data banks and document preparation using expensive word-processing and computer equipment.

Drew visualizes a network composed of either (1) a number of branch clinics, each operated by a partner or an employee, or (2) a franchise arrangement such as the H & R Block tax or Century 21 real estate service, in which the franchising organization provides services the independent franchisee is unable to provide or can only provide at a higher cost.

Questions

1. How would the operation of a legal service franchise system differ from that of a fast-food franchise system?
2. What advice should be given Mr. Drew concerning his marketing efforts?
3. What other types of consumer professional services might be mass-merchandised?

4. What problems might a consumer encounter in using a high-volume, low-cost outlet for legal, dental, or medical services?

15 **Consumers Union of the United States, Inc.**

According to the charter of the Consumers Union of the United States, Inc., it was established in 1936 as a nonprofit organization "to provide for consumer information and counsel on consumer goods and services . . . to give information and assistance on all matters relating to expenditures of family income . . . and to initiate and cooperate with individual and group efforts seeking to create and maintain decent living standards."

Today Consumers Union is the most important and influential organization in the consumer movement. From its inception, CU has concerned itself with a wide range of issues beyond product testing. In recent years it has increasingly come to view the promotion of consumer education as one of its major roles. CU has undertaken to inform consumers about all phases of their relationship with the marketplace, including such topics as interest rates, guarantees and warranties, life insurance, product safety, and the selection of a doctor. It has helped to finance a variety of activities in the consumer movement area, including David Caplovitz's research on the problem of low-income consumers, as well as the development of an international organization of product-testing associations (the International Organization of Consumers Unions), and it has occasionally provided expert testimony at regulatory and legislative hearings.

Most of CU's $20 million income in 1978 came from more than 2 million subscribers and newsstand buyers of *Consumer Reports*, a monthly publication of test results with product ratings and consumer information. The *Buying Guide* issue has in the past consisted of about 450 pages, with more than twenty-three hundred ratings by brand and model. Subscription rates in 1978 were $11 for one year, $20 for two years, $27 for three years. The newsstand price of a single copy was $1.25, and the *Buying Guide* issue was $3.00. Some income was derived from book sales and, on rare occasions, from a government grant. In an effort to protect its independence, CU has not accepted advertising, gifts, donations, subsidies, or private grants. CU defends its impartiality and independence by taking legal action against those who use the name "Consumers Union" or CU test results for commercial purposes. CU members act as watchdogs, and CU has lost few, if any, cases.

In a speech in 1970 Colston E. Warne, president of the Consumers Union of the United States, Inc., mentioned the following as imperfections in the consumer movement:

1. Narrow focus on products, particularly technically complex products
2. Lack of emphasis on nutritional testing

In another speech during the same year, Dr. Warne listed the following as the major complaints of the consumer public regarding Consumers Union's testing methods:

1. Too infrequent testing of major items

2. Inaccessibility of products tested and availability of products yet to be tested
3. Postponement of test results to the point of obsolescence
4. Insufficient coverage of mail-order and door-to-door items
5. Excessive emphasis on minor advantages and disadvantages, and insufficient emphasis on performance and durability

In one of its reports, CU mentions the following priorities:

1. Focus on environmental issues
2. Expansion of the basic staff
3. Coordinated effort to see that legislative, regulatory, and legal actions correct the inequities that CU has exposed
4. Creation and maintenance of a Washington office
5. Experimental research in areas more useful to disadvantaged consumers
6. Formation of a Consumer Interests Foundation, Inc., which will probe more deeply into broader areas of consumer concern

CU's management is reappraising the organization and its operations with an eye to the future. Management is specifically interested in getting recommendations indicating how CU can serve consumers most effectively with its limited resources.

Questions

1. From a marketing point of view, what changes, if any, should CU make in its product-testing service program for consumers, including *Consumer Reports* magazine? Briefly indicate your ideas and reasons for each of the following categories:
   - Target market(s)
   - Product/service line
   - Pricing/fund raising
   - Distribution/place
   - Communication (advertising, publicity, promotion, personal selling)
2. What should be CU's role in the consumer movement?
   - What services should be offered beyond product testing?
   - How should each be financed?
3. Should Consumers Union take an active role in sponsoring causes, as advocated by Ralph Nader when he was a director of the organization?

APPENDIX-1

marketing arithmetic

One aspect of marketing that was not discussed in depth within the text was the computation of business arithmetic. The calculation of sales, costs, and expenses is important for many marketing decisions. Therefore the purpose of this Appendix is to analyze the relevant components of marketing arithmetic. Three major areas are covered: the operating statement, markups and markdowns, and other analytic ratios.

operating statement

The operating statement of a firm presents a summary of the firm's income and expenses over some specified time period. Its primary thrust is to derive the net profit for the organization in dollar terms. The operating statement is sometimes called the income, or profit and loss, statement. From this statement it is possible to calculate ratios that will assist the marketing decision maker.

Table 1 shows an operating statement for Dale Parsons, Ltd., a small menswear specialty store in the Midwest. It should be noted that this statement is for the 1980 calendar year. Operating statements can also be computed monthly, quarterly, and semiannually. This statement is for a retailer; the operating statement for a manufacturer would be somewhat different. Specifically, the section on purchases within the "cost of goods sold" area would be replaced by "cost of goods manufactured." Otherwise the statements are the same.

The computation of the $5,000 net profit for this firm can easily be seen by breaking down the total statement into the following parts:

Net sales	$60,000
Cost of goods sold	35,000
Gross margin	$25,000
Expenses	20,000
	$ 5,000

In its most basic form, the statement can be reduced to net sales minus all costs (cost of goods sold plus expenses), which equals net profit.

The cost of goods sold for Dale Parsons, Ltd., in 1980 deserves a bit of discussion. Of course, the stock of inventory in the store at the beginning of the year must be included. During the year, $33,000 worth of suits, slacks, shirts, ties, jeans, and so forth, was purchased. One company provided a discount of $3,000 to the store, and thus net purchases were $30,000. Since the store is located in a small town and requires a special delivery route, Mr. Parsons had to pay an

Table 1
Dale Parsons, Ltd.
Operating Statement
For the Year Ending
December 31, 1980

Gross Sales			$65,000
Less: Sales returns and allowances			5,000
Net Sales			$60,000
Cost of Goods Sold:			
Beginning inventory, January 1, at cost		$12,000	
Gross purchases	$33,000		
Less: Purchase discounts	3,000		
Net purchases	$30,000		
Plus: Freight-in	2,000		
Net cost of delivered purchases		32,000	
Cost of goods available for sale		$44,000	
Less: Ending inventory, December 31, at cost		9,000	
Cost of goods sold			35,000
Gross Margin			$25,000
Expenses:			
Selling expenses			
Sales, salaries, and commissions	$ 8,000		
Advertising	1,000		
Delivery	1,000		
Total selling expenses		$10,000	
Administrative expenses			
Office salaries	$ 4,000		
Office supplies	1,000		
Miscellaneous (outside consultant)	1,000		
Total administrative expenses		$ 6,000	
General expenses			
Rent	$ 2,000		
Heat, light, and telephone	1,000		
Miscellaneous (insurance, depreciation)	1,000		
Total general expenses		$ 4,000	
Total expenses			$20,000
Net Profit			$ 5,000

additional $2,000 to get the products delivered to him, giving him a net cost of $32,000. When the beginning inventory was added to this figure, the cost of goods available for sale amounted to $44,000. The $9,000 ending inventory of clothes in the store on December 31 was then subtracted to come up with the $35,000 cost of goods sold figure.

In the "expenses" portion of the operating statement, there are several categories important to this store. The selling expenses for Dale Parsons, Ltd., included two part-time employees; local newspaper, radio, and television advertising; and the cost of delivering merchandise to consumers after alterations. In total, this amounted to $10,000 for the year. Administrative expenses encompassed the salary for a part-time bookkeeper, office supplies such as stationery and business cards, and a miscellaneous expense of an administrative audit conducted by an outside consultant. These expenses were $6,000 in 1980. Finally, the general expenses of rent, utilities, insurance, and depreciation came to $4,000. Total expenses were therefore $20,000 for the year.

markups and markdowns

For retailers such as Mr. Parsons and for wholesalers, an understanding of the concepts of markup and markdown is essential. Naturally the marketer must make a profit to stay in business, and thus the markup percentage is an important strategic consideration. Both markups and markdowns are expressed in percentage terms.

There are two different ways to compute markups—on cost or on selling price:

$$\text{Markup percentage on cost} = \frac{\text{Dollar markup}}{\text{Cost}}$$

$$\text{Markup percentage on selling price} = \frac{\text{Dollar markup}}{\text{Selling price}}$$

It is imperative that Mr. Parsons or any other marketer decide which one of these bases the business is going to use. Otherwise much confusion may result. For example, if Mr. Parsons bought shirts for \$8 and wanted to mark them up \$4, his markup percentage on cost would be $\$4/\$8 = 50\%$. However, if it were figured on selling price, the percentage would be $\$4/\$12 = 33.3\%$. In figuring markup percentage, most retailers use the selling price rather than the cost.

Sometimes a retailer would like to be able to convert markups based on selling price to cost, and vice versa. The formulas are:

$$\text{Markup percentage on selling price} = \frac{\text{Markup percentage on cost}}{100\% + \text{Markup percentage on cost}}$$

$$\text{Markup percentage on cost} = \frac{\text{Markup percentage on selling price}}{100\% - \text{Markup percentage on selling price}}$$

As an illustration with regard to men's suits, suppose Mr. Parsons found out that his competitor was using a markup percentage of 30 percent based on cost and he wanted to know what this would be as a percentage of selling price. The calculation would be

$$\frac{30\%}{100\% + 30\%} = \frac{30\%}{130\%} = 23\%$$

Since Mr. Parsons was using a 25 percent markup on the selling price for suits, he felt that his price should be comparable to that of his competitor.

Near the end of the summer Mr. Parsons found that he had an inventory of summer slacks in stock. Thus he knew that a markdown, a reduction from the original selling price, was necessary. He had purchased twenty pairs originally at \$10 each and had sold ten pairs at \$20 each. He marked down the other pairs to \$15 and sold five pairs. His markdown ratio (percentage) is computed as follows:

$$\text{Markdown percentage} = \frac{\text{Dollar markdown}}{\text{Total net sales in dollars}}$$

The dollar markdown is \$25 (5 pairs × \$5 each) and total net sales are \$275, that is, (10 pairs × \$20) + (5 pairs × \$15). The ratio, then, is \$25/\$275 = 9%.

The markdown formula can be further refined by including sales allowances:

$$\text{Markdown percentage} = \frac{\text{Dollar markdown} + \text{Dollar sales allowance}}{\text{Total net sales in dollars}}$$

One of the customers who bought the slacks for \$20 noticed a flaw in them and complained to Mr. Parsons. The customer was given a \$5 sales allowance because he still wanted to keep the slacks. The markdown percentage would now be

$$\frac{\$25 + \$5}{\$275} = \frac{\$30}{\$275} = 11\%$$

analytic ratios

Several additional ratios can be computed by using the operating statement. They are as follows:

RATIO	FORMULA	COMPUTATION FROM TABLE 1
Gross margin percentage	$= \frac{\text{Gross margin}}{\text{Net sales}}$	$= \frac{\$25{,}000}{\$60{,}000} = 42\%$
Net profit percentage	$= \frac{\text{Net profit}}{\text{Net sales}}$	$= \frac{\$5{,}000}{\$60{,}000} = 8\%$
Operating expense percentage	$= \frac{\text{Total expenses}}{\text{Net sales}}$	$= \frac{\$20{,}000}{\$60{,}000} = 33\%$

These ratios may prove useful when Mr. Parsons and other marketers evaluate their marketing programs. The ratios can be compared against industry or historical standards to determine the overall success of the firm.

One other ratio that is useful for analytical purposes is the stockturn rate. The stockturn rate is the number of times that an inventory turns over or is sold during a specified time period (often one year). It may be computed on a cost or a selling price basis. Thus the formula can be

$$\text{Stockturn rate} = \frac{\text{Cost of goods sold}}{\text{Average inventory at cost}}$$

or

$$\text{Stockturn rate} = \frac{\text{Selling price of goods sold}}{\text{Average selling price of inventory}}$$

Returning to the operating statement (Table 1) for Dale Parsons, Ltd., the stockturn rate based on costs can be computed. It is equal to

$$\frac{\$35{,}000 \text{ (Cost of goods sold)}}{\frac{\$12{,}000 + \$9{,}000}{2} \text{ (Average inventory)}} = \frac{\$35{,}000}{\$10{,}500} = 3.3$$

That is, Mr. Parsons's inventory turned over 3.3 times in 1980.

conclusion

This analysis of marketing arithmetic shows that there are several important statements and ratios that marketing managers can use in making marketing decisions. The operating statement, markups and markdowns, and other analytic ratios were discussed in this Appendix. These certainly do not represent an exhaustive list of relevant computations, but they do exhibit the value of a strong analytical approach to evaluating marketing programs.

APPENDIX-2

a career in marketing?

Now that you have read this textbook and completed your first course in marketing, you have some knowledge of what this field entails. You may still be somewhat uncertain, however, as to whether you should seek a career in marketing. The purpose of this Appendix is to acquaint you more fully with entry-level as well as higher-level marketing opportunities that are available within an organization. Before discussing these specific job prospects, a few general facts about marketing and recent trends in marketing need to be stated.

facts about marketing

First, there are many career opportunities within the field of marketing. It is estimated that between one-fourth and one-third of the civilian labor force is employed in a marketing-related position. Consequently, the diversity of tasks to be performed is enormous. The jobs of Kim Kelley of Honeywell and Dr. John McLaren of Evanston Hospital described at the beginning of Chapters 18 and 20 are examples of the divergent career possibilities.

Second, since marketing deals with the exchange of products and services between the marketer and the consumer, marketing jobs are crucial to the success of any organization. Therefore a career in the marketing area offers significant challenges and opportunities that do not usually exist in finance, personnel, accounting, or other fields. In particular, marketing managers need to understand the intricacies of the marketplace and must be able to react quickly to the frequent changes. It may seem trite to say that marketing is an "exciting" area, but this is the way it is often described. If a sense of uncertainty and a challenge are things you are looking for in a career, marketing may be for you.

Although the salary level and financial remuneration should not be the major criterion in selecting a field of study and a potential career, they are nonetheless important. Starting salaries for marketing usually rank slightly below those for engineering, chemistry, and accounting but are higher than those for economics/finance, general business, and the liberal arts. Also, if you are successful in the entry-level marketing position, you will probably be promoted quickly to higher levels of responsibility and salary. Positions in marketing are also thought to be excellent training for the highest levels (president, vice-president) in the organization because of the knowledge of products and consumers gained in these jobs. Remuneration in the marketing area of the firm will usually depend on your level of productivity. The sales and sales management positions with the emphasis on commissions are particularly good illustrations of this procedure.

recent trends in marketing

Several occurrences in the past few years have made marketing a more attractive career for some individuals who have not traditionally considered this field. An area of growing importance to many firms is the "internationalization" of their organizations. As was discussed in Chapter 19, business activity is increasingly being conducted outside the United States. Therefore firms are actively seeking qualified persons who are willing to travel and/or relocate in foreign cities. Of course, fluency in one or more languages other than English is a necessity. It appears that international marketing will continue to be a growth area for many firms in the future. Thus there should be an increasing number of career opportunities available. Many of the specific jobs discussed in the next two sections are available in an international as well as a domestic setting.

A second recent trend is the growing number of women entering the field of marketing. Women have historically been employed primarily in the retail sector of marketing. However, they are now moving into all types of sales jobs. A *Business Week* article stated that in insurance, women accounted for 2 percent of sales recruits in 1971 and 12 percent in 1978. Also, women are increasingly being sought for the more lucrative industrial selling jobs.[1] Apparently it will be only a matter of time before many of these women are promoted to higher levels in their respective organizations.

A third recent trend that may increase marketing career possibilities is the growing acceptance of marketing by nonprofit organizations. Universities, arts organizations, libraries, and hospitals and other health-care institutions are beginning to apply marketing principles and concepts to solve their problems. For example, colleges and universities employ admissions personnel to recruit high-school students. As the field of marketing becomes more broadly accepted by these organizations, jobs will probably open up for persons trained in marketing. Nonprofit marketing may allow you to combine your avocation with a career. Specifically, some arts organizations are increasingly hiring individuals who have an interest and expertise in the arts but have a marketing academic background.

Although emerging areas such as marketing energy conservation will undoubtedly demand marketing talent, the trends discussed above seem to be the most dominant today. The specific entry-level jobs available in marketing are discussed in the following section.

entry-level jobs in marketing

Table 1 lists the major entry-level jobs that are available to individuals entering the field of marketing. The personal characteristics necessary, number of available jobs, type of organization hiring, and other relevant courses are listed for each job. Marketing students should realize that there are more marketing jobs available in personal selling than in any other area. Students often complain that a college degree is not required for a sales job. However, this is getting to be less true, and more companies are listing a college degree as a minimum hiring requirement.

[1]"The Industrial Salesman Becomes a Salesperson, *Business Week,* February 19, 1978, pp. 104–10.

Table 1
Entry-level Jobs in Marketing

	PERSONAL CHARACTERISTICS	NUMBER OF AVAILABLE JOBS	TYPE OF ORGANIZATION HIRING	OTHER RELEVANT NONBUSINESS COURSES*
Personal selling	Empathy Gregariousness Energy	Most	Consumer products Services (e.g., insurance) Industrial firms	Psychology Speech
Retailing	Supervisory abilities	Many	Department stores Specialty shops Discount chains	Sociology Urban Economics Urban Geography
Advertising	Creativity	Some	Ad agencies Retailers	Journalism
Public relations	Interpersonal skills	Some	Consulting firms Nonprofit organizations	Speech Mass Communication
Marketing research	Analytical abilities	Some	Research agencies Firms Retailers	Statistics Computer Science
Industrial purchasing	Technical skills	Some	Manufacturing firms Wholesalers	Engineering

*It is assumed that the marketing graduate will take general business courses in accounting, finance, management, etc.

Companies also provide sales training programs to new members of the sales force. Corporations like Procter & Gamble and IBM provide such excellent sales-training programs and experience that their employees are routinely sought by other firms. Thus, personal selling may be a rewarding first job for you.

The second most prevalent area for initial marketing jobs is in retailing. Major department stores, specialty shops, and discount chains are always seeking individuals who have an interest in merchandising and the ability to supervise others. Retailing, like personal selling, is a people-oriented profession. Although the hours are often long and the financial rewards are not always high, retailing enables the individual to gain a lot of diverse experience in marketing in a relatively short time.

The fields of advertising and public relations also contain jobs for the marketing graduate. The openings are not as common as for selling and retailing, but individuals who are interested in mass-media promotion and account executive work (i.e., developing PR or advertising programs for a client organization) will find that these two fields offer good possibilities. Advertising has historically sought primarily creative people, but those with marketing and management expertise are now being actively recruited. Public relations practitioners currently recognize that PR activities must be consumer oriented. Therefore marketing graduates should be in more demand by these firms.

Two other entry-level job opportunities available in marketing are marketing research and industrial purchasing. Marketing research is a field that requires strong analytical capabilities and statistical expertise. Although research jobs are not plentiful, they are intrinsically rewarding because of the satisfaction gained from developing and carrying out a project from beginning to end. Industrial-purchasing positions often require a technical background such as engineering or hard science. The ability to combine marketing with a more technical field is often not easy to attain. However, if you have this ability, there are manufacturers and wholesalers who have need for your talents.

The above list is certainly not an exhaustive one. There are other entry-level marketing jobs, such as those dealing with physical distribution, warehousing, credit and collections, and pricing, but they are not as prevalent as the ones discussed.

higher-level jobs in marketing

If you continue in the field of marketing and decide to make it a career, there are various other possible positions that you might hold. Table 2 lists several of these. The first column of the table shows that five jobs have the word *management* in their title, and therefore general managerial skills such as organization, leadership, and a strong sense of responsibility are prerequisites for success in these areas.

Table 2
Higher-level Jobs in Marketing

	PERSONAL CHARACTERISTICS	NUMBER OF AVAILABLE JOBS	TYPE OF ORGANIZATION HIRING	PREREQUISITES
Marketing management	Leadership Responsibility Organization skills	Some	Consumer, industrial, and nonprofit organizations	Several years' experience Success in marketing job
Product management	Leadership Responsibility Organization skills	Many	Consumer products marketers	M.B.A. required
Advertising management	Leadership Responsibility Organization skills	Some	Ad agencies Retailers	Account executive and general advertising experience
Sales management	Leadership Responsibility Organization skills	Some	Consumer and industrial firms	Sales experience
Store (retail) management	Leadership Responsibility Organization skills	Many	Retailers	Experience and success in several retailing jobs
Marketing consultant	Leadership Responsibility Organization skills Independence	Some		General marketing background
Customer affairs representative	Empathy	Few	Consumer products marketers	Experience within the organization
Marketing education	Perseverance	Few	Colleges and universities	Ph.D. required

Marketing management positions refer to those medium- to high-level ones that require a coordination of all the marketing mix components. Therefore experience in several other marketing areas, such as sales and product management, is probably needed. The ultimate marketing management position in most organizations is that of vice-president of marketing.

Product management was discussed in Chapter 6 of the text. Most product management organizations have several levels within this structure. For instance, a recent M.B.A. graduate will assume an assistant product manager job and will later be promoted to associate product manager. Large consumer products marketers, such as Procter and Gamble, Carnation, and Johnson Wax, have this type of organization. It is also possible to move into product management positions within some firms after several years' experience in sales. However, this is not the usual path.

Advertising, sales, and store managers are those individuals who have direct responsibility for the entry-level positions in their area, which were analyzed previously. Although persons who are successful in their previous jobs are normally promoted to these management positions, it is important to recognize the "Peter principle." That is, a person rises to his or her level of incompetence in an organization. An individual who is a good sales representative may not necessarily make an effective sales manager. It is hoped that you will not be a victim of the "Peter principle."

The other jobs listed in the first column of Table 2 require somewhat different interests and skills but are nevertheless areas of opportunity within the marketing field. The marketing consultant must combine expertise and past experience to offer services that will be demanded by those in need of marketing advice. Consultants have the flexibility of not being limited to a specific job within an organization, but they must also be able to cope with uncertainty and pressure from clients. Customer affairs representatives are relatively recent additions to many firms as a response to the consumerism movement. A thorough understanding of the organization and an empathy for consumer needs are prerequisites for this position. Finally, the study and teaching of marketing is another career possibility. One course in marketing, however, is probably not enough to enable you to decide whether the field of marketing education is for you. Marketing education requires several years of graduate training, and in most instances a Ph.D. is a necessity. However, it does provide certain psychological rewards. Check with your professor for more information about marketing education.

conclusion

This discussion of marketing careers was necessarily limited. It was the intent of this Appendix to briefly familiarize you with potential avenues within the field of marketing. Some of these careers are discussed in greater depth elsewhere.[2] Good luck on your career decision!

[2] J. Donald Weinrauch and William E. Piland, *Applied Marketing Principles* (Englewood Cliffs, N.J.: Prentice-Hall, 1979), Chap. 2.

GLOSSARY

Absolute product failure. A product failure that loses money and whose sales do not cover the variable costs. [p. 338]

Accelerator principle. A small change in consumer demand leads to a large increase in industrial demand. [p. 269]

Administered vertical marketing system. Achieves coordination of successive stages of production and distribution not through common ownership but through the size and power of one of the parties within the system. [p. 431]

Advertising. The use of paid media by a seller to communicate persuasive information about its products, services, or organization. [p. 519]

Advertising goal. A specific communication task, to be accomplished among a defined audience, in a given period of time. [p. 525]

Agent middlemen. Business firms—such as manufacturer's representatives and brokers—that are hired by producers and find buyers and negotiate sales but do not take title to the merchandise. [p. 47]

Attitude. A person's enduring favorable or unfavorable cognitive evaluations, emotional feelings, and action tendencies toward some object or idea. [p. 251]

Backward integration. The term refers to a company's seeking ownership or increased control of its supply systems. [p. 79]

Belief. A descriptive thought that a person holds about something. [p. 251]

*__Brand.__ A name, term, sign, symbol, or design, or a combination of them which is intended to identify the goods or services of one seller or group of sellers and to differentiate them from those of competitors. [p. 374]

*__Brand mark.__ That part of a brand which can be recognized but is not utterable, such as a symbol, design, or distinctive coloring or lettering. [p. 374]

*__Brand name.__ That part of a brand which can be vocalized—the utterable. [p. 374]

Buyer. Anyone who might conceivably buy a given product. [p. 232]

†**Buying center.** All those individuals and groups who participate in the purchasing decision-making process, who share some common goals and the risks arising from the decisions. [p. 271]

Closed-end question. A question in which the possible answers are supplied. [p. 148]

Cognitive dissonance theory. Almost every purchase is likely to lead to some postpurchase discomfort, and the issues are how much discomfort and what will the consumer do about it. [p. 259]

Company demand. The company's sales resulting from its share of market demand. [p. 155]

*The definitions preceded by an asterisk are from *Marketing Definitions: A Glossary of Marketing Terms* (Chicago: American Marketing Association, 1960).

†The definitions preceded by a dagger are from Frederick E. Webster, Jr., and Yoram Wind, *Organizational Buying Behavior* (Englewood Cliffs, N.J.: Prentice-Hall, 1972).

Company marketing opportunity. An attractive arena of relevant marketing action in which a particular company is likely to enjoy superior competitive advantages. [p. 71]

Company marketing system. The set of major participants, markets, and forces that make up the company's marketing environment. [p. 44]

Company sales forecast. The expected level of company sales based on a chosen marketing plan and assumed marketing environment. [p. 155]

Company sales potential. The limit approached by company demand as company marketing expenditure increases in relation to competitors. [p. 156]

Concentration strategy. A marketing strategy in which the firm concentrates its resources only in the strongest markets and channels while phasing out its efforts elsewhere. [p. 313]

Concentric diversification. The term refers to the company's seeking to add new products that have technological and/or marketing synergies with the existing product line; these products will normally appeal to new classes of customers. [p. 80]

Conglomerate diversification. The term refers to the company's seeking to add new products that have no relationship to the company's current technology, products, or markets; these products will normally appeal to new classes of customers. [p. 80]

Consumerism. An organized social movement seeking to strengthen the rights and power of consumers vis-à-vis sellers. [p. 661]

Consumer markets. The set of individuals and households that buy products intended for personal consumption. [p. 232]

Containerization. The putting of goods in boxes or trailers that can easily be transferred between two or more modes of transportation. [p. 451]

Continuation strategy. A marketing strategy in which the firm continues to use the same market segments, channels, pricing, and promotion.

Contractual vertical marketing system. A system in which independent firms at different levels of production and distribution integrate their programs on a contractual basis to obtain more economies and/or sales impact than they could achieve alone. [p. 430]

*__Convenience goods.__ Consumer goods that the customer usually purchases frequently, immediately, and with the minimum of effort in comparison and buying. [p. 370]

Copyright. The exclusive legal right to reproduce, publish, and sell the matter and form of a literary, musical, or artistic work. [p. 374]

Corporate vertical marketing system. The combining of successive stages of production and distribution under a single ownership. [p. 430]

Cues. Minor stimuli that determine when, where, and how the person responds. [p. 250]

Discretionary income. The amount of money a person has left after paying for his or her basic food, clothing, shelter, insurance, and other necessaries. [p. 209]

Disposable personal income. The amount of money a person has left after paying taxes. [p. 209]

Distribution channel. The set of all the firms and individuals that take title, or assist in transferring title, to the particular good or service as it moves from the producer to the consumer. Thus a distribution channel primarily includes the merchant middlemen (because they take title) and the agent middlemen (because they assist in transferring title). The distribution channel does not include suppliers, facilitators, and marketing firms. [p. 423]

Distribution structure. All available arrangements in a particular industry to get products from the producers to the consumers. [p. 43]

Diversification growth opportunities. Those opportunities lying outside the current marketing channel system. [p. 78–80]

Drive. A strong internal stimulus impelling action. A drive becomes a motive when it is directed toward a particular drive-reducing stimulus object. [p. 250]

DROP-error. Occurs when the company dismisses an otherwise good idea because of a lack of vision of its potentialities. [p. 338]

Durable goods. Tangible goods that normally survive many uses. [p. 370]

Embargo. The ultimate form of quota in that imports in prescribed categories are totally banned. [p. 603]

Environmentalism. An organized social movement seeking to minimize the harm done by marketing practices to the environment and quality of life. [p. 662]

Environmental threat. A challenge posed by an unfavorable trend or specific disturbance in the environment which would lead, in the absence of purposeful marketing action, to the stagnation or demise of a company, product, or brand. [p. 70]

Evoked set. The set of alternatives that the buyer might or did consider at that stage of the decision process. [p. 236]

Exchange. The act of obtaining a desired object from someone by offering something in return. [p. 13]

Expectations-performance theory. A consumer's satisfaction is a function of the consumer's product expectations and the product's perceived performance. [p. 258]

Facilitators. Business firms—such as transportation companies, warehouses, banks, and insurance companies—that assist in the logistical and financial tasks of distribution but do not take title to goods or negotiate purchases or sales. [p. 47]

Fads. Particular fashions that come quickly into the public eye, are adopted with great zeal, peak early, and decline very fast. [p. 349]

Fashion. A currently accepted or popular style in a given field. Fashions tend to pass through four stages: distinctiveness, emulation, mass fashion, and decline. [p. 349]

Forecasting. The art of anticipating what buyers are likely to do under a given set of conditions. [p. 160]

Forward integration. The term refers to a company's seeking ownership or increased control of some of its dealers or distributors. [p. 79]

Functional marketing organization. A form of marketing organization in which the various marketing functions are headed by separate managers who report to the marketing vice-president. [p. 174]

GO-error. Occurs when the company lets a poor idea proceed to development and commercialization. [p. 338]

Government market. Governmental units of all types—federal, state, and local—who purchase or rent goods for carrying out the main functions of government. [p. 284]

Harvesting strategy. A marketing strategy in which the firm sharply reduces its expenses to increase its current profits, knowing that this will accelerate the rate of sales decline and ultimate demise of the product. [p. 82]

Horizontal diversification. The term refers to the company's seeking to add new products that could appeal to its current customers though technically unrelated to its current product line. [p. 80]

Horizontal integration. The term refers to a company's seeking ownership or increased control of some of its competitors. [p. 79]

Human need. A state of felt deprivation in a person. [p. 10]

Image. The set of beliefs that a person or a group holds of an object. [p. 631]

Image persistence. The result of people's continuing to see what they expect to see, rather than what is.

International markets. The set of buyers found in other countries. This set includes foreign consumers, producers, resellers, and governments. [p. 50]

Learning. Changes in an individual's behavior arising from experience. [p. 250]

Line stretching. The act of lengthening the company's product line beyond its current range. [p. 365]

Macroenvironment. The totality of major institutions and forces that are external and potentially relevant to the firm. [p. 203]

Market. The set of all actual and potential buyers of a product. [p. 231]

Market demand. The term refers to the **total volume** that would be **bought** by a defined **customer group** in a defined **geographical area** in a defined **time period** in a defined **marketing environment** under a defined **marketing program.** [p. 152]

Market development. The term refers to the company's seeking increased sales by taking its current products into new markets. [p. 79]

Market forecast. The market forecast shows the expected level of market demand for the expected level of industry marketing effort and the given environment. [p. 154]

Marketing. Human activity directed at satisfying needs and wants through exchange processes. [p. 10]

Marketing audit. A comprehensive, systematic, independent, and periodic examination of a company's—or a business unit's—marketing environment, objectives, strategies, and activities with a view to determining problem areas and opportunities and recommending a plan of action to improve the company's marketing performance. [p. 124]

Marketing channel. A method of organizing the work that has to be done to move goods from producers to consumers. [p. 47]

Marketing concept. A management orientation that holds that the key to achieving organizational goals consists of the organization's determining the needs and wants of target markets and adapting itself to delivering the desired satisfactions more effectively and efficiently than its competitors. [p. 22]

Marketing firms. Business firms—such as advertising agencies, marketing research firms, and marketing consulting firms—that assist in targeting and promoting the sellers' products to the right markets. [p. 47]

Marketing information system. A continuing and interacting structure of people, equipment, and procedures designed to gather, sort, analyze, evaluate, and distribute pertinent, timely, and accurate information for use by marketing decision makers to improve their marketing planning, execution, and control. [p. 136]

Marketing intelligence system. The set of sources and procedures by which marketing executives obtain their everyday information about developments in the external marketing environment. [p. 138]

Marketing management. The analysis, planning, implementation, and control of programs designed to create, build, and maintain mutually beneficial exchanges and relationships with target markets for the purpose of achieving organizational objectives. Effective marketing management involves a disciplined analysis of the needs, wants, perceptions, and preferences of consumer and intermediary markets as the basis for effective product design, pricing, communication, and distribution. [p. 19]

Marketing mix. The particular blend of controllable marketing variables that the firm uses to achieve its objectives in the target market. [p. 88]

Marketing process. The managerial process of identifying, analyzing, choosing, and exploiting marketing opportunities to fulfill the company's mission and objectives. [p. 85]

Marketing research. The systematic design, collection, analysis, and reporting of data and findings relevant to a specific marketing situation facing the company. [p. 139]

Marketing strategy. The fundamental marketing logic by which the business unit intends to achieve its marketing objectives. Marketing strategy consists of a coordinated set of decisions on (1) target markets, (2) marketing mix, and (3) marketing expenditure level. [p. 107]

Marketing system. A set of interacting participants, markets, and flows that are involved in an organized arena of exchange. [p. 36]

Market management organization. A form of marketing organization in which major markets are the responsibility of market managers who work with the various functional specialists to develop and achieve their plans for the market. [p. 179]

Market penetration. The term refers to the company's seeking increased sales for its current products in its current markets through more aggressive marketing effort. [p. 78–79]

Market potential. The limit approached by market demand as industry marketing expenditure goes to infinity, for a given set of competitive prices and a given environment. [p. 154]

Market segmentation. The act of dividing a market into distinct and meaningful groups of buyers who might merit separate products and/or marketing mixes. [p. 50]

Mass marketing. A style of marketing in which the seller mass-produces and mass-distributes one product and attempts to attract everyone to its purchase. [p. 293]

Merchant middlemen. Business firms—such as wholesalers and retailers—that buy, take title to, and resell merchandise. [p. 47]

Micro-sales analysis. An attempt to determine the specific products, territories, and so forth, that failed to produce their expected share of sales. [p. 116]

Model bank. A collection of models that will help marketers develop better marketing decisions. [p. 143]

Motive. A stimulated need which is sufficiently pressing to direct the person toward the goal of satisfying the need. After the need is satisfied, the person's tension is discharged and he or she returns to a state of equilibrium. [p. 246]

***Nondurable goods.** Tangible goods that normally are consumed in one or a few uses. [p. 370]

Open-end question. A question that the respondent is free to answer in his or her own words. [p. 370]

Organization. A social unit characterized by explicit goals, definite rules and regulations, a formal status structure, and clear lines of communication and authority. [p. 67]

†**Organizational buying.** The decision-making process by which formal organizations establish the need for purchased products and services, and identify, evaluate, and choose among alternative brands and suppliers. [p. 267]

Organization marketing. Those activities undertaken to create, maintain, or alter attitudes and/or behavior of target audiences toward particular organizations. [p. 630]

Partial product failure. A product failure that loses money but its sales cover all the variable costs and some of the fixed costs. [p. 338]

‡**Perception.** The process by which an individual selects, organizes, and interprets information inputs to create a meaningful picture of the world. [p. 249]

Physical distribution. The tasks involved in planning and implementing the physical flows of materials and final goods from points of origin to points of use or consumption to meet the needs of customers at a profit. [p. 443]

Political system. The term refers to the forms and institutions by which a nation is governed. It consists of an interacting set of laws, government agencies, and pressure groups that influence and constrain the conduct of various organizations and individuals in the society. [p. 217]

Price leader. A product that is priced below its normal markup or even below cost. It is used to attract customers to the store in the hope that they will buy other things at normal markups.

Price-taking market. A market where each seller must charge the going price. [p. 399]

Pricing strategy. The task of defining the rough initial price range and planned price movement through time that the company will use to achieve its marketing objectives in the target market. [p. 402]

Primary data. Data that are originally collected for the specific purpose at hand. [p. 145]

Producer markets. The set of organizations that buy products for the purpose of using them in the production process to make profits or achieve other objectives. [p. 267]

Product. Anything that can be offered to a market for attention, acquisition, use, or consumption that might satisfy a need. It includes physical objects, services, persons, places, organizations, and ideas. [p. 368]

Product assortment. *See* Product mix.

Product concept. (1) A management orientation that assumes that consumers will favor those products that offer the most quality for the price, and therefore the organization should devote its energy to improving product quality. (2) A particular subjective consumer meaning that a company tries to build into a product idea. [p. 21]

Product development. The term refers to the company's seeking increased sales by developing new or improved products for its current markets. [p. 79]

Product-differentiated marketing. A style of marketing in which the seller produces two or more products designed to look different from each other and competitors' products. [p. 293]

Product idea. A possible product, described in objective and functional terms, that the company can see itself offering to the market. [p. 335]

Product image. The particular subjective picture that consumers actually acquire of the product.

Production concept. A management orientation that assumes that consumers will favor those products that are available and affordable, and therefore the major task of management is to pursue improved production and distribution efficiency. [p. 20]

***Product item.** A distinct unit within a product line that is distinguishable by size, price, appearance, or some other attribute. The item is sometimes called a stockkeeping unit, a product variant, or subvariant. [p. 362]

***Product line.** A group of products within a product mix that are closely related, either because they function in a similar manner, are sold to the same customer groups, are marketed through the same types of outlets, or fall within the given price ranges. [p. 362]

‡This definition is from Bernard Berelson and Gary A. Steiner, *Human Behavior: An Inventory of Scientific Findings* (New York: Harcourt Brace Jovanovich, 1964), p. 88.

Product management organization. A form of marketing in which products are the responsibility of product managers who work with the various functional specialists in the company to develop and achieve their plans for the product. [p. 175]

***Product mix.** The set of all product lines and items that a particular seller offers for sale to buyers. [p. 362]

Public. Any group that has an actual or potential interest in or impact on an organization's ability to achieve its objectives. [p. 39]

Publicity. The securing of free editorial space or time. [p. 549]

Pull strategy. A strategy that calls for spending a lot of money on advertising and consumer promotion aimed at the final consumer to build up demand for the product. [p. 512]

Push strategy. A strategy that calls for using the sales force and trade promotion to push the product through the channels. [p. 512]

Quota. Sets limits on the amount of goods that can be imported in certain product categories. [p. 603]

Relative product failure. A product failure that yields a profit that is less than the company's normal rate of return. [p. 338]

Reseller market. All the individuals and organizations who acquire goods for the purpose of reselling or renting them to others at a profit. [p. 280]

Resellers. *See* Merchant middlemen.

Retailer. Any business enterprise whose sales volume primarily comes from retailing. [p. 459]

Retailing. All the activities involved in selling goods or services directly to final consumers for their personal, nonbusiness use. [p. 458]

Role. A set of activities that the individual is supposed to perform according to the definition and expectations of the individual and the persons around him or her. [p. 243]

Sales analysis. The effort to measure and evaluate the actual sales being achieved in relation to the sales goals set for different managers. [p. 115]

Sales budget. A conservative estimate of the expected volume of sales. It is used primarily for making current purchasing, production, and cash-flow decisions. [p. 156]

Sales quota. A sales goal set for a product line, company division, or sales representative. It is primarily a management tool for defining and stimulating sales effort. [p. 155]

Sales-response function. The likely sales volume during a specified time period associated with different possible levels of a marketing mix element holding constant the other marketing mix elements. [p. 111]

Sales variance analysis. An attempt to determine the relative contribution of different factors to a gap in sales performance. [p. 115]

Secondary data. Data that already exist somewhere, having been collected for another purpose. [p. 145]

Selective distortion. Name given to the tendency of people to twist information into personal meanings. [p. 250]

Selling concept. A management orientation that assumes that consumers will either not buy or not buy enough of the organization's products unless the organization makes a substantial effort to stimulate their interest in its products. [p. 21]

Service. Any activity or benefit that one party can offer to another, is essentially intangible, and does not result in the ownership of anything. Its production may or may not be tied to a physical product. [p. 370]

*__Shopping goods.__ Goods that the customer, in the process of selection and purchase, characteristically compares on such bases as suitability, quality, price, and style. [p. 371]

Social classes. Relatively homogeneous and enduring divisions in a society which are hierarchically ordered and whose members share similar values, interests, and behavior. [p. 240]

Social marketing. The design, implementation, and control of programs seeking to increase the acceptability of a social idea, cause, or practice in a target group. It utilizes market segmentation, consumer research, concept development, communications, facilitation, incentives, and exchange theory to maximize target group response. [p. 640]

Societal marketing concept. A management orientation that holds that the key task of the organization is to determine the needs, wants, and interests of target markets and to adapt the organization to delivering the desired satisfactions more effectively and efficiently than its competitors in a way that preserves or enhances the consumer's and the society's well-being. [p. 25]

*__Specialty goods.__ Goods with unique characteristics and/or brand identification for which a significant group of buyers are habitually willing to make a purchasing effort. [p. 371]

Standard Industrial Classification (S.I.C.). A U.S. Bureau of the Census classification of industries based on the product produced or operation performed by the industry.

Statistical bank. A collection of advanced statistical procedures for learning more about the relationships within a set of data and their statistical reliability. [p. 142]

Statistical demand analysis. A set of statistical procedures designed to discover the most important real factors affecting sales and their relative influence. [p. 163]

Strategic business unit (SBU). Any business making up the company. [p. 80]

Strategic planning. The managerial process of developing and maintaining a strategic fit between the organization and its changing market opportunities. It relies on developing a clear company mission, objectives and goals, growth strategies, and product portfolio plans. [p. 74]

Style. A basic and distinctive mode of expression appearing in a field of human endeavor. [p. 349]

Suppliers. Business firms and individuals who supply resources needed by the producer to produce the particular good or service. [p. 47]

Systems selling. The act of offering a buyer a complete system solution rather than some isolated products. [p. 271]

Target market. A well-defined set of customers whose needs the company plans to satisfy. [p. 87]

Target marketing. The act of selecting one or more of the market segments and developing a positioning and mix strategy for each. [p. 294]

Tariff. A tax levied by the foreign government against designated imported products. [p. 603]

Time-series analysis. A company forecast prepared on the basis of a statistical-mathematical analysis of past data. [p. 162]

Total market potential. The maximum amount of sales (in units or dollars) that might be available to all the firms in an industry during a given period under a given level of industry marketing expenditures and given environmental conditions. [p. 156]

***Trademark.** A brand or part of a brand that is given legal protection because it is capable of exclusive appropriation. A trademark protects the seller's exclusive rights to use the brand name and/or brand mark. [p. 374]

Transaction. A trade of values between two parties. [p. 14]

***Unsought goods.** Goods that the customer either does not know about or knows about but does not have an interest in purchasing. [p. 371]

Value analysis. An approach to cost reduction through the careful study of which components can be redesigned or standardized or made by cheaper methods of production. [p. 276]

Wholesaling. All the activities involved in selling goods or services to those who are buying for the purpose of resale or for business use. [p. 494]

NAME INDEX

A

Abell, Derek F., 94
Abler, Ronald, 453
Abrams, Bill, 591
Acker, David A., 167
Ackoff, Russell L., 131, 530, 557
Adams, John S., 453
Adelman, Morris, 679
Adler, Lee, 453
Aharoni, Yair, 645
Albaum, Gerald S., 618
Alderson, Wroe, 36, 42, 57, 424, 453
Alexander, Ralph S., 394
Allvine, Fred C., 465, 558
Alpert, Mark I., 263
Ames, B. Charles, 190
Anderson, Ralph E., 264
Andreasen, Alan R., 679
Ansoff, H. Igor, 94
Arpan, Jeffrey, 618
Aspinwall, Leo V., 394

B

Bachrach, Arthur J., 264
Backhaus, Klaus, 290
Bailey, Earl L., 356, 679
Baker, George L., 557
Ballachey, Egerton L., 263
Banes, Seymour, 167
Banting, Peter, 33, 394
Barban, Arnold M., 539
Barksdale, Hiram C., 627, 644
Bartels, Robert, 142
Bartos, Rena, 262
Bass, Frank M., 316, 589
Bass, Stephen J., 496
Bates, Albert D., 496
Bauer, Raymond A., 228, 262–63, 658, 679
Beach, Frank, 566
Behling, Orlando, 645
Behrens, William W., III, 227, 679
Belden, Marva, 566
Belden, Thomas, 566
Bell, Alexander Graham, 216
Bell, Martin L., 33, 316
Belshaw, Cyril S., 32
Benson, Lissa, 34
Berelson, Bernard, 263, 516
Berg, Thomas L., 394
Berman, Phyllis, 495–96
Bernstein, Peter W., 316
Berry, Leonard L., 228, 289
Black, George, 558
Blackwell, Roger D., 240, 263, 516
Blattberg, Robert, 356
Blau, Peter, 94
Bogart, Leo, 495
Boiko, Karen, 556
Bonoma, Thomas U., 558
Borch, Fred J., 33
Borden, Neil H., 290
Boulding, Kenneth, 211
Bourne, Francis S., 262
Bowen, Howard R., 669, 679
Bowman, Russell D., 558
Boyd, Harper W., Jr., 130, 167, 245, 262–63, 393
Bradford, Ernest S., 166
Bramel, Dana, 264
Branch, Melville C., 130
Brien, Richard H., 168
Britt, Steuart Henderson, 393
Brooks, John, 334
Brown, George H., 316
Brozen, Yale, 228
Bucklin, Louis P., 394, 453
Buell, Victor P., 190, 618
Burger, Philip C., 142
Buskirk, Richard, 566
Butler, Rhett W., 310
Buzzell, Robert D., 290, 357, 394, 495, 557
Bybee, H. Malcolm, 557

C

Calder, Bobby J., 167
Canfield, Bertrand, 566
Caplovitz, David, 655, 678
Cardozo, Richard, 316
Carroll, Daniel T., 644
Carson, Rachel, 211, 660, 662, 679
Cash, Harold C., 516
Cavanaugh, Suzette, 558
Center, Allen H., 558, 645
Choate, Robert B., 653, 664
Churchill, Sir Winston, 32
Clarke, Darral G., 337
Clayton, Alden G., 557
Clewett, Richard M., 32, 190
Cohen, Mitchell, 679
Cohen, Stanley E., 290
Coleman, Richard P., 316
Colley, Russell H., 525, 557
Combs, Linda Jones, 263
Connor, Richard A., Jr., 644
Coogle, Joseph M., Jr., 558
Cooney, John E., 644
Corey, E. Raymond, 190, 308, 316
Cort, Stanton G., 495
Cox, Donald F., 166, 263
Cox, Keith, 32, 167
Cox, Reavis, 453
Cox, William E., 357
Craig, C. Samuel, 516
Cravens, David W., 481
Cribbin, James, 589
Crissy, William J. E., 317, 516, 589
Crutchfield, Richard S., 263
Cunningham, Isabella C. M., 589
Cunningham, Scott M., 262
Cunningham, William H., 589
Cutlip, Scott M., 558, 645

D

Dalkey, Norman, 167
Daltas, Arthur J., 131
Darden, Donna K., 645
Darden, William R., 645
Davidson, William R., 496
Davis, Harry L., 262
Davis, Robert T., 130
Dawson, Leslie M., 33
Day, George S., 95
Day, Ralph L., 317
Dean, Joel, 418
Denenberg, Herbert S., 664
Dewhurst, J. Frederick, 678
Dhalla, Nariman K., 357

Diamond, Steven L., 671
Diaz, Octavio, 223
Dichter, Ernest, 263, 247, 289
Dickinson, Roger A., 290, 496
Dixon, Paul Rand, 655
Dixon, William R., 567, 588
Dodson, Joe A., 549, 558
Dolich, Ira J., 262
Donnelly, James H., 264
Dougherty, Philip H., 557
Douglas, Susan P., 618
Doyle, Peter, 354
Drucker, Peter, 5, 69, 94, 203, 227, 454, 668, 679
Dunn, S. Watson, 539
Durda, Matthew, 59

E

Edison, Thomas, 216
Ehrich, Thomas, 588
Ehrlich, Ann H. and Paul R., 662, 679
Ehrlich, D., 264
El-Ansary, Adel I., 454
Elsner, David, 496
Emery, C. William, 33
Emshoff, James R., 131, 530, 557
Engel, Ernst, 210
Engel, James F., 240, 263, 516
Enis, Ben M., 645
Evans, Franklin B., 316

F

Faris, Charles W., 289
Farley, John U., 263
Farmer, Richard N., 32
Farris, Paul W., 557
Feldman, Laurence P., 33
Fenn, Dan H., Jr., 228
Festinger, Leon, 264
Field, Louis, 678
Fishbein, Martin, 263
Fisher, Dennis D., 228
Fisk, George, 33
Ford, Henry, 20, 334, 338
Frank, Ronald, 316
Freud, Sigmund, 247
Frey, Albert Wesley, 95, 557
Fromm, Erich, 636, 645
Fu, Marilyn Y. C., 618
Fuss, Norman H., Jr., 419

G

Gabor, Dennis, 228
Gainer, Marion, 645
Galbraith, John Kenneth, 657, 660, 679
Gamble, Theodore R., 394
Gardner, Burleigh, 317
Garman, E. T., 262
Gaudet, H., 516
Gaw, Walter A., 558
Gelb, Betsy D., 316, 645
Gensch, Dennis H., 557
George, William R., 204, 627, 644
Gist, Ronald R., 461, 475, 495–96
Glick, E., 644
Goffman, Erving, 636, 645
Golanty, John, 357
Goldman, Arieh, 618
Goldstucker, Jac L., 357
Gonik, Jacob, 167
Good, Robert E., 166
Goodman, Sam R., 120
Goodrich, Jonathan N., 495
Gootnick, David, 637, 645
Gottlieb, Maurice, 316
Gould, Peter, 453
Gould, Roger, 262
Graf, Franklin, 290
Graham, Ellen, 227
Granger, Charles H., 94
Grathwohl, Harrison L., 262
Gray, Frank B., 190
Green, Paul E., 263, 303
Greenberg, Herbert M., 573, 589
Greenland, Leo, 228
Greer, Thomas V., 32
Gregory, William, 131
Greyser, Stephen A., 262, 454, 658, 671, 679
Groenveld, Leonard, 290
Grubb, Edward L., 262
Gubar, George, 244
Guttman, I., 264
Guzzardi, Walter, Jr., 289

H

Haire, Mason, 150
Haley, Russell J., 304
Hamelman, Paul W., 357
Hanan, Mark, 190, 356, 393, 589, 679
Haner, F. T., 618
Harding, Harold F., 356
Harding, Murray, 279, 289
Harper, Marion, 134, 166
Harris, John S., 356
Hartley, William D., 618
Harvey, Michael G., 357, 391
Hawkins, Edward R., 418
Hayden, Sterling, 32
Haydon, Harold, 496
Heany, Donald F., 394
Heckert, J. B., 589
Heiser, Herman, 589
Helitzer, Melvin, 262
Helmer, Olaf, 167
Henion, Karl E., II, 228, 645
Henry, Carl F. H., 644
Hensel, James S., 228
Hermann, Paul, 565–66
Herzberg, Frederick, 247–48, 263
Heskett, James L., 451
Hess, Sidney W., 167
Heyel, Carl, 262
Hills, Gerald D., 481
Hlavac, T. E., Jr., 167
Hofer, Charles W., 95
Hoffman, Jo Ann, 495
Hollander, Stanley C., 496
Holton, Richard H., 393
Honomichl, Jack J., 142, 166
Hopkins, David S., 335, 356
Hostage, G. M., 644
House, Robert J., 263
Hovland, Carl I., 516
Howard, John A., 236, 262
Howell, Charles D., 447, 454
Hughes, G. David, 228
Hulbert, James M., 131

I-J

Ingrassia, Paul, 59
Ivancevich, John M., 264
Ivie, Robert J., 451
Jackson, Barbara, 393

K

Kangun, Norman, 679
Karrass, Chester L., 589
Kaven, William H., 588
Keegan, Warren J., 612, 618
Keith, Robert J., 33
Kelley, Eugene J., 95, 394
Keough, Donald R., 576
Kerin, Roger A., 357, 391
Kinnear, Thomas C., 167
Kizilbash, A. H., 262
Klein, Frederick C., 262
Kollat, David T., 240, 263, 516
Kotrba, R. William, 317
Krech, David, 263
Kroc, Ray A., 24, 493
Kronholz, June, 227
Krugman, Herbert E., 534, 557
Kuehn, Alfred A., 317

L

Labovitz, George, 645
LaLonde, B. J., 444, 454
Lambin, Jean-Jacques, 131
Lancaster, Kelvin, 11, 32

Landon, E. Laird, Jr., 263
Larson, Carl M., 482
Lazarsfeld, P. F., 516
Lazarus, George, 378
Lazer, William, 95, 394
Leighton, David S. R., 618
Levitt, Theodore, 33, 94, 357, 368–69, 387, 393–94, 511, 513, 644, 652, 678
Levy, Sidney J., 32, 245, 262, 317, 393, 556, 588
Linn, Ed, 555
Little, John D. C., 167, 530, 557
Lodish, L. M., 167
Longman, Donald R., 131
Lonsdale, Ronald T., 316
Lopata, Richard S., 492, 496
Luck, David E., 190
Luick, John F., 557
Lumsdaine, A. A., 516

M

MacDonald, Morgan B., 344
McCammon, Bert C., Jr., 433, 440–41, 453–54, 465, 484, 495
McCarthy, E. Jerome, 95
McDonald, John Dennis, 495
McGarrity, Richard A., 31
McGarry, Edmund D., 453
McGinness, Joseph, 32, 644
McGregor, Douglas, 130
McGuire, E. Patrick, 671
McKay, Edward S., 192
McKelvy, Natalie, 317
McKitterick, John B., 32
McLaren, John, 622–23
McMurry, Robert N., 564, 572–73, 588–89
McNair, Malcolm P., 32, 496
McNamara, Carlton P., 33
McVey, Phillip, 440, 454
Magee, John F., 589
Majur, Paul, 32
Maloney, John C., 516, 531, 557
Mandell, Wallace, 516
Marcuse, Herbert, 679
Maricle, Kenneth E., 289
Markin, Rom J., 262, 264
Maslow, Abraham, 247–48, 263
Massy, William, 167, 316
Matthews, H. Lee, 290
May, Eleanor G., 496
Mayer, David, 573, 589
Mazze, Edward M., 357
Meadows, Dennis L. and Donnella H., 211, 227, 662, 679
Menkus, Belden, 495–96
Merims, Arthur M., 558
Meteja, James, 654
Meyerhoff, Arthur E., 639, 645
Mills, J., 264
Mindak, William A., 557, 644
Miracle, Gordon E., 394, 618
Mitford, Jessica, 678
Monroe, Kent B., 419
Montgomery, David B., 290, 540, 557
Moore, John L., 323
Morein, Joseph H., 190
Morgenroth, William M., 419
Morrill, John E., 511
Mossman, Frank H., 317
Moyer, Reed, 289
Mueller, Robert W., 290
Murphy, Patrick E., 31
Myers, James H., 263

N

Nader, Ralph, 221, 654, 662
Narayana, Chem L., 262
Neidell, Lester A., 558
Nicosia, Francesco M., 263
Nierenberg, Gerald I., 589
Nimer, Daniel A., 418
Nimmo, Dan, 644

O

O'Meara, John T., Sr., 356
Oppenheim, Carol, 644
Osborn, Alex F., 356
Osgood, C. E., 644
Oxenfeldt, Alfred R., 131, 419

P-Q

Packard, Vance, 660
Painter, John J., 316
Parker, Donald D., 454
Parnes, Sydney J., 356
Patterson, John Henry, 566
Paul, Bill, 394
Pearce, Michael R., 495
Pearson, Andrall E., 190
Pegram, Roger M., 588
Pehrson, Gordon O., 679
Perlmutter, Howard V., 618
Perreault, William D., 645
Pessemier, Edgar A., 263
Philiotis, Rob, 215
Pike, Donald L., 32,
Piland, William E., 696
Plummer, Joseph T., 262
Pohl, Frederick, 27
Posner, Ronald S., 588
Prentice, Robert M., 543, 557
Preston, Lee E., 418
Qualter, Terence H., 645

R

Randers, Jorgen, 227, 679
Rankin, Deborah, 32
Ray, Michael L., 263, 503–4, 516
Redinbaugh, Larry D., 460
Reif, Rita, 495
Rein, Irwin J., 32
Revzan, David A., 496
Reynolds, William H., 334, 350
Richman, Barry M., 339
Ricks, David A., 618
Rienow, Leona, 57
Rienow, Robert, 57
Ries, Al, 556
Rigaux, Benny P., 262
Ring, L. Winston, 263
Ringer, Jurgen F., 447, 454
Riso, Ovid, 587
Roberto, Eduardo, 645
Roberts, Alan A., 317
Robertson, Thomas S., 516
Robinson, Dwight E., 350
Robinson, Patrick J., 289
Rodgers, William, 131
Rogers, Everett M., 346
Rosenbloom, Bert, 454
Rothe, James T., 33, 357
Ruffin, M. D., 356
Russell, Frederic, 566

S

Salancik, Gerald R., 222, 228
Salmon, Walter J., 495
Samhaber, Ernest, 495
Sasser, W. Earl, 644
Schendel, Dan, 95
Schiele, George W., 262
Schiff, Michael, 131
Schlinger, Mary Jane, 262
Schoeffler, Sidney, 394
Schonback, P., 264
Schreiber, G. R., 496
Schwartz, David J., 418
Scott, Richard, 94
Seipel, Carl-Magnus, 558
Seligman, Daniel, 557
Seton, Charles, 635
Severs, Richard, 337
Sexton, Donald E., Jr., 131
Shapiro, Benson P., 393, 588
Sheffield, F. D., 516
Sheehy, Gail, 262
Sheth, Jagdish N., 262–63, 679
Shoemaker, F. Floyd, 346
Shostack, G. Lynn, 644
Siegler, William Lee, 557
Silk, Alvin J., 540, 557
Sinclair, Upton, 659–60

Slater, Charles C., 394
Smith, A. B., 496
Smith, Adam, 14, 32, 666
Smith, Samuel V., 160
Smith, Wendell R., 317
Snyder, Watson, Jr., 190
Soloman, Paul J., 204
Sorenson, Howard C., 391
Sorenson, Ralph Z., 32, 618
Stafford, James E., 166
Stanton, William J., 32, 429, 453
Star, Steven H., 190, 337
Starch, Daniel, 540
Stasch, Stanley F., 190
Steinbrink, John, 588
Steiner, Gary A., 263
Stern, Arthur, 558
Stern, Louis W., 454
Sternthal, Brian, 516, 549, 558
Stevens, Charles W., 654
Stewart, John B., 357
Stewart, Paul W., 678
Stigler, George, 418
Stockman, Lynn H., 316
Stone, Bob, 496
Strang, Roger A., 548, 557–58
Strong, Edward C., 263
Suci, C. J., 644
Swan, John E., 263
Sweeney, James K., 618

T

Talley, Walter J., 588
Tallman, Gerald B., 678
Tannenbaum, P. H., 644
Tauber, Edward M., 344
Thomas, Dan R. E., 644
Thompson, Donald L., 589
Thompson, Jacqueline A., 645
Tigert, Douglas J., 316, 461
Tillman, Rollie, 432, 453, 496
Tippet, K. J., 356
Toffler, Alvin, 203, 214, 227–28
Toy, Norman E., 131
Trout, Jack, 556
Tucker, W. T., 316
Twedt, Dik Warren, 166, 305, 531, 557
Tybout, Alice M., 549, 558

U

Ule, G. Maxwell, 529, 557
Upah, Gregory D., 222, 228
Urban, Glen L., 167
Uttal, Bro, 190

V

Veeck, Bill, 555
Vidale, M. I., 530, 557
Vizza, Robert, 580

W

Wadinambiaratchi, 618
Wall, Kevin A., 262
Wanamaker, John, 508
Warne, Colston E., 683
Warner, Daniel S., 522
Warshaw, Martin R., 588
Wasson, Chester R., 350
Waters, Elmer E., 190
Webster, Frederick E., 289, 454
Weigand, Robert E., 454, 482
Weinrauch, J. Donald, 696
Weiss, Doyle L., 130
Weiss, E. B., 394
Wells, Louis T., Jr., 618
Wells, Mary, 144
Wells, William D., 244
Werner, Ray O., 228
Westfall, Ralph, 167, 316
White, Theodore, 644
Whyte, William H., Jr., 589
Widgor, L., 263
Wiebe, G. D., 640, 645
Wieckmann, Ulrich E., 618
Wilkie, William L., 263, 516, 557
Wilson, David T., 290
Wilson, Ian H., 204
Wilson, Thomas W., Jr., 190
Wind, Yoram, 263, 289, 316, 618
Winter, Willis L., Jr., 522
Wolfe, H. B., 530, 557
Woodruff, Robert R., 481
Wright, John S., 357, 482, 522
Wright, Peter L., 679
Wyden, Peter, 558

Y

Yankelovich, Daniel, 316
Young, Robert W., 394
Yuseph, Sonia, 357

Z

Zaltman, Gerald, 142, 357, 558, 645
Zeigler, Sherilyn K., 522
Ziff, Ruth, 301, 316
Zikmund, William G., 429, 453
Zinszer, P. H., 444, 454

SUBJECT INDEX

A

Accelerator principle, 269
Accessory equipment, 373
Accounting, 185
Acquisitions, 659
Action program, 108
Adoption stages, 346
Advertising, 500, 513, 519–41, 546
Advertising agencies, 523–24
Advertising appeals, 504
Advertising budgets, 520, 527–30
Advertising commissions, 524
Advertising continuity and pulsing, 538
Advertising, history of, 521–22
Advertising media, 533–38
Advertising messages, 530–33
Advertising objectives, 524–27
Advertising reach, frequency, and impact, 533–34
Advertising regulation, 27, 541
Advertising testing and evaluation, 538–41
Advertising timing, 536–38
Age, 205, 243–44, 298
Agents, 47, 488–89
Agricultural assemblers, 490
AIDA model, 404, 578
Analytical marketing system, 142–43
Annual plan control, 114–20
Assortment decisions, 280, 480–81, 491
Atmospheres, 481, 506
Attitudes, 251–52
Auction companies, 490
Augmented product, 369
Automatic vending, 472–74
Automobile market, 292–93, 302–4, 333–34
Awareness set, 236

B

Backward channels, 429
Backward integration, 79
Bank marketing, 98, 188, 667
Barriers to entry, 659–60
Barter, 14
Beer market, 319–23, 383
Behavioristic segmentation, 301–2
Beliefs, 251
Benefits and features, 368, 578
Benefit segmentation, 302–4
Bidding, 286, 408–9
Black consumers, 233
Blanket contracts, 278
Boston Consulting Group, 80–82
Brainstorming, 338
Brand decisions, 26, 374–83
Brand extension decision, 382
Brand image, 255, 301
Brand loyalty, 305–06
Brand management, 175–79
Breakeven cost chart, 438
Brokers, 488
Budgeting and budgets, 100, 108–10
Business analysis and planning, 100–3, 341–43
Business portfolio planning, 80–85
Business strength, 83–84
Buyclasses, 270
Buyer intentions survey, 160–61
Buyer readiness stages, 306, 502–4, 512–13
Buyer types, 283, 300
Buyflow, 278–80
Buying allowance, 545
Buying center, 271
Buying committees, 281–82
Buying decisions, 233–37, 270–71, 280–81, 284
Buying influences, 238–52, 272–75, 282–83, 285–86
Buying participants, 237–38, 271–72, 281–82, 284–85
Buying power index, 159–60
Buying process, 252–60, 275–80, 283–84, 286–87
Buying roles, 237–38, 271–72
Buying service, 474
Buying situations, 234, 270
Buyphases, 275–80

C

Cannibalization, 367
Cash-and-carry wholesalers, 487
Cash cows, 81
Catalog selling, 471–72
Catalog showroom, 470
Celebrity marketing, 634–35
Central business district, 478–79
Centralized purchasing, 274
Chain ratio method, 156
Chain store, 475–76
Channel captain, 433
Channel cooperation, conflict, and competition, 433–34
Channel member selection, motivation, and evaluation, 439–41
Choice set, 236
Citizen action publics, 53–54
Closing the sale, 579
Cognitive dissonance theory, 259
College marketing, 628–30
Combination store, 466
Command-directed system, 37
Commercialization decision, 345–47
Commission merchants, 489
Communication model, 501–2
Company demand, 155
Company growth strategy, 77–80
Company marketing system, 44–56
Company mission, 74–76
Comparison advertising, 525–26
Competitive positioning, 89–90
Competitors, 51–52
Complaint and suggestion systems, 118–19, 390
Concentrated marketing, 313–14
Concept development and testing, 339–41
Conglomerchant, 478
Conjunctive model, 255
Consideration set, 236
Consumer buying behavior, 229–60
Consumer cooperative, 476–77
Consumer expenditure patterns, 210
Consumer information sources, 253

Consumerism, 26, 54, 218, 648, 653, 660–62, 668–69, 671, 676–77
Consumer market, 50, 232–33
Consumer panels, 549
Consumer risk taking, 258
Consumer satisfaction, 27–28, 258–60, 388
Consumer sovereignty, 23, 29, 222
Consumer surveys, 549
Consumers Union, 683–84
Consumer testing, 343
Consumption maximization, 27
Consumption system, 369
Contests, sweepstakes, and games, 546
Contingency plans, 102
Contracts, 286–87
Control chart, 117
Convenience goods, 370–71
Convenience store, 466
Copy strategy statement, 532
Corrective action, 119–20
Countermarketing, 19
Coupons, 544
Creativity techniques, 336–38
Credit, 185–86, 390
Criticisms of marketing, 6–7, 377, 649–64
Cues, 250, 343
Cultural environment, 222–26
Culture, 56, 239, 606
Customer attitude tracking, 118–19
Customer orientation, 183
Customer panels and surveys, 119
Customer problem analysis, 337
Customer satisfaction measurement, 388
Customer size, 307

D

DAGMAR, 525
Debt, 210
Deceptive practices, 651–52
Decline stage, 352–55
Delphi method, 162
Demand, 11
Demand function, 111
Demarketing, 19
Demographic environment, 55, 204–9
Demographic segmentation, 295, 298
Demonstration, 545, 577–78
Department store, 462–63
Derived demand, 268
Desire competitors, 51–52
Determinance model, 256
Differential advantage, 86
Differentiated marketing, 312–13
Direct marketing, 472
Disadvantaged consumers, 41–42, 655–56, 674–75
Discounts and allowances, 411–12
Discount store, 468–69
Discrepancy of assortment, 49
Disjunctive competences, 86
Disjunctive model, 256
Distribution channels, 43–44, 47–48, 423–42
Distribution programming, 440–41
Distribution structure, 43
Diversification, 79–80
Division of labor, 36
Dogs, 81
Door-to-door retailing, 474
Drive, 250
Drop shippers, 488
Dual distribution, 432–33
Dumping, 614
Durable goods, 370

E

Early adopters, 346
Ecological environment, 56, 211–12
Economic efficiency, 675
Economic environment, 209–11
Economic influences on buying, 245
Economics and marketing, 29–30
Economy, 55–56
Elasticity of demand, 413
End use segmentation, 307
Energy, 212, 663
Engineering, 184
Environmental analysis, 55–56, 201–26
Environmental change, 69–70
Environmentalism, 552–63
Ethics in marketing, 669
Event creation and management, 506, 553
Evoked set, 236
Exchange, 13–14
Exclusive distribution, 436
Expectancy-value model, 256
Expectations-performance theory, 258–59
Experience curve, 351
Experimental method, 112, 149–51
Exploratory research, 145–46
Export agents and merchants, 609
Exporting, 608–10

F

Facilitators, 47
Fads, 349–50
Family characteristics, 205–6
Family influence on buying, 242–43
Family life cycle, 243–44
Fashion cycle, 349
Feature improvement, 352
Federal Trade Commission, 221
Finance and financial analysis, 46, 102, 185
Financial public, 53
Focus groups, 146
Forcasting, 104–5, 152–64, 203–4
Form utility, 49
Forward integration, 79
Four P's, 89
Franchising, 24, 431, 477–78
Freud's theory of motivation, 247–48
Functions of marketing, 29
Fundraising, 15

G

Gatekeepers, 271–72, 507
General public, 54
Generic brands, 378
Generic competitors, 51–52
Geographical shifts in population, 206–7
Geographical strategy, 345
Geographic segmentation, 296–99
Goals of marketing system, 26–28
Goods and services classification, 369–73
Government legislation and regulation (also see Public policy and marketing), 38, 53, 212, 216–21
Government market, 50, 284–88
Growth share matrix, 80–82
Growth stage, 350–51

H

Heavy users, 304–5
Herzberg's theory of motivation, 248–49
High-pressure selling, 575, 652–53
Horizontal integration, 79
Horizontal marketing systems, 432
Hospital marketing, 622–23
Households, 206
Hypermarche, 466–67

I-J

Idea generation, 335–38
Ideal product, 12, 256
Idea marketing, 639–42
Idea screening, 338–39
Image measurement and planning, 481, 631–34

Income characteristics, 209–10, 299, 604
Industrial distributors, 487
Industrial marketing, 265–87
Industrial markets, 307–08
Industry attractiveness, 82–83
Industry marketing system, 42–44
Inflation, 210
Inflation pricing, 412–13
Information evaluation, 254–57
Information search, 253–54
Innovation, 212–17, 675–76
Innovation diffusion, 346
Innovators, 346
Installations, 373
Institutional marketing, 266
Intensive distribution, 436
Intention-to-buy, 340
Internal publics, 55
International marketing, 8, 39–42, 50, 599–617
International trade, 603–4
Introduction stage, 348–50
Inventory, 185, 448–49

Joint venturing, 610

L

Labeling, 384
Learning, 250–51
Learning curve, 83
Leasing, 269
Lexicographic model, 256
Licensing, 610
Life cycle pricing, 286
Life style, 245, 300–301
Local publics, 54
Loss leaders, 482
Loyal buyers, 305–6

M

Macroenvironment, 55–56, 203
Mail-and-telephone retailing, 471–72
Major accounts, 307, 562–63, 568
Majority fallacy, 312
Management by objectives, 115
Manufacturer's agents, 489
Manufacturing, 46, 184
Market-buildup method, 157–59
Market capacity, 155
Market coverage strategies, 88
Market, definition of, 16–17, 231–32
Market demand measurement, 152–60
Market development, 79
Market-directed systems, 37
Market evolution, 73
Market flows, 37
Market forecasting, 154, 160–64
Market growth rate, 81
Market logistics, 445
Market management, 179–80
Market modification, 351–52
Market participants, 37
Market penetration, 78–79
Market potential, 154–60
Market response function, 153
Market rollout, 345
Market segmentation, 50–51, 87–88, 291–314
Market selection, 607–8
Market-share analysis, 81, 116–17, 399
Market testing, 162, 343–45
Market types, 297
Marketing, definition of, 4, 9–10, 17
Marketing audit, 124–29
Marketing channels, 47, 423–42
Marketing communications mix, 500
Marketing concept, 22–24
Marketing control, 109, 114–29
Marketing controller, 120
Marketing culture, 46–47
Marketing department, 169–88
Marketing environment, 201–26
Marketing expenditure level, 108
Marketing expense-to-sales analysis, 117–18
Marketing firms, 47
Marketing functions, 425, 485
Marketing information systems, 92, 135–36
Marketing intelligence system, 138–39
Marketing management, definition of, 18–19
Marketing management philosophies, 20–26
Marketing management systems, 91–92
Marketing mix, 88–91, 107–8, 352
Marketing opportunity analysis, 68–69, 85–86
Marketing organization, 92, 169–88, 186–87
Marketing planning, 91, 99–114
Marketing plans, 102–14
Marketing process, 73, 85–92
Marketing profitability analysis, 120–24
Marketing research procedure, 143–52
Marketing research system, 139–42, 164
Marketing's interface with other functions, 45–46, 182–86
Marketing strategy, 107–14, 256–57, 341
Marketing systems, 35–36
Marketing tasks, 19
Markets, 49–50
Markup pricing, 402–4, 651
Maslow's theory of motivation, 248
Mass marketing, 293, 311–12
Mass media, 506–7
Materialism, 656
Matrix organization, 181
Maturity stage, 351–52
Media, 53, 506
Merchandise allowance, 546
Merchant middlemen, 47
Merchant wholesalers, 487–88
Message development, 504–6
Micro-sales analysis, 116
Military market, 285, 307
Mission statements, 74–76
Model bank, 143
Motivation and motivational research, 246–49
Motives, 246–50
Multibrand decision, 382
Multichannel marketing systems, 432–33
Multinational companies, 601–02, 617

N

National accounts, 568
National marketing systems, 36–42
Needs and wants, 10–11, 248, 656–57
Need-satisfaction selling approach, 578
Negotiated contract, 286
New product committees and departments, 335
New product development, 58–59, 79, 332–46
Nielsen, A. C., Company, 138
Nondurable goods, 370
Nonprofit organization marketing, 8–9, 68, 630–42

O

Objections, 578–79
Objective-and-task method, 509, 529–30
Objectives and goals, 76–77, 82, 105–6
Occupation, 244–45
Opinion leaders, 242, 507
Opportunity and threat analysis, 70–72, 85–86, 105–06
Optimization planning, 110–13

Order processing, 446–47
Organizational buying behavior, 265–87
Organization/environment adaptation, 68–74
Organization marketing, 630–34
Organizations, types of, 67–68

P

Packaging decisions, 384–86
Party selling, 474
Peddlers, 565–66
Perceived-value pricing, 406–7
Perception, 249–50
Personal influence, 346
Personality, 245–46, 301
Personal selling, 500, 565–66
Person marketing, 634–38
Petroleum bulk plants and terminals, 490
Physical distribution, 443–52
Physical distribution costs, 444
Physical distribution organization, 451–52
Place marketing, 638–39
Place utility, 49
Point-of-purchase displays, 545
Political candidate marketing, 22, 635–36
Political environment, 56, 217–22
Pollution, 212
Population size and growth, 204
Portfolio planning, 80–85
Possession utility, 49
Postpurchase behavior, 258–60
Preference segments, 295
Premiums, 544–45
Presentation, 577–78
Prestige pricing, 410
Price discrimination, 403–4, 407
Price packs, 544
Pricing decisions, 395–417
Primary data, 145
Primary demand, 154, 525
Private brands, 377–78
Problem recognition, 252–53, 276
Producer market, 50, 267–80
Producers' cooperatives, 488
Product, definition of, 11–13
Product, meaning of, 368–69
Product attributes, 254
Product classes, 348
Product concept, 21, 339
Product decisions, 361–73
Product-differentiated marketing, 293
Product failures, 332, 335, 338
Product form competitors, 51–52, 348
Product item, 362
Product life cycle, 331, 347–55, 513–14, 613
Product line decisions, 362–68
Product line pricing, 416–17
Product line stretching, 365–67
Product management, 175–79
Product map, 364, 383
Product/market grid, 87
Product mix, 361–63
Product modification, 337, 352
Product obsolescence, 654–55
Product proliferation, 28
Product recalls, 654
Product safety, 653–54
Product space map, 89–90
Product specification, 276
Product use test, 344
Production concept, 20
Profit gap, 77–78
Profit planning, 109–14, 399
Profitability analysis and control, 114, 120–24
Projective techniques, 247
Promotional pricing, 410
Promotion budget, 508–9
Promotion mix, 509–14
Promotools, 500
Proposal solicitation, 277
Prospecting, 345, 577
Psychographic segmentation, 300
Public advertising, 640
Public interest, 6, 221
Publicity, 500, 549–55
Public policy and marketing, 24–26, 386, 391, 403, 442, 541, 587, 663–65
Public relations, 225, 550, 631
Publics, 39, 52–55
Pull strategy, 512
Purchase decision, 257–58
Purchase occasion, 302
Purchase probability scale, 161
Purchasing, 46, 184, 489–90
Push strategy, 512

Q

Quality, 352, 380
Quality of life, 28, 662–63
Question marks, 81
Questionnaires, 147–48

R

R & D, 46, 184, 215–16, 343
Rack jobbers, 488
Reciprocity, 13–14, 269
Recycling, 429
Reference groups, 241–42
Remarketing, 19
Repositioning, 352, 382–83
Resale price maintenance, 403
Reseller market, 50, 280–84
Resource markets, 37
Retailer cooperatives, 431, 476
Retailer marketing decisions, 480–83
Retailing, 42, 458–84
Retail life cycles, 484
Robinson-Patman Act, 281
Roles and statuses, 243

S

Sales analysis, 115–16
Sales branches and offices, 489–90
Sales budget, 156
Sales call norms, 580–81
Sales contests, 583
Sales estimation, 341–42
Sales force, 561–87
Sales force compensation, 570–72
Sales force efficiency, 580–81
Sales force evaluation, 583–86
Sales force motivation, 582–83
Sales force objectives, 566–67
Sales force opinion forecasting, 161–62
Sales force recruitment, selection, and training, 572–75
Sales force size, 570
Sales force structure, 568–70
Sales force supervision, 579–83
Sales forecasting, 155, 160–64
Sales management, 561–87
Salesmanship, 575–79
Sales meetings, 583
Sales promotion, 500, 541–49
Sales quotas, 155–56, 582–83
Sales reports, 136–38, 584
Sales representatives, 563–65
Sales response function, 110–13
Sales variance analysis, 115–16
Sales wave research, 344
Samples, 544
Satisfiers and dissatisfiers, 248–49
Savings, 210
Scale economies, 83
Secondary data, 143
Selective demand, 154, 525
Selective distribution, 436–37
Selective distortion, 250
Selective exposure, 249–50
Selective retention, 250
Self-concept, 245–46
Self-service, 384, 459–60
Selling agents, 489
Selling concept, 21–22
Selling vs. marketing, 23, 173

Semantic differential, 632
Sensations, 249
Service attributes, 387
Service decisions, 387–90
Service department, 390
Service retailers, 467
Services, 370, 373, 427, 429, 481–82, 623–30
Sex, 298–99
Shopping centers, 479–80
Shopping goods, 371
Shortages, 211
Simulated store technique, 344
Situational factors, 257–58
Situation analysis, 103–5
Skimming pricing, 401
Social audits, 225
Social class, 209, 239–41, 300
Social goods, 657–58
Social marketing, 640–42
Societal marketing concept, 24–26, 668–69
Source credibility, 507
Specialty advertising, 546
Specialty goods, 371
Specialty store, 461–62
Standard Metropolitan Statistical Areas, 207, 227–28
Starch readership scores, 540
Stars, 81
Statistical bank, 142–43
Statistical demand analysis, 163–64
Stockless purchase plan, 278
Strategic business planning grid, 82–83
Strategic business unit (SBU), 80–85
Strategic control, 124–29
Strategic planning, 73–85, 101–2
Strength and weakness analysis, 105–6
Style improvement, 352
Styles, 349
Subcontracting, 287
Subculture, 223, 239
Success requirements, 86
Supermarket, 463–66
Superstore, 466
Supplier attributes, 277
Suppliers, 47
Supplies, 373
Survey research, 146–49
Symbiotic marketing, 432
Synchromarketing, 19
Systems selling, 271, 393

T

Target markets, 86–88, 107, 293, 309–14
Target pricing, 404–5
Task system, 38
Technological environment, 56, 212–17
Telephone selling, 472
Test marketing, 344
Threat analysis, 70–71
Time series analysis, 162–63
Time utility, 49
Trade, origin of, 15–16
Trade promotion, 545–46
Trade relations mix, 437
Trade shows, 344, 546
Trading stamps, 545
Traffic builders, 368
Transactions, 14–15
Transfers, 15
Transportation, 449–51
Truck wholesalers, 487–88
Turnkey operation, 271

U

Undifferentiated marketing, 311–12
Unsought goods, 371
Utilities created by marketing, 49, 425
Utility function, 255

V

Value analysis, 276
Values, 222–26
Vending machines, 472–74
Venture terms, 335
Vertical marketing systems, 429–32
Volume segmentation, 304–5
Voluntary chain, 476

W

Warehouse store, 469–70
Warehousing, 447–48
Weak products, 353–55
Weber's Law, 367
Wheel of retailing, 483
Wholesale merchants, 487
Wholesaler-sponsored voluntary chains, 431
Wholesaling, 484–92
Word-of-mouth influence, 506
Working wives, 206

Y

Youth market, 233